¡Así se dice!

Experience Spanish like never before!

Everything you need to teach Spanish is at your fingertips.

Choose your approach:
- **Go completely digital**
- **Blend print and digital**
- **Move between devices**

ENGAGING

Students experience online learning at its best!

- Interact with online student edition which includes audio, videos, games, and more.
- Record oral responses to activities with record-and-playback tool.
- Build proficiency with carefully organized vocabulary.
- Discover culture integrated throughout program.
- Extend interactive text lessons with ConnectEd resources.

EFFECTIVE

Ensure students are mastering language and enriching their understanding of culture.

- Motivate students with self-check quizzes and games that provide instant feedback.
- View student answers and monitor progress with eBook technology.
- Create, assign, and evaluate assessment all in one place.
- Customize your instruction and assessment.
- Track student results, assess progress with benchmark tests, and remediate as needed.

EASY-TO-USE

Manage your time and resources!

- Access all of your digital resources organized at point-of-use.
- Select the perfect mix of planning and instruction, whether digital or print, to meet the needs of your students.
- Assign and manage student work online.

Go Online! **connectED.mcgraw-hill.com**

¡Así se dice!

Teacher Edition

SPANISH 2

Conrad J. Schmitt

McGraw Hill Education

Bothell, WA • Chicago, IL • Columbus, OH • New York, NY

Information on featured companies, organizations, and their products and services is included for educational purposes only and does not present or imply endorsement of the **¡Así se dice!** program. Permission to use all business logos has been granted by the businesses represented in this text.

connectED.mcgraw-hill.com

Send all inquiries to:
McGraw-Hill Education
8787 Orion Place
Columbus, OH 43240-4027

ISBN: 978-0-02-141265-5
MHID: 0-02-141265-0

Printed in the United States of America.

3 4 5 6 7 8 9 DOR 19 18 17 16

Contenido en breve

Teacher Edition

Student Edition

Dear Spanish Teacher,

Welcome to Glencoe's **¡Así se dice!** Spanish program. We hope that our presentation of the Spanish language and Hispanic cultures will make the Spanish language more teachable for you and more learnable for your students.

Upon completion of each chapter of **¡Así se dice!** your students will be able to communicate in Spanish in real-life situations. The high-frequency, productive vocabulary presented at the beginning of the chapter focuses on a specific communicative and cultural theme. The grammar points that follow the vocabulary section enable students to put their new words together to communicate coherently.

After students acquire the essential vocabulary and grammar needed to function in a given situation, we present a realistic conversation that uses natural, colloquial Spanish and, most importantly, Spanish that students can readily understand. To introduce students to the cultures of the Hispanic world, the chapter theme is subsequently presented in a cultural milieu in narrative form. The **Lectura cultural** and the **Lectura Un poco más** recombine known language and enable students to read and learn—in Spanish—about the fascinating cultures of the people who speak Spanish.

Any one of us who has taught Spanish realizes the importance of giving students the opportunity to practice, a factor so often overlooked in many textbooks today. Throughout **¡Así se dice!** we provide students with many opportunities to use their Spanish in activities with interesting and varied, but realistic, formats. The activities within each chapter progress from simple, guided practice to more open-ended activities that may use all forms of the particular grammar point in question. Finally, activities that encourage completely free communication enable students to recall and reincorporate all the Spanish they have learned up to that point. Toward the end of each chapter, students are given ample opportunity to demonstrate both their oral and written proficiency. Since students need constant reinforcement of material to keep their language skills alive, each chapter includes both its own review and a cumulative review that covers all previously learned material.

We are aware that your students have varied learning styles and abilities. For this reason we have provided a great deal of optional material in **¡Así se dice!** to permit you to pick and choose material appropriate for the needs of your classes. In this Teacher Wraparound Edition we have clearly outlined the material that is required, recommended, or optional.

Many resources accompany **¡Así se dice!** to help you vary and enliven your instruction. We hope you will find these materials not only useful but an integral part of the program. However, we trust you will agree that the Student Edition is the lifeline of any program; the supporting materials can be used to reinforce and expand upon the themes of the main text.

We sincerely hope that you and your students experience much success and enjoyment using **¡Así se dice!**

Atentamente,
Conrad J. Schmitt

LEVEL 1	Preliminary Lessons	Chapter 1	Chapter 2
TOPICS	• Greeting people • Saying good-bye • Speaking politely • Counting • Finding out the price • Days of the week • Months of the year • Finding out and giving the date • Asking and telling time • Seasons and weather	• Physical descriptions and personality traits • Nationalities • School subjects	• Families and pets • Houses and apartments • Rooms and furniture 
CULTURE	• Spanish names • Formality • Currencies • Spanish calendar • 24-hour clock 	• Punta Arenas, Chile • School children in Spain and Latin America • Elementary school in Saquisili, Ecuador • Independence Monument, Mexico City • Colonial plaza in Santo Domingo, Dominican Republic • Windmills in La Mancha, Spain • St. Augustine, Florida • San Juan, Puerto Rico • Spanish speakers in the United States • Characters from the novel *El Quijote*	• Families and homes in the Spanish-speaking world • Pets in the Spanish-speaking world • Tenerife, Canary Islands, Spain • Plaza de Armas in Trujillo, Peru • Quito, Ecuador • **El sato,** a Puerto Rican dog • Galapagos Islands
FUNCTIONS	• How to greet people • How to say good-bye • How to speak politely • How to count from 0–100 • How to find out and tell days of the week • How to tell time • How to find out and tell the months and seasons	• How to describe people and things • How to tell where someone is from • How to tell what subjects you take and express opinions about them	• How to talk about families and pets • How to describe a house or apartment • How to describe rooms and some furnishings
GRAMMAR		• Nouns, adjectives, and articles • The verb **ser** • **Tú** and **usted**	• The verb **tener** • Possessive adjectives

(l)Larry Hamill, (r)Andrew Payti

LEVEL 1	Chapter 3	Chapter 4	Chapter 5
TOPICS	• In the classroom • School clothes and school supplies • After-school activities	• Foods and beverages • Eating at a café	• Soccer • Baseball • Basketball • Tennis • Uniforms • Colors
CULTURE	• Library in Barranco, Peru • School uniforms in Spain and Latin America • Barcelona, Spain, and its languages • Plaza de Armas in Arequipa, Peru • Home in Antigua, Guatemala • School and after-school activities in Spanish-speaking countries and the United States • Working habits of young people in the Spanish-speaking world	• Eating habits in the Spanish-speaking world compared to the United States • Eating times in the Spanish-speaking world compared to the United States • Spanish tapas • **Tunos** in Spain and Mexico • Typical dishes from the Spanish-speaking world • Argentine beef • Popular beverages, such as Inca Kola and mate • Simón Bolívar, a Latin American hero	• Various soccer stadiums in Spain and Latin America • Copán, Honduras • Jai alai • San Pedro de Macoris, Dominican Republic • Nicaragua and the earthquake of 1972 • Sports in Spanish-speaking countries compared to the United States • Baseball player Roberto Clemente
FUNCTIONS	• How to talk about what you do in school • How to identify some school clothes and school supplies • How to talk about what you and your friends do after school	• How to identify food • How to describe breakfast, lunch, and dinner • How to find a table at a café • How to order in a café • How to pay the bill in a café	• How to talk about sports • How to describe a soccer uniform • How to identify colors
GRAMMAR	• Present tense of -**ar** verbs • The verbs **ir**, **dar**, and **estar** • The contractions **al** and **del**	• Present tense of -**er** and -**ir** verbs • Expressions with the infinitive—**ir a**, **tener que**, **acabar de**	• Present tense of stem-changing verbs • **Interesar**, **aburrir**, and **gustar**

LEVEL 1	Chapter 6	Chapter 7	Chapter 8
TOPICS	• Personality, conditions, and emotions • A visit to the doctor's office • Illnesses	• Summer weather and activities • Winter weather and activities	• Celebrating a birthday • Attending concerts, movies, and museums
CULTURE	• Pharmacies in the Spanish-speaking world • Homes of the Embera people of Panama • Canary Islands • Salamanca, Spain • The Plaza Grande in Merida, Mexico • Literary genre, the picaresque novel	• El Yunque • Skiing in the Pyrenees Mountains • Beaches in Spain and Latin America • Vacationing in Argentina • Summer and winter resorts in Spanish-speaking countries	• Mexican artist, Frida Kahlo • Andean musical instrument, **la zampoña** • La Boca, an artistic neighborhood of Buenos Aires • Museums throughout the Spanish-speaking world • El Museo del Barrio and the Hispanic Institute in New York • Shakira, a Colombian singer • *Zapatistas,* by José Clemente Orozco • Hispanic art and music • Art and music in Mexico City
FUNCTIONS	• How to describe people's personality, conditions, and emotions • How to explain minor illnesses • How to talk about a doctor's appointment	• How to talk about summer and winter weather • How to talk about summer and winter activities	• How to talk about a birthday party • How to discuss concerts, movies, and museums
GRAMMAR	• **Ser** and **estar** • Indirect object pronouns	• Preterite tense of regular **-ar** verbs • Preterite of **ir** and **ser** • Direct object pronouns	• Preterite tense of **-er** and **-ir** verbs • The verbs **oír** and **leer** • Affirmative and negative expressions

LEVEL 1	Chapter 9	Chapter 10*	Chapter 11*
TOPICS	• Shopping for clothes • Shopping for food	• Packing for a trip • Getting to the airport • At the airport • On board an airplane	• Parts of the body • Daily routine • Backpacking and camping
CULTURE	• Shopping centers, markets, and food stands in Spain and Latin America • Shopping in Spanish-speaking countries compared to the United States • Indigenous open-air markets • Moorish influence in Spanish architecture	• Airports in Spain and Latin America • Plaza de Armas in Quito, Ecuador • Air travel in South America • Nazca lines in Peru • A beach in Palma de Mallorca • **Casa Rosada** in Buenos Aires • San Juan, Puerto Rico	• Backpackers in the Spanish-speaking world • Camping in the Spanish-speaking world • Nerja Beach, Spain • Petrohue Falls, Chile • Hostals in the Spanish-speaking world
FUNCTIONS	• How to talk about buying clothes • How to talk about buying foods	• How to talk about packing for a trip and getting to the airport • How to speak with a ticket agent • How to buy an airplane ticket • How to talk about being on an airplane	• How to talk about your daily routine • How to talk about camping • How to talk about the contents of your backpack
GRAMMAR	• Numbers over 100 • The present tense of **saber** and **conocer** • Comparatives and superlatives • Demonstrative adjectives and pronouns	• Verbs that have **g** in the **yo** form of the present tense • The present progressive tense	• Reflexive verbs • Commands with **favor de**

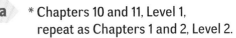

Nota * Chapters 10 and 11, Level 1, repeat as Chapters 1 and 2, Level 2.

LEVEL 2	Repaso	Chapter 1*	Chapter 2*
TOPICS	• Friends, students, and relatives • At home and at school • Personality and health • Sports • Shopping for food and clothing • Summer and winter vacations and activities	• Packing for a trip • Getting to the airport • At the airport • On board an airplane 	• Parts of the body • Daily routine • Backpacking and camping
CULTURE	• Plaza Mayor, Madrid, Spain • Caracas, Venezuela • Central Market in Valencia, Spain • A beach in Gijón, Asturias • Skiing in Portillo, Chile	• Airports in Spain and Latin America • Plaza de Armas in Quito, Ecudor • Air travel in South America • Nazca lines in Peru • A beach in Palma de Mallorca • Casa Rosada in Buenos Aires • San Juan, Puerto Rico	• Backpackers in the Spanish-speaking world • Camping in the Spanish-speaking world • Nerja Beach, Spain • Petrohue Falls, Chile • Hostals in the Spanish-speaking world
FUNCTIONS	• How to talk about friends, family, and home • How to talk about activities at home and at school • How to talk about personality, health, and general well-being • How to talk about sports • How to describe food and clothing • How to talk about vacations	• How to talk about packing for a trip and getting to the airport • How to speak with a ticket agent • How to buy an airplane ticket • How to talk about being on an airplane	• How to talk about your daily routine • How to talk about camping • How to talk about the contents of your backpack
GRAMMAR	• The verb **ser** • Nouns, articles, and adjectives • The verb **tener** • Possessive adjectives • The present tense of verbs • The present tense of **ir**, **dar**, **estar** • Contractions • Uses of **ser** and **estar** • The verbs **aburrir**, **interesar**, **gustar** • The verbs **saber** and **conocer** • Comparatives and superlatives • The preterite of regular verbs • The preterite of **ir** and **ser** • Direct and indirect object pronouns	• Verbs that have **g** in the **yo** form of the present tense • The present progressive tense	• Reflexive verbs • Commands with **favor de** 

(t)David H. Brennan, (b)Andrew Payti

Nota * Chapters 1 and 2, Level 2, repeat Chapters 10 and 11, Level 1.

LEVEL 2	Chapter 3	Chapter 4	Chapter 5
TOPICS	• Train travel • Train trips in Peru and Mexico	• Restaurants and types of food • Utensils	• Various festivals • Traditional carnival costumes
CULTURE	• Atocha train station in Madrid • Plaza de la Independencia in Montevideo, Uruguay • Indigenous market in Peru • Cordoba and the Guadalquivir River • Plaza de Armas in Cuzco, Peru • Machu Picchu • The Barranca del Cobre • Panama Canal and the Panama Canal Railway • Atacama Desert	• Restaurants in Spain and Latin America • **Paella**, a typical Spanish dish • **El casado**, a typical Costa Rican dish • San Telmo and Recoleta, unique neighborhoods of Buenos Aires • Sidewalk cafés in the Spanish-speaking world • Fruit stand in Tepoztlan, Mexico • Famous Argentine beef • Spanish tapas	• Festivals and celebrations in the Spanish-speaking world • Patron saints • **Papel picado** • The use of the piñata in Hispanic celebrations • **El Día de San Juan** • **El Día de los Muertos** • **La Navidad** and **Hanuka** • New Year's Eve in Madrid • Parade in Mexico City
FUNCTIONS	• How to use vocabulary related to train travel • How to discuss interesting train trips in Peru and Mexico	• How to order and pay for a meal at a restaurant • How to identify more foods • How to identify eating utensils and dishes • How to discuss restaurants in Spain and Latin America	• How to talk about several Hispanic holidays • How to compare holidays in the U.S. with those in some Spanish-speaking countries
GRAMMAR	• The preterite of irregular verbs • The verb **decir** • Prepositional pronouns	• Stem-changing verbs in the present and preterite • Adjectives of nationality • The passive voice with **se**	• Regular and irregular forms of the imperfect tense

LEVEL 2	Chapter 6	Chapter 7	Chapter 8
TOPICS	• Computers and e-mail • Cameras and MP3s • Making and receiving phone calls • Technology in Hispanic countries	• Checking into hotels or hostels • Hotels and hostels in Spanish-speaking countries	• City life • Transportation in the city • Country life • Farm animals
CULTURE	• Park Güell in Barcelona, Spain • Buenos Aires, Argentina • Antigua, Guatemala • An **encierro** in San Sebastian de los Reyes, Spain • Public telephones in the Spanish-speaking world	• Guadalajara, Mexico • Indigenous market in Otavalo, Ecuador • Hotel overlooking Lake Atitlan in Guatemala • The Camino de Santiago in Navarre, Spain • Santiago de Compostela in Spain • Arica, Chile • Market in Catarina, Nicaragua	• Avenida 9 de Julio in Buenos Aires, Argentina • Plaza de la Independencia in Montevideo, Uruguay • Panama City, Panama • Bosque de Chapultepec in Mexico City • A cattle ranch in Argentina • Hispanic influence in Miami, Florida • Taquile Island in Lake Titicaca, Peru
FUNCTIONS	• How to talk about computers, the Internet, and e-mail • How to talk about digital cameras and MP3 players • How to make and receive phone calls • How to discuss technology in Hispanic countries	• How to check into a hotel or hostel • How to ask for things you may need while at a hotel or hostel • How to discuss hotel stays in Latin America and Spain	• How to describe life in the city • How to describe life in the country • How to discuss the differences between the city and the country in Latin America
GRAMMAR	• The preterite and imperfect tenses	• The present perfect tense • Double object pronouns	• The future tense • Object pronouns with infinitives and gerunds

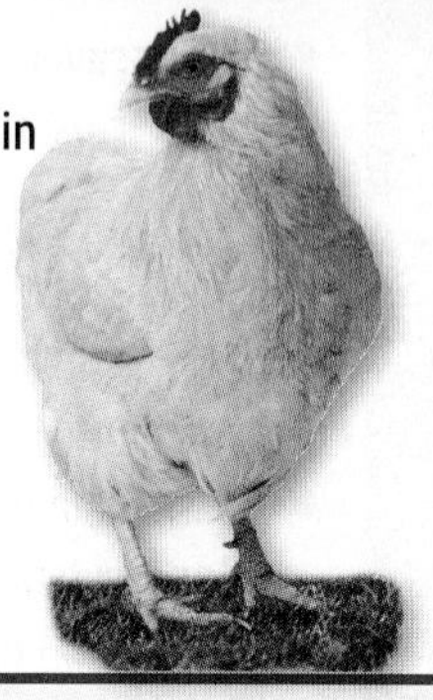

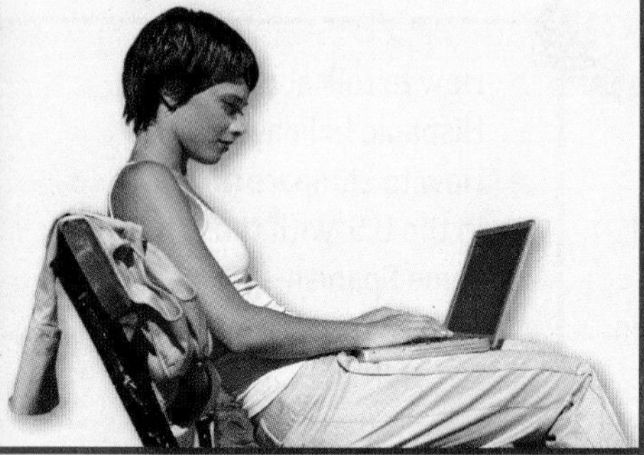

LEVEL 2	Chapter 9	Chapter 10*	Chapter 11*
TOPICS	• Driving on the highway • Driving in the city • Cars • Gas stations	• The kitchen • Cooking • Types of food • Using a recipe	• Parts of the body • Exercise and physical activity • Minor medical problems • The emergency room
CULTURE	• The **Gran Vía** in Madrid, Spain • Traffic signs • Independence Monument in Mexico City • Pan American Highway • Traffic in Spanish-speaking countries • Roller coaster in Chapultepec Park in Mexico City	• Recipe for **paella** and paella utensils • Various foods from Spanish-speaking countries • Recipe for **sopa de pollo** • The metric system • Good nutrition • Recipe for **arroz con pollo** • Recipe for **la ropa vieja**	• Hospitals in the Spanish-speaking world • Physical activity and good health • *Doctors Without Borders*
FUNCTIONS	• How to talk about cars and driving • How to give directions • How to discuss the Pan American Highway	• How to talk about foods and food preparation • How to talk about a Hispanic recipe	• How to identify more parts of the body • How to talk about exercise • How to talk about having a minor accident and a trip to the emergency room • How to discuss physical fitness
GRAMMAR	• **Tú** affirmative commands • The conditional	• The subjunctive • Formal commands • Negative informal commands	• The subjunctive with impersonal expressions • **Ojalá**, **quizás**, **tal vez** • The subjunctive of stem-changing verbs • The comparison of like things

Nota * Chapters 10 and 11, Level 2, repeat as Chapters 1 and 2, Level 3.

LEVEL 3	Repaso	Chapter 1*	Chapter 2*
TOPICS	• At home and at school • Sports and daily routine • Vacations • Shopping and celebrations • City and country • Hotels and restaurants	• The kitchen • Cooking • Types of food • Using a recipe	• Parts of the body • Exercise and physical activity • Minor medical problems • The emergency room
CULTURE	• School in Cienfuegos, Cuba • A school in San Pablo, Ecuador • Skateboarding in Barcelona, Spain • A soccer game in Valparaiso, Chile • Puerto de la Cruz, Tenerife, Canary Islands • Ushuaia, Argentina	• Recipe for **paella** and paella utensils • Various foods from Spanish-speaking countries • Recipe for **sopa de pollo** • The metric system • Good nutrition • Recipe for **arroz con pollo** • Recipe for **la ropa vieja**	• Hospitals in the Spanish-speaking world • Physical activity and good health • *Doctors Without Borders*
FUNCTIONS	• How to discuss home and school • How to discuss sports and daily routine • How to discuss vacations and summer and winter activities • How to discuss shopping and celebrations • How to discuss city and country life • How to discuss hotels and restaurants	• How to talk about foods and food preparation • How to talk about a Hispanic recipe	• How to identify more parts of the body • How to talk about exercise • How to talk about having a minor accident and a trip to the emergency room • How to discuss physical fitness
GRAMMAR	• Present tense of regular and irregular verbs • The verbs **ir**, **dar**, **estar** • Preterite and imperfect of regular and irregular verbs • The verbs **interesar**, **aburrir**, **gustar** • Indirect and direct object pronouns • Uses of the preterite and imperfect • The present perfect tense • Regular and irregular past participles • Double object pronouns	• The subjunctive • Formal commands • Negative informal commands	• The subjunctive with impersonal expressions • **Ojalá**, **quizás**, **tal vez** • The subjunctive of stem-changing verbs • The comparison of like things

Nota * Chapters 1 and 2, Level 3, repeat Chapters 10 and 11, Level 2.

LEVEL 3

	Chapter 3	Chapter 4	Chapter 5
TOPICS	• Weddings • Baptisms • Birthdays • Funerals	• The hair salon • Washing clothes • Mailing letters and packages • The bank	• Courtesies • Manners
CULTURE	• **Quinceañera** celebrations • Wedding ceremonies and customs throughout the Spanish-speaking world • Recoleta cemetery in Buenos Aires, Argentina • Baptism ceremonies throughout the Spanish-speaking world • Atacama Desert • Mariachis • Madrid, Spain • *El hermano ausente en la cena de Pascua* by Abraham Valdelomar	• Palacio de Telecomunicaciones in Madrid, Spain • European currency • ATMs in Spanish-speaking countries • Police officers in Málaga, Spain • Hair salons, laundromats, and banks in Spanish-speaking countries • Baños, Ecuador • A beach in Santa Marta, Colombia • *El mensajero de San Martín* by Ada María Elflein • A statue of General José de San Martín • Santiago, Chile • Plaza de España, Seville, Spain	• Typical greetings throughout Spanish-speaking countries • Typical gestures used among many Spanish speakers • Gardens at the Royal Palace in Madrid, Spain • Toledo, Spain • Segovia, Spain • *El conde Lucanor* by Don Juan Manuel • El AVE at the train station in Madrid
FUNCTIONS	• How to talk about passages of life: weddings, baptisms, birthdays, and funerals • How to read a poem by the Peruvian writer Abraham Valdelomar	• How to talk about errands • How to discuss preparing for a trip through Andalusia • How to read a short story from Argentina	• How to discuss manners • How to compare manners in Spanish-speaking countries to manners in the U.S. • How to read an excerpt from a work by the Spanish writer Don Juan Manuel
GRAMMAR	• The subjunctive to express wishes • The subjunctive to express emotions • Possessive pronouns	• The subjunctive with expressions of doubt • The subjunctive with adverbial clauses • The pluperfect, conditional perfect, and future perfect tenses	• The imperfect subjunctive • The subjunctive vs. the infinitive • Suffixes

NO SE PERMITE
EL USO DEL
MOVIL

LEVEL 3	Chapter 6	Chapter 7	Chapter 8
TOPICS	• Air travel • Train travel • Car travel and rental	• Art • Literature	• History of Latinos in the United States • Spanish speakers in the United States • Spanish-language television and press in the United States
CULTURE	• Various airports throughout the Spanish-speaking world • The Panama Canal Railway • Atocha train station in Madrid • Lake Titicaca in Bolivia • Quito, Ecuador • A trip to Bolivia • La Paz, Bolivia • *Temprano y con sol* by Emilia Pardo Bazán • La Coruña, Spain • Avila, Spain	• Frida Kahlo home and museum in Coyoacan, Mexico • Federico García Lorca • Mayan ruins in Copán, Honduras • *Las meninas* by Diego Velázquez • *El oso y el madroño* in Madrid, Spain • Don Quijote and Sancho Panza • La Boca, an artistic neighborhood in Buenos Aires • *La liberación del peón* by Diego Rivera • *Al partir* by Gertrudis de Avellaneda • Havana, Cuba	• Street festivals in the U.S. honoring Latino heritage and culture • César Chávez • Univisión and Telemundo • Hernando de Soto • Francisco Pizarro, conqueror of Peru • A statue of Ponce de León in St. Augustine, Florida • San Juan, Puerto Rico • *A Julia de Burgos* by Julia de Burgos • Capitolio Nacional in Havana, Cuba • A plaza in Guadalajara, Mexico • Arch of the Revolution, Mexico City
FUNCTIONS	• How to discuss several modes of travel • How to talk about a trip to Bolivia • How to read a short story by the Spanish author Emilia Pardo Bazán	• How to discuss fine art and literature • How to talk about a mural by the Mexican artist Diego Rivera • How to read a sonnet by the Spaniard Federico García Lorca • How to read a poem by the Cuban poet Gertrudis de Avellaneda	• How to talk about the history of Spanish speakers in the U.S. • How to discuss the experience of Latinos in the U.S. • How to read a poem by the Puerto Rican poet Julia de Burgos
GRAMMAR	• The subjunctive with conjunctions of time • The subjunctive to express commands and advice • Irregular nouns	• The present perfect and pluperfect subjunctive • **Si** clauses • Adverbs ending in -**mente**	• The subjunctive with **aunque** • The subjunctive with -**quiera** • Definite and indefinite articles (special uses) • Apocopated adjectives

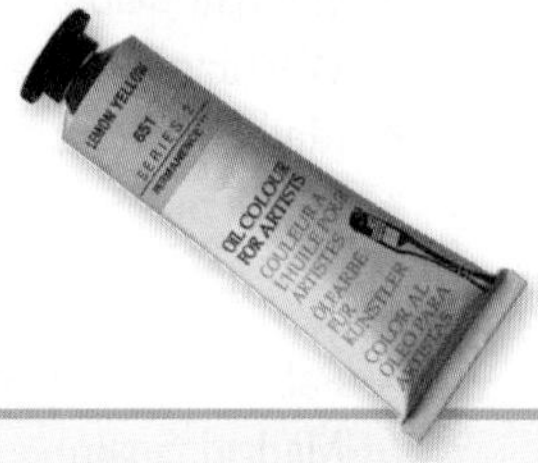

LEVEL 3	Chapter 9	Chapter 10
TOPICS	• Food and food preparation • History of food	• Careers • Job applications and interviews • Second languages and the job market
CULTURE	• Various foods popular throughout Spain and Latin America • Olive groves in Andalusia • History of the potato and the tomato • Taco de carne • History of spices • Arabic influence in Latin cuisine • *Las aceitunas* by Lope de Rueda	• Mexico City, Mexico • Plaza de Armas in Quito, Ecuador • Mayan ruins at Chichén Itzá • Mezquita de Córdoba and other Arabic influences throughout Spain • *El hijo* by Horacio Quiroga • Panama City, Panama • A library in Barranquilla, Colombia
FUNCTIONS	• How to identify more foods • How to describe food preparation • How to discuss the history of foods from Europe and the Americas • How to read an excerpt from a work by the Spanish writer Lope de Rueda	• How to talk about professions and occupations • How to have a job interview • How to discuss the importance of learning a second language • How to read a short story by the Uruguayan writer Horacio Quiroga
GRAMMAR	• Passive voice • Relative pronouns • Expressions of time with **hace** and **hacía**	• **Por** and **para** • The subjunctive with relative clauses

LEVEL 4	Chapter 1	Chapter 2
TOPICS	• The geography of Spain • The history of Spain • Spanish culture	• The geography of Ecuador, Peru, and Bolivia • The history of Ecuador, Peru, and Bolivia • The culture of Ecuador, Peru, and Bolivia
CULTURE	• The invasion of the Moors • Basque country • The Catholic Kings • Christopher Columbus • Roman influence and architecture • Spanish foods • Sevilla, Spain • Plaza Mayor in Trujillo, Spain • Valencia, Spain • Palma de Mallorca, Spain • *Canción del pirata* by José de Espronceda • *La primavera besaba* by Antonio Machado • *El Quijote*	• Quipu, an Incan accounting system • Geography of Peru and Ecuador • Land-locked Bolivia • The Andes Mountains • The Incas • Machu Picchu • Francisco Pizarro, conqueror of the Incan Empire • South American liberators Simón Bolívar and José de San Martín • Otavalo market in Ecuador • Food in Ecuador, Peru, and Bolivia • *¡Quién sabe!* by José Santos Chocano • *Los comentarios reales* by the Inca Garcilaso de la Vega
FUNCTIONS	• How to express past actions • How to refer to specific things 	• How to describe habitual past actions • How to talk about past events • How to describe actions in progress • How to make comparisons
GRAMMAR	• Preterite of regular verbs • Preterite of stem-changing verbs • Preterite of irregular verbs • Nouns and articles	• The imperfect of regular and irregular verbs • The imperfect and the preterite to describe the past and to indicate past actions • The progressive tenses • The comparative and superlative • Comparison of equality

Emma Lee/Life File/Getty Images

LEVEL 4	Chapter 3	Chapter 4
TOPICS	• The geography of Chile, Argentina, Paraguay, and Uruguay • The history of Chile, Argentina, Paraguay, and Uruguay • The culture of Chile, Argentina, Paraguay, and Uruguay	• The geography of Central American countries • The history of Central American countries • The culture of Central American countries
CULTURE	• Atacama Desert • Patagonia and Tierra del Fuego • Guarani • Argentine gauchos and the pampas • Evita and Juan Perón • Ushuaia, Argentina • Argentine beef, Chilean seafood • Casa Rosada in Buenos Aires • *Martín Fierro* by José Hernández • *Historia de dos cachorros de coatí y dos cachorros de hombre* by Horacio Quiroga	• The Central American isthmus • The Mayans • Capital cities of Central America • Tikal, Guatemala, largest ancient ruined city of the Maya civilization • Copán, Honduras, and its famous stelae • Islas de San Blas in Panama • Central American cuisine • *Lo fatal* by Rubén Darío • *Canción de otoño en primavera* by Rubén Darío • *Mis primeros versos* by Rubén Darío
FUNCTIONS	• How to describe actions in the present • How to state location and origin • How to refer to people and things already mentioned • How to express surprise, interest, and annoyance • How to express affirmative and negative ideas	• How to form the present subjunctive • How to express necessity, possibility, and doubt using the subjunctive • How to express emotion using the subjunctive • How to give commands
GRAMMAR	• The present tense of regular and irregular verbs • **Ser** and **estar** • Object pronouns • **Gustar** and verbs like **gustar** • Affirmative and negative expressions	• The present subjunctive • Uses of the subjunctive • Direct and indirect commands

LEVEL 4	Chapter 5	Chapter 6
TOPICS	• The geography of Mexico • The history of Mexico • The culture of Mexico	• The geography of Cuba, Puerto Rico, and the Dominican Republic • The history of Cuba, Puerto Rico, and the Dominican Republic • The culture of Cuba, Puerto Rico, and the Dominican Republic
CULTURE	• Indigenous civilizations • Hernán Cortés and the conquest of the Aztec Empire • September 16, Mexican Independence Day • Cinco de Mayo • Mexican Revolution of 1910 • El Zócalo • Teotihuacán • Chichén Itzá • Mexican cuisine • Bosque de Chapultepec • *Para entonces* by Manuel Gutiérrez Nájera • *Historia verdadera de la conquista de la Nueva España* by Bernal Díaz del Castillo	• Mountain ranges in Cuba, Puerto Rico, and the Dominican Republic • The climate of the Greater Antilles • The exploration of Christopher Columbus • The Taino culture • Fidel Castro • José Martí • Santo Domingo • Havana, Cuba • Caribbean food • Caves of Camuy • *Versos sencillos* by José Martí • *El ave y el nido* by Salomé Ureña • *Perico Paciencia* by Manuel A. Alonso
FUNCTIONS	• How to express what people do for themselves • How to tell what was done or what is done in general • How to express what you have done recently • How to describe actions completed prior to other actions • How to express opinions and feelings about what has happened • How to place object pronouns in a sentence	• How to express future events • How to express what you will have done and what you would have done • How to refer to specific things • How to express ownership 
GRAMMAR	• Reflexive verbs • Passive voice • Present perfect • Pluperfect • Present perfect subjunctive • Object pronouns	• The future and conditional • The future perfect and conditional perfect • Demonstrative pronouns • Possessive pronouns • Relative pronouns

LEVEL 4	Chapter 7	Chapter 8
TOPICS	• The geography of Venezuela and Colombia • The history of Venezuela and Colombia • The culture of Venezuela and Colombia	• Latinos in the United States, past and present • Your own ethnicity
CULTURE	• Angel Falls in Venezuela • Orinoco River • Petroleum industry • Four geographic regions of Colombia • Simón Bolívar and the fight for independence • Typical foods of Venezuela and Colombia • Cartagena, Colombia • *Los maderos de San Juan* by José Asunción Silva • *Cien años de soledad* by Gabriel García Márquez	• Various street festivals and parades celebrating Latinos in the U.S. • History of the term **hispano** • Hispanic celebrities in the U.S. • Hispanic cuisine in the U.S. • Latin and Spanish architectural influences • San Juan, Puerto Rico • St. Augustine, Florida • San Antonio, Texas • *Desde la nieve* by Eugenio Florit • *El caballo mago* by Sabine Ulibarrí
FUNCTIONS	• How to form the imperfect subjunctive • How to use the subjunctive in adverbial clauses • How to express *although* and *perhaps* • How to use **por** and **para**	• How to form the pluperfect subjunctive • How to discuss contrary-to-fact situations • How to use definite and indefinite articles
GRAMMAR	• The imperfect subjunctive • The subjunctive with adverbs of time • The subjunctive with **aunque** • The subjunctive with **quizá(s)**, **tal vez**, **ojalá (que)** • **Por** and **para**	• Pluperfect subjunctive • Clauses with **si** • Subjunctive in adverbial clauses • Shortened forms of adjectives • Definite and indefinite articles

The What, Why, and How of Reading

Reading is a learned process. Your students have been reading in their first language for a long time and now their challenge is to transfer what they know to enable themselves to read fluently in Spanish. Reading will help them improve their vocabulary, cultural knowledge, and productive skills in Spanish. Students are probably familiar with the reading strategies in the chart. Have students review these strategies and apply them as they continue to improve their Spanish reading skills.

What Is It?	Why It's Important	How To Do It
Preview Previewing is looking over a selection before you read.	Previewing lets you begin to see what you already know and what you'll need to know. It helps you set a purpose for reading.	Look at the title, illustrations, headings, captions, and graphics. Look at how ideas are organized. Ask questions about the text.
Skim Skimming is looking over an entire selection quickly to get a general idea of what the piece is about.	Skimming tells you what a selection is about. If the selection you skim isn't what you're looking for, you won't need to read the entire piece.	Read the title of the selection and quickly look over the entire piece. Read headings and captions and maybe part of the first paragraph to get a general idea of the selection's content.
Scan Scanning is glancing quickly over a selection in order to find specific information.	Scanning helps you pinpoint information quickly. It saves you time when you have a number of selections to look at.	As you move your eyes quickly over the lines of text, look for key words or phrases that will help you locate the information you're looking for.
Predict Predicting is taking an educated guess about what will happen in a selection.	Predicting gives you a reason to read. You want to find out if your prediction comes true, don't you? As you read, adjust or change your prediction if it doesn't fit what you learn.	Combine what you already know about an author or subject with what you learned in your preview to guess what will be included in the text.
Summarize Summarizing is stating the main ideas of a selection in your own words and in a logical sequence.	Summarizing shows whether you've understood something. It teaches you to rethink what you've read and to separate main ideas from supporting information.	Ask yourself: What is this selection about? Answer who, what, where, when, why, and how? Put that information in a logical order.

What Is It?	Why It's Important	How To Do It
Clarify Clarifying is looking at difficult sections of text in order to clear up what is confusing.	Authors will often build ideas one on another. If you don't clear up a confusing passage, you may not understand main ideas or information that comes later.	Go back and reread a confusing section more slowly. Look up words you don't know. Ask questions about what you don't understand. Sometimes you may want to read on to see if further information helps you.
Question Questioning is asking yourself whether information in a selection is important. Questioning is also regularly asking yourself whether you've understood what you've read.	When you ask questions as you read, you're reading strategically. As you answer your questions, you're making sure that you'll get the gist of a text.	Have a running conversation with yourself as you read. Keep asking yourself: Is this idea important? Why? Do I understand what this is about?
Visualize Visualizing is picturing a writer's ideas or descriptions in your mind's eye.	Visualizing is one of the best ways to understand and remember information in fiction, nonfiction, and informational texts.	Carefully read how a writer describes a person, place, or thing. Then ask yourself: What would this look like? Can I see how the steps in this process would work?
Monitor Comprehension Monitoring your comprehension means thinking about whether you understand what you are reading.	The whole point of reading is to understand a piece of text. When you don't understand a selection, you're not really reading it.	Keep asking yourself questions about main ideas, characters, and events. When you can't answer a question, review, read more slowly, or ask someone to help you.

The What, Why, and How of Reading

What Is It?	Why It's Important	How To Do It
Identify Sequence Identifying sequence is finding the logical order of ideas or events.	In a work of fiction, events usually happen in chronological order. With nonfiction, understanding the logical sequence of ideas in a piece helps you follow a writer's train of thought. You'll remember ideas better when you know the logical order a writer uses.	Think about what the author is trying to do. Tell a story? Explain how something works? Present information? Look for clues or signal words that might point to time order, steps in a process, or order of importance.
Determine the Main Idea Determining an author's main idea is finding the most important thought in a paragraph or selection.	Finding main ideas gets you ready to summarize. You also discover an author's purpose for writing when you find the main ideas in a selection.	Think about what you know about the author and the topic. Look for how the author organizes ideas. Then look for the one idea that all of the sentences in a paragraph or all of the paragraphs in a selection are about.
Respond Responding is telling what you like, dislike, or find surprising or interesting in a selection.	When you react in a personal way to what you read, you'll enjoy a selection more and remember it better.	As you read, think about how you feel about story elements or ideas in a selection. What's your reaction to the characters in a story? What grabs your attention as you read?
Connect Connecting means linking what you read to events in your own life or to other selections you've read.	You'll "get into" your reading and recall information and ideas better by connecting events, emotions, and characters to your own life.	Ask yourself: Do I know someone like this? Have I ever felt this way? What else have I read that is like this selection?
Review Reviewing is going back over what you've read to remember what's important and to organize ideas so you'll recall them later.	Reviewing is especially important when you have new ideas and a lot of information to remember.	Filling in a graphic organizer, such as a chart or diagram, as you read helps you organize information. These study aids will help you review later.
Interpret Interpreting is using your own understanding of the world to decide what the events or ideas in a selection mean.	Every reader constructs meaning on the basis of what he or she understands about the world. Finding meaning as you read is all about interacting with the text.	Think about what you already know about yourself and the world. Ask yourself: What is the author really trying to say here? What larger idea might these events be about?
Infer Inferring is using your reason and experience to guess what an author does not come right out and say.	Making inferences is a large part of finding meaning in a selection. Inferring helps you look more deeply at characters and points you toward the theme or message in a selection.	Look for clues the author provides. Notice descriptions, dialogue, events, and relationships that might tell you something the author wants you to know.

What Is It?	Why It's Important	How To Do It
Draw Conclusions Drawing conclusions is using a number of pieces of information to make a general statement about people, places, events, and ideas.	Drawing conclusions helps you find connections between ideas and events. It's another tool to help you see the larger picture.	Notice details about characters, ideas, and events. Then make a general statement on the basis of these details. For example, a character's actions might lead you to conclude that he or she is kind.
Analyze Analyzing is looking at separate parts of a selection in order to understand the entire selection.	Analyzing helps you look critically at a piece of writing. When you analyze a selection, you discover its theme or message, and you learn the author's purpose for writing.	To analyze a story, think about what the author is saying through the characters, setting, and plot. To analyze nonfiction, look at the organization and main ideas. What do they suggest?
Synthesize Synthesizing is combining ideas to create something new. You may synthesize to reach a new understanding or you may actually create a new ending to a story.	Synthesizing helps you move to a higher level of thinking. Creating something new on your own goes beyond remembering what you learned from someone else.	Think about the ideas or information you've learned in a selection. Ask yourself: Do I understand something more than the main ideas here? Can I create something else from what I now know?
Evaluate Evaluating is making a judgment or forming an opinion about something you read. You can evaluate a character, an author's craft, or the value of the information in a text.	Evaluating helps you become a wise reader. For example, when you judge whether an author is qualified to speak about a topic or whether the author's points make sense, you can avoid being misled by what you read.	As you read, ask yourself questions such as: Is this character realistic and believable? Is this author qualified to write on this subject? Is this author biased? Does this author present opinions as facts?

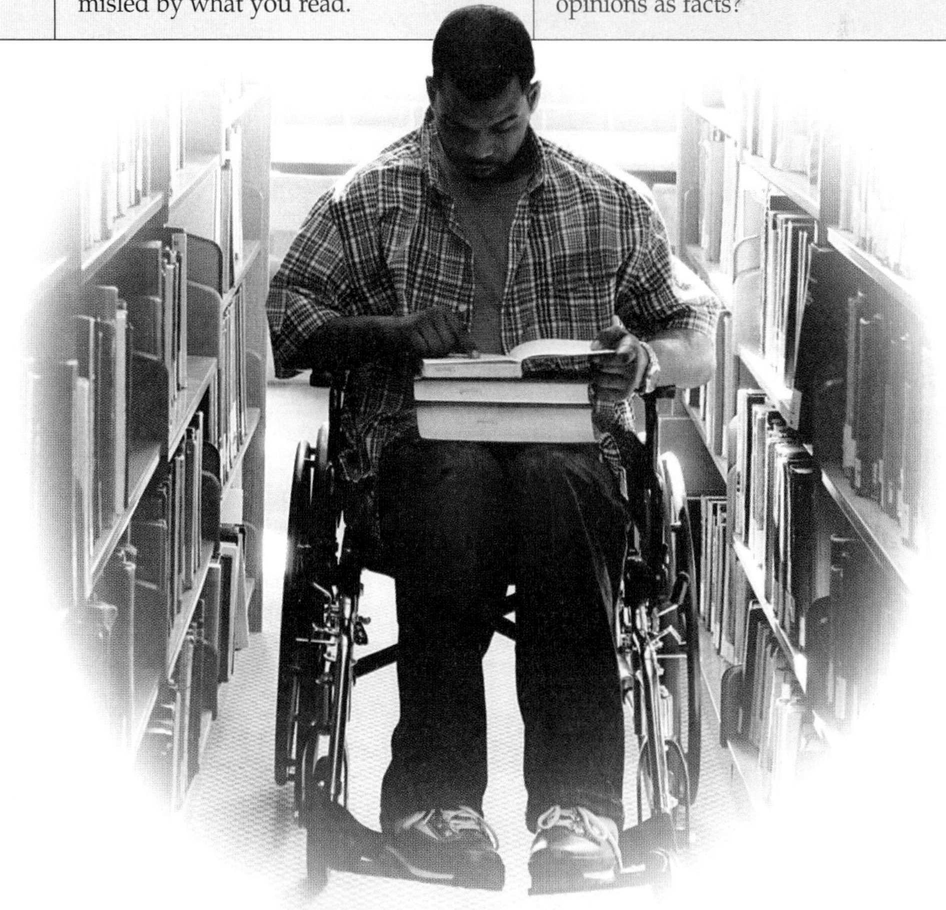

Plan for teaching the chapter.

Preview tells you the theme and content of the chapter.

Spotlight on Culture expands on the comparison presented in **Aquí y Allí** and often gives you further information about the chapter opener photograph.

CAPÍTULO 5

Preview

In this chapter, students will learn the vocabulary they need to discuss some very important holidays celebrated in Spain and Latin America. They will also learn the regular and irregular forms of the imperfect tense. This will be reinforced as students read about the memories of some Latino friends who discuss how they spent different holidays as children in their home countries.

Pacing

It is important to note that once you reach **¡Bravo!** in the chapter, there is no more new material for the students to learn. The rest of the chapter recycles what has already been covered. The suggested pacing listed here leaves two to three days for review, assessment, and enrichment activities such as the chapter project.

Vocabulario 1	1–2 days
Vocabulario 2	1–2 days
Gramática	2–3 days
Conversación	1 day
Lectura cultural	1 day
Lectura Un poco más	1 day

134

CAPÍTULO 5

¿Qué se celebra?

Aquí y Allí

El mundo hispano es famoso por sus ferias y fiestas. Hay ferias para celebrar muchas ocasiones. Algunas duran solamente un día y otras una semana entera. ¿Hay ferias y fiestas donde tú vives? ¿Qué celebran o conmemoran? ¿Tienes una fiesta favorita? ¿Cuál es?

Objetivos

You will:

- talk about several Hispanic holidays
- compare holidays that you celebrate with those in some Spanish-speaking countries

You will use:

- regular and irregular forms of the imperfect tense

Los jóvenes están tomando parte en las celebraciones para Carnaval en Puerto Plata en la República Dominicana

134 **Go Online!** connectED.mcgraw-hill.com Audio Video Práctica Repaso Diversiones eScape ePals

ciento treinta y cinco 135

Go Online!

- **Audio** Listen to spoken Spanish.
- **Video** Watch and learn about the Spanish-speaking world.
- **Práctica** Practice your skills.
- **Repaso** Review what you've learned.
- **Diversiones** Go beyond the classroom.
- **eScape** Read about current events in the Spanish-speaking world.
- **Interactive Whiteboard** Present or practice with interactive whiteboard activities.
- **Assessment** Check student progress.
- **ePals** Connect with Spanish-speaking students around the world.

CAPÍTULO 5

SPOTLIGHT ON CULTURE

Cultural Comparison
In this chapter, students will learn about specific Hispanic holidays such as the Day of the Dead, Patron Saint's Day, etc. They will also learn about Christmas, Hanukkah, and New Year's Day celebrations, noting both similarities and differences in the ways these holidays are celebrated across cultures.

Cultural Snapshot
Carnaval is a very happy celebration that takes place just before Ash Wednesday in preparation for the Lenten fasting that starts on Ash Wednesday. Probably the most noted **Carnaval** festivities are those in La Habana and Rio de Janeiro, followed by the rest of the Caribbean and New Orleans. This is not to say **Carnaval** festivities don't also take place in many other cities.

135

Pacing suggests daily scheduling options to help you budget your time.

Introduce the chapter theme.

Present provides suggestions about how you can make the most out of the photographs and information in **Introducción al tema.**

Questions are suggested to increase students' cultural awareness and to give them practice speaking.

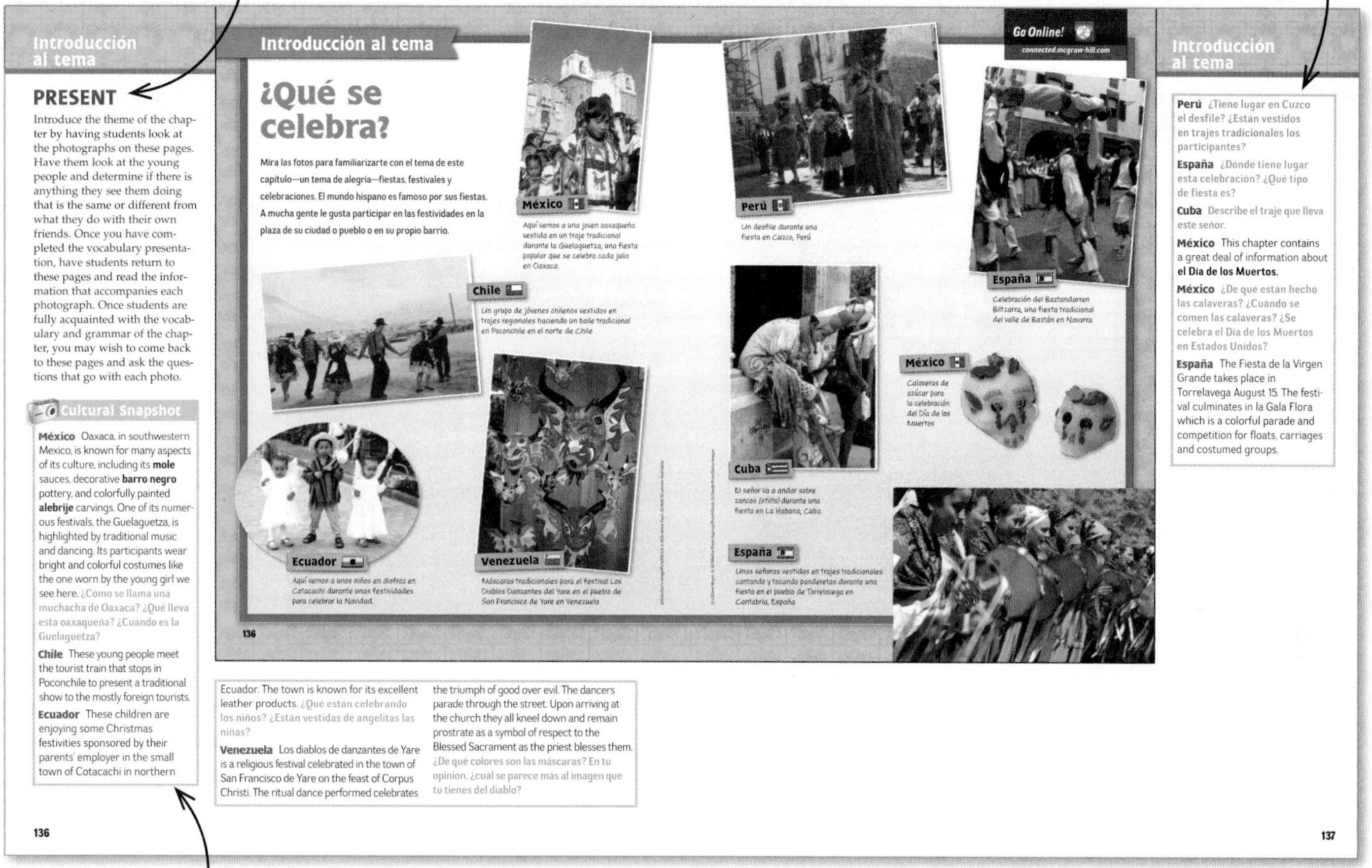

Introducción al tema

PRESENT

Introduce the theme of the chapter by having students look at the photographs on these pages. Have them look at the young people and determine if there is anything they see them doing that is the same or different from what they do with their own friends. Once you have completed the vocabulary presentation, have students return to these pages and read the information that accompanies each photograph. Once students are fully acquainted with the vocabulary and grammar of the chapter, you may wish to come back to these pages and ask the questions that go with each photo.

Cultural Snapshot

México Oaxaca, in southwestern Mexico, is known for many aspects of its culture, including its **mole** sauces, decorative **barro negro** pottery, and colorfully painted **alebrije** carvings. One of its numerous festivals, the Guelaguetza, is highlighted by traditional music and dancing. Its participants wear bright and colorful costumes like the one worn by the young girl we see here. ¿Como se llama una muchacha de Oaxaca? ¿Qué lleva esta oaxaqueña? ¿Cuándo es la Guelaguetza?

Chile These young people meet the tourist train that stops in Poconchile to present a traditional show to the mostly foreign tourists.

Ecuador These children are enjoying some Christmas festivities sponsored by their parents' employer in the small town of Cotacachi in northern Ecuador. The town is known for its excellent leather products. ¿Qué están celebrando los niños? ¿Están vestidas de angelitas las niñas?

Venezuela Los diablos de danzantes de Yare is a religious festival celebrated in the town of San Francisco de Yare on the feast of Corpus Christi. The ritual dance performed celebrates the triumph of good over evil. The dancers parade through the street. Upon arriving at the church they all kneel down and remain prostrate as a symbol of respect to the Blessed Sacrament as the priest blesses them. ¿De qué colores son las máscaras? En tu opinión, ¿cuál se parece más al imagen que tú tienes del diablo?

Introducción al tema

¿Qué se celebra?

Mira las fotos para familiarizarte con el tema de este capítulo—un tema de alegría—fiestas, festivales y celebraciones. El mundo hispano es famoso por sus fiestas. A mucha gente le gusta participar en las festividades en la plaza de su ciudad o pueblo o en su propio barrio.

México Aquí vemos a una joven oaxaqueña vestida en un traje tradicional durante la Guelaguetza, una fiesta popular que se celebra cada julio en Oaxaca.

Chile Un grupo de jóvenes chilenos vestidos en trajes regionales haciendo un baile tradicional en Poconchile en el norte de Chile

Ecuador Aquí vemos a unos niños en disfraz en Cotacachi durante unas festividades para celebrar la Navidad.

Venezuela Máscaras tradicionales para el festival Los Diablos Danzantes del Yare en el pueblo de San Francisco de Yare en Venezuela

Perú Un desfile durante una fiesta en Cuzco, Perú

Go Online! connected.mcgraw-hill.com

España Celebración del Baztandarren Biltzarra, una fiesta tradicional del valle de Baztán en Navarra

México Calaveras de azúcar para la celebración del Día de los Muertos

Cuba El señor va a andar sobre zancos (*stilts*) durante una fiesta en La Habana, Cuba.

España Unas señoras vestidas en trajes tradicionales cantando y tocando panderetas durante una fiesta en el pueblo de Torrelavega en Cantabria, España

Introducción al tema

Perú ¿Tiene lugar en Cuzco el desfile? ¿Están vestidos en trajes tradicionales los participantes?

España ¿Dónde tiene lugar esta celebración? ¿Qué tipo de fiesta es?

Cuba Describe el traje que lleva este señor.

México This chapter contains a great deal of information about **el Día de los Muertos.**

México ¿De qué están hecho las calaveras? ¿Cuándo se comen las calaveras? ¿Se celebra el Día de los Muertos en Estados Unidos?

España The Fiesta de la Virgen Grande takes place in Torrelavega August 15. The festival culminates in la Gala Flora which is a colorful parade and competition for floats, carriages and costumed groups.

136 137

Cultural Snapshot gives you additional information about the cultural photos.

Use helpful suggestions to present and practice the new vocabulary.

Quick Start provides a brief check of previously taught material as a way to begin the class session.

Resources lists the tools you will need to teach, practice, and assess each section of the chapter.

Differentiation offers alternate activities to meet the diverse learning styles and needs of your students.

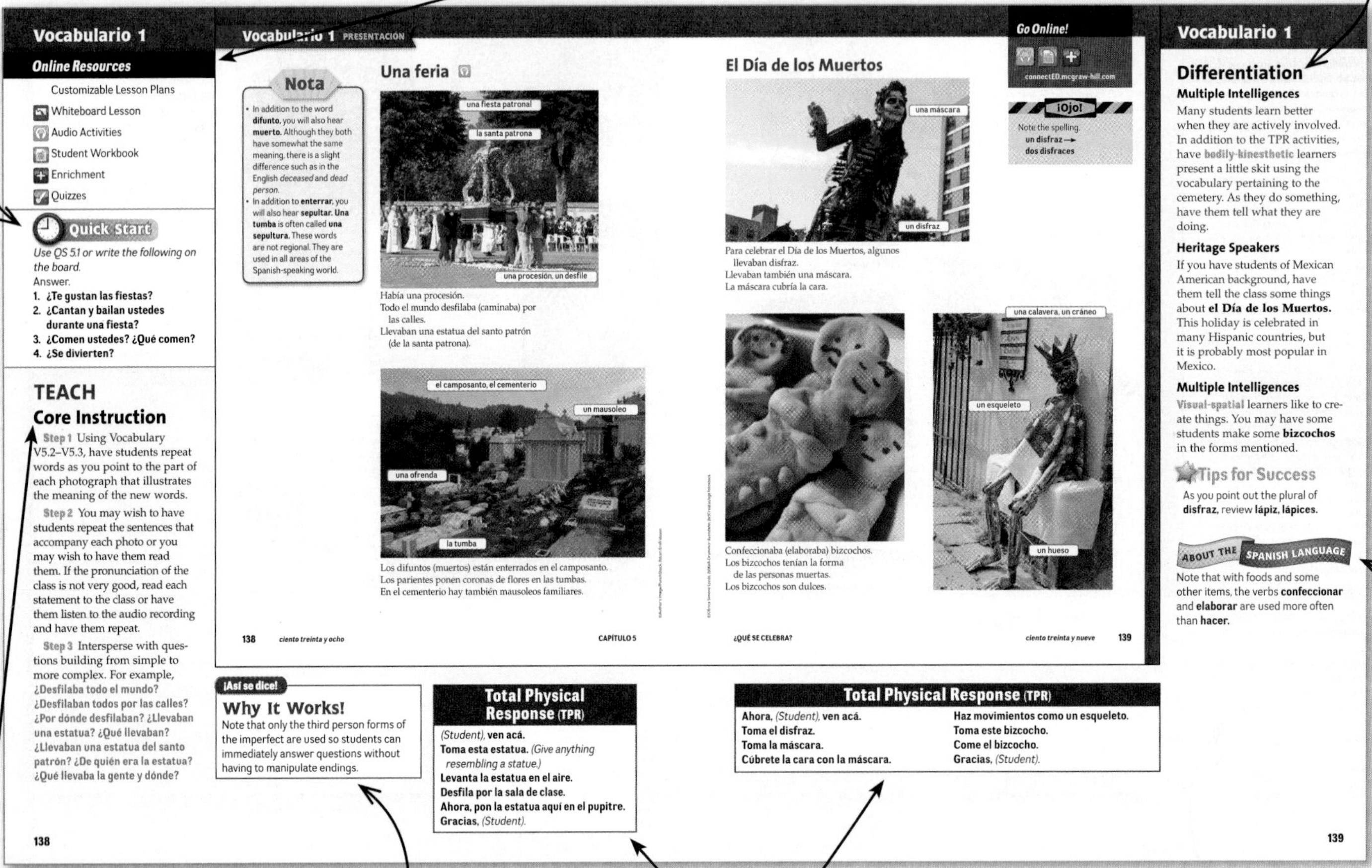

Vocabulario 1

Online Resources

- Customizable Lesson Plans
- Whiteboard Lesson
- Audio Activities
- Student Workbook
- Enrichment
- Quizzes

Quick Start

Use QS 5.1 or write the following on the board.
Answer.

1. **¿Te gustan las fiestas?**
2. **¿Cantan y bailan ustedes durante una fiesta?**
3. **¿Comen ustedes? ¿Qué comen?**
4. **¿Se divierten?**

TEACH

Core Instruction

Step 1 Using Vocabulary V5.2–V5.3, have students repeat words as you point to the part of each photograph that illustrates the meaning of the new words.

Step 2 You may wish to have students repeat the sentences that accompany each photo or you may wish to have them read them. If the pronunciation of the class is not very good, read each statement to the class or have them listen to the audio recording and have them repeat.

Step 3 Intersperse with questions building from simple to more complex. For example, **¿Desfilaba todo el mundo? ¿Desfilaban todos por las calles? ¿Por dónde desfilaban? ¿Llevaban una estatua? ¿Qué llevaban? ¿Llevaban una estatua del santo patrón? ¿De quién era la estatua? ¿Qué llevaba la gente y dónde?**

Vocabulario 1 PRESENTACIÓN

Nota

- In addition to the word **difunto**, you will also hear **muerto**. Although they both have somewhat the same meaning, there is a slight difference such as in the English *deceased* and *dead person*.
- In addition to **enterrar**, you will also hear **sepultar. Una tumba** is often called **una sepultura**. These words are not regional. They are used in all areas of the Spanish-speaking world.

Una feria

una fiesta patronal
la santa patrona
una procesión, un desfile

Había una procesión.
Todo el mundo desfilaba (caminaba) por las calles.
Llevaban una estatua del santo patrón (de la santa patrona).

el camposanto, el cementerio
un mausoleo
una ofrenda
la tumba

Los difuntos (muertos) están enterrados en el camposanto.
Los parientes ponen coronas de flores en las tumbas.
En el cementerio hay también mausoleos familiares.

138 *ciento treinta y ocho* CAPÍTULO 5

El Día de los Muertos

una máscara
un disfraz

Para celebrar el Día de los Muertos, algunos llevaban disfraz.
Llevaban también una máscara.
La máscara cubría la cara.

Confeccionaba (elaboraba) bizcochos.
Los bizcochos tenían la forma de las personas muertas.
Los bizcochos son dulces.

una calavera, un cráneo
un esqueleto
un hueso

Go Online!
connectED.mcgraw-hill.com

¡Ojo!
Note the spelling.
un disfraz → dos disfraces

¿QUÉ SE CELEBRA? *ciento treinta y nueve* 139

Vocabulario 1

Differentiation

Multiple Intelligences
Many students learn better when they are actively involved. In addition to the TPR activities, have **bodily-kinesthetic** learners present a little skit using the vocabulary pertaining to the cemetery. As they do something, have them tell what they are doing.

Heritage Speakers
If you have students of Mexican American background, have them tell the class some things about **el Día de los Muertos.** This holiday is celebrated in many Hispanic countries, but it is probably most popular in Mexico.

Multiple Intelligences
Visual-spatial learners like to create things. You may have some students make some **bizcochos** in the forms mentioned.

Tips for Success
As you point out the plural of **disfraz**, review **lápiz, lápices.**

ABOUT THE SPANISH LANGUAGE
Note that with foods and some other items, the verbs **confeccionar** and **elaborar** are used more often than **hacer.**

¡Así se dice!
Why It Works!
Note that only the third person forms of the imperfect are used so students can immediately answer questions without having to manipulate endings.

Total Physical Response (TPR)

(Student), **ven acá.**
Toma esta estatua. *(Give anything resembling a statue.)*
Levanta la estatua en el aire.
Desfila por la sala de clase.
Ahora, pon la estatua aquí en el pupitre.
Gracias, *(Student).*

Total Physical Response (TPR)

Ahora, *(Student),* **ven acá.**
Toma el disfraz.
Toma la máscara.
Cúbrete la cara con la máscara.
Haz movimientos como un esqueleto.
Toma este bizcocho.
Come el bizcocho.
Gracias, *(Student).*

138 139

Core Instruction offers a clear, step-by-step guide for your presentation of the lesson.

Total Physical Response (TPR) activities engage students by having them respond to language with gestures or actions.

About the Spanish Language enriches students' vocabulary and points out nuances in the Spanish language.

Why It Works! explains the **¡Así se dice!** pedagogy at point of use so you can offer the best possible instruction to your students.

Reach your students through clear presentation of grammar.

Leveling of vocabulary and grammar activities according to difficulty helps you individualize instruction.

Gramática

Online Resources

Customizable Lesson Plans
- Whiteboard Lesson
- Audio Activities
- Video (Gramática)
- Student Workbook
- Enrichment
- Quizzes

Quick Start

Use QS 54 or write the following on the board.

Change **yo** to **nosotros**.

1. **Yo me despierto a las seis y media.**
2. **Yo me levanto enseguida.**
3. **Yo me lavo la cara.**
4. **Yo me cepillo los dientes.**
5. **Yo me acuesto a las once de la noche.**

TEACH

Core Instruction

Step 1 Read Item 1 to students.

Step 2 Write the infinitives of the verbs **leer** and **escribir** on the board. Cross out the infinitive endings, leaving just the stems.

Step 3 Write the forms of **leer** and **escribir** in the imperfect on the board. Underline the endings.

Step 4 Have students read all the verb forms aloud.

Step 5 Write all the imperfect forms of **querer** and **volver** on the board. Have students repeat them.

Step 6 Now go over Item 2. Explain to students that the form **había** never changes.

Gramática

¡Ojo!

There are no verbs with a stem change in the imperfect.

PRESENTE		IMPERFECTO
quiero	→	quería
vuelvo	→	volvía

Imperfecto de los verbos en -er, -ir

1. Regular **-er** and **-ir** verbs have the same endings in the imperfect tense.

infinitive	leer	escribir
stem	le-	escrib-
yo	leía	escribía
tú	leías	escribías
Ud., él, ella	leía	escribía
nosotros(as)	leíamos	escribíamos
vosotros(as)	*leíais*	*escribíais*
Uds., ellos, ellas	leían	escribían

2. The imperfect of **hay** is **había.** Note that either a singular or plural noun follows **había.**

Había un concierto durante la fiesta.
Había fuegos artificiales durante la fiesta.

CULTURA

Un grupo de jóvenes haciendo un baile folklórico en el desierto de Atacama en el norte de Chile

Práctica

HABLAR • ESCRIBIR

6 Personaliza. Da respuestas personales.

1. ¿Vivías en la misma casa cuando tenías doce años?
2. ¿A qué escuela asistías?
3. ¿Recibías buenas o malas notas?
4. ¿Tenías muchos amigos donde vivías?
5. ¿Leías muchos libros de bolsillo?
6. ¿Aprendías mucho?
7. ¿Sabías usar la computadora?
8. ¿Escribías muchos correos electrónicos?
9. ¿Recibías muchos también?

EXPANSIÓN

Ahora, sin mirar las preguntas, relata en tus propias palabras lo que dijo tu compañero(a). Si no recuerdas algo o si no comprendiste algo que te dijo, tu compañero(a) te puede ayudar.

LEER • ESCRIBIR

7 Completa con el imperfecto.

Yo recuerdo que durante la fiesta __1__ (haber) fuegos artificiales que __2__ (iluminar) el cielo. Todo el mundo __3__ (divertirse). Todos nosotros __4__ (beber) y __5__ (comer). __6__ (Haber) muchos puestos de comida donde se __7__ (vender) perros calientes, hamburguesas, pizza y papas fritas.

__8__ (Haber) un desfile. Durante el desfile algunos __9__ (ponerse) máscaras. Yo no __10__ (poder) reconocer a varios amigos porque __11__ (llevar) disfraces.

Nosotros __12__ (tener) mucha suerte. Durante la fiesta __13__ (hacer) buen tiempo y no __14__ (llover).

Yo tengo muy buenos recuerdos (memorias) de esta fiesta.

CULTURA

Grupos de músicos se reúnen los sábados y domingos para dar conciertos en las calles de San Telmo en Buenos Aires, Argentina.

Go Online!

connectED.mcgraw-hill.com

FOLDABLES Study Organizer

MINIBOOK

See the Foldables section of the Student Handbook at the beginning of this book for help with making this foldable. Use this foldable to illustrate and tell about things you did frequently. On each page, draw a picture of an activity you enjoyed. Below each picture, write a few sentences in Spanish describing what was happening. Remember to use the imperfect tense and to stick to the words that you already know in Spanish.

HABLAR • ESCRIBIR

8 Forma frases en el imperfecto con los siguientes verbos.

comer	beber	aprender	conocer	saber	volver
vivir	subir	recibir	salir	escribir	tener

9 *Comunicación*

Dile a un(a) compañero(a) las cosas que hacías a menudo cuando eras alumno(a) en la escuela primaria. Tu compañero(a) va a hacerte preguntas para saber más.

Gramática

Leveling EACH Activity

Easy Activity 6
Average Activities 7, 8, 9
CHallenging Activity 6 **Expansión**

PRACTICE

Activity 6 This activity should be gone over orally in class. Call on several students to do the **Expansión**. Note that Activity 6 can also be done as a paired activity.

Activity 7 This activity should be prepared and then gone over in class.

Activity 8 You may wish to do Activity 8 as an entire class activity or a group activity. You may have students prepare it or do it extemporaneously.

ASSESS

Students are now ready to take Quiz 4.

Differentiation

If you have only non-Spanish speakers in class, it is better not to mention that **n** is not added to **había** when followed by a plural noun. Non-native speakers usually do not bother to add the **n.**

Heritage Speakers

If you have heritage speakers in class, it is important to point out that **había** never takes the **n.** Some may argue that it is **habían dos** because this is a frequently made error.

Answers

6

1. Sí, (No, no) vivía en la misma casa cuando tenía doce años.
2. Asistía a ___
3. Recibía buenas (malas) notas.
4. Sí, (No, no) tenía muchos amigos donde vivía.
5. Sí, (No, no) leía muchos libros de bolsillo.
6. Sí, (No, no) aprendía mucho.
7. Sí, (No, no) sabía usar la computadora.
8. Sí, (No, no) escribía muchos correos electrónicos.
9. Sí, (No, no) recibía muchos también (tampoco).

7

1. había
2. iluminaban
3. se divertía
4. bebíamos
5. comíamos
6. Había
7. vendían
8. Había
9. se ponían
10. podía
11. llevaban
12. teníamos
13. hacía
14. llovía

8 *Answers will vary.*

9 *Answers will vary.*

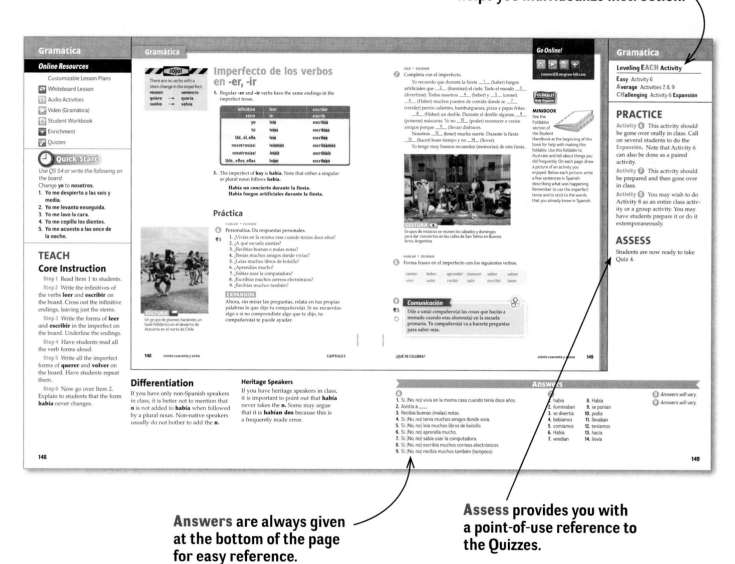

Answers are always given at the bottom of the page for easy reference.

Assess provides you with a point-of-use reference to the Quizzes.

Help your students feel confident about their speaking and writing skills.

Tips for Success presents ideas that will help students master the activities.

Pre-AP explains how activities offer students practice for different portions of the AP exam.

Preparáte para el examen

Tips for Success

Encourage students to say as much as possible when they do these open-ended activities. Tell them not to be afraid to make mistakes, since the goal of the activities is real-life communication. Encourage students to self-correct and to use words and phrases they know to get their meaning across. If someone in the group makes an error that impedes comprehension, encourage the others to ask questions to clarify or, if necessary, to politely correct the speaker. Let students choose the activities they would like to do.

Tell students to feel free to elaborate on the basic theme and to be creative. They may use props, pictures, or posters if they wish.

Pre-AP These oral activities will give students the opportunity to develop and improve their speaking skills so that they may succeed on the speaking portion of the AP exam.

Note: You may want to use the rubric below to help students prepare their speaking activities.

Practice for ORAL PROFICIENCY

Prepárate para el examen

1 Una fiesta latina
Describe a Hispanic holiday
Escoge una de las siguientes fiestas. Describe la fiesta a un(a) amigo(a).

el Día de los Muertos **el Día de los Reyes**
el Día de San Juan **la Nochevieja**

2 Mi fiesta favorita
Talk about your favorite holiday
De todas las fiestas en la lectura, ¿cuál es tu predilecta (favorita)? Explica por qué.

3 Comparaciones
Compare holidays in the United States with Hispanic holidays
Compara el Día de los Muertos con *Halloween*. También compara el día de Navidad con el Día de los Reyes.

4 Recuerdos
Talk about your childhood
Relata unos recuerdos placenteros (agradables) que tienes de los años de tu niñez. Empieza con «Cuando yo era niño(a)… ».

CULTURA
Estas niñas de Cotacachi, Ecuador, llevan trajes para celebrar las Navidades.

162 *ciento sesenta y dos* CAPÍTULO 5

Practice for WRITTEN PROFICIENCY

Go Online! connectED.mcgraw-hill.com

Tarea

Write a journal entry in which you reminisce about a holiday you enjoyed as a youngster. Describe the general characteristics of that holiday, such as when you would celebrate it, how it was celebrated, what would often happen, who would always be there, and why you always enjoyed it.

Writing Strategy
Reminiscing One technique frequently used in journal writing is reminiscing. When you reminisce, you use your memory to recall how things were in the past. The primary source of information will be the thoughts and images that your mind produces of "the way things were back then." Use what you have learned about the imperfect and the vocabulary from this chapter to make your journal entry as descriptive and lively as possible.

1 Prewrite

Make a list of the thoughts and images that come to mind when you reminisce about your favorite holiday. Think about when it would take place, who would be there, what the scene would be like, what would often happen, why it was always fun, how you felt, etc.

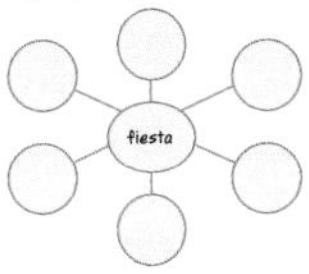

2 Write

- Be sure to stick to vocabulary that you already know.
- Remember to incorporate time expressions often used to indicate habitual or repeated actions in the past, such as **siempre, cada, a menudo, con mucha frecuencia, a veces,** etc.
- Use descriptive adjectives and include as many details as possible to make the memory of your favorite holiday come alive.

It is important to keep in mind that you are not writing about specific events that took place one time during your favorite holiday. Your goal is to capture the overall essence of this habitual or repeated event from your childhood as you remember it.

Evaluate
Don't forget that your teacher will evaluate you on use of vocabulary, correctness of grammar, and the vivid description of details.

¿QUÉ SE CELEBRA? *ciento sesenta y tres* 163

Prepárate para el examen

Pre-AP This **tarea** will give students the opportunity to develop and improve their writing skills so that they may succeed on the writing portion of the AP exam.

ASSESS

Students are now ready to take any of the Listening, Speaking, Reading, Writing Tests you choose to administer.

Note: You may want to use the rubric below to help students prepare their writing task.

Scoring Rubric for Speaking

	4	3	2	1
vocabulary	extensive use of vocabulary, including idiomatic expressions	adequate use of vocabulary and idiomatic expressions	limited vocabulary marked with some anglicisms	limited vocabulary marked by frequent anglicisms that force interpretation by the listener
grammar	few or no grammatical errors	minor grammatical errors	some serious grammatical errors	serious grammatical errors
pronunciation	good intonation and largely accurate pronunciation with slight accent	acceptable intonation and pronunciation with distinctive accent	errors in intonation and pronunciation with heavy accent	errors in intonation and pronunciation that interfere with listener's comprehension
content	thorough response with interesting and pertinent detail	thorough response with sufficient detail	some detail, but not sufficient	general, insufficient response

162

Scoring Rubric for Writing

	4	3	2	1
vocabulary	precise, varied	functional, fails to communicate complete meaning	limited to basic words, often inaccurate	inadequate
grammar	excellent, very few or no errors	some errors, but do not hinder communication	numerous errors interfere with communication	many errors, little sentence structure
content	thorough response to the topic	generally thorough response to the topic	partial response to the topic	insufficient response to the topic
organization	well organized, ideas presented clearly and logically	loosely organized, but main ideas present	some attempts at organization, but with confused sequencing	lack of organization

163

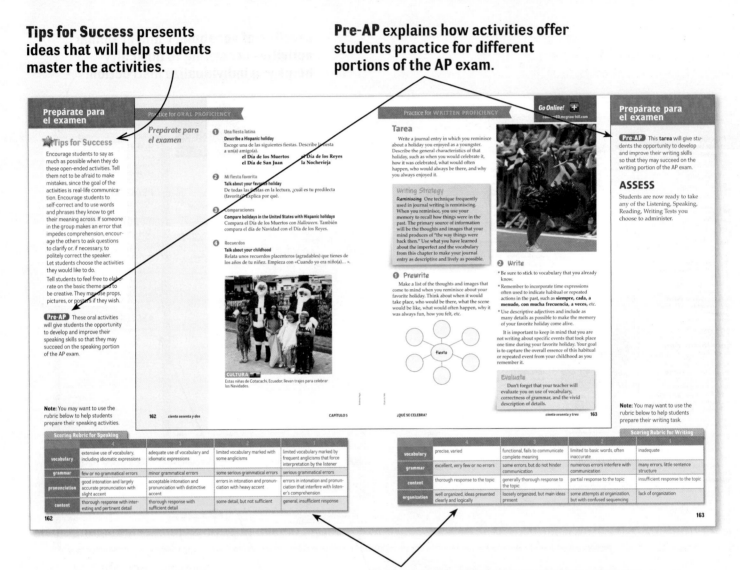

Rubrics not only help you evaluate your students' work but also serve as a guide to help students with their preparation, organization, and presentation.

Help your students review what they have learned.

References to activities tell you what is being reviewed and the section where the information is taught.

Technology calls attention to the numerous audio activities for each chapter.

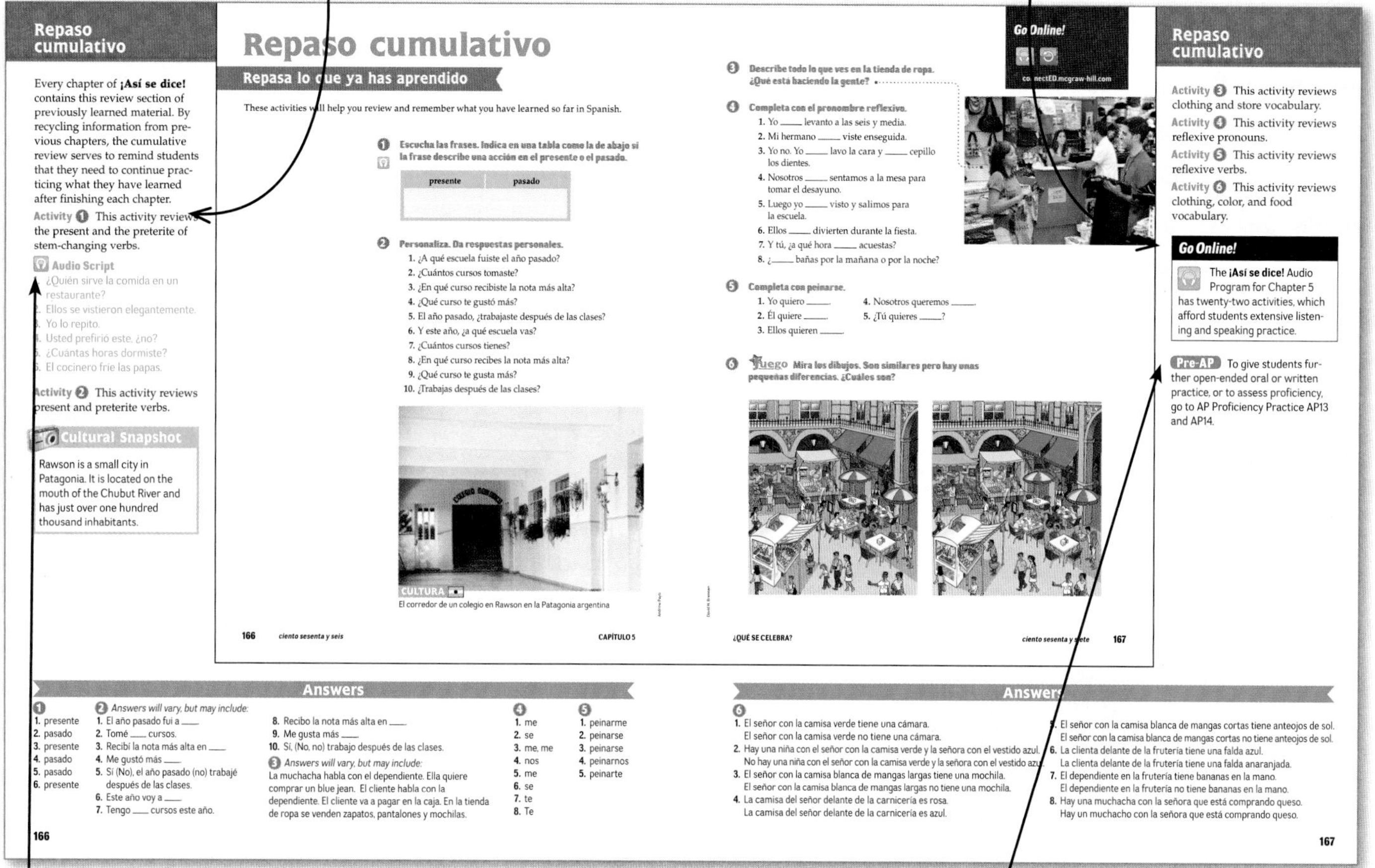

Repaso cumulativo

Every chapter of **¡Así se dice!** contains this review section of previously learned material. By recycling information from previous chapters, the cumulative review serves to remind students that they need to continue practicing what they have learned after finishing each chapter.

Activity 1 This activity reviews the present and the preterite of stem-changing verbs.

Audio Script
1. ¿Quién sirve la comida en un restaurante?
2. Ellos se vistieron elegantemente.
3. Yo lo repito.
4. Usted prefirió este, ¿no?
5. ¿Cuántas horas dormiste?
6. El cocinero fríe las papas.

Activity 2 This activity reviews present and preterite verbs.

Cultural Snapshot
Rawson is a small city in Patagonia. It is located on the mouth of the Chubut River and has just over one hundred thousand inhabitants.

Repaso cumulativo

Repasa lo que ya has aprendido

These activities will help you review and remember what you have learned so far in Spanish.

1 **Escucha las frases. Indica en una tabla como la de abajo si la frase describe una acción en el presente o el pasado.**

presente	pasado

2 **Personaliza. Da respuestas personales.**
1. ¿A qué escuela fuiste el año pasado?
2. ¿Cuántos cursos tomaste?
3. ¿En qué curso recibiste la nota más alta?
4. ¿Qué curso te gustó más?
5. El año pasado, ¿trabajaste después de las clases?
6. Y este año, ¿a qué escuela vas?
7. ¿Cuántos cursos tienes?
8. ¿En qué curso recibes la nota más alta?
9. ¿Qué curso te gusta más?
10. ¿Trabajas después de las clases?

CULTURA
El corredor de un colegio en Rawson en la Patagonia argentina

166 *ciento sesenta y seis* CAPÍTULO 5

3 **Describe todo lo que ves en la tienda de ropa. ¿Qué está haciendo la gente?**

4 **Completa con el pronombre reflexivo.**
1. Yo ___ levanto a las seis y media.
2. Mi hermano ___ viste enseguida.
3. Yo no. Yo ___ lavo la cara y ___ cepillo los dientes.
4. Nosotros ___ sentamos a la mesa para tomar el desayuno.
5. Luego yo ___ visto y salimos para la escuela.
6. Ellos ___ divierten durante la fiesta.
7. Y tú, ¿a qué hora ___ acuestas?
8. ¿___ bañas por la mañana o por la noche?

5 **Completa con peinarse.**
1. Yo quiero ___.
2. Él quiere ___.
3. Ellos quieren ___.
4. Nosotros queremos ___.
5. ¿Tú quieres ___?

6 Juego **Mira los dibujos. Son similares pero hay unas pequeñas diferencias. ¿Cuáles son?**

Go Online!
connectED.mcgraw-hill.com

¿QUÉ SE CELEBRA? *ciento sesenta y siete* 167

Repaso cumulativo

Activity 3 This activity reviews clothing and store vocabulary.
Activity 4 This activity reviews reflexive pronouns.
Activity 5 This activity reviews reflexive verbs.
Activity 6 This activity reviews clothing, color, and food vocabulary.

Go Online!
The **¡Así se dice!** Audio Program for Chapter 5 has twenty-two activities, which afford students extensive listening and speaking practice.

Pre-AP To give students further open-ended oral or written practice, or to assess proficiency, go to AP Proficiency Practice AP13 and AP14.

Answers

1
1. presente
2. pasado
3. presente
4. pasado
5. pasado
6. presente

2 *Answers will vary, but may include:*
1. El año pasado fui a ___
2. Tomé ___ cursos.
3. Recibí la nota más alta en ___
4. Me gustó más ___
5. Sí (No), el año pasado (no) trabajé después de las clases.
6. Este año voy a ___
7. Tengo ___ cursos este año.
8. Recibo la nota más alta en ___
9. Me gusta más ___
10. Sí, (No, no) trabajo después de las clases.

3 *Answers will vary, but may include:*
La muchacha habla con el dependiente. Ella quiere comprar un blue jean. El cliente habla con la dependiente. El cliente va a pagar en la caja. En la tienda de ropa se venden zapatos, pantalones y mochilas.

4
1. me
2. se
3. me, me
4. nos
5. me
6. se
7. te
8. Te

5
1. peinarme
2. peinarse
3. peinarse
4. peinarnos
5. peinarte

166

Answers

6
1. El señor con la camisa verde tiene una cámara.
   El señor con la camisa verde no tiene una cámara.
2. Hay una niña con el señor con la camisa verde y la señora con el vestido azul.
   No hay una niña con el señor con la camisa verde y la señora con el vestido azul.
3. El señor con la camisa blanca de mangas largas tiene una mochila.
   El señor con la camisa blanca de mangas largas no tiene una mochila.
4. La camisa del señor delante de la carnicería es rosa.
   La camisa del señor delante de la carnicería es azul.
5. El señor con la camisa blanca de mangas cortas tiene anteojos de sol.
   El señor con la camisa blanca de mangas cortas no tiene anteojos de sol.
6. La clienta delante de la frutería tiene una falda azul.
   La clienta delante de la frutería tiene una falda anaranjada.
7. El dependiente en la frutería tiene bananas en la mano.
   El dependiente en la frutería no tiene bananas en la mano.
8. Hay una muchacha con la señora que está comprando queso.
   Hay un muchacho con la señora que está comprando queso.

167

Audio Script is a quick reference at point of use for the listening activities. This gives you the option of reading the script yourself.

Pre-AP gives you enrichment opportunities to prepare your students for the AP exam.

Connect with Digital Natives

Go Online! connectED.mcgraw-hill.com

Today's students have an unprecedented access to and appetite for technology and new media. They perceive technology as their friend and rely on it to study, work, play, relax, and communicate.

Your students are accustomed to the role that computers play in today's world. They may well be the first generation whose primary educational tool is a computer or a cell phone. The eStudent Edition allows your students to access their Spanish curriculum anytime, anywhere. Along with your Student Edition, **¡Así se dice!** provides a blended instructional solution for your next-generation students.

Present

ebook

Interactive Whiteboard Present with interactive whiteboard lessons.

Audio Listen to spoken Spanish.

Video Watch and learn about the Spanish-speaking world.

Practice

Audio
Listen to spoken Spanish.

Video
Watch and learn about the Spanish-speaking world.

Práctica
Practice your skills.

Repaso
Review what you've learned.

Diversiones
Go beyond the classroom.

Assess

Check student progress.

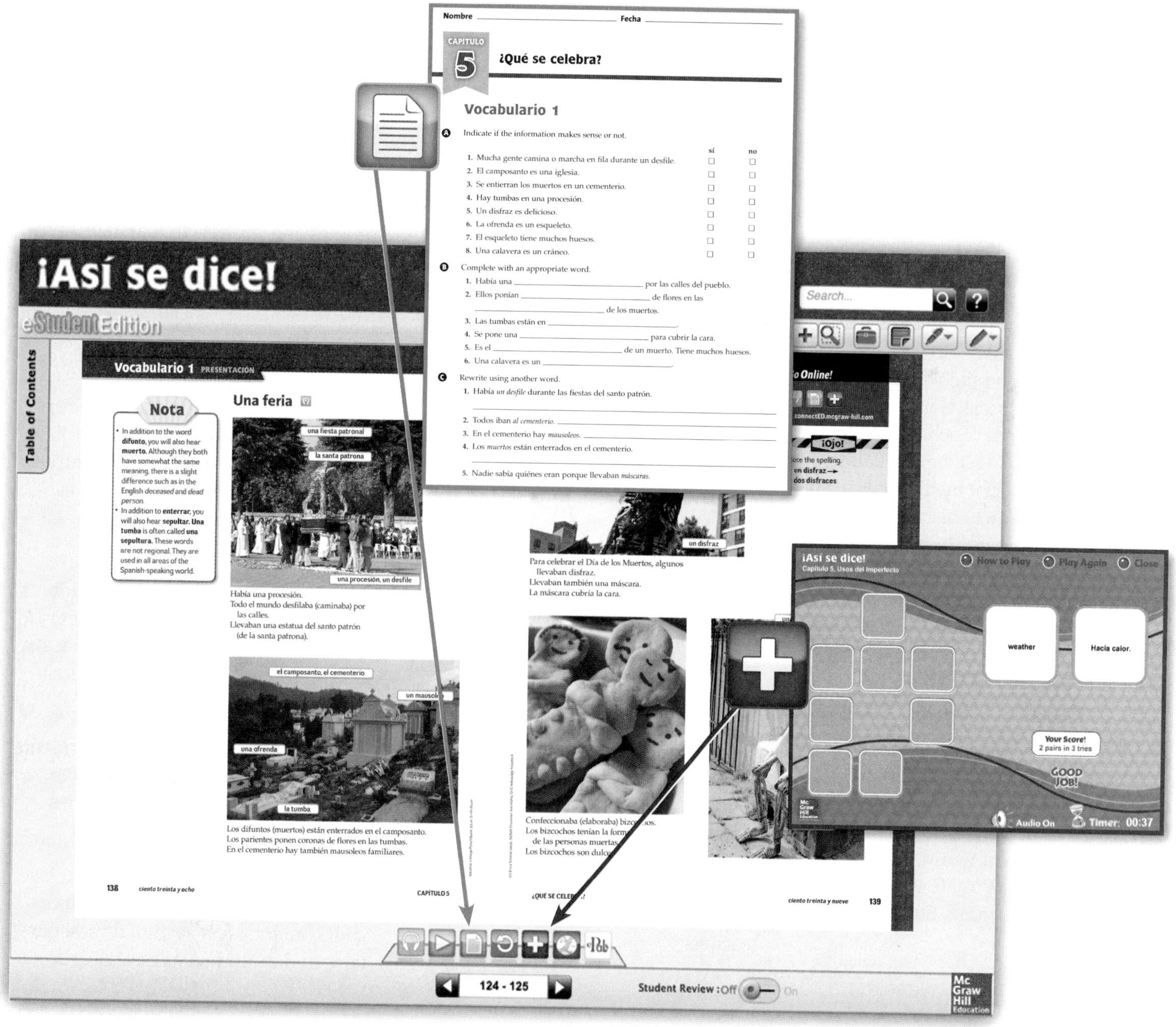

Go Online! www.epals.com/learningcenter

ePals GlobalCommunity
Where learners connect™

ePals®, a global community of more than one million K-12 classrooms in 200 countries and territories, provides teachers with the opportunity to facilitate safe, authentic, and dynamic exchanges with other classrooms. McGraw-Hill Education, The Smithsonian Institution, International Baccalaureate, and leading educators around the globe have partnered with ePals® to help make learning dynamic for students, improve academic achievement, and meet multiple standards.

What Is Global Collaboration?

Global collaboration leverages the power of social media to connect classrooms around the world for real-life lessons and projects in virtual study groups, in and out of school. Students can safely work together on ePals® using familiar social media tools to collaborate on research, discussions, and multimedia projects. By connecting with peers in other parts of the world, students can discover people, places, and cultures far beyond the classroom.

Why Collaboration Is Crucial

Research shows that collaborative learning has a positive effect on student achievement. Collaborative, project-based experiences inspire students with real-world problems and bring lessons to life with dynamic, participatory learning. Students are more motivated and try harder because they're communicating with a real person, for a real purpose. ePals® collaboration benefits students and educators in a variety of ways:

- Facilitates classroom-led delivery of standards-aligned, project-based learning experiences
- Demonstrates student knowledge and progress in level of proficiency in Spanish by publishing written projects to share ideas and receive feedback from an international audience
- Develops core academic, college and career skills such as critical thinking, problem solving, communication and global awareness

Connect Globally

On ePals®, teachers can browse hundreds of thousands of classroom profiles and projects by location, age range, language, and subject matter, to find collaboration partners. Classrooms then partner in virtual project workspaces for digital collaboration around tailored projects, activities, and content. Each project workspace enables roundtable classroom collaboration and includes a suite of safe social media tools (private to that workspace and controlled by the teacher), including blogs, wikis, forums, and media galleries. ePals® also provides safe student e-mail accounts for one-on-one student exchanges that can be monitored by teachers.

ePals® is specifically designed for safe K-12 communication and collaboration, compliant with the Children's Online Privacy Protection Act (COPPA), Family Educational Rights and Privacy Act (FERPA) and Children's Internet Protection Act (CIPA). A team of ePals® educators moderates all classroom profiles and projects to maintain a robust education community safe for K-12 students.

Tips for Collaborating Globally on ePals®

Pair Students With Global Peers: Pair students within a project workspace with peers from other countries to accomplish specific goals, such as completing joint-inquiry projects.

Host Online Discussions: Host dynamic discussions between students by posting forum topics for students to build on one another's ideas and learn to express their own thoughts clearly and persuasively.

Share Student Work: Have students publish their work and ideas to the project group using media galleries and encourage peer review.

Create Collaborative Content: Use wikis to have student groups author joint content, such as digital presentations and multimedia research reports.

eScape

McGraw-Hill Education Spanish blog

Take students on a virtual journey through the Spanish-speaking world by connecting to eScape, where geography and target cultures come alive with fascinating articles, beautiful color photos and slideshows, and enrichment activities related to the readings.

At school, at home, or on the go, students can learn about a country's people, geography, traditions, food, and much more.

Newsstand Read varied news articles in Spanish and English.

Library Connect with all eleven regions of the Hispanic world through photos and informational text.

Museum Explore the history and culture of each region using timelines and informative reading selections.

Poll Provide opinions on topics of interest and see live results.

Travel Agency Take a virtual field trip through your favorite region.

ATM Convert currencies.

Students can interact with classmates and further their cultural awareness through engaging **Explore more** and **Share what you know** activities related to each article.

Spanish Names

The following are some Spanish boys' and girls' names that you may wish to give to your students.

Chicos			Chicas		
Adán	Julio	Patricio	Adela	Luisa	Pilar
Alberto	Justo	Pedro	Alejandra	Lupe	Raquel
Alejandro	Leonardo	Rafael	Alicia	Luz	Rosa
Alfonso	Luis	Ramón	Ana	Margarita	Rosalinda
Álvaro	Manuel	Raúl	Andrea	María	Rosana
Andrés	Marcos	Ricardo	Anita	Mariana	Rosario
Antonio	Mateo	Roberto	Bárbara	Marilú	Sandra
Armando	Miguel	Rubén	Beatriz	Marisa	Sara
Arturo	Nicolás	Santiago	Carlota	Marisol	Silvia
Benito	Octavio	Teodoro	Carmen	Marta	Sofía
Benjamín	Omar	Timoteo	Carolina	Mercedes	Susana
Camilo	Óscar	Tomás	Catalina	Micaela	Teresa
Carlos	Pablo	Vícente	Cecilia	Mónica	Verónica
César	Paco	Víctor	Claudia	Natalia	Victoria
Cristóbal		Wilfredo	Consuelo	Nidia	Yolanda
Daniel			Cristina	Olivia	
David			Diana	Patricia	
Diego			Dolores		
Eduardo			Dulce		
Efraín			Elena		
Emilio			Elisa		
Enrique			Emilia		
Ernesto			Estefanía		
Esteban			Estela		
Federico			Eva		
Felipe			Evangelina		
Fernando			Felicia		
Francisco			Francisca		
Gabriel			Gabriela		
Gerardo			Gloria		
Gilberto			Graciela		
Guillermo			Guadalupe		
Gustavo			Inés		
Héctor			Isabel		
Ignacio			Juana		
Jaime			Juanita		
Javier			Julia		
Jorge			Laura		
José			Lucía		
Juan					

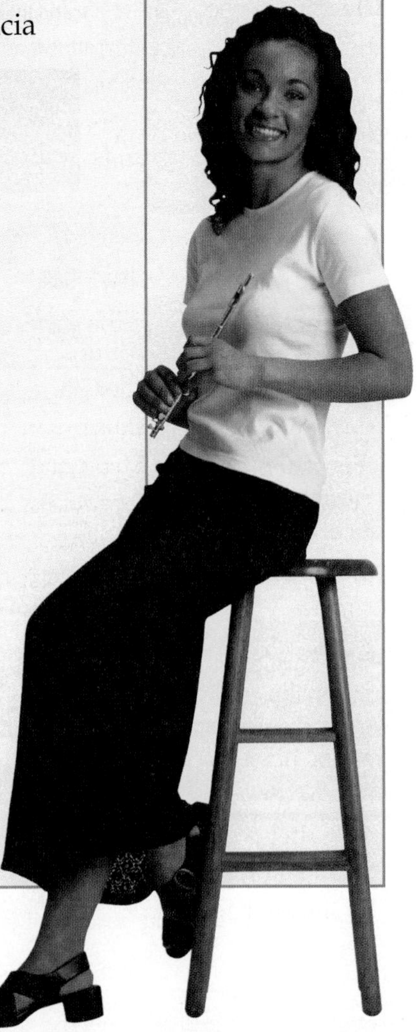

Classroom Expressions

Below is a list of words and expressions frequently used when conducting a Spanish class.

Useful Verbs and Commands		
Ven.	**Vengan.**	Come.
Ve.	**Vayan.**	Go.
Entra.	**Entren.**	Enter.
Sal.	**Salgan.**	Leave.
Espera.	**Esperen.**	Wait.
Pon.	**Pongan.**	Put.
Dame.	**Denme.**	Give me.
Dime.	**Díganme.**	Tell me.
Repite.	**Repitan.**	Repeat.
Practica.	**Practiquen.**	Practice.
Estudia.	**Estudien.**	Study.
Contesta.	**Contesten.**	Answer.
Aprende.	**Aprendan.**	Learn.
Escoge.	**Escojan.**	Choose.
Prepara.	**Preparen.**	Prepare.
Mira.	**Miren.**	Look at.
Describe.	**Describan.**	Describe.
Empieza.	**Empiecen.**	Begin.
Pronuncia.	**Pronuncien.**	Pronounce.
Escucha.	**Escuchen.**	Listen.
Habla.	**Hablen.**	Speak.
Lee.	**Lean.**	Read.
Escribe.	**Escriban.**	Write.
Pregunta.	**Pregunten.**	Ask.
Sigue el modelo.	**Sigan el modelo.**	Follow the model.
Abre.	**Abran.**	Open.
Cierra.	**Cierren.**	Close.
Continúa.	**Continúen.**	Continue.
Siéntate.	**Siéntense.**	Sit.
Levántate.	**Levántense.**	Get up.
Cállate.	**Cállense.**	Be quiet.
Presta atención.	**Presten atención.**	Pay attention.

Su atención, por favor.	Your attention, please.
Silencio.	Quiet.
Otra vez.	Again.
Todos juntos.	All together.
En voz alta.	Out loud.
Más alto, por favor.	Louder, please.
En español, por favor.	In Spanish, please.
En inglés, por favor.	In English, please.

Classroom Supplies	
el papel	paper
la hoja de papel	sheet of paper
el cuaderno	notebook, workbook
el libro	book
el diccionario	dictionary
la regla	ruler
la cinta	tape
el bolígrafo, la pluma	pen
el lápiz	pencil
el sacapuntas	pencil sharpener
la goma	eraser
la tiza	chalk
la pizarra, el pizarrón	chalkboard
el borrador	chalkboard eraser
el escritorio, el pupitre	desk
la silla	chair
la fila	row
el CD	CD
la computadora, el ordenador	computer
el DVD	DVD
la pantalla	screen
el video	video

BananaStock/PictureQuest/Jupiter Images

ACTFL National Standards

¡Así se dice! has been written to help you meet the ACTFL World-Readiness Standards for Learning Languages. Elements throughout the book, identified by the National Standards icon, address all the National Standards. The text also provides students with the interpersonal, interpretive, and presentational skills they need to create language for communication. Culture is integrated throughout the text, from the basic introduction of vocabulary, to the authentic photographs, to the cultural readings. Connections to other disciplines are addressed, not only in the GeoVista and Introduction to Theme pages, but also in the readings and project suggestions. Linguistic and cultural comparisons are made throughout the text. Suggestions are made for ways students may use their language skills in the immediate and more distant communities. Students who complete the **¡Así se dice!** series are prepared to participate in the Spanish-speaking world. Specific correlations to each chapter are provided on the pages preceding each chapter in the Teacher Edition.

World-Readiness Standards for Learning Languages

Goal Areas	Standards		
Communication Communicate effectively in more than one language in order to function in a variety of situations and for multiple purposes	**Interpersonal Communication:** Learners interact and negotiate meaning in spoken, signed, or written conversations to share information, reactions, feelings, and opinions.	**Interpretive Communication:** Learners understand, interpret, and analyze what is heard, read, or viewed on a variety of topics.	**Presentational Communication:** Learners present information, concepts, and ideas to inform, explain, persuade, and narrate on a variety of topics using appropriate media and adapting to various audiences of listeners, readers, or viewers.
Cultures Interact with cultural competence and understanding	**Relating Cultural Practices to Perspectives:** Learners use the language to investigate, explain, and reflect on the relationship between the practices and perspectives of the cultures studies.		**Relating Cultural Products to Perspectives:** Learners use the language to investigate, explain, and reflect on the relationship between the products and perspectives of the cultures studied.
Connections Connect with other disciplines and acquire information and diverse perspectives in order to use the language to function in academic and career-related situations	**Making Connections:** Learners build, reinforce, and expand their knowledge of other disciplines while using the language to develop critical thinking and to solve problems creatively.		**Acquiring Information and Diverse Perspectives:** Learners access and evaluate information and diverse perspectives that are available through the language and its cultures.
Comparisons Develop insight into the nature of language and culture in order to interact with cultural competence	**Language Comparisons:** Learners use the language to investigate, explain, and reflect on the nature of language through comparisons of the language studied and their own.		**Cultural Comparisons:** Learners use the language to investigate, explain, and reflect on the concept of culture through comparisons of the cultures studied and their own.
Communities Communicate and interact with cultural competence in order to participate in multilingual communities at home and around the world	**School and Global Communities:** Learners use the language both within and beyond the classroom to interact and collaborate in their community and the globalized world.		**Lifelong Learning:** Learners set goals and reflect on their progress in using languages for enjoyment, enrichment, and advancement.

¡Así se dice!

SPANISH 2

Conrad J. Schmitt

McGraw Hill Education

Bothell, WA • Chicago, IL • Columbus, OH • New York, NY

Information on featured companies, organizations, and their products and services is included for educational purposes only and does not present or imply endorsement of the **¡Así se dice!** program. Permission to use all business logos has been granted by the businesses represented in this text.

connectED.mcgraw-hill.com

Mc Graw Hill Education

Send all inquiries to:
McGraw-Hill Education
8787 Orion Place
Columbus, OH 43240-4027

ISBN: 978-0-02-141264-8
MHID: 0-02-141264-2

Printed in the United States of America.

2 3 4 5 6 7 8 9 DOW 19 18 17 16 15 14

About the Author

Conrad J. Schmitt

Conrad J. Schmitt received his B.A. degree magna cum laude from Montclair State University, Upper Montclair, New Jersey. He received his M.A. from Middlebury College, Middlebury, Vermont, and did additional graduate work at New York University. He also studied at the Far Eastern Institute at Seton Hall University, Newark, New Jersey.

Mr. Schmitt has taught Spanish and French at all academic levels—from elementary school to graduate courses. He served as Coordinator of Foreign Languages for the Hackensack, New Jersey, public schools. He also taught courses in Foreign Language Education as a visiting professor at the Graduate School of Education at Rutgers University, New Brunswick, New Jersey.

Mr. Schmitt has authored or co-authored more than one hundred books, all published by The McGraw-Hill Companies. He was also editor-in-chief of foreign languages, ESL, and bilingual education for The McGraw-Hill Companies.

Mr. Schmitt has traveled extensively throughout Spain and all of Latin America. He has addressed teacher groups in all fifty states and has given seminars in many countries including Japan, the People's Republic of China, Taiwan, Egypt, Germany, Spain, Portugal, Mexico, Panama, Colombia, Brazil, Jamaica, and Haiti.

Contributing Writers

Louise M. Belnay

Teacher of World Languages
Adams County School District 50
Westminster, Colorado

Reina Martínez

Coordinator/Teacher of Foreign Languages
North Rockland Central School District
Thiells, New York

Student Handbook

Andrew Payti

Student Handbook

GeoVistas
Explorando el mundo hispanohablante

Repaso

Capítulo 1 En avión

Objetivos

You will:

- talk about packing for a trip and getting to the airport
- tell what you do at the airport
- talk about being on an airplane
- discuss air travel in South America

You will use:

- verbs that have **g** in the **yo** form of the present tense
- the present progressive tense

David H Brennan

Contenido

Capítulo 2 ¡Una rutina diferente!

Objetivos

You will:
- identify more parts of the body
- talk about your daily routine
- talk about backpacking and camping

You will use:
- reflexive verbs
- commands with **favor de**

Capítulo 3 En tren

Objetivos

You will:
- use vocabulary related to train travel
- discuss interesting train trips in Peru and Mexico

You will use:
- the preterite of irregular verbs
- the verb **decir**
- prepositional pronouns

Pixtal/AGE Fotostock

Capítulo 4 En el restaurante

Objetivos

You will:

- order and pay for a meal at a restaurant
- identify more foods
- identify eating utensils and dishes
- discuss restaurants in Spain and Latin America

You will use:

- stem-changing verbs in the present and preterite
- adjectives of nationality
- the passive voice with **se**

(l)Westend61/age fotostock (r)David H. Brennan

Capítulo 5 ¿Qué se celebra?

Objetivos

You will:
- talk about several Hispanic holidays
- compare holidays that you celebrate with those in some Spanish-speaking countries

You will use:
- regular and irregular forms of the imperfect tense

Capítulo 6 Tecnomundo

Objetivos

You will:
- talk about computers, the Internet, and e-mail
- talk about a digital camera and an MP3 player
- make and receive phone calls
- discuss technology in Hispanic countries

You will use:
- the preterite and imperfect tenses

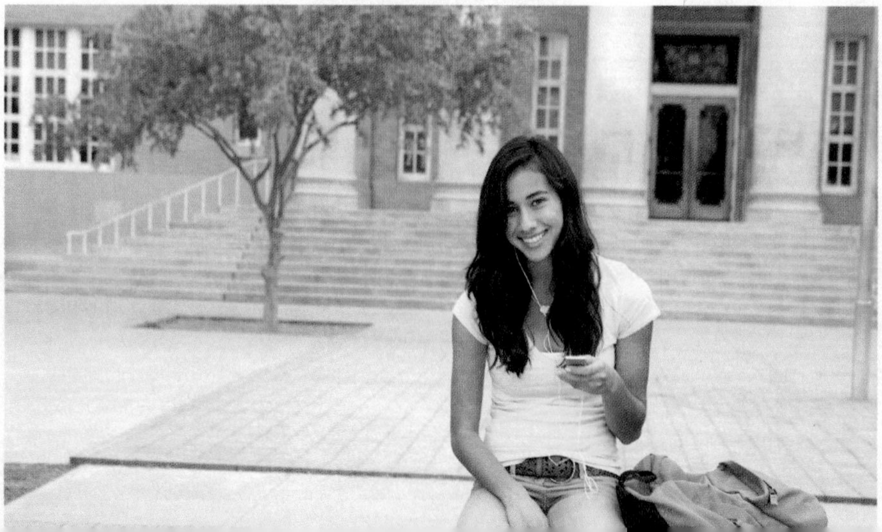

Yellow Dog Productions/Getty Images

Capítulo 7 En el hotel

Objetivos

You will:
- check into a hotel or hostel
- ask for things you may need while at a hotel or hostel
- discuss hotel stays in Latin America and Spain

You will use:
- the present perfect tense
- double object pronouns

Andrew Payti

Contenido

Capítulo 8 Ciudad y campo

Objetivos

You will:
- describe life in the city
- describe life in the country
- discuss the differences between the city and the country in Latin America

You will use:
- the future tense
- object pronouns with infinitives and gerunds

(l)Glowimages/age fotostock, (r)Richard Brommer

Capítulo 9 ¿Vas en carro?

Objetivos

You will:
- talk about cars and driving
- give directions
- discuss the Pan American Highway

You will use:
- **tú** affirmative commands
- the conditional

JUPITERIMAGES/Creatas/Alamy

Capítulo 10 Cocina hispana

Objetivos

You will:
- talk about foods and food preparation
- talk about a Hispanic recipe

You will use:
- the subjunctive
- formal commands
- negative informal commands

Andrew Payti

Capítulo 11 ¡Cuídate bien!

Objetivos

You will:
- identify more parts of the body
- talk about exercise
- talk about having a little accident and a trip to the emergency room
- discuss physical fitness

You will use:
- the subjunctive with impersonal expressions
- **ojalá, quizás, tal vez**
- the subjunctive of stem-changing verbs
- the comparison of like things

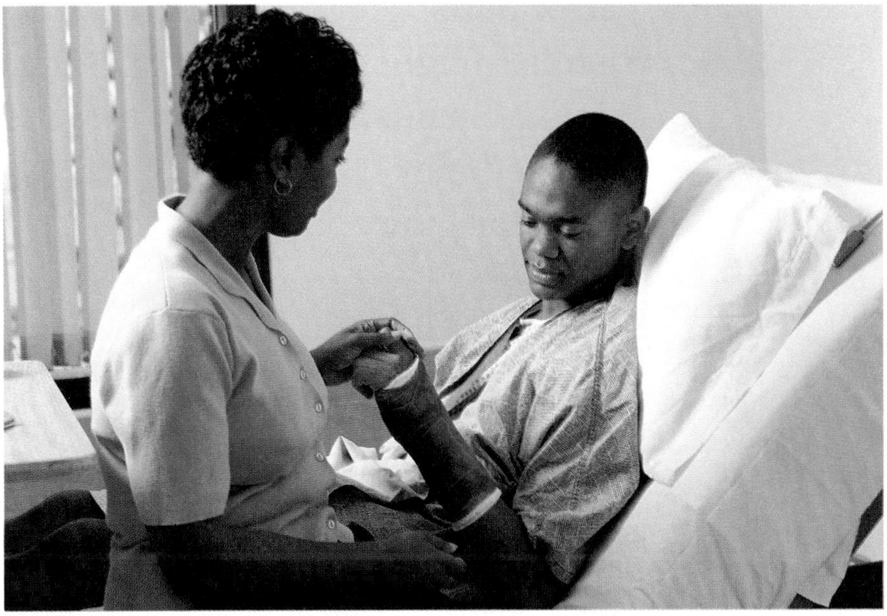

Literary Reader

Language Arts Practice

Student Resources

Guide to Symbols

Throughout **¡Así se dice!** you will see these symbols, or icons. They will tell you how to best use the particular part of the chapter or activity they accompany. Following is a key to help you understand these symbols.

Audio link This icon indicates material in the chapter that is recorded.

Recycling This icon indicates sections that review previously introduced material.

Paired activity This icon indicates activities that you can practice orally with a partner.

Group activity This icon indicates activities that you can practice together in groups.

Critical thinking This icon indicates activities that require critical thinking.

InfoGap **InfoGap** This icon refers to additional paired activities at the end of the book.

¡Bravo! **¡Bravo!** This icon indicates the end of new material in each chapter. All remaining material is recombination and review.

Literary Reader This icon lets you know that you are prepared to read the indicated literature selection.

LA PRACTICE **Language Arts Practice** This icon refers to additional practice at the end of the book that will help you practice Language Arts skills while using your Spanish.

Why Learn Spanish?

¡Viva el español!

Spanish is currently the fourth-most-spoken language in the world. Studying Spanish will help you explore other cultures, communicate with Spanish speakers, and increase your career possibilities.

It's fascinating!

Culture Hispanic culture is full of diverse expressions of music, art, and literature. From dancing the tango or salsa to admiring a modern painting by Salvador Dalí, your studies will introduce you to an array of what the culture has to offer. You'll learn about the various customs, traditions, and values in Latin America and Spain. From food and family to school and sports, you'll learn all about life in the Hispanic world.

CULTURA

Dancers of the tango on the streets of Argentina

It's all around us!

Communication The United States is home to more than fifty million Hispanics or Latinos. Whether on the radio, in your community or school, or in your own home, the Spanish language is probably part of your life in some way. Understanding Spanish allows you to sing along with Latin music on the radio or chat with Spanish speakers in your school, community, or family. No matter who you are, Spanish can enrich your life in some way.

If you plan to travel outside the United States, remember that Spanish is the official language of many countries. Experiencing another country is more fun and meaningful when you can understand restaurant menus, read newspapers, follow street signs, watch TV, and better yet converse with the locals.

Andrew Payti

A Spanish-speaking dentist

It's a lifelong skill!

Career Do you know what career you plan to pursue? Medicine, business, social work, teaching? What will you do if you have a Spanish-speaking patient, client, or student? Speak Spanish, of course! Whatever your career, you will be able to reach more people if you are able to converse in Spanish. After all, it's spoken by more than 16 percent of the U.S. population. You will also be open to many more career opportunities if you know Spanish. Businesses, government agencies, and educational institutions are always looking for people with the ability to speak and read more than one language.

It's an adventure!

Challenge When you study a language, you not only learn about the language and its speakers but also about yourself. Studying a language requires that you challenge yourself and more fully develop your skills. When you know about the customs and values of another culture, you are better able to reflect upon your own. Language is a means of self-discovery. Enjoy!

Reading in a New Language

Following are skills and strategies that can help you understand what you read in a language you have just begun to learn. *Reading and Succeeding* will help you build skills and strategies that will make it easier to understand what you are reading in your exciting new language.

The strategies you use frequently depend on the purpose of your reading. You do not read a textbook or standardized testing questions the same way you read a novel or a magazine article. You read a textbook for information. You read a novel or magazine article for fun.

In the early stages of second-language learning, your vocabulary is, of course, very limited in comparison to the vast number of words you already know in English. The material presented to you to read in the early stages must accommodate this reality. Your limited knowledge of the language does not have to deter you from enjoying what you are reading. Most of what you read, however, will come from your textbook, since original novels and magazine articles are not written for people who have limited exposure to the language.

As you develop your reading ability in Spanish, you will encounter basically two types of readings.

Intensive Readings

These readings are short. They are very controlled, using only language you have already learned. You should find these readings easy and enjoyable. If you find them difficult, it means you have not sufficiently learned the material presented in the chapter of the textbook. The vast majority of these informative readings will introduce you to the fascinating cultures of the Spanish-speaking world.

A very important aspect of reading in Spanish is to give you things to "talk about" in the language. The more you read, speak, and use the language, the more proficient you will become. Whenever you finish reading one of the intensive reading selections, you should be able to talk about it; that is, you should be able to retell it in your own words.

Extensive Readings

Since it is unrealistic to assume that you will never encounter new words as you branch out and read material in Spanish, you will also be presented with extensive readings. The goal of these extensive readings is to help you develop the tools and skills you need in order to read at some future date an original novel or magazine article. They do indeed contain some words and structures that are unfamiliar to you. In this *Reading and Succeeding* section, you will learn to develop many skills that will enable you to read such material with relative ease.

BananaStock/Jupiter Images

Use *Reading and Succeeding* to help you:

- adjust the way you read to fit the type of material you are reading
- identify new words and build your vocabulary
- use specific reading strategies to better understand what you read
- improve your ability to speak by developing strategies that enable you to retell orally what you have read
- use critical thinking strategies to think more deeply about what you read

Identifying New Words and Building Vocabulary

What do you do when you come across a word you do not know as you read? Do you skip the word and keep reading? You might if you are reading for fun. If it hinders your ability to understand, however, you might miss something important. When you come to a word you don't know, try the following strategies to figure out what the word means.

Reading Aloud

In the early stages of learning a second language, a good strategy is to sit by yourself and read the selection aloud. This can help you understand the reading because you once again hear words that you have already practiced orally in class. Hearing them as you read them can help reinforce meaning.

Identifying Cognates

As you read you will come across many cognates. Cognates are words that look alike in both English and Spanish. Not only do they look alike but they mean the same thing. Recognizing cognates is a great reading strategy. Examples of cognates are:

cómico	**nacionalidad**	**entra**
popular	**secundaria**	**clase**
cubano	**matemática**	**prepara**
video	**blusa**	**televisión**

Identifying Roots and Base Words

The main part of a word is called its root. From a root, many new words can be formed. When you see a new word, identify its root. It can help you pronounce the word and figure out its meaning.

For example, if you know the word **importante,** there is no problem determining the meaning of **importancia.** The verb **importar** becomes a bit more problematic, but with some intelligent guessing you can get its meaning. You know it has something to do with importance so it means *it is important,* and by extension it can even carry the meaning *it matters.*

Identifying Prefixes

A prefix is a word part added to the beginning of a root or base word. Spanish as well as English has prefixes. Prefixes can change, or even reverse, the meaning of a word. For example, the prefixes **in-, im-,** and **des-** mean *not.*

estable/inestable **posible/imposible**
honesto/deshonesto

Using Syntax

Like all languages, Spanish has rules for the way words are arranged in sentences. The way a sentence is organized is called its syntax. Spanish syntax, however, is a bit more flexible than English. In a simple English sentence someone or something (its subject) does something (the predicate or verb) to or with another person or thing (the object). This word order can vary in Spanish and does not always follow the subject/verb/object order.

Because Spanish and English syntax vary, you should think in Spanish and not try to translate what you are reading into English. Reading in Spanish will then have a natural flow and follow exactly the way you learned it. Trying to translate it into English confuses the matter and serves no purpose.

Example

English always states: *John speaks to me.*
Spanish can state: *John to me speaks.* or
To me speaks John.

The latter leaves the subject to the end of the sentence and emphasizes that it is John who speaks to me.

Using Context Clues

This is a very important reading strategy in a second language. You can often figure out the meaning of an unfamiliar word by looking at it in context (the words and sentences that surround it). Let's look at the example below.

Example

The glump ate it all up and flew away.

You have no idea what a *glump* is. Right? But from the rest of the sentence you can figure out that it's a bird. Why? Because it flew away and you know that birds fly. In this way you guessed the meaning of an unknown word using context. Although you know it is a bird, you cannot determine the specific meaning such as a robin, a wren, or a sparrow. In many cases it does not matter because that degree of specificity is not necessary for comprehension.

Let's look at another example:
The glump ate it all up and phlumped.

In this case you do not know the meaning of two key words in the same sentence—*glump* and *phlumped.* This makes it impossible to guess the meaning and this is what can happen when you try to read something in a second language that is beyond your proficiency level. This makes reading a frustrating experience. For this reason all the readings in your textbook control the language to keep it within your reach. Remember, if you have studied the vocabulary in your book, this will not happen.

Understanding What You Read

Try using some of the following strategies before, during, and after reading to understand and remember what you read.

Previewing

When you preview a piece of writing, you are looking for a general idea of what to expect from it. Before you read, try the following.

- Look at the title and any illustrations that are included.
- Read the headings, subheadings, and anything in bold letters.
- Skim over the passage to see how it is organized. Is it divided into many parts? Is it a long poem or short story?
- Look at the graphics—pictures, maps, or diagrams.
- Set a purpose for your reading. Are you reading to learn something new? Are you reading to find specific information?

Using What You Know

Believe it or not, you already know quite a bit about what you are going to read. Your own knowledge and personal experience can help you create meaning in what you read. There is, however, a big difference in reading the information in your Spanish textbook. You already have some knowledge about what you are reading from a United States-oriented base. What you will be reading about takes place in a Spanish-speaking environment and thus you will be adding an exciting new dimension to what you already know. Comparing and contrasting are important critical skills to put to use when reading material about a culture other than your own. This skill will be discussed later.

Visualizing

Creating pictures in your mind about what you are reading—called visualizing—will help you understand and remember what you read. With the assistance of the many accompanying photos, try to visualize the people, streets, cities, homes, etc., you are reading about.

Identifying Sequence

When you discover the logical order of events or ideas, you are identifying sequence. Look for clues and signal words that will help you find how information is organized. Some signal words are **primero, al principio, antes, después, luego, entonces, más tarde, por fin, finalmente.**

Determining the Main Idea

When you look for the main idea of a selection, you look for the most important idea. The examples, reasons, and details that further explain the main idea are called supporting details.

Reviewing

When you review in school, you go over what you learned the day before so that the information is clear in your mind. Reviewing when you read does the same thing. Take time now and then to pause and review what you have read. Think about the main ideas and organize them for yourself so you can recall them later. Filling in study aids such as graphic organizers can help you review.

Monitoring Your Comprehension

As you read, check your understanding by summarizing. Pause from time to time and state the main ideas of what you have just read. Answer the questions: **¿Quién?** *(Who?)* **¿Qué?** *(What?)* **¿Dónde?** *(Where?)* **¿Cuándo?** *(When?)* **¿Cómo?** *(How?)* **¿Por qué?** *(Why?)*. Summarizing tests your comprehension because you state key points in your own words. Remember something you read earlier: reading in Spanish empowers your ability to speak by developing strategies that enable you to retell orally what you have read.

BananaStock/PictureQuest

Thinking About Your Reading

Sometimes it is important to think more deeply about what you read so you can get the most out of what the author says. These critical thinking skills will help you go beyond what the words say and understand the meaning of your reading.

Compare and Contrast

To compare and contrast shows the similarities and differences among people, things, and ideas. Your reading experience in Spanish will show you many things that are similar and many others that are different depending upon the culture groups and social mores.

As you go over these culturally oriented readings, try to visualize what you are reading. Then think about the information. Think about what you know about the topic and then determine if the information you are reading is similar, somewhat different, or very different from what you know.

Continue to think about it. In this case you may have to think about it in English. Determine if you find the similarities or the differences interesting. Would you like to experience what you are reading about? Analyzing the information in this way will most certainly help you remember what you have read.

- Signal words and phrases that indicate similarity are **similar, semejante, parecido, igual.**
- Signal words and phrases that indicate differences are **diferente, distinto, al contrario, contrariamente, sin embargo.**

Cause and Effect

Just about everything that happens in life is the cause or the effect of some other event or action. Writers use cause-and-effect structure to explore the reasons for something happening and to examine the results of previous events. This structure helps answer the question that everybody is always asking: Why? Cause-and-effect structure is about explaining things.

- Signal words and phrases are **así, porque, por consiguiente, resulta que.**

Using Reference Materials

In the early stages of second-language learning, you will not be able to use certain types of reference materials that are helpful to you in English. For example, you could not look up a word in a Spanish dictionary as you would not be able to understand many of the words used in the definition.

You can, however, make use of the glossary that appears at the end of your textbook. A glossary includes only words that are included in the textbook. Rather than give you a Spanish definition, the glossary gives you the English equivalent of the word. If you have to use the glossary very frequently, it indicates to you that you have not studied the vocabulary sufficiently in each chapter. A strategy to use before beginning a reading selection in any given chapter is to quickly skim the vocabulary in the **Vocabulario 1** and **Vocabulario 2** sections of the chapter.

Expand your view of the Spanish-speaking world.

¡Así se dice! will show you the many places where you will be able to use your Spanish.

Cultural and geographic information is at your fingertips with GeoVistas, your virtual field trip to the Spanish-speaking countries.

Start your journey into language and culture.

Opening photo provides a cultural backdrop for the chapter.

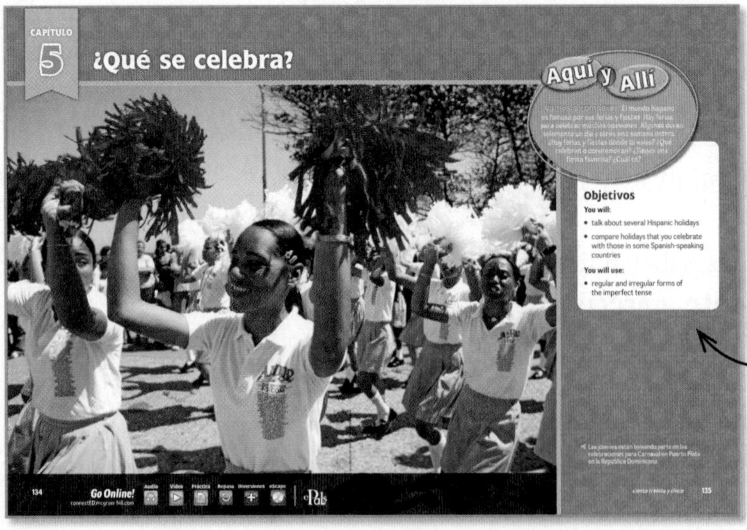

Aquí y Allí introduces you to the chapter theme and invites you to make connections between your culture and the cultures of Spanish-speaking countries.

Objectives let you know what you will be able to do by the end of the chapter.

Use your online resources to enhance learning.

Get acquainted with the chapter theme.

Explore each chapter's theme with vivid cultural photos and informative captions.

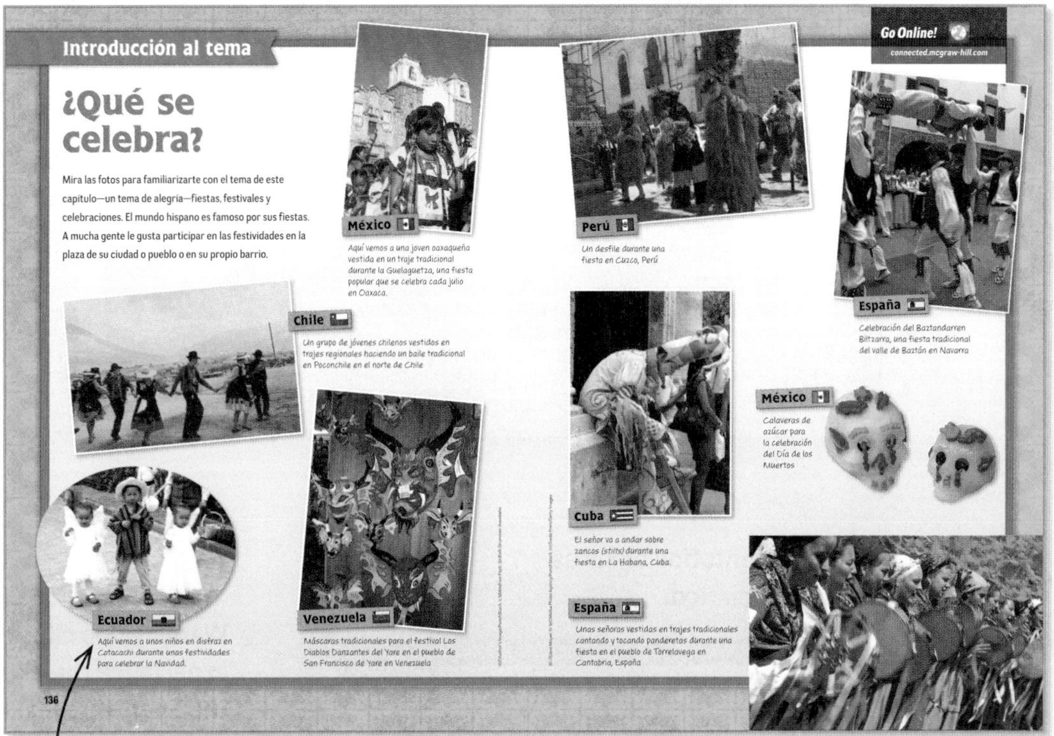
Introducción al tema

¿Qué se celebra?

Mira las fotos para familiarizarte con el tema de este capítulo—un tema de alegría—fiestas, festivales y celebraciones. El mundo hispano es famoso por sus fiestas. A mucha gente le gusta participar en las festividades en la plaza de su ciudad o pueblo o en su propio barrio.

México
Aquí vemos a una joven oaxaqueña vestida en un traje tradicional durante la Guelaguetza, una fiesta popular que se celebra cada julio en Oaxaca.

Chile
Un grupo de jóvenes chilenos vestidos en trajes regionales haciendo un baile tradicional en Poconchile en el norte de Chile

Ecuador
Aquí vemos a unos niños en disfraz en Cotacachi durante unas festividades para celebrar la Navidad.

Venezuela
Máscaras tradicionales para el festival Los Diablos Danzantes del Yare en el pueblo de San Francisco de Yare en Venezuela

136

Go Online!
connected.mcgraw-hill.com

Perú
Un desfile durante una fiesta en Cuzco, Perú

España
Celebración del Baztandarren Biltzarra, una fiesta tradicional del valle de Baztán en Navarra

México
Calaveras de azúcar para la celebración del Día de los Muertos

Cuba
El señor va a andar sobre zancos (*stilts*) durante una fiesta en La Habana, Cuba.

España
Unas señoras vestidas en trajes tradicionales cantando y tocando panderetas durante una fiesta en el pueblo de Torrelavega en Cantabria, España

See how the theme relates to different countries in the Spanish-speaking world.

Talk about the chapter theme with your new vocabulary.

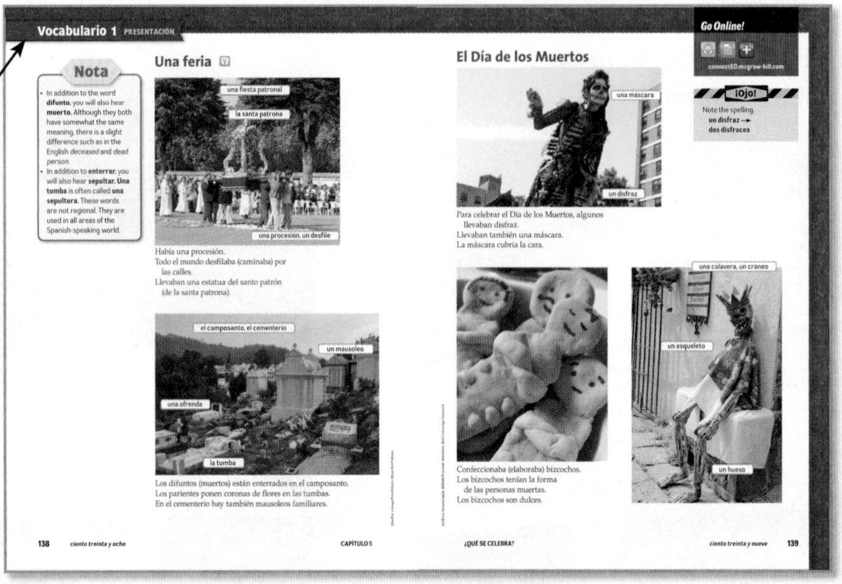

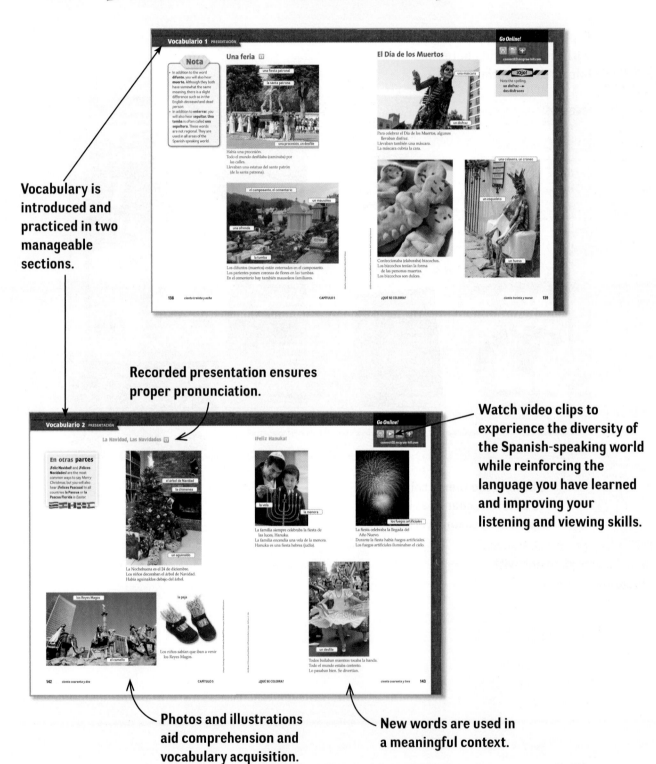

Vocabulary is introduced and practiced in two manageable sections.

Recorded presentation ensures proper pronunciation.

Watch video clips to experience the diversity of the Spanish-speaking world while reinforcing the language you have learned and improving your listening and viewing skills.

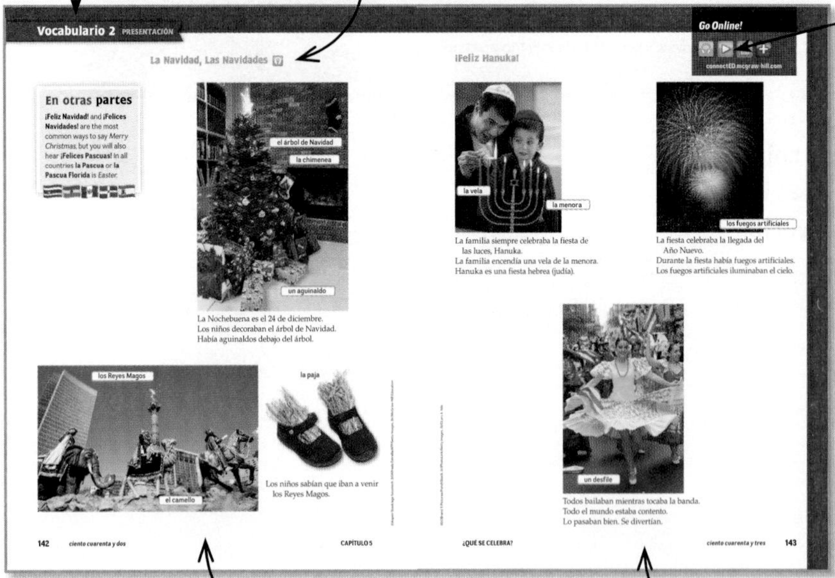

Vocabulario 2 PRESENTACIÓN
La Navidad, Las Navidades
En otras partes
¡Feliz Navidad! and **¡Felices Navidades!** are the most common ways to say *Merry Christmas*, but you will also hear **¡Felices Pascuas!** In all countries **la Pascua** or **la Pascua Florida** is *Easter*.
el árbol de Navidad
la chimenea
un aguinaldo
La Nochebuena es el 24 de diciembre.
Los niños decoraban el árbol de Navidad.
Había aguinaldos debajo del árbol.
los Reyes Magos
el camello
la paja
Los niños sabían que iban a venir los Reyes Magos.
142 ciento cuarenta y dos
CAPÍTULO 5
¡Feliz Hanuka!
Go Online!
connectED.mcgraw-hill.com
la vela
la menora
La familia siempre celebraba la fiesta de las luces, Hanuka.
La familia encendía una vela de la menora.
Hanuka es una fiesta hebrea (judía).
los fuegos artificiales
La fiesta celebraba la llegada del Año Nuevo.
Durante la fiesta había fuegos artificiales.
Los fuegos artificiales iluminaban el cielo.
un desfile
Todos bailaban mientras tocaba la banda.
Todo el mundo estaba contento.
Lo pasaban bien. Se divertían.
¿QUÉ SE CELEBRA?
ciento cuarenta y tres 143

Photos and illustrations aid comprehension and vocabulary acquisition.

New words are used in a meaningful context.

Practice and master new vocabulary.

Look for this symbol to find additional information to help you meet the ACTFL World-Readiness Standards for Learning Languages.

Practice authentic communication with InfoGap activities.

Practice and master your new vocabulary with your Workbook.

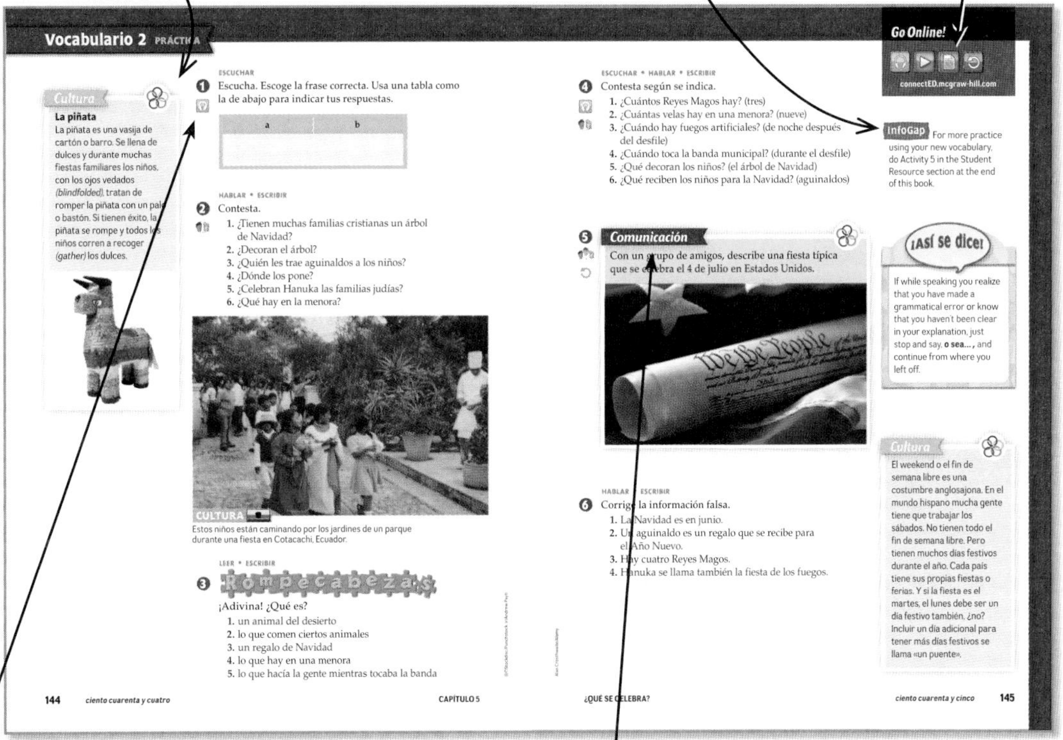

Vocabulario 2 PRÁCTICA

Cultura

La piñata

La piñata es una vasija de cartón o barro. Se llena de dulces y durante muchas fiestas familiares los niños, con los ojos vedados *(blindfolded)*, tratan de romper la piñata con un palo o bastón. Si tienen éxito, la piñata se rompe y todos los niños corren a recoger *(gather)* los dulces.

ESCUCHAR

1 Escucha. Escoge la frase correcta. Usa una tabla como la de abajo para indicar tus respuestas.

a	b

HABLAR • ESCRIBIR

2 Contesta.

1. ¿Tienen muchas familias cristianas un árbol de Navidad?
2. ¿Decoran el árbol?
3. ¿Quién les trae aguinaldos a los niños?
4. ¿Dónde los pone?
5. ¿Celebran Hanuka las familias judías?
6. ¿Qué hay en la menora?

CULTURA

Estos niños están caminando por los jardines de un parque durante una fiesta en Cotacachi, Ecuador.

LEER • ESCRIBIR

3 Rompecabezas

¡Adivina! ¿Qué es?

1. un animal del desierto
2. lo que comen ciertos animales
3. un regalo de Navidad
4. lo que hay en una menora
5. lo que hacía la gente mientras tocaba la banda

ESCUCHAR • HABLAR • ESCRIBIR

4 Contesta según se indica.

1. ¿Cuántos Reyes Magos hay? (tres)
2. ¿Cuántas velas hay en una menora? (nueve)
3. ¿Cuándo hay fuegos artificiales? (de noche después del desfile)
4. ¿Cuándo toca la banda municipal? (durante el desfile)
5. ¿Qué decoran los niños? (el árbol de Navidad)
6. ¿Qué reciben los niños para la Navidad? (aguinaldos)

5 *Comunicación*

Con un grupo de amigos, describe una fiesta típica que se celebra el 4 de julio en Estados Unidos.

HABLAR • ESCRIBIR

6 Corrige la información falsa.

1. La Navidad es en junio.
2. Un aguinaldo es un regalo que se recibe para el Año Nuevo.
3. Hay cuatro Reyes Magos.
4. Hanuka se llama también la fiesta de los fuegos.

Go Online!

connectED.mcgraw-hill.com

InfoGap For more practice using your new vocabulary, do Activity 5 in the Student Resource section at the end of this book.

¡Así se dice!

If while speaking you realize that you have made a grammatical error or know that you haven't been clear in your explanation, just stop and say, **o sea...**, and continue from where you left off.

Cultura

El weekend o el fin de semana libre es una costumbre anglosajona. En el mundo hispano mucha gente tiene que trabajar los sábados. No tienen todo el fin de semana libre. Pero tienen muchos días festivos durante el año. Cada país tiene sus propias fiestas o ferias. Y si la fiesta es el martes, el lunes debe ser un día festivo también, ¿no? Incluir un día adicional para tener más días festivos se llama «un puente».

144 *ciento cuarenta y cuatro* CAPÍTULO 5 ¿QUÉ SE CELEBRA? *ciento cuarenta y cinco* 145

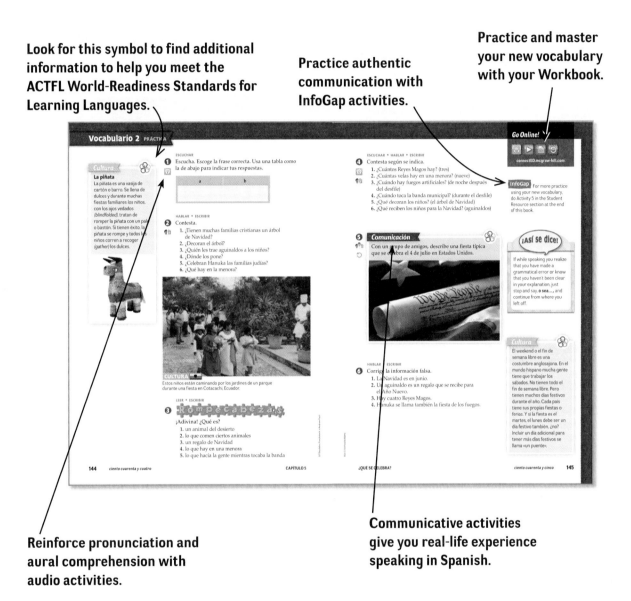

Reinforce pronunciation and aural comprehension with audio activities.

Communicative activities give you real-life experience speaking in Spanish.

Learn grammar within the context of the chapter theme.

Useful tips help you avoid language pitfalls.

New grammar is presented in simple terms with familiar vocabulary.

Foldables® study organizers give you a hands-on tool for learning and studying chapter material.

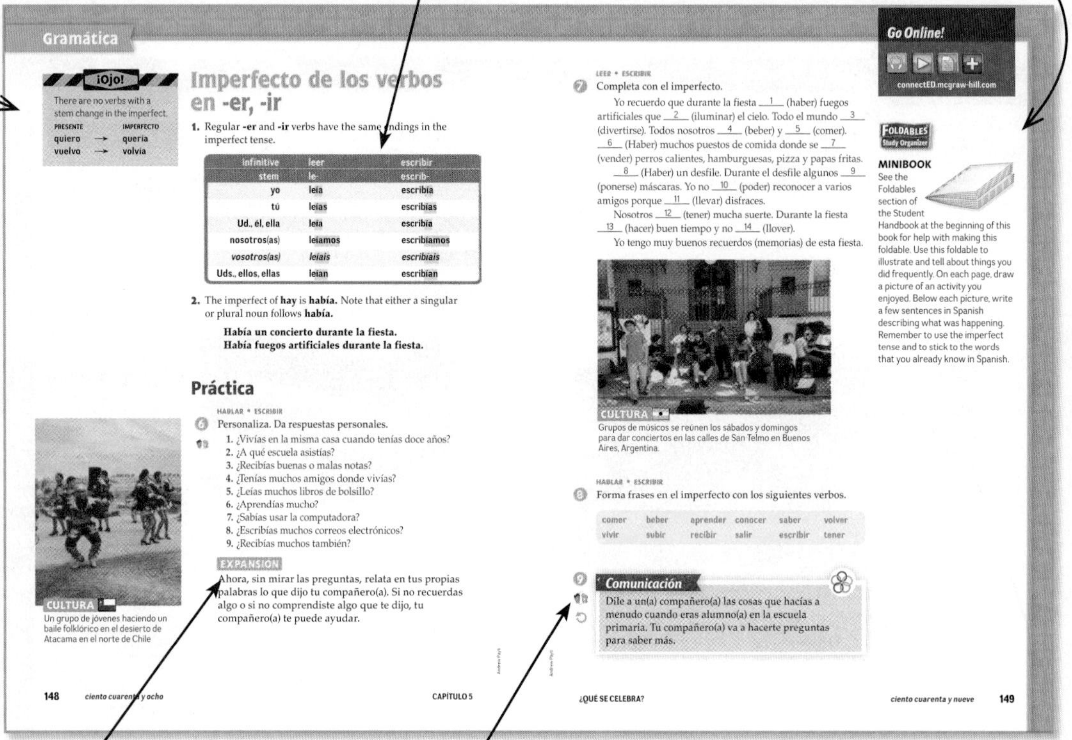

Gramática

¡Ojo!

There are no verbs with a stem change in the imperfect.

PRESENTE		IMPERFECTO
quiero	→	quería
vuelvo	→	volvía

Imperfecto de los verbos en -er, -ir

1. Regular **-er** and **-ir** verbs have the same endings in the imperfect tense.

infinitive	leer	escribir
stem	le-	escrib-
yo	leía	escribía
tú	leías	escribías
Ud., él, ella	leía	escribía
nosotros(as)	leíamos	escribíamos
vosotros(as)	*leíais*	*escribíais*
Uds., ellos, ellas	leían	escribían

2. The imperfect of **hay** is **había.** Note that either a singular or plural noun follows **había.**

Había un concierto durante la fiesta.
Había fuegos artificiales durante la fiesta.

Práctica

HABLAR • ESCRIBIR

6 Personaliza. Da respuestas personales.

1. ¿Vivías en la misma casa cuando tenías doce años?
2. ¿A qué escuela asistías?
3. ¿Recibías buenas o malas notas?
4. ¿Tenías muchos amigos donde vivías?
5. ¿Leías muchos libros de bolsillo?
6. ¿Aprendías mucho?
7. ¿Sabías usar la computadora?
8. ¿Escribías muchos correos electrónicos?
9. ¿Recibías muchos también?

EXPANSIÓN

Ahora, sin mirar las preguntas, relata en tus propias palabras lo que dijo tu compañero(a). Si no recuerdas algo o si no comprendiste algo que te dijo, tu compañero(a) te puede ayudar.

CULTURA

Un grupo de jóvenes haciendo un baile folklórico en el desierto de Atacama en el norte de Chile

148 *ciento cuarenta y ocho* CAPÍTULO 5

Go Online!

connectED.mcgraw-hill.com

LEER • ESCRIBIR

7 Completa con el imperfecto.

Yo recuerdo que durante la fiesta __1__ (haber) fuegos artificiales que __2__ (iluminar) el cielo. Todo el mundo __3__ (divertirse). Todos nosotros __4__ (beber) y __5__ (comer). __6__ (Haber) muchos puestos de comida donde se __7__ (vender) perros calientes, hamburguesas, pizza y papas fritas.

__8__ (Haber) un desfile. Durante el desfile algunos __9__ (ponerse) máscaras. Yo no __10__ (poder) reconocer a varios amigos porque __11__ (llevar) disfraces.

Nosotros __12__ (tener) mucha suerte. Durante la fiesta __13__ (hacer) buen tiempo y no __14__ (llover).

Yo tengo muy buenos recuerdos (memorias) de esta fiesta.

CULTURA

Grupos de músicos se reúnen los sábados y domingos para dar conciertos en las calles de San Telmo en Buenos Aires, Argentina.

FOLDABLES Study Organizer

MINIBOOK

See the Foldables section of the Student Handbook at the beginning of this book for help with making this foldable. Use this foldable to illustrate and tell about things you did frequently. On each page, draw a picture of an activity you enjoyed. Below each picture, write a few sentences in Spanish describing what was happening. Remember to use the imperfect tense and to stick to the words that you already know in Spanish.

HABLAR • ESCRIBIR

8 Forma frases en el imperfecto con los siguientes verbos.

comer	beber	aprender	conocer	saber	volver
vivir	subir	recibir	salir	escribir	tener

9 *Comunicación*

Dile a un(a) compañero(a) las cosas que hacías a menudo cuando eras alumno(a) en la escuela primaria. Tu compañero(a) va a hacerte preguntas para saber más.

¿QUÉ SE CELEBRA? *ciento cuarenta y nueve* 149

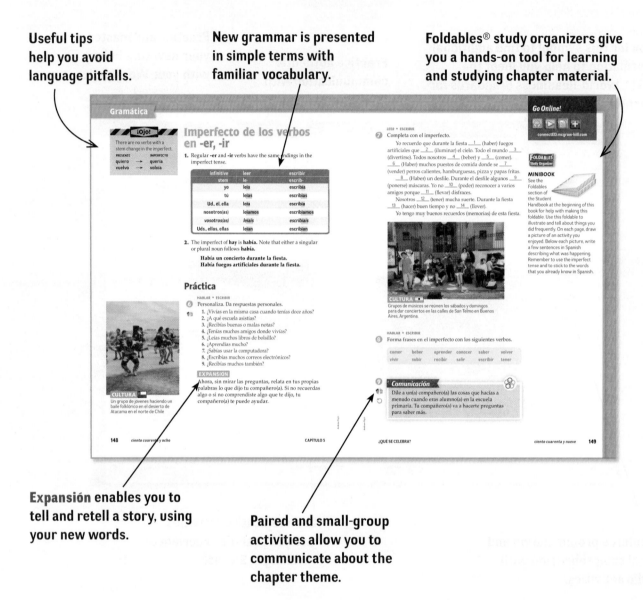

Expansión enables you to tell and retell a story, using your new words.

Paired and small-group activities allow you to communicate about the chapter theme.

Build on what you already know.

You will build confidence as you complete activities that progress from easy to more challenging.

Cultural photos are explained by captions that use grammar and vocabulary that you can understand.

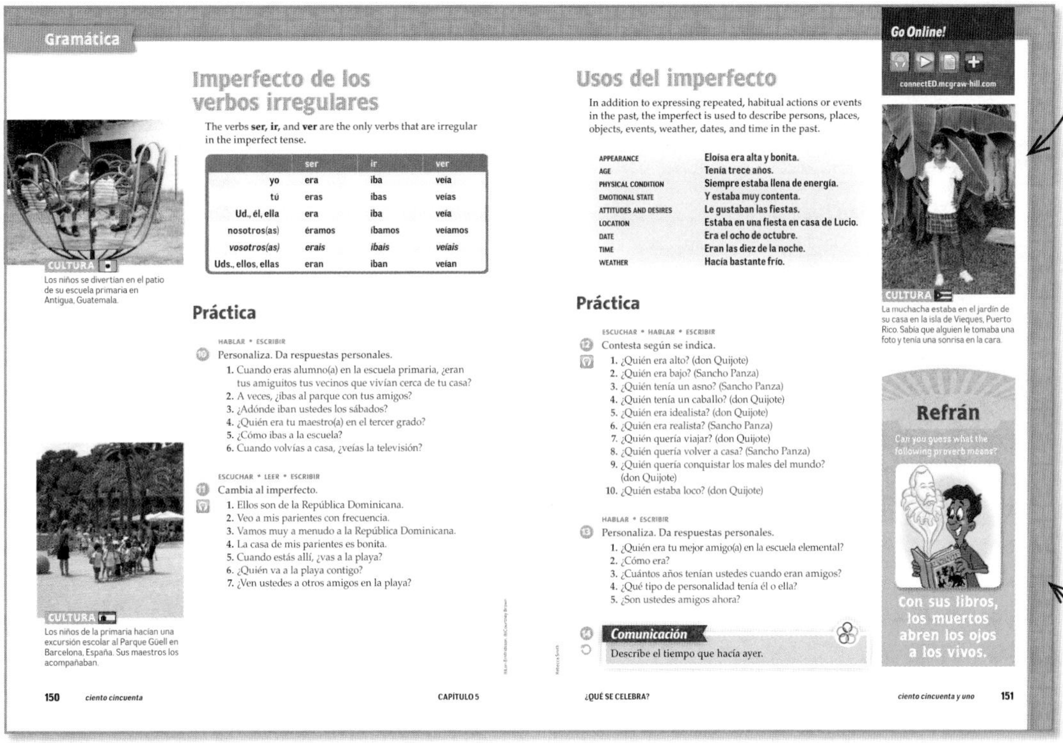

Gramática

Imperfecto de los verbos irregulares

The verbs **ser, ir,** and **ver** are the only verbs that are irregular in the imperfect tense.

	ser	ir	ver
yo	era	iba	veía
tú	eras	ibas	veías
Ud., él, ella	era	iba	veía
nosotros(as)	éramos	íbamos	veíamos
vosotros(as)	*erais*	*ibais*	*veíais*
Uds., ellos, ellas	eran	iban	veían

CULTURA
Los niños se divertían en el patio de su escuela primaria en Antigua, Guatemala.

Práctica

HABLAR • ESCRIBIR

10 Personaliza. Da respuestas personales.

1. Cuando eras alumno(a) en la escuela primaria, ¿eran tus amiguitos tus vecinos que vivían cerca de tu casa?
2. A veces, ¿ibas al parque con tus amigos?
3. ¿Adónde iban ustedes los sábados?
4. ¿Quién era tu maestro(a) en el tercer grado?
5. ¿Cómo ibas a la escuela?
6. Cuando volvías a casa, ¿veías la televisión?

ESCUCHAR • LEER • ESCRIBIR

11 Cambia al imperfecto.

1. Ellos son de la República Dominicana.
2. Veo a mis parientes con frecuencia.
3. Vamos muy a menudo a la República Dominicana.
4. La casa de mis parientes es bonita.
5. Cuando estás allí, ¿vas a la playa?
6. ¿Quién va a la playa contigo?
7. ¿Ven ustedes a otros amigos en la playa?

CULTURA
Los niños de la primaria hacían una excursión escolar al Parque Güell en Barcelona, España. Sus maestros los acompañaban.

150 *ciento cincuenta* CAPÍTULO 5

Usos del imperfecto

In addition to expressing repeated, habitual actions or events in the past, the imperfect is used to describe persons, places, objects, events, weather, dates, and time in the past.

APPEARANCE	Eloísa era alta y bonita.
AGE	Tenía trece años.
PHYSICAL CONDITION	Siempre estaba llena de energía.
EMOTIONAL STATE	Y estaba muy contenta.
ATTITUDES AND DESIRES	Le gustaban las fiestas.
LOCATION	Estaba en una fiesta en casa de Lucio.
DATE	Era el ocho de octubre.
TIME	Eran las diez de la noche.
WEATHER	Hacía bastante frío.

Práctica

ESCUCHAR • HABLAR • ESCRIBIR

12 Contesta según se indica.

1. ¿Quién era alto? (don Quijote)
2. ¿Quién era bajo? (Sancho Panza)
3. ¿Quién tenía un asno? (Sancho Panza)
4. ¿Quién tenía un caballo? (don Quijote)
5. ¿Quién era idealista? (don Quijote)
6. ¿Quién era realista? (Sancho Panza)
7. ¿Quién quería viajar? (don Quijote)
8. ¿Quién quería volver a casa? (Sancho Panza)
9. ¿Quién quería conquistar los males del mundo? (don Quijote)
10. ¿Quién estaba loco? (don Quijote)

HABLAR • ESCRIBIR

13 Personaliza. Da respuestas personales.

1. ¿Quién era tu mejor amigo(a) en la escuela elemental?
2. ¿Cómo era?
3. ¿Cuántos años tenían ustedes cuando eran amigos?
4. ¿Qué tipo de personalidad tenía él o ella?
5. ¿Son ustedes amigos ahora?

14 *Comunicación*
Describe el tiempo que hacía ayer.

Go Online!
connectED.mcgraw-hill.com

CULTURA
La muchacha estaba en el jardín de su casa en la isla de Vieques, Puerto Rico. Sabía que alguien le tomaba una foto y tenía una sonrisa en la cara.

Refrán
Can you guess what the following proverb means?
Con sus libros, los muertos abren los ojos a los vivos.

¿QUÉ SE CELEBRA? *ciento cincuenta y uno* 151

Have fun using your Spanish to figure out the meaning of Spanish proverbs.

Engage classmates in real conversation.

You will have a sense of accomplishment when you are able to comprehend the conversation.

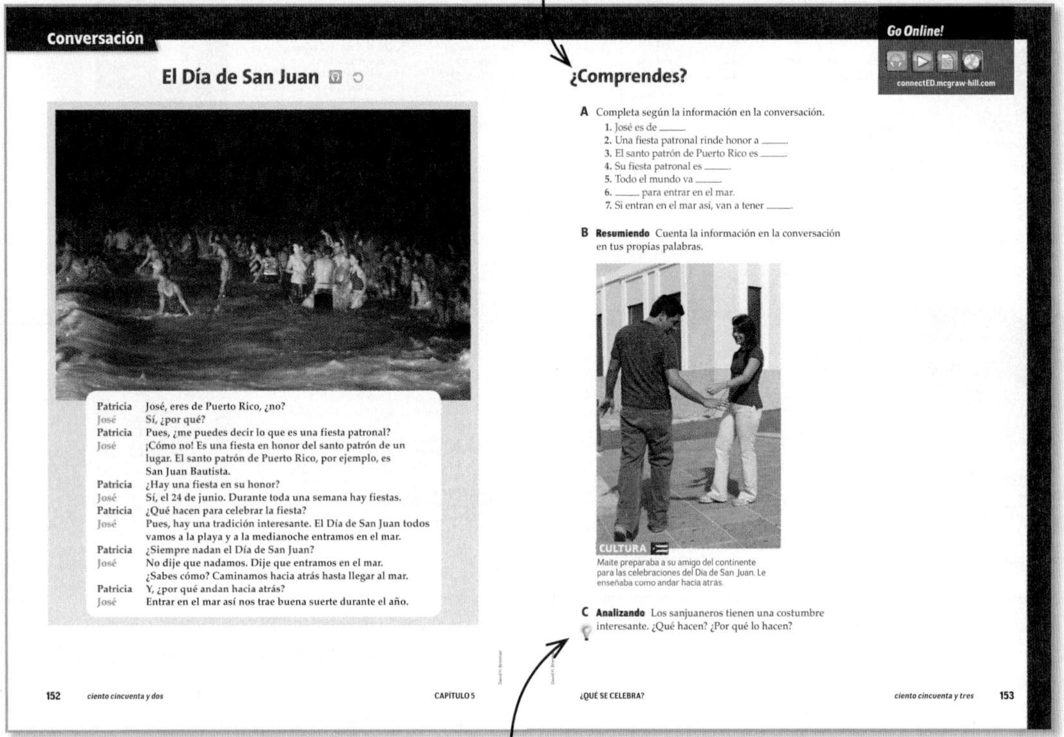

Conversación

El Día de San Juan

Patricia: José, eres de Puerto Rico, ¿no?
José: Sí, ¿por qué?
Patricia: Pues, ¿me puedes decir lo que es una fiesta patronal?
José: ¡Cómo no! Es una fiesta en honor del santo patrón de un lugar. El santo patrón de Puerto Rico, por ejemplo, es San Juan Bautista.
Patricia: ¿Hay una fiesta en su honor?
José: Sí, el 24 de junio. Durante toda una semana hay fiestas.
Patricia: ¿Qué hacen para celebrar la fiesta?
José: Pues, hay una tradición interesante. El Día de San Juan todos vamos a la playa y a la medianoche entramos en el mar.
Patricia: ¿Siempre nadan el Día de San Juan?
José: No dije que nadamos. Dije que entramos en el mar. ¿Sabes cómo? Caminamos hacia atrás hasta llegar al mar.
Patricia: Y, ¿por qué andan hacia atrás?
José: Entrar en el mar así nos trae buena suerte durante el año.

Go Online!
connectED.mcgraw-hill.com

¿Comprendes?

A Completa según la información en la conversación.
1. José es de ____.
2. Una fiesta patronal rinde honor a ____.
3. El santo patrón de Puerto Rico es ____.
4. Su fiesta patronal es ____.
5. Todo el mundo va ____.
6. ____ para entrar en el mar.
7. Si entran en el mar así, van a tener ____.

B **Resumiendo** Cuenta la información en la conversación en tus propias palabras.

CULTURA
Maite preparaba a su amigo del continente para las celebraciones del Día de San Juan. Le enseñaba como andar hacia atrás.

C **Analizando** Los sanjuaneros tienen una costumbre interesante. ¿Qué hacen? ¿Por qué lo hacen?

152 *ciento cincuenta y dos* CAPÍTULO 5 ¿QUÉ SE CELEBRA? *ciento cincuenta y tres* 153

The lightbulb icon indicates a critical thinking activity.

Heighten your cultural awareness.

Cultural reading uses learned language to reinforce chapter theme.

Recorded reading online provides options for addressing various skills and learning styles.

Step-by-step reading strategies help to develop your reading skills.

Verify your comprehension throughout the selection with Reading Checks.

Un poco más reading reinforces the chapter theme and expands your understanding of the Spanish-speaking world.

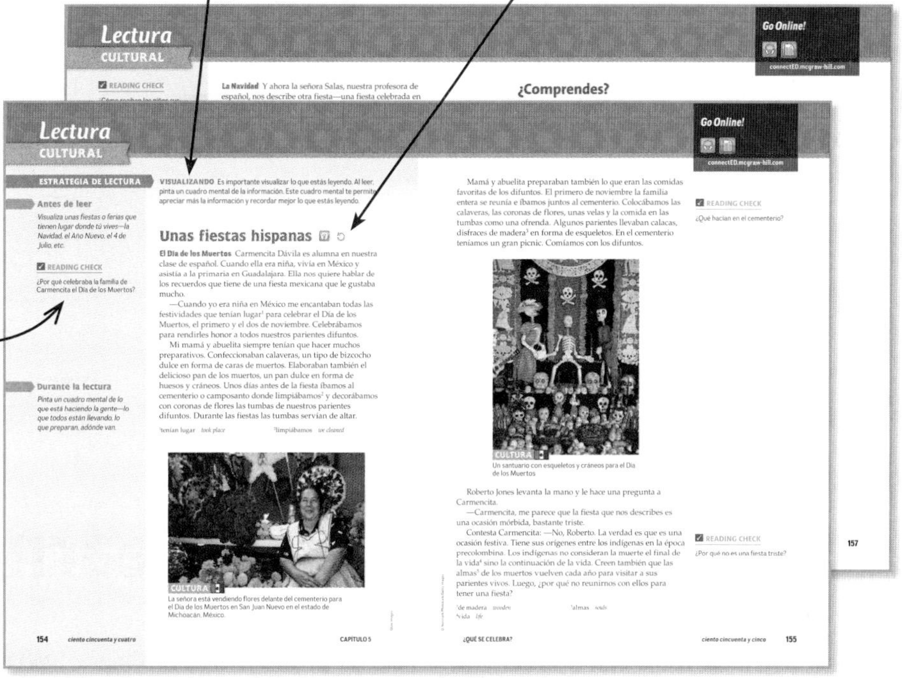

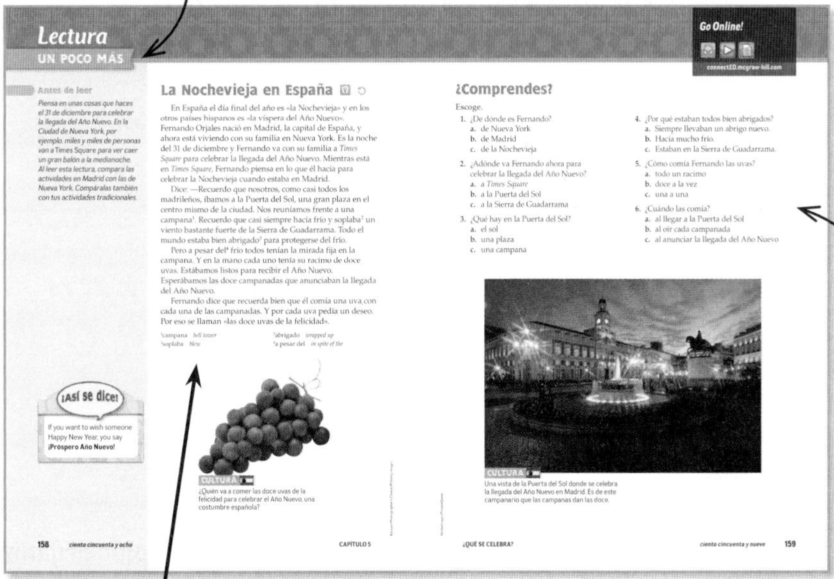

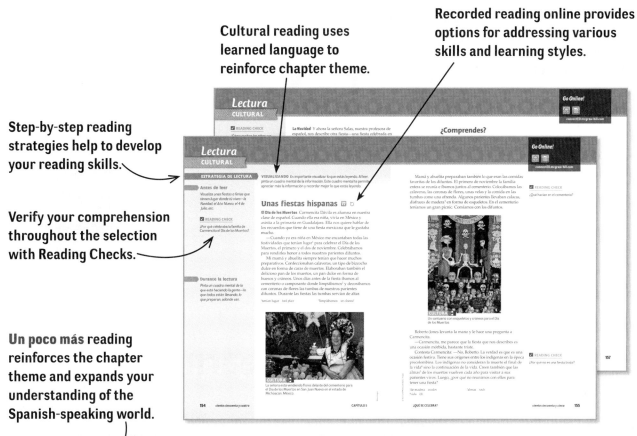

Questions follow the reading to check comprehension and to give you practice with standardized testing format.

An additional reading in each chapter reinforces learned language and chapter theme.

Show what you know!

Review what you have learned and prepare for your chapter test.

Reference notes direct you to the correct section for review.

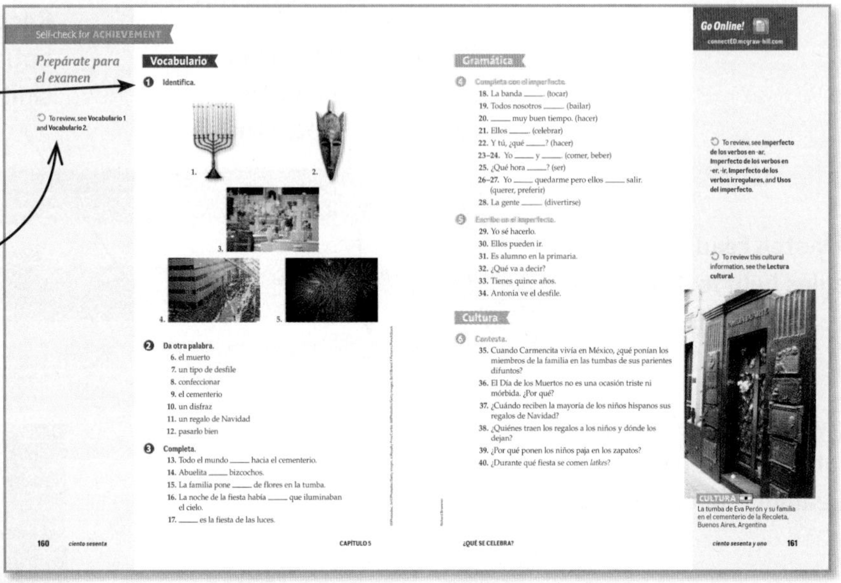
Self-check for ACHIEVEMENT

Prepárate para el examen

To review, see **Vocabulario 1** and **Vocabulario 2.**

Vocabulario

1 **Identifica.**

1. 2. 3. 4. 5.

2 **Da otra palabra.**

6. el muerto
7. un tipo de desfile
8. confeccionar
9. el cementerio
10. un disfraz
11. un regalo de Navidad
12. pasarlo bien

3 **Completa.**

13. Todo el mundo ____ hacia el cementerio.
14. Abuelita ____ bizcochos.
15. La familia pone ____ de flores en la tumba.
16. La noche de la fiesta había ____ que iluminaban el cielo.
17. ____ es la fiesta de las luces.

Gramática

4 Completa con el imperfecto.

18. La banda ____. (tocar)
19. Todos nosotros ____. (bailar)
20. ____ muy buen tiempo. (hacer)
21. Ellos ____. (celebrar)
22. Y tú, ¿qué ____? (hacer)
23–24. Yo ____ y ____. (comer, beber)
25. ¿Qué hora ____? (ser)
26–27. Yo ____ quedarme pero ellos ____ salir. (querer, preferir)
28. La gente ____. (divertirse)

5 Escribe en el imperfecto.

29. Yo sé hacerlo.
30. Ellos pueden ir.
31. Es alumno en la primaria.
32. ¿Qué va a decir?
33. Tienes quince años.
34. Antonia ve el desfile.

Cultura

6 Contesta.

35. Cuando Carmencita vivía en México, ¿qué ponían los miembros de la familia en las tumbas de sus parientes difuntos?
36. El Día de los Muertos no es una ocasión triste ni mórbida. ¿Por qué?
37. ¿Cuándo reciben la mayoría de los niños hispanos sus regalos de Navidad?
38. ¿Quiénes traen los regalos a los niños y dónde los dejan?
39. ¿Por qué ponen los niños paja en los zapatos?
40. ¿Durante qué fiesta se comen *latkes*?

Go Online! connectED.mcgraw-hill.com

To review, see **Imperfecto de los verbos en -ar, Imperfecto de los verbos en -er, -ir, Imperfecto de los verbos irregulares,** and **Usos del imperfecto.**

To review this cultural information, see the **Lectura cultural.**

CULTURA
La tumba de Eva Perón y su familia en el cementerio de la Recoleta, Buenos Aires, Argentina

160 *ciento sesenta* CAPÍTULO 5 ¿QUÉ SE CELEBRA? *ciento sesenta y uno* 161

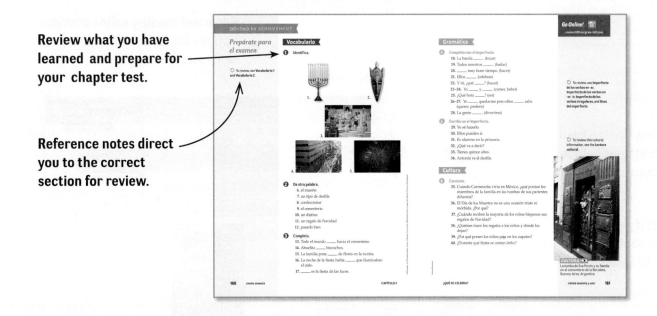

Apply what you have learned!

Use your new skills to communicate orally in meaningful, open-ended activities.

Practice what you have learned while improving your written Spanish.

Writing Strategy gives you the tools you need to develop better writing skills.

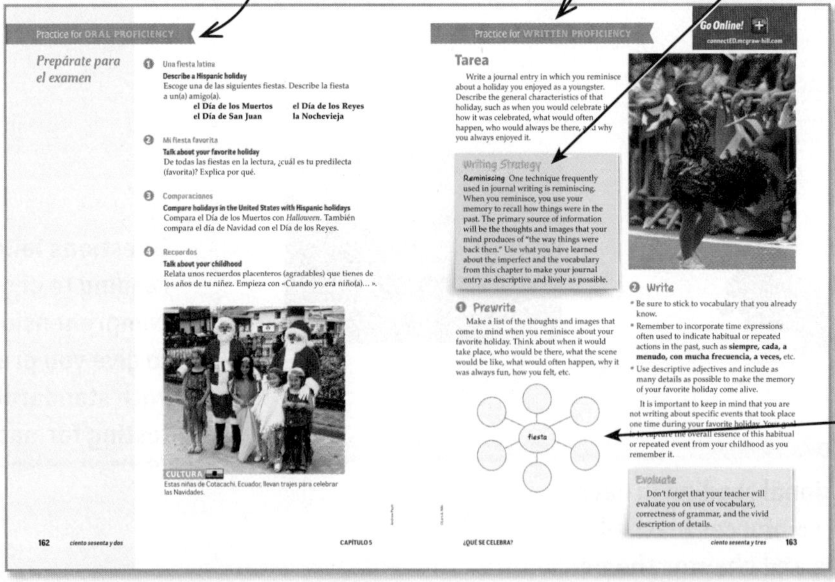
Practice for ORAL PROFICIENCY

Prepárate para el examen

1 Una fiesta latina
Describe a Hispanic holiday
Escoge una de las siguientes fiestas. Describe la fiesta a un(a) amigo(a).
el Día de los Muertos **el Día de los Reyes**
el Día de San Juan **la Nochevieja**

2 Mi fiesta favorita
Talk about your favorite holiday
De todas las fiestas en la lectura, ¿cuál es tu predilecta (favorita)? Explica por qué.

3 Comparaciones
Compare holidays in the United States with Hispanic holidays
Compara el Día de los Muertos con *Halloween*. También compara el día de Navidad con el Día de los Reyes.

4 Recuerdos
Talk about your childhood
Relata unos recuerdos placenteros (agradables) que tienes de los años de tu niñez. Empieza con «Cuando yo era niño(a)... ».

CULTURA
Estas niñas de Cotacachi, Ecuador, llevan trajes para celebrar las Navidades.

Practice for WRITTEN PROFICIENCY

Go Online! connectED.mcgraw-hill.com

Tarea

Write a journal entry in which you reminisce about a holiday you enjoyed as a youngster. Describe the general characteristics of that holiday, such as when you would celebrate it, how it was celebrated, what would often happen, who would always be there, and why you always enjoyed it.

Writing Strategy
Reminiscing One technique frequently used in journal writing is reminiscing. When you reminisce, you use your memory to recall how things were in the past. The primary source of information will be the thoughts and images that your mind produces of "the way things were back then." Use what you have learned about the imperfect and the vocabulary from this chapter to make your journal entry as descriptive and lively as possible.

1 **Prewrite**
Make a list of the thoughts and images that come to mind when you reminisce about your favorite holiday. Think about when it would take place, who would be there, what the scene would be like, what would often happen, why it was always fun, how you felt, etc.

fiesta

2 **Write**
- Be sure to stick to vocabulary that you already know.
- Remember to incorporate time expressions often used to indicate habitual or repeated actions in the past, such as **siempre, cada, a menudo, con mucha frecuencia, a veces,** etc.
- Use descriptive adjectives and include as many details as possible to make the memory of your favorite holiday come alive.

It is important to keep in mind that you are not writing about specific events that took place one time during your favorite holiday. Your goal is to capture the overall essence of this habitual or repeated event from your childhood as you remember it.

Evaluate
Don't forget that your teacher will evaluate you on use of vocabulary, correctness of grammar, and the vivid description of details.

162 *ciento sesenta y dos* CAPÍTULO 5 ¿QUÉ SE CELEBRA? *ciento sesenta y tres* 163

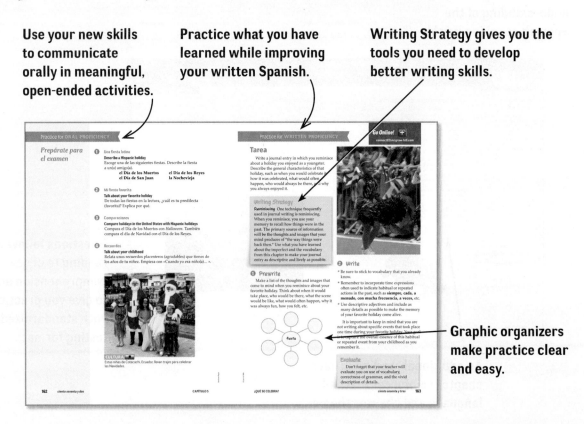

Graphic organizers make practice clear and easy.

Review grammar and vocabulary at a glance.

Succinct grammar notes help you efficiently review chapter material.

Use this vocabulary list to review the vocabulary you have learned in this chapter.

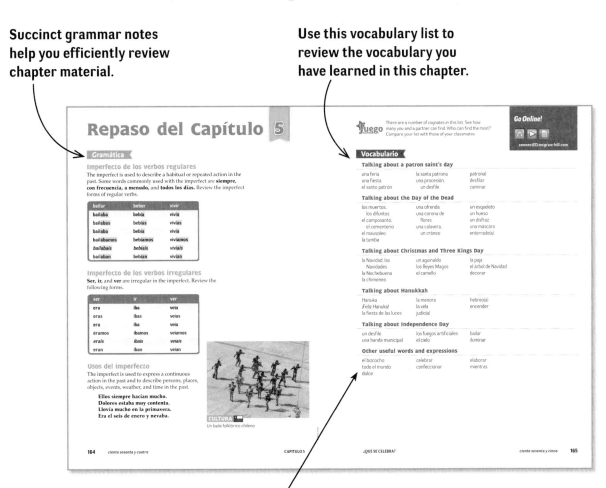

Repaso del Capítulo 5

Gramática

Imperfecto de los verbos regulares

The imperfect is used to describe a habitual or repeated action in the past. Some words commonly used with the imperfect are **siempre, con frecuencia, a menudo,** and **todos los días.** Review the imperfect forms of regular verbs.

bailar	beber	vivir
bailaba	bebía	vivía
bailabas	bebías	vivías
bailaba	bebía	vivía
bailábamos	bebíamos	vivíamos
bailabais	*bebíais*	*vivíais*
bailaban	bebían	vivían

Imperfecto de los verbos irregulares

Ser, ir, and **ver** are irregular in the imperfect. Review the following forms.

ser	ir	ver
era	iba	veía
eras	ibas	veías
era	iba	veía
éramos	íbamos	veíamos
erais	*ibais*	*veíais*
eran	iban	veían

Usos del imperfecto

The imperfect is used to express a continuous action in the past and to describe persons, places, objects, events, weather, and time in the past.

Ellos siempre hacían mucho.
Dolores estaba muy contenta.
Llovía mucho en la primavera.
Era el seis de enero y nevaba.

CULTURA
Un baile folklórico chileno

164 *ciento sesenta y cuatro* CAPÍTULO 5

Juego There are a number of cognates in this list. See how many you and a partner can find. Who can find the most? Compare your list with those of your classmates.

Go Online! connectED.mcgraw-hill.com

Vocabulario

Talking about a patron saint's day

una feria, una fiesta, el santo patrón, la santa patrona, una procesión, un desfile, patronal, desfilar, caminar

Talking about the Day of the Dead

los muertos, los difuntos, el camposanto, el cementerio, el mausoleo, la tumba, una ofrenda, una corona de flores, una calavera, un cráneo, un esqueleto, un hueso, un disfraz, una máscara, enterrado(a)

Talking about Christmas and Three Kings Day

la Navidad, las Navidades, la Nochebuena, la chimenea, un aguinaldo, los Reyes Magos, el camello, la paja, el árbol de Navidad, decorar

Talking about Hanukkah

Hanuka, ¡Feliz Hanuka!, la fiesta de las luces, la menora, la vela, judío(a), hebreo(a), encender

Talking about Independence Day

un desfile, una banda municipal, los fuegos artificiales, el cielo, bailar, iluminar

Other useful words and expressions

el bizcocho, todo el mundo, dulce, celebrar, confeccionar, elaborar, mientras

¿QUÉ SE CELEBRA? *ciento sesenta y cinco* 165

Vocabulary is categorized to help recall.

Practice what you have learned so far in Spanish.

Cumulative activities allow you to practice what you have learned so far in Spanish class.

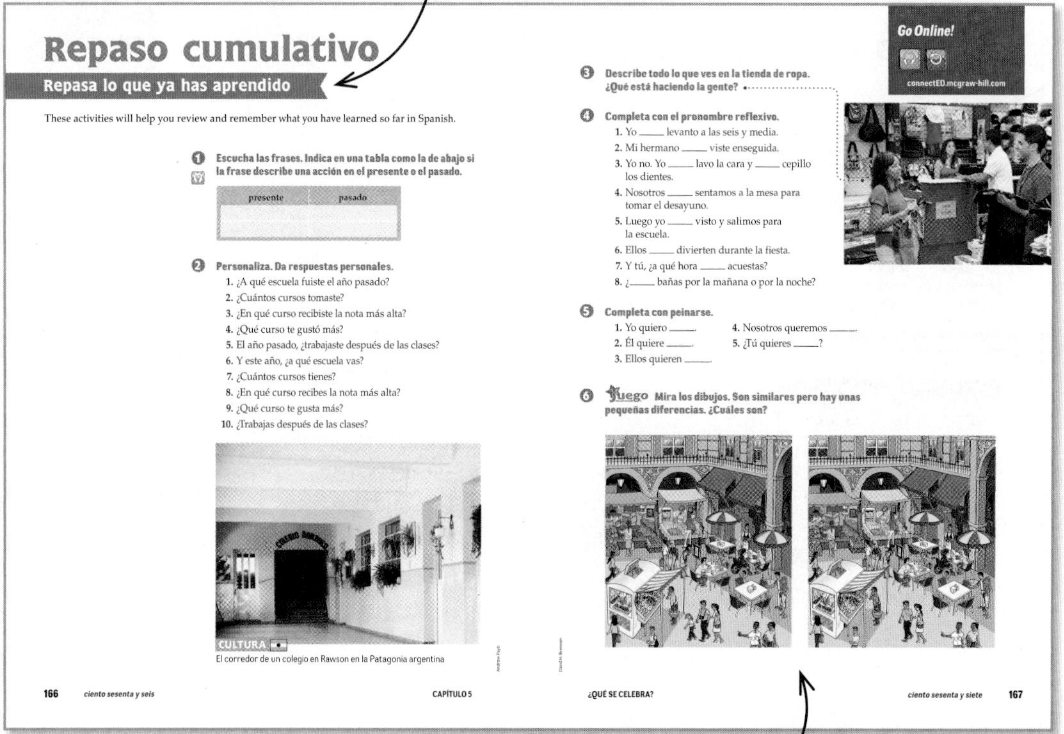

Repaso cumulativo

Repasa lo que ya has aprendido

These activities will help you review and remember what you have learned so far in Spanish.

1 Escucha las frases. Indica en una tabla como la de abajo si la frase describe una acción en el presente o el pasado.

presente	pasado

2 Personaliza. Da respuestas personales.

1. ¿A qué escuela fuiste el año pasado?
2. ¿Cuántos cursos tomaste?
3. ¿En qué curso recibiste la nota más alta?
4. ¿Qué curso te gustó más?
5. El año pasado, ¿trabajaste después de las clases?
6. Y este año, ¿a qué escuela vas?
7. ¿Cuántos cursos tienes?
8. ¿En qué curso recibes la nota más alta?
9. ¿Qué curso te gusta más?
10. ¿Trabajas después de las clases?

CULTURA
El corredor de un colegio en Rawson en la Patagonia argentina

Go Online!
connectED.mcgraw-hill.com

3 Describe todo lo que ves en la tienda de ropa. ¿Qué está haciendo la gente?

4 Completa con el pronombre reflexivo.

1. Yo ____ levanto a las seis y media.
2. Mi hermano ____ viste enseguida.
3. Yo no. Yo ____ lavo la cara y ____ cepillo los dientes.
4. Nosotros ____ sentamos a la mesa para tomar el desayuno.
5. Luego yo ____ visto y salimos para la escuela.
6. Ellos ____ divierten durante la fiesta.
7. Y tú, ¿a qué hora ____ acuestas?
8. ¿____ bañas por la mañana o por la noche?

5 Completa con peinarse.

1. Yo quiero ____.
2. Él quiere ____.
3. Ellos quieren ____.
4. Nosotros queremos ____.
5. ¿Tú quieres ____?

6 Juego Mira los dibujos. Son similares pero hay unas pequeñas diferencias. ¿Cuáles son?

166 *ciento sesenta y seis* CAPÍTULO 5 ¿QUÉ SE CELEBRA? *ciento sesenta y siete* 167

Illustrations recombine material to remind you what you have already learned in Spanish. Use the illustration as a prompt to demonstrate how much you can say or write.

Enhance your appreciation of literature and culture.

Literary Reader gives you another opportunity to apply your reading skills in Spanish.

Literary selections present another view of Hispanic culture.

Level-appropriate literature selections make reading fun.

Practice your Language Arts skills.

Informational and authentic texts will provide you with the opportunity to improve your Language Arts skills while using your Spanish.

Dear Student,

Foldables are interactive study organizers that you can make yourself. They are a wonderful resource to help you organize and retain information. Foldables have many purposes. You can use them to remember vocabulary words or to organize more in-depth information on any given topic, such as keeping track of what you know about a particular country.

You can write general information, such as titles, vocabulary words, concepts, questions, main ideas, and dates, on the front tabs of your Foldables. You view this general information every time you look at a Foldable. This helps you focus on and remember key points without the distraction of additional text. You can write specific information—supporting ideas, thoughts, answers to questions, research information, empirical data, class notes, observations, and definitions—under the tabs. Think of different ways in which Foldables can be used. Soon you will find that you can make your own Foldables for study guides and projects. Foldables with flaps or tabs create study guides that you can use to check what you know about the general information on the front of tabs. Use Foldables without tabs for projects that require information to be presented for others to view quickly. The more you make and use graphic organizers, the faster you will become able to produce them.

To store your Foldables, turn one-gallon freezer bags into student portfolios which can be collected and stored in the classroom. You can also carry your portfolios in your notebooks if you place strips of two-inch clear tape along one side and punch three holes through the taped edge. Write your name along the top of the plastic portfolio with a permanent marker and cover the writing with two-inch clear tape to keep it from wearing off. Cut the bottom corners off the bag so it won't hold air and will stack and store easily. The following figures illustrate the basic folds that are referred to throughout this book.

Good luck!

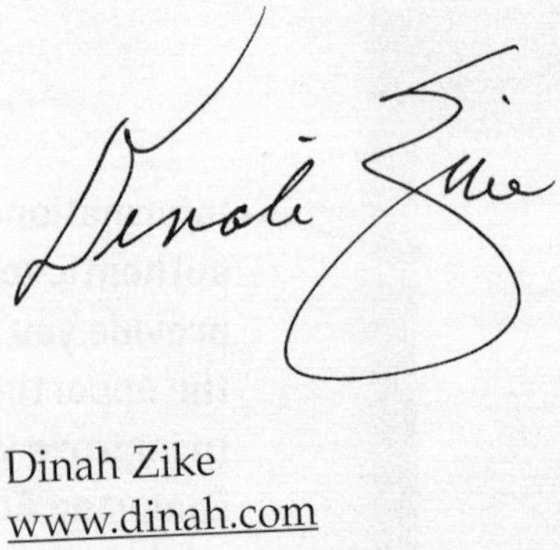

Dinah Zike
www.dinah.com

Doug Martin

Category Book

Los números Use this *category book* organizer as you learn dates and numbers.

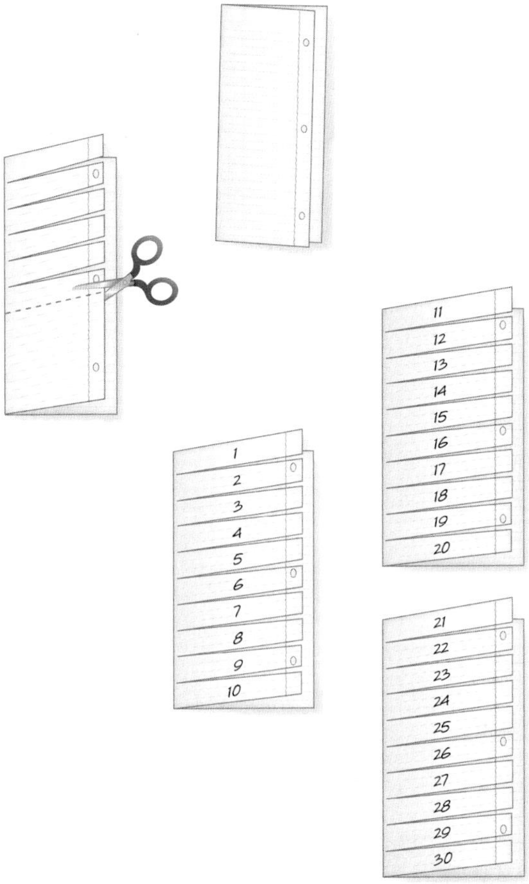

Step 1 **Fold** a sheet of paper (8½" x 11") in half like a *hot dog.*

Step 2 On one side, **cut** every third line. This usually results in ten tabs. Do this with three sheets of paper to make three books.

Step 3 **Write** one Arabic number on the outside of each of the tabs. On the inside write out the respective number. As you learn more numbers, use *category books* to categorize numbers in this way.

Other Suggestions for a *Category Book* Foldable

A *category book* foldable may be used to practice conjugating Spanish verbs. On the top tab, write the infinitive form of a verb. On the following tabs, write the subject pronouns: **yo, tú, él, ella, Ud., nosotros(as), ellos, ellas, Uds.** Then open each tab and write the corresponding form of the verb.

Forward-Backward Book

Las estaciones Use this *forward-backward book* to compare and contrast two seasons of your choice.

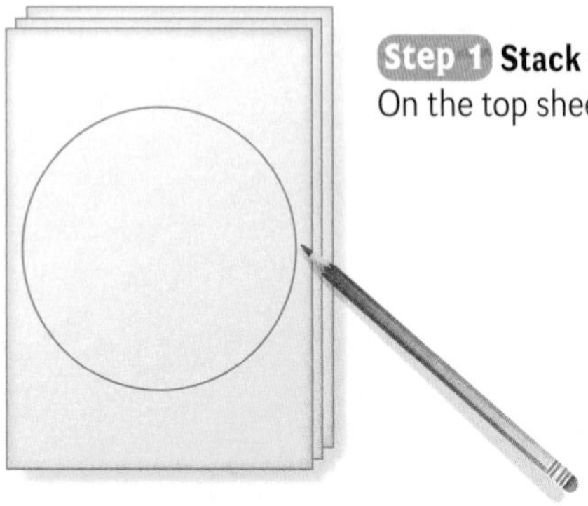

Step 1 **Stack** three sheets of paper. On the top sheet, trace a large circle.

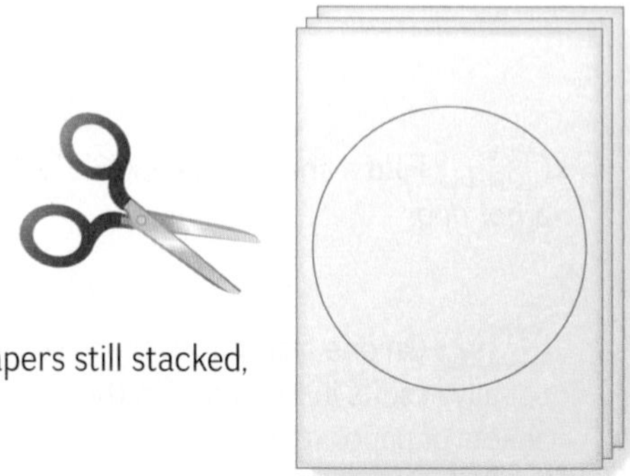

Step 2 With the papers still stacked, **cut out** the circles.

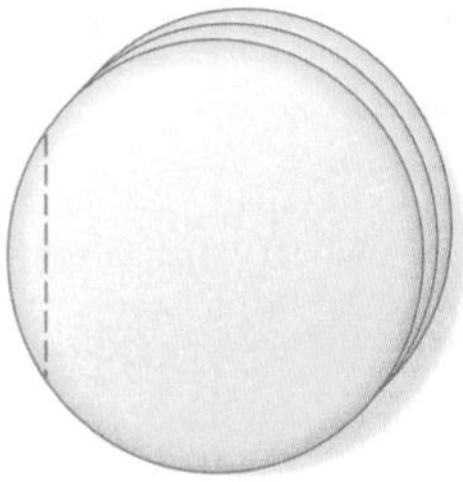

Step 3 **Staple** the paper circles together along the left-hand side to create a circular booklet.

Step 4 **Write** the name of a season on the cover. On the page that opens to the right list the months of the year in that particular season. On the following page draw a picture to illustrate the season.

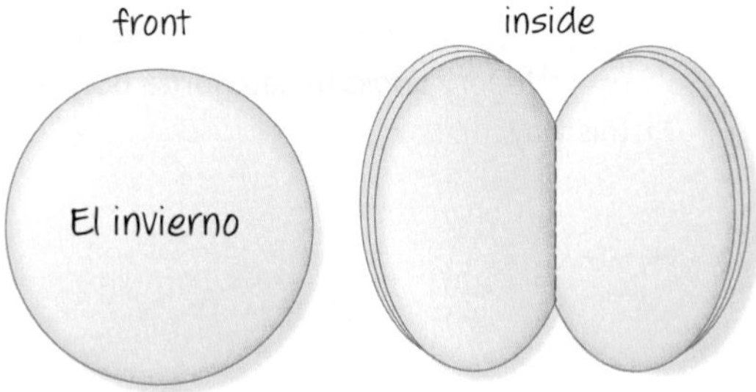

Step 5 **Turn the book upside down** and write the name of a season on the cover. On the page that opens to the right list the months of the year in that particular season. On the following page draw a picture to illustrate the season.

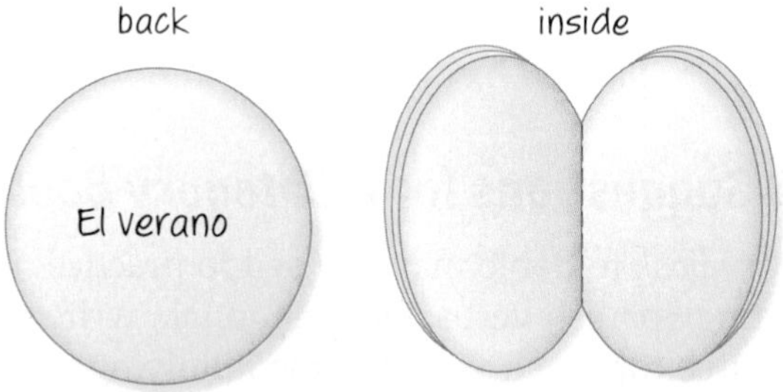

Other Suggestions for a *Forward-Backward Book* Foldable

You may wish to use a *forward-backward book* foldable to organize vocabulary pertaining to the city and the country. On the front cover write **la ciudad.** Open your book. On the right-hand page list words you have learned that pertain to the city. On the next right-hand page, draw a picture illustrating the words on your list. Close your book and flip it over. On the back cover write **el campo** and do the same.

It may be helpful to use a *forward-backward book* foldable to organize the food groups. You could use the name of a food group in Spanish (meat, vegetable, fruit, etc.) as the title. On the inside, list as many foods in this food group as you can on the right-hand page and illustrate these foods on the opposite page. Give the same information for a second food group by reversing the book.

Pocket Book

La geografía Use this *pocket book* organizer in your ongoing study of all the countries in the Spanish-speaking world.

Step 1 **Fold** a sheet of paper (8½" x 11") in half like a *hamburger*.

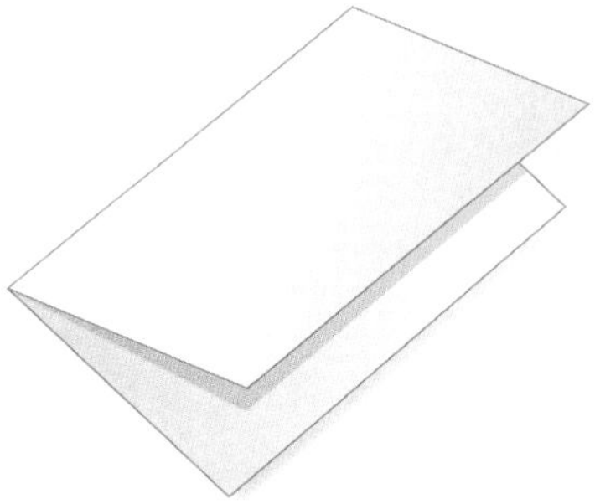

Step 2 **Open** the folded paper and fold one of the long sides up two inches to form a pocket. Refold the *hamburger* fold so that the newly formed pockets are on the inside.

Step 3 **Glue** the outer edges of the two-inch fold with a small amount of glue.

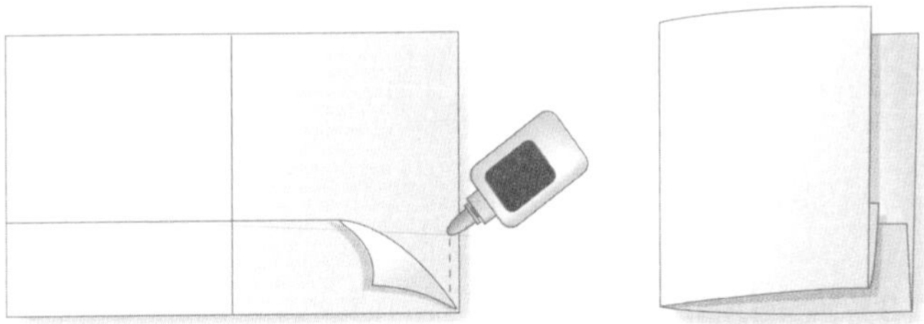

Step 4 **Make a multipaged booklet** by gluing six pockets side-by-side. Glue a cover around the multipaged *pocket book*.

Step 5 **Label** five pockets with the following geographical areas: **Europa, la América del Norte, la América del Sur, la América Central,** and **Islas del Caribe.** Use index cards inside the pockets to record information each time you learn something new about a specific country. Be sure to include the name of the country (in Spanish, of course) and its capital.

Other Suggestions for a *Pocket Book* Foldable

You may wish to use a *pocket book* foldable to organize masculine and feminine nouns or singular and plural forms. You can make an index card to put in the correct pocket each time you learn a new word.

A *pocket book* foldable may be used to organize information about several subjects. For example, to organize information about airplane travel, label pockets with topics such as *preparing for a trip, getting to the airport, at the airport,* and *on the airplane* in Spanish. Make cards for all the words and phrases you know that go with each topic.

If you wish to organize what you are learning about important people, works of art, festivals, and other cultural information in countries that speak Spanish, a *pocket book* foldable may be helpful. You can make a card for each person, work of art, or event that you study, and you can add cards and even add categories as you continue to learn about cultures that speak Spanish.

Vocabulary Book

Sinónimos y antónimos Use this *vocabulary book* to practice your vocabulary through the use of synonyms and antonyms.

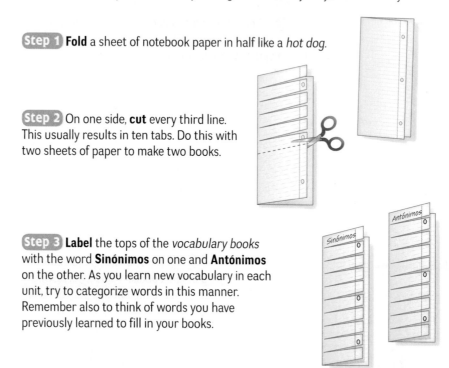

Step 1 **Fold** a sheet of notebook paper in half like a *hot dog.*

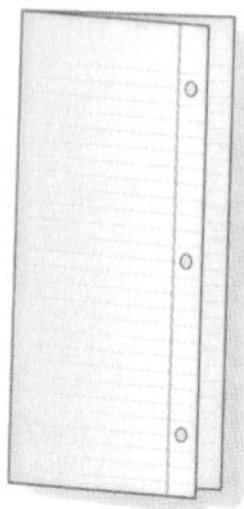

Step 2 On one side, **cut** every third line. This usually results in ten tabs. Do this with two sheets of paper to make two books.

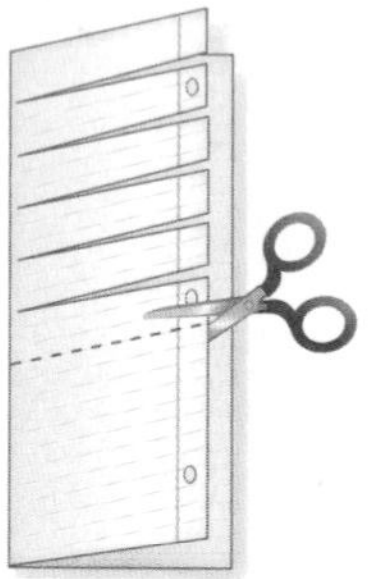

Step 3 **Label** the tops of the *vocabulary books* with the word **Sinónimos** on one and **Antónimos** on the other. As you learn new vocabulary in each unit, try to categorize words in this manner. Remember also to think of words you have previously learned to fill in your books.

Other Suggestions for a *Vocabulary Book* Foldable

You may wish to use a *vocabulary book* foldable to help you practice your informal commands. On the front of each flap, write the infinitive form of a verb. Then open each flap and write the informal **(tú)** command of the verb.

You can use a *vocabulary book* foldable to help remember any verb conjugation in Spanish. Write the infinitive at the top. If you know several tenses of a verb, you should also write what tense or tenses are being practiced. On the outside of the foldable, write the pronouns and, on the inside, write the corresponding verb form. You can use this as a quick study and review tool for any verb. At a more advanced level, you may wish to write many verbs on the outside and entire conjugations on the inside.

You may wish to use a *vocabulary book* foldable to help organize different kinds of clothing. Come up with categories in Spanish to list on the outside, such as *school, casual, men's, women's, summer, winter,* etc. On the inside, list as many articles of clothing fitting the category as you can in Spanish.

You can use *vocabulary book* foldables to practice adjective forms. Create two *vocabulary book* foldables, one for singular forms and the other for plural forms. On the singular book, write either masculine or feminine singular adjective forms on the outside and the other forms on the inside. To make this more challenging, write a mix of masculine and feminine forms on the outside, with the corresponding form on the inside. Repeat this process on the second book for the plural forms.

Tab Book

Preguntas Use this *tab book* to practice asking and answering questions.

Step 1 **Fold** a sheet of paper (8½" x 11") like a *hot dog* but fold it so that one side is one inch longer than the other.

Step 2 On the shorter side only, **cut** five equal tabs. On the front of each tab, **write** a question word you have learned. For example, you may wish to write the following.

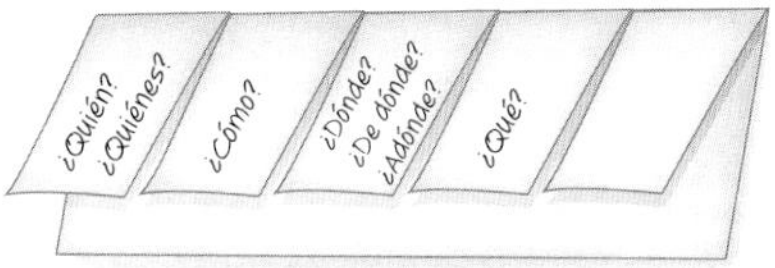

Step 3 On the bottom edge, **write** any sentence you would like.

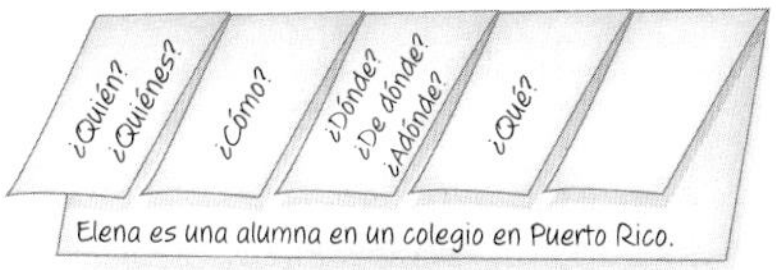

Step 4 Under each tab, **write** the word from your sentence that answers the question on the front of the tab.

Other Suggestions for a *Tab Book* Foldable

You may also use a *tab book* foldable to practice verb conjugations. You would need to make six tabs instead of five. Write a verb and a tense on the bottom edge and write the pronouns on the front of each tab. Under each tab, write the corresponding verb form.

You may wish to use a *tab book* foldable to practice new vocabulary words. Leave extra space on the bottom edge. Choose five or six vocabulary words and write each one on a tab.

You may also use a *tab book* to practice the subjunctive. On the top of each tab, write an expression that requires the subjunctive, for example **Es imposible que...** . Then open each tab and write a sentence using that expression with the subjunctive.

Miniature Matchbook

Descripciones Use this *miniature matchbook* to help communicate in an interesting and more descriptive way.

Step 1 **Fold** a sheet of paper (8½" x 11") in half like a *hot dog*.

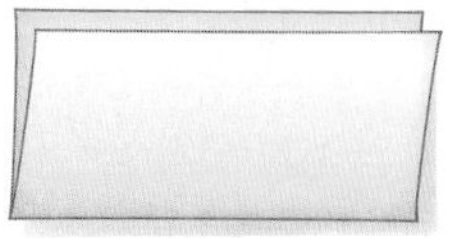

Step 2 **Cut** the sheet in half along the fold line.

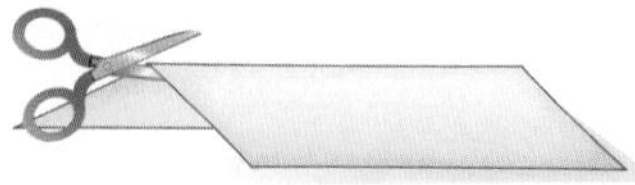

Step 3 **Fold** the two long strips in half like *hot dogs*, leaving one side ½" shorter than the other side.

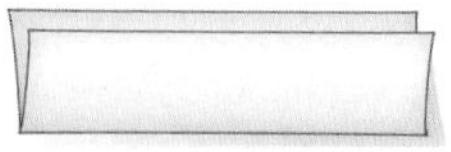

Step 4 **Fold** the ½" tab over the shorter side on each strip.

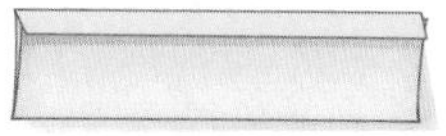

Step 5 **Cut** each of the two strips in half forming four halves. Then cut each half into thirds, making twelve *miniature matchbooks*.

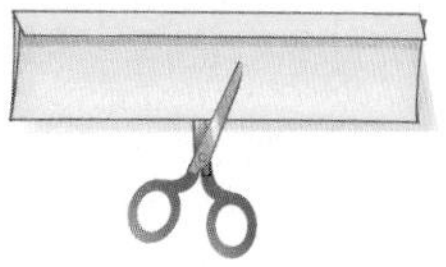

Step 6 **Glue** the twelve small *matchbooks* inside a *hamburger* fold (three rows of four each).

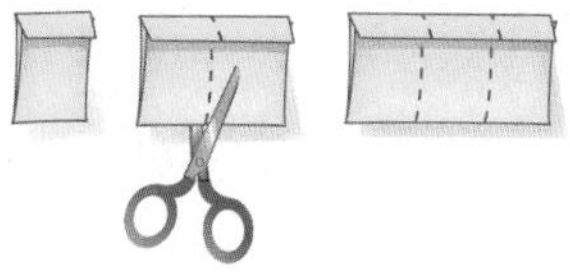

Step 7 On the front of each *matchbook*, **write** a subject you are going to tell or write about, for example, **la escuela.** Open up the tab and list any words you think you could use to make your discussion more interesting. You can add topics and words as you continue with your study of Spanish. If you glue several sections together, this foldable will "grow."

Other Suggestions for a *Miniature Matchbook* Foldable

You may use a *miniature matchbook* foldable to test each other on your knowledge of the vocabulary. Work in pairs with each partner making a blank *miniature matchbook* foldable. Each partner writes a topic related to the subjects you have just studied on the front of each *matchbook*. You may use categories of vocabulary, verbs you have recently learned to conjugate, or the subject of a reading. Your partner then writes as much as he or she can about that topic under the flap. This can alert you if you need to go back and review a topic.

A *miniature matchbook* foldable may help you organize and remember information you have read. After doing a cultural or literary reading, write down a concept presented in the reading on the front of each *matchbook*. Open up each tab and write down supporting details that support the idea.

Single Picture Frame

Dibujar y escribir Use this *single picture frame* to help you illustrate the stories you write.

Step 1 **Fold** a sheet of paper (8½" x 11") in half like a *hamburger*.

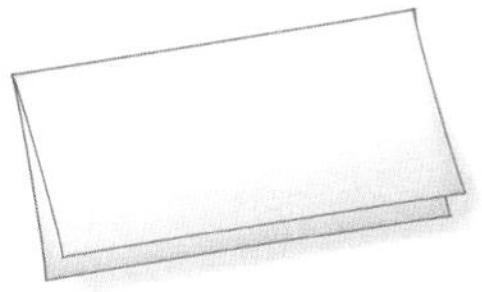

Step 2 **Open** the *hamburger* and gently roll one side of the *hamburger* toward the valley. Try not to crease the roll.

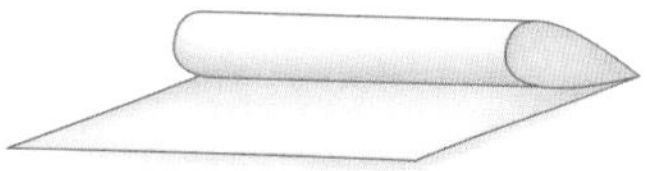

Step 3 **Cut** a rectangle out of the middle of the rolled side of paper, leaving a ½" border and forming a frame.

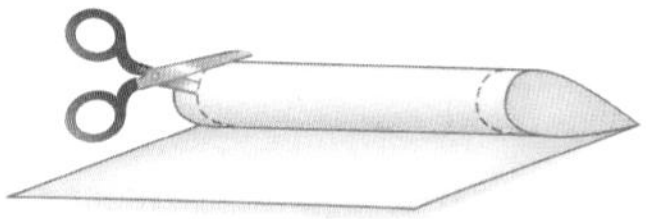

Step 4 **Fold** another sheet of paper (8½" x 11") in half like a *hamburger*.

Step 5 **Apply** glue to the picture frame and place it inside the *hamburger* fold.

Variation:

- Place a picture behind the frame and glue the edges of the frame to the other side of the *hamburger* fold. This locks the picture in place.
- Cut out only three sides of the rolled rectangle. This forms a window with a cover that opens and closes.

Other Suggestions for a *Single Picture Frame* Foldable

You may wish to write about a shopping trip using a *single picture frame* foldable. Before you begin, organize what you will say by drawing your path through the shops at the market, through the supermarket, or through the mall. You can then write about the shopping trip using your drawings as a guide.

Work in small groups. Each student should create a *single picture frame* foldable with a picture glued into it. You may either cut out a magazine picture or draw your own, although it should be fairly complex. Then give your foldable to another member of the group who will write sentences about what is in the picture and what people in the picture are doing. That student will pass it on to a third student who will write sentences about what is not in the picture and what people in the picture are not doing. The foldables can be passed to additional students to see if they can add more sentences.

Minibook

Mi autobiografía Use this *minibook* organizer to write and illustrate your autobiography. Before you begin to write, think about the many things concerning yourself that you have the ability to write about in Spanish. On the left pages, draw the events of your life in chronological order. On the right, write about your drawings.

Step 1 **Fold** a sheet of paper (8½" x 11") in half like a *hot dog.*

Step 2 **Fold** it in half again like a *hamburger.*

Step 3 Then **fold** in half again, forming eight sections.

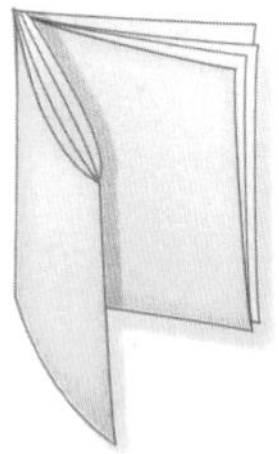

Step 4 **Open** the fold and **cut** the eight sections apart.

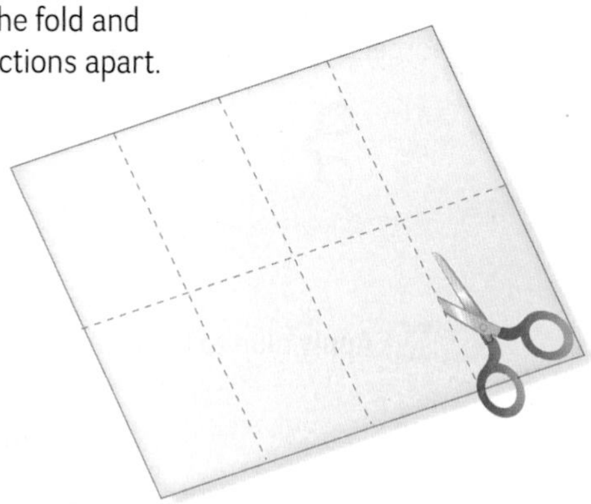

Step 5 **Place** all eight sections in a stack and fold in half like a *hamburger.*

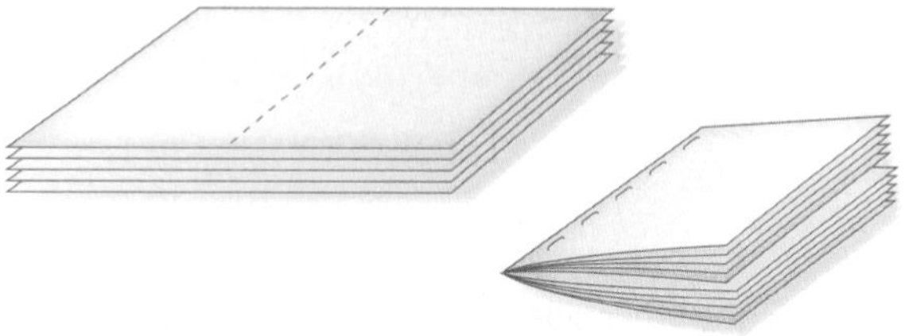

Step 6 **Staple** along the center fold line. **Glue** the front and back sheets into a construction paper cover.

Other Suggestions for a *Minibook* Foldable

Work in pairs to practice new verbs and verb forms using a *minibook* foldable. Illustrate different verbs on the left pages. If it is not clear what pronoun is required, you should write the pronoun under the drawing, for instance to differentiate between *we* and *they*. Then trade *minibooks* and write sentences to go with each picture on the right pages, using the new verb and the pronoun illustrated or indicated.

A *minibook* foldable can be used to help practice the imperfect tense. On each page, draw a picture of an activity that you enjoyed doing frequently. Below each picture, write a sentence describing what was happening. Remember to use the imperfect and to stick to the words you already know in Spanish.

Paper File Folder

Las emociones Use this *paper file folder* organizer to keep track of happenings or events that cause you to feel a certain way.

Step 1 **Fold** four sheets of paper (8½" x 11") in half like a *hamburger*. Leave one side one inch longer than the other side.

Step 2 On each sheet, **fold** the one-inch tab over the short side, forming an envelopelike fold.

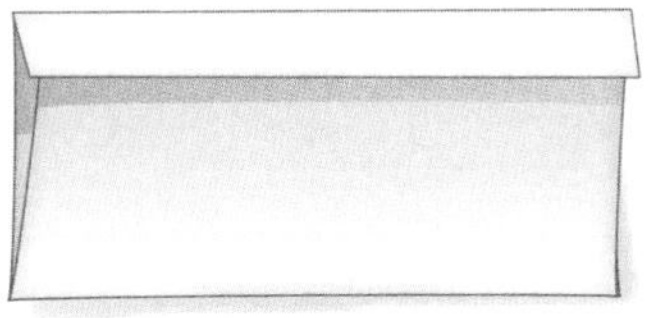

Step 3 **Place** the four sheets side-by-side, then move each fold so that the tabs are exposed.

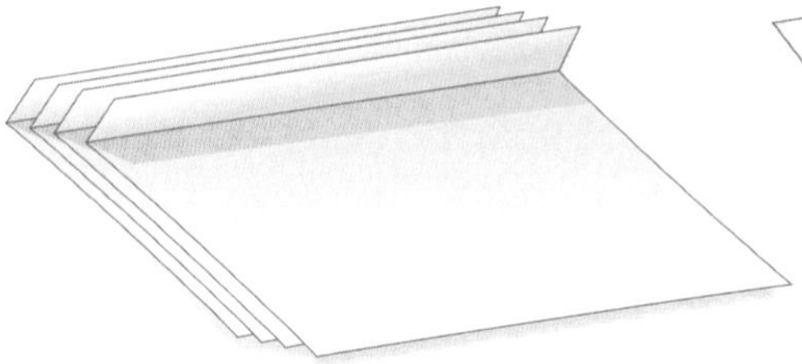

Step 4 Moving left to right, **cut** staggered tabs in each fold, 2⅛" wide. Fold the tabs upward.

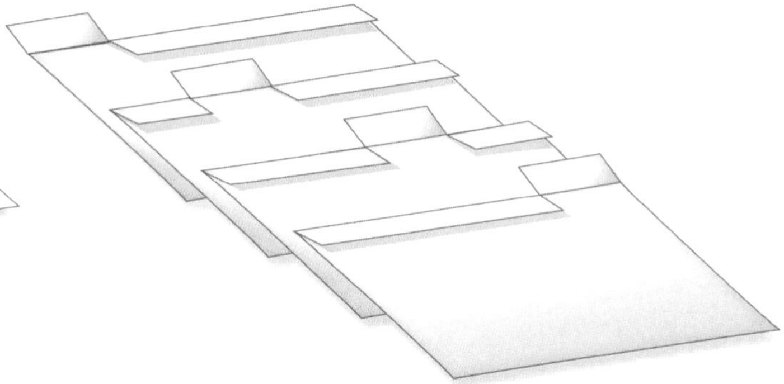

Step 5 **Glue** the ends of the folders together. On each tab, write an emotion you sometimes feel. Pay attention to when it is that you feel happy, sad, nervous, etc. Describe the situation in Spanish and file it in the correct pocket.

Other Suggestions for a *Paper File Folder* Foldable

You may use a *paper file folder* organizer to keep track of verbs and verb forms. You should make a folder for each type of regular verb and for each type of irregular verb. Write the conjugations for some important verbs in each category and file them in the *paper file folder* organizer. Add new tenses to the existing cards and new verbs as you learn them.

A *paper file folder* organizer can be useful for keeping notes on the cultural information that you will learn. You may wish to make categories for different types of cultural information and add index cards to them as you learn new facts and concepts about the target cultures.

Envelope Fold

Un viaje especial Use this *envelope fold* to make a hidden picture or to write secret clues about a city in the Spanish-speaking world you would like to visit.

Step 1 **Fold** a sheet of paper into a *taco* to form a square. Cut off the leftover piece.

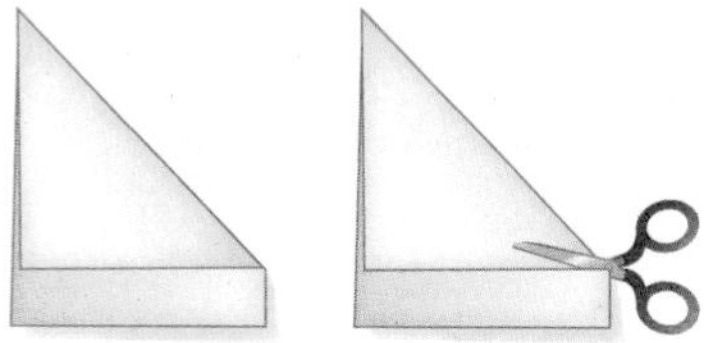

Step 2 **Open** the folded *taco* and refold it the opposite way, forming another *taco* and an X-fold pattern.

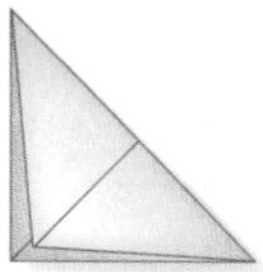

Step 3 **Open** the *taco fold* and fold the corners toward the center point of the X, forming a small square.

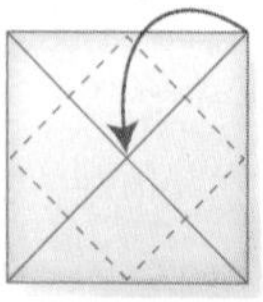

Step 4 **Trace** this square onto another sheet of paper. Cut and glue it to the inside of the envelope. Pictures can be drawn under the tabs.

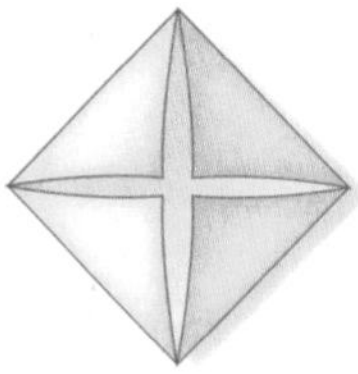

Step 5 Use this foldable to **draw** a picture of the city you would like to visit. Or if you prefer, **write** clues about the city and have your classmates raise one tab at a time until they can guess what city the picture represents. Number the tabs in the order in which they are to be opened.

Other Suggestions for an *Envelope Fold* Foldable

An *envelope fold* can be useful for practicing vocabulary related to airports, trains, technology, or driving. Draw a scene that depicts many of the vocabulary words. Then write on each of the four flaps the new words that are represented under that flap. You could also give the picture to a partner and have the partner fill in the words.

You may want to use an *envelope fold* to review a selection you have read. Depict a scene from the selection on the paper covered by the tabs. Number the tabs in the order they are to be opened and have a partner open the tabs one at a time to guess what scene is illustrated. The partner should then write a description of the scenes.

Large Sentence Strips

El presente y el pasado Use these *large sentence strips* to help you compare and contrast activities in the past and in the present.

Step 1 Take two sheets of paper (8½" x 11") and **fold** into *hamburgers*. Cut along the fold lines, making four half sheets. (Use as many half sheets as necessary for additional pages in your book.)

Step 2 **Fold** each half sheet in half like a *hot dog*.

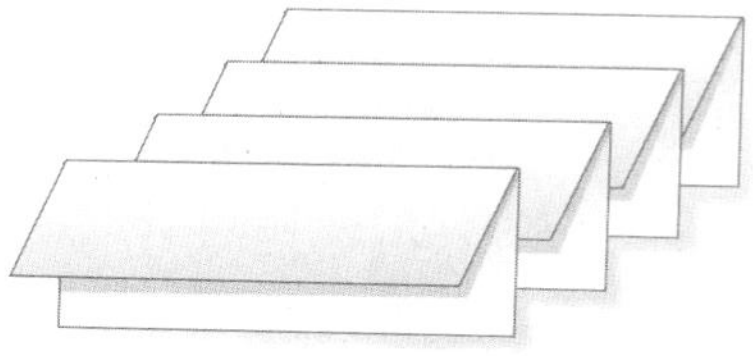

Step 3 Place the folds side-by-side and **staple** them together on the left side.

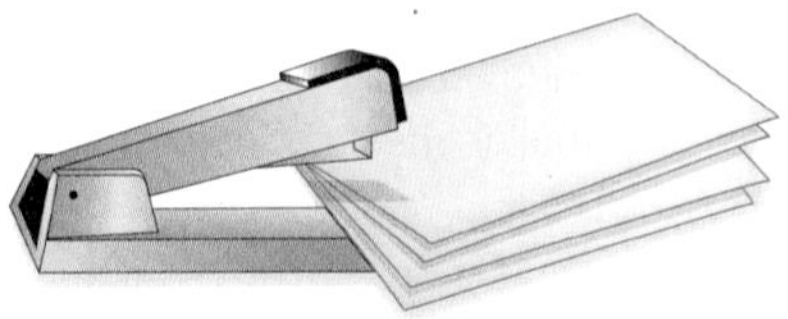

Step 4 About one inch from the stapled edge, **cut** the front page of each folded section up to the top. These cuts form flaps that can be raised and lowered.

Step 5 To make a half-cover, use a sheet of construction paper one inch longer than the book. **Glue** the back of the last sheet to the construction paper strip, leaving one inch on the left side to fold over and cover the original staples. Staple this half-cover in place.

Step 6 With a friend, **write** sentences on the front of the flap, either in the present tense or in the past tense. Then switch your books of sentence strips and write the opposite tense inside under the flaps.

Other Suggestions for a *Large Sentence Strips* Foldable

You may work in pairs to use *large sentence strips* to practice using direct and/or indirect object pronouns. On the front of each flap, write full sentences that have direct or indirect objects or both. Then trade sentence strips. You and your partner will each write sentences under the flaps replacing the direct or indirect objects with object pronouns.

Large sentence strips can help you contrast summer and winter activities. On the front of each flap, write sentences about activities that you do in either summer or winter. Under each flap, you should write that in the other season you do not do that activity, and you should tell what you do instead. This may be done as an individual or a partner activity.

You may use *large sentence strips* to practice using verbs that can be used reflexively and nonreflexively. Write a sentence using a reflexive verb on the outside of each flap. Under the flap, write a sentence using the same verb nonreflexively.

Project Board With Tabs

Diversiones favoritas Use this *project board with tabs* to display a visual about your favorite movie or event. Be sure to make it as attractive as possible to help convince others to see it.

Step 1 **Draw** a large illustration, a series of small illustrations, or write on the front of a sheet of paper.

Step 2 **Pinch** and slightly fold the sheet of paper at the point where a tab is desired on the illustrated piece of paper. Cut into the paper on the fold. Cut straight in, then cut up to form an L. When the paper is unfolded, it will form a tab with the illustration on the front.

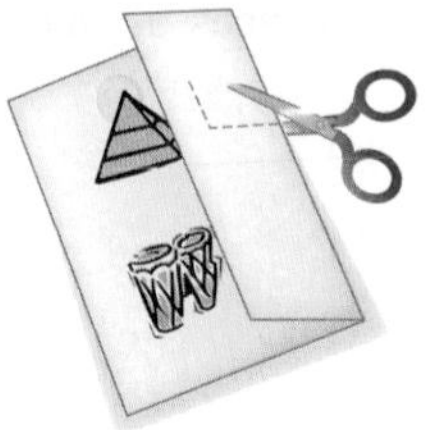

Step 3 After all tabs have been cut, **glue** this front sheet onto a second sheet of paper. Place glue around all four edges and in the middle, away from tabs.

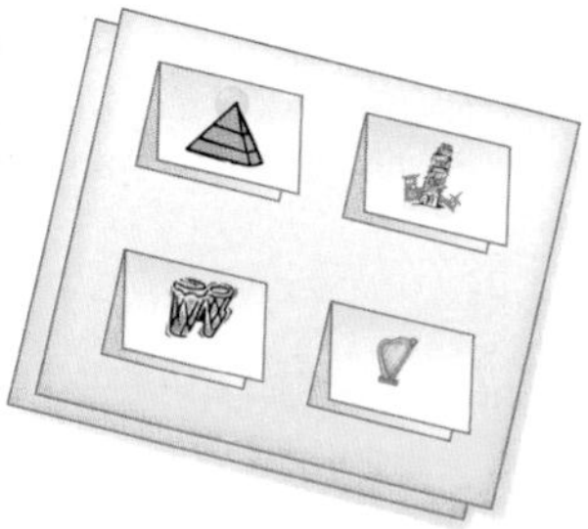

Step 4 **Write** or draw under the tabs. If the project is made as a bulletin board using butcher paper, tape or glue smaller sheets of paper under the tabs.

Think of favorite scenes from a movie or cultural event that you enjoyed and draw them on the front of the tabs. Underneath the tabs write a description of the scene or tell why you liked it. It might be fun to not put a title on the project board and just hang it up and let classmates guess the name of the movie or event you are describing.

Other Suggestions for a *Project Board With Tabs* Foldable

You may wish to use a *project board with tabs* to practice your formal commands. Think of the food words you know in Spanish and use them to create a recipe of your own. Draw a small picture of each ingredient in the order you will use it in your recipe. Next, lift each tab and write instructions about how to prepare each ingredient for your recipe using formal commands. For a more complex recipe, combine two or more *project boards with tabs.*

You may also use a *project board with tabs* to illustrate a party, museum, sport, or concert. Draw one aspect of it on the outside of the tab and write a description of your drawing under the tab.

You may work in pairs to practice the comparative and superlative. Each of you will make a *project board with tabs.* On the outside of each tab, draw a different comparison or superlative. Then trade with your partner and under each tab write a sentence describing the other's illustrations.

You may also wish to use a *project board with tabs* to practice the use of object pronouns. Draw a series of scenes involving two or more people on the outside of the tabs. Write sentences using object pronouns describing the people's conversations.

Sentence Strip Holder

Para practicar más Use this *sentence strip holder* to practice your vocabulary, your verbs, or anything else you might feel you need extra help with.

Step 1 **Fold** a sheet of paper (8½" x 11") in half like a *hamburger*.

Step 2 **Open** the *hamburger* and fold the two outer edges toward the valley. This forms a shutter fold.

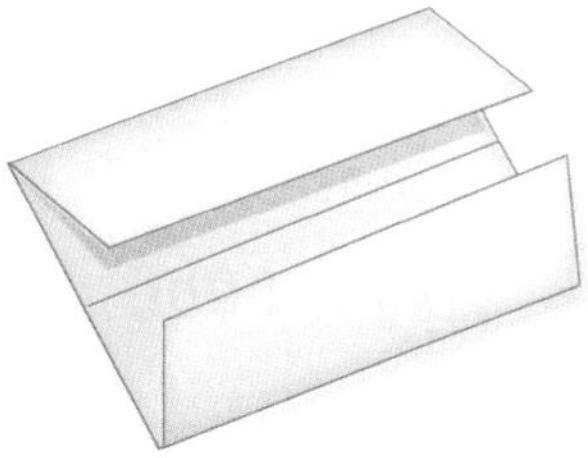

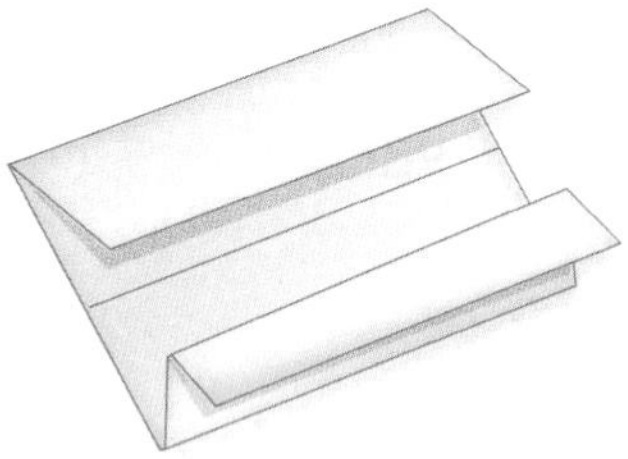

Step 3 **Fold** one of the inside edges of the shutter back to the outside fold. This fold forms a floppy L.

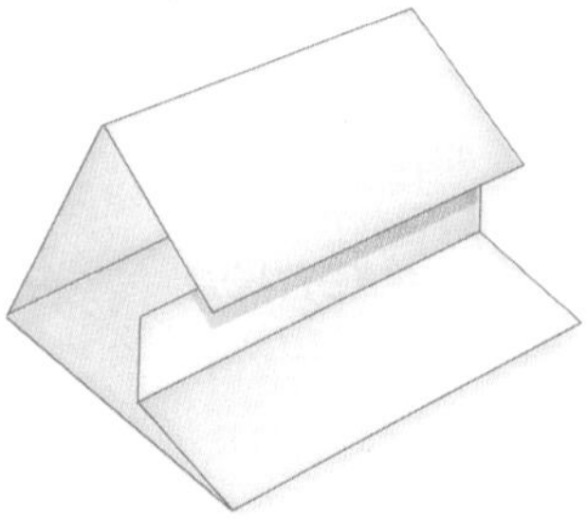

Step 4 **Glue** the floppy L tab down to the base so that it forms a strong straight L tab.

Step 5 **Glue** the other shutter side to the front of this L tab. This forms a tent that is the backboard for the flashcards or student work to be displayed.

Step 6 **Fold** the edge of the L up ¼" to ½" to form a lip that will keep the sentence strips from slipping off the holder.

Vocabulary and verbs can be stored inside the "tent" formed by this fold.

Other Suggestions for a *Sentence Strip Holder* Foldable

You may wish to practice new or irregular verbs using a *sentence strip holder*. Work in pairs. Make flash cards showing the infinitives of the verbs to practice in Spanish. You should each take half of the cards and take turns setting one verb on the *sentence strip holder*. One partner will then say as many sentences as possible using different forms of that verb, and the other will write down the subject and conjugated verb form (or just the verb form) for each sentence. Partners should check to make sure each verb form is spelled correctly. You can repeat this activity for each verb.

You may practice food vocabulary working in small groups and using a *sentence strip holder*. Groups may make flash cards containing the names of local restaurants that everyone will be familiar with, making sure to include different types of restaurants. Put the cards up on the *sentence strip holder* one at a time. Students will spend several minutes writing about what they like to eat at that restaurant. After writing about each restaurant on the list, share your favorite foods with the group.

El alfabeto español

a *avión* 

b *bebé* 

c *cesta* 

d *dedo* 

e *elefante* 

f *foto* 

g *gemelas* 

h *hamaca* 

i *iglesia* 

j *jabón* 

k *kilo* 

l *lago* 

m *mono* 

n *nariz* 

ñ *ñame* 

o *oso* 

p *pelo* 

q *queso* 

r *rana* 

s *sala* 

t *té* 

u *uva* 

v *vaca* 

w *Washington, D.C.* 

x *examen* 

y *yeso* 

z *zapato* 

ch *chicle* 

ll *lluvia* 

rr *guitarra* 

Ch, ll, *and* ***rr*** *are not letters of the Spanish alphabet. However, it is important for you to learn the sounds they represent.*

Spanish is the language of almost 400 million people around the world. Spanish had its origin in Spain. It is sometimes fondly called the "language of Cervantes," the author of the famous novel *El Quijote*. The Spanish **conquistadores** and **exploradores** brought their language to the Americas in the fifteenth and sixteenth centuries. Spanish is the official language of almost all the countries of Central and South America. It is the official language of Mexico and several of the larger islands in the Caribbean. Spanish is also the heritage language of more than fifty million people in the United States.

CULTURA

México

CULTURA

Perú

CULTURA

Puerto Rico

CULTURA

España

(bl)Rebecca Smith, (others)Andrew Payti

El mundo

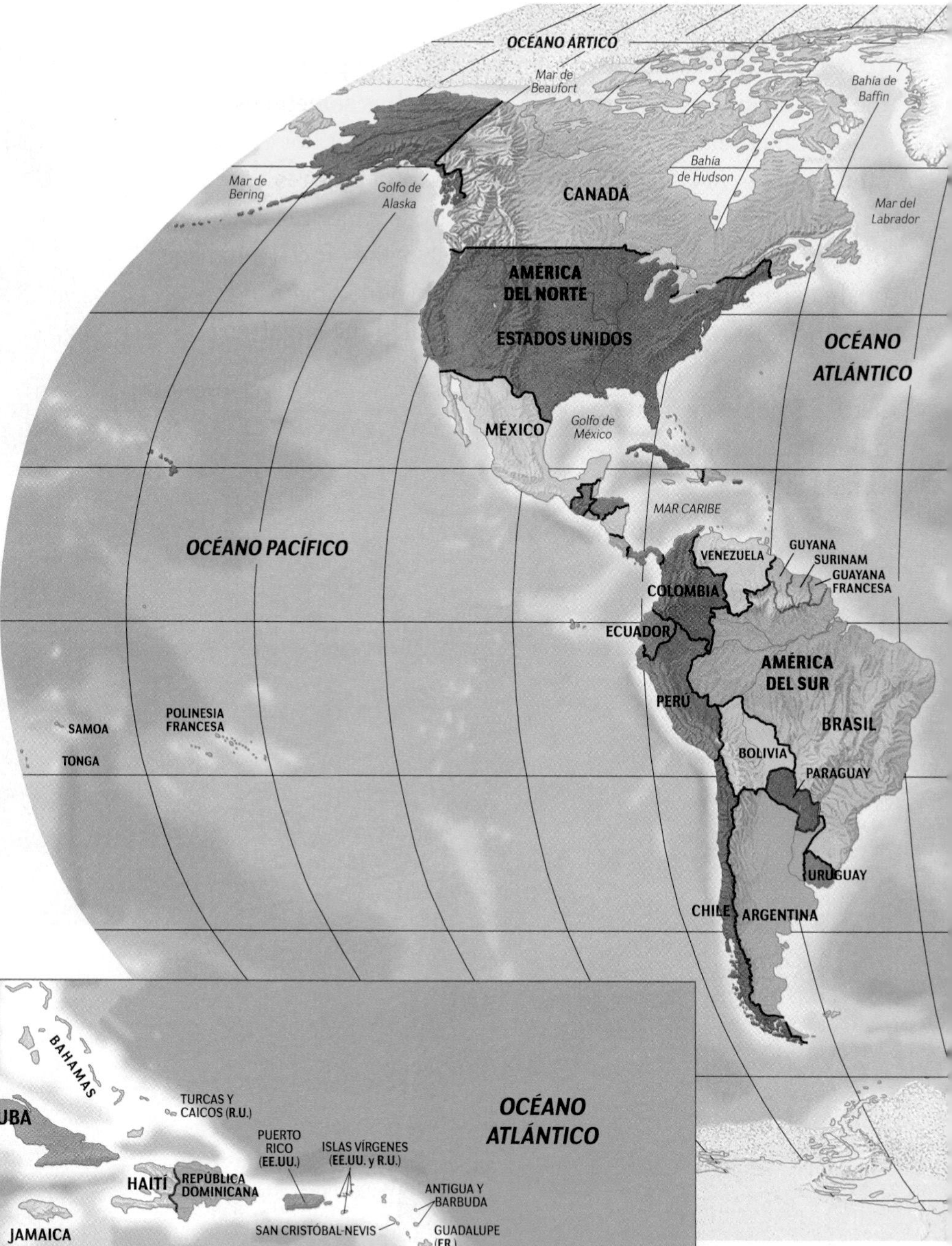
OCÉANO ÁRTICO
Mar de Beaufort
Bahía de Baffin
Mar de Bering
Golfo de Alaska
Bahía de Hudson
CANADÁ
Mar del Labrador
AMÉRICA DEL NORTE
ESTADOS UNIDOS
OCÉANO ATLÁNTICO
MÉXICO
Golfo de México
MAR CARIBE
OCÉANO PACÍFICO
VENEZUELA
GUYANA
SURINAM
GUAYANA FRANCESA
COLOMBIA
ECUADOR
AMÉRICA DEL SUR
PERÚ
BRASIL
SAMOA
POLINESIA FRANCESA
TONGA
BOLIVIA
PARAGUAY
URUGUAY
CHILE
ARGENTINA

GOLFO DE MÉXICO
BAHAMAS
TURCAS Y CAICOS (R.U.)
CUBA
OCÉANO ATLÁNTICO
PUERTO RICO (EE.UU.)
ISLAS VÍRGENES (EE.UU. y R.U.)
MÉXICO
HAITÍ
REPÚBLICA DOMINICANA
ANTIGUA Y BARBUDA
BELICE
JAMAICA
SAN CRISTÓBAL-NEVIS
GUADALUPE (FR.)
GUATEMALA
DOMINICA
HONDURAS
MARTINICA (FR.)
SANTA LUCÍA
MAR CARIBE
EL SALVADOR
SAN VICENTE Y GRENADINES
BARBADOS
ARUBA
NICARAGUA
GRANADA
TRINIDAD Y TOBAGO
COSTA RICA
PANAMÁ
VENEZUELA
GUYANA
OCÉANO PACÍFICO
COLOMBIA
SURINAM

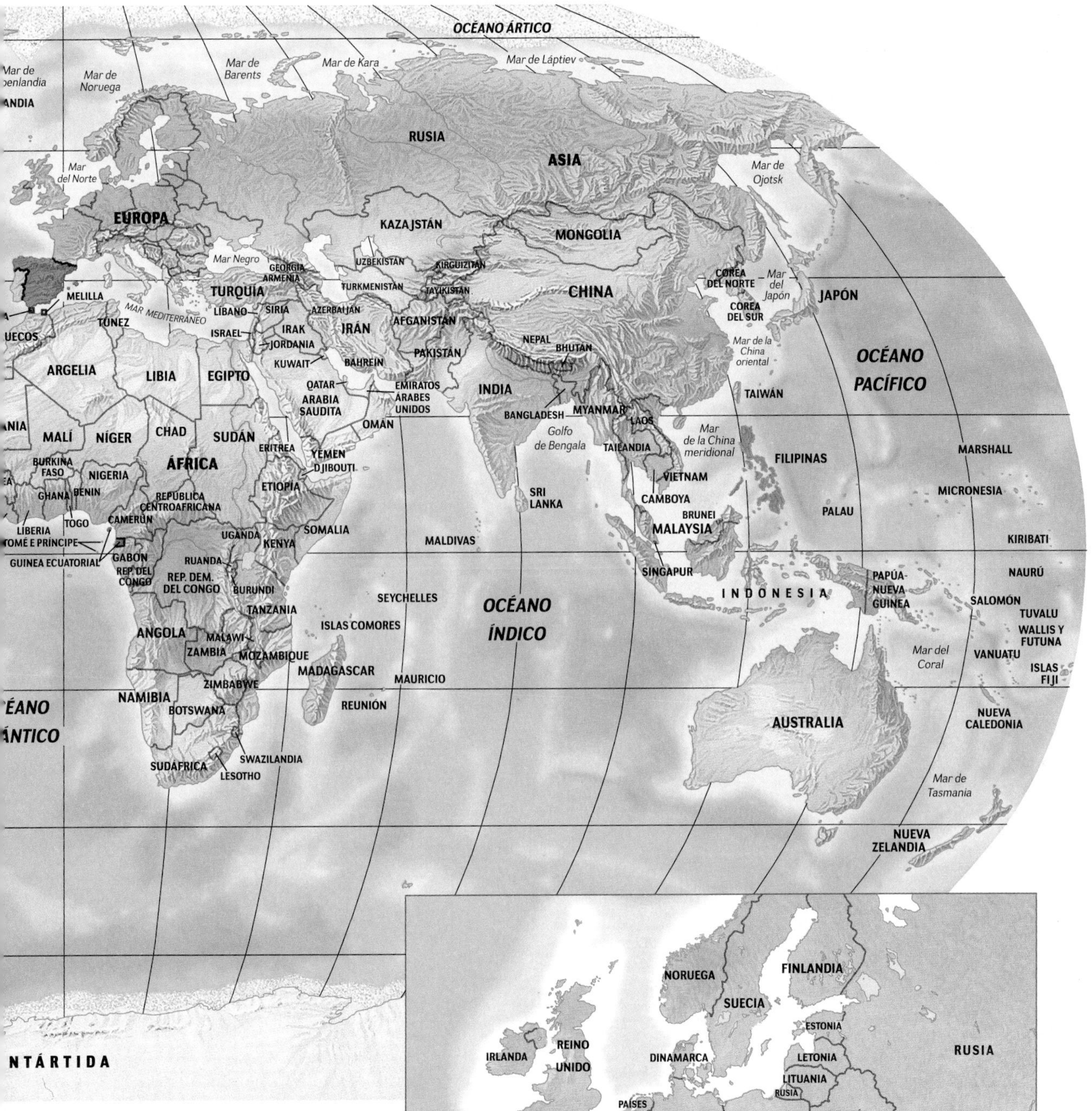
OCÉANO ÁRTICO
Mar de Barents
Mar de Kara
Mar de Láptiev
Mar de Noruega
Mar del Norte
RUSIA
ASIA
Mar de Ojotsk
EUROPA
KAZAJSTÁN
MONGOLIA
Mar Negro
GEORGIA
ARMENIA
UZBEKISTÁN
KIRGUIZISTÁN
TURKMENISTÁN
TAYIKISTÁN
CHINA
COREA DEL NORTE
Mar del Japón
JAPÓN
COREA DEL SUR
MELILLA
TURQUÍA
LÍBANO
SIRIA
AZERBAIJÁN
AFGANISTÁN
TÚNEZ
MAR MEDITERRÁNEO
ISRAEL
IRAK
IRÁN
JORDANIA
NEPAL
BHUTÁN
Mar de la China oriental
KUWAIT
BAHREIN
PAKISTÁN
OCÉANO PACÍFICO
ARGELIA
LIBIA
EGIPTO
QATAR
ARABIA SAUDITA
EMIRATOS ÁRABES UNIDOS
INDIA
TAIWÁN
BANGLADESH
MYANMAR
LAOS
OMÁN
MALÍ
NÍGER
CHAD
SUDÁN
ERITREA
YEMEN
Golfo de Bengala
TAILANDIA
Mar de la China meridional
FILIPINAS
MARSHALL
BURKINA FASO
NIGERIA
ÁFRICA
DJIBOUTI
VIETNAM
GHANA
BENIN
ETIOPÍA
REPÚBLICA CENTROAFRICANA
SRI LANKA
CAMBOYA
MICRONESIA
TOGO
CAMERÚN
BRUNEI
PALAU
LIBERIA
SOMALIA
MALAYSIA
UGANDA
KENYA
MALDIVAS
KIRIBATI
GABÓN
GUINEA ECUATORIAL
RUANDA
REP. DEL CONGO
REP. DEM. DEL CONGO
BURUNDI
SINGAPUR
NAURÚ
INDONESIA
PAPÚA-NUEVA GUINEA
SEYCHELLES
OCÉANO ÍNDICO
TANZANIA
SALOMÓN
TUVALU
ISLAS COMORES
ANGOLA
MALAWI
WALLIS Y FUTUNA
ZAMBIA
MOZAMBIQUE
Mar del Coral
VANUATU
MADAGASCAR
ISLAS FIJI
MAURICIO
ZIMBABWE
NAMIBIA
BOTSWANA
REUNIÓN
AUSTRALIA
NUEVA CALEDONIA
SWAZILANDIA
SUDÁFRICA
LESOTHO
Mar de Tasmania
NUEVA ZELANDIA
NTÁRTIDA

NORUEGA
FINLANDIA
SUECIA
ESTONIA
REINO UNIDO
IRLANDA
DINAMARCA
LETONIA
RUSIA
LITUANIA
RUSIA
PAÍSES BAJOS
BELARÚS
ALEMANIA
POLONIA
BÉLGICA
LUXEMBURGO
OCÉANO ATLÁNTICO
REPÚBLICA CHECA
UCRANIA
ESLOVAQUIA
FRANCIA
SUIZA
AUSTRIA
HUNGRÍA
MOLDOVA
ESLOVENIA
CROACIA
RUMANIA
ANDORRA
BOSNIA-HERZEGOVINA
GEORGIA
PORTUGAL
ESPAÑA
MÓNACO
YUGOSLAVIA (Fed. Rep.)
Mar Negro
ITALIA
BULGARIA
ALBANIA
MACEDONIA
MELILLA
Mar Mediterráneo
CEUTA
GRECIA
TURQUÍA
ÁFRICA
MALTA
CHIPRE
SIRIA
LÍBANO

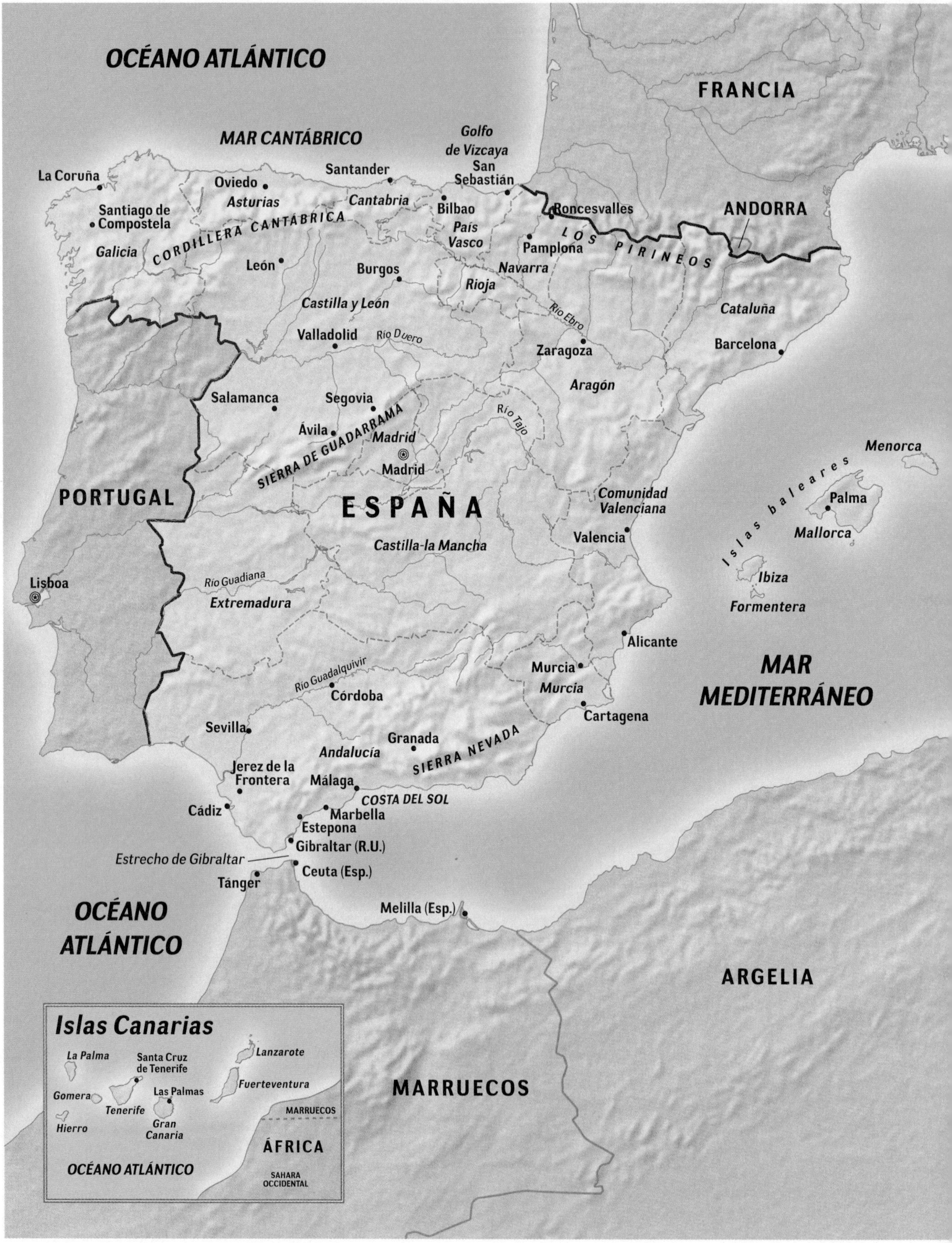
OCÉANO ATLÁNTICO
FRANCIA
MAR CANTÁBRICO
Golfo de Vizcaya
La Coruña
Oviedo
Asturias
Santander
Cantabria
San Sebastián
Bilbao
País Vasco
Roncesvalles
ANDORRA
Santiago de Compostela
Galicia
CORDILLERA CANTÁBRICA
León
Burgos
Pamplona
LOS PIRINEOS
Navarra
Rioja
Castilla y León
Río Ebro
Cataluña
Valladolid
Río Duero
Zaragoza
Barcelona
Aragón
Salamanca
Segovia
Ávila
SIERRA DE GUADARRAMA
Madrid
Río Tajo
Madrid
Menorca
Islas baleares
Palma
Mallorca
Ibiza
Formentera
PORTUGAL
ESPAÑA
Comunidad Valenciana
Valencia
Castilla-la Mancha
Lisboa
Río Guadiana
Extremadura
Alicante
Murcia
Murcia
Cartagena
Río Guadalquivir
Córdoba
MAR MEDITERRÁNEO
Sevilla
Granada
SIERRA NEVADA
Andalucía
Jerez de la Frontera
Málaga
COSTA DEL SOL
Cádiz
Marbella
Estepona
Gibraltar (R.U.)
Estrecho de Gibraltar
Ceuta (Esp.)
Tánger
Melilla (Esp.)
OCÉANO ATLÁNTICO
ARGELIA
MARRUECOS
Islas Canarias
La Palma
Santa Cruz de Tenerife
Lanzarote
Fuerteventura
Las Palmas
Gomera
Tenerife
Hierro
Gran Canaria
MARRUECOS
ÁFRICA
OCÉANO ATLÁNTICO
SAHARA OCCIDENTAL

La América del Sur

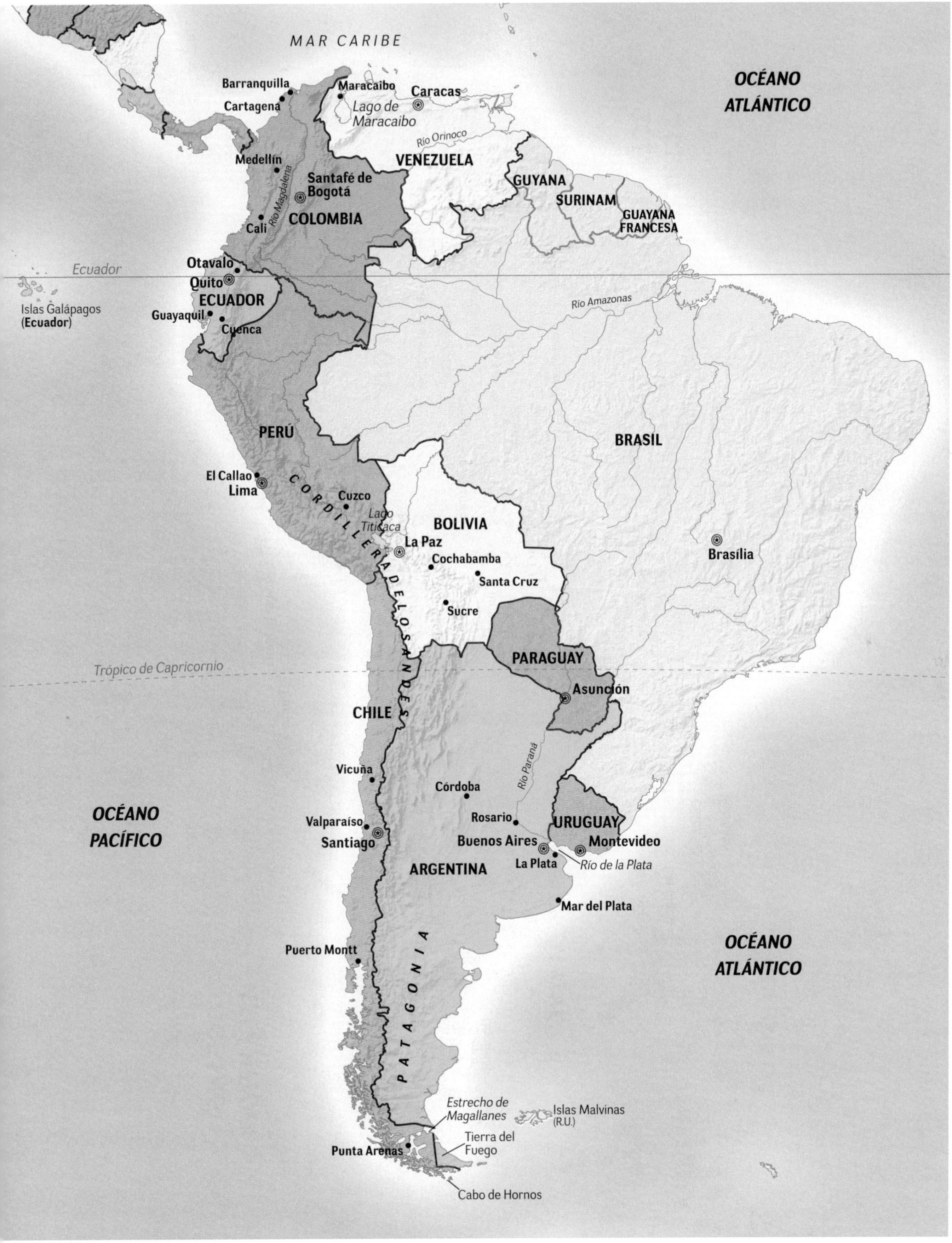

MAR CARIBE
OCÉANO ATLÁNTICO
Barranquilla
Cartagena
Maracaibo
Caracas
Lago de Maracaibo
Río Orinoco
VENEZUELA
Medellín
Santafé de Bogotá
Río Magdalena
COLOMBIA
Cali
GUYANA
SURINAM
GUAYANA FRANCESA
Ecuador
Otavalo
Quito
ECUADOR
Islas Galápagos (Ecuador)
Guayaquil
Cuenca
Río Amazonas
PERÚ
BRASIL
El Callao
Lima
CORDILLERA DE LOS ANDES
Cuzco
Lago Titicaca
BOLIVIA
La Paz
Cochabamba
Santa Cruz
Sucre
Brasília
PARAGUAY
Trópico de Capricornio
Asunción
CHILE
Río Paraná
Vicuña
Córdoba
OCÉANO PACÍFICO
Rosario
URUGUAY
Valparaíso
Santiago
Buenos Aires
Montevideo
La Plata
Río de la Plata
ARGENTINA
Mar del Plata
Puerto Montt
PATAGONIA
OCÉANO ATLÁNTICO
Estrecho de Magallanes
Islas Malvinas (R.U.)
Tierra del Fuego
Punta Arenas
Cabo de Hornos

México, la América Central y el Caribe

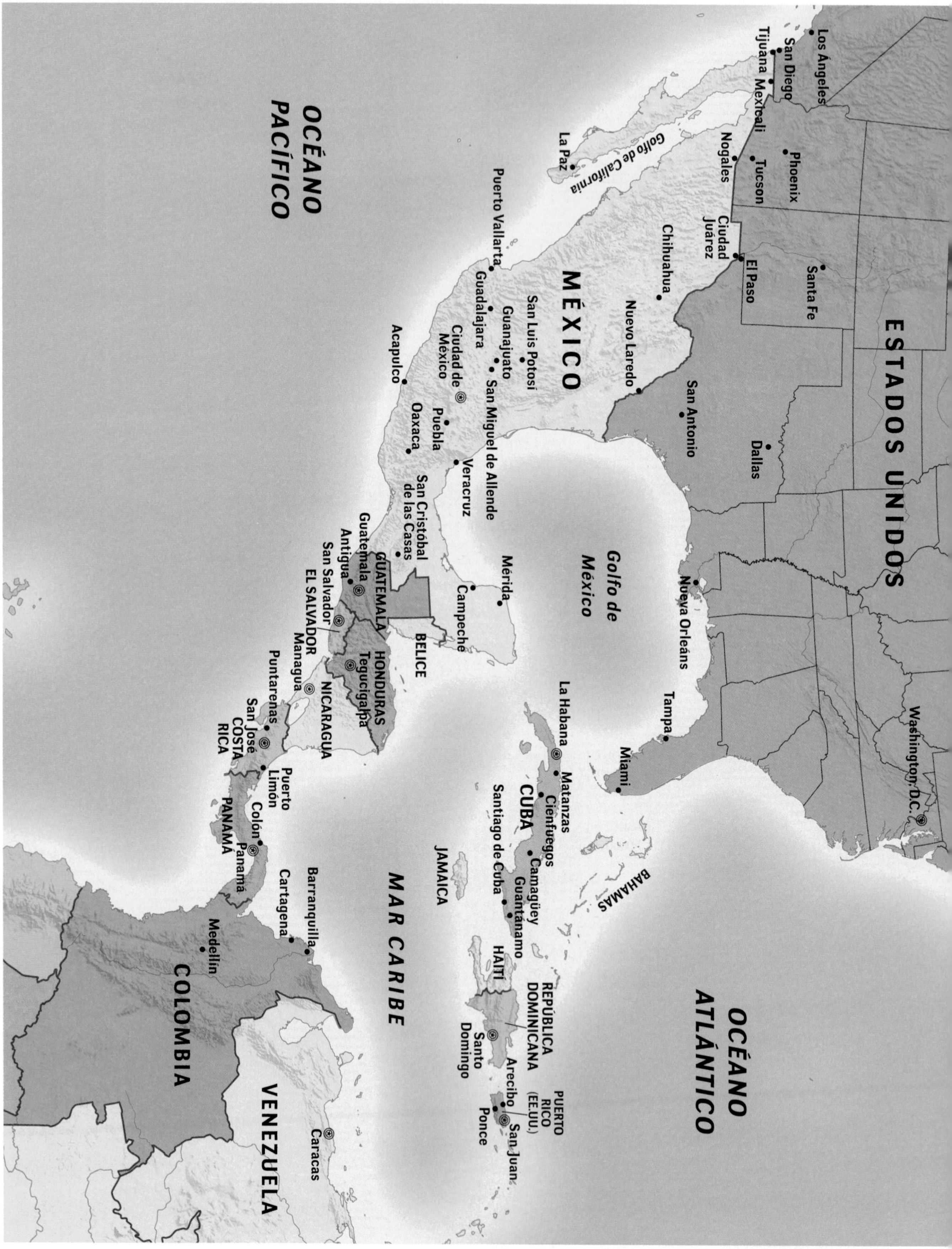

Estados Unidos

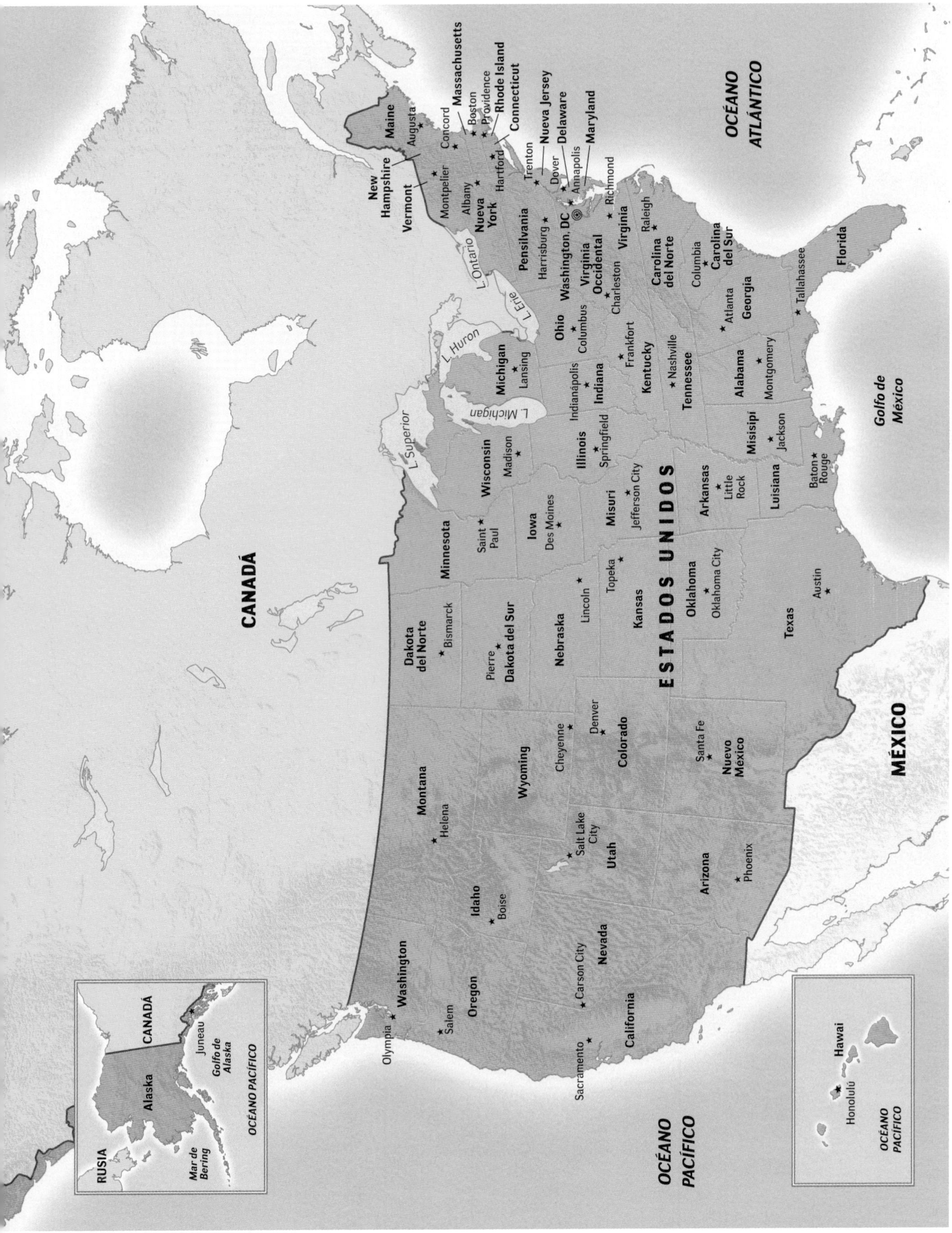

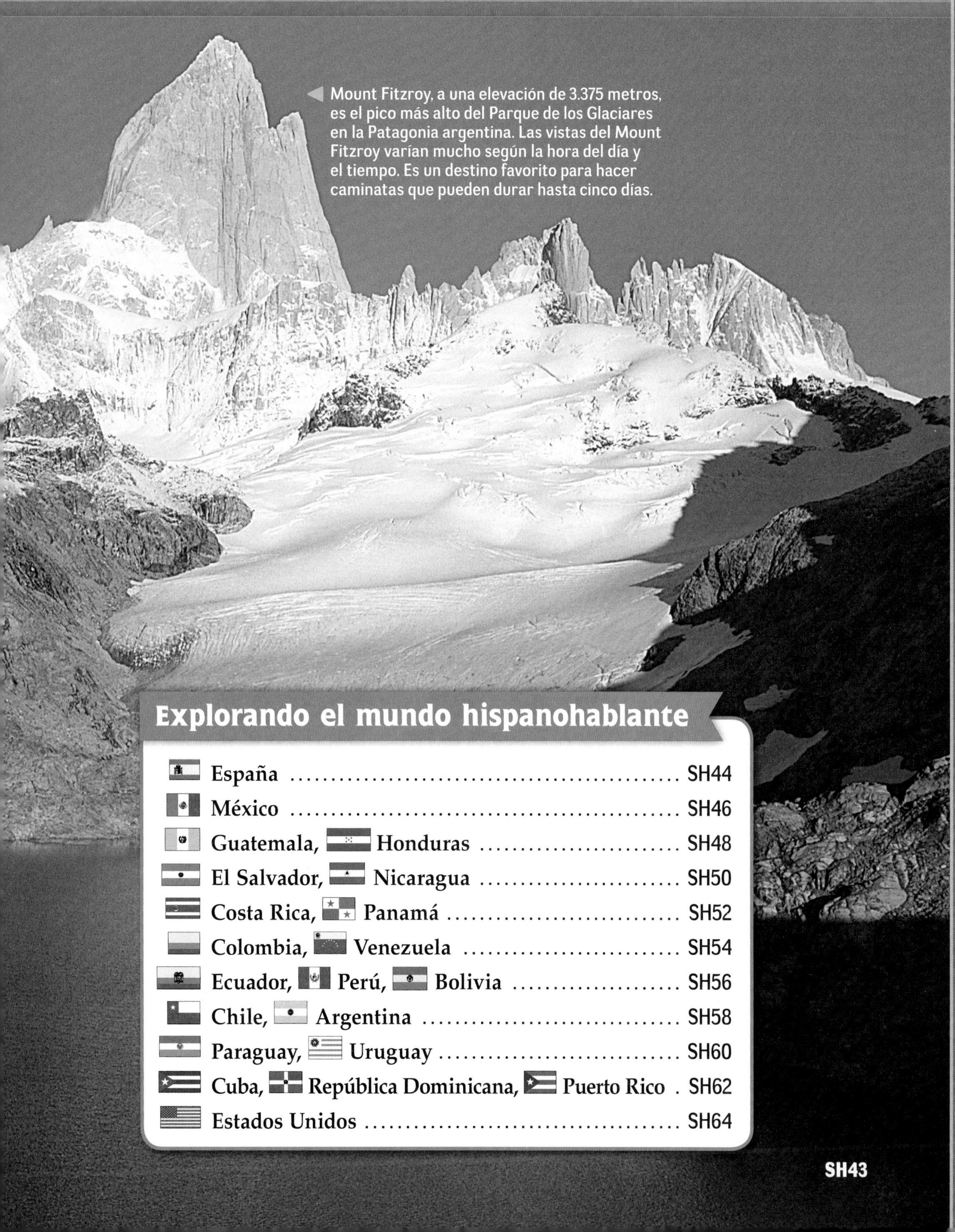

Mount Fitzroy, a una elevación de 3.375 metros, es el pico más alto del Parque de los Glaciares en la Patagonia argentina. Las vistas del Mount Fitzroy varían mucho según la hora del día y el tiempo. Es un destino favorito para hacer caminatas que pueden durar hasta cinco días.

Explorando el mundo hispanohablante

GeoVista

España

España

Mezquita de Córdoba

España

Palacio de Comunicaciones en la Plaza de Cibeles en Madrid, la capital de España

España

Una pescadería en Gijón, Asturias

España

Bailarinas de flamenco en Estepona, España

España

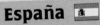

Casares, un pueblo típico en las montañas de Andalucía en el sur de España

Go Online!
connectED.mcgraw-hill.com

España

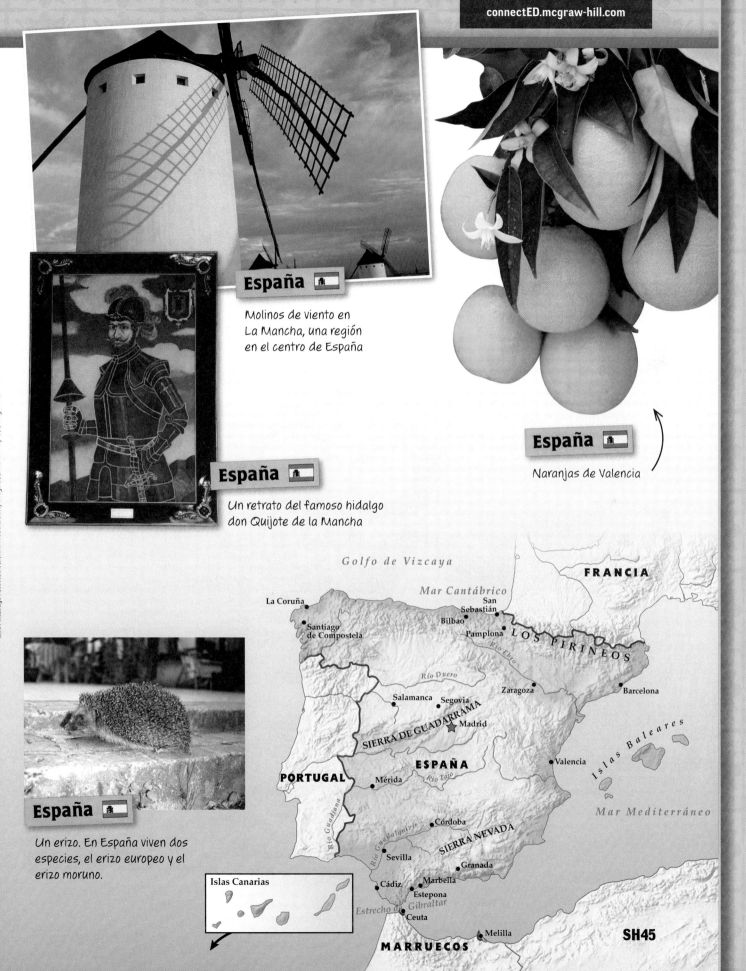

Molinos de viento en La Mancha, una región en el centro de España

España

Naranjas de Valencia

España

Un retrato del famoso hidalgo don Quijote de la Mancha

España

Un erizo. En España viven dos especies, el erizo europeo y el erizo moruno.

GeoVista

México

México

Una vista de la catedral en Tepoztlán en Morelos, México

México

Edificios modernos en la Ciudad de México

México

La mariposa monarca es famosa por su migración anual desde el norte de Estados Unidos hasta el sur de California y los estados de México y Michoacán.

México

Una máscara típica para el Día de los Muertos

México

El balneario de Cancún en la península de Yucatán en la costa del Caribe

(tl tr)Andrew Payti, (c)Kelli Drummer-Avendaño, (bl)U.S. Fish & Wildlife Service/Gene Nieminen, (br)Radius Images/Alamy

México

El monumento de la Independencia en el famoso Paseo de la Reforma en la Ciudad de México, la capital

México

Una tienda de artesanía en isla Mujeres cerca de la costa de la península de Yucatán en México

México

Un mercado en Mérida, México

México

Ruinas famosas de varias civilizaciones indígenas de México en Monte Albán en el estado de Oaxaca en el sur de México

GeoVista

Guatemala Honduras

Honduras

Un puesto de artesanía en una playa de Honduras

Guatemala

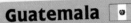

El lago Atitlán y el volcán San Pedro en Guatemala

Guatemala

Una calle de la ciudad colonial de Antigua, Guatemala

Es un coatí. Los coatíes pasan la mayor parte de su tiempo encima de los árboles pero están cómodos también en el suelo.

Honduras

Una cancha de pelota y una estela en Copán, Honduras

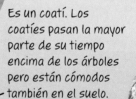

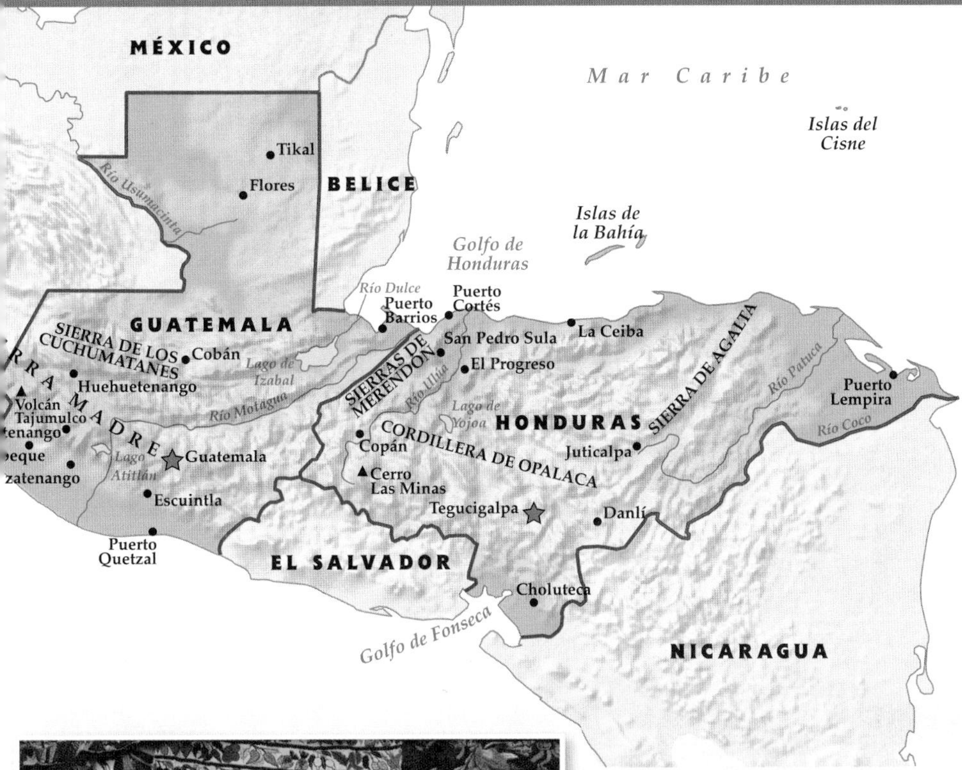

Guatemala

Un quetzal—el pájaro nacional de Guatemala

Guatemala

Se aprecian los tejidos guatemaltecos en el mundo entero. Estos tejidos se venden en un mercado de Santiago de Atitlán.

Guatemala

Dos muchachas llevando una típica falda tejida en Chichicastenango

Honduras

La Plaza Morazán y la Catedral de San Miguel en Tegucigalpa, la capital de Honduras

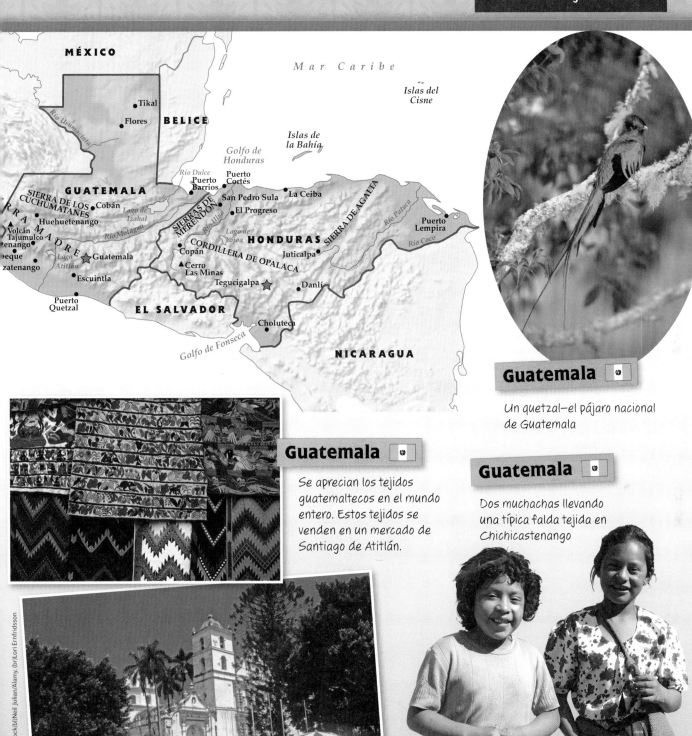

GeoVista

El Salvador Nicaragua

Nicaragua

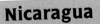

Una vista de Managua, la capital de Nicaragua

Nicaragua

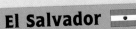

La Catedral de Granada

Nicaragua

El Palacio Nacional de Cultura en Managua que sirve hoy día de Museo Nacional

El Salvador

El mono araña sigue habitando unas regiones de El Salvador.

El Salvador

El volcán Izalco, a unos 45 kilómetros de la capital, San Salvador

El Salvador

La Catedral Metropolitana domina la Plaza Barrios en San Salvador.

Nicaragua

Bueyes en un camino rural del Viejo León

Nicaragua

Un joven pescador en el lago Nicaragua

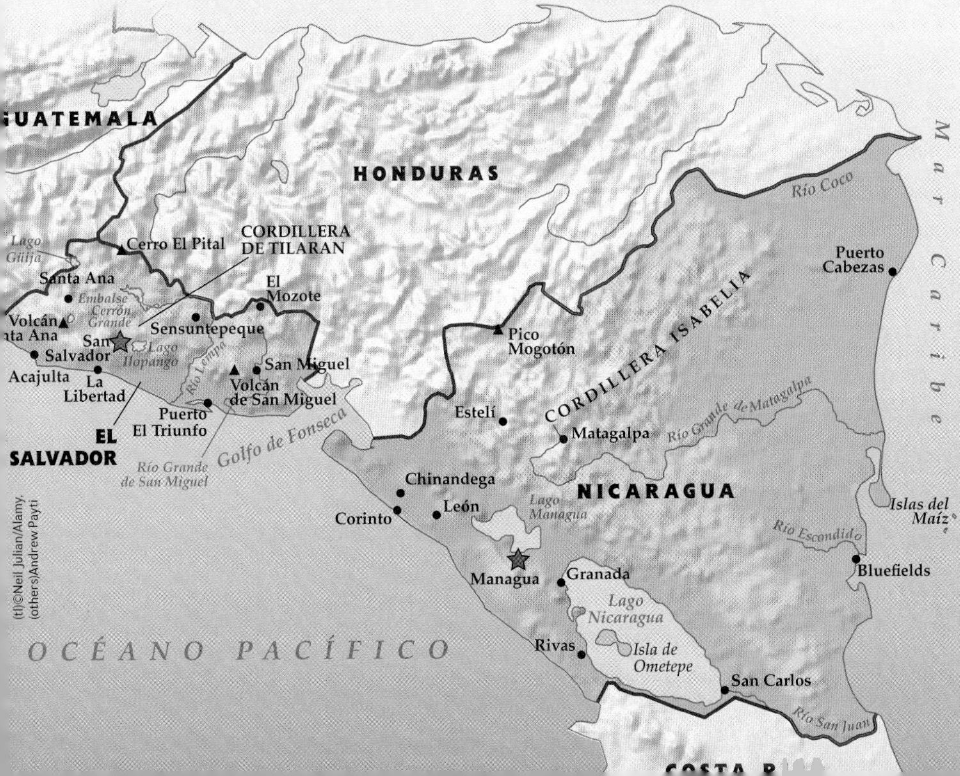

Nicaragua

Cerámicas de mujeres nicaragüenses

GeoVista

Costa Rica Panamá

Panamá

Una vista de los rascacielos modernos de la Ciudad de Panamá

Costa Rica

Un grupo de turistas visitando uno de los muchos lugares de turismo ecológico en Costa Rica

Costa Rica

Un papagayo en una selva costarricense

Panamá

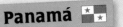

La Iglesia de San Francisco de Asís en el barrio histórico de la Ciudad de Panamá

Panamá

Una vista del canal de Panamá

Go Online!

connectED.mcgraw-hill.com

Panamá

Jóvenes del grupo indígena emberá de la selva tropical cerca de la Ciudad de Panamá

Panamá

El monumento de Vasco Núñez de Balboa en la Ciudad de Panamá

Costa Rica

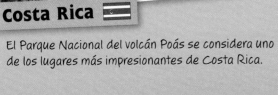

El Parque Nacional del volcán Poás se considera uno de los lugares más impresionantes de Costa Rica.

GeoVista

Colombia Venezuela

Colombia

Aquí vemos un cafeto, la planta que produce el café—un producto importantísimo de Colombia.

Venezuela

El Salto Angel en el Parque Nacional Canaima

Venezuela

Uno de los miles de flamencos que se ven en las lagunas o en vuelo en un parque nacional en Venezuela

Sancocho, un plato tradicional venezolano, tiene variaciones en Colombia también. Aquí hay un sancocho de carne.

Go Online!

connectED.mcgraw-hill.com

Venezuela

Una vista de Caracas, la capital de Venezuela

Venezuela

Un excursionista andino en Venezuela

(tl)Hisham Ibrahim/Getty Images, (tr cr)Kelli Drummer-Avendaño. (cl)Glowimages/Getty Images, (b)Lissa Harrison

Colombia

Una típica callejuela en la zona colonial de Cartagena, Colombia

Venezuela

Un teleférico en las montañas de Mérida

Colombia

La Catedral Primada de Bogotá y su Capilla del Sagrario en la Plaza de Bolívar en Bogotá

GeoVista

Ecuador Perú Bolivia

Perú

Una vista parcial de las ruinas de la ciudad imperial de los incas, Machu Picchu

Perú

Una vista de la catedral y la Plaza de Armas en Cuzco

Perú

Una señora vendiendo tejidos en las orillas del lago Titicaca

Ecuador

La Iglesia de San Francisco en el centro del barrio colonial de Quito

Ecuador

Una playa en la ciudad portuaria de Manta

Go Online!

connectED.mcgraw-hill.com

Ecuador

Unos indígenas en un mercado de Otavalo. Los otavaleños tienen fama mundial por sus tejidos.

Bolivia

Un señor en su balsa en el lago Titicaca

Bolivia

La salina más grande del mundo se encuentra en el Salar de Uyuni ubicado a más de 3.800 metros sobre el nivel del mar.

GeoVista

Chile Argentina

Argentina

Una pareja joven bailando el tango en San Telmo, un barrio de Buenos Aires, la capital de Argentina

Argentina

El Puente de la Mujer es un puente giratorio en Puerto Madero, Buenos Aires. Fue diseñado por el español Santiago Calatrava. El diseño es una imagen de una pareja bailando el tango.

Argentina

La Casa Rosada en la Plaza de Mayo en Buenos Aires

Chile

Una pescadería en Puerto Montt

Chile

Arica, la ciudad más norteña de Chile, con una vista del desierto de Atacama

Andrew Payti

Go Online!
connectED.mcgraw-hill.com

Chile

Caballos en el Parque Nacional Torres del Paine en la Patagonia chilena

Chile

Una vista del valle del Elqui en el norte de Chile

Argentina

Los lobos marinos están tomando el sol en las rocas de Punta Loma cerca de Puerto Madryn. Aquí hay una gran colonia de lobos marinos durante todo el año.

Argentina

Casas típicas del pintoresco barrio La Boca en Buenos Aires

GeoVista

Paraguay Uruguay

Uruguay

Una vista de la Plaza de la Independencia con el monumento al héroe uruguayo José Gervasio Artigas en el centro de Montevideo, la capital de Uruguay

Uruguay

Un guitarrista tocando en una calle de Colonia

Paraguay

Un joven de ascendencia guaraní

Uruguay

Una vista de Pocitos, un bonito barrio playero de Montevideo

Paraguay

Un jaguar, el felino más grande de la América del Sur

Paraguay

La iguana verde se ve en México, Centroamérica y una gran parte de Sudamérica hasta Paraguay y Argentina.

Uruguay

Una vista del puerto deportivo en el balneario famoso de Punta del Este

Paraguay

Las cataratas del Iguazú en la frontera entre Paraguay, Argentina y Brasil

GeoVista

Cuba · República Dominicana · Puerto Rico

Cuba

Músicos tocando en la Casa de las Tradiciones en Santiago de Cuba

República Dominicana

Una plaza en Puerto Plata, un balneario famoso

Cuba

El campanario de la Iglesia y Convento de San Francisco en Trinidad, Cuba

Puerto Rico

Unos alumnos en su uniforme escolar en Fajardo

Cuba

Una vista panorámica de La Habana, la capital de Cuba

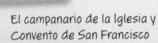

Go Online!
connectED.mcgraw-hill.com

Puerto Rico

La flor—leche de gallina—en el Bosque Nacional El Yunque

Puerto Rico

Muchas especialidades de la cocina puertorriqueña llevan jueyes (cangrejos de tierra).

Puerto Rico

El Yunque, una famosa selva tropical

República Dominicana

Bañadores en la Playa de Cabarete, una favorita entre los surfistas

GeoVista

Estados Unidos

New York

Un señor boricua con su bicicleta y bandera puertorriqueña en el desfile que celebra el día puertorriqueño en la Ciudad de Nueva York

Michigan

Mexicanoamericanos celebrando el Cinco de Mayo en Port Huron, Michigan

Washington

Anclas latinos de televisión en Seattle

Texas

El Paseo del Río en San Antonio

Florida

Una vista del centro de San Agustín, la primera ciudad europea en EE.UU. fundada en 1565 por el español Pedro Menéndez de Avilés

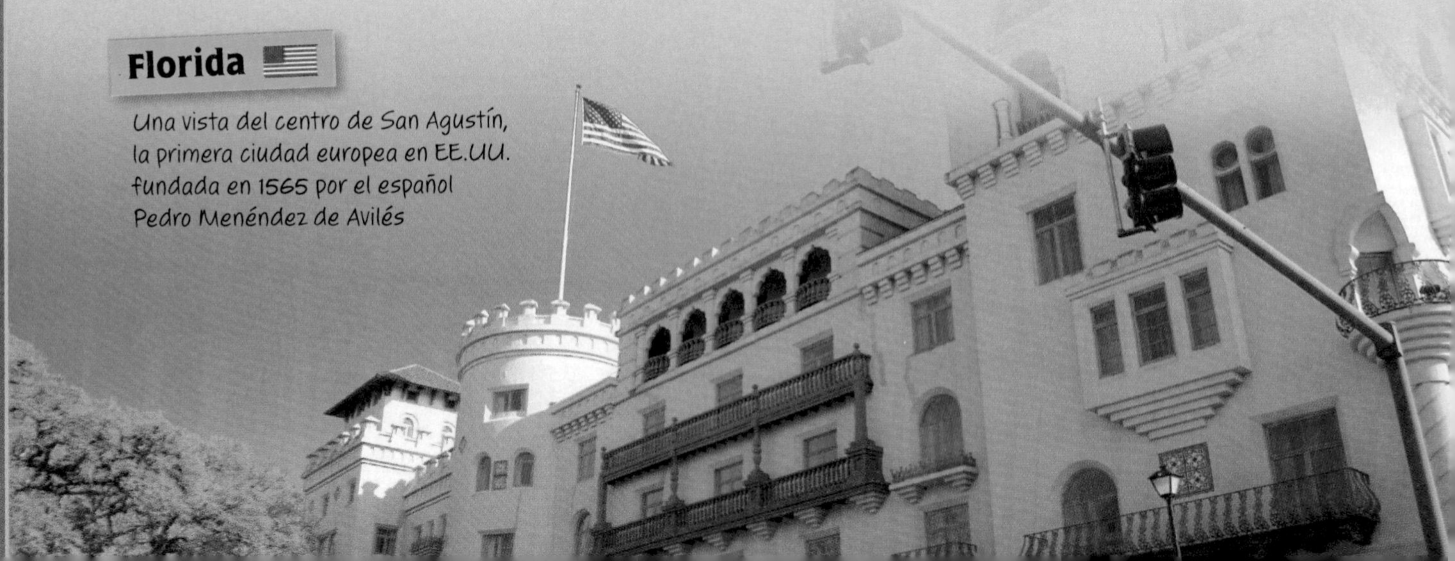

Go Online!

connectED.mcgraw-hill.com

Arizona

Una quinceañera celebrando con su familia

Florida

Un mercado en una calle de la Pequeña Habana en Miami

Florida

El Festival de la Calle Ocho se celebra cada año en marzo en la Pequeña Habana en Miami.

California

La Misión de San Antonio de Padua en Monterey

Preview

In Repaso A, students will review the vocabulary they learned in Level 1 associated with friends, family, and their home. They will also review the verbs **ser** and **tener,** nouns, articles, adjectives, and possessive adjectives.

Leveling EACH Activity

The vocabulary and grammar activities within each chapter are marked according to level of difficulty: **E**asy, **A**verage, and **CH**allenging. Some activities cover a range of difficulty. For example, advanced students will be able to produce more extensive responses while students who learn at a different rate may give less detailed responses. The leveling indicators will help you individualize instruction to best meet your students' needs.

Maria Tejeiro/Getty Images

Go Online! connectED.mcgraw-hill.com — Audio | Video | Práctica | Repaso | Diversiones | eScape | ePals

Go Online!

Audio
Listen to spoken Spanish.

Video
Watch and learn about the Spanish-speaking world.

Práctica
Practice your skills.

Repaso
Review what you've learned.

Diversiones
Go beyond the classroom.

eScape
Read about current events in the Spanish-speaking world.

Repaso

A

Amigos, alumnos y parientes

Objetivos

In this chapter you will review:

- vocabulary associated with friends, family, and home
- the verb **ser**
- the use of nouns, articles, and adjectives
- the verb **tener**
- possessive adjectives

◀ Estos jóvenes están usando su móvil mientras toman un refresco en Asunción, Paraguay.

Interactive Whiteboard
Present or practice with interactive whiteboard activities.

Assessment
Check student progress.

ePals
Connect with Spanish-speaking students around the world.

Online Resources

Customizable Lesson Plans

Audio Activities

Student Workbook

Quick Start

Use QS R.1 or write the following on the board.

Complete.

1. **El hermano de mi padre es mi ___.**
2. **La hija de mis tíos es mi ___.**
3. **Yo soy ___ de los padres de mis padres.**
4. **Los padres de mis padres son mis ___.**

TEACH

Core Instruction

Step 1 As you review the vocabulary, have students repeat the words and sentences after you.

Step 2 Ask questions such as **¿Cómo es Mariana? ¿De dónde es ella? ¿Dónde es alumna?**

Step 3 Once you have asked your questions about all the illustrations, have students say whatever they can about them.

Differentiation

Slower Paced Learners

Have slower paced learners make up sentences about what they see in the photos.

Advanced Learners

Have advanced learners give complete descriptions of what they see.

Multiple Intelligences

Have **visual-spatial** learners draw a picture of a friend. Have them describe their picture.

Vocabulario

¡Hola! Soy Mariana Valdéz. Soy mexicana.

Mariana es morena y bastante alta.
Ella es de Guanajuato.
Es alumna en el Colegio Rivera.

¡Hola! Somos Manuel y Adela.
No somos hermanos. Somos amigos.

Manuel y Adela son alumnos en la misma escuela.
Son alumnos buenos. Son muy inteligentes.
Los dos son bastante cómicos.

¡Hola! Soy Santiago Barros. Soy de Puerto Rico. Tengo dos hermanos.

Santiago tiene dieciséis años.
Su hermano menor tiene catorce.
Y su hermano mayor tiene dieciocho.
Ellos tienen una mascota—Chispa.

La familia Solís tiene una casa privada.
La casa tiene siete cuartos.

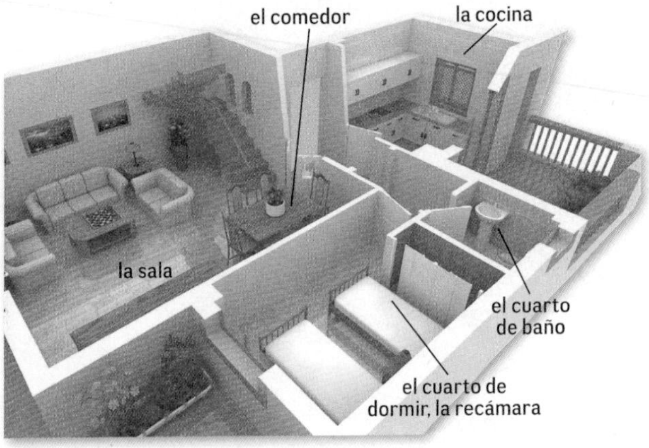
el comedor
la cocina
la sala
el cuarto de baño
el cuarto de dormir, la recámara

Additional Vocabulary

In Level 1 students also learned **el cuarto, el dormitorio, la habitación,** and **la alcoba** as alternate words for **el cuarto de dormir.**

Go Online!

You may wish to remind students to go online for additional vocabulary practice. They can also download audio files of all vocabulary.

Go Online!

connectED.mcgraw-hill.com

Práctica

HABLAR • ESCRIBIR

1 Parea y forma frases basado en la información en el vocabulario.

1. Santiago	**a.** amigos
2. Mariana	**b.** de Puerto Rico
3. Manuel y Adela	**c.** dos hermanos
4. Santiago	**d.** de nacionalidad mexicana

HABLAR

2 Contesta. Presta atención a la palabra interrogativa.

1. ¿De qué nacionalidad es Mariana Valdéz?
2. ¿De dónde es?
3. ¿Cómo es?
4. ¿Dónde es alumna?

LEER • ESCRIBIR

3 Corrige la información falsa.

1. Manuel y Adela son hermanos.
2. Son muy serios.
3. Son alumnos malos.
4. No son muy inteligentes.
5. Son alumnos en escuelas diferentes.

LEER • ESCRIBIR

4 Completa con una palabra apropiada.

1. Santiago Barros es de _____.
2. Tiene dos _____.
3. _____ hermano menor tiene catorce años.
4. Su hermano mayor tiene dieciocho _____.
5. Santiago y sus hermanos tienen una _____.
6. Su perro es _____.

5 **Rompecabezas**

Cambia una letra en cada palabra para formar una palabra nueva.

1. dos
2. hola
3. buen
4. tengo
5. baño

CULTURA

Estos señores mayores pasan un rato agradable sentado en el Parque de la Independencia en Quito, Ecuador. Tienen una conversación interesante.

Richard Brommer

Repaso A

Leveling EACH Activity

Easy Activities 1, 2
Average Activities 3, 4, 5
CHallenging Activities 6, 7

PRACTICE

Activity 2 After going over this activity, you may wish to call on some students to tell all about themselves starting with **(Yo) soy...**

Teaching Options

Go over the **Práctica** activities as quickly as possible. If students appear to have a good command of the vocabulary, it is not necessary that they write the activities.

If, however, you feel students need additional reinforcement of the vocabulary, have them write the activities after you go over them orally in class.

Answers

1
1. Santiago es de Puerto Rico. (Santiago tiene dos hermanos.)
2. Mariana es mexicana.
3. Manuel y Adela son amigos.
4. Santiago tiene dos hermanos. (Santiago es de Puerto Rico.)

2
1. Mariana Valdéz es mexicana.
2. Es de Guanajuato, México.
3. Es morena y bastante alta.
4. Es alumna en el Colegio Rivera.

3
1. Manuel y Adela son amigos.
2. Son bastante cómicos.
3. Son alumnos buenos.
4. Son muy inteligentes.
5. Son alumnos en la misma escuela.

4
1. Puerto Rico
2. hermanos
3. Su
4. años
5. mascota
6. Chispa

5 *Answers will vary but may include:*
1. los, tos
2. cola, sola, hora
3. bien
4. vengo, tango
5. bajo, daño

Activity 6 After going over this activity, you may have students describe their house or the house of their dreams.

Differentiation

Advanced Learners

Activity 7 Call on advanced learners to give a description of each house or apartment in the advertisements.

HABLAR • ESCRIBIR

6 Describe la casa de los Solís.

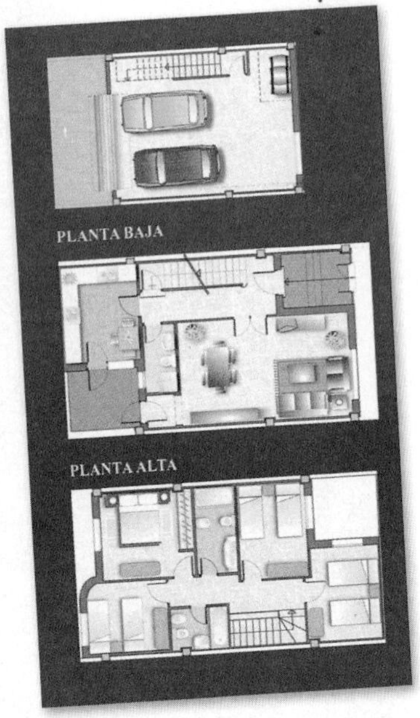

7 ***Comunicación***

With a classmate, look at these real estate ads. Describe your family and housing needs to your real estate agent (your partner). He or she will recommend a dwelling and will describe it to you. Take turns.

PROMOCIONES, FINANCIACION Y VENTAS, S.L.
MILENIUM
VALDELAGRANA
Piso 3 dormitorios, 2 baños, coc. amueb. 3 arm. empotr. parking privado. Ref.- 7151
FUENTEBRAVÍA
Apartamento 1 dormitorio, 1 baño, coc. amueb. jardines, aparc. cerrado. A 100 metros de la playa. Ref.- 7000
VALDELAGRANA
Unifamiliar 160 m2, 3 dormitorios, 2 baños, cocina amueb., aseo, buhardilla, trastero, piscina. Ref.- 7083
FUENTEBRAVÍA
Unifamiliar 3 dormitorios, 1 baño, aseo, cocina amueblada, chimenea, cerca de la playa. Ref,- 7009
C/ Almirante Cañas Trujillo, 17 B (Junto Avd. Libertad)
11500 El Puerto de Santa María

Answers

6 *Answers will vary.*

7 *Answers will vary.*

Go Online!

connectED.mcgraw-hill.com

Conversación

¿De dónde son?

Julio	¡Hola!
Rosa	¡Hola! ¿Qué tal?
Julio	Bien, ¿y tú?
Rosa	Bien. Oye, eres un amigo de Teresa Irizarry, ¿no?
Julio	Sí, soy Julio Arenal.
Rosa	¿De dónde eres, Julio?
Julio	¿Yo? Soy de la Ciudad de México. Y tú eres de Puebla como Teresa, ¿no?
Rosa	Sí.
Julio	¿Cuántos años tienes, Rosa?
Rosa	Tengo dieciséis años.
Julio	¿Dieciséis? Tenemos la misma edad.

¿Comprendes?

A Contesta según la información en la conversación.

1. ¿Son mexicanos los dos muchachos?
2. ¿De dónde es Julio?
3. ¿Son amigos los dos muchachos?
4. ¿Quién es amigo de Teresa Irizarry?
5. ¿De dónde es Rosa?
6. ¿Cuántos años tiene ella?
7. Y, ¿cuántos años tiene Julio?
8. ¿Tienen ellos la misma edad?

B **Resumiendo** Cuenta toda la información sobre las tres personas en la conversación en tus propias palabras.

CULTURA

Rascacielos modernos en la Ciudad de México

Repaso A

Online Resources

Customizable Lesson Plans

Audio Activities

TEACH

Core Instruction

Step 1 Call on students to read the **Conversación** aloud.

Step 2 Have two students read it together as a dramatization—using the proper gestures and intonation.

Teaching Options

Have students make up and ask one another questions about the conversation.

Tips for Success

Since students are reviewing the verbs **ser** and **tener** in this **Repaso**, have them find all forms of these verbs in the **Conversación**.

Go Online!

You may wish to remind students to go online for additional conversation practice.

Answers

A

1. Sí, los dos muchachos son mexicanos.
2. Julio es de la Ciudad de México.
3. No, los dos muchachos no son amigos.
4. Julio es amigo de Teresa Irizarry.
5. Rosa es de Puebla.
6. Elena tiene dieciséis años.
7. Julio tiene dieciséis años.
8. Sí, ellos tienen la misma edad.

B *Answers will vary.*

Online Resources

Customizable Lesson Plans

Audio Activities

Video (Gramática)

Student Workbook

Quick Start

Use QS R.2 or write the following on the board.

Answer.

1. **¿Quién eres?**
2. **¿De dónde eres?**
3. **¿De qué nacionalidad eres?**

TEACH

Core Instruction

Quickly go over the forms of **ser** and have students do the activities.

PRACTICE

Leveling EACH Activity

Easy Activity 1
Average Activity 2
CHallenging Activity 3

Activity 1 You may wish to do this as an entire class activity or you may wish to do it as a paired activity.

Activity 2 This activity can be prepared and then gone over in class. You can call on two students, each will read one completed paragraph to the class.

Tips for Success

When students do an activity such as Activity 3, allow them to feel relaxed and speak as much as they can. If they make an error, you may ignore it. Allow them to feel they are speaking on their own in a natural situation.

Repaso A

Gramática

Presente del verbo ser

Review the forms of the irregular verb **ser.**

ser	
soy	somos
eres	*sois*
es	son

Práctica

HABLAR

1 Personaliza. Da respuestas personales.

1. ¿Quién eres?
2. ¿De qué nacionalidad eres?
3. ¿Dónde eres alumno(a)?
4. ¿Cómo es tu escuela?

LEER • ESCRIBIR

2 Completa con las formas apropiadas de **ser.**

Yo __1__ un amigo de Andrés. Andrés __2__ muy simpático. Y él __3__ gracioso. Andrés y yo __4__ dominicanos. __5__ de la República Dominicana.

La capital de la República Dominicana __6__ Santo Domingo. Nosotros __7__ alumnos en un colegio en Santo Domingo. Nosotros __8__ alumnos de inglés. La profesora de inglés __9__ la señorita White. Ella __10__ norteamericana. __11__ de Estados Unidos.

CULTURA

¿De qué nacionalidad son los jóvenes? Son dominicanos, ¿no?

3 ***Comunicación***

You are key pals with an exchange student from Peru (your partner). He or she wants to know about your school, your schedule, and your classes. Tell as much as you can about your school and then ask him or her about school life in Peru.

Larry Hamill

Answers

1 *Answers will vary but may include:*

1. Yo soy ___.
2. Soy ___.
3. Soy alumno en ___.
4. Mi escuela es ___.

2

1. soy
2. es
3. es
4. somos
5. Somos
6. es
7. somos
8. somos
9. es
10. es
11. Es

3 *Answers will vary.*

Sustantivos, artículos y adjetivos

1. Spanish nouns are either masculine or feminine. Most nouns ending in **o** are masculine and most nouns ending in **a** are feminine. The definite articles **el** and **los** accompany masculine nouns; **la** and **las** accompany feminine nouns.

SINGULAR	PLURAL	SINGULAR	PLURAL
el alumno	**los alumnos**	**la amiga**	**las amigas**
el curso	**los cursos**	**la escuela**	**las escuelas**

2. An adjective must agree with the noun it describes or modifies. Adjectives that end in **o** have four forms.

el amigo sincero	**los amigos sinceros**
la amiga sincera	**las amigas sinceras**

3. Adjectives that end in **e** or a consonant have only two forms.

el curso interesante	**los cursos interesantes**
la clase interesante	**las clases interesantes**
el curso difícil	**los cursos difíciles**
la clase difícil	**las clases difíciles**

Go Online!

connectED.mcgraw-hill.com

Julia es una alumna seria, muy estudiosa.

Práctica

HABLAR • ESCRIBIR

4 Describe a Julia.

HABLAR • ESCRIBIR

5 Describe al grupo de amigos.

HABLAR • ESCRIBIR

6 Describe tu clase favorita.

7 *Comunicación*

Work in groups of three or four. In each group, rate your courses as **fácil, difícil, regular, aburrido, fantástico.** Tally the results and report the information to the class.

CULTURA

Los amigos están en el patio de su escuela en Santo Domingo.

Answers

4 *Answers will vary.*
5 *Answers will vary.*
6 *Answers will vary.*
7 *Answers will vary.*

Go Online!

Gramática en vivo: *Nouns, Articles, and Adjectives* Enliven learning with the animated world of Professor Cruz! **Gramática en vivo** is a fun and effective tool for additional instruction and/or review.

Quick Start

Use QS R.3 or write the following on the board.

Rewrite in the plural.

1. **Él es americano.**
2. **La muchacha es bonita.**
3. **El colegio es moderno.**
4. **El curso es fácil.**

TEACH

Core Instruction

As you go over Items 1 through 3, have students repeat the words and phrases after you. Point to a specific person or object as you use the definite article.

Teaching Options

Since this is all review, ask students questions to determine how much they remember. **¿Cuál es el artículo que va con «alumno» (alumna, curso, clase)? ¿Qué forma de «simpático» usas con «un amigo» (una amiga, unos amigos, unas amigas)?** Do the same with **curso interesante** and **curso fácil.**

PRACTICE

Leveling EACH Activity

Average Activities 4, 5, 6, 7

Note: Since all these activities are review, they are average in difficulty level.

Online Resources

Customizable Lesson Plans

Audio Activities

Student Workbook

TEACH

Core Instruction

Step 1 Have students repeat the forms of the verb **tener.**

Step 2 Read the information about **tener que** to the class.

Step 3 Have students make up additional sentences using **tener que.**

PRACTICE

Leveling EACH Activity

Average Activities 8, 9, Activity 9 **Expansión**

Activity 8 This activity can also be done as a paired activity.

Tips for Success

If students need any additional help with one of the grammar points reviewed, you can refer to the original presentation in **¡Así se dice!** Level 1.

Repaso A

El verbo tener

1. Review the forms of the irregular verb **tener.**

tener	
tengo	**tenemos**
tienes	***tenéis***
tiene	**tienen**

2. You use **tener** to express age.

¿Cuántos años tienes?

3. Note that the expression **tener que** followed by an infinitive means *to have to.*

Tenemos que estudiar y aprender mucho.

CULTURA
Una familia española en una placita en Palma de Mallorca, España

Práctica

HABLAR

8 Personaliza. Da respuestas personales sobre tu familia.

1. ¿Tienes una familia grande o pequeña?
2. ¿Cuántos hermanos tienes?
3. ¿Cuántos años tienen ellos?
4. ¿Y cuántos años tienes tú?
5. ¿Tienen ustedes un perro o un gato?
6. ¿Tiene tu padre o tu madre un carro?
7. En la escuela, ¿tienes que estudiar mucho?
8. ¿Y tienen que trabajar mucho tus padres?

LEER • ESCRIBIR

9 Completa con las formas apropiadas de **tener.**

La familia Bravo __1__ un piso o apartamento en Madrid. Su piso __2__ seis cuartos. Está en Salamanca, una zona muy bonita de la ciudad. Muchas calles en la zona Salamanca __3__ los nombres de artistas famosos—la calle Goya, la calle Velázquez.

Hay cuatro personas en la familia Bravo. Teresa __4__ diecisiete años y su hermano __5__ quince años. Ellos __6__ un gato adorable.

EXPANSIÓN

Ahora, sin mirar el párrafo, cuenta toda la información sobre la familia Bravo en tus propias palabras. Si no recuerdas algo, un(a) compañero(a) te puede ayudar.

Andrew Payti

Answers

8 *Answers will vary but may include:*

1. Tengo una familia grande (pequeña).
2. Tengo ___ hermanos(as). (No tengo hermanos.)
3. Tiene(n) ___ años.
4. Tengo ___ años.
5. Tenemos un perro (un gato). (No tenemos una mascota.)
6. Mi padre (madre) tiene un carro. (No tienen un carro.)
7. Sí (No), en la escuela (no) tengo que estudiar mucho.
8. No, mis padres (no) tienen que trabajar mucho.

9

1. tiene
2. tiene
3. tienen
4. tiene
5. tiene
6. tienen

Adjetivos posesivos

1. Review the forms of the possessive adjectives **mi, tu,** and **su.** These adjectives have only two forms.

¿Dan una fiesta tu hermana y tus primos?
Sí, mi hermana y mis primos dan una fiesta.
Todos sus amigos van a recibir una invitación a su fiesta.

2. The possessive adjective **nuestro** has four forms.

Nuestro primo, nuestra tía, nuestras sobrinas y nuestros abuelos viven todos en Madrid.

Go Online!

connectED.mcgraw-hill.com

Práctica

HABLAR

10 Personaliza. Da respuestas personales sobre tu familia y casa.

1. ¿Dónde está tu casa o departamento?
2. ¿Cuántas personas hay en tu familia?
3. ¿Cuántos cuartos tiene tu casa o departamento?
4. ¿De dónde son tus abuelos?
5. ¿Tienes muchos primos?
6. ¿Quiénes son los padres de tus primos?

LEER • ESCRIBIR

11 Completa con el adjetivo posesivo apropiado.

—La casa de mi familia está en la calle Independencia. __1__ casa tiene siete cuartos. Detrás de __2__ casa hay un jardín.

—José, ¿tienen __3__ padres un carro?

—Sí, y __4__ carro es bastante nuevo. __5__ carro está en el garaje. Y nosotros tenemos un perro. __6__ perro no está en el garaje. Está en el jardín.

CULTURA

Un parque en el centro de San Juan, Venezuela

Kelli Drummer-Avendano

Comunicación

12 You are spending the summer with a family in Venezuela. Tell your Venezuelan "brother" or "sister" (your partner) all you can about your family. Answer any questions he or she may have. Then reverse roles.

13 Work with a classmate. Be good interviewers. Make up questions with the following question words.

¿Qué? ¿Quién? ¿Quiénes? ¿Dónde? ¿De dónde? ¿Cómo? ¿Cuánto(s)?

Online Resources

Customizable Lesson Plans
Audio Activities
Student Workbook
Enrichment
Listening, Speaking, Reading, Writing Tests

Quick Start

Use QS R.4 or write the following on the board.

Answer.

1. **¿Dónde vives?**
2. **¿Tienes una familia grande o pequeña?**
3. **¿Cuántos años tienes?**
4. **Y tu hermano(a), ¿cuántos años tiene?**
5. **¿Tienen ustedes un perro o gato?**

PRACTICE

Leveling EACH Activity

Easy Activity 10
Average Activity 11
CHallenging Activities 12, 13

Activity 11 You may wish to have students do this activity silently and then tell about it in their own words.

Activity 12 Have **verbal-linguistic** learners do this activity as if they were having a real conversation. Have **bodily-kinesthetic** learners actually conduct an interview using other class members as the interviewees.

Answers

10 *Answers will vary but may include:*

1. Mi casa (departamento) está ___.
2. Hay ___ personas en mi familia.
3. Mi casa (departamento) tiene ___ cuartos.
4. Mis abuelos son de ___.
5. Sí, (No, no) tengo muchos primos.
6. Los padres de mis primos son mis tíos.

11

1. Nuestra
2. nuestra
3. tus
4. su
5. Su
6. Nuestro

12 *Answers will vary.*

13 *Answers will vary.*

Preview

In Repaso B, students will review the important vocabulary they learned associated with both home and school activities. To be able to talk about these activities, they will review the present tense of regular verbs, **ir, dar,** and **estar,** and the contractions **al** and **del.**

¡Así se dice!

Why It Works!

- Note how language is grouped together in **¡Así se dice!** to enable students to put their words together and speak immediately.
  En la escuela: estudiar, escuchar al profesor, levantar la mano, contestar una pregunta, hablar, prestar atención, tomar el bus escolar, aprender mucho, comprender, leer, escribir
  En casa: hablar con la familia, mirar la televisión, preparar la comida, escuchar música, usar la computadora, enviar un correo electrónico, navegar la red, comer, leer, escribir
- Note that grammar is always made as easy as possible. After reviewing **-ar** verbs, students review **voy, doy, estoy.** The remaining forms are all the same as those of a regular **-ar** verb.

Go Online! connectED.mcgraw-hill.com — Audio | Video | Práctica | Repaso | Diversiones | eScape | ePals

Go Online!

Audio
Listen to spoken Spanish.

Video
Watch and learn about the Spanish-speaking world.

Práctica
Practice your skills.

Repaso
Review what you've learned.

Diversiones
Go beyond the classroom.

eScape
Read about current events in the Spanish-speaking world.

Repaso

B

En casa y en la escuela

Objetivos

In this chapter you will review:

- vocabulary associated with home and school activities
- the present tense of regular verbs
- the present tense of **ir, dar, estar**
- contractions

◀ Unas casas bonitas en Mallorca, España—una de las islas Baleares en el mar Mediterráneo

Interactive Whiteboard
Present or practice with interactive whiteboard activities.

Assessment
Check student progress.

ePals
Connect with Spanish-speaking students around the world.

Online Resources

Customizable Lesson Plans

Audio Activities

Student Workbook

Quick Start

Use QS R.5 or write the following on the board.

1. **Write in Spanish four things a student does in school.**
2. **Write in Spanish four things a person does at home.**

TEACH

Core Instruction

Step 1 Review the vocabulary presented here. Ask questions building from easy to difficult: **¿Están los alumnos en la escuela? ¿Quiénes están en la escuela? ¿Dónde están los alumnos?**

Step 2 You can follow this procedure with each photograph.

Teaching Options

Rather than presenting the review vocabulary as suggested above, you may wish to have students look at the photos and make up sentences about them using any vocabulary they learned in Level 1.

Vocabulario

Los alumnos están en la escuela.
Ellos prestan atención al profesor.
El profesor habla.
Ramón tiene una pregunta y levanta la mano.

Después de las clases los alumnos van a casa.
Toman el bus escolar.

La familia de Andrés Salinas vive en Nicaragua.
Su familia está en la sala.
La señora Salinas lee un libro.
Su esposo (marido) ve la tele.
Andrés escucha música en su MP3.

La hermana de Andrés está en su cuarto (de dormir).
Ella recibe un correo electrónico. Ella usa su computadora.
Lee su e-mail.

Go Online!

You may wish to remind students to go online for additional vocabulary practice. They can also download audio files of all vocabulary.

Práctica

Go Online!

connectED.mcgraw-hill.com

ESCUCHAR

1 Escucha las frases. Usa una tabla como la de abajo para indicar si la acción tiene lugar en casa o en la escuela.

casa	escuela

HABLAR • ESCRIBIR

2 Contesta.

1. ¿Cómo llegan los alumnos a la escuela? ¿Toman el bus, van en carro o van a pie?
2. ¿Con quién hablan los alumnos cuando entran en la sala de clase?
3. ¿Prestan ellos atención cuando el/la profesor(a) habla?
4. ¿Qué levanta un(a) alumno(a) cuando tiene una pregunta?
5. Los alumnos que estudian mucho, ¿sacan notas buenas o malas?
6. En la escuela, ¿quién da los exámenes y quiénes toman los exámenes?

LEER • ESCRIBIR

3 Parea para formar expresiones.

1. leer	a. mucho en la escuela
2. escribir	b. al quinto piso
3. vivir	c. una novela
4. aprender	d. un alumno bueno y serio
5. vender	e. la orden
6. comer	f. una limonada
7. ser	g. en una casa particular
8. subir	h. CDs en una tienda
9. beber	i. carne, ensalada y papas

HABLAR • ESCRIBIR

4 **Juego** Divide the class into two teams. Your teacher will ask each team to give a word that pertains to a category: **cosas que comemos, bebemos, leemos o escribimos.** Your teacher will keep asking for words until one team is unable to think of a word that pertains to the given category.

CULTURA

Los jóvenes comen y conversan en la cafetería de su escuela en Barranquilla, Colombia. Una de las muchachas chequea mensajes en su móvil.

Repaso B

Leveling EACH Activity

Easy Activities 1, 2, 3
Average Activity 4

PRACTICE

Activity 1

Audio Script

1. Aprenden mucho.
2. Comprenden cuando la profesora habla.
3. Ven la televisión en la sala.
4. Comen en la cafetería.
5. Preparan la comida en la cocina.
6. Toman un examen.
7. Reciben y envían correos electrónicos.

Activity 2 This activity can be done orally in class, asking questions of individual students, or you may wish to do it as a paired activity.

Differentiation

Advanced Learners

Activity 3 After students match the verb with the expression, call on advanced learners to make up original sentences.

ABOUT THE SPANISH LANGUAGE

You may wish to remind students that **el ordenador** is used in Spain and **la computadora** is used in Latin America. In addition to **el bocadillo,** you will hear **el bocata** in Spain, **sándwich** in many areas, and **la torta** in Mexico.

Answers

1

1. escuela
2. escuela
3. casa
4. escuela
5. casa
6. escuela
7. casa

2 *Answers will vary but may include:*

1. Los alumnos toman el bus (van en carro, van a pie).
2. Cuando entran en la sala de clase, los alumnos hablan con ___.
3. Sí (No), ellos (no) prestan atención cuando el/la profesor(a) habla.
4. Un(a) alumno(a) levanta la mano cuando tiene una pregunta.
5. Los alumnos que estudian mucho sacan notas buenas.
6. En la escuela el/la profesor(a) da los exámenes y los alumnos toman los exámenes.

3

1. c
2. e
3. g
4. a
5. h
6. i
7. d
8. b
9. f

4 *Answers will vary.*

Online Resources

Customizable Lesson Plans

Audio Activities

TEACH

Core Instruction

Step 1 Have students listen to the **Conversación.**

Step 2 Have them make up *true/false* statements about the conversation.

Step 3 Call on individual students to read their statements. Have the student call on a classmate to answer *true* or *false* and to correct false statements.

Teaching Options

You may also wish to use the suggestions from Repaso A to present the **Conversación.**

Differentiation

Advanced Learners

Call on advanced learners to retell the information in the **Conversación** in their own words.

Go Online!

You may wish to remind students to go online for additional conversation practice.

Conversación

Otro año en la escuela

Paco	**Claudia, ¿cómo estás?**
Claudia	**Muy bien, Paco. ¿Y tú?**
Paco	**Bien. ¿Qué tal la escuela este año?**
Claudia	**Muy bien. Pero un poco difícil. Tengo seis cursos.**
Paco	**¡Seis cursos! Estudias mucho, ¿no?**
Claudia	**Sí, bastante. Y, a propósito, Paco, ¿dónde están tus primos Enrique y Sara? ¿Dónde viven ahora?**
Paco	**Pues, viven en la misma casa. ¿Por qué?**
Claudia	**Pues, no los veo casi nunca.**

¿Comprendes?

Contesta según la información en la conversación.

1. ¿Quiénes hablan?
2. ¿Cómo está Paco?
3. ¿Y Claudia?
4. ¿Cuántos cursos toma Claudia?
5. ¿Tiene que estudiar mucho?
6. ¿Quiénes son los primos de Paco?
7. ¿Ve Claudia mucho a sus primos?
8. ¿Viven ellos en la misma casa que antes o no?

Answers

1. Paco y Claudia hablan.
2. Está bien.
3. Está muy bien.
4. Claudia toma seis cursos.
5. Sí, tiene que estudiar mucho.
6. Enrique y Sara son los primos de Paco.
7. No, Claudia no los ve casi nunca.
8. Sí, ellos viven en la misma casa que antes.

Go Online!

connectED.mcgraw-hill.com

Gramática

Presente de los verbos regulares

1. Review the present tense forms of regular **-ar, -er,** and **-ir** verbs.

infinitive	mirar	comer	vivir
stem	mir-	com-	viv-
yo	miro	como	vivo
tú	miras	comes	vives
Ud., él, ella	mira	come	vive
nosotros(as)	miramos	comemos	vivimos
vosotros(as)	*miráis*	*coméis*	*vivís*
Uds., ellos, ellas	miran	comen	viven

2. Note that the **-er** and **-ir** verbs have the same endings except **nosotros(as)** and ***vosotros(as).***

comemos — **vivimos**
coméis — ***vivís***

3. Remember, to make a sentence negative, you put **no** before the verb.

No habla francés.
No vivimos en Francia.

4. Remember to use **tú** when talking to a friend, family member, or person your own age. Use **usted** when speaking to an adult, a person you do not know well, or someone to whom you wish to show respect. You use **ustedes** when talking to two or more people.

¿Tú estudias español, Roberto?
¿Y usted, señora? ¿Usted también estudia español?
Ustedes viven aquí, ¿no?

CULTURA

Un puesto de comida en una calle de Oaxaca, México. ¿Qué forma usa la mamá con su hijito? ¿Tú o usted?

Online Resources

Customizable Lesson Plans
Audio Activities
Video (Gramática)
Student Workbook

TEACH

Core Instruction

Step 1 Have students read the verb forms as you write them on the board.

Step 2 Have students read each verb down.

Step 3 Have them read across to compare the endings.

Step 4 Review the difference between **tú, usted,** and **ustedes.**

Differentiation

Multiple Intelligences

You can use stick figures or cutouts with names to review **tú** versus **usted.** This is very helpful for **visual-spatial** learners.

Cultural Snapshot

Street vendors selling food are very common throughout many areas of Latin America.

Go Online!

You may wish to remind students to go online for additional grammar review and practice.

Leveling EACH Activity

Easy Activity 4
Average Activities 1, 2, 3
CHallenging Activity 5, Activity 1 **Expansión**

PRACTICE

Note: Many of the activities are actually quite easy since they are review. However, we have rated them **Average** since students have to use the different forms in each activity.

Activities 1 and 3 These activities can be done as whole class activities orally in class or you can do them as paired activities.

Activity 2 This activity can be prepared and then gone over in class.

Additional Vocabulary

A new term for **biblioteca** is **centro (de recursos) de medios.**

Práctica

HABLAR • ESCRIBIR

1 Personaliza. Da respuestas personales.

1. ¿En qué escuela estudias?
2. ¿Cómo llegas a la escuela por la mañana?
3. ¿Cuántos cursos tomas?
4. ¿En qué llevas los materiales escolares?
5. ¿Estudian mucho los alumnos de tu escuela?
6. ¿Sacan ustedes notas buenas?
7. ¿Toman ustedes muchos exámenes?
8. ¿Escuchan ustedes cuando el/la profesor(a) habla?

EXPANSIÓN

Ahora, sin mirar las preguntas, cuenta toda la información en tus propias palabras. Si no recuerdas algo, un(a) compañero(a) te puede ayudar.

LEER • ESCRIBIR

2 Completa con la forma apropiada del verbo.

1. Durante la fiesta todos nosotros ____. (bailar)
2. Felipe ____ el piano. (tocar)
3. Mientras él ____ el piano, Paz y Jaime ____. (tocar, cantar)
4. ¿____ ustedes refrescos durante la fiesta? (preparar)
5. ¿____ ustedes fotos durante la fiesta? (tomar)
6. Sí, y todos nosotros ____ las fotografías. (mirar)

HABLAR • ESCRIBIR

3 Personaliza. Da respuestas personales.

1. ¿Qué comes cuando tienes hambre?
2. ¿Qué bebes cuando tienes sed?
3. ¿Qué aprenden tú y tus amigos en la escuela?
4. ¿Qué leen ustedes en la clase de inglés?
5. ¿Qué escriben ustedes?
6. ¿Comprenden los alumnos cuando el/la profesor(a) de español habla?
7. ¿Reciben ustedes notas buenas en todos sus cursos?

CULTURA

Un cartel anunciando cursos de verano en un instituto de idiomas en Ceuta, una ciudad española en el norte de África

Andrew Payti

Answers

1 *Answers will vary but may include:*

1. Estudio en ____.
2. Llego a la escuela por la mañana a pie (en bus, en carro).
3. Tomo ____ cursos.
4. Llevo los materiales escolares en mi mochila.
5. Sí, (No, no) estudian mucho los alumnos de mi escuela.
6. Sí, (No, no) sacamos notas buenas.
7. Sí, (No, no) tomamos muchos exámenes.
8. Sí, (No, no) escuchamos cuando el/la profesor(a) habla.

2

1. bailamos
2. toca
3. toca, cantan
4. Preparan
5. Toman
6. miramos

3 *Answers will vary but may include:*

1. Cuando tengo hambre, como ____.
2. Cuando tengo sed, bebo ____.
3. Mis amigos y yo aprendemos ____ en la escuela.
4. En la clase de inglés leemos ____.
5. Escribimos ____.
6. Sí (No), los alumnos (no) comprenden cuando el/la profesor(a) de español habla.
7. Sí, (No, no) recibimos notas buenas en todos nuestros cursos.

LEER • ESCRIBIR

4 Completa sobre una visita a un café.

En el café los clientes __1__ (ver) al mesero. Ellos __2__ (hablar) con el mesero. Los clientes __3__ (leer) el menú y __4__ (decidir) lo que van a tomar. Los meseros __5__ (tomar) la orden y __6__ (escribir) la orden en un cuaderno pequeño. Los meseros no __7__ (leer) el menú. Y los clientes no __8__ (escribir) la orden.

CULTURA

Los clientes toman un refresco en un café al aire libre en Valencia, España.

5 *Comunicación*

Tell all the things you do in a typical school day. Present your information to the class. Do you or your classmates do anything different?

Andrew Payti

CULTURA

El exterior del Colegio Francisco Febres Cordero La Salle en Quito, la capital de Ecuador

Go Online!

connectED.mcgraw-hill.com

Repaso B

Activity 4 This activity can be prepared and then gone over in class.

Comunicación

Have students look at the photographs and describe everything they see, including the people. They can use a great deal of vocabulary they learned in Level 1.

Go Online!

Gramática en vivo: *Present Tense of Regular Verbs* Enliven learning with the animated world of Professor Cruz! **Gramática en vivo** is a fun and effective tool for additional instruction and/or review.

Answers

4

1. ven
2. hablan
3. leen
4. deciden
5. toman
6. escriben
7. leen
8. escriben

5 *Answers will vary.*

Online Resources

Customizable Lesson Plans
Audio Activities
Student Workbook
Enrichment
Listening, Speaking, Reading, Writing Tests

Quick Start

Use QS R.6 or write the following on the board.

Complete.

1. **Ellos ____ mucho. (hablar)**
2. **Tú ____ atención cuando la profesora ____, ¿no? (prestar, hablar)**
3. **A veces nosotros ____ la computadora en clase. (usar)**
4. **¿____ ustedes música latina? (escuchar)**

TEACH

Core Instruction

Step 1 Have students look at the verbs. Point out to them that the endings are the same as regular **-ar** verbs except for the **yo** form.

Step 2 Have students repeat **voy, doy, estoy.** Then have them repeat all the forms.

Step 3 Have students give you more examples of the **ir a** + *infinitive* construction.

PRACTICE

Leveling EACH Activity

Easy Activities 6, 7
CHallenging Activities 8, 9

Activity 6 This activity can be done orally as an entire class activity or as a paired activity.

Los verbos ir, dar, estar

1. Note that the verbs **ir, dar,** and **estar** are the same as regular **-ar** verbs in all forms except **yo.**

	ir	dar	estar
yo	voy	doy	estoy
tú	vas	das	estás
Ud., él, ella	va	da	está
nosotros(as)	vamos	damos	estamos
vosotros(as)	*vais*	*dais*	*estáis*
Uds., ellos, ellas	van	dan	están

2. The preposition **a** often follows the verb **ir.** Remember that **a** contracts with **el** to form one word—**al.**

   Voy al café. No voy a la tienda.

3. Remember, you can use **ir a** + infinitive to express a future idea.

   Voy a tomar el bus.

Práctica

HABLAR

6 Personaliza. Da respuestas personales.

1. ¿Vas a la escuela?
2. ¿A qué hora vas a la escuela?
3. ¿Con quién vas a la escuela?
4. ¿Están ustedes en la escuela ahora?
5. ¿Cómo van ustedes a la escuela?
6. ¿Da el/la profesor(a) muchos exámenes?
7. ¿Dan los alumnos exámenes también?

CULTURA
Unos jóvenes atraviesan la plaza en San Pablo, Ecuador.

Andrew Payti

Answers

6 *Answers will vary but may include:*

1. Sí, (No, no) voy a la escuela.
2. Voy a la escuela a ____.
3. Voy a la escuela con ____.
4. Sí, (No, no) estamos en la escuela ahora.
5. Vamos a la escuela a pie (en bus, en carro).
6. Sí (No), el/la profesor(a) (no) da muchos exámenes.
7. No, los alumnos no dan exámenes.

Go Online!

connectED.mcgraw-hill.com

LEER • ESCRIBIR

7 Completa.

Yo __1__ (ir) a la tienda de ropa. Emilio __2__ (ir) también. Él y yo __3__ (estar) en la tienda. Yo __4__ (comprar) una camiseta y él __5__ (comprar) un blue jean. Nosotros no __6__ (necesitar) mucha ropa porque __7__ (llevar) uniforme a la escuela.

Laura y Tomás __8__ (llevar) uniforme a la escuela también. Ellos __9__ (ir) a una escuela en las afueras de Lima, en Miraflores.

Comunicación

8 Tell some things you're not going to do now because you have to do something else.

9 Work in groups of three or four. You're all friends from Mexico. After school you go to a café where you talk about lots of things—school, teachers, friends, home, family, etc. One of you will be the server. You have to interrupt the conversation once in a while to take the orders and serve. Take turns.

CULTURA

Los jóvenes están delante de un café Internet en Tepoztlán, México.

Andrew Payti

Activity 7 Have students prepare this activity and then retell all the information in their own words.

Activity 9 Before groups do this activity, you may wish to have them make up a list of things they can talk about to help refresh their memories.

Comunidades

In Spanish, ask students if there is an Internet café in your town. If so, ask them to tell where it is and whether or not they go there.

Answers

7

1. voy
2. va
3. estamos
4. compro
5. compra
6. necesitamos
7. llevamos
8. llevan
9. van

8 *Answers will vary.*

9 *Answers will vary.*

Preview

In Repaso C, students will review vocabulary related to personality, health and their general well-being. In order to be able to discuss these topics in Spanish, they will review the uses of **ser** and **estar** and the indirect object pronouns.

R20 **Go Online!** connectED.mcgraw-hill.com Audio Video Práctica Repaso Diversiones eScape ePals

Go Online!

Audio
Listen to spoken Spanish.

Video
Watch and learn about the Spanish-speaking world.

Práctica
Practice your skills.

Repaso
Review what you've learned.

Diversiones
Go beyond the classroom.

eScape
Read about current events in the Spanish-speaking world.

Repaso

C

Personalidad y salud

Objetivos

In this chapter you will review:

- vocabulary related to personality, health, and general well-being
- uses of **ser** and **estar**
- indirect object pronouns

◀ Estos jóvenes están jugando un juego de tira con una cuerda en Santa Marta, Colombia.

Interactive Whiteboard
Present or practice with interactive whiteboard activities.

Assessment
Check student progress.

ePals
Connect with Spanish-speaking students around the world.

Online Resources

Customizable Lesson Plans

Audio Activities

Student Workbook

Quick Start

Use QS R.7 or write the following on the board.

Write a list in Spanish of adjectives you could use to describe yourself or a friend.

TEACH

Core Instruction

Step 1 Have students call out all the review words.

Step 2 As students look at the visuals, ask questions such as **¿Cómo está Alberto? ¿Qué tiene? ¿Por qué tiene que guardar cama?**

Teaching Options

Just have students look at the photos and tell what they see.

Differentiation

Multiple Intelligences

Have **bodily-kinesthetic** learners dramatize the following: **contento, triste, cansado, de mal humor, lleno de energía, de buen humor, me molesta.**

Cultura

Have students note the thumbs-up gesture the young man uses to indicate all is "A-OK."

Vocabulario

Alberto no está bien.
Está enfermo.
Tiene fiebre y tiene que guardar cama.

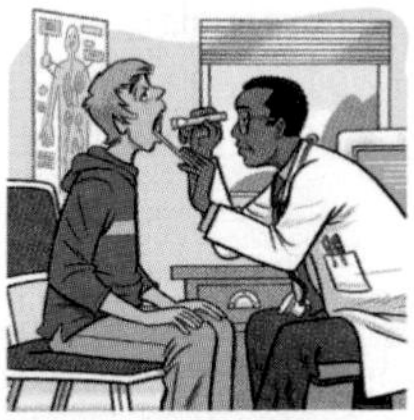

El médico está en su consulta (consultorio).
Examina al paciente (enfermo).

El médico le da una receta.

Arturo está de mal humor. Algo le molesta (enoja).
Felipe está de buen humor.

Go Online!

You may wish to remind students to go online for additional vocabulary practice. They can also download audio files of all vocabulary.

Práctica

Go Online!

connectED.mcgraw-hill.com

ESCUCHAR

1 Escucha. Escoge la frase correcta. Usa una tabla como la de abajo para indicar tus respuestas.

a	b

HABLAR • ESCRIBIR

2 Contesta sobre una consulta médica.

1. César está enfermo. Tiene la temperatura alta. ¿Qué tiene?
2. ¿Adónde tiene que ir?
3. ¿Le da un examen físico el médico?
4. ¿Abre la boca César?
5. ¿Le examina la garganta el médico?
6. ¿Está roja la garganta?
7. ¿Tiene César dolor de garganta?
8. ¿Le duele mucho?

EXPANSIÓN

Ahora, sin mirar las preguntas, cuenta toda la información en tus propias palabras. Si no recuerdas algo, un(a) compañero(a) te puede ayudar.

LEER

3 Parea.

1. Es bien educado.	a. Nunca trabaja.
2. Es muy terco.	b. Nunca presta atención.
3. Tiene una sonrisa en la cara.	c. Tiene buena conducta.
4. Tiene dolor de cabeza.	d. Está contento.
5. Él es perezoso.	e. Le duele mucho.

HABLAR • ESCRIBIR

4 ¿Cuáles son todas las partes del cuerpo que puedes identificar en español? Usa la foto como guía.

5 ***Comunicación***

Work with a classmate and discuss some traits or characteristics you look for in a good friend.

Ryan McVay/Getty Images

Answers

1
1. b
2. a
3. b
4. a
5. b
6. b
7. a
8. b

2
1. Tiene fiebre.
2. Tiene que ir al médico.
3. Sí (No), el médico (no) le da un examen físico.
4. Sí (No), César (no) abre la boca.
5. Sí (No), el médico (no) le examina la garganta.
6. Sí (No), la garganta (no) está roja.
7. Sí (No), César (no) tiene dolor de garganta.
8. Sí, (No, no) le duele mucho.

3
1. c
2. b
3. d
4. e
5. a

4
1. la cabeza
2. el brazo
3. la mano
4. los dedos
5. la pierna
6. la rodilla
7. el pie

5 *Answers will vary.*

Repaso C

Leveling EACH Activity

Easy Activities 2, 3, 5
Average Activities 1, 4
CHallenging Activity 2 **Expansión**

PRACTICE

Activity 1

Audio Script

1. **a.** Una persona de mal humor está contenta.
   b. Una persona de buen humor está contenta.
2. **a.** Cuando una persona está enojada, está de mal humor.
   b. Cuando una persona está enojada, está de buen humor.
3. **a.** Una persona está contenta cuando recibe malas noticias.
   b. Una persona está contenta cuando recibe buenas noticias.
4. **a.** Una persona ambiciosa trabaja mucho.
   b. Una persona perezosa trabaja mucho.
5. **a.** Una persona que tiene mucho estrés está muy calma.
   b. Una persona que tiene mucho estrés está muy nerviosa.
6. **a.** Él va al médico porque está bien.
   b. Él va al médico porque está enfermo.
7. **a.** El médico le da una receta.
   b. El médico le da una fiebre.
8. **a.** El paciente va a la consulta con la receta.
   b. El paciente va a la farmacia con la receta.

Activity 3 This activity can be done in class without previous preparation.

Tips for Success

Play **Simón dice** to review other parts of the body. **Simón dice: indícame tu rodilla,** etc.

Online Resources

Customizable Lesson Plans

Audio Activities

TEACH

Core Instruction

Instead of having students read the **Conversación,** you may wish to have them listen to the recorded audio and then ask the **¿Comprendes?** questions that follow.

Comunicación

Have students describe the young people in the photograph.

Differentiation

Advanced Learners

Have advanced learners make up similar conversations on their own. There are many other expressions students can use that they learned in Level 1.

Go Online!

You may wish to remind students to go online for additional conversation practice.

Conversación

¿Qué le pasa a Ana?

Michel Touraine/age fotostock

Enrique	**¿Qué te pasa, Ana? Tienes la cara triste. ¿Estás enferma?**
Ana	**Sí, me parece que sí. Tengo dolor de garganta y estoy muy cansada.**
Enrique	**Pues, ¿por qué no vas a ver al médico?**
Ana	**No, no tengo que ir al médico. Voy a tomar una siesta.**
Enrique	**Eres muy terca, Ana. Debes ir al médico.**

¿Comprendes?

A Contesta según la información en la conversación.

1. ¿Qué le pregunta Enrique a Ana?
2. ¿Cómo tiene la cara?
3. ¿Qué le duele a Ana?
4. ¿Está llena de energía?
5. ¿Debe ir a ver al médico?
6. ¿Va a ir?
7. ¿Qué va a tomar?
8. Según Enrique, ¿cómo es Ana?

B **Resumiendo** Resume toda la información en la conversación en tus propias palabras.

Answers

A

1. Enrique le pregunta qué le pasa.
2. Tiene la cara triste.
3. A Ana le duele la garganta.
4. No, no está llena de energía.
5. Sí, debe ir a ver al médico.
6. No va a ir.
7. Va a tomar una siesta.
8. Según Enrique, Ana es terca.

B *Answers will vary.*

Gramática

Ser y estar

1. The verbs **ser** and **estar** both mean *to be*. **Ser** is used to tell where someone or something is from. It is also used to describe an inherent trait or characteristic.

   Roberto es de Miami.
   Él es inteligente y guapo.

2. **Estar** is used to tell where someone or something is located. It is also used to describe a temporary state or condition.

   Roberto es de Miami pero ahora está en Madrid.
   Madrid está en España.
   Roberto está muy contento en Madrid.

CULTURA
La Plaza Mayor en el centro del barrio viejo en Madrid.
La estatua de bronce que está en la plaza es de Felipe III.

Daniel Salsgiver

Go Online!

connectED.mcgraw-hill.com

Online Resources

Customizable Lesson Plans
Audio Activities
Video (Gramática)
Student Workbook

Quick Start

Use QS R.8 or write the following on the board.

Complete with the correct form of **ser**.

1. **Yo ____ de aquí.**
2. **Mis abuelos no ____ de aquí.**
3. **¿____ (tú) alumno aquí en nuestra escuela?**
4. **Nuestra escuela ____ grande, ¿no?**
5. **Nosotros ____ todos alumnos de español.**

TEACH

Core Instruction

Step 1 Have students listen as you read the explanation to them.

Step 2 Have students give additional examples for each use of **ser** and **estar.**

Step 3 Write some of their examples on the board and have the class read them aloud.

Teaching Options

Have students take the adjectives from QuickStart R7 and use them in sentences with **ser** or **estar.**

Go Online!

You may wish to remind students to go online for additional grammar review and practice.

Leveling EACH Activity

Easy Activity 1
Average Activities 2, 3
CHallenging Activity 4

PRACTICE

Activity 1 This activity can be done orally with the entire class or it can be done as a paired activity.

Activity 2 This activity can be prepared and then gone over in class.

Activity 3 This activity can be done with or without previous presentation.

Comunicación

Have students look at the photo of Caracas and say as much as they can about it.

Go Online!

Gramática en vivo: *Ser* *and estar* Enliven learning with the animated world of Professor Cruz! **Gramática en vivo** is a fun and effective tool for additional instruction and/or review.

Repaso C

Práctica

CULTURA
Una vista de los rascacielos y montañas en Caracas, la capital de Venezuela

HABLAR

1 Personaliza. Da respuestas personales.

1. ¿Estás en la escuela ahora?
2. ¿Dónde está la escuela?
3. ¿En qué clase estás?
4. ¿Está tu profesor(a) en clase también?
5. ¿Cómo es él o ella?
6. Y, ¿cómo es la clase de español?
7. ¿De dónde es el/la profesor(a)?
8. Y tú, ¿de dónde eres?
9. ¿Cómo estás hoy?

LEER • ESCRIBIR

2 Completa con **ser** o **estar.**

Ángel __1__ de Caracas. Él __2__ muy simpático. __3__ gracioso también. Ahora Ángel __4__ en Nueva York. __5__ estudiante en la universidad allí. Ángel __6__ muy contento en Nueva York.

Nueva York __7__ en el nordeste de Estados Unidos. La Ciudad de Nueva York __8__ muy grande y __9__ muy interesante. A Ángel le gusta mucho Nueva York.

HABLAR • ESCRIBIR

3 Forma frases completas con **es** o **está.**

1. contento
2. de buen humor
3. serio
4. inteligente
5. lleno de energía
6. cansado
7. enfermo
8. estudioso
9. ambicioso
10. enojado

El muchacho está contento y tiene una sonrisa agradable. Y es guapo, ¿no?

4 **Comunicación**

Tell some things about yourself. Where are you from? What kind of personality do you have? Are you a good student?

Answers

1 *Answers will vary but may include:*

1. Sí, (No, no) estoy en la escuela ahora.
2. La escuela está en ____.
3. Estoy en la clase de ____.
4. Sí, mi profesor(a) está en clase también. (No, mi profesor[a] no está en clase.)
5. Él/Ella es ____.
6. La clase de español es ____.
7. Él/La profesor(a) de español es de ____.
8. Yo soy de ____.
9. Estoy ____ hoy.

2

1. es
2. es
3. Es
4. está
5. Es
6. está
7. está
8. es
9. es

3

1. Está contento.
2. Está de buen humor.
3. Es (Está) serio.
4. Es inteligente.
5. Está lleno de energía.
6. Está cansado.
7. Está enfermo.
8. Es estudioso.
9. Es ambicioso.
10. Está enojado.

4 *Answers will vary.*

Go Online!

connectED.mcgraw-hill.com

Pronombres de complemento indirecto

1. An indirect object is the indirect receiver of the action of a verb.

   El médico me da la receta.
   Yo le doy la receta al farmacéutico.

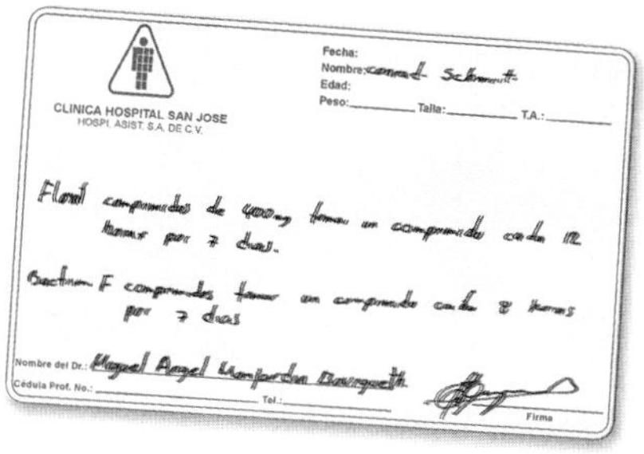

2. Review the indirect object pronouns.

me	**nos**
te	***os***
le	**les**

3. Since **le** and **les** can refer to different people they are often clarified with a prepositional phrase.

   Le hablo { **a él.** / **a ella.** / **a usted.** }
   Les hablo { **a ellos.** / **a ellas.** / **a ustedes.** }

Práctica

HABLAR

5 Personaliza. Da respuestas personales.

1. ¿Te habla en español el/la profesor(a) de español?
2. ¿Les da (a ustedes) muchos exámenes el/la profesor(a)?
3. ¿Te envían correos electrónicos tus amigos?
4. Cuando hablas, ¿te prestan atención tus amigos?

La muchacha les lee algo a los otros miembros de su clase de español. El profesor y los otros alumnos le prestan atención.

LEER • ESCRIBIR

6 Completa.

1. _____ hablo casi todos los días a mis abuelos.
2. _____ explico la lección a él.
3. Guillermo _____ da un regalo a sus abuelos.
4. La empleada _____ habla a sus clientes.
5. Al pobre José _____ duele mucho la garganta.

7 ***Comunicación***

Work with a classmate and describe people who have the following personality traits. Be creative!

Está lleno(a) de energía.	**Es dinámico(a) y ambicioso(a).**
Tiene mucha paciencia.	**Es bien educado(a).**
Es bastante perezoso(a).	**Siempre les enoja a sus amigos.**

Answers

5
1. Sí (No), el/la profesor(a) de español (no) me habla en español.
2. Sí (No), el/la profesor(a) (no) nos da muchos exámenes.
3. Sí (No), mis amigos (no) me envían muchos correos electrónicos.
4. Cuando hablo, mis amigos (no) me prestan atención.

6
1. Les
2. Le
3. les
4. les
5. le

7 *Answers will vary.*

Repaso C

Online Resources

Customizable Lesson Plans
Audio Activities
Student Workbook
Enrichment
Listening, Speaking, Reading, Writing Tests

TEACH

Core Instruction

Read Items 1, 2, and 3 to students. You may also wish to give some more examples.
Él (me, te) envía el correo. Ella (me, te) toma una foto. Ellos (me, te) hablan español.

Differentiation

Multiple Intelligences

Have one student throw a ball to another. When a person catches the ball, indicate that it is the direct object. Point to the person who caught it and show that he or she was not the object thrown (direct object) but rather the receiver of the object thrown (indirect object). This is a difficult concept and this visualization can help **visual-spatial** and **bodily-kinesthetic** learners.

PRACTICE

Leveling EACH Activity

Average Activities 5, 6
CHallenging Activity 7

Activity 5 This activity can be done as an oral activity with the entire class or as a paired activity.

Activity 6 This activity can be prepared in advance or gone over without prior preparation.

Preview

In Repaso D, students will review vocabulary related to team sports such as soccer (football), and baseball. In order to speak about these, they will review the present tense of stem-changing verbs and verbs such as **interesar** and **gustar.**

R28 **Go Online!** connectED.mcgraw-hill.com Audio Video Práctica Repaso Diversiones eScape

Go Online!

Audio
Listen to spoken Spanish.

Video
Watch and learn about the Spanish-speaking world.

Práctica
Practice your skills.

Repaso
Review what you've learned.

Diversiones
Go beyond the classroom.

eScape
Read about current events in the Spanish-speaking world.

Repaso

D

Los deportes

Objetivos

In this chapter you will review:

- vocabulary related to sports
- the present tense of stem-changing verbs
- the verbs **aburrir, interesar, gustar**

◀ Estos jóvenes están jugando béisbol en un parque de La Habana, la capital de Cuba.

¡Así se dice!

Why It Works!

The communicative theme of sports goes together beautifully with stem-changing verbs: **El juego empieza. El equipo vuelve al campo. Los jugadores juegan bien. Gómez devuelve el balón. Los dos equipos quieren ganar pero uno no puede. Uno pierde. Gustar** is presented here since students always like to tell what sports they like. Note that to make **gustar** easier, it is introduced with **me interesa(n)** to give students a comparable construction.

Interactive Whiteboard
Present or practice with interactive whiteboard activities.

Assessment
Check student progress.

ePals
Connect with Spanish-speaking students around the world.

Online Resources

Customizable Lesson Plans

Audio Activities

Student Workbook

Quick Start

Use QS R.9 or write the following on the board.

1. **Write six words in Spanish associated with soccer.**
2. **Write five words in Spanish associated with baseball.**
3. **Write four words in Spanish associated with tennis.**

TEACH

Core Instruction

Have students repeat the words and sentences and ask questions using the words being reviewed. **¿Quiénes juegan? ¿Qué juegan? ¿Qué empieza? ¿Adónde vuelven los jugadores?**

Teaching Options

Have students look at the photos and make up questions. Have students ask their questions of other members of the class.

Differentiation

Multiple Intelligences

Have **bodily-kinesthetic** learners present the short dialogue using proper gestures and intonation. Gestures and intonation can assist with comprehension.

Vocabulario

Los dos equipos juegan (al) fútbol.
Empieza el segundo tiempo.
Los jugadores vuelven al campo de fútbol.

Los dos equipos quieren ganar.
Pero no pueden.
Un equipo pierde.

Es un partido de béisbol.
El jugador batea la pelota.
Luego corre de una base a otra.

Luisa, ¿te gusta el béisbol?
Sí, me gusta mucho. ¿Y a ti?
Sí, me gusta. Pero me gusta más el fútbol.
A mí, no. Me aburre.

Go Online!

You may wish to remind students to go online for additional vocabulary practice. They can also download audio files of all vocabulary.

Go Online!

connectED.mcgraw-hill.com

Práctica

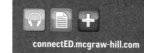

ESCUCHAR • HABLAR

1 Contesta según se indica.

1. ¿Cuántos tiempos hay en un juego de fútbol? (dos)
2. ¿Cuántos jugadores hay en un equipo de fútbol? (once)
3. ¿Dónde juegan fútbol? (en el campo de fútbol)
4. ¿Quién guarda la portería? (el portero)
5. ¿Qué bloquea? (el balón)
6. ¿Quieren perder los dos equipos? (no, ganar)

LEER

2 **Juego** **Cada uno en su sitio** Determina el deporte que cada frase describe.

1. El jugador lanza el balón con el pie.
2. Hay cinco jugadores en el equipo.
3. La pelota pasa por encima de la red.
4. El jugador corre de una base a otra.
5. Es un deporte de invierno.
6. El portero para o bloquea el balón.
7. El jugador tira el balón y encesta.
8. La jugadora usa una raqueta.

EL FÚTBOL	EL BÁSQUETBOL	EL BÉISBOL	EL TENIS	EL PATINAJE SOBRE EL HIELO

HABLAR

3 Personaliza. Da respuestas personales.

1. ¿Cuáles son los deportes que a ti te gustan?
2. ¿Cuáles son los comestibles que te gustan?
3. ¿Cuáles son los cursos que te interesan?
4. ¿Cuáles son algunas cosas que no te gustan, que te aburren?

4 **Juego** Work with a classmate. Give him or her some information about a sport. He or she has to guess what sport you're talking about. Take turns.

Repaso D

Leveling EACH Activity

Easy Activities 1, 3
Average Activity 2
CHallenging Activity 4

PRACTICE

Activity 1 This activity can be done with the whole class as an oral activity or you may do it as a paired activity.

Activity 2 This activity can be prepared outside of class or it can be done as a group activity.

Activity 3 This activity can be expanded a great deal when a student says **me gusta...** or **no me gusta...** This gives classmates an opportunity to disagree and give the reverse opinion. Each student then has to defend his or her opinion.

Differentiation

Multiple Intelligences

Activity 4 **Bodily-kinesthetic** learners may wish to dramatize different sports. Call on other students to guess the sport being depicted.

Answers

1

1. Hay dos tiempos en un juego de fútbol.
2. Hay once jugadores en un equipo de fútbol.
3. Juegan fútbol en el campo de fútbol.
4. El portero guarda la portería.
5. Bloquea el balón.
6. No, los dos equipos quieren ganar.

2

1. el fútbol
2. el básquetbol
3. el tenis
4. el béisbol
5. el patinaje sobre el hielo
6. el fútbol
7. el básquetbol
8. el tenis

3 *Answers will vary but may include:*

1. A mí me gustan ____.
2. A mí me gustan ____.
3. A mí me interesan ____.
4. No me gustan ____. Me aburren ____.

4 *Answers will vary.*

Online Resources

Customizable Lesson Plans

Audio Activities

TEACH

Core Instruction

Step 1 Call on two students to read the **Conversación** aloud with as much expression as possible.

Step 2 After students have read the conversation, do the **¿Comprendes?** activity.

ABOUT THE SPANISH LANGUAGE

When referring to a sports team, one says **el Real** or **el Valencia** for example, because the word **equipo** is understood.

Go Online!

You may wish to remind students to go online for additional conversation practice.

Conversación

Un partido importante

Tadeo	**Isabel y Marta, ¿quieren ir al Café Selma?**
Isabel	**Gracias, Tadeo, pero no podemos. Queremos ver el partido.**
Tadeo	**¿De qué partido hablas?**
Isabel	**El Real juega contra el Valencia.**
Tadeo	**¿Cuál es tu equipo favorito? ¿Cuál te gusta más?**
Isabel	**Mi equipo favorito es el Real porque soy madrileña.**

¿Comprendes?

Contesta según la información en la conversación.

1. ¿Adónde va Tadeo?
2. ¿Quieren ir con él Isabel y Marta?
3. ¿Por qué no pueden ir?
4. ¿Qué equipos juegan?
5. ¿Cuál es el equipo favorito de Isabel?

David H. Brennan

Answers

1. Tadeo va al Café Selma.
2. Isabel y Marta no quieren (pueden) ir con él.
3. No pueden ir porque ellas quieren ver el partido.
4. El Real juega contra el Valencia.
5. El Real es el equipo favorito de Isabel.

Gramática

Verbos de cambio radical

1. Review the following forms of the stem-changing verbs. Remember that the **e** changes to **ie** in all forms except **nosotros(as)** and ***vosotros(as).***

	empezar	perder
yo	empiezo	pierdo
tú	empiezas	pierdes
Ud., él, ella	empieza	pierde
nosotros(as)	empezamos	perdemos
vosotros(as)	*empezáis*	*perdéis*
Uds., ellos, ellas	empiezan	pierden

2. The following verbs change the **o** to **ue** in all forms except **nosotros(as)** and ***vosotros(as).***

	volver	poder
yo	vuelvo	puedo
tú	vuelves	puedes
Ud., él, ella	vuelve	puede
nosotros(as)	volvemos	podemos
vosotros(as)	*volvéis*	*podéis*
Uds., ellos, ellas	vuelven	pueden

3. The verb **jugar** also has a stem change.

jugar			
yo	juego	nosotros(as)	jugamos
tú	juegas	*vosotros(as)*	*jugáis*
Ud., él, ella	juega	Uds., ellos, ellas	juegan

Go Online!

connectED.mcgraw-hill.com

Nota

- Other verbs with the **e → ie** stem change like **empezar** and **perder** are: **sentarse, comenzar, pensar.**
- Other **o → ue** verbs like **volver** and **poder** are: **acostarse, recordar, encontrar.**
- **Sentir** is conjugated like **preferir.**

CULTURA

Los jóvenes juegan fútbol en una playa de Gijón, Asturias, en el norte de España.

Andrew Payti

Online Resources

Customizable Lesson Plans
Audio Activities
Video (Gramática)
Student Workbook
Enrichment

Quick Start

Use QS R.10 or write the following on the board.
Answer.

1. **¿Quién eres?**
2. **¿Dónde estás?**
3. **¿Qué estudias?**
4. **¿Qué aprendes?**
5. **¿A qué hora sales de la escuela?**
6. **¿Qué pones en tu mochila?**
7. **¿Conduces un carro?**

TEACH

Core Instruction

Step 1 Have students repeat all the verb forms after you.

Step 2 Then have students repeat all the **nosotros** forms.

Step 3 Now have them repeat all the **yo** forms to contrast the stem change.

Go Online!

You may wish to remind students to go online for additional grammar review and practice.

Leveling EACH Activity

Easy Activity 1
Average Activity 2
Average-CHallenging Activity 3
CHallenging Activity 4

PRACTICE

Activity 1 This activity can be done as an oral activity with the entire class or it can be done as a paired activity. You may also wish to write the verb forms on the board.

Activity 2 This activity can be prepared and then gone over in class.

Activity 3 You may wish to convert this activity into a competitive game.

Tips for Success

To review even more vocabulary, have students describe the young girl in the photograph.

Comunicación

Interpersonal

Activity 4 Let students speak on their own as if they were communicating in an actual conversation. If someone makes an error you may prefer not to correct it.

Go Online!

Gramática en vivo: *Stem-changing verbs* Enliven learning with the animated world of Professor Cruz! **Gramática en vivo** is a fun and effective tool for additional instruction and/or review.

Práctica

HABLAR • ESCRIBIR

1 Contesta.

1. ¿Quieres ir a la fiesta?
2. ¿Quieren ustedes bailar durante la fiesta?
3. ¿A qué hora empieza la fiesta?
4. ¿Puedes llegar a tiempo?
5. ¿Pueden ustedes tomar el bus a la fiesta?
6. ¿A qué hora vuelven ustedes a casa?

LEER • ESCRIBIR

2 Completa con la forma apropiada del verbo.

El juego de béisbol __1__ (empezar) a las tres y media. Habla Teresa:

—Hoy yo __2__ (querer) ser la pícher.

La verdad es que Teresa __3__ (ser) una pícher muy buena. Ella __4__ (jugar) muy bien. Nosotros __5__ (tener) un equipo bueno. Todos nosotros __6__ (jugar) bien. Nuestro equipo no __7__ (perder) mucho.

HABLAR

3 **¡Te toca a ti!**

1. **Puedo...** Tell all that you can do.
2. **Quiero...** Tell all that you want to do.
3. **Quiero pero no puedo...** Tell all that you want to do but for some reason you cannot do.
4. **No quiero porque prefiero...** Tell something you don't want to do because you prefer to do something else.

4 **Comunicación**

Work with a classmate. Tell him or her what sport you don't want to play because you don't like it. Tell him or her what you prefer to play. Then ask your classmate questions to find out what sports he or she likes.

Una beisbolista que quiere ganar

Carson Ganci/age fotostock

Answers

1

1. Sí, (No, no) quiero ir a la fiesta.
2. Sí, (No, no) queremos bailar durante la fiesta.
3. La fiesta empieza a ____.
4. Sí, (No, no) puedo llegar a tiempo.
5. Sí, (No, no) podemos tomar el bus a la fiesta.
6. Volvemos a casa a ____.

2

1. empieza
2. quiero
3. es
4. juega
5. tenemos
6. jugamos
7. pierde

3 *Answers will vary.*

4 *Answers will vary.*

Verbos como aburrir, interesar y gustar

1. The verbs **aburrir** and **interesar** function the same in Spanish and English.

¿Te aburre el arte?	*Does art bore you?*
¿Te aburren los deportes?	*Do sports bore you?*
No, los deportes me interesan.	*No, sports interest me.*

2. The verb **gustar** functions the same as **aburrir** and **interesar.** **Gustar** conveys the meaning *to like,* but it actually means *to be pleasing to.*

—¿Te gusta el béisbol?
—Sí, me gusta mucho.

—¿Te gustan los deportes?
—Sí, me gustan.

¿Te gustan los camarones?

¿Te gustan los mejillones?

ESCUCHAR • HABLAR

5 Sigue el modelo.

MODELO **¿A mí? ¿Los tomates? →**
—Me gustan mucho los tomates.
Y, ¿a ti te gustan también?

1. ¿A mí? ¿El pescado?
2. ¿A mí? ¿Los vegetales?
3. ¿A mí? ¿La carne?
4. ¿A mí? ¿El jamón?
5. ¿A mí? ¿Los mariscos?

HABLAR • ESCRIBIR

6 Personaliza. Da respuestas personales.

1. ¿Te interesan o te aburren las matemáticas? ¿Te gustan o no?
2. ¿Te interesa o te aburre la historia? ¿Te gusta o no?
3. ¿Te interesan o te aburren las ciencias? ¿Te gustan o no?
4. ¿Te interesa o te aburre la literatura? ¿Te gusta o no?
5. ¿Te interesa o te aburre la geografía? ¿Te gusta o no?

7 ***Comunicación***

Work with a classmate. Tell him or her about your favorite team. Tell all about the sport and tell why you really like this team in particular. Then ask your classmate about his or her favorite team. Do you by chance have the same favorite team?

CULTURA

Los jóvenes celebran la victoria de su equipo. Marchan por una calle de Madrid.

Go Online!

connectED.mcgraw-hill.com

Repaso D

Online Resources

Customizable Lesson Plans
- Audio Activities
- Student Workbook
- Enrichment
- Listening, Speaking, Reading, Writing Tests

TEACH

Core Instruction

Step 1 Have students read the model sentences aloud.

Step 2 Have them point to themselves as they say **me** and point to their friend as they say **te.**

PRACTICE

Leveling EACH Activity

Easy Activity 6
Average Activity 5
CHallenging Activity 7

Activity 5 This activity can be done as a paired activity.

Activity 6 This activity should be done as an oral activity with the entire class. You may wish to have students compare their answers. You can also ask them to expand by explaining why they answered **sí** or **no.**

Answers

5

1. Me gusta mucho el pescado. Y, ¿a ti te gusta también?
2. Me gustan mucho los vegetales. Y, ¿a ti te gustan también?
3. Me gusta mucho la carne. Y, ¿a ti te gusta también?
4. Me gusta mucho el jamón. Y, ¿a ti te gusta también?
5. Me gustan mucho los mariscos. Y, ¿a ti te gustan también?

6

1. Me interesan (Me aburren) las matemáticas. Me gustan. (No me gustan.)
2. Me interesa (Me aburre) la historia. Me gusta. (No me gusta.)
3. Me interesan (Me aburren) las ciencias. Me gustan. (No me gustan.)
4. Me interesa (Me aburre) la literatura. Me gusta. (No me gusta.)
5. Me interesa (Me aburre) la geografía. Me gusta. (No me gusta.)

7 *Answers will vary.*

Preview

In Repaso E, students will review vocabulary related to shopping for food and clothing. They will also review the verbs **saber** and **conocer** and the comparative and superlative forms of adjectives.

Andrew Payti

R36 **Go Online!** connectED.mcgraw-hill.com Audio Video Práctica Repaso Diversiones eScape ePals

Go Online!

Audio
Listen to spoken Spanish.

Video
Watch and learn about the Spanish-speaking world.

Práctica
Practice your skills.

Repaso
Review what you've learned.

Diversiones
Go beyond the classroom.

eScape
Read about current events in the Spanish-speaking world.

Repaso

E

De compras

Objetivos

In this chapter you will review:

- vocabulary related to shopping for food and clothing
- the verbs **saber** and **conocer**
- comparatives and superlatives

◀ Una vista del Mercado Central de Valencia, España. En el mercado hay puestos donde se vende todo tipo de comestibles—legumbres, frutas, carnes, pescado, mariscos. ¡Y todo está muy fresco!

Interactive Whiteboard
Present or practice with interactive whiteboard activities.

Assessment
Check student progress.

ePals
Connect with Spanish-speaking students around the world.

Online Resources

Customizable Lesson Plans

Audio Activities

Student Workbook

Quick Start

Use QS R.11 or write the following on the board.

1. **Write a list in Spanish of foods you have learned.**
2. **Write a list in Spanish of articles of clothing you have learned.**

TEACH

Core Instruction

Step 1 Have students look at each item and repeat it.

Step 2 Call on two boys to dramatize the **Para conversar** section.

Step 3 Ask questions about the market. **¿Qué hay en el mercado? ¿A quién conoce la señora? ¿Qué vende ella en el mercado? ¿Dónde son más baratas las legumbres y las frutas?**

Go Online!

You may wish to remind students to go online for additional vocabulary practice. They can also download audio files of all vocabulary.

Vocabulario

Una tienda de ropa

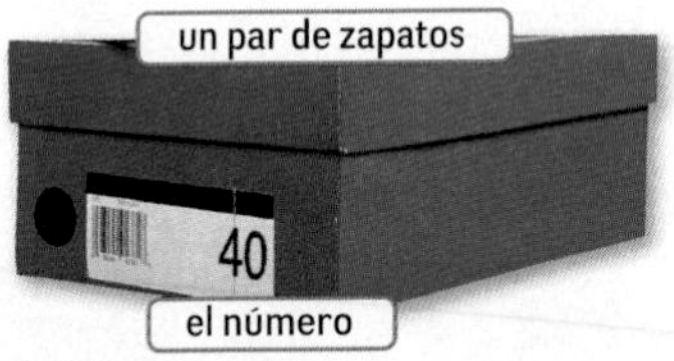

Para conversar
¿Qué te parece? ¿Me queda bien?
No. Te queda grande. ¿No sabes tu talla?
No.

Un mercado

Hay muchos puestos en el mercado.
La señora conoce a la vendedora.
En el mercado venden frutas y legumbres.
Las frutas y legumbres son más baratas en el mercado que en el supermercado.
Cuestan menos.

Práctica

Go Online!

connectED.mcgraw-hill.com

HABLAR

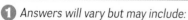

1 Personaliza. Da respuestas personales.

1. ¿Qué llevas a la escuela?
2. ¿Prefieres una camisa o una blusa de mangas largas o de mangas cortas?
3. ¿Llevas un pantalón corto en verano o en invierno?
4. Cuando compras ropa, ¿cuáles son tus colores favoritos?
5. Si necesitas una camiseta, ¿qué talla usas?
6. Si necesitas zapatos, ¿qué número calzas?
7. ¿Te sale todo más barato o más caro cuando una tienda tiene una liquidación?

CULTURA

El escaparate de una tienda de ropa en Valencia, España

Andrew Payti

HABLAR • ESCRIBIR

2 Completa una tabla como la de abajo. ¡A ver cuántas palabras recuerdas o sabes!

ropa	colores	frutas	vegetales

Leveling EACH Activity

Easy Activity 2
Average Activity 1

PRACTICE

Activity 1 This activity contains many important words and should be done orally with the entire class. It can also be done as a paired activity.

Activity 2 You may wish to modify this activity into a competitive individual or group game.

Answers

1 *Answers will vary but may include:*

1. Llevo ___ a la escuela.
2. Prefiero una camisa (una blusa de mangas largas, una blusa de mangas cortas).
3. Llevo un pantalón corto en verano.
4. Cuando compro ropa, mis colores favoritos son ___.
5. Si necesito una camiseta, uso la talla ___.
6. Si necesito zapatos, calzo el número ___.
7. Cuando una tienda tiene una liquidación, me sale todo más barato.

2 *Answers will vary.*

Leveling EACH Activity

Easy Activity 3
Average Activity 4
CHallenging Activities 5, 6

PRACTICE *(continued)*

Activity 3 This activity can be gone over in class without prior preparation.

Differentiation

Advanced Learners

Activity 4 You may wish to call on advanced learners to use all the words in original sentences.

Comunicación

Presentational

Activity 6 You may wish to have students prepare this activity as a skit in a clothing store.

LEER

3 Escoge la palabra apropiada.

1. En un mercado indígena hay muchos (puestos, carritos).
2. Los clientes conocen a los vendedores en el (supermercado, mercado).
3. En el supermercado los clientes llenan (un bote, un carrito) de todas sus compras.
4. —¿Quieres algo más?
   —No, (algo, nada) más, gracias.
5. Las sandalias y cerámicas son ejemplos de (utensilios domésticos, artesanía).

HABLAR • ESCRIBIR

4 Parea los antónimos.

1. blanco	a. barato
2. largo	b. aburrir
3. interesar	c. corto
4. algo	d. comprar
5. clientes	e. negro
6. caro	f. invierno
7. verano	g. nada
8. vender	h. empleados

LEER • ESCRIBIR

5 Completa con la palabra apropiada.

1. _____ de atún
2. _____ de agua mineral
3. _____ de zanahorias congeladas
4. _____ de mayonesa

6 **Comunicación**

Work with a classmate. Discuss whether or not you like to go shopping for clothes. Also discuss the type of clothing you like and dislike. What's your favorite outfit? Do you know what size you wear?

¡Mira lo que acabo de comprar!

Elena acaba de comprar una camiseta. ¿Qué piensas? ¿A Antonio le gusta la camiseta?

Glowimages/age fotostock

Answers

3
1. puestos
2. mercado
3. un carrito
4. nada
5. artesanía

4
1. e
2. c
3. b
4. g
5. h
6. a
7. f
8. d

5
1. un bote (una lata)
2. una botella
3. un paquete
4. un frasco

6 *Answers will vary.*

Conversación

En una tienda de ropa

¿Comprendes?

A Contesta según la información en la conversación.

1. ¿Dónde está Jorge?
2. ¿Con quién va de compras?
3. ¿Qué quiere comprar Jorge?
4. ¿Necesita una talla más grande o más pequeña?
5. ¿Qué color prefiere Mariluz?
6. ¿Tienen una chaqueta en la talla que necesita Jorge?
7. ¿Cuánto cuesta?

B **Llegando a conclusiones** ¿Qué piensas? ¿Compra Jorge la chaqueta o no? ¿Por qué?

Repaso E

Online Resources

Customizable Lesson Plans

Audio Activities

TEACH

Core Instruction

Step 1 Call on three individuals to read the **Conversación** to the class as a skit.

Step 2 Before going over the **¿Comprendes?** activities, have students ask one another questions about the **Conversación.**

Teaching Options

Students can make up false statements about the conversation and call on another student to correct them.

Go Online!

You may wish to remind students to go online for additional conversation practice.

Answers

A

1. Jorge está en una tienda de ropa.
2. Va de compras con su amiga Mariluz.
3. Jorge quiere comprar una chaqueta.
4. Necesita una talla más grande.
5. Prefiere el azul.
6. Sí, tienen una chaqueta en la talla que necesita Jorge.
7. Cuesta mil quinientos pesos.

B *Answers will vary.*

Online Resources

Customizable Lesson Plans

Audio Activities

Student Workbook

Quick Start

Use QS Transparency R.12 or write the following on the board.

Write a list in Spanish of all the things you know such as addresses, names, art, music, etc.

TEACH

Core Instruction

Step 1 Tell students they will once again review two verbs that have regular forms with all subjects except **yo.**

Step 2 Have students repeat the **sé, conozco** forms several times.

Step 3 Read the information in Items 2 and 3 aloud and have students repeat the example sentences.

Step 4 Have students look at their words from the Quick Start activity and determine if they should be used with **saber** or **conocer.**

Go Online!

You may wish to remind students to go online for additional grammar review and practice.

Repaso E

Gramática

Saber y conocer

1. The verbs **saber** and **conocer** both mean *to know.* Like many Spanish verbs, they have an irregular **yo** form in the present tense. All other forms are regular.

saber			
yo	sé	nosotros(as)	sabemos
tú	sabes	*vosotros(as)*	*sabéis*
Ud., él, ella	sabe	Uds., ellos, ellas	saben

conocer			
yo	conozco	nosotros(as)	conocemos
tú	conoces	*vosotros(as)*	*conocéis*
Ud., él, ella	conoce	Uds., ellos, ellas	conocen

2. The verb **saber** means *to know a fact* or *to have information about something.* It also means *to know how to do something.*

Yo sé donde está el mercado.
No sabemos a qué hora sale el vuelo.
Ellos saben regatear.

3. The verb **conocer** means *to know* in the sense of *to be acquainted with.* It is used to talk about people and complex or abstract concepts rather than simple facts.

Yo conozco a Luis.
Ella conoce a su hermano.
Los alumnos conocen bien la literatura mexicana.

Andrew Payti

CULTURA
Estos jóvenes saben disfrutar de sus momentos libres jugando un juego espontáneo de fútbol en una playa de Puerto Madryn, Argentina.

Go Online!

connectED.mcgraw-hill.com

Práctica

HABLAR • ESCRIBIR

1 Personaliza. Da respuestas personales.

1. ¿Sabes el número que calzas?
2. ¿Sabes la talla que usas cuando compras ropa?
3. ¿Sabes el número del celular de tu mejor amigo(a)?
4. ¿Sabes su dirección de correo electrónico también?
5. ¿Conoces a la familia de tu mejor amigo(a)?
6. ¿Conoces la cultura hispana?

HABLAR

2 Trabajen en grupos de tres. Indiquen todo lo que saben hacer.

HABLAR • ESCRIBIR

3 Completa cada frase con **saber** o **conocer.**

1. Yo ____ la palabra.
2. Nosotros ____ a María.
3. Carlos ____ esquiar.
4. Ellos ____ la lección.
5. Yo ____ leer.
6. ¿____ tú a Enrique?
7. Ella ____ el arte de México.
8. Nosotros ____ que París es la capital de Francia.

ESCRIBIR

4 Escribe frases originales.

1. yo / saber...
2. y ellos / saber...
3. tú / conocer...
4. y nosotros / conocer...

5 *Comunicación*

You are now beginning a new year in your study of Spanish. Think about what you have learned so far in Spanish, and tell what you know. Be sure to use **saber** or **conocer** as appropriate.

CULTURA

Los clientes saben que todo lo que se vende en esta tienda del Mercado Central en Valencia está fresco. Ellos conocen a la empleada.

Leveling EACH Activity

Easy Activity 1

Average Activities 2, 3

Average - CHallenging Activities 4, 5

PRACTICE

Activities 3 and 4 These are the only activities that should be prepared before being gone over in class.

Answers

1

1. Sí (No), yo (no) sé el número que calzo.
2. Sí (No), yo (no) sé la talla que uso cuando compro ropa.
3. Sí (No), yo (no) sé el número del celular de mi mejor amigo(a).
4. Sí (No), yo (no) sé su dirección de correo electrónico también (tampoco).
5. Sí (No), yo (no) conozco a la familia de mi mejor amigo(a).
6. Sí (No), yo (no) conozco la cultura hispana.

2 *Answers will vary.*

3

1. sé
2. conocemos
3. sabe
4. saben
5. sé
6. Conoces
7. conoce
8. sabemos

4 *Answers will vary.*

5 *Answers will vary.*

Online Resources

Customizable Lesson Plans
Audio Activities
Student Workbook
Listening, Speaking, Reading, Writing Tests

Quick Start

Use QS R.13 or write the following on the board.

Make a list in Spanish of adjectives you can use to describe people and things.

people
things
people and things

TEACH

Core Instruction

Step 1 Use three stick figures with names and a series of adjectives to show comparative and superlative. **José, Pablo, Luis. José es bajo. Pablo es más bajo que José. Luis es el más bajo de los tres.** Use other adjectives as well.

Step 2 Read the information about the irregular forms and have individuals read the example sentences.

Teaching Options

Using the photo, have students make up sentences comparing Teresa and Paco.

Comparativo y superlativo

1. To form the comparative in Spanish you put **más** or **menos** before the adjective or adverb and **que** after it.

Ella es más (menos) ambiciosa que su hermana.
Ella es más (menos) ambiciosa que yo y la verdad es que ella sabe más (menos) que nadie.

Note that after **que** you use subject pronouns (**yo, tú,** etc.) or **nadie.**

2. You form the superlative by using the appropriate definite article plus **más** or **menos** and the adjective or adverb. The preposition **de** follows the superlative.

Es el joven más (menos) inteligente del grupo.
Es el más (menos) inteligente del grupo.

3. Study the following irregular comparative and superlative forms.

COMPARATIVE		SUPERLATIVE	
bueno	**mejor**	**el/la mejor**	**los/las mejores**
malo	**peor**	**el/la peor**	**los/las peores**
bien	**mejor**		
mal	**peor**		

Esta chaqueta te queda mejor que las otras.
Elena es la mejor alumna de la clase.

4. The adjectives **mayor** and **menor** most often refer to age.

Yo soy menor que mi hermana.
Yo soy el/la menor de la familia.
Mi abuelo es el mayor.

Comparaciones

El inglés

To form the comparative in English, you add *-er* to short adjectives or adverbs. You put *more* before longer adjectives or adverbs.

He is smarter than the others.
She is more intelligent than the others.

To form the superlative in English, you add *-est* to short adjectives or adverbs and you put *most* before longer ones.

This is the largest size.
This is the most popular color.

Según Teresa, el libro que ella tiene es más interesante que los libros que tiene Paco.

Go Online!

connectED.mcgraw-hill.com

Práctica

HABLAR • ESCRIBIR

6 Compara.

1. tu clase de español y tu clase de inglés
2. el equipo de fútbol y el equipo de béisbol
3. tu mejor amigo(a) y tu hermano(a)
4. tu escuela secundaria y tu escuela primaria

HABLAR • ESCRIBIR

7 Forma frases según el modelo.

MODELO **inteligente**
José / Carlos / Diego →
José es inteligente. Carlos es más inteligente que José y Diego es el más inteligente de los tres.

1. graciosa
   Julia / Eva / Carla
2. simpático
   Enrique / Tadeo / Alfonso
3. interesante
   el curso de biología / el curso de historia / el curso de español

HABLAR • ESCRIBIR

8 Personaliza. Da respuestas personales.

1. ¿Quiénes en tu familia son mayores que tú?
2. Y, ¿quiénes son menores?
3. ¿Quién es el/la menor de tu familia? ¿Quién es el/la mayor?
4. ¿En qué curso sacas la mejor nota?
5. ¿En qué curso sacas la peor nota?

HABLAR

9 **Juego** Work in groups of four. Create a sentence that compares two people or things. Have your classmates guess who or what you are comparing. Take turns.

CULTURA

Unas muchachas en un bote de remos en el lago de Nicaragua—el lago de agua dulce *(freshwater)* más grande de Nicaragua

Andrew Payti

Repaso E

Leveling EACH Activity

Easy Activities 6, 8
Average Activities 7, 9

PRACTICE

Activity 6 In this activity, students can give as many answers as possible.

Activity 7 This activity can be done as a paired activity.

Activity 8 Average and advanced learners can give additional information such as ages and grades. You may also have them describe family members more fully.

Answers

6 *Answers will vary.*

7

1. Julia es graciosa. Eva es más graciosa que Julia y Carla es la más graciosa de las tres.
2. Enrique es simpático. Tadeo es más simpático que Enrique y Alfonso es el más simpático de los tres.
3. El curso de biología es interesante. El curso de historia es más interesante que el curso de biología y el curso de español es el más interesante de los tres.

8 *Answers will vary but may include:*

1. En mi familia, ___ son mayores que yo.
2. ___ son menores que mí.
3. ___ es el/la menor de mi familia. ___ es el/la mayor.
4. Saco la mejor nota en ___.
5. Saco la peor nota en ___.

9 *Answers will vary.*

Preview

In Repaso F, students will review the vocabulary they need to talk about vacations they take in the winter and summer. To be able to talk about such activities, they will review the preterite tense of regular verbs, the preterite of **ir** and **ser,** and the direct and indirect object pronouns.

Andrew Payti

R46 **Go Online!** connectED.mcgraw-hill.com Audio Video Práctica Repaso Diversiones eScape ePals

Go Online!

Audio
Listen to spoken Spanish.

Video
Watch and learn about the Spanish-speaking world.

Práctica
Practice your skills.

Repaso
Review what you've learned.

Diversiones
Go beyond the classroom.

eScape
Read about current events in the Spanish-speaking world.

Repaso

F

De vacaciones

Objetivos

In this chapter you will review:

- vocabulary related to summer resorts and activities
- vocabulary related to winter resorts and activities
- the preterite of regular verbs
- the preterite of **ir** and **ser**
- direct and indirect object pronouns

◀ Mucha gente está disfrutando de un día soleado en la playa de Gijón en Asturias. Aquí el agua del mar Cantábrico está un poco fría.

Interactive Whiteboard
Present or practice with interactive whiteboard activities.

Assessment
Check student progress.

ePals
Connect with Spanish-speaking students around the world.

Online Resources

Customizable Lesson Plans

Audio Activities

Student Workbook

Quick Start

Use QS Transparency R.14 or write the following on the board.
Write in Spanish at least five things you do when you are on vacation.

TEACH

Core Instruction

Step 1 Review the vocabulary using suggestions given for previous review lessons.

Step 2 After reviewing the specific vocabulary on this page, have students give additional vocabulary they remember that deals with summer and winter activities.

Teaching Options

Have students look at the photos. Inform them that they will review the preterite forms of regular verbs. Have them write the verbs used in the vocabulary presentation sentences in a list. See if they can separate the **-ar**, **-er**, and **-ir** verbs into separate lists.

Repaso F

Vocabulario

Raúl pasó el verano en la playa.
Nadó en el mar.

Tomó el sol.
Volvió a casa muy bronceado.

Susana pasó una semana en una estación de esquí.
Tomó el telesilla para subir la montaña.
Subió en el telesilla.

Ella bajó la pista para expertos.
No bajó la pista para principiantes.

¡Así se dice!

Why It Works!

Note that all the preterite forms in the vocabulary presentation are in the third person so students can immediately make up and answer questions without having to manipulate the verb endings. They will review the endings in the following grammar section.

Go Online!

You may wish to remind students to go online for additional vocabulary practice. They can also download audio files of all vocabulary.

Go Online!

connectED.mcgraw-hill.com

Práctica

HABLAR • ESCRIBIR

1 Contesta sobre un día en la playa.

1. ¿Fue Francisco a la playa?
2. ¿Nadó en el mar?
3. ¿Esquió en el agua?
4. ¿Tomó el sol?
5. ¿Volvió a casa muy bronceado?

EXPANSIÓN

Ahora, sin mirar las preguntas, cuenta toda la información en tus propias palabras. Si no recuerdas algo, un(a) compañero(a) te puede ayudar.

CULTURA

Esquiadores en Portillo, Chile

HABLAR • ESCRIBIR

2 Contesta sobre una estación de esquí.

1. ¿Fueron a una estación de esquí los amigos?
2. ¿Salieron ellos muy temprano por la mañana?
3. ¿Pasaron el día entero en las pistas?
4. ¿Subieron la montaña en el telesilla?
5. ¿Bajaron la pista para expertos o para principiantes?
6. ¿Volvieron a casa el mismo día?

EXPANSIÓN

Ahora, sin mirar las preguntas, cuenta toda la información en tus propias palabras. Si no recuerdas algo, un(a) compañero(a) te puede ayudar.

3 ***Comunicación***

Work with a classmate. Look at these photos. Tell where you prefer to go and why. Take turns.

Repaso F

Leveling EACH Activity

Easy Activities 1, 2
Average Activity 1 **Expansión**, Activity 2 **Expansión**
CHallenging Activity 3

PRACTICE

Activities 1 and 2 These activities can both be done as oral activities with the entire class or they can be done as paired activities. Call on several students to do the **Expansión** activities.

Differentiation

Advanced Learners

Activity 3 After doing this activity, you may wish to have advanced learners prepare a debate about the advantages and disadvantages of these vacation destinations.

Answers

1

1. Sí (No), Francisco (no) fue a la playa.
2. Sí, (No, no) nadó en el mar.
3. Sí, (No, no) esquió en el agua.
4. Sí, (No, no) tomó el sol.
5. Sí, (No, no) volvió a casa muy bronceado.

2

1. Sí (No), los amigos (no) fueron a una estación de esquí.
2. Sí (No), ellos (no) salieron muy temprano por la mañana.
3. Sí, (No, no) pasaron el día entero en las pistas.
4. Sí, (No, no) subieron la montaña en el telesilla.
5. Bajaron la pista para expertos (principiantes).
6. Sí, (No, no) volvieron a casa el mismo día.

3 *Answers will vary.*

Online Resources

Customizable Lesson Plans

Audio Activities

TEACH

Core Instruction

Step 1 Have two students read the **Conversación** to the class, using as much expression as possible.

Step 2 Go over the **¿Comprendes?** activity.

¿Comprendes?

Differentiation

Advanced Learners

Have advanced learners correct the false information.

Go Online!

You may wish to remind students to go online for additional conversation practice.

Repaso F

Conversación

¿Adónde fueron los amigos?

Nando	¿Adónde fuiste ayer, Teresa?
Teresa	Fui a casa de Sofi.
Nando	¿Y… ?
Teresa	Jugamos tenis.
Nando	¿Tiene Sofi una cancha de tenis?
Teresa	No. Hay canchas en un parque cerca de su casa. Pero Sofi tiene una piscina.
Nando	¿Sí? ¿Nadaron ustedes?
Teresa	Sí, nadamos después de jugar tenis.

¿Comprendes?

Usa una tabla como la de abajo para indicar si la información es correcta o no.

	correcta	incorrecta
1. Nando fue con Teresa a casa de Sofi.		
2. La casa de Sofi tiene una cancha de tenis.		
3. Teresa y Sofi jugaron tenis.		
4. Jugaron en una cancha en un parque.		
5. Nadaron también.		
6. Nadaron en una piscina en el parque.		

Steve Mason/AGE Fotostock

Answers

1. incorrecta
2. incorrecta
3. correcta
4. correcta
5. correcta
6. incorrecta

Gramática

El pretérito

1. Review the forms of the preterite of regular verbs.

	nadar	comer	subir
yo	nadé	comí	subí
tú	nadaste	comiste	subiste
Ud., él, ella	nadó	comió	subió
nosotros(as)	nadamos	comimos	subimos
vosotros(as)	*nadasteis*	*comisteis*	*subisteis*
Uds., ellos, ellas	nadaron	comieron	subieron

Note that **-er** and **-ir** verbs have the same endings in the preterite.

2. The forms of the verbs **ir** and **ser** are the same in the preterite. The meaning is made clear by the context of the sentence.

ir, ser			
yo	fui	nosotros(as)	fuimos
tú	fuiste	*vosotros(as)*	*fuisteis*
Ud., él, ella	fue	Uds., ellos, ellas	fueron

3. The preterite is used to express an event or action that began and ended at a definite time in the past.

Ellos pasaron el verano pasado en México.
Fueron a Acapulco.

4. Note the forms of the verbs **ver** and **dar.**

VER	vi	viste	vio	vimos	*visteis*	vieron
DAR	di	diste	dio	dimos	*disteis*	dieron

Go Online!

connectED.mcgraw-hill.com

InfoGap For more practice with the preterite, do Activity R in the Student Resource section at the end of this book.

CULTURA

Ellos pasaron el verano pasado en México y fueron a la Ciudad de México.

Repaso F

Online Resources

Customizable Lesson Plans

Audio Activities

Video (Gramática)

Student Workbook

Quick Start

Use QS R.15 or write the following on the board.

Write in Spanish four beach activities and four skiing activities.

TEACH

Core Instruction

Step 1 Have students repeat the verbs in Items 1 and 2 after you.

Step 2 Write one form of a verb on the board and challenge volunteers to fill in the rest of the paradigm.

Step 3 Read Items 3 and 4 to the class aloud.

Step 4 Have students make up additional sentences using the preterite. They can use the activities they wrote in the Quick Start activity for this section.

Go Online!

You may wish to remind students to go online for additional grammar review and practice.

Leveling EACH Activity

Easy Activity 1
Average Activities 2, 3, 4
CHallenging Activity 5

PRACTICE

Activities ❶ and ❷ These activities can be done orally with the entire class or they may be done as paired activities.

Activity ❷ It is suggested that you have students write answers in complete sentences. You may, however, wish to have them write only the verb form as follows:

1. fuiste → fui; viste → vi; tomaste → tomé; etc.

Comunicación

Interpersonal

Activities ❸, ❹, and ❺ Have students say as much as they can. Note that the directions are carefully written so as not to "trap" students into having to use the imperfect, which they have not yet learned.

Práctica

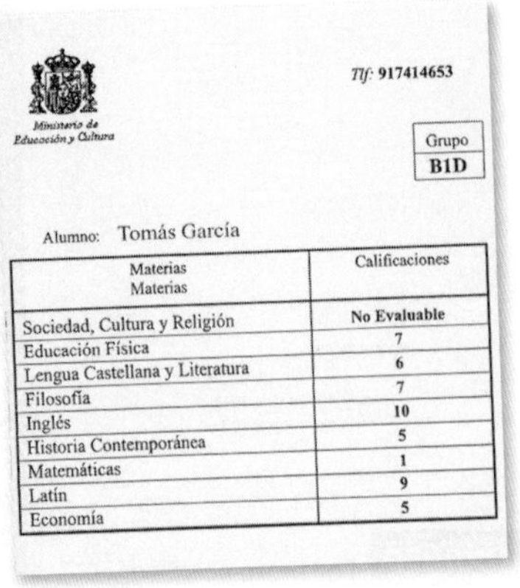

Ministerio de Educación y Cultura

Tlf: 917414653

Grupo
B1D

Alumno: Tomás García

Materias Materias	Calificaciones
Sociedad, Cultura y Religión	No Evaluable
Educación Física	7
Lengua Castellana y Literatura	6
Filosofía	7
Inglés	10
Historia Contemporánea	5
Matemáticas	1
Latín	9
Economía	5

HABLAR • ESCRIBIR

❶ Personaliza. Da respuestas personales.

1. ¿Fuiste a la escuela ayer?
2. ¿A qué hora llegaste a la escuela?
3. ¿Hablaste con el/la profesor(a) de español?
4. ¿Tomaste un examen?
5. ¿En qué curso tomaste el examen?
6. ¿Saliste bien en el examen?
7. ¿Comiste en la cafetería de la escuela?
8. ¿A qué hora volviste a casa?

HABLAR • ESCRIBIR

❷ Contesta.

1. ¿Fuiste al cine ayer?
¿Viste una película?
¿Tomaste un refresco en el cine?
2. ¿Salieron ustedes anoche?
¿Fueron a una fiesta?
¿Bailaron y cantaron durante la fiesta?
3. ¿Esquió Sandra?
¿Subió la montaña en el telesilla?
¿Bajó la pista para expertos?
4. ¿Pasaron los amigos el fin de semana en la playa?
¿Te escribieron una tarjeta postal?
¿Nadaron y esquiaron en el agua?

Comunicación

❸ Tell what you and your friends did last Friday night.

❹ Tell what you did last night.

❺ Tell what you or you and your family or friends did during your last vacation.

CULTURA

Una escuela de esquí y snowboard en la estación de esquí en Cerro Catedral en Bariloche, Argentina

Andrew Payti

Answers

❶ *Answers will vary but may include:*

1. Sí, (No, no) fui a la escuela ayer.
2. Llegué a la escuela a ____.
3. Sí, (No, no) hablé con el/la profesor(a) de español.
4. Sí, (No, no) tomé un examen.
5. Tomé el examen en ____.
6. Sí, (No, no) salí bien en el examen.
7. Sí, (No, no) comí en la cafetería de la escuela.
8. Volví a casa a ____.

❷

1. Sí, (No, no) fui al cine ayer. / Sí, (No, no) vi una película. / Sí, (No, no) tomé un refresco en el cine.
2. Sí, (No, no) salimos anoche. / Sí, (No, no) fuimos a una fiesta. / Sí, (No, no) bailamos y cantamos durante la fiesta.
3. Sí, (No, no) esquió Sandra. / Sí, (No, no) subió la montaña en el telesilla. / Sí, (No, no) bajó la pista para expertos.
4. Sí, (No, no) pasaron los amigos el fin de semana en la playa. / Sí, (No, no) me escribieron una tarjeta postal. / Sí, (No, no) nadaron y esquiaron en el agua.

❸ *Answers will vary.*

❹ *Answers will vary.*

❺ *Answers will vary.*

Go Online!

connectED.mcgraw-hill.com

Los pronombres de complemento

1. The object pronouns **me, te,** and **nos** can be either direct or indirect objects. Note that the object pronoun precedes the conjugated verb.

DIRECT	INDIRECT
Él me miró.	**Él me habló por teléfono.**
¿Te invitó Carlos?	**¿Te dio una invitación?**
Ella nos vio.	**Mónica nos envió algo.**

2. **Lo, los, la,** and **las** function as direct objects only. They can replace either persons or things.

Pablo compró el boleto.	**Pablo lo compró.**
Pablo compró los boletos.	**Pablo los compró.**
Teresa compró la raqueta.	**Teresa la compró.**
Teresa compró las raquetas.	**Teresa las compró.**
Yo vi a los muchachos.	**Yo los vi.**

3. **Le** and **les** function as indirect objects only.

Yo le escribí un correo electrónico (a él, a ella, a usted).
Yo les escribí (a ellos, a ellas, a ustedes).

CULTURA
Una farmacia en Baños, Ecuador

Práctica

HABLAR

6 Contesta.

1. ¿Fuiste al médico?
2. ¿Te habló el médico?
3. ¿Te examinó?
4. ¿Te dio una diagnosis?
5. ¿Te recetó medicina?

ESCUCHAR • HABLAR

7 Sigue el modelo.

MODELO la toalla →
Aquí la tienes.

1. el anorak
2. la crema bronceadora
3. el traje de baño
4. los anteojos de sol
5. los boletos para el telesilla
6. las raquetas

LEER • ESCRIBIR

8 Completa con **le, lo** o **la.**

Pepe está en el consultorio del médico. Pepe __1__ explica al médico que __2__ duele el estómago. El médico __3__ examina. __4__ da una receta. En la farmacia el farmacéutico __5__ lee y __6__ da los medicamentos a Pepe.

R53

Answers

6
1. Sí, (No, no) fui al médico.
2. Sí, (No, no) me habló el médico.
3. Sí, (No, no) me examinó.
4. Sí, (No, no) me dio una diagnosis.
5. Sí, (No, no) me recetó medicina.

7
1. Aquí lo tienes.
2. Aquí la tienes.
3. Aquí lo tienes.
4. Aquí los tienes.
5. Aquí los tienes.
6. Aquí las tienes.

8
1. le
2. le
3. lo
4. Le
5. la
6. le

Repaso F

Online Resources

Customizable Lesson Plans
- Audio Activities
- Video (Gramática)
- Student Workbook
- Listening, Speaking, Reading, Writing Tests

TEACH
Core Instruction

When you present Item 2, have students pay particular attention to the arrow from the noun to the object pronoun.

ABOUT THE SPANISH LANGUAGE

The use of **le** is made even more confusing due to **leísmo.** Students often see **le, les** used as masculine direct objects. **Le vi, le miré, le invité, le llamé.** This use is not isolated.

Go Online!

Gramática en vivo: *The Preterite* Enliven learning with the animated world of Professor Cruz! **Gramática en vivo** is a fun and effective tool for additional instruction and/or review.

PRACTICE

Leveling EACH Activity

Easy Activities 6, 7
CHallenging Activity 8

Activities 6 and 7 These activities can be gone over in class without prior preparation.

Activity 8 This activity should be prepared before going over it in class.

Chapter Overview

En avión

Scope and Sequence

Topics

- Packing for a trip
- Getting to the airport
- At the airport
- On board an airplane

Culture

- Discuss air travel in South America

Functions

- How to talk about packing for a trip and getting to the airport
- How to tell what you do at the airport
- How to talk about being on an airplane

Structure

- Verbs that have **-g** in the **yo** form of the present tense
- The present progressive tense

Lori Ernfridsson

Planning Guide

	required	recommended	optional
Vocabulario 1 Antes de salir para el aeropuerto Al aeropuerto En el aeropuerto	✓		
Vocabulario 2 En el control de seguridad En la puerta de salida Abordo del avión	✓		
Gramática Presente de **hacer, poner, traer, salir** El presente progresivo	✓		
Pronunciación Las consonante **r**		✓	
Conversación En el aeropuerto		✓	
Lectura cultural El avión en la América del Sur		✓	
Lectura Un poco más Un viaje interesante			✓
Prepárate para el examen			✓
Repaso cumulativo			✓

Correlations to ACTFL World-Readiness Standards for Learning Languages

Page numbers in light print refer to the Student Edition.
Page numbers in bold print refer to the Teacher Edition.

COMMUNICATION Communicate effectively in more than one language in order to function in a variety of situations and for multiple purposes		
Interpersonal Communication	Learners interact and negotiate meaning in spoken, signed, or written conversations to share information, reactions, feelings, and opinions.	pp. **2–3, 4, 5,** 6, 7, **8,** 11, 13, 14, **14,** 16, 17, 18, **20,** 28
Interpretive Communication	Learners understand, interpret, and analyze what is heard, read, or viewed on a variety of topics.	pp. **4,** 6, **6,** 7, **7, 8, 9,** 10, **10,** 11, **12,** 13, 14, 16, **16,** 17, **17,** 18, 20, **20,** 21, **21,** 23, **23, 24,** 25, **26,** 26–27, 32–33, **33**
Presentational Communication	Learners present information, concepts, and ideas to inform, explain, persuade, and narrate on a variety of topics using appropriate media and adapting to various audiences of listeners, readers, or viewers.	pp. **1C, 5,** 6, **8, 9, 11,** 14, 16, **17,** 18, **18, 20, 21, 23,** 29, **30, 31**
CULTURES Interact with cultural competence and understanding		
Relating Cultural Practices to Perspectives	Learners use the language to investigate, explain, and reflect on the relationship between the practices and perspectives of the cultures studied.	pp. 2–3, 5, **5, 25**
Relating Cultural Products to Perspectives	Learners use the language to investigate, explain, and reflect on the relationship between the products and perspectives of the cultures studied.	pp. **1C, 1D,** 2–3, **2–3, 7, 13, 14, 15,** 17, 19, **19, 21, 22, 24,** 24–25, **25**
CONNECTIONS Connect with other disciplines and acquire information and diverse perspectives in order to use the language to function in academic and career-related situations		
Making Connections	Learners build, reinforce, and expand their knowledge of other disciplines while using the language to develop critical thinking and to solve problems creatively.	pp. **1C, 1D, 6, 7, 13,** 16, **16, 21, 22,** 22–23, **23, 24,** 24–25, **25,** 27, 28
Acquiring Information and Diverse Perspectives	Learners access and evaluate information and diverse perspectives that are available through the language and its cultures.	pp. 8, **8,** 15, **15,** 19, **19**
COMPARISONS Develop insight into the nature of language and culture in order to interact with cultural competence		
Language Comparisons	Learners use the language to investigate, explain, and reflect on the nature of language through comparisons of the language studied and their own.	pp. **5, 9,** 19, **19, 30,** 31
Cultural Comparisons	Learners use the language to investigate, explain, and reflect on the concept of culture through comparisons of the cultures studied and their own.	pp. **1D,** 1, 2–3, **22,** 24
COMMUNITIES Communicate and interact with cultural competence in order to participate in multilingual communities at home and around the world		
School and Global Communities	Learners use the language both within and beyond the classroom to interact and collaborate in their community and the globalized world.	pp. **1C,** 6, 13, 16, 18, **18, 30**
Lifelong Learning	Learners set goals and reflect on their progress in using languages for enjoyment, enrichment, and advancement.	pp. 8, **8,** 15, **15**

Chapter Project

Un mapa

In this project, students will create large physical maps of Spanish-speaking countries in Latin America.

1. Divide the class into groups of three or four students and have each group pick a Latin American Spanish-speaking country. If possible, each group should pick a different country so that no country is repeated.
2. Each group will then use encyclopedias, the Internet, and/or other references to gather information for their map. Each group will be required to include the country's capital and at least five other cities, as well as major rivers, lakes, mountains, deserts, etc.
3. Students should make the maps visually appealing by using color and adding graphic elements to represent the landscape features. Each group will decide what their graphic elements will be and how they will apply them.
4. After the groups have compiled their lists of information for their maps, they should then begin creating the map on poster board or a large sheet of paper. A transparency and overhead projector can be used to produce a large map image if students don't want to draw the map freehand.
5. When the maps are completed, each group should also turn in a list of all the cities and landforms included on the map, divided into the appropriate categories.

Expansion: Students can brainstorm other types of information that can be mapped (natural resources, historic monuments and landmarks, indigenous population centers, etc.). Students can then do additional research on the countries they have chosen, design additional graphic elements, and add the new information to their maps.

Scoring Rubric for Project

	5	3	1
Evidence of planning	Corrected draft and layout are provided.	Draft and layout are provided, but draft is not corrected.	Draft and layout are not provided.
Use of illustrations	Use of several visual elements.	Use of few visual elements.	No use of any visual elements.
Presentation	Memory book page contains all of the required elements.	Memory book page contains some of the required elements.	Memory book page contains few of the required elements.

Culture

Recipe

SUSPIRO LIMEÑO

Ingredients: (makes 6 servings)
1 14-ounce can sweetened condensed milk
1 12-ounce can evaporated milk
1 tablespoon vanilla extract
2 eggs, separated
1 cup confectioners' sugar
¼ teaspoon cinnamon (optional)

Whisk together sweetened condensed milk, evaporated milk, vanilla, and egg yolks in a saucepan. Gently cook on medium-low heat for 30 minutes until the mixture thickens, stirring constantly. When finished, pour into one large heatproof serving dish or six smaller dishes and set aside. Then whip the egg whites and confectioners' sugar until it forms stiff peaks. Spread meringue on top of the milk mixture. Refrigerate the dessert until cold and sprinkle with cinnamon before serving.

Un lugar misterioso

In this chapter's **Lectura Un poco más,** students will have the opportunity to learn about the Nazca lines in Peru. The purpose of these large geoglyphs is still unknown and may never be discovered. Have students do further research on the Nazca lines and share the information they find with the class. You may wish to divide the class into groups to debate some of the current theories regarding why the Nazca lines were created (could they have been maps?). To further expand the research, have students identify other places in the world where there are unexplained constructions and have them compare the mysteries surrounding those places with that of the Nazca lines.

Connection to Fine Art

Have students look online or in an art text to find *San Francisco to New York in One Hour,* by Alexander Aramburo Maldonado. Students may be surprised to realize that an artist who is illustrating rockets powered by nuclear energy came to the United States as a child at the beginning of the Mexican Revolution. Some students might be interested in researching Maldonado on the Internet and reporting their findings to the class.

50-Minute Lesson Plans

	Objective	Present	Practice	Assess/Homework
Day 1	Talk about packing for a trip and getting to the airport	Chapter Opener (5 min.) Introducción al tema (10 min.) Core Instruction/Vocabulario 1 (20 min.)	Activities 1–3 (15 min.)	Student Workbook Activities A–C **ConnectEd** Vocabulary Practice
Day 2	Talk about packing for a trip and getting to the airport	Quick Start (5 min.) Review Vocabulario 1 (10 min.)	Activities 4–7 (15 min.) Total Physical Response (5 min.) InfoGap (5 min.) Audio Activities A–C (10 min.)	Student Workbook Activities D–E **ConnectEd** Vocabulary Practice
Day 3	Tell what you do at the airport and talk about being on an airplane	Core Instruction/Vocabulario 2 (15 min.) Video, Vocabulario en vivo (10 min.)	Activities 1–3 (15 min.)	Quiz 1 (10 min.) Student Workbook Activities A–C **ConnectEd** Vocabulary Practice
Day 4	Tell what you do at the airport and talk about being on an airplane	Quick Start (5 min.) Review Vocabulario 2 (10 min.)	Activities 4–7 (15 min.) Total Physical Response (5 min.) Audio Activities D–G (15 min.)	Student Workbook Activities D–E **ConnectEd** Vocabulary Practice
Day 5	Verbs that have **-g** in the **yo** form of the present tense	Core Instruction/Gramática, Presente de **hacer, poner, traer, salir** (20 min.)	Activities 1–3 (10 min.) Audio Activities A–B (10 min.)	Quiz 2 (10 min.) Student Workbook Activities A–C **ConnectEd** Grammar Practice
Day 6	Verbs that have **-g** in the **yo** form of the present tense	Quick Start (5 min.) Review Gramática, Presente de **hacer, poner, traer, salir** (20 min.)	Activities 4–6 (15 min.) Audio Activity C (10 min.)	Student Workbook Activities D–E **ConnectEd** Grammar Practice
Day 7	The present progressive tense	Core Instruction/Gramática, El presente progresivo (15 min.) Video, Diálogo en vivo (10 min.)	Activities 7–10 (10 min.) Foldables (5 min.)	Quiz 3 (10 min.) Student Workbook Activities A–B **ConnectEd** Grammar Practice
Day 8	The present progressive tense	Quick Start (5 min.) Review Gramática, El presente progresivo (10 min.) Pronunciación (10 min.)	Activities 11–13 (10 min.) Dictado (5 min.) Audio Activities D–F (10 min.)	Student Workbook Activity C **ConnectEd** Grammar Practice
Day 9	Develop reading and listening comprehension skills	Quick Start (5 min.) Core Instruction/Conversación (20 min.)	¿Comprendes? A–B (15 min.)	Quiz 4 (10 min.) ¿Comprendes? B–C **ConnectEd** Conversation
Day 10	Discuss air travel in South America	Core Instruction/Lectura cultural (20 min.)	¿Comprendes? A–B (15 min.)	Listening Comprehension Test (15 min.) ¿Comprendes? C–D **ConnectEd** Reading Practice
Day 11	Develop reading comprehension skills	Core Instruction/Lectura Un poco más (15 min.)	¿Comprendes? (10 min.) Prepárate para el examen (25 min.)	Prepárate para el examen, Practice for written proficiency **ConnectEd** Reading Practice
Day 12	Chapter review	Repaso del Capítulo 1 (10 min.)	Prepárate para el examen, Practice for oral proficiency (25 min.)	Test for Writing Proficiency (15 min.) Review for chapter test
Day 13	Chapter 1 Tests (50 min.) Reading and Writing Test Speaking Test		Test for Oral Proficiency Test for Reading Comprehension	

90-Minute Lesson Plans

	Objective	Present	Practice	Assess/Homework
Block 1	Talk about packing for a trip and getting to the airport	Chapter Opener (5 min.) Introducción al tema (10 min.) Quick Start (5 min.) Core Instruction/Vocabulario 1 (20 min.)	Activities 1–7 (25 min.) Total Physical Response (5 min.) InfoGap (5 min.) Audio Activities A–C (15 min.)	Student Workbook Activities A–E **ConnectEd** Vocabulary Practice
Block 2	Tell what you do at the airport and talk about being on an airplane	Quick Start (5 min.) Core Instruction/Vocabulario 2 (20 min.) Video, Vocabulario en vivo (10 min.)	Activities 1–7 (25 min.) Total Physical Response (5 min.) Audio Activities D–G (15 min.)	Quiz 1 (10 min.) Student Workbook Activities A–E **ConnectEd** Vocabulary Practice
Block 3	Verbs that have **-g** in the **yo** form of the present tense	Quick Start (5 min.) Core Instruction/Gramática, Presente de **hacer, poner, traer, salir** (20 min.)	Activities 1–6 (30 min.) Audio Activities A–C (20 min.)	Quiz 2 (15 min.) Student Workbook Activities A–E **ConnectEd** Grammar Practice
Block 4	The present progressive tense	Quick Start (5 min.) Core Instruction/Gramática, El presente progresivo (15 min.) Video, Diálogo en vivo (10 min.) Pronunciación (10 min.)	Activities 7–13 (20 min.) Foldables (5 min.) Dictado (5 min.) Audio Activities D–F (10 min.)	Quiz 3 (10 min.) Student Workbook Activities A–C **ConnectEd** Grammar Practice
Block 5	Discuss air travel in South America	Quick Start (5 min.) Core Instruction/Conversación (20 min.) Core Instruction/Lectura cultural (20 min.)	¿Comprendes? A–C (15 min.) ¿Comprendes? A–D (20 min.)	Quiz 4 (10 min.) Prepárate para el examen, Practice for written proficiency **ConnectEd** Conversation, Reading Practice
Block 6	Develop reading comprehension skills	Core Instruction/Lectura Un poco más (15 min.)	¿Comprendes? (10 min.) Prepárate para el examen (20 min.) Prepárate para el examen, Practice for oral proficiency (30 min.)	Listening Comprehension Test (15 min.) Review for chapter test **ConnectEd** Reading Practice
Block 7	Chapter 1 Tests (50 min.) Reading and Writing Test Speaking Test Test for Oral Proficiency Test for Writing Proficiency Test for Reading Comprehension Chapter Project (40 min.)			

Preview

In this chapter, students will be able to talk about preparing for a trip and traveling by air. Students will also discuss air travel in South America. In doing this, students will use the present progressive tense and verbs that have **g** in the **yo** form of the present tense.

Pacing

It is important to note that once you reach **¡Bravo!** in the chapter, there is no further new material for students to learn. The rest of the chapter recycles what has already been covered. The suggested pacing listed here leaves two to three days for review, assessment, and enrichment activities such as the chapter project.

Vocabulario 1	1–2 days
Vocabulario 2	1–2 days
Gramática	2–3 days
Conversación	1 day
Lectura cultural	1 day
Lectura Un poco más	1 day

CAPÍTULO 1

En avión

Go Online! connectED.mcgraw-hill.com

Audio Video Práctica Repaso Diversiones eScape ePals

Go Online!

Audio
Listen to spoken Spanish.

Video
Watch and learn about the Spanish-speaking world.

Práctica
Practice your skills.

Repaso
Review what you've learned.

Diversiones
Go beyond the classroom.

eScape
Read about current events in the Spanish-speaking world.

Aquí y Allí

Vamos a comparar Los medios de transporte más importantes varían de una región del mundo a otra. En España, por ejemplo, el servicio de trenes es excelente. No lo es en Latinoamérica donde mucha gente toma un autobús para ir de un lugar a otro. Pero vas a aprender por qué el avión es el medio de transporte más importante. Donde tú vives, ¿qué medios de transporte públicos hay? ¿Tienen muchos usuarios?

Objetivos

You will:

- talk about packing for a trip and getting to the airport
- tell what you do at the airport
- talk about being on an airplane
- discuss air travel in South America

You will use:

- verbs that have **g** in the **yo** form of the present tense
- the present progressive tense

◀ El avión está despegando de la pista del aeropuerto de La Romana en la República Dominicana.

Interactive Whiteboard
Present or practice with interactive whiteboard lessons.

Assessment
Check student progress.

ePals
Connect with Spanish-speaking students around the world.

SPOTLIGHT ON CULTURE

Cultural Comparison

While this chapter focuses on air travel, it can serve as a springboard to get students thinking about the differences in transportation between Spanish-speaking countries and their own. **Aquí y Allí** encourages students to look at the kinds of transportation found in their own community in comparison to what is common in parts of the Spanish-speaking world and why.

Cultural Snapshot

This plane is taking off from a small international airport in La Romana in the Dominican Republic. The single terminal is built in the style of an old sugar mill. La Romana is a very popular resort and there are many charter flights.

¡Así se dice!

Why It Works!

More than fifty million Spanish speakers live in the United States, and Spanish-speaking countries are not far away. In this chapter, students will learn the vocabulary needed at an airport or on a flight. They may use their Spanish at an airport in Spain, Latin America, or even the United States. Some students may never have been to an airport or flown. In these cases, the information will be one more enrichment experience. The theme of air travel will spark their interest in exploring the Spanish-speaking world, thus furthering their knowledge outside of the classroom.

PRESENT

Find out which students have flown in an airplane and ask if any have flown out of the country. Call on individuals to answer the question **¿Adónde fuiste?** Then tell them about your own travel experience to Spanish-speaking countries. Ask students what countries they would like to visit and why, and what would be their preferred mode of transportation. Then instruct them to read the paragraph and look at the photos on these pages. Once you have completed the vocabulary presentation, have students return to these pages and read the information that accompanies each photograph. Later, when students are fully acquainted with the vocabulary and grammar of the chapter, you may wish to come back to these pages and ask the questions that go with each photo.

Cultural Snapshot

Estados Unidos **¿Cuáles son los vuelos con destino a ciudades latinoamericanas? ¿En qué país está cada una de las ciudades?**

Perú **A la entrada del aeropuerto de Arequipa en el sur de Perú los viajeros ven esta estatua de unos indígenas que las dan una bienvenida cordial a su ciudad bonita. ¿Qué mensaje hay en la estatua?**

Introducción al tema

En avión

Look at these photographs to acquaint yourself with the theme of this chapter. Air travel is the most important means of transportation in the world today. As you learn to use your Spanish in an airport and on an airplane, you will also learn why air travel is so extremely important in Latin America.

DEPARTING TO
AIRLINE
FLIGHT
GATE
TIME
CARACAS American 935 C7 12:30P
HOUSTON-IAH American 1391 C3 12:07P
SANTO DOMINGO American 783 C5 1:20P
KEY WEST American 4987 2:00P
BALTIMORE American 1060 C7 4:19P
QUITO American 967 C5 4:30P
INDIANAPOLIS, IN American 1682 C9 6:21P
SAN JOSE, C.R. American 2171 C7 6:24P

Estados Unidos

Aquí vemos una pantalla de salidas. ¿Para qué ciudades latinoamericanas hay vuelos?

Perú

¡Qué bienvenida más simpática reciben los pasajeros que llegan al aeropuerto de Arequipa en el sur de Perú!

España

Pasajeros en el nuevo aeropuerto de Barajas en Madrid

Guatemala

El mostrador de una línea aérea centroamericana en el aeropuerto de la Ciudad de Guatemala. Es de noche y hay muy poca gente.

2

España El aeropuerto de Madrid-Barajas is located to the northeast of Madrid. The largest airport in Spain, it is the fourth largest in Europe. It has four terminals and it is often necessary to have to go from one terminal to another when making a connecting flight. Distances between gates can be time-consuming. **¿Es nuevo o viejo el aeropuerto de Madrid? ¿Salen vuelos internacionales y nacionales del aeropuerto?**

Guatemala The international airport serving Guatemala City is called La Aurora and is located 6 km from the center of the city. Most of the airport was remodeled in 2010. **¿Por qué hay muy poca gente en el aeropuerto de Guatemala?**

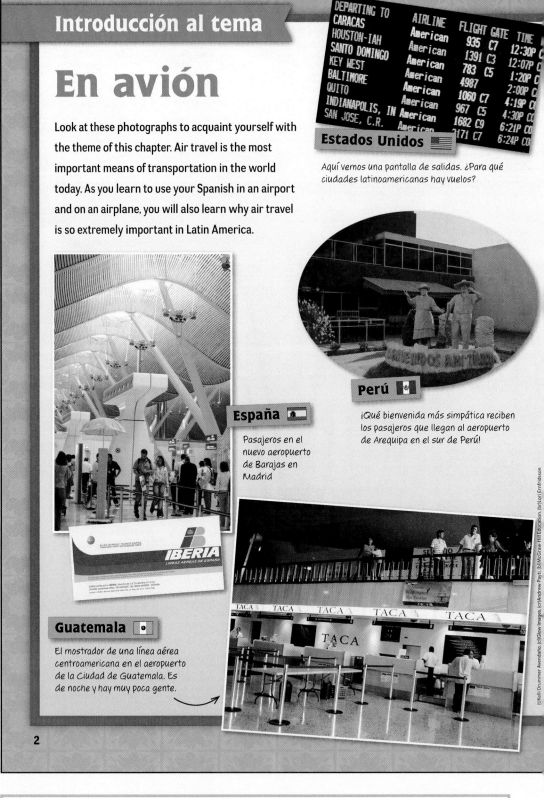

Perú

El avión está en el aeropuerto de Arequipa en el sur de Perú. En el fondo vemos los Andes.

Argentina

Es una experiencia aterrizar o despegar en el aeropuerto de Ushuaia debido a la proximidad del mar, las montañas y los vientos fuertes que a veces son casi violentos.

Perú

De esta parte del aeropuerto Jorge Chávez de Lima salen y llegan los vuelos que sirven las otras ciudades y pueblos de Perú. En la mayoría de los países se llaman «vuelos nacionales» pero a veces se oye «vuelos internos» o «vuelos domésticos». En Argentina son «vuelos de cabotaje».

Introducción al tema

Perú *(top)* Arequipa is a beautiful city in southern Peru. It is one of the few places that truly enjoys perpetual spring. ¿Qué opinas? ¿Es grande o pequeño el aeropuerto de Arequipa?

Argentina Landing or taking off from the airport in Ushuaia is quite an experience because of the high winds and proximity to the water. It is the world's southernmost international airport. ¿Dónde está situado el aeropuerto de Ushuaia? ¿Por qué es difícil aterrizar o despegar de este aeropuerto?

Perú ¿Llegan y salen de aquí vuelos internacionales o vuelos de otros destinos en Perú? ¿Cuál es el término que se usa en Estados Unidos para un vuelo dentro del país?

Online Resources

Customizable Lesson Plans

- Whiteboard Lesson
- Audio Activities
- Student Workbook
- Enrichment
- Quizzes

Quick Start

Use QS 1.1 or write the following on the board.
José is going to pack his suitcase. Give each item that he packs a color.

una camisa ___
un pantalón ___
una corbata ___
zapatos ___
un traje de baño ___
una camiseta ___
calcetines ___

TEACH

Core Instruction

Step 1 Using Vocabulary V1.2–V1.3, introduce the words on the vocabulary pages. Have students repeat after you or the audio recording as you point to the illustrations.

Step 2 As you present the vocabulary, ask contextualized sentences that alternate in difficulty level. **¿Es la maleta? ¿Hace Juan la maleta? ¿Hace Juan su maleta porque hace un viaje? ¿Pone ropa en la maleta? ¿Qué ropa pone en la maleta?**

Antes de salir para el aeropuerto

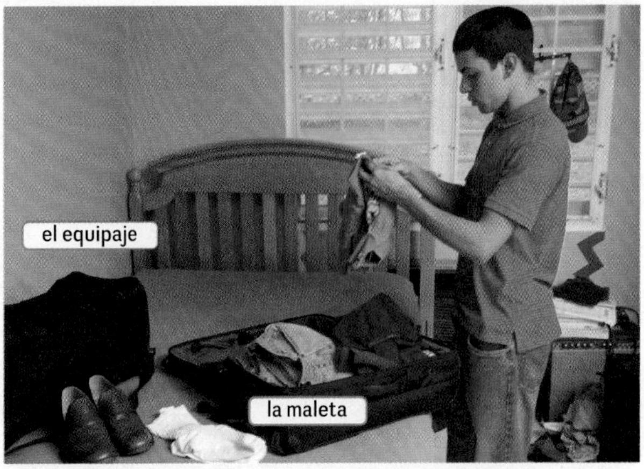

Juan va a hacer un viaje. Antes hace la maleta. ¿Qué pone en la maleta?

Pone la ropa que necesita para el viaje.

¿Te acuerdas?

You will want to be able to discuss packing a suitcase. To review summer and winter clothing, see Repaso E.

Al aeropuerto

Juan sale para el aeropuerto en taxi. Trae su equipaje.

Pone su equipaje en la maletera del taxi. El taxista lo ayuda con su equipaje.

Total Physical Response (TPR)

You may want to bring in props.
(Student), **ven acá. Imagínate que vas a hacer un viaje en avión.**
Pon tu maleta en la cama.
Ahora, haz tu maleta. Pon la ropa en la maleta.
Llama un taxi.
Ahora llega el taxi.
Pon tu maleta en la maletera.
Abre la puerta del taxi.
Siéntate en el taxi.
El taxi llega al aeropuerto. Baja (Bájate) del taxi.
Dale el dinero al taxista.
Busca el mostrador de tu línea aérea.
Habla con el agente.
Dale tu pasaporte o identidad con una fotografía.

En el aeropuerto

Go Online!

connectED.mcgraw-hill.com

Su tarjeta de embarque sale de un distribuidor automático.

Juan está en el mostrador de la línea aérea.
Está haciendo un viaje internacional en avión.
Tiene que facturar su equipaje.
Pero no tiene que facturar su equipaje de mano.

¡Así se dice!

When you are in a crowded area and you want to get by someone, you can politely say **¡Con permiso!**

En otras partes

In addition to **la tarjeta de embarque** you will also hear **la tarjeta de abordar** and **el pasabordo.**

Differentiation

Multiple Intelligences

- To encourage **verbal-linguistic** learners, you may wish to have students create their own boarding pass and present the information to the class.
- Read the **¡Así se dice!** information to the class. Engage **bodily-kinesthetic** learners by having them get up and try to get by one another, saying **¡Con permiso!** in a realistic way.

Teaching Options

To reinforce the airport vocabulary, you may wish to have students come up to your desk individually and act out an authentic exchange with an airline agent (you). Ask questions such as **¿Cuál es su nombre, señor (señorita)? ¿Está usted haciendo un viaje nacional o internacional? ¿Adónde va? ¿Tiene su pasaporte? ¿Cuántas maletas tiene que facturar?** You may then wish to hand them a fake or imaginary boarding pass and have them return to their seats.

About the Spanish Language

In English we often say *a domestic flight.* In Spanish it is far more common to say *a national flight*—**un vuelo nacional.** In Argentina you will also hear **vuelo de cabotaje.**

Go Online!

You may wish to use the whiteboard presentation for additional vocabulary instruction and practice.

Cultural Snapshot

All the photos on these two vocabulary pages were taken in Puerto Rico.

Leveling EACH Activity

Easy Activities 1, 6
Average Activities 2, 3, 4, 7
CHallenging Activity 2
Expansión, Activity 5

PRACTICE

Activity 1

Audio Script

1. Juan pone sus zapatos y calcetines en la maleta.
2. Juan mira su boleto electrónico.
3. Juan pone su equipaje en la maletera.
4. Juan lleva mucho equipaje.
5. Juan factura su equipaje.
6. Juan hace un vuelo internacional.

Cultural Snapshot

(bottom) The Galapagos Islands were discovered by explorer Tomás de Berlanga in 1535. The islands are named after **los galápagos**—the giant, lethargic tortoises that sun themselves on the rocks. Scientists point to the fact that animals evolved there in isolation without natural predators to explain the extraordinary diversity of animal species on the islands.

Go Online!

You may wish to remind students to go online for additional vocabulary practice. They can also download audio files of all vocabulary.

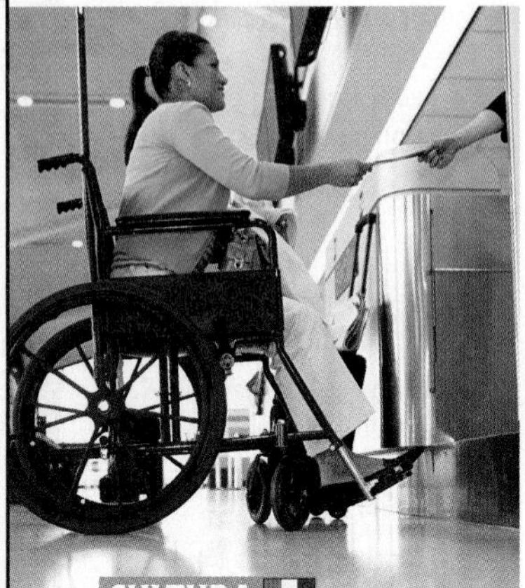

CULTURA
La señora está en el mostrador de la línea aérea. Va a volar a México.

CULTURA
Una vista de las islas Galápagos, Ecuador

ESCUCHAR

1 Escucha las frases. Parea cada frase con el dibujo que describe.

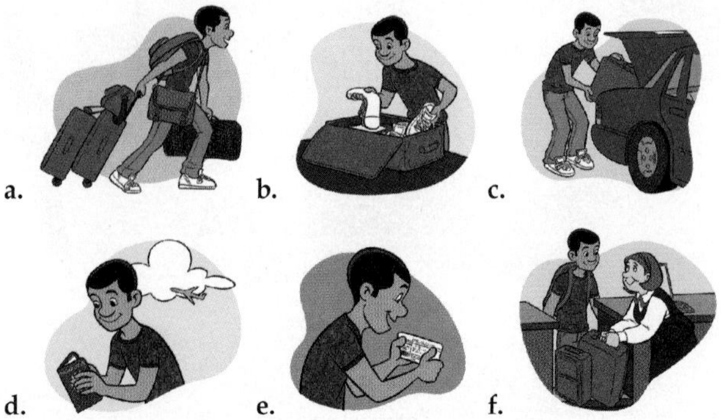

HABLAR • ESCRIBIR

2 Contesta sobre un viaje que Teresa va a hacer a México.

1. ¿Hace Teresa un viaje a México?
2. Antes de hacer su viaje, ¿qué pone en la maleta?
3. ¿Para dónde sale Teresa para empezar su viaje?
4. ¿Cómo va al aeropuerto?
5. ¿Quién la ayuda con su equipaje?
6. ¿Dónde lo pone?

EXPANSIÓN

Ahora, sin mirar las preguntas, relata toda la información en tus propias palabras. Si no recuerdas algo, un(a) compañero(a) te puede ayudar.

LEER • ESCRIBIR

3 Elisa está en el aeropuerto. Va a las Galápagos. Completa con una palabra apropiada.

1. En el aeropuerto Elisa tiene que _____ su equipaje.
2. Va al mostrador de la _____.
3. Elisa tiene un _____ electrónico.
4. El agente le da su _____ para poder abordar el avión.

Answers

1
1. b
2. e
3. c
4. a
5. f
6. d

2
1. Sí, Teresa hace un viaje a México.
2. Antes de hacer su viaje, pone la ropa que necesita para el viaje en la maleta.
3. Teresa sale para el aeropuerto para empezar su viaje.
4. Va al aeropuerto en taxi.
5. El taxista la ayuda con su equipaje.
6. Lo pone en el baúl (la maletera).

3
1. facturar
2. línea aérea
3. boleto (billete)
4. tarjeta de embarque

LEER • ESCRIBIR

❹ Completa. Escoge del **banco de palabras.**

pone	sale	trae	hace

1. Eduardo _____ un viaje a España.
2. Él _____ su ropa en la maleta.
3. Eduardo no _____ mucho equipaje.
4. _____ solamente una maleta y una mochila.
5. _____ el equipaje en la maletera del taxi.
6. _____ para el aeropuerto.
7. Su vuelo para España _____ a las ocho y media de la tarde.

HABLAR • ESCRIBIR

❺ Prepara una pregunta sobre cada frase en la Actividad 4. Usa las siguientes palabras.

¿quién? ¿cuándo? ¿adónde? ¿qué? ¿dónde?

LEER • ESCRIBIR

❻ Completa la tarjeta de embarque.

❼ **Rompecabezas**

Unscramble the letters to reveal words related to airplane travel.

1. a l t a m e
2. n o t i s e a
3. j a q u e p i e
4. r a d o r o m t s
5. s o a r j e p a

Go Online!

connectED.mcgraw-hill.com

InfoGap For more practice using your new vocabulary, do Activity 1 in the Student Resource section at the end of the book.

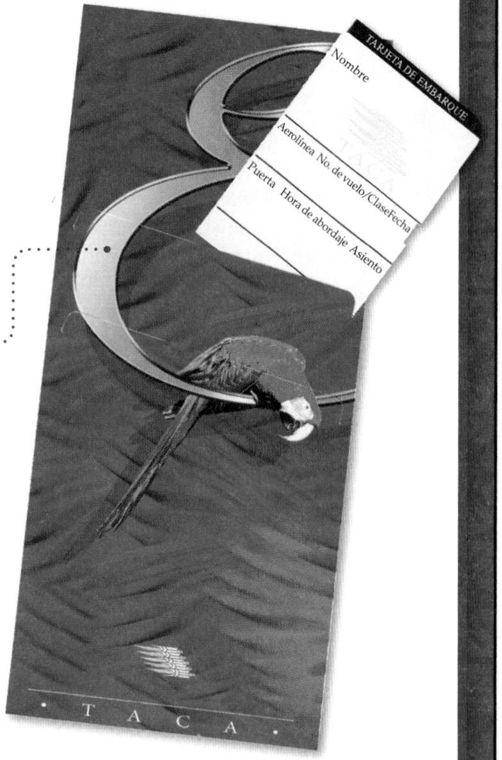

Activity ❻ Have students write the information on a separate sheet of paper. Then, have some students tell the class the information on their boarding card.

InfoGap The *InfoGap* activity will allow students to practice in pairs. This will help interpersonal learners, who learn well through interaction and collaboration. The activity should be very manageable since all vocabulary and grammar are familiar to students.

Go Online!

You may wish to use the whiteboard presentation for additional vocabulary instruction and practice.

ASSESS

Students are now ready to take Quiz 1.

Answers

❹
1. hace
2. pone
3. trae
4. Trae
5. Pone
6. Sale
7. sale

❺ *Answers will vary but may include:*
1. ¿Quién hace un viaje a España?
2. ¿Qué pone en la maleta?
3. ¿Quién no trae mucho equipaje?
4. ¿Qué trae?
5. ¿Dónde pone el equipaje?
6. ¿Adónde sale?
7. ¿Cuándo sale su vuelo para España?

❻ *Answers will vary.*

❼
1. maleta
2. asiento
3. equipaje
4. mostrador
5. pasajero

Online Resources

Customizable Lesson Plans
- Whiteboard Lesson
- Audio Activities
- Video (Vocabulario)
- Student Workbook
- Enrichment
- Quizzes

Quick Start

Use QS 1.2 or write the following on the board.

Complete about yourself.

1. **Soy ___.**
2. **Soy de ___.**
3. **Tengo ojos ___.**
4. **Tengo el pelo ___.**
5. **Tengo ___ años.**

TEACH

Core Instruction

Step 1 Have students look at Vocabulary V1.4–V1.5 as they repeat each word or expression after you or the audio recording.

Step 2 As you present the sentences, you may intersperse comprehension questions building from simple to more complex. For example: **¿Los pasajeros tienen que pasar por el control de seguridad? ¿Por dónde tienen que pasar? ¿Tienen que tener una forma de identidad? ¿Qué le tienen que mostrar al agente?**

Step 3 Have students now read the new material for reinforcement.

Step 4 Go over the expressions taught in the **¡Así se dice!** box. Ask questions using these expressions and have students respond.

En el control de seguridad

Los pasajeros están pasando por el control de seguridad.
Su equipaje de mano tiene que pasar por el control de seguridad.
Hay que mostrar una forma de identidad con una fotografía.

En otras partes

Another word for **cola** is **fila** and the expression is **estar en fila.**

En la puerta de salida

La pasajera está en la puerta de salida.
Está esperando la salida de su vuelo.
El avión está saliendo a tiempo. No sale tarde.
No hay un retraso (una demora).
Ella va a embarcar (abordar) dentro de poco.

¡Así se dice!

- **Hay que** is a useful expression that means **Es necesario.**
- **A veces** and **de vez en cuando** are expressions to tell what you do every so often.

David H. Brennan

Differentiation

Advanced Learners

Have advanced learners make up sentences using the expressions in the **¡Así se dice!** box.

Go Online!

Vocabulario en vivo Join Nora as she gives some advice about traveling by plane.

Go Online!

connectED.mcgraw-hill.com

Abordo del avión

Los pasajeros tienen que poner su equipaje de mano en el compartimiento superior o debajo del asiento.
Durante el despegue y el aterrizaje, los pasajeros tienen que tener sus cinturones abrochados.

El avión está despegando.
Está despegando con destino a Madrid.
El avión acaba de despegar de la pista.

El avión está aterrizando.
Es un vuelo (procedente) de Lima.

Differentiation

Multiple Intelligences

Engage **logical-mathematical** learners by asking students to use the new vocabulary to create a chronological order of events from the moment of arriving at the airport to the final landing of the plane. You may wish to give them the expressions **primero, segundo, tercero, luego,** and **por último.**

About the Spanish Language

El/La asistente(a) de vuelo is today the most common way to express *flight attendant.* In the feminine it is more common to hear **asistenta,** but some use **la asistente.** The word **azafata** is used for a *female flight attendant* in Spain. You will also hear **el/la subrecargo(a). La tripulación** is used for *flight crew.* You may also wish to point out the relationship between **aterrizar** and **tierra** as well as that between **despegar** and **pegar** *(to stick* or *adhere).*

Cultural Snapshot

The photos in the airport on the previous page and on the airplane on this page were taken in San Juan, Puerto Rico.

Go Online!

You may wish to use the whiteboard presentation for additional vocabulary instruction and practice.

Total Physical Response (TPR)

Have students use gestures and props to dramatize the following actions.

Los pasajeros tienen su forma de identidad en las manos.

El avión no está saliendo a tiempo. Está saliendo tarde.

Los pasajeros están poniendo su equipaje de mano en el compartimiento superior.

Los pasajeros están poniendo su equipaje de mano debajo del asiento delante de ellos.

Los pasajeros se están abrochando el cinturón de seguridad.

El avión está despegando.

El avión está aterrizando.

Leveling EACH Activity

Easy Activity 2
Average Activities 1, 3, 5, 7
CHallenging Activities 4, 6

PRACTICE

Tips for Success

Have students go over all these activities orally in class before assigning them for homework.

Activity 3 You may wish to have more advanced students correct the false statements.

Go Online!

You may wish to remind students to go online for additional vocabulary practice. They can also download audio files of all vocabulary.

ESCUCHAR • HABLAR • ESCRIBIR

1 Personaliza. Da respuestas personales.

1. ¿Tomas un vuelo de vez en cuando?
2. ¿Te gusta volar?
3. ¿Quieres tomar un vuelo un día?
4. ¿Quieres hacer un viaje nacional o internacional?
5. ¿Adónde quieres ir?
6. ¿Hay un aeropuerto cerca de tu casa? ¿Cuál?
7. ¿Es un aeropuerto nacional o internacional?
8. Si tienes que tomar un vuelo, ¿prefieres un asiento en el pasillo o en la ventanilla?

CULTURA
Una señora está para abordar una avioneta en el aeropuerto de San José, Costa Rica.

Richard Brommer

LEER

2 Escoge la palabra apropiada.

1. Los pasajeros hacen cola en (el asiento, la puerta) de salida.
2. Están (esperando, haciendo) la salida del vuelo.
3. El avión sale con un retraso de cinco minutos. Sale (tarde, a tiempo).
4. Los pasajeros toman su (pasillo, asiento) en el avión.
5. El avión despega de la (cola, pista).
6. Un vuelo (procedente de, con destino a) Panamá llega ahora.

LEER

3 Verifica. ¿Sí o no?

1. Los pasajeros tienen que pasar por el control de seguridad abordo del avión.
2. Los pasajeros esperan la salida de su vuelo en la puerta de salida.
3. Los pasajeros embarcan después del aterrizaje.
4. Los pasajeros desembarcan después del aterrizaje.
5. Los pasajeros pueden poner su equipaje en el pasillo.
6. Los pasajeros tienen que tener sus cinturones de seguridad abrochados durante el despegue y el aterrizaje.
7. Un vuelo que sale tarde sale a tiempo.
8. En una cola o fila hay mucha gente.

Answers

1

1. Sí, (No, no) tomo un vuelo de vez en cuando.
2. Sí, (No, no) me gusta volar.
3. Sí, (No, no) quiero tomar un vuelo un día.
4. Quiero hacer un viaje nacional (internacional). (No quiero hacer un viaje.)
5. Quiero ir a ____.
6. Sí, (No, no) hay un aeropuerto cerca de mi casa. Es el aeropuerto ____.
7. Es un aeropuerto nacional (internacional). (No hay un aeropuerto cerca de mi casa.)
8. Prefiero un asiento en el pasillo (en la ventanilla).

2

1. la puerta
2. esperando
3. tarde
4. asiento
5. pista
6. procedente de

3

1. no
2. sí
3. no
4. sí
5. no
6. sí
7. no
8. sí

4 **Comunicación**

Habla con un(a) compañero(a). Discutan todo lo que necesitan si hacen un viaje internacional.

LEER • ESCRIBIR

5 Pon las actividades en orden.

Llega al aeropuerto.
Toma su asiento.
Pone su ropa en la maleta.
Factura su equipaje y toma su tarjeta de embarque.
Sale de casa para ir al aeropuerto.
Espera el avión en la puerta de salida.
Pone su equipaje en la maletera del taxi.
Pasa por el control de seguridad.
Embarca el avión.
El avión despega.

6 **Comunicación**

You are flying to Mexico to visit your key pal. You have never flown before. Once on the plane, you have some questions for the flight attendant (your partner) about the flight and where to put your things. Take turns.

7 ¡Manos a la obra! Make up a name for a Spanish airline. Create a fun and colorful travel poster advertising the airline and where it flies. See how many new words you can include.

Andrew Payti

Vocabulario 2

Comunicación

Interpersonal, Presentational

Activity 6 You may want to have pairs perform their role-plays for the class.

Differentiation

Advanced Learners

Have students look in newspapers and magazines for articles about air travel. Ask them to report some of the information to the class in Spanish, if possible.

ASSESS

Students are now ready to take Quiz 2.

Answers

4 *Answers will vary.*

5
Pone su ropa en la maleta.
Pone su equipaje en la maletera del taxi.
Sale de casa para ir al aeropuerto.
Llega al aeropuerto.
Factura su equipaje y toma su tarjeta de embarque.
Pasa por el control de seguridad.
Espera el avión en la puerta de salida.
Embarca el avión.
Toma su asiento.
El avión despega.

6 *Answers will vary.*

7 *Answers will vary.*

Online Resources

Customizable Lesson Plans
Whiteboard Lesson
Audio Activities
Video (Gramática)
Student Workbook
Quizzes

Quick Start

Use QS 1.3 or write the following on the board.

Complete in the present.

1. **Ellos ___ mucho. (aprender)**
2. **Tú ___ todo lo que ___, ¿no? (comprender, aprender)**
3. **Nosotros ___ a veces en la cafetería de la escuela. (comer)**
4. **¿Qué ___ ustedes en la tele? (ver)**
5. **Nosotros ___ muchos correos electrónicos. (recibir)**
6. **Yo ___ cerca de Nueva York. (vivir)**

TEACH

Core Instruction

Step 1 Say the infinitives from Item 1 aloud to students.

Step 2 Point to yourself as you say **hago, pongo, traigo, salgo.**

Step 3 Write the **yo** forms on the board and ask students what they have in common.

Step 4 Have students repeat the **yo** forms as they point to themselves.

Step 5 Write the other forms on the board and indicate to students that they are the same as any regular **-er** or **-ir** verb.

Step 6 For Item 2, have students repeat the forms of **tener** and **venir.** Point out the **g** in the **yo** form; they also have a stem change, the same as **querer** or **preferir.**

Presente de hacer, poner, traer, salir

Nota

The verbs **oír** and **caer** *(to fall)* also have a **g** in the **yo** form.
oigo **caigo**

1. The verbs **hacer** *(to do, to make)*, **poner** *(to put, to place)*, **traer** *(to bring)*, and **salir** *(to leave)* have an irregular **yo** form. The **yo** form has a **g.** All the other forms are regular.

	hacer	poner	traer	salir
yo	**hago**	**pongo**	**traigo**	**salgo**
tú	haces	pones	traes	sales
Ud., él, ella	hace	pone	trae	sale
nosotros(as)	hacemos	ponemos	traemos	salimos
vosotros(as)	*hacéis*	*ponéis*	*traéis*	*salís*
Uds., ellos, ellas	hacen	ponen	traen	salen

2. Remember that the verb **tener** has a **g** in the **yo** form. The verb **venir** *(to come)* follows the same pattern. Note the **g** and the stem change.

venir			
yo	vengo	nosotros(as)	venimos
tú	vienes	*vosotros(as)*	*venís*
Ud., él, ella	viene	Uds., ellos, ellas	vienen

Rebecca Smith

CULTURA

Las señoritas tienen equipaje porque van a hacer un viaje de Puerto Rico a Nueva York. Salen pronto pero antes toman un refresco en un café en San Juan.

ABOUT THE SPANISH LANGUAGE

Explain to students that they will often hear the general questions **¿Qué haces?** or **¿Qué hacen?** and they will have to answer with a different verb.

¿Qué haces? → Miro la tele.
Estudio.
¿Qué hacen ustedes? → Comemos.

Go Online!

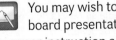

You may wish to remind students to go online for additional grammar review and practice.

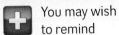

You may wish to use the whiteboard presentation for additional grammar instruction and practice.

Práctica

HABLAR • ESCRIBIR

1 Imagina que vas a hacer un viaje a Ecuador. Contesta las preguntas.

1. ¿Haces un viaje?
2. ¿Haces un viaje a Ecuador?
3. ¿Haces el viaje con un grupo de tu escuela?
4. ¿Sales para el aeropuerto con tus padres?
5. ¿Traes mucho equipaje?
6. ¿Traes tu cámara digital?
7. ¿Pones tu boleto y tu pasaporte en tu mochila?

EXPANSIÓN

Ahora, sin mirar las preguntas, relata toda la información en tus propias palabras. Si no recuerdas algo, un(a) compañero(a) te puede ayudar.

HABLAR • ESCRIBIR

2 Personaliza. Da respuestas personales.

Cuando haces un viaje a la playa donde hace calor, ¿qué pones en la maleta? Y cuando haces un viaje a una estación de esquí, ¿qué pones en la maleta?

CULTURA

La Plaza de Armas en el casco antiguo de Quito, Ecuador

ESCUCHAR • HABLAR • ESCRIBIR

3 Sigue el modelo. Presta atención a las terminaciones **-emos, -imos.**

MODELO **Ellos hacen un viaje.** →
Sí, ellos hacen un viaje y nosotros también hacemos un viaje.

1. Ellos hacen un viaje a España.
2. Ellos salen para el aeropuerto.
3. Ellos traen mucho equipaje.
4. Ellos salen en el mismo vuelo.
5. Ellos vienen al aeropuerto en autobús.

Richard Brommer

Gramática

Leveling EACH Activity

Easy Activities 1, 2
Average Activity 1
Expansión, Activity 3

PRACTICE

Cultural Snapshot

Quito, the capital of Ecuador, has the largest **casco antiguo o histórico** in all of the Americas and is considered by many to be the best preserved. It is the second-most populated city in Ecuador, after Guayaquil. Have students find Quito and Guayaquil on the map on the pages featuring Ecuador in the **GeoVistas** section at the beginning of this book.

¡Así se dice!

Why It Works!

In **¡Así se dice!** we want students to focus their attention on any new form such as the **g** in these verbs. For this reason, the very first activity has students hear the **tú** form and then actively use **hago, pongo, traigo,** and **salgo.**

Go Online!

Gramática en vivo
Present tense of irregular verbs Enliven learning with the animated world of Professor Cruz! **Gramática en vivo** is a fun and effective tool for additional instruction and/or review.

Answers

1

1. Sí, hago un viaje.
2. Sí, hago un viaje a Ecuador.
3. Sí, (No, no) hago el viaje con un grupo de mi escuela.
4. Sí, (No, no) salgo para el aeropuerto con mis padres.
5. Sí, (No, no) traigo mucho equipaje.
6. Sí, (No, no) traigo mi cámara digital.
7. Sí, (No, no) pongo mi boleto y mi pasaporte en mi mochila.

2 *Answers will vary.*

3

1. Sí, ellos hacen un viaje a España y nosotros también hacemos un viaje a España.
2. Sí, ellos salen para el aeropuerto y nosotros también salimos para el aeropuerto.
3. Sí, ellos traen mucho equipaje y nosotros también traemos mucho equipaje.
4. Sí, ellos salen en el mismo vuelo y nosotros también salimos en el mismo vuelo.
5. Sí, ellos vienen al aeropuerto en autobús y nosotros también venimos al aeropuerto en autobús.

Leveling EACH Activity

Average Activities 5, 6
CHallenging Activity 4

PRACTICE *(continued)*

Differentiation

Students with Learning Difficulties

Making grammar relevant is an important way to help students with learning difficulties. Provide a series of personalized questions to which students can relate, such as: **¿Haces la tarea? ¿Dónde pones los libros? ¿Qué traes a la escuela? ¿Cuándo sales para la escuela?** You may also wish to identify students having the same answer and switch to the plural. (**¿Hacen ustedes la tarea por la mañana o por la noche?**)

Activity 4 Call on several students to read a section of this activity after they have completed it.

Cultural Snapshot

The island of Mallorca is known for its beautiful beaches, many of which are set in coves. Like other summer resort areas of Spain, many locals are complaining about the overdevelopment.

ASSESS

Students are now ready to take Quiz 3.

Gramática

LEER • ESCRIBIR

4 Completa con la forma correcta del presente del verbo. Ahora tienes que usar todas las formas.

Yo ___1___ (hacer) un viaje a Palma. Palma ___2___ (estar) en la isla de Mallorca en el Mediterráneo. ___3___ (Estar) al este de España no muy lejos de Barcelona. Mi amiga Luisa ___4___ (hacer) el viaje también. Nosotros ___5___ (hacer) el viaje en avión hasta Barcelona y luego ___6___ (ir) en barco, un ferry, desde Barcelona a Palma. Claro que podemos ___7___ (hacer) el viaje en avión pero preferimos tomar el barco.

—¡Ay, Luisa! Pero tú ___8___ (traer) mucho equipaje.

—No, yo no ___9___ (traer) mucho. ___10___ (Tener) solo dos maletas. Tú exageras. Tú también ___11___ (venir) con mucho equipaje.

—¡Oye! ¿A qué hora ___12___ (salir) nuestro vuelo para Barcelona?

—No ___13___ (salir) hasta las seis y media. Nosotros ___14___ (tener) mucho tiempo.

—¡Vamos ya! ¡Con permiso, señora!

5 ***Comunicación***

Tell a friend all the things you do the day of a flight from packing your suitcase to boarding the plane. Your friend will then ask you questions.

HABLAR

6 **Juego** Play this **Diez preguntas** game with a partner. Think of something related to airline travel for your partner to guess. If your partner guesses in ten questions or less, he or she wins. Take turns.

Andrew Payti

CULTURA
Una playa en Palma de Mallorca. Mallorca es una de las islas Baleares en el mar Mediterráneo.

Answers

4
1. hago
2. está
3. Está
4. hace
5. hacemos
6. vamos
7. hacer
8. traes
9. traigo
10. Tengo
11. vienes
12. sale
13. sale
14. tenemos

5 *Answers will vary.*

6 *Answers will vary.*

El presente progresivo

Go Online!

connectED.mcgraw-hill.com

1. You use the present progressive tense in Spanish to express an action in progress, an action that is currently taking place.

2. To form the present progressive you use the verb **estar** and the present participle. Study the forms of the present participle.

INFINITIVE	**hablar**	**comer**	**vivir**	**hacer**	**salir**
STEM	**habl-**	**com-**	**viv-**	**hac-**	**sal-**
PARTICIPLE	**hablando**	**comiendo**	**viviendo**	**haciendo**	**saliendo**

The verbs **leer, traer, oír,** and **caer** have a **y.**

leyendo **trayendo** **oyendo** **cayendo**

3. Study the following examples of the present progressive.

José está haciendo un viaje a México.
Ahora está esperando la salida de su vuelo.
José está mirando su tarjeta de embarque.

CULTURA

Una pantalla de llegadas y salidas en el aeropuerto de la Ciudad de Guatemala. Hace buen tiempo hoy y la mayoría de los vuelos salen a tiempo. ¡Qué suerte para todos!

Lori Ernfridsson

Gramática

Online Resources

Customizable Lesson Plans
- Whiteboard Lesson
- Audio Activities
- Video (Diálogo)
- Student Workbook
- Enrichment
- Quizzes

Quick Start

Use QS 1.4 or write the following on the board.

Answer.

1. **¿Eres gemelo(a)?**
2. **¿Eres hijo(a) único(a)?**
3. **¿Cuántos hermanos tienes?**
4. **¿Tienes que ir a casa después de las clases?**
5. **¿Tienen tus amigos un móvil?**

TEACH

Core Instruction

Step 1 Have students discuss Items 1 and 2.

Step 2 Give students other **-ar, -er,** and **-ir** verbs they know and have them give the present participle after they have seen how it is formed.

Step 3 Read aloud the sentences in Item 3 and have students repeat them after you.

Differentiation

Slower Paced Learners

Quickly review the forms of the verb **estar.**

Go Online!

Diálogo en vivo In this episode, Julián tells Francisco about an inexpensive plane ticket he bought. Ask students what proverb Francisco tells Julián. What does it mean?

You may wish to use the whiteboard presentation for additional grammar instruction and practice.

Leveling EACH Activity

Easy Activities 7, 9
Average Activity 8
CHallenging Activity 8
Expansión, Activity 10

PRACTICE

Differentiation

Multiple Intelligences

Allow **bodily-kinesthetic** learners to dramatize the Activity 7 conversation in front of the class, using appropriate expression, intonation, and body language.

Teaching Options

Once students have practiced the conversation, you may wish to have them change the verbs from the present progressive to the present tense. This may provide an opportunity to point out the subtle difference in meaning between the two present tense forms.

Conexiones

In the conversation in Activity 7, Julia tells Sandra that she and her family are going to Costa Rica to visit her grandparents. Have students look at the photos and map of Costa Rica in the **GeoVistas** section at the front of the book and choose a town or area they would like to visit. Invite them to do further research on the place and present their findings to the class.

Práctica

ESCUCHAR • HABLAR

7 Con un(a) compañero(a), practica la conversación en voz alta. Presta atención a todos los verbos en el tiempo progresivo.

Sandra, ¡qué sorpresa! ¿Qué estás haciendo aquí en el aeropuerto?
Estoy esperando a mi padre. Está volviendo de Puerto Rico. ¿Y tú, Julia? ¿Qué estás haciendo aquí?

Pues, estoy viajando a Costa Rica.
¡A Costa Rica! ¡Qué suerte tienes!

Sí, toda mi familia está haciendo el viaje para visitar a nuestros abuelos.
Ah, tus abuelos son de Costa Rica.
No, no. Son de aquí pero ahora están viviendo en Costa Rica. Les gusta mucho.

HABLAR • ESCRIBIR

8 Contesta según la conversación.

1. ¿Por qué está en el aeropuerto Sandra?
2. ¿De dónde está volviendo el padre de Sandra?
3. Y, ¿para dónde está saliendo Julia?
4. ¿Quién está viajando con ella?
5. ¿A quiénes van a visitar?
6. ¿Qué están haciendo sus abuelos en Costa Rica?

EXPANSIÓN

Ahora, sin mirar las preguntas, relata toda la información en tus propias palabras. Si no recuerdas algo, un(a) compañero(a) te puede ayudar.

David H. Brennan

Answers

8

1. Sandra está en el aeropuerto porque está esperando a su padre.
2. El padre de Sandra está volviendo de Puerto Rico.
3. Julia está saliendo para Costa Rica.
4. Toda su familia está viajando con ella.
5. Van a visitar a sus abuelos.
6. Sus abuelos están viviendo en Costa Rica.

Go Online!

connectED.mcgraw-hill.com

ESCUCHAR • HABLAR • ESCRIBIR

9 Contesta según se indica.

1. ¿Adónde están llegando los pasajeros? (al aeropuerto)
2. ¿Cómo están llegando? (en taxi)
3. ¿Adónde están viajando? (a Argentina en la América del Sur)
4. ¿Cómo están haciendo el viaje? (en avión)
5. ¿Dónde están facturando el equipaje? (en el mostrador de la línea aérea)
6. ¿Qué está mirando el agente? (los boletos y los pasaportes)
7. ¿De qué puerta están saliendo los pasajeros para Buenos Aires? (número siete)
8. ¿Qué están abordando? (el avión)

10 **Comunicación**

Use the conversation between Julia and Sandra as a guide to role-play a conversation between two friends who run into each other at an airport. Be sure to use gestures and other nonverbal communication in your conversation.

Richard Brommer

CULTURA

La Casa Rosada en Buenos Aires. Es aquí donde tiene el presidente argentino sus oficinas.

Gramática

Go Online!

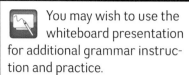

You may wish to use the whiteboard presentation for additional grammar instruction and practice.

Comunicación

Interpersonal, Interpretive, Presentational

Activity 10 After pairs present their conversations, have students answer questions to demonstrate their comprehension. Also, you may want to call on students to interpret or summarize what happened.

Cultural Snapshot

The Casa Rosada houses the office of Argentina's president. It was originally a fortress constructed to protect the city from invasion from the sea via the Río de la Plata. It was from the balcony of the Casa Rosada that Eva Perón delivered one of her stirring speeches to the Argentine masses.

Answers

9

1. Los pasajeros están llegando al aeropuerto.
2. Están llegando en taxi.
3. Están viajando a Argentina en la América del Sur.
4. Están haciendo el viaje en avión.
5. Están facturando el equipaje en el mostrador de la línea aérea.
6. El agente está mirando los boletos y los pasaportes.
7. Los pasajeros para Buenos Aires están saliendo de la puerta número siete.
8. Están abordando el avión.

10 *Answers will vary, but students should include verbs in the present progressive tense.*

Leveling EACH Activity

Average Activities 11, 12
CHallenging Activity 13

PRACTICE *(continued)*

Differentiation

Reaching All Learners

You may gear Activity 13 toward **slower paced** learners by simply asking for a list of the words they see depicted. More **advanced** learners and **verbal-linguistic** learners will be able to say or write complete sentences and put them together in story form as a complete oral or written review. **Bodily-kinesthetic** and **interpersonal** learners may want to work in pairs or small groups and present a skit for the class based on the illustrations.

ASSESS

Students are now ready to take Quiz 4.

FOLDABLES Study Organizer

SINGLE PICTURE FRAME

See the Foldables section of the Student Handbook at the beginning of this book for help with making this foldable. Work in groups. Each member of the group will make a foldable with a drawing (or magazine picture) related to airplane travel. Create a story about each picture by passing the picture around, with each person adding a sentence in the present progressive. An alternative would be to do this same activity as a writing activity.

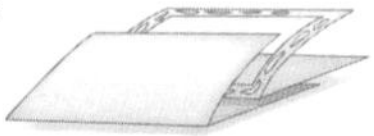

HABLAR • ESCRIBIR

11 Forma frases según el modelo. Escoge palabras del **banco de palabras**.

MODELO viajar →
Sí, estoy viajando.
No, no estoy viajando.

hablar español	usar mi móvil	hacer una tarea
leer una novela	estudiar	jugar fútbol
aprender mucho	salir ahora	comer

HABLAR

12 **Juego** Form small groups. Take turns pantomiming activities that might take place at an airport or on an airplane. The others will guess what you're doing, using the present progressive.

HABLAR • ESCRIBIR

13 Describe lo que ves en los dibujos. Usa el presente progresivo.

Answers

11
Sí, estoy hablando español. (No, no estoy hablando español.)
Sí, estoy leyendo una novela. (No, no estoy leyendo una novela.)
Sí, estoy aprendiendo mucho. (No, no estoy aprendiendo mucho.)
Sí, estoy usando mi móvil. (No, no estoy usando mi móvil.)
Sí, estoy estudiando. (No, no estoy estudiando.)
Sí, estoy saliendo ahora. (No, no estoy saliendo ahora.)
Sí, estoy haciendo una tarea. (No, no estoy haciendo una tarea.)
Sí, estoy jugando fútbol. (No, no estoy jugando fútbol.)
Sí, estoy comiendo. (No, no estoy comiendo.)

12 *Answers will vary, but students should use the present progressive tense.*

13 *Answers will vary, but students should use the present progressive tense and as much vocabulary as possible from* Vocabulario 1 *and* 2.

PRONUNCIACIÓN

La consonante r

When a word begins with **r** (initial position), the **r** is trilled in Spanish. Within a word, this trilled **r** sound is spelled **rr.** The Spanish trilled **r** sound does not exist in English. Repeat the following.

ra	re	ri	ro	ru
rápido	**receta**	**Ricardo**	**Roberto**	**Rubén**
raqueta	**red**	**aterriza**	**rojo**	**rubio**
párrafo	**corre**	**río**	**perro**	

The sound for a single **r** within a word (medial position) does not exist in English either. It is trilled less than the initial **r** or **rr.** Repeat the following.

ra	re	ri	ro	ru
verano	**arena**	**boletería**	**número**	**Perú**
maletera	**quiere**	**consultorio**	**pasajero**	**Aruba**
para		**periódico**	**cinturón**	

Dictado

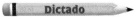

Pronounce the following sentences carefully. Then write them to prepare for a dictation.

El perro de Rubén corre en la arena.
El avión para Puerto Rico aterriza con un retraso de una hora.
El pasajero corre rápido por el aeropuerto.
Ricardo pone su raqueta en la maletera del carro.

CULTURA

El avión está aterrizando en el aeropuerto de Buenos Aires, Argentina.

Andrew Payti

Go Online!

connectED.mcgraw-hill.com

Refrán

Can you guess what the following proverb means?

Mal hace quien nada hace.

¡Bravo!

You have now learned all the new vocabulary and grammar in this chapter. Continue to use and practice all that you know while learning more cultural information. **¡Vamos!**

Gramática

PRONUNCIACIÓN

The following information may help students pronounce the Spanish **r** sound correctly. Remember that this is an extremely difficult sound for Americans to make. Do not frustrate a student who cannot pronounce it perfectly. Any native speaker will understand **"el caro"** as **el carro** even if the **rr** is mispronounced.

Step 1 The Spanish **r** sound does not exist in English. A single **r** in medial position is pronounced like a soft *t* in English. The tongue hits the upper part of the mouth in a position similar to when we say "a lot of" *(a lotta)* very quickly in English.

Step 2 Have students play a game trying to trill the initial **r** or the **rr.** Let them exaggerate as much as they wish, and they may get it right. Some students will not be able to trill the **r.** Tell them that is all right.

Step 3 Have students carefully repeat the sounds and words after you or the audio recording.

Step 4 Next, call on individuals to read the sentences aloud.

Step 5 As noted, all model sentences can be used for dictation. To make the dictation more challenging, you may wish to add the following sentences that students have not seen.

Reina compró arroz y frijoles para el almuerzo.
Roberto y María viven en Barranco, un barrio de Lima, Perú.
En el supermercado hay muchos carritos llenos de compras.

Refrán

Have students recite the proverb aloud. Encourage them to try to give an equivalent expression in English. Although there may not be an exact equivalent, students may be able to think of expressions related to the same theme.

Heritage Speakers

Challenge heritage speakers with the following trabalenguas.

Un burro comía berros y el perro se los robó, el burro lanzó un rebuzno, y el perro al barro cayó.
El perro de Rosa y Roque no tiene rabo, porque Ramón Ramírez se lo ha cortado.

Online Resources

Customizable Lesson Plans
Audio Activities
Student Workbook
Review

Quick Start

Use QS 10.5 or write the following on the board.

Match the related words.

1. embarcar	a. la maletera
2. abordar	b. el asiento
3. despegar	c. la seguridad
4. aterrizar	d. el despegue
5. la maleta	e. el embarque
6. salir	f. el pasillo
7. seguro	g. la salida
8. volar	h. el aterrizaje
9. sentarse	i. abordo
10. pasar	j. el vuelo

TEACH

Core Instruction

Step 1 Tell students they are going to hear a conversation between two friends who are at the airport and about to take a plane trip.

Step 2 Ask students to first listen to the conversation on the audio recording. Ask questions to see how much they understood.

Step 3 Then have students follow along as you read the conversation aloud or have them listen to it again on the audio recording. Ask the same questions to see if they understood more this time.

Step 4 Have several pairs of students role-play the conversation. Encourage them to use facial expressions and body language to help convey the meaning.

Step 5 Go over the **¿Comprendes?** activities together in class or assign them as homework.

En el aeropuerto

Susana	¡Oye, Pedro! Está saliendo nuestro vuelo.
Pedro	Sí, ¡vamos ya! Tenemos que pasar por el control de seguridad y siempre hay una cola larga.
Susana	¿Tienes nuestras tarjetas de embarque?
Pedro	Sí, sí. Las tengo. ¿Necesitas ayuda con tu equipaje de mano?
Susana	No, no traigo mucho. Lo puedo llevar. ¿De qué puerta salimos?
Pedro	De la puerta 11. ¿A qué hora empieza el embarque?
Susana	Ahora mismo. ¡Vamos!

David H Brennan

Differentiation

Multiple Intelligences

To engage **bodily-kinesthetic** learners, extend the activity by having them work in pairs to make up their own dialogues based on the conversation at the airport. Then ask for pairs to volunteer to present their dialogues to the class.

¡Así se dice!

Why It Works!

Although students are still at the elementary level of language acquisition, this conversation uses authentic language in a realistic context that is carefully adapted to what the students know.

¿Comprendes?

connectED.mcgraw-hill.com

A Contesta según la información en la conversación.

1. ¿Dónde están Pedro y Susana?
2. ¿Qué están anunciando?
3. ¿Ya pasaron por el control de seguridad Pedro y Susana?
4. ¿Qué hay siempre en el control de seguridad?
5. ¿Quién tiene las tarjetas de embarque?
6. ¿De qué puerta de salida salen?
7. ¿Está empezando el embarque?

B **Resumiendo** Relata toda la información en la conversación en tus propias palabras.

C **Prediciendo** ¿Piensas que Susana y Pedro van a perder su vuelo? ¿Por qué contestas que sí o que no?

CULTURA

Una vista panorámica de San Juan de Puerto Rico desde el Viejo San Juan hasta el Condado

PRACTICE

¿Comprendes?

C Remind students that they can apply strategies they've learned in their English classes about making predictions.

Writing Development

For Activity B, you may want students to write their summaries in order to help develop their writing skills.

Go Online!

You may wish to remind students to go online for additional conversation practice.

Pre-AP Listening to the audio recording of this conversation will help students develop the skills that they need to be successful on the listening portion of the AP exam.

Cultural Snapshot

Viejo San Juan is the **casco antiguo o histórico** of Puerto Rico's capital and is characterized by narrow streets made of **adoquines** *(cobblestones)*, colorful buildings built in the Spanish colonial style, and numerous plazas, museums, chapels, and a cathedral. In the foreground of the picture, the remnants of the fort El Morro, built between 1540 and 1589, stand in stark contrast to the high-rise buildings of the upscale El Condado district in the background.

Answers

A

1. Pedro y Susana están en el aeropuerto.
2. Están anunciando la salida de su vuelo.
3. No, Pedro y Susana no pasaron por el control de seguridad.
4. Siempre hay una cola larga en el control de seguridad.
5. Pedro tiene las tarjetas de embarque.
6. Salen de la puerta 11.
7. Sí, el embarque está empezando ahora mismo.

B *Answers will vary but may include:*
El vuelo de Pedro y Susana está saliendo. Tienen que pasar por el control de seguridad y siempre hay una cola larga. Pedro tiene sus tarjetas de embarque. Susana no necesita ayuda con su equipaje de mano porque no trae mucho. Salen de la puerta 11. El embarque empieza ahora mismo.

C *Answers will vary but may include:*
Sí, pienso que Susana y Pedro van a perder su vuelo porque tienen que pasar por el control de seguridad y siempre hay una cola larga.

Online Resources

Customizable Lesson Plans

Audio Activities

Student Workbook

TEACH

Core Instruction

Step 1 Ask which members of the class have traveled by air. Did they take a domestic or international flight? What are some of the differences between domestic and international air travel? If they have never flown, would they like to? Why or why not?

Step 2 Discuss the Reading Strategy. Do the **Antes de leer** activity. Then have students study the photo. Have them imagine what it would be like to fly over the landscape they see in this photo.

Step 3 Present the reading in three segments. Call on an individual to read the first section. Then ask the Reading Check question and a few others. **¿Cómo es el continente sudamericano? ¿Toma mucho tiempo viajar de una ciudad a otra? ¿Por qué?** Do the same for the next two sections.

Step 4 Have students explain why air travel is so important in South America.

Step 5 Do the **¿Comprendes?** activities in class or assign them as homework.

Differentiation

Multiple Intelligences

Logical-mathematical and **visual-spatial** learners may benefit from looking at the map of South America in the Student Handbook in the front of this book. Ask them to look for mountain ranges.

Lectura
CULTURAL

READING STRATEGY

IDENTIFYING THE MAIN IDEA It is important to identify the main idea of a reading. Topic sentences—usually the first sentence in a paragraph—help you determine the main idea of a reading.

Antes de leer

Scan the reading to find the most important idea in each section. Look for topic sentences.

READING CHECK

¿Cuál es un medio de transporte muy importante en Sudamérica?

READING CHECK

¿Dónde es muy densa la vegetación? ¿En las montañas o en las selvas?

Durante la lectura

Note each topic sentence. Think about the one idea that all the sentences and sections are about.

Después de leer

What was the main idea of the reading and of each section? What do you think was the author's purpose here?

El avión en la América del Sur

El continente sudamericano es vasto. Las distancias entre ciudades son largas. Por eso el avión es un medio de transporte importante. A veces es imposible viajar por tierra[1] de un lugar a otro. ¿Por qué?

Montañas Una gran parte del oeste del continente es montañosa. Los altos picos nevados de los Andes parecen tocar el cielo[2]. Unas ciudades como Bogotá, Quito y La Paz están en los Andes. Y claro que hay también pequeños pueblos aislados en las montañas.

Selvas Al este de los Andes en Colombia, Ecuador, Perú, Bolivia y Brasil hay grandes selvas tropicales del río Amazonas. En las selvas la vegetación es muy densa y una gran parte de la cuenca[3] amazónica es inhóspita e impenetrable.

Desiertos La región a lo largo de la costa desde Perú hasta el centro de Chile es desierto. El Atacama en Chile es el desierto más árido (seco) del mundo—una región de arena y rocas (piedras).

Día y noche los aviones sobrevuelan los picos, selvas y desiertos para enlazar[4] las ciudades y pueblos de Sudamérica.

[1]por tierra *by land*
[2]cielo *sky*
[3]cuenca *basin*
[4]enlazar *connect*

CULTURA

Un pueblo aislado en los Andes de Venezuela

Kelli Drummer-Avendaño

¡Así se dice!

Why It Works!

The **Lectura cultural,** other than the four footnotes, uses only words the students know, thus making the reading readily accessible to them. Note, too, that the cultural theme of the **Lectura cultural** is always connected to the communicative theme of the chapter.

Cultural Snapshot

This picture captures how the geography of South America makes it difficult to travel by land. Have students take a long look at the image and think about what it might be like to live in that isolated village. How would life there compare with where they live?

¿Comprendes?

A Recordando hechos Contesta.

1. ¿Qué montañas corren del norte al sur a lo largo del océano Pacífico en la América del Sur?
2. ¿Qué hay al este de los Andes?
3. ¿Qué región de Sudamérica es desierto?

B Describiendo Describe.

1. los picos andinos
2. las selvas tropicales
3. el desierto

C Analizando Contesta.

1. ¿Por qué es el avión un medio de transporte muy importante?
2. En muchas regiones de Sudamérica, ¿por qué es difícil viajar por tierra?

D Categorizando Completa la tabla de abajo. Luego, relata la información en la tabla en tus propias palabras.

	a lo largo de la costa peruana y chilena	al este de las montañas	en las montañas
desiertos			
picos cubiertos de nieve			
selvas tropicales			
la cuenca amazónica			
vegetación densa			
tierra árida			
Bogotá, Quito, La Paz			

Lectura

Pre-AP These cultural readings will develop the skills that students need to be successful on the reading and writing sections of the AP exam. Listening to these readings will also help prepare them for the auditory component.

Go Online!

You may wish to remind students to go online for additional reading comprehension and writing skills practice.

Answers

A

1. Los Andes corren del norte al sur a lo largo del océano Pacífico en la América del Sur.
2. Al este de los Andes hay grandes selvas tropicales del río Amazonas.
3. La región a lo largo de la costa desde Perú hasta el centro de Chile es desierto.

B

1. Los picos andinos son los altos picos nevados de los Andes. Están en una gran parte del oeste del continente.
2. Las selvas tropicales están al este de los Andes en Colombia, Ecuador, Perú, Bolivia y Brasil. La vegetación de las selvas es muy densa y una gran parte de la cuenca amazónica es inhóspita e impenetrable.
3. El desierto es una región de arena y rocas a lo largo de la costa desde Perú hasta el centro de Chile.

C

1. Las distancias entre una ciudad y otra son largas y a veces es imposible viajar por tierra.
2. Hay montañas, selvas y desiertos.

D

a lo largo de la costa peruana y chilena: desiertos, tierra árida
al este de las montañas: selvas tropicales, la cuenca amazónica, vegetación densa
en las montañas: picos cubiertos de nieve; Bogotá, Quito, La Paz

Online Resources

Customizable Lesson Plans

Audio Activities

Student Workbook

TEACH

Core Instruction

You may wish to have students read this selection on their own and do the **¿Comprendes?** activities, or you may prefer to present the **Lectura** more in depth. If you choose to present the **Lectura** in class, you may refer to these suggestions.

Step 1 Tell students the general idea of what they will be reading about and discuss the **Antes de leer** questions.

Step 2 Lead students through the **Lectura** by reading it aloud or playing the audio recording.

Step 3 Invite individual students to read aloud a few sentences at a time. After every few sentences, ask questions such as the Reading Check question.

Step 4 Answer the **¿Comprendes?** questions together as a class or assign them as homework.

Differentiation

Multiple Intelligences

Ask **visual-spatial** learners to look at the picture without looking at the words and describe what they see. What is it? Inform students that this image is sometimes referred to as **El astronauta** and then generate a brief discussion about the possible meanings behind the geoglyph.

Lectura

UN POCO MÁS

Antes de leer

Vas a leer sobre un misterio famoso que hay en Perú. ¿Te gustan los misterios? ¿Hay algún misterio donde vives?

READING CHECK

¿Qué son las líneas de Nazca?

Un viaje interesante

Un vuelo interesante Si quieres hacer un viaje interesante en avión tienes que sobrevolar las líneas de Nazca. ¿Qué son las líneas de Nazca? Pues, en el desierto árido del sur de Perú hay una serie de dibujos o figuras misteriosas. Hay figuras geométricas—rectángulos, triángulos y líneas paralelas. Hay también representaciones perfectas de varios animales. A pesar de[1] muchas investigaciones el origen de las líneas o figuras que tienen más de 1.500 años queda[2] un misterio.

Y son tan grandes que la única manera de ver las figuras es tomar un vuelo. Las avionetas salen de Lima o del aeropuerto de la pequeña ciudad de Ica, muy cerca de las figuras.

[1]A pesar de *In spite of* [2]queda *remains*

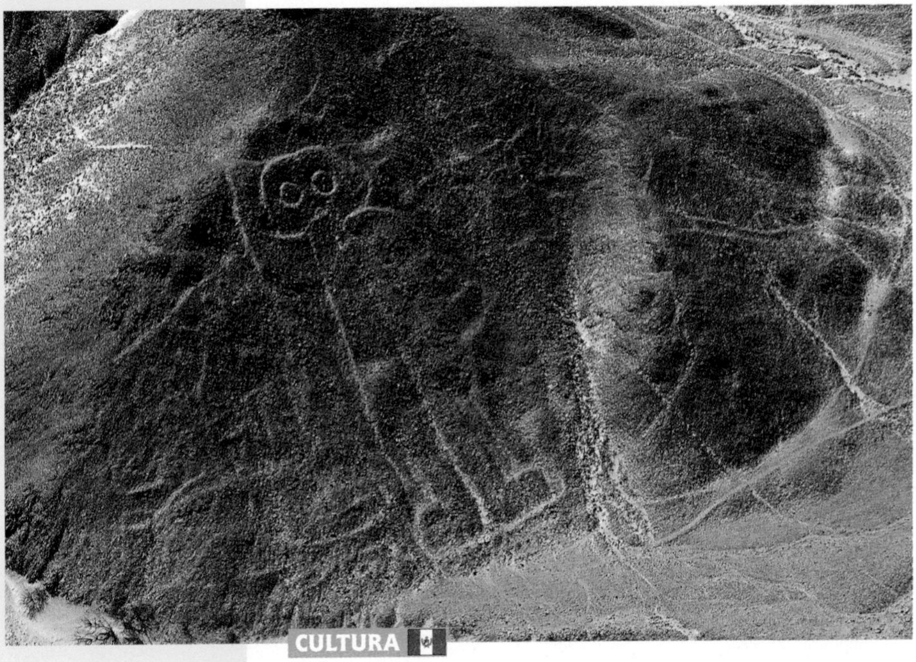

CULTURA

Las líneas de Nazca

Glow Images

Cultural Snapshot

The Nazca lines consist of a series of very large individual figures carved in the sand, many of which are animals, including a spider, a monkey, a hummingbird, a condor, a pelican, a dog, an iguana, a snake, and a whale. Their meaning remains a mystery.

Go Online!

You may wish to remind students to go online for additional reading comprehension and writing skills practice.

Go Online!

connectED.mcgraw-hill.com

¿Comprendes?

Escoge o completa.

1. Las líneas de Nazca están ____.
   a. en el pico de una montaña
   b. en una selva
   c. en un desierto
2. ¿Qué son las líneas?
   a. animales
   b. figuras misteriosas
   c. solamente figuras geométricas
3. El origen de las líneas de Nazca es ____.
4. ¿Por qué es necesario ver las líneas de un avión?
   a. porque hay avionetas que salen de Ica y Lima
   b. porque están en un desierto
   c. porque son tan inmensas
5. Un avión pequeño es ____.

CULTURA

Las líneas de Nazca. Además de las líneas de Nazca los arqueólogos descubrieron otras figuras delineadas en el costado rocoso no muy lejos de Nazca. Se cree que son aún más antiguas que las líneas de Nazca.

CULTURA

Una avioneta que sobrevuela las líneas de Nazca

Tips for Success

The type of multiple-choice comprehension exercises that accompany the second reading selection in each chapter have a format that will help students prepare for standardized tests.

Conexiones

Tell students that the Nazca and Paracas lines are near Ica, Peru. Have them find Ica and Nazca on the map on the pages featuring Peru in the **GeoVistas** section at the beginning of the book. Ask students whether they have studied Peru and the Nazca lines in a world history class. You may suggest that they research the Nazca culture and prepare a written or oral report that includes images. They may want to also present the report to their world history class.

Answers

1. c
2. b
3. un misterio
4. c
5. una avioneta

Prepárate para el examen

Online Resources

Customizable Lesson Plans

Student Workbook

Enrichment

Listening, Speaking, Reading, Writing Tests

Self-check for achievement

This is a pre-test for students to take before you administer the chapter test. Note that each section is cross-referenced so students can easily find the material they feel they need to review. You may wish to use Self-Check Worksheet SC1 to have students complete this assessment in class or at home. You can correct the assessment yourself, or you may prefer to display the answers in class using Self-Check Answers SC1A.

Differentiation

Slower Paced Learners

Have students work in pairs to complete the Self-Check in class. This will allow them to check their answers through collaborative learning.

Multiple Intelligences

To engage **visual-spatial** and **bodily-kinesthetic** learners, number from 1 to 40 on the board and call on a student to go to the board and write a correct answer. (This may be done chronologically or students may choose which question to answer.) Then have the first student call on the next one, and so on, making sure that every student gets to answer at least one question.

Prepárate para el examen

To review, see **Vocabulario 1** and **Vocabulario 2**.

Vocabulario

1 Completa.

1–2. El agente trabaja en el _____ de la línea aérea en el _____.

3. La tarjeta de embarque indica el número del _____ y el número del asiento del pasajero.

4. Antes de ir a la puerta de salida los pasajeros tienen que pasar por el _____ donde inspeccionan su equipaje de mano.

5. El avión no sale a tiempo. Sale _____.

6. Los pasajeros tienen que _____ una forma de identidad.

7. Abordo del avión, hay que poner su equipaje en el _____.

8. Estamos esperando nuestro vuelo en la _____.

9. Antes de facturar mi equipaje, tomo mi tarjeta de embarque del _____.

10. Estás abordo del avión. ¿Sabes el número de tu _____?

2 Identifica.

11.

12.

13.

14.

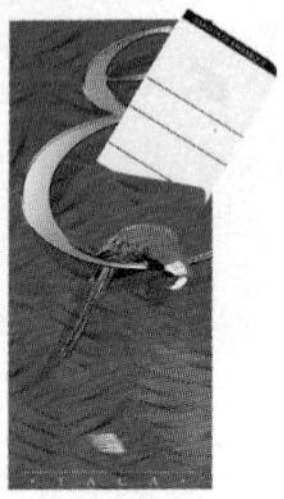
15.

Answers

1

1–2. mostrador, aeropuerto

3. vuelo

4. control de seguridad

5. tarde (con una demora, con un retraso)

6. mostrar

7. compartimiento superior

8. puerta de salida

9. distribuidor automático

10. asiento

2

11. un cinturón de seguridad (una asistenta de vuelo)

12. una maleta (el equipaje)

13. la señal de no fumar

14. el despegue

15. la tarjeta de embarque (el boleto [el billete] electrónico)

Gramática

3 Contesta.

16. ¿Haces un viaje?
17. ¿Vienes en junio para mi cumpleaños?
18. ¿Qué pones en tu maleta o mochila?
19. ¿A qué hora sales?
20. ¿Traes mucho equipaje?

To review, see **Presente de hacer, poner, traer, salir.**

4 Completa con el presente.

21. Ellos ____ mañana. (venir)
22. Nosotros ____ mucho trabajo. (hacer)
23. José ____ su mochila debajo del asiento. (poner)
24. Yo lo ____. (oír)
25. ¿Tú ____ tu equipaje de mano? (traer)
26. Señor, ¿usted ____ esta mañana o esta tarde? (salir)
27. Nosotros ____ al aeropuerto con nuestros padres. (venir)

To review, see **El presente progresivo.**

5 Escribe en el presente progresivo.

28. El avión despega.
29. Nosotros hacemos cola.
30. Ellos salen a tiempo.
31. Los pasajeros esperan en la puerta de salida.
32. Yo leo mi libro favorito.
33. Juan y Marisol, ¡ustedes nadan en el mar!
34. Tú vives cerca de mi casa ahora.
35. ¿Qué oyen tus primos?

CULTURA

Un barquito como este es un medio de transporte importante de la selva tropical en Latinoamérica. El barquito que vemos aquí está en el Amazonas cerca de Iquitos en Perú. Las aguas del Amazonas bajan y suben según la marea.

Cultura

6 Escoge.

36. El continente sudamericano es ____.
    a. pequeño   b. alto   c. inmenso
37. Hay selvas tropicales en ____.
    a. las montañas   b. el desierto   c. la cuenca amazónica
38. El Amazonas es ____.
    a. un pico andino   b. un río   c. un desierto

To review this cultural information, see the **Lectura cultural.**

7 Contesta.

39. ¿Por qué es difícil viajar por tierra en muchas partes de la América del Sur?
40. ¿Cuáles son unas características geográficas de la América del Sur?

Go Online!
connectED.mcgraw-hill.com

Prepárate para el examen

Differentiation

Slower Paced Learners

Encourage students who need extra help to refer to the margin notes and review any section before answering the questions.

Pre-AP Students preparing for the AP exam may benefit from a set time limit when completing this Self-Check. This may also help to identify students with learning difficulties or slower paced students who need extra help.

Go Online!

You may wish to remind students to go online for additional test preparation.

Cultural Snapshot

This photo was taken in the Amazon area of Peru. Notice the thick vegetation along the shores. This dugout canoe is the primary means of transportation for the inhabitants of the tropical Amazon region.

Answers

3

16. Sí, (No, no) hago un viaje.
17. Sí, (No, no) vengo en junio para tu cumpleaños.
18. Pongo ____ en mi maleta (mi mochila).
19. Salgo a las ____.
20. Sí, (No, no) traigo mucho equipaje.

4

21. vienen
22. hacemos
23. pone
24. oigo
25. traes
26. sale
27. venimos

5

28. El avión está despegando.
29. Nosotros estamos haciendo cola.
30. Ellos están saliendo a tiempo.
31. Los pasajeros están esperando en la puerta de salida.
32. Yo estoy leyendo mi libro favorito.
33. Juan y Marisol, ¡ustedes están nadando en el mar!
34. Tú estás viviendo cerca de mi casa ahora.
35. ¿Qué están oyendo tus primos?

6

36. c
37. c
38. b

7

39. Es difícil viajar por tierra en muchas partes de la América del Sur porque hay montañas, selvas y desiertos.
40. La América del Sur tiene montañas, selvas tropicales y desiertos.

Prepárate para el examen

Tips for Success

Encourage students to say as much as possible when they do these open-ended oral activities. Tell them not to be afraid to make mistakes, since the goal of the activities is real-life communication. Students should manipulate all the words and grammar that they have learned up to this point to effectively communicate their message. Let students choose the activities they would like to do.

Tell students to feel free to elaborate on the basic theme and to be creative. They may use props, pictures, or posters if they wish.

Pre-AP These oral activities will give students the opportunity to develop and improve their speaking skills so that they may succeed on the speaking portion of the AP exam.

Note: Some teachers may want to use the rubric below to help students prepare their speaking activities.

Practice for **ORAL PROFICIENCY**

Prepárate para el examen

1. **Preparar para un viaje**

   Tell about packing for a trip

   You're getting ready to leave on a trip. Tell what you're going to pack. Will you use a suitcase, carry-on, or backpack? Does the weather where you're going influence what you are going to pack?

2. **En el mostrador de la línea aérea**

   Converse with a ticket agent

   You are at the ticket counter at the airport. You are talking with the ticket agent (your partner). You want to find out details about the flight and check your luggage. The ticket agent asks for confirmation of your e-ticket and passport and answers any questions you have.

3. **Un billete para Madrid**

   Buy an airplane ticket

   Work with a classmate. You want to fly with your family from somewhere in the United States to Madrid and you will be returning from Barcelona. Call the airline to get a reservation. Your classmate will be the reservation agent. Before you call, think about all the information you will need to provide or get from the airline agent: your name, date of departure, departure time, arrival time in Madrid, flight number, and price.

4. **¿Quién está haciendo qué?**

   Tell what people are doing in your classroom

   Who's doing what? Look around you and tell what everyone is doing.

CULTURA

La profesora está enseñando y los alumnos están prestando atención en una clase de matemáticas en San Juan, Puerto Rico.

David H. Brennan

5. **El continente sudamericano**

   Tell about travel in South America

   Your aunt and uncle are thinking about traveling around South America. You have already been there. Make suggestions about where they should go, how they should get there, and what they should do and see. Tell them why it can be difficult to travel from one place to another by land. They will ask you questions for clarification.

Scoring Rubric for Speaking

	4	3	2	1
vocabulary	extensive use of vocabulary, including idiomatic expressions	adequate use of vocabulary and idiomatic expressions	limited vocabulary marked with some anglicisms	limited vocabulary marked by frequent anglicisms that force interpretation by the listener
grammar	few or no grammatical errors	minor grammatical errors	some serious grammatical errors	serious grammatical errors
pronunciation	good intonation and largely accurate pronunciation with slight accent	acceptable intonation and pronunciation with distinctive accent	errors in intonation and pronunciation with heavy accent	errors in intonation and pronunciation that interfere with listener's comprehension
content	thorough response with interesting and pertinent detail	thorough response with sufficient detail	some detail, but not sufficient	general, insufficient response

Go Online!

connectED.mcgraw-hill.com

Tarea

Write a letter to a service organization interested in international relations. Your goal is to win an all-expense-paid trip to spend two weeks living with a Spanish-speaking family in a country of your choice.

Writing Strategy

Answering an essay question Many types of applications contain or expect you to answer questions concerning your qualifications or reasons for applying. This requires you to write an essay that convinces that you are the right person.

SW Productions/Getty Images

1 Prewrite

- Think of your overall goal—to convince all concerned why you are the right person to be sent to a foreign country.
- Look at the list of some types of questions you may have to answer. **¿Qué quieres visitar? ¿Por qué quieres ir allí? ¿Qué esperas hacer, ver o aprender allí? ¿Cómo quieres viajar? ¿Qué tipo de persona eres? ¿Qué estás haciendo ahora?**
- Think of other information the organization may want to know about you. Add those questions to the list.

2 Write

You really want to go on this trip, so be sure to plan your essay carefully.

- Write an introduction that tells the organization a little about you and makes them want to find out more about you.
- Start a new paragraph for the answer to each question.
- When you finish writing, check your work. Check spelling, grammar, and verb endings. Make sure your sentences are complete and understandable.
- Read over your work again to make sure all errors are corrected and to make sure that you have effectively communicated your message to the organization.

Evaluate

Don't forget that your teacher will evaluate you on your organization, use of vocabulary and grammar, and on how clear, complete, and convincing your essay is.

Prepárate para el examen

Pre-AP This **tarea** will give students the opportunity to develop and improve their writing skills so that they may succeed on the writing portion of the AP exam.

ASSESS

Students are now ready to take any of the Listening, Speaking, Reading, Writing Tests you choose to administer.

Note: Some teachers may want to use the rubric below to help students prepare their writing task.

Scoring Rubric for Writing

	4	3	2	1
vocabulary	precise, varied	functional, fails to communicate complete meaning	limited to basic words, often inaccurate	inadequate
grammar	excellent, very few or no errors	some errors, but do not hinder communication	numerous errors interfere with communication	many errors, little sentence structure
content	thorough response to the topic	generally thorough response to the topic	partial response to the topic	insufficient response to the topic
organization	well organized, ideas presented clearly and logically	loosely organized, but main ideas present	some attempts at organization, but with confused sequencing	lack of organization

Repaso del Capítulo 1

Online Resources

Customizable Lesson Plans
- Whiteboard Lesson
- Audio Activities
- Video (Vocabulario) (Diálogo) (Gramática)
- Student Workbook
- Review
- Enrichment
- Quizzes
- Listening, Speaking, Reading, Writing Tests

Grammar Review

This page provides a quick "at a glance" summary of the grammar points students have learned in this chapter.

Differentiation

Multiple Intelligences

You may want to call on **verbal-linguistic** and **logical-mathematical** learners for whom grammar often comes easily to explain the main concepts to their classmates in their own words. Encourage students to compare and contrast these structures with structures in English. Having students explain the concepts in different ways may also help slower paced students or students with learning difficulties.

Repaso del Capítulo 1

Gramática

Presente de hacer, poner, traer, salir

The verbs **hacer, poner, traer, salir,** and **oír** have a **g** in the **yo** form. All other forms are regular. Review the following forms.

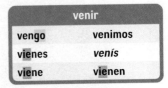

yo **hago** **pongo** **traigo** **salgo** **oigo**

Venir has a **g** in the **yo** form as well as a stem change just like the verb **tener,** which you have already learned.

venir	
vengo	venimos
vienes	*venís*
viene	vienen

Comparaciones

How is the present progressive expressed in English?

El presente progresivo

The present progressive expresses an action that is taking place at the moment. It is formed with the verb **estar** and the present participle. Review the following forms.

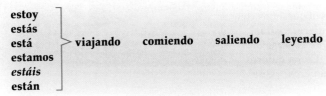

estoy
estás
está
estamos
estáis
están

→ **viajando** **comiendo** **saliendo** **leyendo**

La señorita está escuchando música en su MP3 mientras regresa a casa después de un viaje.

John Flournoy/McGraw-Hill Education

Juego There are a number of cognates in this list. See how many you and a partner can find. Who can find the most? Compare your list with those of your classmates.

Go Online!

connectED.mcgraw-hill.com

Vocabulario

Leaving for a trip

el equipaje de mano
la maleta
el taxi
el/la taxista
la maletera, el baúl
poner
hacer
  un viaje
  la maleta

Describing airport activities

el aeropuerto
el avión
el/la agente
el mostrador
la línea aérea
el boleto, el billete (electrónico)
el distribuidor automático
la tarjeta de embarque
el pasaporte
el nombre
el/la pasajero(a)
el número del vuelo
la hora de salida
la hora de embarque
el número del asiento
la forma de identidad
la puerta de salida
facturar el equipaje
pasar por el control de seguridad
hacer cola
mostrar
esperar
embarcar, abordar

Describing a flight

el/la asistente(a) de vuelo
el asiento
el pasillo
la ventanilla
el compartimiento superior
la máscara de oxígeno
el cinturón de seguridad
la señal de no fumar
el servicio
un retraso, una demora
el despegue
el aterrizaje
la pista
despegar
aterrizar
internacional
abordo
tarde
a tiempo
con destino a
procedente de

Other useful words and expressions

hay que
a veces
de vez en cuando
dentro de poco
debajo de
¡Con permiso!
abrochado(a)

Repaso del Capítulo 1

Vocabulary Review

The words and phrases in **Vocabulario 1** and **2** have been taught for productive use in this chapter. They are summarized here as a resource for both student and teacher. This list also serves as a convenient resource for the **Prepárate para el examen** activities.

¡Así se dice!

Why It Works!

This vocabulary reference list has not been translated into English for two reasons. First, it is recommended that students learn the new vocabulary through direct association with images on the **Vocabulario** pages. Secondly, all vocabulary is reintroduced in the chapter many times and upon completion of the chapter students should be familiar with the meaning of all the words. If there are words that students still do not know, they can refer to the vocabulary presentation in the chapter or the dictionary at the end of the book. If, however, it is your preference to give students the English translations, please refer to Vocabulary V1.1.

Differentiation

Slower Paced Learners

Slower paced learners may benefit from creating their own visual dictionary of words in this list. They can either draw their own depictions or use images from the Internet or magazines.

Don't forget the chapter project and cultural activities. Students have learned all the information from this chapter that they will need to complete these engaging enrichment tasks.

Juego The cognates in this list are: **el taxi, el aeropuerto, el/la agente, electrónico, automático, el pasaporte, el/la pasajero(a), el número, la forma de identidad, el compartimiento, la máscara de oxígeno, internacional.**

Repaso cumulativo

Every chapter of **¡Así se dice!** contains this review section of previously learned material. By recycling information from previous chapters, the cumulative review serves to remind students that they need to continue practicing what they have learned.

Tips for Success

These activities help you determine how much your students are retaining. You may want to skip some of the activities if your students do not need them.

Activity 1 This activity reviews **saber** and **conocer.**

Audio Script

1. la literatura española
2. que Arturo es muy terco
3. a la profesora de biología
4. Buenos Aires
5. navegar la red

Activity 2 This activity reviews a variety of regular and irregular verbs in the present tense.

Activity 3 This activity reviews vocabulary related to clothing.

Repaso cumulativo

Repasa lo que ya has aprendido

These activities will help you review and remember what you have learned so far in Spanish.

1 **Escucha las expresiones. Indica en una tabla como la de abajo si tienes que usar el verbo saber o conocer.**

saber	conocer

2 **Completa con verbos apropiados.**

Álvaro Irizarry __1__ un muchacho alto y guapo. Él __2__ de San Juan, la capital de Puerto Rico. Puerto Rico __3__ una isla tropical en el mar Caribe. En la isla siempre __4__ calor y el tiempo __5__ muy bueno con mucho sol. A Álvaro y a sus amigos les __6__ mucho ir a la playa donde __7__ una tarde agradable. Si __8__ hambre, __9__ a uno de los carritos que __10__ en la playa donde __11__ una empanada deliciosa.

CULTURA

Una playa en la isla de Vieques en Puerto Rico

3 **Repasa tu vocabulario. Prepara una lista de todos los artículos de ropa que ya aprendiste en español.**

4 **Contesta.**

1. Va a hacer calor. ¿Qué vas a llevar?
2. Va a hacer frío. ¿Qué vas a llevar?
3. ¿Qué te gusta comer cuando tienes hambre?
4. ¿Qué te gusta beber cuando tienes sed?

5 **Escribe las frases y cambia las palabras indicadas a pronombres.**

1. Juan vio *a Ana* después de las clases.
2. Él dio *los boletos* a Ana porque es su amiga buena.
3. Habló también *a Mateo y Gabriela.*
4. Ellos compraron un refresco *para Juan.*

Rebecca Smith

Answers

1
1. conocer
2. saber
3. conocer
4. conocer
5. saber

2
1. es
2. es
3. es
4. hace
5. está
6. gusta
7. pasan
8. tienen
9. van
10. están (hay)
11. comen (compran)

3 *Answers will vary.*

4
1. Voy a llevar ___.
2. Voy a llevar ___.
3. Me gusta comer ___ cuando tengo hambre.
4. Me gusta beber ___ cuando tengo sed.

5
1. Juan la vio después de las clases.
2. Él los dio a Ana porque es su amiga buena.
3. Les habló también.
4. Ellos le compraron un refresco.

Go Online!

connectED.mcgraw-hill.com

6 Identifica el deporte.

1. El portero quiere bloquear el balón.
2. Es posible bajar una pista fácil para principiantes o una pista difícil para expertos.
3. Los jugadores corren de una base a otra.
4. El balón tiene que pasar por encima de la red.
5. Juegan con una pelota y una raqueta y la pelota tiene que pasar por encima de la red.

7 Rompecabezas

El intruso Choose the word in each group that does not belong and tell why it is **el intruso.**

1. banda avión carro autobús
2. siempre a veces nunca nadie
3. mar pelota ola piscina
4. cama silla falda mesa
5. leer patinar escribir estudiar

8 Contesta.

1. Ellos están jugando voleibol. ¿Tiene que pasar el balón por encima de la red o debajo de la red?
2. Mi padre está trabajando en nuestro jardín. ¿Él está cerca de nuestra casa o lejos de nuestra casa?
3. La agente trabaja en el mostrador de la línea aérea en el aeropuerto. ¿Está delante del mostrador o detrás del mostrador?
4. La pasajera está facturando su equipaje en el aeropuerto. ¿Está delante del mostrador o detrás del mostrador?
5. Abordo del avión, ¿es necesario poner el equipaje de mano debajo del asiento o sobre el asiento?

CULTURA

Los pasajeros están embarcando un vuelo en el aeropuerto de Bilbao en el País Vasco en el norte de España.

Repaso cumulativo

Activity 4 This activity reviews vocabulary related to weather, clothing, food, and drink.

Activity 5 This activity reviews indirect and direct object pronouns.

Activity 6 This activity reviews sports vocabulary.

Activity 7 This activity reviews a variety of vocabulary from previous chapters.

Activity 8 This activity reviews prepositions.

Go Online!

The **¡Así se dice!** Audio Program for Chapter 1 has twenty-six activities, which afford students extensive listening and speaking practice.

You may wish to remind students to go online for additional cumulative review.

Pre-AP To give students further open-ended oral or written practice, or to assess proficiency, go to AP Proficiency Practice 12.

Answers

6

1. el fútbol
2. el esquí (alpino)
3. el béisbol
4. el voleibol
5. el tenis

7

1. «Banda» es el intruso porque no es un medio de transporte.
2. «Nadie» es el intruso porque no va con las palabras de tiempo.
3. «Pelota» es el intruso porque no es relacionado con nadar.
4. «Falda» es el intruso porque no es un mueble.
5. «Patinar» es el intruso porque no va con los verbos de la escuela.

8

1. El balón tiene que pasar por encima de la red.
2. Él está cerca de nuestra casa.
3. Está detrás del mostrador.
4. Está delante del mostrador.
5. Es necesario poner el equipaje de mano debajo del asiento.

Chapter Overview

¡Una rutina diferente!

Scope and Sequence

Topics
- Parts of the body
- Daily routine
- Backpacking and camping

Culture
- Talk about backpacking and camping in Spanish-speaking countries

Functions
- How to talk about your daily routine
- How to talk about backpacking and camping

Structure
- Reflexive verbs
- Commands with **favor de**

Planning Guide

	required	recommended	optional
Vocabulario 1 El cuerpo humano La rutina diaria	✓		
Vocabulario 2 El camping	✓		
Gramática Verbos reflexivos Verbos reflexivos de cambio radical Mandatos con **favor de**	✓		
Pronunciación La **h**, la **y** y la **ll**		✓	
Conversación De camping		✓	
Lectura cultural Los mochileros		✓	
Lectura Un poco más El camping			✓
Prepárate para el examen			✓
Repaso cumulativo			✓

Andrew Payti

Correlations to ACTFL World-Readiness Standards for Learning Languages

Page numbers in light print refer to the Student Edition.
Page numbers in bold print refer to the Teacher Edition.

COMMUNICATION Communicate effectively in more than one language in order to function in a variety of situations and for multiple purposes		
Interpersonal Communication	Learners interact and negotiate meaning in spoken, signed, or written conversations to share information, reactions, feelings, and opinions.	pp. **34C, 36–37, 40,** 41, 44, 45, **45, 46,** 48, 49, **49,** 51, 52, **52, 57,** 62, **67**
Interpretive Communication	Learners understand, interpret, and analyze what is heard, read, or viewed on a variety of topics.	pp. **38,** 40, **40,** 41, **42,** 44, **44,** 45, **47,** 48, 49, 51, 52, 54, **54,** 55, **55, 56,** 57, **57,** 59, 60–61, **64,** 66–67, **67**
Presentational Communication	Learners present information, concepts, and ideas to inform, explain, persuade, and narrate on a variety of topics using appropriate media and adapting to various audiences of listeners, readers, or viewers.	pp. **34C, 34D, 37, 39,** 41, 44, **45,** 51, 52, 55, **55, 56, 57, 60,** 62, 63, **64, 65,** 67, **67**
CULTURES Interact with cultural competence and understanding		
Relating Cultural Practices to Perspectives	Learners use the language to investigate, explain, and reflect on the relationship between the practices and perspectives of the cultures studied.	pp. **34D,** 35, 36–37, **36–37,** 43, 52, 56–57, 58–59, 61
Relating Cultural Products to Perspectives	Learners use the language to investigate, explain, and reflect on the relationship between the products and perspectives of the cultures studied.	pp. **34C, 34D,** 36, **42,** 45, **51, 57, 58**
CONNECTIONS Connect with other disciplines and acquire information and diverse perspectives in order to use the language to function in academic and career-related situations		
Making Connections	Learners build, reinforce, and expand their knowledge of other disciplines while using the language to develop critical thinking and to solve problems creatively.	pp. **34C, 34D, 36–37, 39,** 46, 48, **48, 51,** 55, **55, 57,** 58, **58, 59**
Acquiring Information and Diverse Perspectives	Learners access and evaluate information and diverse perspectives that are available through the language and its cultures.	pp. **34C, 34D,** 42, 43, **43,** 50, **50,** 53
COMPARISONS Develop insight into the nature of language and culture in order to interact with cultural competence		
Language Comparisons	Learners use the language to investigate, explain, and reflect on the nature of language through comparisons of the language studied and their own.	pp. **43,** 46, 53, **53, 56, 64,** 65
Cultural Comparisons	Learners use the language to investigate, explain, and reflect on the concept of culture through comparisons of the cultures studied and their own.	pp. **34D,** 35, **36,** 36–37, 56, 58
COMMUNITIES Communicate and interact with cultural competence in order to participate in multilingual communities at home and around the world		
School and Global Communities	Learners use the language both within and beyond the classroom to interact and collaborate in their community and the globalized world.	pp. **34C, 41, 43,** 44, **46,** 49, 52, **58, 60, 62, 64, 67**
Lifelong Learning	Learners set goals and reflect on their progress in using languages for enjoyment, enrichment, and advancement.	pp. 35, 42, 43, **43,** 50, **50**

Chapter Project

Los parques nacionales

For this project, students will create travel brochures to promote national parks in Spanish-speaking countries.

1. Have students imagine that they are marketing specialists creating travel brochures for national parks in Spanish-speaking countries. They want to promote the features that appeal to campers and backpackers: spectacular sights, hiking trails, camping facilities, etc.
2. Have each student select and research a park using an atlas or other maps, the Internet, the school or public library, or other resources.
3. Students each create a four-page brochure in Spanish. Each brochure should include at minimum:
   - the name of the park and where it is located (country and city or region)
   - a small-scale map of the country with the park location indicated
   - five sentences promoting camping and backpacking in the park
   - a list of ten essential articles to pack
   - two photos or drawings depicting the park
4. Students should write a first draft of their five sentences and ten essential articles list for peer editing. This first draft should be turned in with the final brochure.

Expansion: Have students role-play visiting a travel agent, using the brochures as props.

Scoring Rubric for Project

	5	3	1
Evidence of planning	Label list is provided and corrections have been made.	Label list is provided but is not corrected.	No label list is provided.
Use of illustrations	Use of several visual elements.	Use of few visual elements.	No use of any visual elements.
Presentation	Collage contains all of the required elements.	Collage contains some of the required elements.	Collage contains few of the required elements.

Culture

Recipe

CHIPAS

Ingredients: (makes 8 servings)
1 egg
2/3 cup milk
6 ounces shredded Italian cheese blend
3 tablespoons butter, melted
$1\frac{3}{4}$ cups tapioca starch
1 cup self-rising flour

Preheat oven to 350° F. Prepare a baking sheet with cooking spray and set aside. Stir together egg, milk, cheese, and butter in a large bowl. Sprinkle in tapioca starch and flour, and then stir to form dough. Knead dough for two minutes on a lightly floured surface. Roll into golf ball-sized balls and place onto baking sheet. Bake 10–15 minutes until golden brown.

Los gauchos

Today Argentina is a popular destination for avid hikers, backpackers, and campers due to the amazing landscapes it houses. From Iguazu Falls to Glaciers National Park, there is plenty of ground to be covered. But Argentina's **pampas** have long been home to a group known for "roughing it"—**gauchos.** During the eighteenth and nineteenth centuries, **gauchos** lived a nomadic life, carrying their few possessions on horseback and living off the land. Their romantic lifestyle was made famous in the epic poem *Martín Fierro* by José Hernández. This poem is written in the style of a **payada,** an improvised folk song that **gauchos** often played. You may wish to share some of this work with your students or have them try to write a short **payada** of their own. Students could then present their **payadas** during National Foreign Language week or at any multicultural fair that takes place in your community.

Andrew Payti

Connection to Fine Art

Have students look online or in an art text to find *Ciudad de Amecameca y el Popocatépetl* by Mexican artist Francisco Díaz de León. Have them identify colors in the painting. Does the landscape represented in the painting look like it would be a good place for hiking and camping? Why or why not?

50-Minute Lesson Plans

	Objective	Present	Practice	Assess/Homework
Day 1	Identify more parts of the body and talk about your daily routine	Chapter Opener (5 min.) Introducción al tema (10 min.) Core Instruction/Vocabulario 1 (20 min.)	Activities 1–4 (15 min.)	Student Workbook Activities A–C **ConnectEd** Vocabulary Practice
Day 2	Identify more parts of the body and talk about your daily routine	Quick Start (5 min.) Review Vocabulario 1 (10 min.)	Activities 5–7 (10 min.) Total Physical Response (5 min.) InfoGap (5 min.) Audio Activities A–D (15 min.)	Student Workbook Activities D–E **ConnectEd** Vocabulary Practice
Day 3	Talk about backpacking and camping	Core Instruction/Vocabulario 2 (10 min.) Video, Vocabulario en vivo (10 min.)	Activities 1–3 (10 min.) Audio Activities E–G (10 min.)	Quiz 1 (10 min.) Student Workbook Activities A–C **ConnectEd** Vocabulary Practice
Day 4	Talk about backpacking and camping	Quick Start (5 min.) Review Vocabulario 2 (10 min.) Video, Diálogo en vivo (10 min.)	Activities 4–6 (10 min.) Total Physical Response (5 min.) Audio Activities H–K (10 min.)	Student Workbook Activities D–E **ConnectEd** Vocabulary Practice
Day 5	Reflexive verbs	Core Instruction/Gramática, Verbos reflexivos (20 min.)	Activities 1–3 (10 min.) Audio Activities A–B (10 min.)	Quiz 2 (10 min.) Student Workbook Activities A–C **ConnectEd** Grammar Practice
Day 6	Reflexive verbs	Quick Start (5 min.) Review Gramática, Verbos reflexivos (10 min.)	Activities 4–7 (20 min.) Audio Activities C–E (15 min.)	Student Workbook Activities D–E **ConnectEd** Grammar Practice
Day 7	Reflexive verbs	Quick Start (5 min.) Core Instruction/Gramática, Verbos reflexivos de cambio radical (10 min.) Video, Gramática en vivo (5 min.)	Activities 8–11 (10 min.) Audio Activities F–G (10 min.)	Quiz 3 (10 min.) Student Workbook Activities F–H **ConnectEd** Grammar Practice
Day 8	Commands with **favor de**	Quick Start (5 min.) Core Instruction/Gramática, Mandatos con **favor de** (10 min.) Pronunciación (10 min.)	Activities 12–13 (10 min.) Dictado (5 min.)	Quiz 4 (10 min.) Student Workbook Activity A **ConnectEd** Grammar Practice
Day 9	Develop reading and listening comprehension skills	Quick Start (5 min.) Core Instruction/Conversación (20 min.)	¿Comprendes? A–B (15 min.)	Quiz 5 (10 min.) ¿Comprendes? C–D **ConnectEd** Conversation
Day 10	Discuss camping and backpacking	Core Instruction/Lectura cultural (20 min.)	¿Comprendes? A–B (15 min.)	Listening Comprehension Test (15 min.) ¿Comprendes? C–D **ConnectEd** Reading Practice
Day 11	Develop reading comprehension skills	Core Instruction/Lectura Un poco más (15 min.)	¿Comprendes? (10 min.) Prepárate para el examen (25 min.)	Prepárate para el examen, Practice for written proficiency **ConnectEd** Reading Practice
Day 12	Chapter review	Repaso del Capítulo 2 (15 min.)	Prepárate para el examen, Practice for oral proficiency (20 min.)	Test for Writing Proficiency (15 min.) Review for chapter test
Day 13	Chapter 2 Tests (50 min.) Reading and Writing Test Speaking Test		Test for Oral Proficiency Test for Reading Comprehension	

90-Minute Lesson Plans

	Objective	Present	Practice	Assess/Homework
Block 1	Identify more parts of the body and talk about your daily routine	Chapter Opener (5 min.) Introducción al tema (10 min.) Quick Start (5 min.) Core Instruction/Vocabulario 1 (20 min.)	Activities 1–7 (25 min.) Total Physical Response (5 min.) InfoGap (5 min.) Audio Activities A–D (15 min.)	Student Workbook Activities A–E **ConnectEd** Vocabulary Practice
Block 2	Talk about backpacking and camping	Quick Start (5 min.) Core Instruction/Vocabulario 2 (10 min.) Video, Vocabulario en vivo (10 min.) Video, Diálogo en vivo (10 min.)	Activities 1–6 (20 min.) Total Physical Response (5 min.) Audio Activities E–K (20 min.)	Quiz 1 (10 min.) Student Workbook Activities A–E **ConnectEd** Vocabulary Practice
Block 3	Reflexive verbs	Quick Start (5 min.) Core Instruction/Gramática, Verbos reflexivos (10 min.) Quick Start (5 min.) Core Instruction/Gramática, Verbos reflexivos de cambio radical (10 min.) Video, Gramática en vivo (10 min.)	Activities 1–7 (10 min.) Activities 8–11 (10 min.) Audio Activities A–E (20 min.)	Quiz 2 (10 min.) Student Workbook Activities A–H **ConnectEd** Grammar Practice
Block 4	Commands with **favor de**	Quick Start (5 min.) Core Instruction/Gramática, Mandatos con **favor de** (15 min.) Pronunciación (10 min.)	Activities 12–13 (15 min.) Foldables (5 min.) Dictado (5 min.) Audio Activities F–G (15 min.)	Quizzes 3–4 (20 min.) Student Workbook Activity A **ConnectEd** Grammar Practice
Block 5	Discuss camping and backpacking	Quick Start (5 min.) Core Instruction/Conversación (20 min.) Core Instruction/Lectura cultural (20 min.)	¿Comprendes? A–D (15 min.) ¿Comprendes? A–D (20 min.)	Quiz 5 (10 min.) Prepárate para el examen, Practice for written proficiency **ConnectEd** Conversation, Reading Practice
Block 6	Develop reading comprehension skills	Core Instruction/Lectura Un poco más (15 min.)	¿Comprendes? (10 min.) Prepárate para el examen (25 min.) Prepárate para el examen, Practice for oral proficiency (25 min.)	Listening Comprehension Test (15 min.) Review for chapter test **ConnectEd** Reading Practice
Block 7	Chapter 2 Tests (50 min.) Reading and Writing Test Speaking Test Test for Oral Proficiency Test for Writing Proficiency Test for Reading Comprehension Chapter Project (40 min.)			

Preview

In this chapter, students will build upon their language skills by learning additional parts of the body as they talk about their daily routine. To put daily chores in a more interesting context, students will also talk about backpacking and camping. To accomplish these goals, students will learn reflexive verbs and the commands with the expression **favor de.**

Pacing

It is important to note that once you reach **¡Bravo!** in the chapter, there is no further new material for students to learn. The rest of the chapter recycles what has already been covered. The suggested pacing listed here leaves two to three days for review, assessment, and enrichment activities such as the chapter project.

Vocabulario 1	1–2 days
Vocabulario 2	1–2 days
Gramática	2–3 days
Conversación	1 day
Lectura cultural	1 day
Lectura Un poco más	1 day

CAPÍTULO 2

¡Una rutina diferente!

Go Online! connectED.mcgraw-hill.com — Audio, Video, Práctica, Repaso, Diversiones, eScape, ePals

Go Online!

Audio
Listen to spoken Spanish.

Video
Watch and learn about the Spanish-speaking world.

Práctica
Practice your skills.

Repaso
Review what you've learned.

Diversiones
Go beyond the classroom.

eScape
Read about current events in the Spanish-speaking world.

Aquí y Allí

Vamos a comparar ¿Qué haces cada día desde el momento que te levantas hasta que te acuestas? Muchas cosas de la rutina diaria pueden ser aburridas, ¿no? Vas a ver si los jóvenes en España y Latinoamérica tienen la misma rutina. Pero vas a observar también que hay maneras de cambiar la rutina—sobre todo si decides viajar con un grupo de jóvenes por un país hispano.

Objetivos

You will:

- identify more parts of the body
- talk about your daily routine
- talk about backpacking and camping

You will use:

- reflexive verbs
- commands with **favor de**

Estos mochileros lo están pasando bien dando una caminata en Costa Rica. Pasan unos días sin tener que seguir su rutina ordinaria.

Interactive Whiteboard
Present or practice with interactive whiteboard lessons.

Assessment
Check student progress.

ePals
Connect with Spanish-speaking students around the world.

SPOTLIGHT ON CULTURE

Cultural Comparison
Students are introduced to the chapter theme in a way that challenges them to think about their own daily routine compared to that of young people in Spanish-speaking cultures. In addition, the information in **Aquí y Allí** serves to encourage them to explore the possibility of visiting a Spanish-speaking country, where they may practice all they have learned by becoming immersed in the culture and the language.

Cultural Snapshot
These young backpackers are traveling through Costa Rica. Your students may be interested in knowing that many young people can be seen backpacking throughout Spain and all of Latin America—in both urban, metropolitan areas and rural, off-the-path isolated areas.

¡Así se dice!

Why It Works!

The focus of this chapter is reflexive verbs. Although reflexive verbs are important, learning to say "I get up, wash, and brush my teeth" is not extremely stimulating. To make it more interesting, we place the daily routine in a campsite since many young people travel as backpackers and carry their own sleeping bag and tent.

PRESENT

Introduce the theme of the chapter by having students look at the photographs on these pages. Have them look at the young people and determine if there is anything they see them doing that is the same or different from what they do. Once you have completed the vocabulary presentation, have students return to these pages and read the information that accompanies each photograph. As soon as students are fully acquainted with the vocabulary and grammar of the chapter, you may wish to come back to these pages and ask the questions that go with each photo.

Cultural Snapshot

México *(top)* **¿Tienes el pelo largo como esta muchacha mexicana? ¿Es bonita ella? ¿Ella se cepilla?**

México *(left)* The historic district of Oaxaca is known for its beauty. It has its own unique style of architecture, and many buildings are covered in beautiful, green volcanic stone. Oaxaca is the capital of the Mexican state of the same name, which is home to two important indigenous groups, the Zapotec and Mixtec peoples. The city is also known as Oaxaca de Juárez, so named in honor of one of Mexico's most beloved presidents, Benito Juárez, who was of Zapotec heritage. Tourism is the most important industry in Oaxaca, and **alebrijes,** fanciful wooden animal figurines painted in vibrant colors, are popular souvenirs. **¿Qué llevan los mochileros? ¿Dónde están?**

Perú The Barranco area where this hostel is located is both interesting and attractive. Not too far from downtown Lima on the coast, it once served as a summer resort.

España Los Picos de Europa are in the Cantabrian Mountains. It was the first of the National Parks of Spain and it covers territory in Castilla, León, Asturias, and Cantabria. The Picos have many beautiful lakes, gorges, and valleys that are wonderful for hiking. The first battle of the Reconquista against the Moors was fought in Covadonga in 718 and Don Pelayo was proclaimed the first king of Spain. **¿Te gusta dar caminatas? ¿Son bonitos los Picos de Europa? ¿Dónde están?**

¡Una rutina diferente!

Look at these photographs to acquaint yourself with the theme of this chapter. What activities are part of your daily routine? What activities do you enjoy doing occasionally? What do you think **una rutina diferente** refers to? In this chapter you will learn to talk about daily activities, but you will also see that many fun opportunities in Spain and Latin America await anyone with a spirit of adventure.

México

La muchacha mexicana se cepilla. Tiene el pelo largo, ¿no?

México

Mochileros en Oaxaca, México

Perú

El cartel que vemos aquí se encuentra delante de un albergue juvenil en Barranco, un barrio de Lima, Perú.

España

Aquí tenemos una vista de los Picos de Europa en Asturias en el norte de España. Es una región muy bonita y mucha gente da paseos o caminatas por la región.

Go Online!

connectED.mcgraw-hill.com

Argentina

Una mochila puede llevar muchas cosas—aun un saco de dormir o, como indica el cartel en una tienda de camping en Buenos Aires, una bolsa de dormir.

Chile

La muchacha tiene su saco de dormir y su carpa en un camping en una reserva natural en Chile.

Chile

El camping es bastante popular en muchas partes de Latinoamérica. Aquí vemos un campamento con muchas carpas o tiendas de campaña y caravanas en una playa de Arica, Chile.

Introducción al tema

Argentina, Chile *(top)* Have students describe in their own words all that they see in the top two photographs.

Chile *(left)* Arica is a city of some 160,000 inhabitants. Once upon a time it was a part of Peru. Arica, on the Pacific coast near the Atacama Desert, has an agreeable, dry, warm climate. Since Bolivia is landlocked, Arica has often served as the port for Bolivia. It is possible to use its beaches year-around.

¿Es popular el camping en Arica?
¿Qué hay en el campamento?
¿Qué tiempo hace en Arica?
¿Dónde está Arica?

Online Resources

Customizable Lesson Plans

Whiteboard Lesson

Audio Activities

Student Workbook

Enrichment

Quizzes

Quick Start

Use QS 2.1 or write the following on the board.

Indicate whether you perform these activities **por la mañana, por la tarde**, and/or **por la noche.**

1. **tomar el desayuno**
2. **cenar con la familia**
3. **llegar a la escuela**
4. **salir de la escuela**
5. **escuchar música**
6. **navegar el Internet**
7. **dormir en la cama**
8. **asistir a tus clases**

TEACH

Core Instruction

Step 1 Using Vocabulary V2.2–V2.3, point to the parts of the body and have students repeat the words after you or the audio recording. Then point to these body parts on your own body and ask **¿Qué es?**

Step 2 Point to each illustration and have students repeat each word or expression.

Step 3 Ask questions using the new verbs. **¿Se despierta el muchacho? ¿Toma una ducha? ¿Se lava la cara la muchacha? ¿Se lava la cara en el cuarto de baño? ¿Qué se lava? ¿Dónde se lava?**

Step 4 Have students repeat the words and sentences on the vocabulary pages.

El cuerpo humano

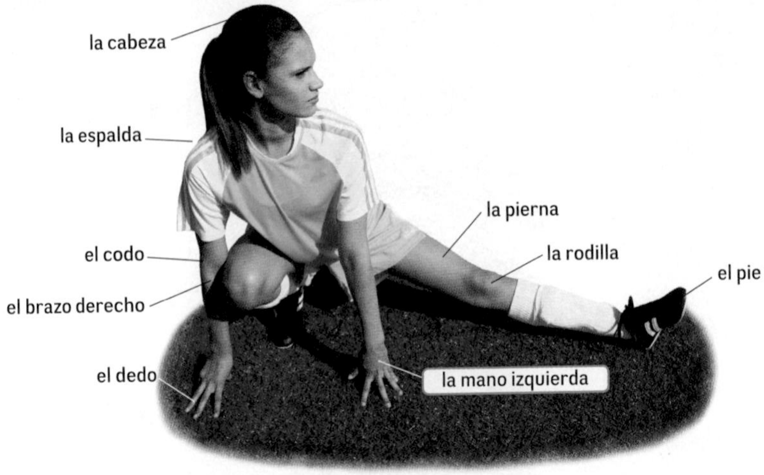

Para mantenerse en forma, Cristina se estira.

La rutina diaria

despertarse

tomar una ducha

lavarse la cara

lavarse el pelo

cepillarse (lavarse) los dientes

peinarse

mirarse

sentarse

Total Physical Response (TPR)

Students can perform this TPR activity in small groups.

Have them act out what Pablo and then Anita are doing.

Pablo se despierta.
No se queda en cama. Se levanta.
Va al cuarto de baño.
Se lava la cara.
Se cepilla los dientes.
Se peina.
Se mira en el espejo cuando se peina.
Baja a la cocina.
Se sienta en la cocina.
Toma el desayuno.

(continued on next page)

Go Online!

connectED.mcgraw-hill.com

¡Hola!
Me llamo Roberto.
¿Y tú? ¿Cómo te llamas?

El muchacho se llama Roberto.

Ana se levanta temprano.
No se queda en la cama.
Se levanta enseguida. Ella es madrugadora.
Le gusta levantarse temprano.

Roberto se acuesta tarde.
Se acuesta a las once y media de la noche.
Él se duerme enseguida.
Él duerme ocho horas.

Elena tiene frío.
Se pone un suéter.

Elena tiene calor.
Se quita el suéter.

Tips for Success

It is recommended that you not contrast **tiene frío (calor)** with **hace** or **está.** When these expressions are grouped together, students tend to become more confused as to which verb to use than when the contrast is not made.

Heritage Speakers

Ask heritage speakers to describe daily routines in their families. Encourage them to expand upon the words taught here and to use gestures to help the others understand.

Additional Vocabulary

You may want to also teach the following words:

maquillarse	*to put on makeup*
el maquillaje	*makeup*
bañarse	*to take a bath*
ducharse	*to take a shower*
afeitarse	*to shave*
la navaja	*razor, shaver*
ponerse la ropa	*to get dressed*

Differentiation

Multiple Intelligences

- Students can have fun dramatizing the verbs on these pages, but it will be especially useful to **bodily-kinesthetic** learners. Other students will say what they're doing, using the infinitive form.
- Motivate **visual-spatial, bodily-kinesthetic,** and **interpersonal** learners by dividing the class into two teams and having them participate in a game of quick sketch drawing.

Total Physical Response (TPR)

(continued from previous page)
Anita toma el desayuno.
Termina el desayuno y se levanta de la mesa.
Sale para la escuela.
Ella tiene frío.
Se pone un suéter.
Ahora tiene calor y se quita el suéter.
Anita vuelve a casa.
Hace sus tareas en la computadora.
Luego se acuesta.
Se duerme enseguida.

Leveling EACH Activity

Easy Activities 1, 5
Average Activities 2, 3, 4, 6

PRACTICE

Activity 1

Audio Script

1. El muchacho se peina.
2. El muchacho se cepilla los dientes.
3. El muchacho se acuesta.
4. El muchacho se despierta.
5. El muchacho se lava el pelo.
6. El muchacho se sienta.

Activity 2 You can also do this activity as a paired activity. One student asks a question and the other one answers it. They should take turns asking and answering.

Go Online!

You may wish to remind students to go online for additional vocabulary practice. They can also download audio files of all vocabulary.

You may wish to use the whiteboard presentation for additional vocabulary instruction and practice.

ESCUCHAR

1 Escucha las frases. Parea cada frase con el dibujo que describe.

a.

b.

c.

d.

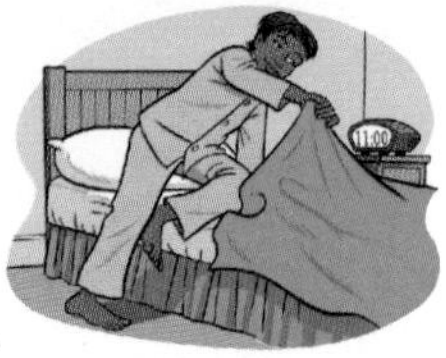
e.

f.

HABLAR • ESCRIBIR

2 Contesta.

1. Cuando Marisol se despierta, ¿se levanta enseguida?
2. Cuando Carlos se despierta, ¿se queda en la cama?
3. Cuando Vicente se peina, ¿se mira en el espejo?
4. Cuando Juanita se lava el pelo, ¿usa agua caliente?
5. Cuando Tomás toma el desayuno, ¿se sienta a la mesa?
6. Cuando Julia se acuesta, ¿se duerme enseguida?
7. ¿Cuándo se levanta un madrugador? ¿Temprano por la mañana o tarde?
8. Cuando Ricardo se levanta, ¿se estira?

3 **Rompecabezas**

Cambia una letra en cada palabra para formar una palabra nueva.

1. como
2. dolor
3. cada
4. coche
5. tocar
6. peso
7. gano
8. hola

Answers

1

1. f
2. c
3. e
4. d
5. a
6. b

2

1. Sí (No), cuando Marisol se despierta, (no) se levanta enseguida.
2. Sí (No), cuando Carlos se despierta, (no) se queda en la cama.
3. Sí (No), cuando Vicente se peina, (no) se mira en el espejo.
4. Sí (No), cuando Juanita se lava el pelo, (no) usa agua caliente.
5. Sí (No), cuando Tomás toma el desayuno, (no) se sienta a la mesa.
6. Sí (No), cuando Julia se acuesta, (no) se duerme enseguida.
7. Un madrugador se levanta temprano por la mañana.
8. Sí (No), cuando Ricardo se levanta, (no) se estira.

3 *Answers will vary but may include:*

1. codo (come, comí)
2. doler
3. cama (cara, casa, nada)
4. noche
5. tomar (tocan, tocas)
6. pero (pelo)
7. gana (gané, ganó)
8. hora (cola)

Go Online!

connectED.mcgraw-hill.com

Vocabulario 1

LEER

4 Parea para hacer una frase larga.

1. Él se pone un suéter	a. porque va a comer.
2. Ella se lava las manos	b. porque se peina.
3. Ella se cepilla los dientes	c. porque tiene calor.
4. Él se mira en el espejo	d. porque acaba de comer.
5. Ella se quita el suéter	e. porque tiene frío.

InfoGap For more practice using your new vocabulary, do Activity 2 in the Student Resource section at the end of this book.

HABLAR • ESCRIBIR

5 **Juego** ¡Corrige todas las frases absurdas!

1. Cada pierna tiene una mano y la mano tiene un dedo.
2. El codo está en la pierna y la rodilla está en el brazo.
3. La cara está en la espalda.
4. Los dientes están en el pelo.
5. La boca y los ojos están en la rodilla.

6 **Comunicación**

Pick someone in your family and describe his or her weekday routine to the class.

LEER

7 **Juego** Race with a partner to see who can be the first to put José's activities in the correct order.

José se levanta.
José se duerme enseguida.
José se lava la cara y los dientes en el cuarto de baño.
José va al comedor y toma el desayuno.
José se despierta.
José se acuesta.
José se quita la ropa.

La muchacha se mira en el espejo para ver si el pantalón le queda bien.

Activity 5 Expansion: Students may want to make up more silly sentences for their classmates to correct.

InfoGap This *InfoGap* activity will allow students to practice in pairs. This will help interpersonal learners, who learn well through interaction and collaboration. The activity should be very manageable since all vocabulary and grammar are familiar to students.

ASSESS

Students are now ready to take Quiz 1.

Answers

4
1. e
2. a
3. d
4. b
5. c

5
1. Cada brazo tiene una mano y la mano tiene dedos.
2. El codo está en el brazo y la rodilla está en la pierna.
3. La cara está en la cabeza.
4. Los dientes están en la boca.
5. La boca y los ojos están en la cara.

6 *Answers will vary, but students should use as many verbs as possible from* Vocabulario 1.

7 *Answers will vary but may include:*
José se quita la ropa.
José se acuesta.
José se duerme enseguida.
José se despierta.
José se levanta.
José se lava la cara y los dientes en el cuarto de baño.
José va al comedor y toma el desayuno.

Online Resources

- Customizable Lesson Plans
- Whiteboard Lesson
- Audio Activities
- Video (Vocabulario) (Diálogo) (Cultura)
- Student Workbook
- Enrichment
- Quizzes

Quick Start

Use QS 2.2 or write the following on the board.

Change the subject in the following sentences to **ellos.**

1. **Mi amiga y yo vamos de compras.**
2. **Doy el suéter a mi madre.**
3. **El mesero nos habla.**
4. **Yo estoy comiendo una merienda.**

TEACH

Core Instruction

Step 1 Present the vocabulary using Vocabulary V2.4–V2.5. Have students repeat after you or the audio recording.

Step 2 As you present the vocabulary, you may wish to ask the following types of questions: **¿Los amigos van de camping? ¿Se divierten mucho? ¿Los jóvenes arman una carpa o un saco de dormir? ¿Qué arman los jóvenes? ¿Llevan el champú en su mochila? ¿Qué llevan en su mochila? ¿Por dónde dan una caminata los amigos?**

Step 3 After you have presented all the vocabulary, have students read the words and sentences for additional reinforcement.

El camping

Los amigos van de camping.
Lo están pasando bien. Se divierten mucho.
Los jóvenes arman (montan) una carpa.

Para conversar

¡Ya voy!
Alex, favor de venir acá. Favor de ayudarme con la carpa.

¿Qué llevan en su mochila?

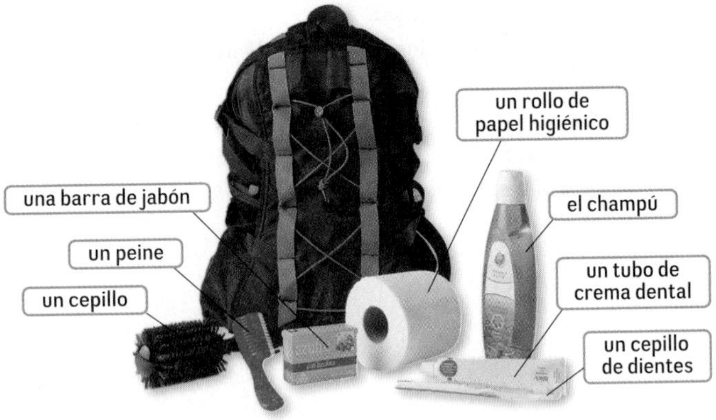

En otras partes

- In addition to **una barra** you will also hear **una pastilla.** You will also hear **pasta dentífrica** as well as **crema dental.**
- Una **tienda de campaña** is more common in Spain, **una carpa** in Latin America.

Differentiation

Reaching All Learners

To practice these new words as well as to review some previously learned ones, bring in a book bag full of toiletries learned in this chapter. Add a few additional items such as school materials and articles of clothing until it is stuffed full. Have the students assemble in a circle and pass the book bag around while listening to Hispanic music. When the music stops, the student holding the bag must open it, take out an object, and identify it. Continue in this manner until the book bag is empty.

Go Online!

connectED.mcgraw-hill.com

Los mochileros dan una caminata.
Dan una caminata por un parque nacional.

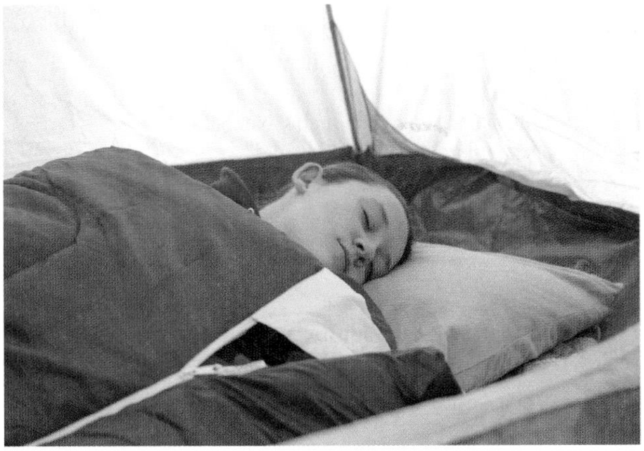

Andrea se acuesta en la carpa.
Duerme en un saco de dormir.

¡Así se dice!

Note that when someone calls and you want to respond *I'm coming* you say: **¡Ya voy!**

Differentiation

Multiple Intelligences

All students, particularly **auditory-musical** learners, will enjoy playing this memory game. Each student adds on to what the previous student says. For example:

(Student 1) **Me levanto.**
(Student 2) **Me levanto y me cepillo los dientes.**
(Student 3) **Me levanto, me cepillo los dientes y me lavo la cara.**

Continue in this manner. The same can be done with items in a backpack.

(Student 1) **Tengo un peine.**
(Student 2) **Tengo un peine y un tubo de crema dental.**

Heritage Speakers

Read **En otras partes** on the previous page and ask heritage speakers in the class to tell the others what words they use for these items and if they can think of other words and expressions related to daily routine and camping that can differ.

Go Online!

Vocabulario en vivo Join Nora as she does something special to give a new twist to her daily routine.

Diálogo en vivo In this episode, students will join Alejandra and Claudia on a hike. Ask students to write down the cognates that they hear.

You may wish to use the whiteboard presentation for additional vocabulary instruction and practice.

Total Physical Response (TPR)

(Student 1), **ven acá.**
Imagínate que estás de camping.
Favor de armar la carpa.
Favor de desenrollar el saco de dormir.
Puedes poner el saco de dormir en la carpa.
(Student 2), **ven acá.**
Te voy a dar el nombre de un artículo.
Dramatiza lo que haces con el artículo.
un peine
el agua
un cepillo (para el pelo)
un cepillo de dientes
una barra de jabón
el champú
un tubo de crema dental

Leveling EACH Activity

Easy Activities 1, 3, 7
Average Activities 2, 4, 5
CHallenging Activity 2
Expansión, Activity 6

PRACTICE

¡Así se dice!

Why It Works!

Students have to practice new words in order to be able to retain them. As in all chapters of **¡Así se dice!**, we present six or more activities for each **Vocabulario** section.

Activity 1

Audio Script

1. Se levanta por la noche y se acuesta por la mañana.
2. Se lava con crema dental.
3. Se lava con jabón y agua.
4. Dormimos en un saco de dormir o en una cama.
5. Se lava el pelo con champú.
6. Se peina con champú.
7. No lo pasan bien. Se divierten mucho.

Go Online!

You may wish to remind students to go online for additional vocabulary practice. They can also download audio files of all vocabulary.

CULTURA

Los amigos están de camping en Chile durante el mes de abril. En Chile es el otoño.

ESCUCHAR

1 Escucha las frases. Indica en una tabla como la de abajo si cada frase es correcta o no.

sí	no

HABLAR • ESCRIBIR

2 Contesta sobre un grupo de amigos que van de camping.

1. ¿Van de camping los amigos?
2. ¿Se divierten en el camping?
3. ¿Qué montan (arman)?
4. ¿En qué duermen?
5. ¿Dónde ponen sus sacos de dormir?
6. ¿Quiere José ayuda para montar la carpa?
7. ¿A ti te gusta el camping?

EXPANSIÓN

Sin mirar las preguntas, da toda la información que recuerdas en tus propias palabras. Si no recuerdas algo, un(a) compañero(a) te puede ayudar.

LEER • HABLAR • ESCRIBIR

3 Completa con una palabra apropiada.

1. María va a cepillarse los dientes. Necesita ____ y ____.
2. Tomás va a tomar una ducha. Necesita ____.
3. Carlos quiere peinarse. Necesita ____.
4. Julia quiere lavarse el pelo. Necesita ____.
5. Claudia va a cepillarse el pelo. Necesita ____.

LEER

4 Parea las palabras que significan lo mismo.

1. la carpa	**a.** los mochileros
2. armar	**b.** se divierte
3. los que llevan una mochila	**c.** la tienda de campaña
4. lo pasa bien	**d.** montar
5. el paseo largo	**e.** la caminata

Answers

1
1. no
2. no
3. sí
4. sí
5. sí
6. no
7. no

2
1. Sí, los amigos van de camping.
2. Sí, (No, no) se divierten en el camping.
3. Montan (Arman) una carpa (una tienda de campaña).
4. Duermen en sacos de dormir.
5. Ponen sus sacos de dormir en la carpa (la tienda de campaña).
6. Sí (No), José (no) quiere ayuda para montar la carpa.
7. Sí (No), a mí (no) me gusta el camping.

3
1. (un tubo de) crema dental, un cepillo de dientes
2. una barra de jabón
3. un peine
4. champú
5. un cepillo

4
1. c
2. d
3. a
4. b
5. e

Go Online!

connectED.mcgraw-hill.com

Comunicación

5 Vas a ir de camping este fin de semana con unos(as) amigos(as). Investiga unos campings que quieres visitar. Luego les debes escribir un e-mail a tus amigos(as) con una descripción de tu lugar preferido y una lista completa de todas las cosas necesarias para tu aventura.

6 Estás en una farmacia. Quieres comprar los siguientes objetos. Conversa con el/la empleado(a).

ESCRIBIR

7 **Rompecabezas**

Join two puzzle pieces to form a word. When you have finished, you should have nine words. Do not use any piece more than once.

CULTURA

El mochilero está esperando un autobús en una parada de buses en Valencia, España.

Comunicación

Interpersonal, Presentational
In Activity 6, have students take turns role-playing each part and ask for volunteers to present their conversations to the class. You may also want to play the role of the clerk to encourage further conversation.

Go Online!

You may wish to use the whiteboard presentation for additional vocabulary instruction and practice.

Cultura en vivo In this video segment, students will learn how **madrileños** relax after a busy week in the city by visiting **el Parque del Retiro** in Madrid. Ask students to research their own city's parks activities and compare and contrast with **el Retiro** in Madrid. Students also may wish to discuss how they spend a typical weekend.

ASSESS

Students are now ready to take Quiz 2.

Answers

5 *Answers will vary.*

6 *Answers will vary, but students should begin their conversation with the customary greetings, followed by* Necesito (Quiero) comprar...

7 espejo, caminata, cepillo, carpa, champú, rodilla, jabón, derecho, dientes

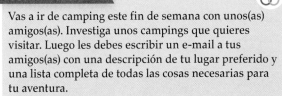

Gramática

Verbos reflexivos

1. Read the following sentences as you look at the illustrations.

Federico lava el carro.
Federico lo lava.

Federico se lava.

Julia cepilla al perro.
Julia lo cepilla.

Julia se cepilla.

Pedro mira a su amigo.
Pedro lo mira.

Pedro se mira en el espejo.

In the sentences to the left, one person performs the action and another person or thing receives the action. In the sentences to the right, the same person performs and receives the action of the verb. For this reason the pronoun **se** must be used. **Se** is called a reflexive pronoun because it refers back to the subject—**Federico, Julia, Pedro.**

Conexiones

El inglés

The reflexive construction exists in English too, but it is used in fewer situations than in Spanish. Here are a few examples of the reflexive in English.

I saw myself in the mirror.
The baby fed herself.
They enjoyed themselves.

Online Resources

Customizable Lesson Plans
- Whiteboard Lesson
- Audio Activities
- Student Workbook
- Enrichment
- Quizzes

Quick Start

Use QS 2.3 or write the following on the board.
Write a list in Spanish of the parts of the body you remember.

TEACH

Core Instruction

Step 1 Have students look at the illustrations.

Step 2 Ask students in which illustrations someone is doing something to himself/herself and in which illustrations the person is doing something to someone/something else.

Step 3 Ask what additional word is used when the person is doing something to himself/herself **(se).**

Step 4 Explain to them that **se** is a reflexive pronoun and refers to the subject.

Step 5 Read the Item 1 explanation on the bottom of the page.

Step 6 Call on students to read the model sentences for each illustration or have the class read them in unison.

Step 7 Read the verb paradigms in Item 2 on the next page and have the class repeat after you. Then write the verbs **lavarse** and **levantarse** on the board. After you say **me lavo,** have students supply **me levanto.** Do the same with each subject.

Step 8 Explain Items 3, 4, and 5 and have the class read the model sentences aloud.

Step 9 You may wish to give additional examples of verbs that can be both reflexive and nonreflexive.

Me pongo un suéter.	**Pongo un suéter en la maleta.**
Él se acuesta.	**Él acuesta al bebé.**
Nos peinamos.	**Peinamos al gato.**

2. Study the forms of a reflexive verb. Pay particular attention to the pronoun that goes with each form of the verb. It is called a "reflexive pronoun."

lavarse			
yo	me lavo	nosotros(as)	nos lavamos
tú	te lavas	*vosotros(as)*	*os laváis*
Ud., él, ella	se lava	Uds., ellos, ellas	se lavan

levantarse			
yo	me levanto	nosotros(as)	nos levantamos
tú	te levantas	*vosotros(as)*	*os levantáis*
Ud., él, ella	se levanta	Uds., ellos, ellas	se levantan

3. In the negative form, **no** is placed before the reflexive pronoun.

¿No te lavas las manos?
La familia Martínez no se levanta tarde.

4. In Spanish, when you refer to parts of the body and articles of clothing in a reflexive sentence, you often use the definite article, not the possessive adjective.

Me lavo la cara.
Ella se cepilla los dientes.
Él se pone el suéter.

5. Note that the reflexive pronoun is added to the infinitive.

El niño quiere acostarse.
Voy a lavarme las manos.
¿Quieres quitarte la chaqueta?

Andrew Payti

CULTURA
Aquí vemos la entrada al parque de atracciones La Feria en el Bosque de Chapultepec en la Ciudad de México. La gente va a divertirse mucho.

One person performs the action & another person or thing receives the action

Same person performs & receives the action
Refer to do must agree with subject

Gramática

Differentiation

Multiple Intelligences

- Engage **bodily-kinesthetic** learners by having them act out different examples of verbs that can be both reflexive and nonreflexive. The other students will say what they are doing.
- Engage **logical-mathematical** learners by having them work in pairs and compare their daily routines in a Venn diagram. Each circle will have the student's name, and where the circles overlap, it will say **Los/Las** ... them to use the ... m in the overlap-

... Success

... except for **se**, the ... ouns are the same ... and direct object ... **te, nos**). Also point ... sed with both sin- ... l subjects.

You may wish to remind students to go online for additional grammar review and practice.

You may wish to use the whiteboard presentation for additional grammar instruction and practice.

Leveling EACH Activity

Easy Activities 1, 2
Average Activities 3, 4, 7
CHallenging Activities 5, 6

PRACTICE

Tips for Success

Show students examples of using reflexive verbs in the past tense by telling them what you did yesterday. Point out that there is nothing new for them to learn here.

Conexiones

Expansion Using the vocabulary they have accumulated, have students brainstorm other measures that can be taken to **mantenerse en buena salud.** Remind them that mental health is just as important as physical health. When they are done, have them point out which verbs are reflexive and which are nonreflexive.

Activity 2 Have partners present these conversations to the class.

Teaching Options

You may wish to have students add more conversation topics to Activity 3, as well as expand on the conversations.

Práctica

Conexiones

La salud
Aquí tienes unas sugerencias importantes para mantenerte en buena salud. Debes
- dormir entre siete y ocho horas cada noche
- tomar un buen desayuno
- lavarte las manos antes de comer
- cepillarte los dientes después de comer

Con un(a) compañero(a), habla de lo que puedes hacer para incorporar estas sugerencias en tu rutina diaria.

ESCUCHAR • HABLAR • ESCRIBIR

1 Contesta.

1. ¿Se levanta tarde o temprano Gregorio?
2. ¿Se lava por la mañana o por la noche?
3. ¿Se lava los dientes antes o después del desayuno?
4. ¿Se pone un suéter cuando hace frío?
5. ¿Se quita el suéter cuando tiene calor?

HABLAR • LEER

2 Completa las conversaciones con un pronombre.

1. ¿A qué hora ____ levantas?
   Soy madrugador(a). ____ levanto temprano, a las seis y media.
2. ¿____ cepillas los dientes con frecuencia?
   Sí, ____ cepillo los dientes unas cuatro veces al día.
3. ¿____ peinas con frecuencia?
   No, no ____ peino con frecuencia.
4. ¿A qué hora ____ despertaste esta mañana?
   ____ desperté a las siete.
5. Y, ¿a qué hora ____ acostaste anoche?
   Anoche ____ acosté a las diez y media.

HABLAR

3 Trabaja con un(a) compañero(a). Preparen una conversación según el modelo.

MODELO  **—¿Te cepillas?**
—Sí, me cepillo.

1. 
2. 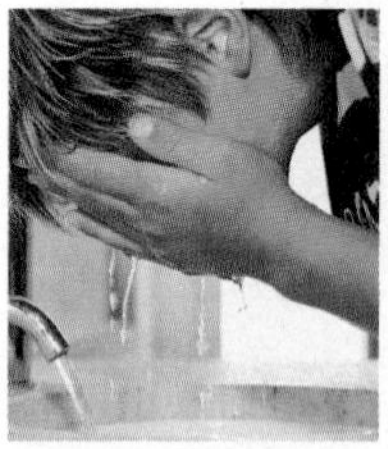
3. 
4. 

(t)Kate Mitchell/Corbis, (bl)Ryan McVay/Getty Images, (bcl)Manchan/Age Fotostock, (bcr)Florian Franke/Purestock/SuperStock, (br)Janis Christie/Getty Images

Answers

1
1. Gregorio se levanta tarde (temprano).
2. Se lava por la mañana (por la noche).
3. Se lava los dientes antes (después) del desayuno.
4. Sí, se pone un suéter cuando hace frío.
5. Sí, se quita el suéter cuando tiene calor.

2
1. te, Me
2. Te, me
3. Te, me
4. te, Me
5. te, me

3
1. —¿Te cepillas los dientes?
   —Sí, me cepillo los dientes.
2. —¿Te lavas la cara?
   —Sí, me lavo la cara.
3. —¿Te lavas el pelo?
   —Sí, me lavo el pelo.
4. —¿Te levantas (estiras)?
   —Sí, me levanto (estiro).

Go Online!

connectED.mcgraw-hill.com

HABLAR • ESCRIBIR

4 Personaliza. Da respuestas personales.

1. ¿Cómo te llamas?
2. Y tu(s) hermano(s), ¿cómo se llama(n)?
3. ¿Cómo se llama tu profesor(a) de español?

CULTURA

Es una clase de español en Santa Fe, Nuevo México. La profesora se llama señora Brown. Parece que los alumnos se divierten mucho en clase, ¿no?

LEER • ESCRIBIR

5 Completa con un pronombre reflexivo y la forma correcta del verbo.

Hola. Yo __1__ llam__2__ Jorge y mi amigo __3__ llam__4__ Felipe. Felipe y yo no __5__ levant__6__ a la misma hora porque él es madrugador y yo no. Él __7__ levant__8__ temprano y yo __9__ levant__10__ tarde. Y tú, ¿__11__ levant__12__ tarde como yo o __13__ levant__14__ temprano como Felipe?

LEER • ESCRIBIR

6 Completa con un pronombre.

1. Quiero levantar___ temprano.
2. Niño, tienes que peinar___.
3. Vamos a lavar___ las manos.
4. ¿No quieres poner___ un suéter? Está haciendo frío.
5. Tienen que cepillar___ los dientes después de cada comida.

HABLAR

7 **Juego** Think of an object from this chapter. Your partner will ask **sí/no** questions which you will answer in complete sentences. If your partner guesses it in five questions or less, he or she wins. If you stump your partner, you win. Then reverse roles.

Gramática

Activity 5 Call on a student to read this activity aloud after completing it.

Teaching Options

Activity 6 is very important as students often want to use **se** whenever they use the infinitive. You may want to give them even more practice by asking the following questions:

¿Te gusta levantarte temprano?
¿Tienes que levantarte en clase cuando hablas?
¿Prefieres acostarte temprano o tarde?
¿Vas a divertirte durante el fin de semana?

You can also ask the same questions with **ustedes.**

Go Online!

You may wish to use the whiteboard presentation for additional grammar instruction and practice.

ASSESS

Students are now ready to take Quiz 3.

Answers

4

1. Me llamo ___.
2. Mi(s) hermano(s) se llama(n) ___.
3. Mi profesor(a) de español se llama ___.

5

1. me
2. -o
3. se
4. -a
5. nos
6. -amos
7. se
8. -a
9. me
10. -o
11. te
12. -as
13. te
14. -as

6

1. -me
2. -te
3. -nos
4. -te
5. -se

7 *Answers will vary.*

Online Resources

Customizable Lesson Plans

Whiteboard Lesson

Audio Activities

Video (Gramática)

Student Workbook

Enrichment

Quizzes

Quick Start

Use QS 2.4 or write the following on the board.

Complete in the present.

1. **Yo ___ la carpa azul. (preferir)**
2. **Ellos ___ ir de camping. (querer)**
3. **Tú ___ jugar con nosotros. (poder)**
4. **Mi primo y yo ___ a comer. (empezar)**
5. **Usted ___ mucho. (dormir)**

¡Así se dice!

Why It Works!

In order not to give students too much to learn at one time, note that the reflexive verbs with a stem change are separated from the regular verbs. Now students are reviewing the pronouns they just learned and the forms of stem-changing verbs, which they learned in Level 1, Chapter 5.

TEACH

Core Instruction

There is actually no new concept here since students are already familiar with the stem-changing verbs and the reflexive pronouns.

Step 1 Model the forms in the verb charts. Have students repeat after you.

Verbos reflexivos de cambio radical

1. The reflexive verbs **acostarse (o → ue), dormirse (o → ue), sentarse (e → ie), despertarse (e → ie),** and **divertirse (e → ie)** are stem-changing verbs.

acostarse			
yo	me acuesto	nosotros(as)	nos acostamos
tú	te acuestas	*vosotros(as)*	*os acostáis*
Ud., él, ella	se acuesta	Uds., ellos, ellas	se acuestan

divertirse			
yo	me divierto	nosotros(as)	nos divertimos
tú	te diviertes	*vosotros(as)*	*os divertís*
Ud., él, ella	se divierte	Uds., ellos, ellas	se divierten

2. Many verbs in Spanish can be used with a reflexive pronoun. Often the reflexive pronoun gives a different meaning to the verb. Study the following examples.

Ana pone su blusa en su mochila.	*Ana puts her blouse in her backpack.*
Ana se pone la blusa.	*Ana puts on her blouse.*
Ana duerme ocho horas.	*Ana sleeps eight hours.*
Ana se duerme enseguida.	*Ana falls asleep immediately.*
Ana llama a Carlos.	*Ana calls Carlos.*
Ella se llama Ana.	*She calls herself Ana. (Her name is Ana.)*
Ana divierte a sus amigos.	*Ana amuses her friends.*
Ana se divierte.	*Ana amuses herself. (Ana has a good time.)*

CULTURA

La joven ciclista se divierte en el Parque de la Ciudadela en Barcelona.

Ask students what other stem-changing verbs they learned in this chapter's vocabulary **(dormirse o→ue, sentarse e→ie, despertarse e→ie).**

Step 2 Go over the examples in Item 2.

Go Online!

Gramática en vivo *Reflexive verbs* Enliven learning with the animated world of Professor Cruz! **Gramática en vivo** is a fun and effective tool for additional instruction and/or review.

Práctica

Go Online!

connectED.mcgraw-hill.com

ESCUCHAR • HABLAR • ESCRIBIR

8 Personaliza. Da respuestas personales.

1. ¿Duermes en una cama o en un saco de dormir?
2. Cuando te acuestas, ¿te duermes enseguida?
3. Por la mañana, ¿te quedas en la cama cuando te despiertas?
4. A veces, ¿despiertas a tus hermanos?
5. ¿Ellos se enfadan cuando los despiertas?
6. ¿Te sientas a la mesa para tomar el desayuno?
7. ¿Te diviertes en la escuela?
8. ¿Diviertes a tus amigos?

LEER • ESCRIBIR

9 Completa sobre un día que María pasa en la playa.

1. María _____ su traje de baño en su mochila. Cuando llega a la playa ella _____ el traje de baño.
2. En la playa María ve a un amigo. Su amigo _____ Luis. Ella _____ a su amigo.
3. María y sus amigos lo pasan muy bien en la playa. Ellos _____ mucho y como María es muy cómica ella también _____ mucho a sus amigos.
4. Después de pasar el día en la playa, María está muy cansada. Cuando ella se acuesta, _____ enseguida y _____ más de ocho horas.

LEER • ESCRIBIR

10 Completa.

Cuando yo __1__ (acostarse), yo __2__ (dormirse) enseguida. Cada noche yo __3__ (dormir) ocho horas. Yo __4__ (acostarse) a las once y __5__ (levantarse) a las siete de la mañana. Cuando yo __6__ (despertarse), __7__ (levantarse) enseguida. Pero cuando mi hermana __8__ (despertarse), ella no __9__ (levantarse) enseguida. Y mi hermano, cuando él __10__ (acostarse), no __11__ (dormirse) enseguida. Él pasa horas escuchando música en la cama. Así él __12__ (dormir) solamente unas seis horas.

11 *Comunicación*

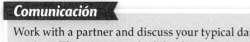

Work with a partner and discuss your typical daily routines. Then create a schedule of your activities for the coming week that includes at least three workouts. Share your results with your classmates.

CULTURA

La playa de Nerja en el sur de España

Andrew Payti

Leveling EACH Activity

Easy Activity 8
Average Activities 9, 11
CHallenging Activity 10

PRACTICE

Activity 8 It is suggested that you go over this activity first orally in class. This can also be done as a paired activity.

Activity 9 You may want to go over this activity orally and then assign it for homework.

Activity 10 This activity should be completed individually and then gone over in class.

Cultural Snapshot

Nerja is about 32 miles east of Malaga in an area overlooking giant cliffs that descend to the sea. In addition to being a beach resort, Nerja is known for its **cuevas de Nerja,** huge caves with Paleolithic paintings and massive stalactite and stalagmite formations. The caves were unknown in modern times until a group of boys discovered them by accident in 1959. Now they serve as a major tourist attraction and there is even a stage that was built inside where cultural performances and music concerts are often held.

ASSESS

Students are now ready to take Quiz 4.

Answers

8

1. Duermo en una cama (un saco de dormir).
2. Cuando me acuesto, (no) me duermo enseguida.
3. Sí, (No,) por la mañana, (no) me quedo en la cama cuando me despierto.
4. Sí, a veces, despierto a mis hermanos. (No, no despierto a mis hermanos.)
5. Sí, (No), ellos (no) se enfadan cuando los despierto.
6. Sí, (No, no) me siento a la mesa para tomar el desayuno.
7. Sí, (No, no) me divierto en la escuela.
8. Sí, (No, no) divierto a mis amigos.

9

1. pone, se pone
2. se llama, llama
3. se divierten, divierte
4. se duerme, duerme

10

1. me acuesto
2. me duermo
3. duermo
4. me acuesto
5. me levanto
6. me despierto
7. me levanto
8. se despierta
9. se levanta
10. se acuesta
11. se duerme
12. duerme

11 *Answers will vary.*

Online Resources

Customizable Lesson Plans
Whiteboard Lesson
Audio Activities
Student Workbook
Enrichment
Quizzes

Quick Start

Use QS 2.5 or write the following on the board.

Complete.

1. **Yo ___ salir ahora. (tener que)**
2. **Nosotros ___ esperar. (ir a)**
3. **Mis amigos ___ llegar. (acabar de)**
4. **Yo ___ ir ahora. (querer)**
5. **Ellos ___ desembarcar ahora. (empezar a)**
6. **Yo ___ hablar con ellos. (deber)**

TEACH

Core Instruction

Read Items 1 and 2 to the class. Have students repeat the model sentences after you.

Tips for Success

Favor de is a very simple way to avoid having to confront the **tú/usted** problem and the complicated command forms. Students hear you use commands, so they are familiar with them in the receptive mode. They do not yet have to use them actively.

Differentiation

Multiple Intelligences

Interpersonal learners will enjoy working in pairs or small groups. Have them practice various commands by politely ordering each other to do this or that. Encourage them to be creative and to try to use vocabulary from different chapters.

FOLDABLES Study Organizer

MINIATURE MATCHBOOK
See the Foldables section of the Student Handbook at the beginning of this book for help with making this foldable. With a partner discuss your daily routines using reflexive verbs. On the front of each matchbook draw something you do every day. On the inside your partner will write a sentence about the picture using the appropriate reflexive verb.

Mandatos con favor de

1. The expression **favor de** followed by the infinitive is a very useful way to give a command to tell someone what to do. It is very polite and you can use **favor de** with a friend, an adult, or any group of people.

   Favor de venir aquí (acá).
   Favor de no hablar.
   Favor de volver pronto.

2. Whenever a pronoun is used with the infinitive, the pronoun is attached to it.

   Favor de ayudarme.
   Favor de traerme el menú.
   Favor de darme el libro.
   Favor de levantarte. *(to a friend)*
   Favor de levantarse. *(to an adult or group of friends)*

Práctica

LEER • HABLAR

12 Escoge.

un amigo — un adulto o un grupo de personas

1. Favor de sentarte.
2. Favor de sentarse aquí.
3. Favor de quitarte las botas.
4. Favor de ponerte los zapatos.
5. Favor de quedarse aquí.
6. Favor de lavarte.
7. Favor de levantarse.

EXPANSIÓN
Ahora, usando la expresión «favor de», puedes decirle a un(a) compañero(a) de clase lo que él o ella debe hacer. Tu compañero(a) tiene que seguir tus mandatos. Luego, cambien de rol.

13 **Comunicación**

You and a friend are planning to do something, for example, take a trip. You need to get ready. Make a diagram similar to the one below and tell your partner what to do to help. Take turns.

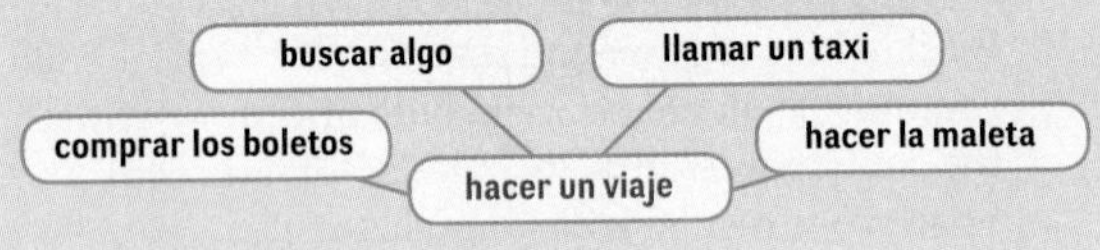

Kerri Galloway

Go Online!

You may wish to use the whiteboard presentation for additional grammar instruction and practice.

ASSESS

Students are now ready to take Quiz 5.

Answers

12
1. un amigo
2. un adulto o un grupo de personas
3. un amigo
4. un amigo
5. un adulto o un grupo de personas
6. un amigo
7. un adulto o un grupo de personas

PRONUNCIACIÓN

La h, la y y la ll

H in Spanish is silent. It is never pronounced. Repeat the following.

hijo	**helado**	**higiénico**	**hola**
hace	**hermano**	**huevos**	**hispano**

Y in Spanish can be either a vowel or a consonant. As a vowel, it is pronounced exactly the same as the vowel **i.** Repeat the following.

el hijo y el hermano
el hotel y el hospital

Y is a consonant when it begins a word or a syllable. As a consonant, **y** is pronounced similarly to the *y* in the English word *yo-yo.* This sound has several variations throughout the Spanish-speaking world. Repeat the following.

ya	**desayuno**	**ayuda**	**playa**
yo	**oye**	**leyó**	

Ll is pronounced as a single consonant in Spanish. In many areas of the Spanish-speaking world, it is pronounced the same as the **y.** It too has several variations. Repeat the following.

llama	**botella**	**taquilla**	**toalla**	**lleva**
llega	**pastilla**	**llueve**	**rollo**	**cepillo**

Dictado

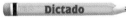

Pronounce the following sentences carefully. Then write them to prepare for a dictation.

La hermana habla hoy con su hermano en el hotel.
Está lloviendo cuando ella llega a la calle Hidalgo.
El hombre lleva una botella de agua a la playa bella.
Él no lo oyó; lo leyó.

Go Online!

connectED.mcgraw-hill.com

Refrán

Can you guess what the following proverb means?

Quien mucho duerme, poco aprende.

¡Bravo!

You have now learned all the vocabulary and grammar in this chapter. Continue to use and practice all that you know while learning more cultural information. **¡Vamos!**

¡Bravo! The remaining pages of the chapter recycle information in a variety of ways, allowing students to build upon their newly acquired language skills as well as to keep track of their own progress. This format also ensures that students are not surprised by vocabulary or grammar that has not yet been introduced or studied.

Teaching Options

To make the dictation more challenging, add sentences that students have not seen:

Los hijos hispanos llegaron a la playa y comieron helado.
Hace mal tiempo y llueve.
Me llamo Luisa y soy honesta.
La mochila está llena.

Gramática

PRONUNCIACIÓN

In all areas of the Spanish-speaking world the **h** is silent. The **ll** and **y** have several variations. In most areas they are pronounced like the *y* in the English word *yo-yo.* In Argentina and Uruguay they are pronounced like the *j* in *Joe.* In Spain you will also hear a *j* sound, similar to the *y* sound Americans make when they pronounce quickly *Did ya…*

Tell students that it is not unusual for Spanish speakers to misspell words with **y** and **ll.** Since the two letters sound the same, they often mix them up. They will also omit the **h** in words that should have it.

Pronunciation Guidelines

Teachers' opinions vary concerning insistence upon correct pronunciation. You may wish to consider the following guidelines concerning three levels of pronunciation.

1. Near-native pronunciation Some students will achieve a near-native pronunciation. This is to be strived for, but it is an unrealistic goal for many students who do not begin their study of Spanish until middle or high school.

2. Accented Many students will speak with an American accent. As long as their accent does not interfere with communication, it should be accepted as they work toward improving.

3. Very accented Some students mispronounce to such an extent that their accent interferes with their ability to be understood. Such pronunciation, of course, cannot be accepted.

Online Resources

Customizable Lesson Plans
Audio Activities
Student Workbook
Review

Quick Start

Use QS 2.6 or write the following on the board.
List five things that you need to bring when you go camping.
Cuando voy de camping, necesito traer...

TEACH

Core Instruction

Step 1 Tell students that they are going to hear a conversation between two friends who have different opinions about camping.

Step 2 Have students follow along as you read the conversation or play the audio recording.

Step 3 Have pairs of students practice reading the conversation aloud. Ask for pairs to volunteer to read the conversation for the class. Remind them to use good expression and gestures to make the conversation more understandable and fun to listen to.

Step 4 Go over the **¿Comprendes?** activities together in class or assign them as homework.

Differentiation

Multiple Intelligences

Have **bodily-kinesthetic** learners stand up and dramatize the conversation for the class.

De camping

Rafael	A ti te gusta mucho el camping, ¿no?
Pablo	A mí, sí.
Rafael	La verdad es que no me interesa mucho. ¿Dónde duermes? ¿Te acuestas al aire libre?
Pablo	No. Siempre voy con uno o dos amigos y montamos una carpa. Y dormimos en un saco de dormir.
Rafael	¿Qué hacen para comer?
Pablo	Muy fácil. Preparamos hamburguesas y salchichas en una barbacoa.
Rafael	Hay muchos insectos, ¿no?
Pablo	Pues, hay. Pero, ¡qué va! No nos molestan.
Rafael	¿Cómo pasan el día entero? ¿No se aburren?
Pablo	Al contrario, damos caminatas y nadamos en el lago. Nos acostamos temprano porque nos levantamos temprano también.
Rafael	Me parece que tienen que levantarse cuando se levanta el sol.
Pablo	Sí, pero no me molesta porque soy madrugador. Pero hay una cosa que no me gusta.
Rafael	¿Verdad? ¿Qué?
Pablo	Lavarme en agua fría.

Fuse

Pre-AP Listening to this conversation will help students develop the skills that they need to be successful on the listening portion of the AP exam.

Go Online!

You may wish to remind students to go online for additional conversation practice.

¿Comprendes?

connectED.mcgraw-hill.com

A Completa según la información en la conversación.

1. A ____ le gusta el camping.
2. A ____ no le interesa mucho.
3. Cuando Pablo y su(s) amigo(s) van de camping, montan ____.
4. Duermen en ____.
5. Comen ____.
6. Las preparan en ____.
7. ____ no les molestan.
8. Durante el día ____.
9. Se acuestan temprano porque ____.
10. A Pablo no le gusta ____.

B **Resumiendo** Relata la información en la conversación en tus propias palabras.

C **Comparando** Compara y contrasta los gustos de Rafael y Pablo.

D **Dando opiniones** ¿Estás de acuerdo con las opiniones de Rafael o de Pablo sobre el camping? Explica.

CULTURA

Saltos del Petrohué cerca del lago Llanquihue en Chile

Andrew Payti

PRACTICE

¿Comprendes?

Writing Development

You may wish to have students write their responses for Activities B and D to help develop their writing skills in Spanish.

B and **C** Remind students that they can apply strategies they've learned in their English classes to summarize and to compare and contrast.

Cultural Snapshot

The Saltos del Petrohué are a series of waterfalls along the Petrohué River in Parque Nacional Vicente Pérez Rosales in southern Chile. Tourists visiting the Saltos del Petrohué marvel at the beautiful cascading emerald and turquoise water with the snowcapped Osorno Volcano rising majestically on the horizon.

Answers

A

1. Pablo
2. Rafael
3. una carpa
4. un saco de dormir
5. hamburguesas y salchichas
6. una barbacoa
7. Los insectos
8. dan caminatas y nadan en el lago
9. se levantan temprano también
10. lavarse en agua fría

B *Answers will vary but may include:*
A Pablo le gusta mucho el camping. A Rafael no le interesa mucho. Pablo siempre va con uno o dos amigos y montan una carpa. Duermen en un saco de dormir. Para comer, preparan hamburguesas y salchichas en una barbacoa. Los insectos no les molestan. Durante el día, dan caminatas y nadan en el lago. Se acuestan temprano y se levantan temprano. A Pablo no le gusta lavarse en agua fría.

C *Answers will vary but may include:*
A Rafael no le interesa el camping pero a Pablo le gusta mucho. A Rafael le molestan los insectos pero a Pablo no. Rafael se aburre en el camping pero Pablo no.

D *Answers will vary.*

Online Resources

Customizable Lesson Plans

Audio Activities

Student Workbook

¡Así se dice!

Why It Works!

This **Lectura cultural** contains only vocabulary that students have already learned. When there are no new words and no unknown grammatical forms, the reading is not only easy, but more importantly it is enjoyable. A reading with lots of unknown material becomes a chore and can be quite frustrating.

TEACH

Core Instruction

Step 1 Read and discuss the Reading Strategy and **Antes de leer.**

Step 2 Have students read the selection quickly and silently.

Step 3 Play the audio recording of the **Lectura** and have students listen while following along.

Step 4 Call on individuals to read aloud a few sentences at a time, after which you may want to ask the Reading Check questions and others of your own to keep students focused on what they are listening to.

Step 5 Discuss the **Durante la lectura** and **Después de leer** questions.

Step 6 Do the **¿Comprendes?** activities together in class or assign them as homework.

Lectura CULTURAL

READING STRATEGY

USING PRIOR KNOWLEDGE Prior knowledge is what you already know. Using what you have read, seen, or experienced will help you understand what you read.

Antes de leer

Have you ever done any backpacking? When and where? If not, do you think you would like to? Think about it. Would you rather go camping or stay in a youth hostel? Explain why.

Los mochileros

Si decides hacer un viaje por España o Latinoamérica con un grupo de amigos, vas a encontrar a muchos jóvenes de muchas nacionalidades haciendo turismo también. Todos tienen el deseo de ver y conocer el mundo. Pero como no tienen mucho dinero, tienen que viajar de una manera económica. ¿Tú no tienes mucho dinero tampoco? Pues, no hay problema. Como los otros aventureros, puedes poner todo lo que necesitas en una mochila grande y salir a ver el mundo.

Vamos a hablar con un mochilero típico. Se llama Antonio. Es de Tejas.

—Me encanta viajar y ver el mundo y lo hago sin mucho dinero. Como en restaurantes económicos y a veces mis compañeros y yo vamos a un mercado donde compramos comida para un picnic. Por lo general pasamos la noche en un albergue juvenil. Son muy económicos pero sus facilidades son limitadas. No tienes baño privado. Te levantas por la mañana y a veces tienes que lavarte en agua fría porque no hay agua caliente. Pero a mí no me importan estas pequeñas inconveniencias. Lo importante es poder hacer nuevos amigos de todas partes del mundo y llegar a apreciar sus costumbres y manera de vivir. ¿Qué te parece? ¿Por qué no nos encontramos un día en México o Chile?

✓ READING CHECK

¿Llevan maletas los jóvenes?

Durante la lectura

How would you like to travel and make new friends from around the world? Would it be fun?

✓ READING CHECK

¿Por qué van a albergues juveniles?

✓ READING CHECK

¿Cuáles son unas inconveniencias?

Después de leer

After reading, are your opinions the same about backpacking around the globe?

—¡Hola! Me llamo Antonio y soy de Texas. Me encanta viajar con mi mochila y ver el mundo. Soy un verdadero trotamundos.

Go Online!

You may wish to remind students to go online for additional reading comprehension and writing skills practice.

ABOUT THE SPANISH LANGUAGE

Un albergue (from **albergar**, *to accommodate*) is usually used to describe what in English is called a youth hostel, although it may take in other people besides youths. **Un hostal** most often refers to a place that offers hotel-like accommodations at a budget price, although it is sometimes used interchangeably with **albergue.**

¿Comprendes?

A Recordando hechos Contesta.

1. ¿De dónde vienen los mochileros que viajan por España o Latinoamérica?
2. ¿Cuál es una cosa que tienen en común?
3. ¿Dónde comen los mochileros?
4. ¿Dónde se quedan los mochileros?

B Describiendo Describe.

1. un albergue juvenil
2. a un mochilero
3. a Antonio

C Analizando Contesta.

¿Cuáles son las ventajas, o conveniencias, y desventajas, o inconveniencias, de quedarse en un albergue juvenil?

D Explicando Antonio piensa que los jóvenes se divierten mucho y al mismo tiempo aprenden a apreciar a gente de muchas culturas. Explica el significado de su opinión.

Andrew Payti

CULTURA

Un hostal o albergue en Punta Arenas en la Patagonia chilena

Differentiation

Reaching All Learners

You may want to have students give an oral review of the reading. To account for individual differences you may:

- Assist average students by asking them to respond to five or six guided questions that review the main points.
- Call on advanced learners to give an oral review with no prompting.
- Ask slower paced learners to repeat a main idea from the reviews they just heard.

Cultural Snapshot

Punta Arenas is a port in lower Patagonia on the Strait of Magellan. Founded in 1848, the city has some mansions that date from the wool boom of the late nineteenth and early twentieth centuries. Many Europeans migrated to Punta Arenas during this period.

Answers

A

1. Los mochileros que viajan por España o Latinoamérica vienen de muchos países.
2. Una cosa que tienen en común es que todos tienen el deseo de ver y conocer el mundo.
3. Los mochileros comen en restaurantes económicos o compran comida para un picnic.
4. Los mochileros se quedan en un albergue juvenil.

B *Answers will vary but may include:*

1. Un albergue juvenil es un hotel para jóvenes. Es económico pero las facilidades son limitadas.
2. Un mochilero es un aventurero que viaja de una manera económica con una mochila grande.
3. Antonio es un mochilero de Tejas. Le encanta viajar y ver el mundo. A Antonio no le importan las inconveniencias del albergue juvenil. Piensa que lo importante es poder hacer nuevos amigos de todas partes del mundo y llegar a apreciar sus costumbres.

C

Ventajas: Son muy económicos y es posible hacer nuevos amigos de todas partes del mundo.
Desventajas: Las facilidades son limitadas. No hay baño privado y a veces no hay agua caliente.

D *Answers will vary but may include:*

Antonio piensa que viajar y ver el mundo es muy divertido, pero también es bueno hacer nuevos amigos de todas partes del mundo y llegar a apreciar sus costumbres y manera de vivir.

Online Resources

Customizable Lesson Plans

Audio Activities

Student Workbook

TEACH
Core Instruction

You may choose any of the following procedures for this second reading.

Independent reading Have students read the selection and answer the **¿Comprendes?** questions as homework, which you collect. This option is least intrusive on class time and requires a minimum of teacher involvement.

Homework with in-class follow-up Assign the reading and **¿Comprendes?** questions as homework. Review and discuss the material in class the next day.

Intensive in-class activity This option includes a discussion of the **Antes de leer** questions, an in-class listening, reading, and discussion, and doing the **¿Comprendes?** questions in class or as homework to go over the next day.

Differentiation
Students with Learning Difficulties

It may be helpful for students with learning difficulties to work with a partner and complete the reading and accompanying activities together. Interpersonal learners will also find this appealing.

Lectura
UN POCO MÁS

Antes de leer

¿Fuiste de camping una vez? Si contestas que sí, ¿te gustó o no? Piensa en tu experiencia. Si contestas que no, que nunca fuiste de camping, ¿qué crees? ¿Te interesa el camping o no? A ver si tienes la misma opinión después de leer esta lectura.

El camping

Hoy en día muchos turistas, sobre todo los mochileros jóvenes, llevan equipo para hacer camping. En Latinoamérica hay campings en los parques nacionales y reservas naturales. Pasar unas noches en un camping puede ser una experiencia agradable. Tienes la oportunidad de conocer a otros turistas y también a familias locales porque a muchas familias les gusta hacer camping. Es una manera económica de viajar.

Los campers se levantan temprano—cuando se levanta el sol. Pasan el día dando caminatas por unas regiones de una belleza natural increíble.

CULTURA

Carpas en una playa de Arica, Chile

Andrew Payti

De noche regresan al camping. Se sientan alrededor de una fogata[1] y preparan comida en la fogata o en una barbacoa. Después de un día de mucha actividad física y una buena comida todos están cansados y van a su carpa. Cada uno desenrolla su saco de dormir y enseguida se duerme. Y, ¿mañana? Otro día de experiencias nuevas.

Con solamente mochila, carpa y saco de dormir es posible disfrutar de[2] unas vacaciones estupendas rodeado de un paisaje espectacular.

[1]fogata *bonfire* [2]disfrutar de *to enjoy*

Go Online!

You may wish to remind students to go online for additional reading comprehension and writing skills practice.

¿Comprendes?

Escoge.

1. ¿Quiénes hacen camping?
   - **a.** solo los mochileros
   - **b.** solo los turistas de otros países
   - **c.** los mochileros y otros turistas
   - **d.** nadie
2. Los campings en Latinoamérica se encuentran en ____.
   - **a.** las ciudades
   - **b.** los alrededores de una ciudad
   - **c.** zonas rurales
   - **d.** caminatas
3. ¿Cuándo se levantan los campers?
   - **a.** temprano por la mañana
   - **b.** cuando regresan al camping
   - **c.** cuando toman el sol
   - **d.** de noche
4. Las montañas y los lagos ofrecen ____.
   - **a.** una experiencia cultural
   - **b.** un paisaje espectacular
   - **c.** un viaje económico
   - **d.** una comida estupenda

CULTURA

Los jóvenes dan una caminata por los Andes no muy lejos de Mérida, Venezuela.

Lectura

Tips for Success

The type of multiple-choice comprehension exercises that accompany the second reading selection in each chapter have a format that will help students prepare for standardized tests.

Cultural Snapshot

These young people are hiking in the Andes. **¿Te parece que hace calor o frío? ¿Por qué piensas así?**

Answers

1. c
2. c
3. a
4. b

Prepárate para el examen

Online Resources

Customizable Lesson Plans

Student Workbook

Enrichment

Listening, Speaking, Reading, Writing Tests

Self-check for achievement

This is a pre-test for students to take before you administer the chapter test. Note that each section is cross-referenced so students can easily find the material they have to review in case they made errors. You may wish to use Self-Check Worksheet SC2 to have students complete this assessment in class or at home. You can correct the assessment yourself, or you may prefer to display the answers in class using Self-Check Answers SC2A.

Differentiation

Slower Paced Learners

Have students work in pairs to complete the Self-Check in class. This will allow them to check their answers through collaborative learning. Once they have finished, call on individual students to give the correct answers as you review together.

Prepárate para el examen

Vocabulario

To review, see **Vocabulario 1**.

1 Escoge la palabra apropiada.

1. Hay cinco (dedos, pies) en cada mano.
2. Escribo con la (mano, pierna) izquierda.
3. Ana se estira (las piernas, los codos) antes de correr.
4. Cuando tengo dolor de (dientes, cabeza) no puedo leer bien.

To review, see **Vocabulario 1** and **Vocabulario 2**.

2 Completa.

5. Los amigos van de camping. Arman una ____.
6. Es mi amiga. ¿Quieres saber su nombre? Ella ____ ____ Susana.

7–8. El joven ____ ____ a las diez y media de la noche. Pero no ____ ____ enseguida porque pasa una hora leyendo en la cama.

9. Necesito ____. Voy a lavarme el pelo.
10. No puedo hacerlo. ¿Me puedes ____?
11. Los mochileros dan una ____ por el parque nacional.

Gramática

To review, see **Verbos reflexivos** and **Verbos reflexivos de cambio radical**.

3 Contesta.

12. ¿Cómo te llamas?
13. ¿A qué hora te levantas?
14. ¿A qué hora te acuestas?

4 Completa.

15. Yo ____ a la mesa. (sentarse)
16. ¿Tú ____ a qué hora? (acostarse)
17. Ellos ____ Raúl y Magdalena. (llamarse)
18. Nosotros ____ enseguida. (dormirse)
19. Yo ____ las manos. (lavarse)
20. Ustedes ____ en la sala. (sentarse)
21. Ellos ____ mucho. (divertirse)
22. Ella ____ temprano cada día. (despertarse)

Answers

1

1. dedos
2. mano
3. las piernas
4. cabeza

2

5. carpa (tienda de campaña)
6. se llama

7–8. se acuesta, se duerme

9. champú
10. ayudar
11. caminata

3

12. Me llamo ____.
13. Me levanto a las ____.
14. Me acuesto a las ____.

4

15. me siento
16. te acuestas
17. se llaman
18. nos dormimos
19. me lavo
20. se sientan
21. se divierten
22. se despierta

Prepárate para el examen

5 Forma frases.

23. tú / sentarse / para comer
24. usted / acostarse / a las diez de la noche
25. mis primos / llamarse / Carlos y Felipe
26. yo / cepillarse / los dientes
27. nosotros / divertirse / durante una fiesta
28. ustedes / ponerse / los guantes

6 Completa con un pronombre si es necesario.

29. Ella ____ mira en el espejo cuando se peina.
30. Ella ____ mira a la profesora.
31. Yo ____ lavo a mi perro.
32. Yo ____ lavo antes de ir a la escuela.

7 Escribe un mandato con favor de. Sigue el modelo.

MODELO **No como. →**
Favor de comer.

33. No salgo.
34. No leo las notas.
35. No escribo la tarea.
36. No paso la sal.

To review, see **Mandatos con favor de.**

Cultura

To review this cultural information, see the **Lectura cultural.**

8 Contesta.

37. ¿Cómo viajan muchos jóvenes en España y Latinoamérica?
38. ¿Dónde pasan la noche?
39. ¿Cómo son los albergues?
40. ¿Por qué a los jóvenes les gustan los albergues juveniles?

CULTURA

Caballito de Totora es un hostal en Huanchaco, Perú. Es un balneario en el océano Pacífico. Un «caballito de totora» es un tipo de embarcación que usan los pescadores.

Differentiation

Slower Paced Learners

Encourage students who need extra help to refer to the margin notes and review any section before answering the questions.

Pre-AP Students preparing for the AP exam may benefit from a set time limit when completing this Self-Check. This may also help to identify students with learning difficulties or slower paced students who need extra help.

Go Online!

You may wish to remind students to go online for additional test preparation.

Answers

5

23. Tú te sientas para comer.
24. Usted se acuesta a las diez de la noche.
25. Mis primos se llaman Carlos y Felipe.
26. Yo me cepillo los dientes.
27. Nosotros nos divertimos durante una fiesta.
28. Ustedes se ponen los guantes.

6

29. se
30. —
31. —
32. me

7

33. Favor de salir.
34. Favor de leer las notas.
35. Favor de escribir la tarea.
36. Favor de pasar la sal.

8

37. Muchos jóvenes en España y Latinoamérica viajan de mochileros.
38. Pasan la noche en un albergue juvenil.
39. Son económicos pero las facilidades son limitadas.
40. Les gustan los albergues juveniles porque pueden tener la oportunidad de hacer nuevos amigos de todas partes del mundo.

Prepárate para el examen

Tips for Success

Encourage students to say as much as possible when they do these activities. Tell them not to be afraid to make mistakes, since the goal of the activities is real-life communication. Encourage students to self-correct and to use words and phrases they know to get their meaning across. If someone in the group makes an error that impedes comprehension, encourage the others to ask questions to clarify or, if necessary, to politely correct the speaker. Let students choose the activities they would like to do.

Tell students to feel free to elaborate on the basic theme and to be creative. They may use props, pictures, or posters if they wish.

Pre-AP These oral activities will give students the opportunity to develop and improve their speaking skills so that they may succeed on the speaking portion of the AP exam.

Note: Some teachers may want to use the rubric below to help students prepare their speaking activities.

Practice for **ORAL PROFICIENCY**

Prepárate para el examen

1 Mi familia

Talk about family routines

Work with a classmate. Discuss your family routines. What things do you and your family typically do and at what times? Do your families have similar routines or are they quite different?

2 No es siempre igual.

Compare your weekday and weekend routines

Most people like a change of pace on the weekend. Compare the things you do or do not do during the week with the things you do or do not do during the weekend.

CULTURA

Están tomando una siesta en hamacas en un camping en las afueras de Santa Marta, Colombia.

3 Una excursión de camping

Talk about a camping trip

Work with a classmate. A friend's family invited you both to join them on a camping trip. Discuss the things you will need to take. Also discuss some of the things you'll probably do during the camping trip.

4 Un día ideal

Talk about your ideal day

Interview a classmate to find out about his or her ideal day. Take turns. See who can come up with the most original ideas. Share the information with the class.

5 Favor de...

Ask someone to do something

Work with a classmate and tell each other to do things. Act out what you're told to do.

Scoring Rubric for Speaking

	4	3	2	1
vocabulary	extensive use of vocabulary, including idiomatic expressions	adequate use of vocabulary and idiomatic expressions	limited vocabulary marked with some anglicisms	limited vocabulary marked by frequent anglicisms that force interpretation by the listener
grammar	few or no grammatical errors	minor grammatical errors	some serious grammatical errors	serious grammatical errors
pronunciation	good intonation and largely accurate pronunciation with slight accent	acceptable intonation and pronunciation with distinctive accent	errors in intonation and pronunciation with heavy accent	errors in intonation and pronunciation that interfere with listener's comprehension
content	thorough response with interesting and pertinent detail	thorough response with sufficient detail	some detail, but not sufficient	general, insufficient response

Go Online! connectED.mcgraw-hill.com

Tarea

For the next week keep **un diario** *(diary)* in Spanish. Write down everything you do in the course of each day.

Writing Strategy

Writing in a journal There are many types of personal writing. One example of personal writing is keeping a journal. One type of journal writing involves writing about what you do each day, along with your thoughts and impressions about these events or activities. It's similar to "thinking out loud."

Brand X Pictures/Alamy

1 Prewrite

- Find a notebook or journal in which you will feel comfortable writing.
- Decide what time of day you will write in your journal, preferably before you go to bed.
- Remember that journal writing is informal, but in this case you still want to use correct vocabulary, grammar, and sentence structure. Use as many reflexive verbs as you can. Don't try to write anything you haven't learned yet.

2 Write

Keeping a diary should be an enjoyable, thoughtful experience.

- Write the date at the top of the page. Write down your activities, thoughts, and feelings for each day. Remember that your teacher will be reading it!
- To help refresh your memory, ask yourself questions such as the following: What did I do when I woke up? Did I go to school? What did I do at school? What did I do after school? Did I eat dinner with my family? What homework did I do? Did I wash my hair? Many activities will be different for the weekend days.
- Read over your diary. Check for correct vocabulary, verb forms, and grammar.
- **Expansion:** If you would like to expand this **Tarea** in order to track your progress, make a list of the goals that you would like to set for yourself with regard to this activity. Continue to write in your journal for as long as you would like or until you achieve the goals you want to achieve. Take note of the improvement you made in your writings. The improvements could include better use of descriptive words, increased use of newly learned vocabulary, or any other aspect of writing that you wish to improve. At the end of your journal writing, review your diary and make a note of the areas in which you have improved most and check that against your list of goals you set for yourself.

Evaluate

Don't forget that your teacher will evaluate you on your sequencing of events and activities, use of vocabulary, correctness of grammar and sentence structure, and the completeness of your message.

Prepárate para el examen

Pre-AP This **tarea** will give students the opportunity to develop and improve their writing skills so that they may succeed on the writing portion of the AP exam.

ASSESS

Students are now ready to take any of the Listening, Speaking, Reading, Writing Tests you choose to administer.

Note: Some teachers may want to use the rubric below to help students prepare their writing task.

Scoring Rubric for Writing

	4	3	2	1
vocabulary	precise, varied	functional, fails to communicate complete meaning	limited to basic words, often inaccurate	inadequate
grammar	excellent, very few or no errors	some errors, but do not hinder communication	numerous errors interfere with communication	many errors, little sentence structure
content	thorough response to the topic	generally thorough response to the topic	partial response to the topic	insufficient response to the topic
organization	well organized, ideas presented clearly and logically	loosely organized, but main ideas present	some attempts at organization, but with confused sequencing	lack of organization

Repaso del Capítulo 2

Online Resources

Customizable Lesson Plans

- Whiteboard Lesson
- Audio Activities
- Video (Vocabulario) (Diálogo) (Gramática) (Cultura)
- Student Workbook
- Enrichment
- Quizzes
- Listening, Speaking, Reading, Writing Tests

Grammar Review

This page provides a quick "at a glance" summary of the grammar points students have learned in this chapter.

Differentiation

Multiple Intelligences

You may want to call on **verbal-linguistic** and **logical-mathematical** learners for whom grammar often comes easily to explain the main concepts to their classmates in their own words. Encourage students to compare and contrast these structures with structures in English. Having students explain the concepts in different ways may also help slower paced learners or students with learning difficulties.

Repaso del Capítulo 2

Gramática

Verbos reflexivos

Review the forms of the reflexive verbs. These verbs have an extra pronoun that refers back to the subject because the subject is both the performer (doer) and receiver of the action of the verb.

lavarse			
yo	me lavo	nosotros(as)	nos lavamos
tú	te lavas	*vosotros(as)*	*os laváis*
Ud., él, ella	se lava	Uds., ellos, ellas	se lavan

Verbos reflexivos de cambio radical

Some reflexive verbs have a stem change in the present. Review the following verbs.

acostarse			
yo	me acuesto	nosotros(as)	nos acostamos
tú	te acuestas	*vosotros(as)*	*os acostáis*
Ud., él, ella	se acuesta	Uds., ellos, ellas	se acuestan

divertirse			
yo	me divierto	nosotros(as)	nos divertimos
tú	te diviertes	*vosotros(as)*	*os divertís*
Ud., él, ella	se divierte	Uds., ellos, ellas	se divierten

Mandatos con favor de

You can use the expression **favor de** followed by the infinitive to tell someone what to do. Review the following.

Favor de empezar ahora.
Favor de no poner la ropa aquí.

Remember that when a pronoun is used with the infinitive, the pronoun is attached to it.

Favor de ayudarme.

CULTURA

Los jóvenes se divierten observando y escuchando la Catarata La Paz en Costa Rica. En el parque hay una serie de senderos y miradores de donde los turistas pueden apreciar el paisaje extraordinario.

Richard Brommer

Juego There are a number of cognates in this list. See how many you and a partner can find. Who can find the most? Compare your list with those of your classmates.

Go Online!

connectED.mcgraw-hill.com

Vocabulario

Stating daily activities

la rutina diaria	lavarse	dormirse
despertarse	cepillarse	ponerse (la ropa)
estirarse	peinarse	quitarse (la ropa)
levantarse	mirarse	llamarse
quedarse	sentarse	
tomar una ducha	acostarse	

Identifying articles for grooming and hygiene

el espejo	el peine	la barra de jabón
el champú	el cepillo de dientes	el rollo de papel higiénico
el cepillo	el tubo de crema dental	

Identifying more parts of the body

el cuerpo humano	el brazo	la pierna
la cabeza	el codo	el pie
los dientes	el dedo	
la espalda	la rodilla	

Describing camping

el parque	el saco (la bolsa) de dormir	montar, armar
el camping	el/la mochilero(a)	dar una caminata
la carpa, la tienda de campaña	ir de camping	divertirse, pasarlo bien

Other useful words and expressions

derecho(a)	el suéter	acá
izquierdo(a)	tener frío (calor)	¡Ya voy!
el/la madrugador(a)	Favor de *(+ infinitive)*	

Repaso del Capítulo 2

Vocabulary Review

The words and phrases in **Vocabulario 1** and **2** have been taught for productive use in this chapter. They are summarized here as a resource for both student and teacher. This list also serves as a convenient resource for the **Prepárate para el examen** activities.

¡Así se dice!

Why It Works!

This vocabulary reference list has not been translated into English for two reasons. First, it is recommended that students learn the new vocabulary through direct association with images on the **Vocabulario** pages. Secondly, all vocabulary is reintroduced in the chapter many times and upon completion of the chapter students should be familiar with the meaning of all the words. If there are words that students still do not know, they can refer to the vocabulary presentation in the chapter or the dictionary at the end of the book. If, however, it is your preference to give students the English translations, please refer to Vocabulary V2.1.

Differentiation

Slower Paced Learners

Slower paced learners may benefit from creating their own visual dictionary of words in this list. They can either draw their own depictions or use images from the Internet, magazines, etc.

Don't forget the chapter project and cultural activities. Students have learned all the information from this chapter that they will need to complete these engaging enrichment tasks.

Juego The cognates in this list are: **la rutina, el champú, el tubo de crema dental, el rollo, humano, el parque, el camping, el suéter.**

Expansion You can also use the vocabulary list to practice proper pronunciation, as well as to make flashcards for a variety of games such as concentration and bingo.

Repaso cumulativo

Every chapter of **¡Así se dice!** contains this review section of previously learned material.

Activity 1 This activity reviews the differences between present tense and past tense.

Audio Script

1. Paco compra un libro en la papelería.
2. Yo fui con mis abuelos a Guatemala el año pasado.
3. Nosotros vamos al parque para jugar fútbol.
4. Luisa escribió una composición fantástica para la clase de inglés.
5. Mis amigos vieron una película fabulosa anoche.
6. Enrique come en casa esta noche.

Activity 2 This activity reviews the present progressive tense.

Activity 3 This activity reviews **ir a, acabar de,** and **tener que** followed by infinitives.

Activity 4 This activity reviews stem-changing verbs.

Activity 5 This activity reviews the differences between **ser** and **estar.**

Repaso cumulativo

Repasa lo que ya has aprendido

These activities will help you review and remember what you have learned so far in Spanish.

1 Escucha las frases. Indica si la frase ocurre en el presente o en el pasado.

en el presente	en el pasado

2 Cambia al presente progresivo.

1. Él compra un juego de computadora.
2. Ellos hacen un álbum de fotografías electrónicas.
3. Compro un regalo para mi papá.
4. ¿Qué lees?
5. No comprendemos nada.
6. Ellos viven en Caracas.
7. ¡Vamos! Sale nuestro vuelo.
8. Hacen cola.

3 Completa con una palabra apropiada.

1. Tengo que ____ una composición para mi clase de inglés.
2. Mañana voy a ____ a la playa donde voy a ____ en el mar.
3. No tengo hambre porque acabo de ____.
4. Mis amigos acaban de ____ de Colombia donde pasaron sus vacaciones.
5. Yo voy a ____ a la tienda porque tengo que ____ un regalo para el cumpleaños de Teresa.

CULTURA

Una playa en la costa del Caribe en Colombia

4 Forma frases en el presente.

1. nosotros / poder
2. nosotros / jugar
3. yo / querer
4. ella / pensar que sí
5. ellos / preferir
6. nosotros / querer
7. nosotros / volver
8. ustedes / volver
9. tú / tener que

Answers

1

1. en el presente
2. en el pasado
3. en el presente
4. en el pasado
5. en el pasado
6. en el presente

2

1. Él está comprando un juego de computadora.
2. Ellos están haciendo un álbum de fotografías electrónicas.
3. Estoy comprando un regalo para mi papá.
4. ¿Qué estás leyendo?
5. No estamos comprendiendo nada.
6. Ellos están viviendo en Caracas.
7. ¡Vamos! Está saliendo nuestro vuelo.
8. Están haciendo cola.

3

1. escribir
2. ir, nadar
3. comer
4. volver (regresar)
5. ir, comprar

4 *Answers will vary but should include the following verbs:*

1. podemos
2. jugamos
3. quiero
4. piensa
5. prefieren
6. queremos
7. volvemos
8. vuelven
9. tienes que

Go Online!

connectED.mcgraw-hill.com

5 Completa con ser o estar.

1. Quiero acostarme. _____ cansado(a).
2. José tiene que prepararse para un examen. _____ un poco nervioso.
3. Teresa no se siente bien. _____ enferma.
4. La muchacha se baña. El jabón que usa _____ muy bueno.
5. Los alumnos se duermen porque el profesor _____ muy aburrido y ellos _____ aburridos.

6 Escribe el contrario.

1. El niño tiene algo en la boca.
2. Ellos siempre se acuestan muy temprano.
3. Yo siempre me duermo enseguida.
4. Alguien va a pie y alguien va en bicicleta.
5. Tenemos algo en la mochila.

7 Mira los dibujos. Describe todo lo que ves.

Answers

5
1. Estoy
2. Está
3. Está
4. es
5. es, están

6
1. El niño no tiene nada en la boca.
2. Ellos no se acuestan nunca muy temprano. (Ellos nunca se acuestan muy temprano.)
3. Yo no me duermo nunca enseguida. (Yo nunca me duermo enseguida.)
4. Nadie va a pie y nadie va en bicicleta.
5. No tenemos nada en la mochila.

7 *Answers will vary.*

Repaso cumulativo

Activity 6 This activity reviews affirmative and negative words.

Activity 7 This open-ended activity reviews the themes of winter activities, attending a concert, and going to the movies.

Differentiation

Reaching All Learners

You may gear Activity 7 toward **slower paced** learners by simply asking for a list of the words they see depicted. More **advanced** learners and **verbal-linguistic** learners will be able to say or write complete sentences and maybe put them together in story form as a complete oral or written review. **Bodily-kinesthetic** learners may want to work in pairs or small groups and present a skit for the class based on one of the illustrations. **Interpersonal** learners may prefer to work in pairs and ask each other questions about the illustrations. This will also allow them to practice using interrogative words.

Go Online!

You may wish to remind students to go online for additional cumulative review.

Pre-AP To give students further open-ended oral or written practice, or to assess proficiency, go to AP Proficiency Practice 13.

Go Online!

The **¡Así se dice!** Audio Program for Chapter 11 has twenty-nine activities, which afford students extensive listening and speaking practice.

Chapter Overview

En tren

Scope and Sequence

Topics
- Train travel
- Train trips in Peru and Mexico

Culture
- El AVE
- Indigenous market in Peru
- Panama Canal and the Panama Canal Railway

Functions
- How to use vocabulary related to train travel
- How to discuss interesting train trips in Peru and Mexico

Structure
- The preterite of irregular verbs
- The verb **decir**
- Prepositional pronouns

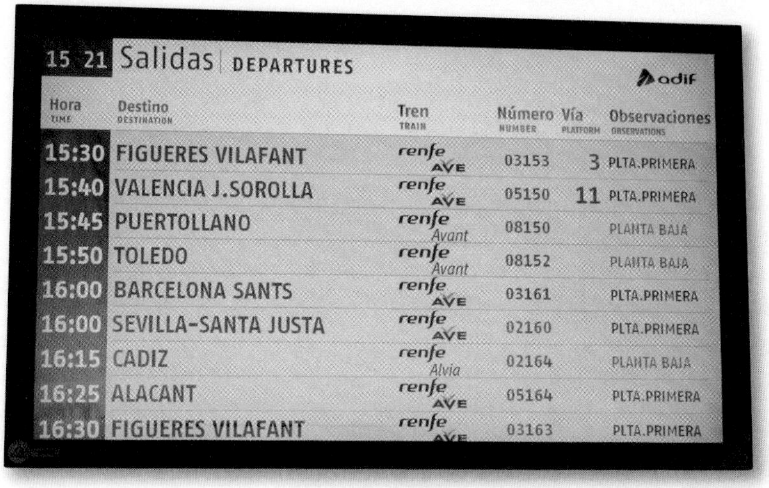
15 21
Salidas
DEPARTURES
adif
Hora
TIME
Destino
DESTINATION
Tren
TRAIN
Número
NUMBER
Vía
PLATFORM
Observaciones
OBSERVATIONS
15:30 FIGUERES VILAFANT renfe AVE 03153 3 PLTA.PRIMERA
15:40 VALENCIA J.SOROLLA renfe AVE 05150 11 PLTA.PRIMERA
15:45 PUERTOLLANO renfe Avant 08150 PLANTA BAJA
15:50 TOLEDO renfe Avant 08152 PLANTA BAJA
16:00 BARCELONA SANTS renfe AVE 03161 PLTA.PRIMERA
16:00 SEVILLA-SANTA JUSTA renfe AVE 02160 PLTA.PRIMERA
16:15 CADIZ renfe Alvia 02164 PLANTA BAJA
16:25 ALACANT renfe AVE 05164 PLTA.PRIMERA
16:30 FIGUERES VILAFANT renfe 03163 PLTA.PRIMERA

Planning Guide

	required	recommended	optional
Vocabulario 1 En la estación de ferrocarril (tren)	✓		
Vocabulario 2 En el tren	✓		
Gramática Pretérito de los verbos irregulares El verbo **decir** Pronombres después de una preposición	✓		
Conversación En la ventanilla		✓	
Lectura cultural Viajes ferroviarios fabulosos		✓	
Lectura Un poco más De Panamá a Colón en tren			✓
Prepárate para el examen			✓
Repaso cumulativo			✓

Daniel Salsgiver

Correlations to ACTFL World-Readiness Standards for Learning Languages

Page numbers in light print refer to the Student Edition.
Page numbers in bold print refer to the Teacher Edition.

COMMUNICATION Communicate effectively in more than one language in order to function in a variety of situations and for multiple purposes		
Interpersonal Communication	Learners interact and negotiate meaning in spoken, signed, or written conversations to share information, reactions, feelings, and opinions.	pp. 75, **75, 81, 83, 86,** 96
Interpretive Communication	Learners understand, interpret, and analyze what is heard, read, or viewed on a variety of topics.	pp. **72, 73,** 74, **74,** 75, **76,** 78, **78,** 79, **79,** 81, 82, **82,** 83, **83,** 84, 85, **85, 86,** 87, **87, 88,** 88–90, **89,** 91, **91, 92,** 93, **95,** 100, **101**
Presentational Communication	Learners present information, concepts, and ideas to inform, explain, persuade, and narrate on a variety of topics using appropriate media and adapting to various audiences of listeners, readers, or viewers.	pp. **68C, 68D, 73, 77,** 81, **81, 83, 87, 88, 91, 94,** 97, **98**
CULTURES Interact with cultural competence and understanding		
Relating Cultural Practices to Perspectives	Learners use the language to investigate, explain, and reflect on the relationship between the practices and perspectives of the cultures studied.	pp. **71,** 88–90, 91
Relating Cultural Products to Perspectives	Learners use the language to investigate, explain, and reflect on the relationship between the products and perspectives of the cultures studied.	pp. **68C, 68D, 69, 70,** 70–71, **71, 74, 75,** 85, 87, **88,** 88–90, **89, 90,** 91, 92, **92,** 93, **93,** 95, 96, **96**
CONNECTIONS Connect with other disciplines and acquire information and diverse perspectives in order to use the language to function in academic and career-related situations		
Making Connections	Learners build, reinforce, and expand their knowledge of other disciplines while using the language to develop critical thinking and to solve problems creatively.	pp. **68D,** 78, 80, **81, 87,** 92
Acquiring Information and Diverse Perspectives	Learners access and evaluate information and diverse perspectives that are available through the language and its cultures.	pp. **68C, 72,** 75, 76, **77,** 84, **84,** 85, **85,** 87, **87,** 99, **99**
COMPARISONS Develop insight into the nature of language and culture in order to interact with cultural competence		
Language Comparisons	Learners use the language to investigate, explain, and reflect on the nature of language through comparisons of the language studied and their own.	pp. 73, 76, **98,** 99, **99**
Cultural Comparisons	Learners use the language to investigate, explain, and reflect on the concept of culture through comparisons of the cultures studied and their own.	pp. **68D,** 69, **69, 70,** 87, **90,** 95
COMMUNITIES Communicate and interact with cultural competence in order to participate in multilingual communities at home and around the world		
School and Global Communities	Learners use the language both within and beyond the classroom to interact and collaborate in their community and the globalized world.	pp. **68C,** 75, 81, **94, 96, 98**
Lifelong Learning	Learners set goals and reflect on their progress in using languages for enjoyment, enrichment, and advancement.	pp. **68C,** 76, **77, 79,** 84, **84,** 87, **87**

Chapter Project

Un recorrido en tren

Students will create their own customized travel itinerary for a seven-day train trip through a Spanish-speaking country.

1. Each student will choose a destination and the time of year they wish to travel. Using resources available in the library and on the Internet, students will plan a week-long trip by train that includes detailed information about the different places they are visiting, such as when they are to arrive and depart, where they are going to stay (hotel, youth hostel, etc.) and what they are going to do at each stop on their trip (sightseeing, museums, food, etc.).
2. The travel itinerary should be organized like a diary or journal, with each entry representing a different day of the trip. You may also wish to have students further organize the activities of each day in terms of **por la mañana, por la tarde,** and **por la noche.**
3. Students should consult travel guidebooks or online travel services to determine the daily schedule of trains running to and from their selected destinations. Each student should also include a visual sketch of the route of his or her train trip, the distance traveled between locations (in miles and kilometers), and the approximate cost of the trip.
4. Have students turn in first drafts of their travel itineraries. After you check them or after they have been peer edited, have the students correct their work and submit final drafts. You may wish to evaluate the travel itineraries as a written assignment and/or have students present them in class.

Expansion: You may wish to have students compose a short description of their trip in the preterite tense, as if they had already taken the trip and were recalling when they went, where they stayed, and what they did.

Horarios

Clase de tren	VALLE	LLANO	LLANO	LLANO	LLANO	VALLE
Número de tren	9114	9118	9124	9128	9136	9140
Observaciones	(1)				(2)	(2)
Días de circulación	LMXJVS•	LMXJVSD	LMXJVSD	LMXJVSD	LMXJVSD	LMXJVSD
MADRID Puerta de Atocha	07:10	09:30	12:25	14:40 ✓	18:30 ✓	20:10
CIUDAD REAL	-	10:30	-	-	19:30	-
PUERTOLLANO	-	10:46 ✓	-	-	19:46	-
CÓRDOBA	09:09 ✓	11:34 ✓	14:24 ✓	16:39 ✓	20:34	22:09 ✓
MONTILLA	-	12:08	-	-	21:08	-
PUENTE GENIL	-	12:25	-	-	21:25 ✓	-
BOBADILLA	10:28	12:56	15:41	18:01	21:52	-
MÁLAGA	11:22	13:50	16:33	18:50	22:39	00:12
Restauración						

Clase de tren	VALLE	LLANO	LLANO	LLANO	LLANO	VALLE
Número de tren	9113	9119	9125	9131	9137	9139
Observaciones	(1)				(2)	(2)
Días de circulación	LMXJVSD	LMXJVSD	LMXJVSD	LMXJVSD	LMXJVSD	LMXJVSD
MÁLAGA	06:45	09:00	12:45	15:00 ✓	18:00	19:45
BOBADILLA	07:30 ✓	09:46	13:32	15:45	-	20:31
PUENTE GENIL	-	10:18	-	16:11	-	-
MONTILLA	-	10:36	-	16:29	-	-
CÓRDOBA	08:54 ✓	11:21 ✓	14:56 ✓	17:13 ✓	20:07 ✓	21:57 ✓
PUERTOLLANO	-	-	-	18:04	-	-
CIUDAD REAL	-	-	-	18:21	-	-
MADRID Puerta de Atocha	10:55	13:22	16:57	19:23	22:14	23:58
Restauración						

Observaciones:

(1) No circula 13/10, 25/12/2001 ni 1/1/2002. También circula 14/10, 4/11, 9/12/2001, 31/3 y 5/5/2002.

(2) No circula 24/12 ni 31/12/2001.

Si su origen/destino es Torremolinos o Fuengirola puede utilizar, gratuitamente y en el margen de 2 horas, el tren de Cercanías presentando su billete de Talgo 200.

Restauración

El servicio de restauración en el asiento se realiza únicamente en las estaciones señaladas ✓.

En los trenes 9128 y 9131, a los viajeros con inicio de viaje en Córdoba se les ofrecerá un Snack.

Desayuno	Snack	Almuerzo	Cena

Scoring Rubric for Project

	5	3	1
Evidence of planning	Corrected draft is provided.	Draft is provided but is not corrected.	No draft is provided.
Written product	Itinerary contains sufficient information and has few errors.	Itinerary contains sufficient information but has some errors.	Itinerary lacks information and has many errors.
Presentation	Itinerary contains all the required elements.	Itinerary contains some of the required elements.	Itinerary contains few of the required elements.

Culture

Recipe

ARROZ TAPADO

Ingredients: (makes 6 servings)
3 cloves garlic, minced
2 tablespoons oil
lemon juice
salt
4 cups water
1 pound washed rice
1 onion, finely chopped
2 pounds ground beef
2 tomatoes, finely chopped
1 tablespoon tomato paste
4 teaspoons raisins
5 black olives, chopped
2 hard-boiled eggs, finely chopped
1 teaspoon parsley, chopped

Sauté the garlic in oil. Add a few drops of lemon juice, salt, and water. Bring to a boil. Add the rice and continue to cook for 20–25 minutes or until rice is done. In another pan, sauté the onions. Add the meat, tomatoes, tomato paste, raisins, olives, egg, and parsley. Mix well. Coat the inside of a 1-cup measuring cup with a little oil or shortening. Fill halfway with rice, add some of the meat mixture, and top off with more rice. Invert onto a plate and carefully remove the measuring cup. Repeat for each serving.

Quipus

This chapter contains a reading about a train trip to famous Machu Picchu, which was constructed by the Incas. The Incas of South America spoke Quechua but also communicated by means of **quipus.** A **quipu** is a series of colorful strings decorated with knots and tied to a main string. Each color represents a different object, event, or other information, while the number or type of knots tied on each string indicates a numeric value. The different strings are often arranged in order of occurrence or importance. **Quipus** were used for counting and for keeping track of information.

You may wish to have students design their own **quipus** based on a variety of topics, such as important life events, information about family, places lived in or traveled to, class schedule, etc. Use black or white for the main string and attach colorful strings to represent different aspects of the theme or topic. The number of knots tied on each colorful strand should correspond to a numeric value, such as time of day or year, date, or age. For example, a red string might stand for a certain place and three knots might mean that the person lived there at the age of three. Once students complete their **quipus,** have them explain the meaning behind them.

Connection to Fine Art

Have students look online or in an art text to find examples of the color plates drawn by Casimiro Castro for the nineteenth-century *Álbum del ferrocarril mexicano.* This album contains twenty-four color plates of Castro's drawings depicting the route between Veracruz and Mexico City. Students can research why the *Álbum del ferrocarril mexicano* was published and investigate the impact of railway construction on the history of Mexico. Encourage students to make comparisons between the expansion of the railways in Mexico and the United States. Students may be able to share their analysis with their social studies class.

50-Minute Lesson Plans

	Objective	Present	Practice	Assess/Homework
Day 1	Talk about train stations	Chapter Opener (5 min.) Introducción al tema (10 min.) Core Instruction/Vocabulario 1 (20 min.)	Activities 1–4 (15 min.)	Student Workbook Activities A–C **ConnectEd** Vocabulary Practice
Day 2	Talk about train stations	Quick Start (5 min.) Review Vocabulario 1 (10 min.)	Activities 5–8 (15 min.) Total Physical Response (5 min.) Audio Activities A–E (15 min.)	Student Workbook Activities D–F **ConnectEd** Vocabulary Practice
Day 3	Talk about traveling by train	Core Instruction/Vocabulario 2 (15 min.) Video, Vocabulario en vivo (10 min.)	Activities 1–3 (15 min.)	Quiz 1 (10 min.) Student Workbook Activities A–C **ConnectEd** Vocabulary Practice
Day 4	Talk about traveling by train	Quick Start (5 min.) Review Vocabulario 2 (5 min.)	Activities 4–6 (15 min.) Total Physical Response (5 min.) InfoGap (10 min.) Audio Activities F–I (10 min.)	Student Workbook Activities D–E **ConnectEd** Vocabulary Practice
Day 5	The preterite of irregular verbs	Core Instruction/Gramática, Pretérito de los verbos irregulares (20 min.)	Activities 1–2 (10 min.) Foldables (10 min.)	Quiz 2 (10 min.) Student Workbook Activities A–C **ConnectEd** Grammar Practice
Day 6	The preterite of irregular verbs	Quick Start (5 min.) Review Gramática, Pretérito de los verbos irregulares (10 min.)	Activities 3–5 (15 min.) Audio Activities A–C (20 min.)	Student Workbook Activities D–F **ConnectEd** Grammar Practice
Day 7	The verb **decir**	Quick Start (5 min.) Core Instruction/Gramática, El verbo **decir** (10 min.) Video, Gramática en vivo (10 min.)	Activities 6–10 (15 min.)	Quiz 3 (10 min.) Student Workbook Activities A–E **ConnectEd** Grammar Practice
Day 8	Prepositional pronouns	Quick Start (5 min.) Core Instruction/Gramática, Pronombres después de una preposición (10 min.)	Activities 11–12 (10 min.) Audio Activities D–F (15 min.)	Quiz 4 (10 min.) Student Workbook Activities A–B **ConnectEd** Grammar Practice
Day 9	Develop reading and listening comprehension skills	Quick Start (5 min.) Core Instruction/Conversación (20 min.) Video, Diálogo en vivo (10 min.)	¿Comprendes? A–B (5 min.)	Quiz 5 (10 min.) ¿Comprendes? C–D **ConnectEd** Conversation
Day 10	Discuss interesting train trips in Peru and Mexico	Core Instruction/Lectura cultural (20 min.)	¿Comprendes? A–C (15 min.)	Listening Comprehension Test (15 min.) ¿Comprendes? D–E **ConnectEd** Reading Practice
Day 11	Develop reading comprehension skills	Core Instruction/Lectura Un poco más (15 min.)	¿Comprendes? (10 min.) Prepárate para el examen (25 min.)	Prepárate para el examen, Practice for written proficiency **ConnectEd** Reading Practice
Day 12	Chapter review	Repaso del Capítulo 3 (15 min.)	Prepárate para el examen, Practice for oral proficiency (20 min.)	Test for Writing Proficiency (15 min.) Review for chapter test
Day 13	Chapter 3 Tests (50 min.) Reading and Writing Test Speaking Test		Test for Oral Proficiency Test for Reading Comprehension	

90-Minute Lesson Plans

	Objective	Present	Practice	Assess/Homework
Block 1	Talk about train stations	Chapter Opener (5 min.) Introducción al tema (15 min.) Quick Start (5 min.) Core Instruction/Vocabulario 1 (20 min.)	Activities 1–8 (25 min.) Total Physical Response (5 min.) Audio Activities A–E (15 min.)	Student Workbook Activities A–F **ConnectEd** Vocabulary Practice
Block 2	Talk about traveling by train	Quick Start (5 min.) Core Instruction/Vocabulario 2 (20 min.) Video, Vocabulario en vivo (10 min.)	Activities 1–6 (20 min.) Total Physical Response (5 min.) InfoGap (5 min.) Audio Activities F–I (15 min.)	Quiz 1 (10 min.) Student Workbook Activities A–E **ConnectEd** Vocabulary Practice
Block 3	The preterite of irregular verbs The verb **decir**	Quick Start (5 min.) Core Instruction/Gramática, Pretérito de los verbos irregulares (20 min.) Core Instruction/Gramática, El verbo **decir** (10 min.)	Activities 1–5 (15 min.) Foldables (5 min.) Activities 6–8 (10 min.) Audio Activities A–C (15 min.)	Quiz 2 (10 min.) Student Workbook Activities A–F Student Workbook Activities A–B **ConnectEd** Grammar Practice
Block 4	The verb **decir** Prepositional pronouns	Quick Start (5 min.) Review Gramática, El verbo **decir** (10 min.) Video, Gramática en vivo (10 min.) Quick Start (5 min.) Core Instruction/Gramática, Pronombres después de una preposición (10 min.)	Activities 9–10 (10 min.) Activities 11–12 (10 min.) Audio Activities D–F (20 min.)	Quiz 3 (10 min.) Student Workbook Activities C–E Student Workbook Activities A–B **ConnectEd** Grammar Practice
Block 5	Discuss interesting train trips in Peru and Mexico	Quick Start (5 min.) Core Instruction/Conversación (15 min.) Video, Diálogo en vivo (10 min.) Core Instruction/Lectura cultural (20 min.)	¿Comprendes? A–B (10 min.) ¿Comprendes? A–C (10 min.)	Quizzes 4–5 (20 min.) ¿Comprendes? C–D ¿Comprendes? D–E Prepárate para el examen, Practice for written proficiency **ConnectEd** Conversation, Reading Practice
Block 6	Develop reading comprehension skills	Core Instruction/Lectura Un poco más (15 min.)	¿Comprendes? (10 min.) Prepárate para el examen (20 min.) Prepárate para el examen, Practice for oral proficiency (30 min.)	Listening Comprehension Test (15 min.) Review for chapter test **ConnectEd** Reading Practice
Block 7	Chapter 3 Tests (50 min.) Reading and Writing Test Speaking Test Test for Oral Proficiency Test for Writing Proficiency Test for Reading Comprehension Chapter Project (40 min.)			

Preview

In this chapter, students will learn the basic vocabulary they need to travel by train in the Spanish-speaking world. They will learn where the train is an important and convenient means of transportation and where train service is nonexistent. Students will come to enjoy some very special train trips in Peru and Mexico. They will also learn the preterite of irregular verbs and the prepositional pronouns.

Pacing

It is important to note that once you reach **¡Bravo!** in the chapter, there is no more new material for the students to learn. The rest of the chapter recycles what has already been covered. The suggested pacing listed here leaves two to three days for review, assessment, and enrichment activities such as the chapter project.

Vocabulario 1	1–2 days
Vocabulario 2	1–2 days
Gramática	2–3 days
Conversación	1 day
Lectura cultural	1 day
Lectura Un poco más	1 day

CAPÍTULO 3

En tren

68 **Go Online!** connectED.mcgraw-hill.com Audio Video Práctica Repaso Diversiones eScape ePals

Go Online!

Audio
Listen to spoken Spanish.

Video
Watch and learn about the Spanish-speaking world.

Práctica
Practice your skills.

Repaso
Review what you've learned.

Diversiones
Go beyond the classroom.

eScape
Read about current events in the Spanish-speaking world.

Aquí y Allí

Vamos a comparar Donde tú vives, ¿hay mucho servicio ferroviario—servicio de trenes? ¿Hay solo trenes locales o hay también trenes de larga distancia? En algunas partes de Estados Unidos, el tren es un medio de transporte importante. En otras no hay servicio ferroviario. Existe la misma situación en el mundo hispano. Vamos a ver donde es importante.

Objetivos

You will:

- use vocabulary related to train travel
- discuss interesting train trips in Peru and Mexico

You will use:

- the preterite of irregular verbs
- the verb **decir**
- prepositional pronouns

El tren azul en los Andes peruanos es un tren de lujo que corre desde Machu Picchu a Cuzco, al lago Titicaca, Puno y otros sitios. Durante estos viajes hay vistas magníficas de los Andes.

SPOTLIGHT ON CULTURE

Cultural Comparison

In addition to observing people in several Spanish-speaking countries using the train services provided, students will read about some fascinating geographical areas accessible by train, notably Cuzco and Machu Picchu, the Copper Canyon, and the Panama Canal. They will also be introduced to some indigenous populations such as the Incas in Peru and the Tarahumara in Mexico.

Cultural Snapshot

PeruRail is now operated by Orient-Express. The company took over in 1999 and has been making constant improvements. They improved services between Cuzco and Machu Picchu and Cuzco, Juliaca and Puno on Lake Titicaca. Between Cuzco and Machu Picchu PeruRail operates several classes of trains: the Backpacker, the Vistadome and the ultra luxurious Hiram Bingham.

Interactive Whiteboard
Present or practice with interactive whiteboard activities.

Assessment
Check student progress.

ePals
Connect with Spanish-speaking students around the world.

Introducción al tema

PRESENT

Introduce the theme of the chapter by having students look at the photographs on these pages. Have them look at the people and determine if there is anything they see them doing that is the same or different from what they do with their own friends. Once you have completed the vocabulary presentation, have students return to these pages and read the information that accompanies each photograph. Once students are fully acquainted with the vocabulary and grammar of the chapter, you may wish to come back to these pages and ask the questions that go with each photo.

Cultural Snapshot

Chile Arica, in northern Chile, is a port on the shores of the Pacific Ocean that serves La Paz, the capital of landlocked Bolivia. Although it is in the Atacama Desert, Arica has a perennial springlike climate and its beaches are quite popular with Chileans and Bolivians. **Hoy en día, ¿de qué sirve la estación de ferrocarril Arica–La Paz? ¿Qué crees? ¿Corre hoy en día el tren o no?**

Panamá **¿Dónde trabajan estas muchachas? ¿Qué ciudades enlaza el ferrocarril? ¿Están bajando (bajándose) o subiendo los pasajeros? ¿Qué observaron a lo largo del canal?**

Introducción al tema

En tren

El tema de este capítulo es el viajar en tren. En unas regiones el tren es un medio de transporte muy importante y en otras no es importante. Sin embargo como vas a ver en este capítulo hay unas excursiones espectaculares que puedes hacer en tren en varias partes del mundo hispanohablante.

Chile

La antigua estación de ferrocarril Arica–La Paz en el norte de Chile es un monumento histórico. Hoy en día la estación sirve de museo ferroviario.

Panamá

Estas jóvenes trabajan en el coche cafetería del tren que enlaza la Ciudad de Panamá y Colón. Los pasajeros que tuvieron la experiencia inolvidable de observar la vegetación tropical a lo largo del canal de Panamá desde las ventanillas del tren hacen cola para bajar(se) en Colón.

Cuba

Qué contraste entre esta locomotora antigua de un tren de turismo en la provincia de Camagüey en Cuba y otros trenes modernos como el AVE.

Nicaragua

Una vieja locomotora en un museo ferroviario en Granada, Nicaragua

(cr)sifa Image Service s.r.o./Alamy, (others)Andrew Payti

Cuba Camagüey is a charming colonial city and, according to the latest information, train service to Camagüey is still available with six trains daily between Camagüey and La Habana. It is the birthplace of the National poet Nicolás Guillén and Carlos J. Finlay, the doctor who discovered the cause of yellow fever (**la fiebre amarilla**). **¿Cómo es la locomotora? ¿Qué tipo de tren es?**

Nicaragua All that is left of the Nicaraguan train system is the small museum in Granada. There is no longer a regular train schedule. **¿Qué vemos aquí, un museo o una estación de ferrocarril? ¿Es una locomotora eléctrica o a vapor?**

Chile

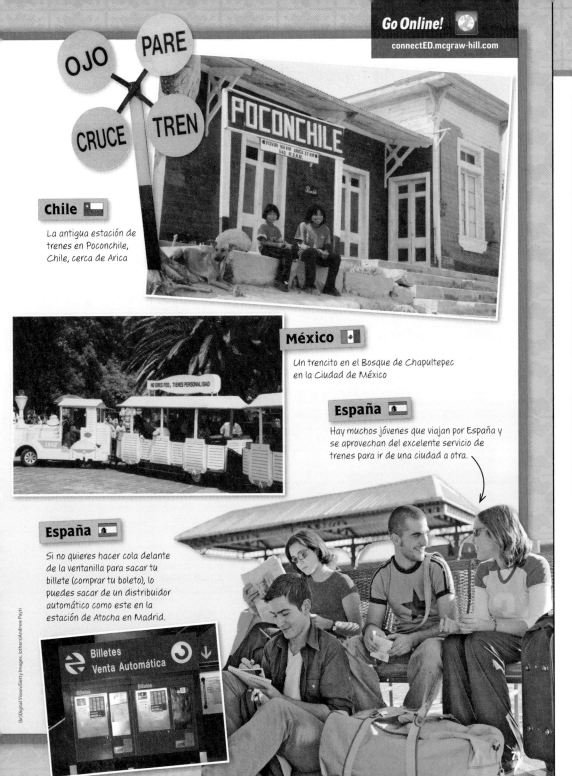

La antigua estación de trenes en Poconchile, Chile, cerca de Arica

México

Un trencito en el Bosque de Chapultepec en la Ciudad de México

España

Hay muchos jóvenes que viajan por España y se aprovechan del excelente servicio de trenes para ir de una ciudad a otra.

España

Si no quieres hacer cola delante de la ventanilla para sacar tu billete (comprar tu boleto), lo puedes sacar de un distribuidor automático como este en la estación de Atocha en Madrid.

Introducción al tema

Chile The Poconchile Station served the train line between Arica, Chile, and La Paz, Bolivia. There is no longer passenger service on this run, but there is a charter tourist service between Arica and Poconchile. **¿Perdieron estos muchachos el tren? ¿Quiénes (se) bajaron del tren en esta estación? ¿Unos usuarios diarios o unos turistas?**

México This little train is a very convenient way to get around and see many parts of the popular Chapultepec Park. It is also a fun tourist attraction. **¿Es el trencito en el Bosque de Chapultepec una parte del sistema urbano de transporte público o más bien una atracción turística?**

España **¿Cómo es el servicio ferroviario en España? ¿Dónde puedes sacar tu billete para el tren si no quieres hacer cola delante de la ventanilla? ¿Cuál es una estación de ferrocarril en Madrid?**

Online Resources

Customizable Lesson Plans
- Whiteboard Lesson
- Audio Activities
- Student Workbook
- Enrichment
- Quizzes

Quick Start

Use QS 3.1 or write the following on the board.

Complete in the preterite.

1. **Ellos ___ en avión. (viajar)**
2. **Yo ___ un vuelo de Miami. (tomar)**
3. **El avión ___ a Lima a tiempo. (llegar)**
4. **Nosotros ___ una merienda durante el vuelo. (tomar)**
5. **Los asistentes de vuelo me ___ en español. (hablar)**
6. **Y tú, ¿___ a Perú? (viajar)**

TEACH

Core Instruction

Step 1 Present the vocabulary first using Vocabulary V3.2–V3.3.

Step 2 Have students repeat each word once or twice. Build to complete sentences. Ask questions such as: **¿Son los pasajeros? ¿Quiénes son? ¿Están en la sala de espera? ¿Dónde están? ¿Esperan el tren? ¿Qué esperan? ¿Dónde esperan el tren?** You can differentiate instruction by asking easy **sí/no** questions of less able learners and the question **¿Dónde esperan el tren?** of more able students who will have to use all the new words to respond—**Los pasajeros esperan el tren en la estación de ferrocarril.**

En la estación de ferrocarril (tren)

el hall
la sala de espera

Los pasajeros esperan su tren en la sala de espera.
El horario indica las llegadas y salidas de los trenes.

Puedes insertar tu tarjeta de crédito o dinero, seleccionar tu destino y tarifa y el billete te sale automáticamente.

el billete sencillo →

el billete de ida y vuelta, el boleto de ida y regreso ⇄

Para conversar

Un billete para Madrid, por favor.
Ventanilla
¿En primera clase o en segunda?
En segunda, por favor, de ida y vuelta.
Ventanilla

Los amigos hicieron un viaje en tren.
Tomaron el tren.
No quisieron tomar el autobús.
Los amigos estuvieron en el andén.
Esperaron el tren en el andén.

La señora hizo un viaje en tren.
No pudo poner su equipaje en el tren.
Un joven la ayudó.

Go Online!

connectED.mcgraw-hill.com

En otras partes

The word **boleto** is used throughout Latin America. **El billete** is used in Spain. **La boletería** is used more frequently in Latin America, while **la ventanilla** is used in Spain. **El boleto de ida y regreso** is common in Latin America for *a round-trip ticket*. In Mexico, however, you will hear **un redondo. El billete de ida y vuelta** is used in Spain. *To buy a ticket* in Latin America is **comprar un boleto**; in Spain it is **sacar un billete.**

Step 3 After the initial presentation, have students read the new vocabulary.

Differentiation

Multiple Intelligences

Have **bodily-kinesthetic** learners actually pretend they are using the automatic ticket dispenser. Have them act out the short **Para conversar.**

¡Así se dice!

Why It Works!

Language is presented in manageable and usable segments: vocabulary—train travel—connected to grammar—irregular preterites. **Hicieron el viaje en tren. No quisieron tomar el bus. Estuvieron en el andén. Pusieron las maletas en el tren.**

Cultural Snapshot

The photos in these train stations were taken in Atocha in Madrid, Belgrano in Buenos Aires, and the Estació Sants (Estación Santos) in Barcelona.

Go Online!

You may wish to use the whiteboard presentation for additional vocabulary instruction and practice.

Total Physical Response (TPR)

(Student), **ven acá, por favor.**
¡Ay! Tu tren va a salir pronto. Corre al distribuidor automático para comprar tu boleto.
Inserta tu tarjeta de crédito.
Pulsa para seleccionar tu destino.
Saca tu boleto o tiquet de la máquina.
Corre al andén.
Párate.
Espera el tren.
Indica que el tren llega.
Antes de subir al tren, ayuda a alguien con su maleta.
Sube al tren.
Gracias, *(Student)*, **y siéntate. Has hecho muy bien.**

Leveling EACH Activity

Easy Activities 1, 5, 6
Average Activities 2, 3, 4
CHallenging Activities 5
Expansión, 7, 8

PRACTICE

Activity 1

Audio Script

1. Hay periódicos delante del quiosco.
2. El tren llega a tiempo.
3. Los pasajeros esperan el tren en el andén.
4. Hay un quiosco en el hall.
5. El pasajero espera el tren y lee un libro de bolsillo.

Activities 2, 4, and 5 It is suggested you go over these activities in class before assigning them for homework. They can also be done as paired activities.

Go Online!

You may wish to remind students to go online for additional vocabulary practice. They can also download audio files of all vocabulary.

Cultural Snapshot

(bottom) The pleasant port city of Málaga has some 700,000 inhabitants. It is considered the capital of the Costa del Sol but most tourists merely use the Málaga airport on their way to the sunny beaches. Picasso was born on the Plaza de la Merced and his house is presently a museum.

ESCUCHAR

1 Escucha las frases. Parea cada frase con la foto que describe.

a. 

b. 

HABLAR • ESCRIBIR

2 Contesta.

1. La señora no sabe a qué hora sale su tren. ¿Qué consulta?
2. La señora quiere sacar un billete para el tren. ¿Adónde va?
3. La señora piensa volver. ¿Qué tipo de billete (boleto) necesita?
4. Los trenes tienen dos clases. ¿En qué clase es más alta la tarifa? ¿En primera o en segunda?
5. La señora no quiere hacer cola delante de la ventanilla. ¿Dónde puede sacar su billete?
6. ¿Dónde esperan los pasajeros el tren?
7. En el hall de la estación de tren hay un quiosco. ¿Qué venden en el quiosco?

CULTURA
En la ventanilla de la estación de ferrocarril en Málaga, España

ESCRIBIR

3 Da una palabra relacionada.

la ventana **esperar** **salir**
ir **llegar** **volver**

Answers

1
1. a
2. b
3. b
4. a
5. b

2
1. La señora consulta el horario.
2. La señora va a la ventanilla. (La señora va al distribuidor automático.)
3. Necesita un billete (boleto) de ida y vuelta (regreso).
4. La tarifa es más alta en primera clase.
5. Puede sacar su billete del distribuidor automático.
6. Los pasajeros esperan el tren en la sala de espera. (Esperan el tren en el andén.)
7. Venden periódicos, revistas y libros de bolsillo en el quiosco.

3
la ventana / la ventanilla
esperar / espera
salir / salidas
ir / ida
llegar / llegadas
volver / vuelta

HABLAR • ESCRIBIR

4 Contesta según la información en el billete.

1. ¿De qué estación en Madrid sale el tren?
2. ¿Cuál es el destino del tren?
3. ¿A qué hora sale?
4. ¿A qué hora llega?
5. ¿Es un billete sencillo o de ida y vuelta?

ESCUCHAR • HABLAR • ESCRIBIR

5 Contesta según se indica.

1. ¿Quiso José hacer el viaje en bus? (no)
2. ¿Cómo hizo el viaje? (en tren)
3. ¿Pudo llevar su equipaje? (no)
4. ¿Quién lo ayudó? (su amigo)
5. ¿Dónde esperó el tren? (en el andén)
6. ¿Estuvo mucho tiempo en el andén? (no)

EXPANSIÓN

Ahora, sin mirar las preguntas, cuenta la información en tus propias palabras. Si no recuerdas algo, un(a) compañero(a) te puede ayudar.

CULTURA

Una vista parcial de la estación de ferrocarril de Atocha en Madrid

LEER • ESCRIBIR

6 **Juego Cada uno en su sitio** Pon cada palabra en el lugar apropiado.

el vagón **el horario** **la vía**
la sala de espera **el distribuidor automático**
el tren **el quiosco** **la ventanilla**

EN EL HALL	EN EL ANDÉN
______	______
______	______
______	______

Comunicación

7 Trabaja con un(a) compañero(a) de clase. Tu compañero(a) va a ser el/la agente en la ventanilla. Preparen una conversación para comprar un billete.

8 Tienes un(a) amigo(a) que está en la estación de Atocha en Madrid. Explícale lo que tiene que hacer para sacar su billete de un distribuidor automático.

¡Así se dice!

If while speaking you realize that you have made a grammatical error, just stop and say, **Perdón, digo...**, and restate correctly what you meant to say.

Go Online!

connectED.mcgraw-hill.com

Vocabulario 1

Comunicación

Interpersonal

As students do Activities 7 and 8 extemporaneously, it is suggested that you not correct all errors since students are speaking and improvising on their own. However, this is up to your own discretion or preference. You may wish to encourage students to self-correct whenever they are aware of having made an error.

Cultural Snapshot

Atocha is a modern, convenient railroad station located in the central part of Madrid, not far from the Prado Museum. The famous high speed train El AVE—**tren de alta velocidad española**—leaves from Atocha. The other main rail station of Madrid is Chamartín.

Go Online!

You may wish to use the whiteboard presentation for additional vocabulary instruction and practice.

ASSESS

Students are now ready to take Quiz 1.

Answers

4
1. El tren sale de Chamartín.
2. El destino del tren es A Coruña.
3. Sale a las 21:45 (11:45).
4. Llega a las 8:45.
5. Es un billete sencillo.

5
1. No, José no quiso hacer el viaje en bus.
2. Hizo el viaje en tren.
3. No, no pudo llevar su equipaje.
4. Su amigo lo ayudó.
5. Esperó el tren en el andén.
6. No, no estuvo mucho tiempo en el andén.

6
en el hall
el horario
la sala de espera
el distribuidor automático
el quiosco
la ventanilla

en el andén
el vagón
la vía
el tren

7 *Answers will vary.*

8 *Answers will vary but may include:* Primero tienes que insertar tu tarjeta de crédito o dinero. Luego, seleccionas tu destino y tarifa. El billete te sale automáticamente.

Online Resources

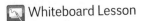

Customizable Lesson Plans
- Whiteboard Lesson
- Audio Activities
- Video (Vocabulario)
- Student Workbook
- Enrichment
- Quizzes

Quick Start

Use QS 3.2 or write the following on the board.

Complete in the preterite.

1. **Yo ___ para Puerto Rico. (salir)**
2. **Antes de salir, nosotros ___ algo en la bufetería en el aeropuerto. (comer)**
3. **¿A qué hora ___ ustedes? (volver)**
4. **Alguien ___ mi mochila. (abrir)**
5. **¿Tú ___ algo? (beber)**

TEACH

Core Instruction

Step 1 Present the vocabulary using Vocabulary V3.4–V3.5.

Step 2 After presenting the vocabulary and asking oral questions as suggested in previous chapters, have students read the material. Following is an example of leveled questions to enable all students to respond. **¿Es el revisor?** *(Easy)* **¿Quién es?** *(Easy)* **¿Son billetes?** *(Easy)* **¿Qué son?** *(Easy)* **¿Es el tren?** *(Easy)* **¿Qué es?** *(Easy)* **¿Revisó los billetes el revisor?** *(Average)* **¿Quién revisó los billetes?** *(Average)* **¿Revisó el revisor los billetes en el tren?** *(Average)* **¿Quién los revisó?** *(Challenging)* **¿Qué revisó?** *(Challenging)* **¿Dónde revisó los billetes?** *(Challenging)*

En el tren

El revisor revisó los billetes.
El tren no está completo. Hay asientos libres.

En otras partes

In Spain **el revisor** is a *train conductor.* The term is used in Latin America as well, but you will also hear **el cobrador,** particularly on buses or trains where one actually pays the fare on board. **El asiento** is used throughout Latin America, and **la plaza** is used in Spain.

El tren salió a tiempo.
No salió tarde.
No salió con retraso (con una demora).

Tips for Success

As students are familiar with the new vocabulary, have them read again the captions in the **Introducción al tema.**

Estos jóvenes estuvieron en México.
Cuando (se) bajaron del tren, alquilaron (rentaron) unos caballos.
Anduvieron a caballo por los riscos del cañón.

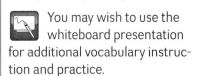

Los pasajeros van a bajar(se) en la próxima parada (estación).

Para conversar

¿Este tren va a Barcelona?
No, señor. Tiene que transbordar (cambiar de tren).
Ay, ¿sí? ¿Dónde?
Puede bajar(se) en la próxima parada (estación).

Tienen que transbordar (cambiar de tren).

Differentiation

Multiple Intelligences

Have **bodily-kinesthetic** learners act out the short **Para conversar** section in front of the class.

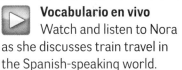

ABOUT THE SPANISH LANGUAGE

You will hear both **bajar del tren** and **bajarse del tren. Subirse al tren** is also used. However, **subir** seems more common. In addition to **revisar** and **verificar, chequear** is also heard.

Go Online!

Vocabulario en vivo Watch and listen to Nora as she discusses train travel in the Spanish-speaking world.

You may wish to use the whiteboard presentation for additional vocabulary instruction and practice.

Total Physical Response (TPR)

(Student), **ven acá.**
Sube al tren.
Busca un asiento libre.
Ay, aquí hay uno. Toma tu asiento.
Mira tu libro de bolsillo.
Ábrelo. Empieza a leer.
Aquí viene el revisor. Dale tu boleto.
El tren está llegando a tu parada.
Levántate, *(Student).*
Ve a la puerta.
Espera. La puerta se está abriendo. Baja (Bájate) del tren, *(Student).*
Gracias, *(Student).*

Leveling EACH Activity

Easy Activities 1, 2
Average Activities 4, 5, 6
Average–CHallenging Activity 3

PRACTICE

Activity 1

Audio Script

1. a. Puede sentarse. Es un asiento libre.
   b. Puede sentarse. Es un asiento ocupado.
2. a. El tren está completo. Hay gente de pie en el pasillo.
   b. Hay muchos asientos libres. Hay gente de pie en el pasillo.
3. a. El revisor revisa los horarios.
   b. El revisor revisa los boletos.
4. a. Los pasajeros tienen que transbordar porque el tren va a la estación donde van a bajar.
   b. Los pasajeros tienen que transbordar porque el tren no hace parada en la estación que quieren.
5. a. Los pasajeros suben al tren en la estación de salida.
   b. Los pasajeros suben al tren en la estación de llegada.
6. a. Los pasajeros (se) bajan del tren cuando terminan su viaje.
   b. Los pasajeros (se) bajan del tren cuando empiezan su viaje.

Activity 2 You can call on students in class to answer the questions as the entire group listens or you can do this as a paired activity.

Differentiation

Slower Paced Learners
Advanced Learners

Activity 3 Have slower paced learners give just the word. Have advanced learners use the word in an original sentence.

ESCUCHAR

1 Escucha. Escoge la frase correcta. Usa una tabla como la de abajo para indicar tus respuestas.

a	b

Conexiones

Las matemáticas

Si tienes que leer un anuncio de un evento o el horario en un país hispano, vas a ver que dan la hora usando las veinticuatro horas. La una es la una de la mañana y las doce es el mediodía. Las trece es una hora después del mediodía—es la una de la tarde. Las veinticuatro horas es la medianoche.

HORARIO DE TRENES

JULIO, JULIOL / JULY, JULI — AGOSTO, AGOST / AUGUST, AUGUST — SEPTIEMBRE, SETEMBRE / SEPTEMBER, SEPTEMBER

SÓLLER - PALMA	PALMA - SÓLLER	
8 00	8 00	
9 15	10 40	TREN TURÍSTICO
11 50	13 00	
14 10	15 15	
19 00	20 05	
19 35		

HABLAR

2 Contesta.

1. Cuando el tren sale a tiempo, ¿hay una demora o no?
2. ¿Pasa el revisor por los pasillos del tren?
3. ¿Revisa los boletos de los pasajeros?
4. Cuando el tren está completo, ¿hay asientos libres?
5. Si los pasajeros tienen hambre, ¿pueden ir a la bufetería?

HABLAR • ESCRIBIR

3 Identifica. Luego usa cada palabra en una frase original.

1.

2.

3.

4.

Answers

1
1. a
2. a
3. b
4. b
5. a
6. a

2
1. No, no hay una demora cuando el tren sale a tiempo.
2. Sí, el revisor pasa por los pasillos del tren.
3. Sí, revisa los boletos de los pasajeros.
4. No, no hay asientos libres cuando el tren está completo.
5. Sí, los pasajeros pueden ir a la bufetería si tienen hambre.

3 *Answers will vary but should include:*
1. un caballo
2. un risco
3. una senda
4. un cañón

LEER

4 Parea las palabras que tienen el mismo significado.

1. una plaza	**a.** la bufetería
2. desocupado	**b.** con una demora
3. el coche cafetería	**c.** cambiar de tren
4. rentar	**d.** un asiento
5. con retraso	**e.** libre
6. transbordar	**f.** alquilar

HABLAR • ESCRIBIR

5 Contesta las preguntas sobre unos amigos que hicieron un viaje interesante por un cañón famoso.

1. ¿Tomaron los amigos el tren?
2. ¿Pagaron una tarifa estudiantil?
3. Cuando (se) bajaron del tren, ¿dieron una caminata?
4. ¿Rentaron caballos?
5. ¿Por dónde anduvieron?
6. ¿Adónde hicieron una excursión?
7. ¿Fueron solos o tuvieron que ir acompañados de un guía?
8. ¿Vieron todo el cañón?

CULTURA

Los jóvenes van a cabalgar.

ESCRIBIR

6 **Rompecabezas**

Forma palabras con las siguientes letras. Luego descubre el mensaje secreto.

1. rfíbuteea
   ◯ ◯ ◯ __ __ ◯ __ __ __
   1 2 3 4
2. ilasplo
   ◯ ◯ __ __ ◯ __ __
   5 6 7
3. rrsantdabor
   ◯ __ __ ◯ __ __ ◯ __ __ __ ◯
   8 9 10 11
4. serrivo
   __ __ ◯ ◯ __ __ __
   12 13

El mensaje secreto

__ __ __ __ __ __ __ __ __,
2 9 1 13 7 7 4 8 4

__ __ __ __ __ __ __ __.
5 10 11 3 6 12 10 11

InfoGap For more practice using your new vocabulary words, do Activity 3 in the Student Resource section at the end of this book.

Go Online!

connectED.mcgraw-hill.com

ImageSource/age fotostock

Vocabulario 2

Additional Vocabulary

If you have some students in class who are interested in horseback riding, you may wish to give them a few additional words:

la brida *bridle*
las riendas *reins*
el freno, el bocado *bit*
el estribo *stirrup*
la silla *saddle*
ensillar *to saddle*
montar a caballo *ride horseback*
subir(se) al caballo *to get on the horse*

Tips for Success

After going over the **Práctica** activities, have students return to the **Vocabulario** section and make up statements and questions about the photos.

Differentiation

Advanced Learners

Advanced learners can make up questions about the photos in the **Vocabulario** section and call on others to answer.

Easily Distracted Learners

The activities have a variety of formats giving students the opportunity to practice the same material in various ways, helping to hold their attention.

ASSESS

Students are now ready to take Quiz 2.

Answers

4

1. d
2. e
3. a
4. f
5. b
6. c

5

1. Sí (No), los amigos (no) tomaron el tren.
2. Sí, (No, no) pagaron una tarifa estudiantil.
3. Sí (No), cuando (se) bajaron del tren, (no) dieron una caminata.
4. Sí, (No, no) rentaron caballos.
5. Anduvieron por el cañón.
6. Hicieron una excursión al cañón.
7. Fueron solos. (Tuvieron que ir acompañados de un guía.)
8. Sí, (No, no) vieron todo el cañón.

6

1. bufetería
2. pasillo
3. transbordar
4. revisor

El mensaje secreto:
Un billete, por favor.

Online Resources

- Customizable Lesson Plans
- Whiteboard Lesson
- Audio Activities
- Video (Gramática)
- Student Workbook
- Quizzes

Quick Start

Use QS 3.3 or write the following on the board.

Complete.

1. **Tengo ___ y quiero comer algo.**
2. **Tengo ___ y quiero beber algo.**
3. **¿Por qué no vamos a un ___?**
4. **¡Buena idea! Pero hay mucha gente. No veo una ___ libre.**
5. **El ___ trabaja en el café.**
6. **Él nos trae el ___ y Sarita lo lee. Decidimos lo que vamos a tomar.**

TEACH

Core Instruction

Step 1 Have the class read each infinitive. Explain to them that these verbs have irregular forms in the preterite.

Step 2 Proceed by having them read aloud each group of verbs across **(hacer, querer, venir; poder poner, saber; estar, andar, tener).** Reading them across focuses on the **i, u, uv.**

Step 3 You may wish to write the verbs on the board, highlighting the **i, u,** or **uv** in each conjugation.

Pretérito de los verbos irregulares

1. The verbs **hacer, querer,** and **venir** are irregular in the preterite. Note that they all have an **i** in the stem. Note too that the endings for **yo** and **usted (él, ella)** are different from the endings of regular verbs.

	hacer	querer	venir
yo	hice	quise	vine
tú	hiciste	quisiste	viniste
Ud., él, ella	hizo	quiso	vino
nosotros(as)	hicimos	quisimos	vinimos
vosotros(as)	*hicisteis*	*quisisteis*	*vinisteis*
Uds., ellos, ellas	hicieron	quisieron	vinieron

2. The verbs **poder, poner,** and **saber** all have a **u** in the stem.

	poder	poner	saber
yo	pude	puse	supe
tú	pudiste	pusiste	supiste
Ud., él, ella	pudo	puso	supo
nosotros(as)	pudimos	pusimos	supimos
vosotros(as)	*pudisteis*	*pusisteis*	*supisteis*
Uds., ellos, ellas	pudieron	pusieron	supieron

3. The verbs **estar, andar,** and **tener** all have a **uv** in the stem.

	estar	andar	tener
yo	estuve	anduve	tuve
tú	estuviste	anduviste	tuviste
Ud., él, ella	estuvo	anduvo	tuvo
nosotros(as)	estuvimos	anduvimos	tuvimos
vosotros(as)	*estuvisteis*	*anduvisteis*	*tuvisteis*
Uds., ellos, ellas	estuvieron	anduvieron	tuvieron

CULTURA

Los peatones anduvieron por la Plaza de la Independencia en Montevideo, Uruguay.

Andrew Payti

¡Así se dice!

Why It Works!

All forms that have a similar irregularity are grouped together to assist students in determining a logical pattern.

Note: Many of the verbs students will be learning in this chapter are not used very frequently in the preterite. For this reason, it is recommended that you not spend a great deal of time on this topic. The most important verbs are **hacer**, **venir**, and **poner.**

4. Many of these verbs are not used frequently in the preterite. When they are, they take on a special meaning. Observe the following.

Quise ayudar.	*I tried to help.*
No quiso ir en carro.	*He refused to go by car.*
Yo lo supe ayer.	*I found out yesterday.*
No pude terminar.	*(I tried but) I couldn't finish.*
Pude terminar.	*(After much effort) I managed to finish.*

Práctica

HABLAR • ESCRIBIR

1 Imagina que estuviste en una estación de tren. Contesta.

1. ¿Cómo viniste a la estación de tren?
2. ¿Hiciste el viaje en tren?
3. ¿Lo hiciste en tren porque no quisiste ir en carro?
4. ¿Pudiste poner todo tu equipaje en el tren?
5. ¿Tuviste que buscar un asiento libre?
6. ¿Anduviste de un vagón a otro para buscar un asiento?

EXPANSIÓN

Ahora, sin mirar las preguntas, cuenta la información en tus propias palabras. Si no recuerdas algo, un(a) compañero(a) te puede ayudar.

LEER • ESCRIBIR

2 Completa las conversaciones en el pretérito.

1. —Ellos no ____ (querer) hacer el viaje.
—¿No lo ____ (querer) hacer?
—No, de ninguna manera.
—Pues, ¿qué pasó entonces? ¿Lo ____ (hacer) o no lo ____ (hacer)?
—No lo ____ (hacer).
2. —¿Por qué no ____ (venir) ustedes esta mañana?
—Nosotros no ____ (venir) porque no ____ (hacer) reservación.
—¿Ustedes no ____ (tener) reservación?
3. —Carlos no ____ (querer) hacer la cama.
—Entonces, ¿quién la ____ (hacer)?
—Pues, la ____ (hacer) yo.
—¡Qué absurdo! ¿Tú la ____ (hacer) porque él no la ____ (querer) hacer?

Go Online!
connectED.mcgraw-hill.com

FOLDABLES Study Organizer

CATEGORY BOOK See the Foldables section of the Student Handbook at the beginning of this book for help with making this foldable. Make a *category book* foldable with ten tabs. On the top tab, write the infinitive of a verb that is irregular in the preterite. On the following tabs, write the subject pronouns: **yo, tú, Ud., él, ella, nosotros(as), Uds., ellos, ellas.** Exchange foldables with your partner. Open each tab and write the correct form of the verb.

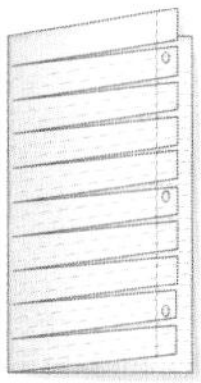

Leveling EACH Activity

Easy Activity 1
Easy-Average Activity 2
Average Activity 1 **Expansión**

PRACTICE

Tips for Success

It is recommended that you go over the grammar activities once in class before they are assigned for homework.

Activity 1 You can do this activity as a class activity or a paired activity, having one student ask the question as the other responds.

Activity 2 After students write this activity at home, call on individuals to read their answers in class.

Conexiones

Have students look at the pages featuring Uruguay in the **GeoVistas** section at the beginning of this book and locate Montevideo on the map. Based on the information in the map, have students guess what industries might be prevalent in this city.

Cultural Snapshot

(previous page) Montevideo is a pleasant South American city on the río Plata and the Atlantic Ocean. On this plaza you can see the equestrian statue of José Gervasio Artigas. He is considered the father of Uruguayan independence, having fought against the Spanish and Portuguese. His mausoleum is beneath the statue.

Answers

1

1. Vine a la estación de tren en carro (en taxi, en bus, a pie).
2. Sí, hice el viaje en tren.
3. Sí, (No, no) lo hice en tren porque no quise ir en carro.
4. Sí, (No, no) pude poner todo mi equipaje en el tren.
5. Sí, (No, no) tuve que buscar un asiento libre.
6. Sí, (No, no) anduve de un vagón a otro para buscar un asiento.

2

1. quisieron, quisieron, hicieron, hicieron, hicieron
2. vinieron, vinimos, hicimos, tuvieron
3. quiso, hizo, hice, hiciste, quiso

Leveling EACH Activity

Average–CHallenging Activity 3
CHallenging Activities 4, 5

PRACTICE *(continued)*

Activity 3 Note that this activity is more challenging because students have to use many different verbs and a variety of forms.

Activity 4 Have students respond orally using proper intonation as in a natural, everyday conversation.

Go Online!

You may wish to remind students to go online for additional grammar review and practice.

You may wish to use the whiteboard presentation for additional grammar instruction and practice.

ASSESS

Students are now ready to take Quiz 3.

LEER • ESCRIBIR

3 Completa con el pretérito del verbo indicado.

El otro día yo __1__ (estar) en un mercado en Perú. Rafael __2__ (estar) allí también. Nosotros __3__ (andar) por el mercado pero no __4__ (poder) comprar nada. No es que no __5__ (querer) comprar nada, es que no __6__ (poder) porque __7__ (ir) al mercado sin dinero.

CULTURA
Un mercado indígena en un pueblo andino de Perú

ESCUCHAR • HABLAR • ESCRIBIR

4 Sigue el modelo.

MODELO **No puedo ahora. →**
No puedo ahora y no pude ayer tampoco.

1. No pueden ahora.
2. No tenemos que hacerlo ahora.
3. No lo haces ahora.
4. Ellos no están ahora.
5. Él no viene ahora.

CULTURA
Carlos es un joven peruano. Como los jóvenes en todas partes, Carlos no pudo salir anoche porque tuvo que estudiar.

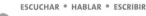

5 ***Comunicación***

Habla con un(a) compañero(a) de clase. Dile lo que no pudiste o no quisiste hacer porque tuviste que hacer otra cosa. Dile lo que hiciste. Luego tu compañero(a) va a decir lo que no pudo o no quiso hacer porque tuvo que hacer otra cosa.

Answers

3
1. estuve
2. estuvo
3. anduvimos
4. pudimos
5. quisimos
6. pudimos
7. fuimos

4
1. No pueden ahora y no pudieron ayer tampoco.
2. No tenemos que hacerlo ahora y no tuvimos que hacerlo ayer tampoco.
3. No lo haces ahora y no lo hiciste ayer tampoco.
4. Ellos no están ahora y no estuvieron ayer tampoco.
5. Él no viene ahora y no vino ayer tampoco.

5 *Answers will vary.*

Go Online!

connectED.mcgraw-hill.com

El verbo decir

The verb **decir** *(to say)* is irregular in the present and preterite tenses. Study the following forms.

PRESENTE			
yo	digo	nosotros(as)	decimos
tú	dices	*vosotros(as)*	*decís*
Ud., él, ella	dice	Uds., ellos, ellas	dicen

PRETÉRITO			
yo	dije	nosotros(as)	dijimos
tú	dijiste	*vosotros(as)*	*dijisteis*
Ud., él, ella	dijo	Uds., ellos, ellas	dijeron

Práctica

HABLAR

6 Personaliza. Da respuestas personales.

1. ¿Qué dices? ¿Quieres dar una caminata? Digo que…
2. ¿Qué dices? ¿Quieres subir hasta las ruinas?
3. ¿Qué dices? ¿Quieres hacer una excursión al cañón?
4. ¿Qué dices? ¿Quieres alquilar un caballo?

LEER • ESCRIBIR

7 Completa con el presente de **decir.**

—Yo __1__ que quiero ir en tren pero Elena me __2__ que prefiere tomar el avión. Ella y Tomás también __3__ que no hay mucha diferencia entre la tarifa del avión y la tarifa del tren. ¿Qué __4__ tú?

—Yo __5__ que es mejor ir en tren.

—Bueno. Tú y yo __6__ la misma cosa. Estamos de acuerdo.

LEER • ESCRIBIR

8 Completa con el presente y el pretérito de **decir.**

1. Yo lo ____ pero ellos no lo ____.
2. Ellos lo ____ pero nosotros no lo ____.
3. Él lo ____ pero ustedes no lo ____.
4. Nosotros lo ____ pero ustedes no lo ____.
5. Tú lo ____ pero yo no lo ____.

Nota

- Note the use of **que** after the verb **decir.**

  Yo digo que sí y ellos dicen que no.

- Note that the verb **traer** follows the same pattern as the verb **decir** in the preterite: **traje.**

Online Resources

Customizable Lesson Plans

- Whiteboard Lesson
- Audio Activities
- Video (Gramática)
- Student Workbook
- Enrichment
- Quizzes

Quick Start

Use QS 3.4 or write the following on the board.

1. Write a list in Spanish of foods you like.
2. Write a list in Spanish of beverages you like.

TEACH

Core Instruction

Step 1 Have students read aloud the present and preterite forms of **decir.**

Step 2 When going over the present you may wish to call students' attention to verbs like **pedir (e → i)** which they have already learned.

Step 3 Tell students to pronounce **dijeron** (and **trajeron**) correctly in the preterite. If they do, they will spell the ending correctly because they hear no **i** sound.

Differentiation

Students with Auditory Impairments

Concentrate on the important **i** and **e** sounds. Allow students to hear **dice, dicen, decimos** several times and then have them repeat.

Answers

6

1. Digo que (no) quiero dar una caminata.
2. Digo que (no) quiero subir hasta las ruinas.
3. Digo que (no) quiero hacer una excursión al cañón.
4. Digo que (no) quiero alquilar un caballo.

7

1. digo
2. dice
3. dicen
4. dices
5. digo
6. decimos

8

1. digo, dijeron
2. dicen, dijimos
3. dice, dijeron
4. decimos, dijeron
5. dices, dije

Multiple Intelligences

Engage **verbal-linguistic** learners by having them debate a topic. Have them use phrases like **«Yo digo… pero tú dices… », «Y ellos dicen… »,** and **«¿Por qué no decimos… ?».**

Leveling EACH Activity

Easy Activity 6
Easy–Average Activity 7
Average Activities 8, 9
CHallenging Activity 10

ASSESS

Students are now ready to take Quiz 4.

Go Online!

Gramática en vivo: *Irregular verbs in the preterite*
Enliven learning with the animated world of Professor Cruz! **Gramática en vivo** is a fun and effective tool for additional instruction and/or review.

You may wish to use the whiteboard presentation for additional grammar instruction and practice.

LEER • ESCRIBIR

9 Completa con el pretérito de **decir.**

1. Tomás me _____ que le gusta mucho la ciudad de Montevideo.
2. Yo le _____ que a mí me gusta también.
3. Nosotros _____ que nos gusta porque es una ciudad bonita.
4. ¿No me _____ (tú) que está cerca del mar?
5. Sí, y (yo) te _____ que en la ciudad misma hay playas.

CULTURA
Montevideo, la capital de Uruguay, es una ciudad cosmopolita. Dentro de la ciudad, hay muchos barrios residenciales.

HABLAR • ESCRIBIR

10 ¿Quién dijo que sí? Contesta usando cada sujeto.

Andrew Payti

Answers

9
1. dijo
2. dije
3. dijimos
4. dijiste
5. dije

10
1. Yo dije que sí.
2. Mi amigo dijo que sí.
3. Tú dijiste que sí.
4. Usted dijo que sí.
5. Nosotros dijimos que sí.
6. Pilar y yo dijimos que sí.
7. Miguel y Andrés dijeron que sí.
8. Ustedes dijeron que sí.

11 *Answers will vary but may include:*
1. Es de él (ella).
2. Es para mí.
3. Pienso bueno (mal) de ti.
4. Sí (No), Julia (no) quiero hacer una caminata con ustedes.
5. Sí, (No, no) quiero ir contigo.
6. _____ van a hacer el viaje conmigo.
7. A mí me gusta más leer libros de bolsillo (artículos de una revista).

12
1. No es para él (ella).
2. Ellos quieren ir conmigo.
3. Es de usted, ¿no?
4. Estamos pensando en ella.
5. ¿Por qué no lo están discutiendo conmigo?

Pronombres después de una preposición

Go Online!

connectED.mcgraw-hill.com

1. You already know all the pronouns you use after a preposition. Remember they are the same as the subject pronouns except for **mí** and **ti. Mí** takes an accent mark to differentiate it from the possessive adjective **mi—mi casa.**

Para	**mí** **ti** **usted** **él** **ella** **nosotros(as)** **ustedes** **ellos** **ellas**	**está bien, ¿no?**

2. Note what happens to **mí** and **ti** when used with **con.**

—¿Vienes conmigo?
—Sí, voy contigo.

—¿Quién hizo el viaje contigo?
—Carolina lo hizo conmigo.

Refrán

Can you guess what the following proverb means?

Querer y poder, hermanos vienen a ser.

Práctica

HABLAR • ESCRIBIR

11 Contesta.

1. ¿De quién es el boleto? ¿Es de él o de ella?
2. ¿Para quién es la cámara digital? ¿Es para ti?
3. ¿Qué piensas de mí? Puedes ser honesto(a).
4. ¿Quiere Julia hacer una caminata con ustedes?
5. ¿Quieres ir conmigo?
6. ¿Quiénes van a hacer el viaje contigo?
7. ¿A ti te gusta más leer libros de bolsillo o artículos en una revista?

ESCRIBIR

12 Escribe en el singular.

1. No es para *ellos.*
2. Ellos quieren ir con *nosotros.*
3. Es de *ustedes,* ¿no?
4. Estamos pensando en *ellas.*
5. ¿Por qué no lo están discutiendo con *nosotros?*

¡Bravo!

You have now learned all the new vocabulary and grammar in this chapter. Continue to use and practice all that you know while learning more cultural information. **¡Vamos!**

Online Resources

Customizable Lesson Plans
- Whiteboard Lesson
- Audio Activities
- Student Workbook
- Quizzes

Quick Start

Use QS 3.5 or write the following on the board.

Complete with the correct subject pronoun.

1. ___ **hablo muy bien el español.**
2. ___ **lo aprendemos en la escuela.**
3. **La señora Gómez es la profesora. ___ es muy buena y aprendemos mucho.**
4. ___ **estudias español también, ¿no?**
5. **¿Son ___ inteligentes?**

TEACH

Core Instruction

Step 1 This point should be very easy for students since most pronouns are the same as the subject pronouns. Note that the subject pronouns are reviewed in the Quick Start activity.

Step 2 Concentrate on the **conmigo** and **contigo** forms.

PRACTICE

Leveling EACH Activity

Easy-Average Activities 11, 12

Activity 11 You can call on class members to respond or you can do this as a paired activity.

ASSESS

Students are now ready to take Quiz 5.

Refrán

Have students recite the proverb aloud. Then see if they can figure out its meaning, and encourage them to try to give an equivalent expression in English such as "Where there is a will, there is a way."

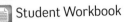

Online Resources

Customizable Lesson Plans

Audio Activities

Video (Diálogo)

Student Workbook

Quick Start

Use QS 3.6 or write the following on the board.

Answer.

1. **¿Está Elena en la estación de ferrocarril?**
2. **¿Necesita ella un boleto?**
3. **¿Es ella estudiante?**
4. **Y tú, ¿estás en la estación también?**
5. **¿Dónde estás?**
6. **¿Eres estudiante también?**

TEACH

Core Instruction

Step 1 Read the conversation to students or play the audio recording.

Step 2 Have the class repeat each line once.

Step 3 Call on two students to read the conversation with as much expression as possible.

Step 4 After completing the conversation, have students summarize it in their own words.

Step 5 After presenting the conversation, go over the **¿Comprendes?** activities. If students can answer the questions with relative ease, move on. Students should not be expected to memorize the conversation.

86 *ochenta y seis* CAPÍTULO 3

¡Así se dice!

Why It Works!

No new material is used in the **Conversación** in order not to confuse students. The **Conversación** recombines only the vocabulary and grammar that students have already learned to understand and manipulate.

Go Online!

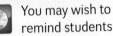

You may wish to remind students to go online for additional conversation practice.

¿Comprendes?

connectED.mcgraw-hill.com

A Completa según la información en la conversación. Indica tus respuestas en una tabla como la de abajo.

el billete				
tipo	clase	destino	tipo de tarifa	precio (tarifa)

B Completa según la información en la conversación. Indica tus respuestas en una tabla como la de abajo.

el viaje		
medio de transporte	hora de salida	andén

C Corrige toda la información falsa.

1. La pasajera compra un billete para Sevilla.
2. Quiere un billete sencillo.
3. Necesita el billete para mañana.
4. Quiere viajar en primera.
5. La pasajera es profesora.
6. El tren sale a las seis y diez de la tarde.

D **Resumiendo** Cuenta todo lo que pasa en la conversación en tus propias palabras.

¿Lo sabes?

Muchos alumnos toman el tren. Hay tarifas escolares (estudiantiles) reducidas.

CULTURA

Córdoba, a orillas del río Guadalquivir, es una ciudad de mucho interés histórico. Aquí vemos el puente romano y la famosa Mezquita.

Answers

A
tipo: ida y vuelta
clase: segunda
destino: Córdoba
tipo de tarifa: reducida (para estudiantes)
precio (tarifa): veintisiete euros

B
medio de transporte: tren
hora de salida: veinte diez
andén: ocho

C
1. La pasajera compra un billete para Córdoba.
2. Quiere un billete de ida y vuelta.
3. Necesita el billete para hoy.
4. Quiere viajar en segunda.
5. La pasajera es estudiante.
6. El tren sale a las veinte diez.

D *Answers will vary.*

PRACTICE

¿Comprendes?

A and **B** Have students complete their charts and report back to the class.

C If you wish, Activity C can be done as a paired activity.

D This activity allows for students of all ability levels to perform.

EXPANSIÓN

You may also wish to ask the following questions of the class: **¿Dónde está la muchacha? ¿Adónde quiere ir? ¿Qué tipo de billete quiere? ¿Cuándo quiere salir? ¿En qué clase quiere viajar? ¿Por qué necesita una tarjeta de identidad estudiantil? ¿Cuánto es el billete (el pasaje) con el descuento? ¿A qué hora sale el próximo tren? ¿De dónde sale?**

Go Online!

Diálogo en vivo In this episode, students will join Claudia and Francisco at a train station as they uncover a mystery. Ask students what they think the **mujer misteriosa** has inside her suitcase.

Cultural Snapshot

Córdoba is on the right bank of the río Guadalquivir and is one of Spain's oldest cities having served as both the Roman and Moorish capital of Spain. During the three hundred years of Moorish rule (eighth to eleventh centuries), Córdoba was a legendary city with a population of about one million, making it the largest city in Europe at the time.

Online Resources

Customizable Lesson Plans

Audio Activities

Student Workbook

TEACH

Core Instruction

Step 1 Have students read the **Estrategia de lectura** and look at the photographs that accompany the **Lectura.**

Step 2 It is up to your discretion as to how thoroughly you wish students to know the information. You may wish to have students learn the material thoroughly enough that they can retell it in their own words—in other words, transfer from a receptive skill (read) to a productive skill (speak and/or write). In this case it is suggested you call on a student to read a few sentences aloud. Then stop and ask questions that other students answer.

Teaching Options

You may have the entire class read all of the **Lectura** or you may wish to divide it into logical parts, assigning each part to a different group. Each group will report to the other concerning what they learned.

Cultural Snapshot

The cathedral in Cuzco took almost one hundred years to build. The cathedral, along with its accompanying churches, **El Triunfo** and **La Sagrada Familia,** is considered by many to be the finest in the Western Hemisphere.

Lectura CULTURAL

ESTRATEGIA DE LECTURA

USANDO VISUALES Antes de empezar a leer una lectura es importante mirar todos los elementos visuales que la acompañan—fotografías, ilustraciones, tablas, etc. Estos visuales te dan una idea del contenido de la lectura y te facilitan la comprensión.

Antes de leer

Mira y estudia todos los visuales que acompañan la lectura.

Viajes ferroviarios fabulosos

El servicio de trenes El tren es un medio de transporte importante y cómodo en España. Hay trenes que sirven casi todas las ciudades y pueblos del país con salidas frecuentes y muy pocas demoras.

En Latinoamérica el bus y el avión son los medios de transporte más importantes. En muchas regiones el servicio ferroviario no existe. No obstante[1] hay unos recorridos o viajes en tren que son fantásticos. Uno es el viaje de Cuzco a Machu Picchu en los Andes de Perú.

READING CHECK

¿Dónde es más importante el servicio de trenes?

De Cuzco a Machu Picchu Cuzco es una ciudad andina famosa por sus magníficos edificios coloniales. Al borde de un cañón en una región remota no muy lejos de Cuzco está Machu Picchu—una ciudad construida por los inca. Un hecho[2] histórico increíble es que los españoles no descubrieron la ciudad durante su conquista de Perú. Fue el senador estadounidense Hiram Bingham quien la descubrió en 1911.

READING CHECK

¿Quién descubrió Machu Picchu?

Durante la lectura

Al leer cierto párrafo, estudia el visual específico que clarifica la información en el párrafo.

[1]No obstante *Nevertheless*

[2]hecho *fact*

CULTURA

Plaza de Armas, Cuzco, Perú

Richard Brommer

Go Online!

You may wish to remind students to go online for additional reading comprehension and writing skills practice.

¡Así se dice!

Why It Works!

This **Lectura,** like all others in **¡Así se dice!,** contains only Spanish that students have already learned with the exception of the footnoted words. The **Lectura** is easy because it is at the students' proficiency level and students are not encumbered with unknown lexicon and grammatical forms.

Go Online!

connectED.mcgraw-hill.com

¿Quiénes toman el tren de Cuzco a Machu Picchu? La mayoría son turistas, entre ellos muchos mochileros jóvenes, que quieren tener la experiencia de visitar las famosas ruinas incaicas. El tren sale de Cuzco y para llegar a Machu Picchu tiene que bajar unos 1.200 metros. Corre al borde mismo de[3] muchos riscos pendientes[4]. Los pasajeros observan que al bajar el clima y la vegetación cambian mucho. A pesar de[5] su altura, Machu Picchu se encuentra en la región amazónica—una región semitropical de densa vegetación. En Machu Picchu es necesario llevar ropa ligera[6] y un impermeable[7] es imprescindible (obligatorio).

La Barranca del Cobre Otra excursión espectacular es la de la línea de ferrocarril Pacífico-Chihuahua por la Sierra Madre de México. El tren hace parada en Divisadero. De allí los pasajeros pueden contemplar la vista de la Barranca del Cobre—un cañón más profundo que el Gran Cañón de Colorado. Si algún día haces el viaje debes bajar(te) del tren en Divisadero y pasar unos días dando caminatas por esta región espectacular. Si eres más aventurero(a) puedes rentar un caballo y con un guía hacer excursiones por los riscos del cañón.

[3]al borde mismo de *right on the edge of*
[4]pendientes *steep*
[5]A pesar de *In spite of*
[6]ligera *light*
[7]impermeable *raincoat*

READING CHECK

¿Dónde hace más frío? ¿En Cuzco o en Machu Picchu?

CULTURA

La Barranca del Cobre en el estado de Chihuahua, México

READING CHECK

¿De dónde pueden ver la Barranca del Cobre los pasajeros del tren?

CULTURA

Ruinas en Machu Picchu

89

Differentiation

There is no doubt that differently paced learners will produce language at different levels. Some techniques you may want to use to get the maximum from each group are:

- Ask a slower paced student three or four questions. He or she answers. The answers to your questions will provide an organized review.
- Call on a more able student to retell what the previous student just said, giving no help with guided questions.
- Call on an advanced learner to retell the entire story in his or her own words with no assistance.
- Ask some questions of a slower paced learner about what the advanced learner said.

Teaching Options

Ask students if they would like to visit one of these exciting places. Which one or both? Why?

Comparaciones

Have students compare train transportation available where they live with the train travel discussed in this chapter.

Lectura CULTURAL

✓ READING CHECK

¿Cómo es la vida de los tarahumara?

En la región del cañón viven los tarahumara. Una vez los tarahumara ocuparon todo el estado de Chihuahua pero muchos de ellos murieron[8] por el duro trabajo forzado que tuvieron que hacer en las minas y más tarde en la construcción del ferrocarril. Para sobrevivir fueron a vivir en los lugares más recónditos (aislados) de la Barranca. Hoy son seminómadas y algunos viven en cuevas. En verano vagan (andan) por las mesetas de la Sierra Madre y en invierno bajan al fondo del cañón.

[8]murieron *died*

Después de leer

Explica como los elementos visuales te ayudaron a comprender la lectura.

CULTURA

Una vista de la Barranca del Cobre en Divisadero, México

Go Online!

connectED.mcgraw-hill.com

¿Comprendes?

A Confirmando información Indica si la información es correcta o no.

	correcta	incorrecta
1. El tren es un medio de transporte importante en España.		
2. El tren es un medio de transporte importante en todas partes de Latinoamérica.		
3. Hay ruinas de una ciudad azteca en Cuzco.		
4. Cuzco es una ciudad colonial en los Andes peruanos.		
5. Machu Picchu se encuentra al borde de un cañón.		
6. Machu Picchu está a una altura más baja que Cuzco.		
7. Por su altura Machu Picchu está en una zona muy fría.		
8. Nunca llueve en Machu Picchu.		

B Describiendo En tus propias palabras describe el viaje en tren de Cuzco a Machu Picchu.

C Infiriendo La lectura no indica de una manera directa que llueve mucho en Machu Picchu. Pero, ¿qué información en la lectura indica que llueve bastante en Machu Picchu?

D Recordando hechos Contesta.

1. ¿Cuál es una excursión espectacular en México?
2. ¿Qué es posible ver de Divisadero?
3. ¿Qué es la Barranca del Cobre?
4. Hay dos maneras de visitar la Barranca del Cobre. ¿Cuáles son?

E Describiendo Contesta.

1. ¿Cuáles son unas características de los tarahumara?
2. ¿Cómo fue su vida en el pasado y cómo es su vida actual?

CULTURA

Un edificio incaico en Machu Picchu

Richard Brommer

Lectura

PRACTICE

Pre-AP These cultural readings will develop the skills that students need to be successful on the reading and writing sections of the AP exam. Listening to these readings will also help prepare them for the auditory component.

¿Comprendes?

A You may wish to have students do this as a paired activity.
B This can be done as both an oral and a written activity.
C This is a higher skills learning activity. It can be done as both an oral and a written activity.
D–E These can be done as both oral and written activities.

Differentiation

Advanced Learners

You can have advanced learners correct the wrong information in Activity A.

Multiple Intelligences

Have **visual-spatial** learners prepare bulletins that advertise these two expeditions by train.

Answers

A
1. correcta
2. incorrecta
3. incorrecta
4. correcta
5. correcta
6. correcta
7. incorrecta
8. incorrecta

B *Answers will vary.*

C En la lectura leemos que un impermeable es imprescindible (obligatorio).

D
1. Una excursión espectacular en México es la línea de ferrocarril Pacífico-Chihuahua por la Sierra Madre.
2. Es posible ver la Barranca del Cobre de Divisadero.
3. La Barranca del Cobre es un cañón más profundo que el Gran Cañón de Colorado.
4. Puedes dar una caminata o rentar un caballo y con un guía hacer excursiones por los riscos del cañón.

E *Answers will vary but may include:*
1. Los tarahumara son seminómadas. Algunos viven en cuevas. Vagan por las mesetas de la Sierra Madre en verano y bajan al fondo del cañón en invierno.
2. La vida de los tarahumara en el pasado fue difícil. Muchos murieron por el duro trabajo forzado que hicieron en las minas y en la construcción del ferrocarril. La vida de los tarahumara hoy también parece difícil. Viven en los lugares más aislados de la Barranca.

Online Resources

Customizable Lesson Plans

Audio Activities

Student Workbook

TEACH

Core Instruction

You may wish to follow any one of the these procedures for the **Un poco más** reading.

Independent reading Have students read the selection and do the post-reading activities as homework which you collect. This option is the least intrusive on class time and requires a minimum of teacher involvement.

Homework with in-class follow-up Assign the reading and post-reading activities as homework. Review and discuss the material in class the next day.

Intensive in-class activity In this option, the teacher presents in Spanish an overview of the reading selection and asks several comprehension questions about his or her summary. This is followed by in-class reading and discussion, assignment of the **¿Comprendes?** activity for homework, and a discussion of the assignment in class the following day.

Go Online!

You may wish to remind students to go online for additional reading comprehension and writing skills practice.

Lectura

UN POCO MÁS

Antes de leer

Utiliza lo que se llama «lo ya aprendido». Piensa en lo que ya aprendiste en el curso de español sobre las regiones tropicales de las Américas. Trata de imaginar el paisaje que ve un(a) pasajero(a) en un viaje a lo largo de un canal en una zona tropical.

De Panamá a Colón en tren

Colón es la segunda ciudad más grande de Panamá. La primera es la capital, la Ciudad de Panamá. Colón está en el Atlántico y Panamá está en el Pacífico.

CULTURA

Vista desde la estación de ferrocarril en Colón, Panamá

Si uno quiere ir de la Ciudad de Panamá a Colón, puede tomar el tren. El boleto o el pasaje es bastante barato y el viaje es interesante. El tren corre a lo largo del famoso canal de Panamá y durante el viaje los pasajeros pueden observar los muchos barcos que usan el canal para hacer la travesía desde el Atlántico hasta el Pacífico o viceversa. Es una zona tropical de vegetación densa y paisaje espectacular.

El tren pasa también por la pequeña isla de Barro Colorado. El Instituto Smithsonian mantiene la isla donde hacen investigaciones importantes sobre enfermedades tropicales.

Es muy fácil hacer el viaje de ida y regreso el mismo día porque dura (toma) solamente una hora y media.

CULTURA

Ferrocarril del canal de Panamá en la estación de Colón

Cultural Snapshot

The Panama Canal Railway leaves Panama City early in the morning and returns in the late afternoon. Tourists use the train, but it is also used by many daily commuters who live in Panama City and work in Colón. The rails are also used for freight trains. If a ship passing through the Panama Canal is over a certain weight, some containers must be taken off. They are carried on freight trains and are reloaded onto the ship at either Panama City or Colón, depending upon the direction in which the ship is traveling.

Go Online!

connectED.mcgraw-hill.com

¿Comprendes?

Escoge.

1. ¿Cómo sabemos que Colón no es la ciudad más grande de Panamá?
   a. No es la capital.
   b. Está en el Atlántico.
   c. La lectura indica que es la segunda ciudad del país.
   d. Hay solo dos ciudades grandes en Panamá.
2. ¿Cómo puede uno ir de Colón a Panamá?
   a. en el canal
   b. en tren
   c. por la isla de Barro Colorado
   d. observando los barcos
3. ¿Por qué es importante el canal de Panamá?
   a. Los barcos pueden hacer la travesía entre el Atlántico y el Pacífico en muy poco tiempo.
   b. Está en una zona tropical con una vegetación densa.
   c. En una de sus islas hay un instituto que hace investigaciones médicas importantes.
   d. Empalma o enlaza la Ciudad de Panamá con Colón.
4. ¿Cuál es la frase que expresa la misma idea que la siguiente?

   Los pasajeros pueden observar los muchos barcos que usan el canal.

   a. Los pasajeros pueden estudiar los muchos barcos que usan el canal.
   b. Los pasajeros pueden servir los muchos barcos que usan el canal.
   c. Los pasajeros pueden ver los muchos barcos que usan el canal.
   d. Los pasajeros pueden describir los muchos barcos que usan el canal.
5. ¿Cuál es un buen título para esta lectura?
   a. La Ciudad de Panamá
   b. El canal de Panamá
   c. Una región tropical
   d. Un viaje interesante en tren

Cultura

Investiga como la construcción del canal de Panamá afectó el comercio internacional.

CULTURA

Vista de unas esclusas del canal de Panamá

Andrew Payti

Cultural Snapshot

Volumes have been written about the construction of the Panama Canal, one of the wonders of the modern world. To transverse the canal is indeed an incredible experience, as gigantic vessels are raised and lowered in three sets of locks. Panama recently voted in favor of widening the canal. Students can click on eScape and select Panama to learn more about the Panama Canal.

Answers

1. c
2. b
3. a
4. c
5. d

Preparate para el examen

Online Resources

Customizable Lesson Plans

Student Workbook

Enrichment

Listening, Speaking, Reading, Writing Tests

Self-check for achievement

This is a pre-test for students to take before you administer the chapter test. Note that each section is cross-referenced so students can easily find the material they feel they need to review. You may wish to use Self-Check Worksheet SC3 to have students complete this assessment in class or at home. You can correct the assessment yourself, or you may prefer to display the answers in class using Self-Check Answers SC3A.

Differentiation

Slower Paced Learners

Have students work in pairs to complete the Self-Check in class. Once they have finished, call on individuals to give the correct answers as you review together.

Multiple Intelligences

To engage **visual-spatial** and **bodily-kinesthetic** learners, number 1 to 40 on the board and call on a student to go to the board and write the correct answer (this may be done chronologically or you may allow students to choose the one they answer). Then have the student who wrote the first answer decide who will write the second, and so on, making sure to remind them not to pick the same person again.

Self-check for ACHIEVEMENT

Prepárate para el examen

CULTURA

Un tren en el desierto de Atacama cerca de Arica, Chile

Andrew Payti

To review, see **Vocabulario 1** and **Vocabulario 2**.

Vocabulario

1 ¿Sí o no?

1. El revisor trabaja en la ventanilla en la estación de ferrocarril.
2. Un boleto sencillo es para un(a) pasajero(a) que no piensa volver al mismo lugar (sitio).
3. Si no sabes la hora de salida de tu tren tienes que consultar el quiosco.
4. Cuando quieres comer en el tren, vas al coche comedor.
5. Venden los boletos en el andén.
6. Un tren que sale tarde tiene una demora.

2 Da otra palabra o expresión.

7. cambiar de tren
8. con retraso
9. de ida y vuelta
10. la bufetería

3 Completa con palabras apropiadas.

11–12. Si quieres leer algo puedes comprar ____ y ____ en el quiosco.

13. El tren está completo. No hay ____ libres.

To review, see **Pretérito de los verbos irregulares.**

Gramática

4 Completa con el pretérito.

14. Yo ____ que salir. (tener)

15. Nosotros no ____ esperar más. (poder)

16–17. Él ____ ir pero no ____. (querer, poder)

18. ¿Cuánto tiempo ____ ustedes allí? (estar)

19. Ellos ____ juntos, ¿no? (venir)

20. ¿Por qué no ____ tú la revista en la mochila? (poner)

21–22. Él no ____ porque no ____ vernos. (estar, querer)

Answers

1
1. no
2. sí
3. no
4. sí
5. no
6. sí

2
7. transbordar
8. con una demora
9. de ida y regreso
10. el coche comedor (el coche cafetería)

3
11. un periódico (una revista, un libro de bolsillo)
12. una revista (un periódico, un libro de bolsillo)
13. asientos (plazas)

4
14. tuve
15. pudimos
16. quiso
17. pudo
18. estuvieron
19. vinieron
20. pusiste
21. estuvo
22. quiso

Go Online!

connectED.mcgraw-hill.com

5 Escribe las frases en el pretérito.

23. Hacemos una excursión interesante.
24. Tengo que hacer las maletas.
25. Ustedes ven todo, ¿no?
26. ¿Por qué no quieres ir?

To review, see **Pretérito de los verbos irregulares.**

6 Completa con la letra que falta.

27–28. Él lo hi_o pero yo no lo hi_e.

7 Completa con decir.

29–30. Yo lo ____ ahora y lo ____ ayer también.
31–32. Ellos lo ____ ahora y lo ____ ayer también.
33–34. Nosotros lo ____ ahora y lo ____ ayer también.

To review, see **El verbo decir.**

Cultura

8 Contesta.

35. ¿Dónde es el tren un medio de transporte importante?
36. ¿Qué hay en Machu Picchu?
37. ¿Cómo van muchos turistas de Cuzco a Machu Picchu?
38. ¿Qué es la Barranca del Cobre?
39. ¿Dónde está?
40. ¿Quiénes son los tarahumara?

To review this cultural information, see the **Lectura cultural.**

CULTURA

Aguas Calientes, la última parada entre Cuzco y Machu Picchu

Richard Brommer

Prepárate para el examen

Differentiation

(continued)

This type of review activity is particularly appealing to interpersonal learners but will also benefit the class as a whole by promoting an inclusive, student-centered learning environment.

Slower Paced Learners

Encourage students who need extra help to refer to the margin notes and review any section before answering the questions.

Pre-AP Students preparing for the AP Exam may benefit from a set time limit when completing this Self-Check. This may also help to identify students with learning difficulties or slower paced students who need extra help.

Go Online!

You may wish to remind students to go online for additional test preparation.

Answers

5

23. Hicimos una excursión interesante.
24. Tuve que hacer las maletas.
25. Ustedes vieron todo, ¿no?
26. ¿Por qué no quisiste ir?

6

27. hizo
28. hice

7

29. digo
30. dije
31. dicen
32. dijeron
33. decimos
34. dijimos

8

35. El tren es un medio de transporte importante en España.
36. Hay ruinas incaicas en Machu Picchu.
37. Muchos turistas van en tren.
38. La Barranca del Cobre es un cañón.
39. La Barranca del Cobre está en la Sierra Madre de México.
40. Los tarahumara son seminómadas que viven en la región de la Barranca del Cobre.

Prepárate para el examen

Tips for Success

Encourage students to say as much as possible when they do these open-ended activities. Tell them not to be afraid to make mistakes, since the goal of the activities is real-life communication. Encourage students to self-correct and to use words and phrases they know to get their meaning across. If someone in the group makes an error that impedes comprehension, encourage the others to ask questions to clarify or, if necessary, to politely correct the speaker. Let students choose the activities they would like to do.

Tell students to feel free to elaborate on the basic theme and to be creative. They may use props, pictures, or posters if they wish.

Pre-AP These oral activities will give students the opportunity to develop and improve their speaking skills so that they may succeed on the speaking portion of the AP exam.

Note: You may want to use the rubric below to help students prepare their speaking activities.

Practice for ORAL PROFICIENCY

Prepárate para el examen

1. **Un viaje en avión o en tren**
   Compare train and plane travel
   Trabaja con un(a) compañero(a) de clase. Van a comparar un viaje en tren con un viaje en avión. Cada uno(a) va a dar su preferencia.

2. **En la boletería**
   Talk about buying a train ticket
   Prepara una conversación en la boletería de una estación de ferrocarril para comprar el tipo de boleto que necesitas.

3. **Un lugar que conozco**
   Talk about a trip you took
   Escoge un lugar que visitaste con unos amigos o parientes. Describe el lugar.

CULTURA
De compras en un mercado al aire libre en San Telmo en Buenos Aires, Argentina

Andrew Payti

4. **El viaje más interesante**
   Discuss train trips in Spanish-speaking countries
   De los viajes en tren en las lecturas de este capítulo, ¿cuál te interesa más? ¿Por qué? Habla con un(a) compañero(a) para determinar si ustedes tienen la misma opinión.

Scoring Rubric for Speaking

	4	3	2	1
vocabulary	extensive use of vocabulary, including idiomatic expressions	adequate use of vocabulary and idiomatic expressions	limited vocabulary marked with some anglicisms	limited vocabulary marked by frequent anglicisms that force interpretation by the listener
grammar	few or no grammatical errors	minor grammatical errors	some serious grammatical errors	serious grammatical errors
pronunciation	good intonation and largely accurate pronunciation with slight accent	acceptable intonation and pronunciation with distinctive accent	errors in intonation and pronunciation with heavy accent	errors in intonation and pronunciation that interfere with listener's comprehension
content	thorough response with interesting and pertinent detail	thorough response with sufficient detail	some detail, but not sufficient	general, insufficient response

Go Online!
connectED.mcgraw-hill.com

Tarea

You are going to write about a fabulous trip you took to a place that you love. The place can be real or imaginary. Be sure to write in such a way that your readers will also want to make that same trip.

Writing Strategy

Describing When writing a descriptive essay, use words that enable your reader to visualize the scene you are describing. Choose details and organize them in a way that creates an impression. Use vivid adjectives to make your writing more alive. Think of some adjectives you know in Spanish that you consider "vivid."

1 Prewrite

Use a diagram like the one below to help you organize your writing.

2 Write

- Read the sentences you wrote in the graphic organizer. Decide the best order for your composition. Each topic could be one paragraph. Give order to the sentences that develop each topic.
- In your description, try to make your readers understand what it is about the place that makes you think it is so great.

Estos dos mochileros en Oaxaca están viajando por México.

Andrew Payti

- **Expansion:** If you are a person who loves to travel and would like to expand this **Tarea** in order to track your progress, make a list of the goals that you would like to set for yourself with regard to this activity. You will learn about many other interesting places you might like to visit as you continue with your study of Spanish. Review this activity and what you wrote and determine how you could improve your writing. Continue to write about other places you might like to visit as you gain more knowledge of Spanish. Take note of the improvement you make in your writings. The improvements could include better use of descriptive words, the use of more newly learned vocabulary, or any other aspect of writing that you wish to improve. When you are ready, review and make a note of the areas in which you have improved most, then check that against the list of goals you set for yourself.

Evaluate

Don't forget that your teacher will evaluate you on organization, use of vocabulary, correctness of grammar, and completeness of information.

Prepárate para el examen

Pre-AP This **tarea** will give students the opportunity to develop and improve their writing skills so that they may succeed on the writing portion of the AP exam.

ASSESS

Students are now ready to take any of the Listening, Speaking, Reading, Writing Tests you choose to administer.

Note: You may want to use the rubric below to help students prepare their writing task.

Scoring Rubric for Writing

	4	3	2	1
vocabulary	precise, varied	functional, fails to communicate complete meaning	limited to basic words, often inaccurate	inadequate
grammar	excellent, very few or no errors	some errors, but do not hinder communication	numerous errors interfere with communication	many errors, little sentence structure
content	thorough response to the topic	generally thorough response to the topic	partial response to the topic	insufficient response to the topic
organization	well organized, ideas presented clearly and logically	loosely organized, but main ideas present	some attempts at organization, but with confused sequencing	lack of organization

Online Resources

- Customizable Lesson Plans
- Whiteboard Lesson
- Audio Activities
- Video (Vocabulario) (Diálogo) (Gramática)
- Student Workbook
- Enrichment
- Quizzes
- Listening, Speaking, Reading, Writing Tests

Grammar Review

This page provides a quick "at a glance" summary of the grammar points students have learned in this chapter.

Differentiation

Multiple Intelligences

You may want to call on **verbal-linguistic** and **logical-mathematical** learners for whom grammar often comes easily to explain the main concepts to their classmates in their own words. Having students explain the concepts in different ways may also help slower paced learners or students with learning difficulties.

Repaso del Capítulo 3

Gramática

Pretérito de los verbos irregulares

Note the irregular preterite stems of the following verbs.

hacer → hic-	**poder → pud-**	**estar → estuv-**
querer → quis-	**poner → pus-**	**andar → anduv-**
venir → vin-	**saber → sup-**	**tener → tuv-**

venir	poner	tener
vine	puse	tuve
viniste	pusiste	tuviste
vino	puso	tuvo
vinimos	pusimos	tuvimos
vinisteis	*pusisteis*	*tuvisteis*
vinieron	pusieron	tuvieron

Remember the spelling of **hacer.**

hice, hizo

El verbo decir

Decir is irregular in the present and in the preterite.

presente		pretérito	
digo	decimos	dije	dijimos
dices	*decís*	dijiste	*dijisteis*
dice	dicen	dijo	dijeron

Traer is conjugated the same as **decir** in the preterite.

Pronombres después de una preposición

Except for **mí** and **ti,** prepositional pronouns are the same as subject pronouns.

mí, ti, usted, él, ella, nosotros(as), ustedes, ellos, ellas

With **con, mí** and **ti** become **conmigo** and **contigo.**

CULTURA

La pantalla de salidas en la estación de ferrocarril de Atocha en Madrid

Daniel Salsgiver

Juego There are a number of cognates in this list. See how many you and a partner can find. Who can find the most? Compare your list with those of your classmates.

Go Online!

connectED.mcgraw-hill.com

Vocabulario

Getting around a train station

la estación de ferrocarril (tren)
el hall
la sala de espera
el horario
la llegada
la salida
la ventanilla, la boletería
el billete, el boleto sencillo
de ida y vuelta
de ida y regreso
en primera (segunda) clase
la tarifa escolar (estudiantil) reducida
la tarjeta de crédito
el distribuidor automático
el tren
el vagón, el coche
el andén
la vía
el destino
subir al tren
bajar(se) del tren

At a kiosk

el quiosco
el periódico
la revista
el libro de bolsillo

On board the train

el pasillo
el asiento, la plaza
el revisor
el coche comedor, el coche cafetería, la bufetería
la parada
libre
ocupado(a)
completo(a)
próximo(a)
revisar los billetes
transbordar (cambiar de tren)

Describing an excursion

el cañón
el risco
una senda
el caballo
andar a caballo
alquilar, rentar

Other useful words and expressions

a tiempo
tarde
insertar
seleccionar

LA PRACTICE Refer to the Language Arts Practice section and use your Spanish to practice Language Arts skills.

Literary Reader

You may wish to read the adaptation of the Spanish classic *El Quijote*, found in the Literary Reader at the end of this book.

Repaso del Capítulo 3

Vocabulary Review

The words and phrases in **Vocabulario 1** and **2** have been taught for productive use in this chapter. They are summarized here as a resource for both student and teacher. This list also serves as a convenient resource for the **Prepárate para el examen** activities.

¡Así se dice!

Why It Works!

This vocabulary reference list has not been translated into English for two reasons. First, it is recommended that students learn the new vocabulary through direct association with images on the **Vocabulario** pages. Secondly, all vocabulary is reintroduced in the chapter many times and upon completion of the chapter students should be familiar with the meaning of all the words. If there are words that students still do not know, they can refer to the vocabulary presentation in the chapter or the dictionary at the end of the book. If, however, it is your preference to give students the English translations, please refer to Vocabulary V3.1.

Literary Reader

It is recommended that students read from the Literary Reader at this stage so that the selections are not presented all at once at the end or skipped entirely due to time restraints.

Don't forget the chapter project and cultural activities. Students have learned all the information that they will need to complete these engaging enrichment tasks.

Juego The cognates in this list are: **la estación, el hall, en primera (segunda) clase, escolar, estudiantil, reducida, crédito, el distribuidor automático, el tren, el vagón, el quiosco, la cafetería, ocupado(a), completo(a), el cañón, rentar, tarde, insertar, seleccionar.**

Repaso cumulativo

Every chapter of **¡Así se dice!** contains this review section of previously learned material. By recycling information from previous chapters, the cumulative review serves to remind students that they need to continue practicing what they have learned after finishing each chapter.

Activity 1 This activity reviews train and plane vocabulary.

Audio Script

1. la maleta
2. la vía
3. la hora de embarque
4. el número del vuelo
5. el pasillo
6. el andén
7. el billete
8. el asiento
9. la pista
10. el revisor
11. el asistente de vuelo
12. la ventanilla

Activity 2 This activity reviews verbs with an irregular **yo** form in the present.

Activity 3 This activity reviews verbs with an irregular **yo** form in the present.

Activity 4 This activity reviews vocabulary related to air travel.

Repaso cumulativo

Repasa lo que ya has aprendido

These activities will help you review and remember what you have learned so far in Spanish.

1 Escucha las palabras. Haz un diagrama como el de abajo. Indica si cada palabra se relaciona con un viaje en tren o en avión o los dos.

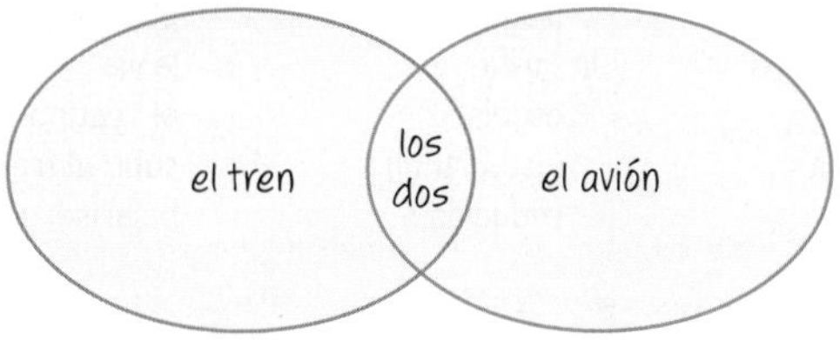

CULTURA

Hay muchos trenes que salen de la estación General Belgrano para los suburbios de Buenos Aires.

Andrew Payti

2 Completa en el presente con la forma yo.

1. ____ un viaje en tren. (hacer)
2. ____ a las ocho. (salir)
3. ____ mucho equipaje. (tener)
4. ____ tres maletas. (traer)
5. ____ mucha ropa en mis maletas. (poner)
6. ____ en tren. (venir)
7. ____ que ____ el viaje en tren. (decir, hacer)
8. ____ que me voy a divertir. (saber)
9. ____ a viajar por Argentina. (ir)
10. ____ Argentina. (conocer)

3 Cambia las frases en la Actividad 2 a María.

4 Parea los contrarios.

1. el despegue	a. largo
2. la llegada	b. subir
3. bajar	c. temprano
4. sentarse	d. el aterrizaje
5. volver, regresar	e. vender
6. corto	f. la salida
7. comprar	g. salir
8. tarde	h. levantarse

Answers

1

1. los dos
2. el tren
3. el avión
4. el avión
5. los dos
6. el tren
7. los dos
8. los dos
9. el avión
10. el tren
11. el avión
12. los dos

2

1. Hago
2. Salgo
3. Tengo
4. Traigo
5. Pongo
6. Vengo
7. Digo, hago
8. Sé
9. Voy
10. Conozco

3

1. Hace un viaje en tren.
2. Sale a las ocho.
3. Tiene mucho equipaje.
4. Trae tres maletas.
5. Pone mucha ropa en sus maletas.
6. Viene en tren.
7. Dice que hace el viaje en tren.
8. Sabe que le voy a divertir.
9. Va a viajar por Argentina.
10. Conoce Argentina.

4

1. d
2. f
3. b
4. h
5. g
6. a
7. e
8. c

Go Online!

connectED.mcgraw-hill.com

5 **Escoge la palabra apropiada del banco de palabras para contestar cada pregunta.**

el mostrador de la línea aérea	el cinturón de seguridad
la tarjeta de embarque	el control de seguridad
el boleto electrónico	en el pasillo
la puerta de salida	en la pista

1. ¿Dónde se presenta Felipe para facturar su equipaje en el aeropuerto?
2. ¿De dónde sale el vuelo?
3. ¿Por dónde tienen que pasar los pasajeros antes de ir a la puerta de salida?
4. ¿Qué necesitan los pasajeros para poder abordar el avión?
5. ¿Qué tienen que abrochar los pasajeros abordo del avión?
6. El asiento de José no está en la ventanilla. ¿Dónde está?

6 **¿Qué pone José en su maleta?**

7 **Personaliza. Da respuestas personales.**

1. Cuando estás de vacaciones, ¿a qué hora te despiertas?
2. ¿Te levantas enseguida?
3. Si vas de camping, ¿duermes en una carpa?
4. ¿Te duermes enseguida si tienes que dormir en un saco de dormir?
5. ¿A qué hora te acuestas?
6. ¿Te diviertes cuando estás de vacaciones?

Repaso cumulativo

Activity 5 This activity reviews vocabulary related to air travel.

Activity 6 This activity reviews vocabulary related to clothing.

Activity 7 This activity reviews reflexive verbs.

Pre-AP To give students further open-ended oral or written practice, or to assess proficiency, go to AP Proficiency Practice AP4 and AP18.

Go Online!

You may wish to remind students to go online for additional cumulative review.

The **¡Así se dice!** Audio Program for Chapter 3 has twenty-six activities, which afford students extensive listening and speaking practice.

Answers

5

1. Felipe se presenta en el mostrador de la línea aérea para facturar su equipaje en el aeropuerto.
2. El vuelo sale de la puerta de salida.
3. Los pasajeros tienen que pasar por el control de seguridad antes de ir a la puerta de salida.
4. Los pasajeros necesitan la tarjeta de embarque para poder abordar el avión.
5. Los pasajeros tienen que abrochar el cinturón de seguridad.
6. El asiento de José está en el pasillo.

6

José pone pantalones cortos, calcetines, una corbata, una camiseta, una camisa, un pantalón, un blue jean, zapatos y un par de tenis en la maleta.

7 *Answers will vary but may include:*

1. Me despierto a las ___.
2. Sí, (No, no) me levanto enseguida.
3. Sí, (No, no) duermo en una carpa.
4. Sí, (No, no) me duermo enseguida.
5. Me acuesto a las ___.
6. Sí, (No, no) me divierto cuando estoy de vacaciones.

Chapter Overview

En el restaurante

Scope and Sequence

Topics
- Restaurants and types of food
- Utensils

Culture
- Restaurants in Spain and Latin America
- Sidewalk cafés in the Spanish-speaking world
- Spanish tapas

Functions
- How to order and pay for a meal at a restaurant
- How to identify more foods
- How to identify eating utensils and dishes
- How to discuss restaurants in Spain and Latin America

Structure
- Stem-changing verbs in the present and preterite
- Adjectives of nationality
- The passive voice with **se**

David H. Brennan

Planning Guide

	required	recommended	optional
Vocabulario 1 En el restaurante Más comestibles	✓		
Gramática Presente de los verbos de cambio radical **e→i** Pretérito de los verbos de cambio radical **e→i, o→u** Adjetivos de nacionalidad La voz pasiva con **se**	✓		
Conversación Una comida muy buena		✓	
Lectura cultural Restaurantes de España y Latinoamérica		✓	
Lectura Un poco más Sé lo que pedí			✓
Prepárate para el examen			✓
Repaso cumulativo			✓

Correlations to ACTFL World-Readiness Standards for Learning Languages

Page numbers in light print refer to the Student Edition.
Page numbers in bold print refer to the Teacher Edition.

COMMUNICATION Communicate effectively in more than one language in order to function in a variety of situations and for multiple purposes		
Interpersonal Communication	Learners interact and negotiate meaning in spoken, signed, or written conversations to share information, reactions, feelings, and opinions.	pp. **102D, 104–105, 107, 108, 111, 115, 122,** 128
Interpretive Communication	Learners understand, interpret, and analyze what is heard, read, or viewed on a variety of topics.	pp. **106,** 108, **108, 109, 110,** 111, **113,** 114, 115, **115,** 116, **116, 118,** 119, **119, 120,** 121, 122, 123, **123, 124,** 125, **125,** 127, **127, 133**
Presentational Communication	Learners present information, concepts, and ideas to inform, explain, persuade, and narrate on a variety of topics using appropriate media and adapting to various audiences of listeners, readers, or viewers.	pp. **102C, 107, 109,** 110, 113, **118,** 119, **120, 121,** 123, **126,** 128, 129, **130, 131**
CULTURES Interact with cultural competence and understanding		
Relating Cultural Practices to Perspectives	Learners use the language to investigate, explain, and reflect on the relationship between the practices and perspectives of the cultures studied.	pp. **102D, 103,** 104, 105, 106, 107, 116, 117, 120, 121, 124, 127
Relating Cultural Products to Perspectives	Learners use the language to investigate, explain, and reflect on the relationship between the products and perspectives of the cultures studied.	pp. **102C, 102D,** 103, **103,** 104, **104–105,** 105, **107,** 117, 119, **119,** 120, 121, 122, 125, 127, 128
CONNECTIONS Connect with other disciplines and acquire information and diverse perspectives in order to use the language to function in academic and career-related situations		
Making Connections	Learners build, reinforce, and expand their knowledge of other disciplines while using the language to develop critical thinking and to solve problems creatively.	pp. **102C, 102D, 104–105,** 113, **113, 117,** 125
Acquiring Information and Diverse Perspectives	Learners access and evaluate information and diverse perspectives that are available through the language and its cultures.	pp. **102C,** 104, 106, **106,** 107, 109, **109,** 111, **111,** 112, **112, 116,** 117, **117,** 119, **119,** 130
COMPARISONS Develop insight into the nature of language and culture in order to interact with cultural competence		
Language Comparisons	Learners use the language to investigate, explain, and reflect on the nature of language through comparisons of the language studied and their own.	pp. **102D,** 106, 107, **114, 120, 130,** 131
Cultural Comparisons	Learners use the language to investigate, explain, and reflect on the concept of culture through comparisons of the cultures studied and their own.	pp. **102D,** 103, **103, 104,** 120, 122, 123, 124, 128
COMMUNITIES Communicate and interact with cultural competence in order to participate in multilingual communities at home and around the world		
School and Global Communities	Learners use the language both within and beyond the classroom to interact and collaborate in their community and the globalized world.	pp. **102C,** 113, **114, 126, 128, 130**
Lifelong Learning	Learners set goals and reflect on their progress in using languages for enjoyment, enrichment, and advancement.	pp. **102C, 102D,** 106, **106,** 112, **112, 117,** 119, **119, 125**

Chapter Project

Libro de cocina hispana

Students will work individually and in small groups to assemble a cookbook showcasing different aspects of Hispanic cuisine.

1. Divide the class into small groups which will each assemble a cookbook. Each group member will create a recipe page for the group cookbook. Each group member should select a dish from a different main category (Appetizers and Snacks, Soups and Salads, Main Courses, Drinks and Refreshments, Desserts) in order to create variety. Group cookbooks will then be combined to form a class cookbook dedicated to the rich diversity of Hispanic cuisine.
2. In addition to the recipe, each student's page will include his or her own description of the dish that includes a brief explanation of its historical and/or cultural significance. The page should be visually appealing and include at least two visual elements (drawings, illustrations, photos, clip art).
3. Remind students that although the recipes themselves may come from another primary source, all other written work must be original. Have each student turn in a first draft. After you check the drafts, have students correct their work and submit final drafts as part of their group's cookbook.
4. After each group presents its cookbook, invite the class to work together to assemble the larger version. If you have multiple classes working on the same project, you may wish to hold a contest for the best Hispanic cookbook, or you can combine material from various classes to form a master volume of food and drink enjoyed throughout the Spanish-speaking world.

LA PAELLA
INGREDIENTES
3 tomates
2 cebollas grandes
2 pimientos (uno verde y uno rojo)
4 dientes de ajo
1/2 kilo de camarones
4 calamares
12 almejas
12 mejillones
langosta (opcional)
1 pollo en partes
3 chorizos
1 paquete de guisantes congelados
1 bote de pimientos morrones
1 1/2 tazas de arroz
3 tazas de consomé de pollo
4 pizcas de azafrán
1/4 taza de aceite de oliva
PREPARACIÓN
1. Pique los tomates, los pimientos, las cebollas y el ajo.
2. Lave las almejas y los mejillones en agua fría.
3. Limpie y pele los camarones.
4. Limpie y corte en rebanadas los calamares.
5. Corte en rebanadas los chorizos.
6. Fría o ase el pollo aparte.

Expansion: Have students share the final cookbook with a home economics/consumer sciences class in your school. If possible arrange a class period when both classes can cook some of the recipes together.

As students progress with their study of Spanish and learn more about foods of the Spanish-speaking world, you may wish to have them create additional recipes for their cookbooks. As a group they might evaluate the cookbook they created originally and discuss how it could be improved and how they could meet language and culture goals they've set. It might be that they could make a cookbook that has more varied recipes or perhaps recipes that reflect better nutrition. Toward the end of the year, have them compare what they've created against their goals, then discuss how they have progressed.

Scoring Rubric for Project

	5	3	1
Evidence of planning	Corrected draft is provided.	Draft is provided but is not corrected.	No draft is provided.
Written product	Description of dish and historical/cultural information are provided.	Only the dish description or the historical/cultural information is provided.	No description of dish or historical/cultural information is provided.
Presentation	Cookbook page contains all of the required elements.	Cookbook page contains some of the required elements.	Cookbook page contains few of the required elements.

Daniel Salsgiver

Culture

Recipe

ENCHILADAS VERDES

Ingredients: (makes 4 servings)
Filling: 2 chicken breast halves with bone
2 cups chicken broth
¼ onion
1 clove garlic
2 teaspoons salt

In a saucepan, combine chicken breasts, chicken broth, onion, garlic clove, and salt. Bring to a boil and continue boiling for 20 minutes. Reserve broth and discard onion and garlic. When cool enough, shred chicken from the bone.

Sauce: 1 pound fresh tomatillos
5 serrano peppers
¼ onion
1 clove garlic
1 pinch salt

Place tomatillos and serrano chiles in a pot with water to cover. Bring to a boil and boil until tomatillos turn a dull green. Strain tomatillos and chiles. Place onion, garlic clove, and salt in a blender with sufficient reserved chicken broth to cover vegetables by about an inch. Blend all ingredients until completely puréed. Pour the salsa into a medium saucepan and bring to a low boil.

12 corn tortillas
¼ cup vegetable oil
1 cup white cheese
½ onion, chopped
1 bunch fresh cilantro, chopped

Heat oil in a frying pan. Fry tortillas slightly one at a time in very hot oil. Set each on a paper towel to soak up oil. Dip the slightly fried tortillas in salsa until tortillas become soft again. Place on plates and fill or top with shredded chicken. Top with shredded cheese, onion, and cilantro.

La sobremesa y la siesta

The expressions **hacer la sobremesa** and **estar de sobremesa** have no exact English equivalent but basically mean *to linger after a meal and engage in conversation.* More than just an after-dinner chat, a typical **sobremesa** might go on for hours in a relaxed atmosphere. The custom of the **sobremesa** is observed throughout Spain and Latin America, although today its practice is becoming less common.

Another after-meal tradition is the **siesta.** The expression **echarse una siesta** refers to the Spanish custom of taking a nap after the midday meal, which is the main meal in Spain. The **siesta** is also observed in parts of Latin America. During **siesta,** shops and businesses close for two or three hours in the afternoon so that everyone can take a short break in order to recharge and prepare for the rest of the day. The **siesta** is not as popular as it once was, especially in big cities where the increasing demands of globalization make taking an afternoon nap impractical.

You may wish to have students participate in their own **sobremesa.** Have them bring in some Hispanic desserts and/or hot beverages and invite them to engage in conversation on an assigned topic or a topic of their choice.

Connection to Fine Art

Have students look online or in an art text to find *Aires Libres Cafe* by Cuban American artist Agustín Gainza. Tell students that the artist was born in Cuba and ask that they guess the setting of the painting. Students can explain what they see in the painting, tell a story about the people and what they might be ordering, or with a partner perform a conversation between customer and server as though they are at this cafe.

50-Minute Lesson Plans

	Objective	Present	Practice	Assess/Homework
Day 1	Talk about dining in a restaurant	Chapter Opener (5 min.) Introducción al tema (10 min.) Core Instruction/Vocabulario (20 min.)	Activities 1–3 (15 min.)	Student Workbook Activities A–C **ConnectEd** Vocabulary Practice
Day 2	Talk about dining in a restaurant	Quick Start (5 min.) Review Vocabulario (5 min.) Video, Vocabulario en vivo (10 min.)	Activities 4–6 (10 min.) Total Physical Response (5 min.) Audio Activities A–F (15 min.)	Student Workbook Activities D–E **ConnectEd** Vocabulary Practice
Day 3	Present tense of stem-changing verbs **e→i**	Quick Start (5 min.) Core Instruction/Gramática, Presente de los verbos de cambio radical **e→i** (10 min.)	Activities 1–6 (15 min.) Audio Activities A–B (10 min.)	Quiz 1 (10 min.) Student Workbook Activities A–E **ConnectEd** Grammar Practice
Day 4	Preterite of stem-changing verbs **e→i, o→u**	Quick Start (5 min.) Core Instruction/Gramática, Pretérito de los verbos de cambio radical **e→i, o→u** (10 min.) Video, Gramática en vivo (5 min.)	Activities 7–9 (10 min.) Audio Activities C–E (10 min.)	Quiz 2 (10 min.) Student Workbook Activities A–E **ConnectEd** Grammar Practice
Day 5	Adjectives of nationality	Quick Start (5 min.) Core Instruction/Gramática, Adjetivos de nacionalidad (15 min.)	Activities 10–11 (10 min.) Audio Activity F (10 min.)	Quiz 3 (10 min.) Student Workbook Activity A **ConnectEd** Grammar Practice
Day 6	The passive voice with **se**	Quick Start (5 min.) Core Instruction/Gramática, La voz pasiva con **se** (10 min.)	Activities 12–14 (15 min.) Audio Activity G (10 min.)	Quiz 4 (10 min.) Student Workbook Activities A–B **ConnectEd** Grammar Practice
Day 7	Develop reading and listening comprehension skills	Quick Start (5 min.) Core Instruction/Conversación (20 min.) Video, Diálogo en vivo (10 min.)	¿Comprendes? A–B (5 min.)	Quiz 5 (10 min.) ¿Comprendes? C–D **ConnectEd** Conversation
Day 8	Discuss restaurants in Spain and Latin America	Core Instruction/Lectura cultural (20 min.)	¿Comprendes? A–B (15 min.)	Listening Comprehension Test (15 min.) ¿Comprendes? C–D **ConnectEd** Reading Practice
Day 9	Develop reading comprehension skills	Core Instruction/Lectura Un poco más (15 min.)	¿Comprendes? (10 min.) Prepárate para el examen (25 min.)	Prepárate para el examen, Practice for written proficiency **ConnectEd** Reading Practice
Day 10	Chapter review	Repaso del Capítulo 4 (15 min.)	Prepárate para el examen, Practice for oral proficiency (20 min.)	Test for Writing Proficiency (15 min.) Review for chapter test
Day 11	Chapter 4 Tests (50 min.) Reading and Writing Test Speaking Test Test for Oral Proficiency Test for Reading Comprehension			

90-Minute Lesson Plans

	Objective	Present	Practice	Assess/Homework
Block 1	Talk about dining in a restaurant	Chapter Opener (5 min.) Introducción al tema (15 min.) Quick Start (5 min.) Core Instruction/Vocabulario (20 min.)	Activities 1–6 (25 min.) Total Physical Response (5 min.) Audio Activities A–F (15 min.)	Student Workbook Activities A–E **ConnectEd** Vocabulary Practice
Block 2	Present tense of stem-changing verbs **e→i** Preterite of stem-changing verbs **e→i, o→u**	Quick Start (5 min.) Core Instruction/Gramática, Presente de los verbos de cambio radical **e→i** (10 min.) Quick Start (5 min.) Core Instruction/Gramática, Pretérito de los verbos de cambio radical **e→i, o→u** (10 min.) Video, Gramática en vivo (5 min.)	Activities 1–6 (15 min.) Foldables (5 min.) Activities 7–9 (10 min.) InfoGap (5 min.) Audio Activities A–E (10 min.)	Quiz 1 (10 min.) Student Workbook Activities A–E Student Workbook Activities A–E **ConnectEd** Grammar Practice
Block 3	Adjectives of nationality The passive voice with **se**	Quick Start (5 min.) Core Instruction/Gramática, Adjetivos de nacionalidad (10 min.) Quick Start (5 min.) Core Instruction/Gramática, La voz pasiva con **se** (10 min.)	Activities 10–11 (10 min.) Activities 12–14 (15 min.) Audio Activities F–G (15 min.)	Quizzes 2–3 (20 min.) Student Workbook Activity A Student Workbook Activities A–B **ConnectEd** Grammar Practice
Block 4	Discuss restaurants in Spain and Latin America	Quick Start (5 min.) Core Instruction/Conversación (15 min.) Video, Diálogo en vivo (10 min.) Core Instruction/Lectura cultural (20 min.)	¿Comprendes? A–B (10 min.) ¿Comprendes? A–B (10 min.)	Quizzes 4–5 (20 min.) ¿Comprendes? C–D ¿Comprendes? C–D Prepárate para el examen, Practice for written proficiency **ConnectEd** Conversation, Reading Practice
Block 5	Develop reading comprehension skills	Core Instruction/Lectura Un poco más (15 min.)	¿Comprendes? (10 min.) Prepárate para el examen (20 min.) Prepárate para el examen, Practice for oral proficiency (30 min.)	Listening Comprehension Test (15 min.) Review for chapter test **ConnectEd** Reading Practice
Block 6	Chapter 4 Tests (50 min.) Reading and Writing Test Speaking Test Test for Oral Proficiency Test for Writing Proficiency Test for Reading Comprehension Chapter Project (40 min.)			

Preview

In this chapter, students will identify more foods as well as the items for a place setting. They will also learn many types of eating venues in the Spanish-speaking world as they consider dining customs that are both similar to and different from their own. To help accomplish this, students will also learn the stem-changing verbs **(e → i; o → u),** adjectives of nationality ending in a consonant, and the passive voice with **se.**

Pacing

It is important to note that once you reach **¡Bravo!** in the chapter, there is no more new material for the students to learn. The rest of the chapter recycles what has already been covered. The suggested pacing listed here leaves two to three days for review, assessment, and enrichment activities such as the chapter project.

Vocabulario	1–2 days
Gramática	2–3 days
Conversación	1 day
Lectura cultural	1 day
Lectura Un poco más	1 day

CAPÍTULO 4

En el restaurante

102

Go Online!
connectED.mcgraw-hill.com

Audio Video Práctica Repaso Diversiones eScape

ePals

Go Online!

Audio
Listen to spoken Spanish.

Video
Watch and learn about the Spanish-speaking world.

Práctica
Practice your skills.

Repaso
Review what you've learned.

Diversiones
Go beyond the classroom.

eScape
Read about current events in the Spanish-speaking world.

Aquí y Allí

Vamos a comparar ¿Come tu familia a veces en un restaurante? ¿Qué tipo de restaurantes hay donde tú vives? ¿Hay restaurantes elegantes y restaurantes económicos? ¿Hay restaurantes étnicos o no? Vamos a ver los muchos tipos de restaurantes que hay en España y Latinoamérica y lo que uno debe esperar cuando come en un restaurante en un país hispano.

Objetivos

You will:

- order and pay for a meal at a restaurant
- identify more foods
- identify eating utensils and dishes
- discuss restaurants in Spain and Latin America

You will use:

- stem-changing verbs in the present and preterite
- adjectives of nationality
- the passive voice with **se**

El restaurante Casa Duque en Segovia, España

SPOTLIGHT ON CULTURE

Cultural Comparison
The material in this chapter is made more personal for the students when they consider the questions in **Aquí y allí.** They will discuss restaurant experiences in the United States and several Spanish-speaking countries, enabling them to observe cultural similarities and differences.

Cultural Snapshot
Casa Duque is a very popular restaurant in Segovia that specializes in cochinillo and cordero asado. It has been in the same family for four generations.

Interactive Whiteboard
Present or practice with interactive whiteboard activities.

Assessment
Check student progress.

ePals
Connect with Spanish-speaking students around the world.

PRESENT

Introduce the theme of the chapter by having students look at the photographs on these pages. Have them look at the people and determine if there is anything they see them doing that is the same or different from what they do with their own friends. Once you have completed the vocabulary presentation, have students return to these pages and read the information that accompanies each photograph. Once students are fully acquainted with the vocabulary and grammar of the chapter, you may wish to come back to these pages and ask the questions that go with each photo.

Cultural Snapshot

México You may wish to remind students that **tortas** are **sándwiches** or **bocadillos** in Mexico. **Panela** is usually a brown sugarloaf sometimes called **chancaca,** which is made from ground corn and honey. **Cueritos** are **chicharrones**—fried pork skins. **Ya sabes que la comida mexicana es muy buena. ¿Qué vas a pedir de esta lista?**

Ecuador **¿Es grande o pequeño el café? ¿Están ocupadas todas las mesas? ¿Ves una mesa libre?**

España **La paella** is also considered a very good leftover dish. It can be made from such a variety of ingredients that many homemakers will throw their leftovers together and make an original paella. **¿Cuáles son unos ingredientes que puedes identificar en la paella? ¿De qué color es el arroz?**

Introducción al tema

En el restaurante

Mira las fotografías para familiarizarte con el tema del capítulo—experiencias en restaurantes en varias partes del mundo hispano. Consulta los menús y observa unos platos deliciosos regionales para decidir los que te apetecen. Y, ¡buen provecho!

México

¿Te apetece comer algo? ¿Qué quieres pedir de esta lista delante de una cafetería en Guadalajara, México?

Ecuador

Es la terraza de un restaurante en Baños, Ecuador. A mucha gente le gusta comer al aire libre.

España

La paella es una especialidad de Valencia. Es un plato rico y como vemos aquí lleva arroz amarillo con un surtido de mariscos. Es el azafrán, un condimento caro, que le da el color amarillo al arroz.

Guatemala

El mesero sirve la comida en un restaurante elegante en la Ciudad de Guatemala.

Unid. Descripción P
recio Total
1 BOC TORTILLA 100G 3,35 3,35
1 AGUA 0,5 L (PC) 1,35 1,35
TOTAL Euro 4,70
ENTREGADO 20,00
CAMBIO 15,30
I.V.A Incluido
GRACIAS POR SU VISITA

(tr)Kerri Galloway, (cl cr)Andrew Paytl, (bl)Lori Ernfridsson, (br)McGraw-Hill Education

104

Guatemala Both Guatemala City and Antigua have many restaurants, from very simple to very elegant. **¿Se vistió de una manera elegante el mesero? ¿Sirvió la comida con cuidado?**

Go Online!

connectED.mcgraw-hill.com

Perú

Entrada a un restaurante en Lima que tiene unas especialidades interesantes. ¿Qué te apetece?

HORCHATERIA
DE
SANTA CATALINA
Casa con dos siglos de tradición

España

El restaurante Horchatería de Santa Catalina en Valencia, España. Este restaurante tiene un menú variado, pero una horchata es una bebida popular en España. Es una bebida hecha a base de almendras machadas con agua y azúcar. Se toma muy fría.

Costa Rica

El casado es una comida típica de los ticos, o costarricenses. Lleva arroz, frijoles, una rodaja de plátano frito y pollo acompañado de una ensalada. El casado puede llevar también yuca y patacones con un filete de carne de res o pescado.

España

¿Quién fue servida en este restaurante?

Chile

Los meseros tienen unos momentos libres para tomar un poco de aire fresco delante de su restaurante en Vicuña, Chile. Vicuña es el pueblo natal de la famosa autora chilena Gabriela Mistral.

Introducción al tema

Perú This restaurant offers a varied menu. Have students match the food items. **tapas variadas** *variety of tapas;* **rabo de toro** *oxtail;* **perdiz** *partridge;* **cochinillo** *roast suckling pig;* **pata de cordero** *leg of lamb*

España *(top)* The exterior of many of the older restaurants in Spain have walls that are tiled—**azulejos.** **¿Es este restaurante viejo o muy viejo? ¿Cómo lo sabes? En el anuncio, ¿a qué se refiere la palabra «casa»?**

España *(bottom)* La Infanta doña Isabel was the first-born of la reina Isabel II and the sister of Alfonso XII. She was born in Madrid in 1851.

Costa Rica **¿Cómo se llaman los habitantes de Costa Rica? ¿Cuál es una comida costarricense típica? ¿Qué ingredientes lleva el casado?**

Chile Some of the dishes served in this restaurant are **pastel de choclo** which is a corn pie.

Choclo is sweet corn or the new corn of the season. The dish is actually more like a layered casserole of corn and beef. It also has some onions, raisins, black olives, paprika, sugar, hard-boiled eggs, etc.

Humitas chilenas are similar, although not identical, to **tamales mexicanos.**

Cabrito asado is roast goat. In some countries **chivo (chivito)** is used rather than **cabrito.**

Porotos granados is a Chilean bean and corn stew with a variety of vegetables and cranberry beans. **¿Qué platos se sirven en este restaurante? ¿Cuál vas a pedir?**

Vocabulario

Online Resources

Customizable Lesson Plans
- Whiteboard Lesson
- Audio Activities
- Video (Vocabulario)
- Student Workbook
- Enrichment
- Quizzes

Quick Start

Use QS 4.1 or write the following on the board.

Write a list in Spanish of the foods you have already learned. Include some **meriendas** and **refrescos.**

TEACH

Core Instruction

Step 1 Present vocabulary first using Vocabulary V4.2–V4.3.

Step 2 Present individual words and build to sentences. **¿Es el menú? ¿Qué es? ¿Es el mesero? ¿Quién es? ¿Es el restaurante? ¿Qué es? ¿Quiénes están en el restaurante? ¿Tiene Alicia el menú? ¿Qué pide Alicia? Y ¿quién va a traer el menú?**

Step 3 You may wish to follow this same procedure with other pictures.

Teaching Options

After presenting the vocabulary orally, then have students read. This is an important learning step for many students.

Go Online!

Vocabulario en vivo
Watch and listen as Nora takes you behind the scenes in a restaurant.

Vocabulario PRESENTACIÓN

En el restaurante

Carlos y Alicia están en el restaurante.
Alicia pide el menú.

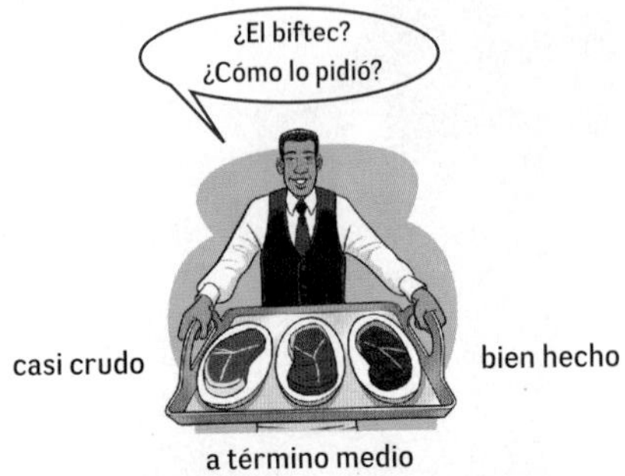

Carlos pidió un biftec.
El mesero lo sirvió.

En otras partes

- **El mesero** is used throughout Latin America. **El camarero** is used in Spain.
- **El cerdo** is the general word for *pork* and **chuletas de cerdo** means *pork chops*. Roast suckling pig is a very popular dish—**el cochinillo asado** in Spain, **el lechón asado** in most of Latin America but particularly in the Caribbean. The word **chancho** is also used in several Latin American countries.
- **El biftec** as well as **el bistec** is used. Both are correct.

Alicia pide la cuenta.
Carlos deja una propina.

David H. Brennan

Total Physical Response (TPR)

(Student 1), **ven acá.**
Y *(Student 2),* **ven acá también.**
Entren en el restaurante.
Busquen una mesa libre.
(Student 1), **indica que ves una mesa libre.**
Tomen sus asientos.
Indica al mesero que quieren su atención.
El mesero llega.
(Student 1), **pide un menú. Toma el menú. Abre el menú. Lee el menú.**
Den su orden al mesero.
Coman.
Después de la comida, *(Student 2)* **pide la cuenta.**
(Student 2) **mira la cuenta. deja una propina en la mesa.**

Más comestibles

La carne

Los mariscos

connectED.mcgraw-hill.com

¡Así se dice!

When you are really starving you can say **Me muero de hambre,** which literally means *I'm dying of hunger.*

Total Physical Response (TPR)

(Student 1), **ven acá.**
Vas a poner la mesa.
Pon el plato en la mesa.
Pon el cuchillo a la derecha del plato.
Luego, pon una cucharita al lado del cuchillo.
Pon un tenedor a la izquierda del plato.
Pon el platillo.
Pon la taza encima del platillo.
Dobla la servilleta.
Pon la servilleta encima del plato.
Gracias, *(Student 1).*
Y ahora *(Student 2),* **ven y levanta la mesa.**

Teaching Options

You may wish to bring in the items necessary to set a table. Using a desk, students can actually set the table and give the name of each item they are placing.

Heritage Speakers

If you have heritage speakers in your class, you may ask them if there are any other words they use for items presented in this section.

Cultura

Salero and **pimentero** are much less frequently used in Spanish-speaking countries. People will tend to say **«Sal, por favor.»** rather than use the word **salero.**

It is not usual to see salt and pepper shakers placed automatically on the table.

Differentiation

Multiple Intelligences

Have **visual-spatial** learners think of other foods they have already learned in Spanish. Have them make a board or a PowerPoint® presentation labeling the foods they know.

Have **bodily-kinesthetic** learners mime the following:

Estás tomando sopa.
Estás cortando la carne.
Estás comiendo ensalada.
Estás tomando café.

Visually Impaired Students

You may wish to have students with visual impairments take an active part in setting a table, naming each item as they touch it.

Students with Learning Difficulties

Students with learning difficulties may benefit from copying the sentences.

Leveling EACH Activity

Easy Activities 1, 2, 4
Average Activities 3, 5
CHallenging Activity 3
Expansión, Activity 6

PRACTICE

Activity 1

Audio Script

1. El mesero trabaja en el restaurante.
2. El mesero pone la mesa.
3. Hay una mesa libre.
4. Hay sal y pimienta en la mesa.
5. Un cliente tiene un menú en la mano.
6. El mesero sirve la carne.

Activities 1, 3, and 6 These activities can be done with the entire class. Read each question and call on students to respond. Each activity should be gone over orally in class and then written for homework.

Teaching Options

You may wish to do Activities 1, 3, and 6 as paired activities. Students can take turns asking and answering the questions.

Activities 2, 3, and 4 These activities can be prepared as homework and then gone over in class the next day.

Cultural Snapshot

Manta, Ecuador, is a port on the Bay of Manta. Its beaches are popular with Ecuadoran vacationers.

CULTURA
El mesero sirve los refrescos que pidieron las jóvenes en un restaurante al aire libre en Manta, Ecuador.

ESCUCHAR

1 Escucha. Indica en una tabla como la de abajo si ves en la foto la información que oyes.

sí	no

ESCRIBIR

2 **Juego Cada uno en su sitio** Determina en qué categoría pertenece cada palabra.

el jamón | la pimienta | el aceite | el cordero | los mejillones | la sal | los camarones | el biftec | el pollo | la langosta

CARNE	MARISCOS	CONDIMENTOS

HABLAR • ESCRIBIR

3 Contesta sobre un restaurante.

1. ¿Quién sirve la comida en un restaurante?
2. ¿Qué pide el cliente para seleccionar o escoger lo que quiere comer?
3. Después de la comida, ¿qué pide para pagar?
4. ¿Deja una propina a veces?
5. ¿Para quién es la propina?

EXPANSIÓN
Ahora, sin mirar las preguntas, cuenta la información en tus propias palabras. Si no recuerdas algo, un(a) compañero(a) te puede ayudar.

4 **¡Te toca a ti!** Vas a poner la mesa. ¿Qué pones en la mesa?

Andrew Payti

Answers

1
1. sí
2. no
3. sí
4. sí
5. no
6. no

2
carne
el jamón
el cordero
el biftec
el pollo
mariscos
los mejillones
los camarones
la langosta
condimentos
la pimienta
el aceite
la sal

3
1. El mesero (El camarero) sirve la comida en un restaurante.
2. El cliente pide el menú para seleccionar o escoger lo que quiere comer.
3. Pide la cuenta para pagar.
4. Sí, a veces deja una propina.
5. La propina es para el mesero (el camarero).

4 *Answers will vary but may include:*
el mantel, la servilleta, la taza, el platillo, la cuchara, el cuchillo, el tenedor, la cucharita, el plato, el vaso

LEER • HABLAR

5 **Rompecabezas**

¡Adivina! ¿Qué es?

1. Se usa para cubrir la mesa.
2. Se usa para tomar agua o leche.
3. Se usa para beber café o té.
4. Se usa para comer sopa.
5. Se usa para cortar la carne.

HABLAR • ESCRIBIR

6 Personaliza. Da respuestas personales.

1. ¿Te gusta comer en un restaurante?
2. ¿Te gusta más la carne o el pescado?
3. ¿Te gustan las legumbres?
4. Para tu ensalada, ¿te gusta una salsa de aceite y vinagre?
5. ¿Te gusta la carne bien hecha, a término medio o casi cruda?
6. En tu casa, ¿quién pone la mesa?
7. ¿Quién lava los platos?
8. Y, ¿quién levanta o quita la mesa?

CULTURA

Un restaurante con una terraza al aire libre en Guadalajara, México

Go Online!

connectED.mcgraw-hill.com

Conexiones

El lenguaje

Ya sabes que en el mundo hispano hay diferencias regionales en cuanto al uso de ciertas palabras. Los nombres de los comestibles tienden a variar de una región a otra. Aquí tenemos unos ejemplos.

- Las judías verdes tienen muchos nombres. Se llaman también «habichuelas tiernas», «chauchas», «vainitas», «ejotes» y «porotos».

- En casi todas partes el maíz es «el maíz» pero en México también se dice «el elote» y en Chile y otros países latinos se dice «el choclo». Un plato chileno delicioso es «el pastel de choclo».

Vocabulario

Conexiones

Students can read the **Conexiones** material silently. However, you may wish to have them repeat aloud the various words for the foods.

Heritage Speakers

If you have heritage speakers in class, ask them if they use or have heard of other terms for *green beans* or *corn.*

Differentiation

Advanced Learners

After doing Activity 6, advanced learners can give a presentation to the class about their eating preferences.

Go Online!

You may wish to remind students to go online for additional vocabulary practice. They can also download audio files of all vocabulary.

You may wish to use the whiteboard presentation for additional vocabulary instruction and practice.

ASSESS

Students are now ready to take Quiz 1.

Answers

5

1. un mantel
2. un vaso
3. una taza
4. una cuchara
5. un cuchillo

6 *Answers will vary but may include:*

1. Sí, (No, no) me gusta comer en un restaurante.
2. Me gusta más la carne (el pescado).
3. Sí, (No, no) me gustan las legumbres.
4. Sí (No), para mi ensalada (no) me gusta una salsa de aceite y vinagre.
5. Me gusta la carne bien hecha (a término medio, casi cruda).
6. En mi casa, ___ pone la mesa.
7. ___ lava los platos.
8. ___ levanta (quita) la mesa.

Online Resources

Customizable Lesson Plans
Whiteboard Lesson
Audio Activities
Video (Gramática)
Student Workbook
Quizzes

Quick Start

Use QS 4.2 or write the following on the board.
Answer.
1. **¿Dices que sí o que no?**
2. **¿Dice José que quiere ir?**
3. **¿Dicen los otros que quieren ir también?**
4. **¿Dicen ustedes que tienen un restaurante favorito?**

TEACH

Core Instruction

Step 1 Write the verb forms on the board. Underline the stem and have students repeat each form after you.

Step 2 When going over the verb **seguir,** review with students the following sound/spelling correspondence: **ga, gue, gui, go, gu.**

Note: Oral practice with these verbs is important, because if students pronounce them correctly, they will spell them correctly.

Differentiation

Students with Auditory Impairments

Help students with auditory impairments distinguish between the sounds **e** and **i: pido, pedimos,** etc.

Presente de los verbos de cambio radical e → i

FOLDABLES Study Organizer

PAPER FILE FOLDER See the Foldables section of the Student Handbook at the beginning of this book for help with making this foldable. Use this foldable to help you review the different tenses of the verbs that you have learned. Make a *paper file folder* for a verb. On separate pieces of paper, write the conjugations of the verb. Continue to file new conjugations in your *paper file folder.*

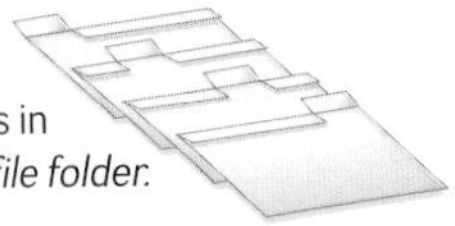

1. The verbs **pedir, servir, repetir, freír** *(to fry),* **seguir** *(to follow),* and **vestirse** *(to get dressed)* are stem-changing verbs. The **e** of the infinitive stem changes to **i** in all forms of the present tense except **nosotros(as)** and ***vosotros(as).*** Study the following forms.

pedir			
yo	pido	nosotros(as)	pedimos
tú	pides	*vosotros(as)*	*pedís*
Ud., él, ella	pide	Uds., ellos, ellas	piden

servir			
yo	sirvo	nosotros(as)	servimos
tú	sirves	*vosotros(as)*	*servís*
Ud., él, ella	sirve	Uds., ellos, ellas	sirven

2. Note the spelling of **seguir.**

   sigo, sigues, sigue, seguimos, *seguís,* siguen

3. Note that the present participle of these verbs also has **i.**

   No estoy pidiendo nada.
   El mesero nos está sirviendo.

CULTURA
Un restaurante callejero en Valencia, España

Práctica

HABLAR • ESCRIBIR

1 Personaliza. Da respuestas personales.

1. ¿Qué pides cuando vas a un restaurante?
2. Si te gusta un plato, ¿lo repites?
3. ¿Sigues una dieta o un régimen?
4. ¿Te vistes antes de salir para la escuela?
5. ¿Sigues un horario fijo en la escuela o varía de un día a otro tu horario?

Andrew Payti

Answers

1 *Answers will vary but may include:*
1. Pido ___ cuando voy a un restaurante.
2. Sí, si me gusta un plato lo repito.
3. Sí, (No, no) sigo una dieta o un régimen.
4. Sí, me visto antes de salir para la escuela.
5. Sí, (No, no) sigo un horario fijo en la escuela. (Mi horario varía de un día a otro.)

Go Online!

You may wish to remind students to go online for additional grammar review and practice.

You may wish to use the whiteboard presentation for additional grammar instruction and practice.

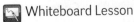

Go Online!

connectED.mcgraw-hill.com

ESCUCHAR • HABLAR

2 Conversa según el modelo.

MODELO **—A Juan le gusta la carne de res. ¿Qué pide él?**
—Él pide carne de res.

1. A Marta le gustan las legumbres. ¿Qué pide ella?
2. A Andrés le gusta el biftec. ¿Qué pide él?
3. A mis amigos les gustan los mariscos. ¿Qué piden ellos?
4. A mis padres les gusta mucho el postre. ¿Qué piden ellos?
5. Nos gusta la ensalada. ¿Qué pedimos?
6. Nos gustan las tortillas. ¿Qué pedimos?

ESCRIBIR

3 Completa la tabla.

yo	nosotros	usted	tú	ellos
		pide		
sirvo				
	seguimos			
				se visten
			repites	

HABLAR • ESCRIBIR

4 Personaliza. Da respuestas personales.

1. Cuando vas a un restaurante, ¿qué pides?
2. ¿Pides papas? Si no pides papas, ¿pides arroz?
3. ¿Qué más pides con la carne y las papas o el arroz?
4. ¿Quién te sirve en el restaurante?
5. Si te sirve bien, ¿qué le dejas?

LEER • ESCRIBIR

5 Escribe en el plural.

1. Siempre pido postre.
2. No repito nada.
3. Él se viste bien.
4. Sigo un plan definido.
5. ¿Qué repites?
6. Ella fríe las papas.

6 **Comunicación**

Trabaja con un(a) compañero(a). Preparen una conversación entre un(a) cliente(a) y un(a) camarero(a). El/La cliente(a) va a leer el menú para decidir lo que quiere comer. El/La camarero(a) contesta las preguntas que el/la cliente(a) tiene sobre los platos y luego escribe la orden. Presenten la conversación a la clase.

POTROS
RESTAURANTE-BAR
24-HORAS
MENÚ
Lunes
- Sopa de Pastas
- Pollo al Horno ó Carne ASADA
- Arroz Blanco
- Frijoles
- Patacones ó Yuca
- Ensalada de Lechuga, Zanahoria, Tomate
- Jugos
Martes
Sopa de Guineo -
Chuleta Ahumada ó Corvina - Apanada
Arroz Blanco -
Ensalada de Lechuga -
Torrejas de Trigo ó Patacones -
Jugos -
3.00
Miércoles
- Sopa de Cebada
- Pechuga Apanada o Lomo de Cerdo Jamonado
- Arroz c/guandú
- Lentejas
- Papa hervida picada en trocitos
- Plátano Asado
- Jugos
Jueves
Sopa de Mondongo -
Arroz Blanco -
Muchacho Relleno, -
Carne en su Salsa -
Yuca Frita o Tajadas -
Ensalada Roja -
Jugos -
Viernes
Bandeja PAISA y Sancocho Colombiano
Jugos
4.00
Sábado
Arroz con Pollo (tajada, ensalada de aguacate)
Frijolada, Pollo frito,
arroz blanco y ensalada de aguacate, Jugos
3.00

Gramática

Leveling EACH Activity

Easy Activities 1, 4
Average Activities 3, 5
CHallenging Activities 2, 6

PRACTICE

Activities 1, 2, and 4 These activities can be done with the entire class. Read each question and call on students to respond, or pair students and have them ask each other the questions. These activities should be gone over orally in class and then written for homework.

Activities 3 and 5 Activities 3 and 5 can be prepared beforehand and then gone over in class.

Learning from Realia

Food vocabulary can be limitless. There are some words on the menu that you may want to give to students:
ahumado(a) *smoked*
apanado(a) (or often **empanado[a]**) *breaded*
guineo *type of banana*
torreja (or more commonly **rodaja**) *slice*
patacones (or often called **tostones**) *fried plantains*
mondongo *stew of tripe* (**callos**)

ASSESS

Students are now ready to take Quiz 2.

Answers

2
1. Ella pide legumbres.
2. Él pide biftec.
3. Ellos piden mariscos.
4. Ellos piden postre.
5. Pedimos ensalada.
6. Pedimos tortillas.

3
pedir: pido, pedimos, pides, piden
servir: servimos, sirve, sirves, sirven
seguir: sigo, sigue, sigues, siguen
vestirse: me visto, nos vestimos, se viste, te vistes
repetir: repito, repetimos, repite, repiten

4 *Answers will vary but may include:*
1. Cuando voy a un restaurante pido ____.
2. Sí, pido papas. (Si, pido arroz.)
3. Pido ____.
4. El mesero (El camarero) me sirve en el restaurante.
5. Si me sirve bien, le dejo una propina.

5
1. Siempre pedimos postre.
2. No repetimos nada.
3. Ellos se visten bien.
4. Seguimos un plan definido.
5. ¿Qué repiten ustedes?
6. Ellas fríen las papas.

6 *Answers will vary.*

Online Resources

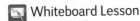

Customizable Lesson Plans
- Whiteboard Lesson
- Audio Activities
- Video (Gramática)
- Student Workbook
- Enrichment
- Quizzes

Quick Start

Use QS 4.3 or write the following on the board.

Complete in the preterite.

1. **El fin de semana pasado (yo) ___ a la playa. (ir)**
2. **Mis amigos ___ un día agradable. (pasar)**
3. **Yo ___, ___ el sol y ___ en el agua. (nadar, tomar, esquiar)**
4. **Nosotros ___ en un chiringuito. (comer)**
5. **Cuando yo ___ en el restaurante ___ una mesa libre. (entrar, ver)**

TEACH

Core Instruction

Step 1 Have students repeat the verb forms shown in the charts, paying particular attention to the stem changes and correct pronunciation.

Step 2 Write the verb forms on the board. Underline the vowel in the stem.

Note: The present tense of verbs like **preferir** and **dormir** was taught previously with other verbs with the **e → ie** and **o → ue** stem changes.

Cultural Snapshot

Outdoor cafés and restaurants with terraces are popular throughout Spain and certain areas of Latin America.

Pretérito de los verbos de cambio radical e → i, o → u

¡Ojo!

If you pronounce the vowels **e** and **i** correctly, you will never make a spelling error.

1. The verbs **pedir, repetir, freír, servir, seguir,** and **vestirse** have a stem change in the preterite. The **e** of the infinitive stem changes to **i** in the **él** and **ellos** forms.

repetir			
yo	repetí	nosotros(as)	repetimos
tú	repetiste	*vosotros(as)*	*repetisteis*
Ud., él, ella	repitió	Uds., ellos, ellas	repitieron

vestirse			
yo	me vestí	nosotros(as)	nos vestimos
tú	te vestiste	*vosotros(as)*	*os vestisteis*
Ud., él, ella	se vistió	Uds., ellos, ellas	se vistieron

2. The verbs **preferir, divertirse,** and **dormir** also have a stem change in the preterite. The **e** in **preferir** and **divertirse** changes to **i** and the **o** in **dormir** changes to **u** in the **él** and **ellos** forms. The verb **morir** *(to die)* follows the same pattern as **dormir—murió, murieron.**

preferir			
yo	preferí	nosotros(as)	preferimos
tú	preferiste	*vosotros(as)*	*preferisteis*
Ud., él, ella	prefirió	Uds., ellos, ellas	prefirieron

dormir			
yo	dormí	nosotros(as)	dormimos
tú	dormiste	*vosotros(as)*	*dormisteis*
Ud., él, ella	durmió	Uds., ellos, ellas	durmieron

CULTURA

Los amigos pasaron un rato en un café en Cádiz, España. Alguien pidió un refresco y el mesero lo está sirviendo ahora.

Andrew Payti

Differentiation

Students with Auditory Impairments

Have students with auditory impairments listen and pay particular attention to the difference between the **e** and **i** and the **o** and **u** sounds.

Go Online!

Gramática en vivo: *Stem-changing verbs in the preterite* Enliven learning with the animated world of Profesor Cruz! **Gramática en vivo** is a fun and effective tool for additional instruction and/or review.

Go Online!

connectED.mcgraw-hill.com

Práctica

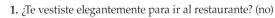

HABLAR • ESCRIBIR

7 Contesta según se indica.

1. ¿Te vestiste elegantemente para ir al restaurante? (no)
2. ¿Qué pediste en el restaurante? (una ensalada)
3. ¿Cómo la pediste? (sin aceite y vinagre)
4. ¿Cuántas veces repetiste sin aceite y vinagre? (dos veces)
5. Y, ¿cómo sirvió el mesero la ensalada? (con aceite y vinagre)
6. ¿Qué hiciste? (pedí otra ensalada)
7. ¿Qué pidió tu amigo? (puré de papas)
8. ¿Y qué pasó? (ellos frieron las papas)
9. ¿Qué sirvió el mesero? (papas fritas)
10. ¿Le dieron ustedes una propina al mesero? (no)

EXPANSIÓN

Ahora, sin mirar las preguntas, cuenta la información en tus propias palabras. Si no recuerdas algo, un(a) compañero(a) te puede ayudar.

Después contesta la pregunta, ¿Por qué no le dieron una propina al mesero?

LEER • ESCRIBIR

8 Completa con el pretérito.

Anoche mi amigo Ángel y yo __1__ (ir) a un restaurante. Ángel __2__ (pedir) pescado—más específicamente __3__ (pedir) corvina, un pescado delicioso del Pacífico. Ángel lo __4__ (pedir) frito y el cocinero lo __5__ (freír) muy bien. El mesero __6__ (servir) la corvina en una salsa de mantequilla y limón.

Yo no __7__ (pedir) pescado. Yo __8__ (pedir) mariscos—un plato delicioso de mejillones, almejas y camarones. El mesero __9__ (servir) el plato muy caliente. Luego nosotros __10__ (pedir) un postre rico, delicioso. Nosotros __11__ (divertirse) mucho.

Cuando yo volví a casa __12__ (dormirse) enseguida. No sé si Ángel __13__ (dormirse) enseguida o no.

CULTURA

Un restaurante popular en una esquina de San Telmo, un barrio interesante de Buenos Aires, la capital de Argentina

Andrew Payti

Gramática

Leveling EACH Activity

Easy Activity 9
Average Activity 7
CHallenging Activity 7
Expansión, Activity 8

PRACTICE

Differentiation

Advanced Learners

Activity 7 After going over this activity with the class or in pairs, you may wish to have advanced learners write a review of this story.

Tips for Success

Have students prepare Activity 8 before going over it in class. It makes students use all preterite forms of these verbs.

Cultural Snapshot

This restaurant in the San Telmo section of Buenos Aires is just off the famous Dorrego Square, which is popular with **tanguistas** and antique shoppers, particularly on Sundays.

Conexiones

Have students locate Buenos Aires on the map on the pages featuring Argentina in the **GeoVistas** section at the beginning of this book. Then have them look for another picture of the San Telmo section of Buenos Aires on these pages. Interested students may want to find out more about the history of the tango in Argentina.

Answers

7

1. No, no me vestí elegantemente para ir al restaurante.
2. Pedí una ensalada.
3. La pedí sin aceite y vinagre.
4. Repetí sin aceite y vinagre dos veces.
5. El mesero sirvió la ensalada con aceite y vinagre.
6. Pedí otra ensalada.
7. Mi amigo pidió puré de papas.
8. Ellos frieron las papas.
9. El mesero sirvió papas fritas.
10. No, no le dimos una propina al mesero.

8

1. fuimos
2. pidió
3. pidió
4. pidió
5. frió
6. sirvió
7. pedí
8. pedí
9. sirvió
10. pedimos
11. nos divertimos
12. me dormí
13. se durmió

Online Resources

Customizable Lesson Plans
Whiteboard Lesson
Audio Activities
Student Workbook
Enrichment
Quizzes

Quick Start

Use QS 4.4 or write the following on the board.
In Spanish, describe a good friend—both his or her physical appearance and some personality traits.

Activity 9 Have students pronounce the words very clearly as they read them aloud.

ASSESS

Students are now ready to take Quiz 3.

TEACH

Core Instruction

Step 1 Write the adjectives on the board. Underline the endings.

Step 2 Explain to students that the only adjectives that deviate from the normal pattern are the adjectives of nationality that end in a consonant. They have four forms. Contrast the following:
un(os) restaurante(s) tradicional(es)
un(os) restaurante(s) español(es)
una(s) comida(s) tradicional(es)
una(s) comida(s) española(s)

Gramática

InfoGap For more practice with stem-changing verbs, do Activity 4 in the Student Resource section at the end of this book.

9 ¡Te toca a ti! Completa la palabra.

1. rep_tió
2. s_rvieron
3. se v_stieron
4. p_dió
5. se div_rtió
6. d_rmieron
7. m_rió
8. pref_rió
9. fr_eron
10. p_dieron

CULTURA
Una joven francesa delante de un monumento francés—la famosa Torre Eiffel

Adjetivos de nacionalidad

1. Adjectives of nationality that end in **o** or **e** follow the same pattern as any other adjective. Those that end in **o** have four forms and those that end in **e** have two forms.

un restaurante cubano	**una comida cubana**
unos restaurantes cubanos	**unas comidas cubanas**
un plato nicaragüense	**una comida nicaragüense**
unos platos nicaragüenses	**unas comidas nicaragüenses**

2. Adjectives of nationality that end in a consonant have four forms rather than two.

un restaurante español	**una comida española**
unos restaurantes españoles	**unas comidas españolas**

3. Adjectives of nationality that end in **s** or **n** have a written accent in the masculine singular. The accent is dropped in all other forms.

francés	**francesa**	**catalán**	**catalana**
franceses	**francesas**	**catalanes**	**catalanas**

Some other common adjectives of nationality that end in a consonant are: **inglés, portugués, irlandés, japonés, alemán.**

4. Note that with an article the adjective becomes a noun.

Los portugueses son de Portugal y los brasileños son de Brasil.

CULTURA
Un plato mexicano

Answers

9
1. repitió
2. sirvieron
3. se vistieron
4. pidió
5. se divirtió
6. durmieron
7. murió
8. prefirió
9. frieron
10. pidieron

Additional Vocabulary

Some nationalities that appear frequently in the newspapers are: **israelí, iraquí, saudí, turquí, lebanés(esa)** *(Lebanese)*, **líbano(a)** *(Libyan)*, **egipto(a).** The plural of **í** is **íes, israelíes.** You may wish to have students look up their own nationality.

Práctica

HABLAR • ESCRIBIR

10 Contesta según el modelo.

MODELO **—¿Son de España las muchachas?**
—Sí, son españolas.

1. ¿Son de España los muchachos?
2. ¿Es de Colombia el café?
3. ¿Son de Nicaragua las profesoras?
4. ¿Son de Inglaterra los libros?
5. ¿Es de Francia tu amigo?

LEER • ESCRIBIR

11 Completa según se indica.

1. En el restaurante sirven comida ____. (mexicano)
2. La cocina ____ no es como la cocina ____. (catalán, francés)
3. Las rosas ____ son las más bonitas. (ecuatoriano)
4. Los pasajeros ____ comprenden el español. (portugués)
5. Los ____ hablan inglés. (irlandés)
6. Hay muchos restaurantes ____ y ____ en Latinoamérica. En Perú los restaurantes ____ se llaman «chifas». (japonés, chino, chino)

CULTURA

Estos jóvenes venezolanos están comiendo comida japonesa auténtica en un restaurante japonés en Caracas, Venezuela.

Leveling EACH Activity

Average Activities 10, 11

PRACTICE

Activity 10 This activity can also be done as a paired activity.

Differentiation

Advanced Learners

Have advanced learners make up original sentences using all types of adjectives of nationality.

Cultural Snapshot

Japanese restaurants are becoming quite popular in Spain and throughout Latin America, particularly, but not exclusively, sushi bars.

Go Online!

You may wish to use the whiteboard presentation for additional grammar instruction and practice.

ASSESS

Students are now ready to take Quiz 4.

Answers

10

1. Sí, son españoles.
2. Sí, es colombiano.
3. Sí, son nicaragüenses.
4. Sí, son ingleses.
5. Sí, es francés.

11

1. mexicana
2. catalana, francesa
3. ecuatorianas
4. portugueses
5. irlandeses
6. japoneses, chinos, chinos

Online Resources

Customizable Lesson Plans
- Whiteboard Lesson
- Audio Activities
- Student Workbook
- Enrichment
- Quizzes

Quick Start

Use QS 4.5 or write the following on the board.
1. Write some articles of clothing you know in Spanish.
2. Write sentences using the following words or expressions: **de manga corta, una talla más grande, el número, calzar, la empleada, la caja.**

TEACH

Core Instruction

Have students pay particular attention to the noun and the verb ending (singular, plural).

PRACTICE

Leveling EACH Activity

Easy Activity 12
Average Activities 13, 14

¡Así se dice!

Why It Works!

Each item of Activity 12 alternates between singular noun/verb and plural noun/verb to help students focus on this important aspect of the concept being taught.

Activity 12 It is suggested that you present Activity 12 as an oral activity in class.

¡Así se dice!

A very useful expression is **¿Cómo se dice en español?**

La voz pasiva con se

1. When you talk about something being done without saying who does it, you use the passive voice in English.

   Fish is sold at the fish market.

2. In Spanish, the pronoun **se** is used to express this idea.

   Se vende pescado en la pescadería.
   Se venden papas en la verdulería.

3. You will often see the **se** construction used to express ideas such as:

   They speak Spanish here.
   Spanish is spoken here.
   One speaks Spanish here.
   People speak Spanish here.
   → **Aquí se habla español.**

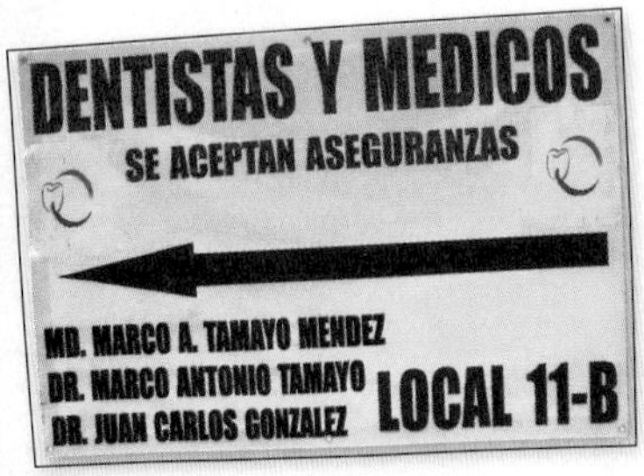

Práctica

ESCUCHAR • HABLAR • ESCRIBIR

12 Contesta. Presta atención a la forma de **vender.**

1. ¿Se vende pan en la panadería?
2. ¿Se venden suéteres en la tienda de ropa?
3. ¿Se vende carne en la carnicería?
4. ¿Se venden guisantes en la verdulería?
5. ¿Se vende fruta en la frutería?
6. ¿Se venden productos congelados en el supermercado?
7. ¿Se vende pescado en la pescadería?
8. ¿Se venden camisas en la tienda de ropa?

CULTURA
Se venden frutas en este puesto en Tepoztlán, México.

Andrew Payti

Learning from Realia

Have students look for this use of **se** in the realia and photo caption.

Cultural Snapshot

As students learned throughout Level 1, markets such as the one seen here are very popular throughout Spain and Latin America.

ABOUT THE SPANISH LANGUAGE

Note that the term **aseguranzas** is used in this realia, but **seguros** is a more commonly used term.

HABLAR • ESCRIBIR

13 ¿Qué se habla y dónde? Sigue el modelo.

MODELO

—¿Qué lengua se habla en España?
—Se habla español en España.

1. 

2. 

3. 

4. 

5. 

6. 

HABLAR • ESCRIBIR

14 Contesta.

1. ¿Se deja una propina (en un restaurante) cuando el servicio está incluido?
2. ¿Se sirve mucha carne en un restaurante argentino?
3. ¿Se usa mucho aceite en España?
4. ¿Se pone el cuchillo a la derecha o a la izquierda del plato?
5. ¿Se pone la taza en un platillo?
6. ¿Se comen muchos mariscos en los restaurantes cerca de la costa?
7. Los tostones son populares en el Caribe. ¿Se sirven tostones con muchas comidas cubanas?
8. ¿Se dice «menú» de la misma manera en inglés y español?

Go Online!

connectED.mcgraw-hill.com

Refrán

Can you guess what the following proverb means?

Con mal vinagre y peor aceite, buen gazpacho no se puede hacer.

¡Bravo!

You have now learned all the new vocabulary and grammar in this chapter. Continue to use and practice all that you know while learning more cultural information. **¡Vamos!**

Differentiation

Multiple Intelligences

Activity 13 You may wish to have **visual-spatial** learners prepare some more maps. Remind them that they will have to know the name of the country and the language. The word for the country is almost always similar to the name of the language except in cases such as **canadiense** and **inglés** or **mexicano** and **español.**

ASSESS

Students are now ready to take Quiz 5.

Refrán

Have students recite the proverb aloud. Then see if they can figure out its meaning. Encourage them to give an equivalent expression in English such as "You can't make a silk purse from a sow's ear."

Go Online!

You may wish to use the whiteboard presentation for additional grammar instruction and practice.

Answers

12

1. Sí, se vende pan en la panadería.
2. Sí, se venden suéteres en la tienda de ropa.
3. Sí, se vende carne en la carnicería.
4. Sí, se venden guisantes en la verdulería.
5. Sí, se vende fruta en la frutería.
6. Sí, se venden productos congelados en el supermercado.
7. Sí, se vende pescado en la pescadería.
8. Sí, se venden camisas en la tienda de ropa.

13

1. Se habla francés en Francia.
2. Se habla italiano en Italia.
3. Se habla alemán en Alemania.
4. Se habla inglés en Irlanda.
5. Se habla inglés en Inglaterra.
6. Se habla árabe en Arabia Saudí.

14

1. No, no se deja una propina cuando el servicio está incluido.
2. Sí, se sirve mucha carne en un restaurante argentino.
3. Sí, se usa mucho aceite en España.
4. Se pone el cuchillo a la derecha del plato.
5. Sí, se pone la taza en un platillo.
6. Sí, se comen muchos mariscos en los restaurantes cerca de la costa.
7. Sí, se sirven tostones con muchas comidas cubanas.
8. No, no se dice «menú» de la misma manera en inglés y en español.

Online Resources

Customizable Lesson Plans

Audio Activities

Video (Diálogo)

Student Workbook

Quick Start

Use QS 4.6 or write the following on the board.

Look at the conversation and write every stem-changing verb you find.

TEACH

Core Instruction

Step 1 Tell students they will hear a conversation between a young man and woman. She and a friend went to an Argentine restaurant. As you hear the conversation, you will learn some interesting things about dining in an Argentine restaurant.

Step 2 Have students repeat the conversation after you or the recorded version. Students who have developed an acceptable pronunciation do not have to repeat aloud.

Teaching Options

You may wish to omit the Core Instruction and merely call on students to read the conversation aloud.

Differentiation

Multiple Intelligences

Call on **bodily-kinesthetic** learners to come to the front of the class and present the conversation. Have them pantomime what they think **«la panza llena»** means.

Una comida muy buena

Adela	Anoche fuimos a un restaurante argentino.
Felipe	Sí, ¿qué pediste?
Adela	Yo pedí un biftec o como dicen en Argentina «bife de lomo».
Felipe	¿Qué tal te gustó?
Adela	Mucho. Lo pedí casi crudo porque yo sé que en Argentina se sirve el bife bien hecho.
Felipe	¿Qué te sirvieron con el bife?
Adela	Papas fritas. Y pedí una ensalada aparte.
Felipe	Se dice que en Argentina se sirven porciones grandes.
Adela	Sí, es verdad. Y después de comer tanto todos pedimos flan.
Felipe	¿Flan? Es un postre español, ¿no?
Adela	Sí, lo es pero es popular en Latinoamérica también.
Felipe	Pues me parece que te divertiste.
Adela	Mucho. Y cuando volví a casa, me dormí enseguida—como se dice «con la panza llena».

David H. Brennan

¡Así se dice!

Why It Works!

This conversation contains no new Spanish. In addition, the grammar taught in this chapter is reintroduced ten times: **pediste, pedí, pedí, se sirve, sirvieron, pedí, se sirven, pedimos, te divertiste, me dormí.** Using the language enables students to retain it.

Go Online!

You may wish to remind students to go online for additional conversation practice.

¿Comprendes?

connectED.mcgraw-hill.com

A Contesta según la información en la conversación.

1. ¿Qué pidió Adela en el restaurante argentino?
2. ¿Le gustó?
3. ¿Cómo pidió el bife?
4. ¿Cómo lo sirven en Argentina?
5. ¿Qué más comió Adela?
6. ¿Cómo son las porciones que se sirven en Argentina?
7. ¿Qué pidió Adela de postre?
8. ¿Qué hizo Adela cuando volvió a casa?

B **Resumiendo** Cuenta la información en la conversación en tus propias palabras.

C **Identificando** Indica todo lo que Adela comió en el restaurante argentino.

D **Llegando a conclusiones** Según la información en la conversación, ¿cuáles son unas características típicas de una comida en Argentina?

CULTURA

El mesero sirve a sus clientes en la terraza de un café en la Recoleta, Buenos Aires, Argentina.

PRACTICE

¿Comprendes?

A You may wish to let students look up the answers in the **Conversación** or you may wish to use this as a factual recall activity.

B Call on students of different ability levels. Some will give a very brief review. Others will give a very complete review.

D This activity involves higher thinking skills.

Go Online!

Diálogo en vivo In this episode Alberto is working at a restaurant in Argentina. Ask students to pay attention to how he treats the two customers. What assumption does Alberto make?

Pre-AP Listening to the audio recording of this conversation will help students develop the skills that they need to be successful on the listening portion of the AP exam.

Answers

A

1. Pidió un biftec (un bife de lomo).
2. Sí, le gustó mucho.
3. Lo pidió casi crudo.
4. Lo sirven bien hecho.
5. Comió papas fritas, una ensalada y flan.
6. Las porciones que se sirven en Argentina son grandes.
7. Pidió flan.
8. Cuando volvió a casa se durmió enseguida.

B *Answers will vary.*

C un biftec, papas fritas, una ensalada, flan

D *Answers will vary but may include:*
Se sirve el bife bien hecho. El biftec se llama «bife de lomo». Se sirven porciones grandes. El flan es un postre popular.

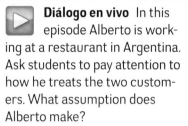

Online Resources

Customizable Lesson Plans

Audio Activities

Student Workbook

TEACH

Core Instruction

Step 1 Have students read the **Estrategia de lectura** and think about it. Then have them read the **Antes de leer.** Have them think about the information and answer the questions silently.

Step 2 Call on individuals to read short sections aloud. Intersperse with comprehension questions. You can use the Reading Checks provided in addition to others you may wish to make up.

Step 3 After every two paragraphs you may wish to call on a student to give a brief review.

Teaching Options

You may have the whole class read the entire **Lectura** or you may wish to assign each part to a different group. Each group will report to the other concerning what they learned.

¡Así se dice!

Why It Works!

This **Lectura**, like all others in **¡Así se dice!**, contains only Spanish students have already learned with the exception of the seven footnoted words. The **Lectura** is easy because it is at the students' proficiency level and they are not encumbered with unknown lexicon and grammatical forms.

Lectura CULTURAL

ESTRATEGIA DE LECTURA

COMPARANDO Cuando lees algo es importante hacer comparaciones. Cuando comparas algo identificas lo que es diferente y lo que es lo mismo o semejante. Hacer comparaciones mentales te ayuda a recordar la información que estás leyendo.

Antes de leer

Piensa en una visita a un restaurante. ¿Qué comes? ¿Quién te sirve? ¿Dejas una propina?

Restaurantes de España y Latinoamérica

Algún día vas a tener la oportunidad de visitar un país hispano. Y como tienes que comer unas tres veces al día, debes saber algo sobre los restaurantes.

¿Comer dónde? En todas las grandes ciudades hay restaurantes elegantes y económicos. Si quieres solamente una merienda puedes ir a un café. Si quieres una comida es mejor ir a un restaurante o una cafetería. Pero una cafetería no es autoservicio[1]. Es un restaurante generalmente modesto donde se sirve comida en una barra[2] igual que en una mesa. Comer en la barra cuesta menos que en una de las mesas.

[1]autoservicio *self-service*
[2]barra *counter*

READING CHECK

¿Dónde se puede comer económicamente?

Durante la lectura

Prepara una lista mental de las cosas que son las mismas en un restaurante aquí en Estados Unidos y las cosas que son diferentes.

CULTURA

Mucha gente pasa un domingo por la tarde en un restaurante como este en Cádiz, España.

Andrew Payti

ABOUT THE SPANISH LANGUAGE

La barra is a *counter* in English. Students will see **el bar** quite often on buildings and awnings. They will frequently see **bar-restaurante.** Although there are true bars in Spain and Latin America where alcohol is the main commodity, they are not as common as in the United States. **El bar** always serves snacks or even more substantial food and probably more wine than hard liquor.

Cultural Snapshot

This café-restaurant is in the old section of Cádiz, just off the square with the main cathedral. Many say the old city has a North African appearance. Columbus left from Cádiz on his second voyage to the Americas.

¿Servir cómo? Por lo general una comida, sobre todo una comida española, consiste en varios platos—primer plato, plato principal y postre. En muchas partes el plato principal se llama «el plato fuerte». En España no se sirve una mezcla[3] de cosas en el mismo plato como aquí en Estados Unidos. Si pides judías verdes o alcachofas salteadas[4], el camarero te va a servir estas legumbres como un primer plato o entrada. Pero como sabemos, siempre hay excepciones. En unos restaurantes modestos o cafeterías se sirve lo que se llama «un plato combinado» que lleva, por ejemplo, carne, papas y una legumbre en el mismo plato.

En Latinoamérica las costumbres varían de país en país. En Puerto Rico y otras islas del Caribe, por ejemplo, la carne o el pescado viene acompañado de arroz blanco o amarillo con frijoles (habichuelas) y tostones o maduros[5]. En México muchos platos llevan arroz y frijoles refritos.

[3]mezcla *mixture*
[4]alcachofas salteadas *sautéed artichokes*
[5]maduros *fried sweet bananas*

✓ READING CHECK

¿Cuál es una característica de una comida española?

✓ READING CHECK

¿Qué acompaña una comida en los países del Caribe?

Go Online!

You may wish to remind students to go online for additional reading comprehension and writing skills practice.

CULTURA

Unos mariscos de un restaurante en Barcelona y una comida de pescado en un restaurante en Maracay, Venezuela.

TEACH

Core Instruction

Have the entire class or small groups discuss their opinions about the **Después de leer** section.

Cultural Snapshot

The Recoleta area in Buenos Aires has many outdoor cafés such as the one seen here, especially on the outskirts of the park.

Lectura CULTURAL

READING CHECK

¿Qué es la sobremesa?

Después de leer

Decide si hay más semejanzas (cosas similares) o diferencias al comer en un restaurante aquí en Estados Unidos y en un restaurante en un país hispano.

¿Tomar el postre? A muchos les gusta terminar una comida con un postre—o una sobremesa. En algunos lugares la palabra «sobremesa» es un sinónimo de postre pero en otros incluye toda la conversación entre los comensales[6] mientras toman el postre. Y en España y Latinoamérica la comida puede durar unas horas—sobre todo una comida en un restaurante o durante una fiesta.

Muchos turistas le preguntan al mesero si el servicio está incluido. La respuesta es casi siempre «sí» y no es necesario dejar una propina.

¿Se puede? ¡Un punto muy importante! Si no comes toda la comida no puedes llevar las sobras[7] a casa. La etiqueta no lo permite.

¡Otro punto importante! Después de comer bien en un restaurante, a mucha gente le gusta ir a otro local para tomar su cafecito—un local que se especializa en el café.

¡Buen apetito!

[6]comensales *diners*
[7]sobras *leftovers*

CULTURA

Los cafés al aire libre son muy populares en la Recoleta, un barrio bonito de Buenos Aires.

Andrew Payti

Go Online!
connectED.mcgraw-hill.com

¿Comprendes?

A Confirmando información Indica si la información es correcta o no.

	correcta	incorrecta
1. En las ciudades españolas y latinoamericanas hay solo restaurantes elegantes.		
2. Una cafetería es siempre autoservicio.		
3. En una cafetería cuesta más comer en una mesa que en la barra.		
4. En España siempre ponen muchas cosas diferentes en el mismo plato.		
5. En España una comida típica comprende (consiste en) varios platos.		

B Describiendo Describe.
1. lo que acompaña una típica comida puertorriqueña
2. lo que acompaña una típica comida mexicana
3. lo que es la sobremesa

C Explicando Explica.
1. la diferencia entre un café, un restaurante y una cafetería
2. como se sirve la comida en España
3. lo que es un plato combinado

D Comparando Compara tu experiencia en restaurantes estadounidenses con lo que aprendiste de los restaurantes en los países hispanos.

E Identificando ¿Cuál es la idea principal de esta lectura? Da unos detalles que apoyan *(support)* esta idea.

F Analizando ¿Qué piensas? ¿Por qué quiere compartir el autor esta información con sus lectores? ¿Cuál es su propósito?

CULTURA
¿Quieres pedir algo del menú de este restaurante en Guatemala?

Richard Brommer

Lectura

PRACTICE

Pre-AP These cultural readings will develop the skills that students need to be successful on the reading and writing sections of the AP exam. Listening to these readings will also help prepare them for the auditory component.

¿Comprendes?

B, C, D Have students be as complete as possible with their answers to Activities B, C, and D. As you go over these activities orally in class, you can have several students respond to the same item.

Answers

A
1. incorrecta
2. incorrecta
3. correcta
4. incorrecta
5. correcta

B
1. arroz blanco o amarillo, frijoles (habichuelas) y tostones o maduros
2. arroz y frijoles refritos
3. el postre o toda la conversación entre los comensales mientras toman el postre

C *Answers will vary but may include:*
1. Un café es un restaurante económico donde uno va para tomar una merienda. Un restaurante es un lugar donde se puede comer una comida. Puede ser elegante o modesto. Una cafetería es un restaurante modesto donde se sirve comida en una barra y a veces en una mesa.
2. Una comida española consiste en el primer plato, el plato principal y el postre. No se sirve una mezcla de cosas en el mismo plato.
3. Un plato combinado es un plato con, por ejemplo, carne, papas y una legumbre. Se sirve en muchos restaurantes modestos o cafeterías.

D *Answers will vary.*

E *Answers will vary.*

F *Answers will vary.*

Online Resources

Customizable Lesson Plans

Audio Activities

Student Workbook

Teaching Options

You may wish to follow any one of the following procedures for the **Un poco más** reading.

Independent reading Have students read the selection and do the post-reading activities as homework which you collect. This option is the least intrusive on class time and requires a minimum of teacher involvement.

Homework with in-class follow-up Assign the reading and post-reading activities as homework. Review and discuss the material in class the next day.

Intensive in-class activity This option includes a discussion of **Antes de leer**, listening to the audio recording of the reading selection, an in-class discussion of the selection, and the **¿Comprendes?** activity. You may also assign **¿Comprendes?** for homework and discuss it in class the next day.

Go Online!

You may wish to remind students to go online for additional reading comprehension and writing skills practice.

Lectura

UN POCO MÁS

Antes de leer

Piensa en unas experiencias personales en un restaurante. ¿Cómo es el servicio? ¿Son corteses los meseros? Una vez, ¿te dio un servicio malo un mesero? Si contestas que sí, recuerda lo que pasó. Si contestas que no, piensa en algunas cosas que pueden pasar.

Sé lo que pedí

Anoche Julio y un grupo de sus amigos fueron a cenar en un restaurante. Se divirtieron porque les gusta estar en su grupo pero la verdad es que no comieron bien. Fue un desastre. Nada anduvo bien. Todo salió mal.

Por ejemplo, Julio pidió un biftec a término medio. Y lo repitió dos veces al mesero—a término medio. Pidió también papas fritas y una ensalada de lechuga y tomates. Y, ¿qué le sirvió el mesero? Es verdad que le sirvió un biftec—pero no a término medio. Le sirvió el biftec casi crudo y a Julio no le gusta la carne muy roja. ¿Le sirvió las papas fritas? No. Le puso un plato de arroz y le dio una ensalada pero sin tomates. ¿Qué piensas? ¿Dejó Julio una buena propina para el mesero? Tú puedes decidir. Pero, te digo una cosa. Cuando salió del restaurante Julio dijo: —¡Increíble! Yo le pedí una cosa y él me sirvió otra. No sé si él me comprendió o no.

¿Fuiste una vez a un restaurante cuando tuviste una mala experiencia como la experiencia de Julio y sus amigos? ¿Te enfadaste? ¿Le dijiste algo al mesero o no?

CULTURA
Es la terraza de un restaurante popular en Miraflores en Lima, Perú.

Andrew Payti

¿Comprendes?

Escoge o completa.

1. ¿Se divirtieron Julio y sus amigos?
   a. Sí, porque fueron a cenar en un restaurante.
   b. Sí, porque el mesero les dio un servicio bueno.
   c. Sí, porque les gusta pasar tiempo juntos.
   d. Sí, porque fue un desastre.
2. ¿Quién o qué causó el problema?
   a. el mesero
   b. Julio
   c. los amigos de Julio
   d. la propina
3. Los comestibles mencionados en la lectura son _____.
4. ¿Qué no comprendió Julio?
   a. por qué no le dio una buena propina al mesero
   b. por qué él pidió una cosa y el mesero le sirvió otra
   c. por qué el mesero no lo comprendió
   d. por qué decidieron ir al restaurante
5. ¿Cuál es un buen título para la lectura?
   a. Mis amigos
   b. Nos gusta pasar tiempo juntos.
   c. Una comida
   d. Una comida desastrosa

CULTURA

Este restaurante en Antigua, Guatemala tiene el nombre de una famosa artista mexicana. ¿Quién es?

Lori Ernfridsson

Differentiation

Multiple Intelligences

To engage **visual-spatial** learners, have them draw at least one caricature of the events in this **Lectura.**

Cultural Snapshot

The beautiful colonial city of Antigua, not far from Guatemala City, has become quite a popular tourist destination. For this reason, there are many new, quaint hotels and small, intimate restaurants such as the one seen here.

Tips for Success

The multiple-choice comprehension activities that accompany the second reading selection in each chapter have a format that will help students prepare for standardized tests.

Answers

1. c
2. a
3. un biftec, papas fritas, una ensalada de lechuga y tomates, arroz, una ensalada sin tomates
4. b
5. d

Prepárate para el examen

Online Resources

Customizable Lesson Plans

Student Workbook

Enrichment

Listening, Speaking, Reading, Writing Tests

Self-check for achievement

This is a pre-test for students to take before you administer the chapter test. Note that each section is cross-referenced so students can easily find the material they feel they need to review. You may wish to use Self-Check Worksheet SC4 to have students complete this assessment in class or at home. You can correct the assessment yourself, or you may prefer to display the answers in class using Self-Check Answers SC4A.

Differentiation

Slower Paced Learners

Have students work in pairs to complete the Self-Check in class. Once they have finished, call on individuals to give the correct answers as you review together.

Multiple Intelligences

To engage **visual-spatial** and **bodily-kinesthetic** learners, number 1 to 40 on the board and call on a student to go to the board and write the correct answer (this may be done chronologically or you may allow students to choose the one they answer). Then have the student who wrote the first answer decide who will write the second, and so on, making sure to remind them not to pick the same person again.

Self-check for **ACHIEVEMENT**

Prepárate para el examen

Vocabulario

1 Identifica.

Jules Frazier/Getty Images

To review, see **Vocabulario**.

2 Completa con una palabra apropiada.

6. Se puede preparar una salsa para una ensalada con _____ y vinagre.

7. El cordero no es un pescado. Es _____.

8. Se sirve el café en _____.

9–10. Los clientes en un restaurante piden _____ antes de comer y piden _____ después de comer.

11. La langosta es _____. No es una carne.

3 ¿Sí o no?

12. Patricia pide el menú porque sabe lo que quiere comer.

13. Si el servicio no está incluido el cliente deja una propina para el mesero.

14. El cerdo es un pescado.

15. El flan es un postre.

16. Tomás necesita un tenedor para tomar la sopa.

17. Levantamos la mesa antes de comer.

18. Antonio pide el biftec casi crudo porque no le gusta la carne muy roja.

Answers

1

1. la servilleta
2. el tenedor
3. el plato
4. el cuchillo
5. la cuchara

2

6. aceite
7. una carne
8. una taza
9. el menú
10. la cuenta
11. un marisco

3

12. no
13. sí
14. no
15. sí
16. no
17. no
18. no

Go Online!

connectED.mcgraw-hill.com

Prepárate para el examen

Gramática

4 Completa con el presente.

19. El mesero les ____ a los clientes en el restaurante. (servir)
20. Yo siempre ____ la misma cosa, un biftec. (pedir)
21. Ellas ____ elegantemente para ir al restaurante. (vestirse)
22. Nosotros no lo ____. (repetir)
23. El cocinero ____ las papas. (freír)
24. El postre ____ el plato principal. (seguir)

To review, see **Presente de los verbos de cambio radical e → i.**

5 Completa con el pretérito.

25. Ellos se divirtieron. Y yo ____ también.
26. Yo dormí bien. Y él ____ bien también.
27. Tú lo repetiste. Y nosotros lo ____ también.
28. Ellos lo prefirieron. Y su amigo lo ____ también.
29. Nos vestimos. Y ellos ____ también.
30. Abuela les sirvió la comida. Y tú les ____ la comida también.

To review, see **Pretérito de los verbos de cambio radical e → i, o → u.**

6 Completa.

31. En los restaurantes ____ se sirve comida ____. (japonés)
32. La blusa ____ es preciosa. (guatemalteco)
33. Unos ____ hablan inglés y francés. (canadiense)

To review, see **Adjetivos de nacionalidad.**

7 Completa.

34. ____ sirv__ el postre después del plato principal.
35. ____ com__ muchos mariscos en Chile y en España.
36. ____ habl__ mucho español en Estados Unidos.

To review, see **La voz pasiva con se.**

Cultura

8 Escoge la información correcta.

37. Se sirven porciones (grandes, pequeñas) de comida en Argentina.
38. En España (ponen, no ponen) muchas cosas en el mismo plato.
39. En España y (Latinoamérica, Estados Unidos) la gente no lleva las sobras a casa.
40. Los tostones o maduros, arroz y frijoles negros acompañan muchas comidas (mexicanas, caribeñas).

To review this cultural information, see the **Lectura cultural.**

Differentiation

(continued)

This type of review activity is particularly appealing to interpersonal learners but will also benefit the class on the whole by promoting an inclusive, student-centered learning environment.

Slower Paced Learners

Encourage students who need extra help to refer to the margin notes and review any section before answering the questions.

Pre-AP Students preparing for the AP exam may benefit from a set time limit when completing this Self-Check. This may also help to identify students with learning difficulties or slower paced students who need extra help.

Go Online!

You may wish to remind students to go online for additional test preparation.

Answers

4
19. sirve
20. pido
21. se visten
22. repetimos
23. fríe
24. sigue

5
25. me divertí
26. durmió
27. repetimos
28. prefirió
29. se vistieron
30. serviste

6
31. japoneses, japonesa
32. guatemalteca
33. canadienses

7
34. Se sirve
35. Se comen
36. Se habla

8
37. grandes
38. no ponen
39. Latinoamérica
40. caribeñas

Prepárate para el examen

Tips for Success

Encourage students to say as much as possible when they do these open-ended activities. Tell them not to be afraid to make mistakes, since the goal of the activities is real-life communication. If someone in the group makes an error, allow the others to politely correct him or her. Let students choose the activities they would like to do.

Tell students to feel free to elaborate on the basic theme and to be creative. They may use props, pictures, or posters if they wish.

Pre-AP These oral activities will give students the opportunity to develop and improve their speaking skills so that they may succeed on the speaking portion of the AP exam.

Note: You may want to use the rubric below to help students prepare their speaking activities.

Practice for **ORAL PROFICIENCY**

Prepárate para el examen

CULTURA

De estas tapas españolas, ¿cuáles te apetecen?

1 ¡Al restaurante!

Order a meal and chat with friends at a restaurant

Imagínate que tu clase de español está en un restaurante donde se sirve comida española y latinoamericana. Todos los meseros hablan español. Pide lo que quieres en español. Con unos compañeros de clase prepara una conversación que tiene lugar en el restaurante. Luego presenta la conversación a la clase.

2 Una comida típica

Talk about foods

Ya sabes mucho sobre las comidas latinas. Habla de un plato o de una comida que te gusta o que quieres probar o comer por primera vez.

3 Preferencias

Discuss where you prefer to eat

Con un(a) compañero(a) indica si prefieres comer en casa o en un restaurante. ¿Por qué? A ver si tu compañero(a) tiene la misma opinión.

4 En casa

Talk about a meal at home

Describe una comida en casa y todo lo que tienes que hacer cuando comes en casa. Mira el diagrama abajo para ayudarte.

5 Semejanzas y diferencias

Compare restaurants where you live with restaurants in Spanish-speaking countries

Compara y contrasta algunas cosas interesantes sobre restaurantes aquí en Estados Unidos y en los países hispanos.

Scoring Rubric for Speaking

	4	3	2	1
vocabulary	extensive use of vocabulary, including idiomatic expressions	adequate use of vocabulary and idiomatic expressions	limited vocabulary marked with some anglicisms	limited vocabulary marked by frequent anglicisms that force interpretation by the listener
grammar	few or no grammatical errors	minor grammatical errors	some serious grammatical errors	serious grammatical errors
pronunciation	good intonation and largely accurate pronunciation with slight accent	acceptable intonation and pronunciation with distinctive accent	errors in intonation and pronunciation with heavy accent	errors in intonation and pronunciation that interfere with listener's comprehension
content	thorough response with interesting and pertinent detail	thorough response with sufficient detail	some detail, but not sufficient	general, insufficient response

Go Online! connectED.mcgraw-hill.com

Tarea

You are going to write a letter of complaint to a restaurant you went to where you had a very bad experience. Write a letter to the management. Include the following details.

¿Cuándo fuiste?
¿Con quiénes?
¿Qué pidieron ustedes?
¿Qué tal la comida?
¿Cómo fue el servicio?

Writing Strategy

Writing a letter of complaint When you write a letter of complaint your goal is to get a problem corrected. You might be angry when you write the letter; however, to be effective, you must control your emotions and use a businesslike tone. Clearly state the problems you had and suggest what the restaurant should do in order to solve each problem. In addition, it is important that the letter be addressed to the person who has the most authority.

1 Prewrite

Use a flow chart like the one below to help you organize the sequence of events in your letter.

¿Cuándo fuiste? → ¿Qué pidieron ustedes? →

¿Qué tal la comida? → ¿Qué tal el servicio?

CULTURA

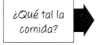

Un restaurante pintoresco en Colonia, Uruguay

2 Write

- An appropriate opening to a business letter in Spanish is **Estimado(a) señor(a)** or **Muy distinguido(a) señor(a).**
- Use the information organized in your prewriting charts to compose your letter.
- An appropriate closing to a business letter is **Atentamente.**

Evaluate

Don't forget that your teacher will evaluate you on the businesslike presentation of your letter, your ability to present solutions to the problems you raise, use of vocabulary, and correctness of grammar.

Richard Brommer

Prepárate para el examen

Pre-AP This **tarea** will give students the opportunity to develop and improve their writing skills so that they may succeed on the writing portion of the AP exam.

Cultural Snapshot

Colonia del Sacramento is just across the río de la Plata from Buenos Aires. Many people make the trip by hydrofoil.

ASSESS

Students are now ready to take any of the Listening, Speaking, Reading, Writing Tests you choose to administer.

Note: You may want to use the rubric below to help students prepare their writing task.

Scoring Rubric for Writing

	4	3	2	1
vocabulary	precise, varied	functional, fails to communicate complete meaning	limited to basic words, often inaccurate	inadequate
grammar	excellent, very few or no errors	some errors, but do not hinder communication	numerous errors interfere with communication	many errors, little sentence structure
content	thorough response to the topic	generally thorough response to the topic	partial response to the topic	insufficient response to the topic
organization	well organized, ideas presented clearly and logically	loosely organized, but main ideas present	some attempts at organization, but with confused sequencing	lack of organization

Repaso del Capítulo 4

Online Resources

Customizable Lesson Plans
- Whiteboard Lesson
- Audio Activities
- Video (Vocabulario) (Diálogo) (Gramática)
- Student Workbook
- Enrichment
- Quizzes
- Listening, Speaking, Reading, Writing Tests

Grammar Review

This page provides a quick "at a glance" summary of the grammar points students have learned in this chapter.

Differentiation

Multiple Intelligences

You may want to call on **verbal-linguistic** and **logical-mathematical** learners for whom grammar often comes easily to explain the main concepts to their classmates in their own words. Having students explain the concepts in different ways may also help slower paced learners or students with learning difficulties.

Repaso del Capítulo 4

Gramática

Presente de los verbos de cambio radical e → i

The verbs **pedir, servir, repetir, freír, seguir,** and **vestirse** have a stem change in the present tense. Review the following forms.

pedir			
yo	pido	nosotros(as)	pedimos
tú	pides	*vosotros(as)*	*pedís*
Ud., él, ella	pide	Uds., ellos, ellas	piden

Pretérito de los verbos de cambio radical e → i, o → u

The verbs **pedir, servir, repetir, seguir, freír, vestirse, preferir, divertirse,** and **dormir** have a stem change in the preterite. Review the following forms.

pedir	preferir	dormir
pedí	preferí	dormí
pediste	preferiste	dormiste
pidió	prefirió	durmió
pedimos	preferimos	dormimos
pedisteis	*preferisteis*	*dormisteis*
pidieron	prefirieron	durmieron

Adjetivos de nacionalidad

Unlike other adjectives, adjectives of nationality that end in a consonant have four forms.

un libro español — **una canción española**
unos libros españoles — **unas canciones españolas**

La voz pasiva con se

The passive voice can be expressed in Spanish with the pronoun **se.**

Se habla español en Chile.
Se venden calcetines en la tienda de ropa.

¿En qué piso se vende?

Andrew Payti

Juego There are a number of cognates in this list. See how many you and a partner can find. Who can find the most? Compare your list with those of your classmates.

Go Online!

connectED.mcgraw-hill.com

Vocabulario

Getting along at a restaurant

el restaurante	el/la mesero(a), el/la camarero(a)	el menú	la propina
la mesa		la cuenta	

Identifying a place setting

la taza	el tenedor	la cuchara
el platillo	el cuchillo	el mantel
el plato	la cucharita	la servilleta

Identifying more foods

los comestibles	los mariscos	el aceite
la carne	los mejillones	el vinagre
la carne de res, el biftec	las almejas	casi crudo
	la langosta	a término medio
la chuleta de cerdo	la sal	bien hecho
el cordero	la pimienta	

Describing some restaurant activities

poner la mesa	pedir	repetir
levantar (quitar) la mesa	servir	freír
	dejar una propina	

Other useful words and expressions

seguir	divertirse	Me muero de hambre.
vestirse	morir	

Juego The cognates in this list are: **el restaurante, el menú, el plato, el vinagre, servir, repetir.**

Don't forget the chapter project and cultural activities. Students have learned all the information that they will need to complete these engaging enrichment tasks.

Repaso del Capítulo 4

Vocabulary Review

The words and phrases in the **Vocabulario** section have been taught for productive use in this chapter. They are summarized here as a resource for both student and teacher. This list also serves as a convenient resource for the **Prepárate para el examen** activities.

¡Así se dice!

Why It Works!

This vocabulary reference list has not been translated into English for two reasons. First, it is recommended that students learn the new vocabulary through direct association with images on the **Vocabulario** pages. Secondly, all vocabulary is reintroduced in the chapter many times and upon completion of the chapter students should be familiar with the meaning of all the words. If there are words that students still do not know, they can refer to the vocabulary presentation in the chapter or the dictionary at the end of the book. If, however, it is your preference to give students the English translations, please refer to Vocabulary V4.1.

Differentiation

Slower Paced Learners

Slower paced learners may benefit from creating their own visual dictionary of nouns and adjectives in this list. They can either draw their own depictions or use images from the Internet, magazines, etc.

Every chapter of **¡Así se dice!** contains this review section of previously learned material. By recycling information from previous chapters, the cumulative review serves to remind students that they need to continue practicing what they have learned after finishing each chapter.

Activity 1 This activity reviews train and airplane vocabulary.

Audio Script

1. Perdón, pero, ¿de qué andén sale?
2. José tiene que facturar su equipaje.
3. Tenemos que mostrar una forma de identidad cuando pasamos por el control de seguridad.
4. El revisor revisa los billetes.
5. Nuestro vuelo sale tarde. No sale a tiempo.
6. Vamos a tomar un refresco en el coche comedor.

Activity 2 This activity reviews vocabulary from Level 1.

Activity 3 This activity reviews vocabulary pertaining to daily routine.

Go Online!

You may wish to remind students to go online for additional cumulative review.

Repaso cumulativo

Repasa lo que ya has aprendido

These activities will help you review and remember what you have learned so far in Spanish.

1 **Escucha las frases. Indica en una tabla como la de abajo si la persona viaja en tren o en avión.**

tren	avión

2 **Parea los contrarios.**

1. grande
2. después
3. alto
4. aburrido
5. gordo
6. siempre
7. debajo de
8. triste
9. cerca
10. detrás
11. fácil
12. corto

a. lejos
b. interesante
c. contento
d. nunca
e. pequeño
f. antes
g. difícil
h. encima de
i. largo
j. flaco
k. bajo
l. delante

3 **Personaliza. Da respuestas personales.**

1. ¿Qué comes cuando tienes hambre?
2. ¿Qué bebes cuando tienes sed?
3. ¿Qué haces cuando estás cansado(a) o tienes sueño?
4. ¿Qué te pones cuando tienes frío?
5. ¿Qué ropa llevas cuando tienes calor?

CULTURA

Una panadería en el patio de comedores en una estación de ferrocarril en Buenos Aires

Andrew Payti

Answers

1

1. tren
2. avión
3. avión
4. tren
5. avión
6. tren

2

1. e
2. f
3. k
4. b
5. j
6. d
7. h
8. c
9. a
10. l
11. g
12. i

3 *Answers will vary but may include:*

1. Cuando tengo hambre, como ___.
2. Cuando tengo sed, bebo ___.
3. Cuando estoy cansado(a) o tengo sueño, ___.
4. Cuando tengo frío, me pongo ___.
5. Cuando tengo calor, llevo ___.

Go Online!

connectED.mcgraw-hill.com

Repaso cumulativo

4 **Escribe una lista de todos los comestibles (alimentos) que puedes decir en español.**

legumbres	frutas	carne	pescado y mariscos	postres

5 **Cambia al pretérito.**

1. Ellos viven en San Francisco.
2. Su hermano asiste a la escuela secundaria en San Francisco.
3. Yo aprendo mucho en la escuela.
4. Nosotros comemos en la cafetería de la escuela.
5. ¿Comprendes lo que lees?

6 **Sigue el modelo.**

MODELO **yo / matemáticas →**
Yo estudié matemáticas y aprendí mucho.

1. tú / biología
2. nosotros / historia
3. Carmen / geografía
4. ellos / álgebra
5. yo / español
6. ustedes / geometría

7 **Escribe en la forma negativa.**

1. Alguien llama a la puerta.
2. Él siempre hace algo.
3. Ella siempre tiene hambre.
4. Quiero comer algo.
5. Siempre quiere decir algo a alguien.

CULTURA

Tapas en un café en Barcelona

Daniel Salsgiver

Activity 4 This activity reviews food vocabulary from Level 1.

Activity 5 This activity reviews the regular preterite **-er** and **-ir** verbs.

Activity 6 This activity reviews regular preterite verbs.

Activity 7 This activity reviews negative words.

Go Online!

The **¡Así se dice!** Audio Program for Chapter 4 has twenty-five activities, which afford students extensive listening and speaking practice.

Pre-AP To give students further open-ended oral or written practice, or to assess proficiency, go to AP Proficiency Practice AP19.

Answers

4 *Answers will vary.*

5

1. Ellos vivieron en San Francisco.
2. Su hermano asistió a la escuela secundaria en San Francisco.
3. Yo aprendí mucho en la escuela.
4. Nosotros comimos en la cafetería de la escuela.
5. ¿Comprendiste lo que leíste?

6

1. Tú estudiaste biología y aprendiste mucho.
2. Nosotros estudiamos historia y aprendimos mucho.
3. Carmen estudió geografía y aprendió mucho.
4. Ellos estudiaron álgebra y aprendieron mucho.
5. Yo estudié español y aprendí mucho.
6. Ustedes estudiaron geometría y aprendieron mucho.

7

1. Nadie llama a la puerta.
2. Él nunca hace nada.
3. Ella nunca tiene hambre.
4. No quiero comer nada.
5. Nunca quiere decir nada a nadie.

Chapter Overview

¿Qué se celebra?

Scope and Sequence

Topics
- The Day of the Dead
- Christmas
- Hanukkah

Culture
- Patron saints
- The use of the piñata in Hispanic celebrations
- New Year's Eve celebration in Spain

Functions
- How to talk about several Hispanic holidays
- How to compare holidays in the U.S. with those in some Spanish-speaking countries

Structure
- Regular and irregular forms of the imperfect tense

Andrew Payti

Planning Guide

	required	recommended	optional
Vocabulario 1 Una feria El Día de los Muertos	✓		
Vocabulario 2	✓		
Gramática Imperfecto de los verbos en **-ar** Imperfecto de los verbos en **-er, -ir** Imperfecto de los verbos irregulares Usos del imperfecto	✓		
Conversación El Día de San Juan		✓	
Lectura cultural Unas fiestas hispanas		✓	
Lectura Un poco más La Nochevieja en España			✓
Prepárate para el examen			✓
Repaso cumulativo			✓

Correlations to ACTFL World-Readiness Standards for Learning Languages

Page numbers in light print refer to the Student Edition.
Page numbers in bold print refer to the Teacher Edition.

COMMUNICATION Communicate effectively in more than one language in order to function in a variety of situations and for multiple purposes		
Interpersonal Communication	Learners interact and negotiate meaning in spoken, signed, or written conversations to share information, reactions, feelings, and opinions.	pp. **136–137,** 141, **141,** 145, 147, **147, 157, 158,** 162, 166
Interpretive Communication	Learners understand, interpret, and analyze what is heard, read, or viewed on a variety of topics.	pp. **138,** 140, **140, 141,** 144, 145, **147,** 148, **148, 149,** 150, 151, **152,** 153, **153,** 154, **154,** 155, **155,** 156, 157, **158,** 159, **161,** 162, **167**
Presentational Communication	Learners present information, concepts, and ideas to inform, explain, persuade, and narrate on a variety of topics using appropriate media and adapting to various audiences of listeners, readers, or viewers.	pp. **134C, 134D, 139, 143,** 147, **147,** 149, 151, **151, 152, 153, 154, 155, 156, 160,** 162, 163, **164, 165**
CULTURES Interact with cultural competence and understanding		
Relating Cultural Practices to Perspectives	Learners use the language to investigate, explain, and reflect on the relationship between the practices and perspectives of the cultures studied.	pp. **134C, 134D,** 135, **135,** 136–137, **136–137,** 142–143, **143,** 144, 145, **152,** 153, 154–156, 156, **156,** 157, 158, 159, 161
Relating Cultural Products to Perspectives	Learners use the language to investigate, explain, and reflect on the relationship between the products and perspectives of the cultures studied.	pp. **134D,** 137, 139, **139,** 140, 141, 144, 151, 157
CONNECTIONS Connect with other disciplines and acquire information and diverse perspectives in order to use the language to function in academic and career-related situations		
Making Connections	Learners build, reinforce, and expand their knowledge of other disciplines while using the language to develop critical thinking and to solve problems creatively.	pp. **134D, 145,** 149, **149**
Acquiring Information and Diverse Perspectives	Learners access and evaluate information and diverse perspectives that are available through the language and its cultures.	pp. 138, 142, **143,** 150, **150,** 151, 153, **153,** 159, **159**
COMPARISONS Develop insight into the nature of language and culture in order to interact with cultural competence		
Language Comparisons	Learners use the language to investigate, explain, and reflect on the nature of language through comparisons of the language studied and their own.	pp. 138, 142, **142, 143, 164,** 165
Cultural Comparisons	Learners use the language to investigate, explain, and reflect on the concept of culture through comparisons of the cultures studied and their own.	pp. **134C, 134D,** 135, **135, 136,** 154, **156,** 158, 159, 162
COMMUNITIES Communicate and interact with cultural competence in order to participate in multilingual communities at home and around the world		
School and Global Communities	Learners use the language both within and beyond the classroom to interact and collaborate in their community and the globalized world.	pp. **134C, 139, 145,** 148, **162, 164**
Lifelong Learning	Learners set goals and reflect on their progress in using languages for enjoyment, enrichment, and advancement.	pp. **134C, 141,** 142, **143, 147,** 150, **150,** 153, **153, 155, 158,** 159, **159**

Chapter Project

Un calendario hispano

Students will work in small groups to design a calendar for the year that includes major Hispanic holidays and information about their Spanish class.

1. Divide the class into groups of three or four and allow the students to assign different months to each group member. Explain that each student will be responsible for designing his or her assigned months, which will then be compiled with the others to form the group's final product.
2. Each student should include the date and days of each week and important events that occur within that month: Hispanic holidays; school holidays; information related to Spanish class (birthdays, test dates, projects deadlines, presentations, etc.); school events such as sports, concerts, or performances. Each month should include at least ten events but must include all major Hispanic holidays.
3. Individually, students will then choose a Hispanic holiday to feature for his or her assigned month. The students will conduct research about the holiday and write at least three sentences briefly describing it and/or how it is celebrated. These sentences will appear with an image of the student's choosing that relates to the holiday.
4. Once students have acquired the necessary information and decided on the image(s) they will use, have them sketch the layout for their calendar pages and draft their sentences.
5. Students will then assemble in groups to peer edit each other's drafts. Once corrections have been made, students should work on the final version to be included in the group's calendar. The initial sketch of the layout and the first draft of the captions should be handed in with the finished product.

noviembre

lunes	martes	miércoles	jueves	viernes	sábado	domingo
					1	2
3	4	5	6	7	8	9
10	11	12	13	14	15	16
17	18	19	20	21	22	23
24	25	26	27	28	29	30

D. Normark/PhotoLink/Getty Images

Scoring Rubric for Project

	5	3	1
Evidence of planning	Layout and corrected draft are provided.	Draft and layout are provided, but draft is not corrected.	Draft and layout are not provided.
Use of illustrations	A visual element accompanies all calendar pages.	A visual element accompanies some calendar pages.	No visual elements accompany calendar pages.
Presentation	Calendar pages contain all the required elements.	Calendar pages contain some of the required elements.	Calendar pages contain few of the required elements.

Culture

Recipe

COLA DE MONO

Ingredients: (makes 16 servings)
20 whole cloves
5 cinnamon sticks
1 cup water
1 gallon cold milk
¼ cup instant coffee
1 cup sugar
1 tablespoon vanilla extract (optional)

Gently simmer the cloves and cinnamon sticks in water for about 30 minutes until reduced by half. Add 1 cup of milk and continue to simmer. Then stir in and dissolve the coffee and sugar. Strain the coffee mixture into the remaining cold milk and discard the cloves and cinnamon sticks. Stir in the optional vanilla extract. Serve cold and store refrigerated.

Papel picado

Papel picado, literally "punched, perforated, or chopped paper," is a popular Mexican tradition of stringing colorful paper cutouts in banners to decorate homes and streets during major festivities and holidays. Although **papel picado** is often associated with the Day of the Dead, it is also displayed during family celebrations such as birthdays, baptisms and weddings, religious holidays, and civic holidays such as Independence Day. The history of **papel picado** may be linked to the Aztec tradition of decorating **amatl,** a form of paper made from the bark of fig trees **(papel amate).** Nowadays, tissue paper, called **papel de seda** *(silk paper)* or **papel de China,** is most commonly used for making these fragile, brightly colored, whimsical decorations.

The procedure for making **papel picado** is fairly simple, and the images will vary depending on the holiday being celebrated. The first step is to create a **patrón** or pattern (like a stencil) depicting the master design, which is then placed on top of layers of tissue paper. Cuts are then made using a pair of scissors or a safety knife, and the resulting paper cutouts are attached to yarn or string and hung like banners.

Connection to Fine Art

Have students do an online image search using the search term **calendario maya.** Ask students to examine the Mayan calendar and give a brief description of it, using a dictionary for help if necessary. Some students may want to choose some of the symbols that they find particularly interesting and describe them in detail. Students should contrast the appearance of this calendar with the one we use. Motivated students can research the Mayan calendar system and prepare a report for the class. They could also share the report with their science, history, or math class.

50-Minute Lesson Plans

	Objective	Present	Practice	Assess/Homework
Day 1	Talk about the Day of the Dead	Chapter Opener (5 min.) Introducción al tema (10 min.) Core Instruction/Vocabulario 1 (20 min.)	Activities 1–3 (15 min.)	Student Workbook Activities A–B **ConnectEd** Vocabulary Practice
Day 2	Talk about the Day of the Dead	Quick Start (5 min.) Review Vocabulario 1 (10 min.)	Activities 4–7 (15 min.) Total Physical Response (5 min.) Audio Activities A–D (15 min.)	Student Workbook Activity C **ConnectEd** Vocabulary Practice
Day 3	Talk about Christmas and Hanukkah	Core Instruction/Vocabulario 2 (15 min.) Video, Vocabulario en vivo (10 min.)	Activities 1–3 (15 min.)	Quiz 1 (10 min.) Student Workbook Activities A–B **ConnectEd** Vocabulary Practice
Day 4	Talk about Christmas and Hanukkah	Quick Start (5 min.) Review Vocabulario 2 (5 min.)	Activities 4–6 (15 min.) Total Physical Response (5 min.) InfoGap (10 min.) Audio Activities E–I (10 min.)	Student Workbook Activity C **ConnectEd** Vocabulary Practice
Day 5	Imperfect of **-ar** verbs	Quick Start (5 min.) Core Instruction/Gramática, Imperfecto de los verbos en **-ar** (15 min.)	Activities 1–5 (20 min.)	Quiz 2 (10 min.) Student Workbook Activities A–E **ConnectEd** Grammar Practice
Day 6	Imperfect of **-er, -ir** verbs	Quick Start (5 min.) Core Instruction/Gramática, Imperfecto de los verbos en **-er, -ir** (10 min.)	Activities 6–9 (10 min.) Foldables (5 min.) Audio Activities A–B (10 min.)	Quiz 3 (10 min.) Student Workbook Activities A–C **ConnectEd** Grammar Practice
Day 7	Imperfect of irregular verbs	Core Instruction/Gramática, Imperfecto de los verbos irregulares (10 min.) Video, Gramática en vivo (10 min.)	Activities 10–11 (10 min.) Audio Activities C–D (10 min.)	Quiz 4 (10 min.) Student Workbook Activities A–C **ConnectEd** Grammar Practice
Day 8	Uses of the imperfect	Quick Start (5 min.) Core Instruction/Gramática, Usos del imperfecto (15 min.)	Activities 12–14 (15 min.) Audio Activities E–F (15 min.)	Student Workbook Activities A–C **ConnectEd** Grammar Practice
Day 9	Develop reading and listening comprehension skills	Quick Start (5 min.) Core Instruction/Conversación (20 min.) Video, Diálogo en vivo (10 min.)	¿Comprendes? A–B (5 min.)	Quiz 5 (10 min.) ¿Comprendes? C **ConnectEd** Conversation
Day 10	Discuss holidays celebrated in Spanish-speaking countries	Core Instruction/Lectura cultural (20 min.)	¿Comprendes? A–C (15 min.)	Listening Comprehension Test (15 min.) ¿Comprendes? D–F **ConnectEd** Reading Practice
Day 11	Develop reading comprehension skills	Core Instruction/Lectura Un poco más (10 min.) Video, Cultura en vivo (10 min.)	¿Comprendes? (5 min.) Prepárate para el examen (25 min.)	Prepárate para el examen, Practice for written proficiency **ConnectEd** Reading Practice
Day 12	Chapter review	Repaso del Capítulo 5 (15 min.)	Prepárate para el examen, Practice for oral proficiency (20 min.)	Test for Writing Proficiency (15 min.) Review for chapter test
Day 13	Chapter 5 Tests (50 min.) Reading and Writing Test Speaking Test		Test for Oral Proficiency Test for Reading Comprehension	

90-Minute Lesson Plans

	Objective	Present	Practice	Assess/Homework
Block 1	Talk about the Day of the Dead	Chapter Opener (5 min.) Introducción al tema (15 min.) Quick Start (5 min.) Core Instruction/Vocabulario 1 (20 min.)	Activities 1–7 (25 min.) Total Physical Response (5 min.) Audio Activities A–D (15 min.)	Student Workbook Activities A–C **ConnectEd** Vocabulary Practice
Block 2	Talk about Christmas and Hanukkah	Quick Start (5 min.) Core Instruction/Vocabulario 2 (20 min.) Video, Vocabulario en vivo (10 min.)	Activities 1–6 (20 min.) Total Physical Response (5 min.) InfoGap (5 min.) Audio Activities E–I (15 min.)	Quiz 1 (10 min.) Student Workbook Activities A–C **ConnectEd** Grammar Practice
Block 3	Imperfect of **-ar, -er, -ir** verbs	Quick Start (5 min.) Core Instruction/Gramática, Imperfecto de los verbos en **-ar** (10 min.) Quick Start (5 min.) Core Instruction/Gramática, Imperfecto de los verbos en **-er, -ir** (10 min.)	Activities 1–5 (15 min.) Activities 6–9 (10 min.) Foldables (5 min.) Audio Activities A–B (20 min.)	Quiz 2 (10 min.) Student Workbook Activities A–E Student Workbook Activities A–C **ConnectEd** Grammar Practice
Block 4	Imperfect of irregular verbs Uses of the imperfect	Core Instruction/Gramática, Imperfecto de los verbos irregulares (10 min.) Video, Gramática en vivo (10 min.) Quick Start (5 min.) Core Instruction/Gramática, Usos del imperfecto (10 min.)	Activities 10–11 (10 min.) Activities 12–14 (10 min.) Audio Activities C–F (15 min.)	Quizzes 3–4 (20 min.) Student Workbook Activities A–C Student Workbook Activities A–C **ConnectEd** Grammar Practice
Block 5	Discuss holidays celebrated in Spanish-speaking countries	Quick Start (5 min.) Core Instruction/Conversación (15 min.) Video, Diálogo en vivo (10 min.) Core Instruction/Lectura cultural (20 min.)	¿Comprendes? A–B (10 min.) ¿Comprendes? A–C (10 min.)	Quiz 5 (10 min.) ¿Comprendes? C ¿Comprendes? D–F Prepárate para el examen, Practice for written proficiency **ConnectEd** Conversation, Reading Practice
Block 6	Develop reading comprehension skills	Core Instruction/Lectura Un poco más (15 min.) Video, Cultura en vivo (10 min.)	¿Comprendes? (5 min.) Prepárate para el examen (20 min.) Prepárate para el examen, Practice for oral proficiency (25 min.)	Listening Comprehension Test (15 min.) Review for chapter test **ConnectEd** Reading Practice
Block 7	Chapter 5 Tests (50 min.) Reading and Writing Test Speaking Test Test for Oral Proficiency Test for Writing Proficiency Test for Reading Comprehension Chapter Project (40 min.)			

Preview

In this chapter, students will learn the vocabulary they need to discuss some very important holidays celebrated in Spain and Latin America. They will also learn the regular and irregular forms of the imperfect tense. This will be reinforced as students read about the memories of some Latino friends who discuss how they spent different holidays as children in their home countries.

Pacing

It is important to note that once you reach **¡Bravo!** in the chapter, there is no more new material for the students to learn. The rest of the chapter recycles what has already been covered. The suggested pacing listed here leaves two to three days for review, assessment, and enrichment activities such as the chapter project.

Vocabulario 1	1–2 days
Vocabulario 2	1–2 days
Gramática	2–3 days
Conversación	1 day
Lectura cultural	1 day
Lectura Un poco más	1 day

CAPÍTULO 5

¿Qué se celebra?

Go Online! connectED.mcgraw-hill.com Audio Video Práctica Repaso Diversiones eScape ePals

Go Online!

Audio
Listen to spoken Spanish.

Video
Watch and learn about the Spanish-speaking world.

Práctica
Practice your skills.

Repaso
Review what you've learned.

Diversiones
Go beyond the classroom.

eScape
Read about current events in the Spanish-speaking world.

Aquí y Allí

Vamos a comparar El mundo hispano es famoso por sus ferias y fiestas. Hay ferias para celebrar muchas ocasiones. Algunas duran solamente un día y otras una semana entera. ¿Hay ferias y fiestas donde tú vives? ¿Qué celebran o conmemoran? ¿Tienes una fiesta favorita? ¿Cuál es?

Objetivos

You will:

- talk about several Hispanic holidays
- compare holidays that you celebrate with those in some Spanish-speaking countries

You will use:

- regular and irregular forms of the imperfect tense

◀ Las jóvenes están tomando parte en las celebraciones para Carnaval en Puerto Plata en la República Dominicana.

SPOTLIGHT ON CULTURE

Cultural Comparison
In this chapter, students will learn about specific Hispanic holidays such as the Day of the Dead, Patron Saint's Day, etc. They will also learn about Christmas, Hanukkah, and New Year's Day celebrations, noting both similarities and differences in the ways these holidays are celebrated across cultures.

Cultural Snapshot
Carnaval is a very happy celebration that takes place just before Ash Wednesday in preparation for the Lenten fasting that starts on Ash Wednesday. Probably the most noted **Carnaval** festivities are those in La Habana and Rio de Janeiro, followed by the rest of the Caribbean and New Orleans. This is not to say **Carnaval** festivities don't also take place in many other cities.

Interactive Whiteboard
Present or practice with interactive whiteboard activities.

Assessment
Check student progress.

ePals
Connect with Spanish-speaking students around the world.

PRESENT

Introduce the theme of the chapter by having students look at the photographs on these pages. Have them look at the young people and determine if there is anything they see them doing that is the same or different from what they do with their own friends. Once you have completed the vocabulary presentation, have students return to these pages and read the information that accompanies each photograph. Once students are fully acquainted with the vocabulary and grammar of the chapter, you may wish to come back to these pages and ask the questions that go with each photo.

Cultural Snapshot

México Oaxaca, in southwestern Mexico, is known for many aspects of its culture, including its **mole** sauces, decorative **barro negro** pottery, and colorfully painted **alebrije** carvings. One of its numerous festivals, the Guelaguetza, is highlighted by traditional music and dancing. Its participants wear bright and colorful costumes like the one worn by the young girl we see here. **¿Cómo se llama una muchacha de Oaxaca? ¿Qué lleva esta oaxaqueña? ¿Cuándo es la Guelaguetza?**

Chile These young people meet the tourist train that stops in Poconchile to present a traditional show to the mostly foreign tourists.

Ecuador These children are enjoying some Christmas festivities sponsored by their parents' employer in the small town of Cotacachi in northern Ecuador. The town is known for its excellent leather products. **¿Qué están celebrando los niños? ¿Están vestidas de angelitas las niñas?**

Venezuela Los diablos de danzantes de Yare is a religious festival celebrated in the town of San Francisco de Yare on the feast of Corpus Christi. The ritual dance performed celebrates the triumph of good over evil. The dancers parade through the street. Upon arriving at the church they all kneel down and remain prostrate as a symbol of respect to the Blessed Sacrament as the priest blesses them. **¿De qué colores son las máscaras? En tu opinión, ¿cuál se parece más al imagen que tú tienes del diablo?**

Introducción al tema

¿Qué se celebra?

Mira las fotos para familiarizarte con el tema de este capítulo—un tema de alegría—fiestas, festivales y celebraciones. El mundo hispano es famoso por sus fiestas. A mucha gente le gusta participar en las festividades en la plaza de su ciudad o pueblo o en su propio barrio.

México

Aquí vemos a una joven oaxaqueña vestida en un traje tradicional durante la Guelaguetza, una fiesta popular que se celebra cada julio en Oaxaca.

Chile

Un grupo de jóvenes chilenos vestidos en trajes regionales haciendo un baile tradicional en Poconchile en el norte de Chile

Ecuador

Aquí vemos a unos niños en disfraz en Cotacachi durante unas festividades para celebrar la Navidad.

Venezuela

Máscaras tradicionales para el festival Los Diablos Danzantes del Yare en el pueblo de San Francisco de Yare en Venezuela

Go Online!
connected.mcgraw-hill.com

Perú

Un desfile durante una fiesta en Cuzco, Perú

España

Celebración del Baztandarren Biltzarra, una fiesta tradicional del valle de Baztán en Navarra

Cuba

El señor va a andar sobre zancos *(stilts)* durante una fiesta en La Habana, Cuba.

México

Calaveras de azúcar para la celebración del Día de los Muertos

España

Unas señoras vestidas en trajes tradicionales cantando y tocando panderetas durante una fiesta en el pueblo de Torrelavega en Cantabria, España

Introducción al tema

Perú ¿Tiene lugar en Cuzco el desfile? ¿Están vestidos en trajes tradicionales los participantes?

España ¿Dónde tiene lugar esta celebración? ¿Qué tipo de fiesta es?

Cuba Describe el traje que lleva este señor.

México This chapter contains a great deal of information about **el Día de los Muertos.** ¿De qué están hecho las calaveras? ¿Cuándo se comen las calaveras? ¿Se celebra el Día de los Muertos en Estados Unidos?

España The Fiesta de la Virgen Grande takes place in Torrelavega August 15. The festival culminates in la Gala Flora which is a colorful parade and competition for floats, carriages and costumed groups.

Online Resources

- Customizable Lesson Plans
- Whiteboard Lesson
- Audio Activities
- Student Workbook
- Enrichment
- Quizzes

Quick Start

Use QS 5.1 or write the following on the board.
Answer.

1. **¿Te gustan las fiestas?**
2. **¿Cantan y bailan ustedes durante una fiesta?**
3. **¿Comen ustedes? ¿Qué comen?**
4. **¿Se divierten?**

TEACH

Core Instruction

Step 1 Using Vocabulary V5.2–V5.3, have students repeat words as you point to the part of each photograph that illustrates the meaning of the new words.

Step 2 You may wish to have students repeat the sentences that accompany each photo or you may wish to have them read them. If the pronunciation of the class is not very good, read each statement to the class or have them listen to the audio recording and have them repeat.

Step 3 Intersperse with questions building from simple to more complex. For example, **¿Desfilaba todo el mundo? ¿Desfilaban todos por las calles? ¿Por dónde desfilaban? ¿Llevaban una estatua? ¿Qué llevaban? ¿Llevaban una estatua del santo patrón? ¿De quién era la estatua? ¿Qué llevaba la gente y dónde?**

Nota

- In addition to the word **difunto,** you will also hear **muerto.** Although they both have somewhat the same meaning, there is a slight difference such as in the English *deceased* and *dead person.*
- In addition to **enterrar,** you will also hear **sepultar. Una tumba** is often called **una sepultura.** These words are not regional. They are used in all areas of the Spanish-speaking world.

Una feria

Había una procesión.
Todo el mundo desfilaba (caminaba) por las calles.
Llevaban una estatua del santo patrón (de la santa patrona).

Los difuntos (muertos) están enterrados en el camposanto.
Los parientes ponen coronas de flores en las tumbas.
En el cementerio hay también mausoleos familiares.

¡Así se dice!

Why It Works!

Note that only the third person forms of the imperfect are used so students can immediately answer questions without having to manipulate endings.

Total Physical Response (TPR)

(Student), **ven acá.**
Toma esta estatua. *(Give anything resembling a statue.)*
Levanta la estatua en el aire.
Desfila por la sala de clase.
Ahora, pon la estatua aquí en el pupitre.
Gracias, *(Student).*

El Día de los Muertos

Para celebrar el Día de los Muertos, algunos llevaban disfraz.
Llevaban también una máscara.
La máscara cubría la cara.

Confeccionaba (elaboraba) bizcochos.
Los bizcochos tenían la forma de las personas muertas.
Los bizcochos son dulces.

Go Online!

connectED.mcgraw-hill.com

¡Ojo!

Note the spelling.
un disfraz → dos disfraces

Differentiation

Multiple Intelligences

Many students learn better when they are actively involved. In addition to the TPR activities, have **bodily-kinesthetic** learners present a little skit using the vocabulary pertaining to the cemetery. As they do something, have them tell what they are doing.

Heritage Speakers

If you have students of Mexican American background, have them tell the class some things about **el Día de los Muertos.** This holiday is celebrated in many Hispanic countries, but it is probably most popular in Mexico.

Multiple Intelligences

Visual-spatial learners like to create things. You may have some students make some **bizcochos** in the forms mentioned.

Tips for Success

As you point out the plural of **disfraz,** review **lápiz, lápices.**

About the Spanish Language

Note that with foods and some other items, the verbs **confeccionar** and **elaborar** are used more often than **hacer.**

Total Physical Response (TPR)

Ahora, *(Student),* ven acá.
Toma el disfraz.
Toma la máscara.
Cúbrete la cara con la máscara.
Haz movimientos como un esqueleto.
Toma este bizcocho.
Come el bizcocho.
Gracias, *(Student).*

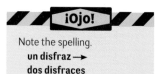

Leveling EACH Activity

Easy Activities 1, 3
Average Activities 2, 5, 7
CHallenging Activities 4, 6

PRACTICE

Activity 1

Audio Script

1. Había una procesión.
2. Había una ofrenda en la tumba.
3. Todo el mundo mira el desfile.
4. Los difuntos están enterrados en las tumbas.

Activity 2 It is suggested that you go over Activity 2 in class before students write it. Note that this activity can also be done as a paired activity.

Activities 3, 4, and 5 Have students prepare these activities before going over them in class.

Go Online!

You may wish to remind students to go online for additional vocabulary practice. They can also download audio files of all vocabulary.

ESCUCHAR

1 Escucha las frases. Parea cada frase con la foto que describe.

a. 

b. 

HABLAR • ESCRIBIR

2 Personaliza. Da respuestas personales.

1. ¿Tiene un santo patrón el pueblo o la ciudad donde ustedes viven?
2. ¿Visitas a veces la tumba de un pariente difunto en el cementerio?
3. ¿Es una costumbre o tradición poner una corona de flores en la tumba?
4. ¿Hay una fiesta cuando se llevan disfraces? ¿Cuál es?
5. A veces, ¿tenemos figuras de cráneos o esqueletos? ¿Cuándo?
6. ¿Tenemos bizcochos o dulces en forma de cráneos o esqueletos?

CULTURA
Bizcochos en forma de calaveras

LEER

3 Completa con una palabra del **banco de palabras**.

elaboraba	llevaba	caminaba	tenía	había

1. ____ una procesión en la calle.
2. Mucha gente ____ un disfraz.
3. Todo el mundo ____ detrás del santo patrón.
4. Abuelita ____ bizcochos.
5. Un bizcocho ____ la forma de una calavera.

Answers

1
1. b 2. a 3. b 4. a

2
1. Sí (No), el pueblo (la ciudad) donde nosotros vivimos (no) tiene un santo patrón.
2. Sí, (No, no) visito a veces (nunca) la tumba de un pariente difunto en el cementerio.
3. Sí, (No, no) es una costumbre poner una corona de flores en la tumba.
4. Sí, hay una fiesta cuando se llevan disfraces. Es el Día de los Muertos *(Halloween)*.
5. Tenemos figuras de cráneos o esqueletos durante *Halloween*.
6. Sí, (No, no) tenemos bizcochos o dulces en forma de cráneos o esqueletos.

3
1. Había
2. llevaba
3. caminaba
4. elaboraba
5. tenía

LEER • ESCRIBIR

4 Expresa de otra manera.

1. Lleva *un disfraz*.
2. Todo el mundo *marchaba* hacia el cementerio.
3. Todo el mundo marchaba hacia *el cementerio*.
4. Todo el mundo *andaba* hacia atrás.
5. La señora *hacía* bizcochos.
6. *Los muertos* están enterrados en el cementerio.
7. Hacía bizcochos en forma de *una calavera*.

ESCRIBIR

5 Completa con la letra que falta.

1. una pro_e_ión
2. un disfra_
3. dos disfra_es
4. un bi_cocho
5. un _ueso

6 *Comunicación*

Habla con un(a) compañero(a) de clase. Describan todo lo que ustedes hacen o no hacen para celebrar *Halloween*. ¿Es una fiesta que les gusta o no?

7 Rompecabezas

Escoge la palabra en cada grupo que no pertenece.

1. el hueso | el esqueleto | el dulce | el cráneo
2. el camposanto | el muerto | el santo patrón | la tumba
3. la ofrenda | la corona de flores | el bizcocho | el mausoleo
4. la procesión | enterrar | desfilar | caminar por la calle

Go Online!

connectED.mcgraw-hill.com

Cultura

Papel picado

Se usa el papel picado para hacer decoraciones para muchas fiestas. Por ejemplo, hay decoraciones de papel picado para los árboles de Navidad. En México usan el papel picado para hacer imágenes de esqueletos para las celebraciones del Día de los Muertos.

Vocabulario 1

Activity 6 Students can work in pairs or larger groups.

Activity 7 This activity can be done as a game. Have students make up original sentences using the words in the **Rompecabezas.** The one (or group) who makes up the most sentences within the time limit you set wins.

Differentiation

Multiple Intelligences

You may wish to have **visual-spatial** learners make some decorations pertaining to the Day of the Dead with papier-mâché.

Go Online!

You may wish to use the whiteboard presentation for additional vocabulary instruction and practice.

ASSESS

Students are now ready to take Quiz 1.

Answers

4
1. una máscara
2. desfilaba (caminaba)
3. el camposanto
4. caminaba
5. elaboraba (confeccionaba)
6. Los difuntos
7. un cráneo

5
1. procesión
2. disfraz
3. difraces
4. bizcocho
5. hueso

6 *Answers will vary.*

7
1. el dulce
2. el santo patrón
3. el bizcocho
4. enterrar

Online Resources

Customizable Lesson Plans
- Whiteboard Lesson
- Audio Activities
- Video (Vocabulario)
- Student Workbook
- Enrichment
- Quizzes

Quick Start

Use QS 5.2 or write the following on the board.

Prepare a list in Spanish of things you could buy for a friend or a family member. Write down some gifts you would like to receive.

TEACH

Core Instruction

You may wish to follow some of the suggestions given in the other Vocabulary sections for the presentation of the new words.

Cultural Snapshot

This display of the Three Wise Men is in Mexico City.

Differentiation

Advanced Learners

You may have advanced learners do some research concerning the animals of the Wise Men. Note that in this photo taken in Mexico City, there is an elephant **(un elefante),** a camel, and a horse. Many such scenes in the United States, Spain, and Latin America have only camels.

La Navidad, Las Navidades

En otras partes

¡Feliz Navidad! and **¡Felices Navidades!** are the most common ways to say *Merry Christmas,* but you will also hear **¡Felices Pascuas!** In all countries **la Pascua** or **la Pascua Florida** is *Easter.*

La Nochebuena es el 24 de diciembre.
Los niños decoraban el árbol de Navidad.
Había aguinaldos debajo del árbol.

Los niños sabían que iban a venir los Reyes Magos.

Total Physical Response (TPR)

(Student), **ven acá.**
Imagínate que es un árbol.
Lo vas a decorar.
Toma esta bolita *(hand student an ornament).*
Cuélgala del árbol.
Aquí tienes unas luces *(make believe you have a string of lights).*
Pon las luces en el árbol.
Toma un aguinaldo de debajo del árbol.
Mira el aguinaldo.
Ábrelo.
Ponte una mirada de sorpresa en la cara.

¡Feliz Hanuka!

Go Online!

connectED.mcgraw-hill.com

La familia siempre celebraba la fiesta de las luces, Hanuka.
La familia encendía una vela de la menora.
Hanuka es una fiesta hebrea (judía).

La fiesta celebraba la llegada del Año Nuevo.
Durante la fiesta había fuegos artificiales.
Los fuegos artificiales iluminaban el cielo.

Todos bailaban mientras tocaba la banda.
Todo el mundo estaba contento.
Lo pasaban bien. Se divertían.

Vocabulario 2

About the Spanish Language

You may wish to explain to students that the word for New Year's Eve in Spain is **la Nochevieja.** Throughout Latin America it is **la víspera de Año Nuevo.**

Additional Vocabulary

You may wish to give students familiar New Year's greetings.
¡Feliz Año Nuevo!
¡Próspero Año Nuevo!

Tips for Success

- As soon as students are familiar with the new vocabulary, have them read again the captions of the **Introducción al tema.**
- After going over the **Práctica** activities, have students return to the vocabulary pages and make up statements and questions about the photos.

Go Online!

Vocabulario en vivo Watch and listen to Nora as she introduces holidays in the Spanish-speaking world.

You may wish to use the whiteboard presentation for additional vocabulary instruction and practice.

Total Physical Response (TPR)

(Student), **ven acá.**
Toma la paja.
Pon la paja en el zapato.
Imagínate que es una menora.
Hay nueve velas en una menora. Cuéntalas.
Enciende una vela.
Imita el ruido que hacen los fuegos artificiales.

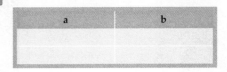

Leveling EACH Activity

Easy Activities 1, 2, 4
Average Activities 3, 6
CHallenging Activity 5

PRACTICE

Activity 1

Audio Script

1. **a.** Todos tenían una sonrisa en la cara. Lo pasaban bien y se divertían.
   b. Todos tenían una sonrisa en la cara. Estaban muy aburridos.
2. **a.** Hay aguinaldos debajo del árbol de Navidad.
   b. Hay aguinaldos para Santa Claus.
3. **a.** Había un desfile militar y tocaba una banda para celebrar la Navidad.
   b. Había un desfile militar y tocaba una banda para celebrar el Día de la Independencia.
4. **a.** Los fuegos artificiales iluminaban la sala.
   b. Los fuegos artificiales iluminaban el cielo.
5. **a.** Los niños ponen paja en los zapatos para los perros de los Reyes Magos.
   b. Los niños ponen paja en los zapatos para los camellos de los Reyes Magos.
6. **a.** La familia judía encendía velas para el Día de los Muertos.
   b. La familia judía encendía velas para Hanuka.
7. **a.** Durante la fiesta una banda tocaba y todos bailaban en la calle.
   b. Durante la fiesta dos bandas bailaban.

Activities 2 and 4 It is suggested you do these activities orally before having students write them.

Cultura

La piñata

La piñata es una vasija de cartón o barro. Se llena de dulces y durante muchas fiestas familiares los niños, con los ojos vedados *(blindfolded)*, tratan de romper la piñata con un palo o bastón. Si tienen éxito, la piñata se rompe y todos los niños corren a recoger *(gather)* los dulces.

ESCUCHAR

1 Escucha. Escoge la frase correcta. Usa una tabla como la de abajo para indicar tus respuestas.

a	b

HABLAR • ESCRIBIR

2 Contesta.

1. ¿Tienen muchas familias cristianas un árbol de Navidad?
2. ¿Decoran el árbol?
3. ¿Quién les trae aguinaldos a los niños?
4. ¿Dónde los pone?
5. ¿Celebran Hanuka las familias judías?
6. ¿Qué hay en la menora?

CULTURA

Estos niños están caminando por los jardines de un parque durante una fiesta en Cotacachi, Ecuador.

LEER • ESCRIBIR

3 Rompecabezas

¡Adivina! ¿Qué es?

1. un animal del desierto
2. lo que comen ciertos animales
3. un regalo de Navidad
4. lo que hay en una menora
5. lo que hacía la gente mientras tocaba la banda

Answers

1
1. a 2. a 3. b 4. b 5. b 6. b 7. a

2
1. Sí, muchas familias cristianas tienen un árbol de Navidad.
2. Sí, decoran el árbol.
3. Santa Claus les trae aguinaldos a los niños.
4. Los pone debajo del árbol.
5. Sí, las familias judías celebran Hanuka.
6. Hay velas en la menora.

3
1. un camello
2. la paja
3. un aguinaldo
4. velas
5. bailaba

ESCUCHAR • HABLAR • ESCRIBIR

4 Contesta según se indica.

1. ¿Cuántos Reyes Magos hay? (tres)
2. ¿Cuántas velas hay en una menora? (nueve)
3. ¿Cuándo hay fuegos artificiales? (de noche después del desfile)
4. ¿Cuándo toca la banda municipal? (durante el desfile)
5. ¿Qué decoran los niños? (el árbol de Navidad)
6. ¿Qué reciben los niños para la Navidad? (aguinaldos)

Go Online!

connectED.mcgraw-hill.com

InfoGap For more practice using your new vocabulary, do Activity 5 in the Student Resource section at the end of this book.

5 ***Comunicación***

Con un grupo de amigos, describe una fiesta típica que se celebra el 4 de julio en Estados Unidos.

¡Así se dice!

If while speaking you realize that you have made a grammatical error or know that you haven't been clear in your explanation, just stop and say, **o sea...**, and continue from where you left off.

HABLAR • ESCRIBIR

6 Corrige la información falsa.

1. La Navidad es en junio.
2. Un aguinaldo es un regalo que se recibe para el Año Nuevo.
3. Hay cuatro Reyes Magos.
4. Hanuka se llama también la fiesta de los fuegos.

Cultura

El weekend o el fin de semana libre es una costumbre anglosajona. En el mundo hispano mucha gente tiene que trabajar los sábados. No tienen todo el fin de semana libre. Pero tienen muchos días festivos durante el año. Cada país tiene sus propias fiestas o ferias. Y si la fiesta es el martes, el lunes debe ser un día festivo también, ¿no? Incluir un día adicional para tener más días festivos se llama «un puente».

Vocabulario 2

Activities 3 and 6 Have students prepare these activities before going over them in class.

Differentiation

Multiple Intelligences

Bodily-kinesthetic learners would love to make, fill, and have the class break a piñata. It is a fun learning activity that you may want to try.

ABOUT THE SPANISH LANGUAGE

You will often hear the English term *weekend* used when people are speaking Spanish. It is probably because the concept of *weekend* is not indigenous to Hispanic cultures. Many people, however, do use the Spanish **el fin de semana.** Have students look up **el puente** and say why it would be an appropriate term to use to describe a day between a weekend and a holiday.

ASSESS

Students are now ready to take Quiz 2.

Answers

4

1. Hay tres Reyes Magos.
2. Hay nueve velas en una menora.
3. Hay fuegos artificiales de noche después del desfile.
4. La banda municipal toca durante el desfile.
5. Los niños decoran el árbol de Navidad.
6. Los niños reciben aguinaldos para la Navidad.

5 *Answers will vary.*

6

1. La Navidad es en diciembre.
2. Un aguinaldo es un regalo que se recibe para la Navidad.
3. Hay tres Reyes Magos.
4. Hanuka se llama también la fiesta de las luces.

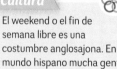

Online Resources

Customizable Lesson Plans
Whiteboard Lesson
Audio Activities
Student Workbook
Quizzes

Quick Start

Use QS 5.3 or write the following on the board.

Complete in the present with a reflexive verb.

1. **Yo ___ a las seis y media.**
2. **Yo ___ enseguida.**
3. **Yo ___ la cara.**
4. **Yo ___ los dientes.**
5. **Yo ___ tarde.**

TEACH

Core Instruction

Step 1 Read to students the definitions of the preterite and imperfect in Items 1 and 2.

Step 2 Write the **-ar** verb forms on the board. Underline the endings and have students read all forms aloud.

Differentiation

Multiple Intelligences

Each time you use a verb in the imperfect, put a shaded line on the board showing that we do not know when the action began or ended. This will help **visual-spatial** learners.

¡Ojo!

It is recommended that you not give students the English equivalents for the imperfect. They must learn that the imperfect expresses an ongoing, continuing action. When students hear that *used to* is an English equivalent of the imperfect, it confuses them because it implies *but no longer*, suggesting an end at some given point in time.

¡Ojo!

There are no verbs with a stem change in the imperfect.

PRESENTE		IMPERFECTO
juego	→	jugaba
empiezo	→	empezaba

Imperfecto de los verbos en -ar

1. In Spanish there are two simple past tenses—the preterite and the imperfect. You have already learned the preterite. You use the preterite to state an action that began and ended at a definite time in the past.
2. You will now learn the imperfect. The imperfect is used to describe a habitual or repeated past action. The exact time the action began and/or ended is not important.
3. Observe the imperfect forms of regular **-ar** verbs.

infinitive	hablar	mirar
stem	habl-	mir-
yo	hablaba	miraba
tú	hablabas	mirabas
Ud., él, ella	hablaba	miraba
nosotros(as)	hablábamos	mirábamos
vosotros(as)	*hablabais*	*mirabais*
Uds., ellos, ellas	hablaban	miraban

4. Some common time expressions used with the imperfect are:

siempre	**con frecuencia**
a veces	**a menudo**
de vez en cuando	**todos los días (años)**

Ellos siempre desfilaban detrás de la banda.
A veces bailaban al son de la banda.
De vez en cuando llevaban disfraces.
Lo pasaban bien.

CULTURA

Esta muchacha guatemalteca regresaba a casa cada día después de sus clases. Siempre llevaba sus materiales escolares en su mochila.

Práctica

HABLAR • ESCRIBIR

1 Contesta.

1. La Nochebuena, ¿se acostaban bastante temprano los niños?
2. ¿Qué esperaban ellos? ¿Esperaban la llegada de Santa Claus?
3. ¿Escuchaban cuando hablaban sus padres?
4. ¿Quiénes decoraban el árbol? ¿Los niños o sus padres?
5. Y en los países hispanos, ¿a quiénes esperaban los niños?

Lori Ernfridsson

¡Así se dice!

Why It Works!

Note that we have separated the **-ar** from the **-er** and **-ir** verbs so students can practice one segment of what they have to know before going on to the next.

Answers

1

1. Sí (No), los niños (no) se acostaban bastante temprano la Nochebuena.
2. Sí (No), los niños (no) esperaban la llegada de Santa Claus.
3. Sí, (No, no) escuchaban cuando hablaban sus padres.
4. Los niños (Los padres) decoraban el árbol.
5. En los países hispanos los niños esperaban a los Reyes Magos.

Go Online!
connectED.mcgraw-hill.com

HABLAR • ESCRIBIR

2 Personaliza. Da respuestas personales.

1. Cuando estabas en la escuela primaria, ¿cómo llegabas a la escuela? ¿Llegabas a pie o tomabas el bus escolar?
2. ¿Estaba tu casa lejos o cerca de tu escuela?
3. ¿Con quiénes jugabas?
4. ¿Qué jugaban ustedes?
5. ¿Tomabas el almuerzo con tus amigos en la cafetería de la escuela?

HABLAR • ESCRIBIR

3 Da la frase con el nuevo sujeto.

Ellas jugaban fútbol.

1. él	4. ustedes
2. nosotros	5. tú
3. yo	6. Javier

LEER • ESCRIBIR

4 Completa con el imperfecto sobre unos veranos en la playa.

Cada año cuando __1__ (llegar) el verano, yo __2__ (estar) contento(a). Mi familia siempre __3__ (pasar) el mes de julio en la playa. Por la mañana mi hermano y yo __4__ (levantarse) y __5__ (tomar) el desayuno. Pero después de tomar el desayuno, no __6__ (caminar) a la escuela. Nosotros __7__ (pasar) el día en la playa.

Yo siempre __8__ (nadar) en el mar. Me __9__ (gustar) las olas altas. De vez en cuando mi hermano __10__ (alquilar) un barquito y nosotros __11__ (esquiar) en el agua.

Cada tarde a eso de las tres __12__ (llegar) algunos amigos y (nosotros) __13__ (formar) un equipo de voleibol. Si digo la verdad (nosotros) __14__ (jugar) muy bien.

El mismo equipo no __15__ (ganar) siempre pero lo importante es que (nosotros) lo __16__ (pasar) bien.

—Y tú, ¿__17__ (pasar) los veranos en la playa o __18__ (quedarse) en casa?

5 **Comunicación**

Trabajen en grupos de cuatro o cinco. Un miembro del grupo es el/la entrevistador(a) que va a preguntar a los otros dónde pasaban los veranos. Presenten las respuestas a la clase.

CULTURA

La muchacha norteamericana jugaba «soccer» con el equipo de su escuela. Su equipo ganaba casi siempre.

Gramática

Leveling EACH Activity

Easy Activities 1, 2, 3
Average Activity 4
CHallenging Activity 5

PRACTICE

Activities 1, 2, and 3 It is recommended that you go over these activities orally in class before students write them.

Activity 4 This activity should be prepared and then read in class.

Activity 5 This activity can be done with many different groups.

Differentiation

When doing an activity like Activity 5, you can have mixed learners in each group. Other members of class listen to each group's discussion. Many students can learn from listening to peers.

Advanced Learners

Have an advanced learner retell all the information in Activity 4 in his or her own words.

Multiple Intelligences

Have **auditory-musical** learners make up a rap using Spanish that they know and inserting many of these imperfect endings.

ASSESS

Students are now ready to take Quiz 3.

Answers

2 *Answers will vary but may include:*

1. Llegaba a pie. (Tomaba el bus escolar.)
2. Mi casa estaba cerca (lejos) de mi escuela.
3. Jugaba con ___.
4. Jugábamos ___.
5. Sí, (No, no) tomaba el almuerzo con mis amigos en la cafetería de la escuela.

3

1. Él jugaba fútbol.
2. Nosotros jugábamos fútbol.
3. Yo jugaba fútbol.
4. Ustedes jugaban fútbol.
5. Tú jugabas fútbol.
6. Javier jugaba fútbol.

4

1. llegaba
2. estaba
3. pasaba
4. nos levantábamos
5. tomábamos
6. caminábamos
7. pasábamos
8. nadaba
9. gustaban
10. alquilaba
11. esquiábamos
12. llegaban
13. formábamos
14. jugábamos
15. ganaba
16. pasábamos
17. pasabas
18. te quedabas

5 *Answers will vary.*

Online Resources

Customizable Lesson Plans
- Whiteboard Lesson
- Audio Activities
- Video (Gramática)
- Student Workbook
- Enrichment
- Quizzes

Quick Start

Use QS 5.4 or write the following on the board.

Change **yo** to **nosotros.**

1. **Yo me despierto a las seis y media.**
2. **Yo me levanto enseguida.**
3. **Yo me lavo la cara.**
4. **Yo me cepillo los dientes.**
5. **Yo me acuesto a las once de la noche.**

TEACH

Core Instruction

Step 1 Read Item 1 to students.

Step 2 Write the infinitives of the verbs **leer** and **escribir** on the board. Cross out the infinitive endings, leaving just the stems.

Step 3 Write the forms of **leer** and **escribir** in the imperfect on the board. Underline the endings.

Step 4 Have students read all the verb forms aloud.

Step 5 Write all the imperfect forms of **querer** and **volver** on the board. Have students repeat them.

Step 6 Now go over Item 2. Explain to students that the form **había** never changes.

¡Ojo!

There are no verbs with a stem change in the imperfect.

PRESENTE		IMPERFECTO
quiero	→	quería
vuelvo	→	volvía

Imperfecto de los verbos en -er, -ir

1. Regular **-er** and **-ir** verbs have the same endings in the imperfect tense.

infinitive	leer	escribir
stem	le-	escrib-
yo	leía	escribía
tú	leías	escribías
Ud., él, ella	leía	escribía
nosotros(as)	leíamos	escribíamos
vosotros(as)	*leíais*	*escribíais*
Uds., ellos, ellas	leían	escribían

2. The imperfect of **hay** is **había.** Note that either a singular or plural noun follows **había.**

Había un concierto durante la fiesta.
Había fuegos artificiales durante la fiesta.

CULTURA

Un grupo de jóvenes haciendo un baile folklórico en el desierto de Atacama en el norte de Chile

Práctica

HABLAR • ESCRIBIR

6 Personaliza. Da respuestas personales.

1. ¿Vivías en la misma casa cuando tenías doce años?
2. ¿A qué escuela asistías?
3. ¿Recibías buenas o malas notas?
4. ¿Tenías muchos amigos donde vivías?
5. ¿Leías muchos libros de bolsillo?
6. ¿Aprendías mucho?
7. ¿Sabías usar la computadora?
8. ¿Escribías muchos correos electrónicos?
9. ¿Recibías muchos también?

EXPANSIÓN

Ahora, sin mirar las preguntas, relata en tus propias palabras lo que dijo tu compañero(a). Si no recuerdas algo o si no comprendiste algo que te dijo, tu compañero(a) te puede ayudar.

Differentiation

If you have only non-Spanish speakers in class, it is better not to mention that **n** is not added to **había** when followed by a plural noun. Non-native speakers usually do not bother to add the **n.**

Heritage Speakers

If you have heritage speakers in class, it is important to point out that **había** never takes the **n.** Some may argue that it is **habían dos** because this is a frequently made error.

LEER • ESCRIBIR

7 Completa con el imperfecto.

Yo recuerdo que durante la fiesta __1__ (haber) fuegos artificiales que __2__ (iluminar) el cielo. Todo el mundo __3__ (divertirse). Todos nosotros __4__ (beber) y __5__ (comer). __6__ (Haber) muchos puestos de comida donde se __7__ (vender) perros calientes, hamburguesas, pizza y papas fritas.

__8__ (Haber) un desfile. Durante el desfile algunos __9__ (ponerse) máscaras. Yo no __10__ (poder) reconocer a varios amigos porque __11__ (llevar) disfraces.

Nosotros __12__ (tener) mucha suerte. Durante la fiesta __13__ (hacer) buen tiempo y no __14__ (llover).

Yo tengo muy buenos recuerdos (memorias) de esta fiesta.

CULTURA

Grupos de músicos se reúnen los sábados y domingos para dar conciertos en las calles de San Telmo en Buenos Aires, Argentina.

HABLAR • ESCRIBIR

8 Forma frases en el imperfecto con los siguientes verbos.

comer	beber	aprender	conocer	saber	volver
vivir	subir	recibir	salir	escribir	tener

9 *Comunicación*

Dile a un(a) compañero(a) las cosas que hacías a menudo cuando eras alumno(a) en la escuela primaria. Tu compañero(a) va a hacerte preguntas para saber más.

Go Online!

connectED.mcgraw-hill.com

FOLDABLES Study Organizer

MINIBOOK

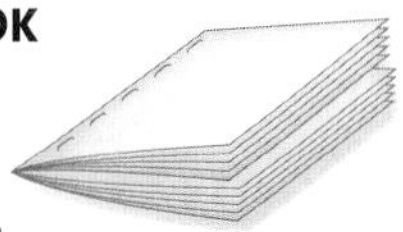

See the Foldables section of the Student Handbook at the beginning of this book for help with making this foldable. Use this foldable to illustrate and tell about things you did frequently. On each page, draw a picture of an activity you enjoyed. Below each picture, write a few sentences in Spanish describing what was happening. Remember to use the imperfect tense and to stick to the words that you already know in Spanish.

Gramática

Leveling EACH Activity

Easy Activity 6
Average Activities 7, 8, 9
CHallenging Activity 6 **Expansión**

PRACTICE

Activity 6 This activity should be gone over orally in class. Call on several students to do the **Expansión.** Note that Activity 6 can also be done as a paired activity.

Activity 7 This activity should be prepared and then gone over in class.

Activity 8 You may wish to do Activity 8 as an entire class activity or a group activity. You may have students prepare it or do it extemporaneously.

ASSESS

Students are now ready to take Quiz 4.

Answers

6

1. Sí, (No, no) vivía en la misma casa cuando tenía doce años.
2. Asistía a ____.
3. Recibía buenas (malas) notas.
4. Sí, (No, no) tenía muchos amigos donde vivía.
5. Sí, (No, no) leía muchos libros de bolsillo.
6. Sí, (No, no) aprendía mucho.
7. Sí, (No, no) sabía usar la computadora.
8. Sí, (No, no) escribía muchos correos electrónicos.
9. Sí, (No, no) recibía muchos también (tampoco).

7

1. había
2. iluminaban
3. se divertía
4. bebíamos
5. comíamos
6. Había
7. vendían
8. Había
9. se ponían
10. podía
11. llevaban
12. teníamos
13. hacía
14. llovía

8 *Answers will vary.*

9 *Answers will vary.*

Online Resources

Customizable Lesson Plans
- Whiteboard Lesson
- Audio Activities
- Video (Gramática)
- Student Workbook
- Enrichment
- Quizzes

TEACH

Core Instruction

Step 1 Write the infinitives of the verbs **ser** and **ir** on the board.

Step 2 Write the verb forms on the board. Have students repeat all the forms after you.

Step 3 When going over the verbs **ser** and **ir,** stress the importance of learning these verbs since they are used very often.

Step 4 Have students read the forms of **ver** once. Students very seldom have a problem with this verb.

PRACTICE

Leveling EACH Activity

Average Activities 10, 11

Go Online!

Gramática en vivo: *The imperfect* Enliven learning with the animated world of Professor Cruz! **Gramática en vivo** is a fun and effective tool for additional instruction and/or review.

ASSESS

Students are now ready to take Quiz 5.

Gramática

CULTURA

Los niños se divertían en el patio de su escuela primaria en Antigua, Guatemala.

Imperfecto de los verbos irregulares

The verbs **ser, ir,** and **ver** are the only verbs that are irregular in the imperfect tense.

	ser	ir	ver
yo	era	iba	veía
tú	eras	ibas	veías
Ud., él, ella	era	iba	veía
nosotros(as)	éramos	íbamos	veíamos
vosotros(as)	*erais*	*ibais*	*veíais*
Uds., ellos, ellas	eran	iban	veían

Práctica

HABLAR • ESCRIBIR

10 Personaliza. Da respuestas personales.

1. Cuando eras alumno(a) en la escuela primaria, ¿eran tus amiguitos tus vecinos que vivían cerca de tu casa?
2. A veces, ¿ibas al parque con tus amigos?
3. ¿Adónde iban ustedes los sábados?
4. ¿Quién era tu maestro(a) en el tercer grado?
5. ¿Cómo ibas a la escuela?
6. Cuando volvías a casa, ¿veías la televisión?

CULTURA

Los niños de la primaria hacían una excursión escolar al Parque Güell en Barcelona, España. Sus maestros los acompañaban.

ESCUCHAR • LEER • ESCRIBIR

11 Cambia al imperfecto.

1. Ellos son de la República Dominicana.
2. Veo a mis parientes con frecuencia.
3. Vamos muy a menudo a la República Dominicana.
4. La casa de mis parientes es bonita.
5. Cuando estás allí, ¿vas a la playa?
6. ¿Quién va a la playa contigo?
7. ¿Ven ustedes a otros amigos en la playa?

Answers

10 *Answers will vary but may include:*

1. Sí (No), cuando era alumno(a) en la escuela primaria mis amiguitos (no) eran mis vecinos.
2. Sí, a veces iba al parque con mis amigos. (No, no iba al parque con mis amigos.)
3. Los sábados íbamos ____.
4. Mi maestro(a) en el tercer grado era ____.
5. Iba a pie (en el bus, en carro) a la escuela.
6. Sí (No), cuando volvía a casa, (no) veía la televisión.

11

1. Ellos eran de la República Dominicana.
2. Veía a mis parientes con frecuencia.
3. Íbamos muy a menudo a la República Dominicana.
4. La casa de mis parientes era bonita.
5. Cuando estabas allí, ¿ibas a la playa?
6. ¿Quién iba a la playa contigo?
7. ¿Veían ustedes a otros amigos en la playa?

Usos del imperfecto

In addition to expressing repeated, habitual actions or events in the past, the imperfect is used to describe persons, places, objects, events, weather, dates, and time in the past.

APPEARANCE	**Eloísa era alta y bonita.**
AGE	**Tenía trece años.**
PHYSICAL CONDITION	**Siempre estaba llena de energía.**
EMOTIONAL STATE	**Y estaba muy contenta.**
ATTITUDES AND DESIRES	**Le gustaban las fiestas.**
LOCATION	**Estaba en una fiesta en casa de Lucio.**
DATE	**Era el ocho de octubre.**
TIME	**Eran las diez de la noche.**
WEATHER	**Hacía bastante frío.**

Práctica

ESCUCHAR • HABLAR • ESCRIBIR

12 Contesta según se indica.

1. ¿Quién era alto? (don Quijote)
2. ¿Quién era bajo? (Sancho Panza)
3. ¿Quién tenía un asno? (Sancho Panza)
4. ¿Quién tenía un caballo? (don Quijote)
5. ¿Quién era idealista? (don Quijote)
6. ¿Quién era realista? (Sancho Panza)
7. ¿Quién quería viajar? (don Quijote)
8. ¿Quién quería volver a casa? (Sancho Panza)
9. ¿Quién quería conquistar los males del mundo? (don Quijote)
10. ¿Quién estaba loco? (don Quijote)

HABLAR • ESCRIBIR

13 Personaliza. Da respuestas personales.

1. ¿Quién era tu mejor amigo(a) en la escuela elemental?
2. ¿Cómo era?
3. ¿Cuántos años tenían ustedes cuando eran amigos?
4. ¿Qué tipo de personalidad tenía él o ella?
5. ¿Son ustedes amigos ahora?

14 **Comunicación**

Describe el tiempo que hacía ayer.

Go Online!

connectED.mcgraw-hill.com

Refrán

Can you guess what the following proverb means?

Con sus libros, los muertos abren los ojos a los vivos.

¡Bravo!

You have now learned all the new vocabulary and grammar in this chapter. Continue to use and practice all that you know while learning more cultural information. ¡Vamos!

Online Resources

Customizable Lesson Plans
- Whiteboard Lesson
- Audio Activities
- Video (Gramática)
- Student Workbook
- Enrichment
- Quizzes

Quick Start

Use QS 5.5 or write the following on the board.

Answer.

1. **¿Quién es tu mejor amigo(a)?**
2. **¿De dónde es?**
3. **¿Cómo es?**
4. **¿De qué color son sus ojos? ¿Y el pelo?**
5. **¿Cuántos años tiene?**
6. **¿Cuál es la fecha de su cumpleaños?**

TEACH

Core Instruction

Step 1 Tell students they are going to read something that describes the past.

Step 2 Have them read the explanation with as much expression as possible.

PRACTICE

Leveling EACH Activity

Easy Activity 12
Average Activities 13, 14

Activities 12 and 13 Both activities can be gone over orally in class before being written. Although these activities have no **Expansion** section, you can call on students to retell all the information in their own words.

Answers

12
1. Don Quijote era alto.
2. Sancho Panza era bajo.
3. Sancho Panza tenía un asno.
4. Don Quijote tenía un caballo.
5. Don Quijote era idealista.
6. Sancho Panza era realista.
7. Don Quijote quería viajar.
8. Sancho Panza quería volver a casa.
9. Don Quijote quería conquistar los males del mundo.
10. Don Quijote estaba loco.

13 *Answers will vary but may include:*
1. Mi mejor amigo(a) era ___.
2. Era ___.
3. Teníamos ___ años.
4. Él/Ella era ___.
5. Sí, (No, no) somos amigos ahora.

14 *Answers will vary.*

Online Resources

Customizable Lesson Plans

Audio Activities

Video (Diálogo)

Student Workbook

Quick Start

Use QS 5.6 or write the following on the board.

Answer.

1. **¿Te gusta la playa?**
2. **¿Juegas en la arena?**
3. **¿Nadas mucho?**
4. **A veces, ¿son grandes las olas?**
5. **¿Corres las olas?**

TEACH

Core Instruction

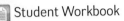

Step 1 Tell students that they are going to learn about a celebration in San Juan, Puerto Rico. There is something rather interesting that takes place during the celebration. Have them listen for it.

Step 2 You may wish to break the conversation into two parts. Have students read it after you or the audio recording.

Step 3 You may ask some questions after every four segments.

Step 4 Call on students to act out the conversation.

Go Online!

You may wish to remind students to go online for additional conversation practice.

El Día de San Juan

Patricia	**José, eres de Puerto Rico, ¿no?**
José	**Sí, ¿por qué?**
Patricia	**Pues, ¿me puedes decir lo que es una fiesta patronal?**
José	**¡Cómo no! Es una fiesta en honor del santo patrón de un lugar. El santo patrón de Puerto Rico, por ejemplo, es San Juan Bautista.**
Patricia	**¿Hay una fiesta en su honor?**
José	**Sí, el 24 de junio. Durante toda una semana hay fiestas.**
Patricia	**¿Qué hacen para celebrar la fiesta?**
José	**Pues, hay una tradición interesante. El Día de San Juan todos vamos a la playa y a la medianoche entramos en el mar.**
Patricia	**¿Siempre nadan el Día de San Juan?**
José	**No dije que nadamos. Dije que entramos en el mar. ¿Sabes cómo? Caminamos hacia atrás hasta llegar al mar.**
Patricia	**Y, ¿por qué andan hacia atrás?**
José	**Entrar en el mar así nos trae buena suerte durante el año.**

David H. Brennan

¡Así se dice!

Why It Works!

No new material is used in the **Conversación** in order not to confuse students. The **Conversación** recombines only the vocabulary and grammar that students have already learned to understand and manipulate.

Go Online!

connectED.mcgraw-hill.com

¿Comprendes?

A Completa según la información en la conversación.

1. José es de ______.
2. Una fiesta patronal rinde honor a ______.
3. El santo patrón de Puerto Rico es ______.
4. Su fiesta patronal es ______.
5. Todo el mundo va ______.
6. ______ para entrar en el mar.
7. Si entran en el mar así, van a tener ______.

B **Resumiendo** Cuenta la información en la conversación en tus propias palabras.

CULTURA

Maite preparaba a su amigo del continente para las celebraciones del Día de San Juan. Le enseñaba como andar hacia atrás.

C **Analizando** Los sanjuaneros tienen una costumbre interesante. ¿Qué hacen? ¿Por qué lo hacen?

Differentiation

Advanced Learners

Call on advanced learners and have them explain if they would like to take part in this celebration and why.

Heritage Speakers

If you have any students of Puerto Rican background, have them give any information they know about **el Día de San Juan.**

PRACTICE

¿Comprendes?

A You may wish to let students review the conversation again to find the information or you may want to use it as a factual recall activity.

B As one student is giving a review, if he/she starts to get confused, call on another to continue. Keep the atmosphere as relaxed as possible so students are not intimidated to speak.

Pre-AP Listening to this conversation will help students develop the skills that they need to be successful on the listening portion of the AP exam.

Go Online!

Diálogo en vivo In this episode, Julián and Francisco prepare to attend a **quinceañera.** Ask students why the two friends are upset when they see each other upon arriving at the party.

Answers

A

1. Puerto Rico
2. un santo patrón de un lugar
3. San Juan Bautista
4. el 24 de junio
5. a la playa
6. Caminan hacia atrás
7. buena suerte

B *Answers will vary.*

C *Answers will vary but may include:*
El Día de San Juan los sanjuaneros caminan hacia atrás para entrar en el mar. Lo hacen para traer buena suerte durante el año que viene.

Online Resources

Customizable Lesson Plans

Audio Activities

Student Workbook

TEACH

Core Instruction

Step 1 Have students read the **Estrategia de lectura** and look at all the illustrative material in the chapter that deals with **el Día de los Muertos.**

Step 2 You may wish to have students listen to the audio recording of the story.

Step 3 Call on a student to read a paragraph. Ask Reading Checks plus any other comprehension questions you wish.

Go Online!

You may wish to remind students to go online for additional reading comprehension and writing skills practice.

Lectura CULTURAL

ESTRATEGIA DE LECTURA

VISUALIZANDO Es importante visualizar lo que estás leyendo. Al leer, pinta un cuadro mental de la información. Este cuadro mental te permite apreciar más la información y recordar mejor lo que estás leyendo.

Antes de leer

Visualiza unas fiestas o ferias que tienen lugar donde tú vives—la Navidad, el Año Nuevo, el Cuatro de Julio, etc.

READING CHECK

¿Por qué celebraba la familia de Carmencita el Día de los Muertos?

Durante la lectura

Pinta un cuadro mental de lo que está haciendo la gente—lo que todos están llevando, lo que preparan, adónde van.

Unas fiestas hispanas

El Día de los Muertos Carmencita Dávila es alumna en nuestra clase de español. Cuando ella era niña, vivía en México y asistía a la primaria en Guadalajara. Ella nos quiere hablar de los recuerdos que tiene de una fiesta mexicana que le gustaba mucho.

—Cuando yo era niña en México me encantaban todas las festividades que tenían lugar[1] para celebrar el Día de los Muertos, el primero y el dos de noviembre. Celebrábamos para rendirles honor a todos nuestros parientes difuntos.

Mi mamá y abuelita siempre tenían que hacer muchos preparativos. Confeccionaban calaveras, un tipo de bizcocho dulce en forma de caras de muertos. Elaboraban también el delicioso pan de los muertos, un pan dulce en forma de huesos y cráneos. Unos días antes de la fiesta íbamos al cementerio o camposanto donde limpiábamos[2] y decorábamos con coronas de flores las tumbas de nuestros parientes difuntos. Durante las fiestas las tumbas servían de altar.

[1]tenían lugar *took place* [2]limpiábamos *we cleaned*

CULTURA

La señora está vendiendo flores delante del cementerio para el Día de los Muertos en San Juan Nuevo en el estado de Michoacán, México.

Tips for Success

Ask students if they know what *reminisce* means. Ask them the kinds of things they often reminisce about. Let them know the older one gets, the more he/she reminisces because there's more to reminisce about. When you reminisce in Spanish, you use the imperfect.

Go Online!

connectED.mcgraw-hill.com

Mamá y abuelita preparaban también lo que eran las comidas favoritas de los difuntos. El primero de noviembre la familia entera se reunía e íbamos juntos al cementerio. Colocábamos las calaveras, las coronas de flores, unas velas y la comida en las tumbas como una ofrenda. Algunos parientes llevaban calacas, disfraces de madera[3] en forma de esqueletos. En el cementerio teníamos un gran picnic. Comíamos con los difuntos.

✓ READING CHECK

¿Qué hacían en el cementerio?

CULTURA

Un santuario con esqueletos y cráneos para el Día de los Muertos

Roberto Jones levanta la mano y le hace una pregunta a Carmencita.

—Carmencita, me parece que la fiesta que nos describes es una ocasión mórbida, bastante triste.

Contesta Carmencita: —No, Roberto. La verdad es que es una ocasión festiva. Tiene sus orígenes entre los indígenas en la época precolombina. Los indígenas no consideran la muerte el final de la vida[4] sino la continuación de la vida. Creen también que las almas[5] de los muertos vuelven cada año para visitar a sus parientes vivos. Luego, ¿por qué no reunirnos con ellos para tener una fiesta?

✓ READING CHECK

¿Por qué no es una fiesta triste?

[3]de madera *wooden*
[4]vida *life*
[5]almas *souls*

Teaching Options

You may wish to break the **Lectura** into parts and read a page a day as you do other parts of the lesson. You may also choose to have the entire class read all of the **Lectura** or divide it into logical parts, assigning each part to a different group. Each group will report to the others concerning what they learned.

¡Así se dice!

Why It Works!

Note that the **Lectura** contains very little new footnoted vocabulary. The students know all the vocabulary and the grammatical point of the chapter is constantly reinforced in a natural manner. Here Carmencita reminisces about her childhood memories of **el Día de los Muertos** when she was in Mexico. Note all the uses of the imperfect: **era, vivía, asistía, le gustaba, era, me encantaban, tenían lugar, celebrábamos, tenían que, confeccionaban, elaboraban, íbamos, limpiábamos, decorábamos, servían de, preparaban, eran, se reunía, íbamos, colocábamos, llevaban, teníamos, comíamos.**

Differentiation

Multiple Intelligences

Verbal-linguistic learners who are interested in philosophy can get involved in some very interesting discussions or debates about Roberto's question and Carmencita's answer to it.

Comunicación

Interpersonal
Call on students to tell about their own Christmas and Hanukkah customs.

Comparaciones

Have advanced learners make comparisons between a Christmas celebration and **el Día de los Reyes.** If you have students of Jewish background you may wish to have those of Ashkenazi background compare their customs with those from a Sephardic background.

Cultura

Among some Sephardic communities, Ladino is still spoken, but not widely. Ladino is similar to fifteenth-century Spanish, the Spanish spoken at the time the Jews were expelled from Spain during the horrible Inquisition.

Lectura
CULTURAL

✓ READING CHECK

¿Cómo reciben los niños sus aguinaldos en los países hispanos?

CULTURA
Los Reyes Magos en el escaparate de una tienda de departamentos durante la temporada navideña en Madrid, España

La Navidad Y ahora la señora Salas, nuestra profesora de español, nos describe otra fiesta—una fiesta celebrada en todos los países hispanos.

Dice la señora Salas: —La mayoría de los niños en los países hispanos no reciben sus regalos de Navidad, sus aguinaldos, el 25 de diciembre. Los reciben el 6 de enero, el Día de los Reyes. La fiesta conmemora la llegada de los tres Reyes Magos al establo en Belén.

Los niños hispanos escriben sus cartas a los Reyes, no a Santa Claus, porque saben que son los Reyes quienes les traen los aguinaldos. Así, en sus cartas ponen una lista de los regalos que quieren recibir. La noche del 5 de enero, antes de acostarse, los niños dejan sus zapatos a la puerta de la casa, delante de la chimenea o debajo de su cama. Llenan sus zapatos de heno, paja o hierba porque saben que los animales de los Reyes van a querer comer. Y saben que los Reyes van a dejar los regalos que quieren en sus zapatos. Pero saben algo más. Si no se comportan bien durante el año los Reyes van a llenar sus zapatos de carbón[6].

Hanuka Isaac del Olmo tiene familia que vive en Panamá.

Dice la señora Salas: —Isaac, ¿sabes cómo celebra tu familia Hanuka en Panamá?

—Sí. Ellos celebran Hanuka de la misma manera que nosotros aquí en Estados Unidos. Es una fiesta alegre que empieza el 25 del mes hebreo de *Kislev* y dura ocho días. La primera noche un miembro de la familia enciende dos velas en la menora. Cada noche después se enciende una vela más. Cada noche los niños reciben regalos y bombones[7]. Y a todos les gusta comer *latkes*, panqueques de papas.

✓ READING CHECK

¿Qué reciben los niños durante Hanuka? ¿Cuántas veces?

[6]carbón *coal* [7]bombones *candies*

Después de leer

De las tres fiestas, ¿cuáles podías visualizar mejor? ¿Por qué?

Go Online!

connectED.mcgraw-hill.com

¿Comprendes?

A **Recordando hechos** Contesta.

1. ¿Dónde vivía Carmencita Dávila cuando era niña?
2. ¿Qué día de fiesta le encantaba?
3. ¿Quiénes hacían muchos preparativos?
4. ¿Adónde iban todos durante la fiesta?

B **Describiendo** Describe.

1. una calavera
2. una calaca

C **Categorizando** Completa la tabla.

lo que hacía la familia de Carmencita en casa	lo que hacía la familia de Carmencita en el cementerio

D **Analizando** Contesta.

¿Por qué no se considera el Día de los Muertos una ocasión mórbida?

E **Recordando hechos** Contesta.

1. ¿Cuándo reciben la mayoría de los niños hispanos sus aguinaldos?
2. ¿Qué conmemora el Día de los Reyes?
3. ¿De quiénes reciben sus aguinaldos los niños hispanos?
4. ¿Qué ponen en sus zapatos?
5. ¿Dónde dejan sus zapatos la noche del 5 de enero?
6. ¿Qué les dan los Reyes a los niños que no se comportan bien durante el año?

F **Buscando información** Completa.

1. Hanuka es ____.
2. Hanuka dura ____.
3. ____ enciende una vela en la menora.
4. Cada una de las ocho noches de Hanuka los niños reciben ____.
5. Los *latkes* son ____.

PRACTICE

Pre-AP These cultural readings will develop the skills that students need to be successful on the reading and writing sections of the AP exam. Listening to these readings will also help prepare them for the auditory component.

¿Comprendes?

Students are afforded a variety of comprehension activities. Encourage them to be as complete as possible in their responses, descriptions, and analysis.

Comunicación

Interpersonal

Have students discuss which holiday they found most interesting to learn about. Why?

Answers

A

1. Vivía en Guadalajara, México.
2. Le encantaba el Día de los Muertos.
3. La mamá y la abuelita de Carmencita hacían muchos preparativos.
4. Todos iban al cementerio.

B

1. Una calavera es un tipo de bizcocho dulce en forma de caras de muertos.
2. Una calaca es un disfraz de madera en forma de esqueleto.

C *Answers will vary.*

D *Answers will vary.*

E

1. La mayoría de los niños hispanos reciben sus aguinaldos el 6 de enero.
2. Conmemora la llegada de los tres Reyes Magos al establo en Belén.
3. Reciben sus aguinaldos de los Reyes Magos.
4. Ponen heno, paja o hierba en sus zapatos.
5. Dejan sus zapatos delante de la chimenea o debajo de su cama.
6. Los Reyes les dan carbón a los niños que no se comportan bien durante el año.

F

1. una fiesta alegre
2. ocho días
3. Un miembro de la familia
4. regalos y bombones
5. panqueques de papas

Online Resources

Customizable Lesson Plans
Audio Activities
Video (Cultura)
Student Workbook

Teaching Options

There are several options for presenting this **Lectura—Un poco más.**

Independent reading Have students read the selection and do the post-reading activities as homework, which you can collect. This option is least intrusive on class time and requires a minimum of teacher involvement.

Homework with in-class follow-up Assign the reading and post-reading activities as homework. Review and discuss the material in class the next day.

Intensive in-class activity In this option, the teacher presents in Spanish an overview of the reading selection and asks several comprehension questions about his or her summary. This is followed by in-class reading and discussion, assignment of the **¿Comprendes?** activity for homework, and a discussion of the assignment in class the following day.

Comunidades

If any students have seen the balloon fall (**se cae el globo; la caída del globo**) in New York's Times Square, you may wish to have them compare this to the celebration on the Plaza Mayor in Madrid. Students can also discuss any other appropriate New Year's celebrations they are familiar with.

Lectura

UN POCO MÁS

Antes de leer

Piensa en unas cosas que haces el 31 de diciembre para celebrar la llegada del Año Nuevo. En la Ciudad de Nueva York, por ejemplo, miles y miles de personas van a Times Square para ver caer un gran balón a la medianoche. Al leer esta lectura, compara las actividades en Madrid con las de Nueva York. Compáralas también con tus actividades tradicionales.

La Nochevieja en España

En España el día final del año es «la Nochevieja» y en los otros países hispanos es «la víspera del Año Nuevo». Fernando Orjales nació en Madrid, la capital de España, y ahora está viviendo con su familia en Nueva York. Es la noche del 31 de diciembre y Fernando va con su familia a *Times Square* para celebrar la llegada del Año Nuevo. Mientras está en *Times Square,* Fernando piensa en lo que él hacía para celebrar la Nochevieja cuando estaba en Madrid.

Dice: —Recuerdo que nosotros, como casi todos los madrileños, íbamos a la Puerta del Sol, una gran plaza en el centro mismo de la ciudad. Nos reuníamos frente a una campana[1]. Recuerdo que casi siempre hacía frío y soplaba[2] un viento bastante fuerte de la Sierra de Guadarrama. Todo el mundo estaba bien abrigado[3] para protegerse del frío.

Pero a pesar del[4] frío todos tenían la mirada fija en la campana. Y en la mano cada uno tenía su racimo de doce uvas. Estábamos listos para recibir el Año Nuevo. Esperábamos las doce campanadas que anunciaban la llegada del Año Nuevo.

Fernando dice que recuerda bien que él comía una uva con cada una de las campanadas. Y por cada uva pedía un deseo. Por eso se llaman «las doce uvas de la felicidad».

[1]campana *bell tower*
[2]soplaba *blew*
[3]abrigado *wrapped up*
[4]a pesar del *in spite of the*

¡Así se dice!

If you want to wish someone Happy New Year, you say **¡Próspero Año Nuevo!**

CULTURA
¿Quién va a comer las doce uvas de la felicidad para celebrar el Año Nuevo, una costumbre española?

Go Online!

You may wish to remind students to go online for additional reading comprehension and writing skills practice.

Go Online!

connectED.mcgraw-hill.com

¿Comprendes?

Escoge.

1. ¿De dónde es Fernando?
   a. de Nueva York
   b. de Madrid
   c. de la Nochevieja
2. ¿Adónde va Fernando ahora para celebrar la llegada del Año Nuevo?
   a. a *Times Square*
   b. a la Puerta del Sol
   c. a la Sierra de Guadarrama
3. ¿Qué hay en la Puerta del Sol?
   a. el sol
   b. una plaza
   c. una campana
4. ¿Por qué estaban todos bien abrigados?
   a. Siempre llevaban un abrigo nuevo.
   b. Hacía mucho frío.
   c. Estaban en la Sierra de Guadarrama.
5. ¿Cómo comía Fernando las uvas?
   a. todo un racimo
   b. doce a la vez
   c. una a una
6. ¿Cuándo las comía?
   a. al llegar a la Puerta del Sol
   b. al oír cada campanada
   c. al anunciar la llegada del Año Nuevo

CULTURA

Una vista de la Puerta del Sol donde se celebra la llegada del Año Nuevo en Madrid. Es de este campanario que las campanas dan las doce.

Go Online!

Cultura en vivo In this episode, students will learn about a festival in Spain called **La Romería.** Ask students if they participate in any family-oriented celebrations like **La Romería.** How are they the same? How do they differ?

Tips for Success

The multiple-choice comprehension activities that accompany the second reading selection in each chapter have a format that will help students prepare for standardized tests.

Answers

1. b
2. a
3. b
4. b
5. c
6. b

Online Resources

Customizable Lesson Plans

Student Workbook

Enrichment

Listening, Speaking, Reading, Writing Tests

Self-check for achievement

This is a pre-test for students to take before you administer the chapter test. Note that each section is cross-referenced so students can easily find the material they feel they need to review. You may wish to use Self-Check Worksheet SC5 to have students complete this assessment in class or at home. You can correct the assessment yourself, or you may prefer to display the answers in class using Self-Check Answers SC5A.

Differentiation

Slower Paced Learners

Have students work in pairs to complete the Self-Check in class. Once they have finished, call on individuals to give the correct answers as you review together.

Multiple Intelligences

To engage **visual-spatial** and **bodily-kinesthetic** learners, number 1 to 40 on the board and call on a student to go to the board and write the correct answer (this may be done chronologically or you may allow students to choose the one they answer). Then have the student who wrote the first answer decide who will write the second, and so on, making sure to remind them not to pick the same person again.

Prepárate para el examen

To review, see **Vocabulario 1** and **Vocabulario 2**.

Vocabulario

1 Identifica.

1.

2.

3.

4.

5.

2 Da otra palabra.

6. el muerto
7. un tipo de desfile
8. confeccionar
9. el cementerio
10. un disfraz
11. un regalo de Navidad
12. pasarlo bien

3 Completa.

13. Todo el mundo _____ hacia el cementerio.
14. Abuelita _____ bizcochos.
15. La familia pone _____ de flores en la tumba.
16. La noche de la fiesta había _____ que iluminaban el cielo.
17. _____ es la fiesta de las luces.

Answers

1
1. la menora
2. la máscara
3. el cementerio (el camposanto)
4. el desfile
5. los fuegos artificiales

2
6. el difunto
7. una procesión
8. elaborar (hacer)
9. el camposanto
10. una máscara
11. un aguinaldo
12. divertirse

3
13. camina
14. elabora (confecciona)
15. coronas
16. fuegos artificiales
17. Hanuka

Gramática

4 Completa con el imperfecto.

18. La banda ____. (tocar)
19. Todos nosotros ____. (bailar)
20. ____ muy buen tiempo. (hacer)
21. Ellos ____. (celebrar)
22. Y tú, ¿qué ____? (hacer)
23–24. Yo ____ y ____. (comer, beber)
25. ¿Qué hora ____? (ser)
26–27. Yo ____ quedarme pero ellos ____ salir. (querer, preferir)
28. La gente ____. (divertirse)

5 Escribe en el imperfecto.

29. Yo sé hacerlo.
30. Ellos pueden ir.
31. Es alumno en la primaria.
32. ¿Qué va a decir?
33. Tienes quince años.
34. Antonia ve el desfile.

Cultura

6 Contesta.

35. Cuando Carmencita vivía en México, ¿qué ponían los miembros de la familia en las tumbas de sus parientes difuntos?
36. El Día de los Muertos no es una ocasión triste ni mórbida. ¿Por qué?
37. ¿Cuándo reciben la mayoría de los niños hispanos sus regalos de Navidad?
38. ¿Quiénes traen los regalos a los niños y dónde los dejan?
39. ¿Por qué ponen los niños paja en los zapatos?
40. ¿Durante qué fiesta se comen *latkes*?

Go Online!
connectED.mcgraw-hill.com

To review, see **Imperfecto de los verbos en -ar, Imperfecto de los verbos en -er, -ir, Imperfecto de los verbos irregulares,** and **Usos del imperfecto.**

To review this cultural information, see the **Lectura cultural.**

CULTURA
La tumba de Eva Perón y su familia en el cementerio de la Recoleta, Buenos Aires, Argentina

Richard Brommer

Prepárate para el examen

Differentiation

(continued)

This type of review activity is particularly appealing to interpersonal learners but will also benefit the class on the whole by promoting an inclusive, student-centered learning environment.

Slower Paced Learners

Encourage students who need extra help to refer to the margin notes and review any section before answering the questions.

Pre-AP Students preparing for the AP exam may benefit from a set time limit when completing this Self-Check. This may also help to identify students with learning difficulties or slower paced students who need extra help.

Cultural Snapshot

In comparison to some of the tombs and mausoleums in the Recoleta Cemetery, the Duarte one is not very grandiose.

Go Online!

You may wish to remind students to go online for additional test preparation.

Answers

4

18. tocaba
19. bailábamos
20. Hacía
21. celebraban
22. hacías
23. comía
24. bebía
25. era
26. quería
27. preferían
28. se divertía

5

29. Yo sabía hacerlo.
30. Ellos podían ir.
31. Era alumno en la primaria.
32. ¿Qué iba a decir?
33. Tenías quince años.
34. Antonia veía el desfile.

6

35. Ponían coronas de flores, calaveras, velas y comida en las tumbas de sus parientes difuntos.
36. Creen que se reúnen con las almas de los muertos y tienen una fiesta. Es una ocasión festiva.
37. Reciben sus regalos de Navidad el 6 de enero.
38. Los Reyes Magos traen los regalos y los dejan en los zapatos de los niños.
39. Ponen paja en los zapatos para los animales de los Reyes Magos.
40. Se comen *latkes* durante Hanuka.

Prepárate para el examen

Tips for Success

Encourage students to say as much as possible when they do these open-ended activities. Tell them not to be afraid to make mistakes, since the goal of the activities is real-life communication. Encourage students to self-correct and to use words and phrases they know to get their meaning across. If someone in the group makes an error that impedes comprehension, encourage the others to ask questions to clarify or, if necessary, to politely correct the speaker. Let students choose the activities they would like to do.

Tell students to feel free to elaborate on the basic theme and to be creative. They may use props, pictures, or posters if they wish.

Pre-AP These oral activities will give students the opportunity to develop and improve their speaking skills so that they may succeed on the speaking portion of the AP exam.

Note: You may want to use the rubric below to help students prepare their speaking activities.

Practice for **ORAL PROFICIENCY**

Prepárate para el examen

1 Una fiesta latina

Describe a Hispanic holiday

Escoge una de las siguientes fiestas. Describe la fiesta a un(a) amigo(a).

el Día de los Muertos	**el Día de los Reyes**
el Día de San Juan	**la Nochevieja**

2 Mi fiesta favorita

Talk about your favorite holiday

De todas las fiestas en la lectura, ¿cuál es tu predilecta (favorita)? Explica por qué.

3 Comparaciones

Compare holidays in the United States with Hispanic holidays

Compara el Día de los Muertos con *Halloween.* También compara el día de Navidad con el Día de los Reyes.

4 Recuerdos

Talk about your childhood

Relata unos recuerdos placenteros (agradables) que tienes de los años de tu niñez. Empieza con «Cuando yo era niño(a)... ».

CULTURA

Estas niñas de Cotacachi, Ecuador, llevan trajes para celebrar las Navidades.

Andrew Payti

Scoring Rubric for Speaking

	4	3	2	1
vocabulary	extensive use of vocabulary, including idiomatic expressions	adequate use of vocabulary and idiomatic expressions	limited vocabulary marked with some anglicisms	limited vocabulary marked by frequent anglicisms that force interpretation by the listener
grammar	few or no grammatical errors	minor grammatical errors	some serious grammatical errors	serious grammatical errors
pronunciation	good intonation and largely accurate pronunciation with slight accent	acceptable intonation and pronunciation with distinctive accent	errors in intonation and pronunciation with heavy accent	errors in intonation and pronunciation that interfere with listener's comprehension
content	thorough response with interesting and pertinent detail	thorough response with sufficient detail	some detail, but not sufficient	general, insufficient response

Go Online! connectED.mcgraw-hill.com

Tarea

Write a journal entry in which you reminisce about a holiday you enjoyed as a youngster. Describe the general characteristics of that holiday, such as when you would celebrate it, how it was celebrated, what would often happen, who would always be there, and why you always enjoyed it.

Writing Strategy

Reminiscing One technique frequently used in journal writing is reminiscing. When you reminisce, you use your memory to recall how things were in the past. The primary source of information will be the thoughts and images that your mind produces of "the way things were back then." Use what you have learned about the imperfect and the vocabulary from this chapter to make your journal entry as descriptive and lively as possible.

1 Prewrite

Make a list of the thoughts and images that come to mind when you reminisce about your favorite holiday. Think about when it would take place, who would be there, what the scene would be like, what would often happen, why it was always fun, how you felt, etc.

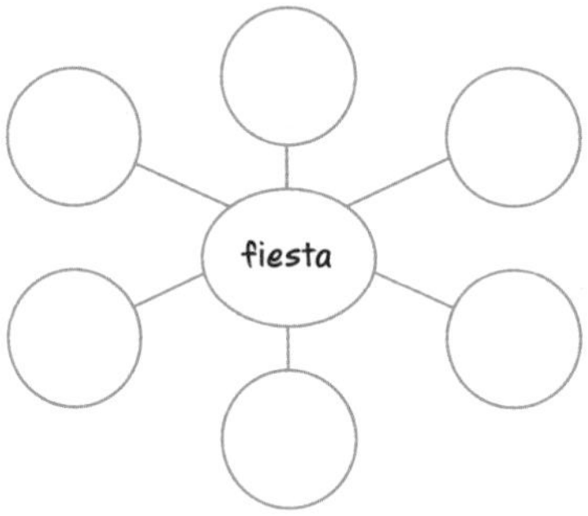

2 Write

- Be sure to stick to vocabulary that you already know.
- Remember to incorporate time expressions often used to indicate habitual or repeated actions in the past, such as **siempre, cada, a menudo, con mucha frecuencia, a veces,** etc.
- Use descriptive adjectives and include as many details as possible to make the memory of your favorite holiday come alive.

It is important to keep in mind that you are not writing about specific events that took place one time during your favorite holiday. Your goal is to capture the overall essence of this habitual or repeated event from your childhood as you remember it.

Evaluate

Don't forget that your teacher will evaluate you on use of vocabulary, correctness of grammar, and the vivid description of details.

Prepárate para el examen

Pre-AP This **tarea** will give students the opportunity to develop and improve their writing skills so that they may succeed on the writing portion of the AP exam.

ASSESS

Students are now ready to take any of the Listening, Speaking, Reading, Writing Tests you choose to administer.

Note: You may want to use the rubric below to help students prepare their writing task.

Scoring Rubric for Writing

	4	3	2	1
vocabulary	precise, varied	functional, fails to communicate complete meaning	limited to basic words, often inaccurate	inadequate
grammar	excellent, very few or no errors	some errors, but do not hinder communication	numerous errors interfere with communication	many errors, little sentence structure
content	thorough response to the topic	generally thorough response to the topic	partial response to the topic	insufficient response to the topic
organization	well organized, ideas presented clearly and logically	loosely organized, but main ideas present	some attempts at organization, but with confused sequencing	lack of organization

Online Resources

Customizable Lesson Plans
Whiteboard Lesson
Audio Activities
Video (Vocabulario) (Diálogo) (Gramática) (Cultura)
Student Workbook
Enrichment
Quizzes
Listening, Speaking, Reading, Writing Tests

Grammar Review

This page provides a quick "at a glance" summary of the grammar points students have learned in this chapter.

Differentiation

Multiple Intelligences

You may want to call on **verbal-linguistic** and **logical-mathematical** learners for whom grammar often comes easily to explain the main concepts to their classmates in their own words. Having students explain the concepts in different ways may also help slower paced students or students with learning difficulties.

Repaso del Capítulo 5

Gramática

Imperfecto de los verbos regulares

The imperfect is used to describe a habitual or repeated action in the past. Some words commonly used with the imperfect are **siempre, con frecuencia, a menudo,** and **todos los días.** Review the imperfect forms of regular verbs.

bailar	beber	vivir
bailaba	bebía	vivía
bailabas	bebías	vivías
bailaba	bebía	vivía
bailábamos	bebíamos	vivíamos
bailabais	*bebíais*	*vivíais*
bailaban	bebían	vivían

Imperfecto de los verbos irregulares

Ser, ir, and **ver** are irregular in the imperfect. Review the following forms.

ser	ir	ver
era	iba	veía
eras	ibas	veías
era	iba	veía
éramos	íbamos	veíamos
erais	*ibais*	*veíais*
eran	iban	veían

Usos del imperfecto

The imperfect is used to express a continuous action in the past and to describe persons, places, objects, events, weather, and time in the past.

Ellos siempre hacían mucho.
Dolores estaba muy contenta.
Llovía mucho en la primavera.
Era el seis de enero y nevaba.

CULTURA
Un baile folklórico chileno

Andrew Payti

Juego There are a number of cognates in this list. See how many you and a partner can find. Who can find the most? Compare your list with those of your classmates.

Go Online!
connectED.mcgraw-hill.com

Vocabulario

Talking about a patron saint's day

una feria	la santa patrona	patronal
una fiesta	una procesión, un desfile	desfilar
el santo patrón		caminar

Talking about the Day of the Dead

los muertos, los difuntos	una ofrenda	un esqueleto
el camposanto, el cementerio	una corona de flores	un hueso
el mausoleo	una calavera, un cráneo	un disfraz
la tumba		una máscara
		enterrado(a)

Talking about Christmas and Three Kings Day

la Navidad, las Navidades	un aguinaldo	la paja
la Nochebuena	los Reyes Magos	el árbol de Navidad
la chimenea	el camello	decorar

Talking about Hanukkah

Hanuka	la menora	hebreo(a)
¡Feliz Hanuka!	la vela	encender
la fiesta de las luces	judío(a)	

Talking about Independence Day

un desfile	los fuegos artificiales	bailar
una banda municipal	el cielo	iluminar

Other useful words and expressions

el bizcocho	celebrar	elaborar
todo el mundo	confeccionar	mientras
dulce		

Repaso del Capítulo 5

Vocabulary Review

The words and phrases in **Vocabulario 1** and **2** have been taught for productive use in this chapter. They are summarized here as a resource for both student and teacher. This list also serves as a convenient resource for the **Prepárate para el examen** activities.

¡Así se dice!

Why It Works!

This vocabulary reference list has not been translated into English for two reasons. First, it is recommended that students learn the new vocabulary through direct association with images on the **Vocabulario** pages. Second, all vocabulary is reintroduced in the chapter many times and upon completion of the chapter students should be familiar with the meaning of all the words. If there are words that students still do not know, they can refer to the vocabulary presentation in the chapter or the dictionary at the end of the book. If, however, it is your preference to give students the English translations, please refer to Vocabulary Transparency V5.1.

Differentiation

Slower Paced Learners

Slower paced learners may benefit from creating their own visual dictionary of nouns and adjectives in this list. They can either draw their own depictions or use images from the Internet, magazines, etc.

Juego The cognates in this list are: **el santo patrón, la santa patrona, una procesión, el cementerio, el mausoleo, la tumba, una ofrenda, un cráneo, un esqueleto, una máscara, la chimenea, el camello, decorar, Hanuka, la menora, hebreo(a), una banda municipal, iluminar, celebrar.**

Don't forget the chapter project and cultural activities. Students have learned all the information that they will need to complete these engaging enrichment tasks.

Repaso cumulativo

Every chapter of **¡Así se dice!** contains this review section of previously learned material. By recycling information from previous chapters, the cumulative review serves to remind students that they need to continue practicing what they have learned after finishing each chapter.

Activity 1 This activity reviews the present and the preterite of stem-changing verbs.

Audio Script

1. ¿Quién sirve la comida en un restaurante?
2. Ellos se vistieron elegantemente.
3. Yo lo repito.
4. Usted prefirió este, ¿no?
5. ¿Cuántas horas dormiste?
6. El cocinero fríe las papas.

Activity 2 This activity reviews present and preterite verbs.

Cultural Snapshot

Rawson is a small city in Patagonia. It is located on the mouth of the Chubut River and has just over one hundred thousand inhabitants.

Repaso cumulativo

Repasa lo que ya has aprendido

These activities will help you review and remember what you have learned so far in Spanish.

1 **Escucha las frases. Indica en una tabla como la de abajo si la frase describe una acción en el presente o el pasado.**

presente	pasado

2 **Personaliza. Da respuestas personales.**

1. ¿A qué escuela fuiste el año pasado?
2. ¿Cuántos cursos tomaste?
3. ¿En qué curso recibiste la nota más alta?
4. ¿Qué curso te gustó más?
5. El año pasado, ¿trabajaste después de las clases?
6. Y este año, ¿a qué escuela vas?
7. ¿Cuántos cursos tienes?
8. ¿En qué curso recibes la nota más alta?
9. ¿Qué curso te gusta más?
10. ¿Trabajas después de las clases?

CULTURA
El corredor de un colegio en Rawson en la Patagonia argentina

Andrew Payti

Answers

1
1. presente
2. pasado
3. presente
4. pasado
5. pasado
6. presente

2 *Answers will vary, but may include:*
1. El año pasado fui a ___.
2. Tomé ___ cursos.
3. Recibí la nota más alta en ___.
4. Me gustó más ___.
5. Sí (No), el año pasado (no) trabajé después de las clases.
6. Este año voy a ___.
7. Tengo ___ cursos este año.
8. Recibo la nota más alta en ___.
9. Me gusta más ___.
10. Sí, (No, no) trabajo después de las clases.

3 *Answers will vary, but may include:*
La muchacha habla con el dependiente. Ella quiere comprar un blue jean. El cliente habla con la dependiente. El cliente va a pagar en la caja. En la tienda de ropa se venden zapatos, pantalones y mochilas.

4
1. me
2. se
3. me, me
4. nos
5. me
6. se
7. te
8. Te

5
1. peinarme
2. peinarse
3. peinarse
4. peinarnos
5. peinarte

Go Online!

connectED.mcgraw-hill.com

3 **Describe todo lo que ves en la tienda de ropa. ¿Qué está haciendo la gente?**

4 **Completa con el pronombre reflexivo.**

1. Yo ____ levanto a las seis y media.
2. Mi hermano ____ viste enseguida.
3. Yo no. Yo ____ lavo la cara y ____ cepillo los dientes.
4. Nosotros ____ sentamos a la mesa para tomar el desayuno.
5. Luego yo ____ visto y salimos para la escuela.
6. Ellos ____ divierten durante la fiesta.
7. Y tú, ¿a qué hora ____ acuestas?
8. ¿____ bañas por la mañana o por la noche?

5 **Completa con peinarse.**

1. Yo quiero ____.
2. Él quiere ____.
3. Ellos quieren ____.
4. Nosotros queremos ____.
5. ¿Tú quieres ____?

6 **Juego** **Mira los dibujos. Son similares pero hay unas pequeñas diferencias. ¿Cuáles son?**

David H. Brennan

Repaso cumulativo

Activity 3 This activity reviews clothing and store vocabulary.

Activity 4 This activity reviews reflexive pronouns.

Activity 5 This activity reviews reflexive verbs.

Activity 6 This activity reviews clothing, color, and food vocabulary.

Go Online!

The **¡Así se dice!** Audio Program for Chapter 5 has twenty-two activities, which afford students extensive listening and speaking practice.

Pre-AP To give students further open-ended oral or written practice, or to assess proficiency, go to AP Proficiency Practice AP13 and AP14.

Answers

6

1. El señor con la camisa verde tiene una cámara.
   El señor con la camisa verde no tiene una cámara.
2. Hay una niña con el señor con la camisa verde y la señora con el vestido azul.
   No hay una niña con el señor con la camisa verde y la señora con el vestido azul.
3. El señor con la camisa blanca de mangas largas tiene una mochila.
   El señor con la camisa blanca de mangas largas no tiene una mochila.
4. La camisa del señor delante de la carnicería es rosa.
   La camisa del señor delante de la carnicería es azul.
5. El señor con la camisa blanca de mangas cortas tiene anteojos de sol.
   El señor con la camisa blanca de mangas cortas no tiene anteojos de sol.
6. La clienta delante de la frutería tiene una falda azul.
   La clienta delante de la frutería tiene una falda anaranjada.
7. El dependiente en la frutería tiene bananas en la mano.
   El dependiente en la frutería no tiene bananas en la mano.
8. Hay una muchacha con la señora que está comprando queso.
   Hay un muchacho con la señora que está comprando queso.

Chapter Overview
Tecnomundo
Scope and Sequence

Topics
- Computers and e-mail
- Digital cameras and MP3s
- Making and receiving phone calls
- Technology in Hispanic countries

Culture
- Public telephones in the Spanish-speaking world

Functions
- How to talk about computers, the Internet, and e-mail
- How to talk about a digital camera and an MP3 player
- How to make and receive phone calls
- How to discuss technology in Hispanic countries

Structure
- The preterite
- The imperfect

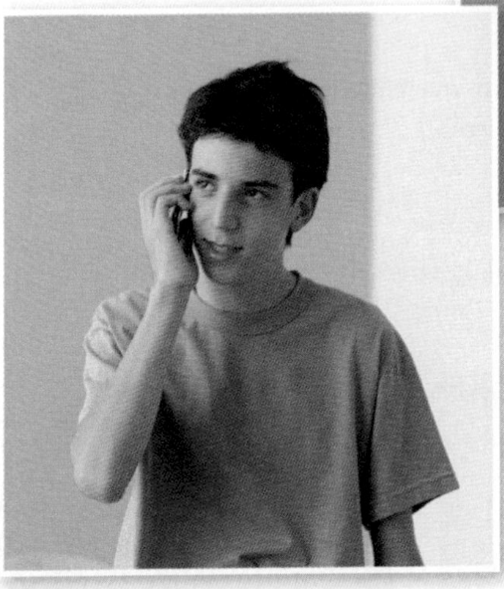

Planning Guide

	required	recommended	optional
Vocabulario 1 La computadora, El ordenador	✔		
Vocabulario 2 Fotos y música Llamadas telefónicas	✔		
Gramática Verbos como **querer, creer** en el pasado El pretérito y el imperfecto Dos acciones pasadas en la misma frase	✔		
Conversación Se cortó la línea.		✔	
Lectura cultural En un mundo tecnológico		✔	
Lectura Un poco más La tecnología de hoy y ayer			✔
Prepárate para el examen			✔
Repaso cumulativo			✔

Correlations to ACTFL World-Readiness Standards for Learning Languages

Page numbers in light print refer to the Student Edition.
Page numbers in bold print refer to the Teacher Edition.

COMMUNICATION Communicate effectively in more than one language in order to function in a variety of situations and for multiple purposes		
Interpersonal Communication	Learners interact and negotiate meaning in spoken, signed, or written conversations to share information, reactions, feelings, and opinions.	pp. **168C, 168D, 170–171, 173,** 175, **175, 177, 178,** 179, **182, 183,** 185, **185, 189, 190,** 194
Interpretive Communication	Learners understand, interpret, and analyze what is heard, read, or viewed on a variety of topics.	pp. **172,** 174, **174, 176,** 178, 179, **179,** 181, 182, **185, 186,** 187, **187,** 188, **188,** 189, **189, 190,** 191, 193, **193,** 198, **199**
Presentational Communication	Learners present information, concepts, and ideas to inform, explain, persuade, and narrate on a variety of topics using appropriate media and adapting to various audiences of listeners, readers, or viewers.	pp. **168C, 173, 174, 176, 177,** 178, 180, 183, **185, 187, 188, 192,** 194, 195, **196**
CULTURES Interact with cultural competence and understanding		
Relating Cultural Practices to Perspectives	Learners use the language to investigate, explain, and reflect on the relationship between the practices and perspectives of the cultures studied.	pp. 170–171, **170–171,** 172, 173, 177, **177,** 188, 189, 190, 193
Relating Cultural Products to Perspectives	Learners use the language to investigate, explain, and reflect on the relationship between the products and perspectives of the cultures studied.	pp. **168D,** 179, **180,** 191
CONNECTIONS Connect with other disciplines and acquire information and diverse perspectives in order to use the language to function in academic and career-related situations		
Making Connections	Learners build, reinforce, and expand their knowledge of other disciplines while using the language to develop critical thinking and to solve problems creatively.	pp. **168C, 168D, 170–171,** 194, 198, **198**
Acquiring Information and Diverse Perspectives	Learners access and evaluate information and diverse perspectives that are available through the language and its cultures.	pp. **168D,** 172, **173,** 176, **176,** 177, 183, 185, **185,** 191, **191,** 195, 197, **197**
COMPARISONS Develop insight into the nature of language and culture in order to interact with cultural competence		
Language Comparisons	Learners use the language to investigate, explain, and reflect on the nature of language through comparisons of the language studied and their own.	pp. 172, 173, **196,** 197
Cultural Comparisons	Learners use the language to investigate, explain, and reflect on the concept of culture through comparisons of the cultures studied and their own.	pp. 169, **169, 170,** 185, 187, 188, 190
COMMUNITIES Communicate and interact with cultural competence in order to participate in multilingual communities at home and around the world		
School and Global Communities	Learners use the language both within and beyond the classroom to interact and collaborate in their community and the globalized world.	pp. **168C, 174,** 178, **183, 192,** 194, **194, 196**
Lifelong Learning	Learners set goals and reflect on their progress in using languages for enjoyment, enrichment, and advancement.	pp. **168C, 168D,** 176, **176, 187,** 191, **191**

Chapter Project

Un sitio Web

Students will work individually and in small groups to design a Web site for their Spanish class. At the end, a contest will be held in which students will vote on the top three designs.

Note: This project does not require that students create a live Web site. They will imagine what the content of a Web site would be and how it would appear.

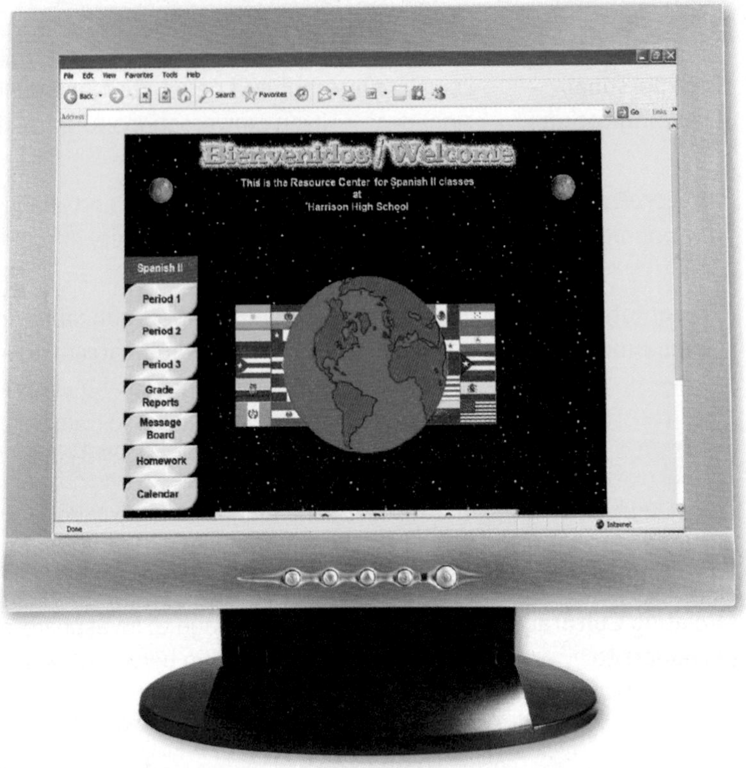

1. Divide the class into small groups of three or four and have each group brainstorm ideas for a Web site design. You may wish to give students a list of basic elements to be included in their sites, such as the time and location that the class meets, information about their teacher and class members, a syllabus or schedule of the due dates for tests and other major assignments, a calendar of the school year, a photo gallery, and links to important or useful Web sites. Remind students that all possible text should be in Spanish.
2. Each group member will be responsible for designing a portion of the Web site. Individual students should include at least three visual elements, sketch the layout, and draft any text to be included in his or her portion. Students will then get together in their groups to peer edit each other's drafts and make any final adjustments to the Web site's overall layout and design.
3. Once corrections have been made, students should work together to create the final version of their group's Web site. All drafts and visual representations should be handed in along with the finished product, with a list of who worked on each portion.

Technology Expansion: If your school provides you with the capabilities, have students put the winning Web site design up live on the Internet. You may wish to give students the opportunity to earn extra credit by helping to maintain and update the Web site throughout the remainder of the school year.

Scoring Rubric for Project

	5	3	1
Evidence of planning	Corrected layout and text draft are provided.	Layout and first text draft are provided but are not corrected.	Layout and first text draft are not provided.
Use of illustrations	Web site design uses several visual elements.	Web site design uses few visual elements.	Web site design does not use any visual elements.
Presentation	Web site design contains all the required elements.	Web site design contains some of the required elements.	Web site design contains few of the required elements.

Culture

Recipe

ARROZ CON LECHE

Ingredients: (makes 6–8 servings)
1 cup long-grain white rice
1½ cups water
1 cinnamon stick
lemon or orange zest (optional)
1 can condensed milk
1 can evaporated milk
1 cup whole milk
½ cup raisins
ground cinnamon for garnish

In a saucepan bring water, rice, cinnamon stick, and fruit zest to a boil. Reduce heat, cover, and simmer until most of the water has been absorbed. Stir in condensed, evaporated, and whole milk and continue to cook on low heat, stirring constantly until the mixture thickens (about 15 minutes). Remove cinnamon stick and fruit zest and stir in raisins. Sprinkle with ground cinnamon before serving.

Música latina

As technology has advanced, music from other countries and cultures has become more accessible. In recent years, music from the Spanish-speaking world has become more popular and influential in the music industry. Although the term **música latina** is often used to describe Latin pop music, the musical expressions of Spanish speakers are as diverse and varied as the people and cultures of the countries they inhabit, as these examples demonstrate: **bachata, bolero, chachachá, cumbia, flamenco, jazz latino, mambo, mariachi, merengue, música andina, música clásica, pop latino, ranchera, reggaetón, rock en español, rumba, salsa, son cubano, tango,** and **tejano.** You may wish to play samples of different styles of Hispanic music and have students guess what kind of music it is and where it originated or is most popular. Such an activity could then serve as a springboard for students to use Spanish-language entertainment resources to learn more about Hispanic musical styles or famous Hispanic musicians. You can teach students songs that demonstrate different aspects of the vocabulary and grammar being studied. Or, you can present various songs along with a cloze lyrics activity and have the class listen to fill in missing words. Lastly, ask students to determine what the song is about and what message the songwriter was trying to convey.

Connection to Fine Art

Have students look online or in an art text to find *Nueva visión* by Argentine painter Ernesto Bertani. Have students describe this painting in Spanish. Then elicit their interpretations of what the painting and its title mean. Why is the book painted like a rainbow? Why is the computer wearing a suit and tie? Does the artist have a positive or negative opinion of modern technology? Ask students to sketch some ideas for their own *Nueva visión* painting and label items in Spanish.

50-Minute Lesson Plans

	Objective	Present	Practice	Assess/Homework
Day 1	Talk about computers	Chapter Opener (5 min.) Introducción al tema (10 min.) Core Instruction/Vocabulario 1 (20 min.)	Activities 1–4 (15 min.)	Student Workbook Activities A–C **ConnectEd** Vocabulary Practice
Day 2	Talk about computers	Quick Start (5 min.) Review Vocabulario 1 (10 min.)	Activities 5–8 (15 min.) Total Physical Response (5 min.) Audio Activities A–C (15 min.)	Student Workbook Activities D–F **ConnectEd** Vocabulary Practice
Day 3	Talk about electronic devices	Core Instruction/Vocabulario 2 (15 min.) Video, Vocabulario en vivo (10 min.)	Activities 1–3 (10 min.) Foldables (5 min.)	Quiz 1 (10 min.) Student Workbook Activities A–C **ConnectEd** Vocabulary Practice
Day 4	Talk about electronic devices	Quick Start (5 min.) Review Vocabulario 2 (5 min.)	Activities 4–7 (15 min.) Total Physical Response (5 min.) InfoGap (10 min.) Audio Activities D–G (10 min.)	Student Workbook Activities D–E **ConnectEd** Vocabulary Practice
Day 5	Verbs like **querer, creer** in the past tense The preterite and the imperfect	Quick Start (5 min.) Core Instruction/Gramática, Verbos como **querer, creer** en el pasado (10 min.) Core Instruction/Gramática, El pretérito y el imperfecto (10 min.)	Activities 1–3 (10 min.) Activity 4 (5 min.)	Quiz 2 (10 min.) Student Workbook Activities A–B **ConnectEd** Grammar Practice
Day 6	The preterite and the imperfect	Quick Start (5 min.) Review Gramática, El pretérito y el imperfecto (10 min.)	Activities 5–10 (20 min.) Audio Activities A–C (15 min.)	Student Workbook Activities C–D **ConnectEd** Grammar Practice
Day 7	Two past actions in the same sentence	Quick Start (5 min.) Core Instruction/Gramática, Dos acciones pasadas en la misma frase (10 min.)	Activities 11–15 (15 min.) Audio Activity D (10 min.)	Quiz 3 (10 min.) Student Workbook Activities A–B **ConnectEd** Grammar Practice
Day 8	Develop reading and listening comprehension skills	Quick Start (5 min.) Core Instruction/Conversación (20 min.)	¿Comprendes? A–C (15 min.)	Quiz 4 (10 min.) **ConnectEd** Conversation
Day 9	Discuss technology in Hispanic countries	Core Instruction/Lectura cultural (20 min.)	¿Comprendes? A–B (15 min.)	Listening Comprehension Test (15 min.) ¿Comprendes? C–D **ConnectEd** Reading Practice
Day 10	Develop reading comprehension skills	Core Instruction/Lectura Un poco más (10 min.) Video, Diálogo en vivo (10 min.)	¿Comprendes? (5 min.) Prepárate para el examen (25 min.)	Prepárate para el examen, Practice for written proficiency **ConnectEd** Reading Practice
Day 11	Chapter review	Repaso del Capítulo 6 (15 min.)	Prepárate para el examen, Practice for oral proficiency (20 min.)	Test for Writing Proficiency (15 min.) Review for chapter test
Day 12	Chapter 6 Tests (50 min.) Reading and Writing Test Speaking Test		Test for Oral Proficiency Test for Reading Comprehension	

90-Minute Lesson Plans

	Objective	Present	Practice	Assess/Homework
Block 1	Talk about computers	Chapter Opener (5 min.) Introducción al tema (15 min.) Quick Start (5 min.) Core Instruction/Vocabulario 1 (20 min.)	Activities 1–8 (25 min.) Total Physical Response (5 min.) Audio Activities A–C (15 min.)	Student Workbook Activities A–F **ConnectEd** Vocabulary Practice
Block 2	Talk about electronic devices	Quick Start (5 min.) Core Instruction/Vocabulario 2 (20 min.) Video, Vocabulario en vivo (10 min.)	Activities 1–7 (15 min.) Total Physical Response (5 min.) Foldables (5 min.) InfoGap (5 min.) Audio Activities D–G (15 min.)	Quiz 1 (10 min.) Student Workbook Activities A–E **ConnectEd** Grammar Practice
Block 3	Verbs like **querer, creer** in the past tense The preterite and the imperfect	Quick Start (5 min.) Core Instruction/Gramática, Verbos como **querer, creer** en el pasado (10 min.) Core Instruction/Gramática, El pretérito y el imperfecto (15 min.)	Activities 1–3 (15 min.) Activities 4–7 (20 min.) Audio Activities A–B (15 min.)	Quiz 2 (10 min.) Student Workbook Activities A–B **ConnectEd** Grammar Practice
Block 4	The preterite and the imperfect Two past actions in the same sentence	Quick Start (5 min.) Review Gramática, El pretérito y el imperfecto (10 min.) Quick Start (5 min.) Core Instruction/Gramática, Dos acciones pasadas en la misma frase (15 min.)	Activities 8–10 (20 min.) Activities 11–15 (20 min.) Audio Activities C–D (15 min.)	Student Workbook Activities C–D Student Workbook Activities A–B **ConnectEd** Grammar Practice
Block 5	Discuss technology in Hispanic countries	Quick Start (5 min.) Core Instruction/Conversación (20 min.) Core Instruction/Lectura cultural (20 min.)	¿Comprendes? A–C (15 min.) ¿Comprendes? A–B (10 min.)	Quizzes 3–4 (20 min.) ¿Comprendes? C–D Prepárate para el examen, Practice for written proficiency **ConnectEd** Conversation Reading Practice
Block 6	Develop reading comprehension skills	Core Instruction/Lectura Un poco más (15 min.) Video, Cultura en vivo (10 min.)	¿Comprendes? (5 min.) Prepárate para el examen (20 min.) Prepárate para el examen, Practice for oral proficiency (25 min.)	Listening Comprehension Test (15 min.) Review for chapter test **ConnectEd** Reading Practice
Block 7	Chapter 6 Tests (50 min.) Reading and Writing Test Speaking Test Test for Oral Proficiency Test for Writing Proficiency Test for Reading Comprehension Chapter Project (40 min.)			

Preview

In this chapter, students will learn the vocabulary they need to talk about modern technology such as computers and e-mail. They will also learn to communicate when speaking on a telephone or cell phone. Students will observe how their counterparts in Spain and Latin America make use of these technological advancements. They will also learn the difference between the preterite and imperfect.

Pacing

It is important to note that once you reach **¡Bravo!** in the chapter, there is no more new material for students to learn. The rest of the chapter recycles what has already been covered. The suggested pacing listed here leaves two to three days for review, assessment, and enrichment activities such as the chapter project.

Vocabulario 1	1–2 days
Vocabulario 2	1–2 days
Gramática	2–3 days
Conversación	1 day
Lectura cultural	1 day
Lectura Un poco más	1 day

CAPÍTULO 6

Tecnomundo

Daniel Salsgiver

168 **Go Online!** connectED.mcgraw-hill.com Audio Video Práctica Repaso Diversiones eScape ePals

Go Online!

Audio
Listen to spoken Spanish.

Video
Watch and learn about the Spanish-speaking world.

Práctica
Practice your skills.

Repaso
Review what you've learned.

Diversiones
Go beyond the classroom.

eScape
Read about current events in the Spanish-speaking world.

Aquí y Allí

Vamos a comparar ¿Puedes imaginar el mundo sin computadoras? ¿Usas tu computadora con frecuencia? ¿Para qué la usas? ¿Qué piensas? ¿Tienen computadora los jóvenes de España y Latinoamérica? Vamos a ver la influencia de la tecnología en su vida diaria.

Objetivos

You will:

- talk about computers, the Internet, and e-mail
- talk about a digital camera and an MP3 player
- make and receive phone calls
- discuss technology in Hispanic countries

You will use:

- the preterite and imperfect tenses

La gente está usando sus aparatos electrónicos para sacar fotos de unas obras arquitectónicas de Antoni Gaudí en el Parque Güell en Barcelona, España. Aquí vemos una serie de viaductos que construyó Gaudí para poder andar por el parque.

SPOTLIGHT ON CULTURE

Cultural Comparison
The photographs in the **Introducción al tema** section of this chapter give students a more personal view of students using their cell phones, digital cameras, and computers in Spain and Latin America. Throughout the chapter, students can compare and contrast their reliance on and use of today's technology with that of their Spanish-speaking counterparts.

Cultural Snapshot
Parc Güell in Barcelona was first built to be a model type English village, but it was never completed as such and became a beautiful park.

Interactive Whiteboard
Present or practice with interactive whiteboard activities.

Assessment
Check student progress.

ePals
Connect with Spanish-speaking students around the world.

Introducción al tema

PRESENT

Introduce the theme of the chapter by having students look at the photographs on these pages. Have them look at the young people and determine if there is anything they see them doing that is the same or different from what they do with their own friends. Once you have completed the vocabulary presentation, have students return to these pages and read the information that accompanies each photograph. Once students are fully acquainted with the vocabulary and grammar of the chapter, you may wish to come back to these pages and ask the questions that go with each photo.

Cultural Snapshot

Venezuela Estas dos jóvenes en San Juan, Venezuela, ¿andaban a pie o iban en bici? ¿Llevaban una camiseta? ¿Tienen un emblema las camisetas? ¿Hablaba una muchacha en su móvil? ¿Le gustó la conversación? ¿Qué tenía en su cara?

España Lanzarote is the fourth largest of the Canary Islands and it is almost completely made of solidified lava. It hardly ever rains on Lanzarote and there are no springs or lakes. Still, it has become quite a destination for European tourists. ¿Qué sigue siendo un medio de comunicación importante en muchas partes del mundo hispanohablante? ¿Cuál es la capital y ciudad más grande de la isla de Lanzarote?

Introducción al tema

Tecnomundo

Mira estas fotos para familiarizarte con el tema de este capítulo—la tecnología hoy en día. No hay duda que los avances tecnológicos en el campo de la informática cambian rápidamente y siguen influyendo la vida de muchos en todos los rincones del mundo.

Venezuela

Las dos jóvenes están caminando en San Juan, Venezuela. A una le gusta la conversación en su móvil.

España

El teléfono público sigue siendo un medio de comunicación corriente en muchas partes del mundo hispano. Aquí vemos unos teléfonos públicos en Arrecife, Lanzarote, en las islas Canarias.

Estados Unidos

Esta joven de ascendencia mexicana se divertía escuchando música en su MP3 después de las clases.

Panamá

De este centro de llamadas en Panamá se puede hacer llamadas telefónicas a muchas partes del mundo. ¿Qué tal te parecen las tarifas? ¿Son altas o no?

(tr)Kelli Drummer-Avendaño, (bl)Yellow Dog Productions/Getty Images, (others)Andrew Payti

Estados Unidos ¿Es mexicanoamericana esta muchacha? ¿Qué tiene en la mano? ¿Tiene los auriculares en los oídos? ¿Qué escucha ella en su MP3?

Panamá This type of calling center is popular in many areas of Latin America. Note that U.S. currency is used in Panama. A tu parecer, ¿son caras o baratas las llamadas telefónicas de Panamá?

Go Online!

connectED.mcgraw-hill.com

Argentina

Una muchacha argentina usa su computadora portátil en un parque de Buenos Aires.

México

Estas carteleras en la Ciudad de México tienen muchos anuncios de publicidad.

Nicaragua

Esta tienda en León, Nicaragua, ofrece muchos servicios.

Nicaragua

Los jóvenes están jugando juegos de video en este salón de videos en León, Nicaragua.

171

Introducción al tema

Argentina This park is located just in front of the Casa Rosada, or Pink House, which houses the offices of the President of the Republic. **¿De qué nacionalidad es la muchacha? ¿Qué está usando? ¿Dónde?**

Nicaragua Have students guess the services available in this store.

México Central Mexico City has many attactive, rather modern high-rise buildings sporting money and advertisements.

Nicaragua **¿Qué estaban mirando los jóvenes? ¿Los veían en la pantalla de un televisor?**

Online Resources

Customizable Lesson Plans
Whiteboard Lesson
Audio Activities
Student Workbook
Enrichment
Quizzes

Quick Start

Use QS 6.1 or write the following on the board.
Answer.

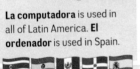

1. **¿Estudias español en la escuela?**
2. **¿Usan ustedes la computadora en clase?**
3. **¿Levantas la mano cuando tienes una pregunta?**
4. **¿Contesta la profesora tu pregunta?**
5. **¿Hablas mucho en la clase de español?**

TEACH

Core Instruction

Step 1 Present the vocabulary first using Vocabulary V6.2–V6.3.

Step 2 As suggested in previous chapters, ask students questions to enable them to use their new words. Ask easier questions first, calling on slower paced learners and then ask more difficult questions of advanced learners. This allows students of different abilities to respond and participate while keeping the classroom pace moving.

Step 3 After the initial presentation, have students read the new vocabulary words.

La computadora, El ordenador

Cristina estaba sentada delante de su computadora.
Prendió la computadora.
Quería entrar en línea.
Por eso, hizo clic con el ratón.
Cuando terminó, apagó la computadora.

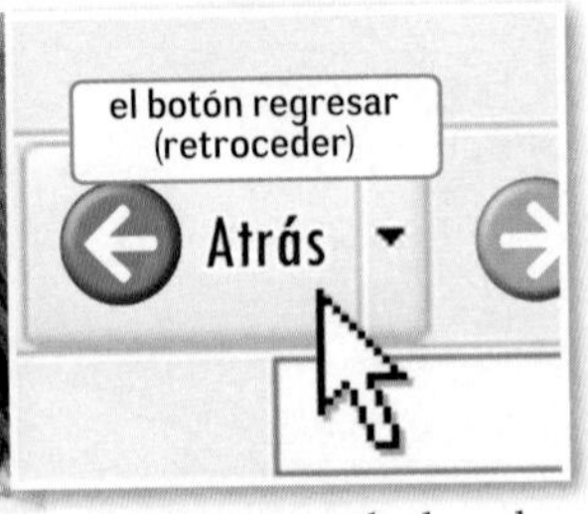

Cristina navegaba la red (el Internet).
Quería regresar a un sitio Web anterior.
Hizo clic en el botón regresar.

En otras partes

La computadora is used in all of Latin America. **El ordenador** is used in Spain.

José no quería guardar cierto archivo.
Ya no lo necesitó y lo borró.
Oprimió (Pulsó) el botón borrador.

Step 4 Read **En otras partes** aloud to students, especially if you have heritage speakers in your class.

Teaching Options

You may wish to present vocabulary by referring to an actual computer in the classroom.

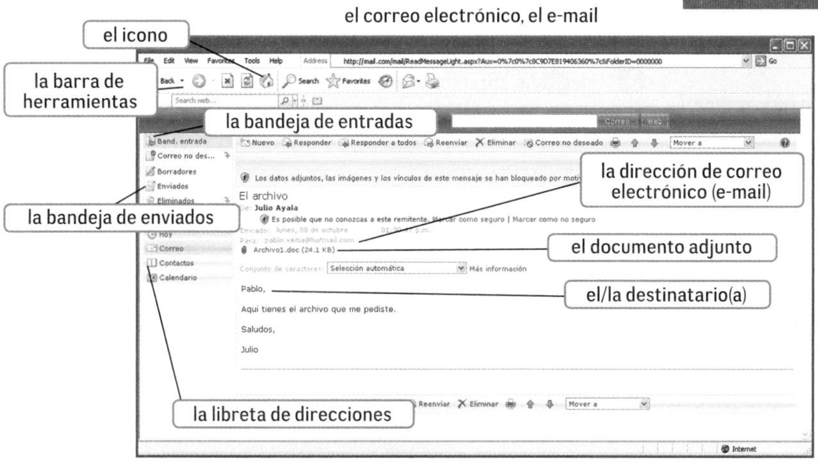

Hoy Paco recibió muchos correos electrónicos.
Los leyó todos pero no contestó todos.
Había tres que no le interesaron y los borró.
Enviaba un correo cuando sonó su móvil (celular).

¿Lo sabes?

Así se lee o se da una dirección de e-mail en español.

josésalas@terra.es
José Salas arroba terra punto España

Observa que además de *com, net, org,* etc., se usa el país.

El padre de José Luis recibió un boleto aéreo electrónico por correo electrónico.
Quería una copia dura de su boleto y lo imprimió.
La sacó de la impresora.

Differentiation

Multiple Intelligences

Have **visual-spatial** and **bodily-kinesthetic** learners watch as you demonstrate and describe computer procedures on a classroom computer. Have them repeat the same procedure and tell what they are doing using their new vocabulary.

About the Spanish Language

The word **ordenador** is used in Spain. It comes from the French *ordinateur.*

Cultural Snapshot

The photos on these pages were taken in Puerto Rico.

Comunicación

Interpersonal
Have students say their e-mail addresses in Spanish.

Go Online!

You may wish to use the whiteboard presentation for additional vocabulary instruction and practice.

Total Physical Response (TPR)

(Student 1), **ven acá, por favor.**
Siéntate delante de tu computadora.
Toma el ratón.
Haz clic.
Entra unos datos.
Oprime el botón para borrar algo.
Gracias, *(Student 1).*
(Student 2), **ven acá.**
Siéntate delante de tu computadora.
Ve en línea.
Quieres reservar un vuelo.
Mira la información sobre el vuelo en la pantalla.
Oprime el botón para imprimir tu boleto.
Saca tu boleto de la impresora.

Leveling EACH Activity

Easy Activities 1, 2, 3
Average Activities 4, 6, 7
CHallenging Activity 3
Expansión, Activities 5, 8, 9

PRACTICE

Activities ①, ②, and ③
These activities can be done orally in class.

Go Online!

You may wish to remind students to go online for additional vocabulary practice. They can also download audio files of all vocabulary.

Comunicación

Presentational

Heritage Speakers
After going over these activities, have heritage speakers give a brief presentation about how they use their computers. Through their presentation, the other students may learn some additional vocabulary.

HABLAR • ESCRIBIR

1 Identifica las partes de la computadora.

LEER

2 Verifica. ¿Sí o no?

	sí	no
1. Cada sitio Web tiene su página inicial.		
2. Si quieres volver a un sitio, haz clic en el botón retroceder.		
3. Dentro de (En) un archivo hay varias carpetas.		
4. Si quieres guardar un documento lo tienes que borrar.		
5. Cada correo electrónico tiene un documento adjunto.		
6. Para hacer una copia dura de un documento necesitas una impresora.		
7. Si quieres leer de nuevo (una vez más) un correo electrónico que enviaste ayer tienes que abrir tu bandeja de entradas.		

HABLAR • ESCRIBIR

3 Personaliza. Da respuestas personales.

1. ¿Tienes una computadora portátil?
2. ¿Eres muy aficionado(a) a la computadora?
3. ¿Usas la computadora para hacer tus tareas escolares? ¿Cómo?
4. ¿Para qué navegas el Internet (la red)?
5. ¿Recibes y envías muchos correos electrónicos?
6. ¿Cuál es tu dirección de e-mail?
7. ¿Recibes muchos correos electrónicos que borras enseguida?
8. ¿Cuándo tienes que consultar tu libreta de direcciones?
9. ¿Apagas la computadora cuando no la usas?

EXPANSIÓN

Ahora, sin mirar las preguntas, cuenta la información en tus propias palabras. Si no recuerdas algo, un(a) compañero(a) te puede ayudar.

CULTURA
Una cartelera divertida en Buenos Aires

Andrew Payti

Answers

1 *Answers will vary but may include:*
la pantalla de escritorio, el ratón, el teclado

2
1. sí
2. sí
3. no
4. no
5. no
6. sí
7. no

3 *Answers will vary but may include:*
1. Sí, (No, no) tengo una computadora portátil.
2. Sí, (No, no) soy muy aficionado(a) a la computadora.
3. Sí, (No, no) uso la computadora para hacer mis tareas escolares.
4. Navego el Internet (la red) para ___.
5. Sí, (No, no) recibo y (no) envío muchos correos electrónicos.
6. Mi dirección de e-mail es ___.
7. Sí, (No, no) recibo muchos correos electrónicos que borro enseguida.
8. Tengo que consultar mi libreta de direcciones cuando ___.
9. Sí, (No, no) apago la computadora cuando no la uso.

Go Online!

connectED.mcgraw-hill.com

LEER

4 **¡Te toca a ti!** Parea cada verbo con una palabra o expresión apropiada.

1. sonar	**a.** en línea
2. imprimir	**b.** el correo electrónico
3. enviar	**c.** el botón
4. borrar	**d.** una copia
5. entrar	**e.** el archivo
6. oprimir	**f.** el móvil

HABLAR • ESCRIBIR

5 Usa cada expresión de la Actividad 4 en una frase original.

LEER • ESCRIBIR

6 Completa con una palabra apropiada.

1. César quería abrir su bandeja de entradas e hizo clic con el ____.
2. Había muchos ____ nuevos en su bandeja de entradas. Los recibió hoy.
3. Él los leyó. Había tres que no le interesaron y los ____.
4. Recibió uno de un buen amigo. Él lo contestó enseguida y guardó la respuesta en su ____.
5. César ____ la computadora cuando empezó a trabajar y la ____ cuando terminó.

LEER • ESCRIBIR

7 Expresa de otra manera.

1. Ella siempre está sentada delante de su *ordenador.*
2. El sitio tiene una página *de inicio* interesante.
3. Ella navegaba *el Internet.*
4. Tienes que *pulsar* el botón borrador.
5. ¿Cuál es tu dirección de *e-mail*?

Comunicación

8 Trabaja con un(a) compañero(a) de clase. Usando el vocabulario y expresiones que ya conocen, discutan lo que hacen con su computadora. ¿Quién la usa más?

9 Usa el Internet para buscar eventos y actividades culturales de la región donde vives. Luego, busca eventos y actividades de una ciudad hispanohablante. Comparte lo que descubriste con tus compañeros(as) de clase. ¿Quién descubrió el evento cultural más interesante? ¿Dónde y cuándo tiene lugar?

Vocabulario 1

Activities 3 and 5 These activities can also be done as paired activities.

Activities 4, 5, 6, and 7 These activities should be prepared first and then gone over in class.

Activity 8 Encourage students to use only words and expressions they know as they describe how they use their computers.

¡Así se dice!

Why It Works!

Vocabulary is an extremely important tool in language acquisition. To enable students to learn and use the language with relative ease we have presented thirty-nine vocabulary practice items in the Student Edition, forty-two in the Workbook, and twelve on the Audio Activities. This is in addition to the open-ended communication activity. Students learn a language by using it and we help them use it!

ASSESS

Students are now ready to take Quiz 1.

Answers

4
1. f
2. d
3. b
4. e
5. a
6. c

5 *Answers will vary.*

6
1. ratón
2. correos electrónicos (e-mails)
3. borró
4. bandeja de enviados
5. prendió, apagó

7
1. computadora
2. inicial (frontal)
3. la red
4. oprimir
5. correo electrónico

8 *Answers will vary.*

9 *Answers will vary.*

Online Resources

Customizable Lesson Plans
Whiteboard Lesson
Audio Activities
Video (Vocabulario)
Student Workbook
Enrichment
Quizzes

Quick Start

Use QS 6.2 or write the following on the board.

Rewrite using an object pronoun.

1. **Estudio *español* en la escuela.**
2. **Leo *el artículo.***
3. **Escribo *la biografía de San Martín.***
4. **Pongo *las fotografías* en un álbum.**
5. **Veo *a mis amigos.***

TEACH

Core Instruction

Step 1 Present the vocabulary using Vocabulary V6.4–V6.5.

Step 2 Here are some examples of leveled questions from easy to challenging concerning the first photograph. **¿Descarga fotos Cristina? ¿Qué descarga ella? ¿Quién descarga fotos? ¿Las descarga en su computadora? ¿Toma Cristina las fotos con su cámara digital? ¿Las toma con su móvil? ¿Con qué las toma Cristina?** This enables students to hear and use the same word many times.

Differentiation

Multiple Intelligences

Step 3 Call on **bodily-kinesthetic** learners to present the short **Para conversar** section using as much animation and intonation as possible.

Fotos y música

una cámara digital

A Cristina le encanta la fotografía.
Siempre descarga (baja) las fotos que toma con su cámara digital o su móvil a su computadora.

A Anita le encanta la música.
Siempre baja sus canciones favoritas a su MP3.

Llamadas telefónicas

¡Ah! Es mi amigo Paco.
el timbre (sonoro)
un móvil, un (teléfono) celular

Sonó el móvil de Patricia.
Sabía quien la llamaba por el timbre.
Es el timbre que asignó a su mejor amigo.

Para conversar
¡Hola! Pepe, ¿eres tú? No te oigo bien. Estás cortando. ¿Me escuchas?
¡Hola!
Ah, se nos cortó la línea. Una llamada perdida (caída).

David H. Brennan

Go Online!

Vocabulario en vivo Watch and listen to Nora as she discusses and uses everyday technology.

Total Physical Response (TPR)

(Student), **ven acá.**
Toma tu móvil. Está sonando.
Contesta el móvil.
Habla. Te está cortando la línea.
Termina la llamada.
Ves algo y quieres una foto.
Toma la foto con tu móvil.

Juan y Teresa estaban en España. Usaron un teléfono público para llamar a casa.
Para llamar a Estados Unidos, tenían que marcar el prefijo del país.

Go Online!

connectED.mcgraw-hill.com

En otras partes

- Regional terms you may hear when someone answers a telephone are: **¡Diga! ¡Dígame! ¡Hola! ¡Aló! ¡Bueno!**
- Another word for **un mensaje** is **un recado.**

Descolgó (el auricular).

Introdujo su tarjeta en la ranura.

Esperó el tono.

Marcó el número que deseaba.

Como contestar el teléfono

¡Hola!
¿Está Teresa, por favor?
Sí, está. ¿De parte de quién, por favor?
De Rafael. Rafael Lugones.
Un momento, por favor.

¡Hola!
¿Está Teresa, por favor?
Lo siento, pero no está.
¿Le puedo dejar un mensaje?
Cómo no, Señor.

Differentiation

Multiple Intelligences

If possible, use a toy public telephone to present vocabulary. This approach can help **visual-spatial** and **bodily-kinesthetic** learners.

Have **bodily-kinesthetic** learners act out the conversation at the bottom of the page.

Go Online!

You may wish to use the whiteboard presentation for additional vocabulary instruction and practice.

Cultura

Although the public telephone is seldom used in the United States, the public phone is still commonly used in Spain and Latin America in both rural and urban areas. In most cases people use a telephone card. The telephone card contains a number of units. When the units are finished the phone goes dead. Cards can be used for local, long distance, and international calls. Each type of call deducts its particular number of units per minute.

Tips for Success

- As soon as students are familiar with the new vocabulary, have them read again the captions of the **Introducción al tema.**
- After going over the **Práctica** activities, have students return to the vocabulary presentation pages and make up statements and questions about the photos.

Total Physical Response (TPR)

(Student), **ven acá.**
Vas a hacer una llamada telefónica.
Descuelga el auricular.
Toma tu tarjeta telefónica.
Introduce la tarjeta en la ranura.
Espera el tono.
Marca el número que deseas.
Está sonando. Alguien contesta. Dile «Hola».
Habla.
Termina la conversación y cuelga.
Gracias, *(Student).*

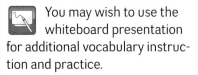

Leveling EACH Activity

Easy Activities 1, 2, 3
Average Activity 4
CHallenging Activities 5, 6, 7

PRACTICE

Activity 1

Audio Script

1. Se puede tomar fotos con un móvil.
2. Cada móvil o celular tiene el mismo timbre.
3. Al hablar en tu móvil, no puedes oír bien cuando se te corta la línea.
4. Cuando haces una llamada de larga distancia, hay que marcar la clave de área.
5. Si haces una llamada dentro de Estados Unidos tienes que marcar el prefijo del país.
6. En vez de usar monedas para hacer una llamada de un teléfono público mucha gente usa una tarjeta telefónica.
7. Antes de marcar un número es necesario descolgar.
8. Antes de marcar un número es necesario esperar el tono.

Activity 2 This activity should be gone over in class. Ask questions and call on students at random. Enabling all students to hear the answers reinforces the new vocabulary. This activity can also be done as a paired activity.

FOLDABLES Study Organizer

ENVELOPE FOLD

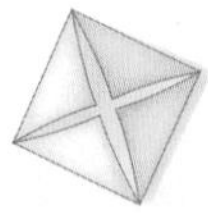

See the Foldables section of the Student Handbook at the beginning of this book for help with making this foldable. Use this study organizer with a partner to help you practice your new words. Draw a picture of a word on the top of each flap. Then pass the foldable to your partner who will write the word that corresponds with each picture on the reverse side of each flap. Take turns.

ESCUCHAR

1 Escucha y decide. Escucha cada frase y decide si la información es correcta o no. Usa una tabla como la de abajo para indicar tus respuestas.

correcta	incorrecta

HABLAR

2 Personaliza. Da respuestas personales.

1. ¿Tienes una cámara digital?
2. A veces, ¿bajas (descargas) las fotos que tomas en tu computadora?
3. ¿Qué bajas más en tu computadora? ¿Fotografías o canciones?
4. ¿Te gusta jugar videojuegos? ¿Cuál es tu favorito?
5. ¿Tienes un móvil?
6. ¿Cuál es el número de tu móvil?
7. ¿Tiene tu móvil un solo timbre o varios timbres?
8. ¿Tienes a veces llamadas perdidas cuando usas tu móvil?
9. ¿Hay muchos teléfonos públicos donde vives?
10. ¿Tiene tu familia un teléfono en casa? ¿Cuál es el número de su teléfono?

LEER • ESCRIBIR

3 Parea los sinónimos.

1. un celular
2. un ordenador
3. le gusta mucho
4. bajar
5. el código de área
6. una llamada perdida
7. ¡Bueno! (al contestar el teléfono)

a. descargar
b. una llamada caída
c. un móvil
d. le encanta
e. ¡Dígame!
f. la clave de área
g. una computadora

LEER • HABLAR

4 Contesta.
¿Para qué producto es el anuncio? ¿Qué significa **prepago**?

Andrew Payti

Answers

1
1. sí
2. no
3. sí
4. sí
5. no
6. sí
7. sí
8. sí

2 *Answers will vary but may include:*
1. Sí, (No, no) tengo una cámara digital.
2. Sí, (No, no) bajo (descargo) las fotos que tomo en mi computadora.
3. Bajo más fotografías (canciones) en mi computadora.
4. Sí, (No, no) me gusta jugar videojuegos. Mi favorito es ____.
5. Sí, (No, no) tengo un móvil.
6. El número de mi móvil es ____. (No tengo móvil.)
7. Mi móvil tiene un solo timbre (varios timbres). (No tengo móvil.)
8. Sí, (No, no) tengo unas llamadas perdidas cuando uso mi móvil.
9. Sí, (No, no) hay muchos teléfonos públicos donde vivo.
10. Sí (No), mi familia (no) tiene un teléfono en casa. El número de teléfono es ____.

3
1. c
2. g
3. d
4. a
5. f
6. b
7. e

4 *Answers will vary but may include:*
Es de Perú. **Prepago** significa que se paga antes de hacer la llamada.

HABLAR • ESCRIBIR

5 Estás hablando por teléfono. ¿Qué vas a decir?

1. Quieres saber si alguien está.
2. Quieres saber quién está llamando.
3. Quieres saber si la persona con quien hablas (tu interlocutor) te puede oír.
4. Quieres decirle que la conexión es mala.
5. Quieres decirle a la persona con quien hablas que alguien no está.
6. Quieres dejarle un mensaje a una persona que no está.
7. Quieres decirle a otra persona que tuviste una llamada perdida.

LEER • ESCRIBIR

6 Completa.

Para hacer una llamada de un teléfono público en España o Latinoamérica debes comprar una __1__. Primero tienes que __2__ el auricular y luego __3__ la tarjeta en la ranura. Es necesario esperar __4__ antes de __5__ el número que deseas. Si haces una llamada de larga distancia tienes que marcar primero __6__ y si haces una llamada internacional tienes que marcar __7__ también. Si no sabes un número de teléfono lo puedes buscar en __8__.

7 **Comunicación**

Trabaja con un(a) compañero(a) de clase. Uno(a) de ustedes hace una llamada telefónica y el/la otro(a) contesta. Conversen. Recuerda, si cometes un error gramatical, puedes decir, **«Perdón, digo... »** para clarificar.

Go Online!

connectED.mcgraw-hill.com

CULTURA

Mamá está haciendo una llamada telefónica en Miraflores, Perú. ¿Está introduciendo el niño una tarjeta en la ranura o está jugando?

InfoGap For more practice using your new vocabulary, do Activity 6 in the Student Resource section at the end of this book.

Una joven hablaba en su móvil mientras la otra leía un mensaje de texto.

Vocabulario 2

Activities 3, 4, 5, and 6 You may wish to have students prepare these activities before going over them in class.

Activity 5 Call on a student to read the activity in class as the others follow along and correct their papers.

Cultural Snapshot

(top) Miraflores is an attractive residential and commercial area of Lima.

Go Online!

You may wish to remind students to go online for additional vocabulary practice. They can also download audio files of all vocabulary.

ASSESS

Students are now ready to take Quiz 2.

Answers

5

1. ¿Está ___, por favor?
2. ¿De parte de quién, por favor?
3. ¿Me escucha(s)?
4. Está(s) cortando.
5. Lo siento, pero no está.
6. ¿Le puedo dejar un mensaje?
7. Se nos cortó la línea.

6

1. tarjeta telefónica
2. decolgar
3. introducir
4. el tono
5. marcar
6. la clave de área
7. el prefijo del país
8. la guía telefónica

7 *Answers will vary.*

Online Resources

Customizable Lesson Plans

Whiteboard Lesson

Student Workbook

Quick Start

Use QS 6.3 or write the following on the board.

Complete. Remember to use an infinitive.

1. **Quiero ___.**
2. **Siento ___.**
3. **Tengo ganas de ___.**
4. **Puedo ___.**
5. **Sé ___.**
6. **Me gusta ___.**

TEACH

Core Instruction

This point is quite easy and if students know their imperfect verb forms, they should have no trouble.

PRACTICE

Leveling EACH Activity

Easy Activity 1

Average Activity 2

CHallenging Activity 3

Cultural Snapshot

The colonial town of Antigua has many **talleres** and **galerías.**

Go Online!

You may wish to use the whiteboard presentation for additional grammar instruction and practice.

Verbos como querer, creer en el pasado

Since most mental processes involve duration or continuance, verbs that deal with mental activities or conditions are most often expressed in the imperfect tense in the past. The most common of these verbs are:

creer	**pensar**
desear	**preferir**
querer	**poder**
tener ganas de *(to feel like)*	**saber**
sentir	**gustar**

Él sabía lo que preferíamos.
Yo tenía ganas de salir.

CULTURA

Esta señorita guatemalteca siempre tenía ganas de ser artista y ahora tiene su propio taller en Antigua, Guatemala.

Práctica

HABLAR • ESCRIBIR

1 Personaliza. Da respuestas personales.

1. ¿Te gustaba jugar videojuegos cuando eras joven?
2. ¿Sabías usar la computadora cuando eras muy joven?
3. ¿Siempre querías salir o preferías quedarte en casa?
4. ¿Siempre sabías lo que preferías hacer?
5. ¿Creías que siempre tenías razón o no?

LEER • ESCRIBIR

2 Completa en el pasado con el imperfecto del verbo indicado.

1. Yo ___ que sí pero no sé por qué, pero ellos ___ que no. (creer, creer)
2. Yo ___ que a ellos les ___ mucho hablar en su móvil. (saber, gustar)
3. Ella ___ lo mismo. (pensar)
4. Nosotros ___ ganas de hacer el viaje. (tener)
5. Nosotros ___ que ellos ___ salir. (saber, preferir)

3 ***Comunicación***

Cuenta algunas cosas que tú siempre querías hacer pero que tu hermano(a) o mejor amigo(a) casi nunca quería hacer. Casi siempre prefería hacer otra cosa. ¿Qué prefería hacer él o ella?

Lori Ernfridsson

Answers

1 *Answers will vary but may include:*

1. Sí, (No, no) me gustaba jugar videojuegos cuando era joven.
2. Sí, (No, no) sabía usar la computadora cuando era muy joven.
3. Siempre quería salir. (Prefería quedarme en casa.)
4. Sí, siempre sabía lo que prefería hacer. (No, nunca sabía lo que prefería hacer.)
5. Sí, creía que siempre tenía razón. (No, nunca creía que tenía razón.)

2

1. creía, creían
2. sabía, gustaba
3. pensaba
4. teníamos
5. sabíamos, preferían

3 *Answers will vary.*

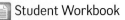

Go Online!

connectED.mcgraw-hill.com

El pretérito y el imperfecto

1. The choice of whether to use the preterite or imperfect depends upon whether the speaker is describing an action completed in the past or a continuous, recurring action in the past.

2. You use the preterite to express actions or events that began and ended at a specific time in the past.

 Anoche volví a casa y envié unos correos electrónicos.
 Luego pasé un rato navegando la red.
 Y a eso de las nueve fui a ver la tele.

3. You use the imperfect to talk about a continuous, habitual, or repeated action in the past. The moment when the action began or ended is unimportant.

 Cada noche volvía a casa y enviaba unos correos electrónicos.
 Luego pasaba un rato navegando la red.
 Y después iba a la sala donde veía la tele.

4. Compare the following sentences.

REPEATED, HABITUAL ACTION	COMPLETED ACTION
Él hablaba con sus abuelos cada semana.	**Él habló con sus abuelos la semana pasada.**
Ella siempre navegaba la red.	**Ella navegó la red anoche.**
Yo siempre me acostaba tarde.	**Pero anoche me acosté temprano.**

Práctica

ESCUCHAR

4 Escucha. Usa una tabla como la de abajo para indicar si es una acción repetida o terminada.

repetida	terminada

CULTURA

El señor hablaba en su móvil mientras caminaba hacia la playa en Cádiz, España.

Andrew Payti

Gramática

Online Resources

Customizable Lesson Plans
- Whiteboard Lesson
- Audio Activities
- Student Workbook
- Enrichment
- Quizzes

Quick Start

Use QS 6.4 or write the following on the board.

Complete with the definite article.

1. **Sonó ___ teléfono.**
2. **Tomé ___ fotografías.**
3. **Escuché ___ música.**
4. **Vi ___ televisión.**
5. **Abrí ___ regalos.**

TEACH

Core Instruction

Step 1 Lead students through Items 1–4.

Step 2 As you go over the model sentences in Item 2, draw a timeline on the board. Each time you give a verb in the preterite, draw an abrupt slash through the timeline to indicate completion or termination of the action in the past.

Step 3 As you go over the model sentences in Item 3, draw another timeline on the board. Each time you give a verb in the imperfect, draw a long shaded box alongside it to indicate duration.

PRACTICE

Leveling EACH Activity

Easy Activity 4

Answers

4
1. repetida
2. terminada
3. terminada
4. repetida
5. terminada
6. repetida
7. terminada
8. terminada

Activity 4

Audio Script

1. Leía sus correos electrónicos.
2. Recibió cinco.
3. Guardó el archivo.
4. Me hablaba en su móvil.
5. Yo lo llamé. Él no me llamó.
6. Siempre hacían copias duras.
7. Hicimos una copia.
8. Abriste el documento adjunto.

Leveling EACH Activity

Easy to Average Activity 5
Average Activities 6, 7, 8
CHallenging Activities 9, 10, Activity 8 **Expansión**

PRACTICE *(continued)*

Activity 5 It is suggested that you go over Activity 5 orally in class. Emphasize the time expression to help students understand the concept. This activity can also be done as a paired activity.

Activity 6 This activity should be prepared and then gone over in class.

Differentiation

Multiple Intelligences

Activity 7 As you go over this activity, draw a timeline on the board. Every time the verb indicates a complete action, mark the timeline with a slash. When the verb indicates a continuous action, mark the timeline with a shaded area. This will help **visual-spatial** learners.

Go Online!

You may wish to use the whiteboard presentation for additional grammar instruction and practice.

ESCUCHAR • HABLAR

5 Contesta. Presta atención a la expresión de tiempo.

1. ¿Jugaron los niños un videojuego anoche?
   ¿Cuándo jugaron un videojuego?
   ¿Jugaban los niños videojuegos todos los días?
   ¿Cuándo jugaban videojuegos?
2. ¿Compraste algo en línea ayer? ¿Qué compraste?
   ¿Cuándo lo/la compraste?
   ¿Siempre hacías compras en línea?
   ¿Cuándo hacías compras en línea?
3. ¿Fue José a España el año pasado?
   ¿Cuándo fue a España?
   ¿Iba José a España cada año?
   ¿Cuándo iba a España?

LEER • ESCRIBIR

6 Cambia **todos los sábados** a **el sábado pasado** y haz los cambios necesarios.

Todos los sábados Juan Antonio se levantaba muy temprano. Bajaba a la cocina y él mismo preparaba el desayuno. Después de comer, subía a su cuarto y prendía su computadora. Cuando hacía la conexión a Internet mandaba un correo electrónico a un buen amigo en España. En pocos segundos se comunicaba con su amigo. Los dos escribían de muchas cosas durante horas.

HABLAR • ESCRIBIR

7 Contesta.

1. Por lo general, ¿guardabas la mayoría de los correos electrónicos que recibías o los borrabas?
2. ¿Guardaste el correo que recibiste anoche o lo borraste?
3. ¿Abría Teresa su bandeja de entradas con frecuencia?
4. ¿La abrió ayer o no?
5. ¿Enviabas mensajes de texto a tus amigos muy a menudo?
6. ¿A quién le enviaste un mensaje de texto ayer?
7. ¿Usabas el Internet muy a menudo?
8. ¿Usaste el Internet anoche?

CULTURA

Muchos españoles recuerdan que visitaban molinos de viento cuando eran jóvenes. Les interesaban los molinos porque pensaban en la aventura de don Quijote con los molinos de viento.

Andrew Payti

Answers

5 *Answers will vary but may include:*

1. Sí, los niños jugaron un videojuego anoche. / Jugaron un videojuego anoche. / Sí, los niños jugaban videojuegos todos los días. / Jugaban todos los días.
2. Sí, compré algo en línea ayer. / Compré ____. / Lo (La) compré ayer. / Sí, siempre hacía compras en línea. / Siempre hacía compras en línea.
3. Sí, José fue a España el año pasado. / Fue a España el año pasado. / Sí, José iba a España cada año. / Iba a España cada año.

6

El sábado pasado Juan Antonio se levantó muy temprano. Bajó a la cocina y él mismo preparó el desayuno. Después de comer, subió a su cuarto y prendió su computadora. Cuando hizo la conexión a Internet, mandó un correo electrónico a un buen amigo en España. En pocos segundos se comunicó con su amigo. Los dos escribieron de muchas cosas durante horas.

Go Online!

connectED.mcgraw-hill.com

HABLAR • ESCRIBIR

8 Mira la fotografía y contesta las preguntas.

1. ¿Había muchos espectadores que asistían al encierro?
2. ¿Corrían los toros en una plaza o en una calle?
3. ¿Corrían detrás de los toros o delante de los toros los corredores?
4. Mira bien la foto. ¿Tocó uno de los corredores a un toro?
5. ¿Obedecieron todos los corredores?
6. ¿Eran jóvenes los corredores?
7. ¿Qué opinas? ¿Eran bravos también? ¿Tenían miedo algunos?
8. ¿Querían impresionar a sus amigos?

EXPANSIÓN

Se dice que las personas como estas son fanfarrones. ¿Qué significa «fanfarrón»?

CULTURA

¿Qué piensas? ¿Eran fanfarrones los que tomaban parte en este encierro durante las fiestas en San Sebastián de los Reyes, España?

HABLAR • ESCRIBIR

9 Personaliza. Da respuestas personales.

¿Conocías a un niño fanfarrón cuando eras más joven? ¿Qué hacía? ¿Veías lo que hacía? ¿Qué hacías tú mientras él cometía sus tonterías? Una vez, ¿hizo algo que le causó un problema? ¿Qué hizo y qué pasó? Y, ¿qué hiciste (tú)?

Cultura

El encierro

El encierro se celebra durante muchas fiestas en España. Generalmente los toros corren en un área cerrada pero a veces corren en la calle misma. Durante un encierro no les hacen daño a los toros. Según las reglas aun no deben tocarlos.

10 *Comunicación*

Di algunas cosas que hacías con frecuencia cuando eras niño(a) y que hiciste ayer también.

Daniel Salsgiver

Gramática

Activities 8 and 9 These activities can also be done as paired activities.

Activity 9 This activity can be done as a group activity. Have students who come up with funny stories relate them to the class.

Comunicación

Interpersonal

Activity 10 When having students do a completely open-ended activity with no learning prompts, they are actually functioning as if they were communicating in a real-life situation. In such a situation, it is normal for early learners to make mistakes. For this reason, you may decide not to interrupt and correct each error a student makes. This is up to your discretion.

ASSESS

Students are now ready to take Quiz 3.

Answers

7

1. Por lo general, guardaba (borraba) la mayoría de los correos electrónicos que recibía.
2. Sí, guardé el correo que recibí anoche. (No, no lo guardé. Lo borré.)
3. Sí (No), Teresa (no) abría su bandeja de entradas con frecuencia.
4. Sí, (No, no) la abrió ayer.
5. Sí, (No, no) enviaba mensajes de texto a mis amigos muy a menudo.
6. Ayer envié un mensaje de texto a ____.
7. Sí, (No, no) usaba el Internet muy a menudo.
8. Sí, (No, no) usé el Internet anoche.

8

1. Sí, había muchos espectadores que asistían al encierro.
2. Los toros corrían en una plaza.
3. Algunos corredores corrían delante de los toros y otros corrían detrás.
4. Sí, uno de los corredores tocó a un toro.
5. No, no todos los corredores obedecieron.
6. Sí, los corredores eran jóvenes.
7. *Answers will vary.*
8. *Answers will vary.*

9 *Answers will vary.*

10 *Answers will vary.*

Online Resources

Customizable Lesson Plans
Whiteboard Lesson
Audio Activities
Video (Gramática)
Student Workbook
Enrichment
Quizzes

Quick Start

Use QS 6.5 or write the following on the board.

1. **Escribe tres cosas que hiciste ayer.**
2. **Escribe tres cosas que hacías con mucha frecuencia.**

TEACH
Core Instruction

Step 1 When explaining the difference between the preterite and the imperfect, you may wish to have students think of a play. Explain that the scenery, props, and the description are in the imperfect. What the actors and actresses actually did on stage is in the preterite.

Step 2 Give some examples and show the difference between background information and acting. Background: **Él era muy guapo. Había una fiesta. Había una mesa en la sala. Todo el mundo se divertía. José y Elena bailaban.** Acting: **En ese momento Carlos entró. Dijo «Buenos días» a todo el mundo. Saludó a todos.**

Step 3 Now use two verbs in one sentence to contrast the background information with the actions on stage. For example: **Ana y Paco bailaban cuando Carlos entró.**

Dos acciones pasadas en la misma frase

1. Often a sentence may have two or more verbs in the past. The verbs may be in the same tense or in different tenses. In the sentence below, both verbs are in the preterite. Both describe simple actions that began and ended at a specific time in the past.

   Laura llegó ayer y Pepe la vio.

2. In the sentence below, the two verbs are in the imperfect because they both describe habitual or continuous actions. The moment when the actions began or ended is unimportant.

   Durante el invierno, Adela iba a las montañas a esquiar, pero yo trabajaba.

3. In the sentence below, the verb **estudiaba** is in the imperfect; it describes the background—what was going on. The verb in the preterite, **entró,** expresses the action or event that interrupted the ongoing action.

   Yo estudiaba cuando Julia entró.

El joven estudiaba mientras su hermana hablaba por teléfono.

Answers

11

1. Sí (No), José (no) enviaba un correo electrónico cuando sonó su móvil. Sí, (No, no) contestó el móvil.
2. Sí, (No, no) estaba cortando la línea mientras ellos hablaban.
3. Sí, (No, no) se les cortó la línea mientras ellos hablaban.
4. Sí (No), Teresa (no) estaba en casa cuando Rafael la llamó.
5. Sí (No), Anita (no) navegaba el Internet cuando su hermanito apagó la computadora.
6. Sí (No), Anita (no) se puso furiosa cuando él la apagó.

12

1. se enfadó, hablaba (habló)
2. leía, llamó
3. era, Estaba, cortó
4. sabía, usaba, salí, apagó

13 *Answers will vary.*

14 *Answers will vary.*

15 *Answers will vary.*

Práctica

HABLAR • ESCRIBIR

11 Contesta.

1. ¿Enviaba José un correo electrónico cuando sonó su móvil? ¿Contestó el móvil?
2. Mientras ellos hablaban, ¿estaba cortando la línea?
3. Mientras ellos hablaban, ¿se les cortó la línea?
4. ¿Estaba Teresa en casa cuando Rafael la llamó?
5. ¿Navegaba Anita el Internet cuando su hermanito apagó la computadora?
6. ¿Se puso furiosa Anita cuando él la apagó?

LEER • ESCRIBIR

12 Completa con la forma apropiada del pretérito o imperfecto.

1. Él _____ cuando yo le _____. (enfadarse, hablar)
2. Yo _____ su e-mail cuando él me _____ en mi móvil. (leer, llamar)
3. La conexión no _____ muy buena. _____ cortando y por fin se nos _____ la línea. (ser, estar, cortar)
4. Mi hermanita no _____ que yo _____ la red y cuando (yo) _____ de mi cuarto ella _____ la computadora. (saber, usar, salir, apagar)

HABLAR • ESCRIBIR

13 Di lo que hacías cuando algo te interrumpió. Forma frases según el modelo.

MODELO **leer →**
Yo leía cuando sonó el teléfono.

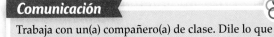

leer	correr	ver	jugar	beber	hablar	sonar
llamar	bailar	comer	subir	servir	llover	pagar

Comunicación

14 Trabaja con un(a) compañero(a) de clase. Dile lo que hacía cada miembro de tu familia anoche mientras tú hacías otra cosa. Di también lo que tú hacías. Luego comparen sus actividades.

15 Habla con un(a) compañero(a) de clase. Dile algo que hacías ayer. Tu compañero(a) te va a decir algo que ocurrió e interrumpió lo que hacías. Luego en una sola frase, describe lo que hacías y lo que pasó (ocurrió).

Go Online!

connectED.mcgraw-hill.com

Refrán

Can you guess what the following proverb means?

No me importa nada. No están maduras.

Así dijo la zorra a las uvas: que no estaban maduras.

¡Bravo!

You have now learned all the new vocabulary and grammar in this chapter. Continue to use and practice all that you know while learning more cultural information. **¡Vamos!**

Leveling EACH Activity

Easy–Average Activities 11, 12
CHallenging Activities 13, 14, 15

PRACTICE

Activity 11 This activity can also be done as a paired activity.

Activities 12 and 13 It is suggested that students prepare these activities before going over them in class. Call on students to read their sentences to the class.

Tips for Success

While doing these activities you may wish to call on a student to put a slash on the board every time he or she hears a verb that is a completed action. Have the student draw a shaded box each time the verb form indicates a continuous or not necessarily completed action.

ASSESS

Students are now ready to take Quiz 4.

Refrán

Have students recite the proverb aloud. Then see if they can figure out its meaning, and encourage them to try to give an equivalent expression in English. Some students may point out that this **Refrán** refers to Aesop's classic fable, "The Fox and the Grapes."

Go Online!

Gramática en vivo *Preterite versus imperfect* Enliven learning with the animated world of Professor Cruz! **Gramática en vivo** is a fun and effective tool for additional instruction and/or review.

You may wish to use the white-board presentation for additional grammar instruction and practice.

¡Bravo! The remaining pages of the chapter recycle information in a variety of ways, allowing students to build upon their newly acquired language skills as well as to keep track of their own progress. This format also ensures that students are not surprised by vocabulary or grammar that has not yet been introduced or studied.

Online Resources

Customizable Lesson Plans

Audio Activities

Student Workbook

Quick Start

Use QS 6.6 or write the following on the board.

1. **Write all the expressions in Spanish you know to greet someone.**
2. **Write all the expressions in Spanish you know to take leave of someone.**

TEACH

Core Instruction

Step 1 Have students listen to and repeat after you or the audio recording.

Step 2 Call on students with good pronunciation skills to read the conversation aloud to the class.

Step 3 Go over the **¿Comprendes?** activities.

Se cortó la línea.

Perdón, José. Es el timbre de Alejandra y le quiero hablar. ¿Alejandra?

Sí, ¿qué tal, Andrés?
Mira, ¿qué hacías anoche? Te llamé dos veces y no contestaste.

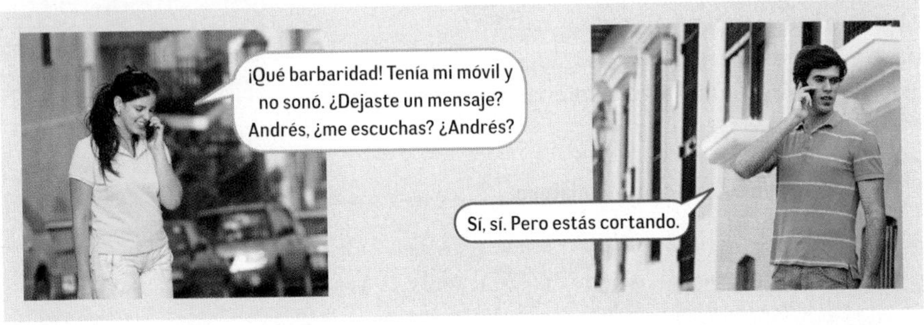

¡Qué barbaridad! Tenía mi móvil y no sonó. ¿Dejaste un mensaje? Andrés, ¿me escuchas? ¿Andrés?
Sí, sí. Pero estás cortando.

¿Ahora?
No. Estás cortando más. ¡Alejandra! Ah, se nos cortó la línea.

David H. Brennan

Go Online!

You may wish to remind students to go online for additional conversation practice.

¡Así se dice!

Why It Works!

No new material is used in the **Conversación** in order not to confuse students. The **Conversación** recombines only the vocabulary and grammar that students have already learned to understand and manipulate.

¿Comprendes?

A Contesta según la información en la conversación.

1. ¿Cómo sabe Andrés que es Alejandra quien lo llama cuando suena su móvil?
2. ¿Qué pasó anoche?
3. ¿Por qué no contestó ella?
4. ¿Sabemos si Andrés dejó un mensaje?
5. ¿Qué problema están teniendo?
6. ¿Cómo terminó la llamada?

B **Analizando** ¿Por qué es conveniente dar un timbre diferente a cada uno de tus amigos o miembros de la familia que te llaman con frecuencia?

C **Personalizando** ¿Tienes a veces unos problemas con tu móvil como los que tenían (experimentaban) Andrés y Alejandra en la conversación? Describe los problemas. Luego habla con tus compañeros para ver si ellos tienen las mismas dificultades.

Yo despertar
mis sentidos
Nuevo teléfono S500
Encuentra la armonía en un diseño slider, único y deslumbrante, gracias a sus efectos de luces y temas cambiantes del día a la noche y de acuerdo a las estaciones del año.
S500
Atención a clientes y venta de accesorios: 01 800 000 4722
www.telcel.com
telcel

Differentiation

Multiple Intelligences

To engage **bodily-kinesthetic** learners, call on students to come to the front of the room and dramatize the conversation using gestures, facial expressions, and proper intonation.

Visual-spatial learners might also enjoy creating their own cartoon strips. They can either imitate the characters in the conversation or create new ones. They may want to share their cartoons with others in the class.

PRACTICE

¿Comprendes?

A You may allow students to look up answers or you may wish to do this as a factual recall activity.

B Students can have fun with this activity and come up with many different answers.

Writing Development

You may want students to write their answers to Activity B to help develop their writing skills.

Pre-AP Listening to this conversation will help students develop the skills that they need to be successful on the listening portion of the AP exam.

Answers

A

1. Andrés sabe que es Alejandra quien lo llama porque tiene un timbre especial en su móvil para Alejandra.
2. Anoche Andrés le llamó a Alejandra dos veces y ella no contestó.
3. No contestó porque su móvil no sonó.
4. No, no sabemos si Andrés dejó un mensaje.
5. Alejandra está cortando.
6. Se les cortó la línea.

B *Answers will vary.*

C *Answers will vary.*

Online Resources

Customizable Lesson Plans

Audio Activities

Student Workbook

TEACH

Core Instruction

Step 1 Read and discuss the **Estrategia de lectura.**

Step 2 Have students scan the reading quickly and silently.

Step 3 Have students listen as you read the selection to them or play the audio recording. Then have them listen again as they follow along.

Step 4 Ask the Reading Check questions as you read the selection. Call on a student to read several sentences of the **Lectura.** Ask questions after every three sentences.

Step 5 Have students do the **¿Comprendes?** activities. Call on several students to give some information in their own words about the technology discussed in the **Lectura.**

Differentiation

Advanced Learners

Have advanced learners read the story and then write a summary of it in their own words.

Lectura CULTURAL

ESTRATEGIA DE LECTURA

PERSONALIZANDO Una buena estrategia de lectura es personalizar la información que estás leyendo. Determina cuáles son cosas que tú también haces o cosas que no haces. Cuando personalizas puedes identificarte más con la información.

Antes de leer

Piensa en todo lo que tú haces con tu computadora y otros aparatos electrónicos.

Durante la lectura

Compara las actividades de los jóvenes hispanos en la lectura con tus propias actividades.

READING CHECK

¿Qué información buscaba Manuel?

READING CHECK

¿Cuál es un pasatiempo favorito de Julia?

READING CHECK

¿Por qué es interesante la información que envió el hermano de Raúl?

Después de leer

¿Con qué actividades podías identificar más? ¿Usan estos jóvenes sus computadoras y otros aparatos de la misma manera que tú?

En un mundo tecnológico

Vamos a hablar con unos amigos hispanohablantes.

—¡Hola! Me llamo Manuel Ramos. Tengo dieciséis años y vivo en la Ciudad de México. Anoche navegaba el Internet para buscar información sobre Simón Bolívar para mi clase de historia. Yo no sabía que Bolívar era de una familia acomodada, una familia que tenía mucho dinero, y que desde su niñez le interesaban mucho las condiciones en que vivían los pobres. Creo que esta información es correcta pero antes de incluirla en mi composición tengo que verificar su confiabilidad[1]. Todos sabemos que hay sitios que no son confiables.

—¡Hola! Me llamo Julia González y soy de Ponce, Puerto Rico. A mí me encanta la música. Anoche bajé (descargué) unas ocho canciones más en mi computadora y en mi MP3. Me encanta escuchar mis canciones favoritas en cualquier[2] momento del día. ¡Una cosa importante! Siempre verifico si es legal bajar las canciones.

— ¡Hola! Soy Raúl Torres. Soy de Málaga, España. Anoche recibí una noticia interesante. Mi hermano mayor está estudiando en la Universidad de Salamanca. Me envió un correo electrónico y me dijo que algunos de sus profesores ponen sus conferencias en el Internet. Si un(a) estudiante no puede asistir a clase puede escuchar la conferencia en su MP3. ¿Qué piensas de tal idea? Vale, ¿no?

David H. Brennan

[1]confiabilidad *reliability* [2]cualquier *any*

Go Online!

You may wish to remind students to go online for additional reading comprehension and writing skills practice.

¿Comprendes?

A Hojeando Hojea la lectura para determinar quién hace las siguientes actividades.

	Manuel Ramos	Julia González	Raúl Torres
1. descarga su música favorita			
2. navega el Internet buscando datos para una tarea escolar			
3. lee un correo electrónico que acaba de recibir			

B Buscando información Da la información para cada persona—Manuel, Julia, Raúl—usando frases completas.

1. de donde es
2. lo que tiene
3. detalles sobre sus actividades

C Recordando hechos Contesta.

1. ¿Qué aprendió Manuel Ramos mientras navegaba el Internet?
2. ¿Qué tiene que verificar Manuel? ¿Por qué?
3. Y Julia, ¿qué tiene ella que verificar?
4. ¿Qué noticia interesante recibió Raúl Torres de su hermano?

D Identificando ¿Cuál es la idea principal de esta lectura? Identifica unos detalles que apoyan *(support)* esta idea.

E Pronosticando Contesta.

1. ¿Cuáles son unos avances tecnológicos no mencionados en esta lectura?
2. ¿Cuáles son otros avances que piensas que van a ocurrir en el futuro?

PRACTICE

Pre-AP These cultural readings will develop the skills that students need to be successful on the reading and writing sections of the AP exam. Listening to these readings will also help prepare them for the auditory component.

¿Comprendes?

Teaching Options

- You can decide when you wish to allow students to look up answers and when you prefer to check their factual recall.
- You may wish to reverse roles and have students play the role of the teacher by asking questions about the information in the **Lectura** section.

Comunicación

Interpersonal
Have students tell what they did last night with their computers.

Answers

A
1. Julia González 2. Manuel Ramos 3. Raúl Torres

B
1. Manuel Ramos es de la Ciudad de México. Tiene una computadora. Navega el Internet para buscar información sobre Simón Bolívar para una tarea escolar.
2. Julia González es de Ponce, Puerto Rico. Tiene un MP3. Descarga canciones en su computadora igual que en su MP3 porque le encanta escuchar sus canciones favoritas.
3. Raúl Torres es de Málaga, España. Tiene una computadora. Usa su computadora para escribir y leer correos electrónicos.

C
1. Manuel aprendió que Bolívar era de una familia acomodada y que le interesaban las condiciones en que vivían los pobres.
2. Tiene que verificar la confiabilidad de la información porque hay sitios que no son confiables.
3. Julia tiene que verificar si es legal bajar las canciones.
4. Raúl Torres aprendió que algunos profesores ponen sus conferencias en el Internet. Si un(a) estudiante no puede asistir a clase puede escuchar la conferencia en su MP3.

D *Answers will vary.*

E *Answers will vary.*

Online Resources

Customizable Lesson Plans

Audio Activities

Video (Diálogo)

Student Workbook

TEACH

Core Instruction

You may wish to have students merely read this selection on their own and do the **¿Comprendes?** activities, or you may prefer to present the **Un poco más** reading more in depth since this selection contains some very useful contemporary vocabulary.

Tips for Success

You can have students get together in small groups to ask one another questions about each major paragraph of this reading selection.

Lectura

UN POCO MÁS

Antes de leer

Piensa en como la tecnología moderna te afecta casi a diario (todos los días). ¿Cuáles son unos aparatos que usas tanto que los consideras indispensables? ¿Cómo te ayudan estos aparatos? En tu opinión, ¿cómo era la vida de tus abuelos sin la tecnología que tienes a tu disposición?

La tecnología de hoy y ayer

Tomás Navarro vive en Martínez, un suburbio de Buenos Aires, la capital de Argentina. Nos va a hablar de su nuevo juguete[1] que le gusta mucho.

—Ayer me compré un móvil. Es increíble la cantidad de opciones que tiene. Claro que puedo hacer y recibir llamadas y para saber quién me está llamando puedo personalizar los timbres asignando canciones u otros sonidos a mis amigos y familiares. Además mi móvil me permite enviar mensajes de texto, acceder mi correo electrónico y bajar música y videojuegos. Tiene otra opción que se llama fotomensajería. Puedo tomar fotografías digitales con mi móvil y enviarlas instantáneamente a mis amigos. Y puedo grabar y enviar un videomensaje con sonido. Las opciones no tienen límite.

Tú tienes un móvil, ¿no? ¿Te ofrece otras opciones que no me ofrece el mío? ¿Cuáles?

Sí, la tecnología está cambiando el mundo de una manera rápida y radical. Si no lo crees, debes hablar con tus abuelos. Cuando ellos eran niños, ¿tenían computadora y móvil? De ninguna manera. Si querían escuchar música ponían la radio o ponían un disco[2] en un tocadiscos. Cuando querían comunicarse con alguien escribían una carta o usaban el teléfono. Hoy día, en Estados Unidos, España y Latinoamérica la gente se comunica por medio de la comunicación electrónica. Pero en España y Latinoamérica, además de los móviles, sigue siendo popular y conveniente el teléfono público. Para usarlo compras una tarjeta telefónica que contiene una cantidad de unidades. La tarjeta que se introduce en la ranura del teléfono te permite hacer llamadas locales, interurbanas, de larga distancia y hasta[3] internacionales. Mientras hablas, se deduce automáticamente el número apropiado de unidades. ¡Otro ejemplo de la tecnología!

[1]juguete *toy*
[2]disco *record*
[3]hasta *even*

Go Online!

You may wish to remind students to go online for additional reading comprehension and writing skills practice.

Go Online!

connectED.mcgraw-hill.com

¿Comprendes?

A Escoge.

1. ¿Qué compró Tomás?
   a. un juguete
   b. un móvil
   c. una cámara
2. Tomás asigna timbres personales para ____.
   a. poder hacer y recibir llamadas
   b. poder oír sus canciones favoritas
   c. poder identificar quien lo está llamando
3. ¿Qué no puede hacer Tomás con su móvil?
   a. escuchar la radio
   b. tomar fotos
   c. enviar mensajes de texto
4. ¿Cómo se comunicaban nuestros abuelos cuando eran jóvenes?
   a. Usaban la radio.
   b. Usaban su tocadiscos.
   c. Usaban el teléfono.
5. ¿Qué contiene una tarjeta telefónica?
   a. números de teléfono
   b. unidades que te permiten hacer una llamada de un teléfono público
   c. un teléfono público
6. Una llamada interurbana es una llamada ____.
   a. local, dentro de la misma ciudad
   b. de una ciudad a otra en la misma región
   c. de larga distancia

B Prepara una presentación visual que compara y contrasta la manera en que Tomás emplea la tecnología con tu uso de la tecnología.

CULTURA

Es un teléfono público en una calle de Buenos Aires, la capital de Argentina. ¿Qué se puede usar para hacer una llamada de este teléfono?

Andrew Payti

Lectura

Tips for Success

The multiple-choice comprehension activities that accompany the second reading selection in each chapter have a format that will help students prepare for standardized tests.

Go Online!

Diálogo en vivo In this episode, Julián and Alejandra attempt to use the wonders of technology in an Internet café. Ask students if they think Julián is qualified to work at the Internet café. Why or why not?

Answers

A
1. b
2. c
3. a
4. c
5. b
6. b

B *Answers will vary.*

Prepárate para el examen

Online Resources

Customizable Lesson Plans

Student Workbook

Listening, Speaking, Reading, Writing Tests

Self-check for achievement

This is a pre-test for students to take before you administer the chapter test. Note that each section is cross-referenced so students can easily find the material they feel they need to review. You may wish to use Self-Check Worksheet SC6 to have students complete this assessment in class or at home. You can correct the assessment yourself, or you may prefer to display the answers in class using Self-Check Answers SC6A.

Differentiation

Slower-Paced Learners

Have students work in pairs to complete the Self-Check in class. Once they have finished, call on individuals to give the correct answers as you review together.

Multiple Intelligences

To engage **visual-spatial** and **bodily-kinesthetic** learners, number from 1 to 40 on the board and call on a student to go to the board and write the correct answer (this may be done chronologically or you may allow students to choose the one they answer). Then have the student who wrote the first answer decide who will write the second, and so on, making sure to remind them not to pick the same person again.

Prepárate para el examen

Vocabulario

1 Identifica.

To review, see **Vocabulario 1.**

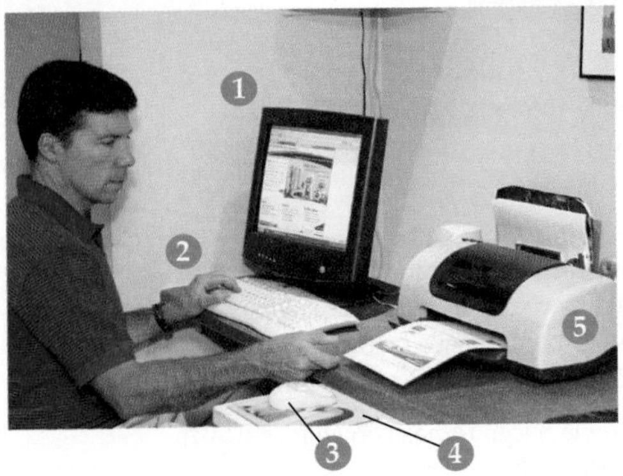

2 Completa.

To review, see **Vocabulario 1** and **Vocabulario 2.**

6. La muchacha quiere entrar en línea y ____ con su ratón.
7–8. Si estás navegando y quieres regresar a un sitio anterior tienes que ____ en el ____ regresar.
9. Una ____ contiene varios archivos.
10. Si quieres saber si tienes correos electrónicos tienes que abrir tu ____.
11. No quiero guardar el correo. Lo voy a ____.
12. Si necesitas una copia dura de un correo o de una página del Internet, tienes que tener ____.
13. Puedes tener diferentes ____ en tu móvil para identificar quienes te llaman.

3 Parea.

14. un móvil	a. bajar
15. la computadora	b. punto
16. descargar	c. guardar
17. llamada perdida	d. un celular
18. @	e. pulsar
19. regresar	f. llamada caída
20. oprimir	g. el ordenador
	h. arroba
	i. retroceder

CULTURA

A esta pareja les gusta usar su móvil pero no tenían móvil cuando eran jóvenes.

Answers

1
1. la pantalla de escritorio
2. el teclado
3. el ratón
4. la alfombrilla
5. la impresora

2
6. hace clic
7. hacer clic
8. botón
9. carpeta
10. bandeja de entradas
11. borrar
12. una impresora
13. timbres

3
14. d
15. g
16. a
17. f
18. h
19. i
20. e

Gramática

4 Escribe en el pasado.

21. Quiero comprarme un nuevo móvil.
22. A mis abuelos les gusta usar un teléfono fijo.
23. Él está contento cuando recibe la buena noticia.

5 Completa con el imperfecto o el pretérito.

24–25. Él ____ muy a menudo y ____ ayer también. (ir, ir)

26–27. Ellos me ____ correos casi todos los días pero ayer yo no ____ ninguno. (enviar, recibir)

28–29. Cuando yo ____ niño(a) mis abuelos siempre me ____ en español. (ser, hablar)

6 Completa con el imperfecto o el pretérito.

30–31. Teresa ____ en el supermercado cuando ____ su móvil. (estar, sonar)

32–33. Yo ____ en mi móvil cuando el empleado me ____ una pregunta. (hablar, hacer)

34–35. Él ____ canciones en su MP3 mientras yo ____ fotografías en el mío. (bajar, bajar)

36–37. Mientras ellos ____ nosotros ____. (divertirse, trabajar)

Cultura

7 Corrige las frases falsas.

38. En algunas universidades si un(a) estudiante no puede ir a clase, puede mirar las conferencias de sus profesores en la televisión.
39. Siempre sabemos que la información que leemos en el Internet es correcta.
40. Se puede bajar canciones sin permiso.

Kerri Galloway

Go Online!

connected.mcgraw-hill.com

To review, see **Verbos como querer, creer en el pasado.**

To review, see **El pretérito y el imperfecto.**

To review, see **Dos acciones pasadas en la misma frase.**

To review this cultural information, see the **Lectura cultural.**

Prepárate para el examen

Differentiation

(continued)

This type of review activity is particularly appealing to interpersonal learners but will also benefit the class on the whole by promoting an inclusive, student-centered learning environment.

Slower Paced Learners

Encourage students who need extra help to refer to the margin notes and review any section before answering the questions.

Pre-AP Students preparing for the AP exam may benefit from a set time limit when completing this Self-Check. This may also help to identify students with learning difficulties or slower paced students who need extra help.

Go Online!

You may wish to remind students to go online for additional test preparation.

Answers

4

21. Quería comprarme un nuevo móvil.
22. A mis abuelos les gustaba usar un teléfono fijo.
23. Él estaba contento cuando recibió la buena noticia.

5

24. iba
25. fue
26. enviaban
27. recibí
28. era
29. hablaban

6

30. estaba
31. sonó
32. hablaba
33. hizo
34. bajaba
35. bajaba
36. se divertían
37. trabajábamos

7

38. En algunas universidades si un(a) estudiante no puede ir a clase, puede escuchar las conferencias en su MP3.
39. Tenemos que verificar la información que leemos en el Internet porque hay sitios que no son confiables.
40. No se puede bajar canciones sin permiso.

Prepárate para el examen

Tips for Success

Encourage students to say as much as possible when they do these open-ended activities. Tell them not to be afraid to make mistakes, since the goal of the activities is real-life communication. Encourage students to self-correct and to use words and phrases they know to get their meaning across. If someone in the group makes an error that impedes comprehension, encourage the others to ask questions to clarify or, if necessary, to politely correct the speaker. Let students choose the activities they would like to do. Tell the students to feel free to elaborate on the basic theme and to be creative. They may use props, pictures, or posters if they wish.

Pre-AP These oral activities will give students the opportunity to develop and improve their speaking skills so that they may succeed on the speaking portion of the AP exam.

Note: You may want to use the rubric below to help students prepare their speaking activities.

Practice for **ORAL PROFICIENCY**

Prepárate para el examen

1 La tecnología

Talk about your opinion of technology

¿A ti te gusta la tecnología? Explica por qué dices que sí o que no. Si conoces a alguien que habla español, puedes preguntarle su opinión. ¿Tiene la misma opinión que tú?

2 Mi móvil

Discuss your new cell phone

Imagínate que acabas de comprar un nuevo móvil con todas las opciones más avanzadas. Dile a un(a) compañero(a) todo lo que puedes hacer con tu móvil. Luego discutan las opciones que les gustan más o que consideran las más interesantes.

3 El uso de los celulares

Debate the use of cell phones

Trabajen en grupos y debatan sus ideas sobre el uso de los celulares. ¿Deben permitir el uso de celulares en la escuela, abordo de un avión, mientras uno maneja (conduce) un carro, en el teatro o cine, etc.? Defiendan sus opiniones.

4 Cuando mis abuelos eran jóvenes

Tell about what your grandparents had and didn't have

Habla con tus abuelos. Ellos te van a decir las muchas cosas que tú tienes que ellos no tenían cuando eran niños. Te van a decir lo que tenían. Comparte los resultados de tus conversaciones con unos(as) compañeros(as) de clase y decidan si sus abuelos dicen más o menos la misma cosa.

CULTURA

Estas dos señoras mayores están disfrutando del tiempo con una conversación importante en una calle de Gijón en Asturias.

Andrew Payti

5 Interrupciones

Talk about one activity interrupting another in the past

Trabaja con un(a) compañero(a) de clase. Ayer ustedes hacían muchas cosas. Pero siempre había interrupciones. Hablen de todo lo que hacían y todo lo que interrumpió lo que hacían.

Scoring Rubric for Speaking

	4	3	2	1
vocabulary	extensive use of vocabulary, including idiomatic expressions	adequate use of vocabulary and idiomatic expressions	limited vocabulary marked with some anglicisms	limited vocabulary marked by frequent anglicisms that force interpretation by the listener
grammar	few or no grammatical errors	minor grammatical errors	some serious grammatical errors	serious grammatical errors
pronunciation	good intonation and largely accurate pronunciation with slight accent	acceptable intonation and pronunciation with distinctive accent	errors in intonation and pronunciation with heavy accent	errors in intonation and pronunciation that interfere with listener's comprehension
content	thorough response with interesting and pertinent detail	thorough response with sufficient detail	some detail, but not sufficient	general, insufficient response

Practice for **WRITTEN PROFICIENCY**

Go Online!
connected.mcgraw-hill.com

Prepárate para el examen

Tarea

You have just received an e-mail message from a Spanish-speaking friend who hasn't heard from you in awhile and wants to know what's up. Write a reply informing him or her of how you are doing and what you did today. Use this opportunity to impress your friend with some of the grammar and vocabulary that you have learned recently, and don't forget to follow the rules of *netiquette.*

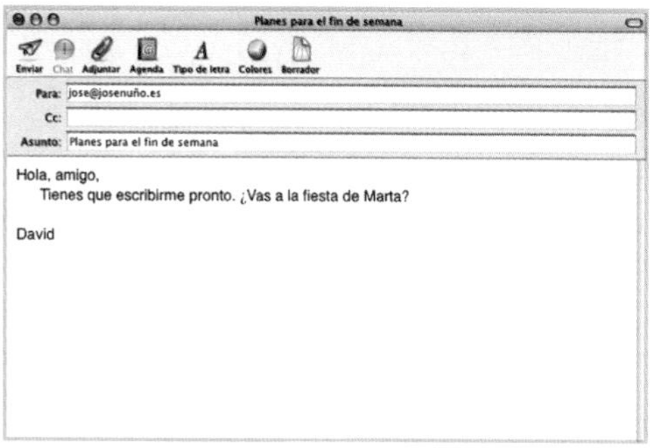
Planes para el fin de semana
Enviar Chat Adjuntar Agenda Tipo de letra Colores Borrador
Para: jose@josenuño.es
Cc:
Asunto: Planes para el fin de semana
Hola, amigo,
Tienes que escribirme pronto. ¿Vas a la fiesta de Marta?
David

Writing Strategy

Netiquette E-mail is a quick and fun way to communicate with friends all over the world. Still, it is important to ensure that your message is not carelessly written. Tone of voice can easily be misunderstood, especially when sarcasm is used, and misspelled words or incorrect grammar can lead to confusion. To avoid hurt feelings and misunderstandings, it is important to adhere to net etiquette, or *netiquette,* and to always check your message for errors before sending it.

1 Prewrite

Although e-mail between friends is an informal means of expression, your message should still follow a logical structure so that it is both easy to understand and fun to read. As you think about what you want your message to contain, categorize the information in terms of whether it belongs in the introduction, in the body or main part of the text, or in the conclusion.

2 Write

Be sure to adhere to the following rules of *netiquette.*

- Be certain that you have typed the correct e-mail address. Sending a personal message to the wrong person can be embarrassing!
- Make sure that your subject line reflects the content of your e-mail.
- Use the correct spelling of words and proper grammar.
- Be cautious when using sarcasm as it can easily be misunderstood.
- Use capital letters appropriately. Words with all capital letters are read as SHOUTING and can be interpreted as rude.
- Remember that good manners are just as important in cyberspace as they are in real life.
- Always re-read your message carefully before sending it.

Evaluate

Don't forget that your teacher will evaluate you on correct use of vocabulary, proper spelling and grammar, logical structure, and good *netiquette.*

Pre-AP This **tarea** will give students the opportunity to develop and improve their writing skills so that they may succeed on the writing portion of the AP exam.

ASSESS

Students are now ready to take any of the Listening, Speaking, Reading, Writing Tests you choose to administer.

Note: You may want to use the rubric below to help students prepare their writing task.

Scoring Rubric for Writing

	4	3	2	1
vocabulary	precise, varied	functional, fails to communicate complete meaning	limited to basic words, often inaccurate	inadequate
grammar	excellent, very few or no errors	some errors, but do not hinder communication	numerous errors interfere with communication	many errors, little sentence structure
content	thorough response to the topic	generally thorough response to the topic	partial response to the topic	insufficient response to the topic
organization	well organized, ideas presented clearly and logically	loosely organized, but main ideas present	some attempts at organization, but with confused sequencing	lack of organization

Online Resources

Customizable Lesson Plans
- Whiteboard Lesson
- Audio Activities
- Video (Vocabulario) (Diálogo) (Gramática)
- Student Workbook
- Enrichment
- Quizzes
- Listening, Speaking, Reading, Writing Tests

Grammar Review

This page provides a quick "at a glance" summary of the grammar points students have learned in this chapter.

Differentiation

Multiple Intelligences

You may want to call on **verbal-linguistic** and **logical-mathematical** learners for whom grammar often comes easily to explain the main concepts to their classmates in their own words. Having students explain the concepts in different ways may also help slower paced learners or students with learning difficulties.

Repaso del Capítulo 6

Gramática

Verbos como querer, creer en el pasado

Verbs that express mental processes or conditions in the past are usually expressed in the imperfect tense.

Tenía ganas de ver a mis amigos.
Mi abuela sabía lo que preferíamos comer.

El pretérito y el imperfecto

The choice of whether to use the preterite or imperfect depends upon whether the action began and ended at a specific time in the past or if it was a continuous, habitual, or repeated action in the past. Compare the following sentences.

PRETERITE	IMPERFECT
Ella habló con su madre anoche.	**Ella hablaba con su madre cada día.**
El sábado fuiste al cine.	**Siempre ibas al cine.**
Comieron en el restaurante una vez.	**Comían en el restaurante a menudo.**

Dos acciones pasadas en la misma frase

A sentence may have two or more verbs in the past. In the sentence below, both verbs are in the preterite because they both tell of events that began and ended at a specific point in the past.

Pablo escribió el e-mail y lo envió.

In the following sentence, both verbs are in the imperfect because they describe continuous actions in the past.

En el verano Tito siempre iba a la playa y yo me quedaba en casa.

Some sentences contain both the preterite and the imperfect. In this case, the preterite expresses an action that interrupted an ongoing action in the past.

Mamá y papá hablaban cuando sonó el teléfono.

CULTURA

Los jóvenes venezolanos se divertían mientras una amiga les leía un textomensaje que alguien le envió en su móvil. ¿Qué crees? ¿Es gracioso o serio el mensaje que recibió?

Juego There are a number of cognates in this list. See how many you and a partner can find. Who can find the most? Compare your list with those of your classmates.

Go Online!

connectED.mcgraw-hill.com

Vocabulario

Describing a computer

la computadora, el ordenador
la pantalla de escritorio
la alfombrilla
el ratón
el teclado
el icono
la barra de herramientas
un sitio Web
la página de inicio, (inicial, frontal)
el botón regresar (retroceder)
el botón borrador
el archivo
la carpeta
la impresora
una copia dura

Discussing e-mail

el correo electrónico, el e-mail
el/la destinatario(a)
la dirección de correo electrónico (de e-mail)
arroba
punto
la libreta de direcciones
la bandeja de entradas
la bandeja de enviados
el documento adjunto

Describing computer activities

prender
apagar
entrar en línea
hacer clic
oprimir, pulsar
guardar
borrar
navegar la red (el Internet)
bajar, descargar
imprimir

Discussing cell phones and other technology

el móvil, el celular
el timbre (sonoro)
una llamada perdida (caída)
la cámara digital
el MP3
sonar
asignar

Making a phone call

el teléfono público
la ranura
un mensaje
llamar
descolgar (el auricular)
introducir la tarjeta telefónica
esperar el tono
marcar el número
¿Está...?
¿De parte de quién?

Discussing telephone numbers

la guía telefónica
el número de teléfono
el prefijo del país
la clave de área

Other useful words and expressions

Estás cortando.
¿Me escuchas?
Se nos cortó la línea.
anterior
cierto(a)
encantar

LA PRACTICE Refer to the Language Arts Practice section for activities that will strengthen your Language Arts skills as you continue to use your Spanish.

Literary Reader
You may wish to read the excerpts from the famous poem *Versos sencillos*, found in the Literary Reader at the end of this book.

Juego The cognates in this list are: **la computadora, el icono, un sitio Web, una copia, electrónico(a), el e-mail, el documento, el botón, en línea, navegar, el Internet, el celular, la cámara digital, el MP3, asignar, el teléfono público, el tono, el número de teléfono.**

Don't forget the chapter project and cultural activities. Students have learned all the information that they will need to complete these engaging enrichment tasks.

Repaso del Capítulo 6

Vocabulary Review

The words and phrases in **Vocabulario 1** and **2** have been taught for productive use in this chapter. They are summarized here as a resource for both student and teacher. This list also serves as a convenient resource for the **Prepárate para el examen.**

¡Así se dice!

Why It Works!

This vocabulary reference list has not been translated into English for two reasons. First, it is recommended that students learn the new vocabulary through direct association with images on the **Vocabulario** pages. Second, all vocabulary is reintroduced in the chapter many times and upon completion of the chapter students should be familiar with the meaning of all the words. If there are words that students still do not know, they can refer to the vocabulary presentation in the chapter or the dictionary at the end of the book. If, however, it is your preference to give students the English translations, please refer to Vocabulary V6.1.

Literary Reader

It is recommended that students read from the Literary Reader at this stage so that the selections are not presented all at once at the end or skipped entirely due to time restraints.

Repaso cumulativo

Every chapter of **¡Así se dice!** contains this review section of previously learned material. By recycling information from previous chapters, the cumulative review serves to remind students that they need to continue practicing what they have learned after finishing each chapter.

Activity 1 This activity reviews vocabulary pertaining to summer and winter activities.

Audio Script

1. La joven pasó el día en la playa.
2. Llevó anteojos de sol.
3. Hay pistas para expertos y otros para principiantes.
4. Hace mucho calor.
5. Los amigos llevaron anorak.
6. Los amigos fueron a la estación de esquí.

Activity 2 This activity reviews the regular forms of the imperfect.

Activity 3 This activity reviews the preterite.

Activity 4 This activity reviews stem-changing verbs in the preterite.

Conexiones

Have students work in small groups or individually to design a poster or computerized slideshow related to the theme of Puerto Rico and then give brief presentations. Topics can be based on demographic, historical, geographic, or cultural information.

Repaso cumulativo

Repasa lo que ya has aprendido

These activities will help you review and remember what you have learned so far in Spanish.

1 Escucha las frases. Parea cada frase con el dibujo que describe.

a. 

b. 

2 Completa con el imperfecto.

1. ____ una fiesta. (haber)
2. Todo el mundo ____ durante la fiesta. (bailar)
3. Una banda ____. (tocar)
4. Nosotros ____. (divertirse)
5. Yo no ____ ir a casa. (querer)
6. Me ____ los fuegos artificiales. (gustar)
7. Mucha gente ____ mientras ____ los fuegos artificiales. (comer, mirar)

3 Completa con cada verbo que falta.

1. Él lo hizo y tú lo ____ pero ellos no lo ____.
2. Ellos vinieron y nosotros ____ pero tú no ____.
3. Yo estuve y él ____ pero tú no ____.
4. Tú lo supiste y yo lo ____ pero los otros no lo ____.

4 Sigue el modelo.

MODELO **Lo pido. →**
Lo pedí.

1. Juan lo pide.
2. Tú lo sirves.
3. Nosotros lo repetimos.
4. Ella lo prefiere así.
5. El cocinero fríe las papas.
6. Usted lo sigue.

Answers

1
1. a
2. a
3. b
4. a
5. b
6. b

2
1. Había
2. bailaba
3. tocaba
4. nos divertíamos
5. quería
6. gustaban
7. comía, miraba

3
1. hiciste, hicieron
2. vinimos, viniste
3. estuvo, estuviste
4. supe, supieron

4
1. Juan lo pidió.
2. Tú lo serviste.
3. Nosotros lo repetimos.
4. Ella lo prefirió así.
5. El cocinero frió las papas.
6. Usted lo siguió.

5 **Identifica. Usa un diagrama como el de abajo para escribir palabras relacionadas con una estación de tren.**

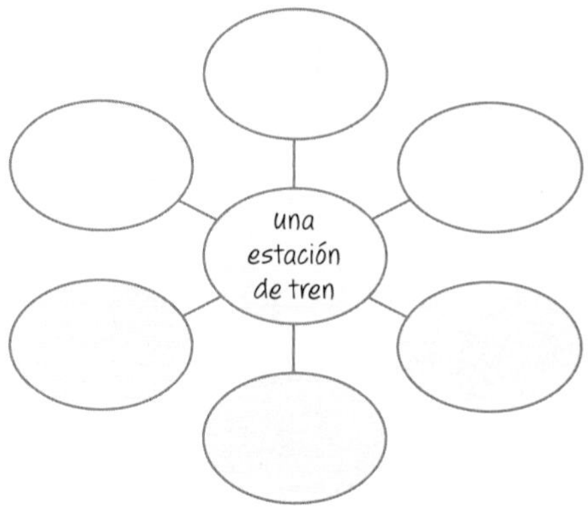

6 **Escribe una frase original con cada una de las palabras de la Actividad 5.**

7 **Escribe una pregunta.**

1. *Juan* fue al restaurante.
2. Juan fue *al restaurante.*
3. El mesero trabajaba *en el restaurante.*
4. Juan pidió *un menú.*
5. El mesero era *de México.*
6. El mesero era *muy simpático.*
7. *Todos* comieron muy bien.
8. Todos comieron *mucho.*
9. Juan volvió a casa *en bus.*
10. Juan volvió *tarde.*

8 **Rompecabezas**

Cambia una letra en cada palabra para formar una nueva palabra.

1. base
2. peso
3. jamón
4. piso
5. llenar
6. fue
7. hay
8. cada

Go Online! connectED.mcgraw-hill.com

Repaso cumulativo

Activity 5 This activity reviews train vocabulary.

Activity 6 This activity reviews train vocabulary.

Activity 7 This activity reviews interrogative words.

Activity 8 This activity reviews a variety of vocabulary.

Go Online!

You may wish to remind students to go online for additional cumulative review.

The **¡Así se dice!** Audio Program for Chapter 6 has seventeen activities, which afford students extensive listening and speaking practice.

Pre-AP To give students further open-ended oral or written practice, or to assess proficiency, go to AP Proficiency Practice AP4 and AP18.

Answers

5 *Answers will vary.*

6 *Answers will vary.*

7
1. ¿Quién fue al restaurante?
2. ¿Adónde fue Juan?
3. ¿Dónde trabajaba el mesero?
4. ¿Qué pidió Juan?
5. ¿De dónde era el mesero?
6. ¿Cómo era el mesero?
7. ¿Quiénes comieron muy bien?
8. ¿Cuánto comieron todos?
9. ¿Cómo volvió Juan a casa?
10. ¿Cuándo volvió Juan?

8 *Answers will vary but may include:*
1. bate
2. piso, paso
3. jabón
4. paso, peso
5. llevar
6. fui
7. hoy
8. casa, cama, nada

Chapter Overview

En el hotel

Scope and Sequence

Topics
- Checking into hotels or hostels
- Hotels and hostels in Spanish-speaking countries

Culture
- The Camino de Santiago in Navarre, Spain
- Santiago de Compostela in Spain

Functions
- How to check into a hotel or hostel
- How to ask for things you may need while at a hotel or hostel
- How to discuss hotel stays in Latin America and Spain

Structure
- The present perfect tense
- Double object pronouns

Planning Guide

	required	recommended	optional
Vocabulario 1 Una estadía en un hotel	✓		
Gramática El presente perfecto Participios irregulares Dos complementos **me lo, te lo, nos lo** Dos complementos con **se**	✓		
Conversación En la recepción		✓	
Lectura cultural Un hostal y un parador		✓	
Lectura Un poco más El Camino de Santiago			✓
Prepárate para el examen			✓
Repaso cumulativo			✓

Andrew Payti

Correlations to ACTFL World-Readiness Standards for Learning Languages

Page numbers in light print refer to the Student Edition.
Page numbers in bold print refer to the Teacher Edition.

COMMUNICATION Communicate effectively in more than one language in order to function in a variety of situations and for multiple purposes		
Interpersonal Communication	Learners interact and negotiate meaning in spoken, signed, or written conversations to share information, reactions, feelings, and opinions.	pp. **200C, 202–203, 206,** 209, **209,** 210, 212, **212,** 213, **216, 217,** 222, **222**
Interpretive Communication	Learners understand, interpret, and analyze what is heard, read, or viewed on a variety of topics.	pp. **204,** 206, **206, 207, 208,** 209, 210, 211, 212, 213, **214,** 215, **215,** 216, **216,** 217, **217, 218,** 219, 221, **221,** 226, **227**
Presentational Communication	Learners present information, concepts, and ideas to inform, explain, persuade, and narrate on a variety of topics using appropriate media and adapting to various audiences of listeners, readers, or viewers.	pp. **200C, 200D, 204, 209,** 211, **214, 216, 217, 218, 219, 220,** 222, **224, 225**
CULTURES Interact with cultural competence and understanding		
Relating Cultural Practices to Perspectives	Learners use the language to investigate, explain, and reflect on the relationship between the practices and perspectives of the cultures studied.	pp. **200D,** 207, **208,** 215, 218, 219, 221
Relating Cultural Products to Perspectives	Learners use the language to investigate, explain, and reflect on the relationship between the products and perspectives of the cultures studied.	pp. **200C, 200D,** 202–203, **202–203,** 207, **209,** 212, 215, 216, 217, 221
CONNECTIONS Connect with other disciplines and acquire information and diverse perspectives in order to use the language to function in academic and career-related situations		
Making Connections	Learners build, reinforce, and expand their knowledge of other disciplines while using the language to develop critical thinking and to solve problems creatively.	pp. **200C, 200D,** 202, **202, 209,** 210, 217, **217,** 218
Acquiring Information and Diverse Perspectives	Learners access and evaluate information and diverse perspectives that are available through the language and its cultures.	pp. **200C,** 204, **204,** 205, 212, **212,** 215, **215**
COMPARISONS Develop insight into the nature of language and culture in order to interact with cultural competence		
Language Comparisons	Learners use the language to investigate, explain, and reflect on the nature of language through comparisons of the language studied and their own.	pp. 205, **205,** 208, **213, 224,** 225
Cultural Comparisons	Learners use the language to investigate, explain, and reflect on the concept of culture through comparisons of the cultures studied and their own.	pp. **200D,** 201, **201, 202,** 215, 216
COMMUNITIES Communicate and interact with cultural competence in order to participate in multilingual communities at home and around the world		
School and Global Communities	Learners use the language both within and beyond the classroom to interact and collaborate in their community and the globalized world.	pp. **200C,** 207, **207,** 209, 211, **220, 222,** 223, **224**
Lifelong Learning	Learners set goals and reflect on their progress in using languages for enjoyment, enrichment, and advancement.	pp. **200C, 200D, 201,** 204, **204,** 215, **215, 218**

Chapter Project

Un cartel publicitario

In this project, students will each create a poster advertising a luxury hotel or a youth hostel in a Spanish-speaking country.

1. Each student will decide which type of accommodation to feature—luxury hotel or youth hostel—and choose its name and location. (You may wish to have students research the names of hotels and hostels in specific locations throughout the Spanish-speaking world or come up with original names and select their own locations.)
2. To create the poster, students should pick two items for each of the following categories to be represented visually in the advertisement: **desayuno, cuarto o habitación, cuarto de baño, otros servicios o actividades.** Each student should write a short description for each illustration.
3. Have students peer edit each other's descriptions and correct their mistakes before they create their posters. Students should turn in corrected first drafts with the final product. You may wish to remind students that one of the defining features of an advertising poster is its visual appeal. Text should be bold, eye-catching, and easy to read. Illustrations should be bright, crisp, and full of color. Everything should be arranged in a way that is pleasing and inviting to view.

Expansion: Students could also work in groups to write and perform television commercials for hotels or hostels based on their posters and on other information presented in the textbook. Students can share their observations regarding ways in which a knowledge of Spanish might benefit careers in advertising or the travel industry.

Scoring Rubric for Project

	5	3	1
Evidence of planning	Corrected draft is provided.	Draft is provided but is not corrected.	No draft is provided.
Use of illustrations	Illustrations are identifiable, colorful, and fully relate to text.	Illustrations are identifiable but lack color and do not fully relate to text.	Illustrations are unidentifiable or unrelated to text.
Presentation	Poster contains all the required elements.	Poster contains some of the required elements.	Poster contains few of the required elements.

Culture

Recipe

ARROZ CON CAMARONES

Ingredients: (makes 6 servings)
3 tablespoons olive oil
2 medium onions, finely chopped
2 cloves garlic, chopped
2 cups long-grain rice
4½ cups chicken stock
1 cup tomatoes, peeled, seeded, and chopped
2 tablespoons fresh coriander, chopped
1 bay leaf
Salt and pepper
1 pound cooked shrimp, chopped into ½-inch pieces

In a large frying pan, sauté the onion and garlic in olive oil over medium heat until the onion is tender but not browned. Stir in the rice and cook it until it has absorbed all the oil. Do not allow it to brown. Add the chicken stock, tomatoes, coriander, and bay leaf. Salt and pepper to taste. Cover and cook over very low heat until the rice is tender and all the liquid has been absorbed. Fold the shrimp into the rice and cook covered for several minutes until heated through.

Pensiones

When traveling around the United States, tourists usually stay at hotels or motels because they are easy to find, they are relatively affordable, and there are few, if any, other options. However, throughout Latin America and Spain tourists have a wider range of accommodations from which to choose. Although motels are uncommon in Hispanic countries, there are alternatives to staying at expensive hotels. In large cities, one of these alternatives is the **pensión.** These smaller, family-run hotels offer more personal service than that of larger hotels. They usually accommodate fewer than fifty guests at one time, may occupy only one floor of a multipurpose building, and often include breakfast. **Pensiones** may not offer the luxurious amenities that large hotels do, but they do offer a visitor the opportunity to experience more of the country's culture. Have students find information about a **pensión** and a hotel in a Spanish-speaking city and compare and contrast them. Where would they choose to stay if they were visiting that city? Why?

Connection to Fine Art

Have students look online or in an art text to find *De mi Buenos Aires,* painted by the Argentine Norberto Russo. Encourage them to identify colors and items in the painting and discuss what they like or do not like about the work. Do they think one of the buildings in the painting is a hotel? Why? Does anyone in class want to visit Buenos Aires? Has anyone traveled to Buenos Aires in the past?

50-Minute Lesson Plans

	Objective	Present	Practice	Assess/Homework
Day 1	Talk about staying at a hotel or hostel	Chapter Opener (5 min.) Introducción al tema (10 min.) Core Instruction/Vocabulario (20 min.)	Activities 1–3 (15 min.)	Student Workbook Activities A–E **ConnectEd** Vocabulary Practice
Day 2	Talk about staying at a hotel or hostel	Quick Start (5 min.) Review Vocabulario (10 min.) Video, Vocabulario en vivo (10 min.)	Activities 4–5 (10 min.) Total Physical Response (5 min.) Audio Activities A–G (10 min.)	Student Workbook Activities F–I **ConnectEd** Vocabulary Practice
Day 3	The present perfect	Quick Start (5 min.) Core Instruction/Gramática, El presente perfecto (10 min.)	Activities 1–4 (10 min.) InfoGap (5 min.) Audio Activities A–D (10 min.)	Quiz 1 (10 min.) Student Workbook Activities A–D **ConnectEd** Grammar Practice
Day 4	Irregular participles	Quick Start (5 min.) Core Instruction/Gramática, Participios irregulares (10 min.)	Activities 5–8 (15 min.) Audio Activities E–F (10 min.)	Quiz 2 (10 min.) Student Workbook Activities A–C **ConnectEd** Grammar Practice
Day 5	Double object pronouns	Quick Start (5 min.) Core Instruction/Gramática, Dos complementos **me lo, te lo, nos lo** (10 min.)	Activities 9–11 (10 min.) Foldables (5 min.) Audio Activities G–H (10 min.)	Quiz 3 (10 min.) Student Workbook Activities A–C **ConnectEd** Grammar Practice
Day 6	Double object pronouns	Quick Start (5 min.) Review Gramática, Dos complementos **me lo, te lo, nos lo** (5 min.) Core Instruction/Gramática, Dos complementos con **se** (10 min.)	Activities 12–13 (10 min.) Activities 14–16 (10 min.) Audio Activity I (10 min.)	Student Workbook Activities A–C **ConnectEd** Grammar Practice
Day 7	Develop reading and listening comprehension skills	Quick Start (5 min.) Core Instruction/Conversación (15 min.) Video, Diálogo en vivo (10 min.)	¿Comprendes? A–B (10 min.)	Quiz 4 (10 min.) ¿Comprendes? C–D **ConnectEd** Conversation
Day 8	Discuss hotel stays in Latin America and Spain	Core Instruction/Lectura cultural (20 min.)	¿Comprendes? A–C (15 min.)	Listening Comprehension Test (15 min.) ¿Comprendes? D–E **ConnectEd** Reading Practice
Day 9	Develop reading comprehension skills	Core Instruction/Lectura Un poco más (15 min.)	¿Comprendes? (10 min.) Prepárate para el examen (25 min.)	Prepárate para el examen, Practice for written proficiency **ConnectEd** Reading Practice
Day 10	Chapter review	Repaso del Capítulo 7 (15 min.)	Prepárate para el examen, Practice for oral proficiency (20 min.)	Test for Writing Proficiency (15 min.) Review for chapter test
Day 11	Chapter 7 Tests (50 min.) Reading and Writing Test Speaking Test Test for Oral Proficiency Test for Reading Comprehension			

90-Minute Lesson Plans

	Objective	Present	Practice	Assess/Homework
Block 1	Talk about staying at a hotel or hostel	Chapter Opener (5 min.) Introducción al tema (10 min.) Quick Start (5 min.) Core Instruction/Vocabulario (20 min.) Video, Vocabulario en vivo (10 min.)	Activities 1–5 (20 min.) Total Physical Response (5 min.) Audio Activities A–G (15 min.)	Student Workbook Activities A–I **ConnectEd** Vocabulary Practice
Block 2	The present perfect Irregular participles	Quick Start (5 min.) Core Instruction/Gramática, El presente perfecto (15 min.) Quick Start (5 min.) Core Instruction/Gramática, Participios irregulares (10 min.)	Activities 1–4 (10 min.) Activities 5–8 (10 min.) InfoGap (5 min.) Audio Activities A–F (20 min.)	Quiz 1 (10 min.) Student Workbook Activities A–D Student Workbook Activities A–C **ConnectEd** Grammar Practice
Block 3	Double object pronouns	Quick Start (5 min.) Core Instruction/Gramática, Dos complementos **me lo, te lo, nos lo** (10 min.) Quick Start (5 min.) Core Instruction/Gramática, Dos complementos con **se** (10 min.)	Activities 9–13 (15 min.) Activities 14–16 (10 min.) Audio Activities G–I (15 min.)	Quizzes 2–3 (20 min.) Student Workbook Activities A–C Student Workbook Activities A–C **ConnectEd** Grammar Practice
Block 4	Discuss hotel stays in Latin America and Spain	Quick Start (5 min.) Core Instruction/Conversación (20 min.) Video, Diálogo en vivo (10 min.) Core Instruction/Lectura cultural (20 min.)	¿Comprendes? A–D (15 min.) ¿Comprendes? A–C (10 min.)	Quiz 4 (10 min.) ¿Comprendes? D–E Prepárate para el examen, Practice for written proficiency **ConnectEd** Conversation, Reading Practice
Block 5	Develop reading comprehension skills	Core Instruction/Lectura Un poco más (15 min.)	¿Comprendes? (10 min.) Prepárate para el examen (20 min.) Prepárate para el examen, Practice for oral proficiency (30 min.)	Listening Comprehension Test (15 min.) Review for chapter test **ConnectEd** Reading Practice
Block 6	Chapter 7 Tests (50 min.) Reading and Writing Test Speaking Test Test for Oral Proficiency Test for Writing Proficiency Test for Reading Comprehension Chapter Project (40 min.)			

Preview

In this chapter, students will learn the vocabulary they need during a hotel or hostel stay. They will learn the present perfect tense as they explore some interesting experiences students their age have enjoyed while traveling economically in Spain and in Latin America. They will also learn how to use double object pronouns in a sentence.

Pacing

It is important to note that once you reach **¡Bravo!** in the chapter, there is no more new material for students to learn. The rest of the chapter recycles what has already been covered. The suggested pacing listed here leaves two to three days for review, assessment, and enrichment activities such as the chapter project.

Vocabulario	1–2 days
Gramática	2–3 days
Conversación	1 day
Lectura cultural	1 day
Lectura Un poco más	1 day

CAPÍTULO 7

En el hotel

Go Online! connectED.mcgraw-hill.com

Audio Video Práctica Repaso Diversiones eScape ePals

Go Online!

Audio
Listen to spoken Spanish.

Video
Watch and learn about the Spanish-speaking world.

Práctica
Practice your skills.

Repaso
Review what you've learned.

Diversiones
Go beyond the classroom.

eScape
Read about current events in the Spanish-speaking world.

Aquí y Allí

Vamos a comparar ¿Has pasado una noche en un hotel aquí en Estados Unidos? ¿Cuándo? Y, ¿cómo era el hotel? ¿Hay muchas categorías de hoteles en Estados Unidos? En este capítulo vas a aprender algo sobre los muchos tipos de hoteles que hay en los países hispanos. Algunos son muy interesantes.

Objetivos

You will:

- check into a hotel or hostel
- ask for things you may need while at a hotel or hostel
- discuss hotel stays in Latin America and Spain

You will use:

- the present perfect tense
- double object pronouns

Aquí ves la piscina o la alberca del Hotel Atitlán en el lago Atitlán en Guatemala. Desde la terraza de la alberca hay vistas estupendas del lago y de los volcanes Tolimán, San Pedro y Atitlán.

SPOTLIGHT ON CULTURE

Cultural Comparison In this chapter, students will learn many types of accommodations available to them as they travel through Spain and Latin America. They will learn about the fun they can have staying with people their own age from all over the world at the many types of youth hostels available to them. They can also experience a big "splurge."

Cultural Snapshot
The area around Lake Atitlán in Guatemala offers some spectacular scenery with the lake, mountains, and volcanoes. The major town in the lake area is Panajachel which has undergone a great deal of expansion in the past decade. There are many new hotels of various categories as well as other tourist attractions. The lake area has become a popular vacation destination for people from the capital and it is particularly popular on weekends.

Interactive Whiteboard
Present or practice with interactive whiteboard activities.

Assessment
Check student progress.

ePals
Connect with Spanish-speaking students around the world.

Introducción al tema

PRESENT

Introduce the theme of the chapter by having students look at the photographs on these pages. Have them look at the young people and determine if there is anything they see them doing that is the same or different from what they do with their own friends. Once you have completed the vocabulary presentation, have students return to these pages and read the information that accompanies each photograph. Once students are fully acquainted with the vocabulary and grammar of the chapter, you may wish to come back to these pages and ask the questions that go with each photo.

Cultural Snapshot

Perú Huanchaco is a beach resort area on the Pacific Coast not far from the city of Trujillo and the famous Mochica ruins. It is quite a popular resort. Huanchaco has many rather inexpensive **hostales** such as the one seen here. **¿Has ido una vez a un balneario? ¿Qué es un balneario? ¿Has nadado en un balneario o solamente en una alberca o piscina?**

España **¿Has tenido que usar una llave como esta? ¿Es más conveniente que una llave magnética o no? ¿Por qué?**

Introducción al tema

En el hotel

¿Te has alojado una vez en un hotel? ¿Por cuántas noches? Mira estas fotos para familiarizarte con el tema de este capítulo—una estadía en un hotel en un país hispano. Como vas a observar hay muchos tipos de hoteles—de los más económicos a los más elegantes.

HOSTAL
LA RIVERA

Perú

El hostal La Rivera en el balneario de Huanchaco en el norte de Perú

España

Una antigua llave que se usaba mucho antes de las llaves magnéticas. En unos hoteles pequeños siguen usando llaves como esta y los clientes siempre tienen que dejarlas en la recepción.

25
Favor
de Arreglar
la Habitación
Please Make Up room
Prière De Faire La Chambre
Hoteles Calinda

Venezuela

El hotel Los Frailes en las montañas de Mérida en Venezuela. ¿Qué tal te parece pasar una hora andando a caballo?

Ecuador

La recepción y el hall en un hotel en Manta, Ecuador

Venezuela The state of Mérida is Venezuela's most popular destination for foreign backpackers. El hotel Los Frailes is a converted monastery. It is in a beautiful location high in the Andes, but it is not convenient to the city of Mérida. **¿Cuál es tu opinión? ¿Cuáles serán algunas actividades disponibles en el hotel? ¿A quiénes se las ofrece el hotel?**

Ecuador Manta es Ecuador's second most important port. It is on the Río Manta. It is the center of the Ecuadoran tuna industry. It is not a major tourist center, but nevertheless many hotels are being built there. **Alguien ha decorado la recepción de este hotel. ¿Por qué? ¿Qué fiesta llega?**

Go Online!
connectED.mcgraw-hill.com

Puerto Rico

Es un hotel bonito en la isla de Vieques.

España

Es el patio de un hotel en la Costa de la Luz en la provincia de Huelva. La provincia está en Andalucía en el suroeste de España.

Nicaragua

El hall de entrada de un hotel bonito en Granada

México

Un hotel elegante en Tepoztlán adonde va mucha gente de la Ciudad de México a pasar el fin de semana

Introducción al tema

Puerto Rico Vieques is a peaceful island off the coast of Puerto Rico. ¿Está cerca del mar el hotel? ¿Hay muchas palmas en la isla de Vieques?

España Today there are many hotels of all categories on the Costa de la Luz. ¿Dónde está la provincia de Huelva? ¿Cómo es el hotel? ¿Es posible nadar en este hotel?

Nicaragua Granada is a very attractive, conservative city on Lake Nicaragua. It is once again becoming fairly popular with tourists. This is the lobby of the Hotel Alhambra on the Parque Central in Granada. ¿Es bonito el hall de entrada de este hotel? ¿Qué hay en el hall?

México Tepoztlán is just 45 miles south of Mexico City. It is located in a lush valley surrounded by unusually shaped mountains. This is the Posada Tepostеco. ¿Tiene jardines bonitos este hotel? ¿Tienen balcones o terrazas muchos de los cuartos?

Vocabulario

Online Resources

Customizable Lesson Plans
- Whiteboard Lesson
- Audio Activities
- Video (Vocabulario)
- Student Workbook
- Enrichment
- Quizzes

Quick Start

Use QS 7.1 or write the following on the board.

Make a list of the things that you would order at a café when traveling through a Spanish-speaking country. Don't forget all you learned about **tapas** and **antojitos**, etc.

TEACH

Core Instruction

Step 1 Present the vocabulary first using Vocabulary V7.2–V7.3.

Step 2 Point to items that have been called out and ask **¿Qué es? ¿Quién es?**

Step 3 Intersperse differentiated questions from easy to more difficult such as: **¿Ha hecho una reservación José? ¿Quién la ha hecho? ¿Ha hecho la reservación en línea? ¿Cómo la ha hecho? ¿Ha reservado un cuarto doble o sencillo? ¿Qué tipo de cuarto ha reservado?**

Step 4 After the oral presentation, call on individuals to read.

Cultural Snapshot

The photos of these hotels were taken in Puerto Rico (**la recepción** and **el mozo**) and Granada, Nicaragua. The hostal is in Huanchaco, Peru.

Una estadía en un hotel

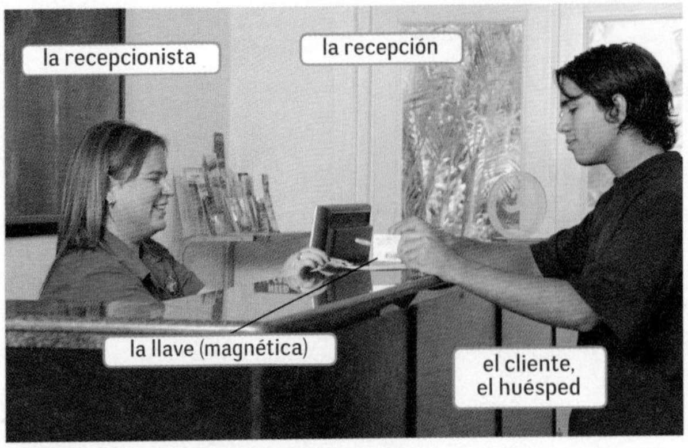

José está en la recepción.
Él ha hecho una reservación en línea.
Ha reservado un cuarto sencillo, no doble.
El huésped va a hospedarse en el hotel.

El mozo ha subido el equipaje en el ascensor.

Un desayuno continental

Un desayuno americano

Comunicación

Presentational

Have groups of students prepare several short impromptu skits about staying at a hotel. Scenes could include a conversation about checking in at the reception desk, taking the elevator with luggage, speaking with the housekeeper, and departing.

Go Online!

Vocabulario en vivo Watch and listen as Nora discusses staying in a hotel in the Spanish-speaking world.

Go Online!

connectED.mcgraw-hill.com

El cuarto, La habitación

La camarera ha limpiado el cuarto.
Ha hecho la cama.

Para conversar

Necesitamos toallas limpias. ¿Nos las ha cambiado la camarera?
No, no nos las ha cambiado.

El cuarto de baño

El huésped va a salir.
Ha abandonado el cuarto.

En otras partes

In addition to **la camarera**, you will also hear **la mucama**, especially in Mexico.

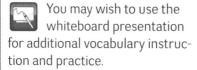

Vocabulario

About the Spanish Language

- In addition to **el ascensor** you will also hear **el elevador.**
- There are many terms for **cuarto de baño.** Technically the term **cuarto de baño** must include **el baño.** Other terms are: **los servicios, el servicio para señores(as), los sanitarios, el retrete, el excusado, el tocador, el aseo.**

Go Online!

You may wish to use the whiteboard presentation for additional vocabulary instruction and practice.

Total Physical Response (TPR)

(Student 1), **ven acá, por favor.**
Estás en la recepción del hotel. Toma tu llave.
Ve al ascensor.
Pon tu maleta en el ascensor.
Empuja el botón para subir.
Sal del ascensor.
Pon la llave en la puerta de tu cuarto.
Abre la puerta.
Entra en el cuarto.
Pon tu equipaje sobre la cama.
(Student 2), **ven acá, por favor.**
Estás en un hotel.
Estás en tu cuarto.
Abre la puerta del armario.
Toma una percha.
Cuelga tu abrigo y ponlo en el armario.
Cierra la puerta del armario.
Ve al baño.
Mírate en el espejo.
Toma el jabón. Lávate la cara.
Toma una toalla.
Sécate la cara con la toalla.
Gracias, *(Student 2)*. **Bien hecho.**

Leveling EACH Activity

Easy Activities 1, 2, 3
Average Activity 2
Expansión, Activity 4
CHallenging Activity 5

PRACTICE

Activity 1

Audio Script

1. El huésped está en la recepción.
2. El mozo ha subido el equipaje.
3. El señor va a hospedarse en el hotel.
4. Hay dos lavabos en el cuarto de baño.
5. El señor habla con la recepcionista.

Activity 2 It is suggested that you go over this activity orally. Call on individuals to answer and then have students write the answers. This activity can also be done as a paired activity.

Comunicación

Interpersonal
You may wish to ask the general question: **¿Qué haces para mantenerte en forma?**

Go Online!

You may wish to remind students to go online for additional vocabulary practice. They can also download audio files of all vocabulary.

ESCUCHAR

1 Escucha las frases. Parea cada frase con la foto que describe.

a.

b.

c.

Nota

Hoy en día muchos hoteles tienen un gimnasio y una sauna para sus clientes. A mucha gente le gusta ir al gimnasio por la mañana antes de ir a su trabajo o por la tarde después de volver de su trabajo. Todos quieren mantenerse en forma.

HABLAR • ESCRIBIR

2 Contesta sobre la llegada a un hotel.

1. ¿Ha reservado el señor un cuarto?
2. ¿Adónde va el cliente cuando llega al hotel?
3. ¿Quién lo saluda en la recepción?
4. ¿Quién lo va a ayudar con sus maletas?
5. ¿Qué le da el recepcionista para abrir la puerta de su cuarto?

EXPANSIÓN

Ahora, sin mirar las preguntas, cuenta la información en tus propias palabras. Si no recuerdas algo, un(a) compañero(a) te puede ayudar.

Answers

1

1. c
2. b
3. c
4. a
5. c

2

1. Sí (No), el señor (no) ha reservado un cuarto.
2. El cliente va a la recepción.
3. El/La recepcionista lo saluda en la recepción.
4. El mozo lo va a ayudar con sus maletas.
5. El recepcionista le da una llave (magnética) para abrir la puerta de su cuarto.

Go Online!

connectED.mcgraw-hill.com

LEER

3 Escoge la palabra apropiada.

1. (Una manta, Una almohada) cubre la cama.
2. Hay (perchas, sábanas) en el armario.
3. (El mozo, La camarera) ha hecho la cama.
4. Me gusta dormir con dos (camas, almohadas).
5. Es necesario cambiar las toallas (limpias, sucias).
6. El desayuno (continental, americano) incluye huevos.
7. La huéspeda ha (abandonado, reservado) el cuarto porque va a salir.
8. Necesito (jabón, champú) para lavarme la cara.

CULTURA

Es una habitación en un hotel en Madrid, España. Identifica todo lo que ves en la habitación.

ESCRIBIR

4 **Rompecabezas**

Usa las letras en la tabla para formar palabras de este capítulo. Puedes usar unas letras más de una vez. Luego, escribe frases originales con tus palabras.

a	r	e
p	i	s
t	d	v
l	n	c
o	b	m

HABLAR • ESCRIBIR

5 Describe.

1. el cuarto de un hotel
2. un desayuno continental
3. un desayuno americano
4. las actividades en la recepción de un hotel

Carreras

Si conoces el español y lo sabes hablar por lo menos un poquito, hay muchas oportunidades para trabajar en la industria hotelera. Además de los muchos hispanohablantes que viven aquí, hay miles de turistas de España y Latinoamérica que visitan Estados Unidos cada año. Si es posible, visita un hotel en tu ciudad y observa a los clientes y habla con los empleados. ¿Hablan español?

Differentiation

Advanced Learners

Activity 3 You may wish to have advanced learners make up original sentences, putting into proper context the words that do not belong.

Activity 5 Have students give complete descriptions.

¡Así se dice!

Why It Works!

Note that in addition to the many activities in the Student Edition, students are given many activities in the Workbook and Audio Activities to practice their new words in a variety of formats leveled from easy to challenging.

Comunidades

Have students think of some hotels or motels in your area where the personnel may be able to use some Spanish.

Cultural Snapshot

Have students describe all they see in this hotel room in the Gran Vía of Madrid.

ASSESS

Students are now ready to take Quiz 1.

Answers

3
1. Una manta
2. perchas
3. La camarera
4. almohadas
5. sucias
6. americano
7. abandonado
8. jabón

4 *Answers will vary but may include:* la recepción, el/la recepcionista, la llave, el/la cliente(a), el ascensor, el panecillo, la mermelada, el tocino, el bacón, el lacón, la manta, la sábana, la cama, la camarera, el armario, el lavabo, la toalla, el váter, el inodoro, el aire acondicionado

5 *Answers will vary.*

Online Resources

Customizable Lesson Plans
Whiteboard Lesson
Audio Activities
Student Workbook
Quizzes

Quick Start

Use QS 7.2 or write the following on the board.
Answer.

1. **¿Qué bebes cuando tienes sed?**
2. **¿Qué comes cuando tienes hambre?**
3. **¿Cuál es un almuerzo típico que tomas en la cafetería de la escuela?**

TEACH

Core Instruction

Step 1 Go over the presentation of the past participle as you write the examples on the board. Have students repeat them.

Step 2 As you go over the conjugations you may wish to give students just the forms of the verb **haber.** Then go over the present perfect forms presented here and have the students repeat them in unison.

Step 3 Call on students to read Activity 3 aloud.

Cultural Snapshot

Guadalajara, the capital of the state of Jalisco, is the second-largest city in Mexico with a population of some four million. Guadalajara is the home of the **mariachi** and the **jarabe tapatío,** the famous Mexican hat dance.

Gramática

El presente perfecto

1. The present perfect tense is called a compound tense because it consists of two parts—the present tense of the verb **haber** and the past participle.

2. The past participle is formed by adding **-ado** to the stem of **-ar** verbs and **-ido** to the stem of **-er** and **-ir** verbs.

llegar → llegado | **comer → comido** | **subir → subido**
cambiar → cambiado | **tener → tenido** | **vivir → vivido**

3. Study the forms of regular present perfect verbs.

	llegar	comer	salir
yo	he llegado	he comido	he salido
tú	has llegado	has comido	has salido
Ud., él, ella	ha llegado	ha comido	ha salido
nosotros(as)	hemos llegado	hemos comido	hemos salido
vosotros(as)	*habéis llegado*	*habéis comido*	*habéis salido*
Uds., ellos, ellas	han llegado	han comido	han salido

4. The present perfect tense is used when speaking of a past event without reference to any particular time. It brings the action right up to the present. Some time expressions frequently used with the present perfect are:

ya — *already, yet*
todavía no — *not yet*
hasta ahora — *until now, so far*
jamás — *ever, never*
nunca — *never*

—En tu vida, ¿has viajado a México?
—No. No he ido nunca a México.
—Yo sí. Hasta ahora he estado tres veces.

5. The verb **haber** and the past participle are never separated.

Ella ha llegado pero sus amigos no han llegado.
Y ella no les ha hablado.

CULTURA
Es una calle peatonal en Guadalajara, México. ¿Jamás has viajado a México?

Kerri Galloway

Go Online!

ePals You may wish to remind students to go online for additional grammar review and practice.

You may wish to use the whiteboard presentation for additional grammar instruction and practice.

Go Online!
connectED.mcgraw-hill.com

Práctica

ESCUCHAR • HABLAR • ESCRIBIR

1 Contesta sobre la visita de Sofía a un hotel.

1. ¿Ha llegado Sofía al hotel?
2. ¿Ha ido a la recepción?
3. ¿Ha hablado con la recepcionista?
4. ¿Le ha dado su llave la recepcionista?
5. ¿Ha subido a su cuarto?
6. ¿Ha subido la escalera o ha tomado el ascensor?
7. ¿La ha ayudado el mozo?

EXPANSIÓN

Ahora, sin mirar las preguntas, cuenta la información en tus propias palabras. Si no recuerdas algo, un(a) compañero(a) te puede ayudar.

HABLAR

2 Personaliza. Da respuestas personales.

1. ¿Has viajado por Ecuador?
2. ¿Te has hospedado en un albergue juvenil?
3. ¿Jamás has comido tacos o enchiladas?
4. ¿Has asistido a un concierto de rock?
5. Tú y tus amigos, ¿han ido a un museo?
6. ¿Han viajado ustedes en avión?

LEER • ESCRIBIR

3 Completa con el presente perfecto.

Los huéspedes __1__ (llegar) al hotel y __2__ (presentarse) en la recepción. El recepcionista les __3__ (dar) su llave pero (ellos) no __4__ (subir) a su cuarto todavía. ¿Tú __5__ (ir) a un hotel recientemente?

4 ***Comunicación***

Tus tíos y primos están visitando tu ciudad. Están hospedándose en un hotel. Llama al hotel por teléfono y habla con el/la recepcionista (tu compañero[a]). Quieres saber si ya han llegado tus parientes y si ya han subido a su cuarto. Después cambien de rol.

Si quieres estar cerca del mercado en Otavalo, Ecuador, puedes hospedarte en este hostal.

InfoGap For more practice using the present perfect, do Activity 7 in the Student Resource section at the end of this book.

Richard Brommer

Gramática

Leveling EACH Activity

Easy Activities 1, 2
Average Activity 1
Expansión, Activity 3
CHallenging Activity 4

PRACTICE

Activities 1 and 2 These activities should be gone over orally in class with individual members of the class responding. These same activities can also be done as paired activities.

Differentiation

Multiple Intelligences

Bodily-kinesthetic learners can act out each of Sofía's actions in Activity 1.

Cultural Snapshot

Otavalo is known for its market. Its weavers are considered the best of all Latin America.

Conexiones

Have students make up some sentences in the present perfect in English. If they use incorrect participles, have them correct one another.

ASSESS

Students are now ready to take Quiz 2.

Answers

1

1. Sí (No), Sofía (no) ha llegado al hotel.
2. Sí, (No, no) ha ido a la recepción.
3. Sí, (No, no) ha hablado con la recepcionista.
4. Sí (No), la recepcionista (no) le ha dado su llave.
5. Sí, (No, no) ha subido a su cuarto.
6. Ha subido la escalera. (Ha tomado el ascensor.)
7. Sí (No), el mozo (no) la ha ayudado.

2

1. Sí, (No, no) he viajado por Ecuador.
2. Sí, (No, no) me he hospedado en un albergue juvenil.
3. Sí, (No, no) he comido tacos o enchiladas.
4. Sí, (No, no) he asistido a un concierto de rock.
5. Sí (No), mis amigos y yo (no) hemos ido a un museo.
6. Sí, (No, no) hemos viajado en avión.

3

1. han llegado
2. se han presentado
3. ha dado
4. han subido
5. has ido

4 *Answers will vary.*

Online Resources

Customizable Lesson Plans

Whiteboard Lesson

Audio Activities

Student Workbook

Quizzes

Quick Start

Use QS 7.3 or write the following on the board.

Answer.

1. **¿Ves una mesa libre en el café?**
2. **¿Ves al mesero?**
3. **¿Pone el mesero la mesa?**
4. **¿Qué pone en la mesa?**
5. **Y tú, ¿tienes mucha hambre? ¿Te mueres de hambre?**

TEACH

Core Instruction

Have students repeat the irregular past participles several times.

PRACTICE

Leveling EACH Activity

Easy Activity 5

Average Activities 6, 8

CHallenging Activity 7

¡Así se dice!

Why It Works!

In this chapter we first present students with the pronouns that do *not* change form when used together. Once they grasp this position, we present the pronoun **se** in the next section to plateau the difficulty level of the structure. All forms will then be used together in the Cumulative Review section.

Gramática

Conexiones

El inglés

There are very few verbs that have an irregular past participle in Spanish. Such is not the case in English. There are many verbs with irregular past participles and many people learning English, as well as native speakers, have trouble with them. Can you give the past participle of the following verbs? *be, begin, bite, break, bring, buy, catch, come, eat, fall, find, fly, go, hear, hide, leave, make, meet, ride, run, see, sing, sit, speak, stand, swim, throw, write*

Participios irregulares

The following verbs have irregular past participles.

decir → dicho	**volver → vuelto**
hacer → hecho	**devolver → devuelto**
ver → visto	**morir → muerto**
escribir → escrito	**abrir → abierto**
poner → puesto	**cubrir → cubierto** *(covered)*
romper → roto *(broken)*	**freír → frito**

Práctica

HABLAR

5 Conversa según el modelo.

MODELO —**¿Van a verlo?**
—**Pero, ya lo hemos visto.**

1. ¿Van a abrirlo?
2. ¿Van a ponerlo?
3. ¿Van a devolverlo?
4. ¿Van a escribirlo?
5. ¿Van a decirlo?
6. ¿Van a cubrirlo?

HABLAR

6 Contesta según el modelo.

MODELO **¿Hacer tal cosa? →**
¿Hacer tal cosa? ¡Vaya, hombre! ¿Yo? En mi vida he hecho tal cosa.

1. ¿Ver tal cosa?
2. ¿Decir tal cosa?
3. ¿Leer tal cosa?
4. ¿Escribir tal cosa?

HABLAR • ESCRIBIR

7 Contesta según se indica.

1. ¿Ustedes se han ayudado? (sí)
2. ¿Quién ha hecho la cama? (yo)
3. ¿Quién ha frito los huevos? (Elena y Tomás)
4. ¿Quién ha abierto la lata? (yo)
5. ¿Quién ha puesto la mesa? (yo)
6. ¿Quién no ha hecho nada? (tú)

CULTURA

¿Quién ha puesto esta mesa en un restaurante en Guatemala?

8 *Comunicación*

Hay muchas cosas que queremos hacer algún día que hasta ahora no hemos hecho. Con un(a) compañero(a) de clase, hablen de las cosas que quieren hacer pero que todavía no han hecho. Cuando posible, expliquen por qué no las han hecho o no las han podido hacer.

Lori Ernfridsson

Answers

5

1. Pero, ya lo hemos abierto.
2. Pero, ya lo hemos puesto.
3. Pero, ya lo hemos devuelto.
4. Pero, ya lo hemos escrito.
5. Pero, ya lo hemos dicho.
6. Pero, ya lo hemos cubierto.

6

1. ¿Ver tal cosa? ¡Vaya, hombre! ¿Yo? En mi vida he visto tal cosa.
2. ¿Decir tal cosa? ¡Vaya, hombre! ¿Yo? En mi vida he dicho tal cosa.
3. ¿Leer tal cosa? ¡Vaya, hombre! ¿Yo? En mi vida he leído tal cosa.
4. ¿Escribir tal cosa? ¡Vaya, hombre! ¿Yo? En mi vida he escrito tal cosa.

7

1. Sí, nos hemos ayudado.
2. Yo he hecho la cama.
3. Elena y Tomás han frito los huevos.
4. Yo he abierto la lata.
5. Yo he puesto la mesa.
6. Tú no has hecho nada.

8 *Answers will vary.*

Dos complementos me lo, te lo, nos lo

1. Many sentences have both a direct and an indirect object pronoun. In Spanish the indirect object pronoun always precedes the direct object pronoun. Both pronouns precede the conjugated form of the verb.

2. Study the following sentences.

Ella nos sirvió el helado.	**Ella nos lo sirvió.**
El mozo me dio la llave.	**El mozo me la dio.**
Él me vendió los libros.	**Él me los vendió.**
Papá te hizo las reservaciones.	**Papá te las hizo.**

Práctica

HABLAR

9 Conversa según el modelo.

MODELO los videos →
—¿Quién te dio los videos?
—Mi tío Julio me los dio.

1. la raqueta
2. los esquís
3. las botas
4. el boleto
5. las gafas para el sol
6. la computadora

HABLAR • ESCRIBIR

10 Contesta con **la camarera** o **el mozo** y los pronombres apropiados.

1. ¿Quién te ha traído las perchas?
2. ¿Quién te ha cambiado las toallas?
3. ¿Quién te ha limpiado el baño?
4. ¿Quién te ha subido el equipaje?
5. ¿Quién te ha abierto la puerta?
6. ¿Quién te ha servido el desayuno?

Go Online!

connectED.mcgraw-hill.com

FOLDABLES Study Organizer

LARGE SENTENCE STRIPS

See the Foldables section of the Student Handbook at the beginning of this book for help with making this foldable. Use this study organizer to help you practice object pronouns. Write a sentence with a direct and indirect object on the front of each flap. Then pass the foldable to your partner who will open each flap and rewrite the sentences using pronouns. When you're finished, switch roles.

CULTURA

Es un cuarto con dos camas en un hotel bonito en Cotacachi, Ecuador. La camarera ha limpiado el cuarto y ha puesto las batas en la cama para los huéspedes.

Andrew Payti

Online Resources

Customizable Lesson Plans
- Whiteboard Lesson
- Audio Activities
- Video (Gramática)
- Student Workbook
- Enrichment
- Quizzes

Quick Start

Use QS 7.4 or write the following on the board.

Answer.

1. **¿Quién te sirve en un restaurante o un café?**
2. **¿Te trae el menú?**
3. **¿Abres el menú?**
4. **¿Lo lees?**
5. **¿Quién escribe la orden? ¿Tú la escribes o la escribe el mesero?**

TEACH

Core Instruction

Step 1 Lead students through Items 1 and 2.

Step 2 Call on volunteers to read the model sentences aloud.

Step 3 You may wish to write the model sentences on the board. Highlight the objects as is done in Item 2. Draw an arrow from the pronoun to the noun it replaces. Have students note that the second pronoun comes after the one that was already there.

Answers

9

1. ¿Quién te dio la raqueta? Mi tío Julio me la dio.
2. ¿Quién te dio los esquís? Mi tío Julio me los dio.
3. ¿Quién te dio las botas? Mi tío Julio me las dio.
4. ¿Quién te dio el boleto? Mi tío Julio me lo dio.
5. ¿Quién te dio las gafas para el sol? Mi tío Julio me las dio.
6. ¿Quién te dio la computadora? Mi tío Julio me la dio.

10

1. La camarera me las ha traído.
2. La camarera me las ha cambiado.
3. La camarera me lo ha limpiado.
4. El mozo me lo ha subido.
5. El mozo me la ha abierto.
6. La camarera me lo ha servido.

Leveling EACH Activity

Easy Activity 9
Average Activity 10

Leveling EACH Activity

Average Activities 11, 12
CHallenging Activity 13

PRACTICE

Activities 11 and 12 These activities can also be done as paired activities.

Refrán

Proverbs, adages, idiomatic expressions, and other popular sayings provide a wealth of opportunities for students to learn about different cultural perspectives as well as perspectives shared by different cultures. They also serve to enrich students' overall understanding of language.

Have students recite the proverb aloud. Then see if they can figure out its meaning, and encourage them to try to give an equivalent expression in English such as "To each his own."

Go Online!

Gramática en vivo *Double object pronouns* Enliven learning with the animated world of Professor Cruz! **Gramática en vivo** is a fun and effective tool for additional instruction and/or review.

You may wish to use the whiteboard presentation for additional grammar instruction and practice.

Gramática

Refrán

Can you guess what the following proverb means?

Sobre gustos no hay nada escrito.

HABLAR

11 Conversa según el modelo.

MODELO **cámara nueva →**
—¿Quieres ver mi cámara nueva?
—¿Quién te la compró?
—Me la compró mi tía Adela.

1. zapatos nuevos
2. casco nuevo
3. mochila nueva
4. botas nuevas

ESCUCHAR • HABLAR • ESCRIBIR

12 Contesta con **nuestra profesora** y los pronombres apropiados.

MODELO **—¿Quién les dio (a ustedes) el examen?**
—Nuestra profesora nos lo dio.

1. ¿Quién les explicó (a ustedes) la regla?
2. ¿Quién les enseñó la gramática?
3. ¿Quién les explicó las diferencias?
4. ¿Quién les presentó el vocabulario?
5. ¿Quién les leyó los poemas?

13 ***Comunicación***

Habla con un(a) compañero(a) de clase. Tu compañero(a) está llevando unas cosas que te gustan y quieres saber quién se las dio. Sigue el modelo.

MODELO **—_____, me gusta mucho tu camisa. ¿Quién te la dio?**
—_____ me la dio. *or* **No me la dio nadie. Me la compré.**

Andrew Payti

CULTURA

El Hospedaje Sunset en Huanchaco, Perú. Este hospedaje tiene tarifas económicas.

Answers

11

1. —¿Quieres ver mis zapatos nuevos?
   —¿Quién te los compró?
   —Me los compró mi tía Adela.
2. —¿Quieres ver mi casco nuevo?
   —¿Quién te lo compró?
   —Me lo compró mi tía Adela.
3. —¿Quieres ver mi mochila nueva?
   —¿Quién te la compró?
   —Me la compró mi tía Adela.
4. —¿Quieres ver mis botas nuevas?
   —¿Quién te las compró?
   —Me las compró mi tía Adela.

12

1. Nuestra profesora nos la explicó.
2. Nuestra profesora nos la enseñó.
3. Nuestra profesora nos las explicó.
4. Nuestra profesora nos lo presentó.
5. Nuestra profesora nos los leyó.

13 *Answers will vary.*

Dos complementos con se

Go Online!
connectED.mcgraw-hill.com

1. The indirect object pronouns **le** and **les** change to **se** when used with **lo, la, los,** or **las.** Note that the indirect object **se** always precedes the direct object.

El mozo les subió el equipaje. → **El mozo se lo subió.**

El recepcionista le dio las llaves a José. → **El recepcionista se las dio.**

2. Because the pronoun **se** can refer to many different people, it is often clarified with a prepositional phrase.

Yo se lo di { **a él. / a ella. / a usted.**

Yo se lo di { **a ellos. / a ellas. / a ustedes.**

Práctica

ESCUCHAR • HABLAR

14 Conversa según el modelo.

MODELO —**¿Quién le compró el regalito?**
—**Su abuela se lo compró.**

1. ¿Quién le compró la bicicleta?
2. ¿Quién le compró las entradas?
3. ¿Quién le compró la tabla hawaiana?
4. ¿Quién le compró los esquís acuáticos?
5. ¿Quién le compró el balón?

LEER • ESCRIBIR

15 Contesta con los pronombres apropiados.

1. ¿Les abrió la puerta a los huéspedes el mozo?
2. ¿Les subió las maletas el mozo?
3. ¿Le dio la llave a la cliente el recepcionista?
4. ¿Le dieron su nombre al recepcionista los huéspedes?
5. ¿Les ha cambiado las toallas sucias la camarera?

16 ***Comunicación***

Alguien que conoces acaba de recibir algo nuevo. Decide lo que es. Con un(a) compañero(a) de clase, prepara una conversación como la siguiente.

MODELO —**¿Viste el carro nuevo de Isabel?**
—**Sí, lo vi. ¿Quién se lo dio?**
—**No sé si alguien se lo dio o si se lo compró.**

CULTURA
Parece que a la niña le gusta mucho el dulce. ¿Quién se lo compró?

Andrew Payti

¡Bravo!
You have now learned all the new vocabulary and grammar in this chapter. Continue to use and practice all that you know while learning more cultural information. **¡Vamos!**

Answers

14
1. Su abuelita se la compró.
2. Su abuelita se las compró.
3. Su abuelita se la compró.
4. Su abuelita se los compró.
5. Su abuelita se lo compró.

15
1. Sí (No), el mozo (no) se la abrió.
2. Sí (No), el mozo (no) se las subió.
3. Sí (No), el recepcionista (no) se la dio.
4. Sí (No), los huéspedes (no) se lo dieron.
5. Sí (No), la camarera (no) se las ha cambiado.

16 *Answers will vary.*

Online Resources

Customizable Lesson Plans
- Whiteboard Lesson
- Audio Activities
- Video (Gramática)
- Student Workbook
- Enrichment
- Quizzes

Quick Start

Use QS 7.5 or write the following on the board.

Complete with the correct pronoun.

1. **Yo veo al mesero. Yo ___ veo y ___ hablo.**
2. **Yo ___ doy la orden y él ___ escribe.**
3. **Cuando los meseros me dan un buen servicio yo ___ dejo una propina.**
4. **Yo ___ pongo en la mesa.**

TEACH

Core Instruction

Step 1 Lead students through Items 1 and 2.

Step 2 You may want to write the model sentences on the board to reinforce this concept. Draw an arrow from the pronoun to the noun it replaces.

About the Spanish Language

You may wish to explain to students that **le** changes to **se** strictly for the sake of pronunciation. It would be both difficult and awkward to say **le lo, le la.**

ASSESS

Students are now ready to take Quiz 4.

Online Resources

Customizable Lesson Plans
Audio Activities
Video (Diálogo)
Student Workbook

Quick Start

Use QS 7.6 or write the following on the board.

Match the word in the first column with a related word in the second column.

1. **limpio**	a. **la reservación**
2. **bañar**	b. **la llegada**
3. **reservar**	c. **la recepción**
4. **recibir**	d. **la limpieza**
5. **llegar**	e. **el baño**

TEACH

Core Instruction

Step 1 Tell students they are going to hear a conversation between a hotel clerk and guests.

Step 2 Have students follow along as you play the audio recording.

Step 3 Have pairs of students create hotel-centered skits based on the conversation. Then have them present their skits to the class. They can make any changes they wish.

Step 4 Now go over the **¿Comprendes?** activities. If students can answer the questions with relative ease, move on. Students should not be expected to memorize the conversation.

¡Así se dice!

Why It Works!

Note that this realistic, lifelike conversation contains no new language to confuse students. They are already familiar with all of the Spanish—both vocabulary and grammar.

Go Online!

You may wish to remind students to go online for additional conversation practice.

connectED.mcgraw-hill.com

¿Comprendes?

A Contesta según la información en la conversación.

1. ¿Con quién están hablando las muchachas? ¿Dónde?
2. ¿Han hecho una reservación las dos muchachas?
3. ¿Hay una habitación disponible?
4. ¿Cuál es la tarifa?
5. ¿Cuánto tiempo piensan estar en el hotel las muchachas?
6. ¿Por qué están cansadas?
7. ¿Han abandonado la habitación los otros clientes?
8. ¿Qué está incluido en la tarifa?

B **Resumiendo** Cuenta la información en la conversación en tus propias palabras.

C **Llegando a conclusiones** ¿Qué piensas? ¿Van a tomar un desayuno continental o un desayuno americano las muchachas? ¿Por qué has llegado a esta conclusión?

D **Investigando** En línea o en el periódico busca el tipo de cambio del dólar al euro. Luego, calcula el precio de la habitación en dólares.

Andrew Payti

CULTURA
La entrada a un hotel en Gijón, Asturias

Comparaciones

Los hoteles
En España y Latinoamérica todavía hay hoteles económicos que no tienen baño privado pero menos que en el pasado. Hasta recientemente había muchos que no lo tenían y un cuarto con baño privado costaba mucho. Cuando vas a un hotel, ¿prefieres un baño privado?

Pre-AP Listening to this conversation will help students develop the skills that they need to be successful on the listening portion of the AP exam.

PRACTICE

¿Comprendes?

A You can allow students to refer to the **Conversación** to look up answers or you may use this as a factual recall activity and not let them look up the information.

Differentiation

Slower Paced Learners

B Call on a less able student to review what was said by a more able student.

Advanced Learners

Have advanced learners take three minutes to write a review.
C and **D** These activities deal with higher skills development.

Comparaciones

Have students make some comparisons concerning hotels in your area.

Go Online!

Diálogo en vivo In this episode, Francisco visits an unusual hotel. Ask students why Francisco chooses this hotel over others in his guide book.

Answers

A

1. Están hablando con la recepcionista en la recepción del hotel.
2. No, las dos muchachas no han hecho una reservación.
3. Sí, hay una habitación disponible.
4. Noventa euros la noche.
5. Esperan estar tres noches en el hotel.
6. Están cansadas porque han pasado toda la noche en el avión.
7. No, los otros clientes no han abandonado la habitación.
8. El desayuno continental está incluido en la tarifa.

B *Answers will vary.*

C *Answers will vary.*

D *Answers will vary.*

Online Resources

Customizable Lesson Plans

Audio Activities

Student Workbook

TEACH

Core Instruction

Step 1 As suggested in the **Estrategia de lectura,** have students sit back and enjoy this selection.

Step 2 Ask questions as you progress in the reading. Have students relate information about their own ideas from the **Antes de leer** and **Durante la lectura.**

Step 3 After every five or six sentences, you may want to call on a student to give a review of the information.

Differentiation

Multiple Intelligences

Have a group of **verbal-linguistic** learners respond to Phil's declaration as "king of the castle." Ask them if Phil should be expected to pay for his share of the room like his companions.

Comunicación

Interpersonal

If any students in class have already traveled in a Spanish-speaking country, have them tell something about a hotel experience.

Lectura CULTURAL

ESTRATEGIA DE LECTURA

LEYENDO ALGO PERSONAL Un e-mail de un(a) amigo(a) es un tipo de lectura personal. Una estrategia sencilla es simplemente gozar o disfrutar de lo que tu amigo(a) te está diciendo.

Antes de leer

Imagina que tienes unos amigos que están disfrutando de un viaje en un país hispano pero no tienen mucho dinero. ¿Cuáles son unas cosas que pueden hacer para economizar?

Durante la lectura

Identifícate con lo que tus amigos están haciendo. ¿Encuentras unas cosas bastante graciosas? ¿Cuáles?

✓ READING CHECK

¿Por qué se hospedan los viajeros en un albergue juvenil?

CULTURA

Un hostal en la estación de esquí Los Penitentes en Argentina, no muy lejos de Mendoza

Andrew Payti

✓ READING CHECK

¿Cómo han botado la casa por la ventana los amigos? Y, ¿por qué?

Un hostal y un parador

De: Verónica Valverde
A: maripaz.contador@estrella.com
Asunto: Viaje a Latinoamérica

Queridos amigos,

Ya hemos viajado bastante y no pueden imaginar todo lo que hemos visto y hecho. ¡El Perú! ¡Una maravilla! Y aquí estamos en Bariloche—después de un vuelo de cinco horas de Lima a Buenos Aires y dos más a Bariloche. Son largos, ¿no? Como siempre, hemos decidido hospedarnos en un albergue juvenil porque cuestan mucho menos que en un hotel. La mayoría de los albergues son bastante cómodos pero en algunos hasta ocho personas duermen en un solo cuarto. A veces no hay agua caliente pero nos hemos acostumbrado a tomar una ducha en agua fría. Todos han estado limpios—y baratos. Además hemos conocido a estudiantes de todas partes del mundo.

Besitos,
Verónica

De: Agustín Echevarría
A: maripaz.contador@estrella.com
Asunto: Viaje por España

Queridos amigos,

Saludos de Galicia en el norte de España. Ya hemos visitado a lo menos diez ciudades españolas y después de muchas noches en albergues juveniles hemos decidido botar la casa por la ventana. Estamos pasando una noche en el parador de los Reyes Católicos en Santiago de Compostela. En España, los paradores son del gobierno. Casi todos son antiguos castillos o monasterios. Son elegantes y NO baratos. Somos los únicos clientes del hotel con mochilas. Pero, ¡qué va!

Hemos elegido a Phil rey del castillo. Como él es rey él va a pagar la cuenta. ¡Ja, ja! Dice Phil que si él es el rey es también el dueño del castillo y no tiene que pagar nada. Ustedes conocen a Phil, ¿no?

Agustín

Go Online!

You may wish to remind students to go online for additional reading comprehension and writing skills practice.

Go Online!

connectED.mcgraw-hill.com

¿Comprendes?

A Buscando información Da la siguiente información.

Verónica y sus amigos
por donde viajan
donde están ahora
donde se hospedan
por qué les gustan los albergues
como son los albergues

Agustín, Phil y sus amigos
por donde viajan
donde están ahora
donde se hospedan en este momento
cuantas noches van a estar
como son los paradores

B Explicando Explica lo que es un parador nacional en España.

C Comparando Compara un albergue juvenil con un parador nacional.

D Resumiendo En tus propias palabras, cuenta el episodio entre Phil y sus compañeros de viaje en el parador de los Reyes Católicos.

E Llegando a conclusiones Basado en el episodio entre Phil y sus compañeros, ¿qué concluyes sobre la personalidad de Phil? ¿Qué tipo de persona es?

CULTURA

El exterior de un parador en Cáceres, España. Los paradores son del gobierno español y muchos de ellos son joyas arquitectónicas como conventos, monasterios y palacios.

Andrew Payti

Lectura

PRACTICE

Pre-AP These cultural readings will develop the skills that students need to be successful on the reading and writing sections of the AP exam. Listening to these readings will also help prepare them for the auditory component.

¿Comprendes?

A Have students fill in the information and then have individuals report it to the class.

B, C, D, E You can have students work in pairs or small groups or you may wish to have the entire class take part in the discussions.

Writing Development

You may also want to have students develop written responses to Activities B and C.

Conexiones

Have students locate Santiago de Compostela on the maps at the beginning of this book in the **GeoVista** section that features Spain. Ask students what body of water is near Santiago de Compostela. What are some names for the waters off the coast of northern Spain?

Answers

A

Verónica y sus amigos

por donde viajan: por Latinoamérica

donde están ahora: en Bariloche, Argentina

donde se hospedan: en un albergue juvenil

por qué les gustan los albergues: porque son económicos y es posible conocer a estudiantes de todas partes del mundo

como son los albergues: La mayoría son bastante cómodos pero en algunos hasta ocho personas duermen en un cuarto y en unas ocasiones no hay agua caliente. Todos están limpios.

Agustín, Phil y sus amigos

por donde viajan: por España

donde están ahora: en Santiago de Compostela

donde se hospedan en este momento: en el Parador de los Reyes Católicos

cuantas noches van a estar: una noche

como son los paradores: Son antiguos castillos y monasterios y son muy lujosos.

B *Answers will vary but may include:* Un parador nacional en España es un antiguo castillo o monasterio del gobierno. Es elegante y no barato.

C *Answers will vary.*

D *Answers will vary.*

E *Answers will vary.*

Online Resources

Customizable Lesson Plans

Audio Activities

Student Workbook

TEACH

Core Instruction

You may wish to have students go over this **Lectura—Un poco más** selection somewhat thoroughly since there is quite a bit of renewed interest in the **Camino de Santiago,** much of which is due to tourists who are interested in history or staying in shape.

Differentiation

Multiple Intelligences

You may wish to have **visual-spatial** learners interested in this topic prepare a map that traces the entire route of the **Camino de Santiago.**

Teaching Options

Call on some students to read aloud individually. After a student has read three or four sentences, ask questions of other students to check comprehension.

Lectura

UN POCO MÁS

Antes de leer

¿Te interesa hacer un viaje si tienes que caminar muchos kilómetros cada día por una semana entera o más? ¿Por qué contestas que sí o que no? Luego decide si el viaje en la lectura es para ti o no.

El Camino de Santiago

Durante la Edad Media[1] había unas peregrinaciones[2] importantes. Una era la peregrinación a Santiago de Compostela.

Santiago de Compostela está en Galicia, una región en el noroeste de España que se parece mucho a Irlanda. Llueve mucho en Galicia y todo es muy verde. Además hay mucha influencia de los celtas—como en Irlanda. Muchos gallegos son rubios o pelirrojos y tienen ojos azules o verdes.

Los peregrinos de la Edad Media iban a Santiago porque creían que allá estaba enterrado el apóstol Santiago. El Camino empezaba en Francia. Cruzaba los Pirineos y todo el norte de España—una región de altos picos montañosos. Los peregrinos viajaban a pie de un pueblo a otro. Cada día cubrían un trecho[3] fijo. Al final de cada trecho había un hostal donde los peregrinos podían comer y pasar la noche. Aun[4] en el siglo XI había industria hotelera.

Hoy en día el Camino de Santiago es una vez más muy popular. A muchos turistas les gusta seguir el mismo camino que los peregrinos de la Edad Media. Muchos de ellos son mochileros jóvenes. Unos siguen andando a pie pero hay también quienes van en bicicleta o aun en carro.

[1]Edad Media *Middle Ages*
[2]peregrinaciones *pilgrimages*
[3]trecho *stretch*
[4]Aun *Even*

CULTURA

Una escena idílica en Navarra, España. Navarra es la puerta del Camino de Santiago en la Península ibérica.

Go Online!

You may wish to remind students to go online for additional reading comprehension and writing skills practice.

¿Comprendes?

Escoge.

1. ¿Qué es una peregrinación?
   a. un viaje al extranjero
   b. un viaje de motivo religioso
   c. un viaje por las montañas
2. ¿Por qué son rubios y pelirrojos muchos gallegos?
   a. Son de ascendencia celta.
   b. Son irlandeses.
   c. Tienen ojos azules.
3. ¿Por qué hacían los peregrinos el viaje?
   a. Querían ver la catedral de Santiago de Compostela.
   b. Querían ver la tumba del apóstol Santiago.
   c. Querían cruzar el norte de España.
4. ¿Qué hay hoy en día?
   a. un interés nuevo en el Camino de Santiago
   b. un nuevo Camino de Santiago
   c. hostales del siglo XI
5. ¿Cuál es una diferencia entre la peregrinación durante la Edad Media y hoy?
   a. Hoy no hay hostales.
   b. Hoy todos los peregrinos no van a pie.
   c. La ruta ha cambiado.

CULTURA
Una vista de Burgos, España

Lectura

Tips for Success

The multiple-choice comprehension activities that accompany the second reading selection in each chapter have a format that will help students prepare for standardized tests.

Comunicación

Presentational
Have students take a class survey polling how many would like to travel the **Camino de Santiago.** Of those who respond affirmatively, ask how they would like to travel—on foot, on bike, in a car. Have a group of students tally the results and present them to the class. You may wish to follow up the survey by asking individual students why they would like or dislike this trip.

Answers

1. b
2. a
3. b
4. a
5. b

Prepárate para el examen

Online Resources

Customizable Lesson Plans

Student Workbook

Enrichment

Listening, Speaking, Reading, Writing Tests

Self-check for achievement

This is a pre-test for students to take before you administer the chapter test. Note that each section is cross-referenced so students can easily find the material they feel they need to review. You may wish to use Self-Check Worksheet SC7 to have students complete this assessment in class or at home. You can correct the assessment yourself, or you may prefer to display the answers in class using Self-Check Answers SC7A.

Differentiation

Slower Paced Learners

Have students work in pairs to complete the Self-Check in class. Once they have finished, call on individuals to give the correct answers as you review together.

Multiple Intelligences

To engage **visual-spatial** and **bodily-kinesthetic** learners, number from 1 to 40 on the board and call on a student to go to the board and write the correct answer (this may be done chronologically or you may allow students to choose the one they answer). Then have the student who wrote the first answer decide who will write the second, and so on, making sure to remind them not to pick the same person again.

Prepárate para el examen

To review, see **Vocabulario**.

Vocabulario

1 **Identifica siete cosas que están en una habitación y en un cuarto de baño de un hotel.**

Andrew Payti

2 **Completa.**

8. Cecilia y Gloria han llegado al hotel. Han reservado un cuarto doble con ____.
9. Necesito ____ para abrir la puerta.
10. ____ te puede ayudar con tu equipaje en un hotel.
11. La camarera tiene que cambiar las toallas porque están ____.
12. Los clientes del hotel tienen que ____ su cuarto al mediodía.
13. Es más caro pasar una noche en un hotel que en un ____.
14. Para subir al piso doce de un hotel, los clientes usan ____.

3 **Describe.**

15–16. un desayuno continental

17–18. un desayuno americano

Answers

1

1. la almohada
2. la sábana
3. la manta
4. la ducha
5. la bañera
6. la toalla
7. el váter (el inodoro)

2

8. un baño
9. una llave
10. El mozo
11. sucias
12. abandonar
13. albergue juvenil (un hostal)
14. el ascensor

3

15–16. Un desayuno continental contiene panecillos, panes dulces, mermelada, mantequilla y café.

17–18. Un desayuno americano contiene huevos revueltos, pan tostado, tocino (bacón, lacón) y jugo de naranja.

Go Online!

connectED.mcgraw-hill.com

Gramática

4 Completa con el presente perfecto.

19. Ellos _____ al hotel. (llegar)
20. ¿Todavía no _____ (tú) el desayuno? (tomar)
21. ¿_____ ustedes en el hotel? (comer)
22. No, (nosotros) no _____ todavía. (salir)
23. Yo _____ en tres estados. (vivir)
24. Mónica ya _____ con este libro. (terminar)

To review, see **El presente perfecto.**

5 Sigue el modelo.

MODELO **¿Hacerlo? →**
Ya lo he hecho.

25. ¿Decirlo?
26. ¿Verlo?
27. ¿Escribirlo?
28. ¿Abrirlo?
29. ¿Devolverlo?

To review, see **Participios irregulares.**

6 Contesta con pronombres.

30. ¿Te ha devuelto el dinero Tomás?
31. ¿Te ha dado las llaves la recepcionista?
32. ¿Le has enviado el correo electrónico a Tomás?
33. ¿Les has escrito la carta a tus padres?
34. ¿Les has dicho la información a tus tíos?

To review, see **Dos complementos me lo, te lo, nos lo,** and **Dos complementos con se.**

7 Completa con pronombres.

35. El profesor les explicó la gramática a los alumnos. El profesor _____ explicó _____.
36. Yo le di los boletos a Teresa. Yo _____ di _____.
37. ¿Te ha cambiado las toallas la camarera? Sí, _____ ha cambiado.
38. ¿Les ha abierto la puerta el mozo a ustedes? Sí, el mozo _____ ha abierto.

Cultura

8 Contesta.

39. ¿Por qué a muchos viajeros jóvenes les gustan los albergues juveniles?
40. ¿Qué es un parador nacional en España?

To review this cultural information, see the **Lectura cultural.**

Prepárate para el examen

Differentiation

(continued)

This type of review activity is particularly appealing to interpersonal learners but will also benefit the class on the whole by promoting an inclusive, student-centered learning environment.

Slower Paced Learners

Encourage students who need extra help to refer to the margin notes and review any section before answering the questions.

Pre-AP Students preparing for the AP exam may benefit from a set time limit when completing this Self-Check. This may also help to identify students with learning difficulties or slower paced students who need extra help.

Go Online!

You may wish to remind students to go online for additional test preparation.

Answers

4
19. han llegado
20. has tomado
21. Han comido
22. hemos salido
23. he vivido
24. ha terminado

5
25. Ya lo he dicho.
26. Ya lo he visto.
27. Ya lo he escrito.
28. Ya lo he abierto.
29. Ya lo he devuelto.

6
30. Sí (No), Tomás (no) me lo ha devuelto.
31. Sí (No), la recepcionista (no) me las ha dado.
32. Sí, (No, no) se lo he enviado.
33. Sí, (No, no) se la he escrito.
34. Sí, (No, no) se la he dicho.

7
35. se la, a ellos
36. se los, a ella
37. me las
38. nos la

8 *Answers will vary but may include:*
39. A muchos viajeros jóvenes les gustan los albergues juveniles porque cuestan menos que un hotel y es posible conocer a estudiantes de todas partes del mundo.
40. Los paradores son del gobierno. Muchos son antiguos castillos o monasterios. Son elegantes y no baratos.

Prepárate para el examen

Tips for Success

Encourage students to say as much as possible when they do these open-ended activities. Tell them not to be afraid to make mistakes, since the goal of the activities is real-life communication. Encourage students to self-correct and to use words and phrases they know to get their meaning across. If someone in the group makes an error that impedes comprehension, encourage the others to ask questions to clarify or, if necessary, to politely correct the speaker. Let students choose the activities they would like to do.

Tell students to feel free to elaborate on the basic theme and to be creative. They may use props, pictures, or posters if they wish.

Pre-AP These oral activities will give students the opportunity to develop and improve their speaking skills so that they may succeed on the speaking portion of the AP exam.

Note: You may want to use the rubric below to help students prepare their speaking activities.

Practice for **ORAL PROFICIENCY**

Prepárate para el examen

1 Una extravagancia

Discuss a time when you splurged on something

En tu vida, ¿has botado la casa por la ventana? ¿Qué has hecho?

2 Experiencias interesantes

Talk about interesting experiences you have had

Habla con un(a) compañero(a). Dile a tu compañero(a) las cosas que tú has hecho en la vida que consideras interesantes. Tu compañero(a) te va a decir lo que ha hecho él/ella. Van a llegar a una conclusión. ¿Quién ha tenido las experiencias más interesantes?

3 Ya no lo he hecho.

Talk about things you have not done yet

Habla con un(a) compañero(a). Los dos van a hablar de algunas cosas que todavía no han hecho pero que quieren hacer un día.

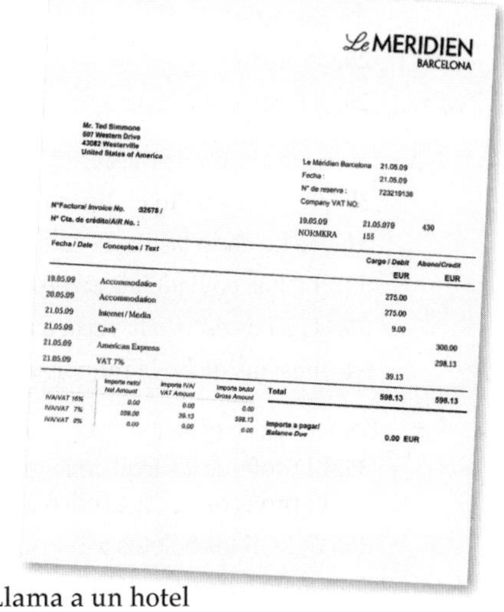

4 Una estadía personal

Describe a stay at a hotel

¿Te has hospedado o pasado unas vacaciones en un hotel? ¿En qué hotel? Describe tu experiencia. Si nunca has estado en un hotel, da una descripción ficticia.

5 Una habitación, por favor.

Make a hotel reservation

Tú has llegado a Burgos, España. Necesitas una habitación en un hotel. Llama a un hotel y habla con el/la recepcionista (tu compañero[a]). Quieres saber si tienen una habitación disponible, la tarifa, lo que está incluido en la tarifa, etc.

6 Las preferencias de un(a) viajero(a) joven

Compare and contrast travel preferences

Por lo general un viaje fabuloso para una persona joven no es un viaje fabuloso para una persona mayor y viceversa. Describe lo que para ti es un viaje ideal. ¿Cuáles son las necesidades que tú consideras importantes y las que no son importantes? ¿Qué buscas en un hotel? ¿Qué piensas? ¿Tienen tus abuelos las mismas opiniones que tú? ¿Tienen ellos los mismos deseos o las mismas necesidades que tú?

Scoring Rubric for Speaking

	4	3	2	1
vocabulary	extensive use of vocabulary, including idiomatic expressions	adequate use of vocabulary and idiomatic expressions	limited vocabulary marked with some anglicisms	limited vocabulary marked by frequent anglicisms that force interpretation by the listener
grammar	few or no grammatical errors	minor grammatical errors	some serious grammatical errors	serious grammatical errors
pronunciation	good intonation and largely accurate pronunciation with slight accent	acceptable intonation and pronunciation with distinctive accent	errors in intonation and pronunciation with heavy accent	errors in intonation and pronunciation that interfere with listener's comprehension
content	thorough response with interesting and pertinent detail	thorough response with sufficient detail	some detail, but not sufficient	general, insufficient response

Go Online! connectED.mcgraw-hill.com

Tarea

You and your classmates are on an educational tour of a Spanish-speaking country and your teacher has given everyone the assignment of keeping a travel journal in Spanish. Write about everything you have done since you arrived there. You will need to use the library and/or the Internet to find out more about the country you have chosen to visit.

Writing Strategy

Transition Words To make your writing flow more smoothly, it is a good idea to use a variety of transition words, because they help connect different ideas. Some useful transition words in Spanish are listed below:

antes (de)	**luego**
después (de)	**por último**
primero	**también**
segundo	**sobre todo**
tercero	**por eso**

1 Prewrite

Create a rough outline using the following questions.

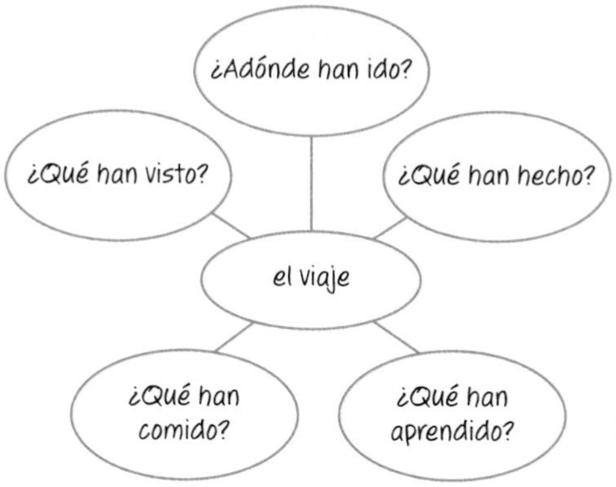

Digital Vision/age fotostock

As you research, answer the questions with information you want to include in your travel narrative. You should consult multiple sources to ensure that your information is accurate.

2 Write

- Use the present perfect tense and vocabulary from the textbook to describe what you and your classmates have done on the trip.
- Use your outline as a guide to help keep your information organized.
- Incorporate transition words so that your writing flows smoothly.

Evaluate

Your teacher will evaluate you on correct use of vocabulary and grammar, organization, accuracy and completeness of information, and effective use of transition words.

Prepárate para el examen

Pre-AP This **tarea** will give students the opportunity to develop and improve their writing skills so that they may succeed on the AP exam.

ASSESS

Students are now ready to take any of the Listening, Speaking, Reading, Writing Tests you choose to administer.

Note: You may want to use the rubric below to help students prepare their writing task.

Scoring Rubric for Writing

	4	3	2	1
vocabulary	precise, varied	functional, fails to communicate complete meaning	limited to basic words, often inaccurate	inadequate
grammar	excellent, very few or no errors	some errors, but do not hinder communication	numerous errors interfere with communication	many errors, little sentence structure
content	thorough response to the topic	generally thorough response to the topic	partial response to the topic	insufficient response to the topic
organization	well organized, ideas presented clearly and logically	loosely organized, but main ideas present	some attempts at organization, but with confused sequencing	lack of organization

Online Resources

Customizable Lesson Plans
- Whiteboard Lesson
- Audio Activities
- Video (Vocabulario) (Diálogo) (Gramática)
- Student Workbook
- Enrichment
- Quizzes
- Listening, Speaking, Reading, Writing Tests

Grammar Review

This page provides a quick "at a glance" summary of the grammar points students have learned in this chapter.

Differentiation

Multiple Intelligences

You may want to call on **verbal-linguistic** and **logical-mathematical** learners for whom grammar often comes easily to explain the main concepts to their classmates in their own words. Encourage students to compare and contrast these structures with similar structures in English. Having students explain the concepts in different ways may also help slower paced learners or students with learning difficulties.

Repaso del Capítulo 7

Gramática

El presente perfecto

The present perfect tense is used to speak about a past event without reference to any particular time. It is formed with the present tense of the verb **haber** and a past participle. The past participle of an **-ar** verb is formed by adding **-ado** to the stem, and the past participle of an **-er** or **-ir** verb is formed by adding **-ido** to the stem. Review the following forms.

hablar	beber	asistir
he hablado	he bebido	he asistido
has hablado	has bebido	has asistido
ha hablado	ha bebido	ha asistido
hemos hablado	hemos bebido	hemos asistido
habéis hablado	*habéis bebido*	*habéis asistido*
han hablado	han bebido	han asistido

CULTURA

Los huéspedes han pasado unos días agradables en la piscina de este hotel en Manta, Ecuador.

Andrew Payti

Participios irregulares

Review the verbs that have irregular past participles.

decir → dicho
hacer → hecho
romper → roto
escribir → escrito
freír → frito
ver → visto
poner → puesto
volver → vuelto
devolver → devuelto
morir → muerto
abrir → abierto
cubrir → cubierto

Dos complementos en la misma frase

When a sentence has two object pronouns, the indirect object always precedes the direct object. The indirect object pronouns **le, les** change to **se** when used with **lo, la, los,** or **las.**

Teodoro me vendió el carro. — **Teodoro me lo vendió.**
Tu padre te dio los regalos. — **Tu padre te los dio.**
El cliente le devolvió las llaves a la recepcionista. — **El cliente se las devolvió.**

![Juego] There are a number of cognates in this list. See how many you and a partner can find. Who can find the most? Compare your list with those of your classmates.

Go Online!

connectED.mcgraw-hill.com

Vocabulario

Making a hotel reservation

una reservación	un cuarto sencillo	reservar
un cuarto, una habitación	un cuarto doble	

Arriving at/leaving a hotel

el hotel	el/la recepcionista	el mozo
el albergue juvenil, el hostal	el/la cliente(a), el/la huésped(a)	el ascensor
		hospedarse
la recepción	la llave (magnética)	abandonar el cuarto

Having breakfast in a hotel

el desayuno continental	la mantequilla	el pan tostado
el panecillo	el café	el tocino, el bacón, el lacón
el pan dulce	el desayuno americano	
la mermelada	los huevos revueltos	el jugo de naranja

Talking about a hotel room

la cama	la almohada	la percha, el colgador
la sábana	el armario	el aire acondicionado
la manta, la frazada		

Talking about a bathroom

el cuarto de baño	el inodoro, el váter	una toalla
la bañera	el lavabo	sucio(a)
la ducha	el jabón	limpio(a)

Talking about cleaning a hotel room

la camarera	hacer la cama	cambiar
limpiar		

David H. Brennan

Repaso del Capítulo 7

Vocabulary Review

The words and phrases in the **Vocabulario** section have been taught for productive use in this chapter. They are summarized here as a resource for both student and teacher. This list also serves as a convenient resource for the **Prepárate para el examen** activities.

¡Así se dice!

Why It Works!

This vocabulary reference list has not been translated into English for two reasons. First, it is recommended that students learn the new vocabulary through direct association with images on the **Vocabulario** pages. Second, all vocabulary is reintroduced in the chapter many times and upon completion of the chapter students should be familiar with the meaning of all the words. If there are words that students still do not know, they can refer to the vocabulary presentation in the chapter or the dictionary at the end of the book. If, however, it is your preference to give students the English translations, please refer to Vocabulary V7.1.

Differentiation

Slower Paced Learners

Slower paced learners may benefit from creating their own visual dictionary of nouns and adjectives in this list. They can either draw their own depictions or use images from the Internet, magazines, etc.

Juego The cognates in this list are: **una reservación, doble, reservar, el hotel, el hostal, la recepción, el/la recepcionista, el/la cliente(a), magnético(a), continental, americano(a), tostado(a), la mermelada, el bacón, el aire acondicionado.**

Don't forget the chapter project and cultural activities. Students have learned all the information that they will need to complete these engaging enrichment tasks.

Repaso cumulativo

Every chapter of **¡Así se dice!** contains this review section of previously learned material. By recycling information from previous chapters, the cumulative review serves to remind students that they need to continue practicing what they have learned after finishing each chapter.

Activity 1 This activity reviews vocabulary related to cultural events.

Audio Script

1. La gente va al teatro.
2. La película empieza a las diecinueve y treinta.
3. No hay cola.
4. La gente hace cola para comprar entradas.
5. Están comprando entradas en la taquilla.
6. La gente sale del cine.

Activity 2 This activity reviews vocabulary related to daily routines.

Activity 3 This activity reviews reflexive pronouns.

Activity 4 This activity reviews reflexive pronouns.

Cultural Snapshot

Arica is in northern Chile and it is a popular vacation spot for Chileans and Bolivians. It has a rather mild climate year-round.

Repaso cumulativo

Repasa lo que ya has aprendido

These activities will help you review and remember what you have learned so far in Spanish.

1 Escucha las frases. Indica si la frase describe el dibujo o no.

CULTURA

Unos *campers* con sus caravanas y carpas en una playa cerca de Arica, Chile

2 Imagina que vas de camping por una noche. ¿Qué vas a poner en tu mochila?

3 Completa con el pronombre reflexivo.

1. Cuando voy de camping, ____ acuesto en una carpa.
2. Marcos ____ duerme enseguida en su saco de dormir.
3. Nosotros ____ lavamos con agua fría.
4. Ellos ____ divierten mucho cuando van de camping.
5. ¿Por qué no ____ peinas? Tienes el pelo desarreglado.

4 Completa con el pronombre apropiado.

1. Él tiene que levantar____.
2. Voy a cepillar____ los dientes.
3. Y yo voy a vestir____.
4. ¿A qué hora tenemos que reunir____?
5. Ellos quieren acostar____ temprano porque tienen que levantar____ mañana a las cinco y media.
6. ¿Quieres sentar____ aquí?

Answers

1

1. no
2. sí
3. no
4. sí
5. sí
6. no

2 *Answers will vary but may include:*
Voy a poner en mi mochila un tubo de crema dental, un cepillo de dientes, un peine, un cepillo, una barra de jabón, un rollo de papel higiénico y el champú.

3

1. me
2. se
3. nos
4. se
5. te

4

1. se
2. me
3. me
4. nos
5. se, se
6. te

Go Online!
connectED.mcgraw-hill.com

5 Escoge.

1. ______ llave que tengo no es para mi puerta.
   a. Esta b. Esa c. Aquella
2. ______ muchacho que ves allá es el primo de Esteban.
   a. Este b. Ese c. Aquel
3. Carlos, ______ novela que estás leyendo, ¿te gusta?
   a. esta b. esa c. aquella

6 Cambia al plural.

1. ¿De quién es *este libro de bolsillo*?
2. ¿Quiénes han dejado *aquella mochila* allí?
3. Me gusta mucho *ese juego* que tiene José.
4. ¿Es caro *aquel carro*?

7 ¿Sí o no?

1. Hay muchas tiendas en un centro comercial.
2. Los precios son más bajos cuando hay un saldo.
3. Si una camisa no te queda bien necesitas otra talla.
4. Venden objetos de artesanía en una tienda de ropa.
5. Mucha gente regatea en una tienda elegante.
6. En un mercado municipal hay muchos puestos diferentes.

CULTURA
Una tienda en un mercado callejero en Catarina, Nicaragua

8 Tienes que comprar mucho. Decide en qué tienda vas a comprar las siguientes cosas. Puedes comprar algunas cosas en más de una tienda.

lo que necesitas	la tienda de ropa	la frutería	la verdulería	el supermercado	el mercado indígena
1. el papel higiénico					
2. la artesanía					
3. el maíz					
4. un vestido					
5. un paquete de judías verdes congeladas					
6. un racimo de uvas					

Andrew Payti

Repaso cumulativo

Activity 5 This activity reviews demonstrative adjectives.

Activity 6 This activity reviews demonstrative adjectives.

Activity 7 This activity reviews shopping vocabulary.

Activity 8 This activity reviews shopping vocabulary.

Go Online!

You may wish to remind students to go online for additional cumulative review.

The **¡Así se dice!** Audio Program for Chapter 7 has twenty-five activities, which afford students extensive listening and speaking practice.

Pre-AP To give students further open-ended oral or written practice, or to assess proficiency, go to AP Proficiency Practice AP5 and AP20.

Answers

5
1. a
2. c
3. b

6
1. ¿De quién son estos libros de bolsillo?
2. ¿Quiénes han dejado aquellas mochilas allí?
3. Me gustan mucho esos juegos que tiene José.
4. ¿Son caros aquellos carros?

7
1. sí
2. sí
3. sí
4. no
5. no
6. sí

8
1. el supermercado
2. el mercado indígena
3. la verdulería, el supermercado
4. la tienda de ropa
5. el supermercado
6. la frutería, el supermercado

Chapter Overview

Ciudad y campo

Scope and Sequence

Topics
- City life
- Transportation in the city
- Country life
- Farm animals

Culture
- A cattle ranch in Argentina
- Hispanic influence in Miami, Florida

Functions
- How to describe life in the city
- How to describe life in the country
- How to discuss the differences between the city and the country in Latin America

Structure
- The future tense
- Object pronouns with infinitives and gerunds

Andrew Payti

Planning Guide

	required	recommended	optional
Vocabulario 1 En el centro de la ciudad	✔		
Vocabulario 2 En el campo	✔		
Gramática Futuro de los verbos regulares; Futuro de los verbos irregulares; Los pronombres con el infinitivo y el gerundio	✔		
Conversación Un verano en el campo		✔	
Lectura cultural La ciudad y el campo		✔	
Lectura Un poco más Una ciudad interesante			✔
Prepárate para el examen			✔
Repaso cumulativo			✔

Correlations to ACTFL World-Readiness Standards for Learning Languages

Page numbers in light print refer to the Student Edition.
Page numbers in bold print refer to the Teacher Edition.

COMMUNICATION Communicate effectively in more than one language in order to function in a variety of situations and for multiple purposes		
Interpersonal Communication	Learners interact and negotiate meaning in spoken, signed, or written conversations to share information, reactions, feelings, and opinions.	pp. **230–231, 237, 238,** 239, **239, 241,** 243, **243, 245, 246, 247, 251, 252,** 256
Interpretive Communication	Learners understand, interpret, and analyze what is heard, read, or viewed on a variety of topics.	pp. **228D, 232,** 234, **235,** 238, 239, **239, 240,** 241, **241,** 243, 244, 245, **246,** 247, 248, **248,** 249, **249,** 250, 251, **252,** 253, 255, **255,** 260, **261**
Presentational Communication	Learners present information, concepts, and ideas to inform, explain, persuade, and narrate on a variety of topics using appropriate media and adapting to various audiences of listeners, readers, or viewers.	pp. **228C,** 235, 238, **239, 248, 249, 250, 253, 254,** 256, 257, **258, 259**
CULTURES Interact with cultural competence and understanding		
Relating Cultural Practices to Perspectives	Learners use the language to investigate, explain, and reflect on the relationship between the practices and perspectives of the cultures studied.	pp. **228D,** 230–231, 238, 243, 247, **249,** 251
Relating Cultural Products to Perspectives	Learners use the language to investigate, explain, and reflect on the relationship between the products and perspectives of the cultures studied.	pp. **228C, 228D, 229, 230–231, 233, 238,** 245, 248–250, **249,** 251, 252, **252,** 253, **253,** 255
CONNECTIONS Connect with other disciplines and acquire information and diverse perspectives in order to use the language to function in academic and career-related situations		
Making Connections	Learners build, reinforce, and expand their knowledge of other disciplines while using the language to develop critical thinking and to solve problems creatively.	pp. **228C, 228D,** 234, 240, 253, **253**
Acquiring Information and Diverse Perspectives	Learners access and evaluate information and diverse perspectives that are available through the language and its cultures.	pp. **228C,** 232, 236, **236,** 237, 244, **244,** 245, 247, **247**
COMPARISONS Develop insight into the nature of language and culture in order to interact with cultural competence		
Language Comparisons	Learners use the language to investigate, explain, and reflect on the nature of language through comparisons of the language studied and their own.	pp. 232, **232, 233,** 237, **237,** 240, **258,** 259
Cultural Comparisons	Learners use the language to investigate, explain, and reflect on the concept of culture through comparisons of the cultures studied and their own.	pp. **228C, 228D,** 229, **229, 230, 232, 234,** 244, **247,** 248, **248,** 252, 256, 257
COMMUNITIES Communicate and interact with cultural competence in order to participate in multilingual communities at home and around the world		
School and Global Communities	Learners use the language both within and beyond the classroom to interact and collaborate in their community and the globalized world.	pp. **237,** 250, **254, 256, 258**
Lifelong Learning	Learners set goals and reflect on their progress in using languages for enjoyment, enrichment, and advancement.	pp. **228C, 234,** 236, **236,** 244, **244,** 247, **247, 251, 253,** 256

Chapter Project

El casco antiguo

Students will design and label a map of the historic district of a major city in Spain or Latin America.

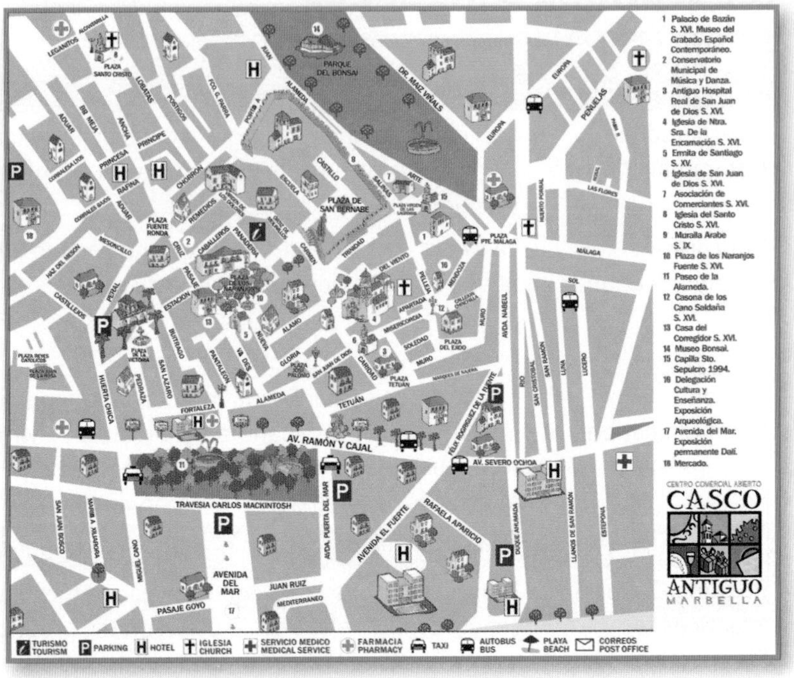

1. Each student will conduct preliminary research to find a city with a historic district known as the **casco antiguo** *(old town)*. Since this is a feature of many cities throughout the Spanish-speaking world, you may wish to have each student in the class focus on a different city. They can either make an original drawing of the historic district based on maps found in the library or online or trace an outline of a map and fill in the necessary information.
2. In addition to labeling major streets, students should locate and name important structures, such as government buildings, churches and cathedrals, theaters, museums, monuments, and other historical landmarks. Color should be used to differentiate items on the map, indicating natural spaces such as parks or gardens and geographic features such as oceans or mountains. A compass rose should be included to show the district's orientation.
3. Students should submit a sketch of the layout of their map along with a paragraph providing a brief history of the historic district and describing its main characteristics or points of interest. They will then revise their paragraphs and turn in both drafts along with a final version of the map.

Expansion: You may wish to have students present their maps and then discuss the common aspects shared by the historic districts presented. These characteristics could then be compared and contrasted with historic districts in U.S. cities. This might lead to further discussion regarding similarities or differences in colonial architecture in Latin America and the United States.

Scoring Rubric for Project

	5	3	1
Evidence of planning	Layout and corrected draft are provided.	Draft and layout are provided, but draft is not corrected.	Draft and layout are not provided.
Use of illustrations	Map is colorful and well labeled.	Map contains some color and some labeling.	Map contains no color and very little labeling.
Presentation	Map contains all the required elements.	Map contains some of the required elements.	Map contains few of the required elements.

Culture

Recipe

EMPANADAS

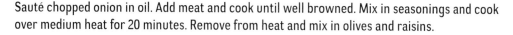

Ingredients: (makes 8 8-inch servings)

This recipe is divided into two parts: the pastry shell and the filling. If you desire, you may wish to find other filling recipes and make several varieties of **empanadas.**

Filling:
- ½ pound ground beef
- 1 tablespoon vegetable oil
- 1 small onion, chopped
- ½ teaspoon ground cumin
- ½ teaspoon paprika
- ½ teaspoon salt
- ½ teaspoon pepper
- 10 green olives, sliced
- ¼ cup raisins

Sauté chopped onion in oil. Add meat and cook until well browned. Mix in seasonings and cook over medium heat for 20 minutes. Remove from heat and mix in olives and raisins.

Shell:
- 1½ cups flour
- 1 teaspoon baking powder
- 3 tablespoons cold butter or margarine
- 2 tablespoons cooking oil
- 1 teaspoon water
- 3 eggs, beaten

Sift flour and baking powder into a medium bowl. With two knives, cut in butter and oil until coarsely blended. Add water and eggs and mix until dough holds together. Roll dough to ⅛-inch thickness on a lightly floured surface. Using a saucepan cover or plate, cut 8-inch circles from dough and place them on a lightly greased baking sheet. Place ⅓ to ½ cup filling in the center of each circle. Fold each circle in half, moisten edges with water, and firmly press edges together with a fork. Bake at 400° for 25 minutes.

Cascarones

Cascarón means *eggshell,* but one meaning of **cascarones** refers to the Mexican tradition of filling colorful, hollow eggshells with confetti and breaking them above the heads of unsuspecting friends, so that confetti drops all over them, showering them with good luck. Popular at Easter, **cascarones** are also used during birthday and other celebrations as a playful way to liven up the festivities. This custom is also common throughout the southwestern United States, especially in places with large Mexican American populations.

While it is possible to purchase ready-made **cascarones** online, you might want students to make them. Have students bring in emptied eggs from home. (Tell them to cut a hole about the size of a dime in one end of an egg, shake out the contents, rinse out the inside, allow the shell to drain and dry, and pack it safely.) In class, students can decorate their shells with dye, paint, or markers, fill them halfway with confetti, and glue a small piece of tissue paper over the hole. Now they are ready to spread cheer and good fortune!

Connection to Fine Art

Have students look online or in an art text to find *Small Farmers* painted by Cuban artist Leopoldo Romanach. Have students discuss what they like or do not like about the work and identify as many colors and items as they can in Spanish. Students can talk about what they think life in the country is like for the family in the painting.

50-Minute Lesson Plans

	Objective	Present	Practice	Assess/Homework
Day 1	Talk about city life	Chapter Opener (5 min.) Introducción al tema (10 min.) Core Instruction/Vocabulario 1 (20 min.)	Activities 1–3 (15 min.)	Student Workbook Activities A–B **ConnectEd** Vocabulary Practice
Day 2	Talk about city life	Quick Start (5 min.) Review Vocabulario 1 (10 min.)	Activities 4–6 (15 min.) Total Physical Response (5 min.) Audio Activities A–E (15 min.)	Student Workbook Activity C **ConnectEd** Vocabulary Practice
Day 3	Talk about country life	Core Instruction/Vocabulario 2 (15 min.) Video, Vocabulario en vivo (10 min.)	Activities 1–4 (10 min.) Foldables (5 min.)	Quiz 1 (10 min.) Student Workbook Activities A–C **ConnectEd** Vocabulary Practice
Day 4	Talk about country life	Quick Start (5 min.) Review Vocabulario 2 (10 min.)	Activities 5–8 (15 min.) Total Physical Response (5 min.) InfoGap (5 min.) Audio Activities F–J (10 min.)	Student Workbook Activities D–E **ConnectEd** Vocabulary Practice
Day 5	Future tense of regular verbs	Quick Start (5 min.) Core Instruction/Gramática, Futuro de los verbos regulares (10 min.)	Activities 1–4 (15 min.) Audio Activities A–D (10 min.)	Quiz 2 (10 min.) Student Workbook Activities A–D **ConnectEd** Grammar Practice
Day 6	Future tense of irregular verbs	Quick Start (5 min.) Core Instruction/Gramática, Futuro de los verbos irregulares (10 min.)	Activities 5–8 (15 min.) Audio Activities E–H (10 min.)	Quiz 3 (10 min.) Student Workbook Activities A–E **ConnectEd** Grammar Practice
Day 7	Object pronouns with infinitives and gerunds	Quick Start (5 min.) Core Instruction/Gramática, Los pronombres con el infinitivo y el gerundio (10 min.) Video, Cultura en vivo (5 min.)	Activities 9–13 (10 min.) Audio Activities I–M (10 min.)	Quiz 4 (10 min.) Student Workbook Activities A–B **ConnectEd** Grammar Practice
Day 8	Develop reading and listening comprehension skills	Quick Start (5 min.) Core Instruction/Conversación (15 min.) Video, Diálogo en vivo (10 min.)	¿Comprendes? A–B (10 min.)	Quiz 5 (10 min.) ¿Comprendes? C **ConnectEd** Conversation
Day 9	Discuss the differences between the city and the country in Latin America	Core Instruction/Lectura cultural (20 min.)	¿Comprendes? A–C (15 min.)	Listening Comprehension Test (15 min.) ¿Comprendes? D–E **ConnectEd** Reading Practice
Day 10	Develop reading comprehension skills	Core Instruction/Lectura Un poco más (15 min.)	¿Comprendes? (10 min.) Prepárate para el examen (25 min.)	Prepárate para el examen, Practice for written proficiency **ConnectEd** Reading Practice
Day 11	Chapter review	Repaso del Capítulo 8 (15 min.)	Prepárate para el examen, Practice for oral proficiency (20 min.)	Test for Writing Proficiency (15 min.) Review for chapter test
Day 12	Chapter 8 Tests (50 min.) Reading and Writing Test Speaking Test		Test for Oral Proficiency Test for Reading Comprehension	

90-Minute Lesson Plans

	Objective	Present	Practice	Assess/Homework
Block 1	Talk about city life	Chapter Opener (5 min.) Introducción al tema (10 min.) Quick Start (5 min.) Core Instruction/Vocabulario 1 (20 min.)	Activities 1–6 (20 min.) Total Physical Response (10 min.) Audio Activities A–E (20 min.)	Student Workbook Activities A–C **ConnectEd** Vocabulary Practice
Block 2	Talk about country life	Quick Start (5 min.) Core Instruction/Vocabulario 2 (20 min.) Video, Vocabulario en vivo (10 min.)	Activities 1–8 (20 min.) Total Physical Response (5 min.) Foldables (5 min.) InfoGap (5 min.) Audio Activities F–J (10 min.)	Quiz 1 (10 min.) Student Workbook Activities A–E **ConnectEd** Vocabulary Practice
Block 3	Future tense of regular verbs Future tense of irregular verbs	Quick Start (5 min.) Core Instruction/Gramática, Futuro de los verbos regulares (15 min.) Core Instruction/Gramática, Futuro de los verbos irregulares (15 min.)	Activities 1–4 (15 min.) Activities 5–6 (10 min.) Audio Activities A–G (20 min.)	Quiz 2 (10 min.) Student Workbook Activities A–D Student Workbook Activities A–B **ConnectEd** Grammar Practice
Block 4	Future tense of irregular verbs Object pronouns with infinitives and gerunds	Quick Start (5 min.) Review Gramática, Futuro de los verbos irregulares (10 min.) Quick Start (5 min.) Core Instruction/Gramática, Los pronombres con el infinitivo y el gerundio (15 min.)	Activities 7–8 (10 min.) Activities 9–13 (20 min.) Audio Activities H–M (15 min.)	Quiz 3 (10 min.) Student Workbook Activities C–E Student Workbook Activities A–B **ConnectEd** Grammar Practice
Block 5	Discuss the differences between the city and the country in Latin America	Quick Start (5 min.) Core Instruction/Conversación (15 min.) Video, Diálogo en vivo (10 min.) Core Instruction/Lectura cultural (20 min.)	¿Comprendes? A–B (10 min.) ¿Comprendes? A–C (10 min.)	Quizzes 4–5 (20 min.) ¿Comprendes? C ¿Comprendes? D–E Prepárate para el examen, Practice for written proficiency **ConnectEd** Conversation, Reading Practice
Block 6	Develop reading comprehension skills	Core Instruction/Lectura Un poco más (15 min.)	¿Comprendes? (10 min.) Prepárate para el examen (20 min.) Prepárate para el examen, Practice for oral proficiency (30 min.)	Listening Comprehension Test (15 min.) Review for chapter test **ConnectEd** Reading Practice
Block 7	Chapter 8 Tests (50 min.) Reading and Writing Test Speaking Test Test for Oral Proficiency Test for Writing Proficiency Test for Reading Comprehension Chapter Project (40 min.)			

Preview

In this chapter, students will learn about city and rural life in Latin America and how one impacts the other. They will also become familiar with the future tense as they are made aware that the tense is more frequently expressed with either the **ir a** + *infinitive* construction or the present tense. Students will also learn the placement of object pronouns with infinitives and gerunds.

Pacing

It is important to note that once you reach **¡Bravo!** in the chapter, there is no more new material for students to learn. The rest of the chapter recycles what has already been covered. The suggested pacing listed here leaves two to three days for review, assessment, and enrichment activities such as the chapter project.

Vocabulario 1	1–2 days
Vocabulario 2	1–2 days
Gramática	2–3 days
Conversación	1 day
Lectura cultural	1 day
Lectura Un poco más	1 day

CAPÍTULO 8

Ciudad y campo

Andrew Payti

228

Go Online! connectED.mcgraw-hill.com

Audio Video Práctica Repaso Diversiones eScape

ePals

Go Online!

Audio
Listen to spoken Spanish.

Video
Watch and learn about the Spanish-speaking world.

Práctica
Practice your skills.

Repaso
Review what you've learned.

Diversiones
Go beyond the classroom.

eScape
Read about current events in the Spanish-speaking world.

Aquí y Allí

Vamos a comparar La vida en el campo es muy diferente que la vida en una ciudad. Los problemas que existen en el campo y en la ciudad son diferentes también. Piensa en las zonas urbanas y rurales donde tú vives. Vas a observar si en Latinoamérica hay muchas diferencias entre la vida en una ciudad y la vida en el campo. Y aprenderás también si hay diferencias entre Latinoamérica y Estados Unidos.

Objetivos

You will:

- describe life in the city
- describe life in the country
- discuss the differences between the city and the country in Latin America

You will use:

- the future tense
- object pronouns with infinitives and gerunds

◀ Un gaucho joven con su caballo trabajando en la estancia Ombú en las pampas argentinas

Interactive Whiteboard
Present or practice with interactive whiteboard activities.

Assessment
Check student progress.

ePals
Connect with Spanish-speaking students around the world.

SPOTLIGHT ON CULTURE

Cultural Comparison

The material in this chapter introduces students to the many currents at play that impact life in both the urban and rural areas of Latin America. They will visit some beautiful Latin American cities as well as some spectacular areas in the countryside. Students will also be exposed to some of the real socioeconomic issues confronting Latin America today. Throughout the chapter they can draw conclusions concerning some interesting differences between Latin America and the United States.

Cultural Snapshot

This estancia is about a ninety-minute drive from Buenos Aires. It is a working ranch and it has provisions for about ten people to spend a night or two to experience life on the pampas. It gets its name—Ombú—from an indigenous tree that grows only in the pampas.

PRESENT

Introduce the theme of the chapter by having students look at the photographs on these pages. Have them look at the young people and determine if there is anything they see them doing that is the same or different from what they do with their own friends. Once you have completed the vocabulary presentation, have students return to these pages and read the information that accompanies each photograph. Once students are fully acquainted with the vocabulary and grammar of the chapter, you may wish to come back to these pages and ask the questions that go with each photo.

Cultural Snapshot

Perú El Jirón de la Unión has been a pedestrian-only thoroughfare for many years. Throughout the years, government officials have made many efforts to keep street vendors, **vendedores ambulantes,** out of the area. **¿Qué tipo de calle es el Jirón de la Unión? ¿Dónde está?**

España Have students note the various ways to say *juice* and *orange.* **Jugo** and **naranja** are the most common. **Zumo** is used only in Spain. **China** is used in Puerto Rico and some other areas of the Caribbean and it is a slightly different orange. Note the following:

la naranja—la fruta
el naranjo—el árbol
el naranjal—lugar donde crecen naranjos

Limón and **lima** can be somewhat problematic. **Limón** can be used for either a lemon or a lime; **una lima** is more often used for just a lime.

Ciudad y campo

Perú

El Jirón de la Unión en el centro de Lima es una calle peatonal comercial.

Mira estas fotos para familiarizarte con el tema de este capítulo—ciudad y campo. Vas a observar que hay unas diferencias interesantes entre la vida urbana y la vida rural en las muchas regiones del mundo hispanohablante.

España

Se cultivan deliciosas naranjas en los naranjos de los naranjales de Andalucía. A los españoles les gusta beber «zumo de naranja» y a los latinoamericanos les gusta tomar un «jugo de naranja» o, en Puerto Rico, «jugo de china».

Venezuela

Santo Domingo es un pueblo idílico en los Andes venezolanos. Las casas se parecen a los chalets en los Alpes suizos.

Ecuador

Unos niños andan con su rebaño de ovejas. Están al lado de una carretera en un pueblo en las afueras de Riobamba, Ecuador.

(bl)Kelli Drummer-Avendaño, (others)Andrew Payti

Venezuela By night the **páramos,** seen in the upper part of the photo, resemble a moonscape. The area can also be quite eerie when the fog rolls in. Santo Domingo, however, is a beautiful town that lies in a wooded valley not far from the **páramo. ¿Qué tipo de pueblo es Santo Domingo? ¿Cuáles son unas características de un pueblo idílico? ¿Dónde está Santo Domingo?**

Ecuador These youngsters are walking with a herd of sheep on the **Carretera panamericana** on the outskirts of Riobamba. Riobamba serves as a trading station for the south-central sierra. The name of the city Riobamba reflects its indigenous/Spanish heritages: **Río** (Spanish for *river*) and **bamba** (Quechua for *valley*). **¿Dónde están estos niños? Mira como están vestidos. ¿Qué opinas? ¿Hace frío o calor en esta región? ¿Están ellos en un campo o en una carretera?**

Go Online!
connectED.mcgraw-hill.com

Argentina

La famosa Avenida 9 de Julio en Buenos Aires tiene fama de ser la avenida más ancha del mundo.

España

Un mimo vestido de oro entretiene a los peatones en una calle de Madrid en espera de recibir una propina por su talento.

Argentina

El gaucho conduce (lleva) al caballo por las riendas. En muchas estancias los visitantes tienen la oportunidad y el placer de andar (montar) a caballo.

México

La Ciudad de México tiene cada día más y más rascacielos modernos de un estilo arquitectónico reconocido y apreciado en el mundo entero.

Costa Rica

Los bueyes están tirando una carreta llena de café. Están tirándola por un pueblo de Costa Rica. El pueblo de Sarchí cerca de Alajuela tiene fama por la fábrica de estas carretas de diferentes colores y diseños.

(tl)Glowimages/age fotostock, (bl)Emily Lowry, (others)Andrew Payti

Introducción al tema

Argentina The **Avenida 9 de Julio** is supposedly the widest avenue in the world. The famous **obelisco** is at the intersection of **Avenida 9 de Julio** and **Calle Corrientes**, an area with rather active nightlife. ¿Cómo se llama esta avenida ancha?

España ¿Dónde está trabajando el mimo? ¿A quiénes está entreteniendo? ¿Qué quiere recibir? ¿Has visto a muchos mimos trabajando en las calles de las ciudades de Estados Unidos?

Argentina ¿Está ensillado el caballo? ¿Está montado a caballo el gaucho? ¿Pueden cabalgar los turistas en la estancia? ¿Cómo conduce el gaucho al caballo?

México ¿Te interesa la arquitectura moderna? ¿Cuáles son algunas características de la arquitectura moderna que puedes ver en la foto? Explícalas a un(a) compañero(a).

Costa Rica Very close to Alajuela in the small town of Sarchí is the birthplace of **artesanía tica.** For more than a century they have been manufacturing these colorful carts that in days past were pulled by oxen. They were used to transport sugar. Every year there is **un desfile de carretas** in Sarchí.

Online Resources

- Customizable Lesson Plans
- Whiteboard Lesson
- Audio Activities
- Student Workbook
- Enrichment
- Quizzes

Quick Start

Use QS 8.1 or write the following on the board.

Separate the following words into two categories: **el avión** y **el tren.**

el asistente de vuelo
el revisor
el coche cama
el andén
la puerta de salida
la estación
el aeropuerto
la vía
la pista
el aterrizaje
la cabina

TEACH

Core Instruction

You may wish to use some of the suggestions presented in previous chapters for the presentation of the new vocabulary.

Differentiation

Multiple Intelligences

Have **bodily-kinesthetic** learners make hand motions to indicate the following: **ancho, estrecho, esquina, tiovivo, noria, la montaña rusa.**

Comparaciones

Have students make a comparison between **una avenida ancha** and **una calle angosta o estrecha.**

En el centro de la ciudad

¿Vas al centro mañana? Es viernes y habrá mucho tráfico. Si tomas el carro, no podrás aparcar en la calle. Tendrás que buscar un parking.
Para conversar

En otras partes

- In Spain you will hear both **estacionar** and **aparcar.** These terms are also used in Latin America as well as **parquear.** A parking spot or lot can be **el parking, el parqueo, el aparcamiento,** or **el estacionamiento.**
- There are many words used for **autobús.** It is not necessary for you to learn them all. In general **el autobús** is used in Spain, **el camión** in Mexico, and **la guagua** in the Caribbean and in the Canary Islands. You will also frequently hear **el bus.**

About the Spanish Language

In some Latin American countries, particularly Peru, a parking lot is **una playa de estacionamiento.**

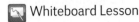

Go Online!

connectED.mcgraw-hill.com

Medios de transporte urbanos

El señor no subirá la escalera.
Tomará la escalera mecánica.

Los pasajeros esperan el autobús en la parada de autobús.

El parque de atracciones

El sábado los jóvenes irán al parque de atracciones.

Vocabulario 1

ABOUT THE SPANISH LANGUAGE

- In some areas **el colectivo** is another term used for *bus.* However, it is more often a public taxi that permits people to get on and off as they need.
- **El cobrador** collects money for a bus. **El revisor** checks tickets. **El cobrador** is more common on a bus and **el revisor** is more common on a train.

Cultura

In many cities and small towns a bus has both a driver, **un conductor,** and a conductor, **el cobrador,** who collects the money.

Go Online!

You may wish to use the whiteboard presentation for additional vocabulary instruction and practice.

Total Physical Response (TPR)

(Student 1), **ven acá, por favor.**
Quieres cruzar la calle, pero, ¡espera!
Ha cambiado el semáforo. Ahora puedes cruzar.
Quédate en el cruce.
Despacio. Levanta el pie porque aquí está la acera.
Sigue andando derecho.
Cuenta—una esquina—dos esquinas.
Ahora llegas a la tercera esquina. Dobla a la izquierda.
Gracias, *(Student 1).*
(Student 2), **ven acá, por favor.**
Estás en el metro. Están acercándose a la estación.
Agárrate. El tren está parando.
Baja (Bájate).
Busca el ascensor.
Toma el ascensor.
(Student 3), **ven acá, por favor.**
Imita como te sientes en una montaña rusa.
Imita como te sientes en un tiovivo.
Imita como te sientes en una noria.

Vocabulario 1

Leveling EACH Activity

Easy Activity 1
Easy–Average Activity 4
Average Activities 2, 3, 5
CHallenging Activity 6

PRACTICE

Activity 1

Audio Script

1. Los peatones deben cruzar la calle en el cruce.
2. No puede entrar el tráfico en una calle peatonal—es decir, una calle solo para peatones.
3. El señor no puede aparcar en la calle. Tendrá que buscar un parqueo.
4. En muchas estaciones de metro hay una escalera mecánica para bajar a la estación.
5. En el casco antiguo hay muchas calles anchas y rascacielos.
6. Hay muchas oficinas en el rascacielos.
7. A los niños les gusta ir al zoológico para ver los animales.
8. La noria y el tiovivo son atracciones.

Comunidades

Ask students to discuss the pollution present in their community.

Comparaciones

Have students look at the photograph. Ask them if cities near where they live have many parks such as this one in Buenos Aires. Parks are very common and popular in the cities of Latin America.

ESCUCHAR

1 Escucha cada frase y decide si la información es correcta o no. Usa una tabla como la de abajo para indicar tus respuestas.

correcta	incorrecta

Conexiones

La ecología
El término «ecología» significa el equilibrio entre los seres humanos y la naturaleza. Hoy en día hay grandes problemas ecológicos en todas partes del mundo. Muchos consideran la contaminación del aire el número uno. En las zonas urbanas el aire que se respira está contaminado principalmente por las emisiones de gases que escapan de los automóviles, los camiones y las chimeneas de las fábricas.

HABLAR

2 Contesta sobre unos jóvenes en un parque en Latinoamérica.

1. ¿Está en la ciudad el parque?
2. ¿Irán los jóvenes al parque el sábado?
3. ¿Caminarán por las sendas del parque?
4. ¿Irán al parque de atracciones?
5. ¿Subirán a la montaña rusa?
6. ¿Visitarán el zoológico?
7. ¿Verán los animales?
8. ¿Les darán de comer a los animales?

CULTURA
Las jóvenes están mirando a sus perros en un parque de Buenos Aires, Argentina.

Andrew Payti

Answers

1

1. correcta
2. correcta
3. correcta
4. correcta
5. incorrecta
6. correcta
7. correcta
8. correcta

2

1. Sí, el parque está en la ciudad.
2. Sí (No), los jóvenes (no) irán al parque el sábado.
3. Sí, (No, no) caminarán por las sendas del parque.
4. Sí, (No, no) irán al parque de atracciones.
5. Sí, (No, no) subirán a la montaña rusa.
6. Sí, (No, no) visitarán el zoológico.
7. Sí, (No, no) verán los animales.
8. Sí, (No, no) les darán de comer a los animales.

Go Online!

connectED.mcgraw-hill.com

LEER • ESCRIBIR

3 Expresa de otra manera.

1. una avenida ancha
2. el casco antiguo
3. parquear
4. un parking
5. el autobús
6. una calle estrecha

LEER • ESCRIBIR

4 Completa con una palabra del **banco de palabras.**

la esquina	mimos	peatones	el parque de atracciones
un rascacielos	estrechas	la escalera	
el zoológico	la parada	la boca	

1. Hay un semáforo en ____ de la calle para controlar la circulación del tráfico.
2. Una calle peatonal es solo para ____.
3. La entrada al metro en la calle se llama ____.
4. Él bajó ____ para ir a la estación de metro.
5. Un edificio muy alto de muchos pisos es ____.
6. Hay calles ____ en el casco antiguo de la ciudad.
7. Mucha gente está esperando el bus en ____.
8. Muchas veces los ____ tienen la cara pintada.
9. Hay una montaña rusa y una noria en ____.
10. Hay elefantes, tigres, leones y cocodrilos en ____ en el parque.

CULTURA

Un edificio interesante con una torre alta en la Plaza de la Independencia en el centro de Montevideo, la capital de Uruguay

ESCRIBIR

5 **Rompecabezas**

Join two puzzle pieces to form a word. When you have finished you should have six words. Do not use any piece more than once.

6 **Comunicación**

Describe la ciudad en que vives. Si no vives en una ciudad describe una que está cerca de donde tú vives.

Andrew Payti

Vocabulario 1

Activities 3 and 4 These activities can be prepared before going over them in class.

Tips for Success

Have students actively use the interrogative words as frequently as possible. Have them make up as many questions as they can about each of the sentences in Activity 4. Some examples for the first sentence are:
1. **¿Qué hay en la esquina?**
2. **¿Dónde está el semáforo?**
3. **¿Qué controla el semáforo?**
4. **¿Por qué hay un semáforo en la esquina de la calle?** Another excellent activity is to have students respond using only the specific information requested in the question word.
1. **un semáforo** 2. **en la esquina**
3. **la circulación del tráfico**
4. **para controlar la circulación del tráfico**

Go Online!

You may wish to remind students to go online for additional vocabulary practice. They can also download audio files of all vocabulary.

ASSESS

Students are now ready to take Quiz 1.

Answers

3
1. un paseo
2. el barrio antiguo
3. aparcar (estacionar)
4. un parqueo (el aparcamiento, el estacionamiento)
5. el camión (la guagua)
6. una calle angosta

4
1. la esquina
2. peatones
3. la boca
4. la escalera
5. un rascacielos
6. estrechas
7. la parada
8. mimos
9. el parque de atracciones
10. el zoológico

5
estación, parada, esquina, peatones, rascacielos, autobús

6 *Answers will vary.*

Online Resources

Customizable Lesson Plans

Whiteboard Lesson

Audio Activities

Video (Vocabulario) (Cultura)

Student Workbook

Enrichment

Quizzes

Quick Start

Use QS 8.2 or write the following on the board.

Rewrite in the present progressive.

1. **Salgo para Costa Rica.**
2. **Paso por el control de seguridad.**
3. **Mucha gente espera.**
4. **Llegamos a la puerta de salida.**
5. **El agente anuncia la salida.**
6. **Abordamos.**
7. **Andrea, ¿buscas nuestros asientos?**

TEACH

Core Instruction

You may wish to use suggestions from previous chapters for the presentation of this new vocabulary.

Teaching Options

If your students live in a rural area you may wish to emphasize this vocabulary. If, on the other hand, they are from an urban, industrial area you may wish to de-emphasize it.

En el campo

Los peones cultivan (labran, trabajan) la tierra.
Están cultivando trigo.
Siembran el trigo en la primavera.
¿Cuándo será la cosecha?
Cosecharán el trigo en el otoño.

En una huerta cultivan legumbres o frutas.

Go Online!

Vocabulario en vivo Watch and listen as Nora discusses the attributes of the city and the country.

Total Physical Response (TPR)

(Student), **estás en el campo. Siembra el trigo.**
Cosecha el maíz y unas frutas.
Dale heno al caballo.
Ensilla al caballo. (Ask students what they think **ensilla** means. Also point to a chair.)
Monta al caballo.

Go Online!

connectED.mcgraw-hill.com

Los caballos están en el corral.
Las muchachas montarán (andarán) a caballo.
Les gusta mucho la equitación.

En otras partes

- The words **finca** and **granja** both mean *farm* and are used in Spain and many areas of Latin America. **Chacra** is used only in certain areas of Latin America. In many areas of Latin America, **la hacienda** is *a ranch*. In Spain it is **una finca. El rancho** is used in Mexico. In Chile, Argentina, and Uruguay **una estancia** is *a cattle ranch*.
- Another word for **cosechar (la cosecha)** is **recolectar (la recolección)**.

El ganado pace en el campo.

El verano que viene Enrique y su hermana visitarán a sus primos en el campo.
Pasarán un mes con ellos.

(t)David H Brennan, (bl br)Andrew Payti

About the Spanish Language

The word **el campo** can mean *country* or *countryside* as well as *field*, as in **campo de trigo.** People who work on farms are also called **labradores. El ganado** is the generic word for *livestock*. More specific terms are: **ganado vacuno:** *beef or dairy cattle;* **ganado porcino:** *hogs;* **ganado orino:** *sheep.*

Tips for Success

- As soon as students are familiar with the new vocabulary, have them read again the captions of the **Introducción al tema.**
- After going over the **Práctica** activities, have students return to the vocabulary presentation pages and make up statements and questions about the photos.

Go Online!

You may wish to use the whiteboard presentation for additional vocabulary instruction and practice.

Differentiation

Heritage Speakers

If you have heritage speakers in class you may wish to have them give some of the farming terms with which they are familiar.

Leveling EACH Activity

Easy Activities 1, 2
Average Activities 3, 5, 8
Average-CHallenging Activity 4
CHallenging Activities 6, 7

PRACTICE

Activity 1

Audio Script

1. El ganado pace en un establo.
2. En muchas partes del mundo, la siembra es en la primavera y la cosecha en el otoño.
3. Los campesinos labran la tierra.
4. Los cerdos nunca comen hierba.
5. Las gallinas ponen huevos.
6. El deporte de andar a camello es la equitación.
7. La vaca da leche.

Activities 2 and 4 These activities can be prepared before going over them in class.

Activity 3 This activity can be done as a paired activity.

Go Online!

Cultura en vivo Students will be introduced to the **gauchos** of Argentina. Have them explain what **la pampa** refers to.

FOLDABLES Study Organizer

FORWARD-BACKWARD BOOK See the Foldables section of the Student Handbook at the beginning of this book for help with making this foldable. On the front cover, write **la ciudad.** Open your book. On the right-hand page list words that you have learned that pertain to the city. On the next right-hand page, draw a picture illustrating the words on your list. Close your book and flip it over. On the back cover, write **el campo** and do the same.

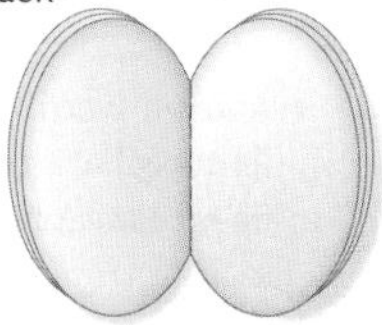

CULTURA

Estos caballos están comiendo heno en una granja cerca de Córdoba, España.

Emily Lowry

ESCUCHAR

1 Escucha cada frase y decide si la información es correcta o no. Usa una tabla como la de abajo para indicar tus respuestas.

correcta	incorrecta

LEER

2 Parea los sinónimos.

1. cultivar la tierra
2. persona del campo
3. practicar la equitación
4. una finca grande
5. recoger o recolectar el trigo
6. el rancho

a. cosechar
b. una estancia
c. trabajar, labrar la tierra
d. la hacienda
e. montar a caballo
f. un(a) campesino(a)

HABLAR • ESCRIBIR

3 Contesta.

1. ¿Dónde trabajan los campesinos?
2. ¿Qué hay en una finca?
3. ¿Qué hay en una huerta?
4. ¿Cuáles son algunos animales que producen carne?
5. Ella es aficionada a la equitación. ¿Qué hace ella?

LEER • ESCRIBIR

4 Completa con una palabra apropiada.

1. La ____ es verde y el trigo es amarillo.
2. El ganado ____ en el campo.
3. Las ____ ponen huevos.
4. Las ____ dan leche.
5. Cuando los caballos no están en el establo, están en ____.
6. Guardan el trigo y el heno en ____.
7. Los ____ trabajan la tierra.
8. Una ____ produce vegetales y frutas.

Answers

1
1. incorrecta
2. correcta
3. correcta
4. incorrecta
5. correcta
6. incorrecta
7. correcta

2
1. c
2. f
3. e
4. b (d)
5. a
6. d (b)

3 *Answers will vary but may include:*
1. Los campesinos trabajan en el campo.
2. Hay animales, campos y huertas en una finca.
3. Hay frutas y legumbres en una huerta.
4. Algunos animales que producen carne son la vaca, la gallina, el cordero y el cerdo.
5. Ella monta (anda) a caballo.

4
1. hierba
2. pace
3. gallinas
4. vacas
5. el corral
6. un granero
7. campesinos (peones)
8. huerta

Go Online!

connectED.mcgraw-hill.com

ESCRIBIR

5 Usa diagramas como los de abajo para categorizar las palabras que ya sabes en español.

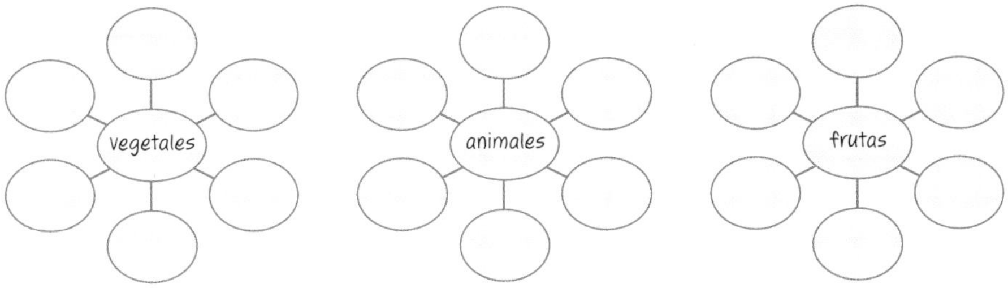

HABLAR • ESCRIBIR

6 Utiliza cada palabra en una frase original.

la finca · una estancia · el ganado · una casa de campo · la huerta · cosechar · el corral

7 **Comunicación**

Con unos compañeros de clase, preparen una encuesta *(survey)* para determinar si la mayoría de los alumnos en su clase aprecian más o conocen mejor la vida urbana o la vida rural. Basado en los resultados de su encuesta, analicen y expliquen el porqué.

LEER

8 **Rompecabezas**

Choose the word in each group that does not belong. Then switch the wrong words to make each group correct.

1. la vaca · la gallina · la hacienda
2. el trigo · una granja · el heno
3. el rancho · el cordero · la estancia
4. una finca · una chacra · sembrar
5. la hierba · cosechar · labrar

InfoGap For more practice using your new vocabulary, do Activity 8 in the Student Resource section at the end of this book.

Activities 5 and 6 These activities can be done as paired activities.

Comunicación

Presentational

Activity 7 After doing the survey in this activity, have several students present the results to the class.

Differentiation

Advanced Learners

Have advanced learners make up definitions of vocabulary words and call on volunteers in class to give the word(s) they have defined.

Go Online!

You may wish to remind students to go online for additional vocabulary practice. They can also download audio files of all vocabulary.

ASSESS

Students are now ready to take Quiz 2.

Answers

5 *Answers will vary but may include:*

1. la lechuga, los tomates, las papas (las patatas), los guisantes, las judías verdes, las zanahorias, las cebollas, los pimientos, el maíz
2. el perro, el gato, el caballo, el ganado, la vaca, el cerdo, el cordero, la gallina
3. las naranjas, las manzanas, los plátanos, las uvas, la piña

6 *Answers will vary.*

7 *Answers will vary.*

8

1. la hacienda / la vaca, la gallina, el cordero
2. una granja / el trigo, el heno, la hierba
3. el cordero / el rancho, la estancia, la hacienda
4. sembrar / una finca, una chacra, una granja
5. la hierba / cosechar, labrar, sembrar

Online Resources

Customizable Lesson Plans
- Whiteboard Lesson
- Audio Activities
- Student Workbook
- Enrichment
- Quizzes

Quick Start

Use QS 8.3 or write the following on the board.

Complete with an infinitive.

1. **No tengo que ___ mañana porque trabajé ayer.**
2. **No tengo que ___ mañana porque asistí ayer.**
3. **No tengo que ___ mañana porque fui ayer.**
4. **No tengo que ___ temprano porque volví temprano ayer.**

TEACH

Core Instruction

Step 1 You may wish to indicate to students that the endings are from the verb **haber** or you may wish to skip it.

Step 2 Have students read the verb forms down and across. Reading them across shows them the similarities.

Step 3 Read Item 3 to students, which explains the use of the future tense and substitutions for it.

Gramática

Conexiones

El inglés

English, the same as Spanish, very often uses the present tense or the expression *to be going to* to express the future.

They leave tomorrow.
They're (They are) leaving tomorrow.
They are going to leave tomorrow.
They'll (They will) leave tomorrow.

Futuro de los verbos regulares

1. The future tense is used to tell what will take place in the future. The endings for the future tense come from the verb **haber.**

   he has ha hemos habéis han

2. You add these endings to the entire infinitive to form the future tense of regular verbs.

infinitive	estudiar	leer	escribir
stem	estudiar-	leer-	escribir-
yo	estudiaré	leeré	escribiré
tú	estudiarás	leerás	escribirás
Ud., él, ella	estudiará	leerá	escribirá
nosotros(as)	estudiaremos	leeremos	escribiremos
vosotros(as)	*estudiaréis*	*leeréis*	*escribiréis*
Uds., ellos, ellas	estudiarán	leerán	escribirán

Algún día él irá a la América del Sur.
Visitará Perú y otros países.
Yo estaré en Bogotá en el mes de julio.

3. The future tense is not used a great deal in Spanish. It is more common to use **ir a** + *the infinitive* or the present tense.

Voy a salir mañana.	**Salgo mañana.**
Ellos van a volver en dos meses.	**Ellos vuelven en dos meses.**

4. The future tense can be used to express what is called the future of probability.

¿Cuántos años tendrá él? No sé.	*How old can he be? I don't know.*
¿Qué hora será? Serán las once.	*What time can it be? It must be about eleven o'clock.*

CULTURA
Los peatones cruzan la calle en Buenos Aires, Argentina. ¿Adónde irán?

Andrew Payti

Teaching Options

It is up to your discretion as to how thoroughly you wish to present the future tense. Students should be able to recognize the future but as stated in the grammatical explanation, they will not have to use it with a great deal of frequency.

¡Así se dice!

Why It Works!

Note that no lesson is burdened with too many grammatical points. In this chapter students learn the future, a low-frequency grammar point, and just one more grammatical concept—location of pronouns with infinitives and gerunds.

Go Online!

You may wish to remind students to go online for additional grammar review and practice.

Go Online!
connectED.mcgraw-hill.com

Práctica

HABLAR

1 Contesta sobre un viaje futuro de Mónica.

1. ¿Irá Mónica a Quito el año que viene?
2. ¿Pasará unos días en Quito?
3. ¿Visitará el casco antiguo?
4. ¿Irá al Museo de Arte Moderno?
5. ¿Caminará por el parque el Ejido?
6. ¿Verá una exposición de arte en el parque?
7. ¿Comerá ceviche?
8. ¿Asistirá a un concierto?

CULTURA

¿Caminarás un día por una de estas pintorescas calles en el barrio de Panecillo en Quito, Ecuador?

ESCUCHAR • HABLAR • ESCRIBIR

2 Sigue el modelo.

MODELO **Tomaré el carro. →**
Voy a tomar el carro.

1. Aparcaré el carro en un parking.
2. Tomaremos el metro para llegar al centro.
3. ¿Visitarán ustedes el barrio viejo?
4. ¿Andarás por las calles estrechas del barrio viejo?
5. ¿Tú irás al parque de atracciones?
6. Pasaré unas horas en el zoológico.

ESCUCHAR • HABLAR • ESCRIBIR

3 Sigue el modelo.

MODELO **Voy a ir al campo. →**
Iré al campo.

1. Van a cultivar trigo.
2. Vamos a comer vegetales de la huerta.
3. ¿Vas a montar a caballo?
4. ¿Quién va a limpiar el establo?
5. Voy a visitar una estancia.

LEER • ESCRIBIR

4 Completa con el futuro.

1. Ellos _____ dentro de poco. (volver)
2. Yo los _____. (ver)
3. Nosotros _____ de muchas cosas. (hablar)
4. ¿Tú los _____ a tu casa? (invitar)
5. Sí, (yo) _____ una comida y (nosotros) _____ juntos. (preparar, comer)
6. El postre _____ el plato principal. (seguir)

Leveling EACH Activity

Easy Activity 1
Average Activities 2, 3
CHallenging Activity 4

PRACTICE

Activity 1 This activity can be done as an entire class activity.

Differentiation

Advanced Learners

Call on one or more advanced learners to retell all the information in Activity 1.

Activities 2 and 3 These activities can be done as paired activities.

Activity 4 This activity should be prepared and then gone over in class.

Cultural Snapshot

The police and officials of Quito are trying to alleviate a crime problem that exists in the area of el Panecillo. The Panecillo Hill close to the colonial section is considered unsafe for visitors, particularly at night.

ASSESS

Students are now ready to take Quiz 3.

Answers

1

1. Sí (No), Mónica (no) irá a Quito el año que viene.
2. Sí, (No, no) pasará unos días en Quito.
3. Sí, (No, no) visitará el casco antiguo.
4. Sí, (No, no) irá al Museo de Arte Moderno.
5. Sí, (No, no) caminará por el parque el Ejido.
6. Sí, (No, no) verá una exposición de arte en el parque.
7. Sí, (No, no) comerá ceviche.
8. Sí, (No, no) asistirá a un concierto.

2

1. Voy a aparcar el carro en un parking.
2. Vamos a tomar el metro para llegar al centro.
3. ¿Van a visitar ustedes el barrio viejo?
4. ¿Vas a andar por las calles estrechas del barrio viejo?
5. ¿Vas a ir al parque de atracciones?
6. Voy a pasar unas horas en el zoológico.

3

1. Cultivarán trigo.
2. Comeremos vegetales de la huerta.
3. ¿Montarás a caballo?
4. ¿Quién limpiará el establo?
5. Visitaré una estancia.

4

1. volverán
2. veré
3. hablaremos
4. invitarás
5. prepararé, comeremos
6. seguirá

Online Resources

Customizable Lesson Plans
- Whiteboard Lesson
- Audio Activities
- Video (Gramática)
- Student Workbook
- Enrichment
- Quizzes

Quick Start

Use QS 8.4 or write the following on the board.
Answer.
Cuando sales de tu hotel, ¿tienes que devolver la llave a la recepción o la puedes poner en tu mochila?

TEACH

Core Instruction

Call on students to read the verbs aloud. You may wish to have groups read them.

Teaching Options

It is up to your discretion as to how thoroughly you want to teach and present this particular point.

¡Así se dice!

Why It Works!

Note that verbs are grouped according to their sound to make irregularities appear as regular as possible.

Cultural Snapshot

This sign is located about ninety minutes north of Quito.

Futuro de los verbos irregulares

1. Study the following forms of verbs that have an irregular stem in the future tense. Note that the endings for all irregular verbs are the same as those for the regular verbs.

infinitive	tener	salir	venir
stem	tendr-	saldr-	vendr-
yo	tendré	saldré	vendré
tú	tendrás	saldrás	vendrás
Ud., él, ella	tendrá	saldrá	vendrá
nosotros(as)	tendremos	saldremos	vendremos
vosotros(as)	*tendréis*	*saldréis*	*vendréis*
Uds., ellos, ellas	tendrán	saldrán	vendrán

2. Other verbs that follow the same pattern are **poner, saber,** and **poder.**

poner → pondré **saber → sabré** **poder → podré**

3. The verbs **decir, hacer,** and **querer** also have an irregular future stem.

infinitive	decir	hacer	querer
stem	dir-	har-	querr-
yo	diré	haré	querré
tú	dirás	harás	querrás
Ud., él, ella	dirá	hará	querrá
nosotros(as)	diremos	haremos	querremos
vosotros(as)	*diréis*	*haréis*	*querréis*
Uds., ellos, ellas	dirán	harán	querrán

4. Note that the future of **hay (haber)** is **habrá.**

¿Cuántos habrá?
Habrá más de uno.
Habrá por lo menos cuatro.

CULTURA
¿Harás un viaje a Ecuador algún día para conocer mejor el país?

Richard Brommer

Go Online!

Gramática en vivo *Future and conditional tenses* Enliven learning with the animated world of Professor Cruz! **Gramática en vivo** is a fun and effective tool for additional instruction and/or review.

Go Online!

connectED.mcgraw-hill.com

Práctica

HABLAR

5 Personaliza. Da respuestas personales.

1. Algún día, ¿tendrás la oportunidad de viajar a Latinoamérica?
2. ¿Podrás visitar varias ciudades?
3. ¿Harás el viaje en avión?
4. ¿Podrás tomar fotos digitales?
5. ¿Las podrás descargar a tu computadora?
6. ¿Las imprimirás y las pondrás en un álbum?

ESCUCHAR • HABLAR

6 Conversa según el modelo.

MODELO **—Beatriz no vino hoy.**
—No, pero vendrá mañana.

1. Ella no salió de casa a tiempo.
2. Él no me lo dijo.
3. No lo hice.
4. No tuvimos tiempo.
5. Antonio no sabía hacerlo.
6. Ellos no podían decirlo.

Un paseo en el casco histórico de la Ciudad de Panamá

LEER • ESCRIBIR

7 Completa sobre Ricardo en Panamá.

El invierno que viene Ricardo Rojas __1__ (tener) dos semanas de vacaciones. Él y su familia __2__ (hacer) un viaje a Panamá. Allí ellos __3__ (poder) pasar unos días con sus parientes. El padre de Ricardo __4__ (llamar) a Panamá y les __5__ (decir) a sus parientes la hora de su llegada. Todos los parientes de Ricardo __6__ (querer) ir al aeropuerto a recibirlos. Ricardo y sus padres __7__ (salir) en el vuelo de las once. El vuelo __8__ (hacer) escala en Miami antes de llegar a Panamá.

8 ***Comunicación***

Tu familia va a hacer un viaje a un país latinoamericano. Trabajando en pequeños grupos, (o sea, con los miembros de tu «familia») hagan investigaciones para escribir un plan detallado para su viaje. Incluyan detalles esenciales sobre las necesidades y deseos específicos de los varios miembros de su grupo. Luego compartan su plan e itinerario con otros grupos.

Leveling EACH Activity

Easy Activity 5
Average-CHallenging
Activities 6, 7, 8

PRACTICE

Activities 5 and 6 These activities can also be done as paired activities.

Teaching Options

Note that the response in Activity 6 can also be **No, pero va a venir (viene) mañana.**

Activities 7 This activity should be prepared before going over it in class.

Go Online!

You may wish to use the whiteboard presentation for additional grammar instruction and practice.

ASSESS

Students are now ready to take Quiz 4.

Answers

5

1. Sí, (No, no) tendré la oportunidad de viajar a Latinoamérica algún día.
2. Sí, (No, no) podré visitar varias ciudades.
3. Sí, (No, no) haré el viaje en avión.
4. Sí, (No, no) podré tomar fotos digitales.
5. Sí, (No, no) las podré descargar en mi computadora.
6. Sí, (No, no) las imprimiré y pondré en un álbum.

6

1. No, pero saldrá de casa a tiempo mañana.
2. No, pero me lo dirá mañana.
3. No, pero lo haré mañana.
4. No, pero tendremos tiempo mañana.
5. No, pero sabrá hacerlo mañana.
6. No, pero podrán decirlo mañana.

7

1. tendrá
2. harán
3. podrán
4. llamará
5. dirá
6. querrán
7. saldrán
8. hará

8 *Answers will vary.*

Online Resources

Customizable Lesson Plans

- Whiteboard Lesson
- Audio Activities
- Student Workbook
- Enrichment
- Quizzes

Quick Start

Use QS 8.5 or write the following on the board.

Rewrite each sentence in the present progressive.

1. **Salen.**
2. **Ponen las maletas en la maletera.**
3. **Llegan al aeropuerto.**
4. **Los asistentes sirven una merienda.**
5. **Volvemos de nuestras vacaciones.**

TEACH

Core Instruction

Step 1 Read each item to the class.

Step 2 As you go over each item, underline the noun, circle the pronoun, and draw arrows to show the location of each.

Differentiation

Slower Paced Learners

With the exception of the **favor de** construction, the pronoun(s) can always precede the auxiliary. Students should realize that the pronouns are often attached. For productive purposes, however, you may allow slower paced learners to always put the pronoun(s) before the auxiliary.

Los pronombres con el infinitivo y el gerundio

1. You have already learned that the pronoun is attached to the infinitive in the expression **favor de** and with the reflexive verbs.

Favor de darme el menú.	**¿Quieres levantarte?**
Favor de pasarle el pan.	**¿Puedo sentarme aquí?**
Favor de decírmelo.	**Vamos a divertirnos.**

2. When the object pronouns are used with the infinitive and a helping verb, the object pronouns can either be placed before the helping verb or attached to the infinitive.

Voy a tomar el metro.	**Quiero mostrar la finca a mi primo.**
Lo voy a tomar.	**Se la quiero mostrar a él.**
Voy a tomarlo.	**Quiero mostrársela a él.**

3. When the object pronouns are used with the present participle, they may also precede the helping verb or they may be attached to the present participle.

Está visitando el parque de atracciones.
Lo está visitando.
Está visitándolo.

4. To maintain the same stress, a participle carries a written accent with either one or two attached pronouns. The infinitive carries a written accent only when two pronouns are attached to it.

PARTICIPLE	INFINITIVE
Está sirviéndolo.	**Quiero darle el plano.**
Está sirviéndomelo.	**Quiero dárselo.**

CULTURA

En todas partes, como en esta calle de Buenos Aires, a los niños les fascinan los títeres. Parece que este niño está preguntándose si puede o debe tocarlos o no.

Andrew Payti

Práctica

ESCUCHAR • HABLAR • ESCRIBIR

9 Sigue el modelo.

MODELO **la fecha →**
No la puedo recordar.
No puedo recordarla.

1. el día
2. la hora
3. el número de teléfono
4. las direcciones
5. los nombres

Answers

9

1. No lo puedo recordar. / No puedo recordarlo.
2. No la puedo recordar. / No puedo recordarla.
3. No lo puedo recordar. / No puedo recordarlo.
4. No las puedo recordar. / No puedo recordarlas.
5. No los puedo recordar. / No puedo recordarlos.

10

1. Sí, (No, no) acabo de comprarlo. (Sí, [No, no] lo acabo de comprar.)
2. Sí, (No, no) acabo de leerlo. (Sí, [No, no] lo acabo de leer.)
3. Sí, (No, no) acabo de dárselo (a él). (Sí, [No, no] se lo acabo de dar [a él].)
4. Sí, (No, no) acabo de hacerlos. (Sí, [No, no] los acabo de hacer.)
5. Sí, (No, no) acabo de comunicárselos (a ellos). (Sí, [No, no] se los acabo de comunicar [a ellos]).

ESCUCHAR • HABLAR • ESCRIBIR

10 Contesta con pronombres.

1. ¿Acabas de comprar el periódico?
2. ¿Acabas de leer el periódico?
3. ¿Acabas de dar el periódico a Pedro?
4. ¿Acabas de hacer tus planes finales?
5. ¿Acabas de comunicarlos a tus padres?

LEER • ESCRIBIR

11 Sigue el modelo.

MODELO **Los campesinos están labrando la tierra. →**
Los campesinos están labrándola.
Los campesinos la están labrando.

1. Están cultivando el trigo.
2. Están cosechando las legumbres.
3. Están limpiando el corral.
4. Los corderos están comiendo la hierba.
5. Los caballos están comiendo el heno.

LEER • ESCRIBIR

12 Escribe las frases con pronombres.

1. En la clase de español los alumnos están aprendiendo *la gramática.*
2. Ahora algunos están escuchando *los CDs.*
3. Todos están prestando atención *a la profesora.*
4. Carlos está revisando *su composición.*
5. León está enviando *el correo electrónico a un amigo.*
6. El profesor está devolviendo *los exámenes a los alumnos.*

ESCUCHAR • HABLAR • ESCRIBIR

13 Contesta con **sí** usando pronombres.

1. ¿Quiere ver la película Marisol?
2. ¿Va a ver la película?
3. ¿Está comprando las entradas ahora?
4. ¿Está comprando las entradas en la taquilla del cine?
5. ¿Quiere Marisol ver la película desde la primera fila o está demasiado cerca de la pantalla?
6. Desde la primera fila, ¿puede ver bien la película?

Go Online!

connectED.mcgraw-hill.com

Refrán

Can you guess what the following proverb means?

Alegría ten, y vivirás bien.

¡Bravo!

You have now learned all the new vocabulary and grammar in this chapter. Continue to use and practice all that you know while learning more cultural information. ¡Vamos!

Gramática

Leveling EACH Activity

Average Activities 9, 10, 11
CHallenging Activities 12, 13

PRACTICE

Activities 9, 10, and 11 These activities can be done as paired activities.

Teaching Options

Activities 9, 10, and 11 can be **Easy** if the students only put pronouns before the auxiliary. Similarly, Activities 12 and 13 become **Average.**

Activity 12 This activity should be prepared before going over it in class.

Activity 13 This activity can be done with the entire class or it can be done as a paired activity.

ASSESS

Students are now ready to take Quiz 5.

Answers

11

1. Están cultivándolo. / Lo están cultivando.
2. Están cosechándolas. / Las están cosechando.
3. Están limpiándolo. / Lo están limpiando.
4. Los corderos están comiéndola. / Los corderos la están comiendo.
5. Los caballos están comiéndolo. / Los caballos lo están comiendo.

12

1. En la clase de español los alumnos están aprendiéndola. (En la clase de español los alumnos la están aprendiendo.)
2. Ahora algunos están escuchándolos. (Ahora algunos los están escuchando.)
3. Todos están prestándole atención. (Todos le están prestando atención.)
4. Carlos está revisándola. (Carlos la está revisando.)
5. León está enviándoselo. (León se lo está enviando.)
6. El profesor está devolviéndoselos. (El profesor se los está devolviendo.)

13

1. Sí, Marisol quiere verla. (Sí, Marisol la quiere ver.)
2. Sí, va a verla. (Sí, la va a ver.)
3. Sí, está comprándolas ahora. (Sí, las está comprando ahora.)
4. Sí, está comprándolas en la taquilla del cine. (Sí, las está comprando en la taquilla del cine.)
5. Sí, Marisol quiere verla desde la primera fila. (Sí, Marisol la quiere ver desde la primera fila.)
6. Sí, desde la primera fila, puede verla bien. (Sí, desde la primera fila la puede ver bien.)

Online Resources

Customizable Lesson Plans

- Audio Activities
- Video (Diálogo)
- Student Workbook

Quick Start

Use QS 8.6 or write the following on the board.

Write in Spanish a list of summer activities and a list of winter activities.

TEACH

Core Instruction

Step 1 Have two students with good pronunciation read the conversation to the class. One can take the part of Clara and the other the part of Julio. If you wish, you can change the names to the names of the students in your class.

Step 2 Have students listen to the audio recording.

Step 3 Call on individuals to read parts of the conversation aloud.

Step 4 After a student reads, you can intersperse some questions. You can make up questions or use those from the **¿Comprendes?** section.

Step 5 After presenting the conversation in class, have students write answers to the **¿Comprendes?** questions for homework.

¡Así se dice!

Why It Works!

No new material is used in the **Conversación.** The **Conversación** recombines only the vocabulary and grammar that students have already learned to understand and manipulate.

Un verano en el campo

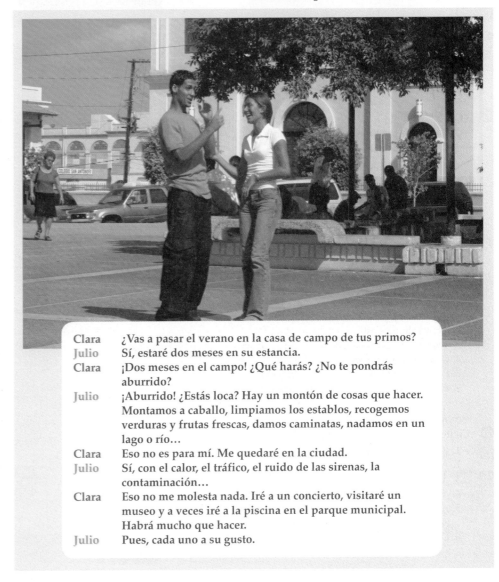

Clara	¿Vas a pasar el verano en la casa de campo de tus primos?
Julio	Sí, estaré dos meses en su estancia.
Clara	¡Dos meses en el campo! ¿Qué harás? ¿No te pondrás aburrido?
Julio	¡Aburrido! ¿Estás loca? Hay un montón de cosas que hacer. Montamos a caballo, limpiamos los establos, recogemos verduras y frutas frescas, damos caminatas, nadamos en un lago o río...
Clara	Eso no es para mí. Me quedaré en la ciudad.
Julio	Sí, con el calor, el tráfico, el ruido de las sirenas, la contaminación...
Clara	Eso no me molesta nada. Iré a un concierto, visitaré un museo y a veces iré a la piscina en el parque municipal. Habrá mucho que hacer.
Julio	Pues, cada uno a su gusto.

Larry Hamill

Comunicación

Interpersonal

Remind students that people often form personal opinions about what others say during a conversation. They may agree with some points and disagree with others. Have students think about their own opinions as they go over the conversation. Then allow them to give their opinions. You may wish to wait until after you have finished the **¿Comprendes?** activities.

Go Online!

You may wish to remind students to go online for additional conversation practice.

¿Comprendes?

Go Online!

connectED.mcgraw-hill.com

A Contesta según la información en la conversación.

1. ¿Quién va a pasar el verano en el campo?
2. ¿A quiénes visitará?
3. ¿Qué tienen sus primos en el campo?
4. ¿Por qué a Julio no le gusta la ciudad en el verano?
5. ¿Se aburrirá Clara en el campo?

B Completa la tabla según la conversación.

actividades en el campo	actividades en la ciudad

C **Explicando** Contesta.

1. ¿Cuál es la diferencia de opinión entre Clara y Julio?
2. ¿Qué significa «Cada uno a su gusto»?

CULTURA

Los alumnos están esperando un bus en una parada en una esquina de Quito, Ecuador. ¿Qué piensas? ¿Tomarán el bus que está pasando ahora?

Conversación

PRACTICE

¿Comprendes?

B You may call on students to read their list of activities.

C Have students discuss whether they agree with Clara or Julio.

Go Online!

Diálogo en vivo In this episode, Julián and Claudia discuss the advantages of living in the city and in the country. Ask students to identify the disadvantages of living in both places.

Comparaciones

Have students look at the photo. Ask them to compare their experience traveling to and from school with that of the students in the photo.

Pre-AP Listening to this conversation will help students develop the skills that they need to be successful on the listening portion of the AP exam.

Answers

A

1. Julio va a pasar el verano en el campo.
2. Visitará a sus primos.
3. Sus primos tienen una casa de campo.
4. A Julio no le gusta la ciudad en el verano porque hay demasiado calor, tráfico, ruido y contaminación.
5. Sí, Clara se aburrirá en el campo.

B

actividades en el campo: montar a caballo, limpiar los establos, recoger verduras y frutas frescas, dar caminatas, nadar en un lago o río
actividades en la ciudad: ir a un concierto, visitar un museo, ir a la piscina en el parque municipal

C *Answers will vary but may include:*

1. Clara piensa que pasar el verano en el campo es aburrido. A Julio le gusta mucho pasar el verano en el campo. Para él no es aburrido.
2. «Cada uno a su gusto» significa que la gente puede tener opiniones diferentes.

Online Resources

Customizable Lesson Plans

Audio Activities

Student Workbook

TEACH

Core Instruction

Step 1 Have students look at the photographs that accompany this **Lectura** to familiarize themselves even more with some areas of Latin America.

Step 2 Call on a student to read three or four sentences aloud. Then stop and ask other members of the class questions about the material that was just read.

Step 3 As you go over the paragraph **Las afueras,** you may wish to ask students to compare the location of many of the poorer areas in the United States with those in Latin America.

Step 4 Go over the Reading Checks.

Step 5 The information, although briefly stated here, gives students some important background about some basic facts concerning some of Latin America's current problems. Ask questions about the information and call on individuals to respond.

Teaching Options

You may have the entire class read all of the **Lectura** or you may wish to divide it into logical parts, assigning each part to a different group. Each group will report to the others concerning what they learned.

Lectura CULTURAL

ESTRATEGIA DE LECTURA

REPASANDO Al leer una selección que tiene muchos detalles, es importante volver a leer unos trozos (la misma parte) para ayudarte a recordar los detalles.

Antes de leer

Reflexiona sobre lo que ya sabes de la vida urbana y rural según tus experiencias personales.

La ciudad y el campo

La ciudad Si vas algún día a una ciudad latinoamericana, observarás que en el centro mismo de casi todas hay un casco antiguo. En el centro del casco antiguo se encuentra una gran plaza que muchas veces se llama «la Plaza de Armas». En la plaza verás la catedral y algunos edificios gubernamentales que datan de la época colonial. De la plaza salen callecitas pintorescas.

Cada ciudad tiene también barrios modernos con grandes rascacielos que tienen oficinas y condominios donde vive la gente de las clases media y alta. En los barrios modernos hay avenidas anchas y paseos bonitos. Hay también calles peatonales donde no se permite entrar el tráfico vehicular.

CULTURA

Plaza de Armas, Quito

READING CHECK

¿Cuáles son características del casco viejo y del barrio moderno?

CULTURA

Hay muchos peatones en la Plaza de Armas en Lima. Les gusta andar por la plaza sobre todo cuando hace buen tiempo.

Andrew Payti

Cada ciudad tiene uno o más parques donde los habitantes disfrutan del aire libre y espacio abierto. Los fines de semana dan un paseo por el parque y se divierten mirando a los mimos. En muchos parques hay un parque de atracciones y a veces un zoológico.

Las afueras Desafortunadamente en las afueras de casi todas las ciudades verás los barrios bajos. Sus nombres varían de país en país—ranchos, villas miseria, pueblos jóvenes, etc. No importa el nombre. En todos viven los pobres en chozas o casuchas[1] sin luz (electricidad), gas ni agua corriente[2]. Para saber una de las razones que tanta gente vive en tales condiciones iremos al campo.

[1]chozas, casuchas *shacks* [2]agua corriente *running water*

Durante la lectura

Al leer, toma notas o apuntes sobre los detalles que consideras importantes y que crees que debes recordar.

READING CHECK

¿Qué hay en las afueras de las ciudades?

CULTURA

Mucha gente va al Bosque de Chapultepec los domingos. Es un parque muy grande en la Ciudad de México.

Andrew Payti

¡Así se dice!

Why It Works!

This **Lectura,** like all others in **¡Así se dice!,** contains only vocabulary Spanish students have already learned with the exception of the five footnoted words. The **Lectura** is easy because it is at the students' proficiency level and they are not encumbered with unknown lexical and grammatical forms.

Writing Development

You may wish to ask students to read **Durante la lectura** and to take notes as they read. Then have them write a summary based on their notes.

Go Online!

You may wish to remind students to go online for additional reading comprehension and writing skills practice.

Cultural Snapshot

The **Bosque de Chapultepec** is a very beautiful and popular park. On weekends thousands of families can be seen taking advantage of the many activities available in the park.

Differentiation

Advanced Learners

Have advanced learners explain the meaning of the following terms in their own words: **latifundio, terratenientes, reforma agraria, sobrepoblación.**

Heritage Speakers

If you have any heritage speakers in class, have them explain to the other members of the class the urban/rural situation in their home country. Have students from different countries explain similarities and differences.

Pre-AP These cultural readings will develop the skills that students need to be successful on the reading and writing sections of the AP exam. Listening to these readings will also help prepare them for the auditory component.

Lectura
CULTURAL

CULTURA

El cultivo de flores, como estas orquídeas, es una industria importante en Ecuador.

El campo La vida de muchos campesinos es difícil. Los problemas rurales tienen una larga historia. Desde la época de los españoles había grandes extensiones de tierras llamadas latifundios. Sus dueños o propietarios eran grandes terratenientes[3] ricos y más tarde grandes compañías de Estados Unidos y Europa. Debido a reformas agrarias estos latifundios han sido divididos en parcelas pequeñas y distribuidas entre los campesinos pobres que antes las tenían que trabajar para los terratenientes. Pero los campesinos no tienen suficiente dinero para comprar lo que necesitan para labrar la tierra de una manera productiva. Así toman la decisión de salir para la ciudad en busca de una vida mejor y añaden al problema de la sobrepoblación[4] que ya existe en las ciudades latinoamericanas.

Sí, hay problemas pero hay que señalar[5] que al viajar por Latinoamérica verás paisajes de una belleza increíble—montañas, volcanes, jardines, estancias o ranchos—todo.

[3]terratenientes *landowners*
[4]sobrepoblación *overpopulation*
[5]señalar *point out*

✓ READING CHECK

¿Siguen existiendo problemas económicos en las zonas rurales?

CULTURA

Una campesina cuidando de sus ovejas en el campo en Sabandía, Perú

Después de leer

Los detalles pueden ser interesantes o aburridos. De los detalles en esta lectura, ¿cuáles consideras interesantes? ¿Cuáles te interesan menos?

Answers

A

1. Casi todas las ciudades latinoamericanas tienen un casco antiguo.
2. La gran plaza que se encuentra en el centro de muchas ciudades de Latinoamérica se llama «la Plaza de Armas».
3. Casi todos los edificios del casco viejo datan de la época colonial.
4. Los barrios bajos donde viven los pobres se encuentran en las afueras de las ciudades.

B *Answers will vary but may include:* En muchos parques latinoamericanos, hay un parque de atracciones y a veces un zoológico. Los parques son importantes y populares porque los habitantes pueden disfrutar del aire libre y espacio abierto. También pueden dar un paseo y mirar a los mimos.

C

1. La vida de muchos campesinos es difícil.
2. Un latifundio es una extensión grande de tierra.
3. Sus dueños eran terratenientes ricos o grandes compañías de Estados Unidos o Europa.
4. El resultado de muchas reformas agrarias es que los latifundios han sido divididos en parcelas pequeñas y distribuidas entre los campesinos.
5. No tienen suficiente dinero para labrar la tierra en una manera productiva.

¿Comprendes?

A Confirmando información Corrige la información falsa.

1. Muy pocas ciudades latinoamericanas tienen un casco antiguo.
2. La gran plaza que se encuentra en el centro de muchas ciudades latinoamericanas se llama la Catedral.
3. Casi todos los edificios en el casco viejo datan de la época de las civilizaciones indígenas o precolombinas.
4. Los barrios bajos donde viven los pobres se encuentran en el centro de las ciudades.

B Describiendo y analizando Describe un parque de una ciudad latinoamericana y explica por qué los parques son importantes y populares.

CULTURA

Es la entrada a un rancho en Cozumel, México.

C Recordando hechos Contesta.

1. ¿Cómo es la vida de muchos campesinos?
2. ¿Qué es un latifundio?
3. ¿Quiénes eran sus dueños o propietarios?
4. ¿Cuál es el resultado de muchas reformas agrarias?
5. ¿Por qué no pueden labrar bien la tierra?
6. ¿Adónde van?
7. ¿Cuál es un problema que ya existe en muchas ciudades latinoamericanas?

D Describiendo y categorizando Completa las tablas.

la ciudad en Latinoamérica		
el barrio antiguo	el barrio moderno	problemas en las afueras

el campo en Latinoamérica		
distribución de la tierra en el pasado	distribución de la tierra actualmente	problemas en las zonas rurales

E Explicando Completa.

Visitar el campo en Latinoamérica puede ser una experiencia fabulosa porque...

PRACTICE

¿Comprendes?

A and **C** You may allow students to look up answers in the reading or you may wish to hold them responsible for giving the answers without such assistance.
D You may wish to have students do this as a paired or group activity.

Writing Development

You may wish to have students individually or in groups pick an area in Latin America and prepare a research report on it.

Cultural Snapshot

Cozumel is an island in the Caribbean, just off the coast of the Yucatan peninsula.

Answers

6. Van a las ciudades.
7. La sobrepoblación es un problema que ya existe en las ciudades latinoamericanas.

D

la ciudad en Latinoamérica

el barrio antiguo: Hay uno en casi todas las ciudades; en el centro de muchos de los barrios hay una plaza que se llama «la Plaza de Armas».

el barrio moderno: Tiene grandes rascacielos con oficinas y condominios; viven aquí las clases media y alta; hay avenidas anchas, paseos bonitos y calles peatonales.

problemas en las afueras: Muchos pobres viven en los barrios bajos donde no hay electricidad, gas ni agua corriente. Hay también sobrepoblación.

el campo en Latinoamérica

distribución de la tierra en el pasado: latifundios cuyos dueños eran grandes terratenientes o compañías grandes

distribución de la tierra actualmente: parcelas pequeñas distribuidas entre los campesinos pobres

problemas en las zonas rurales: Los campesinos pobres no pueden labrar la tierra en una manera productiva y así toman la decisión de salir para la ciudad.

E *Answers will vary but may include:* ... verás paisajes de una belleza increíble.

Online Resources

Customizable Lesson Plans

Audio Activities

Student Workbook

Teaching Options

You may wish to follow any one of these procedures for the **Lectura—Un poco más.**

Independent reading Have students read the selection and do the post-reading activities as homework, which you collect. This option is least intrusive on class time and requires a minimum of teacher involvement.

Homework with in-class follow-up Assign the reading and post-reading activities as homework. Review and discuss the material in class the next day.

Intensive in-class activity This option includes a discussion of **Antes de leer**, listening to the audio recording of the reading selection, an in-class discussion of the selection, and the **¿Comprendes?** activity. You may also assign **¿Comprendes?** for homework and discuss it in class the next day.

Lectura

UN POCO MÁS

Antes de leer

Durante toda la historia de Estados Unidos ha habido ciudades con grandes poblaciones de gente de otros países. ¿Conoces tal ciudad?

Una ciudad interesante

La ciudad de Miami en la Florida empezó a desarrollarse[1] en 1895 cuando Henry Flagler tomó la decisión de extender el ferrocarril hacia el sur. Hoy la aglomeración de Miami tiene casi dos millones quinientos mil habitantes y está aumentándose cada día. Es uno de los grandes focos latinos de Estados Unidos. Empezó una gran migración de cubanos a fines de los años cincuenta cuando Fidel Castro derrocó[2] la dictadura de Fulgencio Batista. Hoy en día sigue llegando y estableciéndose en Miami gente de casi todas partes de Centroamérica, Sudamérica y del Caribe.

Una zona típicamente cubana de Miami se llama «la Pequeña Habana». Aquí se oye más español que inglés. El corazón[3] de la Pequeña Habana es la calle Ocho. Aquí hay muchos cafés, restaurantes y tiendas cubanas tradicionales. Si quieres comprarte una guayabera no hay problema. Hay una cantidad de tiendas de ropa. Si tienes sed, puedes sentarte en un café para tomar un guarapo, un café con leche o un típico cafecito cubano—un expreso muy fuerte con mucho azúcar. A los cubanos les gusta su cafecito muy dulce.

En una calle llamada *Cuban Memorial Boulevard*, hay una serie de monumentos dedicados a patriotas cubanos que lucharon[4] por la libertad de su país. Hay también un mapa de relieve de Cuba. Es imposible pasar un día en Miami sin observar la influencia y las contribuciones de los cubanos y otros hispanos o latinos a la vitalidad y personalidad de esta gran ciudad cosmopolita.

[1]desarrollarse *develop*
[2]derrocó *brought down*
[3]corazón *heart*
[4]lucharon *fought*

CULTURA

El parque de Máximo Gómez se conoce como el Parque Dominó porque a muchos cubanos de mayor edad les gusta reunirse allí para jugar dominó.

Go Online!

You may wish to remind students to go online for additional reading comprehension and writing skills practice.

Go Online!

connectED.mcgraw-hill.com

¿Comprendes?

A Escoge o completa.

1. ¿Cuál es el mejor título para esta lectura?
   - **a.** El establecimiento de Miami
   - **b.** Un parque interesante
   - **c.** La Pequeña Habana
   - **d.** Miami, ayer y hoy
2. ¿Qué tuvo mucha importancia en el desarrollo de Miami?
   - **a.** el Parque Dominó
   - **b.** el ferrocarril
   - **c.** la calle Ocho
   - **d.** Cuba
3. ¿Por qué es Miami uno de los grandes focos hispanos o latinos de Estados Unidos?
   - **a.** Hay muchos inmigrantes de Cuba y de todo Latinoamérica.
   - **b.** Castro derrocó la dictadura de Fulgencio Batista.
   - **c.** Está en el mar Caribe.
   - **d.** Ya había muchos hispanos en Miami cuando llegó Henry Flagler.
4. ¿Cuál es una característica de la Pequeña Habana?
   - **a.** Está en el corazón de la ciudad.
   - **b.** Es la única zona donde hay restaurantes y cafés.
   - **c.** Allí se oye más español que inglés.
   - **d.** Nadie habla inglés.
5. Sabemos que podemos comprar una guayabera porque la lectura dice ____.
6. ¿Cuál de los siguientes es una bebida?
   - **a.** un dominó
   - **b.** un guarapo
   - **c.** el azúcar
   - **d.** una guayabera

B Analiza.

¿Por qué quiere compartir el autor esta información con sus lectores? En tu opinión, ¿cuál es su propósito?

CULTURA

Una vista bonita de la ciudad de Miami

Lectura

Comunidades

If you have students in class who have been to Miami, have them tell about and share their experiences.

Comunicación

Presentational

You may have students prepare a brief historical overview of where they live that could be of interest to Spanish-speaking visitors. You might also have them create an itinerary of interesting places to visit.

Conexiones

Have students look at the photographs of Spanish-speaking communities in the United States featured in the **GeoVistas** section at the beginning of the book. Then have them locate some of these cities on the map of the United States. Ask students why they think there are such large Spanish-speaking communities in the cities mentioned.

Tips for Success

The multiple-choice comprehension activities that accompany the second reading selection in each chapter have a format that will help students prepare for standardized tests.

Answers

A

1. d
2. b
3. a
4. c
5. que hay una cantidad de tiendas de ropa
6. b

B *Answers will vary.*

Prepárate para el examen

Online Resources

Customizable Lesson Plans

Student Workbook

Listening, Speaking, Reading, Writing Tests

Self-check for achievement

This is a pre-test for students to take before you administer the chapter test. Note that each section is cross-referenced so students can easily find the material they feel they need to review. You may wish to use Self-Check Worksheet SC8 to have students complete this assessment in class or at home. You can correct the assessment yourself, or you may prefer to display the answers in class using Self-Check Answers SC8A.

Differentiation

Slower-Paced Learners

Have students work in pairs to complete the Self-Check in class. Once they have finished, call on individuals to give the correct answers as you review together.

Prepárate para el examen

Vocabulario

1 Completa con una palabra apropiada.

To review, see **Vocabulario 1**.

1. Puedes aparcar en la calle o en un ____.
2. Los peatones deben cruzar la calle en ____.
3. Hay ____ para bajar a la estación de metro.
4. Un ____ es un edificio alto que tiene muchos pisos.
5–6. ____ y ____ son dos atracciones en el parque de atracciones.
7. Hay animales exóticos en el ____.

CULTURA

Llamas en una hacienda cerca de Puerto Montt, Chile

2 Corrige.

To review, see **Vocabulario 1** and **Vocabulario 2**.

8. El semáforo está en la boca del metro.
9. Un paseo es una calle angosta.
10. Tienes que aparcar el carro en la parada de autobús.
11. El ganado cosecha en el campo.
12. Los caballos están en el granero.
13. Los campesinos cultivan trigo en la huerta.

3 Identifica.

To review, see **Vocabulario 2**.

14. contrario de «sembrar»
15. los que cultivan o trabajan la tierra
16–17. dos cosas que comen unos animales

Andrew Payti

Answers

1
1. parking (parqueo)
2. el cruce
3. una escalera mecánica (una escalera)
4. rascacielos
5. El tiovivo (La noria, La montaña rusa)
6. La noria (La montaña rusa, El tiovivo)
7. zoológico

2
8. El semáforo está en la esquina.
9. Un paseo es una calle ancha.
10. Tienes que aparcar el carro en la calle (el parking, un parqueo).
11. El ganado pace en el campo.
12. Los caballos están en el corral.
13. Los campesinos cultivan legumbres y frutas en la huerta.

3
14. cosechar
15. los campesinos (los peones)
16. la hierba (el heno)
17. el heno (la hierba)

4
18. Visitaremos Lima.
19. Él irá a la Plaza de Armas.
20. Ellos comerán en el Café Haití.
21. ¿Tú nos reservarás un cuarto en el hotel?
22. No viviré en Lima.
23. Ellos no rentarán un departamento.

5
24. saldré
25. pondrán
26. podrás
27. dirá
28. haremos
29. tendré

Go Online!
connectED.mcgraw-hill.com

Prepárate para el examen

Gramática

4 Escribe en el futuro.

18. Visitamos Lima.
19. Él va a la Plaza de Armas.
20. Ellos comen en el Café Haití.
21. ¿Tú nos reservas un cuarto en el hotel?
22. No vivo en Lima.
23. Ellos no rentan un departamento.

To review, see **Futuro de los verbos regulares**.

5 Completa con el futuro.

24. Yo ___ mañana. (salir)
25. Ellos ___ todo en orden. (poner)
26. ¿Tú me ___ ayudar? (poder)
27. Él me lo ___. (decir)
28. Nosotros ___ el viaje juntos. (hacer)
29. Yo ___ que recordar los billetes. (tener)

To review, see **Futuro de los verbos irregulares**.

6 Escribe con pronombres.

30. Acabo de comprar el plano de la ciudad.
31. ¡Bueno! Ahora puedes consultar el plano.
32. Estoy mirando el plano ahora.
33. Voy a darte las direcciones.
34. Estoy escribiendo las direcciones.
35. Tenemos que llamar a nuestros amigos.
36. Quiero darles la hora de nuestra llegada.

To review, see **Los pronombres con el infinitivo y el gerundio**.

Cultura

7 Describe.

37. el casco antiguo de una ciudad latinoamericana
38. un parque típico en una ciudad latinoamericana
39. un barrio bajo
40. el problema agrario en el campo

To review this cultural information, see the **Lectura cultural**.

CULTURA
Una calle típica del Casco Viejo en la Ciudad de Panamá

Andrew Payti

Differentiation

(continued)

Slower Paced Learners

Encourage students who need extra help to refer to the margin notes and review any section before answering the questions.

Pre-AP Students preparing for the AP exam may benefit from a set time limit when completing this Self-Check. This may also help to identify students with learning difficulties or slower paced students who need extra help.

Cultural Snapshot

The **Casco Viejo** of Panama City is presently undergoing major restoration work.

Go Online!

You may wish to remind students to go online for additional test preparation.

Answers

6

30. Acabo de comprarlo. (Lo acabo de comprar.)
31. ¡Bueno! Ahora puedes consultarlo. (¡Bueno! Ahora lo puedes consultar.)
32. Estoy mirándolo ahora. (Lo estoy mirando ahora.)
33. Voy a dártelas. (Te las voy a dar.)
34. Estoy escribiéndolas. (Las estoy escribiendo.)
35. Tenemos que llamarlos. (Los tenemos que llamar.)
36. Quiero dársela. (Se la quiero dar.)

7 *Answers will vary but may include:*

37. El casco antiguo de muchas ciudades latinoamericanas tiene una plaza que muchas veces se llama «la Plaza de Armas». En la plaza hay una catedral y edificios gubernamentales que datan de la época colonial. De la plaza salen calles pintorescas.
38. Un parque típico en una ciudad latinoamericana tiene mimos, un parque de atracciones y un zoológico. Los habitantes de la ciudad disfrutan del aire libre y espacio abierto del parque.
39. Un barrio bajo se encuentra en las afueras de muchas ciudades latinoamericanas. Es el barrio donde viven los pobres en chozas o casuchas sin luz, gas ni agua corriente.
40. Los campesinos pobres no tienen suficiente dinero para labrar la tierra de una manera productiva. Así toman la decisión de ir a la ciudad y añaden al problema de la sobrepoblación.

Preparate para el examen

Tips for Success

Encourage students to say as much as possible when they do these open-ended activities. Tell them not to be afraid to make mistakes, since the goal of the activities is real-life communication. Encourage students to self-correct and to use words and phrases they know to get their meaning across. If someone in the group makes an error that impedes comprehension, encourage the others to ask questions to clarify or, if necessary, to politely correct the speaker. Let students choose the activities they would like to do.

Tell students to feel free to elaborate on the basic theme and to be creative. They may use props, pictures, or posters if they wish.

Pre-AP These oral activities will give students the opportunity to develop and improve their speaking skills so that they may succeed on the speaking portion of the AP exam.

Cultural Snapshot

(bottom) There are many small islands in Lake Titicaca. Not all are inhabited.

Note: You may want to use the rubric below to help students prepare their speaking activities.

Practice for ORAL PROFICIENCY

Prepárate para el examen

CULTURA

El bus local de León a Managua, Nicaragua

1 La ciudad

Describe a city that you know

Describe una ciudad que has visitado y que te gusta. Explica por qué volverás a esta ciudad.

2 Una ciudad hispana

Describe a Latin American city

Describe una típica ciudad latinoamericana. Luego mira las fotos que salen en el libro o en el Internet y escoge la ciudad que a ti te gusta más. Explica por qué te gusta.

3 Transporte público

Talk about modes of transportation

Describe los medios de transporte que existen en muchas ciudades.

4 El campo

Describe what you like about the country

Describe algunos aspectos del campo que a ti te gustan.

5 ¿El campo o la ciudad?

Compare and contrast the city and the country

Trabajen en grupos. Van a preparar una encuesta *(survey)* contestando las siguientes preguntas:

¿Prefieres vivir en la ciudad o en el campo? ¿Por qué?
¿Cuáles son las ventajas y desventajas de cada lugar?

Después de terminar las entrevistas para la encuesta, presentarán los resultados a la clase.

6 En el futuro

Talk about what you will do in the future

Habla de todo lo que harás en el futuro. Luego habla con un(a) compañero(a) y comparen sus deseos o planes.

CULTURA

La campesina está cosechando heno a mano en la isla Taquile en el lago Titicaca en Perú.

(t)Andrew Payti, (b)Richard Brommer

Scoring Rubric for Speaking

	4	3	2	1
vocabulary	extensive use of vocabulary, including idiomatic expressions	adequate use of vocabulary and idiomatic expressions	limited vocabulary marked with some anglicisms	limited vocabulary marked by frequent anglicisms that force interpretation by the listener
grammar	few or no grammatical errors	minor grammatical errors	some serious grammatical errors	serious grammatical errors
pronunciation	good intonation and largely accurate pronunciation with slight accent	acceptable intonation and pronunciation with distinctive accent	errors in intonation and pronunciation with heavy accent	errors in intonation and pronunciation that interfere with listener's comprehension
content	thorough response with interesting and pertinent detail	thorough response with sufficient detail	some detail, but not sufficient	general, insufficient response

Go Online!
connectED.mcgraw-hill.com

Tarea

Think about all you have learned so far about the countryside and the city in parts of Latin America. Using vocabulary and information contained in the textbook, write a short essay comparing and contrasting life in the countryside with life in the city. Conclude your essay with a paragraph in which you predict what the city and the countryside will be like in fifty years. In what ways do you think they will change and why?

Writing Strategy

Comparing and contrasting When you write an essay that compares and contrasts, you write about similarities and differences between two things. To start organizing the main ideas of your essay, ask yourself a few questions. How does life in the countryside differ from life in the city? What similarities are there? What aspects of city and country life do I want to focus on and do I have enough information to compare and contrast them?

1 Prewrite

Create a Venn diagram like the one below to help you illustrate the similarities and differences between the city and the countryside. List the similarities in the area where the two circles intersect. List the differences in the main body of each circle.

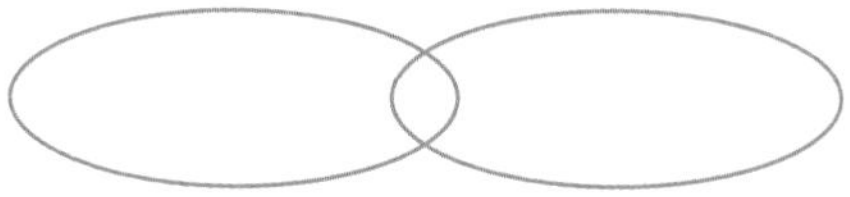

Try to maintain a balance of the details that you would like to include in your essay. In other words, for each detail that you provide for life in the city, you should also provide a detail about the countryside.

2 Write

- Be sure to include a topic sentence that presents the purpose of your essay to the reader.
- Use the information from your Venn diagram to present the similarities and differences in an organized way.
- Use the future tense in your concluding paragraph to predict what you think the city and the countryside will be like in fifty years.

Evaluate

Your teacher will evaluate you on correct use of vocabulary and grammar, organization, completeness of information, and presence of comparable and contrastable details.

Andrew Payti

Prepárate para el examen

Pre-AP This **tarea** will give students the opportunity to develop and improve their writing skills so that they may succeed on the writing portion of the AP exam.

ASSESS

Students are now ready to take any of the Listening, Speaking, Reading, Writing Tests you choose to administer.

Note: You may want to use the rubric below to help students prepare their writing task.

Scoring Rubric for Writing

	4	3	2	1
vocabulary	precise, varied	functional, fails to communicate complete meaning	limited to basic words, often inaccurate	inadequate
grammar	excellent, very few or no errors	some errors, but do not hinder communication	numerous errors interfere with communication	many errors, little sentence structure
content	thorough response to the topic	generally thorough response to the topic	partial response to the topic	insufficient response to the topic
organization	well organized, ideas presented clearly and logically	loosely organized, but main ideas present	some attempts at organization, but with confused sequencing	lack of organization

Repaso del Capítulo 8

Online Resources

Customizable Lesson Plans

Whiteboard Lesson

Audio Activities

Video (Vocabulario) (Diálogo) (Gramática) (Cultura)

Student Workbook

Enrichment

Quizzes

Listening, Speaking, Reading, Writing Tests

Grammar Review

This page provides a quick "at a glance" summary of the grammar points students have learned in this chapter.

Differentiation

Multiple Intelligences

You may want to call on **verbal-linguistic** and **logical-mathematical** learners for whom grammar often comes easily to explain the main concepts to their classmates in their own words. Having students explain the concepts in different ways may also help slower paced learners or students with learning difficulties.

Repaso del Capítulo 8

Gramática

Futuro de los verbos regulares

Review the forms of regular **-ar, -er,** and **-ir** verbs in the future tense.

bailar	comer	vivir
bailaré	comeré	viviré
bailarás	comerás	vivirás
bailará	comerá	vivirá
bailaremos	comeremos	viviremos
bailaréis	*comeréis*	*viviréis*
bailarán	comerán	vivirán

Futuro de los verbos irregulares

The following verbs have irregular stems in the future.

tener → tendr-
salir → saldr-
venir → vendr-
poner → pondr-
saber → sabr-
poder → podr-
decir → dir-
hacer → har-
querer → querr-

Los pronombres con el infinitivo y el gerundio

Note that object pronouns can be added to an infinitive or present participle, or they can precede the helping verb.

Voy a comer la manzana.
Voy a comerla.
La voy a comer.

Estoy preparando la comida.
Estoy preparándola.
La estoy preparando.

Andrew Payti

CULTURA

Los jóvenes están comprando entradas. Están comprándolas en las taquillas a la entrada del parque de atracciones en el Bosque de Chapultepec en la Ciudad de México.

Juego There are a number of cognates in this list. See how many you and a partner can find. Who can find the most? Compare your list with those of your classmates.

Go Online!

connectED.mcgraw-hill.com

Vocabulario

Talking about the city

la ciudad el centro el casco (el barrio) antiguo la plaza	la avenida, el paseo la calle el semáforo la esquina	el/la peatón(ona) el cruce el rascacielos la oficina el tráfico la acera	el parking, el parqueo ancho(a) angosto(a), estrecho(a) urbano(a) aparcar, estacionar

Talking about public transportation

el medio de transporte la estación de metro	la boca del metro la escalera la escalera mecánica	el autobús, el camión, la guagua la parada de autobús

Talking about an amusement park and a zoo

el parque de atracciones	el tiovivo la noria	la montaña rusa el mimo	el zoológico

Talking about the country

el campo la finca, la granja, la chacra la casa de campo	el/la campesino(a), el peón el establo el corral	el granero el heno la hierba la equitación	la hacienda, el rancho, la estancia montar (andar) a caballo

Talking about farming

la tierra el trigo	la huerta la cosecha	cosechar sembrar	cultivar, labrar

Talking about some farm animals

el cerdo el cordero	la gallina la vaca	el ganado	pacer

Repaso del Capítulo 8

Vocabulary Review

The words and phrases in **Vocabulario 1** and **2** have been taught for productive use in this chapter. They are summarized here as a resource for both student and teacher. This list also serves as a convenient resource for the **Prepárate para el examen** activities.

¡Así se dice!

Why It Works!

This vocabulary reference list has not been translated into English for two reasons. First, it is recommended that students learn the new vocabulary through direct association with images on the **Vocabulario** pages. Second, all vocabulary is reintroduced in the chapter many times and upon completion of the chapter students should be familiar with the meaning of all the words. If there are words that students still do not know, they can refer to the vocabulary presentation in the chapter or the dictionary at the end of the book. If, however, it is your preference to give students the English translations, please refer to Vocabulary V8.1.

Differentiation

Slower Paced Learners

Slower paced learners may benefit from creating their own visual dictionary of nouns and adjectives in this list. They can either draw their own depictions or use images from the Internet, magazines, etc.

Juego The cognates in this list are: **el centro, la plaza, la avenida, la oficina, el tráfico, el parking, el parqueo, urbano(a), aparcar, el medio de transporte, la estación de metro, el autobús, el parque de atracciones, el mimo, el zoológico, el peón, el establo, el corral, el rancho, cultivar.**

Don't forget the chapter project and cultural activities. Students have learned all the information that they will need to complete these engaging enrichment tasks.

Every chapter of **¡Así se dice!** contains this review section of previously learned material. By recycling information from previous chapters, the cumulative review serves to remind students that they need to continue practicing what they have learned after finishing each chapter.

Activity 1 This activity reviews past and future tenses.

Audio Script

1. Yo envié un correo electrónico a Cecilia.
2. Alejandra y Manolo fueron al cine.
3. Corrías en el parque todos los sábados.
4. El profesor te hablará a las once y media.
5. Mis primos vendrán a la fiesta.
6. Asistiremos al concierto mañana.
7. Hacía mucho calor.
8. Llegaremos a las siete.

Activity 2 This activity reviews previous vocabulary.

Activity 3 This activity reviews the imperfect and the preterite.

Go Online!

You may wish to remind students to go online for additional cumulative review.

Repaso cumulativo

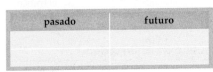

Repasa lo que ya has aprendido

These activities will help you review and remember what you have learned so far in Spanish.

1 **Escucha las frases. Indica en una tabla como la de abajo si la acción ocurrió en el pasado o si va a ocurrir en el futuro.**

pasado	futuro

2 **Parea los antónimos.**

1. derecho
2. sencillo
3. guardar
4. detrás
5. bajar
6. ancho
7. largo
8. joven
9. debajo

a. delante
b. viejo
c. izquierdo
d. encima, sobre
e. de ida y vuelta
f. estrecho
g. borrar
h. subir
i. corto

CULTURA

Pastoras con su oveja en la isla Taquile en el lago Titicaca en Perú

Richard Brommer

3 **Completa con el imperfecto o el pretérito.**

1. Yo ____ ayer pero él ____ todos los días. (ir, ir)
2. Él lo ____ ayer pero nosotros lo ____ todos los días. (ver, ver)
3. Tú le ____ ayer pero yo le ____ todos los días. (hablar, hablar)
4. Ellas lo ____ con frecuencia y tú lo ____ solamente una vez. (hacer, hacer)
5. Yo ____ el verano pasado en el campo y él ____ todos los veranos allí. (pasar, pasar)
6. Mi abuelita ____ todo lo que ____ cada día. (comprar, necesitar)
7. Yo ____ hablar con José y lo ____ ayer pero él no ____. (querer, llamar, contestar)
8. ¿____ tú hacer lo que ____ el profesor? (poder, querer)

Answers

1

1. pasado
2. pasado
3. pasado
4. futuro
5. futuro
6. futuro
7. pasado
8. futuro

2

1. c
2. e
3. g
4. a
5. h
6. f
7. i
8. b
9. d

3

1. fui, iba
2. vio, veíamos
3. hablaste, hablaba
4. hacían, hiciste
5. pasé, pasaba
6. compraba, necesitaba
7. quería, llamé, contestó
8. Podías, quería

4 Cambia al pasado.

1. Hace buen tiempo.
2. Hay sol.
3. La niña es adorable.
4. Tiene solo quince meses.
5. Está muy contenta.
6. Tiene una sonrisa grande.
7. Su papá la adora.
8. Él sabe que yo los conozco.

5 Usa cada palabra en una frase original.

1. el cine
2. el museo
3. un concierto

6 Describe el dibujo.

Repaso cumulativo

¡Así se dice!

Why It Works!

Note that the forms of the imperfect are reviewed to prepare students for the formation of the conditional.

Activity 4 This activity reviews the imperfect.

Activity 5 This activity reviews previous vocabulary and grammar.

Activity 6 This activity reviews previous vocabulary and grammar.

Go Online!

The **¡Así se dice!** Audio Program for Chapter 8 has thirty-two activities, which afford students extensive listening and speaking practice.

Pre-AP To give students further open-ended oral or written practice, or to assess proficiency, go to AP Proficiency Practice AP21.

Answers

4

1. Hacía buen tiempo.
2. Había sol.
3. La niña era adorable.
4. Tenía solo quince meses.
5. Estaba muy contenta.
6. Tenía una sonrisa grande.
7. Su papá la adoraba.
8. Él sabía que yo los conozco (conocía).

5 *Answers will vary.*

6 *Answers will vary.*

Chapter Overview

¿Vas en carro?

Scope and Sequence

Topics
- Driving on the highway
- Driving in the city
- Cars
- Gas stations

Culture
- The Bridge of the Americas in Panama
- Pan American Highway
- Traffic in Spanish-speaking countries

Functions
- How to talk about cars and driving
- How to give directions
- How to discuss the Pan American Highway

Structure
- **Tú** affirmative commands
- The conditional

Andrew Payti

Planning Guide

	required	recommended	optional
Vocabulario 1 En la carretera En la ciudad	✔		
Vocabulario 2 El coche, El carro En la estación de servicio (la gasolinera)	✔		
Gramática Imperativo familiar—formas regulares Imperativo familiar—formas irregulares El condicional	✔		
Conversación Un sitio para aparcar		✔	
Lectura cultural La panamericana		✔	
Lectura Un poco más Tráfico y más tráfico			✔
Prepárate para el examen			✔
Repaso cumulativo			✔

Correlations to ACTFL World-Readiness Standards for Learning Languages

Page numbers in light print refer to the Student Edition.
Page numbers in bold print refer to the Teacher Edition.

COMMUNICATION Communicate effectively in more than one language in order to function in a variety of situations and for multiple purposes		
Interpersonal Communication	Learners interact and negotiate meaning in spoken, signed, or written conversations to share information, reactions, feelings, and opinions.	pp. **262C, 262D, 264–265, 268,** 269, **270, 272,** 273, 275, **275, 276,** 277, **277, 278,** 279, **285,** 290
Interpretive Communication	Learners understand, interpret, and analyze what is heard, read, or viewed on a variety of topics.	pp. **266,** 268, **268, 269, 273,** 274, 275, **275,** 276, 278, 279, **280,** 281, **282,** 282, 283, 284, 285, **285, 286,** 287, 289, **289,** 290, 294, **294, 295**
Presentational Communication	Learners present information, concepts, and ideas to inform, explain, persuade, and narrate on a variety of topics using appropriate media and adapting to various audiences of listeners, readers, or viewers.	pp. **262C, 262D, 267, 269, 275,** 276, **280,** 281, **283, 284, 288,** 290, 291, **292**
CULTURES Interact with cultural competence and understanding		
Relating Cultural Practices to Perspectives	Learners use the language to investigate, explain, and reflect on the relationship between the practices and perspectives of the cultures studied.	pp. **262C, 279**
Relating Cultural Products to Perspectives	Learners use the language to investigate, explain, and reflect on the relationship between the products and perspectives of the cultures studied.	pp. **262D, 263,** 264, **264–265,** 265, 268, 269, **276,** 278, 279, 282, 282–284, 283, **283,** 284, 285, 286, 287, 289, 290
CONNECTIONS Connect with other disciplines and acquire information and diverse perspectives in order to use the language to function in academic and career-related situations		
Making Connections	Learners build, reinforce, and expand their knowledge of other disciplines while using the language to develop critical thinking and to solve problems creatively.	pp. **262C, 262D,** 268, 272, **272,** 273, 285, **285,** 290
Acquiring Information and Diverse Perspectives	Learners access and evaluate information and diverse perspectives that are available through the language and its cultures.	pp. 266, 267, **267,** 268, 269, 270, **270, 272,** 273, **274,** 278, **278,** 279, **279,** 281, **281,** 287, **287,** 290, 293, **293**
COMPARISONS Develop insight into the nature of language and culture in order to interact with cultural competence		
Language Comparisons	Learners use the language to investigate, explain, and reflect on the nature of language through comparisons of the language studied and their own.	pp. 266, **267, 271, 272, 277,** 287, **292,** 293
Cultural Comparisons	Learners use the language to investigate, explain, and reflect on the concept of culture through comparisons of the cultures studied and their own.	pp. **262D,** 263, **263, 264,** 282–284, 286, 287
COMMUNITIES Communicate and interact with cultural competence in order to participate in multilingual communities at home and around the world		
School and Global Communities	Learners use the language both within and beyond the classroom to interact and collaborate in their community and the globalized world.	pp. **262C, 271,** 273, 276, **277, 288, 290, 292**
Lifelong Learning	Learners set goals and reflect on their progress in using languages for enjoyment, enrichment, and advancement.	pp. **262D, 267,** 270, **270,** 278, **278,** 281, **281,** 287, **287**

Chapter Project

Un manual de conducir

Students will work individually and in small groups to create a driver's manual in Spanish that outlines basic driving rules and gives instructions for safe driving.

1. Working together in groups of four to six, students will determine the different parts of a driver's manual and divide the sections among the group members. Students can use their state's driver's manual as a guide, but they should not translate word for word. You may wish to provide them with a list of categories to choose from, such as **señales y letreros, límites de velocidad, cinturones de seguridad y asientos de seguridad para niños, conducir a la defensiva, conducir bajo los efectos del alcohol, la condición del vehículo,** and **vehículos de emergencia y autobuses escolares.**
2. Students should be cautioned not to attempt to include all the possible information for each section—the purpose of the assignment is to give a brief overview or summary of basic driving rules and safe driving techniques. Each student will be responsible for creating one section of the group's manual, and each section should contain at least four illustrations. Students will sketch their section layout and draft at least ten sentences of accompanying text to be checked for mistakes and corrected.
3. Once students have been given an opportunity to revise their drafts, they should compile the final versions of all sections to create a complete driver's manual. Each student should turn in his or her layout sketch and first draft along with the group's final manual.

Expansion: You may wish to have groups present their driver's manuals to the class. This could lead to further investigation into driving rules and regulations in Spanish-speaking countries and additional discussion regarding the benefits of knowing Spanish for a traveler driving in a Spanish-speaking country.

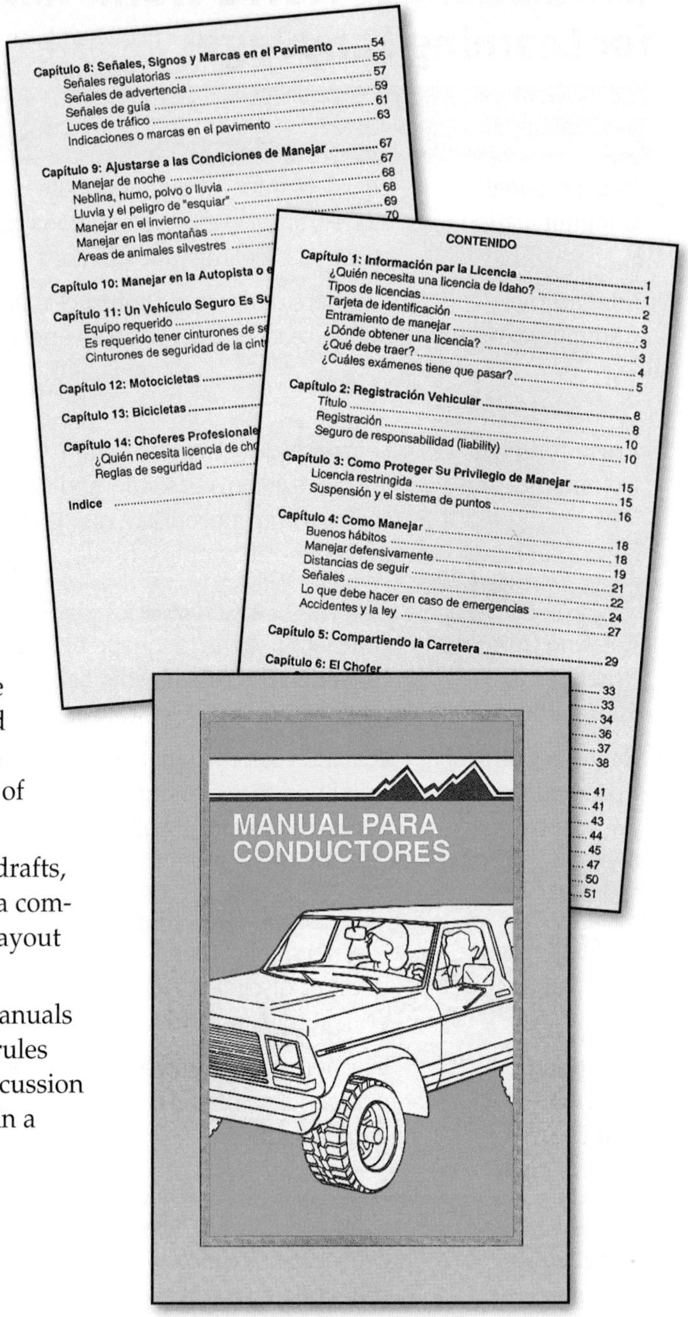

Scoring Rubric for Project

	5	3	1
Evidence of planning	Layout and corrected draft are provided.	Draft and layout provided but draft is not corrected.	Draft and layout are not provided.
Use of illustrations	Manual contains several visual elements.	Manual contains few visual elements.	Manual contains no visual elements.
Presentation	Manual contains all the required elements.	Manual contains some of the required elements.	Manual contains few of the required elements.

Culture

Recipe

LOCRO

Ingredients: (makes 6–8 servings)
4 tablespoons butter
1 teaspoon sweet paprika
1 medium onion, finely chopped
4 pounds potatoes, peeled and sliced
1 cup milk
1 cup light cream
½ pound Muenster cheese, grated
salt
avocado for garnish

Heat the butter in a large saucepan. When melted, stir in the paprika. Add the onion and sauté over moderate heat until the onion is softened. Add 4 cups water and increase heat to a boil. Add the potatoes and reduce heat. Allow to simmer uncovered 20–25 minutes. Stir occasionally. Just before the potatoes are cooked through, add the cream and milk, stirring from time to time until the potatoes start to break up. Stir in the cheese. Salt to taste and serve right away. This dish can be garnished with slices of avocado.

Las señales de tráfico

One of the first steps in learning how to drive is learning to recognize road signs and what they mean. Many road signs found in Spain and Latin America differ from signs in the United States. You may wish to have students research online pictures of road signs in Spanish-speaking countries and see if they can figure out what each sign means. You may also wish to present the signs depicted on this page for additional examples. Students can use the Internet or other resources to look up a list of road signs used in the United States for comparison. Ask students to describe how the signs are different from the signs found in Spanish-speaking countries. Are there general differences they can point out (shapes, colors)? Which signs are the same or similar? As a fun activity, you may wish to have students create signs depicting rules for Spanish class in the style of traffic signs and hang them up around the classroom.

Connection to Fine Art

Have students look online or in an art text to find *Calle 14* by Ecuadoran painter Camilo Egas. Egas painted this scene while he lived in New York City. Ask students if they can name cities in Spanish-speaking countries and in the United States that have metro trains. Encourage students to say whatever they can in Spanish to discuss reasons for and against taking the train versus driving a car and to express opinions regarding urban transportation in this country.

Andrew Payti

50-Minute Lesson Plans

	Objective	Present	Practice	Assess/Homework
Day 1	Talk about driving	Chapter Opener (5 min.) Introducción al tema (10 min.) Core Instruction/Vocabulario 1 (20 min.)	Activities 1–3 (15 min.)	Student Workbook Activities A–D **ConnectEd** Vocabulary Practice
Day 2	Talk about driving	Quick Start (5 min.) Review Vocabulario 1 (10 min.)	Activities 4–6 (15 min.) Total Physical Response (5 min.) Audio Activities A–E (15 min.)	Student Workbook Activities E–G **ConnectEd** Vocabulary Practice
Day 3	Talk about cars	Core Instruction/Vocabulario 2 (20 min.) Video, Vocabulario en vivo (10 min.)	Activities 1–3 (10 min.)	Quiz 1 (10 min.) Student Workbook Activities A–B **ConnectEd** Vocabulary Practice
Day 4	Talk about cars	Quick Start (5 min.) Review Vocabulario 2 (10 min.)	Activities 4–6 (15 min.) Total Physical Response (5 min.) Audio Activities F–I (15 min.)	Student Workbook Activities C–D **ConnectEd** Vocabulary Practice
Day 5	**Tú** affirmative commands	Quick Start (5 min.) Core Instruction/Gramática, Imperativo familiar—formas regulares (10 min.)	Activities 1–6 (15 min.) Audio Activities A–C (10 min.)	Quiz 2 (10 min.) Student Workbook Activities A–E **ConnectEd** Grammar Practice
Day 6	**Tú** affirmative commands	Core Instruction/Gramática, Imperativo familiar—formas irregulares (10 min.)	Activities 7–10 (10 min.) Foldables (5 min.) InfoGap (5 min.) Audio Activities D–F (10 min.)	Quiz 3 (10 min.) Student Workbook Activity A **ConnectEd** Grammar Practice
Day 7	The conditional	Core Instruction/Gramática, El condicional (15 min.) Video, Gramática en vivo (10 min.)	Activities 11–13 (15 min.)	Quiz 4 (10 min.) Student Workbook Activities A–B **ConnectEd** Grammar Practice
Day 8	The conditional	Quick Start (5 min.) Review Gramática, El condicional (10 min.)	Activities 14–16 (15 min.) Audio Activities G–J (20 min.)	Student Workbook Activity C **ConnectEd** Grammar Practice
Day 9	Develop reading and listening comprehension skills	Quick Start (5 min.) Core Instruction/Conversación (15 min.) Video, Diálogo en vivo (10 min.)	¿Comprendes? A–B (10 min.)	Quiz 5 (10 min.) ¿Comprendes? C **ConnectEd** Conversation
Day 10	Discuss the Pan American Highway	Core Instruction/Lectura cultural (20 min.)	¿Comprendes? A–C (15 min.)	Listening Comprehension Test (15 min.) ¿Comprendes? D–E **ConnectEd** Reading Practice
Day 11	Develop reading comprehension skills	Core Instruction/Lectura Un poco más (15 min.)	¿Comprendes? (5 min.) Video, Cultura en vivo (5 min.) Prepárate para el examen (25 min.)	Prepárate para el examen, Practice for written proficiency **ConnectEd** Reading Practice
Day 12	Chapter review	Repaso del Capítulo 9 (15 min.)	Prepárate para el examen, Practice for oral proficiency (20 min.)	Test for Writing Proficiency (15 min.) Review for chapter test
Day 13	Chapter 9 Tests (50 min.) Reading and Writing Test Speaking Test		Test for Oral Proficiency Test for Reading Comprehension	

90-Minute Lesson Plans

	Objective	Present	Practice	Assess/Homework
Block 1	Talk about driving	Chapter Opener (5 min.) Introducción al tema (10 min.) Quick Start (5 min.) Core Instruction/Vocabulario 1 (20 min.)	Activities 1–6 (20 min.) Total Physical Response (10 min.) Audio Activities A–E (20 min.)	Student Workbook Activities A–G **ConnectEd** Vocabulary Practice
Block 2	Talk about cars	Quick Start (5 min.) Core Instruction/Vocabulario 2 (20 min.) Video, Vocabulario en vivo (10 min.)	Activities 1–6 (20 min.) Total Physical Response (5 min.) Audio Activities F–I (20 min.)	Quiz 1 (10 min.) Student Workbook Activities A–D **ConnectEd** Vocabulary Practice
Block 3	**Tú** affirmative commands	Quick Start (5 min.) Core Instruction/Gramática, Imperativo familiar—formas regulares (10 min.) Core Instruction/Gramática, Imperativo familiar—formas irregulares (10 min.)	Activities 1–6 (15 min.) Activities 7–10 (15 min.) Foldables (5 min.) InfoGap (5 min.) Audio Activities A–F (15 min.)	Quiz 2 (10 min.) Student Workbook Activities A–E Student Workbook Activity A **ConnectEd** Grammar Practice
Block 4	The conditional	Quick Start (5 min.) Core Instruction/Gramática, El condicional (20 min.) Video, Gramática en vivo (10 min.)	Activities 11–16 (20 min.) Audio Activities G–J (15 min.)	Quizzes 3–4 (20 min.) Student Workbook Activities A–C **ConnectEd** Grammar Practice
Block 5	Discuss the Pan American Highway	Quick Start (5 min.) Core Instruction/Conversación (15 min.) Video, Diálogo en vivo (10 min.) Core Instruction/Lectura cultural (20 min.)	¿Comprendes? A–C (15 min.) ¿Comprendes? A–C (15 min.)	Quiz 5 (10 min.) ¿Comprendes? D–E Prepárate para el examen, Practice for written proficiency **ConnectEd** Conversation, Reading Practice
Block 6	Develop reading comprehension skills	Core Instruction/Lectura Un poco más (15 min.)	¿Comprendes? (5 min.) Video, Cultura en vivo (10 min.) Prepárate para el examen (20 min.) Prepárate para el examen, Practice for oral proficiency (25 min.)	Listening Comprehension Test (15 min.) Review for chapter test **ConnectEd** Reading Practice
Block 7	Chapter 9 Tests (50 min.) Reading and Writing Test Speaking Test Test for Oral Proficiency Test for Writing Proficiency Test for Reading Comprehension Chapter Project (40 min.)			

Preview

In this chapter, students will learn to identify parts of an automobile and expressions necessary to drive both in town and on the highway. They will also learn the familiar affirmative commands and the conditional.

Pacing

It is important to note that once you reach **¡Bravo!** in the chapter, there is no more new material for students to learn. The rest of the chapter recycles what has already been covered. The suggested pacing listed here leaves two to three days for review, assessment, and enrichment activities such as the chapter project.

Vocabulario 1	1–2 days
Vocabulario 2	1–2 days
Gramática	2–3 days
Conversación	1 day
Lectura cultural	1 day
Lectura Un poco más	1 day

CAPÍTULO 9

¿Vas en carro?

Go Online! connectED.mcgraw-hill.com
Audio · Video · Práctica · Repaso · Diversiones · eScape · ePals

Go Online!

Audio
Listen to spoken Spanish.

Video
Watch and learn about the Spanish-speaking world.

Práctica
Practice your skills.

Repaso
Review what you've learned.

Diversiones
Go beyond the classroom.

eScape
Read about current events in the Spanish-speaking world.

Aquí y Allí

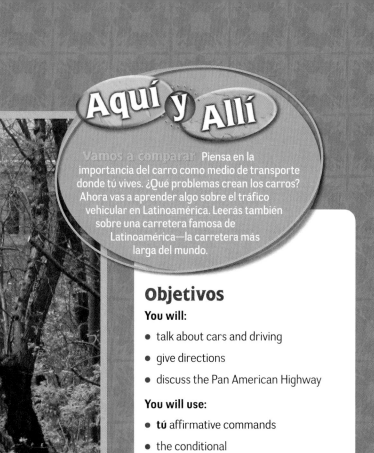

Vamos a comparar Piensa en la importancia del carro como medio de transporte donde tú vives. ¿Qué problemas crean los carros? Ahora vas a aprender algo sobre el tráfico vehicular en Latinoamérica. Leerás también sobre una carretera famosa de Latinoamérica—la carretera más larga del mundo.

Objetivos

You will:

- talk about cars and driving
- give directions
- discuss the Pan American Highway

You will use:

- **tú** affirmative commands
- the conditional

Intersección donde convergen la Castellana, el Paseo de Recoletos, la calle de Alcalá y la Gran Vía en el centro de Madrid en la famosa Plaza de Cibeles

SPOTLIGHT ON CULTURE

Cultural Comparison In addition to discussing what it's like to drive in the United States, students will learn about traffic and driving in Spain and Latin America. They will read about the world's longest highway, endearingly referred to by many Latin Americans as **la panamericana.** Students will take a vicarious trip along this fascinating road that varies a great deal from place to place.

Cultural Snapshot
This is a beautiful, main intersection in Madrid. In the center of the roundabout (**glorieta**) is the famous statue of Cibeles. Straight ahead is **la calle de Alcalá** and shortly after passing the statue one bears right to take **la Gran Vía** which during the Civil War and Franco era was called **la Avenida de José Antonio.** Both to the left and the right the streets are bordered by beautiful parks and fountains.

Interactive Whiteboard
Present or practice with interactive whiteboard activities.

Assessment
Check student progress.

ePals
Connect with Spanish-speaking students around the world.

PRESENT

Introduce the theme of the chapter by having students look at the photographs on these pages. Have them look at the young people and determine if there is anything they see them doing that is the same or different from what they do with their own friends. Once you have completed the vocabulary presentation, have students return to these pages and read the information that accompanies each photograph. Once students are fully acquainted with the vocabulary and grammar of the chapter, you may wish to come back to these pages and ask the questions that go with each photo.

Cultural Snapshot

España The arid plains of La Mancha, south of Madrid, were made famous by Don Quijote and Sancho Panza. **¿Qué recuerdas de la novela *El Quijote*? ¿Qué hizo don Quijote con los molinos de viento?**

Venezuela Recently the traffic problem has been so severe there have been revolts to have the government do something about it.

¿Vas en carro?

Mira las fotos para familiarizarte con el tema del capítulo—el carro y la carretera. Como observarás hay mucho tráfico vehicular en todas partes del mundo hispanohablante. Hay autopistas modernas y pintorescos caminos rurales.

España

Un camino rural en la Mancha

Venezuela

Hay mucho tráfico en Caracas, ¿no? Los embotellamientos como este que ves aquí son frecuentes.

Argentina

Estos dos turistas jóvenes (se) bajan de un taxi en Buenos Aires.

(bl)JUPITERIMAGES/Brand X/Alamy, (cl)Andrew Payti, (tcr)Rebecca Smith, (bcr)Kelli Drummer-Avendano, (b)JUPITERIMAGES/Creatas/Alamy

Go Online!
connectED.mcgraw-hill.com

España

Muchos peatones están cruzando la calle en el Passeig de Grácia en Barcelona. En esta avenida bonita se puede ver muchos ejemplos de la arquitectura modernista de Barcelona.

España

Esta gasolinera en Estepona ofrece un servicio excelente a los dueños de mascotas—un lugar donde pueden lavar su perro mientras llenan de gasolina el tanque de su coche.

Ecuador

Si uno no tiene carro y no quiere tomar el bus, puede tomar un taxi.

Introducción al tema

España **Passeig de Grácia—Pasajo de Gracia**—in Spanish, is one of the most elegant streets in Barcelona where some of the city's most elegant shops and cafés are found. It is also the street to visit to enjoy examples of modernist architecture like those to the right in the photograph.

España ¿Hay una gasolinera cerca de donde tú vives donde puedes lavar a tu perro(a)?

Ecuador ¿Qué significará «Turismo dentro y fuera de la ciudad»?

Online Resources

Customizable Lesson Plans
- Whiteboard Lesson
- Audio Activities
- Student Workbook
- Enrichment
- Quizzes

Quick Start

Use QS 9.1 or write the following on the board.
Write a list in Spanish of things you could see in a large city.

TEACH

Core Instruction

Step 1 Present vocabulary using Vocabulary V9.2–V9.3. Have students repeat called-out words.

Step 2 Ask questions about sentences building from easy to more complex.

Cultural Snapshot

(bottom) This highway is in Zafra, Extremadura, Spain.

Go Online!

You may wish to use the whiteboard presentation for additional vocabulary instruction and practice.

En la carretera

En otras partes

- **La autopista, la autovía, la garita,** and **la cabina** are widely used.
- **El peaje** is the most common word for *toll* but you will also hear **la cuota.**
- The word for *lane*, **el carril,** has many variations.
- Another word for **derecho** is **recto.**

el rótulo

la garita (la cabina) de peaje
la autopista, la autovía

Para conversar
Carolina, paga el peaje. Después de pagar el peaje, sal de la autopista en la próxima salida.
PEAJE

una línea continua
km
68
el carril
la velocidad máxima
el arcén, el acotamiento

En la carretera nacional hay solo un carril en cada sentido.
Está prohibido pasar (adelantar, rebasar) otro carro cuando hay una línea continua.
Hay que quedarse en su carril.

Para conversar
Yo tomaría la autopista porque llegaríamos en menos tiempo.
Yo la tomaría también, pero José no. Él no pagaría el peaje. Es muy tacaño.

(t)Lori Ernfridsson, (tr,b)Andrew Payti

Total Physical Response (TPR)

(Student), **ven acá.**
Siéntate en el carro.
Pon la llave aquí. *(Indicate.)*
Prende el motor.
Vas a ir a la autopista. Estás acercándote a la garita de peaje.
Reduce la velocidad.
Párate.
Abre la ventanilla.
Dale el peaje al cobrador.
Continúa.
Ahora estás en la autopista. Hay un carro delante de ti que va muy despacio.
Ve al carril izquierdo.
Cambia de carril.
Adelanta el carro.
Y ahora, vuelve al carril derecho.

En la ciudad

connectED.mcgraw-hill.com

Al llegar a una bocacalle (donde se cruzan dos calles) debes reducir la velocidad. Debes ir más despacio.

Para conversar

—Mete una moneda en el parquímetro. Te saldrá un tiquete. Pon el tiquete en el parabrisas. ¡Ten cuidado! Si no metes el tiquete, te clavarán con (darán) una multa.

Pidiendo direcciones

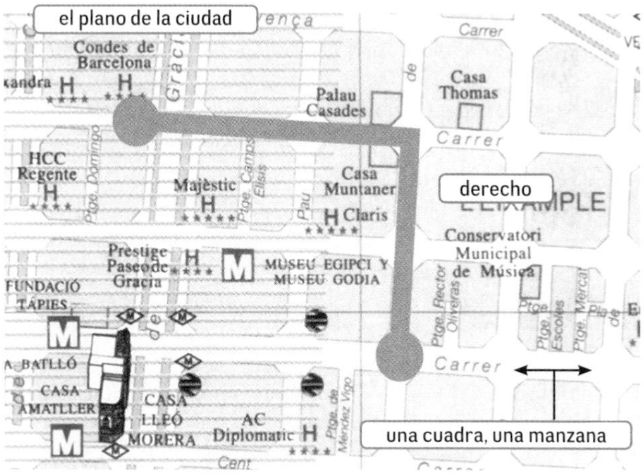

Para llegar al Hotel Condes de Barcelona:
Da la vuelta.
Sigue derecho dos cuadras.
En el segundo cruce (la segunda bocacalle), dobla a la izquierda.
A cien metros, verás el Hotel Condes de Barcelona.

Differentiation

Multiple Intelligences

Have **verbal-linguistic** learners present the **Para conversar** section to the class. Have them read each miniconversation with as much expression as possible.

Teaching Options

Play a game. See how quickly the class can guess the meaning of **tacaño** based on the context in **Para conversar** on the previous page.

About the Spanish Language

Note that the **plano** is in Catalan because it is from Barcelona—**carrer** is **carrera; palau** is **palacio;** and **museú** is **museo.**

Total Physical Response (TPR)

(Student), **ven acá.**
Toma la moneda.
Ve al parquímetro.
Mete la moneda en la ranura.
Saca el tiquete.
Pon el tiquete en el parabrisas de tu carro.

Leveling EACH Activity

Easy Activities 1, 2, 4
Average Activity 3
Average-CHallenging Activity 5
CHallenging Activity 6

PRACTICE

Activity 1

Audio Script

1. Una autopista es una carretera de solo un carril en cada sentido.
2. En muchas autopistas hay que pagar un peaje.
3. La velocidad máxima es más alta en el centro de la ciudad que en las afueras.
4. Hay que quedarse en el carril derecho para adelantar otro carro.
5. No se puede adelantar otro carro si hay una línea continua entre los carriles.
6. Tienes que dar la vuelta cuando has pasado la salida que querías.
7. Hay un parquímetro en el parabrisas de un carro.
8. Hay muchos semáforos en las autopistas.
9. Tienes que pagar el peaje después de pasar la garita de peaje.
10. Cuando el semáforo tiene una luz roja tienes que parar.

Activity 2 This activity can be done orally, calling on individuals to respond or having students respond to each other in pairs.

Activity 3 This activity can be prepared before going over it in class.

Conexiones

Have students discuss environmental problems that exist in your area. What might be done to solve these issues?

Conexiones

La ecología

La contaminación del aire es un problema serio en casi todas las áreas urbanas del mundo. España y Latinoamérica no son ninguna excepción. El aire de muchas de sus ciudades está contaminado. Los gases que salen de los tubos de escape de los automóviles, camiones y buses son una causa principal de la contaminación. ¿Está contaminado el aire donde tú vives? Si contestas que sí, ¿cuál es la causa de la contaminación?

ESCUCHAR

1 Escucha cada frase y decide si la información es correcta o no. Usa una tabla como la de abajo para indicar tus respuestas.

correcta	incorrecta

HABLAR • ESCRIBIR

2 Contesta.

1. ¿Tiene varios carriles en cada sentido una autopista?
2. Por lo general, ¿hay que pagar un peaje para tomar la autopista?
3. ¿Dónde se paga el peaje?
4. Si hay una línea continua en el medio de una carretera de solo dos carriles, ¿es posible adelantar un carro que anda despacio?
5. En las autopistas, ¿hay rótulos que indican la velocidad máxima?

LEER • ESCRIBIR

3 Completa con una palabra apropiada.

1. Hay _____ en muchas esquinas de una ciudad.
2. Donde se cruzan dos calles es _____.
3. Para aparcar el carro, debes tomar el tiquete que sale del _____ y ponerlo en el _____ del carro.
4. Si excedes la velocidad máxima o si no pagas para aparcar el carro, el policía te dará _____.
5. No puedes entrar porque es una calle de _____ único.
6. Si buscas una calle en la ciudad debes consultar _____.
7. José no tomaría la autopista porque tendría que pagar _____.
8. No lo (la) pagaría porque es muy _____. No le gusta gastar dinero.

CULTURA

Aquí ves un rótulo en una esquina de Quito, Ecuador. ¿Cómo se dice «sentido único» en Ecuador?

Andrew Payti

Answers

1

1. incorrecta
2. correcta
3. incorrecta
4. incorrecta
5. correcta
6. correcta
7. incorrecta
8. incorrecta
9. incorrecta
10. correcta

2

1. Sí, una autopista tiene varios carriles en cada sentido.
2. Sí, por lo general hay que pagar un peaje para tomar la autopista.
3. Se paga el peaje en la garita (cabina) de peaje.
4. No, si hay una línea continua en el medio de una carretera de solo dos carriles, no es posible adelantar un carro que anda despacio.
5. Sí, en las autopistas hay rótulos que indican la velocidad máxima.

3

1. semáforos
2. una bocacalle (un cruce)
3. parquímetro, parabrisas
4. una multa
5. sentido
6. el plano de la ciudad
7. el peaje (la cuota)
8. tacaño

Go Online!

connectED.mcgraw-hill.com

LEER

4 Parea las expresiones que tienen el mismo significado.

1. ir en el sentido contrario	**a.** derecho
2. ni a la izquierda ni a la derecha	**b.** rebasar
3. una cuadra	**c.** una manzana
4. un cruce	**d.** la dirección
5. el arcén	**e.** dar la vuelta
6. adelantar	**f.** el acotamiento
7. el sentido	**g.** una bocacalle

LEER • ESCRIBIR

5 Escribe de otra manera.

1. Tienes que pagar *el peaje* en *la cabina*.
2. El rótulo indica que estamos llegando a la entrada de *la autovía*.
3. *El arcén* está a cada lado de la carretera.
4. No se puede *rebasar* cuando hay una línea continua entre los carriles.
5. Debes reducir la velocidad al llegar a *un cruce*.
6. Debes *reducir la velocidad*.
7. Tienes que seguir *unas* cinco *manzanas* más.
8. Te *darán* una multa.

6 ***Comunicación***

Conversa con un(a) compañero(a) sobre las reglas de la calle—lo que uno puede y no puede hacer. Luego imaginen que están en la carretera. Inventen unos escenarios en que tú y tu compañero(a) discuten lo que pasa y lo que ven—rótulos, señales, etc. Usen voz animada y gestos al describir las situaciones. Presenten los escenarios a la clase.

(bl)Daniel Salsgiver; (others)Andrew Payti

Vocabulario 1

Activities 4 and 5 These activities can also be prepared before going over them in class. Call on individuals to read each new sentence in Activity 5.

Differentiation

Advanced Learners

Have advanced learners make up an original sentence using either the words from the first or second column in Activity 4.

Go Online!

You may wish to remind students to go online for additional vocabulary practice. They can also download audio files of all vocabulary.

ASSESS

Students are now ready to take Quiz 1.

Answers

4

1. e
2. a
3. c
4. g
5. f
6. b
7. d

5

1. Tienes que pagar la cuota en la garita (de peaje).
2. El rótulo indica que estamos llegando a la entrada de la autopista.
3. El acotamiento está a cada lado de la carretera.
4. No se puede pasar (adelantar) cuando hay una línea continua entre los carriles.
5. Debes reducir la velocidad al llegar a una bocacalle.
6. Debes ir más despacio.
7. Tienes que seguir unas cinco cuadras más.
8. Te clavarán con una multa.

6 *Answers will vary.*

Online Resources

Customizable Lesson Plans
- Whiteboard Lesson
- Audio Activities
- Video (Vocabulario)
- Student Workbook
- Enrichment
- Quizzes

Quick Start

Use QS 9.2 or write the following on the board.
Write a list in Spanish of all the means of transportation you have learned so far.

TEACH

Core Instruction

The vocabulary in this section is easy and of high interest to most students. You may wish to follow suggestions from previous chapters for presentation.

Tips for Success

- As soon as students are familiar with the new vocabulary, have them read again the captions of the **Introducción al tema.**
- After going over the **Práctica** activities have students return to the vocabulary presentation pages and make up statements and questions about the photos.

Go Online!

Vocabulario en vivo Watch and listen to Nora as she discusses cars and traffic.

El coche, El carro

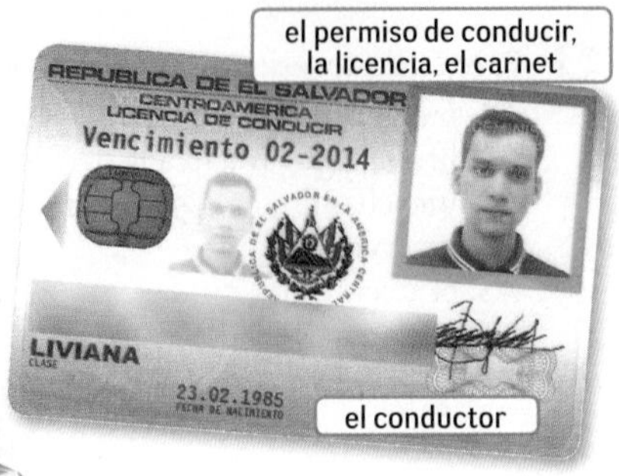

el permiso de conducir, la licencia, el carnet

el conductor

un descapotable, un convertible

un coche deportivo

un sedán a cuatro puertas

un SUV

un camión

Para conversar

Total Physical Response (TPR)

Have students draw a car on the board or use Vocabulary Transparency V9.4.
(Student), **indícame la puerta.**
Indícame el capó.
Indícame la maletera.
Indícame el volante.
Indícame las luces.
Y ahora, abre la maletera.
Saca la gata.
Saca la rueda de repuesto.
Cambia la llanta.
Ahora llena el tanque de gasolina.

Go Online!

connectED.mcgraw-hill.com

En la estación de servicio (la gasolinera)

El tanque está casi vacío.
La señorita llena el tanque.

¡Ay! Tengo un pinchazo. Tengo que cambiar la llanta. Tengo una rueda de repuesto y un(a) gato(a) en la maletera.

Differentiation

Heritage Speakers

If you have any heritage speakers in the class, have them share the terms they use for the vocabulary in this chapter. Most often people from different areas recognize various terms for a word but have one that they use more commonly. At times, however, they do not recognize all the terms.

ABOUT THE SPANISH LANGUAGE

Vocabulary associated with vehicles, driving, and highways can vary quite a bit. We have, however, tried to include the most commonly used terms. Another word for **pinchazo** is **neumático (goma) desinflado(a)** or **ponchado(a).** In addition to **de repuesto (recambio),** you will also see and hear **de refacción.** Note that both **los** and **las** are used with **intermitentes** and **direccionales.** The gender depends upon whether the speaker is thinking about ***las* luces** or ***los* faros.**

Go Online!

You may wish to use the whiteboard presentation for additional vocabulary instruction and practice.

Leveling EACH Activity

Easy Activities 1, 2, 3
Average Activities 4, 5
CHallenging Activity 6, Activity 5 **Expansión**

PRACTICE

Conexiones

You may wish to have all students read this **Conexiones** section. Although some may not be immediately interested in this topic, they may be interested shortly if they wish to purchase a car or get a college loan.

Learning from Realia

Have students read **Calculadora de Pagos Mensuales** and look for the following words in Spanish: *enter, estimate, monthly payment, charges, payments, down payment.*

ABOUT THE SPANISH LANGUAGE

Other terms for *down payment* are: **el pronto, el pie, el pago inicial.**

Activity 3 This activity can be done as a paired activity or an entire-class activity.

Conexiones

Las finanzas
Muchas veces cuando uno quiere comprar un carro no tiene suficiente dinero para pagar el precio total. Así tiene que pedir un préstamo. Pero hay que tener cuidado porque la tasa de interés de un préstamo a corto plazo (por poco tiempo) es más alta que la tasa de interés de un préstamo a largo plazo. Un(a) consumidor(a) inteligente siempre tiene que verificar la tasa de interés que tiene que pagar.

Calculadora de Pagos Mensuales

Ingresa el precio del vehículo que estás considerando y otras variables para calcular una estimación del pago mensual. Este cálculo refleja montos en dólares aproximados al valor entero más cercano. Esta estimación de pagos mensuales no incluye licencia, documentación, cobros por emisiones u otros posibles pagos extra.

Precio 25000
Pago adelantado 5000
Tasa de interés 6.0 %
Calcular

HABLAR • ESCRIBIR

1 Identifica.

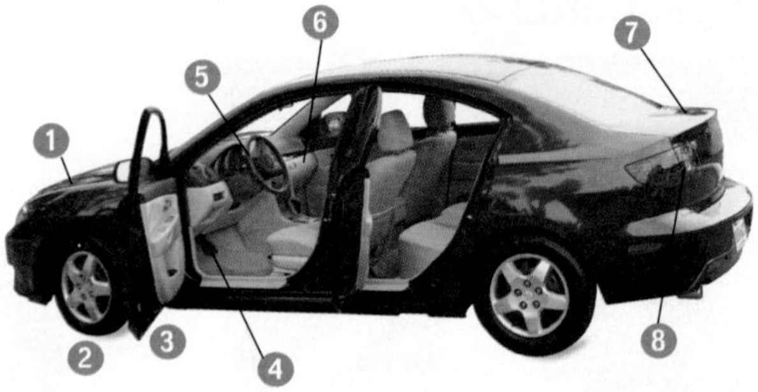

David H. Brennan

LEER

2 Indica si la información es correcta o no.

	correcta	incorrecta
1. Para conducir (manejar) un carro es necesario tener un permiso de conducir.		
2. Un descapotable es más bien un coche deportivo.		
3. Antes de doblar el conductor debe poner las direccionales.		
4. Por si acaso tienes un pinchazo, siempre debes tener una gata y una rueda de repuesto en la guantera.		
5. Para parar el carro tienes que poner los frenos.		
6. El motor del carro está en la maletera.		
7. Tienes que llenar el tanque de gasolina cuando está lleno.		

HABLAR • ESCRIBIR

3 Personaliza. Da respuestas personales.

1. ¿Tienes un carro?
2. ¿Tienes tu permiso de conducir?
3. En tu estado, ¿a qué edad puedes conseguir (tener) un permiso de conducir?
4. En tu estado, ¿son de autoservicio las gasolineras?

Answers

1
1. el capó
2. la llanta (la goma, el neumático)
3. la puerta
4. los frenos
5. el volante
6. la guantera
7. la maletera (el baúl)
8. las luces (las direccionales, las intermitentes)

2
1. correcta
2. correcta
3. correcta
4. incorrecta
5. correcta
6. incorrecta
7. incorrecta

3 *Answers will vary but may include:*
1. Sí, (No, no) tengo un carro.
2. Sí, (No, no) tengo mi permiso de conducir.
3. En mi estado tienes que tener ___ años para conseguir (tener) un permiso de conducir.
4. Sí (No), en mi estado las gasolineras (no) son de autoservicio.

Go Online!

connectED.mcgraw-hill.com

4 **Conexiones**

El lenguaje Como el mundo hispano es tan grande, hay muchas maneras de decir la misma cosa. Puedes familiarizarte con los siguientes términos relacionados con un carro o una carretera pero no tienes que aprenderlos todos. En esta lista debes saber por lo menos la primera palabra.

- el carril, la pista, la vía, la banda, el canal
- el arcén, el acotamiento, la banquina, la berma, el hombrillo
- adelantar, pasar, rebasar
- el tráfico, el tránsito
- estacionar, aparcar, parquear
- el permiso de conducir, la licencia, el carnet
- la llanta, el neumático, la goma, el caucho
- el pinchazo, la llanta desinflada, la llanta pinchada
- de repuesto, de recambio, de refacción
- la gasolina, la nafta, la benzina

Si hay unos alumnos latinos en tu clase, pregúntales cuáles son las palabras que ellos usan. Pregúntales también si usan otra palabra para expresar la misma idea.

LEER

5 Parea para crear una historia.

1. A Alejandra le gustaría tener
2. Lo compraría pero
3. No puede porque
4. Para comprarlo
5. Para ganar bastante dinero

a. necesitaría mucho dinero.
b. no tiene bastante dinero.
c. un carro nuevo.
d. tendría que trabajar mucho.
e. no puede.

EXPANSIÓN

Ahora, sin mirar las frases, cuenta la historia en tus propias palabras. Si no recuerdas algo, tu compañero(a) te puede ayudar.

HABLAR

6 **Juego** Trabaja con un(a) compañero(a). Piensa en una palabra relacionada con los carros. Tu compañero(a) te va a hacer unas preguntas para adivinar la palabra en que estás pensando. Después, cambien de rol. ¡A ver quién hace menos preguntas antes de adivinar la palabra!

CULTURA

Entrada a un servicio para autos en la Ciudad de México

Andrew Payti

Activity 4 This activity can be read aloud quickly to help familiarize students with the many terms. The first entry is usually the most commonly used term, but there are exceptions.

ASSESS

Students are now ready to take Quiz 2.

Go Online!

You may wish to remind students to go online for additional vocabulary practice. They can also download audio files of all vocabulary.

Answers

5

1. c
2. e
3. b
4. a
5. d

6 *Answers will vary.*

Online Resources

Customizable Lesson Plans
Whiteboard Lesson
Audio Activities
Student Workbook
Quizzes

Quick Start

Use QS 9.3 or write the following on the board.

Complete in the present.

1. **Usted ___ bien. (conducir)**
2. **Usted ___ el semáforo. (ver)**
3. **Usted ___ la velocidad. (reducir)**
4. **Usted ___ el peaje. (pagar)**
5. **Usted ___ pronto. (volver)**

TEACH

Core Instruction

Step 1 Have students read the **usted** form of the verb and the affirmative command to establish that they are the same forms. When students read the imperative form, insist that they use a command intonation.

Step 2 You may wish to give some more examples of commands with pronouns. **Háblame. Escríbela. Mírame. Cómpramelo. Termínalo. Explícamelo. Léelo. Véndemelo.**

Learning from Realia

(top) Have students read this sign from **el parque Chapultepec** in Mexico City. Tell them to pay attention to the following **tú** commands: **evita, deposita, respeta.** See if students can determine the meaning and purpose of what they read.

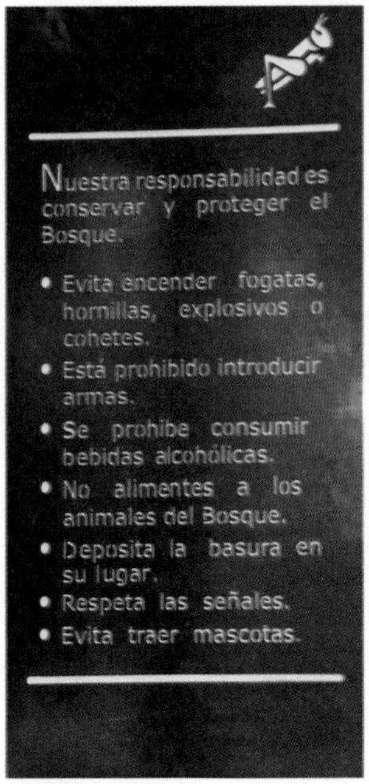

Nuestra responsabilidad es conservar y proteger el Bosque.
• Evita encender fogatas, hornillas, explosivos o cohetes.
• Está prohibido introducir armas.
• Se prohibe consumir bebidas alcohólicas.
• No alimentes a los animales del Bosque.
• Deposita la basura en su lugar.
• Respeta las señales.
• Evita traer mascotas.

Imperativo familiar—formas regulares

1. Just as in English, you use the imperative in Spanish to give a command. You use the **tú** command when speaking to a friend, a family member, someone you know well, or a child. The regular **tú** form of the command is the same as the **usted** form of the present tense of the verb.

PRESENT (UD.)	IMPERATIVE (TÚ)
Usted habla.	**¡Habla!**
Usted conduce.	**¡Conduce!**
Usted escribe.	**¡Escribe!**
Usted comienza.	**¡Comienza!**
Usted vuelve.	**¡Vuelve!**
Usted sigue.	**¡Sigue!**

2. The object pronouns are added to this command form and the verb takes a written accent.

Quédate en el carril izquierdo.
El plano, por favor. Dámelo.

¿Qué es el programa Hoy No Circula?

Si visitas la Ciudad de México o el Área Metropolitana, tienes que cumplir con el Programa Hoy No Circula, el cual prohibe la circulación de vehículos algunos días de la semana. Opera de lunes a viernes de las 05:00 a las 22:00 horas, de acuerdo con el último número de placa de tu vehículo. Revisa qué día no circula tu auto:

Lunes 5 y 6
Martes 7 y 8
Miércoles 3 y 4
Jueves 1 y 2
Viernes 9 y 0, así como permisos y placas personalizadas que no cuenten con números.

Práctica

ESCUCHAR • HABLAR

1 Conversa según el modelo.

MODELO —¿Debo hablar?
—Sí, Pepe. ¡Habla!

1. ¿Debo parar?
2. ¿Debo doblar?
3. ¿Debo dar la vuelta?
4. ¿Debo doblar a la derecha?
5. ¿Debo leer el rótulo?
6. ¿Debo seguir derecho?
7. ¿Debo volver?
8. ¿Debo pedir direcciones?

Muévete
en bici, patineta o caminando
Domingo 13 de mayo
7 Am a 2 Pm
Disfruta el Paseo de la Reforma desde la Puerta de los leones de Chapultepec hasta el Zócalo
Llega en bici o llévala en metro o metrobús
Ciudad México

Andrew Payti

¡Así se dice!

Why It Works!

Students have already heard the **tú** command form in direction lines and in TPR activities. They also know how to give a polite command with **favor de.** Now they will learn to actively use and produce the **tú** command. The commands in Spanish are not easy for English speakers to use with ease. For this reason, in this chapter we introduce only the affirmative **tú** command. Students use the **-a** or **-e** form of the verb with which they are already completely familiar. In the next chapter, students will learn to use the formal commands and the negative familiar, all of which take the opposite vowel.

LEER • ESCRIBIR

2 Completa con el imperativo familiar del verbo indicado.

1. Oye, Magda, _____ a la derecha. (doblar)
2. _____ derecho. (seguir)
3. _____ derecho hasta el tercer cruce. (seguir)
4. _____ a la izquierda. (mirar)
5. A mano izquierda, verás la tienda. _____. (entrar)
6. _____ el ascensor. (tomar)
7. _____ al sexto piso. (subir)
8. _____ allí. (esperar)

HABLAR

3 Mira las ilustraciones. Usa el imperativo para decirle a tu compañero(a) lo que debe hacer.

1. 
2. 
3. 
4. 

HABLAR

4 **Juego** Escoge a un(a) compañero(a) para jugar «Simón dice».

ESCUCHAR • HABLAR • ESCRIBIR

5 Sigue el modelo.

MODELO **la mantequilla →**
Pásame la mantequilla, por favor.

1. el pan
2. el vaso
3. la taza
4. la botella
5. los panecillos

ESCUCHAR • HABLAR • ESCRIBIR

6 Sigue el modelo.

MODELO **la toalla →**
Ramón, dámela, por favor.

1. la cámara
2. el jabón
3. el peine
4. los boletos
5. las entradas

Gramática

Leveling EACH Activity

Easy Activity 1
Average Activities 2, 4, 5
CHallenging Activities 3, 6

PRACTICE

Activities 1, 5, and 6 These activities can be done as paired activities.

Activity 2 Have students read their answers to the class.

Go Online!

You may wish to remind students to go online for additional grammar review and practice.

You may wish to use the whiteboard presentation for additional grammar instruction and practice.

Comunicación

Interpersonal, Presentational
Have students write a short conversation based on each illustration in Activity 3. Then have students present their conversation with a partner to the rest of the class.

ASSESS

Students are now ready to take Quiz 3.

Answers

1
1. Sí, Pepe. ¡Para!
2. Sí, Pepe. ¡Dobla!
3. Sí, Pepe. ¡Da la vuelta!
4. Sí, Pepe. ¡Dobla a la derecha!
5. Sí, Pepe. ¡Lee el rótulo!
6. Sí, Pepe. ¡Sigue derecho!
7. Sí, Pepe. ¡Vuelve!
8. Sí, Pepe. ¡Pide direcciones!

2
1. dobla
2. Sigue
3. Sigue
4. Mira
5. Entra
6. Toma
7. Sube
8. Espera

3
1. Levántate.
2. Siéntate.
3. Lávate la cara y las manos.
4. Acuéstate.

4 *Answers will vary.*

5
1. Pásame el pan, por favor.
2. Pásame el vaso, por favor.
3. Pásame la taza, por favor.
4. Pásame la botella, por favor.
5. Pásame los panecillos, por favor.

6
1. Ramón, dámela, por favor.
2. Ramón, dámelo, por favor.
3. Ramón, dámelo, por favor.
4. Ramón, dámelos, por favor.
5. Ramón, dámelas, por favor.

Online Resources

Customizable Lesson Plans
- Whiteboard Lesson
- Audio Activities
- Student Workbook
- Enrichment
- Quizzes

TEACH

Core Instruction

Step 1 Have students repeat aloud each of these irregular commands at least twice.

Step 2 You may also wish to give students additional practice by having them repeat the following: **Ve, Roberto. Sal ahora. Sal con Elena. Haz el trabajo. Haz la tarea. Ten cuidado. Ten paciencia. Ven acá. Ven conmigo. Pon tu mochila aquí. Pon la mesa.**

PRACTICE

Leveling EACH Activity

Easy Activity 8
Easy-Average Activity 7
CHallenging Activities 9, 10

Activity 7 This activity can be done orally with the entire class or as a paired activity.

Activity 8 Have pairs make up the short conversations.

Cultural Snapshot

The gold-plated bronze angel on top of this statue was cast in Florence, Italy, at a cost of $2.5 million when it was completed in 1906.

FOLDABLES Study Organizer

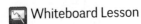

VOCABULARY BOOK See the Foldables section of the Student Handbook at the beginning of this book for help with making this foldable. Use this study organizer to practice your informal commands. On the front of each flap, write the infinitive form of a verb. Then open each flap and write the informal **(tú)** command of the verb. For extra practice, exchange *vocabulary book* foldables with a partner.

InfoGap For more practice with affirmative commands, do Activity 9 in the Student Resource section at the end of this book.

CULTURA
El monumento de la Independencia en el famoso Paseo de la Reforma en la Ciudad de México

Imperativo familiar—formas irregulares

The following verbs are irregular in the **tú** form of the command.

INFINITIVE	IMPERATIVE (TÚ)
decir	**di**
ir	**ve**
ser	**sé**
salir	**sal**
hacer	**haz**
tener	**ten**
venir	**ven**
poner	**pon**

Práctica

ESCUCHAR • HABLAR • ESCRIBIR

7 Contesta con **sí** y el imperativo.

1. ¿Debo venir mañana?
2. ¿Debo salir temprano?
3. ¿Debo hacer el viaje en carro?
4. ¿Debo poner aire en las llantas?
5. ¿Debo decir «adiós» a mi hermano?
6. ¿Debo ir por la carretera vieja?
7. ¿Debo tener cuidado?

ESCUCHAR • HABLAR

8 Tu compañero(a) no sabe lo que debe hacer. Conversa según el modelo.

MODELO **ir →**
—No sé si debo ir.
—Sí, ve.

1. hacer el viaje
2. salir de la ciudad
3. manejar
4. ir por la autopista
5. pedir un día libre
6. volver tarde

Andrew Payti

Answers

7
1. Sí, ven mañana.
2. Sí, sal temprano.
3. Sí, haz el viaje en carro.
4. Sí, pon aire en las llantas.
5. Sí, di «adiós» a tu hermano.
6. Sí, ve por la carretera vieja.
7. Sí, ten cuidado.

8
1. No sé si debo hacer el viaje. / Sí, haz el viaje.
2. No sé si debo salir de la ciudad. / Sí, sal de la ciudad.
3. No sé si debo manejar. / Sí, maneja.
4. No sé si debo ir por la autopista. / Sí, ve por la autopista.
5. No sé si debo pedir un día libre. / Sí, pide un día libre.
6. No sé si debo volver tarde. / Sí, vuelve tarde.

9 *Answers will vary.*

10 *Answers will vary.*

Comunicación

9 Escríbele las direcciones a un(a) amigo(a) diciéndole como llegar a tu casa del aeropuerto. Tu amigo(a) leerá las direcciones y preparará un mapa para verificar que las comprendió.

10 Habla con un(a) compañero(a) de clase. Dale direcciones para ir de la escuela a tu casa. Luego tu compañero(a) te dirá como ir a su casa. Deben hacerse preguntas si no comprenden algo.

El condicional

1. As with the future, the infinitive serves as the stem for the conditional of regular verbs. The endings added to the infinitive to form the conditional are the same endings you use for the imperfect of **-er** and **-ir** verbs.

	llegar	ver	ir
yo	llegaría	vería	iría
tú	llegarías	verías	irías
Ud., él, ella	llegaría	vería	iría
nosotros(as)	llegaríamos	veríamos	iríamos
vosotros(as)	*llegaríais*	*veríais*	*iríais*
Uds., ellos, ellas	llegarían	verían	irían

¿Te gustaría nadar en esta alberca en Tepoztlán, México?

Andrew Payti

Go Online!

connectED.mcgraw-hill.com

Gramática

Online Resources

Customizable Lesson Plans
Whiteboard Lesson
Audio Activities
Video (Gramática)
Student Workbook
Enrichment
Quizzes

Quick Start

Use QS 9.4 or write the following on the board.

Indicate where you find or use the following.

en la mesa **en la cama**

1. **la manta**
2. **la almohada**
3. **las servilletas**
4. **las sábanas**
5. **las cucharas**

Comunicación

Activities 9 and 10 When having students do an open-ended activity with no learning prompts, they are actually communicating as if they were in a real-life situation. In such a situation, it is normal for early learners to make mistakes. For this reason you may decide not to interrupt and correct each error a student makes. You may instead encourage students to self-correct when they are aware of errors. This is up to your discretion.

¡Así se dice!

Why It Works!

Note that the forms of the imperfect were reviewed in the Cumulative Review section of the previous chapter to prepare students for the formation of the conditional.

Tips for Success

The conditional should be relatively easy for all students to learn since they are already familiar with the endings and the stems. In addition, the conditional is used the same way in Spanish as it is in English.

ASSESS

Students are now ready to take Quiz 4.

TEACH

Core Instruction

Step 1 Write the three infinitives on the board. Quickly review the **-ía** endings.

Step 2 Add the appropriate endings to the infinitive and have students repeat.

Tips for Success

Remind students that they already learned these irregular stems in Chapter 8 when they learned the future tense.

Leveling EACH Activity

Easy Activities 11, 12, 13
Average Activity 14
CHallenging Activities 15, 16

PRACTICE

Activity 11

Audio Script

1. Iremos pronto.
2. Ellos lo harían.
3. Saldremos dentro de poco.
4. No te lo devolverían.
5. ¿Cómo lo sabríamos?
6. Venderé el carro.
7. Vendrían con nosotros.
8. Lo terminará.

Activity 12 This activity can be gone over with the entire class or as a paired activity.

Go Online!

Gramática en vivo: *Future and conditional tenses* Enliven learning with the animated world of Professor Cruz! **Gramática en vivo** is a fun and effective tool for additional instruction and/or review.

You may wish to use the whiteboard presentation for additional grammar instruction and practice.

2. Verbs that have an irregular stem in the future have the same irregular stem in the conditional.

INFINITIVE	FUTURE STEM	CONDITIONAL
tener	**tendr-**	**tendría**
poner	**pondr-**	**pondría**
salir	**saldr-**	**saldría**
venir	**vendr-**	**vendría**
poder	**podr-**	**podría**
saber	**sabr-**	**sabría**
hacer	**har-**	**haría**
decir	**dir-**	**diría**
querer	**querr-**	**querría**

3. You use the conditional in Spanish the same as you do in English. The conditional expresses what would take place under certain conditions.

Ellos podrían llegar en menos tiempo, pero no quieren tomar la autopista.
Él adelantaría el otro carro, pero no quiere exceder el límite de velocidad.
No excederíamos el límite porque no queremos tener una multa.

4. You can also use the conditional to soften requests.

¿Me pasaría usted la sal, por favor?
¿Me dirías cómo llegar a la Plaza de Armas?

CULTURA

Una joven está conduciendo su moto en una calle de Madrid. Esta joven es muy sabia porque está llevando casco. No es el caso entre muchos motociclistas en España y Latinoamérica.

Práctica

ESCUCHAR

11 Escucha. Indica el tiempo del verbo.

futuro	condicional

HABLAR • ESCRIBIR

12 Personaliza. Da respuestas personales.

1. ¿Te gustaría ser millonario(a) o no?
2. ¿Vivirías en el campo o en la ciudad?
3. ¿Tendrías una casa de verano?
4. ¿Viajarías mucho?
5. ¿Adónde irías?
6. ¿Con quién harías tus viajes?

Andrew Payti

Answers

11

1. futuro
2. condicional
3. futuro
4. condicional
5. condicional
6. futuro
7. condicional
8. futuro

12 *Answers will vary but may include:*

1. Sí, (No, no) me gustaría ser millonario(a).
2. Viviría en el campo (la ciudad).
3. Sí, (No, no) tendría una casa de verano.
4. Sí, (No, no) viajaría mucho.
5. Iría a ____.
6. Haría mis viajes con ____.

LEER • ESCRIBIR

13 Completa con el condicional.

1. Yo sé que él no lo hará, pero yo lo ______.
2. Yo sé que a ellos les gustará la idea, pero a mí no me ______ nada.
3. Yo sé que ellos no lo dirán, pero tú se lo ______ a todos.
4. Yo sé que ella irá, pero ustedes no ______.
5. Yo sé que tú contestarás, pero ella no ______.
6. Nosotros sabemos que él comerá el pescado pero nosotros no lo ______.

ESCUCHAR • HABLAR

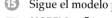

14 Conversa según el modelo.

MODELO **—¿Se quedará tu hermano?**
—Dijo que se quedaría.

1. ¿Estará tu hermano?
2. ¿Hará el viaje?
3. ¿Vendrá mañana?
4. ¿Saldrá con Elena?
5. ¿Tendrá mucho tiempo?

ESCUCHAR • HABLAR • ESCRIBIR

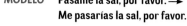

15 Sigue el modelo para ser más cortés.

MODELO **Pásame la sal, por favor. →**
Me pasarías la sal, por favor.

1. Pásame el pan, por favor.
2. Ayúdame, por favor.
3. Llámame mañana, por favor.
4. Repítelo, por favor.

16 ***Comunicación***

¿Hay muchas cosas que te gustaría hacer pero que no puedes porque tienes otras obligaciones? Ten una conversación con un(a) compañero(a). Discutan todo lo que les gustaría hacer pero que no pueden. Expliquen por qué no pueden.

Go Online!

connectED.mcgraw-hill.com

Refrán

Can you guess what the following proverb means?

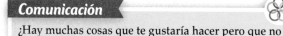

Si ves las estrellas brillar, sal, marinero, a la mar.

¡Bravo!

You have now learned all the new vocabulary and grammar in this chapter. Continue to use and practice all that you know while learning more cultural information. **¡Vamos!**

Answers

13
1. haría
2. gustaría
3. dirías
4. irían
5. contestaría
6. comeríamos

14
1. Dijo que estaría.
2. Dijo que haría el viaje.
3. Dijo que vendría mañana.
4. Dijo que saldría con Elena.
5. Dijo que tendría mucho tiempo.

15
1. Me pasarías el pan, por favor.
2. Me ayudarías, por favor.
3. Me llamarías mañana, por favor.
4. Lo repetirías, por favor.

16 *Answers will vary.*

Gramática

Activity 13 Students should read their answers aloud.

Activities 14 and 15 All students should listen to these short conversations for aural practice.

ABOUT THE SPANISH LANGUAGE

Note that Activity 14 has students use the conditional after the preterite, which is a grammatical rule that is still very much in existence. The reality is, however, that the future is frequently replacing the conditional even in well-respected newspapers. It may be some time before language purists will accept this.

ASSESS

Students are now ready to take Quiz 5.

Refrán

Have students recite the proverb aloud. Then see if they can figure out its meaning, and encourage them to try to give an equivalent expression in English. Although in many cases there may not be an exact match, students may be able to think of expressions related to the same theme.

¡Bravo! The remaining pages of the chapter recycle information in a variety of ways, allowing students to build upon their newly acquired language skills as well as to keep track of their own progress. This format also ensures that students are not surprised by vocabulary or grammar that has not yet been introduced or studied.

Online Resources

Customizable Lesson Plans
Audio Activities
Video (Diálogo)
Student Workbook

Quick Start

Use QS 9.5 or write the following on the board.
Answer.

1. **¿Adónde vas cuando tienes que comprar carne?**
2. **¿Adónde vas cuando tienes que comprar ropa?**
3. **¿Adónde vas cuando tienes que comprar legumbres?**
4. **¿Adónde vas cuando tienes que comprar pescado?**
5. **¿Adónde vas cuando tienes que comprar pan?**
6. **¿Adónde vas cuando tienes que comprar productos congelados?**

TEACH

Core Instruction

Step 1 Have students listen to the audio recording of the conversation.

Step 2 Have the class repeat the conversation after you.

Step 3 Call on two students to read the conversation aloud.

Step 4 After students read a few lines, ask corresponding questions from the **¿Comprendes?** section.

Differentiation

Multiple Intelligences

Have **bodily-kinesthetic** learners present this conversation to the class. Encourage them to improvise and give it a comical twist.

Conversación

Go Online!

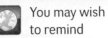

You may wish to remind students to go online for additional conversation practice.

¡Así se dice!

Why It Works!

The **Conversación** recombines only the vocabulary and grammar that students have already learned to understand and manipulate.

¿Comprendes?

connectED.mcgraw-hill.com

A Contesta según la información en la conversación.

1. ¿Por qué no puede Gregorio aparcar el carro donde lo quiere aparcar?
2. ¿Qué hay en la esquina donde tiene que doblar a la derecha?
3. ¿Hasta dónde debe seguir derecho?
4. ¿Qué hay en la plaza?
5. ¿Qué indica su entrada?

B Busca todas las direcciones que Carmen le da a Gregorio para llegar a la plaza.

C **Resumiendo** Cuenta la información en la conversación en tus propias palabras.

CULTURA

Es la caja de un parking en Tenerife en las islas Canarias de España.

Andrew Payti

PRACTICE

¿Comprendes?

A You may wish to allow students to look up the answers or do this as a factual recall activity.

Differentiation

Advanced Learners

C Call on more able students to do this activity.

Go Online!

Diálogo en vivo In this episode, Claudia and Alejandra take a road trip through the countryside. Ask students if the police officer believes the girls when they claim to have a tragedy in the family.

Pre-AP Listening to this conversation will help students develop the skills that they need to be successful on the listening portion of the AP exam.

Answers

A

1. Gregorio no puede aparacar el carro donde lo quiere aparcar porque hay un cruce de peatones.
2. Hay una gasolinera en la esquina donde tiene que doblar a la derecha.
3. Debe seguir derecho hasta el primer semáforo.
4. Hay un parqueo subterráneo en la plaza.
5. Un rótulo indica su entrada.

B

Toma la calle Mayor. A dos cuadras de aquí dobla a la derecha. Sigue derecho hasta el primer semáforo. Al semáforo, dobla a la izquierda.

C *Answers will vary.*

Online Resources

Customizable Lesson Plans

Audio Activities

Student Workbook

TEACH
Core Instruction

Step 1 Have students read the **Estrategia de lectura.**

Step 2 Then have them read the **Antes de leer** to start thinking about different types of highways.

Step 3 Tell students they are going to read about the longest and possibly most interesting highway in the world.

Step 4 You may wish to have all students read the entire **Lectura** or you may break it into parts having each group report to the other.

Step 5 Have students do the Reading Checks as they read.

Step 6 After each paragraph, have a student give a review.

Teaching Options

You may have the entire class read all of the **Lectura** or you may wish to divide it into logical parts, assigning each part to a different group. Each group will report to the other concerning what they learned.

Lectura CULTURAL

ESTRATEGIA DE LECTURA

RESUMIENDO Hacer un resumen de lo que estás leyendo te permite recordar información. Tomando notas o apuntes también te puede ayudar a preparar para una prueba o un examen.

Antes de leer

Piensa en las carreteras donde vives. ¿Son anchas con muchos carriles en cada sentido o son más bien caminos estrechos con solo un carril en cada sentido?

La panamericana

¿Te gustaría rentar un carro y explorar a lo menos una o más regiones de Latinoamérica? Sería una experiencia que no olvidarías nunca. Pues, ¡al volante! ¡Empieza tu aventura! Tendrías que tomar, sin duda, una parte de la carretera panamericana—pero solo una parte pequeña porque la panamericana es la carretera más larga del mundo—cubre 47.516 kilómetros.

La panamericana es una red o sistema de carreteras y caminos que se extiende desde la frontera de Estados Unidos y México hasta la ciudad de Puerto Montt en la Patagonia chilena. En unos lugares la carretera enlaza también la costa occidental con la costa oriental de la América del Sur. La carretera es una ruta importante para el transporte de todo tipo de mercancías y productos agrícolas. Muchos camiones están tan cargados que parecen[1] que van a volcar[2]. Cuando llegan a una pendiente[3] su peso[4] no les permite agarrar velocidad[5] y los sigue una larga cola (fila) de vehículos que querrían adelantarlos.

[1]parecen *they seem*
[2]volcar *flip over*
[3]pendiente *incline*
[4]peso *weight*
[5]agarrar velocidad *to pick up speed*

READING CHECK

¿Entre qué países se extiende la carretera panamericana?

READING CHECK

¿Por qué es muy importante la carretera panamericana?

Durante la lectura

Escribe a lo menos dos frases sobre cada párrafo. Al terminar cada párrafo lee todos tus apuntes.

Andrew Payti

CULTURA

Una garita de peaje en la carretera panamericana en Perú

Cultural Snapshot

This is the toll booth of the Pan American Highway in Ica in southern Peru. This area was heavily damaged during an earthquake in 2007.

¡Así se dice!

Why It Works!

This **Lectura**, like all others in **¡Así se dice!**, contains only Spanish students have already learned with the exception of the eleven footnoted words. The **Lectura** is easy because it is at the students' proficiency level and they are not encumbered with unknown lexicon and grammatical forms.

Go Online!

connectED.mcgraw-hill.com

Unas partes de la panamericana son modernas con dos o más carriles en cada sentido. La mayor parte de la carretera está pavimentada—a veces en buenas condiciones y otras veces no. Por eso tendrías que manejar con mucho cuidado sobre todo de noche. En las áreas remotas no hay luces pero hay baches[6] que frecuentemente no puedes ver. De repente puede terminar el pavimento y la carretera se convierte en un camino de rocas, piedras[7] y lodo[8].

[6]baches *ruts*
[7]piedras *stones*
[8]lodo *mud*

✓ **READING CHECK**

¿Cómo cambia la carretera de una región a otra?

CULTURA

Este rótulo en el centro de Cotacachi indica como ir a Quito vía la panamericana.

CULTURA

Un tramo de la carretera panamericana al llegar a Buenos Aires, Argentina

Andrew Payti

Go Online!

You may wish to remind students to go online for additional reading comprehension and writing skills practice.

Cultural Snapshot

Have students look at the various photographs of **la panamericana** in this selection.

Differentiation

Multiple Intelligences

Have **bodily-kinesthetic** learners dramatize the following.

Ay, tienes una avería.
Abre la puerta.
Bájate del carro.
Verifica las gomas.
Tienes un pinchazo.
Abre la maletera.
Quita la gata.
Ah. Ve a buscar una rama.
Pon la rama detrás del carro.
Cambia la llanta.
Devuelve todo en la maletera.
Y, ¿la rama? ¿La vas a dejar allí?

¡Ten cuidado! Hay otro peligro[9] posible. Una gran parte de la carretera no tiene acotamiento. Cuando un carro, camión o bus tiene una avería[10], el conductor coloca unas ramas de árboles o plantas unos metros detrás del vehículo. Estas ramas les avisan a los otros conductores que hay cerca un vehículo averiado que está bloqueando el camino. Y después de cambiar una llanta o reparar el vehículo, ¿qué hace el conductor? Pues, sale y deja en su lugar las ramas. Y de noche es difícil verlas.

Como te he dicho, en muchas áreas la panamericana es una carretera moderna y conveniente. Pero en unas zonas remotas, tomar la panamericana es una aventura.

[9]peligro *danger*
[10]avería *breakdown*

✓ READING CHECK

¿Qué pone el conductor en la carretera cuando hay una avería?

Después de leer

Lee todos tus apuntes. Añade algunos detalles o descripciones que quieres recordar. Puedes consultar tus apuntes antes de tomar un examen.

Andrew Payti

CULTURA

Es un rótulo en el sur de Perú. Hay que ir derecho (recto) si quieres ir a Pisco. Pero si quieres seguir la panamericana tienes que doblar a la derecha en el siguiente cruce.

Go Online!

connectED.mcgraw-hill.com

¿Comprendes?

A Recordando hechos Contesta.

1. ¿Cuál es la carretera más larga del mundo?
2. ¿Qué es la panamericana?
3. ¿Dónde empieza (nace) y dónde termina (muere) la panamericana?
4. ¿Cómo es la carretera en algunas partes?
5. ¿Cómo es en otras partes?

B Confirmando información Verifica. ¿Sí o no?

1. Toda la carretera panamericana es una carretera moderna con muchos carriles en cada sentido.
2. De noche la carretera está bien iluminada.
3. Una gran parte de la panamericana no tiene acotamiento.
4. No se puede usar la panamericana en ninguna parte para viajar de la costa occidental a la costa oriental de la América del Sur.
5. La panamericana es una ruta usada exclusivamente por razones turísticas.

C Describiendo Describe.

1. unas características de la panamericana
2. los posibles peligros en la panamericana

D Analizando Contesta.

¿Por qué es muy importante la carretera panamericana?

E Describiendo y categorizando Completa la tabla.

la panamericana		
por donde pasa	su condición	unos peligros

PRACTICE

Pre-AP These cultural readings will develop the skills that students need to be successful on the reading and writing sections of the AP exam. Listening to these readings will also help prepare them for the auditory component.

¿Comprendes?

Differentiation

Advanced Learners

Have the advanced learners correct all the wrong information in Activity B.

Tips for Success

When students finish the reading, have them write questions to ask other members of the class.

Conexiones

Using the world map in the Student Handbook pages at the beginning of this book, show students the route the Pan American Highway takes.

Answers

A

1. La carretera más larga del mundo es la carretera panamericana.
2. La panamericana es una red o un sistema de carreteras y caminos que se extiende desde la frontera de Estados Unidos y México hasta la ciudad de Puerto Montt en la Patagonia chilena.
3. Empieza en la frontera de Estados Unidos y México y termina en la ciudad de Puerto Montt en la Patagonia chilena.
4. En algunas partes la carretera es una carretera moderna con dos o más carriles pavimentados en cada sentido.
5. En otras partes no hay luces y hay baches. De repente la carretera pavimentada se convierte en un camino de rocas, piedras y lodo.

B

1. no **2.** no **3.** sí **4.** no **5.** no

C *Answers will vary.*

D *Answers will vary but may include:*
Es muy importante porque es una carretera que se usa para el transporte de todo tipo de mercancías y productos agrícolas.

E *Answers will vary.*

Online Resources

Customizable Lesson Plans

Audio Activities

Video (Cultura)

Student Workbook

TEACH

Core Instruction

You may wish to have students read this selection on their own and do the **¿Comprendes?** activities, or you may prefer to present the **Lectura** in more depth. If you choose to present the **Lectura** in class, you may wish to refer to suggestions given in previous chapters.

Teaching Options

Call on some students to read aloud individually. After a student has read about three sentences, ask questions of other students to check comprehension.

Go Online!

You may wish to remind students to go online for additional reading comprehension and writing skills practice.

Lectura

UN POCO MÁS

Antes de leer

Piensa en el tráfico donde tú vives. ¿Hay mucho o no? ¿Es un problema o no? ¿Tiene la mayoría de las familias carros que usan casi siempre o hay un buen sistema de transporte público?

CULTURA

Hay mucho tráfico en las calles en el centro de Caracas, Venezuela.

Tráfico y más tráfico

Hay muchos que dicen que hay más tráfico en Caracas, Buenos Aires o México que en Chicago, Jacksonville o Dallas, y puede ser verdad. En estas ciudades el tráfico es denso y hay muchos embotellamientos o tapones[1]. Se observará también que muchos carros son bastante viejos. Son viejos pero en su mayoría están en buenas condiciones. En Latinoamérica los carros suelen ser muy caros. Los gobiernos les imponen impuestos[2] altos a los automóviles. Un carro de ocasión, es decir un carro usado, que ya tiene más de diez años puede costar unos quince mil dólares o más. ¿Cuánto cuesta un carro nuevo? Depende, pero puede costar casi el doble de lo que cuesta en Estados Unidos. Por eso, los dueños de los carros los cuidan bien y los reparan frecuentemente para mantenerlos en excelentes condiciones.

No hay duda que los vehículos viejos contaminan el aire. Por eso, la contaminación del aire es un problema serio en muchas ciudades latinoamericanas. Tan grave es el problema que en algunas ciudades el gobierno no permite circular todos los vehículos todos los días. Algunos pueden circular los días pares[3] y otros los días impares[4].

Como los carros cuestan tanto, los autobuses son el medio de transporte más popular en los países latinoamericanos. Viajar en bus, sea en bus municipal o en el de una compañía privada, resulta muy barato. Y es interesante notar que la palabra «autobús» no es universal en el mundo hispanohablante. Otros términos son el autocar, el bus, el camión, la guagua, el ómnibus, la camioneta, el micro y el colectivo.

[1]tapones *traffic jams*
[2]impuestos *taxes*
[3]pares *even*
[4]impares *odd*

CULTURA

El bus es un medio de transporte importante en Latinoamérica. El bus que vemos aquí está en la Ciudad de Panamá.

(l)Kelli Drummer-Avendaño, (r)Andrew Payti

Go Online!

connected.mcgraw-hill.com

¿Comprendes?

Escoge o completa.

1. ¿Por qué hay muchos carros viejos en Latinoamérica?
   - a. Nadie tiene el dinero para comprarse un carro nuevo.
   - b. Los carros son muy caros.
   - c. La gente prefiere carros de ocasión.
   - d. A mucha gente le gusta repararlos.
2. ¿Por qué cuestan tanto dinero los carros en Latinoamérica?
   - a. Los gobiernos les imponen impuestos altos.
   - b. La mayoría de la gente es muy rica.
   - c. Pueden costar hasta el doble de lo que cuestan en Estados Unidos.
   - d. Los dueños los cuidan bien.
3. Los carros viejos causan mucha ____.
4. ¿Qué hacen algunos gobiernos para tratar de eliminar la contaminación del aire?
   - a. Imponen impuestos altos cada vez que el dueño usa su vehículo.
   - b. No permiten circular todos los vehículos todos los días.
   - c. Imponen impuestos altos para los carros viejos.
   - d. No permiten circular los carros en malas condiciones.
5. En inglés se dice *bottleneck* al hablar de un problema de mucho tráfico. Hay dos palabras en español que también tienen que ver con una botella y que expresan la misma idea. Estas dos palabras son ____.

CULTURA

Muchos carros y taxis pasan delante del monumento a la Revolución en la Ciudad de México.

Tips for Success

The multiple-choice comprehension activities that accompany the second reading selection in each chapter have a format that will help students prepare for standardized tests.

Go Online!

Cultura en vivo In this episode, students will learn about modes of transportation in Peru. Ask students why the narrator says that sometimes the oldest forms of transportation are the best.

Answers

1. b
2. a
3. contaminación del aire
4. b
5. embotellamientos, tapones

Prepárate para el examen

Online Resources

Customizable Lesson Plans

Student Workbook

Enrichment

Listening, Speaking, Reading, Writing Tests

Self-check for achievement

This is a pre-test for students to take before you administer the chapter test. Note that each section is cross-referenced so students can easily find the material they feel they need to review. You may wish to use Self-Check Worksheet SC9 to have students complete this assessment in class or at home. You can correct the assessment yourself, or you may prefer to display the answers in class using Self-Check Answers SC9A.

Differentiation

Slower Paced Learners

Have students work in pairs to complete the Self-Check in class. Once they have finished, call on individuals to give the correct answers as you review together.

Multiple Intelligences

To engage **visual-spatial** and **bodily-kinesthetic** learners, number from 1 to 40 on the board and call on a student to go to the board and write the correct answer (this may be done chronologically or you may allow students to choose the one they answer). Then have the student who wrote the first answer decide who will write the second, and so on, making sure to remind them not to pick the same person again.

Prepárate para el examen

Vocabulario

To review, see **Vocabulario 1.**

1 Completa.

1–2. En una autopista hay varios ____ en cada ____.

3. El ____ indica donde está la salida.

4. Quiero ____ el carro delante de mí porque va muy despacio.

5. En muchas autopistas hay que pagar ____.

6. Hay ____ en el cruce que indica que tienes que pararte.

7. El museo está a tres ____ de aquí.

8. Para llegar al hotel tienes que ____ a la derecha en el segundo cruce.

To review, see **Vocabulario 2.**

2 Identifica.

9. donde se ponen las maletas en el carro

10. lo que se usa en el carro de noche

11. lo que se usa para indicar a otros conductores que vas a doblar

12. un vehículo que transporta muchas cosas

13. adonde vas cuando necesitas llenar el tanque de gasolina

14. lo que se usa para levantar el carro cuando hay un pinchazo

15. cada carro tiene cuatro y uno de recambio

16. lo que necesitas para conducir un carro; tiene una foto del/de la conductor(a)

Gramática

To review, see **Imperativo familiar—formas regulares.**

3 Completa con el imperativo familiar.

17. José, ____ la vuelta. (dar)

18. ____ dos cuadras. (seguir)

19. Luego ____ a la izquierda. (doblar)

20. Si te pierdes, ____ el plano de la ciudad. (consultar)

21. ____ una moneda en el parquímetro. (introducir)

22. ____ si necesitas gasolina. (verificar)

23. ____ antes de las seis de la tarde. (volver)

24. ____ con el agente de policía. (hablar)

Answers

1

1. carriles
2. sentido
3. rótulo
4. pasar (rebasar, adelantar)
5. un peaje
6. un semáforo
7. cuadras (manzanas)
8. doblar

2

9. la maletera (el baúl)
10. las luces
11. las direccionales (las intermitentes)
12. un camión
13. la estación de servicio (la gasolinera)
14. un(a) gato(a)
15. las llantas (las ruedas, las gomas, los neumáticos)
16. el permiso de conducir (la licencia, el carnet)

3

17. da
18. Sigue
19. dobla
20. consulta
21. Introduce
22. Verifica
23. Vuelve
24. Habla

Go Online!
connectED.mcgraw-hill.com

4 Completa con el imperativo familiar.

25. _____ cuidado. (tener)
26. _____ las direccionales para indicar que vas a doblar. (poner)
27. _____ de la autopista en la próxima salida. (salir)
28. _____ el viaje en carro. (hacer)
29. _____ la verdad. (decir)

To review, see **Imperativo familiar—formas irregulares.**

5 Completa con el condicional.

30. Yo tomaré la autovía, pero Lupe no la _____ porque no quiere pagar el peaje.
31. Estaremos muy cansados, pero Nando y Eduardo no _____ cansados porque siempre se acuestan temprano.
32. Aunque no debes exceder la velocidad máxima, yo sé que ella la _____.
33. Mis padres no asistirán al concierto, pero yo sí _____.
34. Luis no lo hará, pero tú lo _____.
35. El niño le tendrá miedo al perro, pero nosotros no _____ miedo.
36. Yo iré pero sé que tú no _____.

To review, see **El condicional.**

Cultura

6 Contesta.

37. ¿Qué es la panamericana?
38. ¿Cómo es la panamericana en algunas áreas remotas?
39–40. ¿Por qué tienes que tener cuidado cuando conduces en la carretera panamericana? Puedes dar más de una respuesta.

To review this cultural information, see the **Lectura cultural.**

CULTURA

Un tramo de la carretera panamericana en un área muy árida en el sur de Perú cerca de Ica. ¿Cuántos carriles tiene la carretera aquí en cada sentido o dirección?

Andrew Payti

Differentiation

(continued)

This type of review is particularly appealing to interpersonal learners but will also benefit the class on the whole by promoting an inclusive, student-centered learning environment.

Slower Paced Learners

Encourage students who need extra help to refer to the margin notes and review any section before answering the questions.

Pre-AP Students preparing for the AP exam may benefit from a set time limit when completing this Self-Check. This may also help to identify students with learning difficulties or slower paced students who need extra help.

Go Online!

You may wish to remind students to go online for additional test preparation.

Answers

4
25. Ten
26. Pon
27. Sal
28. Haz
29. Di

5
30. tomaría
31. estarían
32. excedería
33. asistiría
34. harías
35. tendríamos
36. irías

6 *Answers will vary but may include:*
37. Es la carretera más larga del mundo.
38. En algunas áreas remotas, la carretera se convierte en un camino de rocas, piedra y lodo.
39–40. Tienes que tener cuidado porque de noche no hay luces y hay baches. Los conductores de vehículos averiados ponen ramas detrás del vehículo para advertir a los conductores que se acercan a un vehículo averiado. De noche es difícil verlas.

Prepárate para el examen

Tips for Success

Encourage students to say as much as possible when they do these open-ended activities. Tell them not to be afraid to make mistakes, since the goal of the activities is real-life communication. Encourage students to self-correct and to use words and phrases they know to get their meaning across. If someone in the group makes an error that impedes comprehension, encourage the others to ask questions to clarify or, if necessary, to politely correct the speaker. Let students choose the activities they would like to do.

Tell students to feel free to elaborate on the basic theme and to be creative. They may use props, pictures, or posters if they wish.

Pre-AP These oral activities will give students the opportunity to develop and improve their speaking skills so that they may succeed on the speaking portion of the AP exam.

Note: You may want to use the rubric below to help students prepare their speaking activities.

Practice for **ORAL PROFICIENCY**

Prepárate para el examen

CULTURA

Un tapón en una calle del centro de la Ciudad de Panamá

1 Leyendo el mapa

Create and describe a travel route through Spain

Con un(a) compañero(a), mira un mapa de España. Han alquilado un coche y quieren ir de Madrid a otra ciudad que ustedes dos han escogido. Discutan como van a ir y las carreteras que van a tomar. ¡A ver si pueden adivinar cuánto tiempo tardará *(will take)* el viaje!

2 Las carreteras de tu estado

Describe highways in your state

Describe las carreteras de tu estado. ¿Cómo son? ¿Adónde van? ¿Hay mucho tráfico?

3 ¿Qué piensas de la panamericana?

Explain your opinion

Algún día, ¿quieres tener la experiencia de tomar la panamericana? Explica por qué dices que sí o que no.

4 Uno de tus padres te habla.

Tell what needs to be done

Imagínate que eres tu madre o padre. Imita como habla él o ella. Dile a un(a) compañero(a) las tareas que te da con frecuencia. Usa el imperativo familiar.

5 ¿Yo? ¿Millonario(a)?

Talk about what you would do with a million dollars

Tú y un(a) compañero(a) acaban de recibir un millón de dólares. Cada uno de ustedes hará una lista de todo lo que haría con tal cantidad de dinero. Comparen sus listas y decidan quién haría las cosas más interesantes.

6 Una encuesta

Prepare a survey and present the results

Trabaja con un(a) compañero(a). Van a hacer una encuesta. Esta es la situación. Hay un billete de cien dólares en la calle. Cada uno(a) de ustedes preguntará a cinco compañeros lo que harían al encontrar los cien dólares. Luego organicen las respuestas para informar a la clase sobre los resultados.

Andrew Payti

Scoring Rubric for Speaking

	4	3	2	1
vocabulary	extensive use of vocabulary, including idiomatic expressions	adequate use of vocabulary and idiomatic expressions	limited vocabulary marked with some anglicisms	limited vocabulary marked by frequent anglicisms that force interpretation by the listener
grammar	few or no grammatical errors	minor grammatical errors	some serious grammatical errors	serious grammatical errors
pronunciation	good intonation and largely accurate pronunciation with slight accent	acceptable intonation and pronunciation with distinctive accent	errors in intonation and pronunciation with heavy accent	errors in intonation and pronunciation that interfere with listener's comprehension
content	thorough response with interesting and pertinent detail	thorough response with sufficient detail	some detail, but not sufficient	general, insufficient response

Go Online!
connectED.mcgraw-hill.com

Tarea

A Spanish-speaking friend who is always getting lost calls to tell you he or she is coming to visit but doesn't remember how to get to your house. Write a dialogue of a phone conversation between you and your friend in which you are trying to give directions but he or she keeps getting mixed up.

Writing Strategy

Dialogue Composing a dialogue between two or more people is a good way to practice the way language is naturally spoken. Although a conversation between friends involves informal speech, when writing dialogue, it is important to use correct spelling and punctuation, appropriate vocabulary, and proper grammar. This is especially true in the context of giving directions, because you don't want misunderstandings or confusion to cause your friend to get lost!

1 Prewrite

Give your Spanish-speaking friend an identity and decide where he or she will be coming from. Then use the vocabulary from this chapter to make a list of the information you will need to know in order to give accurate directions. Break the information down in steps.

Step 1 → Step 2 → Step 3

2 Write

- Be sure to review the information in Chapter 6 on how to make and receive phone calls.
- Use the affirmative **tú** commands when giving directions.
- Make sure your phone conversation flows smoothly and sounds natural.
- Remember that your friend keeps getting mixed up. Be creative!

Evaluate

Your teacher will evaluate you on correct spelling and punctuation, proper vocabulary and grammar, organization, and completeness of information.

Prepárate para el examen

Pre-AP This **tarea** will give students the opportunity to develop and improve their writing skills so that they may succeed on the writing portion of the AP exam.

ASSESS

Students are now ready to take any of the Listening, Speaking, Reading, Writing Tests you choose to administer.

Note: You may want to use the rubric below to help students prepare their writing task.

Scoring Rubric for Writing

	4	3	2	1
vocabulary	precise, varied	functional, fails to communicate complete meaning	limited to basic words, often inaccurate	inadequate
grammar	excellent, very few or no errors	some errors, but do not hinder communication	numerous errors interfere with communication	many errors, little sentence structure
content	thorough response to the topic	generally thorough response to the topic	partial response to the topic	insufficient response to the topic
organization	well organized, ideas presented clearly and logically	loosely organized, but main ideas present	some attempts at organization, but with confused sequencing	lack of organization

Repaso del Capítulo 9

Online Resources

- Customizable Lesson Plans
- Whiteboard Lesson
- Audio Activities
- Video (Vocabulario) (Diálogo) (Gramática) (Cultura)
- Student Workbook
- Enrichment
- Quizzes
- Listening, Speaking, Reading, Writing Tests

Grammar Review

This page provides a quick "at a glance" summary of the grammar points students have learned in this chapter.

Differentiation

Multiple Intelligences

You may want to call on **verbal-linguistic** and **logical-mathematical** learners for whom grammar often comes easily to explain the main concepts to their classmates in their own words. Having students explain the concepts in different ways may also help slower paced learners or students with learning difficulties.

Repaso del Capítulo 9

Gramática

Imperativo familiar—formas regulares

You use the **tú** command when speaking to a friend, family member, a child, or someone you know well. The **tú** form of the command is the same as the **usted** form of the present tense.

PRESENT (UD.)	IMPERATIVE (TÚ)
Usted habla.	**¡Habla!**
Usted come.	**¡Come!**
Usted sigue.	**¡Sigue!**

Object pronouns are added to the imperative.

Dame la mano. **Devuélvemelo.**

Imperativo familiar—formas irregulares

Review the following irregular forms of the **tú** command.

decir → di	**venir → ven**	**salir → sal**
ir → ve	**tener → ten**	**hacer → haz**
ser → sé	**poner → pon**	

El condicional

To form the conditional of regular verbs, you add the endings of the imperfect tense of **-er** and **-ir** verbs to the infinitive.

pagar	comer	seguir
pagaría	comería	seguiría
pagarías	comerías	seguirías
pagaría	comería	seguiría
pagaríamos	comeríamos	seguiríamos
pagaríais	*comeríais*	*seguiríais*
pagarían	comerían	seguirían

Verbs that have an irregular stem in the future tense have the same irregular stem in the conditional. Review the following forms.

tener → tendría	**poner → pondría**	**hacer → haría**
salir → saldría	**venir → vendría**	**decir → diría**
poder → podría	**saber → sabría**	**querer → querría**

The conditional is used the same in Spanish as in English.

Juego There are a number of cognates in this list. See how many you and a partner can find. Who can find the most? Compare your list with those of your classmates.

Go Online!

connectED.mcgraw-hill.com

Vocabulario

Talking about driving on the highway

la carretera	el sentido	la salida	el arcén, el acotamiento
la autopista, la autovía	el peaje	el rótulo	una línea continua
el carril	la garita (la cabina) de peaje	la velocidad máxima	conducir

Giving directions

el plano de la ciudad	quedarse en el carril	adelantar, rebasar, pasar	estar prohibido
dar la vuelta	doblar	parar(se)	
seguir derecho			

Talking about the city

la cuadra, la manzana	el parquímetro	una calle de sentido único	reducir la velocidad
el cruce, la bocacalle	una moneda	despacio	cruzar
la luz roja	el tiquete	clavar	
	una multa		

Talking about cars

el coche, el carro	el SUV	la estación de servicio, la gasolinera	llenar
el descapotable, el convertible	el camión	el/la gato(a)	cambiar la llanta
el coche deportivo	el/la conductor(a)	el tanque	vacío(a)
el sedán a cuatro puertas	el permiso de conducir, la licencia, el carnet	un pinchazo	

Identifying parts of a car

el capó	las luces	la guantera	la llanta (la rueda) de repuesto (de recambio)
la puerta	los frenos	el volante	
la maletera, el baúl	las direccionales, las intermitentes	la llanta, la goma, el neumático	
el parabrisas			

Other useful words and expressions

tacaño(a)	tener cuidado

LA PRACTICE Refer to the Language Arts Practice section for activities that will strengthen your Language Arts skills as you continue to use your Spanish.

Literary Reader
You may wish to read the adapted version of *Marianela*, found in the Literary Reader at the end of this book.

Repaso del Capítulo 9

Vocabulary Review

The words and phrases in **Vocabulario 1** and **2** have been taught for productive use in this chapter. They are summarized here as a resource for both student and teacher. This list also serves as a convenient resource for the **Prepárate para el examen.**

¡Así se dice!

Why It Works!

This vocabulary reference list has not been translated into English for two reasons. First, it is recommended that students learn the new vocabulary through direct association with images on the **Vocabulario** pages. Second, all vocabulary is reintroduced in the chapter many times and upon completion of the chapter students should be familiar with the meaning of all the words. If there are words that students still do not know, they can refer to the vocabulary presentation in the chapter or the dictionary at the end of the book. If, however, it is your preference to give students the English translations, please refer to Vocabulary V9.1.

Literary Reader

It is recommended that students read from the Literary Reader at this stage so that the selections are not presented all at once at the end or skipped entirely due to time restraints.

Juego The cognates in this list are: **una línea continua, pasar, prohibido, el tiquete, reducir, cruzar, el carro, el convertible, el sedán, el SUV, la licencia, la estación de servicio, el tanque.**

Don't forget the chapter project and cultural activities. Students have learned all the information that they will need to complete these engaging enrichment tasks.

Every chapter of **¡Así se dice!** contains this review section of previously learned material. By recycling information from previous chapters, the cumulative review serves to remind students that they need to continue practicing what they have learned after finishing each chapter.

Activity 1 This activity reviews vocabulary related to air travel.

Audio Script

1. Los pasajeros hacen un viaje en tren.
2. Los pasajeros compran un periódico en el quiosco.
3. Algunos pasajeros pasan por el control de seguridad con su equipaje de mano.
4. Hay flores en el mostrador.
5. Los pasajeros van a Madrid.
6. Algunos pasajeros facturan el equipaje.
7. Hay un avión que despega.

Activity 2 This activity reviews verbs with an irregular **yo** form.

Activity 3 This activity reviews verbs with an irregular **yo** form.

Activity 4 This activity reviews food vocabulary.

Go Online!

You may wish to remind students to go online for additional cumulative review.

Repaso cumulativo

Repasa lo que ya has aprendido

These activities will help you review and remember what you have learned so far in Spanish.

1 **Escucha las frases. Indica si la frase describe el dibujo o no.**

2 **Personaliza. Da respuestas personales.**

1. ¿Cuántos años tienes?
2. ¿Haces mucho trabajo cada día?
3. ¿Te pones un suéter cuando hace frío?
4. ¿A qué hora sales de casa por la mañana?
5. ¿Conoces a muchos compañeros de clase?
6. ¿Conduces un carro?

3 **Da la forma de yo en el presente.**

1. hacer
2. poner
3. traer
4. salir
5. tener
6. decir
7. venir
8. conocer
9. conducir
10. oír

4 **Categoriza las siguientes palabras.**

	legumbres	frutas	carnes	productos lácteos	pescado o mariscos
1. el jamón					
2. el queso					
3. la lechuga					
4. el helado					
5. la naranja					
6. el pollo					
7. los camarones					
8. las judías verdes					
9. la piña					
10. las almejas					

Answers

1

1. no
2. no
3. sí
4. no
5. no
6. sí
7. sí

2 *Answers will vary but may include:*

1. Tengo ___ años.
2. Sí, (No, no) hago mucho trabajo cada día.
3. Sí, (No, no) me pongo un suéter cuando hace frío.
4. Salgo de casa a las ___ por la mañana.
5. Sí, (No, no) conozco a muchos compañeros de clase.
6. Sí, (No, no) conduzco un carro.

3

1. hago
2. pongo
3. traigo
4. salgo
5. tengo
6. digo
7. vengo
8. conozco
9. conduzco
10. oigo

4

1. carnes
2. productos lácteos
3. legumbres
4. productos lácteos
5. frutas
6. carnes
7. pescado o mariscos
8. legumbres
9. frutas
10. pescado o mariscos

Go Online!
connectED.mcgraw-hill.com

5 Personaliza. Da respuestas personales.

1. ¿A qué escuela ibas cuando tenías siete años?
2. ¿Quiénes eran algunos de tus maestros en la escuela primaria?
3. ¿Te gustaba ir a un parque de atracciones cuando eras niño(a)?
4. ¿Había un parque de atracciones cerca de donde vivías?
5. ¿Qué atracciones te gustaban más?
6. ¿Ibas de vez en cuando a un zoológico?
7. ¿Qué animales veías?
8. ¿Podías darles de comer a los animales o estaba prohibido?

CULTURA
Mucha gente está haciendo cola para comprar tickets para montar a la montaña rusa en el Parque de Chapultepec en la Ciudad de México.

6 Completa con el adjetivo posesivo.

1. La hermana de mi padre es ____ tía y ____ hermano es ____ tío.
2. Los hijos de mis tíos son ____ primos y ____ hijos son los sobrinos de mis padres.
3. Mi hermano y yo queremos mucho a los abuelos. Los adoramos. ____ abuelos son los padres de ____ padres.
4. Dime algo de ____ familia. ¿Tienes hermanos? ¿Cuántos años tienen ____ hermanos?

Repaso cumulativo

Activity 5 This activity reviews the imperfect.

Activity 6 This activity reviews possessive adjectives.

Go Online!

The **¡Así se dice!** Audio Program for Chapter 9 has twenty-seven activities, which afford students extensive listening and speaking practice.

Pre-AP To give students further open-ended oral or written practice, or to assess proficiency, go to AP Proficiency Practice AP6 and AP22.

Answers

5 *Answers will vary but may include:*

1. Iba a la escuela ____ cuando tenía siete años.
2. Algunos de mis maestros en la escuela primaria eran ____.
3. Sí, (No, no) me gustaba ir a un parque de atracciones cuando era niño(a).
4. Sí, (No, no) había un parque de atracciones cerca de donde yo vivía.
5. Me gustaban más ____.
6. Sí, (No, no) iba de vez en cuando a un zoológico.
7. Veía ____.
8. Sí, (No, no) podía darles de comer a los animales. (Estaba prohibido.)

6

1. mi, su, mi
2. mis, sus
3. Nuestros, nuestros
4. tu, tus

Chapter Overview
Cocina hispana
Scope and Sequence

Topics
- The kitchen
- Cooking
- Types of food
- Using a recipe

Culture
- Various foods from Spanish-speaking countries
- The metric system
- Good nutrition

Functions
- How to talk about foods and food preparation
- How to talk about a Hispanic recipe

Structure
- The subjunctive
- Formal commands
- Negative informal commands

Planning Guide

	required	recommended	optional
Vocabulario La cocina	✔		
Gramática El subjuntivo; El imperativo formal; El imperativo familiar—formas negativas	✔		
Conversación ¿Yo? ¿En la cocina?		✔	
Lectura cultural Una receta hispana		✔	
Lectura Un poco más Una receta para «la ropa vieja»			✔
Prepárate para el examen			✔
Repaso cumulativo			✔

Getty Images/Blend Images

Correlations to ACTFL World-Readiness Standards for Learning Languages

Page numbers in light print refer to the Student Edition.
Page numbers in bold print refer to the Teacher Edition.

COMMUNICATION Communicate effectively in more than one language in order to function in a variety of situations and for multiple purposes		
Interpersonal Communication	Learners interact and negotiate meaning in spoken, signed, or written conversations to share information, reactions, feelings, and opinions.	pp. **298–299, 300,** 303, **303,** 306, 309, 318
Interpretive Communication	Learners understand, interpret, and analyze what is heard, read, or viewed on a variety of topics.	pp. **300,** 302, **302,** 305, **305,** 306, 307, 308, 309, **310,** 311, 312, 313, **314,** 315, 317, **317,** 322, **323**
Presentational Communication	Learners present information, concepts, and ideas to inform, explain, persuade, and narrate on a variety of topics using appropriate media and adapting to various audiences of listeners, readers, or viewers.	pp. **296C, 296D, 300, 301,** 302, **303,** 307, **308, 312, 316,** 318, 319, **319, 320, 321**
CULTURES Interact with cultural competence and understanding		
Relating Cultural Practices to Perspectives	Learners use the language to investigate, explain, and reflect on the relationship between the practices and perspectives of the cultures studied.	pp. **296D, 310, 314**
Relating Cultural Products to Perspectives	Learners use the language to investigate, explain, and reflect on the relationship between the products and perspectives of the cultures studied.	pp. **296C, 296D, 297,** 298–299, **298–299,** 303, **303, 305, 306,** 308, 309, 311, **311,** 312, **312,** 313, 314, **315,** 317, 318, 319, 323
CONNECTIONS Connect with other disciplines and acquire information and diverse perspectives in order to use the language to function in academic and career-related situations		
Making Connections	Learners build, reinforce, and expand their knowledge of other disciplines while using the language to develop critical thinking and to solve problems creatively.	pp. **296C, 296D,** 302, 306, **306**
Acquiring Information and Diverse Perspectives	Learners access and evaluate information and diverse perspectives that are available through the language and its cultures.	pp. 301, **301, 307,** 309, **309,** 311, **311,** 312, 313, 314, 315, **315,** 317
COMPARISONS Develop insight into the nature of language and culture in order to interact with cultural competence		
Language Comparisons	Learners use the language to investigate, explain, and reflect on the nature of language through comparisons of the language studied and their own.	pp. **296C,** 301, 304, **309, 315, 320,** 321
Cultural Comparisons	Learners use the language to investigate, explain, and reflect on the concept of culture through comparisons of the cultures studied and their own.	pp. **296D,** 297, **297, 298,** 315
COMMUNITIES Communicate and interact with cultural competence in order to participate in multilingual communities at home and around the world		
School and Global Communities	Learners use the language both within and beyond the classroom to interact and collaborate in their community and the globalized world.	pp. **296C, 311, 312, 316, 318, 320**
Lifelong Learning	Learners set goals and reflect on their progress in using languages for enjoyment, enrichment, and advancement.	pp. 301, **301,** 311, **311,** 315, **315**

Chapter Project

Un programa de cocina

Students will prepare and present a Hispanic dish as if they were on a cooking show.

1. Pair students up to conduct preliminary research on Hispanic cuisine and to select a recipe to prepare and present—or have them choose from a predetermined list of recipes. Each pair should pick a name for their show, make a list of the ingredients they will need, and schedule a time outside of class to practice their presentation.
2. Each pair will draft a script in Spanish to use as a guideline for the presentation. You may wish to provide the class with a short list of cooking vocabulary and to encourage students to use a dictionary to find any additional words for utensils, measurements, or other cooking terms required to present their dish.
3. Although it is important for students to prepare for their episode in advance, students should not memorize their scripts word for word. You might allow them to use note cards as prompts—but remind them that reading their note cards and failing to maintain eye contact with the audience will result in a lower score.
4. In order to avoid mess and waste, or if you do not have cooking facilities available, you may want students to pantomime the preparation of their dish without using real ingredients. Have students gather props to use while presenting their cooking show to the class: bowls, utensils, measuring cups and spoons, etc. Each presentation should incorporate several visual aids in addition to the kitchen items. Students can use visuals, gestures, or circumlocution to illustrate meaning of any new cooking vocabulary. Encourage students to be creative.
5. Have each pair submit a draft of their script to be checked or peer edited and corrected accordingly. Each pair should turn in their original draft along with the final corrected version, as well as a copy of the recipe they followed, when they present their show to the class. For additional cultural enrichment, you may wish to have students share actual dishes they have prepared in class or at home with the rest of the class.

Technology Expansion: If you are able, take a video of students' presentations and then allow the students to edit their video clips. Using video editing software, they can add Spanish titles, credits, and music to make their video more like an actual television show. Post the video clips to the class Web site to share them with Spanish-speaking members of the community and student key pals.

Scoring Rubric for Project

	5	3	1
Evidence of planning	Corrected draft of script is provided.	Draft of script is provided but is not corrected.	Draft of script is not provided.
Use of visual aids	Cooking show contains several visual aids.	Cooking show contains few visual aids.	Cooking show contains no visual aids.
Presentation	Cooking show contains all the required elements.	Cooking show contains some of the required elements.	Cooking show contains few of the required elements.

Culture

Recipe

DULCE DE LECHE

This delicious sauce is popular throughout Latin America and is used in various desserts as flavoring or filling. You may wish for students to research recipes that call for the use of **dulce de leche** so they can use this recipe to create another dish.

Ingredients:

4 cups whole milk
1⅓ cup sugar
1 vanilla bean
½ teaspoon baking soda

Combine all the ingredients in a large saucepan and bring to a boil over high heat. Stir to dissolve the sugar. Simmer over medium heat, stirring often, until the milk begins to thicken and turns a caramel color (about 45 minutes). Once the mixture has reached the consistency of condensed milk, remove and discard the vanilla bean. Transfer the mixture to a serving bowl or jar and allow to cool.

La dieta

How we cook and what we cook is a reflection of our diet. The kinds of food one family eats may not be the same as those eaten by another family, especially if they live in another region or country. Diet is very much influenced by the surrounding culture and environment and often reflects the types of products found in a certain region of the world. The following is a list of foods that are part of a typical diet of inhabitants of Spain and Latin America.

Meat	• very little red meat • more chicken, lamb, veal, fish, and shellfish • fish and shellfish three to four times a week, perhaps
Vegetables	• beans, chickpeas, lentils • fresh vegetables such as peppers, tomatoes, and onions
Fruit	• as dessert and throughout day
Dairy	• no butter in cooking • no milk as adult beverage (babies and small children only) • much cheese, often at meal's end
Grains	• much unbuttered bread with meals • bread for breakfast, not cereal • rice

After sharing this chart with your students, have them come up with a typical diet for someone living in North America. How do the two diets differ? Which typical diet do students think is healthier, North American or Hispanic? Have students give reasons to support their responses.

Connection to Fine Art

Have students look online or in an art text to find *Preparando tortillas* painted in 1926 by Diego Rivera. The tortilla maker boils corn with lime to make **nixtamal,** grinds that mixture into **masa** dough using a stone **mano** and **metate,** pats the dough into tortillas, and bakes the tortillas on a dish called a **comal.** Encourage students to investigate modern issues affecting these traditional techniques (such as alternative technology design) and to share their report with their social studies class.

50-Minute Lesson Plans

	Objective	Present	Practice	Assess/Homework
Day 1	Talk about foods and food preparation	Chapter Opener (5 min.) Introducción al tema (10 min.) Core Instruction/Vocabulario (20 min.)	Activities 1–4 (15 min.)	Student Workbook Activities A–D **ConnectEd** Vocabulary Practice
Day 2	Talk about foods and food preparation	Quick Start (5 min.) Review Vocabulario (10 min.) Video, Vocabulario en vivo (10 min.)	Activities 5–7 (10 min.) Total Physical Response (5 min.) Audio Activities A–E (10 min.)	Student Workbook Activities E–G **ConnectEd** Vocabulary Practice
Day 3	The subjunctive	Core Instruction/Gramática, El subjuntivo (20 min.)	Activities 1–2 (10 min.) Audio Activities A–B (10 min.)	Quiz 1 (10 min.) Student Workbook Activities A–B **ConnectEd** Grammar Practice
Day 4	The subjunctive	Quick Start (5 min.) Review Gramática, El subjuntivo (15 min.)	Activities 3–5 (20 min.) InfoGap (10 min.)	Student Workbook Activities C–D **ConnectEd** Grammar Practice
Day 5	Formal commands	Quick Start (5 min.) Core Instruction/Gramática, El imperativo formal (10 min.)	Activities 6–10 (10 min.) Foldables (5 min.) Audio Activities C–F (10 min.)	Quiz 2 (10 min.) Student Workbook Activities A–E **ConnectEd** Grammar Practice
Day 6	Negative informal commands	Quick Start (5 min.) Core Instruction/Gramática, El imperativo familiar—formas negativas (15 min.)	Activities 11–13 (10 min.) Audio Activities G–J (10 min.)	Quiz 3 (10 min.) Student Workbook Activities A–C **ConnectEd** Grammar Practice
Day 7	Develop reading and listening comprehension skills	Quick Start (5 min.) Core Instruction/Conversación (15 min.) Video, Diálogo en vivo (10 min.)	¿Comprendes? A–B (10 min.)	Quiz 4 (10 min.) ¿Comprendes? C–D **ConnectEd** Conversation
Day 8	Talk about a Hispanic recipe	Core Instruction/Lectura cultural (20 min.)	¿Comprendes? A–C (15 min.)	Listening Comprehension Test (15 min.) **ConnectEd** Reading Practice
Day 9	Develop reading comprehension skills	Core Instruction/Lectura Un poco más (15 min.) Video, Cultura en vivo (10 min.)	¿Comprendes? (5 min.) Prepárate para el examen (20 min.)	Prepárate para el examen, Practice for written proficiency **ConnectEd** Reading Practice
Day 10	Chapter review	Repaso del Capítulo 10 (15 min.)	Prepárate para el examen, Practice for oral proficiency (20 min.)	Test for Writing Proficiency (15 min.) Review for chapter test
Day 11	Chapter 10 Tests (50 min.) Reading and Writing Test Speaking Test Test for Oral Proficiency Test for Reading Comprehension			

90-Minute Lesson Plans

	Objective	Present	Practice	Assess/Homework
Block 1	Talk about foods and food preparation	Chapter Opener (5 min.) Introducción al tema (10 min.) Quick Start (5 min.) Core Instruction/Vocabulario (20 min.) Video, Vocabulario en vivo (10 min.)	Activities 1–7 (20 min.) Total Physical Response (5 min.) Audio Activities A–E (15 min.)	Student Workbook Activities A–G **ConnectEd** Vocabulary Practice
Block 2	The subjunctive	Quick Start (5 min.) Core Instruction/Gramática, El subjuntivo (20 min.)	Activities 1–5 (25 min.) InfoGap (10 min.) Audio Activities A–B (20 min.)	Quiz 1 (10 min.) Student Workbook Activities A–D **ConnectEd** Grammar Practice
Block 3	Formal commands Negative informal commands	Quick Start (5 min.) Core Instruction/Gramática, El imperativo formal (10 min.) Quick Start (5 min.) Core Instruction/Gramática, El imperativo familiar—formas negativas (10 min.)	Activities 6–10 (15 min.) Activities 11–13 (10 min.) Foldables (5 min.) Audio Activities C–J (20 min.)	Quiz 2 (10 min.) Student Workbook Activities A–E Student Workbook Activities A–C **ConnectEd** Grammar Practice
Block 4	Talk about a Hispanic recipe	Quick Start (5 min.) Core Instruction/Conversación (20 min.) Video, Diálogo en vivo (10 min.) Core Instruction/Lectura cultural (20 min.)	¿Comprendes? A–B (5 min.) ¿Comprendes? A–C (10 min.)	Quizzes 3–4 (20 min.) ¿Comprendes? C–D Prepárate para el examen, Practice for written proficiency **ConnectEd** Conversation , Reading Practice
Block 5	Develop reading comprehension skills	Core Instruction/Lectura Un poco más (15 min.) Video, Cultura en vivo (10 min.)	¿Comprendes? (10 min.) Prepárate para el examen (20 min.) Prepárate para el examen, Practice for oral proficiency (20 min.)	Listening Comprehension Test (15 min.) Review for chapter test **ConnectEd** Reading Practice
Block 6	Chapter 10 Tests (50 min.) Reading and Writing Test Speaking Test Test for Oral Proficiency Test for Writing Proficiency Test for Reading Comprehension Chapter Project (40 min.)			

Preview

In this chapter, students will learn the way in which several popular Latino dishes are prepared. They will also read a recipe for the popular **arroz con pollo.** In order to do this, students will learn the command forms of the verbs. They will also be introduced to the subjunctive.

Pacing

It is important to note that once you reach **¡Bravo!** in the chapter, there is no more new material for students to learn. The rest of the chapter recycles what has already been covered. The suggested pacing listed here leaves two to three days for review, assessment, and enrichment activities such as the chapter project.

Vocabulario	1–2 days
Gramática	2–3 days
Conversación	1 day
Lectura cultural	1 day
Lectura Un poco más	1 day

CAPÍTULO 10

Cocina hispana

Go Online! connectED.mcgraw-hill.com

Audio Video Práctica Repaso Diversiones eScape ePals

Go Online!

Audio
Listen to spoken Spanish.

Video
Watch and learn about the Spanish-speaking world.

Práctica
Practice your skills.

Repaso
Review what you've learned.

Diversiones
Go beyond the classroom.

eScape
Read about current events in the Spanish-speaking world.

Aquí y Allí

Vamos a comparar Ya has aprendido que las sobras son la comida que queda después de comer. Has aprendido también que las sobras de una comida en un restaurante de Latinoamérica o España no se llevan a casa «para el perrito». Ahora vamos a ver si las familias hispanas elaboran unos platos sirviéndose de las sobras en vez de botarlas. Y en tu casa, ¿hay unos platos que llevan sobras?

Objetivos

You will:

- talk about foods and food preparation
- talk about a Hispanic recipe

You will use:

- the subjunctive
- formal commands
- negative informal commands

◀ Esta señora está preparando una salsa de mole en Puebla, México. El mole es una exquisita salsa confeccionada con varios chiles, especias y condimentos. Se sirve típicamente sobre pollo o cerdo asado.

SPOTLIGHT ON CULTURE

Cultural Comparison As students go through this chapter, they will be able to make comparisons between the preparation of foods in Spain, Latin America, and the United States. They will also learn some interesting information about leftovers and doggie bags.

Cultural Snapshot
There is no doubt about the fact that mole is a well known Mexican "salsa" having a variety of recipes. Three Mexican states claim to be the origin of mole—Parabla, Oaxaca, and Tlaxcala. The two most famous are **mole poblano** and **mole oaxaqueño.** Legend has it that the first mole made was by the nuns at the Convento de Santa Rosa in Puebla. The nuns heard the Archbishop was coming to visit and since they were poor they had nothing to prepare. They threw together what they had and one nun declared, "I made a mole,"—mole being an ancient word for *mix.*

Interactive Whiteboard
Present or practice with interactive whiteboard activities.

Assessment
Check student progress.

ePals
Connect with Spanish-speaking students around the world.

PRESENT

Introduce the theme of the chapter by having students look at the photographs on these pages. Have them look at the young people and determine if there is anything they see them doing that is the same or different from what they do with their own friends. Once you have completed the vocabulary presentation, have students return to these pages and read the information that accompanies each photograph. Once students are fully acquainted with the vocabulary and grammar of the chapter, you may wish to come back to these pages and ask the questions that go with each photo.

Cultural Snapshot

Costa Rica There are many types of peppers and chiles. They are used in many cuisines of Latin America. **¿Para qué se usan los chiles?**

Cuba Ask students if their family ever fries some kind of pastry for breakfast. Who does? What is it called? **¿Cuándo se comen churros? ¿Dónde se comen? ¿Qué beben los adultos con los churros?¿Y los niños? ¿Qué toman?**

Guatemala Meat grilled on a barbecue is very popular in many areas of Latin America. **A ti, ¿cómo te gusta la carne? ¿Casi cruda, a término medio o bien hecha?**

Introducción al tema

Cocina hispana

Mira estas fotos para familiarizarte con el tema de este capítulo—la cocina hispana. Al mirar las fotos, ¿qué piensas? Hay una gran variedad de platos. ¿Hay algunos que quieres probar?

Costa Rica

Un cuenco de chiles—un tipo de pimiento o ají. Se usan los chiles para añadir un sabor picante a muchas comidas.

Cuba

Un vendedor o cocinero callejero está haciendo churros en La Habana Vieja. A muchos españoles y a mucha gente de varias partes de Latinoamérica les encanta comer churros frescos para el desayuno. Los adultos los comen con café y los niños con chocolate.

México

Un plato de chiles rellenos acompañado de arroz y aguacate en un restaurante en Tepoztlán

Guatemala

El señor está asando carne en Tikal, Guatemala. ¿Quieres que él te prepare la carne bien hecha o a término medio?

(t)Dave Moyer, (cl)Richard Brommer, (cr)Andrew Payti, (bl)Lori Ernfridsson

Go Online!
connectED.mcgraw-hill.com

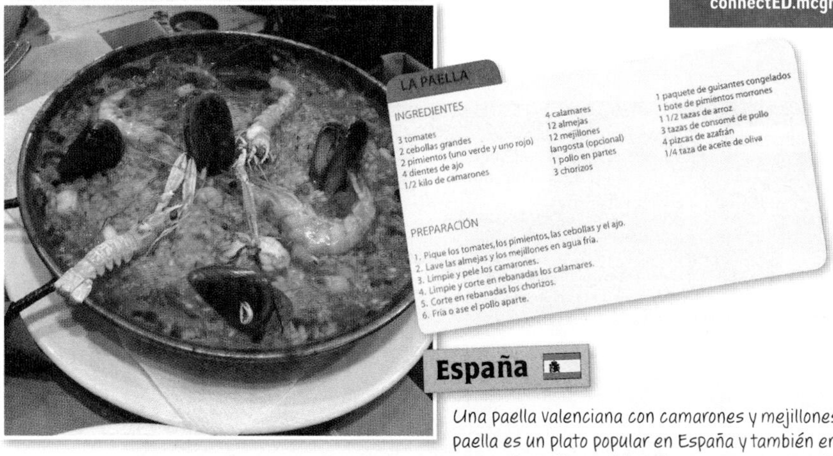

LA PAELLA
INGREDIENTES
3 tomates
2 cebollas grandes
2 pimientos (uno verde y uno rojo)
4 dientes de ajo
1/2 kilo de camarones
4 calamares
12 almejas
12 mejillones
langosta (opcional)
1 pollo en partes
3 chorizos
1 paquete de guisantes congelados
1 bote de pimientos morrones
1 1/2 tazas de arroz
3 tazas de consomé de pollo
4 pizcas de azafrán
1/4 taza de aceite de oliva
PREPARACIÓN
1. Pique los tomates, los pimientos, las cebollas y el ajo.
2. Lave las almejas y los mejillones en agua fría.
3. Limpie y pele los camarones.
4. Limpie y corte en rebanadas los calamares.
5. Corte en rebanadas los chorizos.
6. Fría o ase el pollo aparte.

España

Una paella valenciana con camarones y mejillones. La paella es un plato popular en España y también en muchas partes de Latinoamérica. Hay muchas recetas diferentes para preparar una paella deliciosa.

Perú

Aquí vemos dos teteras sobre un tipo de estufa u horno de barro colocado sobre una superficie de piedras en el pueblo de Uros en una de las islas flotantes cerca de Puno, Perú.

España

El cocinero está asando cochinillos y corderos en un horno viejo de un restaurante muy antiguo y famoso de Madrid.

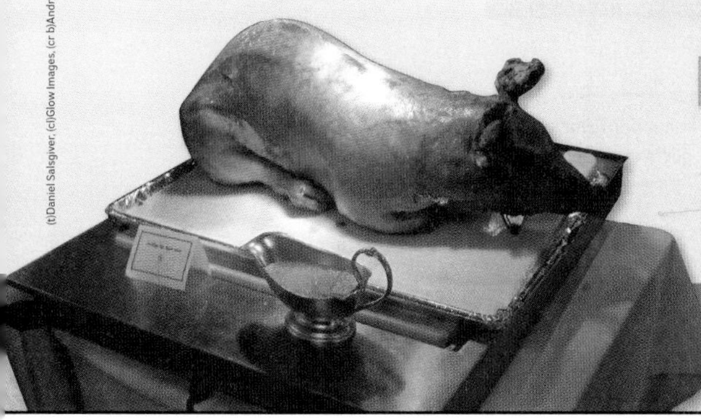

Latinoamérica y España

El cochinillo asado en España o el lechón asado en muchas partes de Latinoamérica es un plato muy apreciado. Se sirve durante una gran variedad de fiestas—fiestas populares y fiestas elegantes—para celebrar eventos familiares.

Introducción al tema

España Students will learn about a paella from the conversation in this chapter. Since paella started out as **una comida casera,** it has many variations. Have students tell what they already know about paella.

Perú You may wish to have students go online to see the many types of **teteras peruanas artesenales** that are made. Some are quite expensive.

Latinoamérica y España As stated here, **el lechón** or **el cochinillo** is a specialty in many countries. It can be cooked outside and served at picnics, or it can be prepared for fancy parties. It is interesting to note the **chancho** *(pig)* is an animal that is very important in poor, rural areas. It is an excellent food source because there is no waste. **¡Se puede comerlo todo!**

Online Resources

- Customizable Lesson Plans
- Whiteboard Lesson
- Audio Activities
- Video (Vocabulario)
- Student Workbook
- Enrichment
- Quizzes

Quick Start

Use QS 10.1 or write the following on the board.

In Spanish, write the names of the rooms of a house. Add to this list any items you would find in each room.

TEACH

Core Instruction

Step 1 Present the vocabulary using Vocabulary V10.2–V10.3.

Step 2 Have students repeat each word two or three times. You may wish to use some of your own props such as photos of kitchens and actual kitchenware.

Step 3 Intersperse the presentation with questions.

Step 4 Have students read the new vocabulary.

Differentiation

Multiple Intelligences

Call on **bodily-kinesthetic** learners to read aloud and dramatize the **Para conversar** sections.

La cocina

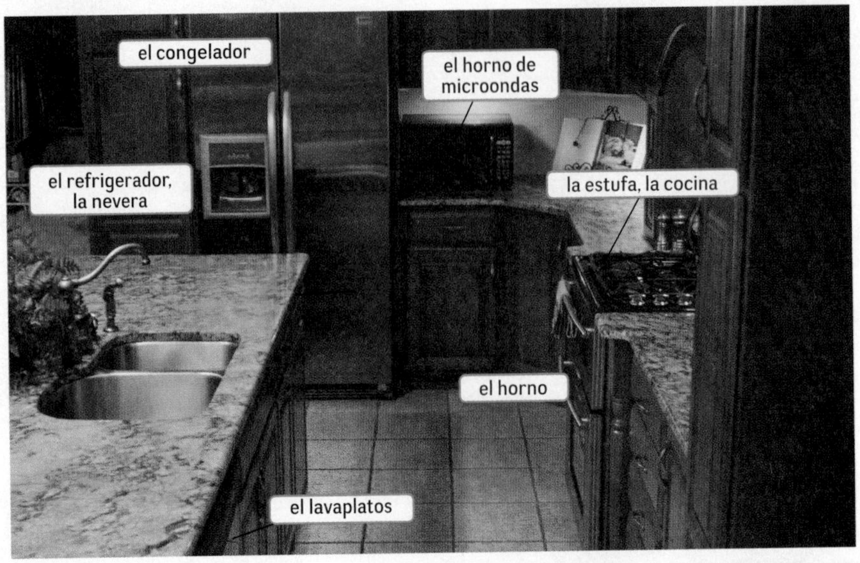

En otras partes

- **El aguacate** is **la palta** in Chile.
- There are many terms that mean *slice*. Some general guidelines are:
  rebanada (de pan, pastel)
  tajada (de carne)
  lonja, loncha (de jamón)
  rodaja (de limón, pepino)
  raja (de melón)
- **Pedazos** and **trozos** (**trocitos**) refer to pieces.

Para conversar

¿Quiere usted que yo ase el pollo o que lo fría?
Fríalo, por favor. Me gusta el pollo frito.

Tips for Success

- As soon as students are familiar with the new vocabulary, have them read again the captions of the **Introducción al tema.**
- After going over the **Práctica** activities, have students return to the vocabulary presentation pages and make up statements and questions about the photos.

Go Online!

connectED.mcgraw-hill.com

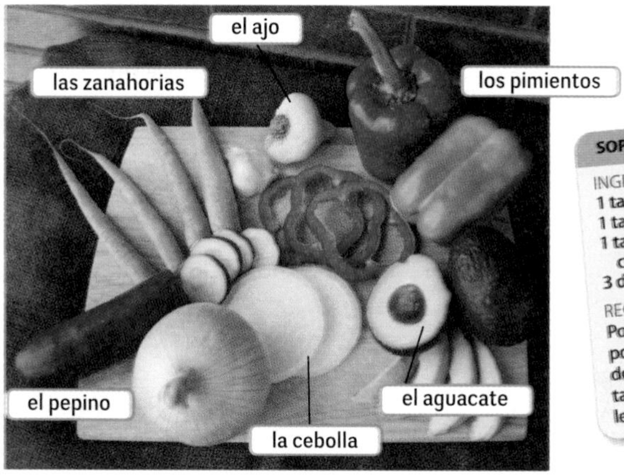

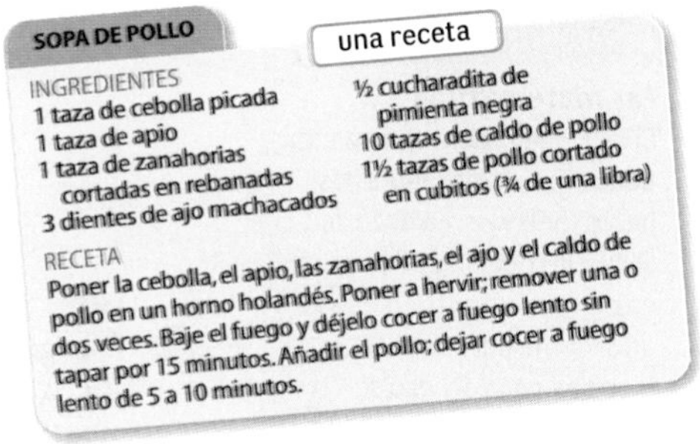
una receta

SOPA DE POLLO

INGREDIENTES
1 taza de cebolla picada
1 taza de apio
1 taza de zanahorias cortadas en rebanadas
3 dientes de ajo machacados
½ cucharadita de pimienta negra
10 tazas de caldo de pollo
1½ tazas de pollo cortado en cubitos (¾ de una libra)

RECETA
Poner la cebolla, el apio, las zanahorias, el ajo y el caldo de pollo en un horno holandés. Poner a hervir; remover una o dos veces. Baje el fuego y déjelo cocer a fuego lento sin tapar por 15 minutos. Añadir el pollo; dejar cocer a fuego lento de 5 a 10 minutos.

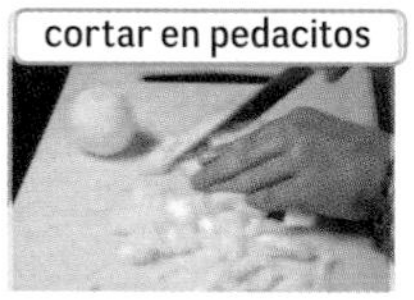
cortar en pedacitos

cortar en rebanadas

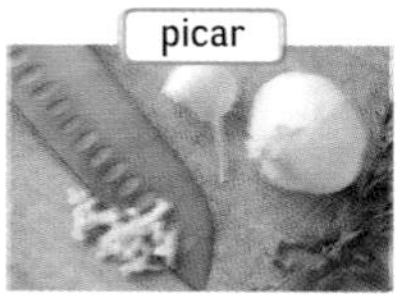
picar

Pique usted el ajo.

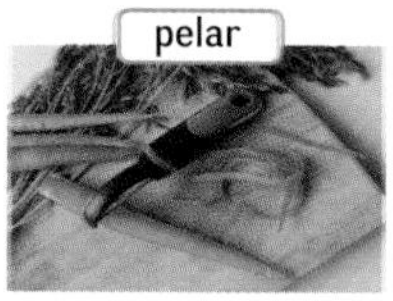
pelar

Pele usted las zanahorias.

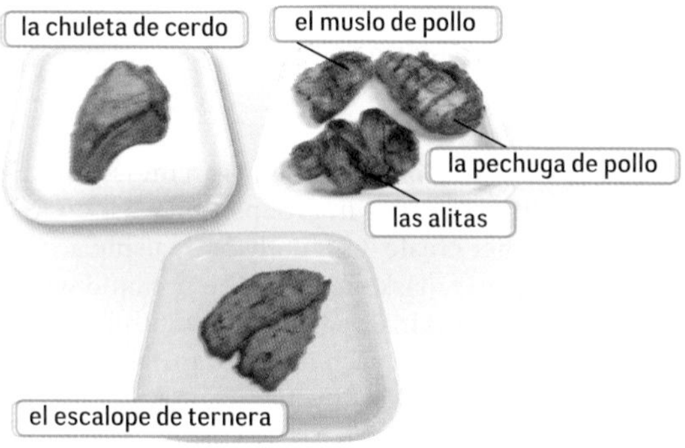

Cuando el cocinero cocina algo tiene que añadir condimentos.
Los condimentos le dan sabor a la comida.

Tips for Success

Some students are motivated by competition. Have students work in small teams. Give them a time limit to write the names of as many foods as they can. The team that writes the largest number in the time limit wins.

Go Online!

Vocabulario en vivo Watch and listen to Nora as she discusses cooking in the Spanish-speaking world.

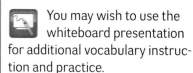

You may wish to use the whiteboard presentation for additional vocabulary instruction and practice.

Total Physical Response (TPR)

(Student 1) **y** *(Student 2)*, **vengan acá.**
Imagínense en una cocina. Están preparando una comida.
Aquí tienen unas papas. Córtenlas en rebanadas.
Pongan las papas en una sartén y fríanlas.
Ahora están haciendo una salsa. No quieren que se queme.
Revuelven la salsa.
¡Cuidado! Quiten la cacerola del fuego.
Bajen el fuego.
Pongan la cacerola en la estufa.
Revuélvanla de nuevo.
Añadan un poco de sal a la salsa.
Gracias, *(Student 1)* **y** *(Student 2)*.

Leveling EACH Activity

Easy Activities 1, 2, 4, 5
Average Activity 3
CHallenging Activities 6, 7

PRACTICE

Activity 1

Audio Script

1. Se puede freír el agua.
2. Se puede freír las papas.
3. Se puede freír o asar el pollo.
4. Se puede pelar la lechuga.
5. Se puede pelar las zanahorias y las papas.
6. Se puede asar la carne a la parrilla.
7. Se debe poner la carne cruda en el refrigerador.
8. Si se cocina algo a fuego lento se quema.
9. La sal y la pimienta son frutas.
10. Los condimentos dan sabor a una comida.

Activity 2 Call on students to read the answers aloud.

Go Online!

You may wish to remind students to go online for additional vocabulary practice. They can also download audio files of all vocabulary.

Conexiones

Las matemáticas
Si lees una receta en español tienes que comprender los pesos métricos. La onza, la libra y la tonelada no existen en el sistema métrico que es un sistema decimal. Las medidas para el peso se basan en el kilogramo o kilo. Hay mil gramos en un kilo. El kilo es igual a 2,2 libras. Una libra inglesa o estadounidense es un poco menos de medio kilo.

ESCUCHAR

1 Escucha cada frase y decide si la información es correcta o no. Usa una tabla como la de abajo para indicar tus respuestas.

correcta	incorrecta

LEER

2 Escoge.

1. Antes de hervirlas, debes (freír, pelar) las zanahorias.
2. Puedes freír las pechugas de pollo en (una cacerola, una sartén).
3. Tienes que (revolver, asar) la salsa.
4. Favor de poner los vasos sucios en (la nevera, el lavaplatos).
5. Si lo quieres cocinar rápido lo debes poner en (el horno, el horno de microondas).
6. ¿Quiere usted que yo ponga la olla (al agua, al fuego)?
7. ¿Quiere usted que yo pele (las zanahorias, los pimientos)?
8. Voy a cortar el pan en (rebanadas, pedacitos).

ESCRIBIR

3 **¡Manos a la obra!** Good nutrition is an important part of staying healthy. Working in groups, make a food pyramid. You can either create it digitally or by using a piece of poster board and markers. Label the pyramid with each of the food groups: grains, vegetables, fruits, oils, milk, and meat/beans. Within each food group, label the foods that you know. Then present your pyramid to the class and suggest a healthy meal based on the foods you listed in each group.

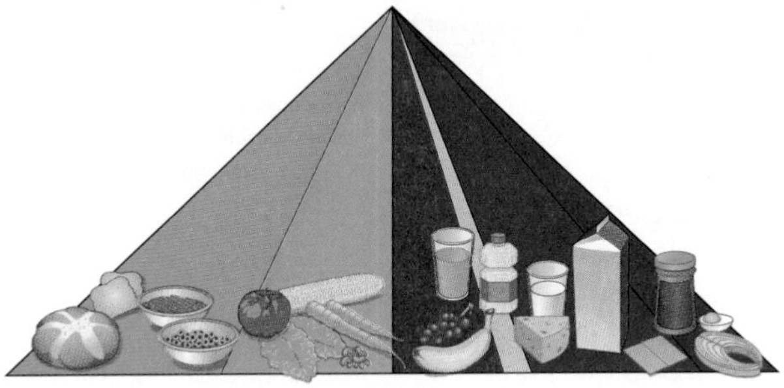

Kerri Galloway

Answers

1
1. incorrecta
2. correcta
3. correcta
4. incorrecta
5. correcta
6. correcta
7. correcta
8. incorrecta
9. incorrecta
10. correcta

2
1. pelar
2. una sartén
3. revolver
4. el lavaplatos
5. el horno de microondas
6. al fuego
7. las zanahorias
8. rebanadas

3 *Answers will vary.*

4
1. Cuando como pollo, prefiero el muslo (la pechuga).
2. Me gusta más una chuleta de cerdo (un escalope de ternera).
3. Prefiero el pescado asado (frito).
4. Prefiero mis legumbres muy cocidas (casi crudas).
5. Me gusta la carne con una salsa (sin salsa).
6. Sí, (No, no) me gusta la comida salada. Sí, (No, no) añado mucha sal.

Go Online!

connectED.mcgraw-hill.com

HABLAR • ESCRIBIR

4 Personaliza. Da respuestas personales.

1. Cuando comes pollo, ¿prefieres el muslo o la pechuga?
2. ¿Te gusta más una chuleta de cerdo o un escalope de ternera?
3. ¿Prefieres el pescado asado o frito?
4. ¿Prefieres tus legumbres muy cocidas o casi crudas?
5. ¿Te gusta la carne con una salsa o sin salsa?
6. ¿Te gusta la comida salada o no? ¿Añades mucha sal?

LEER

5 Usa una tabla como la de abajo para indicar si se puede poner los siguientes ingredientes en una ensalada.

sí	no

1. la lechuga
2. el ajo
3. la carne cruda
4. el aguacate
5. las zanahorias
6. el aceite
7. el café
8. una cebolla

HABLAR • ESCRIBIR

6 Describe.

1. tu comida favorita
2. las legumbres que te gustan
3. los ingredientes de una buena ensalada
4. algunos alimentos que pones en el refrigerador
5. unas cosas que se preparan a la parrilla
6. una cocina moderna

7 *Comunicación*

Trabajen en grupos de cuatro y discutan sus platos o comidas favoritas. ¿Tienen ustedes los mismos gustos o no?

CULTURA

El señor está asando carne en un puesto de comida en una calle de la Ciudad de Panamá.

▲ Unos platos populares ▼

Vocabulario

Activity 4 This activity can also be done as a paired activity.

Activity 5 Students can make up additional foods and decide whether or not they can be used in a salad.

Comunicación

Interpersonal

Activity 7 As students do this activity extemporaneously, it is suggested that you not correct all errors since students are speaking and improvising on their own. This, however, is up to your own discretion or preference.

Tips for Success

Humor is an excellent way to engage students. Have them work in small groups to create recipes for ridiculous sand-wiches, salads, or meals. Have them share their "inventions" with the class.

ASSESS

Students are now ready to take Quiz 1.

Cultural Snapshot

Puestos or **tenderetes de comida** are very popular in almost all areas of Latin America. Some of them have a little stand-up counter and many have some tables and chairs. People use them most frequently for a snack or lunch.

Hamburgers with french fries as well as pizza are popular foods throughout the Spanish-speaking world.

Answers

5
1. sí
2. no (sí)
3. no
4. sí
5. sí
6. no (sí)
7. no
8. no (sí)

6 *Answers will vary but may include:*
1. Mi comida favorita es ____.
2. Las legumbres que me gustan son ____.
3. Los ingredientes de una ensalada buena son ____.
4. Algunos alimentos que pongo en el refrigerador son ____.
5. Unas cosas que se preparan a la parrilla son ____.
6. Una cocina moderna tiene ____.

7 *Answers will vary.*

Online Resources

Customizable Lesson Plans
- Whiteboard Lesson
- Audio Activities
- Video (Gramática)
- Student Workbook
- Enrichment
- Quizzes

Quick Start

Use QS 10.2 or write the following on the board.

Complete with the correct form of **querer** in the present.

1. **Yo ___ salir.**
2. **Pero ellos no ___ ir.**
3. **¿Tú ___ ir o quedarte aquí?**
4. **¿Por qué no ___ (nosotros) hacer la misma cosa?**

TEACH

Core Instruction

Step 1 Have students read aloud the information in Items 1 and 2. It is important for students to understand this basic concept.

Step 2 Go over the formation of the subjunctive. Point out to students that the vowel is the opposite of what they are familiar with in the indicative.

Step 3 Have students read the verb forms in Item 3 aloud.

Step 4 Have students read the verb conjugations in Items 4 and 5 aloud.

Go Online!

You may wish to use the whiteboard presentation for additional grammar instruction and practice.

El subjuntivo

1. All verbs you have learned so far are in the indicative mood. The indicative mood is used to express actions that actually do, did, or will take place. The indicative is used to express real events.

Juan es un alumno bueno.
Estudia mucho.
Recibe buenas notas.

All the preceding information is factual.

Juan is a good student, he studies a lot, and he gets good grades.

2. You are now going to learn the subjunctive mood. The subjunctive is used to express something that is not necessarily factual or real. It expresses things that might happen. Compare the following.

Juan estudia mucho y recibe buenas notas.
Los padres de Juan quieren que él estudie mucho y que reciba buenas notas.

The first sentence tells you that Juan studies a lot and gets good grades. The information is factual, and for this reason you use the indicative. The second sentence states that Juan's parents want him to study a lot and get good grades, but that doesn't mean that Juan will actually do it even though his parents want him to. The second sentence tells what may happen. It does not present facts, and for this reason you must use the subjunctive in the clause that depends upon **quieren.** Such a clause is called a dependent clause.

3. To form the present tense of the subjunctive of regular verbs, you drop the **o** ending of the **yo** form of the present indicative. This is also true for verbs that have an irregular form in the present tense of the indicative. Add **e** endings to all **-ar** verbs and **a** endings to all **-er** and **-ir** verbs.

INFINITIVE	PRESENT (YO)	STEM	PRESENT SUBJUNCTIVE (YO)
mirar	**miro**	**mir-**	**mire**
comer	**como**	**com-**	**coma**
vivir	**vivo**	**viv-**	**viva**
salir	**salgo**	**salg-**	**salga**
hacer	**hago**	**hag-**	**haga**
decir	**digo**	**dig-**	**diga**
conducir	**conduzco**	**conduzc-**	**conduzca**

La profesora ayuda a una alumna porque quiere que salga bien en su examen y que tenga éxito.

¿Te acuerdas?

Remember that you just reviewed the present tense in the previous chapter.

Tips for Success

The basic concept for students to understand is that the subjunctive is used when we do not know if the action will take place. If we know that it is or will be a reality, the indicative is used. If students understand this, it will not be necessary for them to memorize lists of phrases that are followed by the subjunctive. You may give students the following simple outline:

Indicative: indicates or points something out; is factual; is objective; stands alone; is independent.

Subjunctive: is subjective; is not objective; is not factual; cannot stand alone; is dependent on something else; may or may not happen.

Go Online!

connectED.mcgraw-hill.com

4. Study the forms for the present tense of the subjunctive.

	mirar	comer	vivir	salir
yo	mire	coma	viva	salga
tú	mires	comas	vivas	salgas
Ud., él, ella	mire	coma	viva	salga
nosotros(as)	miremos	comamos	vivamos	salgamos
vosotros(as)	*miréis*	*comáis*	*viváis*	*salgáis*
Uds., ellos, ellas	miren	coman	vivan	salgan

5. The following are the only verbs that do not follow the regular pattern for the formation of the present subjunctive.

	dar	estar	ir	saber	ser
yo	dé	esté	vaya	sepa	sea
tú	des	estés	vayas	sepas	seas
Ud., él, ella	dé	esté	vaya	sepa	sea
nosotros(as)	demos	estemos	vayamos	sepamos	seamos
vosotros(as)	*deis*	*estéis*	*vayáis*	*sepáis*	*seáis*
Uds., ellos, ellas	den	estén	vayan	sepan	sean

Práctica

ESCUCHAR • HABLAR • ESCRIBIR

1 Sigue el modelo.

MODELO **estudiar mucho →**
Los padres de Mateo quieren que él estudie mucho.

1. trabajar
2. leer mucho
3. comer bien
4. aprender mucho
5. asistir a la universidad
6. recibir buenas notas
7. hacer el trabajo
8. poner todo en orden
9. salir bien en todo
10. ir a clase
11. estar aquí
12. ser bueno

CULTURA

Los señores están preparando una paella grande en Tenerife, España. Quieren que salga deliciosa y que a todos les guste.

Gramática

¡Así se dice!

Why It Works!

In this chapter, students are introduced to the subjunctive. As an introduction they will use the subjunctive after the verb **querer** only. This allows students to focus on the subjunctive verb forms themselves. Since the affirmative of formal commands and the negative of informal commands are all subjunctive forms, they are presented at the same time.

Go Online!

You may wish to remind students to go online for additional grammar review and practice.

Leveling EACH Activity

Easy Activity 1

PRACTICE

Activity 1 Have students read the sentences aloud to accustom their ears to hearing the subjunctive forms.

Cultural Snapshot

Large paellas such as the one seen here are made at some fairs and beachside restaurants.

Answers

1

1. Los padres de Mateo quieren que él trabaje.
2. Los padres de Mateo quieren que él lea mucho.
3. Los padres de Mateo quieren que él coma bien.
4. Los padres de Mateo quieren que él aprenda mucho.
5. Los padres de Mateo quieren que él asista a la universidad.
6. Los padres de Mateo quieren que él reciba buenas notas.
7. Los padres de Mateo quieren que él haga el trabajo.
8. Los padres de Mateo quieren que él ponga todo en orden.
9. Los padres de Mateo quieren que él salga bien en todo.
10. Los padres de Mateo quieren que él vaya a clase.
11. Los padres de Mateo quieren que él esté aquí.
12. Los padres de Mateo quieren que él sea bueno.

Leveling EACH Activity

Easy Activity 2
Average Activities 3, 5
CHallenging Activity 4

PRACTICE *(continued)*

Activities 2 and 3 It is suggested that you go over these activities orally in class and then have students write them.

Activity 4 This activity can be prepared as homework and then gone over in class.

ASSESS

Students are now ready to take Quiz 2.

Go Online!

Gramática en vivo *Introduction to the subjunctive* Enliven learning with the animated world of Professor Cruz! **Gramática en vivo** is a fun and effective tool for additional instruction and/or review.

CULTURA

Esta muchacha está preparando tortillas en Chichicastenango, Guatemala. La tortilla sirve de base de muchas comidas en México y Centroamérica. ¿Quieres que ella te prepare una tortilla?

Lori Ernfridsson

LEER • ESCRIBIR

2 Forma una frase completa usando el subjuntivo.

Yo quiero que Luis...

1. preparar la comida
2. cortar las cebollas
3. asar la carne
4. leer la receta
5. pelar los tomates
6. picar el ajo
7. poner la mesa
8. hacer una ensalada

HABLAR • ESCRIBIR

3 Completa la frase con tus propias ideas usando los siguientes nombres y pronombres.

Yo quiero que...

1. tú
2. Justina y Roberto
3. todos ustedes
4. ella
5. todos nosotros
6. mi profesor

LEER • ESCRIBIR

4 Completa con la forma apropiada del verbo.

1. Yo quiero que tú le ____ y ellos quieren que nosotros le ____. (hablar)
2. Yo quiero que él ____ el postre y él quiere que yo lo ____. (comer)
3. Ellos quieren que yo ____ el paquete y yo quiero que ellos lo ____. (abrir)
4. Tú quieres que yo lo ____ y yo quiero que tú lo ____. (hacer)
5. Ellos quieren que nosotros ____ la mesa y nosotros queremos que ellos la ____. (poner)
6. Él quiere que yo lo ____ pero no quiere que tú lo ____. (saber)
7. Ellos quieren que tú ____ pero no quieren que yo ____. (ir)
8. Yo quiero que ustedes se lo ____ y ellos quieren que nosotros se lo ____. (dar)

InfoGap For more practice with the subjunctive, do Activity 10 in the Student Resource section at the end of this book.

5 ***Comunicación***

Trabajen en grupos y discutan todo lo que tu profesor(a) de español quiere que ustedes hagan.

Answers

2

1. Yo quiero que Luis prepare la comida.
2. Yo quiero que Luis corte las cebollas.
3. Yo quiero que Luis ase la carne.
4. Yo quiero que Luis lea la receta.
5. Yo quiero que Luis pele los tomates.
6. Yo quiero que Luis pique el ajo.
7. Yo quiero que Luis ponga la mesa.
8. Yo quiero que Luis haga una ensalada.

3 *Answers will vary.*

4

1. hables, hablemos
2. coma, coma
3. abra, abran
4. haga, hagas
5. pongamos, pongan
6. sepa, sepas
7. vayas, vaya
8. den, demos

5 *Answers will vary.*

El imperativo formal

1. The formal commands **(usted, ustedes),** both affirmative and negative, use the subjunctive form of the verb.

(no) prepare usted	**(no) preparen ustedes**
(no) lea usted	**(no) lean ustedes**
(no) sirva usted	**(no) sirvan ustedes**
(no) haga usted	**(no) hagan ustedes**
(no) salga usted	**(no) salgan ustedes**
(no) conduzca usted	**(no) conduzcan ustedes**
(no) vaya usted	**(no) vayan ustedes**
(no) sea usted	**(no) sean ustedes**

2. You have already learned that object pronouns can be attached to an infinitive or gerund or come before the helping verb. In the case of commands, the object pronouns must be added to the affirmative command, as you already know from the **tú** commands. They must come before the negative command.

AFFIRMATIVE	NEGATIVE
Háblele.	**No le hable usted.**
Démelo.	**No me lo dé usted.**
Levántense.	**No se levanten ustedes.**

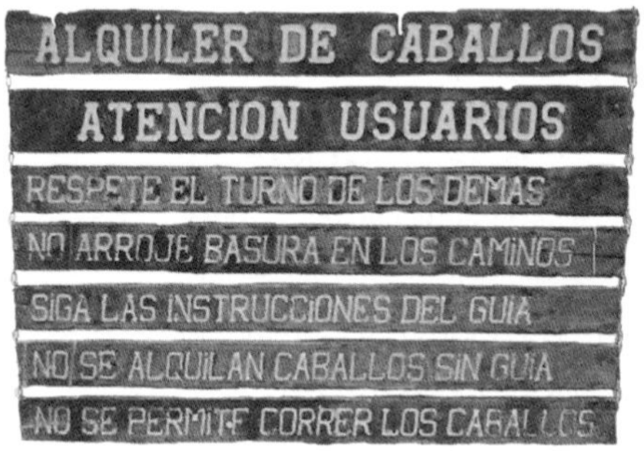

Go Online!

connectED.mcgraw-hill.com

CULTURA
En un parque en San Pablo, Ecuador

Práctica

ESCUCHAR • HABLAR • ESCRIBIR

6 Contesta según el modelo.

MODELO **—¿Preparo la comida?**
—Sí, prepare usted la comida.

1. ¿Preparo el postre?
2. ¿Aso la carne?
3. ¿Pelo los tomates?
4. ¿Pico el ajo?
5. ¿Frío el pollo?
6. ¿Pongo la mesa?
7. ¿Hago la ensalada?
8. ¿Pongo la cacerola al fuego?

FOLDABLES Study Organizer

PROJECT BOARD WITH TABS
See the Foldables section of the Student Handbook at the beginning of the book for help with making this foldable. Think of the food words you know in Spanish and use them to create a recipe of your own. Draw a small picture of each ingredient on the front of each tab in the order you will use it. Next, lift each tab and write instructions about how to prepare your recipe using formal commands.

Gramática

Online Resources

Customizable Lesson Plans
- Whiteboard Lesson
- Audio Activities
- Student Workbook
- Enrichment
- Quizzes

Quick Start

Use QS 10.3 or write the following on the board.
Complete with as many foods as you can think of.
Ase usted ___.
Pele usted ___.
Fría usted ___.
Hierva usted ___.

TEACH

Core Instruction

Although students have not yet actively used formal commands, they have heard the **ustedes** formal command many times when the teacher has given instructions to the entire class or groups.

Step 1 Have students repeat the verb forms aloud. Point out that they are the same subjunctive forms that they just learned.

Step 2 There is no doubt that students find the placement of pronouns with commands very tricky. Even when they understand the concept, they tend to get confused when trying to use them. Students need a lot of practice with this and most will take time before mastering this concept.

Learning from Realia

(bottom) Have students find the command forms on the sign.

Answers

6
1. Sí, prepare usted el postre.
2. Sí, ase usted la carne.
3. Sí, pele usted los tomates.
4. Sí, pique usted el ajo.
5. Sí, fría usted el pollo.
6. Sí, ponga usted la mesa.
7. Sí, haga la ensalada.
8. Sí, ponga la cacerola al fuego.

Differentiation

Slower Paced Learners

Since slower paced learners tend to find the imperative in Spanish quite difficult, you may wish to present this point more for recognition than production. Students can avoid the active use of the commands by using the polite **favor de** + *infinitive.*

Leveling EACH Activity

Easy-Average Activity 6
Average Activities 7, 9
CHallenging Activities 8, 10

PRACTICE *(continued)*

Note: Because of the nature of this grammatical point, no activity is rated easy.

Activity 6 Have students present this activity as a short conversation.

Activities 7, 8, and 9 Have students present these activities as short conversations.

¡Así se dice!

Why It Works!

Note that these forms reinforce and give students additional practice with the subjunctive forms they just learned in the previous section.

Go Online!

You may wish to use the whiteboard presentation for additional grammar instruction and practice.

ASSESS

Students are now ready to take Quiz 3.

Gramática

CULTURA

Esta señora cocina en una calle de Oaxaca, México. Como se ve, tiene un negocio próspero. Muchos clientes quieren saborear sus comidas.

Andrew Payti

¿Te acuerdas?

Remember other polite ways you learned to express a command.

Favor de pasarme la sal.
¿Me pasaría usted la sal, por favor?

ESCUCHAR • HABLAR • ESCRIBIR

7 Contesta según el modelo.

MODELO **—¿Preparamos la comida?**
—No, no preparen ustedes la comida. Yo la voy a preparar.

1. ¿Preparamos el postre?
2. ¿Lavamos la lechuga?
3. ¿Pelamos las papas?
4. ¿Cortamos el pepino?
5. ¿Hacemos la ensalada?
6. ¿Ponemos la mesa?

ESCUCHAR • HABLAR • ESCRIBIR

8 Contesta según el modelo.

MODELO **—¿Quiere usted que yo ase la chuleta?**
—No, no la ase usted. Fríala.

1. ¿Quiere usted que yo ase el pollo?
2. ¿Quiere usted que yo ase las papas?
3. ¿Quiere usted que yo ase las chuletas de cordero?
4. ¿Quiere usted que yo ase los pimientos?
5. ¿Quiere usted que yo ase el pescado?
6. ¿Quiere usted que yo ase los camarones?

ESCUCHAR • HABLAR • ESCRIBIR

9 Sigue el modelo.

MODELO **Páseme la sal, por favor. → Pásemela, por favor.**

1. Páseme la pimienta, por favor.
2. Páseme el pan, por favor.
3. Páseme la ensalada, por favor.
4. Páseme los platos, por favor.
5. Páseme el tenedor, por favor.
6. Páseme las zanahorias, por favor.

LEER • ESCRIBIR

10 Completa la tabla.

sí	no
Démelo.	
	No me lo diga usted.
Cocínelo a fuego lento.	
	No la revuelva usted.
Léamela.	

Answers

7
1. No, no preparen ustedes el postre. Yo lo voy a preparar.
2. No, no laven ustedes la lechuga. Yo la voy a lavar.
3. No, no pelen ustedes las papas. Yo las voy a pelar.
4. No, no corten ustedes el pepino. Yo lo voy a cortar.
5. No, no hagan ustedes la ensalada. Yo la voy a hacer.
6. No, no pongan ustedes la mesa. Yo la voy a poner.

8
1. No, no lo ase usted. Fríalo.
2. No, no las ase usted. Fríalas.
3. No, no las ase usted. Fríalas.
4. No, no los ase usted. Fríalos.
5. No, no lo ase usted. Fríalo.
6. No, no los ase usted. Fríalos.

9
1. Pásemela, por favor.
2. Pásemelo, por favor.
3. Pásemela, por favor.
4. Pásemelos, por favor.
5. Pásemelo, por favor.
6. Pásemelas, por favor.

10
sí: Dígamelo. / Revuélvala.
no: No me lo dé usted. / No lo cocine a fuego lento. / No me la lea usted.

El imperativo familiar—formas negativas

1. The negative **tú** or informal command uses the **tú** form of the verb in the subjunctive.

No hables más.	**No salgas.**
No comas más.	**No vayas.**
No sirvas más.	**No conduzcas.**

2. As with the formal commands, object pronouns are added to the affirmative command and come before the negative command.

Háblame.	**No me hables.**
Dímelo.	**No me lo digas.**

Práctica

ESCUCHAR • HABLAR • ESCRIBIR

11 Contesta según el modelo.

MODELO **—¿Miro ahora o no?**
—No, no mires ahora.

1. ¿Hablo ahora o no?
2. ¿Como ahora o no?
3. ¿Subo ahora o no?
4. ¿Sirvo ahora o no?
5. ¿Salgo ahora o no?
6. ¿Voy ahora o no?

LEER • ESCRIBIR

12 Completa la tabla.

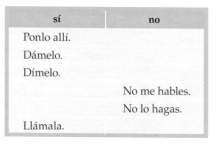

sí	no
Ponlo allí.	
Dámelo.	
Dímelo.	
	No me hables.
	No lo hagas.
Llámala.	

13 ***Comunicación***

Acabas de recibir un gatito para tu cumpleaños. Como todos los gatitos, es muy curioso. Dale un nombre al gatito y dile que no haga cosas peligrosas y destructivas.

Go Online!

connectED.mcgraw-hill.com

¿Te acuerdas?

You have already learned the familiar **tú** command in the affirmative.

Refrán

Can you guess what the following proverb means?

Espinacas, cómelas a sacas.

¡Bravo!

You have now learned all the new vocabulary and grammar in this chapter. Continue to use and practice all that you know while learning more cultural information. **¡Vamos!**

Answers

11
1. No, no hables ahora.
2. No, no comas ahora.
3. No, no subas ahora.
4. No, no sirvas ahora.
5. No, no salgas ahora.
6. No, no vayas ahora.

12
sí: Háblame. / Hazlo.
no: No lo pongas allí. / No me lo des. / No me lo digas. / No la llames.

13 *Answers will vary.*

Gramática

Online Resources

Customizable Lesson Plans
Whiteboard Lesson
Audio Activities
Student Workbook
Enrichment
Quizzes

Quick Start

Use QS 10.4 or write the following on the board.
Answer.

1. **¿Quién te prepara la cena, tu mamá o tu papá?**
2. **¿Quién te sirve la comida en el restaurante?**
3. **¿Te la sirve pronto el mesero?**
4. **¿Le das la propina al mesero?**
5. **¿Se la das antes o después de comer?**

TEACH

Core Instruction

You may wish to follow the same suggestions as given for the formal commands.

PRACTICE

Leveling EACH Activity

Easy–Average Activity 11
Average Activities 12, 13

ASSESS

Students are now ready to take Quiz 4.

Refrán

Have students recite the proverb aloud. Then see if they can figure out its meaning and give an equivalent expression in English such as "Eat your spinach."

Online Resources

Customizable Lesson Plans
Audio Activities
Video (Diálogo)
Student Workbook

Quick Start

Use QS 10.5 or write the following on the board.
Write the names of a few Latino dishes you are familiar with.

TEACH

Core Instruction

Step 1 You may wish to have students listen to the audio recording of the conversation.

Step 2 Call on pairs of students to read the conversation aloud. Insist that they use proper intonation and expression.

Step 3 You may wish to ask the questions from Activity A as you are going over the **Conversación.**

Cultura

You may wish to point out that, historically, chefs were men. Today, however, there are many well-known female chefs in the kitchens of renowned restaurants. This is true in Spain and Latin America as well as in the United States. Have students who watch cooking programs on television talk to the class about any chefs they know and what type of cuisine they are famous for.

¿Yo? ¿En la cocina?

Alicia, ¿te gusta cocinar?
A mí, ¿cocinar? ¿Hablas en serio, Jorge? En la cocina soy un desastre. ¿A ti te gusta cocinar?
Sí, bastante. La verdad es que algún día me gustaría ser cocinero.

¿De veras? Dame una idea de lo que sabes preparar.
Muchas cosas, pero mi plato favorito es la paella.
La paella, dices. ¿Qué es?

Pues, es una especialidad española, de Valencia. Lleva muchos ingredientes—mariscos, arroz. Algún día, ¿quieres que yo te prepare una paella?
Sí, pero no sé si me gustarán los mariscos.
Pues, nosotros los españoles comemos mucho pescado y mariscos. Pero ahora se están poniendo muy caros.

David H. Brennan

¡Así se dice!

Why It Works!

No new material is used in the **Conversación** in order not to confuse students. The **Conversación** recombines only the vocabulary and grammar that students have already learned to understand and manipulate.

Go Online!

You may wish to remind students to go online for additional conversation practice.

¿Comprendes?

connectED.mcgraw-hill.com

A Contesta según la información en la conversación.

1. ¿A quién le gusta cocinar?
2. ¿Quién es un desastre en la cocina?
3. Algún día, ¿qué quiere ser Jorge?
4. ¿Cuál es el plato que más le gusta preparar?
5. ¿De qué región de España es la paella una especialidad?
6. ¿A Alicia le va a gustar una paella?
7. ¿Son caros los mariscos?

B Identifica a quien describe.

	Jorge	Alicia
1. Le gusta cocinar y sabe cocinar.		
2. No sabe si le gustan los mariscos.		
3. Es un desastre en la cocina.		
4. Come mariscos.		

C **Analizando** Contesta.

1. ¿De qué país es Jorge? ¿Cómo lo sabes?
2. ¿Es Alicia de España?

D **Personalizando** ¿Qué piensas? ¿A ti te gustaría la paella o no? ¿Por qué?

Andrew Payti

CULTURA

En esta tienda en Valencia, España, se venden utensilios para elaborar una buena paella.

PRACTICE

¿Comprendes?

A and **B** You may wish to do Activity A as a factual recall activity and permit students to look up the information for Activity B.

Comunidades

There are many cooking shows on the Spanish-speaking TV channels in the United States. You may wish to have students view one at home and present what they learned to the class. Have them comment on how easy or difficult it was to understand the speakers on the program.

Cultural Snapshot

You may wish to point out to students that the large hanging vessels in varying sizes are **paelleras.** Discuss what the image suggests about the importance of **paella** in the Spanish culture.

Go Online!

Diálogo en vivo In this episode, Vicky and Alejandra prepare an Argentine meal. Ask students to note what time dinner will be served. How does this compare with typical dinnertimes in the United States?

Answers

A

1. A Jorge le gusta cocinar.
2. Alicia es un desastre en la cocina.
3. Algún día, Jorge quiere ser cocinero.
4. La paella es el plato que más le gusta preparar.
5. Es una especialidad de Valencia.
6. Alicia no sabe si le va a gustar la paella.
7. Sí, son caros los mariscos.

B

1. Jorge
2. Alicia
3. Alicia
4. Jorge

C

1. Jorge es de España. Dice que en España «comemos» muchos mariscos.
2. No.

D *Answers will vary.*

Online Resources

Customizable Lesson Plans

Audio Activities

Student Workbook

TEACH

Core Instruction

You may wish to have students read this selection silently. When going over the **Preparación** section in the recipe, you may wish to have students read aloud since there are many examples of the command form.

Differentiation

Heritage Speakers

If you have heritage speakers in class, have them tell if they have ever had **arroz con pollo.** Ask them if they are familiar with the ingredients. If so, ask them if they are the same as those listed in the recipe. If not, what are the differences?

Cultural Snapshot

Azafrán is now reported to be the most expensive spice in the world.

Go Online!

You may wish to remind students to go online for additional reading comprehension and writing skills practice.

Lectura CULTURAL

ESTRATEGIA DE LECTURA

LEYENDO INFORMACIÓN DETALLADA A veces cuando lees algo como una receta es necesario prestar atención a muchos detalles. Para hacerlo debes leer o consultar la selección más de una vez siempre concentrando y prestando mucha atención.

Antes de leer

Dale una ojeada a la receta para familiarizarte con los ingredientes y la preparación.

Durante la lectura

Al leer asegúrate que comprendes el orden de cada procedimiento durante la elaboración del plato.

READING CHECK

¿Por qué es amarillo el arroz?

CULTURA

Los ingredientes para hacer arroz con pollo

Después de leer

Trata de contar la receta de la manera más detallada posible a un(a) compañero(a) de clase.

Una receta hispana

Otro plato delicioso y muy apreciado en España y otros países hispanohablantes es el arroz con pollo. Hay muchas variaciones en las recetas para elaborar un buen arroz con pollo pero aquí tiene usted una receta bastante sencilla. Decida si a usted le gustaría comer este plato delicioso.

Antes de leer la receta hay que saber algo más. El arroz en el arroz con pollo igual que el arroz en una paella es amarillo. Es el azafrán, una hierba de origen árabe, que le da al arroz el color amarillo. Pero el azafrán es muy caro y como colorante se puede usar bujol. El bujol se vende en muchos supermercados.

Arroz con pollo

Ingredientes

3 tomates
2 cebollas grandes
2 pimientos (uno verde y uno rojo)
4 dientes[1] de ajo
1 pollo en partes
3 chorizos[2]
1 paquete de guisantes congelados
1 frasco de (pimientos) morrones (rojos)
1 ½ tazas de arroz
3 tazas de consomé de pollo
unas pizcas[3] de azafrán o bujol
¼ (una cuarta) taza de aceite de oliva
una pizca de sal y pimienta

Preparación

1. Pique los tomates, pimientos, cebollas y ajo.
2. Corte en rodajas los chorizos.
3. Fría o ase el pollo aparte (se puede preparar el pollo en partes [muslos, media pechuga, piernas] o se puede cortarlo en pedazos deshuesados[4]).

Elaboración

Se usa una sartén o una olla grande.

1. Fría ligeramente[5] en el aceite los pimientos y las cebollas picadas.
2. Agregue (Añada) a la misma sartén el ajo y los tomates y fría ligeramente a fuego lento unos dos o tres minutos.
3. Agregue el arroz.
4. Revuelva el arroz con los tomates, cebollas, morrones y ajo.
5. Añada el pollo.
6. Agregue el consomé de pollo y llévelo a la ebullición[6].
7. Agregue el azafrán o bujol.
8. Ponga sal y pimienta a su gusto.
9. Tape[7] la sartén o la olla y cocine a fuego lento encima de la estufa unos treinta minutos.
10. Al final agregue los guisantes y pimientos morrones.

[1]dientes *cloves*
[2]chorizos *Spanish sausage*
[3]pizcas *pinches*
[4]deshuesados *deboned*
[5]ligeramente *lightly*
[6]a la ebullición *to a boil*
[7]Tape *Cover*

¿Comprendes?

A **Buscando palabras específicas** ¿Cuál es la palabra? Completa según la receta.

1. una ____ para hacer (elaborar) arroz con pollo
2. un ____ de guisantes congelados
3. cuatro ____ de ajo
4. una ____ de sal
5. tres ____ de consomé de pollo

B **Recordando detalles importantes** Lee la receta una vez más. Luego, sin consultar la receta, escribe una lista de todos los ingredientes necesarios. Luego consulta la receta para verificar si has omitido algo.

C **Confirmando información** Verifica. ¿Sí o no?

	sí	no
1. Se puede cocinar el arroz con pollo encima de la estufa.		
2. El arroz con pollo lleva muchas papas.		
3. Hay muchos mariscos en un arroz con pollo.		
4. El arroz se pone amarillo.		
5. El chorizo es un tipo de salchicha española.		

Comparaciones

La historia y la geografía influyen lo que come la gente de una región. La geografía dicta los productos que pueden crecer en un lugar y la historia indica lo que a los antiguos habitantes les gustaba comer. Investiga estas influencias en varios países latinos y discute como ahora están teniendo un impacto en nuestra propia cultura.

PRACTICE

Pre-AP These cultural readings will develop the skills that students need to be successful on the reading and writing sections of the AP exam. Listening to these readings will also help prepare them for the auditory component.

Answers

A

1. receta
2. paquete
3. dientes
4. pizca
5. tazas

B

3 tomates, 2 cebollas grandes, 2 pimientos (uno verde y uno rojo), 4 dientes de ajo, 1 pollo en partes, 3 chorizos, 1 paquete de guisantes congelados, 1 frasco de (pimientos) morrones (rojos), 1½ tazas de arroz, 3 tazas de consomé de pollo, unas pizcas de azafrán o bujol, ¼ taza de aceite de oliva, una pizca de sal y pimienta

C

1. sí
2. no
3. no
4. sí
5. sí

Online Resources

Customizable Lesson Plans

Audio Activities

Student Workbook

TEACH

Core Instruction

You may wish to have students read this selection on their own and do the **¿Comprendes?** activities. Before having them read it, you may ask them if they remember what they have already learned about **sobras.** In Chapter 4 of Level 2, students learned that it is definitely not a custom in Spanish-speaking countries to ask to take your leftovers home.

Teaching Options

Call on some students to read aloud individually. After a student has read three or four sentences, ask questions of other students to check comprehension.

Go Online!

ePals

You may wish to remind students to go online for additional reading comprehension and writing skills practice.

Lectura

UN POCO MÁS

Antes de leer

A veces no podemos comer todo lo que está en nuestro plato. Lo que no comemos y dejamos en el plato son «las sobras». Piensa en unas recetas que tiene tu familia en que se usan las sobras.

Una receta para «la ropa vieja»

Aquí tienes otra receta para un plato que es popular en muchas partes de Latinoamérica—sobre todo en Cuba. Se llama «ropa vieja»—un nombre divertido, ¿no? Se llama «ropa vieja» porque se puede elaborar con muchas sobras. Este plato tan conocido se originó en las islas Canarias.

Ropa vieja

Ingredientes

- ½ kg de carne (de ternera, bife) picada
- 1 cebolla
- 1 pimiento verde y un pimiento rojo
- 3 dientes de ajo
- 1 cucharadita de orégano
- una pizca de pimienta
- ½ taza de tomate cocido (o enlatado)
- 3 cucharadas de aceite de oliva
- ½ taza de caldo (consomé de pollo)

Preparación o cocción

Corte los pimientos, las cebollas y los ajos en trocitos. Fría los pimientos, las cebollas y los ajos en el aceite de oliva con una pizca de pimienta y el orégano. Añada la carne picada y revuelva todos los ingredientes (unos dos minutos). Añada el caldo y cueza (cocine) a fuego mediano hasta que se evapore el caldo. Sirva con arroz blanco.

Emily Lowry

Go Online!

ePals

connectED.mcgraw-hill.com

¿Comprendes?

Escoge o completa.

1. La ropa vieja viene de ____.
   a. Latinoamérica
   b. Cuba
   c. las islas Canarias
2. Se llama «ropa vieja» porque se puede elaborar (hacer) con ____.
   a. ropa
   b. comida que queda
   c. ingredientes divertidos
3. ____ es una cantidad muy pequeña.
4. Hay que ____ los pimientos verdes y rojos, la cebolla y los dientes de ajo en trocitos.
   a. cortar
   b. picar
   c. freír
5. Dos especias que lleva el plato son ____ y ____.
6. Cueza los ingredientes hasta que se evapore ____.
   a. el aceite
   b. el tomate
   c. el caldo
7. La ropa vieja se sirve acompañada de ____.
   a. caldo
   b. azafrán
   c. arroz blanco
8. Un amigo vegetariano comerá la ropa vieja si no pones ____.

Andrew Payti

Answers

1. c
2. b
3. Una pizca
4. a
5. orégano y pimienta
6. c
7. c
8. carne

Lectura

Cultura

You may wish to have students look for Latino recipes online. They can share them and decide if there is one they would like to try. If you have any students interested in cooking, they may want to prepare the dish.

Go Online!

Cultura en vivo In this episode, students visit a **tortillería** in Mexico. Ask students if there are any food products that they regularly purchase outside of a supermarket.

About the Spanish Language

The word **triturado,** meaning *crushed,* appears on the **lata (el bote) de tomates.** A *garbage disposal unit* is **el triturador de basura** in many areas of Latin America.

Tips for Success

The multiple-choice comprehension activities that accompany the second reading selection in each chapter have a format that will help students prepare for standarized tests.

Prepárate para el examen

Online Resources

Customizable Lesson Plans
Student Workbook
Enrichment
Listening, Speaking, Reading, Writing Tests

Self-check for achievement

This is a pre-test for students to take before you administer the chapter test. Note that each section is cross-referenced so students can easily find the material they feel they need to review. You may wish to use Self-Check Worksheet SC10 to have students complete this assessment in class or at home. You can correct the assessment yourself, or you may prefer to display the answers in class using Self-Check Answers SC10A.

Differentiation

Slower Paced Learners

Have students work in pairs to complete the Self-Check in class. Once they have finished, call on individuals to give the correct answers as you review together.

Multiple Intelligences

To engage **visual-spatial** and **bodily-kinesthetic** learners, number from 1 to 40 on the board and call on a student to go to the board and write the correct answer (this may be done chronologically or you may allow students to choose the one they answer). Then have the student who wrote the first answer decide who will write the second, and so on, making sure to remind them not to pick the same person again.

Prepárate para el examen

To review, see **Vocabulario**.

Vocabulario

1 Parea.

1. hervir
2. freír
3. revolver
4. pelar
5. cortar en rebanadas
6. añadir

a. la salsa
b. el pan
c. las zanahorias
d. el agua
e. sal y pimienta
f. el pollo

2 Identifica.

7.

8.

9.

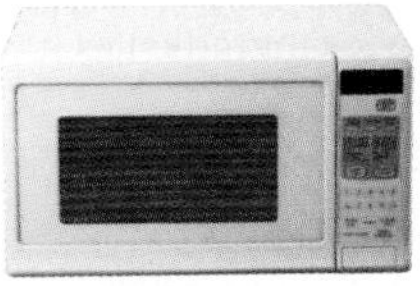
10.

11.

12.

Answers

1
1. d
2. f
3. a
4. c
5. b
6. e

2
7. el lavaplatos
8. la estufa (la cocina, el horno)
9. el aguacate
10. el horno de microondas
11. las chuletas de cerdo
12. el ajo

Go Online!
connectED.mcgraw-hill.com

Gramática

3 Completa.

13–14. Él quiere que yo ____ y yo quiero que él ____. (hablar)

15–16. Tú quieres que nosotros lo ____ y nosotros queremos que tú lo ____. (leer)

17–18. Yo quiero que tú lo ____ y tú quieres que yo lo ____. (escribir)

19–20. Tú quieres que yo lo ____ y él quiere que tú lo ____. (hacer)

21–22. Nosotros queremos que ellos ____ y ellos quieren que nosotros ____. (ir)

To review, see **El subjuntivo.**

4 Completa con el imperativo formal.

23. ____ usted la comida. (preparar)
24. ____ usted la receta. (leer)
25. ____ usted la lata. (abrir)
26. ____ usted ahora. (salir)
27. Y ____ usted mañana. (regresar)
28. No me lo ____ usted. (decir)
29. No ____ usted más. (añadir)

To review, see **El imperativo formal.**

5 Escribe con el pronombre.

30. Prepare usted *la ensalada.*
31. No prepare usted *el postre.*
32. Déme *las direcciones.*

6 Escribe en la forma negativa.

33. Luis, habla.
34. Jacinta, come más.
35. Carlos, levántate.
36. Teresa, ven.

To review, see **El imperativo familiar—formas negativas.**

Cultura

7 Contesta.

37–40. ¿Cuáles son algunos ingredientes que lleva el arroz con pollo?

To review this cultural information, see the **Lectura cultural.**

Differentiation

(continued)

This type of review activity is particularly appealing to interpersonal learners but will also benefit the class on the whole by promoting an inclusive, student-centered learning environment.

Slower Paced Learners

Encourage students who need extra help to refer to the margin notes and review any section before answering the questions.

Pre-AP Students preparing for the AP exam may benefit from a set time limit when completing this Self-Check. This may also help to identify students with learning difficulties or slower paced students who need extra help.

Go Online!

You may wish to remind students to go online for additional test preparation.

Answers

3

13. hable
14. hable
15. leamos
16. leas
17. escribas
18. escriba
19. haga
20. hagas
21. vayan
22. vayamos

4

23. Prepare
24. Lea
25. Abra
26. Salga
27. regrese
28. diga
29. añada

5

30. Prepárela.
31. No lo prepare.
32. Démelas.

6

33. Luis, no hables.
34. Jacinta, no comas más.
35. Carlos, no te levantes.
36. Teresa, no vengas.

7

37–40. *Answers will vary but may include:* el pollo, el arroz, los tomates, las cebollas, los pimientos, el ajo, los chorizos, los guisantes congelados, los morrones, el consomé, el azafrán, el aceite de oliva, la sal, la pimienta.

Prepárate para el examen

Tips for Success

Encourage students to say as much as possible when they do these open-ended activities. Tell them not to be afraid to make mistakes, since the goal of the activities is real-life communication. Encourage students to self-correct and to use words and phrases they know to get their meaning across. If someone in the group makes an error that impedes comprehension, encourage the others to ask questions to clarify or, if necessary, to politely correct the speaker. Let students choose the activities they would like to do.

Tell students to feel free to elaborate on the basic theme and to be creative. They may use props, pictures, or posters if they wish.

Pre-AP These oral activities will give students the opportunity to develop and improve their speaking skills so that they may succeed on the speaking portion of the AP exam.

Note: You may want to use the rubric below to help students prepare their speaking activities.

Practice for **ORAL PROFICIENCY**

Prepárate para el examen

1 Yo en la cocina

Talk about cooking

Habla con un(a) compañero(a) de clase. Dile si te gusta cocinar o no. Explícale por qué. Luego verifica si tu compañero(a) tiene las mismas opiniones que tú.

2 Comidas étnicas

Discuss and describe a restaurant and the food it serves

¿Hay restaurantes étnicos, restaurantes que sirven comida de otras partes del mundo, en tu comunidad? Si hay, con un(a) compañero(a) preparen una lista de estos restaurantes y el tipo de comida que sirven. Luego describan un plato típico de uno de los restaurantes que les gusta.

3 ¡Qué comida más deliciosa!

Describe a delicious meal

Estás viajando por México. Anoche fuiste a cenar en un restaurante y pediste algo que salió delicioso, muy rico. Te gustó mucho. Llama a tus padres y descríbeles el restaurante y el plato que te gustó tanto. Si puedes, explícales como crees que el cocinero preparó el plato.

4 Simón dice...

Give and receive commands

Trabajen ustedes en grupos de cinco. Van a jugar «Simón dice». Cada líder dará cinco órdenes a todos los miembros del grupo y luego escogerá a otro líder.

5 Mis padres

Discuss what your parents want you to do

Tus padres quieren que hagas muchas cosas, ¿no? Dile a un(a) compañero(a) todo lo que quieren tus padres que hagas. Tu compañero(a) te dirá si sus padres quieren que él o ella haga las mismas cosas. Luego discutan como se sienten cuando sus padres quieren que ustedes hagan algo que no quieren hacer.

CULTURA

La gente está sentada en la terraza de un café en Puebla, México.

Andrew Payti

Scoring Rubric for Speaking

	4	3	2	1
vocabulary	extensive use of vocabulary, including idiomatic expressions	adequate use of vocabulary and idiomatic expressions	limited vocabulary marked with some anglicisms	limited vocabulary marked by frequent anglicisms that force interpretation by the listener
grammar	few or no grammatical errors	minor grammatical errors	some serious grammatical errors	serious grammatical errors
pronunciation	good intonation and largely accurate pronunciation with slight accent	acceptable intonation and pronunciation with distinctive accent	errors in intonation and pronunciation with heavy accent	errors in intonation and pronunciation that interfere with listener's comprehension
content	thorough response with interesting and pertinent detail	thorough response with sufficient detail	some detail, but not sufficient	general, insufficient response

Go Online!
connectED.mcgraw-hill.com

Tarea

Your teacher wants to know the recipe for the warm quesadillas and chilled fresh tomato salsa that you brought to the last Spanish Club meeting. Use the ingredients listed below or research other recipes for quesadillas and salsa to give your teacher instructions on how to make this delicious, easy-to-prepare Mexican snack.

Quesadillas
unas tortillas de harina
queso triturado *(shredded cheese)*
aceite de oliva

Salsa de tomate
tomates
pimientos verdes
cebolla
chiles jalapeños
ajo
cilantro
jugo de lima

Getty Images/Blend Images

Writing Strategy

Giving Instructions When giving instructions, it is important to present the details accurately, clearly, and in logical order. This is especially true when writing a recipe because directions that are incorrect, unclear, or out of order could cause the dish to taste bad or be ruined altogether.

1 Prewrite

Make a list of the steps for completing the recipe and put them in chronological order. Also think about what utensils and/or appliances will be used, and remember that timing and presentation are very important. What should be prepared first? What should be prepared last? How will the dish be served?

2 Write

- Use formal commands since this is a recipe for your teacher.
- Make sure all of the steps follow a logical order.
- Use transition words to help you present your information in an organized way.
- Remember to stick to vocabulary you already know and don't attempt to translate from English to Spanish.

Evaluate

Your teacher will evaluate you on accurate and logical presentation of details, correct use of vocabulary and grammar, and completeness of information.

Prepárate para el examen

Pre-AP This **tarea** will give students the opportunity to develop and improve their writing skills so that they may succeed on the writing portion of the AP exam.

ASSESS

Students are now ready to take any of the Listening, Speaking, Reading, Writing Tests you choose to administer.

Note: You may want to use the rubric below to help students prepare their writing task.

Scoring Rubric for Writing

	4	3	2	1
vocabulary	precise, varied	functional, fails to communicate complete meaning	limited to basic words, often inaccurate	inadequate
grammar	excellent, very few or no errors	some errors, but do not hinder communication	numerous errors interfere with communication	many errors, little sentence structure
content	thorough response to the topic	generally thorough response to the topic	partial response to the topic	insufficient response to the topic
organization	well organized, ideas presented clearly and logically	loosely organized, but main ideas present	some attempts at organization, but with confused sequencing	lack of organization

Repaso del Capítulo 10

Online Resources

Customizable Lesson Plans
- Whiteboard Lesson
- Audio Activities
- Video (Vocabulario) (Diálogo) (Cultura) (Gramática)
- Student Workbook
- Enrichment
- Quizzes
- Listening, Speaking, Reading, Writing Tests

Grammar Review

This page provides a quick "at a glance" summary of the grammar points students have learned in this chapter.

Differentiation

Multiple Intelligences

You may want to call on **verbal-linguistic** and **logical-mathematical** learners for whom grammar often comes easily to explain the main concepts to their classmates in their own words. Having students explain the concepts in different ways may also help slower paced learners or students with learning difficulties.

Repaso del Capítulo 10

Gramática

El subjuntivo

The subjunctive expresses that which is not necessarily factual or real. It expresses things that might happen.

El profesor quiere que los alumnos lean el libro.

Review the following forms of the present subjunctive.

hablar	beber	escribir	poner
hable	beba	escriba	ponga
hables	bebas	escribas	pongas
hable	beba	escriba	ponga
hablemos	bebamos	escribamos	pongamos
habléis	*bebáis*	*escribáis*	*pongáis*
hablen	beban	escriban	pongan

Review the following irregular verbs in the present subjunctive.

dar	estar	ir	saber	ser
dé	esté	vaya	sepa	sea
des	estés	vayas	sepas	seas
dé	esté	vaya	sepa	sea
demos	estemos	vayamos	sepamos	seamos
deis	*estéis*	*vayáis*	*sepáis*	*seáis*
den	estén	vayan	sepan	sean

El imperativo

The affirmative and negative formal commands and the negative familiar commands use the subjunctive form of the verb.

(no) mire usted	**(no) miren ustedes**	**no mires**
(no) coma usted	**(no) coman ustedes**	**no comas**
(no) asista usted	**(no) asistan ustedes**	**no asistas**
(no) salga usted	**(no) salgan ustedes**	**no salgas**
(no) vaya usted	**(no) vayan ustedes**	**no vayas**

¿Te acuerdas?

You learned the affirmative **tú** command in the previous chapter.

Object pronouns are attached to affirmative commands but must come before negative commands. Review the following sentences.

Mírelo.	**No lo mire usted.**	**No lo mires.**
Démelas.	**No me las dé usted.**	**No me las des.**
Levántenlas.	**No las levanten ustedes.**	**No las levantes.**

Juego There are a number of cognates in this list. See how many you and a partner can find. Who can find the most? Compare your list with those of your classmates.

Go Online!

connectED.mcgraw-hill.com

Vocabulario

Talking about some kitchen appliances and utensils

la cocina	el horno	la olla, la cacerola
el refrigerador, la nevera	el horno de microondas	la tapa
el congelador	el lavaplatos	la cazuela
la estufa, la cocina	el/la sartén	la parrilla

Talking about food preparation

la receta	cortar	quemarse
el/la cocinero(a)	en pedacitos	hervir
el sabor	en rebanadas	freír
pelar	añadir	asar
picar	poner al fuego	revolver
	cocinar, cocer	
	a fuego lento	

Identifying more foods

la chuleta de cerdo	la pechuga de pollo	el aguacate
el escalope de ternera	la cebolla	el ajo
el muslo de pollo	la zanahoria	el condimento
las alitas de pollo	el pepino	
	el pimiento	

Andrew Payti

Juego The cognates in this list are: **el refrigerador, el escalope, el condimento.**

Don't forget the chapter project and cultural activities. Students have learned all the information that they will need to complete these engaging enrichment tasks.

Repaso del Capítulo 10

Vocabulary Review

The words and phrases in the **Vocabulario** section have been taught for productive use in this chapter. They are summarized here as a resource for both student and teacher. This list also serves as a convenient resource for the **Prepárate para el examen.**

¡Así se dice!

Why It Works!

This vocabulary reference list has not been translated into English for two reasons. First, it is recommended that students learn the new vocabulary through direct association with images on the **Vocabulario** pages. Second, all vocabulary is reintroduced in the chapter many times and upon completion of the chapter students should be familiar with the meaning of all the words. If there are words that students still do not know, they can refer to the vocabulary presentation in the chapter or the dictionary at the end of the book. If, however, it is your preference to give students the English translations, please refer to Vocabulary V10.1.

Differentiation

Slower Paced Learners

Slower paced learners may benefit from creating their own visual dictionary of nouns in this list. They can either draw their own depictions or use images from the Internet, magazines, etc.

Every chapter of **¡Así se dice!** contains this review section of previously learned material. By recycling information from previous chapters, the cumulative review serves to remind students that they need to continue practicing what they have learned after finishing each chapter.

Activity 1 This activity reviews comparatives and superlatives.

Audio Script

1. Miguel tiene ocho años. Su hermana tiene diez años. Miguel es mayor que su hermana.
2. La blusa cuesta veinte pesos. La falda cuesta treinta pesos. La falda cuesta más que la blusa.
3. Tú recibiste una A en español, una B en inglés y una D en matemáticas. Tú recibiste la mejor nota en inglés.
4. Un carro es rápido, un avión es más rápido, pero el tren es el más rapido de todos.
5. Mi casa tiene ocho cuartos. La casa de Elena tiene catorce cuartos. Mi casa es más pequeña que la casa de Elena.

Activity 2 This activity reviews vocabulary related to foods.

Repaso cumulativo

Repasa lo que ya has aprendido

These activities will help you review and remember what you have learned so far in Spanish.

1 Escucha las frases. Indica en una tabla como la de abajo si la información en cada frase es correcta o no.

sí	no

2 Identifica.

1. todas las legumbres que ya conoces en español
2. todas las carnes que ya conoces en español
3. todo lo que necesitas para poner la mesa
4. la diferencia entre un desayuno continental y un desayuno americano

3 Completa con el presente.

1. Yo ____ bife y Anita ____ pescado y nosotros dos ____ flan. (pedir)
2. Nosotros no nos ____. El mesero nos ____. (servir)
3. Yo ____ esto y él ____ el otro. Nosotros nunca ____ la misma cosa. (preferir)

4 Describe las siguientes fiestas.

1. el Día de los Muertos
2. el Día de los Reyes
3. el Cuatro de Julio en Estados Unidos

CULTURA

Una barbacoa para celebrar el Cuatro de Julio en Estados Unidos

5 Completa con el imperativo.

1. José, ____ más. (comer)
2. Rosario, ____ el correo electrónico. (leer)
3. Manuel, ____ tu regalo. (abrir)
4. Adela, ____ acá. (venir)
5. Alberto, ____ pronto. (volver)
6. Federico, ____ la mesa. (poner)
7. Magda, ____ la verdad. (decir)
8. Gabriel, ____ la comida. (servir)

Answers

1
1. no
2. sí
3. no
4. no
5. sí

2 *Answers will vary but may include:*
1. la lechuga, los tomates, las papas (las patatas), los guisantes, las judías verdes, las zanahorias, las cebollas, los pimientos, el maíz, el pepino, el aguacate
2. el tocino (el bacón, el lacón), el pollo, el jamón, el biftec, la carne de res, el cerdo, el cordero, la ternera
3. los platos, el tenedor, la cuchara, la cucharita, el cuchillo, la taza, el platillo, el vaso, el mantel, la servilleta
4. **un desayuno continental:** panecillos, panes dulces, mermelada, mantequilla y café
un desayuno americano: los huevos revueltos, el bacón (el tocino, el lacón), el pan tostado, la mantequilla, la mermelada, el café

3
1. pido, pide, pedimos
2. servimos, sirve
3. prefiero, prefiere, preferimos

4 *Answers will vary.*

5
1. come
2. lee
3. abre
4. ven
5. vuelve
6. pon
7. di
8. sirve

Go Online!

connectED.mcgraw-hill.com

6 **Categoriza según el deporte.**

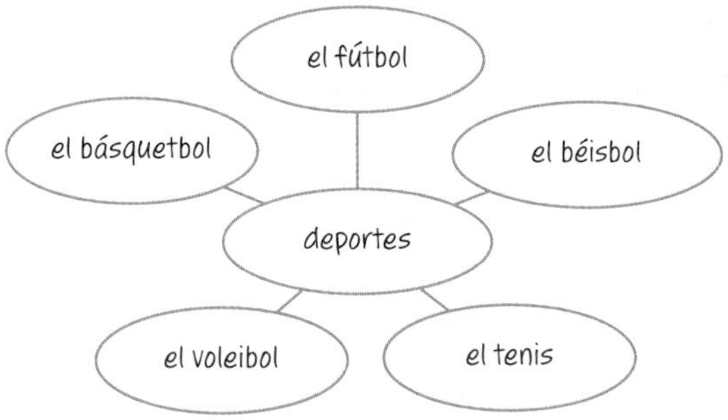

1. Un jugador lanza el balón y quiere que entre en la portería.
2. El portero no pudo bloquear el balón y el balón entró en la portería.
3. Un jugador corre de una base a otra.
4. Para marcar un tanto hay que meter el balón en el cesto.
5. El jugador corre y dribla con el balón.
6. La jugadora atrapa la pelota con el guante.
7. El balón o la pelota tiene que pasar por encima de la red.
8. Podemos jugar dobles o individuales.
9. Los jugadores juegan con un balón.
10. Los jugadores juegan con una pelota.

7 **Usa las siguientes palabras en frases originales.**

el campo la cancha **el balón**
la pelota **el segundo tiempo**
el tanto
lanzar **devolver** marcar

8 **Prepara una lista de lo que tienes que comprar para preparar un plato favorito. Da las cantidades también.**

CULTURA

Un mercado en Tepoztlán, México

Repaso cumulativo

Activity 3 This activity reviews stem-changing verbs.

Activity 4 This activity reviews vocabulary related to holidays.

Activity 5 This activity reviews familiar commands.

Activity 6 This activity reviews vocabulary related to sports.

Activity 7 This activity reviews vocabulary related to sports.

Activity 8 This activity reviews vocabulary related to food.

Go Online!

You may wish to remind students to go online for additional cumulative review.

The **¡Así se dice!** Audio Program for Chapter 10 has twenty-one activities, which afford students extensive listening and speaking practice.

Pre-AP To give students further open-ended oral and written practice, or to assess proficiency, go to AP Proficiency Practice AP23.

Answers

6

1. el fútbol
2. el fútbol
3. el béisbol
4. el básquetbol
5. el básquetbol
6. el béisbol
7. el voleibol y el tenis
8. el tenis
9. el fútbol, el voleibol, el básquetbol
10. el béisbol

7 *Answers will vary.*

8 *Answers will vary.*

Chapter Overview
¡Cuídate bien!
Scope and Sequence

Topics
- Parts of the body
- Exercise and physical activity
- Minor medical problems
- The emergency room

Culture
- Hospitals in the Spanish-speaking world
- Physical activity and good health
- *Doctors Without Borders*

Functions
- How to identify more parts of the body
- How to talk about exercise
- How to talk about having a minor accident and a trip to the emergency room
- How to discuss physical fitness

Structure
- The subjunctive with impersonal expressions
- **Ojalá, quizás, tal vez**
- The subjunctive of stem-changing verbs
- The comparison of like things

RubberBall Productions/Getty Images

Planning Guide

	required	recommended	optional
Vocabulario 1 Más partes del cuerpo	✓		
Vocabulario 2 Unos accidentes En la sala de emergencia	✓		
Gramática El subjuntivo con expresiones impersonales **¡Ojalá! ¡Quizás! ¡Tal vez!** El subjuntivo de los verbos de cambio radical Comparación de igualdad	✓		
Conversación Un accidente		✓	
Lectura cultural Vida activa y buena salud		✓	
Lectura Un poco más *Médicos Sin Fronteras*			✓
Prepárate para el examen			✓
Repaso cumulativo			✓

Correlations to ACTFL World-Readiness Standards for Learning Languages

Page numbers in light print refer to the Student Edition.
Page numbers in bold print refer to the Teacher Edition.

COMMUNICATION Communicate effectively in more than one language in order to function in a variety of situations and for multiple purposes		
Interpersonal Communication	Learners interact and negotiate meaning in spoken, signed, or written conversations to share information, reactions, feelings, and opinions.	pp. **324C, 324D, 326–327, 329, 330,** 331, **335,** 337, 338, 341, 350
Interpretive Communication	Learners understand, interpret, and analyze what is heard, read, or viewed on a variety of topics.	pp. **328,** 330, **330, 331, 332,** 334, 335, **335,** 336, **337,** 338, **341, 342,** 343, **344,** 346, **346,** 347, 349, **349,** 354, **355**
Presentational Communication	Learners present information, concepts, and ideas to inform, explain, persuade, and narrate on a variety of topics using appropriate media and adapting to various audiences of listeners, readers, or viewers.	pp. **324C, 324D, 328, 329, 332, 333,** 337, **337,** 343, **343, 344, 348,** 350, 351, **352, 353**
CULTURES Interact with cultural competence and understanding		
Relating Cultural Practices to Perspectives	Learners use the language to investigate, explain, and reflect on the relationship between the practices and perspectives of the cultures studied.	pp. **324D,** 326–327, **326–327, 335,** 343, 344, 344–345, 345, 351
Relating Cultural Products to Perspectives	Learners use the language to investigate, explain, and reflect on the relationship between the products and perspectives of the cultures studied.	pp. **324D,** 336, 341, 344, 344–345, 345, 346, 347, 349
CONNECTIONS Connect with other disciplines and acquire information and diverse perspectives in order to use the language to function in academic and career-related situations		
Making Connections	Learners build, reinforce, and expand their knowledge of other disciplines while using the language to develop critical thinking and to solve problems creatively.	pp. **324C, 324D,** 330, 340, 343, **343, 346, 355**
Acquiring Information and Diverse Perspectives	Learners access and evaluate information and diverse perspectives that are available through the language and its cultures.	pp. 332, 333, **333,** 334, 340, **340,** 341, **341,** 343, **343**
COMPARISONS Develop insight into the nature of language and culture in order to interact with cultural competence		
Language Comparisons	Learners use the language to investigate, explain, and reflect on the nature of language through comparisons of the language studied and their own.	pp. 333, **351, 352,** 353
Cultural Comparisons	Learners use the language to investigate, explain, and reflect on the concept of culture through comparisons of the cultures studied and their own.	pp. **324D,** 325, **325, 326,** 344–345
COMMUNITIES Communicate and interact with cultural competence in order to participate in multilingual communities at home and around the world		
School and Global Communities	Learners use the language both within and beyond the classroom to interact and collaborate in their community and the globalized world.	pp. **324C,** 334, 337, **337, 348, 350,** 351, **352**
Lifelong Learning	Learners set goals and reflect on their progress in using languages for enjoyment, enrichment, and advancement.	pp. 332, **333,** 340, **340,** 343, **343**

Chapter Project

Un programa de entrevistas (Un talkshow)

Students will work in groups to plan and perform a talk show based on healthy living or other health-related issues.

1. Each group should pick a name for its show and choose a theme or topic to discuss. The group will then assign each member a role, as **el/la presentador(a)/conductor(a)** *(host)*, **los invitados** *(guests)*, **los expertos** *(experts)*, or **miembros del auditorio/del público** *(audience members)*.
2. Students will work together to create an outline of their show and to develop a draft of the show's script. You may wish to establish a minimum number of lines that each group member must have. Then, each member should submit a draft of his or her part to be checked or peer edited and revised accordingly. Corrected drafts should be turned in on the day of the group's performance.
3. Each group should include all members in the discussion and should incorporate several props or visual aids related to the topic of the show. In addition to the interviews between the host and the guests and experts, each program should close with a question-and-answer session in which audience members participate. To add an element of improvisation and to check for comprehension, ask additional follow-up questions or have classmates who are not in the group do so.
4. You may wish to give students a minimum and/or maximum time for each show so that performances can be completed within a few class periods. Encourage students to have fun and be creative with this project, since talk shows are often full of excitement and sometimes controversial.

Scoring Rubric for Project

	5	3	1
Evidence of planning	Corrected draft of script is provided.	Draft of script is provided but is not corrected.	Draft of script is not provided.
Use of props or visual aides	Talk show contains several props or visual aids.	Talk show contains few props or visual aids.	Talk show contains no props or visual aids.
Presentation	Talk show contains all the required elements.	Talk show contains some of the required elements.	Talk show contains few of the required elements.

BananaStock/PictureQuest

Culture

Recipe

GUACAMOLE

Ingredients:
2 medium, ripe avocados
1 small onion, finely chopped
1 clove garlic, minced
1 tomato, chopped
2 tablespoons lime juice

Peel and mash avocados with a fork in a medium bowl. Stir in onion, garlic, tomato, and lime juice. Salt and pepper to taste. Chill for 30 minutes before serving. Can be served with tortilla chips as a dip or as a garnish for other dishes.

¿Caminar o conducir?

In this chapter, students will talk about exercise and fitness activities that can contribute to a healthy lifestyle. While the desire to be fit and healthy is equally evident in the United States and Spanish-speaking countries, getting exercise may be less of a challenge for those who live in Spain and Latin America. In Spain and Latin America, people walk more than we do in the United States, not for recreational or fitness purposes, but as a means of transportation. Because businesses are in close proximity to residences in Hispanic cities, people do not drive to shop and do errands—they walk or ride bikes. Even in the country, it is not unheard of to walk miles to the market or even a friend's home. Ask students to compare how things are done in the United States. How often do they walk instead of going by car? For one week have students keep track of how often they use a vehicle. Then have them try to reduce that frequency the following week by walking or biking more. Students can share this project with other appropriate classes.

Connection to Fine Art

Have students look online or in an art text to find *Hospital visit* by Manuel Jiménez Prieto. Ask students to identify elements of the painting in Spanish. They could recycle vocabulary from Level 1, Chapter 6, **El bienestar**, to explain what might be the matter with the patients. Then using this chapter's vocabulary they can expand by telling what healthy habits can help prevent hospital visits.

50-Minute Lesson Plans

	Objective	Present	Practice	Assess/Homework
Day 1	Identify more parts of the body and talk about exercise	Chapter Opener (5 min.) Introducción al tema (10 min.) Core Instruction/Vocabulario 1 (20 min.)	Activities 1–4 (15 min.)	Student Workbook Activities A–D **ConnectEd** Vocabulary Practice
Day 2	Identify more parts of the body and talk about exercise	Quick Start (5 min.) Review Vocabulario 1 (10 min.)	Activities 5–8 (15 min.) Total Physical Response (5 min.) Audio Activities A–D (15 min.)	Student Workbook Activities E–G **ConnectEd** Vocabulary Practice
Day 3	Talk about having a minor accident and a trip to the emergency room	Core Instruction/Vocabulario 2 (20 min.) Video, Vocabulario en vivo (10 min.)	Activities 1–3 (10 min.)	Quiz 1 (10 min.) Student Workbook Activities A–C **ConnectEd** Vocabulary Practice
Day 4	Talk about having a minor accident and a trip to the emergency room	Quick Start (5 min.) Review Vocabulario 2 (10 min.)	Activities 4–6 (10 min.) Total Physical Response (5 min.) InfoGap (5 min.) Audio Activities E–H (15 min.)	Student Workbook Activities D–F **ConnectEd** Vocabulary Practice
Day 5	The subjunctive with impersonal expressions	Quick Start (5 min.) Core Instruction/Gramática, El subjuntivo con expresiones impersonales (10 min.)	Activities 1–6 (15 min.) Audio Activities A–C (10 min.)	Quiz 2 (10 min.) Student Workbook Activities A–E **ConnectEd** Grammar Practice
Day 6	**Ojalá, quizás, tal vez** The comparison of like things	Quick Start (5 min.) Core Instruction/Gramática, **¡Ojalá! ¡Quizás! ¡Tal vez!** (5 min.) Core Instruction/Gramática, Comparación de igualdad (5 min.)	Activities 7–9 (10 min.) Activity 15 (5 min.) Audio Activities D–H (10 min.)	Quiz 3 (10 min.) Activities 13–14 Student Workbook Activities A–C Student Workbook Activities A–C **ConnectEd** Grammar Practice
Day 7	The subjunctive of stem-changing verbs	Core Instruction/Gramática, El subjuntivo de los verbos de cambio radical (10 min.) Video, Gramática en vivo (10 min.)	Activities 10–12 (10 min.)	Quizzes 4 and 6 (20 min.) Student Workbook Activities A–C **ConnectEd** Grammar Practice
Day 8	Develop reading and listening comprehension skills	Quick Start (5 min.) Core Instruction/Conversación (15 min.) Video, Diálogo en vivo (10 min.)	¿Comprendes? A–B (10 min.)	Quiz 5 (10 min.) ¿Comprendes? C **ConnectEd** Conversation
Day 9	Discuss physical fitness	Core Instruction/Lectura cultural (20 min.)	¿Comprendes? A–C (15 min.)	Listening Comprehension Test (15 min.) **ConnectEd** Reading Practice
Day 10	Develop reading comprehension skills	Core Instruction/Lectura Un poco más (15 min.)	¿Comprendes? (10 min.) Prepárate para el examen (25 min.)	Prepárate para el examen, Practice for written proficiency **ConnectEd** Reading Practice
Day 11	Chapter review	Repaso del Capítulo 11 (15 min.)	Prepárate para el examen, Practice for oral proficiency (20 min.)	Test for Writing Proficiency (15 min.) Review for chapter test
Day 12	Chapter 11 Tests (50 min.) Reading and Writing Test Speaking Test		Test for Oral Proficiency Test for Reading Comprehension	

90-Minute Lesson Plans

	Objective	Present	Practice	Assess/Homework
Block 1	Identify more parts of the body and talk about exercise	Chapter Opener (5 min.) Introducción al tema (10 min.) Quick Start (5 min.) Core Instruction/Vocabulario 1 (20 min.)	Activities 1–8 (20 min.) Total Physical Response (10 min.) Audio Activities A–D (20 min.)	Student Workbook Activities A–G **ConnectEd** Vocabulary Practice
Block 2	Talk about having a minor accident and a trip to the emergency room	Quick Start (5 min.) Core Instruction/Vocabulario 2 (20 min.) Video, Vocabulario en vivo (10 min.)	Activities 1–6 (20 min.) Total Physical Response (5 min.) InfoGap (5 min.) Audio Activities E–H (15 min.)	Quiz 1 (10 min.) Student Workbook Activities A–F **ConnectEd** Vocabulary Practice
Block 3	The subjunctive with impersonal expressions **Ojalá, quizás, tal vez**	Quick Start (5 min.) Core Instruction/Gramática, El subjuntivo con expresiones impersonales (10 min.) Quick Start (5 min.) Core Instruction/Gramática, **¡Ojalá! ¡Quizás! ¡Tal vez!** (10 min.)	Activities 1–6 (20 min.) Activities 7–9 (10 min.) Audio Activities A–F (20 min.)	Quiz 2 (10 min.) Student Workbook Activities A–E Student Workbook Activities A–C **ConnectEd** Grammar Practice
Block 4	The subjunctive of stem-changing verbs The comparison of like things	Core Instruction/Gramática, El subjuntivo de los verbos de cambio radical (10 min.) Video, Gramática en vivo (10 min.) Core Instruction/Gramática, Comparación de igualdad (10 min.)	Activities 10–12 (10 min.) Activities 13–15 (15 min.) Audio Activities G–H (15 min.)	Quizzes 3–4 (20 min.) Student Workbook Activities A–C Student Workbook Activities A–C **ConnectEd** Grammar Practice
Block 5	Discuss physical fitness	Quick Start (5 min.) Core Instruction/Conversación (15 min.) Video, Diálogo en vivo (10 min.) Core Instruction/Lectura cultural (20 min.)	¿Comprendes? A–C (10 min.) ¿Comprendes? A–C (10 min.)	Quizzes 5–6 (20 min.) Prepárate para el examen, Practice for written proficiency **ConnectEd** Conversation, Reading Practice
Block 6	Develop reading comprehension skills	Core Instruction/Lectura Un poco más (15 min.)	¿Comprendes? (10 min.) Prepárate para el examen (25 min.) Prepárate para el examen, Practice for oral proficiency (25 min.)	Listening Comprehension Test (15 min.) Review for chapter test **ConnectEd** Reading Practice
Block 7	Chapter 11 Tests (50 min.) Reading and Writing Test Speaking Test Test for Oral Proficiency Test for Writing Proficiency Test for Reading Comprehension Chapter Project(40 min.)			

Preview

In this chapter, students will discuss some exercises and other physical activities to stay in shape. They will also learn some vocabulary they may need to discuss and get emergency medical attention in the event of an accident. Students will also learn some more uses of the subjunctive.

Pacing

It is important to note that once you reach **¡Bravo!** in the chapter, there is no more new material for students to learn. The rest of the chapter recycles what has already been covered. The suggested pacing listed here leaves two to three days for review, assessment, and enrichment activities such as the chapter project.

Vocabulario 1	1–2 days
Vocabulario 2	1–2 days
Gramática	2–3 days
Conversación	1 day
Lectura cultural	1 day
Lectura Un poco más	1 day

CAPÍTULO 11

¡Cuídate bien!

 Go Online! connectED.mcgraw-hill.com Audio Video Práctica Repaso Diversiones eScape ePals

Go Online!

Audio
Listen to spoken Spanish.

Video
Watch and learn about the Spanish-speaking world.

Práctica
Practice your skills.

Repaso
Review what you've learned.

Diversiones
Go beyond the classroom.

eScape
Read about current events in the Spanish-speaking world.

Aquí y Allí

Vamos a comparar Hoy en día todos quieren cuidarse bien y mantenerse en forma. No importa que sea aquí en Estados Unidos o en España o Latinoamérica—todos van a un parque o gimnasio para hacer ejercicios. Pero, a veces, ¿qué tenemos? ¡Un accidente pequeño!

Objetivos

You will:

- identify more parts of the body
- talk about exercise
- talk about having a minor accident and a trip to the emergency room
- discuss physical fitness

You will use:

- the subjunctive with impersonal expressions
- **ojalá, quizás, tal vez**
- the subjunctive of stem-changing verbs
- the comparison of like things

◀ Todos sabemos que es necesario que nos mantengamos en forma. Estos jóvenes lo saben también y aquí los vemos haciendo jogging en Santa Cruz de Tenerife. El jogging es un ejercicio bueno.

SPOTLIGHT ON CULTURE

Cultural Comparison In the United States, there is significant interest in health and well-being. Students will learn that many people in Spain and Latin America are equally interested in physical activities and keeping in shape. Just as in towns and cities across the United States, there are marathons in the cities of Spain and Latin America, the proceeds of which often benefit a particular health cause or concern.

Cultural Snapshot
Jogging has become a very important form of exercise in both Spain and Latin America. Most cities have parks with pathways for walking and jogging. Note too that people of all ages have become more aware about staying in shape.

Interactive Whiteboard
Present or practice with interactive whiteboard activities.

Assessment
Check student progress.

ePals
Connect with Spanish-speaking students around the world.

PRESENT

Introduce the theme of the chapter by having students look at the photographs on these pages. Have them look at the people and determine if there is anything they see them doing that is the same or different from what they do with their own friends. Once you have completed the vocabulary presentation, have students return to these pages and read the information that accompanies each photograph. Once students are fully acquainted with the vocabulary and grammar of the chapter you may wish to come back to these pages and ask the questions that go with each photo.

Cultural Snapshot

Argentina ¿Por qué toma mucha gente agua mineral?

Chile ¿Anda el joven en bici o en moto? ¿Por dónde anda? ¿Qué lleva? ¿Por qué lo lleva?

Venezuela ¿Es necesario que tomes en cuenta la altitud si decides hacer una caminata por los Andes? ¿Por qué? ¿Hay más o menos oxígeno en el aire?

Introducción al tema

¡Cuídate bien!

Mira estas fotos para familiarizarte con el tema de este capítulo—cuídate bien. ¿Qué haces para cuidarte? ¿Hay algunas actividades que ves aquí que tú también practicas o que te gustan? Y, ¿puedes simpatizar con la joven argentina que ha tenido un accidente?

España

Estos corredores están participando en un maratón en Santa Cruz de Tenerife. En un maratón hay participantes de todas las edades—los mayores y los menores.

Argentina

Mucha gente toma agua mineral porque la consideran buena para la salud.

Chile

El joven anda en bici por las montañas. Nota que él también lleva casco. La seguridad siempre es importante, ¿no?

Venezuela

Estos andinistas pasan un día agradable haciendo una caminata por las montañas en la región de Mérida, Venezuela.

Go Online!
connectED.mcgraw-hill.com

España

Este joven está divirtiéndose andando en monopatín en una calle cerca de las famosas Ramblas de Barcelona.

México

Un hospital privado en Oaxaca, México

Argentina

Siempre es necesario tener cuidado cuando haces ejercicios para evitar tener un accidente como tuvo esta joven en Trelew, Argentina. Acaba de salir de un centro médico y tiene que andar a muletas. ¡Ojalá que se mejore pronto!

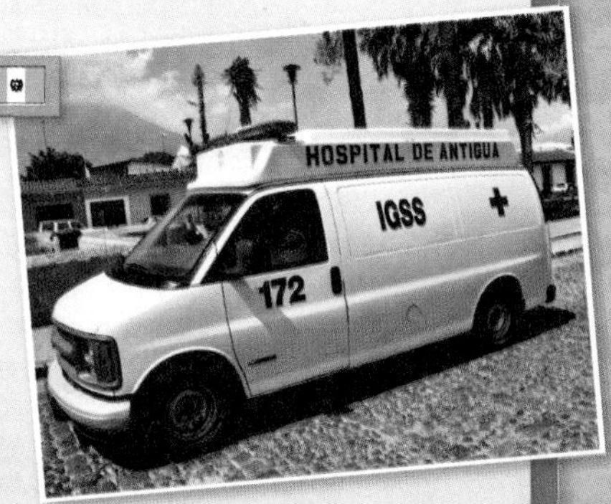

Guatemala

Una ambulancia en Antigua, Guatemala

Argentina

Aquí hay un anuncio en Buenos Aires. ¿Cuál es el significado del juego de palabras? Para ayudarte en la solución te damos una pista: la lengua está en la boca y la lengüeta está en el zapato.

(t)Daniel Salsgiver, (bcr)Lori Ernfridsson, (others)Andrew Payti

Introducción al tema

España Este joven, ¿está haciendo el monopatín o está andando en bici? ¿Se puede alquilar estas bicis que se ven en la foto? ¿Es necesario siempre devolverlo al mismo sitio? Si has dicho que no, tienes razón.

Argentina Trelew is a small town in the Patagonia founded by Welsh settlers. The area is famous for raising sheep.

Argentina En este anuncio, ¿por qué lleva acento escrito el verbo «corré»?

Online Resources

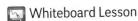

Customizable Lesson Plans
- Whiteboard Lesson
- Audio Activities
- Student Workbook
- Enrichment
- Quizzes

Quick Start

Use QS 11.1 or write the following on the board.
Write a list in Spanish of the parts of the body.

TEACH

Core Instruction

Step 1 As you teach these parts of the body you may wish to have students point to themselves.

Step 2 If the pronunciation of the class is quite good, students do not have to repeat the sentences after you. Have them read them aloud or silently and intersperse the presentation with questions such as **¿Qué están practicando los amigos? Cuando practican yoga, ¿qué tipo de ejercicios hacen? ¿Cómo son los movimientos? ¿Qué efecto tienen estos ejercicios?**

Differentiation

Multiple Intelligences

You can have **bodily-kinesthetic** learners dramatize the meaning of many of the expressions in this vocabulary section.

Más partes del cuerpo

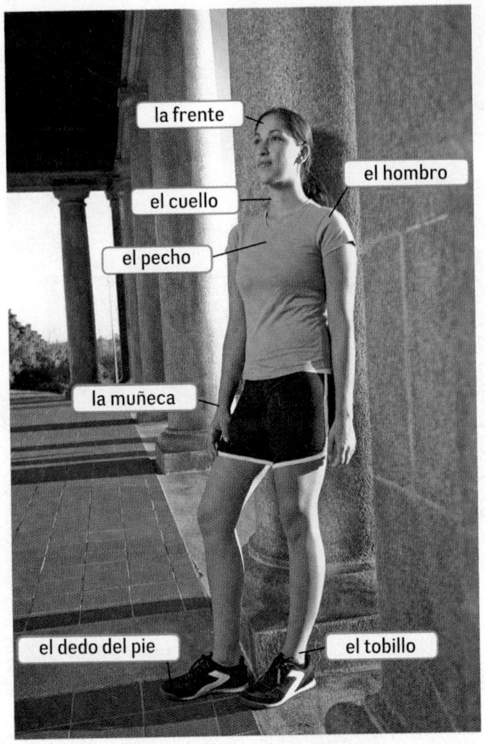

Los amigos están practicando yoga.
Hacen ejercicios de respiración.
Hacen movimientos lentos.
Liberan su espíritu de tensiones.

En el gimnasio

La muchacha está haciendo ejercicios.
El señor anda en bicicleta.
El muchacho levanta pesas.
Es necesario que él tenga cuidado.
Es importante que todos hagamos ejercicios.

Total Physical Response (TPR)

(Student), **ven acá, por favor.**
Vas a hacer unos ejercicios.
Estírate los brazos.
Estírate las piernas.
Levanta una pesa.
Acuéstate en el suelo.
Haz planchas—uno, dos, tres. Muy bien, *(Student)*.

Go Online!

connectED.mcgraw-hill.com

Las jóvenes están patinando en línea.
Es importante que lleven casco y rodilleras.

Los corredores participan en un maratón.

Están corriendo una carrera de relevos.
Cada corredora corre una vuelta.

Es una carrera a campo traviesa.
Una carrera a campo traviesa es de larga distancia.

Vocabulario 1

Tips for Success

You may wish to reinforce the pronunciation and spelling of the sounds **rr** and **r** using words from this section: **rodilleras, corredores, corriendo, carrera, relevos, maratón, espíritu, respiración.**

Comunicación

Interpersonal
Have students sit in groups and discuss which of these activities interest them.

Presentational
Have students create a chart or schedule showing their exercise regimen. Then have them present it to the class, explaining where, when, and how they stay fit.

Go Online!

You may wish to use the whiteboard presentation for additional vocabulary instruction and practice.

Total Physical Response (TPR)

(Student), **ven acá, por favor.**
Vas a indicar que estás haciendo lo siguiente.
Estás poniéndote el casco.
Estás poniéndote las rodilleras.
Estás haciendo el monopatín.
Ahora estás quitándote las rodilleras.
Estás haciendo jogging.
Y ahora, estás corriendo.
Gracias, *(Student).*

Leveling EACH Activity

Easy Activities 1, 2, 4
Average Activities 3, 5, 7
CHallenging Activities 6, 8

PRACTICE

Activity 1

Audio Script

1. Están en el gimnasio.
2. Están corriendo.
3. Están levantando pesas.
4. Se están estirando.
5. Están haciendo ejercicios de respiración.

Activity 2 This activity can be done as an entire-class activity or you may wish to have students work in pairs.

Activity 3 This activity can be prepared in advance and then gone over in class.

Activity 4 This activity can be done in small groups as a game.

Go Online!

You may wish to remind students to go online for additional vocabulary practice. They can also download audio files of all vocabulary.

Conexiones

La anatomía

La anatomía es el estudio de la estructura del cuerpo de un ser viviente y de sus órganos. Ya sabemos las partes del cuerpo humano pero son aun más importantes los órganos vitales—el corazón, los pulmones, los riñones, el hígado y el páncreas.

ESCUCHAR

1 Escucha las frases. Parea cada frase con la foto que describe.

a.  b.  c. 

ESCUCHAR • HABLAR

2 Personaliza. Da respuestas personales.

1. ¿Haces muchos ejercicios?
2. ¿Haces ejercicios aeróbicos o abdominales?
3. ¿Te estiras los brazos y las piernas?
4. ¿Levantas pesas?
5. ¿Andas en bicicleta?
6. ¿Haces jogging?
7. ¿Participas en carreras?
8. ¿Corres vueltas?
9. ¿Practicas yoga?
10. ¿Has participado en un maratón?

LEER • ESCRIBIR

3 Completa con una palabra apropiada.

1. Uno se pone ____ cuando va al gimnasio o cuando hace jogging.
2. Es importante ponerse ____ para proteger el cráneo al andar en bicicleta.
3. Es importante llevar ____ al patinar en línea.
4. ¿Cuántas ____ puedes correr sin descansar?
5. El yoga ayuda a liberar el espíritu de ____.
6. Muchas ciudades y organizaciones tienen ____ que son carreras de muy larga distancia.
7. Dos tipos de carreras son ____ y ____.

LEER • ESCRIBIR

4 Pon las siguientes partes del cuerpo en orden desde la parte más alta del cuerpo hasta la más baja.

el pecho la mano el dedo del pie
la frente el hombro
el tobillo el cuello la rodilla

Answers

1
1. c
2. a
3. c
4. b
5. b

2
1. Sí, (No, no) hago muchos ejercicios.
2. Hago ejercicios aeróbicos (abdominales).
3. Sí, (No, no) me estiro los brazos y las piernas.
4. Sí, (No, no) levanto pesas.
5. Sí, (No, no) ando en bicicleta.
6. Sí, (No, no) hago jogging.
7. Sí, (No, no) participo en carreras.
8. Sí, (No, no) corro vueltas.
9. Sí, (No, no) practico yoga.
10. Sí, (No, no) he participado en un maratón.

3
1. un buzo
2. un casco
3. rodilleras
4. vueltas
5. tensiones
6. maratones
7. una carrera de relevos, una carrera a campo traviesa (un maratón)

4 *Answers will vary.*

HABLAR

5 Dramatiza. Trabajen en grupos. Escojan a un líder. El líder va a dramatizar un ejercicio o un deporte. Los otros miembros del grupo adivinarán la actividad. Cambien de líder.

HABLAR • ESCRIBIR

6 Usa las siguientes expresiones en frases originales.

hacer ejercicios	patinar en línea	hacer jogging
practicar yoga	correr vueltas	hacer planchas

CULTURA

Equipo para hacer ejercicios en un gimnasio en un hotel en Montelimar, Nicaragua

ESCRIBIR

7 Completa con lo que falta.

1. el cue_o
2. las rodi_eras
3. el tobi_o
4. el _imnasio
5. los _óvenes
6. un bu_o
7. el bra_o

8 *Comunicación*

Trabajen en grupos y discutan las actividades que practican en su clase de educación física. Indiquen las actividades que les gustan y que no les gustan. Expliquen por qué.

Go Online!

connectED.mcgraw-hill.com

Differentiation

Multiple Intelligences

Activity 5 This activity is particularly beneficial for **bodily-kinesthetic** learners.

Activity 6 This activity should be prepared in advance and then gone over in class.

Activity 7 You may also wish to give students a dictation with these words.

Activity 8 Depending upon your preference, you may or may not wish to correct all errors as students speak in this open-ended activity.

Cultural Snapshot

Montelimar is a resort area on the Pacific coast of Nicaragua.

ASSESS

Students are now ready to take Quiz 1.

Answers

5 *Answers will vary.*

6 *Answers will vary.*

7
1. el cuello
2. las rodilleras
3. el tobillo
4. el gimnasio
5. los jóvenes
6. un buzo
7. el brazo

8 *Answers will vary.*

Online Resources

Customizable Lesson Plans

- Whiteboard Lesson
- Audio Activities
- Video (Vocabulario)
- Student Workbook
- Enrichment
- Quizzes

Quick Start

Use QS 11.2 or write the following on the board.

Complete in the present.

1. **Él ___ una pierna quebrada. (tener)**
2. **Le ___ mucho. (doler)**
3. **No ___ andar. (poder)**
4. **___ que usar muletas. (tener)**
5. **¡Qué lástima! ___ jugar fútbol. (querer)**
6. **Y no ___ jugar. (poder)**

TEACH

Core Instruction

You may wish to use some suggestions given in previous vocabulary sections for the presentation of these new words.

Differentiation

Multiple Intelligences

Have **bodily-kinesthetic** learners make up and present little skits about these emergency procedures.

Slower Paced Learners

After the presentation of the new vocabulary show Vocabulary V11.4–V11.5 again. Allow slower paced learners to give isolated words indicating what they see in each illustration.

Unos accidentes

Pilar se cortó el dedo.
Tiene una herida.
Pero no es seria. No se ha hecho mucho daño.

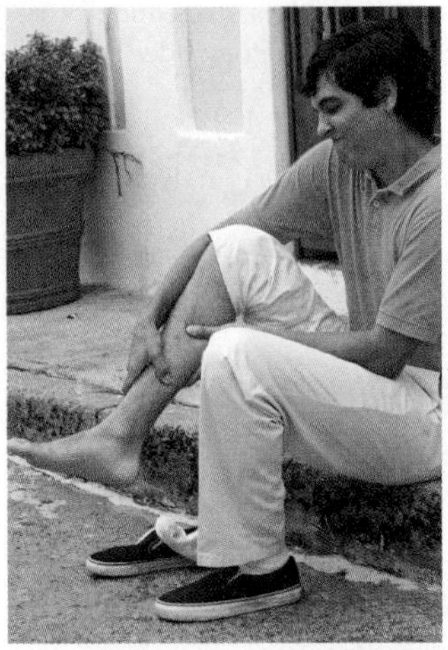

José corría y se torció el tobillo.
El tobillo está hinchado.
Le duele mucho.

El joven se cayó.
¿Se rompió (Se quebró) la pierna?

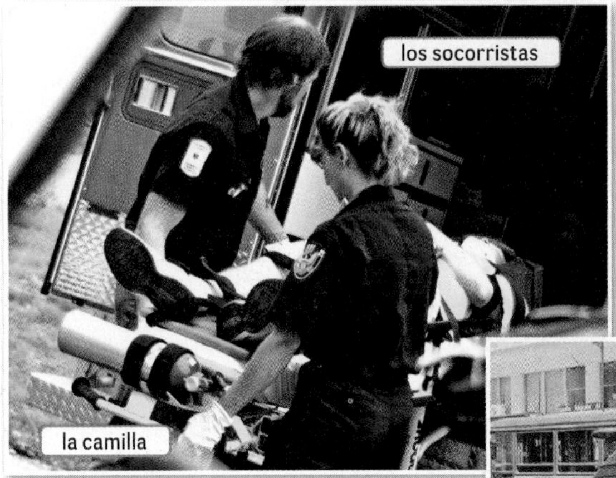

Total Physical Response (TPR)

(Student), **ven acá, por favor.**	*(Do as a group TPR activity.)*
Dramatiza los siguientes accidentes.	**Dramaticen lo siguiente.**
Te cortaste el dedo.	**Me duele el dedo.**
Te torciste el tobillo.	**Me duele el pie.**
Andas con muletas.	**Me duele la cabeza.**
Te duele mucho la muñeca.	**Me duele la garganta.**
Tienes el dedo muy hinchado.	**Me duele el estómago.**

En la sala de emergencia

Go Online!

connectED.mcgraw-hill.com

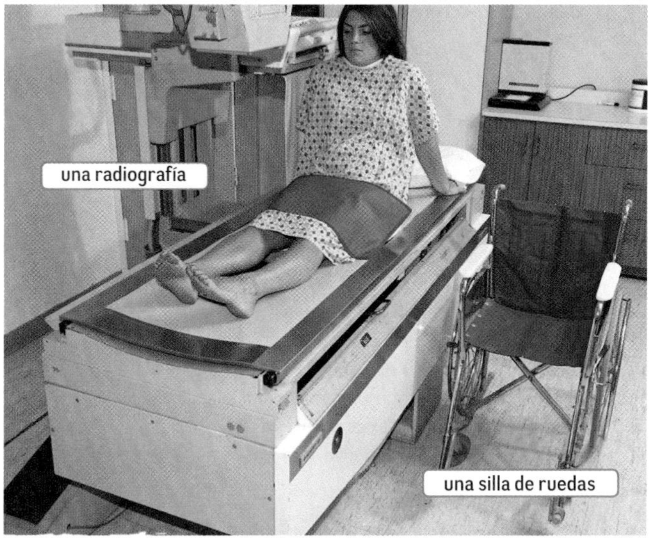

Le toman (hacen) una radiografía.

Nota

In addition to **hacerse daño,** you will hear **lastimarse.** Another term for **radiografía** is **rayos equis.**

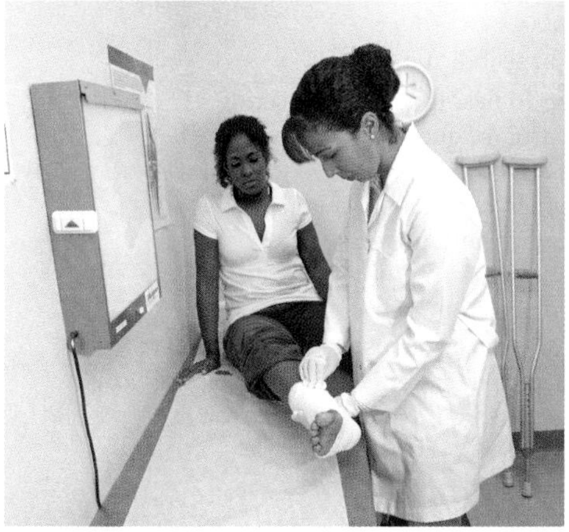

La cirujana ortopédica le ha reducido (acomodado) el hueso.
Le ha puesto la pierna en un yeso.
Paula tendrá que andar con muletas.

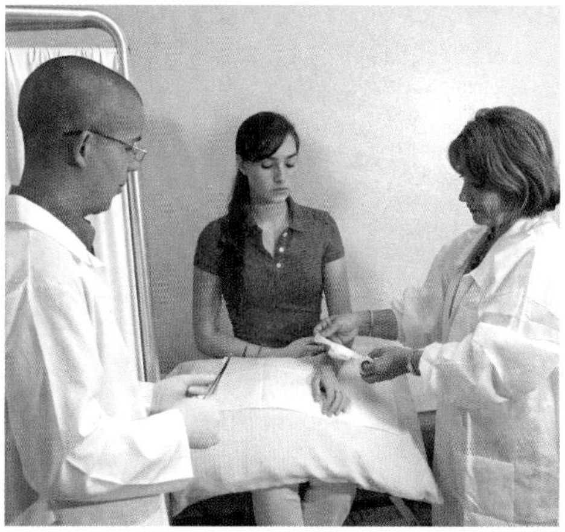

Es necesario que el médico cierre la herida.
El médico pone unos puntos (unas suturas).
La enfermera le va a poner una venda.

David H. Brennan

Differentiation

Advanced Learners

Have advanced learners look at Vocabulary V11.4–V11.5 and make up sentences about what they see.

Tips for Success

- As soon as students are familiar with the new vocabulary, have them read again the captions of the **Introducción al tema.**
- After going over the **Práctica** activities, have students return to the vocabulary presentation pages and make up statements and questions about the photos.

Go Online!

Vocabulario en vivo Watch and listen to Nora as she discusses exercise and staying in shape.

You may wish to use the whiteboard presentation for additional vocabulary instruction and practice.

Leveling EACH Activity

Easy Activities 1, 2, 3
Average Activities 4, 5, Activity 2 **Expansión**, Activity 3 **Expansión**
CHallenging Activity 6

PRACTICE

Activity 1

Audio Script

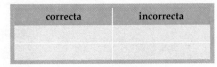

1. Un tobillo torcido se hincha.
2. Si tienes un brazo quebrado tienes que andar con muletas.
3. El cirujano ortopédico le ha puesto la pierna en un yeso porque tiene una fractura.
4. Han puesto al herido en una camilla porque no puede levantarse.
5. Lo han puesto en una silla de ruedas porque no puede sentarse.
6. Le van a suturar porque se cortó el pie.

Activities 2 and 3 These activities should be done orally before they are written.

Cultural Snapshot

This hospital is typical of the many modern, new hospitals throughout Spain.

CULTURA
Un hospital grande y moderno en Barcelona, España

ESCUCHAR

1 Escucha cada frase y decide si la información es correcta o no. Usa una tabla como la de abajo para indicar tus respuestas.

correcta	incorrecta

HABLAR • ESCRIBIR

2 Contesta sobre un accidente que tuvo Mariana.

1. Mariana ha tenido un accidente. ¿Se cayó ella?
2. ¿Se torció el tobillo?
3. ¿Le duele mucho el tobillo?
4. ¿Está hinchado el tobillo?
5. ¿Le duele mucho cuando anda a pie?
6. ¿Tendrá que andar con muletas?
7. ¿Se ha hecho mucho daño o no?

EXPANSIÓN
Ahora, sin mirar las preguntas, cuenta la información en tus propias palabras. Si no recuerdas algo, un(a) compañero(a) te puede ayudar.

ESCUCHAR • HABLAR • ESCRIBIR

3 Contesta según se indica.

1. ¿Qué tuvo Tomás? (un accidente serio)
2. ¿Qué le pasó? (se quebró la pierna)
3. ¿Qué le causó la pierna quebrada? (mucho dolor)
4. ¿Adónde fue? (a la sala de emergencia)
5. ¿Cómo fue? (en ambulancia)
6. ¿Quiénes lo ayudaron? (los socorristas)
7. ¿En qué lo pusieron? (una camilla)
8. ¿Qué le tomaron en el hospital? (radiografías)
9. ¿A qué médico llamaron? (al cirujano ortopédico)
10. Al salir del hospital, ¿qué necesitará Tomás? (una silla de ruedas)

EXPANSIÓN
Ahora, sin mirar las preguntas, cuenta la información en tus propias palabras. Si no recuerdas algo, un(a) compañero(a) te puede ayudar.

Answers

1
1. correcta
2. incorrecta
3. correcta
4. correcta
5. incorrecta
6. correcta

2
1. Sí, se cayó.
2. Sí, se torció el tobillo.
3. Sí, (No, no) le duele mucho el tobillo.
4. Sí (No), el tobillo (no) está hinchado.
5. Sí, (No, no) le duele mucho cuando anda a pie.
6. Sí, (No, no) tendrá que andar con muletas.
7. Sí, (No, no) ha hecho mucho daño.

3
1. Tomás tuvo un accidente serio.
2. Se quebró la pierna.
3. La pierna quebrada le causó mucho dolor.
4. Fue a la sala de emergencia.
5. Fue en ambulancia.
6. Los socorristas lo ayudaron.
7. Lo pusieron en una camilla.
8. Le tomaron radiografías en el hospital.
9. Llamaron al cirujano ortopédico.
10. Al salir del hospital, Tomás necesitará una silla de ruedas.

Go Online!

connectED.mcgraw-hill.com

HABLAR • ESCRIBIR

4 Trabajen en grupos. Describan unas actividades que tienen lugar en esta sala de emergencia.

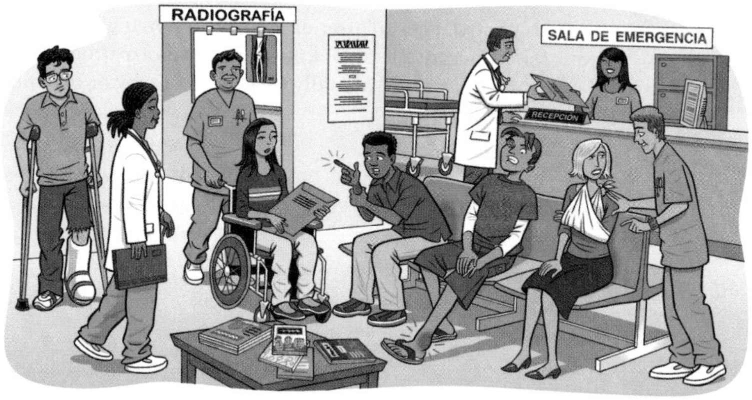

ESCRIBIR

5 Completa con lo que falta.

1. una _erida
2. un tobi_o _inchado
3. el _ospital
4. la cami_a y la si_a de ruedas
5. se ca_ó
6. el _eso
7. el _ueso
8. una _enda

ESCRIBIR

6 Rompecabezas

Pon las palabras en orden para formar frases. Luego, pon las frases en orden para crear una historia.

1. dijo no que le la necesitaba enfermera suturas
2. corrió la de cerca bicicleta perro muy un
3. calle la andaba por en Catalina bicicleta
4. de sala fue la a emergencia
5. rodilla enfermera venda la le en la puso una
6. ella perro a le cayó el se sorprendió y Catalina
7. rodilla cayó cortó se se la cuando

InfoGap For more practice with your new vocabulary, do Activity 11 in the Student Resource section at the end of this book.

Tips for Success

It is important that all students hear the answers to these activities. The answers give them the opportunity to hear their new words in context, thus reinforcing meaning and helping to make the new words an active part of the students' vocabulary.

Activity 4 This activity can be done as a group activity.

Comunicación

Interpersonal

Have students use the illustration that accompanies Activity 4 to make up conversations.

Activity 5 You may also wish to use these words in a dictation.

Cultura

Spain is currently known for its excellent medical services. Its services are reported to have surpassed those of several other countries in the European Union.

Go Online!

You may wish to remind students to go online for additional vocabulary practice. They can also download audio files of all vocabulary.

Answers

4 *Answers will vary.*

5

1. una herida
2. un tobillo hinchado
3. el hospital
4. la camilla y la silla de ruedas
5. se cayó
6. el yeso
7. el hueso
8. una venda

6 *Correct order of sentences:* 3, 2, 6, 7, 4, 1, 5

1. La enfermera le dijo que no necesitaba suturas.
2. Un perro corrió muy cerca de la bicicleta.
3. Catalina andaba en bicicleta por la calle.
4. Fue a la sala de emergencia.
5. La enfermera le puso una venda en la rodilla.
6. El perro le sorprendió a Catalina y ella se cayó.
7. Cuando se cayó se cortó la rodilla.

ASSESS

Students are now ready to take Quiz 2.

Online Resources

- Customizable Lesson Plans
- Whiteboard Lesson
- Audio Activities
- Student Workbook
- Enrichment
- Quizzes

Quick Start

Use QS 11.3 or write the following on the board.

Rewrite with **nosotros.**

1. **Me acuesto.**
2. **Me despierto.**
3. **No quiero.**
4. **Me siento aquí.**
5. **No puedo.**
6. **No vuelvo.**
7. **No pierdo.**

TEACH

Core Instruction

Step 1 As you go over the use of the subjunctive in impersonal expressions, point out that the subjunctive is used because it is not known if the information in the clause will actually take place or not. Indicate to students that the rationale for using the subjunctive with these expressions is the same as the rationale for using the subjunctive after **querer,** which they learned in Chapter 10.

Step 2 Have students read the expressions aloud as well as the example sentences.

PRACTICE

Leveling EACH Activity

Easy Activities 1, 4
Average Activities 2, 3, Activity 4 **Expansión**
CHallenging Activities 5, 6

El subjuntivo con expresiones impersonales

The subjunctive is used after each of the following impersonal expressions because it is not known if the information in the clause that follows will actually take place. It may or may not.

es importante	**es fácil**
es necesario	**es difícil**
es imposible	**es bueno**
es posible	**es probable**
es mejor	**es improbable**

Es probable que él esté bien.
Pero es necesario que vea al médico.
Es importante que sepa lo que tiene.

CULTURA
Papi corre en un maratón con sus dos niños en Tenerife en las islas Canarias. Es posible que ganen, ¿no?

Práctica

ESCUCHAR • HABLAR • ESCRIBIR

1 Sigue el modelo.

MODELO **Tú haces ejercicios. →**
Es necesario que tú hagas ejercicios.

1. Hablas con el entrenador.
2. Vas al gimnasio.
3. Haces jogging.
4. Corres por lo menos cinco vueltas.
5. Participas en el maratón.

HABLAR • ESCRIBIR

2 Prepara una lista de cosas que es probable que tú hagas con frecuencia porque es fácil hacerlas. Prepara otra lista que indica lo que es difícil que tú hagas. Luego compara tus listas con las listas que ha preparado un(a) compañero(a).

LEER • ESCRIBIR

3 Sigue el modelo.

MODELO **es necesario / saber la receta →**
Es necesario que el cocinero sepa la receta.

1. es importante / lavar las ollas
2. es fácil / pelar las papas
3. es probable / freír el pescado
4. es mejor / asar el cordero
5. es posible / servir la comida

CULTURA
¿Es posible que el cocinero esté aprendiendo a cocinar algo en esta escuela culinaria en España?

(t)Andrew Payti, (b)Javier Larrea/age fotostock

Answers

1
1. Es necesario que tú hables con el entrenador.
2. Es necesario que tú vayas al gimnasio.
3. Es necesario que tú hagas jogging.
4. Es necesario que tú corras por lo menos cinco vueltas.
5. Es necesario que tú participes en el maratón.

2 *Answers will vary.*

3
1. Es importante que el cocinero lave las ollas.
2. Es fácil que el cocinero pele las papas.
3. Es probable que el cocinero fría el pescado.
4. Es mejor que el cocinero ase el cordero.
5. Es posible que el cocinero sirva la comida.

Go Online!

connectED.mcgraw-hill.com

HABLAR

4 Contesta.

1. ¿Es importante que los jóvenes de Estados Unidos estudien una lengua?
2. ¿Es necesario que ellos sepan hablar otra lengua?
3. ¿Es bueno que ellos hablen otra lengua?
4. ¿Es necesario que ellos conozcan otra cultura?
5. ¿Es posible que algún día ellos tengan la oportunidad de visitar otros países?
6. ¿Es probable que ellos vayan a otros países?

EXPANSIÓN

Ahora, sin mirar las preguntas, cuenta la información en tus propias palabras. Si no recuerdas algo, un(a) compañero(a) te puede ayudar.

LEER • ESCRIBIR

5 Completa.

Abuelito está un poco nervioso. Es posible que sus nietos __1__ (llegar) mañana por la mañana. Es importante que Abuelito __2__ (saber) cuándo van a llegar. Pero es difícil que Abuelita le __3__ (decir) la hora precisa de la llegada de los nietos. Es posible que mañana __4__ (hacer) mal tiempo. Como los nietos vienen en carro será necesario que __5__ (conducir) despacio y con mucho cuidado si hay nieve. Es mejor que ellos __6__ (llegar) un poco tarde. Abuelito no quiere que ellos __7__ (tener) un accidente. Es mejor que __8__ (llegar) tarde pero sanos y salvos.

6 ***Comunicación***

Trabaja con un(a) compañero(a) de clase. Dile cosas que haces. Tu compañero(a) te dará su opinión sobre las cosas que haces usando las siguientes expresiones: **es importante, es bueno, es necesario, es mejor.**

FOLDABLES Study Organizer

TAB BOOK See the Foldables section of the Student Handbook at the beginning of this book for help with making this foldable. Use this study organizer to help you practice the subjunctive. On the top of each tab, write an expression that requires the subjunctive, for example, **Es imposible que...** Then open each tab and write a sentence using that expression with the subjunctive.

Answers

4

1. Sí, (No, no) es importante que los jóvenes de Estados Unidos estudien una lengua.
2. Sí, (No, no) es necesario que ellos sepan hablar otra lengua.
3. Sí, (No, no) es bueno que ellos hablen otra lengua.
4. Sí, (No, no) es necesario que ellos conozcan otra cultura.
5. Sí, (No, no) es posible que algún día ellos tengan la oportunidad de visitar otros países.
6. Sí, (No, no) es probable que ellos vayan a otros países.

5

1. lleguen
2. sepa
3. diga
4. haga
5. conduzcan
6. lleguen
7. tengan
8. lleguen

6 *Answers will vary.*

Gramática

Activity 1 Have students use the correct intonation as they give the sentence with **es necesario.** The proper intonation can indicate that it is necessary but maybe it won't happen.

Activity 2 After students read their lists, you may wish to expand the activity by having them make up additional sentences such as: ___ **y yo hemos decidido que es difícil que (nosotros) ___.**

Activity 3 This activity can be prepared in advance and then gone over orally in class.

Tips for Success

Have students read the captions that accompany the photographs since they reinforce the grammar point they are learning.

Activity 4 This activity can be done orally in class.

Activity 5 This activity can be prepared before being gone over in class.

Differentiation

Advanced Learners
Slower Paced Learners

Have students make up sentences telling what they think is important, necessary, etc., for others to do. For example: **Es necesario que tú (yo, ustedes)...** After a student gives his or her sentence to the class, he or she will call on classmates to indicate whether or not they agree. Advanced learners will be capable of making up many sentences while slower paced learners will make up just a few. The important point is that all students will be working to capacity.

Online Resources

Customizable Lesson Plans
Whiteboard Lesson
Audio Activities
Student Workbook
Enrichment
Quizzes

Quick Start

Use QS 11.4 or write the following on the board.

Complete in the present.

1. **Ellos siempre ___ más. (pedir)**
2. **El mesero nos ___. (servir)**
3. **Yo no ___ el pescado. (freír)**
4. **Tú ___ la misma cosa. (repetir)**
5. **Yo no ___ más. (seguir)**

TEACH

Core Instruction

Step 1 Read the explanation to the class.

Step 2 Call on students to read the example sentences aloud. This point should be rather easy.

PRACTICE

Leveling EACH Activity

Easy Activities 7, 8, 9
Average-CHallenging Activities 7, 8, 9

Note: Activities 7, 8, and 9 are all Easy for students who are not having difficulty with the subjunctive verb forms. Those students who are still having problems with the verb forms will find them Average–Challenging.

ASSESS

Students are now ready to take Quiz 4.

¡Ojalá! ¡Quizás! ¡Tal vez!

The expression **¡Ojalá!** or **¡Ojalá que!** comes from Arabic and it means *Would that . . .* Since the information that follows **ojalá** may or may not happen, it is followed by the subjunctive. The expressions **¡Quizás!** and **¡Tal vez!** mean *perhaps* or *maybe* and can also be followed by the subjunctive.

¡Ojalá que vengan!
¡Quizás lleguen mañana!
¡Tal vez estén aquí!

CULTURA
¡Quizás te guste tener una golosina! ¿Qué color o sabor prefieres?

Andrew Payti

Práctica

ESCUCHAR • HABLAR

7 Contesta con **quizás** según el modelo.

MODELO **¿Carla lo va a saber? →**
¡Quizás lo sepa!

1. ¿Carla va a estar aquí?
2. ¿Va a ir al parque?
3. ¿Va a participar en la carrera?
4. ¿Va a salir primero?
5. ¿Va a romper un récord?
6. ¿Va a ganar un trofeo?

LEER • ESCRIBIR

8 Sigue el modelo.

MODELO **tener cuidado →**
¡Ojalá que tengan cuidado!

1. prestar atención
2. no tomar una decisión ridícula
3. ponerse el casco
4. llevar rodilleras
5. no tener ningún accidente
6. no ir al hospital

9 ***Comunicación***

Trabajaja con un(a) compañero(a). Los dos van a hablar de eventos que quieren que ocurran durante su vida. Introduzcan sus ideas con **¡ojalá!**

Differentiation

Many activities can serve as diagnostic tools. If students have problems with these activities it indicates they do not know the subjunctive verb forms. If this is the case, it is suggested that you go over the forms again. Slower paced students will need quite a bit more practice.

Answers

7

1. ¡Quizás esté aquí!
2. ¡Quizás vaya al parque!
3. ¡Quizás participe en la carrera!
4. ¡Quizás salga primero!
5. ¡Quizás rompa un récord!
6. ¡Quizás gane un trofeo!

El subjuntivo de los verbos de cambio radical

1. Verbs that have a stem change in the present indicative also have a stem change in the present subjunctive.

E → IE			
cerrar			
yo	cierre	nosotros(as)	cerremos
tú	cierres	*vosotros(as)*	*cerréis*
Ud., él, ella	cierre	Uds., ellos, ellas	cierren

O → UE			
encontrar			
yo	encuentre	nosotros(as)	encontremos
tú	encuentres	*vosotros(as)*	*encontréis*
Ud., él, ella	encuentre	Uds., ellos, ellas	encuentren

2. The verbs **preferir (e → ie), dormir (o → ue),** and **pedir (e → i)** have a stem change in every person of the present subjunctive.

	E → IE, I	O → UE, U	E → I
	preferir	dormir	pedir
yo	prefiera	duerma	pida
tú	prefieras	duermas	pidas
Ud., él, ella	prefiera	duerma	pida
nosotros(as)	prefiramos	durmamos	pidamos
vosotros(as)	*prefiráis*	*durmáis*	*pidáis*
Uds., ellos, ellas	prefieran	duerman	pidan

HABLAR • ESCRIBIR

10 Contesta.

1. ¿Dónde quieres que yo me siente?
2. ¿Es importante que yo no pierda el juego?
3. ¿Quieres que yo vuelva temprano?
4. ¿Es posible que yo duerma aquí?
5. ¿Es necesario que yo se lo repita?

Go Online!

connectED.mcgraw-hill.com

Nota

- Other verbs with the **e → ie** stem change like **cerrar** are: **perder, sentarse, comenzar, empezar, pensar.**
- Other **o → ue** verbs like **encontrar** are: **acostarse, recordar, poder, volver.**
- **Sentir** is conjugated like **preferir.**
- Other verbs with the **e → i** stem change like **pedir** are: **repetir, freír, seguir, servir.**

Según los jóvenes, es importante que todos sigamos una dieta sana.

Olive/age fotostock

Gramática

Online Resources

Customizable Lesson Plans
Whiteboard Lesson
Audio Activities
Video (Gramática)
Student Workbook
Enrichment
Quizzes

TEACH

Core Instruction

Step 1 Have students repeat the forms of the verbs as you write them on the board.

Step 2 Remind students that if they pronounce the forms correctly, they will have no problem spelling them.

Differentiation

Students with Auditory Impairments

Tell students to pay very close attention to the difference in sound between: **ie** and **e; ue** and **u; ie** and **ue; i** and **u.**

PRACTICE

Leveling EACH Activity

Average Activities 10, 11, 12

Activity 10 It is suggested that you go over this activity orally in class. Then have students write the activity.

Go Online!

You may wish to use the whiteboard presentation for additional grammar instruction practice.

Answers

8

1. ¡Ojalá que presten atención!
2. ¡Ojalá que no tomen una decisión ridícula!
3. ¡Ojalá que se pongan el casco!
4. ¡Ojalá que lleven rodilleras!
5. ¡Ojalá que no tengan ningún accidente!
6. ¡Ojalá que no vayan al hospital!

9 *Answers will vary.*

10 *Answers will vary but may include:*

1. Yo quiero que tú te sientes ___.
2. Sí, (No, no) es importante que tú no pierdas el juego.
3. Sí, (No, no) quiero que tú vuelvas temprano.
4. Sí, (No, no) es posible que tú duermas aquí.
5. Sí, (No, no) es necesario que tú se lo repitas.

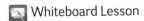

Online Resources

Customizable Lesson Plans
- Whiteboard Lesson
- Audio Activities
- Video (Gramática)
- Student Workbook
- Enrichment
- Quizzes

PRACTICE *(continued)*

Activities 11 and 12 These activities can be gone over orally in class with or without previous presentation.

ASSESS

Students are now ready to take Quiz 5.

TEACH

Core Instruction

Step 1 Lead students through the explanation.

Step 2 Have them repeat all the example sentences after you.

Conexiones

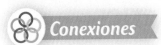

Point out to students some problems non-English speakers have when learning English. They have great difficulty contrasting *as many as* and *as much as*. They are told to think of "count nouns," nouns that can have a numeral before them (like *dollars*), and "noncount nouns," words that cannot be preceded by a numeral (like *money*). You use *as many as* with "count nouns," for example, *She has as many dollars as I have*. You use *as much as* with "noncount nouns"—*She has as much money as I have*. It sounds easy but it's not easy for many non-English speakers.

Práctica

LEER • ESCRIBIR

11 Sigue el modelo.

MODELO **Quiere que tú lo cierres. →**
Quiere que nosotros lo cerremos.

1. Quiere que te sientes aquí.
2. Quiere que tú pierdas.
3. Quiere que tú lo encuentres.
4. Quiere que tú vuelvas pronto.
5. Quiere que duermas aquí.
6. Quiere que lo pidas.
7. Quiere que lo sigas.
8. Quiere que tú no lo repitas.

HABLAR • LEER • ESCRIBIR

12 Cambia el segundo verbo al verbo indicado.

1. Yo quiero que ellos lo cierren. (empezar, perder, encontrar, recordar, devolver, preferir, pedir, repetir)
2. Es posible que yo lo encuentre. (cerrar, perder, recordar, devolver, servir, pedir, repetir)
3. Es necesario que nosotros volvamos. (comenzar, sentarnos, recordar, dormir, seguir)

Comparación de igualdad

1. In Spanish you use **tanto... como** to compare quantities. Because **tanto** is an adjective, it has to agree with the noun it modifies.

   Elena tiene tanta energía como yo.
   Pero ella no tiene tantos accidentes como yo.

2. In Spanish you use **tan... como** to compare qualities with either an adjective or adverb.

   Él está tan enfermo como su amiga.
   Él se va a curar tan rápido como ella.

3. The subject pronoun always follows the comparison of equality.

   Él es tan bueno como tú.
   Y tiene tanto dinero como yo.

Conexiones

El inglés
To compare equal quantities in English you use:
as much money as I
as many problems as I
To compare equal qualities you use:
as smart as she
as tall as he

Go Online!

Gramática en vivo: *Introduction to the subjunctive* Enliven learning with the animated world of Professor Cruz! **Gramática en vivo** is a fun and effective tool for additional instruction and/or review.

Answers

11
1. Quiere que nosotros nos sentemos aquí.
2. Quiere que nosotros perdamos.
3. Quiere que nosotros lo encontremos.
4. Quiere que nosotros volvamos pronto.
5. Quiere que nosotros durmamos aquí.
6. Quiere que nosotros lo pidamos.
7. Quiere que nosotros lo sigamos.
8. Quiere que nosotros no lo repitamos.

Práctica

HABLAR

13 Personaliza. Da respuestas personales.

1. ¿Eres tan inteligente como tus amigos?
2. ¿Eres tan cómico(a) como tus amigos?
3. ¿Eres tan ambicioso(a) como tus amigos?
4. ¿Eres tan aficionado(a) a los deportes como tus amigos?
5. ¿Tienes tanta paciencia como tus amigos?
6. ¿Tienes tanto éxito como tus amigos?
7. ¿Tienes tanto trabajo como tus amigos?
8. ¿Tienes tantas ambiciones como tus amigos?

LEER • ESCRIBIR

14 Completa con **tan... o tanto... como**.

1. Ella corre en _____ carreras _____ yo.
2. Y ella va _____ rápido _____ yo.
3. Él puede levantar _____ pesas _____ yo.
4. Pero él no es _____ fuerte _____ yo.
5. Yo no hago _____ ejercicios _____ tú.
6. Yo no soy _____ aficionado(a) a los ejercicios físicos _____ tú.

CULTURA

Un grupo de gente mayor (de la tercera edad) está jugando voleibol en un gimnasio en Oaxaca, México.

15 *Comunicación*

Trabaja con un(a) compañero(a). Piensen en algunas personas que ustedes conocen que, en su opinión, tienen mucho en común o que tienen las mismas características físicas. Comparen a estas personas.

Go Online!

connectED.mcgraw-hill.com

Refrán

Can you guess what the following proverb means?

La mejor almohada es la conciencia sana.

¡Bravo!

You have now learned all the new vocabulary and grammar in this chapter. Continue to use and practice all that you know while learning more cultural information. **¡Vamos!**

Gramática

Leveling EACH Activity

Easy Activity 13
Average Activity 14
CHallenging Activity 15

PRACTICE

Activity 13 You may wish to have students write the answers.

Activity 14 This activity may be done with or without prior preparation.

Cultural Snapshot

This volleyball group gets together several days a week. All team members are over 55 years old.

Refrán

Have students recite the proverb aloud. Then see if they can figure out its meaning, and encourage them to try to give an equivalent expression in English such as "A clean conscience is a good pillow." Students may be able to think of expressions related to the same theme.

Answers

12

1. Yo quiero que ellos lo empiecen (pierdan, encuentren, recuerden, devuelvan, prefieran, pidan, repitan).
2. Es posible que yo lo cierre (pierda, recuerde, devuelva, sirva, pida, repita).
3. Es necesario que nosotros comencemos (nos sentemos, recordemos, durmamos, sigamos).

13

1. Sí, (No, no) soy tan inteligente como mis amigos.
2. Sí, (No, no) soy tan cómico(a) como mis amigos.
3. Sí, (No, no) soy tan ambicioso(a) como mis amigos.
4. Sí, (No, no) soy tan aficionado(a) a los deportes como mis amigos.
5. Sí, (No, no) tengo tanta paciencia como mis amigos.
6. Sí, (No, no) tengo tanto éxito como mis amigos.
7. Sí, (No, no) tengo tanto trabajo como mis amigos.
8. Sí, (No, no) tengo tantas ambiciones como mis amigos.

14

1. tantas, como
2. tan, como
3. tantas, como
4. tan, como
5. tantos, como
6. tan, como

15 *Answers will vary.*

Online Resources

Customizable Lesson Plans
- Audio Activities
- Video (Diálogo)
- Student Workbook

Quick Start

Use QS 11.5 or write the following on the board.

Answer.

1. **¿Te sientes bien cuando tienes fiebre?**
2. **¿Te sientes bien cuando tienes catarro?**
3. **¿Vas a la consulta del médico cuando estás enfermo(a)?**
4. **¿Te examina el médico?**
5. **A veces, ¿te da una receta?**
6. **¿Vas a la farmacia con la receta?**

TEACH

Core Instruction

Step 1 Ask students to listen and repeat as you read the conversation aloud or play the audio recording.

Step 2 Call on volunteers to read the conversation in parts with as much expression as possible.

Step 3 Go over the **¿Comprendes?** activities.

Go Online!

You may wish to remind students to go online for additional conversation practice.

¡Así se dice!

Why It Works!

No new material is used in the **Conversación** in order not to confuse students. The **Conversación** recombines only the vocabulary and grammar that students have already learned to understand and manipulate.

connectED.mcgraw-hill.com

¿Comprendes?

A Contesta según la información en la conversación.

1. ¿Qué hacía Enrique cuando se cayó?
2. ¿Qué le duele?
3. ¿Cómo está el tobillo?
4. ¿Qué crees? ¿Quiere Enrique que Catalina lo lleve a la sala de emergencia? ¿Le gusta la idea?
5. Según Catalina, ¿por qué debe ir Enrique a la sala de emergencia?
6. ¿Es posible que no tenga el tobillo quebrado?

B **Resumiendo** Cuenta todo lo que pasó en la conversación en tus propias palabras.

C **Prediciendo** Predice lo que va a pasar a Enrique y Catalina en la sala de emergencia. Prepara una conversación que tiene lugar en el hospital. Debes incluir a otros en la conversación como el médico o el enfermero. ¡Usa tanta imaginación posible!

CULTURA
Entrada a la sala de emergencias en un hospital en la Ciudad de Panamá

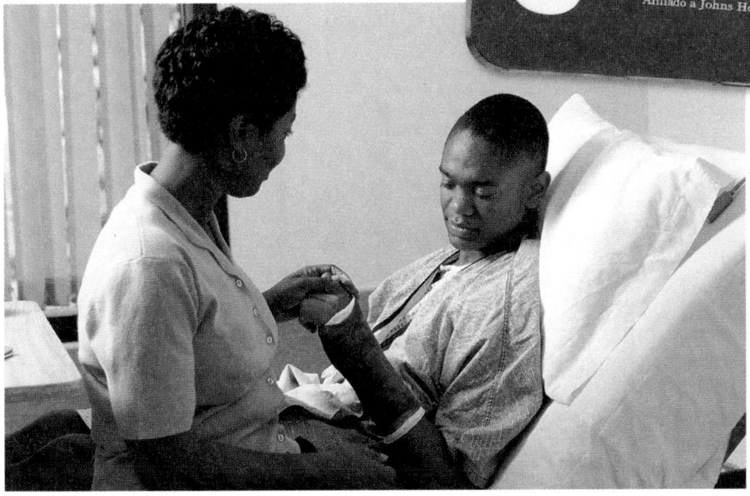

Es necesario que él se cuide bien.
Es posible que le duela mucho el brazo, ¿no?

Answers

A

1. Hacía jogging cuando se cayó.
2. Le duele el tobillo.
3. Está muy hinchado.
4. No, Enrique no quiere que Catalina lo lleve a la sala de emergencia. No le gusta la idea.
5. Según Catalina, Enrique debe ir a la sala de emergencia porque le pueden tomar una radiografía y él sabrá si el tobillo está roto o torcido.
6. Sí, es posible que no tenga el tobillo quebrado.

B *Answers will vary.*

C *Answers will vary.*

Differentiation

Multiple Intelligences

Have **bodily-kinesthetic** students dramatize this conversation. Using the proper gestures and intonation, students can make it quite humorous. Seeing the dramatization also helps **visual-spatial** learners.

PRACTICE

¿Comprendes?

A You may wish to allow students to look up the information in the conversation as they respond or you may wish to do this as a factual recall activity. Students can also write the answers to the questions.

B If a student is giving a review and appears to be having trouble, call on another to continue. You may also do this as a group activity and have each group present their conversation to the class.

Go Online!

Diálogo en vivo In this episode, Vicky goes skateboarding. Ask students if they think she really hurt herself.

Conexiones

Have students look at the map of Panama in the **GeoVista** featuring Panama at the beginning of this book. Have them locate the Panama Canal and find the picture of the canal. Ask students what geographic features they can observe that allow the canal to have been built in this location.

Lectura

Online Resources

Customizable Lesson Plans

Audio Activities

Student Workbook

TEACH

Core Instruction

Step 1 Have students read the **Estrategia de lectura** and do the **Antes de leer** activity silently.

Step 2 Call on a student to read several sentences aloud. Ask questions about what he or she read. If the pronunciation of the class is good, you can skip this step. Just have students read silently, go over the Reading Checks, and ask students a few more comprehension questions.

Step 3 Go over the **¿Comprendes?** activities.

Differentiation

There is no doubt that differently paced learners will produce language at different levels. Some techniques you may want to use to get the maximum from each group are:

- Ask a slower paced student three or four questions. He or she answers. The answers to your questions will provide an organized review.
- Call on a more able student to retell what the previous student just said, giving no help with guided questions.
- With no assistance, call on an advanced learner to retell the entire story in his/her own words.
- Ask some questions of a slower paced learner about what the previous student said.

Lectura CULTURAL

ESTRATEGIA DE LECTURA

ADIVINANDO Hay dos estrategias que te pueden ayudar a comprender lo que lees en español: reconocer o adivinar el significado de palabras aparentadas con una palabra inglesa y adivinar el significado de una palabra desconocida por medio del contexto en que se usa. Las otras palabras en la frase te pueden ayudar a determinar el significado de la palabra desconocida.

Antes de leer

Dale una ojeada a la lectura y busca palabras que consideres desconocidas. No habrá muchas.

Vida activa y buena salud

Hoy en día el interés que tenemos en nuestra salud y forma física es fenomenal. Y este interés existe en España y Latinoamérica igual que en Estados Unidos.

Como es importante que uno haga ejercicios a lo menos tres veces a la semana, hay una gran proliferación de gimnasios. Estos gimnasios tienen muchos socios[1]. En el gimnasio hacen ejercicios aeróbicos y abdominales. Se estiran los brazos y las piernas. Hacen planchas. Algunos levantan pesas. ¡Todo para mantenerse en forma!

Además de los gimnasios los parques son inmensamente populares, y para ir a un parque no hay que ser socio o miembro. Un parque es un buen lugar para hacer jogging o correr unas vueltas. A muchos les gusta dar un paseo por el parque en bicicleta. Andar en bicicleta es una forma excelente de ejercicio. Otros se sientan en un lugar aislado del parque donde disfrutan del silencio y de la tranquilidad. Se relajan practicando yoga y meditando.

[1]socios *members*

✓ READING CHECK

¿Qué hacen todos en el gimnasio?

Durante la lectura

Busca clarificaciones—si hay una palabra que no sabes, tal vez haya un sinónimo en la frase.

✓ READING CHECK

¿Cuál es la ventaja de los parques?

CULTURA

El ciclista está haciendo ejercicios en un parque en Viña del Mar, Chile.

Andrew Payti

Cultural Snapshot

Viña del Mar is a rather upscale resort about ninety minutes from Santiago, just north of the port of Valparaiso.

Go Online!

You may wish to remind students to go online for additional reading comprehension and writing skills practice.

Muchas ciudades tienen un maratón a lo menos una vez al año. Muchos maratones tienen un propósito benévolo[2] y atraen a muchos participantes. Además atraen a muchos espectadores que animan a los corredores que tienen que correr largas distancias.

Entre los jóvenes el patinaje en línea y el monopatín son muy apreciados. Tienen muchos aficionados. Pero, una advertencia[3]— al practicar estas formas de patinaje hay que tener mucho cuidado porque puedes lastimarte fácilmente. Siempre tienes que llevar casco y rodilleras. Nadie quiere que te hagas daño y que te encuentres en una sala de emergencia.

[2]propósito benévolo *charitable purpose* [3]advertencia *warning*

READING CHECK

¿Quiénes animan a los corredores en el maratón?

READING CHECK

¿Qué hay que tener al practicar el patinaje o el monopatín? ¿Por qué?

Después de leer

Prepara una lista de palabras aparentadas que encontraste en la lectura.

¿Comprendes?

A Categorizando Completa la tabla según la información en la lectura.

actividades en un gimnasio	actividades en el parque	actividades durante un maratón	actividades populares entre los jóvenes

B Personalizando Contesta.
¿En qué actividades de la Actividad A participas? Explica por qué te gustan.

C Analizando Contesta.
¿Por qué son populares los gimnasios y los parques?

Andrew Payti

CULTURA

Los jóvenes están patinando en línea en el Parque de Palermo en Buenos Aires, Argentina.

PRACTICE

Pre-AP These cultural readings will develop the skills that students need to be successful on the reading and writing sections of the AP exam. Listening to these readings will also help prepare them for the auditory component.

¡Así se dice!

Why It Works!

Note that as always in **¡Así se dice!**, readings are geared to the students' proficiency level in Spanish. This reading contains only material, vocabulary, and grammar that students have already learned. The only exceptions are the three footnoted vocabulary items.

Answers

A

actividades en un gimnasio: hacer ejercicios aeróbicos y abdominales, estirarse los brazos y las piernas, hacer planchas y levantar pesas

actividades en el parque: hacer jogging, correr unas vueltas, dar un paseo en bicicleta, practicar yoga

actividades durante un maratón: correr, animar a los corredores

actividades populares entre los jóvenes: practicar el patinaje en línea y el monopatín

B *Answers will vary.*

C *Answers will vary but may include:* Son populares porque todo el mundo quiere mantenerse en forma.

Online Resources

Customizable Lesson Plans

Audio Activities

Student Workbook

Teaching Options

You may wish to follow any one of the following procedures for the **Lectura—Un poco más.**

Independent reading Have students read the selection and do the post-reading activities as homework which you collect. This option is the least intrusive on class time and requires a minimum of teacher involvement.

Homework with in-class follow-up Assign the reading and post-reading activities as homework. Review and discuss the material in class the next day.

Intensive in-class activity This option includes a discussion of **Antes de leer**, listening to the audio recording of the reading selection, an in-class discussion of the selection, and the **¿Comprendes?** activity. You may also assign **¿Comprendes?** for homework and discuss it in class the next day.

Conexiones

Have students find out more about the work of *Médicos Sin Fronteras* and present what they learn to the class. Ask them to consider how knowing a second language could be an advantage for someone doing this kind of work.

Lectura

UN POCO MÁS

Antes de leer

Piensa en unas organizaciones benévolas o caritativas donde vives. ¿Qué tipo de trabajo hacen? ¿Has oído de Médicos Sin Fronteras, *una famosa organización internacional?*

Médicos Sin Fronteras

Hay gente que se cuida bien y también hay gente que cuida de otros como los *Médicos Sin Fronteras.* La organización *Médicos Sin Fronteras* tuvo su origen en Francia en 1971. Un grupo de médicos y periodistas franceses fueron a África con la Cruz Roja donde vieron morir a millones de biafranos[1] de guerra[2] y de hambre. Su situación fue tan desesperada que a su regreso a Francia este grupo de médicos creó una organización pequeña, *Médecins Sans Frontières.* Hoy es una organización internacional independiente con más de dos mil quinientos benévolos (voluntarios) presentes en más de setenta países, incluyendo unos en Latinoamérica. La organización tiene proyectos en zonas de guerra, campos de refugiados y en regiones devastadas por desastres naturales o epidemias de enfermedades como el sida[3].

Entre los benévolos hay médicos, cirujanos, enfermeros y técnicos. Hay también personas que se responsabilizan por los materiales que necesitan y la administración de los proyectos. Todos reciben muy poco dinero por el trabajo maravilloso que hacen.

En 1999 *Médicos Sin Fronteras* ganó el prestigioso Premio Nobel de la Paz.

[1]biafranos *people from Biafra*
[2]guerra *war*
[3]sida *AIDS*

MEDICOS SIN FRONTERAS

Doctors Without Borders/Médecins Sans Frontières (MSF)

Después de leer

Investiga la organización Médicos Sin Fronteras. *Escoge uno de los países hispanohablantes donde hace la organización proyectos de ayuda médico-humanitaria. Prepara un informe sobre el trabajo que hacen los benévolos de* Médicos Sin Fronteras *en aquel país.*

Go Online!

You may wish to remind students to go online for additional reading comprehension and writing skills practice.

¿Comprendes?

A Escoge.

1. Los *Médicos Sin Fronteras* ____.
   a. se cuidan bien
   b. cuidan de otros
   c. no tienen país
   d. son todos franceses
2. La organización *Médicos Sin Fronteras* tuvo su origen en ____.
   a. Francia
   b. Biafra, África
   c. la Cruz Roja
   d. una situación desesperada
3. ¿Quiénes establecieron la organización?
   a. miembros de la Cruz Roja
   b. un grupo internacional independiente
   c. un grupo de médicos y periodistas franceses
   d. un grupo de benévolos
4. Los biafranos morían ____.
   a. de un desastre natural
   b. de una epidemia
   c. de malnutrición y guerra
   d. a causa del calor
5. Por lo general, ¿quiénes toman refugio en los campos de refugiados?
   a. las víctimas de guerra
   b. los benévolos
   c. los enfermos
   d. los soldados
6. Los benévolos que trabajan con la organización ____.
   a. son todos personal médico
   b. tienen un salario
   c. reciben muy poco dinero
   d. viven de proyectos

B **Identifica.**
¿Cuál es la idea principal de esta lectura? Da unos detalles que apoyan *(support)* esta idea.

C **Analiza.**
¿Qué piensas? ¿Por qué quiere compartir el autor esta información con sus lectores? ¿Cuál es su propósito?

CULTURA
Aquí tienes un cartel de los *Médicos Sin Fronteras* en Valencia, España. ¿Cuál es el mensaje en el cartel?

Andrew Payti

Pre-AP These cultural readings will develop the skills that students need to be successful on the reading and writing sections of the AP exam. Listening to these readings will also help prepare them for the auditory component.

Tips for Success

The multiple-choice comprehension activities in the second reading selection of each chapter have a format that will help students prepare for standardized tests.

Answers

A
1. b
2. a
3. c
4. c
5. a
6. c

B *Answers will vary.*

C *Answers will vary.*

Prepárate para el examen

Online Resources

Customizable Lesson Plans

Student Workbook

Enrichment

Listening, Speaking, Reading, Writing Tests

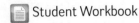

Self-check for achievement

This is a pre-test for students to take before you administer the chapter test. Note that each section is cross-referenced so students can easily find the material they feel they need to review. You may wish to use Self-Check Worksheet SC11 to have students complete this assessment in class or at home. You can correct the assessment yourself, or you may prefer to display the answers in class using Self-Check Answers SC11A.

Differentiation

Slower Paced Learners

Have students work in pairs to complete the Self-Check in class. Once they have finished, call on individuals to give the correct answers as you review together.

Multiple Intelligences

To engage **visual-spatial** and **bodily-kinesthetic** learners, number from 1 to 40 on the board and call on a student to go to the board and write the correct answer (this may be done chronologically or you may allow students to choose the one they answer). Then have the student who wrote the first answer decide who will write the second, and so on, making sure to remind them not to pick the same person again.

Prepárate para el examen

Vocabulario

1 Identifica.

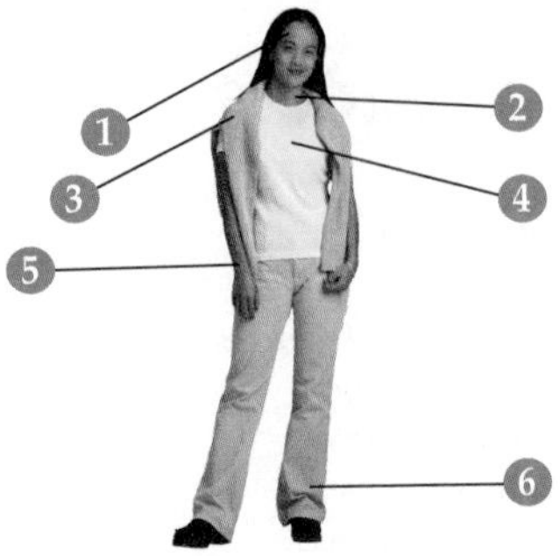

To review, see **Vocabulario 1.**

2 Corrige.

7. Es importante que uno lleve casco y rodilleras si levanta pesas.
8. A mucha gente le gusta andar en monopatín en el hospital.
9. Un maratón es una carrera de corta distancia.
10. Antes de correr, los corredores se estiran los dedos y los pies.
11. Cuando practicas yoga, haces muchas planchas.

3 Identifica.

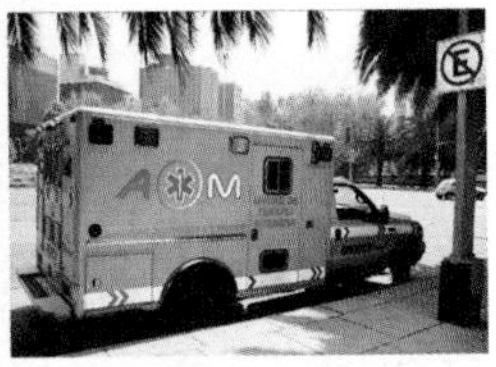

12.

13.

14.

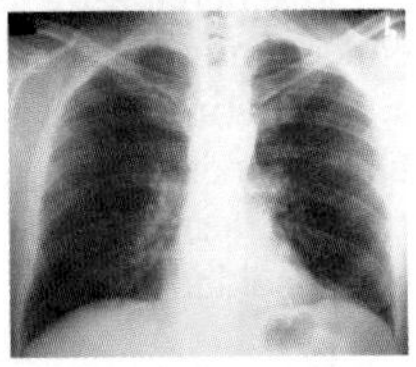

15.

To review, see **Vocabulario 2.**

4 Completa.

16. El niño se _____ el tobillo y lo tiene muy hinchado.
17. Se _____ la pierna y el cirujano ortopédico la tiene que poner en un yeso.
18. Los socorristas pusieron a la víctima en una camilla y la llevaron al hospital en _____.
19. José necesita ayuda para andar. Anda con _____.

Answers

1

1. la frente
2. el cuello
3. el hombro
4. el pecho
5. la muñeca
6. el tobillo

2

7. Es importante que uno lleve casco y rodilleras si hace monopatín o patinaje en línea.
8. A mucha gente le gusta andar en monopatín en el parque.
9. Un maratón es una carrera de larga distancia.
10. Antes de correr, los corredores se estiran las piernas.
11. Cuando practicas yoga, liberas tu espíritu de tensiones.

3

12. la ambulancia
13. la silla de ruedas
14. la camilla
15. la radiografía

Go Online! connectED.mcgraw-hill.com

Prepárate para el examen

Gramática

5 Completa.

20. Es importante que nosotros _____ ejercicios. (hacer)
21. Es necesario que ellos nos _____. (acompañar)
22. Es posible que ella _____. (estar)
23. Es probable que yo _____. (ir)
24. Es imposible que tú lo _____. (saber)

To review, see **El subjuntivo con expresiones impersonales.**

6 Completa formando una frase.

25. Es necesario que…
26. Es posible que…
27. Es difícil que…

7 Completa.

28. ¡Ojalá _____ su equipo! (ganar)
29. ¡Quizás _____ ellos! (venir)
30. ¡Tal vez _____ (ellos) en el gimnasio! (estar)
31. ¡Ojalá _____ (tú) los resultados mañana! (tener)

To review, see **¡Ojalá! ¡Quizás! ¡Tal vez!**

8 Completa las frases con **nosotros**.

32. Ellos quieren que tú se lo pidas a Javier.
    Ellos quieren que nosotros…
33. Ella quiere que yo me siente aquí.
    Ella quiere que nosotros…

To review, see **El subjuntivo de los verbos de cambio radical.**

9 Completa con **tan… como** o **tanto… como**.

34. A veces los hospitales en las zonas rurales no son _____ buenos _____ los de las grandes ciudades.
35. Esta clínica es _____ moderna _____ la otra.
36. Ella tiene _____ paciencia _____ yo.
37. Yo hago _____ ejercicios _____ tú.

To review, see **Comparación de igualdad.**

Cultura

10 Contesta.

38. ¿Por qué hay gimnasios que tienen muchos socios?
39. ¿Cuáles son algunas actividades atléticas que practica la gente en un parque?
40. ¿Qué propósito tienen muchos maratones?

To review this cultural information, see the **Lectura cultural.**

Differentiation

(continued)

This type of review activity is particularly appealing to interpersonal learners but will also benefit the class on the whole by promoting an inclusive, student-centered learning environment.

Slower Paced Learners

Encourage students who need extra help to refer to the margin notes and review any section before answering the questions.

Pre-AP Students preparing for the AP exam may benefit from a set time limit when completing this Self-Check. This may also help to identify students with learning difficulties or slower paced students who need extra help.

Go Online!

You may wish to remind students to go online for additional test preparation.

Answers

4
16. torció
17. rompió (quebró)
18. una ambulancia
19. muletas

5
20. hagamos
21. acompañen
22. esté
23. vaya
24. sepas

6
25–27. *Answers will vary.*

7
28. gane
29. vengan
30. estén
31. tengas

8
32. se lo pidamos a Javier.
33. nos sentemos aquí.

9
34. tan, como
35. tan, como
36. tanta, como
37. tantos, como

10
38. Todo el mundo quiere mantenerse en forma.
39. La gente hace jogging, corre unas vueltas, anda en bicicleta y practica yoga.
40. Tienen un propósito benévolo.

Prepárate para el examen

Tips for Success

Encourage students to say as much as possible when they do these open-ended activities. Tell them not to be afraid to make mistakes, since the goal of the activities is real-life communication. Encourage students to self-correct and to use words and phrases they know to get their meaning across. If someone in the group makes an error that impedes comprehension, encourage the others to ask questions to clarify or, if necessary, to politely correct the speaker. Let students choose the activities they would like to do.

Tell students to feel free to elaborate on the basic theme and to be creative. They may use props, pictures, or posters if they wish.

Pre-AP These oral activities will give students the opportunity to develop and improve their speaking skills so that they may succeed on the speaking portion of the AP exam.

Note: You may want to use the rubric below to help students prepare their speaking activities.

Practice for **ORAL PROFICIENCY**

Prepárate para el examen

1 Actividades atléticas

Discuss which sports you play
Trabajen en grupos de tres o cuatro. Discutan todas las actividades atléticas en que participan ustedes. Determinen si tienen los mismos intereses o no.

2 Peligros

Talk about avoiding danger
Las actividades atléticas pueden ser buenas para la salud pero cuando practicas ciertas actividades hay que tener cuidado de no lastimarte. ¿Cuáles son algunas cosas que debes hacer para evitar (no tener) accidentes?

3 Un accidente

Describe an accident you had when you were young
Explica si tú eres propenso(a) a accidentes o si lo eras de niño(a). ¿Has tenido unos accidentes? Descríbelos. Si nunca has tenido un accidente explica como es posible que tengas tanta suerte.

4 Importante y necesario

Talk about what is important for you to do and what is necessary for you to do
Completa una tabla como la de abajo y presenta la información a tu clase.

Es importante que yo	Y es necesario que yo
porque	

5 En la sala de emergencia

Helping someone out after an accident
Estás en la sala de espera de la sala de emergencia en un hospital. Entran los padres con su hijo que ha tenido un accidente y se ha hecho daño. Los padres están nerviosos y solo hablan español. Ayúdalos.

Andrew Payti

Scoring Rubric for Speaking

	4	3	2	1
vocabulary	extensive use of vocabulary, including idiomatic expressions	adequate use of vocabulary and idiomatic expressions	limited vocabulary marked with some anglicisms	limited vocabulary marked by frequent anglicisms that force interpretation by the listener
grammar	few or no grammatical errors	minor grammatical errors	some serious grammatical errors	serious grammatical errors
pronunciation	good intonation and largely accurate pronunciation with slight accent	acceptable intonation and pronunciation with distinctive accent	errors in intonation and pronunciation with heavy accent	errors in intonation and pronunciation that interfere with listener's comprehension
content	thorough response with interesting and pertinent detail	thorough response with sufficient detail	some detail, but not sufficient	general, insufficient response

Practice for **WRITTEN PROFICIENCY**

Go Online! connectED.mcgraw-hill.com

Tarea

You have learned about many sports in Spanish. You have also learned about the parts of the body and physical fitness. Now you are going to write a research paper that discusses the physical benefits of some sports. Use the library and the Internet to find out more about how your body stays fit by doing each sport. Be sure to cite your sources.

Writing Strategy

Researching As you prepare to write your research paper, you will be consulting many sources for information. It is important that your sources be reliable, especially when they are found on the Internet. It is advisable to consult more than one source for any fact you present. If your two sources disagree, consult a third.

CULTURA

El andinista venezolano tiene todo el equipo necesario para escalar montañas.

Kelli Drummer-Avendaño

1 Prewrite

- Before you begin your research, create a rough outline of your paper. This will help you identify the topics you need to research.

Título
A. El fútbol
1. ¿Cómo se mantiene uno en forma jugando fútbol?
a.
b.
2. ¿Cuáles son algunas desventajas o peligros del fútbol?
a.
b.
B. El jogging
1. ¿Cómo se mantiene uno en forma haciendo jogging?

- As you research, fill the holes in your outline. Make an effort to consult written as well as video resources to practice both your reading and listening skills.

2 Write

- Use your outline as a guide while you write. It will ensure your information is organized and that nothing is omitted.
- It is very important to cite the sources you used to obtain information. This will add validity to your paper and it will also ensure that you do not plagiarize.

Evaluate

Your teacher will evaluate you on organization of information, correctness of grammar, and proper citation.

Prepárate para el examen

Pre-AP This **tarea** will give students the opportunity to develop and improve their writing skills so that they may succeed on the writing portion of the AP exam.

ABOUT THE SPANISH LANGUAGE

Note that the word **alpinista** is often used for *mountain climber.* In South America it is **andinista** for good reason.

ASSESS

Students are now ready to take any of the Listening, Speaking, Reading, Writing Tests you choose to administer.

Note: You may want to use the rubric below to help students prepare their writing task.

Scoring Rubric for Writing

	4	3	2	1
vocabulary	precise, varied	functional, fails to communicate complete meaning	limited to basic words, often inaccurate	inadequate
grammar	excellent, very few or no errors	some errors, but do not hinder communication	numerous errors interfere with communication	many errors, little sentence structure
content	thorough response to the topic	generally thorough response to the topic	partial response to the topic	insufficient response to the topic
organization	well organized, ideas presented clearly and logically	loosely organized, but main ideas present	some attempts at organization, but with confused sequencing	lack of organization

Online Resources

- Customizable Lesson Plans
- Whiteboard Lesson
- Audio Activities
- Video (Vocabulario) (Diálogo) (Gramática)
- Student Workbook
- Enrichment
- Quizzes
- Listening, Speaking, Reading, Writing Tests

Grammar Review

This page provides a quick "at a glance" summary of the grammar points students have learned in this chapter.

Differentiation

Multiple Intelligences

You may want to call on **verbal-linguistic** and **logical-mathematical** learners for whom grammar often comes easily to explain the main concepts to their classmates in their own words. Having students explain the concepts in different ways may also help slower paced learners or students with learning difficulties.

Repaso del Capítulo 11

Gramática

El subjuntivo con expresiones impersonales

The subjunctive is used after many impersonal expressions when it is not known if the information that follows will or will not take place.

Es importante que tengas cuidado cuando levantas pesas.
Es necesario que la niña lleve casco cuando anda en bicicleta.
Es probable que ellos lleguen a tiempo.

¡Ojalá! ¡Quizás! ¡Tal vez!

The expressions **¡Ojalá!**, **¡Quizás!**, and **¡Tal vez!** are also followed by the subjunctive. Review the following sentences.

¡Ojalá no te hagas daño!
Quizás vengan mañana.

El subjuntivo de los verbos de cambio radical

Verbs that have a stem change in the present indicative also have a stem change in the present subjunctive.

cerrar		encontrar	
cierre	cerremos	encuentre	encontremos
cierres	*cerréis*	encuentres	*encontréis*
cierre	cierren	encuentre	encuentren

Preferir and **sentir (e → ie, i)**, **dormir (o → ue, u)**, and **pedir, repetir, freír, seguir,** and **servir (e → i, i)** have a stem change in every person of the subjunctive. Review the following forms.

preferir		dormir		pedir	
prefiera	prefiramos	duerma	durmamos	pida	pidamos
prefieras	*prefiráis*	duermas	*durmáis*	pidas	*pidáis*
prefiera	prefieran	duerma	duerman	pida	pidan

Comparación de igualdad

You use **tanto... como** to compare like quantities and **tan... como** to compare like qualities.

Yo tengo tanta paciencia como mi padre.
Anita hace tantos ejercicios como yo.

La señora Mayo es tan simpática como la señora Hernández.
Manolo corre tan rápido como tú.

CULTURA
Los jóvenes están haciendo jogging en Barcelona, España.

Juego There are a number of cognates in this list. See how many you and a partner can find. Who can find the most? Compare your list with those of your classmates.

Go Online!

connectED.mcgraw-hill.com

Vocabulario

Identifying more parts of the body

la frente	el pecho	el tobillo
el cuello	la muñeca	el dedo del pie
el hombro		

Talking about physical fitness

el gimnasio	la respiración	una vuelta
el buzo	el monopatín	un maratón
el casco	el jogging	estirarse
las rodilleras	el/la corredor(a)	patinar
los ejercicios	una carrera	en línea
las planchas	de relevos	practicar yoga
las pesas	a campo traviesa	descansar
el movimiento	de larga distancia	liberar

Talking about an accident

una herida	torcerse	doler
hinchado(a)	caerse	hacerse daño
cortarse	romperse, quebrarse	

Talking about medical emergencies and a hospital

la ambulancia	la camilla	la silla de ruedas
el/la socorrista	la sala de emergencia	andar con muletas

Talking about medical care

el/la cirujano(a)	una radiografía	los puntos, las suturas
ortopédico(a)	un yeso	una venda
el/la enfermero(a)	un hueso	reducir, acomodar

Other useful words and expressions

el espíritu	la tensión	lento(a)

Repaso del Capítulo 11

Vocabulary Review

The words and phrases in **Vocabulary 1** and **2** have been taught for productive use in this chapter. They are summarized here as a resource for both student and teacher. This list also serves as a convenient resource for the **Prepárate para el examen** activities.

¡Así se dice!

Why It Works!

This vocabulary reference list has not been translated into English for two reasons. First, it is recommended that students learn the new vocabulary through direct association with images on the **Vocabulario** pages. Second, all vocabulary is reintroduced in the chapter many times and upon completion of the chapter students should be familiar with the meaning of all the words. If there are words that students still do not know, they can refer to the vocabulary presentation in the chapter or the dictionary at the end of the book. If, however, it is your preference to give students the English translations, please refer to Vocabulary V11.1.

Differentiation

Slower Paced Learners

Slower paced learners may benefit from creating their own visual dictionary of nouns and adjectives in this list. They can either draw their own depictions or use images from the Internet, magazines, etc.

Juego The cognates in this list are: **el gimnasio, los ejercicios, el movimiento, la respiración, el jogging, la distancia, un maratón, practicar yoga, liberar, la ambulancia, la emergencia, ortopédico(a), el espíritu, la tensión.**

Don't forget the chapter project and cultural activities. Students have learned all the information that they will need to complete these engaging enrichment tasks.

Repaso cumulativo

Every chapter of **¡Así se dice!** contains this review section of previously learned material. By recycling information from previous chapters, the cumulative review serves to remind students that they need to continue practicing what they have learned after finishing each chapter.

Activity 1 This activity reviews formal and informal commands.

Audio Script

1. Invita a Manolo y Sara.
2. Doblen a la derecha en la calle Príncipe.
3. No vayas a clase hoy. ¡Es sábado!
4. Lea usted el correo electrónico.
5. ¡No me dé tantos exámenes!
6. Ayúdenme, por favor.
7. Dámelo.
8. Permítanme asistir al concierto.

Activity 2 This activity reviews double object pronouns.

Activity 3 This activity reviews double object pronouns with **se.**

Go Online!

You may wish to remind students to go online for additional cumulative review.

Repaso cumulativo

Repasa lo que ya has aprendido

These activities will help you review and remember what you have learned so far in Spanish.

1 Escucha las frases. Indica en una tabla como la de abajo a quien habla el joven en cada frase.

a un(a) amigo(a)	a su profesor(a)	a sus padres

2 Sigue el modelo.

MODELO —Son mis zapatos nuevos.
—¿Quién te los compró?

1. Es mi cámara nueva.
2. Es mi casco nuevo.
3. Son mis gafas nuevas.
4. Son mis esquís nuevos.
5. Son mis botas nuevas.

desayuno
buffet100%
Mexicano
Sábados y Domingos de 7:00 a 13:00 hrs.
Buffet de CARNES y cortes
Americanos
Lunes a Viernes de 13:00 a 18:00 hrs.
Comida buffet de Langostas y Mariscos
Sábados y Domingos de 14:00 a 18:00 hrs.
CENA
Buffet
crownewich
Pastas y ensaladas a la plancha
Lunes a Sábados de 19:00 a 23:00 hrs.

3 Completa con los pronombres.

1. Yo le di los CDs a Anita.
   Yo ____ di a ella.
2. Carlos le devolvió el dinero a Juan.
   Carlos ____ devolvió a él.
3. Sara le dio las direcciones a usted.
   Sara ____ dio.
4. Yo le leí la receta a Susana.
   Yo ____ leí a ella.
5. Yo no le preparé la comida.
   Yo no ____ preparé.

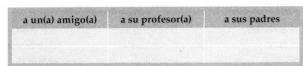

Answers

1

1. a un amigo
2. a sus padres
3. a un amigo
4. a su profesor
5. a su profesor
6. a sus padres
7. a un amigo
8. a sus padres

2

1. ¿Quién te la compró?
2. ¿Quién te lo compró?
3. ¿Quién te las compró?
4. ¿Quién te los compró?
5. ¿Quién te las compró?

3

1. se los
2. se lo
3. se las
4. se la
5. se la

Go Online!

connectED.mcgraw-hill.com

4 **Completa cada serie de frases con el presente, el pretérito y el imperfecto.**

hablar

1. **a.** Yo _____ con Juan todos los días.
   b. Yo _____ con Juan ayer.
   c. Yo _____ mucho con Juan cuando éramos niños.

vender

2. **a.** Mi padre _____ carros.
   b. Ayer él _____ dos.
   c. Pero cuando yo era niño él no _____ carros.

escribir

3. **a.** Ahora nosotros le _____ un correo electrónico todos los días.
   b. Nosotros le _____ un correo electrónico el otro día.
   c. Nosotros le _____ correos electrónicos casi a diario cuando estaba en España.

hacer

4. **a.** No lo _____ yo.
   b. No lo _____ yo ayer.
   c. Yo no lo _____ nunca.

poner

5. **a.** ¿Por qué no _____ (tú) las maletas en la maletera?
   b. ¿Por qué no _____ (tú) las maletas en la maletera cuando fuiste al aeropuerto?
   c. Cada vez que hacías un viaje _____ las maletas en la maletera.

decir

6. **a.** Yo siempre _____ la verdad.
   b. Yo no te _____ una mentira. Fue la verdad.
   c. Yo nunca _____ mentiras—siempre la verdad.

poder

7. **a.** Ellos _____ hacerlo ahora.
   b. Ellos intentaron pero no _____ hacerlo.
   c. Ellos _____ hacerlo cuando eran más jóvenes.

CULTURA

Cada día los señores pasaban mucho tiempo en la terraza de este café en San Juan. Les gustaba leer el periódico y hablar.

Repaso cumulativo

Activity 4 This activity reviews present, preterite, and imperfect verb forms.

Conexiones

Geography

You may wish to say to students: **Este señor lleva abrigo y bufanda. Está bien abrigado. En Buenos Aires, ¿qué mes será?** (note that **abrigo** and **bufanda** are new words). Students have learned about the reverse seasons.

Go Online!

The **¡Así se dice!** Audio Program for Chapter 11 has twenty-six activities, which afford students extensive listening and speaking practice.

Pre-AP To give students further open-ended oral and written practice, or to assess proficiency, go to AP Proficiency Practice AP11 and AP 24.

Answers

4

1. a. hablo
   b. hablé
   c. hablaba
2. a. vende
   b. vendió
   c. vendía
3. a. escribimos
   b. escribimos
   c. escribíamos
4. a. hago
   b. hice
   c. hacía
5. a. pones
   b. pusiste
   c. ponías
6. a. digo
   b. dije
   c. decía
7. a. pueden
   b. pudieron
   c. podían

Literary Reader

¡Así se dice! Level 2 teaches reading skills as it teaches language, culture, and an appreciation of literature. The Literary Reader exposes students to literature from Spain and Cuba.

Preview

You may decide to skip these literary selections, assign them as extra credit, or go over them thoroughly to the point that students can tell about them in their own words.

The selection on *El Quijote* can be done at any time after finishing three or more chapters, *Versos sencillos* after six or more chapters, and *Marianela* after nine or more chapters.

Literary Reader

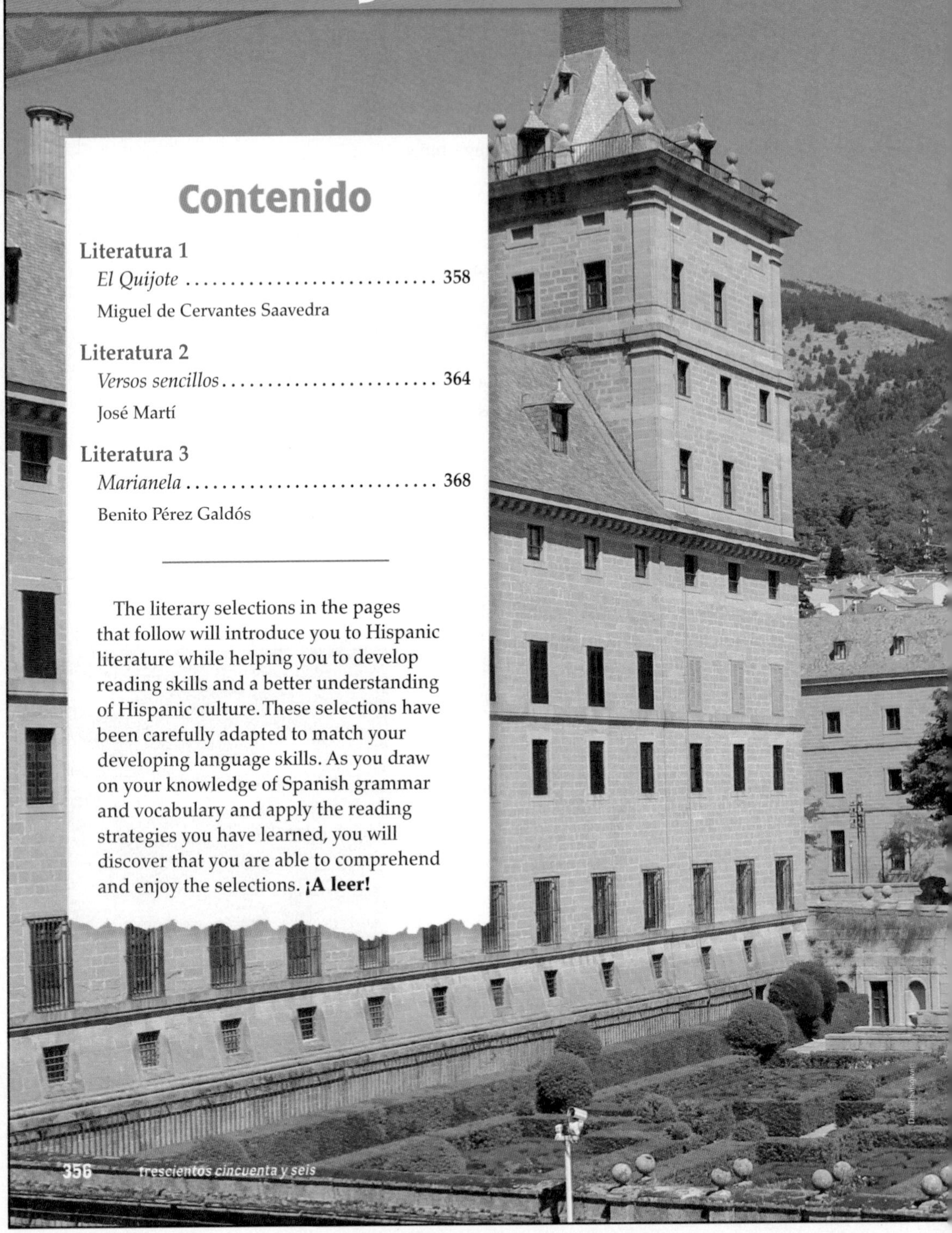

Contenido

The literary selections in the pages that follow will introduce you to Hispanic literature while helping you to develop reading skills and a better understanding of Hispanic culture. These selections have been carefully adapted to match your developing language skills. As you draw on your knowledge of Spanish grammar and vocabulary and apply the reading strategies you have learned, you will discover that you are able to comprehend and enjoy the selections. **¡A leer!**

Una vista exterior de El Escorial con sus jardines. El Escorial es un monasterio y palacio construido en el siglo XVI cerca de Madrid.

Tips for Success

The exposure to literature early in one's study of a foreign language should be a pleasant experience. As students read these selections, it is not necessary that they understand every word. Explain to them that they should try to enjoy the experience of reading literature in a new language. As they read they should look for the following:

- who the main characters are
- what they are like
- what they are doing—the plot
- what happens to them—the outcome of the story

Cultural Snapshot

The austere El Escorial monastery was built by Felipe II from 1563–1584. Second only to the Vatican library, the library at El Escorial holds the writings of San Agustín, Alfonso el Sabio, and Santa Teresa. It also is home to the largest collection of Arabic manuscripts in the world.

Pre-AP Reading these literary selections and doing the activities that accompany them will help students develop the skills that they need to be successful on the reading and writing sections of the AP exam.

This literary selection is optional. You may wish to present it after students have completed Chapters 1–3, as they will have acquired the vocabulary and grammar necessary to read the selection by this point.

Teaching Options

You may present the reading thoroughly as a class activity or you may have some or all students read it on their own. If you present it as a class activity, some options are:

- Students read silently.
- Students read after you in unison.
- Individual students read aloud.

With any of the above procedures, intersperse comprehension questions. Call on a student or students to give a brief synopsis of small sections in Spanish.

Vocabulario

TEACH

Core Instruction

If you wish to have students read this selection in depth in class, have them read each new word and its definition and then ask them a question using the new word. Examples for this section are: **¿Quiere don Quijote conquistar el mal o el bien? Ya conoces un poco a don Quijote. ¿Hace o comete él unas tonterías? ¿Son espantables las guerras? ¿Hay una guerra ahora? ¿Dónde? ¿Hay mucha gente sabia en el mundo? Cuando uno viaja, ¿se desvía de vez en cuando el equipaje? ¿Siempre le haces caso a tu profesor(a)? ¿Tratas de salir a toda prisa de una situación mala?**

Literatura 1

El Quijote

de Miguel de Cervantes Saavedra

CULTURA

Don Quijote es un caballero andante. Sancho Panza es su escudero. Don Quijote tiene una lanza.

Vocabulario

Estudia las siguientes palabras y sus definiciones.

el mal lo contrario de «bien»; una desgracia, un daño
una tontería una cosa absurda
la guerra una larga serie de batallas
espantable horrible
sabio(a) muy inteligente
desviar disuadir, apartar o alejar a alguien de su camino
hacerle caso a alguien prestarle atención
a toda prisa rápido

Práctica

A Contesta.

1. ¿Tiene escudero don Quijote? ¿Quién es su escudero?
2. ¿Monta don Quijote a caballo o en un asno?
3. ¿Existen males en el mundo o es todo bueno?
4. ¿Hay una guerra en este momento?
5. ¿Son espantables las guerras?

B Expresa de otra manera.

1. Él siempre está haciendo *cosas ridículas.*
2. No hay duda. Es un señor *muy inteligente.*
3. Ellos tenían miedo y salieron *rápido.*
4. Él nunca quiere *prestarle atención* a nadie.
5. Cuando quiere hacer algo es difícil *disuadirlo.*

C Da la palabra cuya definición sigue.

1. a toda velocidad
2. de mucha inteligencia
3. una estupidez
4. espantoso, asqueroso
5. vicio, imperfección

Answers

A

1. Sí, tiene escudero. Sancho Panza es su escudero.
2. Don Quijote monta a caballo.
3. Existen males en el mundo.
4. Sí, (No, no) hay una guerra en este momento.
5. Sí, las guerras son espantables.

B

1. Él siempre está haciendo tonterías.
2. No hay duda. Es un señor sabio.
3. Ellos tenían miedo y salieron a toda prisa.
4. Él nunca quiere hacerle caso a nadie.
5. Cuando quiere hacer algo es difícil desviarlo.

C

1. a toda prisa
2. sabio(a)
3. una tontería
4. espantable
5. el mal

INTRODUCCIÓN

La obra más famosa de todas las letras hispanas es la novela *El ingenioso hidalgo don Quijote de la Mancha* de Miguel de Cervantes Saavedra.

A DON MIGUEL DE CERVANTES,
EN EL IV CENTENARIO DE LA PUBLICACIÓN
DE LA PRIMERA PARTE DEL QUIJOTE
(1605 - 2005)
LA REAL ACADEMIA ESPAÑOLA

Los dos personajes principales de la novela son don Quijote y Sancho Panza. Don Quijote, un hombre alto y delgado, es un caballero andante. Es un idealista que quiere conquistar todos los males del mundo. Su escudero, Sancho Panza, es un hombre bajo y gordo. Él es un realista puro. Siempre trata de° desviar a don Quijote de sus ilusiones y aventuras.

trata de *he tries*

El Quijote

1

Un día, don Quijote salió de su pueblo en la región de la Mancha. Un idealista sin par°, don Quijote salió en busca de aventuras para conquistar los males del mundo. Es el trabajo de un verdadero caballero andante. Pero después de unos pocos días, don Quijote volvió a casa porque hizo su primera expedición sin escudero. No hay caballero andante sin escudero—sobre todo un caballero andante de la categoría de don Quijote.

sin par *without equal*

Cuando volvió a su pueblo, empezó a buscar un escudero. Por fin encontró a un vecino, Sancho Panza, un hombre bajo y gordo. Salió por segunda vez, esta vez acompañado de su escudero. Don Quijote montó a su caballo, Rocinante, y Sancho lo siguió montado en su asno.

Conexiones

La literatura
Busca en el Internet algo sobre las obras de Miguel de Cervantes Saavedra. Examina su impacto en la literatura española.

Andrew Payti

CULTURA
El ingenioso hidalgo don Quijote de la Mancha, el famoso caballero andante

PRACTICE

A This activity can be done orally without previous preparation.

B This activity can be prepared beforehand and then gone over in class.

C This activity can also be prepared beforehand.

Differentiation

Advanced Learners

Have advanced learners use each word or expression in Activity C in an original sentence.

Cultura

You may wish to have some students go online or do some research to find out more information about Cervantes.

Core Instruction

Step 1 You may wish to call on students to read some short sections aloud. Others may be read silently.

Step 2 You may wish to intersperse comprehension questions from time to time. **¿Cuál es el trabajo de don Quijote? ¿Quién salió con él para ser su escudero?**

Core Instruction

At times you may want to paraphrase a sentence that seems somewhat difficult. For example, you may wish to rephrase the question **¿Por qué no dejamos con estas tonterías?** as **¿Por qué no decidimos que no vamos a continuar a hacer cosas estúpidas?**

Differentiation

Advanced Learners

After reading a section, you may wish to call on an advanced learner to give a review of the section.

Literatura 1

Vuestra Merced *Your Highness*
loco *crazy*
dejamos con *we put an end to*
consejos *advice*
así como *as soon as*
parecen *appear to be*

2

Los dos hicieron muchas expediciones por la región de la Mancha. El idealista don Quijote hizo muchas cosas que no quiso hacer el realista Sancho Panza. Más de una vez Sancho le dijo: —Pero, don Quijote, noble caballero y fiel compañero, Vuestra Merced° está loco°. ¿Por qué no dejamos con° estas tonterías? ¿Por qué no volvemos a casa? Yo quiero comer. Y quiero dormir en mi cama.

Don Quijote no les hizo mucho caso a los consejos° de Sancho. Uno de los episodios más famosos de nuestro estimado caballero es el episodio de los molinos de viento.

3

Del buen suceso que el valeroso don Quijote tuvo en la espantable y jamás imaginada aventura de los molinos de viento.

En esto descubrieron treinta o cuarenta molinos de viento que hay en aquel campo; y así como° don Quijote los vio, dijo a su escudero: —¡Sancho! ¡Mira! ¿Tú ves lo que veo yo?

—No, Vuestra Merced. No veo nada.

—Amigo Sancho, ¿no ves allí unos treinta o más gigantes que vienen hacia nosotros a hacer batalla?

—¿Qué gigantes?

—Aquellos que allí ves, de los brazos largos.

—Don Quijote. No son gigantes. Son simples molinos de viento. Y lo que en ellos parecen° brazos son aspas.

—Bien parece, Sancho, que tú no sabes nada de aventuras. Ellos son gigantes. Y si tienes miedo...

—¡Don Quijote! ¿Adónde va Vuestra Merced?

CULTURA
Los molinos de viento tienen aspas.

4

¿Adónde fue don Quijote? Él fue a hacer batalla con los terribles gigantes. Gigantes como estos no deben ni pueden existir en el mundo. En nombre de Dulcinea, la dama de sus pensamientos°, don Quijote los atacó. Puso su lanza en el aspa de uno de los molinos. En el mismo instante vino un viento fuerte. El viento movió las aspas. El viento las revolvió con tanta furia que hizo pedazos° de la lanza de don Quijote y levantó a don Quijote en el aire.

A toda prisa el pobre Sancho fue a socorrer° a su caballero andante. Lo encontró en el suelo muy mal herido°.

—Don Quijote, le dije a Vuestra Merced que no vio gigantes. Vio simples molinos de viento. No puedo comprender por qué los atacó.

—Sancho, tú no sabes lo que dices. Son cosas de guerra que tú no comprendes. Tú sabes que tengo un enemigo. Mi enemigo es el horrible pero sabio monstruo Frestón. Te dije las cosas malas que él hace. Y ahora convirtió a los gigantes en molinos de viento.

—Yo no sé lo que hizo vuestro enemigo, Frestón. Pero yo sé lo que le hizo el molino de viento.

Sancho levantó a don Quijote del suelo. Don Quijote subió de nuevo sobre Rocinante. Habló más de la pasada aventura pero Sancho no le hizo caso. Siguieron el camino hacia Puerto Lápice en busca de otras aventuras jamás imaginadas.

dama de sus pensamientos *lady of his dreams*

pedazos *pieces*

socorrer *help*

herido *injured*

Andrew Payti

CULTURA

El letrero de la Calle de Cervantes en el barrio de Lavapiés en Madrid. La calle lleva el nombre del autor porque Cervantes pasó una parte de su vida viviendo en esta calle.

Differentiation

Multiple Intelligences

You may wish to have **bodily-kinesthetic** learners dramatize what Don Quijote is doing as well as Sancho Panza's reactions. They can also dramatize the help Sancho gives to Don Quijote.

¿Comprendes?

These **¿Comprendes?** activities reinforce students' reading comprehension and critical thinking skills.

A In addition to checking students' understanding of specific information, this activity verifies general reading comprehension.

Tips for Success

This multiple-choice activity is good practice for many standardized tests.

Differentiation

Advanced Learners

B Have advanced learners correct the false information.

C and **D** You may wish to allow students to look up information when doing these activities or you may wish to make them responsible for the information.

Literatura 1

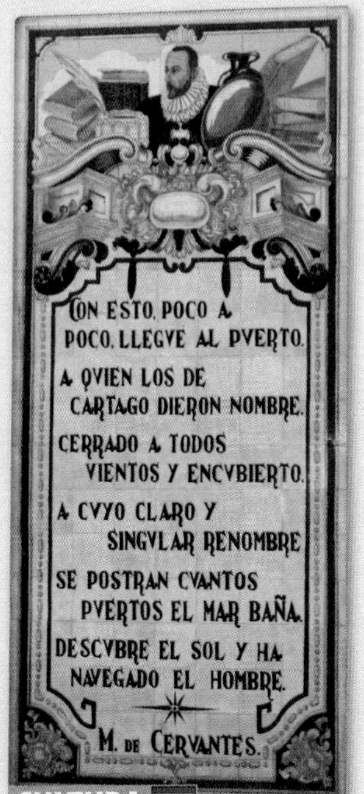

CULTURA

Un azulejo con unos versos de Cervantes en la pared de un edificio en Cartagena, España

Andrew Payti

¿Comprendes?

1

A Recordando hechos Escoge.

1. Don Quijote es _____.
   a. un realista
   b. un idealista
   c. un escudero
2. Don Quijote salió de su pueblo _____.
   a. en busca de la Mancha
   b. en busca de un escudero
   c. en busca de aventuras
3. Don Quijote volvió a casa para _____.
   a. comenzar su primera expedición
   b. buscar un escudero
   c. ver a Dulcinea
4. Sancho Panza es _____.
   a. un caballero andante también
   b. un idealista sin par
   c. un vecino de don Quijote
5. Sancho Panza tiene _____.
   a. un asno
   b. un caballo
   c. una lanza

2

B Confirmando información Usa una tabla como la de abajo para indicar si la información es correcta o no.

	correcta	incorrecta
1. Don Quijote y Sancho Panza hicieron solo dos expediciones.		
2. Sancho le dice a don Quijote que está loco.		
3. Don Quijote siempre quiere volver a casa.		
4. Un episodio famoso del *Quijote* es el episodio de los molinos de viento.		

Answers

A
1. b
2. c
3. b
4. c
5. a

B
1. incorrecta
2. correcta
3. incorrecta
4. correcta

3

C Buscando información Busca la información en la lectura para completar cada frase.

1. Hay unos ___ molinos de viento en el campo.
2. Don Quijote le dice a Sancho que ve unos ___.
3. Estos vienen hacia don Quijote y Sancho para ___.
4. Don Quijote dice que tienen ___.
5. Pero Sancho no ve ___, solamente ___.

4

D Recordando hechos Contesta.

1. ¿Contra quiénes fue don Quijote a hacer batalla?
2. ¿En dónde puso su lanza?
3. ¿Qué hizo mover el aspa?
4. ¿Revolvió rápidamente el aspa?
5. ¿Adónde levantó a don Quijote?
6. ¿Dónde encontró Sancho a don Quijote?
7. ¿Quién convirtió a los gigantes en molinos de viento?
8. Cuando Sancho levantó a don Quijote del suelo, ¿volvieron a casa?
9. Después de este episodio, ¿admite don Quijote que los gigantes son molinos de viento?

E Causa y efecto When an event or action causes other things to happen it is called a *cause-and-effect relationship.* In English, explain the cause and effect of Don Quijote's actions.

F Comparando y contrastando When you describe how two or more things are similar, you are *comparing* them. When you describe how they are different, you are *contrasting* them. Compare and contrast Sancho Panza's reasoning with that of Don Quijote.

CULTURA
Una librería en León, Nicaragua, que lleva el nombre de don Quijote

Answers

C
1. treinta o cuarenta
2. gigantes
3. hacer batalla
4. los brazos largos
5. gigantes, molinos de viento

D
1. Don Quijote fue a hacer batalla contra los terribles gigantes.
2. Puso su lanza en el aspa de uno de los molinos.
3. Un viento fuerte hizo mover el aspa.
4. Sí, revolvió rápidamente el aspa.
5. Levantó a don Quijote en el aire.
6. Sancho encontró a don Quijote en el suelo.
7. Frestón convirtió a los gigantes en molinos de viento.
8. Cuando Sancho levantó a don Quijote del suelo, no volvieron a casa.
9. No, don Quijote no admite que los gigantes son molinos de viento.

E *Answers will vary.*

F *Answers will vary.*

This literary selection is optional. You may wish to present it after students have completed Chapters 4–6, as they will have acquired the vocabulary and the grammar necessary to read the selection at this point.

Teaching Options

You may present the reading thoroughly as a class activity or you may have some or all students read it on their own. If you present it as a class activity, some options are:

- Students read silently.
- Students read after you in unison.
- Individual students read aloud.

With any of the above procedures, intersperse comprehension questions. Call on a student or students to give a brief synopsis of short sections in Spanish.

Vocabulario
Core Instruction

You may wish to follow some of the same suggestions given for *El Quijote.*

Literatura 2

Versos sencillos

de José Martí

CULTURA

Una estatua dedicada a la memoria del héroe cubano José Martí en la Plaza de la Revolución en La Habana, Cuba

Vocabulario

Estudia las siguientes palabras y sus definiciones.

el monte elevación natural de terreno, montaña
las joyas adornos de oro, plata, diamantes, esmeraldas, etc.
el joyero el que vende joyas
el corazón órgano vital muscular que impulsa la sangre
arrancar sacar o quitar con violencia

CULTURA

Montes en Casares, España

Práctica

Completa con la palabra apropiada.

1. Me causó tanto dolor y tristeza que me _____ el corazón.
2. El _____ y los pulmones son órganos vitales.
3. Un anillo de oro con diamantes es una _____.
4. El _____ vende anillos, brazaletes (pulseras) y pendientes (aretes) en su joyería.
5. No hay muchos _____ en un estado como Kansas o Nebraska.

Answers

1. arrancó
2. corazón
3. joya
4. joyero
5. montes

INTRODUCCIÓN

José Martí (1853–1895) nació en Cuba de padres españoles. Dedicó su vida a la causa de la independencia de su país. Fue deportado dos veces a España por sus actividades políticas. Martí vivió también en México, Guatemala, Honduras y Venezuela. Dice que en cada país se encontró en casa—lo que le hizo proclamar «De América soy hijo». Pasó catorce años en Estados Unidos donde organizó un grupo revolucionario. Martí murió en el campo de batalla en Cuba en 1895. Murió sin realizar su sueño de ver a su Cuba libre e independiente.

Además de ser político y revolucionario, la gran pasión de Martí durante toda su vida era la poesía. Escribió sus famosos *Versos sencillos* durante su estadía en Nueva York.

Las palmas crecen en regiones tropicales.

Versos sencillos

I

Yo soy un hombre sincero
de donde crece la palma;
y antes de morirme, quiero
echar mis versos del alma°.

Yo vengo de todas partes
y hacia todas partes voy:
arte soy entre las artes;
en los montes, monte soy.

. . .

Si dicen que del joyero
tome la joya mejor,
tomo a un amigo sincero
y pongo a un lado el amor°.

alma *soul*

amor *love*

Conexiones

La literatura

Investiga las obras de José Martí. Determina si la época en que escribió influyó sus obras.

Core Instruction

If you decide to present this poem in depth, it is suggested you have students read it aloud. If their pronunciation is not very good, read one or two strophes to them. Then have them repeat after you. As you are presenting the poem, you may wish to incorporate Activity A while reading.

Differentiation

Heritage Speakers

If you have any Cuban American students in class, you may ask them what they know about José Martí and have them give some more information about him.

Literatura 2

La rosa es una flor bonita.

XXXIX

Cultivo una rosa blanca
en julio como en enero,
para el amigo sincero
que me da su mano franca.

Y para el cruel que me arranca
del corazón con que vivo
cardo° ni ortiga° cultivo
cultivo la rosa blanca.

cardo *thistle*
ortiga *nettle*

Andrew Payti

¿Comprendes?

A Interpretando ¿Cómo lo dice José Martí?

1. Soy de un país tropical.
2. Quiero ser poeta.
3. Me siento o me encuentro en casa en muchos lugares diferentes.
4. Quiero ver el mundo.
5. Puedo adaptarme a muchas situaciones.

B Buscando hechos Contesta.

1. ¿Cuál es la mejor joya para Martí?
2. ¿Cuál prefiere? ¿A un amigo sincero o el amor?
3. ¿Qué cultiva para un amigo?
4. ¿Cómo trata a una persona que no lo trata bien?

C Personalizando En estos versos aprendemos mucho sobre la personalidad y las aspiraciones del poeta José Martí. Compara tres ideas y opiniones tuyas con las de José Martí.

Don Tremain/Getty Images

CULTURA
El Morro, La Habana, Cuba

¿Comprendes?

These **¿Comprendes?** activities reinforce students' reading comprehension and critical thinking skills. Particular skills you may wish to focus on in this reading are interpreting, analyzing, and drawing conclusions.

C Have students share their ideas concerning their responses to this activity.

Differentiation

Slow Paced Learners

You may wish to have slower paced learners do the **¿Comprendes?** activities in pairs so they can help each other.

Cultural Snapshot

The famous **Morro** walls, built by the Spaniards to defend their ports and forts, are found in San Juan de Puerto Rico, Santo Domingo, La República Dominicana, La Habana, Cuba, and Cartagena, Colombia.

Answers

A

1. Yo soy un hombre sincero de donde crece la palma;
2. quiero echar mis versos del alma
3. Yo vengo de todas partes y hacia todas partes voy;
4. hacia todas partes voy
5. arte soy entre las artes; en los montes, monte soy

B

1. Para Martí, la mejor joya es un amigo sincero.
2. Prefiere a un amigo sincero.
3. Cultiva una rosa blanca.
4. Trata a la persona como un amigo.

C *Answers will vary.*

This literary selection is optional. You may wish to present it after students have completed Chapters 7–9, as they will have acquired the vocabulary and grammar necessary to read the selection at this point.

Teaching Options

You may present the reading thoroughly as a class activity or you may have some or all students read it on their own. If you present it as a class activity, some options are:

- Students read silently.
- Students read after you in unison.
- Individual students read aloud.

With any of the above procedures, intersperse comprehension questions. Call on a student or students to give a brief synopsis of short sections in Spanish.

Vocabulario

TEACH

Core Instruction

If you plan to present this reading thoroughly, you may wish to present the vocabulary thoroughly. In addition to going over each definition, you may wish to employ one of the following strategies in order to appeal to a variety of learning styles.

- Draw pictures on the board to represent words such as **una colina, una estrella, feliz.**
- Dramatize the following: **una tontería** (do something silly), **feliz** (happy expression), **acercarse a** (go very close to something), **huir** (run away), **ladrar** (bark), **a lo lejos** (point afar), **a solas** (stand alone and look lonely), **lentamente** (move slowly).

Literatura 3

Marianela

de Benito Pérez Galdós

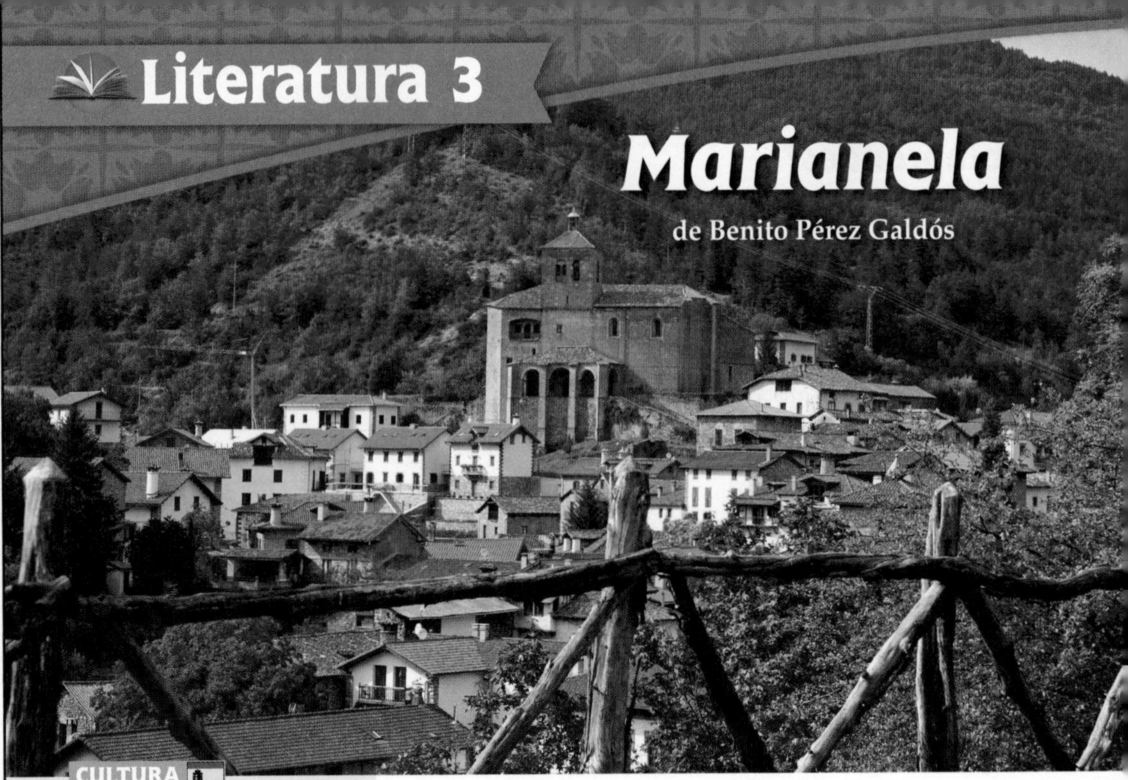

CULTURA
El pueblo de Erronkari en las montañas de Navarra

Vocabulario

Estudia las siguientes palabras y sus definiciones.

una colina elevación de terreno menor que un monte o una montaña
un buen mozo un joven guapo
la estrella lo que brilla en el cielo de noche
una tontería una cosa absurda
bello(a) bonito, hermoso
desconocido(a) no conocido
feliz contento, alegre
acercarse a ir cerca de algo
despedirse de salir y decirles «adiós» a todos
huir escapar
ladrar lo que hace el perro
ponerse a empezar
a lo lejos en la distancia
a menudo con frecuencia
a solas solo, sin nadie, no acompañado
lentamente despacio, no rápido

Práctica

A Contesta.

1. ¿Es el hermano de Teresa un buen mozo?
2. ¿Comete una persona inteligente y sabia muchas tonterías?
3. ¿Te sientes feliz cuando te ocurre algo agradable?
4. ¿Tienes miedo cuando te acerca una persona desconocida?
5. ¿Brillan las estrellas en el cielo de día o de noche?
6. ¿Te despides de tus amigos cuando tienes que salir?
7. ¿Ladra el perro si quiere atención?

B Expresa de otra manera.

1. Ella es una persona *alegre.*
2. Ellos lo hacen *con frecuencia.*
3. Yo sé que van a *escapar.*
4. ¡Qué *cosa más ridícula!*
5. Vi las colinas *en la distancia.*
6. Andaba *despacio.*
7. Él lo hizo *solo.*
8. Tiene paisajes *hermosos.*

C Da el contrario.

1. feo
2. triste
3. famoso
4. rápido
5. de cerca
6. alejarse de

Philip Coblentz/Brand X Pictures/PictureQuest

CULTURA

Las Palmas de Gran Canaria, ciudad natal de Benito Pérez Galdós

PRACTICE

A This activity can be gone over without prior preparation. After going over it in class, you may also have students write it.

B and **C** These activities should be prepared first and then gone over in class.

Differentiation

Advanced Learners

Have advanced learners make up original sentences using words in Activity C.

Answers

A

1. Sí, (No, no) es un buen mozo.
2. No, una persona inteligente y sabia no comete muchas tonterías.
3. Sí, me siento feliz cuando me ocurre algo agradable.
4. Sí, (No, no) tengo miedo cuando me acerca una persona desconocida.
5. Las estrellas brillan en el cielo de noche.
6. Sí, me despido de mis amigos cuando tengo que salir.
7. Sí, el perro ladra si quiere atención.

B

1. Ella es una persona feliz.
2. Ellos lo hacen a menudo.
3. Yo sé que van a huir.
4. ¡Qué tontería!
5. Vi las colinas a lo lejos.
6. Andaba lentamente.
7. Él lo hizo a solas.
8. Tiene paisajes bellos.

C

1. bello
2. feliz
3. desconocido
4. lentamente
5. a lo lejos
6. acercarse a

Conexiones

Literature

You may wish to explain to students that Galdós is compared to such great novelists as Dostoyevsky and Dickens.

Core Instruction

Step 1 Many sections of this abridged novel have dialogue. You can call on students to read these dialogue sections aloud. Encourage them to use proper intonation and gestures.

Step 2 Each time a new character is introduced, call on a student to give a brief description of the character.

Literatura 3

Conexiones

La literatura

Se dice que la influencia de las novelas de Galdós es universal. Haz unas investigaciones para aprender algo de esta idea.

nacimiento *birth*

INTRODUCCIÓN

Benito Pérez Galdós es uno de los mejores novelistas de España. Nació en Las Palmas de Gran Canaria en 1843 pero pasó casi toda su vida en Madrid donde murió en 1920. Un escritor fecundo, Galdós escribió setenta y siete novelas y veintidós obras teatrales. Dijo Galdós en un discurso «la novela es la imagen de la vida y su arte consiste en reproducir sus caracteres humanos; pasiones, debilidades, grandezas y bajezas».

Una de sus novelas más populares es *Marianela*. En esta novela Galdós trata el problema social de la miseria y del trabajo en las minas del norte de España. De todas sus novelas *Marianela* es la más sentimental como observarás al conocer a los dos protagonistas—Pablo Penáguilas y Marianela.

Marianela

1

Un día se acercó cierto Teodoro Golfín al pueblo de Socartes. En el camino él se perdió. Andaban por la región un joven, Pablo Penáguilas, y su perro Choto. Pablo era un muchacho guapo. Tenía unos veinte años. Pablo y Choto oyeron al señor y lo ayudaron a encontrar su camino. Como el pueblo de Socartes está situado en la región de las minas es fácil desorientarse. Para llegar a Socartes hay que bajar y subir muchas colinas y pasar por una cueva misteriosa.

Cuando Pablo y el señor Golfín salieron de la cueva oscura el señor observó algo en el muchacho que le hizo preguntar a Pablo:

—Chico, ¿eres ciego?

—Sí, señor. No tengo vista. No puedo ver. Soy ciego desde mi nacimiento° —contestó Pablo.

—¡Qué pena!—pensó el señor Golfín—un buen mozo como este y no tiene el don de ver.

Los dos seguían el camino de Socartes cuando a lo lejos oyeron una voz muy bella. Era la voz de Marianela. Pablo le explicó al señor Golfín que Marianela era una muchacha muy buena que siempre lo acompañaba por las minas.

Cuando el señor Golfín vio a Marianela observó enseguida que la pobre muchacha era muy fea. Era muy pequeña de estatura. Sus ojos negros le daban una expresión de mujer pero tenía el cuerpo de una niña. Marianela tenía dieciséis años pero parecía° menor.

El señor Golfín le habló a Pablo. Le dijo que era el hermano de Carlos Golfín, el ingeniero de las minas.

—Ah, don Carlos es muy amigo de mi padre y sé que le espera a usted desde ayer—dijo Pablo.

Por fin el joven tuvo que despedirse del grupo para volver a casa. Sabía que su padre le esperaba. El señor Golfín, guiado por Marianela, continuó su viaje hacia la casa de su hermano. Mientras caminaban hacia la casa, Marianela le hablaba al señor Golfín de su vida.

—Soy una muchacha pobre. No tengo ni padre ni madre. Soy huérfana. Mi padre fue el primero que encendía y limpiaba faroles en este pueblo. Cada día él me ponía en un cesto y yo lo acompañaba en su trabajo. Un día tenía que subir a un farol que había en un puente. Puso el cesto sobre el antepecho del puente. Yo me salí fuera° y me caí° al río. Me caí sobre unas piedras. Antes del accidente yo era bonita pero ahora soy fea. Poco después del accidente mi padre se puso enfermo y fue al hospital donde se murió. Mi madre fue a trabajar en las minas y un día ella se cayó en una cueva y no ha vuelto a salir. Y ahora yo vivo con los Centeno. Ellos tienen una casa aquí en las minas.

Después de caminar un rato más, los dos llegaron a la casa del hermano de Teodoro Golfín.

Marianela le dice «adiós» al señor Golfín y vuelve a la casa de los Centeno. Antes de salir el señor le da una moneda.

parecía *she seemed*

Un farol

me salí fuera *fell out*
me caí *I fell*

Un cesto

CULTURA

Un puente en el pueblo de Aribe en la provincia de Navarra

Tips for Success

Have students look at the photographs throughout the **Lectura.** They will give assistance with vocabulary.

Core Instruction

You may wish to select certain paragraphs and have students read them silently. If you do this, it is suggested that you have a student give a brief synopsis.

Teaching Options

Tell students they should empathize with the characters as they read. Tell them to put themselves into the characters' position. An important lesson to learn is that some people are less fortunate than others and face greater hardships. It is the less fortunate, however, who are sometimes the most kind and considerate. Ask students why they think this might be. Example: **Marianela le da la moneda a Pablo y ella no tiene nada.**

Core Instruction

Step 1 You may wish to select one or two paragraphs on this page and read them aloud to the class. Very often your intonation, gestures, etc., can greatly assist students' comprehension.

Step 2 Have students keep a list of all the adversities Marianela faces or endures.

Literatura 3

2

Cuando salió el señor Golfín, Marianela, que se llama también la Nela, fue a la casa de los Centeno.

La casa de los Centeno es bastante humilde. Viven en la casa el señor Centeno, la señora Centeno, sus cuatro hijos y la pobre Marianela. La señora Centeno es una persona cruel. Le encanta contar su dinero pero no se lo da a nadie. Trata a la Nela peor que a un animal. La hace dormir en una cesta en un rincón° de la cocina. A pesar de° toda la miseria en que vive la Nela, ella es muy generosa. En cuanto° vuelve a casa, ella le da la moneda del señor Golfín a Celipín.

rincón *corner*
A pesar de *In spite of*
En cuanto *As soon as*

Celipín es el hijo menor de los Centeno. Él no quiere seguir viviendo como está viviendo ahora. Quiere salir de Socartes para ir a estudiar en Madrid para hacer algo de su vida. Quiere ser un hombre importante. Marianela le dice que siempre tiene que ser bueno para con sus padres y que les debe escribir a menudo.

Al día siguiente, igual que todos los días, Marianela sale de casa y va a buscar a su amigo Pablo Penáguilas. Como el joven no tiene vista hay muchas cosas que le son desconocidas. La pobre Marianela no tiene educación alguna pero siempre quiere explicarle a Pablo como son las cosas del mundo. Mientras andan a diario por los campos discuten muchas tonterías. La Nela le dice que las estrellas en el cielo son las sonrisas de los muertos que están en el cielo.

Durante sus muchas conversaciones Pablo promete a Marianela que un día va a casarse con° ella. Una muchacha tan buena como ella tiene que ser bonita. Cada vez que Pablo le dice a Marianela que es bonita, ella se mira en el agua de un arroyo° y una vez más ve que es fea.

casarse con *marry*
arroyo *brook*

Andrew Payti

CULTURA
Casas con balcones típicos en Gijón, Asturias

Teodoro Golfín es médico y después de observar mucho a Pablo, toma la decisión de operarle de los ojos. No sabe si la operación tendrá éxito o no pero quiere intentar de darle vista al hijo del mejor amigo de su hermano. Pablo le dice a Marianela que después de la operación él se casará con ella.

Todos se preparan para la operación. Llega a Socartes Florentina, la prima de Pablo. Florentina es una muchacha muy bonita y es además una persona buena y generosa. Cuando ve por primera vez a Marianela se pone triste. No puede comprender como algunas personas como ella y su familia tienen mucho y otras no tienen nada. La pobre Marianela no tiene zapatos. Florentina le dice a Marianela que le comprará un vestido y un par de zapatos. Promete que se cuidará° de Marianela para siempre. La Nela cree que Florentina es una santa. Una persona tan buena tiene que ser santa.

se cuidará *she will take care*

3

Ha llegado el día de la operación. Todo el mundo está muy ansioso para saber los resultados. ¿Pablo tendrá vista o no? ¡Es la cuestión! Pasan unos días y el médico decide que ha llegado la hora de quitarle° las vendas a Pablo. ¿Puede ver o no? Sí, puede ver. Todos se alegran° con una sola excepción. La única persona que no es feliz es la Nela. Está contenta porque sabe que Pablo tiene vista pero está triste porque sabe que Pablo querrá casarse con Florentina y no con ella.

quitarle *to take off*
se alegran *rejoices*

La pobre Marianela no sabe qué hacer. No quiere estar con nadie. Quiere estar a solas con sus pensamientos°. Decide vagar por los campos.

pensamientos *thoughts*

A lo lejos, Marianela oye un ruido°. ¿Quién puede ser? Es Florentina.

ruido *noise*

Habla Florentina:

—Pero, Nela, ¿dónde has estado? ¿No sabes que Pablo tiene vista? La operación ha sido un éxito.

—Sí, lo sé—contesta la Nela.

—Pablo te quiere ver. Siempre pregunta dónde está la Nela. Tú sabes que él te quiere mucho.

La pobre Nela se cayó al suelo.

—Florentina, usted ha sido muy buena conmigo. La quiero mucho y no quiero ser ingrata. Y adoro a Pablo. Pero no puedo, no puedo.

—¿No puedes qué?—preguntó Florentina. De repente° la Nela se levantó y empezó a correr.

De repente *Suddenly*

Gritó—No, no puedo, Florentina. Perdóneme, pero no puedo hablar más con usted. ¡Adiós! ¡Adiós!

Core Instruction

Step 1 Explain to students that an author often builds suspense. Ask them what suspense is being built here.

Step 2 You can have students act out a great deal of Part 3 of the **Lectura.** This will appeal to **bodily-kinesthetic** learners.

Core Instruction

Call on two students to read the dialogue between Marianela and Celipín.

Literatura 3

Con estas palabras la Nela desapareció entre los árboles. Tomó la decisión de huir. No quiso pasar más tiempo en Socartes.

Durante la noche la Nela oyó otro ruido. Oyó a Celipín, el hijo de los Centeno.

—¿Adónde vas, Celipín?—preguntó Marianela.

—Nela, por fin voy a Madrid. Pero me tienes que hacer una promesa. No vas a decir nada a mis padres.

—De acuerdo, Celipín. No les voy a decir nada. Pero les escribirás, ¿no? Tienes que ser bueno para con tus padres.

—Sí, les escribiré. Te lo prometo. Pero, Nela, ¿por qué no vienes conmigo a Madrid? No tienes que quedarte aquí en Socartes. Podemos salir juntos.

—¡Buena idea! Te acompaño—contestó la Nela.

Luego se puso a° pensar. La Nela pensó en su madre enterrada en una cueva de Socartes. Por fin le dijo a Celipín:

—Celipín. Lo siento pero no puedo ir contigo. No puedo salir de Socartes. Tengo mis razones. Tú tienes que ir solo. Y, ¡escribe mucho! Adiós, Celipín y ¡buena suerte!

—No me olvidaré° de mis padres ni de ti que me has ayudado tanto… Adiós, Nelilla. Siento pasos°… Me voy—dijo Celipín.

se puso a *she began*

No me olvidaré *I will not forget*

Siento pasos *I hear steps*

CULTURA

Picos de Europa, Asturias

Entrada a una mina

4

Celipín desapareció entre las sombras° de la noche. Los pasos que había sentido eran de Choto, el perro de Pablo. Al ver a Marianela, Choto saltó alrededor de ella acariciándola con sus patas°. Luego empezó a correr hacia la casa de los Penáguilas.

sombras *shadows*

acariciándola con sus patas *caressing her with its paws*

A la misma hora que Choto llegaba a la casa, Teodoro Golfín salía de la casa. Cuando el perro lo vio dio unas cuarenta vueltas en torno de él y no dejó de ladrar. El señor Golfín sabía que el perro trataba de decirle algo. Choto empezó a correr y el doctor Golfín decidió seguirlo. Lo siguió y el perro lo llevó hasta donde estaba la Nela delante de la cueva donde está enterrada su madre.

El doctor gritó:

—Nela, ¿qué haces allí? Te quiero hablar.

—No puedo—contestó la Nela.

—Sí—insistió el doctor.

Marianela subió de la cueva. Le dijo al doctor que quería estar con su madre. No quería ver a Pablo porque él creía que era bonita y ella sabía que no lo era.

Por fin el doctor levantó a la Nela, la puso en sus hombros y la llevó a la casa de Pablo.—¡Ay! Marianela, ¡qué enferma estás!—pensó el médico.

Cuando llegaron a la casa, el doctor puso a la Nela en el sofá. Todos se cuidaron de ella—Florentina, el padre de Pablo, el doctor Golfín.

Tips for Success

Personalization can increase comprehension. Ask students if they have a dog. Can they relate to what is happening here with Choto? Would their dog do something similar?

Core Instruction

As students come to the scene where the disconsolate Nela passes, you may wish to have students discuss immediately Activity Q. Point out to students that at the time this novel was written, the role of science was being questioned. Galdós used his much romanticized and beloved Marianela in order to pose an uncomfortable and complicated question: **¿En qué consiste el éxito, sobre todo el éxito científico?**

Literatura 3

Al día siguiente Pablo salió de su cuarto para hablar con Florentina. Consideró a Florentina la muchacha más bonita del mundo. Cuando vio a Florentina le dijo:

—Florentina, no te vi esta mañana. ¿Por qué no viniste a hablar conmigo?

Pablo vio solo a Florentina—a nadie más. Luego miró hacia el sofá y vio la cara de una pobre muchacha fea con los ojos cerrados y la boca abierta.

—¡Ah!—dijo Pablo. Florentina ha encontrado a una pobre fea y la quiere ayudar. ¡Qué buena es Florentina!

Pablo se acercó al sofá. Extendió una mano hasta tocar aquella cabeza en la cual veía una expresión de dolor y tristeza. Entonces la Nela movió los ojos y los fijó en Pablo. Sacó de entre las mantas una mano flaca y tomó la mano de Pablo. Al sentir° su contacto Pablo se estremeció° de pies a cabeza y gritó.

Con voz temblorosa°, Marianela le dijo:

—Sí, señorito mío, yo soy la Nela.

Lentamente ella llevó a sus secos labios la mano de Pablo y le dio un beso°... después un segundo beso... y al darle el tercero, sus labios se quedaron inertes.

El primero que dijo algo fue Pablo.

—Eres tú... , eres tú.

Pablo la llamó repetidas veces.

—No responde—dijo con terror.

Pablo se inclinó sobre ella y acercando sus labios al oído de Marianela, gritó:

—Nela, Nela, amiga querida°, que tanto me has ayudado y ahora estás muerta. Adiós, Nelilla. Adiós.

Al sentir *Upon feeling*
se estremeció *shook*
temblorosa *trembling*

beso *kiss*

querida *dear, beloved*

Andrew Payti

CULTURA

Fíjate en el montañoso terreno de Extremadura, al sur de Asturias. Aun en las regiones del centro y del sur de España hay montañas. España es el segundo país más montañoso de Europa después de Suiza.

¿Comprendes?

1

A Identificando Identifica quien es.

	Pablo Penáguilas	Teodoro Golfín	don Carlos	los Centeno	Marianela
1. un señor que se perdió un día en el camino de Socartes					
2. un muchacho ciego que vive en Socartes y que le ayudó al señor que se perdió					
3. una muchacha fea que siempre le ayuda al joven ciego y que guió al señor que se perdió					
4. el ingeniero de las minas a quien iba a visitar el señor que se perdió					
5. la familia con quien vive la muchacha					

B Describiendo Escoge las frases que describen a Marianela.

1. Es una muchacha muy buena.
2. Es ciega.
3. Su madre y su padre trabajan en las minas de Socartes.
4. Es muy fea.
5. Tiene ojos azules.
6. Es muy alta.
7. Tiene una estatura baja.
8. Ayuda mucho al muchacho ciego.
9. Sufrió un accidente horrible cuando era niña.

C Describiendo Describe a los siguientes personajes.

1. Pablo Penáguilas
2. Marianela
3. Teodoro Golfín

D Analizando Contesta.

1. El camino de Socartes es un camino difícil y es fácil perderse en el camino. ¿Por qué?
2. ¿Qué indica que el señor Golfín es un hombre generoso?
3. ¿Por qué quiere compartir el autor esta historia con sus lectores? En tu opinión, ¿cuál es su propósito?

¿Comprendes?

These **¿Comprendes?** activities reinforce students' reading comprehension and critical thinking skills. Particular skills you may wish to focus on in this reading are describing, interpreting, analyzing, and drawing conclusions.

Tips for Success

- Students can do any or all of these activities on their own or they can be done as class discussion activities.
- You may also choose to go over these activities as you present each section of the **Lectura.**

A, B, C, and **D** It is suggested that you go over these activities orally as you are reading each particular section.
C and **D** These activities should also be written.

Answers

A

1. Teodoro Golfín
2. Pablo Penáguilas
3. Marianela
4. don Carlos
5. los Centeno

B

1, 4, 7, 8, 9

C

1. Es un muchacho guapo. Es ciego. Es simpático. Tiene veinte años.
2. Es la amiga de Pablo. Tiene una voz bella. Es una muchacha buena. Es fea y baja. Tiene ojos negros. Es simpática. Tiene dieciséis años.
3. Es médico. Es el hermano del ingeniero de las minas. Es simpático.

D

1. Hay que bajar y subir muchas colinas y pasar por una cueva misteriosa.
2. Le da a Marianela una moneda.
3. *Answers will vary.*

E and **F** You may wish to have students prepare these activities before going over them in class.

Literatura 3

E Aumentando tu vocabulario Parea.

1. se perdió
2. andaba
3. está situado
4. oscura
5. ser ciego
6. buen mozo
7. bello
8. huérfano
9. un rato

a. se encuentra
b. guapo
c. sin padres
d. bonito
e. se desorientó
f. caminaba, iba
g. sin luz
h. poco tiempo
i. no tener vista

F Identificando Usa una tabla como la de abajo para indicar quien es.

1. un señor que es médico y que le puede operar a Pablo de los ojos
2. un joven de unos veinte años que es guapo
3. el hijo menor de la familia Centeno que no quiere seguir viviendo como está viviendo ahora
4. una muchacha generosa que no tiene nada pero que siempre quiere ayudar a los otros
5. una muchacha bonita y generosa que viene a Socartes antes de la operación de Pablo
6. una señora cruel que nunca le da nada a nadie

Marianela	Pablo Penáguilas	Celipín	Teodoro Golfín	la Sra. Centeno	Florentina	don Carlos

Answers

E

1. e
2. f
3. a
4. g
5. i
6. b
7. d
8. c
9. h

F

1. Teodoro Golfín
2. Pablo Penáguilas
3. Celipín
4. Marianela
5. Florentina
6. la Sra. Centeno

G, H, and **I** You may wish to go over Activity G orally in class. Have students write Activities H and I.

2

G Recordando hechos Contesta.

1. ¿Con quién vive Marianela?
2. ¿Cómo la trata la señora?
3. ¿En qué cuarto de la casa duerme Marianela?
4. ¿En qué duerme ella?
5. ¿A quién le da Marianela la moneda del señor Golfín?
6. ¿Quién es Celipín?
7. ¿Por qué quiere él ir a Madrid?
8. ¿Qué le dice siempre Marianela?

H Analizando Contesta.

1. El autor dice que Marianela le dice muchas tonterías a Pablo. ¿Por qué son tonterías la información que Marianela le da?
2. Pablo siempre le dice a Marianela que va a casarse con ella. ¿Por qué quiere Pablo casarse con ella?
3. Marianela dice que Florentina es una santa. ¿Por qué?

I Describiendo Describe.
Describe a Florentina. En tu descripción indica por qué se le considera una persona generosa y compasiva.

CULTURA
Paisaje cerca de Santillana del Mar en el norte de España

Neil Beer/Getty Images

Answers

G

1. Marianela vive con los Centeno.
2. La señora la trata peor que a un animal.
3. Marianela duerme en la cocina.
4. Ella duerme en una cesta en el rincón.
5. Ella le da la moneda del señor Golfín a Celipín.
6. Celipín es el hijo menor de los Centeno.
7. Quiere ir a Madrid para estudiar y hacer algo de su vida.
8. Marianela le dice a Celipín que tiene que ser bueno para con sus padres y que les debe escribir a menudo.

H *Answers will vary but may include:*

1. Son tonterías porque la pobre Nela no tiene educación y la información que le da a Pablo es incorrecta.
2. Pablo quiere casarse con Marianela porque es una muchacha buena y una muchacha tan buena tiene que ser bonita.
3. Marianela dice que Florentina es una santa porque es una persona muy buena y la trata muy bien.

I *Answers will vary.*

Literatura 3

3

J Analizando Contesta.

1. Unos días después de la operación, el médico le quita las vendas a Pablo y todos se alegran. ¿Por qué?
2. La única persona que no es feliz es la Nela. ¿Por qué?
3. Florentina le dice a Marianela que Pablo la quiere ver. ¿Por qué quiere verla?
4. La pobre Marianela no puede hablar más con Florentina. ¿Por qué?
5. Cuando Celipín invita a Marianela a acompañarlo a Madrid, Marianela cree que es una buena idea. Luego dice que no, que ella no puede ir con él. ¿Por qué?
6. Marianela le dice a Florentina que no quiere ser ingrata. ¿Por qué le dice tal cosa a Florentina?

K Confirmando información Usa una tabla como la de abajo para indicar si la información es correcta o no.

	correcta	incorrecta
1. Marianela no quiere ir a la casa de Pablo porque sabe que todos son muy felices.		
2. Marianela está triste porque Pablo tiene vista.		
3. Marianela quiere estar sola con sus pensamientos porque está muy triste.		
4. Está muy triste porque sabe que Pablo va a casarse con Florentina.		

L Creando un diálogo El diálogo, una conversación entre dos personas, es un elemento importante en muchas novelas. Prepara una conversación que tiene lugar entre Celipín y Marianela cuando él se despide de ella.

M Llegando a conclusiones ¿Qué opinión tienes? ¿Se casará Pablo con Florentina o no? Explica.

Answers

J *Answers will vary but may include:*

1. Todos se alegran porque Pablo puede ver.
2. La Nela no es feliz porque sabe que Pablo querrá casarse con Florentina y no con ella.
3. Pablo quiere verla porque quiere a la Nela.
4. Marianela no puede hablar más con Florentina porque está muy triste y quiere estar a solas.
5. Marianela dice que no porque no quiere estar lejos de donde se murió su madre.
6. Marianela está triste porque quiere mucho a Pablo pero sabe que Pablo no querrá casarse con ella. Marianela no quiere decírselo y aparecer ingrata porque Florentina ha sido tan buena con ella.

K

1. incorrecta
2. incorrecta
3. correcta
4. correcta

L *Answers will vary.*

M *Answers will vary.*

N You may wish to intersperse questions from this activity as you are going over the reading selection.

P You may wish to have students write their interpretation of this activity.

Q This activity can serve as the basis of an extensive classroom or small group discussion.

4

N Recordando hechos Contesta.

1. ¿De quién eran los pasos que oyó Celipín?
2. ¿Hacia dónde corrió el perro?
3. ¿Qué hizo el perro cuando llegó a la casa de Pablo?
4. ¿Quién siguió al perro?
5. ¿Adónde lo llevó el perro?
6. ¿Quería Marianela hablar con el doctor?
7. ¿Qué hizo el doctor?
8. ¿Adónde la llevó?
9. ¿Dónde la puso?
10. Al día siguiente, ¿quién salió de su cuarto?
11. ¿Con quién habló?

O Confirmando información Usa una tabla como la de abajo para indicar si la información es correcta o no.

	correcta	incorrecta
1. Cuando Pablo mira hacia el sofá, sabe que la muchacha en el sofá es Marianela. La reconoce enseguida.		
2. Pablo cree que la muchacha en el sofá es otra pobre a quien ayudaba Florentina.		
3. Pablo reconoció a Marianela cuando le tocó la cabeza y vio la expresión en su cara.		
4. Pablo no reconoció a Marianela hasta que ella le tomó la mano.		

P Interpretando Explica el significado de la siguiente frase.

«Al sentir su contacto Pablo se estremeció de pies a cabeza y gritó».

Q Interpretando y analizando En la novela *Marianela*, el doctor Teodoro Golfín representa la ciencia. Él da nueva vida a Pablo al darle vista. Pero, ¿qué le pasa a Marianela? Lee el siguiente párrafo. ¿Qué opinión tienes? ¿Han triunfado la ciencia y el progreso? Defiende tu opinión.

> Después de la muerte de Marianela el doctor Teodoro Golfín dice:
> —La realidad ha sido para él nueva vida; para ella ha sido dolor y asfixia, la humillación, la tristeza, el dolor… ¡la muerte!

En realidad, ¿qué nos está diciendo el doctor? ¿Es posible que sea también la opinión del autor Galdós?

Answers

N

1. Los pasos que oyó Celipín eran de Choto.
2. El perro corrió hacia la casa de los Penáguilas.
3. Cuando llegó a la casa de Pablo, Choto vio a Teodoro Golfín y dio cuarenta vueltas en torno de él y no dejó de ladrar.
4. Teodoro Golfín siguió al perro.
5. Lo llevó adonde estaba la Nela.
6. No, Marianela no quería hablar con Teodoro Golfín.
7. El doctor levantó a la Nela.
8. La llevó a la casa de Pablo.
9. La puso en el sofá.
10. Pablo salió de su cuarto.
11. Habló con Florentina.

O

1. incorrecta
2. correcta
3. incorrecta
4. correcta

P *Answers will vary.*

Q *Answers will vary.*

This Language Arts Practice section exposes students to additional practice with their Language Arts skills while using their Spanish.

Preview

You may decide to skip these informational and authentic readings, assign them as extra credit, or go over them thoroughly to the point that students can tell about them in their own words. They could also serve as a source of enrichment for heritage speakers.

The section on **El arte** can be done any time after finishing three or more chapters, **La ecología** can be done after finishing six or more chapters, and **César Chávez** can be done after finishing nine or more chapters.

Language Arts Practice

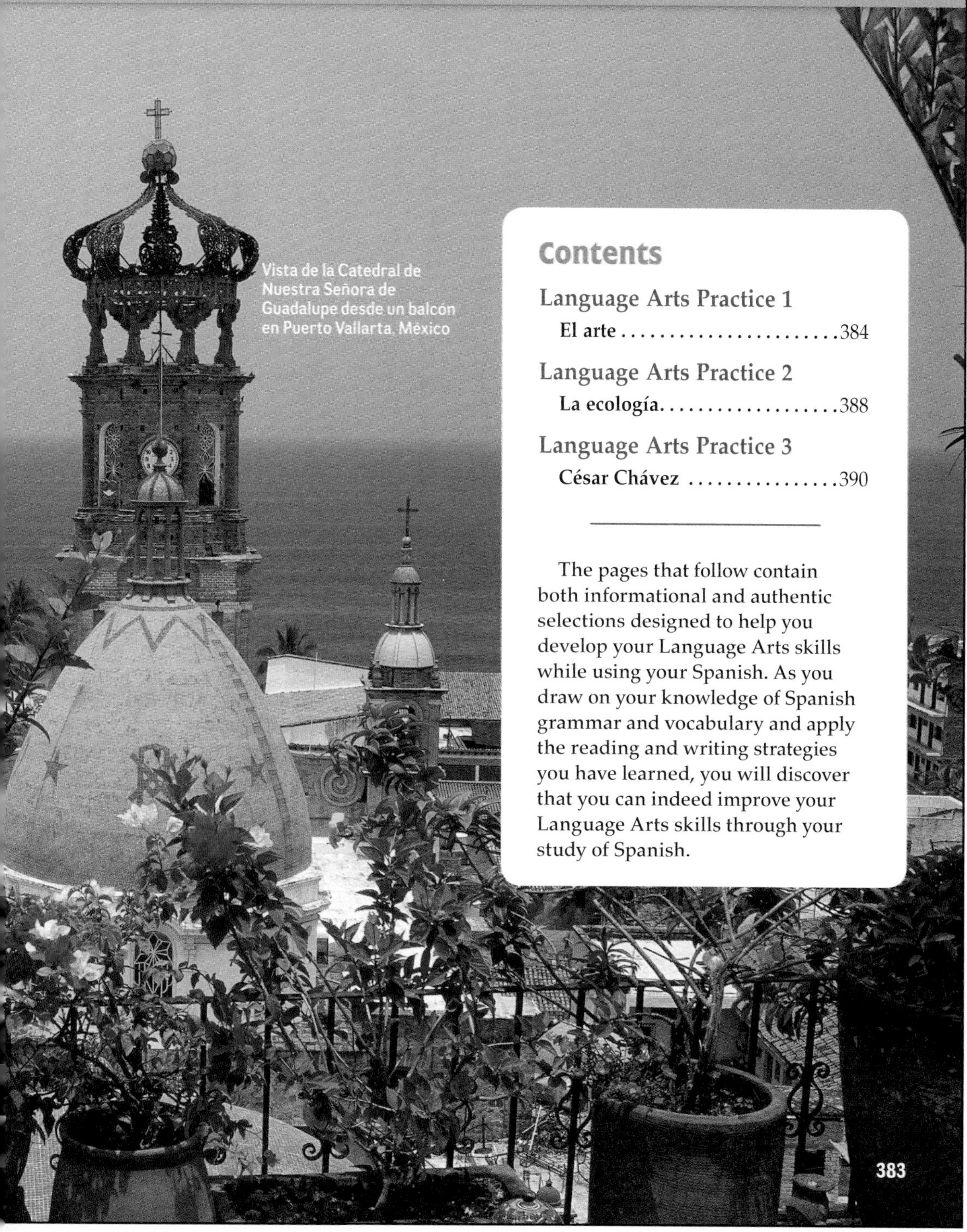

Vista de la Catedral de Nuestra Señora de Guadalupe desde un balcón en Puerto Vallarta, México

Contents

The pages that follow contain both informational and authentic selections designed to help you develop your Language Arts skills while using your Spanish. As you draw on your knowledge of Spanish grammar and vocabulary and apply the reading and writing strategies you have learned, you will discover that you can indeed improve your Language Arts skills through your study of Spanish.

Tips for Success

The exposure to these types of readings early in one's study of a foreign language should be a pleasant experience. As students read these selections, it is not necessary that they understand every word. Explain to them that they should try to enjoy the experience of reading in a new language.

Pre-AP Reading these selections and doing the activities that accompany them will help students develop the skills that they need to be successful on the reading and writing sections of the AP exam.

Language Arts Practice 1

This Language Arts Practice section is optional. You may wish to present it after students have completed at least three chapters, as they will have begun to understand the process of and strategies associated with reading in a second language by this point.

Teaching Options

You may assign the piece as an independent activity, including reading and answering the questions on their own; you may assign it as homework with follow-up in class; or you may present it thoroughly as an in-class activity. This option includes a pre-reading vocabulary presentation, in-class reading and discussion, and going over the activities in class or assigning them for homework with a class discussion the following day. You may also wish to vary the presentation procedures. Some options are:

- Students read silently.
- Students read after you in unison.
- Individual students read aloud.

With any of the above procedures, intersperse comprehension questions. Call on a student or students to give a brief synopsis in Spanish.

Language Arts Practice 1

El arte

Para apreciar una visita al museo o solo para apreciar una obra de arte es necesario tener a lo menos un conocimiento elemental del arte: la pintura, la escultura y el dibujo.

La pintura

Antes de empezar a pintar, el pintor o artista tiene que tener su lienzo[1] preparado. Tiene que tensarlo y colocarlo[2] en el caballete[3]. El pintor escoge su medio. Los tres medios que más emplean los pintores son la acuarela, el óleo y el acrílico. La espátula se usa para mezclar[4] los colores y a veces para aplicarlos. Por lo general el artista aplica los colores con un pincel[5], sobre todo cuando pinta con acuarelas.

Elementos de composición

Al mirar una pintura hay que fijarse en[6] la composición. Hay algunos elementos de composición muy importantes. La perspectiva es la representación de los objetos en tres dimensiones—alto, ancho, profundo—sobre una superficie plana. El pintor tiene que tomar en cuenta su alejamiento—su posición en el espacio con respecto a la del observador.

[1]lienzo *canvas*
[2]colocarlo *place it*
[3]caballete *easel*
[4]mezclar *mix*
[5]pincel *brush*
[6]fijarse en *pay attention to*

Pablo Picasso pintando en su taller

Un sello que conmemora la batalla en el pequeño pueblo de Guernica

El tema o motivo de una obra de arte es el principal elemento de interés para el observador. Es la materia que pinta el artista. El estilo es el modo o la expresión del artista. El estilo puede clasificarse en términos básicos en figurativo y abstracto. A las obras de arte que enfatizan la importancia de los elementos y principios de diseños a favor de asunto o de la materia se les llama obras de arte abstracto. Una obra figurativa presenta una rendición más literal, o sea, más realista de la materia.

La escultura

El escultor crea objetos o formas bellas en tres dimensiones o en relieve. Puede servirse de varios materiales como barro, yeso, madera, piedra o bronce. Unas esculturas, las de piedra o madera, por ejemplo, pueden ser talladas[7] con cincel[8]. Otras, de materiales blandos como el yeso, barro o bronce fundido pueden ser modeladas sobre un esqueleto o armadura. La cocción[9] y la fundición[10] en un horno son dos procesos que prolongan la duración de (hacen más duraderas) las esculturas.

El relieve

Un relieve es cualquier cosa que resalta sobre una superficie plana. Una escultura de relieve es una escultura hecha sobre una superficie de modo que las figuras están talladas solamente en parte. Bajorrelieve significa que la figura tallada es menos de la mitad del bulto[11] natural de la figura. Y altorrelieve significa que es más de la mitad del bulto de la figura. Se ven muchas esculturas de relieve en las catedrales, iglesias y otros edificios monumentales.

[7]talladas *carved*
[8]cincel *chisel*
[9]cocción *cooking*
[10]fundición *melting*
[11]bulto *shape*

Andrew Payti

CULTURA
Esta estatua del oso y del madroño es una escultura de bronce ubicada en la Puerta del Sol en Madrid.

LA PRACTICE Language Arts Practice 1

Actividades

A En forma gráfica indica lo que tiene que hacer el pintor cuando decide pintar algo.

B Si tú tienes interés en el arte, sobre todo la pintura, explica a unos amigos tu medio favorito. Diles por qué.

C Estás hablando con un amigo que no sabe nada del arte. Explícale la diferencia entre el medio y la composición. Explícale también la diferencia entre el medio y el tema o motivo.

D Explica la diferencia entre una obra figurativa y una obra abstracta.

E Determina las ideas centrales sobre la información presentada en el texto. Da un resumen de las ideas más importantes y explica como se desarrollan en el texto.

F Describe en la manera más precisa posible lo que es una escultura.

G Prepara un cartel en el cual divides y presentas el vocabulario específico que se necesita al hablar de la pintura y de la escultura.

H Alguien dice que un relieve es una escultura. Habla con la persona y de una manera cortés y en un tono objetivo explícale que lo que está diciendo no es completamente correcto. Ayúdale a ampliar lo que ha dicho para dar una definición o descripción más precisa de un relieve.

I Trabajando en grupos divídanse una vez más en dos grupos—los que prefieren el arte abstracto y los que prefieren el arte figurativo. Abran la sesión con una definición de cada uno. Presenten sus opiniones sobre sus predilecciones y expliquen por qué ustedes tienen tales opiniones. Si alguien quiere una clarificación de la aserción de otro(a), puede pedirle más información. Todos deben señalar lo que consideran exageraciones o conclusiones erróneas de los otros. Al final, trabajen juntos para presentar una conclusión a las perspectivas e ideas del grupo.

Answers

A *Answers will vary.*

B *Answers will vary but may include:*
la acuarela, el óleo y el acrílico.

- La composición tiene elementos muy importantes. Uno es la perspectiva que es la representación de los objetos en tres dimensiones: alto, ancho y profundo sobre una superficie plana.
- El tema o motivo es el principal elemento de interés para el observador. Es el estilo o expresión del artista. Este puede clasificarse en abstracto y figurativo.

C *Answers will vary.*

D *Answers will vary but may include:*
Una obra figurativa presenta una rendición más literal, o sea, más realista de la materia. Una obra abstracta enfatiza la importancia de los elementos y principios de diseño a favor de la materia.

Las Bellas Artes

UN PROYECTO

Busca y estudia varios cuadros de artistas españoles o latinoamericanos y decide cuales son obras que te interesan, que te pican el interés o que encuentras bonitas.

Escribe un reportaje sobre el cuadro que seleccionas. Luego da tus ideas personales sobre los aspectos de la obra que te pican el interés. Da también una descripción de lo que encuentras bonito en la obra y porque te gusta tanto. Luego, presenta tu proyecto a la clase.

Aquí tienes una lista de algunos artistas famosos.

España	**Latinoamérica**
Murillo	Botero
Goya	Kahlo
El Greco	Rivera
Velázquez	Orozco
Dalí	

San Ildefonso de El Greco

Marquesa de Pontejos de Francisco de Goya.

Answers

E *Answers will vary but may include:* Las ideas centrales son cuatro: La pintura, los elementos de composición, la escultura y el relieve. Las ideas más importantes en la pintura son los tres medios que más emplean los pintores (la acuarela, el óleo y el acrílico). En los elementos de composición son la perspectiva, el estilo figurativo y el abstracto. En la escultura son los diferentes materiales y los diferentes tipos de relieve: el relieve, el bajorrelieve y el altorrelieve.

F *Answers will vary but may include:* Una escultura es un objeto tallado en forma bella. Una escultura puede ser creada en tres diferentes dimensiones o en relieve.

G *Answers will vary but may include:* Vocabulario de la pintura: el lienzo, el caballete, la acuarela, el óleo, el acrílico, la espátula, el pincel. Vocabulario de la escultura: el relieve, las tres dimensiones, los materiales, el yeso, la madera, la piedra, el bronce, el cincel, tallado.

H *Answers will vary but may include:* El relieve es una escultura hecha sobre una superficie plana de modo que las figuras están talladas solamente en parte.

I *Answers will vary.*

Language Arts Practice 2

This Language Arts Practice section is optional. You may wish to present it after students have completed at least six chapters, as they will have acquired much of the vocabulary and grammar necessary to understand the selection by this point and will be able to put into practice the reading strategies they have been learning.

Teaching Options

You may assign the piece as an independent activity, including reading and answering the questions on their own; you may assign it as homework with follow-up in class; or you may present it thoroughly as an in-class activity. This option includes a pre-reading vocabulary presentation, in-class reading and discussion, and going over the activities in class or assigning them for homework with a class discussion the following day. You may also wish to vary the presentation procedures. Some options are:

- Students read silently.
- Students read after you in unison.
- Individual students read aloud.

With any of the above procedures, intersperse comprehension questions. Call on a student or students to give a brief synopsis in Spanish.

La ecología

El medio ambiente

El problema de la contaminación del medio ambiente[1] ha dado lugar al movimiento ecologista. El término «ecología», el equilibrio entre los seres vivientes y la naturaleza, ha llegado a ser[2] sinónimo de supervivencia[3] para muchos seres humanos.

La contaminación del aire

La contaminación de todos tipos es la plaga de nuestros tiempos. Buques[4] petroleros derraman[5] quién sabe cuántos litros de petróleo cada año en nuestros mares y océanos. El aire que respiramos está contaminado, mayormente por las emisiones de gases de los tubos de escape de los automóviles y camiones y de las fábricas[6] que queman[7] sustancias químicas. Es la responsabilidad de todos evitar que se expulsen al aire sustancias tóxicas.

La contaminación del agua

Los ríos son las venas de una gran parte de la humanidad y desgraciadamente muchos de ellos están tan contaminados que son portadores de enfermedades. En las zonas industriales, sobre todo en el este de Europa y China, la situación es catastrófica. Los desechos[8] industriales que las fábricas echan en las aguas cercanas son casi imposibles de eliminar. A estos se añaden los desechos que están enterrados[9] y que son transportados por las corrientes de agua subterráneas o los que simplemente vuelven a la superficie para contaminar la tierra. Siempre volvemos al mismo problema, el de los desechos y la manera de deshacernos de ellos. Hoy en día hay grandes campañas de reciclaje. El reciclaje consiste en recoger los desechos de papel, vidrio e hierro para transformarlos y poder utilizarlos de nuevo.

Como dijo uno de los astronautas, el coronel Jon E. Blaha, «El planeta Tierra es un lugar absolutamente bello. Uno se da cuenta cuando lo ve desde aquí arriba. Ciertamente necesitamos cuidarlo».

[1]medio ambiente *environment*
[2]ha llegado a ser *has become*
[3]supervivencia *survival*
[4]Buques *ships*
[5]derraman *spill*
[6]fábricas *factories*
[7]queman *burn*
[8]desechos *waste*
[9]enterrados *buried*

Richard Brommer

Actividades

A Explica de una manera concisa lo que es el medio ambiente.

B Trabajen en grupos y respondan a diversas perspectivas de lo que sus colegas consideran los problemas más serios en cuanto a la destrucción del medio ambiente. Al terminar su discusión preparen un resumen de los puntos en que hay acuerdo y desacuerdo y preséntenlo a la clase.

C Hoy en día hay artículos casi a diario en los periódicos sobre el medio ambiente. Léelos y después de leer a lo menos tres prepara un reportaje sobre lo que el gobierno está considerando asuntos serios. ¿Hay mucho acuerdo o desacuerdo entre los varios grupos políticos? ¿Cuáles son los asuntos que tú personalmente consideras importantes? ¿Por qué los consideras tan importantes? Y, ¿cuáles para ti no tienen tanta importancia?

D Haz un reportaje en el cual comparas la contaminación del aire y la contaminación del agua. En tu opinión, ¿representa una un problema más serio que otra o no? Busca datos y evidencia para soportar tus opiniones.

E Basado en los recursos sobre el medio ambiente que tienes a tu disponibilidad, escribe una carta a un miembro gubernamental estatal diciéndole lo que tú propones como acciones que él debe soportar para mejorar el medio ambiente en tu estado. Escribe tu carta en un estilo formal y un tono objetivo. Cuando necesario da información para soportar tus ideas y conclusiones.

F Trabajando en grupos preparen y presenten un debate sobre los problemas ambientales que existen en la región donde ustedes viven. Después de identificar los problemas discutan lo que ustedes creen que el gobierno está haciendo o no haciendo para enfrentar los problemas. Al terminar el debate, lleguen a una conclusión. Incluyan materia que soporta su conclusión y que explica de una manera clara el significado y las posibles consecuencias del tema.

POR SIGLOS, EL HOMBRE DE ESTAS TIERRAS
CONVIVIO CON LA NATURALEZA.
RESTABLECER ESA ARMONIA
ES UNA TAREA QUE NOS CORRESPONDE A TOD

Richard Brommer

G Describe la importancia del mensaje en esta cartelera. Explica lo que tú haces personalmente para tratar de conformarte con el aviso. ¿Qué hacen otros que rehúsan seguir el aviso?

Answers

A *Answers will vary but may include:* El medio ambiente es el equilibrio entre los seres vivientes y la naturaleza.

B *Answers will vary but may include:* la contaminación del aire y del agua.

C *Answers will vary.*

D *Answers will vary.*

E *Answers will vary.*

F *Answers will vary.*

G *Answers will vary.*

Language Arts Practice 3

This Language Arts Practice vsection is optional. You may wish to present it after students have completed at least nine chapters, as they will have acquired much of the vocabulary and grammar necessary to understand the selection by this point and will be able to put into practice the reading strategies they have been learning.

Teaching Options

You may assign the piece as an independent activity, including reading and answering the questions on their own; you may assign it as homework with follow-up in class; or you may present it thoroughly as an in-class activity. This option includes a pre-reading vocabulary presentation, in-class reading and discussion, and going over the activities in class or assigning them for homework with a class discussion the following day. You may also wish to vary the presentation procedures. Some options are:

- Students read silently.
- Students read after you in unison.
- Individual students read aloud.

With any of the above procedures, intersperse comprehension questions. Call on a student or students to give a brief synopsis in Spanish.

César Chávez

CULTURA

César Chávez hablando con unos obreros en California

César Chávez nació en 1927 en Yuma, Arizona, en una familia de campesinos. César recibió el nombre de su querido abuelo. Al perder su tierra la familia Chávez se trasladó a California donde el joven César recogía algodón, vegetales y uvas cuando podía encontrar trabajo. Dice Chávez que recuerda haber asistido a sesenta y cinco escuelas elementales en un solo año escolar—a veces por solamente un día.

Durante la Segunda Guerra mundial Chávez sirvió en la Marina. Al salir de la Marina se estableció de nuevo en California con su esposa, Helen Fabela. Cuando tenía solo veinticinco años César empezó a organizarse para ayudar a «su gente» a mejorar las lamentables condiciones laborales que habían aceptado durante generaciones. A principios de los años 60 Chávez fundó el primer sindicato para obreros[1] migratorios. Este sindicato se fusionó más tarde con otro para formar la primera gran organización de campesinos. César incitó a los campesinos mexicanoamericanos a inscribirse para votar e inauguró una huelga[2] contra las grandes empresas vinícolas[3]. La huelga atrajo mucha atención nacional y ayudó a informar a la nación de las grandes injusticias que enfrentaban los campesinos mexicanoamericanos.

Les informó también de las pésimas condiciones en que vivían durante décadas. En su lucha[4] llamada «La Causa», Chávez se aprovechó de algunas tácticas del movimiento de derechos civiles tales como marchas y protestas o manifestaciones pacíficas incluyendo un ayuno[5] de veinticinco días. Pero los cultivadores de uva no sucumbieron. Por fin el modesto pero carismático y determinado Chávez les rogó[6] a todos los americanos a boicotear las empresas cultivadoras de uvas en California. Más de diecisiete millones de habitantes oyeron su petición y apoyaron a La Causa rehusando comprar uvas de California. El boicoteo duró cinco años. Las empresas perdieron millones de dólares y por fin el 30 de julio de 1970 los cultivadores de uvas de California accedieron[7] a firmar un contrato que por primera vez otorgó[8] algunos derechos a los recogedores[9] de uvas y les concedió un pequeño aumento de sueldo[10]. Fue el primero de muchos boicoteos exitosos organizados por Chávez para ayudar a mejorar la vida de todos los obreros agrícolas.

Uvas

Chávez fue un hombre sencillo de una espiritualidad profunda. Era vegetariano. Sus símbolos fueron la virgen de Guadalupe, la santa patrona de México, y un águila azteca negra en un paisaje norteamericano. Su causa enfrentó muchas dificultades y obstáculos pero Chávez no dejó la lucha. Él será para siempre no solo el líder de los campesinos mexicanoamericanos sino de todos los campesinos. Chávez murió tranquilamente en su sueño a los sesenta y seis años en Yuma, no muy lejos de la casita de adobe donde había nacido. Había en su cara una sonrisa y en la mano un libro de artesanía del sudoeste. La muerte de Chávez suscitó elogios[11] de líderes nacionales e internacionales. Robert F. Kennedy describió a este humilde campesino mexicanoamericano con su ideal de justicia e igualdad para todos como *one of the heroic figures of our time.*

¡Qué descanse en paz y que sigamos realizando su sueño!

[1]obreros *workers*
[2]huelga *strike*
[3]empresas vinícolas *wine producers*
[4]lucha *fight*
[5]ayuno *fast*
[6]rogó *begged*
[7]accedieron *agreed*
[8]otorgó *gave*
[9]recogedores *pickers*
[10]sueldo *pay*
[11]elogios *tributes, praises*

Actividades

A Cita razones por las cuales César Chávez se considera, como lo llama Roberto Kennedy, una figura histórica de nuestra época. Después de citar las razones, provee evidencia para soportar las razones.

B Da algunos datos personales sobre la vida de Chávez y describe el tipo de persona que era.

C Según todos los recursos que tienes a tu disponibilidad, defiende o refuta la siguiente declaración «Las grandes empresas estaban muy contentas con el trabajo que hacía César Chávez y sus seguidores». Explica el porqué.

D Hoy en día siguen problemas de inmigración y derechos de los trabajadores. Trabajen en grupos de tres o cuatro y comparen todo lo que saben de estos problemas y den sus opiniones sobre unas soluciones para resolverlos.

CULTURA

Plaza de César Chávez en San José, California

Answers

A César Chávez se considera una figura histórica de nuestra época porque fue un líder de los campesinos. Se enfrentó a muchas dificultades y obstáculos.

B *Answers will vary but may include:*
Él nació en Yuma, Arizona. Él era de una familia de campesinos. Él se trasladó a California. Él sirvió a la Marina. Él fundó el primer sindicato para obreros migratorios. Él era vegetariano. Él asistió a sesenta y cinco escuelas elementales en solo un año escolar. Él era una persona modesta, carismática y determinada. Él fue un hombre sencillo de una espiritualidad profunda.

C *Answers will vary.*

D *Answers will vary.*

Core Instruction

If you decide to present this poem in depth, it is suggested that you have students read it aloud. If their pronunciation is not very good, read several lines to them and have them repeat after you.

¿Quién sabe?

de José Santos Chocano

INTRODUCCIÓN

En muchas partes del mundo ha habido y todavía hay problemas de que sufren los labradores, sobre todo los labradores agrícolas. Muchos de ellos trabajan muchas horas al día y en la mayoría de los casos no son dueños de la tierra que labran. Aquí tenemos un poema de José Santos Chocano (1875–1934), el famoso poeta peruano, en el cual le habla al indígena peruano.

¿Quién sabe?

—Indio que labras[1] con fatiga
tierras que de otros dueños son:
¿Ignoras tú que deben tuyas
ser, por tu sangre y tu sudor[2]?
¿Ignoras tú que audaz codicia[3],
siglos atrás te las quitó?
¿Ignoras tú que eres el Amo[4]?
—¡Quién sabe, señor!

—Indio de frente taciturna
y de pupilas sin fulgor[5]
¿Qué pensamiento es el que escondes
en tu enigmática expresión?
¿Qué es lo que buscas en tu vida?
¿Qué es lo que imploras a tu Dios?
¿Qué es lo que sueña tu silencio?
—¡Quién sabe, señor!

[1]labras *work*
[2]sudor *sweat*
[3]audaz codicia *bold greed*
[4]Amo *owner*
[5]sin fulgor *without sparkle*

Actividades

A Escribe un resumen sobre lo que aprendiste del indígena a quien habla José Santos Chocano. Indica las transiciones que hace el autor en su obra.

B Hablando en grupos discutan por qué usa el autor tantas preguntas en su poema. ¿Tendrá un sentido o mensaje especial? ¿Cuál será? ¿Cuál será la razón?

C Llega a una conclusión sobre el poema explicando la respuesta repetida del indígena: «¡Quién sabe, señor!»

CULTURA

En muchos casos los agricultores se sirven de métodos antiguos para cultivar la tierra como vemos en este campo en Puno, Perú.

Actividades

These activities reinforce students' reading comprehension and critical thinking skills.

Answers

A *Answers will vary.*

B El mensaje especial del poema es que el labrador debe ser el dueño de su propia tierra. La razón es porque él la trabaja.

C *Answers will vary.*

Student Resources

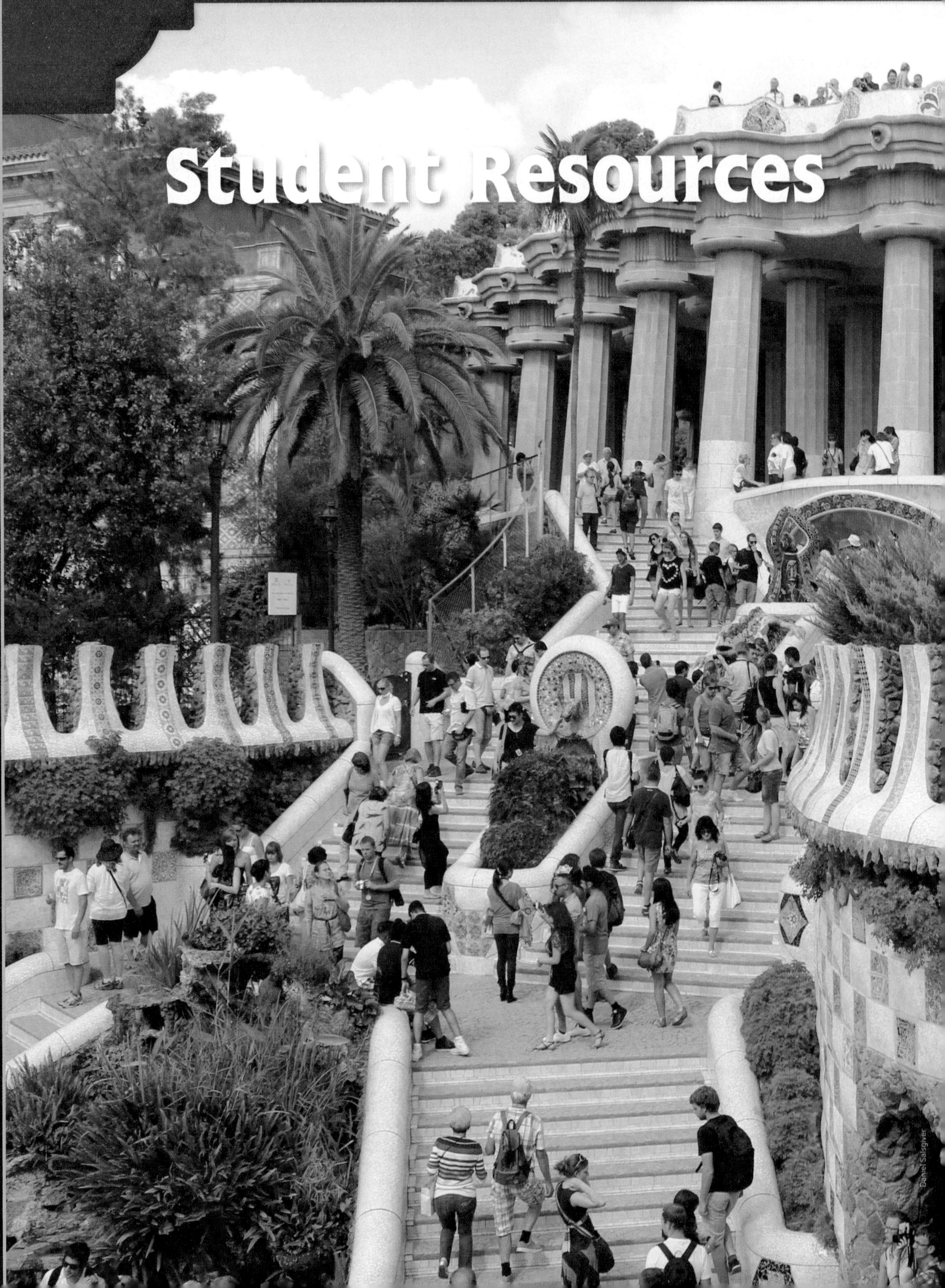

Daniel Salsgiver

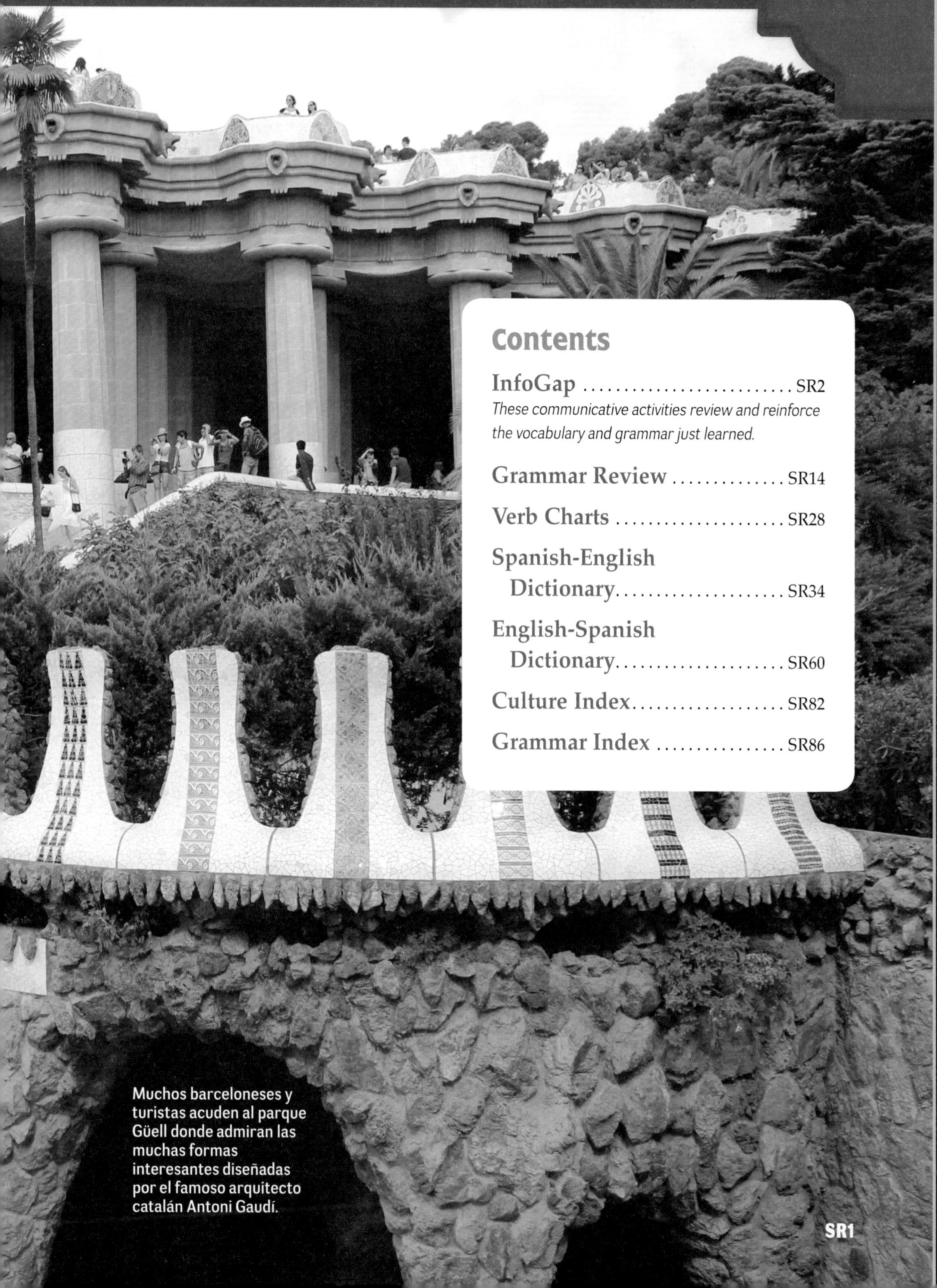

Contents

Muchos barceloneses y turistas acuden al parque Güell donde admiran las muchas formas interesantes diseñadas por el famoso arquitecto catalán Antoni Gaudí.

InfoGap

Activity R

REPASO F, Gramática

Alumno A Ask your partner the following questions. Correct answers are in parentheses.

1. ¿Dónde nadaste? *(Nadé en el mar.)*
2. ¿Adónde fueron ustedes? *(Fuimos al mercado.)*
3. ¿Qué viste? *(Vi una película.)*
4. ¿Qué comieron ustedes? *(Comimos una tortilla a la española.)*
5. ¿Dónde viviste? *(Viví en El Salvador.)*

Alumno A Use the clues below to answer your partner's questions.

1. el telesilla
2. una camisa roja
3. una exposición de arte colombiano
4. yo
5. no

Alumno B Use the clues below to answer your partner's questions.

1. el mar
2. al mercado
3. una película
4. una tortilla a la española
5. El Salvador

Alumno B Ask your partner the following questions. Correct answers are in parentheses.

1. ¿Cómo subieron la montaña ustedes? *(Subimos la montaña en el telesilla.)*
2. ¿Qué le compraste a Sofi? *(Le compré una camisa roja.)*
3. ¿Qué vieron ustedes? *(Vimos una exposición de arte colombiano.)*
4. ¿Quién fue el/la ganador(a)? *(Yo fui el/la ganador[a].)*
5. ¿Tomaron mucho sol ustedes? *(No, no tomamos mucho sol.)*

Activity 1

CAPÍTULO 1, Vocabulario 1

Alumno A Ask your partner the following questions. Correct answers are in parentheses.

1. ¿Es una tarjeta de embarque o un carnet de identidad? *(Es una tarjeta de embarque.)*
2. ¿Qué hace Gil? *(Gil factura su equipaje.)*
3. ¿Quién espera a los pasajeros? *(El taxista espera a los pasajeros.)*
4. ¿Dónde están la madre y su hija? *(La madre y su hija están en el aeropuerto.)*

Alumno A Answer your partner's questions based on the pictures below.

1. 

2. 

3. 

4. 

Alumno B Answer your partner's questions based on the pictures below.

1. 

2. 

3. 

4. 

Alumno B Ask your partner the following questions. Correct answers are in parentheses.

1. ¿Dónde pone el padre el equipaje? *(El padre pone el equipaje en la maletera [el baúl].)*
2. ¿Dónde están las pasajeras? *(Las pasajeras están en el mostrador de la línea aérea.)*
3. ¿El avión acaba de despegar o de aterrizar? *(El avión acaba de aterrizar.)*
4. ¿Cuál es el número del asiento del pasajero? *(El número del asiento del pasajero es 1C.)*

InfoGap

InfoGap

Activity 2

CAPÍTULO 2, Vocabulario 1

Alumno A Ask your partner the following questions. Correct answers are in parentheses.

1. ¿Qué hace Catalina? *(Catalina se cepilla los dientes.)* or *(Catalina se lava los dientes.)*
2. ¿Se acuesta Mateo o se estira? *(Mateo se acuesta.)*
3. ¿Qué hace Celia? *(Celia se pone un suéter.)*
4. ¿Se sienta la joven a la mesa o se cepilla el pelo? *(La joven se sienta a la mesa.)*

Alumno A Answer your partner's questions based on the photos below.

Mateo

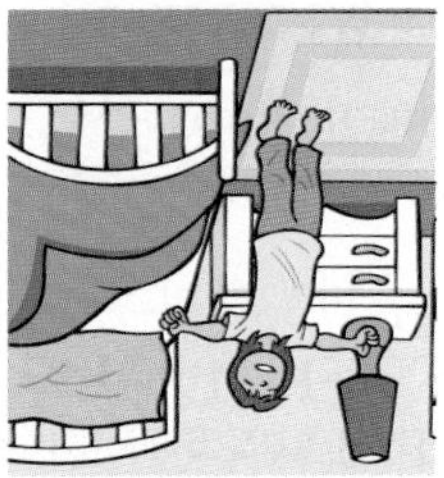

Elisa

Federico

la muchacha

Alumno B Answer your partner's questions based on the photos below.

la joven

Celia

Mateo

Catalina

Alumno B Ask your partner the following questions. Correct answers are in parentheses.

1. ¿Qué hace Elisa? *(Elisa se despierta.)* or *(Elisa se estira.)* or *(Elisa se levanta.)*
2. ¿Qué hace Mateo? *(Mateo se lava la cara.)*
3. ¿Qué hace la muchacha? *(La muchacha se peina.)* or *(La muchacha se mira en el espejo.)*
4. ¿Se mira en el espejo Federico o se lava el pelo? *(Federico se lava el pelo.)*

Activity 3

CAPÍTULO 3, Vocabulario 1, 2

Alumno A Ask your partner the following questions. Correct answers are in parentheses.

1. ¿Dónde compra el señor su billete? *(el señor compra su billete en la ventanilla [la boletería].)*
2. ¿Dónde comen Marcos y Mariana? *(Marcos y Mariana comen en el coche comedor [el coche cafetería].)*
3. ¿Dónde están los pasajeros? *(Los pasajeros están en el vagón [el coche].)* or *(Los pasajeros están en el tren.)*
4. ¿Qué lee el muchacho? *(El muchacho lee una revista.)* or *(El muchacho lee un periódico.)*

Alumno A Answer your partner's questions based on the pictures below.

1.

2–3.

4.

Alumno B Answer your partner's questions based on the pictures below.

1.

3–4.

2.

Alumno B Ask your partner the following questions. Correct answers are in parentheses.

1. ¿Dónde compras tu billete? *(Compro mi billete en el distribuidor automático.)*
2. ¿A quién le da su billete la muchacha? *(La muchacha le da su billete al revisor.)*
3. ¿Está el revisor en la plaza o en el pasillo? *(El revisor está en el pasillo.)*
4. ¿Van a bajar del tren los pasajeros o van a subir al tren? *(Los pasajeros van a subir al tren.)*

InfoGap

Activity 4

CAPÍTULO 4, Gramática

Alumno A Ask your partner the following questions. Correct answers are in parentheses.

1. ¿Qué piden ustedes? *(Nosotros pedimos los mariscos.)*
2. ¿Quién repitió la orden? *(El mesero repitió la orden.)*
3. ¿Cuántas horas durmieron los muchachos? *(Los muchachos durmieron cinco horas.)*
4. ¿Qué prefieres tomar? *(Prefiero tomar jugo.)*
5. ¿Cuántas veces repetí yo «el postre»? *(Tú repetiste «el postre» tres veces.)*

Alumno A Use the clues below to answer your partner's questions.

1. José Luis
2. los tostones
3. el arroz con frijoles
4. sí
5. el cocinero

Alumno B Use the clues below to answer your partner's questions.

1. los mariscos
2. el mesero
3. cinco horas
4. jugo
5. tres veces

Alumno B Ask your partner the following questions. Correct answers are in parentheses.

1. ¿Quién se viste? *(José Luis se viste.)*
2. ¿Qué prefirieron comer tus amigos? *(Mis amigos prefirieron comer los tostones.)*
3. ¿Qué pediste tú? *(Pedí el arroz con frijoles.)*
4. ¿Se divierten ustedes? *(Sí, nosotros nos divertimos.)*
5. ¿Quién frió las papas? *(El cocinero frió las papas.)*

Activity 5

Alumno A Ask your partner the following questions. Correct answers are in parentheses.

1. ¿Qué celebraba la familia? *(La familia celebraba Hanuka [la fiesta de las luces].)*
2. ¿Qué había en el puesto? *(Había esqueletos en el puesto.)*
3. ¿Qué hay en los zapatos? *(Hay paja en los zapatos.)*
4. ¿Qué llevaba la muchacha? *(La muchacha llevaba una máscara.)*

Alumno A Answer your partner's questions based on the pictures below.

1.

2.

3.

4.

Alumno B Answer your partner's questions based on the pictures below.

1.

3.

2.

4.

Alumno B Ask your partner the following questions. Correct answers are in parentheses.

1. ¿Qué hay en la sala? *(Hay un árbol de Navidad en la sala.)* or *(Hay muchos aguinaldos en la sala.)*
2. ¿Qué enciende el joven? *(El joven enciende una vela de la menora.)*
3. ¿Quiénes son ellos? *(Ellos son los Reyes Magos.)*
4. ¿Es un desfile o una tumba? *(Es un desfile.)*

InfoGap

Activity 6

CAPÍTULO 6, Vocabulario 1, 2

Alumno A Ask your partner the following questions. Correct answers are in parentheses.

1. ¿La muchacha navega el Internet o asigna timbres a sus amigos? *(La muchacha navega el Internet.)*
2. ¿Qué compraste ayer? *(Compré un móvil [un (teléfono) celular].)*
3. ¿Cuál es el prefijo del país? *(El prefijo del país es 34.)*
4. ¿Cuál es la clave de área? *(La clave de área es 952.)*

Alumno A Answer your partner's questions based on the pictures below.

1.

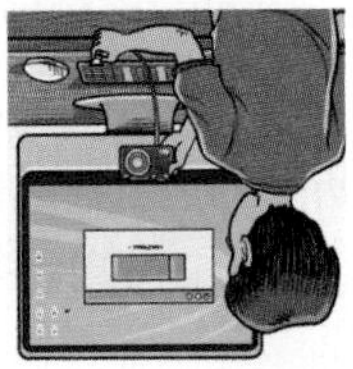

2–3.

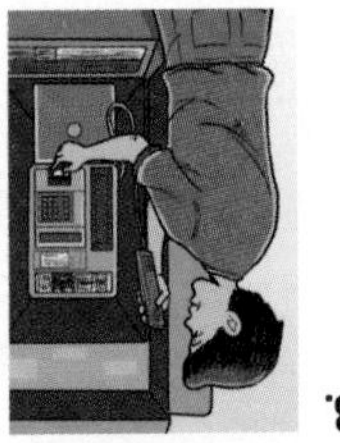

4.

Alumno B Answer your partner's questions based on the pictures below.

1.

3–4.

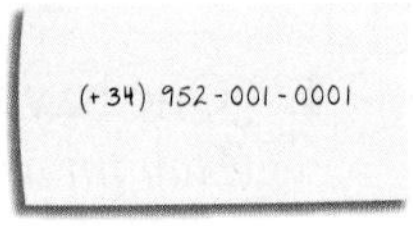

2.

Alumno B Ask your partner the following questions. Correct answers are in parentheses.

1. ¿Qué hace el muchaco? *(El muchacho baja fotos de su cámara digital.)*
2. ¿Qué usa el muchacho? *(El muchacho usa el teléfono público.)*
3. ¿Usa una tarjeta telefónica o unas monedas para hacer la llamada? *(Usa una tarjeta telefónica.)*
4. ¿Qué va a comprar Felipe para su computadora? *(Felipe va a comprar una impresora para su computadora.)*

Activity 7

Alumno A Ask your partner the following questions. Correct answers are in parentheses.

1. ¿Adónde no has ido todavía? *(Todavía no he ido al museo.)*
2. ¿Quién ya ha llegado? *(El mozo ya ha llegado.)*
3. ¿Quién te ha ayudado? *(Mi padre me ha ayudado.)*
4. ¿Qué ha comido Sara? *(Sara ha comido el desayuno continental.)*
5. ¿Qué han bebido ustedes? *(Hemos bebido un café.)*

Alumno A Use the clues below to answer your partner's questions.

1. el huésped
2. Colombia
3. Francisco
4. en el restaurante nuevo
5. Fernando

Alumno B Use the clues below to answer your partner's questions.

1. al museo
2. el mozo
3. mi padre
4. el desayuno continental
5. un café

Alumno B Ask your partner the following questions. Correct answers are in parentheses.

1. ¿Quién ha abandonado el cuarto? *(El huésped ha abandonado el cuarto.)*
2. ¿Adónde ya han viajado ustedes? *(Ya hemos viajado a Colombia.)*
3. ¿Con quién has hablado? *(He hablado con Francisco.)*
4. ¿Dónde hemos comido ya? *(Ya hemos comido en el restaurante nuevo.)*
5. ¿Quién te ha dado un regalo? *(Fernando me ha dado un regalo.)*

InfoGap

Activity 8

CAPÍTULO 8, Vocabulario 1, 2

Alumno A Ask your partner the following questions. Correct answers are in parentheses.

1. ¿Dónde entran los jóvenes?
   (Los jóvenes entran en la boca del metro.)
2. ¿Qué cosecha el campesino?
   (El campesino cosecha el trigo.)
3. ¿Es un cordero o es un cerdo?
   (Es un cerdo.)
4. ¿Dónde está la gente?
   (La gente está en la parada de autobús.)

Alumno A Answer your partner's questions based on the pictures below.

1.
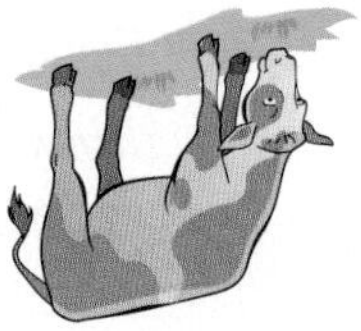

2.

3.
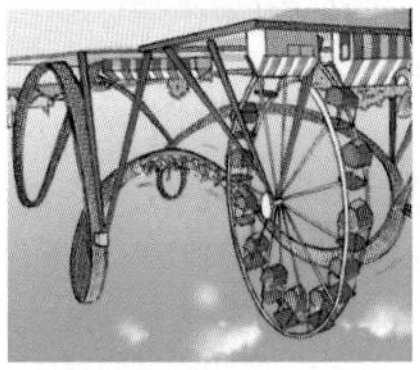

4.

Alumno B Answer your partner's questions based on the pictures below.

1.

2.

3.

4.

Alumno B Ask your partner the following questions. Correct answers are in parentheses.

1. ¿Es una vaca o es una gallina?
   (Es una vaca.)
2. ¿Dónde están los caballos?
   (Los caballos están en el establo.)
3. ¿Adónde van los jóvenes este fin de semana? *(Los jóvenes van al parque de atracciones este fin de semana.)*
4. ¿Dónde vive la familia, en la ciudad o en el campo?
   (La familia vive en el campo.)

Activity 9

Alumno A Ask your partner the following questions. Correct answers are in parentheses.

1. ¿Debo tomar el ascensor o las escaleras? *(Toma el ascensor.)*
2. ¿Quieres el vaso? *(Sí, pásame el vaso, por favor.)* or *(Sí, pásamelo, por favor.)*
3. ¿Quieres saber el secreto? *(Sí, dime el secreto.)* or *(Sí, dímelo.)*
4. ¿Qué hago con los libros? *(Pon los libros en la mesa.)* or *(Ponlos en la mesa.)*
5. ¿Adónde debo ir el viernes? *(Ve a la fiesta.)*

Alumno A Answer your partner's questions with an affirmative command based on the cues and the verbs given below.

1. llevar / a la playa
2. venir / aquí
3. sí / pasarme
4. estudiar / todos los días
5. salir / conmigo

Alumno B Answer your partner's questions with an affirmative command based on the cues and the verbs given below.

1. tomar / el ascensor
2. sí / pasarme
3. sí / decirme
4. poner / en la mesa
5. ir / a la fiesta

Alumno B Ask your partner the following questions. Correct answers are in parentheses.

1. ¿Qué hago con la cámara digital? *(Lleva la cámara digital a la playa.)* or *(Llévala a la playa.)*
2. ¿Adónde debo ir? *(Ven aquí.)*
3. ¿Quieres el pan? *(Sí, pásame el pan, por favor.)* or *(Sí, pásamelo, por favor.)*
4. ¿Qué debo hacer para sacar notas buenas? *(Estudia todos los días.)*
5. ¿Con quién debo salir? *(Sal conmigo.)*

InfoGap

Activity 10

CAPÍTULO 10, Gramática

Alumno A Ask your partner the following questions. Correct answers are in parentheses.

1. ¿Qué quiere Marisa que su primo haga? *(Marisa quiere que su primo se acueste.)*
2. ¿Qué quieren sus amigos que Marta haga? *(Sus amigos quieren que Marta salga este fin de semana.)*
3. ¿Qué quieres que hagamos esta noche? *(Quiero que miremos la tele esta noche.)*
4. ¿Qué quiere la madre de Diego que él haga? *(La madre de Diego quiere que él limpie la casa.)*

Alumno A Answer your partner's questions based on the clues below.

1. jugar tenis
2. preparar la comida
3. conducir con cuidado
4. decir la verdad

Alumno B Answer your partner's questions based on the clues below.

1. acostarse
2. salir este fin de semana
3. mirar la tele
4. limpiar la casa

Alumno B Ask your partner the following questions. Correct answers are in parentheses.

1. ¿Qué quieren los padres que sus hijos hagan? *(Los padres quieren que sus hijos jueguen tenis.)*
2. ¿Qué quieres que yo haga? *(Quiero que tú prepares la comida.)*
3. ¿Qué quiere Olivia que su hermana haga? *(Olivia quiere que su hermana conduzca con cuidado.)*
4. ¿Qué quiere el profesor que sus alumnos hagan? *(El profesor quiere que sus alumnos digan la verdad.)*

Alumno A Ask your partner the following questions. Correct answers are in parentheses.

1. ¿Qué se ha cortado la joven?
   (La joven se ha cortado la frente.)
2. ¿Ella está en la ambulancia?
   (No, ella no está en la ambulancia.)
3. ¿El médico le pone unas suturas?
   (Sí, el médico le pone unas suturas [unos puntos].)
4. ¿Qué le va a poner la enfermera?
   (La enfermera le va a poner una venda.)

Alumno A Answer your partner's questions based on the photo below.

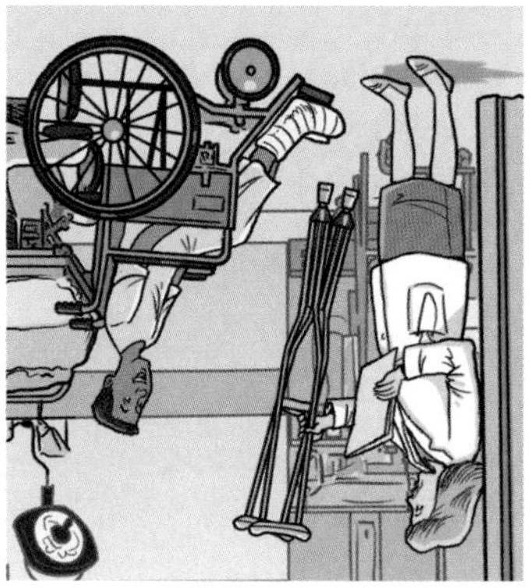

Alumno B Answer your partner's questions based on the photos below.

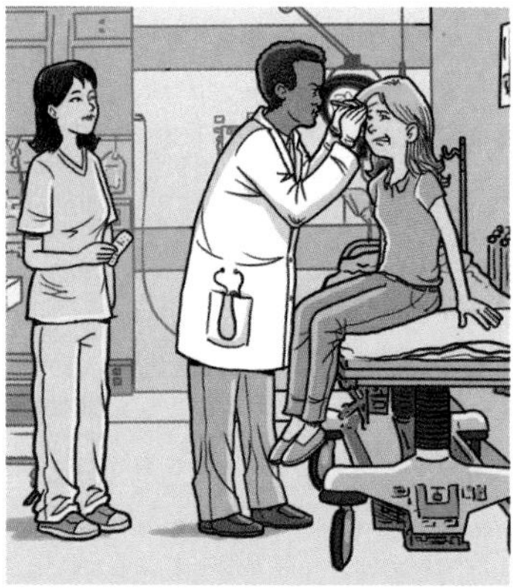

Alumno B Ask your partner the following questions. Correct answers are in parentheses.

1. ¿Qué se rompió el joven?
   (El joven se rompió el tobillo.) or
   (El joven se rompío el pie.)
2. ¿Habla el joven con los socorristas?
   (No, el joven no habla con los socorristas.)
3. ¿Con quién habla el joven?
   (El joven habla con la médica.)
4. ¿Está en una silla de ruedas?
   (Sí, está en una silla de ruedas.)

Grammar Review

Nouns and articles

Nouns and definite articles

A noun is the name of a person, place, or thing. Unlike English, all nouns in Spanish have a gender—either masculine or feminine. Almost all nouns that end in **-o** are masculine and almost all nouns that end in **-a** are feminine. Note that the definite article **el** is used with masculine nouns. The definite article **la** is used with feminine nouns.

MASCULINE	FEMININE
el muchacho	**la muchacha**
el libro	**la escuela**
el curso	**la sala**

Nouns that end in **-e** can be either masculine or feminine. It is necessary for you to learn the gender.

MASCULINE	FEMININE
el padre	**la madre**
el restaurante	**la carne**
el nombre	**la leche**
el norte	**la gente**
el billete	**la nube**

Many nouns that end in **-e** and refer to a person can be either masculine or feminine.

el paciente	**la paciente**

It is also necessary to learn the gender of nouns that end in a consonant.

el comedor	**la flor**
el animal	**la capital**
el jamón	**la mujer**

Note, however, that nouns that end in **-ción, -dad, -tad** are always feminine.

la habitación	**la universidad**	**la dificultad**

Irregular nouns

There are not many irregular nouns in Spanish. The ones you have learned so far are:

la mano	**el problema**	**la foto** (from **la fotografía**)

Plural of nouns

To form the plural of nouns you add **-s** to nouns that end in a vowel. You add **-es** to nouns that end in a consonant. Note, too, that the definite articles **el** and **la** become **los** and **las** in the plural.

MASCULINE PLURAL	FEMININE PLURAL
los libros	**las novelas**
los cuartos	**las casas**
los coches	**las carnes**
los comedores	**las flores**

Nouns that end in **-z** change the **-z** to **-c** and add **-es.**

el lápiz	**los lápices**

Nouns that end in **-ción** drop the accent in the plural.

la estación	**las estaciones**
la conversación	**las conversaciones**

Indefinite articles

The indefinite articles are *a, an,* and *some* in English. They are **un, una, unos, unas** in Spanish. Note that the indefinite article, like the definite article, must agree with the noun it modifies in both gender (masculine or feminine) and number (singular or plural).

SINGULAR		PLURAL	
un alumno	**una alumna**	**unos alumnos**	**unas alumnas**
un café	**una clase**	**unos cafés**	**unas clases**
un árbol	**una flor**	**unos árboles**	**unas flores**

Contractions

The prepositions **a** *(to, at)* and **de** *(of, from)* contract (combine) with the definite article **el** to form one word, **al** or **del.** There is no contraction with **la, los,** or **las.**

Voy al mercado; no vuelvo del mercado.
Es el dinero del empleado, no del cliente.

A personal

Remember that whenever a person is the direct object of the verb, it must be preceded by **a.** This **a personal** also contracts with **el.**

Conozco a Juan.
Pero no conozco al hermano de Juan.

Grammar Review

Nouns and adjectives

Agreement of nouns and adjectives

An adjective is a word that describes a noun. An adjective must agree in gender (masculine or feminine) and number (singular or plural) with the noun it describes or modifies.

Adjectives that end in **-o** have four forms, the same as nouns that end in **-o.**

	SINGULAR	PLURAL
MASCULINE	**el muchacho simpático**	**los muchachos simpáticos**
FEMININE	**la muchacha simpática**	**las muchachas simpáticas**

Adjectives that end in **-e** have only two forms—singular and plural.

	SINGULAR	PLURAL
MASCULINE	**un alumno inteligente**	**los alumnos inteligentes**
FEMININE	**una alumna inteligente**	**las alumnas inteligentes**

Adjectives that end in a consonant have only two forms—singular and plural. Note that the plural ends in **-es.**

	SINGULAR	PLURAL
MASCULINE	**un curso fácil**	**dos cursos fáciles**
FEMININE	**una tarea fácil**	**dos tareas fáciles**

Adjectives of nationality

Adjectives of nationality that end in a consonant have four forms. Observe the following.

un joven francés	**unos jóvenes franceses**
una joven francesa	**unas jóvenes francesas**

Note that adjectives of nationality that end in **-s, -n (francés, inglés, japonés, tailandés, alemán, catalán)** drop the written accent in all forms except the masculine singular.

Possessive adjectives

A possessive adjective tells who owns or possesses something—*my* book and *your* pencil. Like other adjectives in Spanish, possessive adjectives agree with the noun they modify. Note that only **nuestro** and ***vuestro*** have four forms.

MASCULINE SINGULAR	FEMININE SINGULAR	MASCULINE PLURAL	FEMININE PLURAL
mi tío	**mi tía**	**mis tíos**	**mis tías**
tu tío	**tu tía**	**tus tíos**	**tus tías**
su tío	**su tía**	**sus tíos**	**sus tías**
nuestro tío	**nuestra tía**	**nuestros tíos**	**nuestras tías**
vuestro tío	***vuestra tía***	***vuestros tíos***	***vuestras tías***

Since **su** can refer to many different people, it is often accompanied by a phrase that gives clarification.

su familia

la familia de Juan **la familia de él**
la familia de María **la familia de ella**
la familia de Juan y María **la familia de ellos**
la familia de usted
la familia de ustedes

Demonstrative adjectives

Until recently the demonstrative pronoun *(this one, that one, these, those)* had to carry a written accent to differentiate it from a demonstrative adjective. That is no longer the case and the pronouns are the same as the adjectives.

In Spanish there are three demonstrative adjectives (pronouns): **este** *(this)*, **ese** *(that)*, and **aquel** *(that, farther away)*. Each of the demonstratives has four forms and must agree in gender and number with the nouns they modify or replace.

MASCULINE SINGULAR	FEMININE SINGULAR	MASCULINE PLURAL	FEMININE PLURAL
este libro	**esta chaqueta**	**estos libros**	**estas chaquetas**
ese libro	**esa chaqueta**	**esos libros**	**esas chaquetas**
aquel libro	**aquella chaqueta**	**aquellos libros**	**aquellas chaquetas**

Grammar Review

Comparative and superlative

Regular forms

You use the comparative *(more, -er)* and the superlative *(most, -est)* to compare people or things.

To form the comparative in Spanish you use **más** (or **menos**) before the adjective. The comparative is followed by **que: más… que.**

Él es más (menos) inteligente que los otros.
Ella es más ambiciosa que los otros.

To form the superlative you use the definite article with **más.** Note that **de** follows the superlative: **el/la más... de.**

Él es el más ambicioso de todos.
Ella es la alumna más inteligente de todos.

Irregular forms

The adjectives **bueno** and **malo** and the adverbs **bien** and **mal** have irregular comparative and superlative forms.

	COMPARATIVE	SUPERLATIVE
bueno	**mejor**	**el/la mejor**
malo	**peor**	**el/la peor**
bien	**mejor**	**el/la mejor**
mal	**peor**	**el/la peor**

Él es mejor jugador que su hermano.
Pero su hermana Teresa es la mejor jugadora de los tres.
La verdad es que ella juega mejor que nadie.
Ella juega mejor que yo.

Note that the comparative is followed by the subject pronoun or a negative word.

más alto que yo (tú, él, nosotros)
más alto que nadie

(El) mayor and **(el) menor** are also comparative and superlative forms. They most often refer to age and sometimes size.

Mi hermano menor tiene trece años.
Y mi hermana mayor tiene diecisiete.
La Ciudad de México tiene el mayor número de habitantes.

Comparison of equality

To compare things that have equal qualities *as . . . as* you use **tan... como** in Spanish. Note that **tan** can precede an adjective or an adverb.

Ella es tan inteligente como sus hermanos.
Sus hermanos son tan inteligentes como ella.
Ella habla tan rápido como los otros.

To compare equal quantities *as much . . . as, as many . . . as* you use **tanto... como.** Since **tanto** is an adjective it must agree with the noun it modifies.

Él tiene tanta paciencia como su hermana.
Susana no tiene tantos primos como yo.

Note that the subject pronouns follow **como.**

Grammar Review

Pronouns

A pronoun is a word that replaces a noun. Review the forms of the pronouns that you have learned so far.

SUBJECT PRONOUNS	DIRECT OBJECT PRONOUNS	INDIRECT OBJECT PRONOUNS	REFLEXIVE PRONOUNS	PREPOSITIONAL PRONOUNS
yo	**me**	**me**	**me**	**mí**
tú	**te**	**te**	**te**	**ti**
Ud., él, ella	**lo, la**	**le**	**se**	**Ud., él, ella**
nosotros(as)	**nos**	**nos**	**nos**	**nosotros(as)**
vosotros(as)	***os***	***os***	***os***	***vosotros(as)***
Uds., ellos, ellas	**los, las**	**les**	**se**	**Uds., ellos, ellas**

Remember that an object pronoun comes right before the conjugated form of the verb.

Ella me ve. **Ella nos habla.** **Ella lo ha escrito.**

The direct object pronoun is the direct receiver of the action of the verb. The indirect object is the indirect receiver of the action of the verb.

The direct object pronouns **lo, la, los, las** can refer to a person or a thing.

Ellos tiraron la pelota. **Ellos la tiraron.**
Ellos vieron a sus amigos. **Ellos los vieron.**

The indirect object pronouns **le, les** refer to people only. They are often accompanied by a phrase for clarification.

Ella le habló { **a él.** / **a ella.** / **a usted.** }

Yo les hablé { **a ellos.** / **a ellas.** / **a ustedes.** }

Note that the prepositional pronouns **mí** and **ti** form one word with **con.**

Yo voy contigo y tú vas conmigo.

Double object pronouns

When there are two object pronouns in the same sentence, the indirect object pronoun always precedes the direct object pronoun.

Él me lo dijo.
Nuestros padres nos los dan.
¿Quién te lo dio?

The indirect object pronouns **le** and **les** change to **se** when used with a direct object pronoun **(lo, la, los, las).**

El profesor se lo explica muy bien.
¿Quién se las compró?

Se is often accompanied by a prepositional phrase to clarify its meaning.

Yo se lo di {
a usted.
a él.
a ella.
a ustedes.
a ellos.
a ellas.

Position of object pronouns

The object pronouns always precede the conjugated form of the verb.

José me vio.
El profesor se lo explicó a ustedes.
Ellos no lo han hecho.

With the progressive tenses or the infinitive the pronouns can either come before the helping verb or can be added to the present participle or the infinitive.

Ellos nos están ayudando.	**Ella te lo va a explicar.**
Ellos están ayudándonos.	**Ella va a explicártelo.**
Ella se la está vendiendo a ellos.	**Ellos nos quieren ayudar.**
Ella está vendiéndosela a ellos.	**Ellos quieren ayudarnos.**

Note that in order to maintain the same stress you add a written accent mark to the present participle with either one or two pronouns. You add an accent to the infinitive with two pronouns only.

Grammar Review

The object pronouns are added to an affirmative command. They precede the negative command.

AFFIRMATIVE	NEGATIVE
Háblame.	**No me hables.**
Dáselo.	**No se lo des.**
Invítelos usted.	**No los invite.**
Díganmelo.	**No me lo digan.**

Note that in order to maintain the same stress, you add a written accent to the command with a pronoun.

Negative expressions

To make a sentence negative, you merely put **no** before the verb or before the object pronoun that precedes the verb.

El gato no está en el jardín.
No lo veo.

Review the following affirmative and negative expressions.

AFFIRMATIVE	NEGATIVE
algo	**nada**
alguien	**nadie**
siempre	**nunca**

Nadie está aquí.

Note that in Spanish, unlike in English, more than one negative word can be used in the same sentence.

No ves a nadie.
Ellos nunca hablan a nadie de nada.

The negative of **también** is **tampoco.**

A Juan le gusta. A mí también.
A Juan no le gusta. Ni a mí tampoco.

Verbs such as interesar, aburrir, gustar

Note the construction with verbs such as **interesar** and **aburrir.**

La historia me interesa. **Me interesa la historia.**	*History interests me.*
Los deportes no les aburren. **No les aburren los deportes.**	*Sports don't bore them.*

Gustar functions the same as **interesar** and **aburrir.** It conveys the meaning *to like,* but it literally means *to please.*

Me **Te** **Le** **Nos** **Les**	**gusta el helado.**	**Me** **Te** **Le** **Nos** **Les**	**gustan los vegetales.**

Expressions with the infinitive

The infinitive is the form of the verb that ends in **-ar, -er,** or **-ir.** The infinitive often follows another verb.

Ellos quieren salir.
Yo debo estudiar más.
Me gusta leer.

Three very common expressions that are followed by the infinitive are **tener que** *(to have to),* **ir a** *(to be going to),* and **acabar de** *(to have just).*

Tengo que trabajar y estudiar más.
Y voy a trabajar y estudiar más.
Acabo de recibir una nota mala.

You can use the expression **favor de** followed by an infinitive to ask someone in a polite way to do something.

Favor de escribir tu nombre.
Favor de ayudarme.

Note that the object pronoun is added to the end of the infinitive.

Ser and estar

Spanish has two verbs that mean *to be.* They are **ser** and **estar** and each one has distinct uses.

Ser

You use **ser** to express a characteristic, where someone or something is from, or what something is made of.

Él es guapo. Es inteligente también.
Ellos son de Nuevo México.
Su casa es de adobe.

Estar

You use **estar** to express a condition or location.

Él está muy cansado y está triste también.
Madrid está en España.
Sus amigos están en Madrid.

Saber and conocer

Both **saber** and **conocer** mean *to know.*

Saber means to know a fact or to have information about something. With an infinitive it expresses *to know how to do something.*

Yo sé su número de teléfono.
Sabemos que ella va a viajar.
Todos saben usar el Internet.

Conocer means *to know* in the sense of *to be familiar with.* It is used with people or complex, abstract concepts.

Yo conozco a su amigo Tadeo.
Ellos conocen bien la historia de España.

Reflexive verbs

When the subject is both the doer and receiver of the action of the verb, you have to use a reflexive pronoun with the verb. Study the following examples of the reflexive construction.

REFLEXIVE	NONREFLEXIVE
Ella se levanta.	**Ella levanta al niño.**
Él se divierte.	**Él divierte a sus amigos.**
Me cepillo.	**Cepillo a mi perro.**

When the reflexive is followed by an article of clothing or a part of the body, you use a definite article in Spanish. (In English the possessive adjective is used.)

Me lavo la cara y las manos.
Ella tiene frío y se pone el suéter.

Verbs

See the charts on pages SR28–SR33 for the verb forms you have learned.

Verb tense usage

Present

You use the present tense to state what is taking place now or what always takes place.

Hablamos español.
Juegan fútbol en el otoño.
Siempre hacen la misma cosa.

You can also use the present tense to express a future action.

Salen mañana.
Vamos a México en julio.

Preterite

You use the preterite to express an action that began and ended at a specific time in the past.

Ellos salieron la semana pasada.
Nosotros llegamos ayer.
Los árabes invadieron España en 711.

Imperfect

You use the imperfect to describe a continuous, habitual action in the past. The time at which the action began or ended is not important.

Ellos siempre hacían la misma cosa.
Yo los veía de vez en cuando.
Ellos iban a España con frecuencia porque tenían una casa allí.

You use the imperfect to describe things in the past.

Él era joven.
Tenía solo dos años.
Hacía buen tiempo.
Su hermana era muy simpática.

You use the imperfect to reminisce about past events.

Cuando yo era niño vivíamos en Puerto Rico y siempre celebrábamos el Día de los Reyes. Yo recuerdo bien que recibíamos nuestros regalos el seis de enero.

You use the imperfect with verbs to express mental activities or emotions in the past.

Él lo creía.
Querían hacerlo.
Estaban contentos.

Future

The true future *will* is used less frequently in Spanish than in English.

Le hablaré a él mañana.
Volverán la semana que viene.

The present tense and the **ir a** + *infinitive* construction are often used to convey the future.

Le hablo a él mañana.	**Le voy a hablar mañana.**
Vuelven la semana que viene.	**Van a volver la semana que viene.**

Conditional

You use the conditional in Spanish the same as in English. It tells what would or could happen.

¿Iría él?	**Sí, él iría.**
¿Lo sabrían ellos?	**Sí, ellos lo sabrían.**
¿Estarías contento?	**Sí, yo estaría contento.**

Present perfect

The present perfect is used to describe an action without reference to a specific past time. It is accompanied by time expressions such as **ya, todavía no, jamás, nunca.**

Nunca hemos hecho tal cosa.
En mi vida he tenido un accidente.
Todavía no han llegado.

Progressive tense

The progressive tense is formed by using the verb **estar** (or **ir, seguir**) and the present participle. You use the progressive to indicate that the action is actually taking place.

Estamos pasando tiempo en la playa.
Estoy mirando a los niños.
Están nadando en el mar.

Subjunctive

You use the subjunctive in a dependent clause. As the word *subjunctive* implies, it is used to express a subjective action that is not necessarily a fact. It may or may not take place. So far you have learned the following uses of the subjunctive.

You use the subjunctive in a clause introduced by **querer.**

Quiero que ellos salgan ahora.
Ellos quieren que estudiemos y que tengamos éxito.

You use the subjunctive following many impersonal expressions.

Es importante que lleguemos a tiempo.
Es necesario que ellos lo sepan.
Es mejor que tú lo hagas.

The subjunctive follows the expressions **ojalá, quizás,** and **tal vez.**

¡Ojalá vengan a la fiesta!
¡Quizá(s) vayan!
¡Tal vez lo sepan!

Passive voice with se

The pronoun **se** is used to express something being done without saying by whom.

Se habla español en México.
- *Spanish is spoken in Mexico.*
- *One speaks Spanish in Mexico.*
- *They speak Spanish in Mexico.*

¿A qué hora se abre el restaurante?
Se sirven comidas mexicanas y peruanas.

Imperative (commands)

You use the subjunctive form of the verb for all formal **(usted, ustedes)** commands and the negative familiar **(tú)** command.

Hable Ud.	**No hable Ud.**	**Hablen Uds.**	**No hablen Uds.**	**No hables.**
Coma Ud.	**No coma Ud.**	**Coman Uds.**	**No coman Uds.**	**No comas.**

You use the **usted** form of the present indicative for the familiar **(tú)** command.

Habla.
Come.

Note that you add the object pronouns to affirmative commands. The pronouns come before the negative command.

AFFIRMATIVE	NEGATIVE
Prepárelo.	**No lo prepare.**
Escríbanlo Uds.	**No lo escriban Uds.**
Háblame.	**No me hables.**

There are no irregular formal commands. You will find any irregular familiar **(tú)** commands in the following verb charts.

Grammar Review

Verb Charts

Regular verbs			
INFINITIVO	hablar *to speak*	comer *to eat*	vivir *to live*
PARTICIPIO PRESENTE	hablando	comiendo	viviendo
PARTICIPIO PASADO	hablado	comido	vivido
PRESENTE	hablo hablas habla hablamos *habláis* hablan	como comes come comemos *coméis* comen	vivo vives vive vivimos *vivís* viven
PRETÉRITO	hablé hablaste habló hablamos *hablasteis* hablaron	comí comiste comió comimos *comisteis* comieron	viví viviste vivió vivimos *vivisteis* vivieron
IMPERFECTO	hablaba hablabas hablaba hablábamos *hablabais* hablaban	comía comías comía comíamos *comíais* comían	vivía vivías vivía vivíamos *vivíais* vivían
FUTURO	hablaré hablarás hablará hablaremos *hablaréis* hablarán	comeré comerás comerá comeremos *comeréis* comerán	viviré vivirás vivirá viviremos *viviréis* vivirán
CONDICIONAL	hablaría hablarías hablaría hablaríamos *hablaríais* hablarían	comería comerías comería comeríamos *comeríais* comerían	viviría vivirías viviría viviríamos *viviríais* vivirían
PRESENTE PERFECTO	he hablado has hablado ha hablado hemos hablado *habéis hablado* han hablado	he comido has comido ha comido hemos comido *habéis comido* han comido	he vivido has vivido ha vivido hemos vivido *habéis vivido* han vivido

Regular verbs *(continued)*			
SUBJUNTIVO: PRESENTE	hable hables hable hablemos *habléis* hablen	coma comas coma comamos *comáis* coman	viva vivas viva vivamos *viváis* vivan

Stem-changing verbs (-ar and -er verbs)				
INFINITIVO	empezar (e→ie) *to begin*	perder (e→ie) *to lose*	recordar (o→ue) *to remember*	volver (o→ue) *to return*
PRESENTE	empiezo empiezas empieza empezamos *empezáis* empiezan	pierdo pierdes pierde perdemos *perdéis* pierden	recuerdo recuerdas recuerda recordamos *recordáis* recuerdan	vuelvo vuelves vuelve volvemos *volvéis* vuelven
SUBJUNTIVO: PRESENTE	empiece empieces empiece empecemos *empecéis* empiecen	pierda pierdas pierda perdamos *perdáis* pierdan	recuerde recuerdes recuerde recordemos *recordéis* recuerden	vuelva vuelvas vuelva volvamos *volváis* vuelvan

e→ie

Other verbs conjugated like **empezar** and **perder** are: **cerrar**, **comenzar**, **despertar**, **pensar**, **defender**, **entender**, **querer**.

o→ue

Other verbs conjugated like **recordar** and **volver** are: **acordar**, **almorzar**, **contar**, **costar**, **probar**, **acostar**(**se**), **jugar** (**u→ue**), **devolver**, **mover**, **poder**.

Stem-changing verbs (-ir verbs)			
INFINITIVO	preferir (e→ie, i) *to prefer*	dormir (o→ue, u) *to sleep*	pedir (e→i, i) *to ask for*
PARTICIPIO PRESENTE	prefiriendo	durmiendo	pidiendo
PRESENTE	prefiero prefieres prefiere preferimos *preferís* prefieren	duermo duermes duerme dormimos *dormís* duermen	pido pides pide pedimos *pedís* piden

Stem-changing verbs (-ir verbs) *(continued)*			
PRETÉRITO	**preferí** **preferiste** **prefirió** **preferimos** ***preferisteis*** **prefirieron**	**dormí** **dormiste** **durmió** **dormimos** ***dormisteis*** **durmieron**	**pedí** **pediste** **pidió** **pedimos** ***pedisteis*** **pidieron**
SUBJUNTIVO: PRESENTE	**prefiera** **prefieras** **prefiera** **prefiramos** ***prefiráis*** **prefieran**	**duerma** **duermas** **duerma** **durmamos** ***durmáis*** **duerman**	**pida** **pidas** **pida** **pidamos** ***pidáis*** **pidan**

e→ie, i

Other verbs conjugated like **preferir** are: **sentir, sugerir.**

o→ue

Another verb conjugated like **dormir** is **morir.**

e→i, i

Other verbs conjugated like **pedir** are: **repetir, servir, seguir, vestirse.**

Irregular verbs						
	abrir *to open*					
PARTICIPIO PASADO	**abierto**					
	andar *to walk*					
PRETÉRITO	**anduve**	**anduviste**	**anduvo**	**anduvimos**	***anduvisteis***	**anduvieron**
	conocer *to know, to be familiar with*					
PRESENTE	**conozco**	**conoces**	**conoce**	**conocemos**	***conocéis***	**conocen**
	cubrir *to cover*					
PARTICIPIO PASADO	**cubierto**					
	dar *to give*					
PRESENTE	**doy**	**das**	**da**	**damos**	***dais***	**dan**
PRETÉRITO	**di**	**diste**	**dio**	**dimos**	***disteis***	**dieron**
SUBJUNTIVO	**dé**	**des**	**dé**	**demos**	***deis***	**den**

Verb Charts

Irregular verbs *(continued)*						
	decir *to say*					
PARTICIPIO PRESENTE	diciendo					
PARTICIPIO PASADO	dicho					
PRESENTE	digo	dices	dice	decimos	*decís*	dicen
PRETÉRITO	dije	dijiste	dijo	dijimos	*dijisteis*	dijeron
FUTURO	diré	dirás	dirá	diremos	*diréis*	dirán
CONDICIONAL	diría	dirías	diría	diríamos	*diríais*	dirían
IMPERATIVO FAMILIAR	di					
	devolver *to return (bring back)*					
PARTICIPIO PASADO	devuelto					
	escribir *to write*					
PARTICIPIO PASADO	escrito					
	estar *to be*					
PRESENTE	estoy	estás	está	estamos	*estáis*	están
PRETÉRITO	estuve	estuviste	estuvo	estuvimos	*estuvisteis*	estuvieron
SUBJUNTIVO	esté	estés	esté	estemos	*estéis*	estén
	freír *to fry*					
PARTICIPIO PASADO	frito					
	haber *to have (in compound tenses)*					
PRESENTE	he	has	ha	hemos	*habéis*	han
	hacer *to do, to make*					
PARTICIPIO PASADO	hecho					
PRESENTE	hago	haces	hace	hacemos	*hacéis*	hacen
PRETÉRITO	hice	hiciste	hizo	hicimos	*hicisteis*	hicieron
FUTURO	haré	harás	hará	haremos	*haréis*	harán
CONDICIONAL	haría	harías	haría	haríamos	*haríais*	harían
IMPERATIVO FAMILIAR	haz					
	ir *to go*					
PARTICIPIO PRESENTE	yendo					
PRESENTE	voy	vas	va	vamos	*vais*	van
PRETÉRITO	fui	fuiste	fue	fuimos	*fuisteis*	fueron
IMPERFECTO	iba	ibas	iba	íbamos	*ibais*	iban
SUBJUNTIVO	vaya	vayas	vaya	vayamos	*vayáis*	vayan
IMPERATIVO FAMILIAR	ve					
	morir *to die*					
PARTICIPIO PASADO	muerto					

Irregular verbs *(continued)*

	oír *to hear*					
PRESENTE	**oigo**	**oyes**	**oye**	**oímos**	***oís***	**oyen**
	poder *to be able to*					
PARTICIPIO PRESENTE	**pudiendo**					
PRETÉRITO	**pude**	**pudiste**	**pudo**	**pudimos**	***pudisteis***	**pudieron**
FUTURO	**podré**	**podrás**	**podrá**	**podremos**	***podréis***	**podrán**
CONDICIONAL	**podría**	**podrías**	**podría**	**podríamos**	***podríais***	**podrían**
	poner *to put*					
PARTICIPIO PASADO	**puesto**					
PRESENTE	**pongo**	**pones**	**pone**	**ponemos**	***ponéis***	**ponen**
PRETÉRITO	**puse**	**pusiste**	**puso**	**pusimos**	***pusisteis***	**pusieron**
FUTURO	**pondré**	**pondrás**	**pondrá**	**pondremos**	***pondréis***	**pondrán**
CONDICIONAL	**pondría**	**pondrías**	**pondría**	**pondríamos**	***pondríais***	**pondrían**
IMPERATIVO FAMILIAR	**pon**					
	querer *to want*					
PRETÉRITO	**quise**	**quisiste**	**quiso**	**quisimos**	***quisisteis***	**quisieron**
FUTURO	**querré**	**querrás**	**querrá**	**querremos**	***querréis***	**querrán**
CONDICIONAL	**querría**	**querrías**	**querría**	**querríamos**	***querríais***	**querrían**
	romper *to break*					
PARTICIPIO PASADO	**roto**					
	saber *to know (how)*					
PRESENTE	**sé**	**sabes**	**sabe**	**sabemos**	***sabéis***	**saben**
PRETÉRITO	**supe**	**supiste**	**supo**	**supimos**	***supisteis***	**supieron**
FUTURO	**sabré**	**sabrás**	**sabrá**	**sabremos**	***sabréis***	**sabrán**
CONDICIONAL	**sabría**	**sabrías**	**sabría**	**sabríamos**	***sabríais***	**sabrían**
SUBJUNTIVO	**sepa**	**sepas**	**sepa**	**sepamos**	***sepáis***	**sepan**
	salir *to leave, to go out*					
PRESENTE	**salgo**	**sales**	**sale**	**salimos**	***salís***	**salen**
FUTURO	**saldré**	**saldrás**	**saldrá**	**saldremos**	***saldréis***	**saldrán**
CONDICIONAL	**saldría**	**saldrías**	**saldría**	**saldríamos**	***saldríais***	**saldrían**
IMPERATIVO FAMILIAR	**sal**					
	ser *to be*					
PRESENTE	**soy**	**eres**	**es**	**somos**	***sois***	**son**
PRETÉRITO	**fui**	**fuiste**	**fue**	**fuimos**	***fuisteis***	**fueron**
IMPERFECTO	**era**	**eras**	**era**	**éramos**	***erais***	**eran**
SUBJUNTIVO	**sea**	**seas**	**sea**	**seamos**	***seáis***	**sean**
IMPERATIVO FAMILIAR	**sé**					

Irregular verbs *(continued)*

	tener *to have*					
PRESENTE	tengo	tienes	tiene	tenemos	*tenéis*	tienen
PRETÉRITO	tuve	tuviste	tuvo	tuvimos	*tuvisteis*	tuvieron
FUTURO	tendré	tendrás	tendrá	tendremos	*tendréis*	tendrán
CONDICIONAL	tendría	tendrías	tendría	tendríamos	*tendríais*	tendrían
IMPERATIVO FAMILIAR	ten					
	traer *to bring*					
PRESENTE	traigo	traes	trae	traemos	*traéis*	traen
PRETÉRITO	traje	trajiste	trajo	trajimos	*trajisteis*	trajeron
	venir *to come*					
PARTICIPIO PRESENTE	viniendo					
PRETÉRITO	vine	viniste	vino	vinimos	*vinisteis*	vinieron
FUTURO	vendré	vendrás	vendrá	vendremos	*vendréis*	vendrán
CONDICIONAL	vendría	vendrías	vendría	vendríamos	*vendríais*	vendrían
IMPERATIVO FAMILIAR	ven					
	ver *to see*					
PARTICIPIO PASADO	visto					
PRESENTE	veo	ves	ve	vemos	*veis*	ven
PRETÉRITO	vi	viste	vio	vimos	*visteis*	vieron
IMPERFECTO	veía	veías	veía	veíamos	*veíais*	veían
	volver *to return*					
PARTICIPIO PASADO	vuelto					

Verb Charts

Spanish-English Dictionary

The Spanish-English Dictionary contains all productive and receptive vocabulary from Levels 1 and 2. The numbers following each productive entry indicate the chapter and vocabulary section in which the word is introduced. For example, **3.2** *in dark print means that the word was first taught in* **Capítulo 3, Vocabulario 2.** *A light print number means that the word was introduced in* **¡Así se dice!** *Level 1.* LP *refers to the* **Lecciones preliminares** *in Level 1. If there is no number following an entry, this means that the word or expression is there for receptive purposes only.*

A

a at; to
a eso de las tres (cuatro, diez, etc.) at around three (four, ten, etc.) o'clock
a fines de at the end of
a la una (a las dos, a las tres...) at one o'clock (two o'clock, three o'clock), LP
a lo lejos in the distance
a lo menos at least
a menudo often
a pesar de in spite of
a pie on foot, 3.2
¡A propósito! By the way!, 8.2
¿a qué hora? at what time?, LP
a solas alone
a tiempo on time, 10.2; **1.2**
a veces at times, sometimes, 6.1; **1.2**
a ver let's see
abajo down; below
de abajo below
(ir) para abajo (to go) down
abandonar el cuarto to check out *(hotel)*, **7**
el **abono** fertilizer
abordar to board, 10.2; **1.2**
abordo aboard, on board, 10.2; **1.2**
abreviado(a) abbreviated, shortened
abrigado(a) wrapped up
el **abrigo** coat
abril April, LP
abrir to open, 4.2
abrochado(a) fastened, 10.2; **1.2**
la **abuela** grandmother, 2.1
el **abuelo** grandfather, 2.1
los **abuelos** grandparents, 2.1
abundoso(a) abundant
aburrido(a) boring, 1.2
aburrir to bore, 5.2
acá here, 11.2; **2.2**
acabar de to have just (done something), 4.2
la **academia** school
acaso: por si acaso just in case
acceder to access
el **accidente** accident, **11.2**
el **aceite** oil, **4**
la **aceituna** olive, 4.2
el **acento** accent
la **acera** sidewalk, **8.1**
acercarse to approach
acomodado(a) wealthy, well-off
acomodar to set *(bone)*, **11.2**
acordarse (ue) to remember
¿Te acuerdas? Do you remember?
acostarse (ue) to go to bed, 11.1; **2.1**
acostumbrarse to get used to
el **acotamiento** shoulder *(road)*, **9.1**
la **actividad** activity
actual present-day, current
actuar to act, to take action
acudir to go to
acuerdo: estar de acuerdo con to agree with
adelantar(se) to pass *(car)*, **9.1**
adelante ahead
ir hacia adelante to move forward, ahead
además furthermore, what's more; besides
además de in addition to, besides
¡Adiós! Good-bye!, LP
adivinar to guess
adjunto: el documento adjunto attached file, **6.1**
admitir to admit
¿adónde? (to) where?, 3.2
la **advertencia** warning
advertir (ie, i) to warn
aérea: la línea aérea airline, 10.1; **1.1**
aeróbico(a) aerobic
el **aeropuerto** airport, 10.1; **1.1**
aficionado(a): ser aficionado(a) a to like, to be a fan of
el/la **aficionado(a)** fan, 5.1
afine: la palabra afine cognate
las **afueras** suburbs, 2.2; outskirts
agarrar velocidad to pick up speed
el/la **agente** agent, 10.1; **1.1**
la **aglomeración** big city
agosto August, LP
agradable pleasant, friendly, agreeable
agrario(a) agrarian
agresivo(a) aggressive
agrícola agricultural
el **agua** *(f.)* water, 4.1
el agua mineral (con gas) (sparkling) mineral water, 4.2
el agua corriente running water
el **aguacate** avocado, **10**
el **aguinaldo** Christmas gift, **5.2**
ahora now
el **aire** air
al aire libre open-air, outdoor
el **aire acondicionado** air conditioning, **7**
aislado(a) isolated
el **ají** chili pepper
el **ajo** garlic, **10**
al to the, on the, in the
al aire libre open-air, outdoor

Spanish-English Dictionary

al borde mismo de right on the edge of
al contrario on the contrary
al lado de beside, next to, 2.2
la **alberca** swimming pool, 7.1
el **albergue juvenil** youth hostel, **7**
la **albóndiga** meatball, 4.2
el **álbum** album
la **alcachofa** artichoke
las alcachofas salteadas sautéed artichokes
alcanzar to reach
la **alcoba** bedroom
la **aldea** small village
alegrarse to rejoice
alegre happy, 6.1
la **alegría** happiness, joy
alemán(ana) German
los **alemanes** Germans
la **alfombrilla** mouse pad, **6.1**
el **álgebra** algebra
algo something, 4.1; anything, 9.2
¿Algo más? Anything else?, 9.2
alguien someone, somebody, 8.2
algunos(as) some
el **alimento** food
las **alitas** wings, **10**
allá over there, 9.1
allí there
el **alma** *(f.)* soul
las **almejas** clams, **4**
la **almohada** pillow, **7**
el **almuerzo** lunch, 4.1
tomar el almuerzo to have lunch, 4.1
¡Aló! Hello! *(on the phone)*
alpino: el esquí alpino downhill skiing, 7.2
alquilar to rent, 7.1; **3.2**
alrededor de around, 2.2
los **alrededores** outskirts, surroundings
altivo(a) arrogant
alto(a) tall, 1.1; high, 3.1; upper
la clase alta upper class
la nota alta high grade, 3.1
la **altura** altitude
el/la **alumno(a)** student, 1.2
amarillo(a) yellow, 5.1
la **ambición** ambition
ambicioso(a) hard-working, 1.2
el **ambiente** atmosphere, environment
la **ambulancia** ambulance, **11.2**
la **América del Sur** South America
americano(a) American
el/la **amigo(a)** friend, 1.1
el **amor** love
amurallado(a) walled
anaranjado(a) orange *(color)*, 5.1
ancho(a) wide, broad, **8.1**
andar to go, to walk; to ride, **3.2**
andar a caballo to ride a horse, **3.2**
andar en bicicleta to ride a bike, **11.1**
el **andén** *(railway)* platform, **3.1**
andino(a) Andean, of the Andes
angosto(a) narrow, **8.1**
la **angustia** distress, anguish
animado(a) lively
el **animal** animal
animar to cheer (somebody, something) on
anoche last night, 7.1
anónimo(a) anonymous
el **anorak** anorak, ski jacket, 7.2
los **anteojos de sol** sunglasses, 7.1
el **antepecho** parapet
anterior previous, **6.1**
antes de before, 10.1; **1.1**
los **antibióticos** antibiotics
antiguo(a) ancient, old, **8.1;** former
el casco (barrio) antiguo the old city, **8.1**
antipático(a) unpleasant, not nice 1.1
los **antojitos** snacks, nibbles, 4.2
anunciar to announce
el **anuncio** announcement
añadir to add, **10**
el **año** year, LP
el Año Nuevo New Year
el año pasado last year, 7.1
¿Cuántos años tiene? How old is he (she)?, 2.1
cumplir... años to be (turn) . . . years old
apagar to turn off, **6.1**
el **aparato** device
aparcar to park, **8.1**
aparentado(a) related
la **apariencia** appearance, looks
¿Qué apariencia tiene? What does he (she) look like?
el **apartamento** apartment, 2.2
la casa de apartamentos apartment house
el **apartamiento** apartment, 2.2
aparte apart, on the side
apetecer to feel like, to crave
apetito: ¡Buen apetito! Bon appétit! Enjoy your meal!
aplaudir to applaud, to clap, 5.1
el **aplauso** applause, 5.1
recibir aplausos to be applauded, 5.1
apreciado(a) appreciated, liked
aprender to learn, 4.2
apropiado(a) appropriate
aproximadamente approximately
aquel(la) that, 9.1
aquí here, 9.1
Aquí lo (las, etc.) tienes. Here it (they) is (are).
el/la **árabe** Arab
aragonés(esa) from Aragon *(Spain)*
el **árbol** tree, 2.2
el árbol de Navidad Christmas tree, **5.2**
el **arcén** shoulder *(road)*, **9.1**
el **archivo** file, **6.1**
la **arena** sand, 7.1
argentino(a) Argentine
árido(a) dry, arid
la **aritmética** arithmetic
armar to put up *(tent)*, 11.2; **2.2**
el **armario** closet, **7**
la **arqueología** archaeology
el **arroyo** brook
la **arroba** the @ sign, **6.1**
el **arroz** rice, 4.1
el **arte** art, 1.2
arterial: la tensión arterial blood pressure, 6.2
la **artesanía** crafts, 9.2
el/la **artista** artist
asar to grill, to roast, **10**
la **ascendencia** heritage, background
el **ascensor** elevator, **7**
asegurarse to make sure
así thus, so, in this way
el **asiento** seat, 10.1; **1.1**
el número del asiento seat number, 10.1; **1.1**
asignar to assign, **6.2**
la **asistencia médica** medical care
el/la **asistente de vuelo** flight attendant, 10.2; **1.2**

Spanish-English Dictionary

Spanish-English Dictionary

asistir a to attend, 8.1
el **asno** donkey
el **aspa(f.)** sail *(windmill)*
astuto(a) astute, smart
atacar to attack
la **atención** attention
¡Atención! Careful!
prestar atención to pay attention, 3.1
el **aterrizaje** landing, 10.2; **1.2**
aterrizar to land, 10.2; **1.2**
el/la **atleta** athlete
las **atracciones** rides *(amusement park)*, **8.1**
el parque de atracciones amusement park, **8.1**
atraer to attract
atrapar to catch, 5.2
atrás: hacia atrás backwards
el **atún** tuna, 9.2
aumentar to grow, to increase, to enlarge
aun even
aún still
aunque although, even though
el **auricular** (phone) receiver, **6.2**
ausente absent
auténtico(a) authentic, real
el **autobús** bus, 8.1; **8.1**
perder el autobús to miss the bus, 8.1
automático(a) automatic, 10.2; **1.2**
el distribuidor automático boarding pass kiosk, 10.2; **1.2;** automatic dispenser, **3.1**
la **autopista** highway, **9.1**
el/la **autor(a)** author
el **autoservicio** self-service *(restaurant, gas station)*
la **autovía** highway, **9.1**
avanzado(a) difficult, 7.2; advanced
la **avenida** avenue, **8.1**
la **aventura** adventure
la **avería** breakdown
averiado(a) broken down
el **avión** airplane, 10.1; **1.1**
la **avioneta** small airplane
ayer yesterday, 7.1
ayer por la tarde yesterday afternoon, 7.1
la **ayuda** help, assistance
ayudar to help, 10.1; **1.1**

el **azafrán** saffron
el **azúcar** sugar
azul blue, 2.1
el **azulejo** glazed tile, floor tile

B

el **bache** pothole
el **bacón** bacon, 4.1; **7**
el/la **bailador(a)** dancer
bailar to dance, **5.2**
bajar to go down, 7.2; to download, **6.2**
bajar(se) to get off *(train)*, **3.2**
la **bajeza** baseness
bajo(a) short, 1.1; low, 3.1; poor, lower-class
la nota baja low grade, 3.1
el **balcón** balcony
el **balneario** seaside resort, beach resort, 7.1
el **balón** ball, 5.1
el **baloncesto** basketball, 5.2
la **banda** band, 8.1; **5.2;** lane *(highway)*
la banda municipal municipal band, **5.2**
la **bandeja de entradas** inbox *(e-mail)*, **6.1**
la **bandeja de enviados** sent mailbox *(e-mail)*, **6.1**
la **bandera** flag
el **bañador** swimsuit, 7.1
bañarse to take a bath, to bathe oneself
la **bañera** bathtub, **7**
el **baño** bath; bathroom
el cuarto de baño bathroom, 2.2; **7**
barato(a) inexpensive, cheap, 9.1
Todo te sale más barato. It's all a lot cheaper., 9.1
la **barbacoa** barbecue
barbaridad: ¡Qué barbaridad! That's awful!
¡Bárbaro! Great!, Awesome!, 5.2
el **barco** boat
el **barquito** small boat, 7.1
la **barra** bar *(soap)*, 11.2; **2.2;** counter, bar *(restaurant)*
la barra de jabón bar of soap, 11.2; **2.2**
la **barra de herramientas** toolbar, **6.1**

el **barrio** neighborhood, area, quarter, district, **8.1**
la **base** base, 5.2
el **básquetbol** basketball, 5.2
la cancha de básquetbol basketball court, 5.2
bastante rather, quite, 1.2; enough
el **bastón** ski pole, 7.2
la **batalla** battle
el **bate** bat, 5.2
el/la **bateador(a)** batter, 5.2
batear to hit, to bat, 5.2
batear un jonrón to hit a home run, 5.2
el **batido** shake, smoothie, 4.2
el **baúl** trunk *(car)*, 10.1; **1.1**
beber to drink, 4.1
la **bebida** beverage, drink, 4.1
el **béisbol** baseball, 5.2
el/la beisbolista baseball player, 5.2
el campo de béisbol baseball field, 5.2
el/la jugador(a) de béisbol baseball player, 5.2
la **belleza** beauty
bello(a) beautiful
la **benzina** gas(oline)
el **beso** kiss
los **biafranos** people from Biafra
la **biblioteca** library
la **bicicleta** bicycle, 2.2
andar en bicicleta to ride a bike, **11.1**
bien well, fine, LP
bien educado(a) polite, well-mannered, 6.1
bien hecho(a) well-done *(meat)*, **4**
estar bien to be (feel) well, fine, 6.2
Muy bien. Very well., LP
la **bienvenida: dar la bienvenida** to greet, to welcome
bienvenido(a) welcome
el **bife** beef
el **biftec** steak, **4**
el **billete** ticket, 10.1; **1.1**
el billete electrónico e-ticket, 10.1; **1.1**
el billete de ida y vuelta round-trip ticket, **3.1**
el billete sencillo one-way ticket, **3.1**
la **biología** biology
el/la **biólogo(a)** biologist

el **bizcocho** cake, **5.1**
blanco(a) white, 5.1
blando(a) soft
bloquear to block, 5.1
el **blue jean** jeans, 9.1
la **blusa** blouse, 3.1
la **boca** mouth, 6.2
la **boca del metro** subway entrance, **8.1**
la **bocacalle** intersection, **9.1**
el **bocadillo** sandwich, 4.1
los **bocaditos** snacks
la **boda** wedding
la **bodega** grocery store
la **boletería** ticket window, 7.2; **3.1**
el **boleto** ticket, 7.2; **3.1**
el boleto de ida y regreso round-trip ticket, **3.1**
el boleto electrónico e-ticket, 10.1; **1.1**
el boleto sencillo one-way ticket, **3.1**
el **bolígrafo** pen, 3.1
el **bolívar** bolivar *(currency of Venezuela)*
la **bolsa de dormir** sleeping bag, 11.2; **2.2**
bolsillo: el libro de bolsillo paperback, **3.1**
la **bombilla** *(drinking)* container
los **bombones** candy
bonito(a) pretty, 1.1
el **borde** side *(of a street, sidewalk)*
al borde mismo de right on the edge of
borrador: el botón borrador delete key, **6.1**
borrar to delete, **6.1**
el **bosque** woods
la **bota** boot, 7.2
botar to throw out
botar la casa por la ventana to splurge
el **bote** can, 9.2
la **botella** bottle, 9.2
el **botón** button, key *(computer)*, **6.1**
el botón borrador delete key, **6.1**
el botón regresar (retroceder) back button, **6.1**
Brasil Brazil
brasileño(a) Brazilian
bravo(a) rough, stormy
el **brazo** arm, 11.1; **2.1**
brillar to shine
bronce: de bronce bronze *(adj.)*, 8.2
bronceador(a): la loción bronceadora suntan lotion, 7.1
bucear to go snorkeling, 7.1; to scuba dive
el **buceo** snorkeling, 7.1; scuba diving
buen good, LP
estar de buen humor to be in a good mood, 6.1
Hace buen tiempo. The weather is nice., LP
tener un buen sentido de humor to have a good sense of humor, 6.1
bueno(a) good, 1.1; Hello! *(on the phone)*
Buenas noches. Good evening., LP
Buenas tardes. Good afternoon., LP
Buenos días. Good morning., Hello., LP
sacar notas buenas to get good grades, 3.1
la **bufetería** dining car, **3.2**
el **burrito** burrito
el **bus** bus
el bus escolar school bus, 3.2
perder el autobús to miss the bus, 8.1
tomar el autobús to take the bus
busca: en busca de seeking, in search of
buscar to look for, to seek, 3.2
el **buzo** sweat suit, warm-ups, **11.1**

C

el **caballero** gentleman
el caballero andante knight errant
el **caballo** horse, **3.2**
andar a caballo to ride a horse, **3.2**
montar a caballo to go horseback riding, **8.2**
la **cabeza** head, 6.2; **2.1**
tener dolor de cabeza to have a headache, 6.2
la **cabina de mando** cockpit *(airplane)*
la **cabina de peaje** tollbooth, **9.1**
el **cacahuate** peanut, 8.1
el **cacahuete** peanut
la **cacerola** saucepan, **10**
el **cacique** leader, chief
cada each, every, 2.2
caer to fall
caerse to fall, **11.2**
el **café** café, 3.1; coffee, 4.1; **7**
la **cafetería** cafeteria, 4.1
el coche cafetería dining car, **3.2**
la **caída** drop
la llamada caída dropped call *(cell phone)*, **6.2**
la **caja** cash register, 3.2
la **calavera** skull, **5.1;** sweet cake made for the Day of the Dead
los **calcetines** socks, 5.1
la **calculadora** calculator, 3.1
el **caldo** broth
caliente hot, 4.1
el chocolate caliente hot chocolate, 4.1
la **calle** street, **8.1**
la calle de sentido único one-way street, **9.1**
calmo(a) calm, 6.1
el **calor** heat
Hace calor. It's hot., LP
tener calor to be hot, 11.1; **2.1**
calzar to wear, to take *(shoe size)*, 9.1
¿Qué número calzas? What size shoe do you wear (take)?, 9.1
la **cama** bed, 2.2; **7**
guardar cama to stay in bed *(illness)*, 6.2
hacer la cama to make the bed, **7**
quedarse en la cama to stay in bed, 11.1; **2.1**
la **cámara digital** digital camera, 7.1; **6.2**
el/la **camarero(a)** server, waiter (waitress), **4;** *(hotel)* housekeeper, **7**
los **camarones** shrimp, 4.2
cambiar to change, **3.2**
el **camello** camel, **5.2**
la **camilla** stretcher, **11.2**
caminar to walk, **5.1**
la **caminata: dar una caminata** to take a hike, 11.2; **2.2**
el **camino** road
tomar el camino to set out for
el **camión** bus *(Mexico)*, **8.1;** truck, **9.2**
la **camisa** shirt, 3.1
la camisa de manga corta (larga) short- (long-) sleeved shirt, 9.1

Spanish-English Dictionary

la **camiseta** T-shirt, 5.1
la **campana** bell tower
la **campanada** peal of the bell
el/la **campeón(ona)** champion
el/la **campesino(a)** farmer, peasant, **8.2**
el **camping** camping, 11.2; **2.2;** campsite
ir de camping to go camping, 11.2; **2.2**
el **campo** field, 5.1; **8.2;** country, countryside, **8.2**
el campo de béisbol baseball field, 5.2
el campo de fútbol soccer field, 5.1
la carrera a campo traviesa cross-country race, **11.1**
la casa de campo country house, **8.2**
el **camposanto** cemetery, **5.1**
canadiense Canadian
el **canal** lane *(highway)*
la **canasta** basket, 5.2
la **cancha** court, 5.2
la cancha de básquetbol (tenis) basketball (tennis) court, 5.2
la cancha de voleibol volleyball court, 7.1
la **candela** candle
el **cangrejo de río** crayfish
el **cañón** canyon, **3.2**
cansado(a) tired, 6.1
el/la **cantante** singer, 8.1
cantar to sing, 8.1
la **cantidad** quantity, amount, number of
la **cantina** cafeteria
la **capital** capital
el **capítulo** chapter
el **capó** hood *(car)*, **9.2**
la **cara** face, 6.1
la **característica** feature, trait
el **carbón** coal
el **cardo** thistle
cargado(a) thrown (over one's shoulders); loaded
el **Caribe** Caribbean
el mar Caribe Caribbean Sea
cariñoso(a) adorable, affectionate, 2.1
caritativo(a) charitable
la **carne** meat, 4.1; **4**
la **carne de res** beef, **4**
el **carnet** driver's license, **9.2**
el **carnet de identidad** ID card, 10.2; **1.2**
la **carnicería** butcher shop
caro(a) expensive, 9.1
la **carpa** tent, 11.2; **2.2**
armar (montar) una carpa to put up a tent, 11.2; **2.2**
la **carpeta** folder, 3.2; **6.1**
la **carrera** race, **11.1;** career
la carrera a campo traviesa cross-country race, **11.1**
la carrera de larga distancia long-distance race, **11.1**
la carrera de relevos relay race, **11.1**
la **carretera** highway, **9.1**
el **carril** lane *(highway)*, **9.1**
el **carrito** shopping cart, 9.2
el **carro** car, 2.2; **9.2**
en carro by car
la **carta** letter
la **casa** house, 2.2
la casa de apartamentos apartment building, 2.2
la casa de campo country house, **8.2**
en casa at home
regresar a casa to go home, 3.2
casarse to get married
el **casco** helmet, 7.2; **11.1**
el **casco antiguo** the old city, **8.1**
casi almost, practically, 8.2; **4**
casi crudo rare *(meat)*, **4**
el **caso** case
hacer caso to pay attention
castaño(a) brown, chestnut *(eyes, hair)*, 2.1
el **castillo** castle
la **casucha** shack
catarro: tener catarro to have a cold, 6.2
el/la **cátcher** catcher, 5.2
la **catedral** cathedral
la **categoría** category
catorce fourteen, LP
el **caucho** tire
cautivar to captivate, to charm
la **cazuela** saucepan, pot, **10**
el **CD** CD
la **cebolla** onion, 9.2; **10**
celebrar to celebrate, **5.2**
el **celular** cell phone, 3.2; **6.1**
el **cementerio** cemetery, **5.1**
la **cena** dinner, 4.1
cenar to have dinner, 4.1
el **cenote** natural water well
el **centro** downtown, **8.1;** center
el **centro comercial** shopping center, mall, 9.1
cepillarse to brush, 11.1; **2.1**
cepillarse los dientes to brush one's teeth, 11.1; **2.1**
el **cepillo** brush, 11.2; **2.2**
el cepillo de dientes toothbrush, 11.2; **2.2**
las **cerámicas** ceramics, 9.2
cerca (de) near, 3.2
el **cerdo** pig, **8.2**
la chuleta de cerdo pork chop; **4**
el **cereal** cereal, 4.1
cero zero, LP
cerrar (ie) to close, 11.2; **2.2**
la **cesta** basket
el **cesto** basket, 5.2
la **chacra** farm, **8.2**
el **champú** shampoo, 11.2; **2.2**
¡Chao! Good-bye!, Bye!, LP
la **chaqueta** jacket, 9.1
la chaqueta de esquí ski jacket, anorak, 7.2
las **chauchas** green beans
el **chico** boy
chileno(a) Chilean
la **chimenea** fireplace, **5.2**
el **chipotle** smoked jalapeño pepper
el **chiringuito** refreshment stand
el **chisme** rumor, gossip
el **choclo** corn
el **chocolate** chocolate, 4.1
el chocolate caliente hot chocolate, 4.1
el **chorizo** Spanish sausage
la **choza** shack
la **chuleta de cerdo** pork chop, **4**
el **churro** (type of) doughnut
ciego(a) blind
el/la **ciego(a)** blind man (woman)
el **cielo** sky, **5.2**
cien(to) one hundred, LP
la **ciencia** science, 1.2
cierto(a) true, certain, **6.1**
cinco five, LP
cincuenta fifty, LP
el **cine** movie theater, movies, 8.2
ir al cine to go to the movies, 8.2

Spanish-English Dictionary

el **cinturón de seguridad** seat belt, 10.2; **1.2**
el/la **cirujano(a) ortopédico(a)** orthopedic surgeon, **11.2**
la **ciudad** city, 2.2; **8.1**
la **civilización** civilization
claro(a) clear
claro que of course
la **clase** class *(school)*, 1.2; class *(ticket)*, **3.1**
en primera (segunda) clase first-class (second-class), **3.1**
la sala de clase classroom, 3.1
clavar con una multa to give (someone) a ticket, **9.1**
la **clave de área** area code, **6.2**
clic: hacer clic to click *(computer)*, **6.1**
el/la **cliente(a)** customer, 4.2; **7**
el **clima** climate
la **clínica** clinic
la **cocción** cooking
cocer (ue) to cook, **10**
el **coche** car, **9.2;** train car, **3.1**
el coche deportivo sports car, **9.2**
el **coche comedor (cafetería)** dining car, **3.2**
el **cochinillo asado** roast suckling pig
la **cocina** kitchen, 2.2; **10;** stove, **10;** cooking, cuisine
cocinar to cook, **10**
el/la **cocinero(a)** cook, **10**
el **cocodrilo** crocodile
el **codo** elbow, 11.1; **2.1**
la **cola** cola (soda) 4.1; line *(of people)*, 10.2; **1.2**
hacer cola to wait in line, 10.2; **1.2**
el **colegio** secondary school, high school
el **colgador** hanger, **7**
colgar (ue) to hang up
la **colina** hill
la **colocación** placement
colocar to place, to put
colombiano(a) Colombian
colonial colonial
el **color** color, 5.1
de color marrón brown, 5.1
¿De qué color es? What color is it?
el **comando** command
combinado: el plato combinado combination plate
el **comedor** dining room, 2.2
el coche comedor dining car, **3.2**
el/la **comensal** diner
comenzar (ie) to begin
comer to eat, 4.1
dar de comer a to feed
los **comestibles** food, **4**
cómico(a) funny, comical, 1.1
la **comida** meal, 4.1; food
como like, as; since
¿cómo? how?; what?, 1.1
¿Cómo es él? What's he like? What does he look like?, 1.1
¿Cómo está... ? How is...?
¡Cómo no! Sure! Of course!
cómodo(a) comfortable
el/la **compañero(a)** companion
comparar to compare
el **compartimiento superior** overhead bin, 10.2; **1.2**
compartir to share
completar to complete, to fill in
completo(a) full, **3.2**
el **comportamiento** behavior, conduct, 6.1
comportarse to behave
la **composición** composition
la **compra** purchase, 9.2
el/la **comprador(a)** shopper, customer
comprar to buy, 3.2
compras: ir de compras to shop, to go shopping, 9.1
comprender to understand, 4.2; to include
la **computadora** computer, 3.2; **6.1**
comunicarse to communicate with each other
con with
con frecuencia often
con retraso (una demora) late, delayed, 10.2; **1.2**
el **concierto** concert, 8.1
el **condimento** condiment, **10**
el **condominio** condominium
conducir to drive, **9.2**
la **conducta** conduct, behavior, 6.1
tener buena conducta to be well-behaved, 6.1
el/la **conductor(a)** driver, **9.2**
conectado(a) on-line, connected
conectar to connect
la **conexión** connection
confeccionar to make, to prepare, **5.1**
la **conferencia** lecture
confiabilidad reliability
confiable reliable, trustworthy
conforme: estar conforme to agree, to be in agreement
confortar to soothe
congelado(a) frozen, 9.2
los productos congelados frozen food, 9.2
el **congelador** freezer, **10**
el **conjunto** band, musical group, 8.1
conocer to know, to be familiar with, 9.1; to meet
conocido(a) known
el **conquistador** conqueror
conquistar to conquer
consecuencia: por consecuencia as a result, consequently
el/la **consejero(a)** counselor
el **consejo** advice
considerar to consider
consiguiente: por consiguiente consequently
el **consomé** bouillon, consommé
la **consonante** consonant
constar (de) to consist of, to be made up of
la **consulta** doctor's office, 6.2
consultar to consult
el **consultorio** doctor's office, 6.2
el/la **consumidor(a)** consumer
contagioso(a) contagious
la **contaminación del aire** air pollution
contaminar to pollute
contar (ue) to tell, to count
contemporáneo(a) contemporary
el **contenido** contents
contento(a) happy, 6.1
contestar to answer, 3.1
continental: el desayuno continental Continental breakfast, **7**
el **continente** continent
continua: la línea continua solid line *(road)*, **9.1**
continuar to continue
contra against
contrario(a) opposite; opposing
al contrario on the contrary
contrastar to contrast

Spanish-English Dictionary

contribuir to contribute
el control de seguridad security (checkpoint), 10.2; **1.2**
  pasar por el control de seguridad to go through security, 10.2; **1.2**
la **conversación** conversation
conversar to converse
el **convertible** convertible, **9.2**
convertir to convert, to transform
copa: la Copa Mundial World Cup
la **copia** copy, **6.1**
  la copia dura hard copy, **6.1**
el **corazón** heart
la **corbata** tie, 9.1
el **cordero** lamb, **4**
la **corona** wreath, **5.1**
el **corral** corral, **8.2**
el/la **corredor(a)** runner
el **correo electrónico** e-mail, 3.2; **6.1**
correr to run, 5.2
cortar to cut off, **6.2;** to cut, to chop, **10**
  cortar en pedacitos to cut in small pieces, to dice, **10**
  cortar en rebanadas to slice, **10**
  Estás cortando. You're breaking up. *(telephone),* **6.2**
  Se nos cortó la línea. We've been cut off. *(telephone),* **6.2**
cortarse to cut oneself, **11.2**
la **cortesía** courtesy, LP
corto(a) short, 9.1
  de manga corta short-sleeved, 9.1
  el pantalón corto shorts, 5.1
la **corvina** corbina, drumfish
la **cosa** thing, 3.1
la **cosecha** harvest, **8.2**
cosechar to harvest, **8.2**
cosmopolito(a) cosmopolitan
la **costa** coast
costar (ue) to cost, 9.1
  ¿Cuánto cuesta? How much does it cost?, 3.2
costarricense Costa Rican
la **costumbre** custom
el **cráneo** skull, **5.1**
crear to create

crecer to grow
creer to believe, to think
  Creo que sí (que no). I (don't) think so.
la **crema dental** toothpaste, 11.2; **2.2**
la **crema solar** suntan lotion, 7.1
el/la **criado(a)** housekeeper
cristiano(a) Christian
criticar to criticize
el **cruce** crosswalk, pedestrian crossing, **8.1;** intersection, **9.1**
crudo(a) raw, 8.1
  casi crudo rare *(meat),* **4**
  los vegetales crudos raw vegetables, crudités, 8.1
cruzar to cross; to intersect, **9.1**
el **cuaderno** notebook, 3.1
la **cuadra** *(city)* block, **9.1**
el **cuadro** painting, 8.2
¿cuál? which? what?, LP
  ¿Cuál es la fecha de hoy? What is today's date?, LP
¿cuáles? which ones? what?
cualquier(a) any
cualquier otro(a) any other
cuando when, 3.1
¿cuándo? when?, 3.2
cuanto: en cuanto as soon as
cuanto: en cuanto a in terms of, as far as . . . is concerned
¿cuánto? how much?
  ¿A cuánto está(n)... ? How much is (are) . . . ?, 9.2
  ¿Cuánto es? How much is it (does it cost)?, LP
¿cuántos(as)? how many?, 2.1
  ¿Cuántos años tiene? How old is he (she)?, 2.1
cuarenta forty, LP
el **cuarto** room, 2.2; **7;** quarter
  el cuarto de baño bathroom, 2.2; **7**
  el cuarto de dormir bedroom, 2.2
  el cuarto sencillo (doble) single (double) room, **7**
  y cuarto a quarter past (the hour), LP
cuatro four, LP
cuatrocientos(as) four hundred
el/la **cubano(a)** Cuban
el/la **cubanoamericano(a)** Cuban American

cubierto(a) covered; indoor
cubrir to cover
la **cuchara** tablespoon, **4**
la **cucharada** tablespoonful
la **cucharadita** teaspoonful
la **cucharita** teaspoon, **4**
el **cuchillo** knife, **4**
el **cuello** neck, **11.1**
la **cuenca** basin *(river)*
la **cuenta** check *(restaurant),* 4.2; **4;** account
  darse cuenta to realize
  por su cuenta on its own
  tomar en cuenta to take into account
el **cuento** story
el **cuerdo** string
el **cuerpo** body, 11.1; **2.1**
la **cueva** cave
cuidado: con (mucho) cuidado (very) carefully
  tener cuidado to be careful, **9.1**
cuidar to take care of, to care for
  ¡Cuídate! Take care of yourself!
la **culpa** blame, guilt
cultivar to work *(land);* to grow, **8.2**
la **cultura** culture
el **cumpleaños** birthday, 8.1
cumplir... años to be (turn) . . . years old
cumplir un sueño to fulfill a wish, to make a wish come true
la **cuota** toll
curarse to get better, to recover
el **curso** class, course, 1.2
cuyos(as) whose

D

daño: hacerse daño to harm oneself, to get hurt, **11.2**
dar to give, 3.1
  dar de comer a to feed
  dar la vuelta to turn around, **9.1**
  dar un examen (una prueba) to give a test, 3.1
  dar una caminata to take a hike, 11.2; **2.2**

dar una fiesta to throw a party, 8.1
darse cuenta to realize
datar to date *(time)*
los **datos** data, facts
de of, from, LP
¿de dónde? from where?, 1.1
De nada. You're welcome., LP
¿De parte de quién, por favor? Who's calling, please?, **6.2**
¿de qué nacionalidad? what nationality?, 1.1
de vez en cuando from time to time, 10.2; **1.2**
No hay de qué. You're welcome., LP
debajo de below, underneath, 10.2; **1.2**
deber should, 4.2
debido a owing to
la **debilidad** weakness
decidir to decide
decir to say, to tell
la **decisión** decision
tomar una decisión to make a decision
decorar to decorate, **5.2**
dedicado(a) devoted
el **dedo** finger, 11.1; **2.1**
el **dedo del pie** toe, **11.1**
deducirse to deduct
el **defecto** defect
defender (ie) to defend
definido(a) definite
dejar to leave (something), **4;** to let, to allow
dejar con to put an end to
dejar un mensaje to leave a message, **6.2**
dejar una propina to leave a tip, **4**
del of the, from the
delante de in front of, 2.2
delantero(a) front *(adj.)*, **8.1**
delgado(a) thin
demás: lo(s) demás the rest
demasiado too *(adv.)*, too much
la **demora** delay, 10.2; **1.2**
con una demora late, 10.2; **1.2**
dental: el tubo de crema dental tube of toothpaste, 11.2; **2.2**
dentífrica: la pasta dentífrica toothpaste
dentro de within
dentro de poco soon, shortly thereafter, 10.2; **1.2**
el **departamento** apartment, 2.2
el departamento de orientación guidance office
el/la **dependiente(a)** salesperson, employee
el **deporte** sport, 5.1
el deporte de equipo team sport
el deporte individual individual sport
deportivo(a) *(related to)* sports
el coche deportivo sports car, **9.2**
deprimido(a) sad, depressed, 6.1
derecho(a) right, 11.1; **2.1**
a la derecha on the right, **9.1**
derecho straight (ahead), **9.1**
derrocar to bring down
desafortunadamente unfortunately
desagradable unpleasant, not nice
desaparecer to disappear
desarrollarse to develop
el **desastre** disaster
desastroso(a) disastrous, catastrophic
el **desayuno** breakfast, 4.1; **7**
el desayuno americano American breakfast, **7**
el desayuno continental Continental breakfast, **7**
tomar el desayuno to have breakfast, 4.1
descansar to rest, **11.1**
el **descapotable** convertible, **9.2**
descargar to download, **6.2**
descolgar (el auricular) to unhook (the telephone receiver), **6.2**
desconocido(a) unknown
desconsolado(a) very sad
describir to describe
la **descripción** description
el **descuento** discount
desde since; from
desear to want, to wish, 4.2
¿Qué desean tomar? What would you like *(to eat, drink)*?, 4.2
desembarcar to deplane, disembark, 10.2; **1.2**
desembocar to lead, to go (from one street into another), to come out onto
el **deseo** wish, desire
desesperado(a) desperate
desfilar to walk (in a parade or procession), **5.1**
el **desfile** parade, **5.2**
desgraciadamente unfortunately
deshuesado(a) deboned
el **desierto** desert
desinflada: la llanta desinflada flat tire, **9.2**
despacio slow, slowly, **9.1**
despedirse (i, i) to take leave
despegar to take off *(plane)*,10.2; **1.2**
el **despegue** takeoff, 10.2; **1.2**
despertarse (ie) to wake up, 11.1; **2.1**
después (de) after, 3.1; later
el/la **destinatario(a)** addressee, recipient, **6.1**
el **destino** destination, **3.1**
destino: con destino a (going) to; for, 10.2; **1.2**
las **desventajas** disadvantages
el **detalle** detail
detrás de in back of, behind, 2.2
devolver (ue) to return *(something)*, 5.2
el **día** day
Buenos días. Good morning., LP
el Día de los Muertos Day of the Dead, **5.1**
el Día de los Reyes Epiphany (January 6), **5.1**
hoy en día nowadays
¿Qué día es hoy? What day is it today?, LP
el **diablo** devil
el **diagnóstico** diagnosis
el **diálogo** dialogue
diaria: la rutina diaria daily routine, 11.1; **2.1**
el **dibujo** drawing, illustration
diciembre December, LP
el **dictado** dictation
diecinueve nineteen, LP
dieciocho eighteen, LP
dieciséis sixteen, LP
diecisiete seventeen, LP
el **diente** clove (of garlic)
los **dientes** teeth, 11.1; **2.1**
cepillarse (lavarse) los dientes to brush one's teeth, 11.1; **2.1**
la **dieta** diet

Spanish-English Dictionary

diez ten, LP
de diez en diez by tens
la **diferencia** difference
diferente different
difícil difficult, 1.2
la **dificultad** difficulty
sin dificultad easily
difunto(a) dead, deceased, **5.1**
el/la **difunto(a)** deceased, dead person, **5.1**
¡Diga! Hello! *(on the phone)*
¡Dígame! Hello! *(on the phone)*
dinámico(a) dynamic, 6.1
el dinero money, 3.2
la **dirección** address, **6.1;** direction
la dirección de correo electrónico (e-mail) e-mail address, **6.1**
las **direccionales** turn signals, **9.2**
el **disco** record
el **disfraz** disguise, costume, **5.1**
disfrutar (de) to enjoy
disponible available
distancia: de larga distancia long-distance *(race)*, **11.1**
distinto(a) different
el **distribuidor automático** boarding pass kiosk, 10.1; **1.1;** ticket dispenser, **3.1**
el **distrito** district, area, section
divertido(a) fun, funny, amusing
divertir (ie, i) to amuse, 11.2; **2.2**
divertirse (ie, i) to have a good time, to have fun, 11.2; **2.2**
divino(a) divine, heavenly
doblar to turn, **9.1**
doble: el cuarto doble double *(hotel room)*, **7**
dobles doubles *(tennis)*, 5.2
doce twelve, LP
la **docena** dozen
el **documento adjunto** attached file, **6.1**
el **dólar** dollar
doler (ue) to ache, to hurt, 6.2; **11.2**
Le (Me, etc.) duele mucho. It hurts him (me, etc.) a lot., **11.2**
Me duele(n)... My . . . ache(s)., 6.2
el **dolor** pain, ache, 6.2
tener dolor de cabeza to have a headache, 6.2
tener dolor de estómago to have a stomachache, 6.2
tener dolor de garganta to have a sore throat, 6.2
domesticado(a) domesticated
el **domingo** Sunday, LP
dominicano(a) Dominican
la República Dominicana Dominican Republic
el **dominó** dominos
donde where
¿dónde? where?, 1.1
¿de dónde? from where?, 1.1
dormir (ue, u) to sleep
la bolsa de dormir sleeping bag, 11.2; **2.2**
el cuarto de dormir bedroom, 2.2
el saco de dormir sleeping bag, 11.2; **2.2**
dormirse (ue, u) to fall asleep, 11.1; **2.1**
el **dormitorio** bedroom, 2.2
dos two
doscientos(as) two hundred
driblar to dribble, 5.2
la **ducha** shower, 11.1; **2.1**
tomar una ducha to take a shower, 11.1; **2.1**
la **duda** doubt
el/la **dueño(a)** owner
dulce sweet, **5.1**
el pan dulce pastry, 7
el **dulce** sweet
durante during, 3.2
durar to last
duro(a) hard, difficult, 1.2
la copia dura hard copy, **6.1**
el **DVD** DVD, 3.2

E

la **ebullición** boiling
echar to throw, to expel
económico(a) inexpensive
ecuatoriano(a) Ecuadoran, 1.1
la **edad** age
la Edad Media Middle Ages
el **edificio** building, 2.2
la **educación** education
la educación física physical education, 1.2
educado(a) mannered
estar bien (mal) educado(a) to be polite (rude), 6.1
egoísta selfish, egotistical
el **ejemplo** example
por ejemplo for example
los **ejercicios** exercises, **11.1**
ejercicios de respiración breathing exercises, **11.1**
hacer ejercicios to exercise, **11.1**
los **ejotes** green beans
el the *(m. sing.)*, 1.1
él he, 1.1
elaborar to make, to produce, **5.1**
electrónico(a) electronic, 10.1; **1.1**
el boleto (billete) electrónico e-ticket, 10.1; **1.1**
el correo electrónico e-mail, 3.2; **6.1**
el **elefante** elephant
elegante elegant, fancy
elegir (i, i) to elect
elemental elementary
ella she, 1.1
ellos(as) they, 1.2
el **elote** corn
el **e-mail** e-mail, **6.1**
embarcar to board, 10.2; **1.2**
el **embarque** boarding, 10.1; **1.1**
la hora de embarque boarding time, 10.1; **1.1**
el **embotellamiento** traffic jam
emergencia: la sala de emergencia emergency room, **11.2**
emocionante moving; exciting
la **empanada** meat pie, 4.2
empezar (ie) to begin, 5.1
el/la **empleado(a)** salesperson, employee, 3.2
empujar to push
en in; on; at
en casa at home
el/la **enamorado(a)** sweetheart
enamorado(a) de in love with
encantar to love, to adore, **6.2**
encender (ie) to light, **5.2**

encerrar (ie) to enclose
encestar to make a basket *(basketball),* 5.2
la **enchilada** enchilada
encima: por encima de above, over, 5.2
encontrar (ue) to find, to encounter
encontrarse (ue) to be found; to meet
la **encuesta** survey
el/la **enemigo(a)** enemy
energético(a) energetic, 6.1
la **energía** energy, 6.1
enero January, LP
el primero de enero January 1, LP
enfadado(a) angry, mad, 6.1
enfadar to make angry, 6.1
la **enfermedad** sickness, disease
el/la **enfermero(a)** nurse, 6.2; **11.2**
enfermo(a) ill, sick, 6.2
el/la **enfermo(a)** patient, sick person
enfrente de in front of
enlatado(a) canned
enlazar to connect
enojado(a) angry, mad, annoyed, 6.1
enojar to make angry, to annoy, 6.1
enorme enormous
la **ensalada** salad, 4.1
enseguida right away, 4.2
enseñar to teach, 3.1; to show
entender (ie) to understand, 8.2
entero(a) entire, whole
enterrado(a) buried, **5.1**
enterrar (ie) to bury
la **entrada** ticket, 8.1; entrée *(meal);* entrance
entradas: la bandeja de entradas e-mail inbox, **6.1**
entrar to enter, to go into, 5.1
entrar en línea to go online, **6.1**
entre between, among
el/la **entrenador(a)** coach, manager
el/la **entrevistador(a)** interviewer
entusiasmado(a) enthusiastic
el **entusiasmo** enthusiasm, 6.1
enviados: la bandeja de enviados sent mailbox, **6.1**
enviar to send, 3.2
el **episodio** episode
la **época** times, period
el **equilibrio** balance
el **equipaje** luggage, baggage, 10.1; **1.1**
el equipaje de mano hand luggage, carry-on bags, 10.2; **1.2**
el **equipo** team, 5.1; equipment
el deporte de equipo team sport
la **equitación** horseback riding, **8.2**
escala: hacer escala to stop over, to make a stop
la **escalera** stairs, staircase, **8.1**
la escalera mecánica escalator, **8.1**
el **escalope de ternera** veal cutlet, **10**
el **escaparate** store window, 9.1
la **escena** scene
escoger to choose
escolar *(related to)* school
el bus escolar school bus, 3.2
los materiales escolares school supplies, 3.1
la tarifa escolar student fare
escribir to write, 4.2
escrito(a) written
el **escrito** document, paper
escritorio: la pantalla de escritorio *(computer)* screen, **6.1**
escuchar to listen (to), 3.2
¿Me escuchas? Can you hear me? *(telephone),* **6.2**
el **escudero** squire
la **escuela** school, 1.2
la escuela primaria elementary school
la escuela secundaria secondary school, high school, 1.2
el/la **escultor(a)** sculptor
la **escultura** sculpture
ese(a) that, that one
eso: a eso de at about *(time)*
por eso for this reason, that is why
esos(as) those
la **espalda** back, 11.1; **2.1**
espantable horrendous
España Spain
español(a) Spanish *(adj.)*
el/la **español(a)** Spaniard
el **español** Spanish *(language),* 1.2
la **especia** spice
la **especialidad** specialty
especialmente especially
específico(a) specific
espectacular spectacular
el **espectáculo** show, spectacle
el/la **espectador(a)** spectator
el **espejo** mirror, 11.1; **2.1**
espera: la sala de espera waiting room, **3.1**
esperar to wait (for), 10.2; **1.2;** to hope; to expect
el **espíritu** mind, spirit, **11.1**
la **esplendidez** splendor
espontáneo(a) spontaneous
la **esposa** wife, 2.1
el **esposo** husband, 2.1
el **esqueleto** skeleton, **5.1**
el **esquí** ski; skiing, 7.2
el esquí acuático (naútico) waterskiing, 7.1
el esquí alpino downhill skiing
el esquí nórdico cross-country skiing
el/la **esquiador(a)** skier, 7.2
esquiar to ski, 7.2
esquiar en el agua to water-ski, 7.1
la **esquina** corner, **8.1**
¿Está... , por favor? Is . . . there, please?, **6.2**
establecer(se) to establish; to settle
el **establecimiento** establishment, settling
el **establo** stable, **8.2;** manger
la **estación** season, LP; resort, 7.1; station, **3.1**
la estación de esquí ski resort, 7.2
la estación de ferrocarril (tren) railroad (train) station, **3.1**
la estación de metro subway (metro) station, **8.1**
la estación de servicio gas station, **9.2**
¿Qué estación es? What season is it?, LP
estacionar to park
la **estadía** stay
el **estadio** stadium
Estados Unidos United States
estadounidense from the United States
la **estancia** ranch, **8.2**
estar to be, 3.1
¿Está...? Is . . . there?, **6.2**
estar bien to feel fine, 6.2
estar cansado(a) to be tired, 6.1
estar contento(a) (triste, nervioso[a], etc.) to be happy (sad, nervous, etc.), 6.1

Spanish-English Dictionary

Spanish-English Dictionary

estar de buen (mal) humor to be in a good (bad) mood, 6.1
estar enfermo(a) to be sick, 6.2
la **estatua** statue, 8.2
la **estatura** stature, height
este(a) this, this one, 9.1
el **este** east
estereofónico(a) stereo
el **estilo** style
estimado(a) esteemed
estirarse to stretch, 11.1; **2.1**
el **estómago** stomach, 6.2
el dolor de estómago stomachache, 6.2
estos(as) these
la **estrategia** strategy
estrecho(a) narrow, **8.1**
la **estrella** star
estremecerse to shake
el **estrés** stress, 6.2
la **estructura** structure
el/la **estudiante** student
estudiantil: la tarifa estudiantil student fare
estudiar to study, 3.1
el **estudio** study
los estudios sociales social studies, 1.2
la **estufa** stove, **10**
estupendo(a) terrific, stupendous
la **etnia** ethnicity, ethnic group
étnico(a) ethnic
el **euro** euro *(currency of most of the countries of the European Union)*
Europa Europe
el **evento** event
evitar to avoid
el **examen** test, exam, 3.1
el examen físico physical, 6.2
examinar to examine, 6.2
exceder to go over *(speed limit)*
excelente excellent
la **excepción** exception
la **excursión** excursion, outing
el/la **excursionista** hiker
existir exist
el **éxito** success, 6.1
tener éxito to succeed, to be successful, 6.1
exótico(a) exotic
experimentar to try, to try out
el/la **experto(a)** expert
explicar to explain
el/la **explorador(a)** explorer
la **exposición de arte** art show, exhibition, 8.2
la **expresión** expression
extenderse (ie) to extend
extranjero(a) foreign
al extranjero abroad
extraordinario(a) extraordinary

F

la **fábrica** factory
fabuloso(a) fabulous
fácil easy, 1.2
la **factura** bill
facturar el equipaje to check luggage, 10.1; **1.1**
la **falda** skirt, 3.1
falso(a) false
faltar to lack, not to have, 6.1
Le falta paciencia. He (She) has no patience., 6.1
la **familia** family, 2.1
familiar *(related to)* family
los **familiares** family members
famoso(a) famous
la **fantasía** fantasy
fantástico(a) fantastic
el/la **farmacéutico(a)** druggist, pharmacist
la **farmacia** pharmacy, drugstore, 6.2
el **favor** favor
Favor de *(+ infinitive).* Please (do something)., 11.2; **2.2**
por favor please, LP
favorito(a) favorite
febrero February, LP
la **fecha** date, LP
¿Cuál es la fecha de hoy? What is today's date?, LP
fecundo(a) prolific
la **felicidad** happiness
feliz happy, **5.2**
¡Felices Pascuas! Happy Easter!
¡Feliz Hanuka! Happy Hanukkah!, **5.2**
¡Feliz Navidad! Merry Christmas!, **5.2**
feo(a) unattractive, ugly, 1.1
la **feria** festival, fair, **5.1**
ferrocarril: la estación de ferrocarril train station, railroad station, **3.1**
festivo: el día festivo holiday
la **fiebre** fever, 6.2
tener fiebre to have a fever, 6.2
fiel loyal, faithful
la **fiesta** party, 8.1; holiday, **5.1**
dar una fiesta to throw a party, 8.1
la fiesta de las luces festival of lights (Hanukkah), **5.2**
fijo(a) fixed, unchanging
la **fila** line *(of people);* row *(of seats)*
estar en fila to wait in line
el **film** film, movie
el **filme** film, movie, 8.2
el **fin** end
el fin de semana weekend, 7.1
por fin finally
final: al final de at the end of
la **finca** farm, **8.2**
fines: a fines de at the end of
fingir to pretend
físico(a) physical
la apariencia física physical appearance, looks
la educación física physical education, 1.2
flaco(a) thin
el **flan** flan, custard, 4.1
la **flauta** flute
la **flecha** arrow
flexible open-minded, flexible, 6.1
la **flor** flower, 2.2
el **foco** center, focal point
la **fogata** bonfire, campfire
fondo: al fondo to the bottom
los **fondos** funds, money
la **forma** form, piece, 10.2; **1.2;** shape
la forma de identidad piece of ID, 10.2; **1.2**
formar to form, to make up; to put together
el **formulario** form
forzado(a) forced
la **foto(grafía)** photo, 7.1
la **fractura** fracture
el **francés** French, 1.2
el **franciscano** Franciscan
franco(a) frank, sincere, candid

Spanish-English Dictionary

el **frasco** jar, 9.2
la **frase** sentence
la **frazada** blanket, **7**
frecuencia: con frecuencia often, frequently
freír (i, i) to fry, **4**
los **frenos** brakes, **9.2**
la **frente** forehead, **11.1**
frente a in front of
fresco(a) cool, LP
Hace fresco. It's cool *(weather).*, LP
los **frijoles** beans, 4.1
frío(a) cold, 4.2
Hace frío. It's cold *(weather).*, LP
tener frío to be cold, 11.1; **2.1**
el **frío** cold
frito(a) fried
las patatas (papas) fritas french fries, 4.1
frontal: la página frontal home page, **6.1**
la **frontera** border
la **fruta** fruit, 9.2
el puesto de frutas fruit stand, 9.2
la **frutería** fruit stand, 9.2
el **fuego** flame, heat, **10**
a fuego lento on low heat, **10**
los **fuegos artificiales** fireworks, **5.2**
la **fuente** fountain
fuera de outside
fuerte strong; substantial
las **fuerzas** (armed) forces
fumar: la señal de no fumar no-smoking sign, 10.2; **1.2**
el **fútbol** soccer, 5.1
el campo de fútbol soccer field, 5.1
el fútbol americano football
el/la **futbolista** soccer player
el **futuro** future

G

las **gafas para el sol** sunglasses, 7.1
el **galán** elegant man, heartthrob
gallardo(a) brave, dashing
las **galletas** crackers, 8.1
la **gallina** hen, **8.2**
la **gamba** shrimp, prawn
el **ganado** cattle, livestock, **8.2**
ganar to win, 5.1; to earn
ganas: tener ganas de to feel like
el **garaje** garage, 2.2
la **garganta** throat, 6.2
el dolor de garganta sore throat, 6.2
la **garita de peaje** tollbooth, **9.1**
el **gas: el agua mineral con gas** carbonated (sparkling) mineral water, 4.2
la **gaseosa** soda, carbonated drink, 4.2
la **gasolina** gas
la **gasolinera** gas station, **9.2**
gastar to spend; to waste
el/la **gato(a)** cat, 2.1; jack *(car)*, **9.2**
el/la **gemelo(a)** twin, 2.1
general general
en general in general
por lo general usually, as a rule
generalmente usually, generally
generoso(a) generous
la **gente** people, 9.1
la **geografía** geography
la **geometría** geometry
el **gigante** giant
el **gimnasio** gym(nasium), **11.1**
la **gitanilla** little gypsy
el **gobierno** government
el **gol** goal, 5.1
meter un gol to score a goal, 5.1
golpear to hit *(ball)*, 5.2
la **goma** tire, **9.2**
gordo(a) fat
el **gorro** ski hat, 7.2
gozar de to enjoy
grabar to record
Gracias. Thank you., LP
dar gracias a to thank
gracioso(a) funny, 1.1
la **gramática** grammar
gran, grande big, large, 1.2
la **grandeza** greatness, grandeur
el **granero** barn, **8.2**
la **granja** farm, **8.2**
gratis for free
gratuito(a) free
grave serious
gris gray, 5.1
gritar to yell, to shout
el **grupo** group, 8.1
la **guagua** bus *(Puerto Rico, Cuba)*, **8.1**
el **guante** glove, 5.2
la **guantera** glove compartment, **9.2**
guapo(a) attractive, good-looking, 1.1
guardar to guard, 5.1; to save, to keep, **6.1**
guardar cama to stay in bed *(illness)*, 6.2
la **guardería** shelter
guatemalteco(a) Guatemalan
la **guerra** war
el **guerrero** warrior
la **guía** guidebook
la guía telefónica phone book, **6.2**
guiar to guide
el **guisante** pea, 9.2
la **guitarra** guitar
gustar to like, to be pleasing to, 5.1
el **gusto** pleasure; like; taste
Mucho gusto. Nice *(It's a pleasure)* to meet you. 1.2

H

haber to have *(in compound tenses)*
las **habichuelas** beans
las habichuelas tiernas green beans, string beans
la **habitación** bedroom; hotel room, **7**
el/la **habitante** inhabitant
hablar to speak, to talk, 3.1
hablar en el móvil to talk on the cell phone
hablar por teléfono to talk on the phone
¿Hablas en serio? Are you serious?
hace: Hace... años . . . years ago
Hace buen tiempo. The weather is nice., LP
Hace (mucho) calor. It's (very) hot *(weather).*, LP
Hace fresco. It's cool *(weather).*, LP
Hace frío. It's cold *(weather).*, LP
Hace mal tiempo. The weather is bad., LP
Hace sol. It's sunny., LP
Hace viento. It's windy., LP
hacer to do, to make, 10.2; **1.2**
hacer clic to click *(computer)*, **6.1**
hacer cola to stand (wait) in line, 10.2; **1.2**

Spanish-English Dictionary

Spanish-English Dictionary

hacer ejercicios to exercise, **11.1**
hacer jogging to go jogging, **11.1**
hacer la cama to make the bed, **7**
hacer la maleta to pack, 10.1; **1.1**
hacer planchas to do push-ups, **11.1**
hacer un viaje to take a trip, 10.1; **1.1**
hacerse daño to hurt oneself, **11.2**
hacia toward
hacia atrás backwards
la **hacienda** ranch, **8.2**
el **hall** concourse *(train station)*, **3.1**
el **hambre** *(f.)* hunger
Me muero de hambre. I'm starving., **4**
tener hambre to be hungry, 4.1
la **hamburguesa** hamburger, 4.1
el **Hanuka** Hanukkah, **5.2**
¡Feliz Hanuka! Happy Hanukkah!, **5.2**
la **harina** flour
hasta until; up to; as far as; even
¡Hasta luego! See you later!, LP
¡Hasta mañana! See you tomorrow!, LP
¡Hasta pronto! See you soon!, LP
hay there is, there are, 2.2
hay que it's necessary to (do something), one must, 10.2; **1.2**
Hay sol. It's sunny., LP
No hay de qué. You're welcome., LP
¿Qué hay? What's new (up)?
la **hazaña** achievement
hebreo(a) Jewish, Hebrew, **5.2**
el **hecho** fact
hecho(a): bien hecho(a) well-done *(meat)*, **4**
el **helado** ice cream, 4.1
el **heno** hay, **8.2**
la **herida** wound, injury, **11.2**
el/la **herido(a)** injured person
la **hermana** sister, 2.1
la **hermanastra** stepsister, 2.1
el **hermanastro** stepbrother, 2.1
el **hermano** brother, 2.1
hermoso(a) beautiful
el **héroe** hero
la **heroína** heroine
herramientas: la barra de herramientas toolbar, **6.1**
hervir (ie, i) to boil, **10**
el **hielo** ice, 7.2
el patinaje sobre el hielo ice-skating, 7.2
la **hierba** grass, **8.2**
las **hierbas** herbs
el **hígado** liver
higiénico: el rollo de papel higiénico roll of toilet paper, 11.2; **2.2**
la **hija** daughter, 2.1
el **hijo** son, child, 2.1
el hijo único only child, 2.1
los **hijos** children, 2.1
hinchado(a) swollen, **11.2**
hincharse to get swollen, to swell
hispano(a) Hispanic
hispanohablante Spanish-speaking
el/la **hispanohablante** Spanish speaker
la **historia** history, 1.2
el/la **historiador(a)** historian
la **hoja de papel** sheet of paper, 3.1
hojear to skim, to scan
¡Hola! Hello!, LP
el **hombre** man
el **hombro** shoulder, **11.1**
honesto(a) honest
la **hora** hour; time, 10.1; **1.1**
¿a qué hora? at what time?, LP
la hora de embarque boarding time, 10.1; **1.1**
la hora de salida departure time, 10.1; **1.1**
¿Qué hora es? What time is it?, LP
el **horario** *(train)* schedule, timetable, **3.1**
el **horno** oven, **10**
el **horno de microondas** microwave oven, **10**
hospedarse to stay *(in a hotel)*, **7**
el **hospital** hospital
el **hostal** hostel, small (inexpensive) hotel, **7**
el **hotel** hotel, **7**
hoy today, LP
¿Cuál es la fecha de hoy? What's today's date?, LP
hoy en día nowadays
¿Qué día es hoy? What day is it today?, LP
la **huerta** orchard, **8.2**
el **hueso** bone, **5.1**
el/la **huésped(a)** guest, **7**
el **huevo** egg, 4.1; **7**
los huevos pasados por agua soft-boiled eggs
los huevos revueltos scrambled eggs, **7**
huir to flee
humanitario(a) humanitarian
humano(a) human, 11.1; **2.1**
el ser humano human being
humilde humble
el **humor** mood; humor
estar de buen (mal) humor to be in a good (bad) mood, 6.1
tener un buen sentido de humor to have a good sense of humor, 6.1
el **huso horario** time zone

I

el **icono** icon, **6.1**
ida y vuelta (regreso): un boleto (billete) de ida y vuelta (regreso) round-trip ticket, **3.1**
la **idea** idea
la **identidad** identification, 10.2; **1.2**
el carnet de identidad ID card, 10.2; **1.2**
identificar to identify
la **iglesia** church
igual que as well as; like; just as
iluminar to light up, to illuminate, **5.2**
la **imagen** picture, image
impaciente impatient, 6.1
impares odd *(numeric)*
impermeable raincoat
importa: No importa. It doesn't matter.
la **importancia** importance
importante important

imposible impossible
la **impresora** printer, **6.1**
imprimir to print, **6.1**
el **impuesto** tax
incluir to include
¿Está incluido el servicio? Is the tip included?, 4.2
increíble incredible
indicar to indicate
indígena native, indigenous, 9.2
el/la **indígena** indigenous person
individual: el deporte individual individual sport
individuales singles *(tennis),* 5.2
industrializado(a) industrialized
la **infinidad** infinity
la **influencia** influence
la **información** information, 3.2
el **inglés** English, 1.2
el **ingrediente** ingredient
inhóspito(a) inhospitable, desolate
inicial: la página inicial home page, **6.1**
inicio: la página de inicio home page, **6.1**
inmenso(a) immense
el **inodoro** toilet, **7**
insertar to insert, **3.1**
inteligente intelligent, 1.2
el **interés** interest
interesante interesting, 1.2
interesar to interest, 5.1
las **intermitentes** turn signals, **9.2**
el **Internet** Internet, 3.2; **6.1**
navegar el Internet to surf the Net, 3.2; **6.1**
interurbano(a) city-to-city
intervenir (ie) to intervene
la **introducción** introduction
introducir to insert, **6.2**
el **invierno** winter, LP
la **invitación** invitation
el/la **invitado(a)** guest
invitar to invite
ir to go, 3.2
ir a (+ *infinitive*) to be going to (do something), 4.2
ir a casa to go home, 3.2
ir a pie to go on foot, 3.2
ir al cine to go to the movies, 8.2
ir de camping to go camping, 11.2; **2.2**
ir de compras to go shopping, 9.1
irlandés(esa) Irish
la **isla** island
el **istmo** isthmus
italiano(a) Italian
izquierdo(a) left, 11.1; **2.1**
a la izquierda to the left, **9.1**

J

el **jabón** soap, 11.2; **2.2**
la barra (pastilla) de jabón bar of soap, 11.2; **2.2**
jamás never
el **jamón** ham, 4.1
el sándwich de jamón y queso ham and cheese sandwich, 4.1
el **jardín** garden, 2.2
el/la **jardinero(a)** outfielder, 5.2
jogging: hacer jogging to go jogging, **11.1**
el **jonrón** home run
batear un jonrón to hit a home run
joven young
el/la **joven** young person, 1.1
la **joya** jewel, piece of jewelry
las **judías verdes** green beans, 9.2
judío(a) Jewish, **5.2**
el **juego** game, 5.1
el **jueves** Thursday, LP
el/la **jugador(a)** player, 5.1
jugar (ue) to play, 5.1
jugar (al) fútbol (béisbol, básquetbol) to play soccer (baseball, basketball), 5.1
el **jugo** juice, 4.1
el jugo de naranja orange juice, 4.1; **7**
el **juguete** toy
julio July, LP
junio June, LP
juntos(as) together

K

el **kilo** kilogram *(2.2 lbs.),* **9.2**
el **kilómetro** kilometer

L

la the *(f. sing.),* **1.1; it, her** *(pron.)*
el **labio** lip
el **laboratorio** laboratory
laborioso(a) hardworking
labrar to work *(land),* **8.2**
el **lacón** bacon, **7**
lácteo(a): productos lácteos dairy products
el **lado** side
al lado de beside, next to, 2.2
ladrar to bark
el **lago** lake
la **lámpara** lamp, 2.2
la **langosta** lobster, **4**
la **lanza** lance
el/la **lanzador(a)** pitcher, 5.2
lanzar to kick, to throw, 5.1
el **lapicero** ballpoint pen
el **lápiz** pencil, 3.1
largo(a) long, 5.1
a lo largo de along
las the *(f. pl.);* them *(pron.)*
lastimarse to harm oneself, to get hurt
la **lata** can, 9.2
latino(a) Latino
Latinoamérica Latin America
el/la **latinoamericano(a)** Latin American
el **lavabo** washbasin, sink, **7**
el **lavaplatos** dishwasher, **10**
lavar to wash, 11.2; **2.2**
lavarse to wash oneself, 11.1; **2.1**
lavarse el pelo (la cara, las manos) to wash one's hair (face, hands), 11.1; **2.1**
lavarse los dientes to clean *(brush)* one's teeth, 11.1; **2.1**
le to him, to her; to you *(formal) (pron.)*
la **lección** lesson
la **leche** milk, 4.1
el café con leche coffee with milk, café au lait
el **lechón asado** roast suckling pig
la **lechuga** lettuce, 4.1
la **lectura** reading
leer to read, 4.2
la **legumbre** vegetable, 4.1
lejos (de) far (from), 3.2
a lo lejos in the distance
la **lengua** language
lentamente slowly
lento(a) slow, **11.1;** low *(heat),* **10**
a fuego lento on low heat, **10**
el **león** lion
les to them; to you *(formal) (pron.)*

Spanish-English Dictionary

Spanish-English Dictionary

la **letra** letter *(of alphabet)*
las **letras** literature
levantar to raise, 3.1; to clear, **4;** to lift, **11.1**
levantar la mano to raise one's hand, 3.1
levantar la mesa to clear the table, **4**
levantar pesas to lift weights, **11.1**
levantarse to get up, 11.1; **2.1**
la **leyenda** legend
liberar to free, to rid, **11.1**
la **libertad** freedom
la **libra** pound *(weight)*
libre free, unoccupied, 4.2; **3.2**
al aire libre outdoor, open-air
el tiempo libre spare time, 8.1
la **libreta de direcciones** (e-mail) address book, **6.1**
el **libro** book, 3.1
el libro de bolsillo paperback, **3.1**
la **licencia** driver's license, **9.2**
el **líder** leader
la **liga** league
las Grandes Ligas Major Leagues
ligeramente lightly
ligero(a) light
el **límite de velocidad** speed limit
el **limón** lemon
la **limonada** lemonade
limpiar to clean, **7**
limpio(a) clean, **7**
lindo(a) beautiful
la **línea** *(telephone)* line, **6.2;** *(road)* line, **9.1**
la línea continua solid line, **9.1**
Se nos cortó la línea. We've been cut off. *(phone)*, **6.2**
línea: en línea online, **6.1**
entrar en línea to go online, **6.1**
la **línea aérea** airline, 10.1; **1.1**
la **liquidación** sale, 9.1
listo(a) ready
la **litera** bunk
la **literatura** literature
la **llama** llama
la **llamada** *(telephone)* call, **6.2**
la llamada perdida (caída) dropped call *(cell phone)*, **6.2**
llamar to call, 11.2; **2.2**
llamarse to call oneself, to be called, named, 11.1; **2.1**
Me llamo... My name is . . . , 11.1; **2.1**
la **llanta** tire, **9.2**
la llanta de repuesto (recambio) spare tire, **9.2**
la **llave** key, **7**
la llave magnética magnetic key, **7**
la **llegada** arrival, **3.1**
llegar to arrive, 4.1
llenar to fill, **9.2**
lleno(a) de full of, 6.1
llevar to carry; to wear, 3.1; to take; to bear; to have
llorar to cry
llover (ue) to rain
Llueve. It's raining., LP
lluvioso(a) rainy
lo it, him, you *(formal) (pron.)*
lo que what
la **loción bronceadora** suntan lotion, sunblock, 7.1
loco(a) crazy
el **lodo** mud
lógico(a) logical
la **loncha** slice *(ham)*
la **lonja** slice *(ham)*
el **loro** parrot
los them *(m. pl.) (pron.)*
el **lote** lot
las **luces** lights, **5.2;** headlights, **9.2**
la fiesta de las luces festival of lights *(Hanukkah)*, **5.2**
luchar to fight
luego later, LP; then, 3.2
¡Hasta luego! See you later!, LP
el **lugar** place
tener lugar to take place
lujoso(a) luxurious
el **lunes** Monday, LP
la **luz** light, **5.2**
la luz roja red light, **9.1**

M

la **madera** wood
de madera wooden
la **madrastra** stepmother, 2.1
la **madre** mother, 2.1
los **madrileños** citizens of Madrid
el/la **madrugador(a)** early riser, 11.1; **2.1**
los **maduros** fried sweet bananas
magnético(a) magnetic, **7**
magnífico(a) magnificent, splendid
Magos: los Reyes Magos the Three Wise Men, **5.2**
el **maíz** corn, 9.2
mal bad
estar de mal humor to be in a bad mood, 6.1
Hace mal tiempo. The weather is bad., LP
mal educado(a) ill-mannered, rude, 6.1
el **malecón** boardwalk (seafront)
los **males** the evil (things), the ills
la **maleta** suitcase, 10.1; **1.1**
hacer la maleta to pack, 10.1; **1.1**
la **maletera** trunk *(car)*, 10.1; **1.1**
malicioso(a) malicious
malo(a) bad, 1.2
sacar notas malas to get bad grades, 3.1
mamá mom, mommy
mandar to send
el **mandato** command
mando: la cabina de mando cockpit
manejar to drive
la **manera** manner, way
de ninguna manera in no way, by no means
manga: de manga corta (larga) short- (long-) sleeved, 9.1
el **maní** peanut, 8.1
la **mano** hand, 3.1
el equipaje de mano carry-on luggage, 10.2; **1.2**
levantar la mano to raise one's hand, 3.1
manso(a) gentle
la **manta** blanket, **7**
el **mantel** tablecloth, **4**
mantener to maintain
mantenerse en forma to stay in shape
la **mantequilla** butter, 4.1; **7**
la **manzana** apple, 9.2; (city) block, **9.1**

mañana tomorrow, LP
¡Hasta mañana! See you tomorrow!, LP
la **mañana** morning
de la mañana A.M.
por la mañana in the morning
el **mapa** map
la **máquina** machine
la **maquinaria** machinery, equipment
el **mar** sea, ocean, 7.1
el mar Caribe Caribbean Sea
el **maratón** marathon, **11.1**
marcar to score, 5.1; to dial, **6.2**
marcar el número to dial the number, **6.2**
marcar un tanto to score a point, 5.1
la **marcha** march
en marcha working
marchar to march
el **marido** husband, 2.1
el **marinero** sailor
los **mariscos** shellfish, seafood, **4**
marrón: de color marrón brown, 5.1
el **martes** Tuesday, LP
marzo March, LP
más more, 9.1
¡Qué... más...! What a . . . !
la **máscara** mask, **5.1**
la **máscara de oxígeno** oxygen mask, 10.2; **1.2**
la **mascota** pet, 2.1
las **matemáticas** mathematics, math, 1.2
los **materiales escolares** school supplies, 3.1
el **mausoleo** mausoleum, **5.1**
máximo(a) highest, top
la velocidad máxima speed limit, top speed
mayo May, LP
la **mayonesa** mayonnaise, 9.2
mayor older
el/la **mayor** the oldest; the greatest
la **mayoría** majority
mayoritario(a) *(related to)* majority
me me *(pron.)*
mediano(a) medium, medium-size
la **medianoche** midnight
el **medicamento** medicine, 6.2
la **medicina** medicine, 6.2
el/la **médico(a)** doctor, 6.2
la **medida** measurement
las **medidas** measures
medio(a) half; middle
a término medio medium *(meat)*, **4**
la clase media middle class
y media half past (the hour), LP
el **medio** means; middle
el medio de transporte means of transport, **8.1**
el **mediodía** noon
los **mejillones** mussels, **4**
mejor better
el/la **mejor** the best
menor younger; lesser
el/la **menor** the youngest; the least
la **menora** menorah, **5.2**
menos less, 9.1
a lo menos at least
menos cuarto a quarter to (the hour)
el **mensaje** message, **6.2**
el **menú** menu, 4.2; **4**
menudo: a menudo often
el **mercado** market, 9.2
la **mercancía** merchandise
la **merienda** snack, 4.2
la **mermelada** jam, marmalade, **7**
el **mes** month, LP
la **mesa** table, 2.2; **4**
levantar la mesa to clear the table, **4**
poner la mesa to set the table, **4**
quitar la mesa to clear the table, **4**
el/la **mesero(a)** waiter (waitress), server, 4.2; **4**
la **meseta** meseta, plateau
la **mesita** table, 2.2; **4**
meter to put, to place
meter un gol to score a goal, 5.1
el **metro** subway, metro, **8.1;** meter
la boca del metro subway station entrance, **8.1**
la estación de metro subway station, **8.1**
el **metrópoli** metropolis, big city
mexicano(a) Mexican, 1.2
la **mezcla** mixture
mi(s) my
mí me
el **miedo** fear
tener miedo to be afraid, 7.2
el **miembro** member, 2.1
mientras while, **5.2**
el **miércoles** Wednesday, LP
mil (one) thousand
el **millón** million
el/la **millonario(a)** millionaire
mimado(a) spoiled *(person)*
el **mimo** mime, **8.1**
la **mina** mine
el **minuto** minute
¡Mira! Look! 3.1
la **mirada** gaze, look
tener la mirada fijada to keep one's eyes fixed on
mirar to look at, 3.2
mirarse to look at oneself, 11.1; **2.1**
la **miseria** poverty
mismo(a) same, 1.2; own; very
misterioso(a) mysterious
mixto(a) co-ed
la **mochila** backpack, knapsack, 3.1
el/la **mochilero(a)** backpacker, hiker, 11.2; **2.2**
viajar de mochilero to go backpacking, hiking
los **modales** manners, 6.1
tener buenos (malos) modales to have good (bad) manners, to be well-behaved (rude), 6.1
moderno(a) modern
modesto(a) inexpensive
molestar to bother, to annoy, 6.1
el **molino de viento** windmill
el **monasterio** monastery
la **moneda** coin, **9.1**
el **mono** monkey
el **monopatín** skateboard, **11.1**
el **monstruo** monster
la **montaña** mountain, 7.2
la **montaña rusa** roller coaster, **8.1**
montañoso(a) mountainous
montar to put up *(tent)*, 11.2; **2.2;** to ride, **8.2**
montar a caballo to go horseback riding, **8.2**
el **montón** bunch, heap
el **monumento** monument
mórbido(a) morbid
morder (ue) to bite
moreno(a) dark-haired, brunette, 1.1
morir (ue, u) to die, **4**
el **morrón** sweet red pepper
el **mostrador** (ticket) counter, 10.1; **1.1**
mostrar (ue) to show, 10.2; **1.2**

Spanish-English Dictionary

Spanish-English Dictionary

el **motivo** theme; reason, motive
el **móvil** cell phone, 3.2; **6.1**
el **movimiento** movement, **11.1**
el **mozo** bellhop, **7**
el **MP3** MP3 player, **6.2**
la **muchacha** girl, 1.1
el **muchacho** boy, 1.1
mucho a lot, many, much, 2.2; very, LP
Hace mucho calor (frío). It's very hot (cold)., LP
Mucho gusto. Nice to meet you.
los **muebles** furniture, 2.2
la **muerte** death
muerto(a) dead
el/la **muerto(a)** dead person, deceased, **5.1**
el Día de los Muertos the Day of the Dead, **5.1**
la **mujer** wife, 2.1
la **mula** mule
las **muletas** crutches, **11.2**
andar con muletas to walk on crutches, **11.2**
la **multa** fine, **9.1**
mundial: la Copa Mundial World Cup
el **mundo** world
todo el mundo everyone
la **muñeca** wrist, **11.1**
el **mural** mural
el/la **muralista** muralist
el **muro** wall
el **museo** museum, 8.2
la **música** music, 1.2
el/la **músico(a)** musician, 8.1
el **muslo** thigh, **10**
muy very, LP
muy bien very well, LP

N

nacer to be born
el **nacimiento** birth
nacional national
la **nacionalidad** nationality 1.1
¿de qué nacionalidad? what nationality?, 1.1
nada nothing, not anything, 8.2
De nada. You're welcome., LP
Nada más. Nothing else., 9.2
Por nada. You're welcome., LP; for no reason
nadar to swim, 7.1
nadie nobody, not anybody, 8.2
la **nafta** gasoline
la **naranja** orange *(fruit)*, 4.1
natal pertaining to where someone was born
la **naturaleza** nature
navegar la red (el Internet) to surf the Web (the Internet), 3.2; **6.1**
la **Navidad** Christmas, **5.2**
el árbol de Navidad Christmas tree, **5.2**
¡Feliz Navidad! Merry Christmas!
necesario: Es necesario. It's necessary., **11.2**
necesitar to need, 3.2
negativo(a) negative
negro(a) black, 2.1
nervioso(a) nervous, 6.1
el **neumático** tire, **9.2**
nevado(a) snowy, snow-covered
nevar (ie) to snow
Nieva. It's snowing., LP
la **nevera** refrigerator, **10**
ni neither, nor
Ni idea. No idea.
nicaragüense Nicaraguan
la **nieta** granddaughter, 2.1
el **nieto** grandson, 2.1
la **nieve** snow, 7.2
ninguno(a) none, not any
de ninguna manera in no way, by no means
la **niñez** childhood
el/la **niño(a)** boy, girl, child, 6.2
el **nivel** level
no no
No hay de qué. You're welcome., LP
no obstante nevertheless
la **noche** night, evening
Buenas noches. Good evening., LP
esta noche tonight, 4.1
por la noche in the evening
la **Nochebuena** Christmas Eve, **5.2**
la **Nochevieja** New Year's Eve
nombrar to name
el **nombre** name, 2.1; **10.1**
la **noria** Ferris wheel, **8.1**
normal normal, 6.2
el **norte** north
norteamericano(a) American, North American
nos us *(pron.)*
nosotros(as) we
la **nota** grade, mark, 3.1
sacar notas buenas (malas) to get good (bad) grades, 3.1
la(s) **noticia(s)** news, piece of news
novecientos(as) nine hundred, 9.2
la **novela** novel
noventa ninety, LP
noviembre November, LP
la **nube** cloud, 7.1
nublado(a) cloudy, 7.1
nuestro(a) our
nueve nine, LP
nuevo(a) new, 1.1
de nuevo again
el **número** shoe size, 9.1; number, 10.1; **1.1**
el número del asiento seat number, 10.1; **1.1**
el número de teléfono telephone number, **6.2**
el número del vuelo flight number, 10.1; **1.1**
¿Qué número calzas? What size shoe do you wear (take)?, 9.1
nunca never, not ever, 8.2

O

o or
objetivo objective
obligatorio(a) required, obligatory
la **obra** work; work of art
observar to observe, to notice
el **obstáculo** obstacle
obstinado(a) obstinate, stubborn, 6.1
occidental western
el **océano** ocean
ochenta eighty, LP
ocho eight, LP
ochocientos(as) eight hundred, 9.2
octubre October, LP

Spanish-English Dictionary

ocupado(a) occupied, 4.2; **3.2**
el **oeste** west
la **oficina** office, **8.1**
ofrecer to offer
la **ofrenda** offering, **5.1**
el **oído** ear
oír to hear, 8.1
Ojalá que... Would that . . . , I hope . . . , **11.2**
ojeada: dar una ojeada to take a look at
¡Ojo! Watch out! Be careful!
el **ojo** eye, 2.1
tener mucho ojo to be very careful
tener ojos azules (castaños, verdes) to have blue (brown, green) eyes, 2.1
la **ola** wave, 7.1
oliva: el aceite de oliva olive oil
la **olla** pot, **10**
olvidar to forget
once eleven, LP
la **onza** ounce
la **opinión** opinion
la **oportunidad** opportunity
el/la **opresor(a)** oppressor
oprimir to press, to push *(button, key)*, **6.1**
opuesto(a) opposite
la **oración** sentence
la **orden** order *(restaurant)*, 4.2
el **orden** order
el **ordenador** computer, 3.2; **6.1**
la **orfebrería** craftsmanship in precious metals
organizar to organize, to set up
el **órgano** organ
oriental eastern
el **origen** origin, background
originarse to come from
las **orillas** banks, shores
a orillas de on the shores of
el **oro** gold
la **orquesta** orchestra, band
la **orquídea** orchid
ortopédico(a): el/la cirujano(a) ortopédico(a) orthopedic surgeon, **11.2**
oscuro(a) dark
el **otoño** autumn, fall, LP
otro(a) other, another
otros(as) others
el **oxígeno: la máscara de oxígeno** oxygen mask, 10.2; **1.2**
¡Oye! Listen!, 1.2

P

pacer to graze, **8.2**
la **paciencia** patience
paciente patient *(adj.)*, 6.1
el/la **paciente** patient, 6.2
el **padrastro** stepfather, 2.1
el **padre** father, 2.1
los **padres** parents, 2.1
pagar to pay, 3.2
la **página** page
la página de inicio (inicial, frontal) home page, **6.1**
el **país** country
el **paisaje** landscape
la **paja** straw, **5.2**
el **pájaro** bird
la **palabra** word
la palabra afine cognate
el **palacio** palace
la **palma** palm tree
la **paloma** pigeon
la **palta** avocado
el **pan** bread
el pan dulce pastry, **7**
el pan tostado toast, 4.1; **7**
la **panadería** bakery
el **panecillo** roll, 4.1; **7**
el **panqueque** pancake
la **pantalla de escritorio** (computer) screen, monitor, **6.1**
el **pantalón** pants, 3.1
el pantalón corto shorts, 5.1
el pantalón largo long pants, 9.1
la **panza** belly
la **papa** potato, 4.1
las papas fritas french fries, 4.1
el **papel** paper, 3.1; role
la hoja de papel sheet of paper, 3.1
el rollo de papel higiénico roll of toilet paper, 11.2; **2.2**
el **paquete** package, 9.2
el **par** pair, 9.1
el par de zapatos pair of shoes, 9.1
para for; in order to
el **parabrisas** windshield, **9.1**
la **parada** stop, station, **3.2**
la parada de autobús bus stop, **8.1**
el **parador** inn
el **paraíso** paradise
parar(se) to stop, **9.1**
parear to match
parecer to seem, to look like
a mi (tu, su) parecer in my *(your, his)* opinion
¿Qué te parece? What do you think?
pares even *(numeric)*
el/la **pariente** relative, 2.1
el **parking** parking lot, **8.1**
el **parque** park, 11.2; **2.2**
el parque de atracciones amusement park, **8.1**
parquear to park
el **parqueo** parking lot, **8.1**
el **parquímetro** parking meter, **9.1**
el **párrafo** paragraph
la **parrilla** grill, **10**
la **parte** part; place
¿De parte de quién, por favor? Who's calling, please?, **6.2**
en muchas partes in many places
la mayor parte the greatest part, the most
participar to participate, to take part in
el **partido** game, 5.1
el **pasabordo** boarding pass
pasado(a) last, 7.1
el año pasado last year, 7.1
la semana pasada last week, 7.1
el/la **pasajero(a)** passenger, 10.1; **1.1**
el **pasaporte** passport, 10.2; **1.2**
pasar to pass, to go, 5.2; to spend *(time)*, 7.1; to pass *(car)*, **9.1**
pasarlo bien to have a good time, to have fun, 11.2; **2.2**
pasar por el control de seguridad to go through security, 10.2; **1.2**
¿Qué pasa? What's going on? What's happening?
¿Qué te pasa? What's the matter (with you)?
la **Pascua (Florida)** Easter
el **paseo** broad street, avenue, **8.1**
dar un paseo to take a walk
dar un paseo en bicicleta to take a (bike) ride
el **pasillo** aisle, 10.2; **1.2**
la **pasta dentífrica** toothpaste
el **pastel** cake

Spanish-English Dictionary

la **pastilla** bar *(soap)*
los **patacones** slices of fried plantain
la **patata** potato, 4.1
las patatas fritas french fries, 4.1
el **patín** ice skate, 7.2
el/la **patinador(a)** ice-skater, 7.2
el **patinaje** skating, 7.2; **11.1**
el patinaje en línea in-line skating, **11.1**
el patinaje sobre hielo ice-skating, 7.2
patinar to skate, to go skating, 7.2; **11.1**
patinar en línea to go in-line skating, **11.1**
patinar sobre el hielo to ice-skate, 7.2
el/la **patrón(ona)** patron, **5.1**
el/la santo(a) patrón(ona) patron saint, **5.1**
patronal pertaining to a patron saint, **5.1**
pausado(a) slow, deliberate
pavimentado(a) paved
el **pavimento** pavement
el **peaje** toll, **9.1**
la cabina (garita) de peaje tollbooth, **9.1**
el/la **peatón(ona)** pedestrian, **8.1**
peatonal related to pedestrians, **8.1**
el **pecho** chest, **11.1**
la **pechuga (de pollo)** (chicken) breast, **10**
el **pedacito** little piece, **10**
el **pedazo** piece
pedir (i, i) to ask for, to request, **4**
peinarse to comb one's hair, 11.1; **2.1**
el **peine** comb, 11.2; **2.2**
pelar to peel, **10**
la **película** movie, film, 8.2
el **peligro** danger
peligroso(a) dangerous
pelirrojo(a) redheaded, 1.1
el **pelo** hair, 2.1
tener el pelo rubio (castaño, negro) to have blond (brown, black) hair, 2.1
la **pelota** ball *(baseball, tennis),* 5.2
la pelota vasca jai alai
la **pena** pain, sorrow
¡Qué pena! What a shame!, 5.1
pendiente steep
la **pendiente** incline
el **pensamiento** thought
pensar (ie) to think, 5.1
pensar en to think about
¿Qué piensas? What do you think?, 5.1
el **peón** peasant, farm laborer, **8.2**
peor worse
el/la **peor** worst
el **pepino** cucumber, **10**
pequeño(a) small, little, 1.2
la **percha** hanger, **7**
perder (ie) to lose, 5.1; to miss, 8.1
perdida: la llamada perdida dropped call *(cell phone),* **6.2**
perdón pardon me, excuse me
la **peregrinación** pilgrimage
perezoso(a) lazy, 1.2
el **periódico** newspaper, **3.1**
permiso: Con permiso. Excuse me., 10.1; **1.1**
el **permiso de conducir** driver's license, **9.2**
permitir to permit
pero but
el/la **perro(a)** dog, 2.1
la **persona** person
el **personaje** character *(in a novel, play)*
la **personalidad** personality, 6.1
pertenecer to belong
peruano(a) Peruvian
la **pesa** weight, **11.1**
levantar pesas to lift weights, **11.1**
pesar: a pesar de in spite of
la **pescadería** fish market
el **pescado** fish, 4.1
el **peso** peso *(monetary unit of several Latin American countries);* weight
picar to nibble on; to chop; to mince, **10**
picaresco(a) picaresque
el/la **pícher** pitcher, 5.2
el **pico** mountain top, peak, 7.2
el **pie** foot, 5.1; **2.1**
a pie on foot, 3.2
de pie standing
la **piedra** stone
la **pierna** leg, 11.1; **2.1**
la **pieza** bedroom; piece
la **pila** swimming pool
el **pimentón** pepper *(vegetable)*
la **pimienta** pepper *(spice),* **4**
el **pimiento** bell pepper, 9.2; **10**
el **pinchazo** flat tire, **9.2**
los **pinchitos** kebabs, 4.2
pintado(a) painted
pintar to paint
el/la **pintor(a)** painter, artist, 8.2
pintoresco(a) picturesque
la **piña** pineapple, 9.2
la **piscina** swimming pool, 7.1
el **piso** floor, 2.2; apartment *(Spain)*
la **pista** ski slope, 7.2; runway, 10.2; **1.2;** lane *(highway)*
la pista de patinaje ice-skating rink, 7.2
la **pizca** pinch
la **pizza** pizza, 4.1
placentero(a) pleasant
la **plancha de vela** windsurfing; sailboard, 7.1
practicar la plancha de vela to windsurf, to go windsurfing, 7.1
planchas: hacer planchas to do push-ups, **11.1**
el **plano** map, **9.1**
la **planta** plant, 2.2
la **plata** silver
el **plátano** banana, 9.2
el **platillo** home plate, 5.2; saucer, **4**
el **plato** dish *(food);* plate, **4;** course *(meal)*
la **playa** beach, 7.1
la **plaza** square, plaza, **8.1;** seat *(train),* **3.2**
la **pluma** (fountain) pen
la **población** population
pobre poor
el/la **pobre** poor boy (girl)
poco(a) a little; few, 2.2
dentro de poco soon; shortly thereafter
un poco más a little more
poder (ue) to be able, 5.1
el **poema** poem
el/la **policía** police officer
el **pollo** chicken, 4.1; **10**
poner to put, to place, to set, 10.2; **1.2**

Spanish-English Dictionary

poner al fuego to heat, **10**
poner la mesa to set the table, **4**
poner unos puntos (unas suturas) to give (someone) stitches, **11.2**
ponerse to put on *(clothes)*, 11.1; **2.1;** to become
popular popular
por for, by
por ejemplo for example
por encima de over, 5.2
por eso that's why, for this reason
por favor please, LP
por fin finally
por la mañana in the morning
por la noche at night, in the evening
por la tarde in the afternoon
por lo general in general
Por nada. You're welcome., LP; for no reason
¿por qué? why?, 3.2
los **porotos** green beans *(Chile)*
porque because, 3.2
el/la **porrista** cheerleader
portátil: la computadora portátil laptop computer
el/la **porteño(a)** person from Buenos Aires
la **portería** goal *(box)*, 5.1
el/la **portero(a)** goalie, 5.1
portugués(esa) Portuguese
poseer to possess
posible possible
positivo(a) positive
el **postre** dessert, 4.1
practicar to practice *(sport)*
practicar la plancha de vela (la tabla hawaiana) to go windsurfing (surfing), 7.1
practicar yoga to do yoga, **11.1**
el **precio** price, 9.1
precolombino(a) pre-Columbian
la **preferencia** preference
preferir (ie, i) to prefer
el **prefijo del país** country code, **6.2**
la **pregunta** question, 3.1
preguntar to ask (a question)
el **premio** prize, award
prender to turn on, **6.1**
preparar to prepare; to get ready
la **prepa(ratoria)** high school

presentar to introduce
el **préstamo** loan
el préstamo a corto (largo) plazo short- (long-) term loan
prestar: prestar atención to pay attention, 3.1
el **pretendiente** suitor
primario(a): la escuela primaria elementary school
la **primavera** spring, LP
primero(a) first, LP
el primero de enero (febrero, etc.) January (February, etc.) 1, LP
en primera clase first-class, **3.2**
el/la **primo(a)** cousin, 2.1
la **princesa** princess
principal main
el/la **principiante** beginner, 7.2
prisa: de prisa fast, hurriedly
a toda prisa with full speed
privado(a) private, 2.2
probable probable, likely
el **problema** problem
No hay problema. No problem.
procedente de coming, arriving from, 10.2; **1.2**
el **procedimiento** step *(recipe)*
la **procesión** procession, parade, **5.1**
producir to produce
el **producto** product; food, 9.2
los productos congelados frozen food, 9.2
la **profesión** profession, occupation
profesional professional
el/la **profesor(a)** teacher, 1.2
profundo(a) deep
prohibido(a) forbidden, **9.1**
prometer to promise
el **pronombre** pronoun
pronto: ¡Hasta pronto! See you soon!, LP
propenso(a) prone to
la **propina** tip *(restaurant)*, **4**
propio(a) own, 5.1
propósito: ¡A propósito! By the way!, 8.2
el **propósito benévelo** charitable purpose
protectora: la loción protectora suntan lotion, sunblock, 7.1
próximo(a) next, **3.2**
la **prueba** test, exam, 3.1

el **pueblo** town
el **puente** bridge
la **puerta** gate *(airport)*, 10.2; **1.2;** door, **9.2**
la puerta delantera (trasera) front (back) door *(bus)*
la puerta de salida gate *(airport)*, 10.2; **1.2**
el **puerto** port
puertorriqueño(a) Puerto Rican
pues well
el **puesto** market stall, 9.2
los **pulmones** lungs
pulsar to press *(button, key)*, **6.1**
la **pulsera** bracelet
pulso: tomar el pulso to take someone's pulse, 6.2
el **punto** point; dot *(Internet)*, **6.1;** stitch, **11.2**
poner puntos (a alguien) to give (somebody) stitches, **11.2**
el **pupitre** desk, 3.1

Q

que that; who
¿qué? what? how?, LP
¿a qué hora? at what time?, LP
¿de qué nacionalidad? what nationality?
No hay de qué. You're welcome., LP
¿Qué desean tomar? What would you like (to eat)?, 4.2
¿Qué día es hoy? What day is it today?, LP
¿Qué hay? What's new (up)?
¿Qué hora es? What time is it?, LP
¡Qué... más... ! What a . . . !
¿Qué pasa? What's going on? What's happening?
¡Qué pena! What a shame!, 5.1
¿Qué tal? How are things? How are you?, LP
¿Qué tal le gustó? How did you like it? *(formal)*
¿Qué tiempo hace? What's the weather like?, LP
quebrarse to break, **11.2**
quedar (bien) to fit, to look good on, 9.1

Spanish-English Dictionary

Spanish-English Dictionary

Esta chaqueta no te queda bien. This jacket doesn't fit you., 9.1
quedar(se) to remain, to stay, 11.1; **2.1**
quemarse to burn, **10**
querer (ie) to want, to wish, 5.1; to love
querido(a) dear, beloved
el **queso** cheese, 4.1
el sándwich de jamón y queso ham and cheese sandwich, 4.1
el **quetzal** quetzal *(currency of Guatemala)*
¿quién? who?, 1.1
¿De parte de quién, por favor? Who's calling, please?, **6.2**
¿quiénes? who? *(pl.)*, 1.2
quince fifteen, LP
la **quinceañera** fifteen-year-old girl
quinientos(as) five hundred
el **quiosco** kiosk, newsstand, **3.1**
quitar la mesa to clear the table, **4**
quitarse to take off *(clothes)*, 11.1; **2.1**
quizá(s) maybe, perhaps, 7.2

R

el **racimo** bunch *(grapes)*
la **radiografía** X ray, **11.2**
Le toman (hacen) una radiografía. They're taking an X ray of him (her)., **11.2**
la **raja** slice *(melon)*
la **rama** branch
el **rancho** ranch, **8.2**
la **ranura** slot, **6.2**
rápidamente quickly
rápido(a) fast
la **raqueta** *(tennis)* racket, 5.2
raro(a) rare
el **rascacielos** skyscraper, **8.1**
el **rato** time, while
el **ratón** mouse, **6.1**
la **raza** breed
la **razón** reason
tener razón to be right
el/la **realista** realist
rebajar to lower *(prices)*, 9.1
la **rebanada** slice *(bread)*, **10**
cortar en rebanadas to slice, **10**
rebasar to pass *(car)*, **9.1**
la **recámara** bedroom, 2.2
recambio: la rueda (llanta) de recambio spare tire, **9.2**
la **recepción** front desk *(hotel)*, **7**
el/la **recepcionista** hotel clerk, **7**
el/la **receptor(a)** catcher, 5.2
la **receta** prescription, 6.2; recipe, **10**
recetar to prescribe, 6.2
recibir to receive, 4.1; to catch
recibir aplausos to be applauded, 5.1
reclamar to claim
recoger to collect, to gather
reconocer to recognize
recordar (ue) to remember
el **recorrido** trip, route
los **recuerdos** memories
recuperar to claim, to get back
la **red** the Web, 3.2; **6.1**; net, 5.2
navegar la red to surf the Web, 3.2; **6.1**
pasar por encima de la red to go over the net, 5.2
reducido(a) reduced
reducir to reduce; to set *(bone)*, **11.2**
reducir la velocidad to reduce speed, **9.1**
refacción: la rueda (llanta) de refacción spare tire
el **refresco** soft drink, 4.2
el **refrigerador** refrigerator, **10**
refrito(a) refried
el **refugio** refuge
el **regalo** gift, present, 8.1
regatear to bargain, 9.2
el **régimen** diet
la **región** region
la **regla** rule
regresar to go back, to return, 3.2
el botón regresar back button, back key, **6.1**
regresar a casa to go home, 3.2
regreso: el boleto de ida y regreso round-trip ticket, **3.1**
regular regular, average
la **reina** queen
reinar to rule, to reign
relacionado(a) related
relevos: la carrera de relevos relay race, **11.1**
religioso(a) religious
rendir (i, i) honor to honor
renombrado(a) famous
rentar to rent, 7.1; **3.2**
repartido(a) distributed, split up among
repasar to review
el **repaso** review
repente: de repente suddenly, all of a sudden
repetir (i, i) to repeat, to have seconds *(meal)*, **4**
la **república** republic
la República Dominicana Dominican Republic
repuesto: la rueda (llanta) de repuesto spare tire, **9.2**
la **reserva** reservation
la **reservación** reservation, **7**
reservar to reserve, **7**
resfriado(a) stuffed up *(cold)*, 6.2
respetado(a) respected
respetar to respect
la **respiración** breathing, **11.1**
respirar to breathe
responsable responsible
la **respuesta** answer
el **restaurante** restaurant, **4**
resultar to turn out to be
el **retraso** delay, 10.2; **1.2**
con retraso late, 10.2; **1.2**
el **retrato** portrait
retroceder: el botón retroceder back button, back key, **6.1**
la **reunión** meeting, get-together
reunirse to meet, to get together
revisar to check *(ticket)*, **3.2**
el/la **revisor(a)** conductor, **3.2**
la **revista** magazine, **3.1**
revolver (ue) to stir, **10**
revueltos: los huevos revueltos scrambled eggs, **7**
el **rey** king
el Día de los Reyes Epiphany (January 6), **5.2**
los Reyes Magos the Three Wise Men, **5.2**
rico(a) rich; delicious
¡Qué rico! How delicious!
el **rincón** corner
los **riñones** kidneys
el **río** river

el **risco** cliff, **3.2**
el **ritmo** rhythm
robar to steal
la **roca** rock, stone
la **rodaja** slice *(lemon, cucumber)*
rodeado(a) surrounded
la **rodilla** knee, 11.1; **2.1**
la **rodillera** kneepad, **11.1**
rojo(a) red, 5.1
la luz roja red light, **9.1**
el **rol** role
el **rollo de papel higiénico** roll of toilet paper, 11.2; **2.2**
el **rompecabezas** puzzle
romper(se) to break, **11.2**
Se rompió la pierna. He (She) broke his (her) leg., **11.2**
la **ropa** clothing, 9.1
la **rosa** rose
rosado(a) pink, 5.1
roto(a) broken
el **rótulo** sign, **9.1**
rubio(a) blonde, 1.1
la **rueda** tire, **9.2**
la rueda de repuesto (recambio) spare tire, **9.2**
la silla de ruedas wheelchair, **11.2**
el **ruido** noise
las **ruinas** ruins
la **ruta** route
la **rutina diaria** daily routine, 11.1; **2.1**

S

el **sábado** Saturday, LP
la **sábana** sheet, **7**
saber to know, 9.1
sabio(a) wise
el **sabor** flavor, **10**
sacar to get, 3.1; to take, 7.1
sacar fotos to take pictures, 7.1
sacar notas buenas (malas) to get good (bad) grades, 3.1
el **saco de dormir** sleeping bag, 11.2; **2.2**
el **sacrificio** sacrifice
la **sal** salt, **4**
la **sala** living room, 2.2
la sala de clase classroom, 3.1
la sala de emergencia emergency room, **11.2**
la sala de espera waiting room, **3.1**
salado(a) salty
el **saldo** sale, 9.1
la **salida** departure, 10.1; **1.1;** exit, **9.1**
la hora de salida time of departure, 10.1; **1.1**
la puerta de salida gate *(airport),* 10.2; **1.2**
salir to leave; to go out, 8.1; to turn out, to result
Todo te sale más barato. Everything costs a lot less.; It's all a lot less expensive., 9.1
la **salsa** sauce, gravy, **10;** dressing
saltar to jump (over)
salteado(a) sautéed
la **salud** health, 6.1
saludar to greet
el **saludo** greeting
salvar to save
la **sandalia** sandal, 9.2
el **sándwich** sandwich, 4.1
el sándwich de jamón y queso ham and cheese sandwich, 4.1
sano(a) healthy
el/la **santo(a)** saint
el/la santo(a) patrón(ona) patron saint, **5.1**
el **sarape** blanket
el/la **sartén** skillet, frying pan, **10**
satisfacer to satisfy
el **sato** a type of dog from Puerto Rico
seco(a) dry
secundario(a): la escuela secundaria high school, 1.2
la **sed** thirst, 4.1
tener sed to be thirsty, 4.1
el **sedán** sedan, **9.2**
seguir (i, i) to follow, **4;** to continue, **9.1**
según according to
segundo(a) second
el segundo tiempo second half *(soccer),* 5.1
en segunda clase second-class *(ticket),* **3.1**
seguramente surely, certainly
seguridad: el control de seguridad security *(airport),* 10.2; **1.2**
el cinturón de seguridad seat belt, 10.2; **1.2**
seguro(a) sure; safe
seguro que certainly
seis six, LP
seiscientos(as) six hundred
seleccionar to choose, **3.1**
la **selva** jungle, forest
el **semáforo** traffic light, **8.1**
la **semana** week, LP
el fin de semana weekend, 7.1
la semana pasada last week, 7.1
sembrar (ie) to plant, to sow, **8.2**
el **seminómada** seminomad
sencillo one-way, **3.1;** single *(hotel room),* **7;** simple
el billete (boleto) sencillo one-way ticket, **3.1**
el cuarto sencillo single room, **7**
la **senda** path, **3.2**
sentado(a) seated
sentarse (ie) to sit down, 11.1; **2.1**
el **sentido** direction, **9.1;** sense, 6.1
la calle de sentido único one-way street, **9.1**
sentir (ie, i) to be sorry; to feel
Lo siento mucho. I'm very sorry.
sentirse (ie, i) to feel
la **señal** sign, 10.2; **1.2**
la señal de no fumar no-smoking sign, 10.2; **1.2**
señalar to point out
el **señor** sir, Mr., gentleman, LP
la **señora** Ms., Mrs., madam, LP
los **señores** Mr. and Mrs.
la **señorita** Miss, Ms., LP
septiembre September, LP
ser to be
el **ser** being
los seres humanos human beings
los seres vivientes living beings
serio(a) serious, 1.1
¿Hablas en serio? Are you serious?
el **servicio** tip, 4.2; restroom, 10.2; **1.2;** service, **9.2**
¿Está incluido el servicio? Is the tip included?, 4.2
la estación de servicio gas station, **9.2**
la **servilleta** napkin, **4**
servir to serve, **4**
servir de to serve as
sesenta sixty, LP

Spanish-English Dictionary

setecientos(as) seven hundred
setenta seventy, LP
severo(a) harsh, strict
si if
sí yes, LP
siempre always, 8.2
siento: Lo siento mucho. I'm very sorry., 5.1
la **siesta** nap
siete seven, LP
el **siglo** century
significar to mean
siguiente following
la **silla** chair, 2.2
  la silla de ruedas wheelchair, **11.2**
similar similar
simpático(a) nice, 1.1
sin without
sincero(a) sincere
sino but rather
el **síntoma** symptom
el **sistema** system
el **sitio** space *(parking)*
el **sitio Web** Web site, **6.1**
el/la **snowboarder** snowboarder, 7.2
las **sobras** leftovers
sobre on, on top of; about
  sobre todo above all, especially
la **sobremesa** dessert; after-dinner conversation
la **sobrepoblación** overpopulation
sobrevivir to survive
sobrevolar (ue) to fly over
la **sobrina** niece, 2.1
el **sobrino** nephew, 2.1
social social
  los estudios sociales social studies, 1.2
la **sociedad** society
el/la **socio(a)** member
socorrer to help
el/la **socorrista** paramedic, **11.2**
el **sofá** sofa, 2.2
el **sol** sun
  Hace (Hay) sol. It's sunny., LP
  tomar el sol to sunbathe, 7.1
solamente only
solar: la crema solar suntan lotion, 7.1
solas: a solas alone
el **soldado** soldier
soler (ue) to be used to, to do something usually
solo(a) single; alone
solo only
el/la **soltero(a)** single, unmarried person
el **sombrero** hat
sonar (ue) to ring, **6.1**
el **sonido** sound
la **sonrisa** smile, 6.1
la **sopa** soup
soplar to blow *(wind)*
la **sorpresa** surprise, 4.1
su(s) his, her, their, your *(formal)*
subir to go up, 7.2; to get on *(train, etc.)*, **3.1**
subterráneo(a) underground
los **suburbios** suburbs, 2.2
sucio(a) dirty, **7**
Sudamérica South America
sudamericano(a) South American
el/la **suegro(a)** father- (mother-) in-law
el **suelo** ground, floor
el **sueño** dream
  tener sueño to be sleepy
la **suerte** luck
  ¡Buena suerte! Good luck!
  ¡Qué suerte tengo! How lucky I am!, 9.1
el **suéter** sweater, 11.1; **2.1**
sufrir to suffer
superior upper, top
  el compartimiento superior overhead bin *(airplane)*, 10.2; **1.2**
el **supermercado** supermarket, 9.2
el **sur** south
  la América del Sur South America
el **surtido** assortment
sus his, her, their, your *(formal)*
el **susto** fear
la **sutura** stitch, **11.2**
suturar to give (someone) stitches
el **SUV** SUV, **9.2**

T

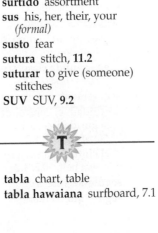

la **tabla** chart, table
la **tabla hawaiana** surfboard, 7.1
  practicar la tabla hawaiana to surf, to go surfing, 7.1
tacaño(a) stingy, cheap, **9.1**
el **taco** taco
la **tajada** slice *(ham, meat)*, 9.2
tal such
  ¿Qué tal? How are things? How are you?, LP
  ¿Qué tal tu clase de español? How's your Spanish class?
tal vez maybe, perhaps, 7.2
la **talla** size, 9.1
  ¿Qué talla usas? What size do you take?, 9.1
el **tamaño** size
también also, too, 1.2
el **tambor** drum
el **tamborín** small drum
tampoco either, neither
tan so
tan... como as . . . as
el **tanque** gas tank, **9.2**
el **tanto** score, point, 5.1
  marcar un tanto to score a point, 5.1
tanto(a) so much
  tanto(a)... como as much . . . as
  tantos(as)... como as many . . . as
la **tapa** lid, **10**
tapar to cover *(pot)*
las **tapas** snacks, nibbles, 4.2
el **tapón** traffic jam
la **taquilla** box office, ticket window, 8.2
tarde late, 10.2; **1.2**
la **tarde** afternoon
  ayer por la tarde yesterday afternoon, 7.1
  Buenas tardes. Good afternoon., LP
la **tarea** homework; task
la **tarifa** fare, **3.1;** price
la **tarjeta** card; pass
  la tarjeta de abordar boarding pass
  la tarjeta de crédito credit card, **3.1**
  la tarjeta de embarque boarding pass, 10.1; **1.1**
  la tarjeta telefónica telephone card, **6.2**
la **tarta** cake, 8.1
la **tasa de interés** interest rate
el **taxi** taxi, 10.1; **1.1**

el/la **taxista** taxi driver, 10.1; **1.1**
la **taza** cup, 4.1; **4**
te you *(fam. pron.)*
el **té** tea
el **teclado** keyboard, **6.1**
el/la **técnico(a)** technician
la **tecnología** technology
tejano(a) Texan
los **tejidos** fabrics, 9.2
la **tele** TV
telefónico(a) *(related to)* phone, **6.2**
la guía telefónica phone book, **6.2**
la tarjeta telefónica phone card, **6.2**
el **teléfono** telephone
el número de teléfono phone number, **6.2**
el teléfono celular cell phone, **6.1**
el teléfono público pay phone, **6.2**
hablar por teléfono to speak on the phone
la **telenovela** serial, soap opera
el **telesilla** chairlift, ski lift, 7.2
el **telesquí** ski lift, 7.2
la **televisión** television
el **tema** theme
tembloroso(a) trembling
la **temperatura** temperature, 7.2
temprano(a) early, 11.1; **1.2**
el **tenderete** market stall, 9.2
el **tenedor** fork, **4**
tener (ie) to have, 2.1
tener... años to be . . . years old, 2.1
tener calor (frío) to be hot (cold), 11.1; **2.1**
tener catarro to have a cold, 6.2
tener cuidado to be careful, **9.1**
tener dolor de... to have a(n) . . . -ache, 6.2
tener el pelo rubio (castaño, negro) to have blond (brown, black) hair, 2.1
tener éxito to be successful, 6.1
tener fiebre to have a fever, 6.2
tener ganas de to feel like
tener hambre to be hungry, 4.1
tener lugar to take place
tener miedo to be afraid, 7.2
tener ojos azules (castaños, verdes) to have blue (brown, green) eyes, 2.1
tener que to have to *(do something)*, 4.2
tener sed to be thirsty, 4.1
el **tenis** tennis
la cancha de tenis tennis court, 5.2
jugar (al) tenis to play tennis, 5.2
los **tenis** sneakers, tennis shoes, 9.1
el/la **tenista** tennis player
la **tensión** tension, stress, **11.1**
la tensión arterial blood pressure, 6.2
tercer(o)(a) third
terco(a) stubborn, 6.1
terminar to end, finish
término: a término medio medium *(meat)*, **4**
el **término** term
la **ternera** veal, **10**
el escalope de ternera veal cutlet, **10**
el/la **terrateniente** landowner
la **terraza** terrace, balcony
el **terremoto** earthquake
el **tesoro** treasure
ti you
la **tía** aunt, 2.1
el **ticket** ticket, 7.2
el **tiempo** weather, LP; half *(soccer)*, 5.1
a tiempo on time, 10.2; **1.2**
a tiempo completo (parcial) full- (part-) time
el segundo tiempo second half *(soccer)*, 5.1
Hace buen (mal) tiempo. The weather is nice (bad)., LP
¿Qué tiempo hace? What's the weather like?, LP
la **tienda** store, 3.2
la tienda de ropa clothing store, 9.1
la **tienda de campaña** tent, 11.2; **2.2**
la **tierra** land, **8.2**
el **tigre** tiger
los **timbales** small drums, kettledrums
el **timbre (sonoro)** ringtone, **6.2**
tímido(a) shy
el **tío** uncle, 2.1
los **tíos** aunt and uncle, 2.1
el **tiovivo** merry-go-round, **8.1**
típico(a) typical
el **tipo** type, 6.1
el **tiquete** ticket, **9.1**
tirar to throw, 5.2
el **título** title
la **toalla** towel, 7.1; **7**
el **tobillo** ankle, **11.1**
el **tocadiscos** record player
tocar to touch, 5.1; to play *(musical instrument)*, 8.1; **5.2**
¡Te toca a ti! It's your turn!
el **tocino** bacon, 4.1; **7**
todavía still; yet
todo(a) everything; all
sobre todo above all, especially
todo el mundo everyone, **5.2**
todos(as) everyone, 8.1; everything; all
en todas partes everywhere
tomar to take, 3.1; to have *(meal)*, 4.1
tomar el almuerzo (el desayuno) to have lunch (breakfast), 4.1
tomar el bus to take the bus
tomar el pulso to take someone's pulse, 6.2
tomar el sol to sunbathe, 7.1
tomar fotos to take pictures, 7.1
tomar la tensión arterial to take someone's blood pressure, 6.2
tomar un examen to take a test, 3.1
tomar una ducha to take a shower, 11.1; **2.1**
tomar una radiografía to take an X ray of someone, **11.2**
el **tomate** tomato, 4.1
la **tonelada** ton
el **tono** dial tone, **6.2**
las **tonterías** foolish things
tonto(a) foolish, crazy
torcerse (ue) to sprain, to twist, **11.2**
Se torció el tobillo. He (She) sprained his (her) ankle., **11.2**
torcido(a) sprained, twisted
la **torta** cake, 4.1; sandwich
la **tortilla** tortilla
la **tos** cough, 6.2
tener tos to have a cough, 6.2
toser to cough, 6.2
la **tostada** tostada

Spanish-English Dictionary

Spanish-English Dictionary

las **tostadas** toast, 4.1
tostado(a) toasted
el pan tostado toast, 4.1; **7**
los **tostones** slices of fried plantain, 4.2
trabajar to work, 3.2; **8.2**
el **trabajo** work
tradicional traditional
traer to carry, to bring, to take, 10.1; **1.1**
el **tráfico** traffic, **8.1**
el **traje** suit
el **traje de baño** swimsuit, 7.1
tranquilo(a) calm, 6.1
transbordar to transfer *(trains)*, **3.2**
el **tránsito** traffic
transporte: los medios de transporte means of transportation, **8.2**
trasero(a) back
el **tratamiento** treatment
tratar to treat
tratar de to try to (do something)
tratar de desviar to try to dissuade
la **travesía** crossing
traviesa: a campo traviesa cross-country *(race)*, **11.1**
el **trayecto** stretch (of road)
trece thirteen, LP
el **trecho** stretch *(distance)*
treinta thirty, LP
treinta y uno thirty-one, LP
el **tren** train, **3.1**
tres three, LP
trescientos(as) three hundred
el **trigo** wheat, **8.2**
triste sad, 6.1
el **trocito** little piece
la **trompeta** trumpet
las **tropas** troops
tropical tropical
el **trotamundos** globe-trotter
el **trozo** piece
el **T-shirt** T-shirt
tu(s) your *(fam.)*
tú you *(sing. fam.)*
el **tubo de crema dental** tube of toothpaste, 11.2; **2.2**
la **tumba** grave, tomb, **5.1**
el **turismo** tourism
el/la **turista** tourist

U

u or *(used instead of o before words beginning with o or ho)*
Ud., usted you *(sing.) (formal)*
Uds., ustedes you *(pl.) (formal)*
último(a) last; final
un(a) a, an, 1.1
la **una** one o'clock, LP
único(a) only, 2.1; one-way, **9.1**
la calle de sentido único one-way street, **9.1**
el/la hijo(a) único(a) only child, 2.1
la **unidad** unit
el **uniforme** uniform, 3.1
la **universidad** university
uno(a) one, LP
unos(as) some
urbano(a) urban, **8.1**
usar to use, 3.2; to wear *(size)*, 9.1
¿Qué talla usas? What size do you wear (take)?, 9.1
el **uso** use
el/la **usuario(a)** user
la **uva** grape, 9.2

V

la **vaca** cow, **8.2**
las **vacaciones** vacation, 7.1
estar de vacaciones to be on vacation
vacante vacant
vacío(a) empty, **9.2**
vagar to wander, to roam
el **vagón** train car, **3.1**
la **vainilla** vanilla
las **vainitas** green beans
Vale. It's a good idea.
No vale. It's not worth it., 7.1
valeroso(a) brave
el **valle** valley
¡Vamos! Let's go!
varios(as) several
el **varón** man, boy
vasco(a) Basque
la pelota vasca jai-alai
el **vaso** glass, 4.1
el **váter** toilet, **7**
veces: a veces at times, sometimes, 6.1
el/la **vecino(a)** neighbor
el **vegetal** vegetable, 4.1
los vegetales crudos raw vegetables, crudités, 8.1
vegetariano(a) vegetarian, 4.1
veinte twenty, LP
veinticinco twenty-five, LP
veinticuatro twenty-four, LP
veintidós twenty-two, LP
veintinueve twenty-nine, LP
veintiocho twenty-eight, LP
veintiséis twenty-six, LP
veintisiete twenty-seven, LP
veintitrés twenty-three, LP
veintiuno twenty-one, LP
la **vela** candle, 8.1; **5.2**
vela: la plancha de vela windsurfing; sailboard, 7.1
la **velocidad** speed, **9.1**
la velocidad máxima speed limit, **9.1**
la **venda** bandage, **11.2**
el/la **vendedor(a)** merchant, 9.2
vender to sell, 6.2
venezolano(a) Venezuelan
venir (ie) to come
el verano (año, mes) que viene next summer (year, month), **8.2**
la **venta** small hotel
las **ventajas** advantages
la **ventanilla** ticket window, 7.2, **3.1**; window *(plane)*, 10.2; **1.2**
ver to see, 4.2
el **verano** summer, LP
el **verbo** verb
la **verdad** truth
Es verdad. That's true (right)., 9.1
¿Verdad? Right?
verdadero(a) real, true
verde green, 2.1
las judías verdes green beans, 9.2
la **verdulería** greengrocer (vegetable) store, 9.2
la **verdura** vegetable, 4.1
verificar to check
el **vestido** dress, 9.1
el vestido de novia wedding dress

Spanish-English Dictionary

vestirse (i, i) to get dressed, to dress, **4**
la **vez** time
a veces at times, sometimes, 6.1; **1.2**
cada vez each time, every time
de vez en cuando from time to time, occasionally, 10.2; **1.2**
en vez de instead of
una vez más (once) again, one more time
la **vía** track, **3.1;** lane *(highway)*
viajar to travel
viajar en avión (tren) to travel by plane (train)
el **viaje** trip, voyage 10.1; **1.1**
hacer un viaje to take a trip, 10.1; **1.1**
la **víctima** victim
la **vida** life
el **video** video
viejo(a) old, 2.2
el **viento** wind, LP
Hace viento. It's windy., LP
el **viernes** Friday, LP
el **vinagre** vinegar, **4**
el **vino** wine
el **violín** violin
visitar to visit, 8.2
la **víspera de Año Nuevo** New Year's Eve
la **vista** view; sight
la **viuda** widow
vivir to live, 4.1
vivo(a) lively
los **vivos** the living
la **vocal** vowel
el **volante** steering wheel, **9.2**
volar (ue) to fly
el **volcán** volcano
volcar to flip over
el **voleibol** volleyball, 7.1
la cancha de voleibol volleyball court, 7.1
volver (ue) to return, 5.1
volver a casa to go back (return) home, 8.1
vosotros(as) you *(pl.)*
la **voz** voice
el **vuelo** flight, 10.1; **1.1**
el número del vuelo flight number, 10.1; **1.1**
vuelta: un boleto (billete) de ida y vuelta round-trip ticket, **3.1**
la **vuelta** lap, **11.1**
Vuestra Merced Your Highness

Y

y and, LP
y cuarto a quarter past (the hour), LP
y media half past (the hour), LP
ya already
¡Ya voy! I'm coming!, 11.2; **2.2**
el **yeso** cast, **11.2**
yo I; me
el **yoga** yoga, **11.1**

Z

la **zanahoria** carrot, 9.2; **10**
las **zapatillas** (sports) shoes, sneakers, 5.1
los **zapatos** shoes, 9.1
la **zona** area, zone
el **zoológico** zoo, **8.1**
el **zumo** juice *(Spain)*

English-Spanish Dictionary

This English-Spanish Dictionary contains all productive and some receptive vocabulary from Levels 1 and 2. The numbers following each productive entry indicate the chapter and vocabulary section in which the word is introduced. For example, ***3.2*** *in dark print means that the word was first taught in* ***Capítulo 3, Vocabulario 2.*** *A light print number means that the word was introduced in* ***¡Asi Se Dice!,*** *Level 1.* LP *refers to the* ***Lecciones preliminares*** *in Level 1. If there is no number following an entry, this means that the word or expression is there for receptive purposes only.*

A

@ la arroba, **6.1**
a, an un(a), 1.1
able: to be able poder (ue), 5.1
aboard abordo (de), 10.2; **1.2**
about sobre; *(time)* a eso de
above por encima de, 5.2
above all sobre todo
abroad al extranjero
accident el accidente, **11.2**
accompanied by acompañado(a) de, **3.2**
according to según
ache el dolor, 6.2
to **ache** doler, 6.2; **11.2**
My . . . ache(s). Me duele(n)... , 6.2
activity la actividad
to **add** añadir, **10**
addition: in addition to además de
address la dirección, **6.1**
address book la libreta de direcciones, **6.1**
e-mail address la dirección de correo electrónico (e-mail), **6.1**
addressee el/la destinatario(a), **6.1**
adorable cariñoso(a), 2.1; adorable
advanced avanzado(a), 7.2
advantage la ventaja
afraid: to be afraid tener miedo, 7.2
after después (de), 3.1; *(time)* y
It's ten after one. Es la una y diez., LP
afternoon la tarde
Good afternoon. Buenas tardes., LP
this afternoon esta tarde, 7.1
yesterday afternoon ayer por la tarde, 7.1
again de nuevo
against contra
age la edad
agent el/la agente, 10.1; **1.1**
agricultural agrícola
air el aire
open-air (outdoor) café (market) el café (mercado) al aire libre
air conditioning el aire acondicionado, **7**
airline la línea aérea, 10.1; **1.1**
airplane el avión, 10.1; **1.1**
airport el aeropuerto, 10.1; **1.1**
aisle el pasillo, 10.2; **1.2**
album el álbum
algebra el álgebra
all todo(a), 6.2; todos(as), 8.1
above all sobre todo
to **allow** dejar
almost casi, 8.2; **4**
alone solo(a); a solas
already ya
also también, 1.2
although aunque
always siempre, 8.2
A.M. de la mañana
ambulance la ambulancia, **11.2**
American americano(a)
among entre
to **amuse** divertir (ie, i), 10.2; **1.2**
amusement park el parque de atracciones, **8.1**
amusement park ride la atracción, **8.1**
amusing divertido(a)
ancient antiguo(a), **8.1**
and y, LP
Andean andino(a)
angry enfadado(a), enojado(a), 6.1
to make angry enfadar, 6.1
animal el animal
ankle el tobillo, **11.1**
to **annoy** molestar, enojar, 6.1
another otro(a)
answer la respuesta
to **answer** contestar, 3.1
any cualquier
any other cualquier otro(a)
anybody alguien, 8.2
anything algo, 9.2
Anything else? ¿Algo más?, 9.2
apartment el apartamento, el apartamiento, el departamento, 2.2; el piso
apartment building la casa de apartamentos, 2.2
appearance la apariencia
to **applaud** aplaudir, 5.1
to be applauded recibir aplausos, 5.1
applause el aplauso, 5.1
apple la manzana, 9.2
appreciated apreciado(a)
to **approach** acercarse a
April abril, LP
archaeology la arqueología
area la zona
area code la clave de área, **6.2**
Argentine argentino(a)
arithmetic la aritmética
arm el brazo, 11.1; **2.1**
around alrededor de, 2.2; *(time)* a eso de
arrival la llegada, **3.1**
to **arrive** llegar, 4.1
arriving from procedente de, 10.2; **1.2**
art el arte, 1.2
art show (exhibition) la exposición de arte, 8.2
artichoke (sautéed) la alcachofa salteada
artist el/la artista; el/la pintor(a), 8.2
as como
as . . . as tan... como
as many . . . as tantos(as)... como
as much . . . as tanto(a)... como
to **ask (a question)** preguntar
to **ask for** pedir (i, i), **4**

English-Spanish Dictionary

assign asignar, **6.2**
assistance la ayuda
at a, en
at (@) sign la arroba, **6.1**
at around ***(time)*** a eso de
at home en casa, 2.2
at night por la noche; de noche
at one o'clock (two o'clock, three o'clock . . .) a la una (a las dos, a las tres…), LP
at times a veces, 6.1; **1.2**
at what time? ¿a qué hora?, LP
athlete el/la atleta
attached file el documento adjunto, **6.1**
to **attend** asistir a, 8.1
attention: to pay attention prestar atención, 3.1
attractive guapo(a), 1.1
August agosto, LP
aunt la tía, 2.1
aunt and uncle los tíos, 2.1
author el/la autor(a)
automatic automático(a), 10.2; **1.2**
automatic dispenser el distribuidor automático, **3.1**
autumn el otoño, LP
available disponible
avenue la avenida, **8.1**
average regular
avocado el aguacate, **10;** la palta
Awesome! ¡Bárbaro!, 5.2

B

back la espalda, 11.1; **2.1**
back ***(adj.)*** trasero(a)
back button ***(key)*** el botón regresar (retroceder), **6.1**
back door la puerta trasera, **8.1**
back: in back of detrás de, 2.2
background la ascendencia
backpack la mochila, 3.1
backpacker el/la mochilero(a), 11.2; **2.2**
backwards hacia atrás
bacon el tocino, el bacón, 4.1; **7;** el lacón, **7**
bad malo(a), 1.2; mal, LP
The weather is bad. Hace mal tiempo., LP
to be in a bad mood estar de mal humor, 6.1
to get bad grades sacar notas malas, 3.1
baggage el equipaje, 10.1; **1.1**
carry-on baggage el equipaje de mano, 10.1; **1.1**
bakery la panadería
balcony el balcón
ball ***(soccer, basketball)*** el balón, 5.1; ***(volleyball)*** el balón, 7.1; ***(baseball, tennis)*** la pelota, 5.2
to hit the ball batear, 5.2; golpear, 5.2
to kick (throw) the ball lanzar el balón, 5.1
ballpoint pen el bolígrafo, 3.1; el lapicero, la pluma
banana el plátano, 9.2
fried sweet bananas los maduros
band ***(music)*** la banda, 8.1; **5.2;** el conjunto, 8.1
city band la banda municipal, **5.2**
bandage la venda, **11.2**
bar: bar of soap la barra de jabón, 11.2; **2.2;** la pastilla de jabón
to **bargain** regatear, 9.2
barn el granero, **8.2**
base ***(baseball)*** la base, 5.2
baseball el béisbol, 5.2
baseball field el campo de béisbol, 5.2
baseball game el juego (partido) de béisbol, 5.2
baseball player el/la jugador(a) de béisbol, el/la beisbolista, 5.2
basket ***(basketball)*** el cesto, la canasta, 5.2
to make a basket encestar, meter el balón en la cesta, 5.2
basketball el básquetbol, el baloncesto, 5.2
basketball court la cancha de básquetbol, 5.2
bat el bate, 5.2
to **bat** batear, 5.2
bath el baño, 2.2; **7**
bathing suit el bañador, el traje de baño, 7.1
bathroom el cuarto de baño, 2.2; **7**
bathtub la bañera, **7**
batter el/la bateador(a), 5.2
to **be** ser, 1.1; estar, 3.1
to be able (to) poder (ue), 5.1
to be afraid tener miedo, 7.2
to be applauded recibir applausos, 8.1
to be born nacer
to be called (named) llamarse, 11.1; **2.1**
to be careful tener cuidado, **9.1**
to be cold (hot) tener frío (calor), 11.1; **2.1**
to be cut off cortar la línea (a alguien), **6.2**
to be familiar with conocer, 9.1
to be fine (well) estar bien, 6.2
to be going to (do something) ir a *(+ infinitive)*, 4.2
to be happy estar contento(a), alegre, 6.1
to be hungry tener hambre, 4.1
to be in a good (bad) mood estar de buen (mal) humor, 6.1
to be pleasing (to someone) gustar, 5.1
to be sad estar triste, deprimido(a), 6.1
to be sick estar enfermo(a), 6.2
to be sorry sentir (ie, i)
to be successful tener éxito, 6.1
to be thirsty tener sed, 4.1
to be tired estar cansado(a), 6.1
to be . . . years old tener… años, 2.1
beach la playa, 7.1
beach resort el balneario, 7.1
beans los frijoles, 4.1
green beans (string beans) las judías verdes, 9.2
beautiful bello(a), hermoso(a)
because porque, 3.2
bed la cama, 2.2; **7**
to go to bed acostarse (ue), 11.1; **2.1**
to make the bed hacer la cama, **7**
to stay in bed guardar cama, 6.2; quedarse en la cama, 11.1; **2.1**
bedroom el cuarto de dormir, la recámara, 2.2; la habitación, **7;** el dormitorio, la alcoba, la pieza
beef la carne de res, **4;** el bife
before antes de, 3.2
beforehand antes, 10.1; **1.1**
to **begin** empezar (ie), 5.1; comenzar (ie)

English-Spanish Dictionary

beginner el/la principiante, 7.2
behaved: to be well-behaved tener buena conducta, 6.1
behavior la conducta, el comportamiento, 6.1
behind detrás de, 2.2
to **believe** creer
bell pepper el pimiento, 9.2
bell tower la campana
bellhop el mozo, **7**
to **belong** pertenecer
below debajo de, 10.2; **1.2**
beside al lado de, 2.2
besides además
best el/la mejor
better mejor
between entre
beverage la bebida, el refresco, 4.1
bicycle la bicicleta, 2.2
  to ride a bicycle andar en bicicleta, **11.1**
big gran, grande, 1.2
bike ride: to go for a bike ride dar un paseo en bicicleta
bike riding: to go bike riding andar en bicicleta, **11.1**
bill la factura
biologist el/la biólogo(a)
biology la biología
bird el pájaro
birthday el cumpleaños, 8.1
black negro(a), 2.1
blanket la manta, la frazada, **7**
block *(city)* la cuadra, la manzana, **9.1**
to **block** bloquear, 5.1
blond(e) rubio(a), 1.1
  to have blond hair tener el pelo rubio, 2.1
blood pressure la tensión arterial, 6.2
blouse la blusa, 3.1
to **blow** *(wind)* soplar
blue azul, 2.1
blue jeans el blue jean, 9.1
board: on board abordo (de), 10.2; **1.2**
to **board** embarcar, abordar, 10.2; **1.2**
boarding el embarque, 10.1; **1.1**
  boarding pass la tarjeta de embarque, 10.1; **1.1;** el pasabordo, la tarjeta de abordar
  boarding pass kiosk el distribuidor automático, 10.1; **1.1**
  boarding time la hora de embarque, 10.1; **1.1**
boat el barquito, 7.1
body *(human)* el cuerpo (humano), 11.1; **2.1**
to **boil** hervir (ie, i), **10**
  boiling la ebullición
bone el hueso, **5.1**
  to set the bone reducir, acomodar el hueso, **11.2**
book el libro, 3.1
boot la bota, 7.2
border la frontera
to **bore** aburrir, 5.2
boring aburrido(a), 1.2
born: to be born nacer
to **bother** molestar, enfadar, enojar, 6.1
bottle la botella, 9.2
box office la taquilla, 8.2
boy el muchacho, 1.1; el niño, 6.2
brakes los frenos, **9.2**
  to put on (apply) the brakes poner los frenos
brave valeroso(a)
Brazilian brasileño(a)
bread el pan
to **break** romper; romperse, quebrarse, **11.2**
  He (She) broke his (her) leg. Se rompió (Se quebró) la pierna., **11.2**
breakdown la avería
breakfast el desayuno, 4.1; **7**
  Continental breakfast el desayuno continental, **7**
  to have breakfast tomar el desayuno, 4.1; desayunarse
breaking: You're breaking up. *(telephone)* Estás cortando., **6.2**
breast *(chicken)* la pechuga, **10**
breathing la respiración, **11.1**
breed la raza
to **bring** traer, 10.1; **1.1**
to **bring down** derrocar
broad ancho(a), **8.1**
broken roto(a); quebrado(a)
bronze *(adj.)* de bronce, 8.2
brother el hermano, 2.1
brown castaño(a), 2.1; de color marrón, 5.1
  to have brown eyes tener ojos castaños, 2.1
  to have brown hair tener el pelo castaño, 2.1
brunette moreno(a), 1.1
brush el cepillo, 11.2; **2.2**
  toothbrush el cepillo de dientes, 11.2; **2.2**
to **brush** cepillar, 11.1; **2.1**
  to brush one's hair cepillarse, 11.1; **2.1**
  to brush one's teeth cepillarse (lavarse) los dientes, 11.1; **2.1**
building el edificio, 2.2
bunk la litera
buried enterrado(a), **5.1**
to **burn** quemarse, **10**
burrito el burrito
to **bury** enterrar (ie)
bus el autobús, el camión, la guagua, **8.1;** el bus
  bus stop la parada de autobús (de camiones, de guaguas), **8.1**
  school bus el bus escolar, 3.2
  to miss the bus perder el autobús, 8.1
but pero
butcher shop la carnicería
butter la mantequilla, 4.1; **7**
button el botón, **6.1**
  back button el botón regresar (retroceder), **6.1**
  delete button el botón borrador, **6.1**
to **buy** comprar, 3.2
by por; en
  by plane (car, bus) en avión (carro, autobús)
  by tens de diez en diez
  By the way! ¡A propósito!, 8.2
Bye! ¡Chao!, LP

C

café el café, 3.1
  outdoor café el café al aire libre
cafeteria la cafetería, 4.1
cake la torta, 4.1; el bizcocho, **5.1;** el pastel, la tarta, 8.1
calculator la calculadora, 3.1
call (phone) la llamada, **6.2**
  dropped call la llamada perdida (caída), **6.2**
to **call** llamar, 11.2; **2.2**
  Who's calling, please? ¿De parte de quién, por favor?, **6.2**
calm calmo(a), tranquilo(a), 6.1

English-Spanish Dictionary

camel el camello, **5.2**
camera la cámara, 7.1; **6.2**
digital camera la cámara digital, 7.1; **6.2**
camping el camping, 11.2; **2.2**
to go camping ir de camping, 11.2; **2.2**
can el bote, la lata, 9.2
Canadian canadiense
candle la vela, 8.1; **5.2**
canned enlatado(a)
canyon el cañón, **3.2**
cap el gorro, 7.2
capital la capital
car el carro, 2.2; **9.2;** el coche, **9.2;** ***(train)*** el coche, el vagón, **3.1**
dining car el coche comedor (cafetería), la bufetería, **3.1**
sports car el coche deportivo, **9.2**
carbonated drink la gaseosa, 4.1
card la tarjeta, 3.1; **6.2;** el carnet, 10.2; **1.2**
credit card la tarjeta de crédito, 3.1
ID card el carnet de identidad, 10.2; **1.2**
phone card la tarjeta telefónica, **6.2**
careful: to be careful tener cuidado, **9.1**
carefully con cuidado
Caribbean Sea el mar Caribe
carrot la zanahoria, 9.2; **10**
to **carry** llevar, 3.1; traer, 10.1; **1.1**
carry-on luggage el equipaje de mano, 10.2; **1.2**
cart el carrito, 9.2; **3.1**
case: in case en caso de; por si acaso
cash register la caja, 3.2
cashier el/la cajero(a)
cast el yeso, **11.2**
castle el castillo
cat el/la gato(a), 2.1
to **catch** atrapar, 5.2
catcher el/la cátcher, el/la receptor(a), 5.2
Catholic católico(a)
cattle el ganado, **8.2**
to **cause** causar
to **celebrate** celebrar, **5.2**
celebration la celebración
cell phone el móvil, el celular, 3.2; **6.1**
cemetery el cementerio, el camposanto, **5.1**
century el siglo
ceramics las cerámicas, 9.2
cereal el cereal, 4.1
certain cierto(a), **6.1**
chair la silla, 2.2
chairlift el telesilla, el telesquí, 7.2
to **change** cambiar, **3.2**
to change trains (transfer) transbordar, **3.2**
chapter el capítulo
character el personaje
charitable purpose el propósito benévolo
cheap barato(a), 9.1
It's all a lot cheaper. Todo te sale más barato., 9.1
check *(restaurant)* la cuenta, 4.2; **4**
to **check *(ticket)*** revisar, **3.2;** ***(facts)*** verificar
to **check luggage** facturar el equipaje, 10.1; **1.1**
to **check out *(hotel room)*** abandonar el cuarto, 7
cheese el queso, 4.1
ham and cheese sandwich el sándwich de jamón y queso, 4.1
chemistry la química
chest el pecho, **11.1**
chicken el pollo, 4.1; **10**
chicken breast la pechuga de pollo, **10**
chicken thigh el muslo de pollo, **10**
chicken wings las alitas de pollo, **10**
child el/la niño(a), 6.2
children los hijos, 2.1
Chilean chileno(a)
chili pepper el ají
chocolate el chocolate, 4.1
hot chocolate el chocolate caliente, 4.1
to **choose** escoger; seleccionar, **3.1**
chop: pork chop la chuleta de cerdo, **10**
to **chop** picar, **10**
Christian cristiano(a)
Christmas la Navidad, las Navidades, **5.2**
Christmas Eve la Nochebuena, **5.2**
Christmas gift el aguinaldo, **5.2**
Christmas tree el árbol de Navidad, **5.2**
Merry Christmas! ¡Feliz Navidad!
church la iglesia
city la ciudad, 2.2; **8.1**
civilization la civilización
clams las almejas, **4**
to **clap** aplaudir, 5.1
clarinet el clarinete
class *(school)* la clase; el curso, 1.2; ***(ticket)*** la clase, **3.1**
first- (second-) class en primera (segunda) clase, **3.1**
classroom la sala de clase, 3.1
clean limpio(a), **7**
to **clean** limpiar, **7**
to **clear the table** levantar la mesa, quitar la mesa, **4**
clerk el/la empleado(a), 3.1; el/la dependiente(a)
to **click *(computer)*** hacer clic, **6.1**
cliff el risco, **3.2**
climate el clima
close (to) cerca (de)
to **close** cerrar (ie), 11.2; **2.2**
closet el armario, **7**
clothes la ropa, 9.1
clothes hanger la percha, el colgador, **7**
clothing la ropa, 9.1
clothing store la tienda de ropa, 9.1
cloud la nube, 7.1
cloudy nublado(a), 7.1
clove (of garlic) el diente
coach el/la entrenador(a)
coast la costa
code: area code la clave de área, **6.2**
country code el prefijo del país, **6.2**
co-ed mixto(a)
coffee el café, 4.1; **7**
cognate la palabra afine
coin la moneda, **9.1**
cola la cola, 4.1
cold el frío; frío(a), 4.2; ***(illness)*** el catarro, 6.2
It's cold (weather). Hace frío., LP
to be cold tener frío, 11.1; **2.1**
to have a cold tener catarro, 6.2
Colombian colombiano(a)
color el color, 5.1
comb el peine, 11.2; **2.2**
to **comb one's hair** peinarse, 11.1; **2.1**
to **come** venir (ie)
I'm coming! ¡Ya voy!, 11.2; **2.2**
to **come out onto** desembocar
comical cómico(a), gracioso(a), 1.1

English-Spanish Dictionary

coming from procedente de, 10.2; **1.2**
companion el/la compañero(a)
to complete completar
completely totalmente
composition la composición
computer la computadora, el ordenador, 3.2; **6.1**
concert el concierto, 8.1
concourse *(train station)* el hall, **3.1**
condiment el condimento, **10**
condo(minium) el condominio
conduct la conducta, el comportamiento, 6.1
conductor *(train)* el revisor, **3.2**
connected conectado(a)
connection la conexión
consonant la consonante
to consult consultar
to contain contener (ie)
continent el continente
Continental breakfast el desayuno continental, **7**
to continue continuar; seguir, **9.1**
contrary: on the contrary al contrario
conversation la conversación
convertible el descapotable, el convertible, **9.2**
to convince convencer
cook el/la cocinero(a), **10**
to cook cocinar, cocer (ue), **10**
cooking la cocción
cool fresco(a), LP
It's cool (weather). Hace fresco., LP
copy la copia, **6.1**
hard copy la copia dura, **6.1**
corn el maíz, 9.2; el elote, el choclo
corner la esquina, **8.1**
corral el corral, **8.2**
to cost costar (ue), 9.1
How much does it cost? ¿Cuánto cuesta?, 3.2
Costa Rican costarricense
costume el disfraz, **5.1**
cough la tos, 6.2
to have a cough tener tos, 6.2
to cough toser, 6.2
counter *(airline)* el mostrador, 10.1; **1.1**
country el país; el campo, **8.2**
country code el prefijo del país, **6.2**
country house la casa de campo, **8.2**
Spanish-speaking countries los países hispanohablantes
countryside el campo, **8.2**
course el curso, 1.2
court la cancha, 5.2
basketball (tennis) court la cancha de básquetbol (tenis), 5.2
volleyball court la cancha de voleibol, 7.1
courtesy la cortesía, LP
cousin el/la primo(a), 2.1
to cover cubrir, tapar
cow la vaca, **8.2**
crackers las galletas, 8.1
crafts la artesanía, 9.2
crazy loco(a)
credit card la tarjeta de crédito, **3.1**
to cross cruzar, **9.1**
cross-country *(skiing)* el esquí nórdico, 7.2; *(race)* la carrera a campo traviesa, **11.1**
crosswalk el cruce, **8.1**
crutches las muletas, **11.2**
to walk on crutches andar con muletas, **11.2**
Cuban cubano(a)
Cuban American cubanoamericano(a)
cucumber el pepino, **10**
cuisine la cocina
culture la cultura
cup la taza, 4.1; **4**
custard el flan, 4.1
custom la costumbre
customer el/la cliente(a), 4.2; **7**
to cut cortar, **10**
to cut (up) in small pieces cortar en pedacitos, **10**
cut off: We've been cut off. *(telephone)* Se nos cortó la línea., **6.2**
to cut oneself cortarse, **11.2**
cutlet: veal cutlet el escalope de ternera, **10**

D

daily diario(a)
daily routine la rutina diaria, 11.1; **2.1**
dairy products los productos lácteos
to dance bailar, **5.2**
danger el peligro
dangerous peligroso(a)
dark-haired moreno(a), 1.1
data los datos
date la fecha, LP
What's today's date? ¿Cuál es la fecha de hoy?, LP
daughter la hija, 2.1
day el día, LP; la fiesta, **5.1**
the Day of the Dead el Día de los Muertos, **5.1**
patron saint's day la fiesta patronal, **5.1**
What day is it (today)? ¿Qué día es hoy?, LP
dead muerto(a), difunto(a), **5.1**
dead person, deceased person el/la muerto(a), el/la disfunto(a), **5.1**
dear querido(a)
death la muerte
deboned deshuesado(a)
December diciembre, LP
to decide decidir
to decorate decorar, **5.2**
deep profundo(a)
definition la definición
delay el retraso, la demora, 10.2; **1.2**
to delete borrar, **6.1**
delete key *(computer)* el botón borrador, **6.1**
delicious delicioso(a); rico(a)
to demand exigir
departure la salida, 10.1; **1.1**
departure gate la puerta de salida, 10.2; **1.2**
departure time la hora de salida, 10.1; **1.1**
to depend depender (ie) (de)
to deplane desembarcar
to describe describir
description la descripción
desert el desierto
desk el pupitre, 3.1
desolate inhóspito(a)
dessert el postre, 4.1
destination el destino, **3.1**
to develop desarrollarse
device el aparato
diagnosis el diagnóstico

to **dial** marcar el número, **6.2**
dial tone el tono, **6.2**
to **dice** cortar en pedacitos, **10**
dictation el dictado
to **die** morir (ue, u), **4**
diet la dieta
difference la diferencia
different diferente, 9.2
difficult difícil; duro(a), 1.2; avanzado(a), 7.2
difficulty la dificultad
digital camera la cámara digital, 7.1; **6.2**
diner el/la comensal
dining car el coche comedor (cafetería), la bufetería, **3.2**
dining room el comedor, 2.2
dinner la cena, 4.1
to have dinner cenar, 4.1
direction ***(road)*** sentido, **9.1**
in each direction en cada sentido, **9.1**
directions las direcciones
dirty sucio(a), **7**
disadvantage la desventaja
disagreeable desagradable
to **disappear** desaparecer
to **discover** descubrir
to **disembark** desembarcar, **1.2**
disguise el disfraz, **5.1**
dish el plato, **4**
dishwasher el lavaplatos, **10**
dispenser: automatic boarding pass dispenser el distribuidor automático, 10.1; **1.1**
distance: long distance de larga distancia
district el casco, el barrio, **8.1**
to **dive** bucear, 7.1
divine divino(a)
to **do** hacer, 10.2; **1.2**
to do homework hacer las tareas
to do push-ups hacer planchas, **11.1**
to do yoga practicar yoga, **11.1**
doctor el/la médico(a), 6.2
doctor's office el consultorio, la consulta, 6.2
document el documento
attached document el documento adjunto, **6.1**
dog el/la perro(a), 2.1
dollar el dólar
Dominican dominicano(a)
Dominican Republic la República Dominicana

door la puerta, **9.2**
front (back) door la puerta delantera (trasera)
dot ***(Internet)*** el punto, **6.1**
double ***(room)*** el cuarto doble, **7**
doubles ***(tennis)*** dobles, 5.2
doubt la duda
to **doubt** dudar
doughnut (type of) el churro
down: to go down bajar, 7.2
downhill skiing el esquí alpino, 7.2
to **download** bajar, descargar, **6.2**
downtown el centro, **8.1**
dozen la docena
drawing el dibujo
dream el sueño
dress el vestido, 9.1
to **dress** vestirse (i, i), **4**
to **dribble** driblar (con el balón), 5.2
drink ***(beverage)*** el refresco, 4.2; la bebida, 4.1
to **drink** beber, 4.1
to **drive** conducir, manejar, **9.2**
driver el/la conductor(a), **9.2**
driver's license el permiso de conducir, la licencia, el carnet, **9.2**
dropped call la llamada caída (perdida), **6.2**
drugstore la farmacia, 6.2
dry seco(a)
during durante, 3.2
DVD el DVD, 3.2
dynamic dinámico(a), 6.1

E

e-mail el correo electrónico, 3.2; **6.1;** el e-mail
e-mail address la dirección de correo electrónico (e-mail), **6.1**
e-mail inbox la bandeja de entradas, **6.1**
e-ticket el boleto (billete) electrónico, 10.1; **1.1**
each cada, 2.2
early temprano, 11.1; **2.1**
early riser el/la madrugador(a), 11.1; **2.1**
to **earn** ganar
easily sin dificultad, 7.2
east el este
easy fácil, 1.2

to **eat** comer, 4.1
to eat breakfast (lunch) tomar el desayuno (el almuerzo), 4.1
to eat dinner cenar, 4.1
Ecuadoran ecuatoriano(a), 1.1
education la educación
physical education la educación física, 1.2
egg el huevo, 4.1; **7**
scrambled eggs los huevos revueltos, **7**
eight ocho, LP
eight hundred ochocientos(as)
eighteen dieciocho, LP
eighty ochenta, LP
either tampoco *(after negation)*
elbow el codo, 11.1; **2.1**
electronic electrónico(a), 10.1; **1.1**
elementary school la escuela primaria
elevator el ascensor, **7**
eleven once, LP
else: Anything else? ¿Algo más?, 9.2
Nothing else. Nada más., 9.2
emergency room la sala de emergencia, **11.2**
employee el/la empleado(a), 3.2; el/la dependiente(a)
empty vacío(a), **9.2**
enchilada la enchilada
end el fin
at the end (of) al final (de); a fines de
to **end** terminar
energetic energético(a), 6.1
energy la energía, 6.1
engine el motor
English ***(language)*** el inglés, 1.2
to **enjoy** disfrutar; gozar
to **enjoy oneself** divertirse (ie, i), 11.2; **2.2**
enormous enorme
enough bastante; suficiente
to **enter** entrar, 5.1
enthusiasm el entusiasmo, 6.1
enthusiastic lleno(a) de entusiasmo, 6.1; entusiasmado(a)
entire entero(a)
entrance la entrada; ***(subway)*** la boca del metro, **8.1**
Epiphany el Día de los Reyes, **5.2**
equal igual

English-Spanish Dictionary

escalator la escalera mecánica, **8.1**
especially especialmente; sobre todo
ethnic étnico(a)
euro el euro
European europeo(a)
even aun; hasta
even *(numeric)* par
evening la noche
Good evening. Buenas noches., LP
in the evening por la noche
yesterday evening anoche, 7.1
every cada, 2.2; todos(as)
every day (year) todos los días (años)
everybody todo el mundo, todos(as), 8.1
everyone todo el mundo, **5.1** todos(as), 8.1
everything todo, 6.2
everywhere en todas partes
exactly exactamente
exam el examen, la prueba, 3.1
physical exam el examen físico, 6.2
to take an exam tomar un examen, 3.1
to **examine** examinar, 6.2
example: for example por ejemplo
to **exceed** exceder
excellent excelente
exception la excepción
Excuse me. Con permiso., 10.1; **1.1**
exercise los ejercicios, **11.1**
to **exercise** hacer ejercicios, **11.1**
exhibition la exposición (de arte), 8.2
to **exist** existir
exit la salida, **9.1**
exotic exótico(a)
expensive caro(a), 9.1
less expensive más barato, 9.1
expert el/la experto(a), 7.2
to **explain** explicar
expressway la autopista, la autovía, **9.1**
extraordinary extraordinario(a)
eye el ojo, 2.1
to have blue (green, brown) eyes tener ojos azules (verdes, castaños), 2.1

F

fabrics los tejidos, 9.2
fabulous fabuloso(a)
face la cara, 6.1
fact el hecho
fair la feria, **5.1**
fall el otoño, LP
to **fall** caerse, **11.2**
to **fall asleep** dormirse (ue, u), 11.1; **2.1**
false falso(a)
family la familia, 2.1
family *(related to)* familiar
famous famoso(a)
fan el/la aficionado(a), 5.1
fantastic fantástico(a)
far lejos (de), 3.2
fare la tarifa, **3.1**
farm la finca, la granja, la chacra, **8.2**
farmer el/la campesino(a), el peón, **8.2**
farmhand el peón, **8.2**
to **fascinate** fascinar
fast rápido(a)
fastened abrochado(a), 10.2; **1.2**
fat gordo(a)
father el padre, 2.1
favor el favor
favorite favorito(a)
fear el miedo
feature la característica
February febrero, LP
to **feel** sentirse (ie, i)
to **feel like (doing something)** tener ganas de *(+ infinitive)*
Ferris wheel la noria, **8.1**
fertilizer el abono
festival la feria, **5.1**
festival of lights (Hanukkah) la fiesta de las luces, **5.2**
fever la fiebre, 6.2
to have a fever tener fiebre, 6.2
few poco(a), pocos(as), 2.2
a few unos(as)
fewer menos
field el campo, 5.1; **8.2**
baseball field el campo de béisbol, 5.2
soccer field el campo de fútbol, 5.1

fifteen quince, LP
fifteen-year-old girl la quinceañera
fifty cincuenta, LP
to **fight** luchar
file el archivo, **6.1;** el documento
attached file el documento adjunto, 6.1
to **fill up *(gas tank)*** llenar el tanque, **9.2**
film el filme, la película, 8.2; el film
finally por fin
to **find** encontrar (ue)
fine la multa, **9.1**
fine *(adj.)* bien, LP
to be fine estar bien, 6.2
finger el dedo, 11.1; **2.1**
to **finish** terminar
fire el fuego, **10**
fireplace la chimenea, **5.2**
fireworks los fuegos artificiales, **5.2**
first primero(a), LP
first-class primera clase, **3.1**
first of January el primero de enero, LP
fish el pescado, 4.1
fish market la pescadería
to **fit** quedar, 9.1
This jacket doesn't fit you. Esta chaqueta no te queda bien., 9.1
five cinco, LP
five hundred quinientos(as)
flame el fuego, **10**
on a low flame (heat) a fuego lento, **10**
flan el flan, 4.1
flat (tire) el pinchazo, **9.2**
flavor el sabor, **10**
flight el vuelo, 10.1; **1.1**
flight attendant el/la asistente(a) de vuelo, 10.2; **1.2**
flight number el número del vuelo, 10.1; **1.1**
to **flip over** volcar
floor el piso, 2.2
flower la flor, 2.2
flute la flauta
to **fly** volar (ue)
folder la carpeta, 3.2; **6.1**
to **follow** seguir (i, i), **4**
following siguiente

English-Spanish Dictionary

food la comida, 4.1; los comestibles, **4;** el alimento
frozen food los productos congelados, 9.2
foot el pie, 5.1; **2.1**
on foot a pie, 3.2
football el fútbol americano
for por, para; con destino a, 10.2; **1.2**
for example por ejemplo
forbidden prohibido(a), **9.1**
forehead la frente, **11.1**
foreign extranjero(a)
to **forget** olvidar
fork el tenedor, **4**
form la forma, 10.2; **1.2**
former antiguo(a)
forty cuarenta, LP
fountain pen la pluma, 5.1
four cuatro, LP
four hundred cuatrocientos(as)
fourteen catorce, LP
fracture la fractura
free libre, 4.2; **3.2**
to **free** liberar, **11.1**
freezer el congelador, **10**
French el francés, 1.2; *(adj.)* francés(esa), **4**
french fries las papas (patatas) fritas, 4.1
frequently con frecuencia, frecuentemente
fresh fresco(a)
Friday el viernes, LP
fried frito(a)
friend el/la amigo(a), 1.1; el/la compañero(a)
friendly agradable, 6.1
from de, LP; desde
from time to time de vez en cuando
from where? ¿de dónde?, 1.1
front *(adj.)* delantero(a), **8.1**
in front of delante de, 2.2
front desk ***(hotel)*** la recepción, **7**
front door ***(car, bus)*** la puerta delantera, **8.1**
frozen congelado(a), 9.2
frozen food los productos congelados, 9.2
fruit la fruta, 9.2
fruit stand la frutería, el puesto de frutas, 9.2
to **fry** freír (i, i), **4**
frying pan el/la sartén, **10**
full completo(a), **3.2**
full of lleno(a) de, 6.1

fun: to have fun divertirse (ie, i), pasarlo bien, 11.2; **2.2**
funny cómico(a); gracioso(a), 1.1; divertido(a)
furious furioso(a)
furniture los muebles, 2.2
future el futuro

G

game el juego; ***(match)*** el partido, 5.1
garage el garaje, 2.2
garden el jardín, 2.2
garlic el ajo, **10**
gasoline la gasolina, la nafta, la benzina
gas station la estación de servicio, la gasolinera, **9.2**
gas tank el tanque, **9.2**
gate ***(airport)*** la puerta de salida, 10.2; **1.2**
general general
generally, in general en general, por lo general
generous generoso(a)
gentle manso(a)
gentleman el señor, LP
geography la geografía
geometry la geometría
German alemán(ana)
to **get** sacar, 3.1
to get good (bad) grades sacar notas buenas (malas), 3.1
to **get dressed** ponerse la ropa, 11.1; **2.1;** vestirse (i, i), **4**
to **get off** ***(train, bus)*** bajar(se), **3.2**
to **get on** ***(train, bus)*** subir, **3.1;** ***(plane)*** abordar, 10.2; **1.2**
to **get together** reunirse
to **get up** levantarse, 11.1; **2.1**
gift el regalo, 8.1; **Christmas gift** el aguinaldo, **5.2**
girl la muchacha, 1.1; la niña, 6.2
to **give** dar, 3.1
to give an exam dar un examen (una prueba), 3.1
to give back devolver (ue)
to give (someone) stitches poner unos puntos (unas suturas) (a alguien)
to give (throw) a party dar una fiesta, 8.1
to give up renunciar
glass (drinking) el vaso, 4.1; **4**
glove el guante, 5.2

glove compartment la guantera, **9.2**
to **go** ir, 3.2; pasar, 5.2; andar, **3.2**
Let's go! ¡Vamos!
to be going (to do something) ir a *(+ infinitive)*, 4.2
to go back regresar, 3.2; volver (ue), 5.1
to go bike riding andar en bicicleta, **11.1**
to go camping ir de camping, 11.2; **2.2**
to go down bajar, 7.2
to go for a hike dar una caminata, 11.2; **2.2**
to go home regresar a casa, ir a casa, 3.2; volver (ue) a casa, 8.1
to go horseback riding andar a caballo, **3.2;** montar a caballo, **8.2**
to go ice-skating patinar sobre el hielo, 7.2
to go jogging hacer jogging, **11.1**
to go on a trip hacer un viaje
to go online entrar en línea, **6.1**
to go out salir, 8.1
to go over the net pasar por encima de la red, 5.2
to go rollerblading (inline skating) patinar en línea, **11.1**
to go scuba diving bucear
to go shopping ir de compras, 9.1
to go skiing esquiar, 7.2
to go snorkeling bucear, 7.1
to go surfing practicar la tabla hawaiana, 7.1
to go swimming nadar, 7.1
to go to bed acostarse (ue), 11.1; **2.1**
to go to the movies ir al cine, 8.2
to go through pasar por, 10.2; **1.2**
to go up subir, 7.2
to go waterskiing esquiar en el agua, 7.1
to go windsurfing practicar la plancha de vela, 7.1
goal el gol, 5.1
to score a goal meter un gol, 5.1
goal (box) la portería, 5.1
goalie el/la portero(a), 5.1

English-Spanish Dictionary

English-Spanish Dictionary

going to con destino a, 10.2; **1.2**
gold el oro
good buen, LP; bueno(a), 1.1
to be in a good mood estar de buen humor, 6.1
to get good grades sacar notas buenas, 3.1
Good afternoon. Buenas tardes., LP
Good evening. Buenas noches., LP
Good morning. Buenos días., LP
Good-bye! ¡Adiós!; ¡Chao!, LP
good-looking guapo(a), bonito(a), 1.1
government el gobierno
grade la nota, 3.1
high grade la nota alta, 3.1
low grade la nota baja, 3.1
to get good (bad) grades sacar notas buenas (malas), 3.1
grandchildren los nietos, 2.1
granddaughter la nieta, 2.1
grandfather el abuelo, 2.1
grandmother la abuela, 2.1
grandparents los abuelos, 2.1
grandson el nieto, 2.1
grape la uva, 9.2
grass la hierba, **8.2**
grave la tumba, **5.1**
gravy la salsa, **10**
gray gris, 5.1
to **graze** pacer, **8.2**
great gran, grande
Great! ¡Bárbaro!, 5.2
greater (greatest) part (la) mayor parte
green verde, 2.1
green beans las judías verdes, 9.2
green pepper el pimiento, 9.2; **10**
greengrocer (vegetable) store la verdulería, 9.2
greeting el saludo, LP
grill la parrilla, **10**
to **grill** asar, **10**
ground el suelo
group *(musical)* el grupo, el conjunto, 8.1
to **grow *(agriculture)*** cultivar, **8.2**
to **guard** guardar, 5.1
Guatemalan guatemalteco(a)
to **guess** adivinar
guest el/la invitado(a), ***(hotel)*** el/la cliente(a), el/la huésped(a), **7**
guitar la guitarra, 8.1
guy el tipo, 6.1
gymnasium el gimnasio, **11.1**

H

hair el pelo, 2.1
to brush one's hair cepillarse, 11.1; **2.1**
to comb one's hair peinarse, 11.1; **2.1**
to have blond (brown, black) hair tener el pelo rubio (castaño, negro), 2.1
half *(soccer)* el tiempo, 5.1
second half *(soccer)* el segundo tiempo, 5.1
half past *(hour)* y media, LP
ham el jamón, 4.1
ham and cheese sandwich el sándwich de jamón y queso, 4.1
hamburger la hamburguesa, 4.1
hand la mano, 3.1
to raise one's hand levantar la mano, 3.1
handsome guapo(a), 1.1
hanger la percha, el colgador, **7**
Hanukkah el Hanuka, **5.2**
to **happen** pasar; ocurrir
What's happening? ¿Qué pasa?
happiness la alegría, la felicidad
happy alegre, contento(a), 6.1; feliz, **5.2**
Happy Hanukkah! ¡Feliz Hanuka!, **5.2**
hard difícil, duro(a), 1.2
hard copy la copia dura, **6.1**
hard-working ambicioso(a), 1.2
harvest la cosecha, **8.2**
to **harvest** cosechar, **8.2**
hat el sombrero; ***(ski)*** el gorro, 7.2
to **have** tener (ie), 2.1; haber *(in compound tenses)*
to have a cold tener catarro, 6.2
to have a cough tener tos, 6.2
to have a fever tener fiebre, 6.2
to have fun pasarlo bien, divertirse (ie, i), 11.2; **2.2**
to have a good time pasarlo bien, divertirse (ie, i), 11.2; **2.2**
to have a headache tener dolor de cabeza, 6.2
to have a party dar una fiesta, 8.1
to have a snack tomar una merienda, 4.2
to have a sore throat tener dolor de garganta, 6.2
to have a stomachache tener dolor de estómago, 6.2
to have blond (brown, black) hair tener el pelo rubio (castaño, negro), 2.1
to have blue (brown, green) eyes tener ojos azules (castaños, verdes), 2.1
to have breakfast (lunch) tomar el desayuno (el almuerzo); 4.1
to have dinner cenar, 4.1
to have fun pasarlo bien, divertirse (ie, i), 11.2; **2.2**
to have just (done something) acabar de *(+ infinitive)*, 4.2
to have to (do something) tener que, 4.2
hay el heno, **8.2**
he él, 1.1
head la cabeza, 6.2; **2.1**
headache: to have a headache tener dolor de cabeza, 6.2
headlights las luces, **9.2**
health la salud, 6.1
to **hear** oír, 8.1
¿Can you hear me? *(telephone)* ¿Me escuchas?, **6.2**
heart el corazón
heat el calor; el fuego, **10**
on low heat a fuego lento, **10**
to **heat** poner en el fuego, **10**
heavy pesado(a)
height la altura
Hello! ¡Hola!, LP; **6.2; *(on the phone)*** ¡Diga!, ¡Dígame!, ¡Aló!, ¡Bueno!
helmet el casco, 7.2; **11.1**
help la ayuda
to **help** ayudar, 10.1; **1.1**
hen la gallina, **8.2**
her *(pron.)* la
to her *(pron.)* le
her su(s)

English-Spanish Dictionary

here aquí, 9.1; acá, 11.2; **2.2**
Here it (they) is (are). Aquí lo (la, los, etc.) tienes.
hero el héroe
heroine la heroína
Hi! ¡Hola!, LP
high alto(a), 3.1
high school la escuela secundaria, 1.2; el colegio
highway la autopista, la autovía, la carretera, **9.1**
hike: to take (go for) a hike dar una caminata, 11.2; **2.2**
hiker el/la mochilero(a), 11.2; **2.2**
him *(pron.)* lo
to him *(pron.)* le
his su(s)
Hispanic hispano(a)
history la historia, 1.2
to **hit** ***(baseball)*** batear; ***(tennis, volleyball)*** golpear, 5.2
to hit a home run batear un jonrón, 5.2
holiday la fiesta, **5.1**
home la casa, 2.2; a casa; 3.2
at home en casa
to go home regresar a casa, 3.2; volver (ue) a casa, 8.1
home page la página de inicio (inicial, frontal), **6.1**
home plate el platillo, 5.2
home run el jonrón, 5.2
to hit a home run batear un jonrón, 5.2
homework las tareas
honest honesto(a)
hood ***(car)*** el capó, **9.2**
to **hope** esperar
I hope . . . Ojalá… , **11.2**
horse el caballo, **3.2**
horseback riding la equitación, **8.2**
to go horseback riding andar a caballo, **3.2;** montar a caballo, **8.2**
hospital el hospital
hostel: youth hostel el albergue juvenil, el hostal, **7**
hot: to be hot tener calor, 11.1; **2.1**
It's (very) hot *(weather).* Hace (mucho) calor., LP
hot caliente, 4.1
hotel el hotel, **7**
small (inexpensive) hotel el hostal, **7**
hotel clerk el/la recepcionista, **7**
hour la hora
house la casa, 2.2
apartment house la casa de apartamentos, 2.2
private house la casa privada, 2.2
housekeeper la camarera, **7**
how? ¿cómo?, 1.1; ¿qué?, LP
How are things going? ¿Qué tal?, LP
How are you? ¿Qué tal?, LP; ¿Cómo estás?
How much does it cost? ¿Cuánto cuesta?, 3.2
How much is (are) . . . ? ¿A cuánto está(n)… ?, 9.2
How much is it? ¿Cuánto es?, LP
How old is he (she)? ¿Cuántos años tiene?, 2.1
how many? ¿cuántos(as)?, 2.1
how much? ¿cuánto?, 3.1
human humano(a), 11.1; **2.1**
human being el ser humano
humble humilde
humor: to have a good sense of humor tener un buen sentido de humor, 6.1
hundred cien(to), LP
hunger el hambre *(f.)*
hungry: to be hungry tener hambre, 4.1
to **hurt** doler, 6.2; **11.2**
It hurts him (me, etc.) a lot. Le (Me, etc.) duele mucho., **11.2**
My head (stomach, etc.) hurts. Me duele la cabeza (el estómago, etc.), **11.2**
to **hurt (oneself)** hacerse daño, **11.2**
husband el esposo, el marido, 2.1

I

I yo
ice el hielo, 7.2
ice cream el helado, 4.1
ice skate el patín, 7.2
to **ice-skate** patinar sobre el hielo, 7.2
ice-skater el/la patinador(a), 7.2
ice-skating el patinaje sobre (el) hielo, 7.2
ice-skating rink la pista de patinaje, 7.2
icon el icono, **6.1**
ID card el carnet de identidad, 10.2; **1.2**
idea la idea
idealist el/la idealista
identification la identidad, 10.2; **1.2**
piece of identification la forma de identidad, 10.2; **1.2**
to **identify** identificar
if si
ill enfermo(a), 6.2
ill-mannered mal educado(a), 6.1
illness la enfermedad
to **imagine** imaginar
immediately enseguida, 4.2; inmediatamente
immense inmenso
impatient impaciente, 6.1
important importante
impossible imposible
in en
in back of detrás de, 2.2
in front of delante de, 2.2
in general por lo general
inbox ***(e-mail)*** la bandeja de entradas, **6.1**
incline la pendiente
to **include** incluir
Is the tip included? ¿Está incluido el servicio?, 4.2
to **increase** aumentar
incredible increíble
to **indicate** indicar
indigenous indígena, 9.2
individual: individual sport el deporte individual
inexpensive barato(a), 9.1
influence la influencia
to **inform** informar
information la información, 3.2
ingredient el ingrediente
inhabitant el/la habitante
inhospitable inhóspito(a)
injured herido(a)
injury la herida, **11.2**
inline skating el patinaje en línea, **11.1**
to go inline skating patinar en línea, **11.1**
inn el parador
to **insert** insertar, **3.1;** introducir, **6.2**
instead of en vez de
instrument el instrumento
intelligent inteligente, 1.2
interest el interés
to **interest** interesar, 5.1
interesting interesante, 1.2
international internacional, 10.1; **1.1**

English-Spanish Dictionary

English-Spanish Dictionary

Internet el Internet, 3.2; **6.1**
to surf the Net navegar el Internet, 3.2; **6.1**
to **interrupt** interrumpir
to **intersect** cruzarse
intersection la bocacalle, el cruce, **9.1**
interview la entrevista
to **interview** entrevistar
interviewer el/la entrevistador(a)
to **invite** invitar
Irish irlandés(esa)
Is . . . there, please? ¿Está… , por favor?, **6.2**
island la isla
it lo, la
Italian italiano(a)

J

jack *(car)* el/la gato(a), **9.2**
jacket la chaqueta, 9.1
ski jacket la chaqueta de esquí, el anorak, 7.2
jam la mermelada, **7**
January enero, LP
Japonese japonés(esa)
jar el frasco, 9.2
jeans el blue jean, 9.1
Jewish judío(a), hebreo(a), **5.2**
jogging: to go jogging hacer jogging, **11.1**
juice el jugo, el zumo, 4.1
orange juice el jugo de naranja, 4.1; **7**
July julio, LP
June junio, LP
just: to have just (done something) acabar de (+ *infinitive)*, 4.2
just as (like) igual que

K

kebabs los pinchitos, 4.2
to **keep** guardar, **6.1**
key la llave, **7;** *(computer)* el botón, **6.1**
back key el botón regresar (retroceder), **6.1**
delete key el botón borrador, **6.1**
magnetic key la llave magnética, **7**
keyboard el teclado, **6.1**
to **kick** lanzar, 5.1
kilogram el kilo, 9.2
kilometer el kilómetro
king el rey
the Three Kings (Wise Men) los Reyes Magos, **5.2**
kiosk *(newsstand)* el quiosco, **3.1;** *(ticket dispenser)* el distribuidor automático, **3.1**
kitchen la cocina, 2.2, **10**
knapsack la mochila, 3.1
knee la rodilla, 11.1, **2.1**
kneepad la rodillera, **11.1**
knife el cuchillo, **4**
to **know** saber; conocer, 9.1
to know how (to do something) saber, 9.1

L

to **lack** faltar, 6.1
He/She lacks . . . Le falta... , 6.1
lamb el cordero, **4**
lamp la lámpara, 2.2
land la tierra, **8.2**
to **land** aterrizar, 10.2; **1.2**
landing el aterrizaje, 10.2; **1.2**
landowner el/la terrateniente
landscape el paisaje
lane *(highway)* el carril, **9.1;** la pista, la vía, la banda, el canal
language la lengua
lap *(track)* la vuelta, **11.1**
laptop computer la computadora portátil
large gran, grande, 1.2
last pasado(a) 7.1; último(a)
last night anoche, 7.1
last week la semana pasada, 7.1
last year el año pasado, 7.1
to **last** durar
late tarde; con retraso (una demora), 10.2; **1.2**
later luego, LP; más tarde; después
See you later! ¡Hasta luego!, LP
Latin America Latinoamérica
Latin American latinoamericano(a)
Latino latino(a)
to **laugh** reír
lazy perezoso(a), 1.2
to **lead** *(from one street into another)* desembocar
league la liga
to **learn** aprender, 4.2
least: at least a lo menos
to **leave** salir, 8.1
to **leave** *(something)* dejar, **4**
to leave a message dejar un mensaje, **6.2**
to leave a tip dejar una propina, **4**
left izquierdo(a), 11.1; **2.1**
to the left a la izquierda, **9.1**
leftovers las sobras
leg la pierna, 11.1; **2.1**
lemon el limón
lemonade la limonada
less menos, 9.1
lesson la lección
to **let** dejar; permitir
letter la carta
letter *(of alphabet)* la letra
lettuce la lechuga, 4.1
lid la tapa, **10**
life la vida
to **lift** levantar
to lift weights levantar pesas, **11.1**
light la luz, **5.2**
red light la luz roja, **9.1**
traffic light el semáforo, **8.1**
to **light** encender, **5.2**
to **light up** iluminar, **5.2**
lightly ligeramente
lights las luces, **5.2;** *(headlights)* las luces, **9.2**
festival of lights (Hanukkah) la fiesta de las luces, **5.2**
like como
to **like** gustar, 5.1; encantar, **6.2**
What would you like *(to eat)?* ¿Qué desean tomar?, 4.2
line *(of people)* la cola, 10.2; **1.2;** la fila
to wait in line hacer cola, 10.2; **1.2;** estar en fila
line la línea, **6.2**
solid line *(road)* la línea continua, **9.1**
to **line up** hacer cola, 10.2; **1.2**
lion el león
lip el labio
to **listen to** escuchar, 3.2
Listen! ¡Oye!, 1.2
literature la literatura, las letras

little pequeño(a), 1.2
- **a little** poco(a), 2.2

to **live** vivir, 4.1
livestock el ganado, **8.2**
living room la sala, 2.2
lobster la langosta, **4**
logical lógico(a)
long largo(a), 5.1
long-distance ***(race)*** de larga distancia, **11.1**
long-sleeved de manga larga, 9.1
Look! ¡Mira!, 3.1
to **look at** mirar, 3.2
to **look at oneself** mirarse, 11.1; **2.1**
to **look for** buscar, 3.2
to **lose** perder (ie), 5.1
lot: a lot mucho(a), LP; muchos(as), 2.1
lotion: suntan lotion la crema solar, la loción bronceadora, 7.1
love el amor
- **in love with** enamorado(a) de
- **loved one** el/la amado(a)

to **love** encantar, **6.2;** querer (ie)
- **Le encanta la música.** She loves the music.

low bajo(a), 3.1
- **low (heat),** a fuego lento, **10**

to **lower** ***(price)*** rebajar, 9.1
luck: How lucky I am! ¡Qué suerte tengo!, 9.1
luggage el equipaje, 10.1; **1.1**
- **carry-on luggage** el equipaje de mano, 10.1; **1.1**
- **luggage cart** el carrito, **3.1**
- **to check luggage** facturar el equipaje, 10.1; **1.1**

lunch el almuerzo, 4.1
- **to have lunch** tomar el almuerzo, 4.1

luxurious lujoso(a)

M

mad enojado(a), enfadado(a), 6.1
madam (la) señora, LP
made hecho(a)
magazine la revista, **3.1**
magnetic magnético(a), **7**
magnificent magnífico(a)
maid la camarera, **7**
mail el correo
- **e-mail** el correo electrónico, **6.1**

main principal
majority la mayoría; *(adj.)* mayoritario(a)
to **make** hacer, 10.2; **1.2;** confeccionar, elaborar, 5.1
- **to make a basket** ***(basketball)*** encestar, 5.2
- **to make the bed** hacer la cama, **7**

mall el centro comercial, 9.1
man el hombre
manners los modales, 6.1
- **to have good (bad) manners** tener buenos (malos) modales, 6.1

many muchos(as), 2.2
- **as many . . . as** tantos(as)... como
- **how many?** ¿cuántos(as)?, 2.1

map el plano, **9.1;** el mapa
marathon el maratón, **11.1**
March marzo, LP
mark la nota, 3.1
- **bad (low) mark** la nota mala (baja), 3.1
- **good (high) mark** la nota buena (alta), 3.1
- **to get good (bad) marks** sacar notas buenas (malas), 3.1

market el mercado, 9.2
- **native market** el mercado indígena, 9.2

market stall el puesto, el tenderete, 9.2
marmalade la mermelada, **7**
mask la máscara, **5.1**
to **match** parear
mathematics las matemáticas, 1.2
mausoleum el mausoleo, **5.1**
maximum máximo(a)
May mayo, LP
maybe quizá, quizás, tal vez, 7.2
mayonnaise la mayonesa, 9.2
me *(pron.)* me
- **to (for) me** a (para) mí

meal la comida, 4.1
to **mean** significar
means of transport el medio de transporte, **8.1**
meat la carne, 4.1; **4**
meatball la albóndiga, 4.2
meat pie la empanada, 4.2
medicine el medicamento, la medicina, 6.2
medium ***(meat)*** a término medio, **4**
medium-sized mediano(a)

to **meet** encontrarse (ue); conocer
member el miembro, 2.1; el/la socio(a)
menorah la menora, **5.2**
menu el menú, 4.2; **4**
merchant el/la vendedor(a), 9.2
Merry Christmas! ¡Feliz Navidad!
merry-go-round el tiovivo, **8.1**
message el mensaje, **6.2**
meter el metro
Mexican mexicano(a)
Mexican American mexicanoamericano(a), 1.2
microwave oven el horno de microondas, **10**
Middle Ages la Edad Media
midnight la medianoche
mile la milla
milk la leche, 4.1
million el millón
- **a million dollars** un millón de dólares

mime el mimo, **8.1**
to **mince** picar, **10**
mind el espíritu, **11.1**
mineral water el agua mineral, 4.2
mirror el espejo, 11.1; **2.1**
Miss (la) señorita, LP
to **miss the bus** perder (ie) el autobús, 8.1
mobile phone el móvil, 3.2; el celular, **6.2**
modern moderno(a)
mom mamá
moment el momento
monastery el monasterio
Monday el lunes, LP
money el dinero, 3.2
monitor ***(computer)*** la pantalla de escritorio, **6.1**
month el mes, LP
monument el monumento
mood el humor, 6.1
- **to be in a good (bad) mood** estar de buen (mal) humor, 6.1

moon la luna
more más, 9.1
morning la mañana
- **Good morning.** Buenos días., LP
- **in the morning** por la mañana; de la mañana

mother la madre, 2.1
motive el motivo

English-Spanish Dictionary

mountain la montaña, 7.2
mountaintop el pico, 7.2
mouse el ratón, **6.1**
mousepad la alfombrilla, **6.1**
mouth la boca, 6.2
to **move** mover (ue)
movement el movimiento, **11.1**
movie la película, el filme, 8.2; el film
movie theater el cine, 8.2
movies: to go to the movies ir al cine, 8.2
MP3 player el MP3, **6.2**
Mr. (el) señor, LP
Mr. and Mrs. (los) señores
Mrs. (la) señora, LP
Ms. (la) señorita, (la) señora, LP
much mucho(a), LP
  as much . . . as tan... como, **11.2**
  How much is it (does it cost)? ¿Cuánto es?, LP; ¿Cuánto cuesta?, 3.2
mud el lodo
museum el museo, 8.2
music la música, 1.2
musician el/la músico(a), 8.1
mussels los mejillones, **4**
my mi
mysterious misterioso(a)

N

name el nombre, 2.1
  My name is . . . Me llamo... , 11.1; **2.1**
  What is your name? ¿Cómo te llamas?, 11.1; **2.1;** ¿Cuál es su nombre? *(formal)*
napkin la servilleta, **4**
narrow angosto(a), estrecho(a), **8.1**
national nacional
nationality la nacionalidad, 1.1
  what nationality? ¿de qué nacionalidad?, 1.1
native indígena, 9.2
native person el/la indígena
nature la naturaleza
near cerca de, 3.2
necessary necesario(a)
  It's necessary. Es necesario., **11.2**
  it's necesssary to (do something) hay que, 10.2; **1.2**
neck el cuello, **11.1**
necktie la corbata, 9.1
to **need** necesitar, 3.2
negative negativo(a)
neighbor el/la vecino(a)
neighborhood el casco, el barrio, **8.1**
neither tampoco
nephew el sobrino, 2.1
nervous nervioso(a), 6.1
net *(World Wide Web)* la red, 3.2; **6.1;** *(tennis)*, 5.2
  to surf the Net navegar el Internet, 3.2; **6.1**
never nunca, 8.2; jamás
new nuevo(a), 1.1
  New Year el Año Nuevo
  New Year's Eve la Nochevieja, la víspera del Año Nuevo
news la(s) noticia(s)
newspaper el periódico, **3.1**
newsstand el quiosco, **3.1**
next próximo(a), **3.2;** que viene, **8.2**
  next stop la próxima parada, **3.2**
  next summer (year, etc.) el verano (año, etc.) que viene, **8.2**
next to al lado de, 2.2
Nicaraguan nicaragüense
nice simpático(a), 1.1; *(weather)* buen (tiempo)
  Nice to meet you. Mucho gusto., 1.2
  The weather is nice. Hace buen tiempo., LP
niece la sobrina, 2.1
night la noche
  at night por la noche
  Good night. Buenas noches., LP
  last night anoche, 7.1
nine nueve, LP
nine hundred novecientos(as), 9.2
nineteen diecinueve, LP
ninety noventa, LP
no no, LP; ninguno(a)
  by no means de ninguna manera
no one nadie, 8.2
nobody nadie, 8.2
none ninguno(a)
noon el mediodía
normal normal, 6.2
north el norte
North American norteamericano(a), 1
no-smoking sign la señal de no fumar, 10.2; **1.2**
not no, 1.2
notebook el cuaderno, 3.1
nothing nada, 8.2
  Nothing else. Nada más., 9.2
novel la novela
November noviembre, LP
now ahora
nowadays hoy en día
number el número, 10.1; **1.1**
  flight number el número del vuelo, 10.1; **1.1**
  seat number el número del asiento, 10.1; **1.1**
  telephone number el número de teléfono, **6.2**
nurse el/la enfermero(a), 6.2; **11.2**

O

object el objeto
objective el objetivo
obligatory obligatorio(a)
to **observe** observar
obstinate obstinado(a), 6.1
occasionally de vez en cuando
occupied ocupado(a), 4.2; **3.2**
ocean el océano
o'clock: It's two o'clock. Son las dos., LP
October octubre, LP
odd *(numeric)* impar
of de LP
  Of course! ¡Cómo no!; ¡Claro!
  of the del, de la
to **offer** ofrecer
offering la ofrenda, **5.1**
office la oficina, **8.1**
  doctor's office la consulta del médico, 6.2
often con frecuencia, a menudo
oil el aceite, **4**
  olive oil el aceite de oliva
OK de acuerdo
old viejo(a), 2.2; antiguo(a), **8.1**
  How old is he (she)? ¿Cuántos años tiene?, 2.1
  old city el casco (barrio) antiguo, **8.1**

English-Spanish Dictionary

older mayor
oldest el/la mayor
olive la aceituna, 4.2
on sobre; en
  on board abordo, 10.2; **1.2**
  on foot a pie, 3.2
  on the edge of al borde mismo de
  on time a tiempo, 10.2; **1.2**
  on top of sobre
one uno; un(a), LP
one hundred cien(to), LP
one thousand mil
one-way (ticket) el boleto (billete) sencillo, **3.1; (street)** la calle de sentido único, **9.1**
onion la cebolla, 9.2; **10**
online: to go online entrar en línea, **6.1**
only único(a), 2.1; solo; solamente
to **open** abrir, 4.2
open-air al aire libre, 7.2
open-minded flexible, 6.1
opinion la opinión
opponents el equipo contrario, 5.2
opposite el contrario
or o, u *(used instead of* **o** *in front of words beginning with* **o** *or* **ho***)*
orange *(color)* anaranjado(a), 5.1
orange *(fruit)* la naranja, 4.1
  orange juice el jugo (zumo) de naranja, 4.1; **7**
orchard la huerta, **8.2**
order *(restaurant)* la orden, 4.2
to **order *(restaurant)*** pedir (i, i)
to **organize** organizar
origin el origen
orthopedic surgeon el/la cirujano(a) ortopédico(a), **11.2**
other otro(a)
  any other cualquier otro(a)
our nuestro(a), nuestros(as)
outdoor al aire libre
outfielder el/la jardinero(a), 5.2
outskirts los alrededores, las afueras
oven el horno, **10**
over por encima de, 5.2
overhead bin el compartimiento superior, 10.2; **1.2**
overpopulation la sobrepoblación
own: propio(a), 5.1
oxygen mask la máscara de oxígeno, 10.2; **1.2**

P

to **pack** hacer la maleta, 10.1; **1.1**
package el paquete, 9.2
page la página
  home page la página de inicio (inicial, frontal), **6.1**
pain el dolor, 6.2
to **paint** pintar
painter el/la pintor(a), 8.2
painting el cuadro, 8.2; la pintura
pair el par, 9.1
  pair of shoes el par de zapatos, 9.1
pants el pantalón, 3.1
  long pants el pantalón largo, 9.1
paper el papel, 3.1
  sheet of paper la hoja de papel, 3.1
  toilet paper el papel higiénico, 11.2; **2.2**
paperback (book) el libro de bolsillo, **3.1**
parade el desfile, **5.2**
  to walk in a parade desfilar, **5.1**
paramedic el/la socorrista, **11.2**
parents los padres, 2.1
park el parque, 11.2; **2.2**
to **park** aparcar, **8.1;** estacionar, parquear
parka el anorak, 7.2
parking lot el parking, el parqueo, **8.1**
parking meter el parquímetro, **9.1**
part la parte
  la mayor parte the greatest part, the majority
party la fiesta, 8.1
  to (have) throw a party dar una fiesta, 8.1
to **pass** pasar, 5.2; ***(car)*** adelantar(se), rebasar, pasar, **9.1**
passenger el/la pasajero(a), 10.1; **1.1**
passport el pasaporte, 10.2; **1.2**
past el pasado
pastry el pan dulce, **7**
path la senda, **3.2**
patience la paciencia, 6.1
patient el/la paciente, 6.2
patient *(adj.)* paciente, 6.1
patron saint el/la santo(a) patrón(ona), **5.1**
  patron saint's day la fiesta patronal, **5.1**
pavement el pavimento
to **pay** pagar, 3.2
  to pay attention prestar atención, 3.1; hacer caso
pay phone el teléfono público, **6.2**
pea el guisante, 9.2
peaceful tranquilo(a), 6.1
peak el pico, 7.2
peanut el cacahuate, el maní, 8.1; el cacahuete
peasant el campesino, el peón, **8.2**
pedestrian el/la peatón(ona), **8.1**
  pedestrian crossing el cruce peatonal, **8.1**
to **peel** pelar, **10**
pen el bolígrafo, 3.1; el lapicero, la pluma
pencil el lápiz, 3.1
people la gente, 9.1
pepper *(spice)* la pimienta, **4; *(bell pepper)*** el pimiento, 9.2; **10;** el pimentón; el ají; el chipotle; el morrón
perhaps quizá, quizás, tal vez, 7.2
to **permit** permitir
person la persona
personality la personalidad, 6.1
Peruvian el/la peruano(a)
peso el peso
pet la mascota, 2.1
pharmacist el/la farmacéutico(a)
pharmacy la farmacia, 6.2
phone el teléfono
  cell phone el móvil, 3.2; el (teléfono) celular, **6.1**
  pay phone el teléfono público, **6.2**
  phone book la guía telefónica, **6.2**
  phone call la llamada telefónica, **6.2**
  phone card la tarjeta telefónica, **6.2**
  phone number el número de teléfono, **6.2**
  phone receiver el auricular, **6.2**

English-Spanish Dictionary

English-Spanish Dictionary

public phone el teléfono público, **6.2**
to pick up the phone descolgar (ue) el auricular, **6.2**
to speak on the phone hablar por teléfono
photo(graph) la foto(grafía), 7.1
to take photos sacar (tomar) fotos, 7.1
physical ***(exam)*** el examen físico, 6.2
physical education la educación física, 1.2
physics la física
piano el piano
to **pick up** ***(phone)*** descolgar (ue) el auricular, **6.2**
to **pick up** ***(speed)*** agarrar velocidad
picture la foto(grafía); la imagen
to take pictures sacar (tomar) fotos, 7.1
picturesque pintoresco(a)
piece el pedazo, el trozo (trocito)
little piece el pedacito, **10**
pig el cerdo, **8.2;** el cochinillo, el lechón, el chancho
pillow la almohada, 7
pinch la pizca
pineapple la piña, 9.2
pink rosado(a), 5.1
pitcher ***(baseball)*** el/la pícher, el/la lanzador(a), 5.2
pizza la pizza, 4.1
place el lugar; el sitio
to **plan** planear
plane el avión, 10.1; **1.1**
plant la planta, 2.2
to **plant** sembrar (ie), **8.2**
plantain: slices of fried plantain los tostones, 4.2; los patacones
plate el plato, **4**
platform ***(railway)*** el andén, **3.1**
to **play** ***(sport)*** jugar (ue), 5.1; ***(musical instrument)*** tocar, 8.1; **5.2**
to play soccer (baseball, etc.) jugar (al) fútbol (béisbol, etc.), 5.1
player el/la jugador(a), 5.1
baseball player el/la jugador(a) de béisbol, el/la beisbolista, 5.2
plaza la plaza, **8.1**
pleasant agradable, placentero(a)
please por favor, LP; favor de (+ *infinitive*), 11.2; **2.2**
pleasure: It's a pleasure to meet you. Mucho gusto.
P.M. de la tarde, de la noche
poem el poema
point el tanto, 5.1; el punto
to score a point marcar un tanto, 5.1
to **point out** señalar
polite bien educado(a), 6.1
polluted contaminado(a)
pollution la contaminación
pool la piscina, la alberca, 7.1; la pila
poor pobre
popular popular
population la población
pork chop la chuleta de cerdo, **4**
portrait el retrato
Portuguese portugués(esa)
to **possess** poseer
possibility la posibilidad
possible posible
pot la olla, la cacerola, **10**
potato la papa, la patata, 4.1
french fried potatoes las papas (patatas) fritas, 4.1
pothole el bache
practically casi, 8.2
to **practice** practicar
to **prefer** preferir (ie, i), 5.2; **4**
to **prepare** preparar; confeccionar, **5.1**
to **prescribe** recetar, 6.2
prescription la receta, 6.2
present el regalo, 8.1
Christmas present el aguinaldo, **5.2**
to **present** presentar
president el/la presidente(a)
to **press** ***(button)*** oprimir, pulsar, **6.1**
pretty bonito(a), 1.1; hermoso(a)
previous anterior, **6.1**
price el precio, 9.1
primary primario(a)
to **print** imprimir, **6.1**
printer la impresora, **6.1**
private privado(a), 2.2
probable probable
problem el problema
procession la procesión, **5.1**
product el producto, 9.2
public público(a)
Puerto Rican puertorriqueño(a)
pulse el pulso, 6.2
purchase la compra, 9.2
to **push** ***(button)*** oprimir, pulsar, **6.1**
push-ups: to do push-ups hacer planchas, 11.1
to **put** poner, 10.2; **1.2;** meter, 5.2
to **put on** ***(clothes)*** ponerse, 11.1; **2.1** ***(brakes)*** poner los frenos
to **put up** ***(tent)*** armar, montar, 11.2; **2.2**
puzzle el rompecabezas

Q

quarter ***(city)*** el casco, el barrio, **8.1;** ***(time)*** el cuarto, LP
a quarter past (the hour) y cuarto, LP
question la pregunta, 3.1
to ask a question preguntar, 3.1
quickly rápidamente
quiet tranquilo(a), calmo(a), 6.1
quite bastante, 1.2

R

race la carrera, **11.1**
cross-country race la carrera a campo traviesa, **11.1**
long-distance race la carrera de larga distancia, **11.1**
relay race la carrera de relevos, **11.1**
racket la raqueta, 5.2
railroad el ferrocarril, **3.1**
railroad platform el andén, **3.1**
railroad station la estación de ferrocarril, **3.1**
to **rain** llover (ue)
It's raining. Llueve., LP
raincoat impermeable

to **raise** levantar, 3.1
to raise one's hand levantar la mano, 3.1
ranch la hacienda, la estancia, el rancho, **8.2**
rare *(meat)* casi crudo, **4**
rate la tarifa; la tasa
rather bastante, 1.2
raw crudo(a), 8.1
raw vegetables los vegetales crudos, 8.1
reaction la reacción
to **read** leer, 4.2
reading la lectura
ready listo(a)
really realmente
reason la razón, el motivo
to **receive** recibir, 4.2
receiver *(telephone)* el auricular, **6.2**
recipe la receta, **10**
recipient el/la destinatario(a), **6.1**
to **recognize** reconocer
record el disco
red rojo(a), 5.1
red light la luz roja, **9.1**
redheaded pelirrojo(a), 1.1
to **reduce *(price)*** rebajar, 9.1
to **reduce *(speed)*** reducir la velocidad, **9.1**
reduced reducido(a)
refrigerator el refrigerador, la nevera, **10**
region la región
relative el/la pariente, 2.1
relay: relay race la carrera de relevos, **11.1**
reliability la confiabilidad
religious religioso(a)
to **remain** quedarse, 11.1; **2.1**
to **remember** recordar (ue)
to **rent** alquilar, rentar, 7.1; **3.2**
to **repeat *(take second helping)*** repetir (i, i), **4**
to **represent** representar
republic la república
Dominican Republic la República Dominicana
to **request** pedir (i, i), **4**
required obligatorio(a)
reservation la reservación, **7;** la reserva
to **reserve** reservar, **7**
resort: seaside resort el balneario, 7.1
ski resort la estación de esquí, 7.2
rest: the rest lo(s) demás
to **rest** descansar, **11.1**
restaurant el restaurante, **4**
restroom el servicio, 10.2; **1.2**
result el resultado
to **return** regresar, 3.2; volver (ue), 5.1
to return *(something)* devolver (ue), 5.2
review el repaso
to **review** repasar
rice el arroz, 4.1
rich rico(a)
to **rid** liberar, **11.1**
ride: to go for a (bike) ride dar un paseo en bicicleta
to **ride *(horse)*** andar a caballo, **3.2;** montar a caballo, **8.2;** *(bicycle)* andar en bicicleta, **11.1**
rides *(amusement park)* las atracciones, **8.1**
right derecho(a), 11.1; **2.1**
right on the edge of al borde mismo de
to the right a la derecha, **9.1**
right: That's right! ¡Verdad!
right away enseguida, 4.2
to **ring** sonar (ue), **6.1**
ringtone el timbre (sonoro), **6.2**
rink *(ice-skating)* la pista de patinaje, 7.2
river el río
roast asado(a)
roast suckling pig el cochinillo asado, el lechón asado, el chancho asado
to **roast** asar, **10**
roll *(bread)* el panecillo, 4.1; **7**
roll of toilet paper el rollo de papel higiénico, 11.2; **2.2**
rollerblading el patinaje en línea, **11.1**
rollerblading: to go rollerblading patinar en línea, **11.1**
roller coaster la montaña rusa, **8.1**
romantic romántico(a)
room el cuarto, 2.2; **7**
bathroom el cuarto de baño, 2.2; **7**
bedroom el cuarto de dormir, la recámara, 2.2; el dormitorio, la habitación, la alcoba, la pieza
classroom la sala de clase, 3.1
dining room el comedor, 2.2
emergency room la sala de emergencia, **11.2**
living room la sala, 2.2
restroom el servicio, 10.2; **1.2**
single (double) room el cuarto sencillo (doble), **7**
waiting room la sala de espera, **3.1**
round-trip (ticket) el boleto (billete) de ida y vuelta (regreso), **3.1**
routine la rutina, 11.1; **2.1**
daily routine la rutina diaria, 11.1; **2.1**
rude mal educado(a), 6.1
ruins las ruinas
rule la regla
to **run** correr, 5.2
running water el agua corriente
runway la pista, 10.2; **1.2**
rural rural

S

sad triste, deprimido(a), 6.1
saffron el azafrán
sailboard la plancha de vela, 7.1
saint el/la santo(a), **5.1**
patron saint el/la santo(a) patrón(ona), **5.1**
salad la ensalada, 4.1
sale el saldo, la liquidación, 9.1
salesperson el/la empleado(a), 3.2; el/la dependiente(a)
salt la sal, **4**
salty salado(a)
same mismo(a), 1.2
sand la arena, 7.1
sandal la sandalia, 9.2
sandwich el sándwich, el bocadillo, 4.1; la torta
ham and cheese sandwich el sándwich de jamón y queso, 4.1
satisfied satisfecho(a)
to **satisfy** satisfacer
Saturday el sábado, LP
sauce la salsa, **10**
saucepan la cacerola, la olla, **10**
saucer el platillo, **4**
sausage el chorizo
to **save** guardar, **6.1**
saxophone el saxófono
to **say** decir, **3.2**
scenery el paisaje
schedule *(train)* el horario, **3.1**
school la escuela, 1.2; el colegio; la academia
elementary school la escuela primaria
high school la escuela secundaria, 1.2; el colegio

English-Spanish Dictionary

school *(related to)* escolar
school bus el bus escolar, 3.2
school supplies los materiales escolares, 3.1
science la ciencia, 1.2
score el tanto, 5.1
to score a goal meter un gol, 5.1
to score a point marcar un tanto, 5.1
scrambled: scrambled eggs los huevos revueltos, **7**
screen *(computer)* la pantalla de escritorio, **6.1**
scuba diving el buceo
to go scuba diving bucear
sculptor el/la escultor(a)
sculpture la escultura, 8.2
sea el mar, 7.1
Caribbean Sea el mar Caribe
seafood los mariscos, **4**
seaside resort el balneario, 7.1
search: in search of en busca de
to **search** buscar, 3.2
season la estación, LP
¿Qué estación es? What season is it?, LP
seat el asiento, 10.1; **1.1;** la plaza, **3.2**
seat number el número del asiento, 10.1; **1.1**
seat belt el cinturón de seguridad, 10.2; **1.2**
second segundo(a), 5.1
second-class segunda clase, **3.1**
second half *(soccer)* el segundo tiempo, 5.1
secondary secundario(a), 1.2
security *(checkpoint)* el control de seguridad, 10.2; **1.2**
to go through security pasar por el control de seguridad, 10.2; **1.2**
sedan el sedán, **9.2**
four-door sedan el sedán a cuatro puertas, **9.2**
to **see** ver, 4.2
let's see a ver
See you later! ¡Hasta luego!, LP
See you soon! ¡Hasta pronto!, LP
See you tomorrow! ¡Hasta mañana!, LP
to **seem** parecer
It seems to me . . . Me parece...
to **select** seleccionar, **3.1**
self-service (restaurant, gas station) el autoservicio
to **sell** vender, 6.2
to **send** enviar, 3.2; mandar
sense: sense of humor el sentido de humor, 6.1
to have a good sense of humor tener un buen sentido de humor, 6.1
sent mailbox la bandeja de enviados, **6.1**
sentence la frase, la oración
September septiembre, LP
serious serio(a), 1.1
to **serve** servir (i, i), **4**
to serve as servir (i, i) de
server el/la mesero(a), 4.2, **4;** el/la camarero(a), **4**
service el servicio, **9.2**
to **set** *(table)* poner la mesa, **4;** *(bone)* reducir, acomodar el hueso, **11.2**
seven siete, LP
seven hundred setecientos(as)
seventeen diecisiete, LP
seventy setenta, LP
several varios(as)
shack la choza, la casucha
shake *(drink)* el batido, 4.2
shame: What a shame! ¡Qué pena!, 5.1
shampoo el champú, 11.2; **2.2**
shape la forma
she ella, 1.1
sheet la sábana, **7**
sheet of paper la hoja de papel
shellfish los mariscos, **4**
shirt la camisa, 3.1
short- (long-) sleeved shirt la camisa de manga corta (larga), 9.1
shoe size el número, 9.1
What size shoe do you wear (take)? ¿Qué número calzas?, 9.1
shoes las zapatillas, 5.1; los zapatos, 9.1
to **shop** ir de compras, 9.1
shopping cart el carrito, 9.2
shopping center el centro comercial, 9.1
short *(person)* bajo(a), 1.1; *(length)* corto(a), 9.1
short-sleeved de manga corta, 9.1
shorts el pantalón corto, 5.1
should deber, 4.2
shoulder *(road)* el acotamiento, el arcén, **9.1;** *(body)* el hombro, **11.1**
to **show** mostrar (ue), 10.2; **1.2**
shower la ducha, 11.1; **2.1**
to take a shower tomar una ducha, 11.1; **2.1**
shrimp los camarones, 4.2
shy tímido(a)
sick enfermo(a), 6.2
sick person el/la enfermo(a)
side el lado
sidewalk la acera, **8.1**
sign la señal, 10.2; **1.2;** *(road)* el rótulo, **9.1**
no-smoking sign la señal de no fumar, 10.2; **1.2**
similar similar
since desde; como
sincere sincero(a); franco(a)
to **sing** cantar, 8.1
singer el/la cantante, 8.1
single solo(a); **(room)** un cuarto sencillo, **7**
singles *(tennis)* individuales, 5.2
sink el lavabo, **7**
sir el señor, LP
sister la hermana, 2.1
to **sit down** sentarse (ie), 11.1; **2.1**
site (Web site) el sitio, **6.1**
six seis, LP
six hundred seiscientos(as)
sixteen dieciséis, LP
sixty sesenta, LP
size *(clothing)* la talla; *(shoes)* el número, 9.1
What size (*clothing*) do you wear (take)? ¿Qué talla usas?, 9.1
What size (*shoe*) do you wear (take)? ¿Qué número calzas?, 9.1
to **skate** patinar, 7.2; **11.1**
to ice-skate patinar sobre el hielo, 7.2
to inline skate (rollerblade) patinar en línea, **11.1**
skateboard el monopatín, **11.1**
skeleton el esqueleto, **5.1**
ski el esquí, 7.2
ski hat el gorro, 7.2
ski jacket la chaqueta de esquí, el anorak, 7.2

English-Spanish Dictionary

ski lift el telesilla, el telesquí, 7.2
ski pole el bastón, 7.2
ski resort la estación de esquí, 7.2
ski slope la pista, 7.2
to ski esquiar, 7.2
to water-ski esquiar en el agua, 7.1
skier el/la esquiador(a), 7.2
skiing el esquí, 7.2
cross-country skiing el esquí nórdico
downhill skiing el esquí alpino, 7.2
waterskiing el esquí acuático (náutico), 7.1
skillet el/la sartén, **10**
skirt la falda, 3.1
skull el cráneo, la calavera, **5.1**
sky el cielo, **5.2**
skyscraper el rascacielos, **8.1**
to sleep dormir (ue, u)
sleeping bag el saco (la bolsa) de dormir, 11.2; **2.2**
sleeved: short- (long-) sleeved de manga corta (larga), 9.1
slice la tajada, 9.2; la rebanada, 10; ***(ham)*** la lonja, la loncha; ***(lemon, cucumber)*** la rodaja; ***(melon)*** la raja
to slice cortar en rebanadas, **10**
slope la pista, 7.2
slot la ranura, **6.2**
slow lento(a), **11.1**
slowly despacio, **9.1**
small pequeño(a), 1.2
smile la sonrisa, 6.1
smoking: no-smoking sign la señal de no fumar, 10.2; **1.2**
smoothie el batido, 4.2
snack la merienda; las tapas, los antojitos, 4.2; los bocaditos
sneakers las zapatillas, 5.1; los tenis, 5.2
to snorkel bucear, **7.1**
snorkeling el buceo **7.1**
snow la nieve, 7.2
to snow nevar (ie), 7.2
It's snowing. Nieva., LP
snowboarder el/la snowboarder, 7.2
so tan; **(thus)** así
soap el jabón, 11.2; **2.2**
bar of soap la barra de jabón, 11.2; **2.2;** la pastilla de jabón
soap opera la telenovela
soccer el fútbol, 5.1
soccer field el campo de fútbol, 5.1
social studies los estudios sociales, 1.2
socks los calcetines, 5.1
soda la cola, la gaseosa, 4.1
sofa el sofá, 2.2
soft blando(a)
soft drink el refresco, 4.2
solid line ***(road)*** la línea continua, **9.1**
some algunos(as); unos(as)
someone alguien, 8.2
something algo, 8.2
sometimes a veces, 6.1; **1.2;** de vez en cuando
son el hijo, 2.1
soon pronto, LP; dentro de poco, 10.2; **1.2**
See you soon! ¡Hasta pronto!, LP
sore throat: to have a sore throat tener dolor de garganta, 6.2
sorry: to be sorry sentir (ie, i)
I'm very sorry. Lo siento mucho., 5.1
soul el alma *(f.)*
soup la sopa
south el sur
South America la América del Sur, la Sudamérica
to sow sembrar (ie), **8.2**
space el espacio; ***(parking)*** el sitio (para estacionar)
Spain España
Spanish ***(language)*** el español, 1.2; ***(person)*** el/la español(a)
Spanish *(adj.)* español(a)
Spanish speaker el/la hispanohablante
Spanish-speaking hispanohablante
spare time el tiempo libre, 8.1
spare tire la rueda (llanta) de repuesto (recambio), 9.2; la rueda de refacción
to speak hablar, 3.1
to speak on the phone hablar por teléfono
special especial
specialty la especialidad
spectator el/la espectador(a)
speed la velocidad, **9.1**
speed limit la velocidad máxima, **9.1;** el límite de velocidad
to spend ***(time)*** pasar, 7.1; ***(money)*** gastar
spice la especia
spirit el espíritu, **11.1**
to splurge botar la casa por la ventana
spoon ***(tablespoon)*** la cuchara, **4; *(teaspoon)*** la cucharita, **4**
sport el deporte, 5.1
individual sport el deporte individual
team sport el deporte de equipo
sports ***(related to)*** deportivo(a)
sports car el coche deportivo, **9.2**
to sprain torcerse, **11.2**
He (She) sprained his (her) ankle. Se torció el tobillo., **11.2**
spring la primavera, LP
square ***(town)*** la plaza, **8.1**
stable el establo, **8.2**
stadium el estadio
stairs la escalera, **8.1**
stall ***(market)*** el puesto, el tenderete, 9.2
to stand in line hacer cola, 10.2; **1.2;** estar en fila
standing de pie
star la estrella
starving: I'm starving. Me muero de hambre., **4**
state el estado
station ***(train)*** la estación de ferrocarril (tren), **3.1; *(subway)*** la estación de metro, **8.1; *(gas)*** la estación de servicio, la gasolinera, **9.2**
statue la estatua, 8.2
stay la estadía
to stay quedarse, 11.1; **2.1**
to stay in bed ***(illness)*** guardar cama, 6.2; ***(idleness)*** quedarse en la cama, 11.1; **2.1**
to stay in a hotel hospedarse, **7**
steak el biftec, **4**
steep pendiente
steering wheel el volante, **9.2**
stepbrother el hermanastro, 2.1
stepfather el padrastro, 2.1
stepmother la madrastra, 2.1
stepsister la hermanastra, 2.1
still todavía
stingy tacaño(a), **9.1**
to stir revolver (ue), **10**
stitch el punto, la sutura, **11.2**
to give (someone) stitches poner unos puntos (unas suturas) (a alguien), **11.2**

English-Spanish Dictionary

English-Spanish Dictionary

stomach el estómago, 6.2
to have a stomachache tener dolor de estómago, 6.2
stone la piedra
stop la parada, **3.2**
next stop la próxima parada, **3.1**
to **stop** parar(se), **9.1**
store la tienda, 3.2
story el cuento, la historia
stove la cocina, la estufa, **10**
straight (ahead) derecho, **9.1**
to go straight (ahead) seguir derecho, **9.1**
straw la paja, **5.2**
street la calle, **8.1**
one-way street la calle de sentido único, 9.1
stress el estrés, 6.2; las tensiones, **11.1**
stretch ***(distance)*** el trecho
to **stretch** estirarse, 11.1; **2.1**
stretcher la camilla, **11.2**
string beans las judías verdes, 9.2
strong fuerte
stubborn obstinado(a), terco(a), 6.1
student el/la alumno(a), 1.2; el/la estudiante; *(adj.)* estudiantil, escolar, **3.1**
study el estudio
stuffed up *(head, cold)* resfriado, 6.2
social studies los estudios sociales, 1.2
to **study** estudiar, 3.1
suburbs las afueras, los suburbios, 2.2
subway el metro, **8.1**
subway entrance la boca del metro, **8.1**
subway station la estación de metro, **8.1**
to **succeed** tener éxito, 6.1
success el éxito, 6.1
successful: to be successful tener éxito, 6.1
such tal
suddenly de repente
to **suffer** sufrir
sugar el azúcar
suitcase la maleta, 10.1; **1.1**
to pack one's suitcase hacer la maleta, 10.1; **1.1**
summer el verano, LP
sun el sol
to **sunbathe** tomar el sol, 7.1
Sunday el domingo, LP
sunglasses los anteojos de sol, las gafas para el sol, 7.1
sunny: It's sunny. Hace (Hay) sol., LP
suntan lotion la crema solar, la loción bronceadora, 7.1
supermarket el supermercado, 9.2
supplies: school supplies los materiales escolares, 3.1
sure seguro(a)
to **surf** practicar la tabla hawaiana, 7.1
to **surf the Web (the Net)** navegar la red (el Internet), 3.2; **6.1**
surfboard la tabla hawaiana, 7.1
surfing la tabla hawaiana, el surfing, 7.1
to go surfing practicar la tabla hawaiana, el surfing, 7.1
surgeon: orthopedic surgeon el/la cirujano(a) ortopédico(a), **11.2**
surprise la sorpresa, 4.1
survey la encuesta
SUV el SUV, **9.2**
sweat suit el buzo, **11.1**
sweater el suéter, 11.1; **2.1**
sweet dulce, **5.1**
to **swim** nadar, 7.1
swimming pool la piscina, la alberca, 7.1; la pila
swimsuit el bañador, el traje de baño, 7.1
swollen hinchado(a), **11.2**
symptom el síntoma

T

T-shirt la camiseta, 5.1; el T-shirt
table la mesa, la mesita, 2.2; **4**
to clear the table levantar (quitar) la mesa, **4**
to set the table poner la mesa, **4**
tablecloth el mantel, 4
tablespoon la cuchara, **4;** *(in recipe)* la cucharada
taco el taco
to **take** tomar, 3.1; traer, 10.1; **1.1;** sacar, 7.1
to take *(size)* usar, calzar, 9.1
to take a bath bañarse
to take a flight tomar un vuelo
to take a hike dar una caminata, 11.2; **2.2**
to take a shower tomar una ducha, 11.1; **2.1**
to take a test tomar un examen, 3.1
to take a trip hacer un viaje, 10.1; **1.1**
to take an X ray of someone tomar una radiografía, **11.2**
to take pictures (photos) sacar (tomar) fotos, 7.1
to take place tener lugar
to take someone's blood pressure tomar la tensión arterial, 6.2
to take someone's pulse tomar el pulso, 6.2
to take the (school) bus tomar el bus (escolar), 3.2
to **take off *(airplane)*** despegar, 10.2; **1.2; *(clothes)*** quitarse, 11.1; **2.1**
to **take out** sacar
taken ocupado(a), 4.2; **3.2**
takeoff el despegue, 10.2; **1.2**
to **talk** hablar, 3.1
to talk on a cell phone hablar en el móvil
to talk on the phone hablar por teléfono
tall alto(a), 1.1
tank *(car)* el tanque, **9.2**
taste el gusto
tax el impuesto
taxi el taxi, 10.1; **1.1**
taxi driver el/la taxista, 10.1; **1.1**
tea el té
to **teach** enseñar, 3.1
teacher el/la profesor(a), 1.2
team el equipo, 5.1
team sport el deporte de equipo
teaspoon la cucharita, **4;** ***(in recipe)*** la cucharadita

English-Spanish Dictionary

teeth los dientes, 11.1; **2.1**
to brush one's teeth cepillarse (lavarse) los dientes, 11.1; **2.1**
telephone el teléfono
pay telephone el teléfono público, **6.2**
(related to) **telephone** telefónico(a), **6.2**
telephone book la guía telefónica, **6.2**
telephone call la llamada telefónica, **6.2**
telephone card la tarjeta telefónica, **6.2**
telephone line la línea, **6.2**
telephone number el número de teléfono, **6.2**
telephone receiver el auricular, **6.2**
to pick up the telephone descolgar (ue) el auricular, 6.2
to speak on the telephone hablar por teléfono
television la televisión, la tele
temperature la temperatura, 7.2
ten diez, LP
tennis el tenis
to play tennis jugar (al) tenis, 5.2
tennis court la cancha de tenis, 5.2
tennis player el/la tenista, 5
tennis racket la raqueta, 5.2
tennis shoes los tenis, 9.1
tension la tensión, **11.1**
tent la carpa, la tienda de campaña, 11.2; **2.2**
to put up a tent armar, montar una carpa (una tienda de campaña), 11.2; **2.2**
terrace la terraza
terrible terrible
test el examen, la prueba, 3.1
to give a test dar un examen (una prueba), 3.1
to take a test tomar un examen, 3.1
Texan tejano(a)
text message el mensaje de texto
Thank you. Gracias., LP
that aquel, aquella, 9.1; ese(a)
that ***(one)*** eso
the el, la, los, las
their su(s)
them las, los, les
to them *(pron.)* les
then luego, 3.2
there allí, allá, 9.1
Is . . . there? ¿Está... ?, **6.2**
there is, there are hay, 2.2
therefore por eso
these estos(as)
they ellos(as), 1.2
thigh el muslo, **10**
thin flaco(a); delgado(a)
thing la cosa, 3.1
to **think** pensar (ie), 5.1
What do you think? ¿Qué piensas?, 5.1
thirsty: to be thirsty tener sed, 4.1
thirteen trece, LP
thirty treinta, LP
thirty-one treinta y uno, LP
this este(a), 9.1
those aquellos(as), esos(as)
thousand mil
three tres, LP
the Three Wise Men los Reyes Magos, **5.2**
three hundred trescientos(as)
throat la garganta, 6.2
to have a sore throat tener dolor de garganta, 6.2
to **throw** tirar, 5.2
to throw (give) a party dar una fiesta, 8.1
Thursday el jueves, LP
thus así
ticket el boleto, el ticket, 7.2; **3.1;** la entrada, 8.1; el billete, 10.1; **1.1;** el tiquet(e); *(car)* la multa, **9.1**
e-ticket el boleto (billete) electrónico, 10.1; **1.1**
one-way ticket el boleto (billete) sencillo, **3.1**
round-trip ticket el boleto (billete) de ida y vuelta (regreso), **3.1**
to give (someone) a ticket clavar con una multa, **9.1**
ticket counter ***(airport)*** el mostrador, 10.1; **1.1**
ticket dispenser el distribuidor automático, **3.1**
ticket window la ventanilla, la boletería, 7.2, **3.1;** la taquilla, 8.2
tie la corbata, 9.1
tiger el tigre
time la hora, LP; 10.1; **1.1;** el tiempo, 8.1; la vez
at times (sometimes) a veces, 6.1; **1.2**
at what time? ¿a qué hora?, LP
boarding time la hora de embarque, 10.1; **1.1**
departure time la hora de salida, 10.1; **1.1**
from time to time de vez en cuando, 10.2, **1.2**
full-time a tiempo completo
on time a tiempo, 10.2; **1.2**
part-time a tiempo parcial
spare time el tiempo libre, 8.1
What time is it? ¿Qué hora es?, LP
timetable el horario, **3.1**
timid tímido(a)
tip el servicio, 4.2; la propina, **4**
Is the tip included? ¿Está incluido el servicio?, 4.2
tire la llanta, la goma, el neumático, la rueda, **9.2;** el caucho
flat tire el pinchazo, **9.2**
spare tire la rueda (llanta) de repuesto (recambio), **9.2**
tired cansado(a), 6.1
to a
toast las tostadas, el pan tostado, 4.1; **7**
today hoy, LP
What day is it today? ¿Qué día es hoy?, LP
What is today's date? ¿Cuál es la fecha de hoy?, LP
toe el dedo del pie, **11.1**
together juntos(as)
toilet el inodoro, el váter, **7**
toilet paper el papel higiénico, 11.2; **2.2**
roll of toilet paper el rollo de papel higiénico, 11.2; **2.2**
toll el peaje, **9.1;** la cuota
tollbooth la cabina (garita) de peaje, **9.1**
tomato el tomate, 4.1
tomb la tumba, **5.1**
tomorrow mañana, LP
See you tomorrow! ¡Hasta mañana!, LP
tonight esta noche, 4.1
too también, 1.2
toolbar la barra de herramientas, **6.1**
toothbrush el cepillo de dientes, 11.2; **2.2**
toothpaste la crema dental, 11.2; **2.2;** la pasta dentífrica
tube of toothpaste el tubo de crema dental, 11.2; **2.2**

English-Spanish Dictionary

to **touch** tocar, 5.1
tourist el/la turista
toward hacia
towel la toalla, 7.1; **7**
town el pueblo
town square la plaza, **8.1**
toy el juguete
track (train) la vía, 3.1
traffic el tráfico, **8.1;** el tránsito
traffic jam el tapón
traffic light el semáforo, **8.1;** la luz roja, **9.1**
track la vía, **3.1**
trail el camino; la senda, **3.2**
train el tren, **3.1**
train car el coche, el vagón, **3.1**
train conductor el/la revisor(a), **3.2**
train station la estación de ferrocarril (tren), **3.1**
to **transfer *(train)*** transbordar, **3.2**
transportation: means of transportation los medios de transporte, **8.2**
to **travel** viajar
tree el árbol, 2.2
trip el viaje, 10.1; **1.1**
to take a trip hacer un viaje, 10.1; **1.1**
trombone el trombono
truck el camión, **9.2**
true *(adj.)* verdadero(a); cierto(a), **6.1**
That's true. Es verdad., 9.1
trunk *(car)* el baúl, la maletera, 10.1; **1.1**
truth la verdad
to **try** tratar de
tube el tubo, 11.2; **2.2**
Tuesday el martes, LP
tuna el atún, 9.2
to **turn** doblar, **9.1**
to **turn around** dar la vuelta, 9.1
to **turn off** apagar, **6.1**
to **turn on** prender, **6.1**
to **turn . . . years old** cumplir… años
turn signals las direccionales, las intermitentes, **9.2**
TV la tele
twelve doce, LP
twenty veinte, LP
twenty-eight veintiocho, LP
twenty-five veinticinco, LP
twenty-four veinticuatro, LP
twenty-nine veintinueve, LP
twenty-one veintiuno, LP
twenty-seven veintisiete, LP
twenty-six veintiséis, LP
twenty-three veintitrés, LP
twenty-two veintidós, LP
twin el/la gemelo(a), 2.1
to **twist** torcerse, **11.2**
two dos, LP
two hundred doscientos(as)
type el tipo, 6.1
typical típico(a)

U

ugly feo(a), 1.1
unattractive feo(a), 1.1
uncle el tío, 2.1
under debajo de, 10.2; **1.2**
underneath debajo de, 10.2; **1.2**
to **understand** comprender, 4.2; entender (ie), 8.2
unfortunately desgraciadamente
to **unhook *(telephone receiver)*** descolgar el auricular, **6.2**
uniform el uniforme, 3.1
United States Estados Unidos
from the United States estadounidense
university la universidad
unless a menos que
unoccupied libre, 4.2; **3.2**
unpleasant antipático(a), 1.1; desagradable
until hasta, LP
up: to go up subir, 7.2
upper superior
urban urbano(a), **8.1**
us *(pron.)* nos
to **use** usar, 3.2

V

vacation las vacaciones, 7.1
vanilla *(adj.)* de vainilla
various varios(as)
veal la ternera, 10
veal cutlet el escalope de ternera, **10**
vegetable la legumbre, la verdura, el vegetal, 4.1
vegetable store (greengrocer) la verdulería, 9.2
vegetarian vegetariano(a), 4.1
Venezuelan venezolano(a)
very muy, LP; mucho, LP
It's very hot (cold). Hace mucho calor (frío)., LP
Very well. Muy bien, LP
view la vista
vinegar el vinagre, 4
violin el violín
to **visit** visitar, 8.2
volcano el volcán
volleyball el voleibol, 7.1
volleyball court la cancha de voleibol, 7.1
vowel la vocal

W

to **wait (for)** esperar, 10.2; **1.2**
to wait in line hacer cola, 10.2; **1.2;** estar en fila
waiter (waitress) el/la mesero(a), 4.2, **4;** el/la camarero(a), **4**
waiting room la sala de espera, **3.1**
to **wake up** despertarse (ie), 11.1; **2.1**
to **walk** caminar, **5.1;** andar
to walk in a procession desfilar, **5.1**
to **want** querer (ie), 5.1; desear, 4.2
war la guerra
warm-ups *(clothing)* el buzo, **11.1**
to **warn** advertir (ie)
warning la advertencia
to **wash** lavar, 11.2; **2.2**
to **wash oneself** lavarse, 11.1; **2.1**
to wash one's hair (face, hands) lavarse el pelo (la cara, las manos), 11.1; **2.1**
washbasin el lavabo, **7**
to **watch** mirar, 3.2; ver, 4.2
water el agua *(f.)*, 4.1
(sparkling) mineral water el agua mineral (con gas), 4.2
running water el agua corriente
waterskiing el esquí acuático (náutico), 7.1
to water-ski esquiar en el agua, 7.1

English-Spanish Dictionary

wave la ola, 7.1
way la manera
to lose one's way perder el camino
we nosotros(as)
to **wear** llevar, 3.1; ***(shoe size)*** calzar, 9.1; ***(clothing size)*** usar, 9.1
weather el tiempo, LP
It's cold *(weather).* Hace frío., LP
It's cool *(weather).* Hace fresco., LP
The weather is bad. Hace mal tiempo., LP
The weather is nice. Hace buen tiempo., LP
What's the weather like? ¿Qué tiempo hace?, LP
Web la red, 3.2; **6.1**
to surf the Web navegar la red, 3.2; **6.1**
Web site el sitio Web, **6.1**
Wednesday el miércoles, LP
week la semana, LP
last week la semana pasada, 7.1
weekend el fin de semana, 7.1
weight el peso
weights: to lift weights levantar pesas, **11.1**
welcome: You're welcome. De nada., Por nada., No hay de qué., LP
well bien, LP; pues
Very well. Muy bien., LP
well-done *(meat)* bien hecho(a), **4**
well-known renombrado(a)
well-mannered bien educado(a), 6.1
west el oeste
what ¿qué?; ¿cuál?, LP; ¿cuáles? ¿cómo?, 1.1
at what time? ¿a qué hora?, LP
What a shame! ¡Qué pena!, 5.1
What day is it (today)? ¿Qué día es hoy?, LP
What does he (she, it) look like? ¿Cómo es?, 1.1
What's happening? What's going on? ¿Qué pasa?, 3.1
What is he (she, it) like? ¿Cómo es?, 1.1
What is today's date? ¿Cuál es la fecha de hoy?, LP
what nationality? ¿de qué nacionalidad?, 1.1
What's new (up)? ¿Qué hay?
What size shoe do you wear (take)? ¿Qué número calzas?, 9.1
What would you like (to eat)? ¿Qué desean tomar?, 4.2
What time is it? ¿Qué hora es?, LP
wheat el trigo, **8.2**
wheelchair la silla de ruedas, **11.2**
when cuando, 3.1
when? ¿cuándo?, 3.2
where donde
where? ¿dónde?, 1.1; **(to) where?** ¿adónde?, 3.2
from where? ¿de dónde?, 1.1
which? ¿cuál?, LP; ¿cuáles?
while mientras, **5.2**
white blanco(a), 5.1
who? ¿quién?, 1.1; ¿quiénes?, 1.2
Who's calling, please? ¿De parte de quién, por favor?, **6.2**
whole entero(a)
whose cuyos(as)
why? ¿por qué?, 3.2
wide ancho(a), **8.1**
wife la esposa, la mujer, 2.1
to **win** ganar, 5.1
wind el viento, LP
window *(store)* el escaparate, 9.1; ***(plane)*** la ventanilla, 10.2; **1.2**
windshield el parabrisas, **9.1**
windsurfing la plancha de vela, 7.1
to go windsurfing practicar la plancha de vela, 7.1
windy: It's windy. Hace viento., LP
wings las alitas, **10**
winter el invierno, LP, 7.2
wise: the Three Wise Men los Reyes Magos, **5.2**
to **wish** desear, 4.2
with con
within dentro de
without sin, 7.2
woman la dama
wooden de madera
word la palabra
work el trabajo; ***(art)*** la obra
to **work** trabajar, 3.2; ***(land)*** cultivar, labrar, **8.2**
world el mundo
World Cup la Copa Mundial
worldwide mundial
worse peor
worst el/la peor
to **be worth: It's not worth it.** No vale., 7.1
Would that . . . Ojalá que… , **11.2**
wound la herida, **11.2**
wreath la corona, **5.1**
wrist la muñeca, **11.1**
to **write** escribir, 4.2
written escrito(a)
wrong erróneo(a)

X

X ray la radiografía, **11.2**
They're taking an X ray (of him or her). Le toman (hacen) una radiografía., **11.2**

Y

year el año, LP
last year el año pasado, 7.1
to be turning . . . years old cumplir... años, 2.1
to be . . . years old tener... años, 2.1
yellow amarillo(a), 5.1
yes sí, LP
yesterday ayer, 7.1
yesterday afternoon ayer por la tarde, 7.1
yesterday evening anoche, 7.1
yet aún; todavía
yoga el yoga, **11.1**
to do yoga practicar yoga, **11.1**
you tú; *(sing. form.)* usted; *(pl. form.)* ustedes; *(pl. fam.)* vosotros(as); *(fam. pron.)* ti; te; *(form. pron.)* le
You're welcome. De (Por) nada., No hay de qué., LP
young person el/la joven, 1.1
younger menor
youngest el/la menor
your *(fam.)* tu(s); *(form.)* su(s)
It's your turn! ¡Te toca a ti!
youth hostel el albergue juvenil, el hostal, **7**

Z

zero cero, LP
zone la zona
zoo el zoológico, **8.1**

Culture Index

A

B

C

D

E

F

G

H

L

Culture Index

U

V

Grammar Index

Certification Contact

Weber, Ryan <RWeber@ssdmo.org>

Tue 1/25/2022 9:16 AM

To: Adkins, Alma <AAdkins@ssdmo.org>

Alma, below is what I received from Angie Vaughn. She was the contact person at central office for certification. If you have further questions I would contact her.

You have to actually log onto DESE's website and apply for the cert by choosing the Additional Cert application and using your tests scores as your proof of eligibility. It'll cost you $35 and then DESE will add it to your current cert status. If you fail to do this part then you'll NEVER get the cert. Now you won't have to send them a copy of your test scores, because they should have received them before you did.

314 989
8291
A Vaughn

Ryan Weber
SPED / Social Studies
North Technical High School
1700 Derhake
Florissant MO 63033
314-989-7733